M000248647

Women, Gender, and Crime
A Text/Reader

3rd Edition

For Jeff, Taylor, and Keegan

Sara Miller McCune founded SAGE Publishing in 1965 to support the dissemination of usable knowledge and educate a global community. SAGE publishes more than 1000 journals and over 800 new books each year, spanning a wide range of subject areas. Our growing selection of library products includes archives, data, case studies and video. SAGE remains majority owned by our founder and after her lifetime will become owned by a charitable trust that secures the company's continued independence.

Los Angeles | London | New Delhi | Singapore | Washington DC | Melbourne

Women, Gender, and Crime
A Text/Reader

3rd Edition

Stacy L. Mallicoat

California State University, Fullerton

Los Angeles | London | New Delhi
Singapore | Washington DC | Melbourne

FOR INFORMATION:

SAGE Publications, Inc.
2455 Teller Road
Thousand Oaks, California 91320
E-mail: order@sagepub.com

SAGE Publications Ltd.
1 Oliver's Yard
55 City Road
London EC1Y 1SP
United Kingdom

SAGE Publications India Pvt. Ltd.
B 1/I 1 Mohan Cooperative Industrial Area
Mathura Road, New Delhi 110 044
India

SAGE Publications Asia-Pacific Pte. Ltd.
3 Church Street
#10-04 Samsung Hub
Singapore 049483

Acquisitions Editor: Jessica Miller
Content Development Editor: Laura Kirkhuff
Editorial Assistant: Rebecca Lee
Production Editor: Karen Wiley
Copy Editor: Kimberly Cody
Typesetter: C&M Digitals (P) Ltd.
Proofreader: Caryne Brown
Indexer: Jeanne Busemeyer
Cover Designer: Janet Kiesel
Marketing Manager: Jillian Oelsen

Copyright © 2019 by SAGE Publications, Inc.

All rights reserved. No part of this book may be reproduced or utilized in any form or by any means, electronic or mechanical, including photocopying, recording, or by any information storage and retrieval system, without permission in writing from the publisher.

Printed in Canada

ISBN 978-1-5063-6686-9

This book is printed on acid-free paper.

MIX
Paper from
responsible sources
FSC® C004071

19 20 21 22 10 9 8 7 6 5 4 3 2

Brief Contents

Detailed Contents

READINGS

READINGS

SECTION VIII. Female Offenders and Their Crimes — 325

READINGS

SECTION IX. Processing and Sentencing of Female Offenders — 375

READINGS

SECTION XII. Women Professionals and the Criminal Justice System: Police, Corrections, and Offender Services

READINGS

SECTION XIII. Women Professionals and the Criminal Justice System: Courts and Victim Services

READINGS

Foreword

You hold in your hands a book that we think is a different approach to this subject matter and to student learning. It is billed a "text/reader." What that means is that we have blended the two most commonly used types of books, the textbook and the reader, in a way that will appeal to both students and faculty.

Our experience as teachers and scholars has been that textbooks for the core classes in criminal justice (or any other social science discipline) leave many students and professors cold. The textbooks are huge and crammed with photographs, charts, highlighted material, and all sorts of pedagogical devices intended to increase student interest. Too often, however, these books end up creating a sort of sensory overload for students and suffer from their focus on "bells and whistles," such as fancy graphics, at the expense of coverage of the most significant and current research on the subject matter. And, in the end, isn't that what matters most? We study crime and justice to better understand why crime happens and how society processes it, and it is research—not pretty pictures—that informs this process. Our students deserve more than a nicely packaged recitation of boring facts; they need to understand what the research says, and this research needs to be presented in a fashion that does not scare them off.

Readers, on the other hand, are typically composed of recent and classic research articles on the subject matter. They generally suffer, however, from an absence of meaningful explanatory material. Articles are simply lined up and presented to the students with little or no context or explanation. Students, particularly undergraduate students, are often confused and overwhelmed by the jargon and detailed statistical analyses presented in the articles. It is unrealistic to expect students to fully grasp criminal justice research if this research is not placed in context and presented in a manner suited to their knowledge level.

This text/reader represents our attempt to take the best of both textbook and reader approaches. The book includes a combination of previously published articles on criminological theory and of textual material introducing the articles and providing structure and context. The text/reader is intended to serve either as a supplement to a core undergraduate textbook or as a stand-alone text.

The book is divided into a number of sections. The sections of the book track the typical content and structure of a textbook on the subject. Each section of the book has an introductory chapter that introduces, explains, and provides context for the readings that follow. The readings are a selection of the best recent research from academic journals, as well as some classic readings where appropriate. The articles are edited as necessary to make them accessible to students. This variety of research and perspectives will provide the student with a grasp of the development of research, as well as an understanding of the current status of research in the subject area. The approach gives the student the opportunity to learn the basics (in the introductory portion of each section) and to read some of the most interesting research on the subject.

There are also a preface and an introductory chapter. The preface explains the organization and content of the book, and the introductory chapter provides a framework for the material that follows and introduces relevant themes, issues, and concepts to assist the student in understanding the articles.

Each section concludes with a summary of the material covered, as well as a set of discussion questions. Discussion questions also appear at the end of each reading. These summaries and discussion questions should facilitate student thought and class discussion of the material.

Ancillary materials, such as PowerPoint slides, a testbank, and lecture outlines, are available to help assist the instructor in moving from a standard textbook to this hybrid approach.

We acknowledge that this approach may be viewed by some as more challenging than the traditional textbook. To that we say "Yes! It is!" But we believe that, if we raise the bar, our students will rise to the challenge. Research shows that students and faculty often find textbooks boring to read. It is our belief that many criminal justice instructors welcome the opportunity to teach without having to rely on a "standard" textbook that covers only the most basic information and that lacks both depth of coverage and an attention to current research. This book provides an alternative for instructors who want more than a basic textbook aimed at the lowest common denominator and filled with flashy but often useless features that merely drive up its cost. This book is intended for instructors who want their students to be exposed to more than the ordinary, basic coverage of criminal justice.

We also believe students will find this approach more interesting. They are given the opportunity to read current, cutting-edge research on the subject while also being provided with background and context for such research. In addition to including the most topical and relevant research, we have included a short entry, "How to Read a Research Article." The purpose of this entry, placed toward the beginning of the book, is to provide students with an overview of the components of a research article. It helps walk them through the process of reading a research article, lessening their trepidation, and increasing their ability to comprehend the material presented therein. Many students will be unfamiliar with reading and deciphering research articles; we hope this feature will help them do so.

In addition, we provide a student study site on the Internet with supplemental research articles, study questions, practice quizzes, and other pedagogical material to assist the student in learning the material. We chose to put these pedagogical tools on a companion study site rather than in the text to allow instructors to focus on the material, while still offering students the opportunity to learn more.

To date, there have been thirteen books published in the text/reader series. Many of them have gone into (or are in the process of going into) multiple editions. The feedback we have received from early adopters has been overwhelmingly positive. Instructors have successfully used these books in community colleges and universities at both the undergraduate and graduate levels. Faculty tell us that they find the books more interesting to use and teach from and that students appreciate the different approach.

We hope that this unconventional approach will be more interesting to students and faculty alike and thus make learning and teaching more fun. Criminal justice is a fascinating subject, and the topic deserves to be presented in an interesting manner. We hope you will agree.

Craig Hemmens, JD, PhD, Series Editor

Department of Criminal Justice and Criminology
Washington State University

Preface

The purpose of this book is to introduce readers to the issues that face women as they navigate the criminal justice system. Regardless of the participation, women have unique experiences that have significant effects on their perspectives of the criminal justice system. Effectively understanding the criminal justice system means that the voices of women must be heard. This book seeks to inform readers on the realities of women's lives as they interact with the criminal justice system. These topics are presented in this book through summary essays highlighting the key terms and research findings and incorporating cutting-edge research from scholars whose works have been published in top journals in criminal justice, criminology, and related fields.

Organization and Contents of the Book

This book is divided into thirteen sections, with each section dealing with a different subject related to women, gender, and crime. Each section begins with an introduction to the issues raised within each topic and summarizes some of the basic themes related to the subject area. Each section also includes Spotlights on critical issues or current events related to the topic. Each introductory essay concludes with a discussion of the policy implications related to each topic. This discussion is followed by selected readings that focus on research being conducted on critical issues within each topical area. These readings represent some of the best research in the field and are designed to expose students to the discussions facing women's issues within contemporary criminal justice. These thirteen sections are as follows:

- Women, Gender, and Crime: Introduction
- Theories of Victimization
- Women, Gender, and Victimization: Rape and Sexual Assault
- Women, Gender, and Victimization: Intimate Partner Abuse and Stalking
- International Issues in Gender-Based Violence
- Women, Gender, and Offending
- Girls, Gender, and Juvenile Delinquency
- Female Offenders and Their Crimes
- Processing and Sentencing of Female Offenders
- The Supervision of Women: Community Corrections, Rehabilitation, and Reentry

- Women, Gender, and Incarceration

- Women Professionals and the Criminal Justice System: Police, Corrections, and Offender Services

- Women Professionals and the Criminal Justice System: Courts and Victim Services

The first section provides an introduction and foundation for the book. In setting the context for the book, this section begins with a review of the influence of feminism on the study of crime. The section looks at the different types of data sources that are used to assess female offending and victimization. The section concludes with a discussion on feminist methodology and how it can contribute to the discussions of women, gender, and crime. The Spotlight in this section highlights the role of gender within the study of criminology. The first article in this section, by Meda Chesney-Lind and Merry Morash, looks at the contributions of feminist criminology in the understanding of gender and crime issues and provides some insights for the future. The second article by Jody Miller focuses on issues of gender in qualitative research.

The second section begins with a review of the victim experience in the criminal justice system. This section highlights the experience of help seeking by victims and the practice of victim blaming. The section then turns to a discussion of victimization and focuses on how fear about victimization is a gendered experience. The section then turns to the discussion of victimization and how theories seek to understand the victim experience and place it within the larger context of the criminal justice system and society in general. The Spotlights in this section looks at the issue of victim rights in Mexico and the femicides of women along the border cities, and cases of kidnapping involving women and girls. The section includes two readings on victimization. The first article in this section, by Bonnie S. Fisher and David May, investigates the effects of gender on the fear of victimization by college students. The second article by Judy L. Postmus, looks at how ethnicity can impact the help-seeking experience.

The third section focuses on the victimization of women by crimes of rape and sexual assault. From historical issues to contemporary standards in the definition of sexual victimization, this section highlights the various forms of sexual assault and the role of the criminal justice system in the reporting and prosecution of these crimes, and the role of victims in the criminal justice system. This section also looks at critical issues such as campus sexual assault, sexual violence in the LGBTQ communities, and racial and ethnic issues in sexual assault. The Spotlights in this section look at issues of rape culture, and sexual assault within the military. The readings in this section highlight some of the critical research on issues related to rape and sexual assault. Beginning with a discussion of campus sexual assault, Rebecca M. Hayes-Smith and Lora M. Levett investigate whether information about these resources altered students' beliefs in rape myths. The second reading, by Clare Gunby, Anna Carline, and Caryl Beynon, investigates how alcohol consumption alters perceptions of rape and sexual assault claims.

The fourth section presents the discussion of victimization of women in cases of intimate partner abuse and stalking. A review of the legal and social research on intimate partner violence addresses a multitude of issues for victims, including the barriers to leaving a battering relationship. This section also highlights how demographics such as race, sexuality, and immigration status impact the abusive experience. The articles in this section address some of the contemporary issues facing victims of intimate partner violence. The section concludes with a discussion of stalking and highlights the issue of cyberstalking. The Spotlights for this section look at issues of intimate partner abuse within the NFL, international issues of IPA, and stalking on college campuses. The readings for this section begin with an essay by Alisa J. Velonis and the issues with nonphysical acts of intimate partner abuse. The second article, by Katie M. Edwards, Christina M. Dardis, and Christine A. Gidycz, investigates the disclosure practices of victims of dating violence.

The fifth section focuses on international issues for women and includes discussions on crimes such as human trafficking, honor-based violence, witch burnings, genital mutilation, and rape as a war crime. The Spotlights in this section looks the issue of witch burnings in Papua New Guinea, and the case of Malala Yousafzai. In the first article in this section, Chenda Keo, Theirry Bouhours, Roderic Broadhurt, and Brigette Bouhours investigate how issues of human trafficking in Cambodia have created a moral panic throughout the region. The second article, by Inger Skjelsbaek, looks at the experiences of women who endured sexual assault during the Bosnia-Herzegovina War.

The sixth section focuses on the theoretical explanations of female offending. The section begins with a review of the classical and modern theories of female criminality. While the classical theories often described women in sexist and stereotypical ways, modern theories of crime often ignored women completely. Recent research has reviewed many of these theories to assess whether they might help explain female offending. The section concludes with a discussion of gender-neutral theories and feminist criminology. The Spotlights in this section look at the Manson Women as a classical example of strain theory. This section includes two articles that involve testing criminological theory on female populations. The first article is by April Bernard, who uses a case study to assess which theories of crime might best explain this offender's criminal behavior. The second article, by Kimberly J. Cook, looks at how classical theories of crime failed to include girls and women and concludes with a discussion on the future opportunities for feminist criminology.

Section VII focuses on girls and the juvenile justice system. Beginning with a discussion on the patterns of female delinquency, this section investigates the historical and contemporary standards for young women in society and how the changing definitions of delinquency have disproportionately and negatively impacted young girls. The Spotlights in this section look at the issue of sexual abuse in confinement, arts programming for at-risk youth, and girls' voices to assess what girls need from the juvenile justice system. The readings for this section begin with an article by Jessica P. Hodge, Kristi Holsinger, and Kristen Maziarka and explores the efficacy of gender specific programs by using juvenile justice staff members. The section concludes with an article by Juliette Noel Graziano and Eric F. Wagner and investigates the role of trauma and LGBTQ girls in the juvenile justice system.

Section VIII deals with women and their crimes. While female crimes of violence are highly sensationalized by the media, these crimes are rare occurrences. Instead, the majority of female offending is made up of crimes that are nonviolent in nature or are considered victimless crimes, such as property-based offenses, drug abuse, and sexually based offenses. The Spotlights in this section look at how a typically masculine crime of bank robbery can be gendered, a discussion of gender and self-defense, and a look at the case of Michelle Carter, who was convicted for using text messages to encourage her boyfriend to commit suicide. The readings for this section include an article by Judith A. Ryder and Regina E. Brisgone that focuses on the experiences of women and girls living and growing up during the era of crack cocaine and an article by Corey Shdaimah and Chrystanthi Leon on how women use their experience in prostitution as a way to assert power and control over their lives

The ninth section details the historical and contemporary patterns in the processing and sentencing of female offenders. This section highlights research on how factors such as patriarchy, chivalry, and paternalism within the criminal justice system impact women. The Spotlight in this section looks at international perspectives in the processing of female offenders. Two articles in this section investigate the effects of gender on the processing of offenders: Tina L. Freiburger and Carly M. Hilinski investigate how race, gender, and age impact decision making in cases of pretrial detention; and Jill K. Doerner and Stephen Demuth look at whether women in the federal courts benefit from chivalrous sentencing practices.

The tenth section looks at the experience of women in the community corrections setting. The section begins with a discussion on gender-specific programming and how correctional agents and programs need to address these unique issues for women. The section then looks at the role of risk assessment instruments and how they need to reflect gender differences between male and female offenders. The section concludes with a discussion on the reentry challenges of women exiting from prison. The Spotlight in this section looks at life after parole. The first article, by Tara D. Opsal, focuses on how women handle experience of being on parole. The second article, by Kelle Barrick, Pamela J. Mattimore, and Christy A. Visher, looks at how social ties during incarceration can prevent recidivism.

Section XI examines the incarceration of women. Here, the text and readings focus on the patterns and practices of the incarceration of women. Ranging from historical examples of incarceration to modern-day policies, this section looks to how the treatment of women in prison varies from that of their male counterparts and how incarcerated women have unique needs based on their differential pathways to prison. The Spotlights in this section looks at how California's experience with realignment has impacted the incarceration of women, the financial challenges for women while they are in prison, and the Girl Scouts Beyond Bars program. The readings in this section begin with a discussion by Andrea Cantora, Jeff Mellow, and Melinda D. Schlager on how issues of trust can impact the rehabilitative process, and conclude with research by Holly M. Harner and Suzanne Riley on the mental health effects of the incarceration experience.

Section XII focuses on women who work within criminal justice occupations within traditionally male-dominated environments: policing and corrections. The readings for this section bring attention to the women who work within the domain of the criminal justice system and how gender impacts their occupational context. Following a discussion of the history of women in these occupations, this section looks at how gender impacts the performance of women in these jobs and the personal toll it has on their lives. The Spotlights in this section looks at issues of pregnancy on policing. The first article, by Robin N. Haarr and Merry Morash, looks at how women in policing cope with discrimination. The section concludes with research by Cassandra Matthews, Elizabeth Monk-Turner, and Melvina Sumter on promotional opportunities for women in corrections.

Section XIII concludes this text with a discussion of women in the legal and victim services fields. The section looks at both women who work as attorneys as well as women in the judiciary. While women are a minority in this realm of the criminal justice system, women are generally overrepresented within victim services agencies. Here, gender also plays a significant role in terms of both the individual's work experiences and the structural organization of the agency. The Spotlights in this section highlight the impact of gender on the U.S. Supreme Court, women in politics, and the value of self-care for victim services' workers. The readings for this section include an article by Christina L. Boyd on whether gender impacts judicial decision making in the trial courts, and conclude with research by Sarah E. Ullman and Stephanie M. Townsend on the barriers that rape crisis workers experience in working with victims.

As you can see, this book provides an in-depth look at the issues facing women in the criminal justice system. From victimization to incarceration to employment, this book takes a unique approach in its presentation by combining a review of the literature on each of these issues followed by some of the key research studies that have been published in academic journals. Each section of this book presents a critical component of the criminal justice system and the role of women in it. As you will soon learn, gender is a pervasive theme that runs deeply throughout our system, and how we respond to it has a dramatic effect on the lives of women in society.

New to the Third Edition

Nearly half of the journal articles have been updated and cover important topics, such as

- Transformative Feminist Criminology
- Women From Different Ethnic Groups and Their Experiences With Victimization
- Intimate Partner Violence
- Human Trafficking
- Social Identities of Women Who Experienced Rape During the War in Bosnia-Herzegovina
- Criminology and Androcentrism
- Gender-Specific Programs for Juveniles
- Resilience Among Women Who Work as Prostitutes

- Women's Experiences of Parole
- The Impact of Social Ties on Long-Term Recidivism
- Social Relationships and Group Dynamics for Female Inmates
- The Impact of Incarceration on Women's Mental Health
- The Effect of Rank on Policewomen Coping With Discrimination and Harassment
- The Effects of Trial Judges' Sex and Race

There is expanded coverage of critical topics, such as

- Representation of women in criminal justice academia
- Victim blaming
- Multiple marginalities and LGBT populations, including LGBTQ sexual violence
- Marital rape and rape as a war crime
- Campus sexual assault
- Economic abuse
- Cyberstalking
- Labor trafficking
- Women and pretrial release
- Challenges faced by female police officers
- The increasing number of women in the legal field

Fourteen new or updated Spotlights cover key issues, such as

- Victims' Rights in Mexico
- Sexual Victimization at Military Academies
- Stalking and College Campuses
- The Manson Women
- Life After Parole
- Financial Challenges for Incarcerated Women
- Pregnancy and Policing
- Women in Politics
- Self-Care for Victim Advocates

Statistics, graphs, and tables have all been updated to demonstrate the most recent trends in criminology.

Digital Resources

http://study.sagepub.com/mallicoat3e

The open-access Student Study Site includes the following:

- Mobile-friendly eFlashcards reinforce understanding of key terms and concepts that have been outlined in the chapters.

- Mobile-friendly web quizzes allow for independent assessment of progress made in learning course material.

- EXCLUSIVE! Access to certain full-text SAGE journal articles that have been carefully selected for each chapter.

- Web resources are included for further research and insights.

- Carefully selected video links feature relevant interviews, lectures, personal stories, inquiries, and other content for use in independent or classroom-based explorations of key topics.

The password-protected Instructor Resource Site includes the following:

- A Microsoft® Word® test bank is available containing multiple choice, true/false, short answer, and essay questions for each chapter. The test bank provides you with a diverse range of prewritten options as well as the opportunity for editing any question and/or inserting your own personalized questions to effectively assess students' progress and understanding.

- Editable, chapter-specific Microsoft® PowerPoint® slides offer you complete flexibility in easily creating a multimedia presentation for your course. Highlight essential content, features, and artwork from the book.

- Lecture notes summarize key concepts on a chapter-by-chapter basis to help with preparation for lectures and class discussions.

- Sample course syllabi for semester and quarter courses provide suggested models for use when creating the syllabus for your courses.

- EXCLUSIVE! Access to certain full-text SAGE journal articles that have been carefully selected for each chapter. Each article supports and expands on the concepts presented in the chapter.

- Web resources are included for further research and insights.

Acknowledgments

I have to give tremendous thanks to Jessica Miller, acquisitions editor for the Criminology and Criminal Justice Division at SAGE Publications. I am also deeply thankful to Jerry Westby and Craig Hemmens, who created the opportunity for me to become involved in this project many years ago. Special thanks as well to the staff at SAGE Publications who have also helped breathe life into this book.

Throughout my career, I have been blessed with amazing colleagues and mentors. I am so appreciative of your love and support. Your wisdom and friendship inspire me every day to be a better scholar, teacher, and human being. I also have to give thanks to my amazing network of friends from the Division on Women and Crime and the Division on People of Color and Crime. I am honored to get to work in an environment that is caring and supportive of my adventures in research and scholarship.

Finally, I am deeply indebted to my family for their love, support, and care and their endless encouragement for my adventures in academia and beyond.

SAGE Publications gratefully acknowledges the contributions of the following reviewers for this third edition:

Dr. Dorinda L. Dowis, Professor, Columbus State University

Leah Grubb, Georgia Southern University

Susan L. Wortmann, Nebraska Wesleyan University

Sandra Pavelka, PhD, Florida Gulf Coast University

Katherine J. Ely, Lock Haven University

Reviewers for the second edition:

Kathleen A. Cameron, Pittsburgh State University

Dorinda L. Dowis, Columbus State University

Katherine J. Ely, Lock Haven University

Allison J. Foley, Georgia Regents University

Bob Lilly, Northern Kentucky University

Johnnie Dumas Myers, Savannah State University

Sue Uttley-Evans, University of Central Lancashire

Women, Gender, and Crime
Introduction

Section Highlights

- Introduction to women as victims, offenders, and workers in the criminal justice system
- The emergence of feminism in criminology
- Data sources that estimate female offending and victimization rates
- The contributions of feminist methodologies in understanding issues about women and crime

Since the creation of the American criminal justice system, the experiences of women either have been reduced to a cursory glance or have been completely absent. **Gendered justice**, or rather injustice, has prevailed in every aspect of the system. The unique experiences of women have historically been ignored at every turn—for victims, for offenders, and even for women who have worked within its walls. Indeed, the criminal justice system is a gendered experience.

Yet the participation of women in the system is growing in every realm. Women make up a majority of the victims for certain types of crimes, particularly when men are the primary offender. These gendered experiences of victimization appear in crimes such as rape, sexual assault, intimate partner abuse, and stalking, to name a few. While women suffer in disproportionate ways in these cases, their cries for help have traditionally been ignored by a system that many in society perceive is designed to help victims. Women's needs as offenders are also ignored because they face a variety of unique circumstances and experiences that are absent from the male offending population. Traditional approaches in criminological theory and practice have been criticized by feminist scholars for their failure to understand the lives and experiences of women (Belknap, 2007). Likewise, the employment of women in the criminal justice system has been limited, because women were traditionally shut out of many of these male-dominated occupations. As women began to enter these occupations, they were faced with a hypermasculine culture that challenged the introduction of women at every turn. While the participation of women in these traditionally male-dominated fields has grown significantly in modern-day times, women continue to struggle for equality in a world where the effects of the "glass ceiling" continue to pervade a system that presents itself as one interested in the notion of justice (Martin, 1991).

1

In setting the context for the book, this section begins with a review of the influence of feminism on the study of crime. Following an introduction of how gender impacts victimization, offending, and employment experiences in the criminal justice system, the section presents a review of the different data sources and statistics within these topics. The section concludes with a discussion on the research methods used to investigate issues of female victimization, offending, and work in criminal justice-related fields.

The Influence of Feminism on Studies of Women, Gender, and Crime

As a student, you may wonder what **feminism** has to do with the topic of women and crime. Feminism plays a key role in understanding how the criminal justice system responds to women and women's issues. In doing so, it is first important that we identify what is meant by the term *woman*. Is "woman" a category of *sex* or *gender*? Sometimes, these two words are used interchangeably. However, *sex* and *gender* are two different terms. *Sex* refers to the biological or physiological characteristics of what makes someone male or female. Therefore, we might use the term *sex* to talk about the segregation of men and women in jails or prison. In comparison, the term *gender* refers to the identification of masculine and feminine traits, which are socially constructed terms. For example, in early theories of criminology, female offenders were often characterized as *masculine*, and many of these scholars believed that female offenders were more like men than women. While sex and gender are two separate terms, the notions of sex and gender are interrelated within the study of women and crime. Throughout this book, you will see examples of how sex and gender both play an important role in the lives of women in the criminal justice system.

The study of women and crime has seen incredible advances throughout the 20th and 21st century. Many of these changes are a result of the social and political efforts of feminism. The 1960s and 1970s shed light on several significant issues that impacted many different groups in society, including women. The momentum of social change as represented by the civil rights and women's movements had significant impacts on society, and the criminal justice system was no stranger in these discussions. Here, the second wave of feminism expanded beyond the focus of the original activists (who were concerned exclusively about women's suffrage and the right to vote) to topics such as sexuality, legal inequalities, and reproductive rights. It was during this time frame that criminology scholars began to think differently about women and offending. Prior to this time, women were largely forgotten in research about crime and criminal behavior. When they were mentioned, they were relegated to a brief footnote or discussed in stereotypical and sexist ways. Given that there were few female criminologists (as well as proportionally few female offenders compared to the number of male offenders), it is not surprising that women were omitted in early research on criminal behavior.

Some of the first feminist criminologists gained attention during the 1960s and 1970s. The majority of these scholars focused primarily on issues of equality and difference between men and women in terms of offending and responses by the criminal justice system. Unfortunately, these liberal feminists focused only on gender and did not include discussions that reflected a multicultural identity. Such a focus resulted in a narrow view of the women that were involved in crime and how the system responded to their offending. As Burgess-Proctor (2006) notes,

▲ **Photo 1.1** The icon of Lady Justice represents many of the ideal goals of the justice system, including fairness, justice, and equality.

©iStock/PatrickPoendl

By asserting that women universally suffer the effects of patriarchy, the dominance approach rests on the dubious assumption that all women, by virtue of their shared gender, have a common "experience" in the first place. . . . It assumes that all women are oppressed by all men in exactly the same ways or that there is one unified experience of dominance experienced by women. (p. 34)

While second-wave feminism focused on the works by these White liberal feminists, third-wave feminism addresses the multiple, diverse perspectives of women, such as race, ethnicity, nationality, and sexuality. With these new perspectives in hand, feminist criminologists began to talk in earnest about the nature of the female offender and began to ask questions about the lives of women involved in the criminal justice system. Who is she? Why does she engage in crime? And, perhaps most important, how is she different from the male offender, and how should the criminal justice system respond to her?

As feminist criminologists began to encourage the criminal justice system to think differently about female offenders, feminism also encouraged new conversations about female victimization. The efforts of second- and third-wave feminism brought increased attention to women who were victims of crime. How do women experience victimization? How does the system respond to women who have been victims of a crime? How have criminal justice systems and policies responded to the victimization of women? Indeed, there are many crimes that are inherently gendered that have historically been ignored by the criminal justice system.

Feminism also brought a greater participation in the workforce in general, and the field of criminal justice was no exception. Scholars were faced with questions regarding how gender impacts the way in which women work within the police department, correctional agencies, and the legal system. What issues do women face within the context of these occupations? How has the participation of women in these fields affected the experiences of women who are victims and offenders?

Today, scholars in criminology, criminal justice, and related fields explore these issues in depth in an attempt to shed light on the population of women in the criminal justice system. While significant gains have been made in the field of **feminist criminology**, scholars within this realm have suggested that "without the rise of feminisms, scholarly concerns with issues such as rape, domestic assault, and sex work—let alone recent emphases on intersectionality and overlapping biases or race, class, sexualities, and gender—would arguably never have happened" (Chancer, 2016, p. 308). Consider the rise of black feminist criminology, which looks at how the relationship between race, gender, and other issues of oppression create multiple marginalities for women of color (Potter, 2015).

Spotlight on Women and the Academy

Like many other fields, the academy has historically been a male-dominated profession. Yet the number of women faculty has grown significantly over the past four decades. This is also true in the academic study of crime and the criminal justice system. While the number of men in senior faculty positions outnumbers women, the presence of women entering the academy is growing. In 2007, 57% of doctoral students were female (Frost & Clear, 2007). This marks a significant trend for a field (practitioners and the academy) that has been historically, and continues to be, dominated by men.

As a national organization, the roots of the American Society of Criminology date back to 1941. The founding members of the organization were all male (ASC, n.d.). It was not until 1975 that the annual conference showcased a panel on women and crime. Even with the growing interest in female crime and victimization, not to mention an increase in the number of female scholars, the majority of the association members questioned whether gender

(Continued)

(Continued)

was a valuable variable to study. In response to these challenges, a small group of female scholars combined their efforts to lobby for more panels on the study of women and crime. In 1984, the Division on Women and Crime was instituted as an official branch of the American Society of Criminology. Today, the Division is the largest division of the ASC, with 384 members in 2012.

As a result of the work of these early female criminologists, the number of panels and papers presented annually on issues related to gender and crime research has grown substantially and includes discussions related to offending, victimization, and employment issues within the criminal justice system. Between 1999 and 2008, there were 3,050 (16.13%) presentations on themes related to the study of women and crime. The top five topic areas of these presentations include (1) domestic violence/intimate partner violence, (2) gender-specific programming and policies, (3) gender differences in criminal behavior, (4) victimization of women, and (5) international perspectives on women and crime (Kim & Merlo, 2012).

While much of the work of feminist criminology involves female scholars, there are also men who investigate issues of gender and crime. At the same time, there are female scholars whose work does not look at issues of gender. Over the past decade, a body of work has looked at the productivity of criminologists and in particular how female scholars compare to male scholars. While men publish more than women, the gender gap on publishing is reduced when we take into account the length of time in the academy, because the men generally report a longer career history (Snell, Sorenson, Rodriguez, & Kuanliang, 2009). However, achieving gender equity is a long road. A review of three of the top publications in criminology and criminal justice from 2013 notes that while women are well represented as first authors in *Justice Quarterly* (45.2%) and *Theoretical Criminology* (40.7%), they are underrepresented in *Criminology* 28.6%) (Chesney-Lind & Chagnon, 2016). Research by female authors is also less likely to be cited. A review of research publications in the field for the past two years notes that white men are most likely to have their work cited in subsequent research (77.1%) compared to white women (12.4%), while both men and women of color are rarely likely to find their research referenced by others (men of color = 1.3%; women of color = 0.7%) (Kim & Hawkins, 2013). Indeed, the rise of female scholars led some researchers to note that the future of the "most productive and influential scholars will have a more markedly feminine quality" (Rice, Terry, Miller, & Ackerman, 2007, p. 379).

Women are also becoming more active in the leadership roles within these academic organizations. What was once a "boys club" now reflects an increase in the participation of women on the executive boards as well as officer positions within the organization. Between 2014 and 2018, four of the five presidents of the American Society of Criminology were women—Joanne Belknap, Candace Kruttschnitt, Ruth Peterson, and Karen Heimer. Women are also being elected to the highest position within the Academy of Criminal Justice Sciences, where four women have served as president since 2000, and Nicole Piquero has been elected for 2018. Female criminologists have also chipped away at the glass ceiling at the national level with the appointment of Nancy Rodriguez as Director of the National Institute of Justice in 2014.

While feminist scholars have made a significant impact on the study of crime over the past 40 years, there are still several areas where additional research is needed.

Women, Gender, and Crime

How does the criminal justice system respond to issues of gender? While there have been significant gains and improvements in the treatment of women as victims, offenders, and workers within the criminal justice system and related fields, there is still work to be done in each of these areas.

Women as Victims of Violence

The experience of victimization is something that many women are intimately familiar with. While men are more likely to be a victim of a crime, women compose the majority of victims of certain forms of violent crime. In addition, women are most likely to be victimized by someone they know. In many cases when they do seek help from the criminal justice system, charges are not always filed or are often reduced through plea bargains, resulting in offenders receiving limited (if any) sanctions for their criminal behavior. Because of the sensitive nature of these offenses, victims can find their own lives put on trial to be criticized by the criminal justice system and society as a whole. Based on these circumstances, it is no surprise that many women have had little faith in the criminal justice system. You'll learn more about the experience of victimization in Section II.

Women who experience victimization have a number of needs, particularly in cases of violent and personal victimization. While these cases can involve significant physical damage, it is often the emotional violence that can be equally, if not more, traumatic for victims to deal with. While significant gains have been made by the criminal justice system, the high needs of many victims, coupled with an increased demand for services, means that the availability of resources by agencies such as domestic violence shelters and rape crisis centers are often limited. You'll learn more about the experience of women in crimes such as rape, sexual assault, intimate partner violence, and stalking in Sections III and IV, while Section V highlights issues of victimization of women around the globe.

Women Who Offend

How do female offenders compare to male offenders? When scholars look at the similarities and differences between the patterns of male and female offending, they are investigating the *gender* gap. What does this research tell us? We know that men are the majority of offenders represented for most of the crime categories, minus a few exceptions. **Gender gap** research tells us that the gender gap, or difference between male and female offending, is larger in cases of serious or violent crimes, while the gap is narrower for crimes such as property and drug related offenses (Steffensmeier & Allan, 1996).

While men are more likely to engage in criminal acts, women offenders dominate certain categories of criminal behavior. One example of this phenomenon is the crime of prostitution. Often called a victimless crime, prostitution is an offense where the majority of arrests involve women. Status offenses are another category where girls are over-represented. Status offenses are acts that are considered criminal only because of the offender's age. For example, the consumption of alcohol is considered illegal only if you are under a designated age (generally 21 in the United States). Section VIII highlights different offense types and how gender is viewed within these offenses. A review of these behaviors and offenders indicates that most female offenders share a common foundation—one of economic need, addiction, and abuse.

Gender also impacts the way that the criminal justice system responds to offenders of crime. Much of this attention comes from social expectations about how women "should" behave. When women engage in crime (particularly violent crimes), this also violates the socially proscribed gender roles for female behavior. As a result, women in these cases may be punished not only for violating the law but also for violating the socially proscribed gender roles. In Section IX, you'll learn more about how women can be treated differently by the criminal justice system as a result of their gender. As more women have come to the attention of criminal justice officials, and as policies and practices for handling these cases have shifted, more women are being sent to prison rather than being supervised in the community. This means that there is a greater demand on reentry programming and services for women. These collateral consequences in the incarceration of women are far reaching, because the identity as an *ex-offender* can threaten a woman's chances for success long after she has served her sentence.

The Intersection of Victimization and Offending

One of the greatest contributions of feminist criminology is the acknowledgment of the relationship between victimization and offending. Research has consistently illustrated that a history of victimization of women is a common factor for many women offenders. Indeed, a review of the literature finds that an overwhelming majority of women in prison have experienced some form of abuse—physical, psychological, or sexual—and in many cases, are victims of long-term multiple acts of violence. Moreover, not only is there a strong relationship that leads from victimization to offending, but the relationship between these two variables continues also as a vicious cycle. For example, a young girl who is sexually abused by a family member runs away from home. Rather than return to her abusive environment, she ends up selling her body as a way to provide food, clothing, and shelter because she has few skills to legitimately support herself. As a result of her interactions with potentially dangerous clients and pimps, she continues to endure physical and sexual violence and may turn to substances such as alcohol and drugs to numb the pain of the abuse. When confronted by the criminal justice system, she receives little if any assistance to address the multiple issues that she faces as a result of her life experiences. In addition, her *criminal* identity now makes it increasingly difficult to find valid employment, receive housing and food benefits, or have access to educational opportunities that could improve her situation. Ultimately, she ends up in a world where finding a healthy and sustainable life on her own is a difficult goal to attain. You will learn more about these challenges in Sections X and XI and how the criminal justice system punishes women for these crimes.

Women and Work in the Criminal Justice System

While much of the study of women and crime focuses on issues of victimization and offending, it is important to consider how issues of sex and gender impact the work environment, particularly for those who work within the justice system. Here, the experiences of women as police and correctional officers, victim advocates, probation and parole case managers, and lawyers and judges provide valuable insight on how sex and gender differences affect women. Just as the social movements of the 1960s and 1970s increased the attention on female offenders and victims of crime, the access to opportunities for work within the walls of criminal justice expanded for women. Prior to this era of social change, few women were granted access to work within these occupations. Even when women were present, their duties were significantly limited compared to those of their male counterparts, and their opportunities for advancement were essentially nonexistent. In addition, these primarily male workforces resented the presence of women in "their" world. Gender also has a significant effect for fields that are connected to criminal justice. One example of this is found within the field of victim services, which has typically been viewed as women's work.

Women continue to face a number of sex- and gender-based challenges directly related to their status as women, such as on-the-job sexual harassment, work-family balance, maternity, and motherhood. In addition, research reflects how women manage the roles, duties, and responsibilities of their positions within a historically masculine environment. The experience of womanhood can impact the work environment, both personally and culturally. You'll learn more about these issues in Sections XII and XIII of this book.

Data Sources on Women as Victims and Offenders

To develop an understanding of how often women engage in offending behaviors or the frequency of victimizations of women, it is important to look at how information about crime is gathered. While there is no one dataset that tells us everything that we want to know about crime, we can learn something from each source because they each represent different points of view. Datasets vary based on the type of information collected (quantitative and/or qualitative), who manages the dataset (such as government agencies, professional scholars, community organizations) and the purpose for the data collection. Finally, each dataset represents a picture of crime for a specific population, region, and time frame, or stage, of the criminal justice system.

The **Uniform Crime Reports** (UCR) represents one of the largest datasets on crime in the United States. The Federal Bureau of Investigation (FBI) is charged with collecting and publishing the arrest data from over 17,000 police agencies in the United States. These statistics are published annually and present the rates and volume of crime by offense type, based on arrests made by police. The dataset includes a number of demographic variables to evaluate these crime statistics, including age, gender, race/ethnicity, location (state), and region (metropolitan, suburban, or rural).[1]

UCR data give us a general understanding of the extent of crime in the United States and are often viewed as the most accurate assessment of crime. In addition, the UCR data allow us to compare how crime changes over time, because it allows for the comparison of arrest

▲ **Photo 1.2** Most official crime statistics such as the Uniform Crime Reports are based on arrest data.

data for a variety of crimes over a specific time frame (e.g., 1990–2000) or from one year to the next. Generally speaking, data from the UCR findings are typically reported to the greater society through news media outlets and form the basis for headline stories that proclaim the rising and falling rates of crime.

A review of arrest data from the UCR indicates that the overall levels of crime for women decreased 11.8% between 2006 and 2015. For the same time period, the number of arrests for men declined 25.6%. Such results might lead us to question why the percentage of men involved in crime decreased at more than twice the percentage of female arrests. To understand this issue, we need to take a deeper look. Table 1.1 illustrates the UCR data on arrest trends for men and women for 2006 and 2015. In 2006, the UCR shows that women made up 23.8% of all arrests (8,676,456 total number of arrests, with women accounting for 2,070,999 arrests). In contrast, 2015 UCR data indicate that 8,739,363 arrests were made, and women accounted for 27.0% of these arrests (2,140,934) (Crime in the United States 2012 [CIUS], 2012. Note that while the number of arrests involving women decreased by approximately almost a quarter of a million arrests (244,835), the total number of arrests over the decade decreased by almost 800,000. This change notes that while both the proportion of men and women decreased, the rate of male arrests decreased at a greater rate than that of women between these two time periods.

When assessing trends in crime data, it is important to consider the time period of evaluation, because this can alter your results. While both the 10-year and 1-year overall arrest trends demonstrate an decrease for both women and men, the data for 2015 demonstrates areas where arrests increased for women compared to men (and vice versa) compared to 2014. Table 1.2 demonstrates the arrest trends for these 2 years. The proportion of crime involving men fell 3.7%, while the proportion for women decreased 2.9%, indicating that the proportion of men arrested is similar to that of women between these two years. While this gives us a picture of overall crime trends, we see the picture differently when we look at the trends for specific crime categories. Here, a deeper look at the data shows that violent crime increased for both men and women while property crime declined for both groups. However, these changes were minor. In addition, there were no gender differences for specific crime categories. When

---

[1]Up-to-date statistical reports on crime data from the Uniform Crime Reports can be accessed at http://www.fbi.gov/ucr/ucr.htm

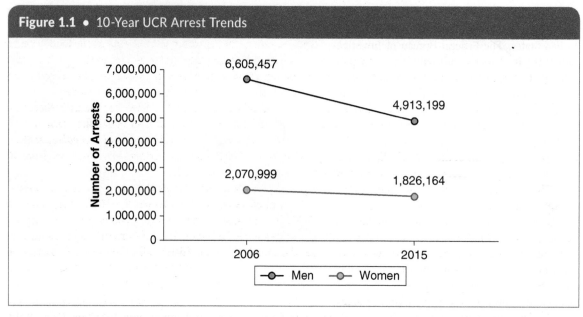

Figure 1.1 • 10-Year UCR Arrest Trends

SOURCE: Crime in the United States 2015 (CIUS), 2015.

Table 1.1 • 10-Year UCR Arrest Trends

	Men			Women		
	2006	2015	% Change	2006	2015	% Change
All arrests	6,605,457	4,913,199	−25.6	2,070,999	1,826,164	−11.8
Violent crime	297,166	244,197	−17.8	64,235	61,780	−3.8
Homicide	6,292	5,463	−13.2	812	738	−9.1
Rape*	13,932	13,546	−	188	409	−
Robbery	60,460	46,060	−23.8	7,977	7,943	−0.4
Aggravated assault	216,482	179,138	−17.3	55,258	52,690	−4.6
Property crime	645,926	576,178	−10.8	304,581	366,152	+20.2
Burglary	159,767	110,416	−30.9	28,355	26,049	−8.1
Larceny-theft	418,187	424,956	+1.6	261,103	328,713	+25.9
Motor vehicle theft	59,234	36,177	−38.9	13,416	10,286	−23.3
Arson	8,738	4,633	−47.0	1,707	1,104	−35.3

SOURCE: Crime in the United States 2015 (CIUS), 2015.

NOTE: 9,581 agencies reporting; 2015 estimated population 199,921,204; 2006 estimated population 186,371,331

*The 2006 rape figures are based on the legacy definition, and the 2015 rape figures are aggregate totals based on both the legacy and revised UCR reporting definition.

the percentage of men involved in burglary decreased, it also decreased for women. When the percentage of men involved in aggravated assault increased for men, it also increased for women.

While the UCR data can illustrate important trends in crime, the reporting of UCR data as the true extent of crime is flawed for the majority of the crime categories (with the exception of homicide), even though these data represent arrest statistics from approximately 95% of the population. Here, it is important to take several issues into consideration. First, the UCR data represent statistics on only those crimes that are reported to the police. As a result, the data are dependent on both what police know about criminal activity and how they use their discretion in these cases. If the police are not a witness to a crime or are not called to deal with an offender, they cannot make an arrest. Arrests are the key variable for UCR data. This means that unreported crimes are not recognized in these statistics. Sadly, many of the victimization experiences of women, such as intimate partner abuse and sexual assault, are significantly underreported and therefore do not appear within the UCR data.

Second, the UCR collects data only on certain types of crime (versus all forms of crime). The classification of crime is organized into two different types of crime: Part 1 offenses and Part 2 offenses. Part 1 offenses, known as *index crimes*, include eight different offenses: aggravated assault, forcible rape, murder, robbery, arson, burglary, larceny-theft, and motor vehicle theft. However, these categories may have limited definitions that fail to capture the true extent of arrests made for these crimes. Consider the category of rape. Historically, the UCR defined forcible rape as "the carnal knowledge of a female forcibly and against her will" (CIUS, 2012, para. 1). While the UCR also collects data on attempted rape by force or threat of force within this category, the definition failed to capture the magnitude of sexual assaults, which may not involve female victims or may involve other sexual acts beyond vaginal penetration. In January 2012, the FBI announced a revised definition for the crime of rape to include "the penetration, no matter how slight, of the vagina or anus with any body part or object, or oral penetration by a sex organ of another person, without the consent of the victim" (FBI, 2012a, para. 1). This new definition went into effect in January 2013. Not only does the new law allow for both males and females to be identified as victims or offenders but it also allows the UCR to include cases where the victim either was unable or unwilling to consent to sexual

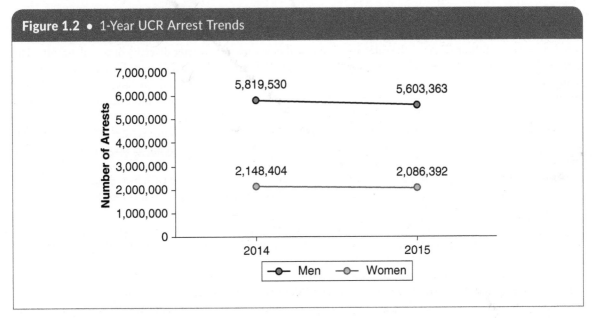

Figure 1.2 ● 1-Year UCR Arrest Trends

SOURCE: Crime in the United States 2012 (CIUS), 2015.

Table 1.2 • 1-Year UCR Arrest Trends

	Men			Women		
	2014	2015	% Change	2014	2015	% Change
All arrests	5,819,530	5,603,363	−3.7	2,148,404	2,086,392	−2.9
Violent crime	283,298	287,487	+1.5%	72,463	73,754	−1.8
Homicide	6,201	6,639	+7.1	843	880	+4.4
Forcible rape	14,563	15,453	+6.1	428	481	+12.4
Robbery	55,379	56,502	+2.0	9,233	9,636	+4.4
Aggravated assault	207,155	208,893	+0.8	61,959	62,757	+1.3
Property crime	686,290	648,880	−5.5	430,517	405,792	−5.7
Burglary	140,035	126,630	−9.6	31,402	29,789	−5.1
Larceny-theft	503,460	475,551	−5.5	388,081	363,323	−6.4
Motor vehicle theft	37,311	41,807	+12.1	9,716	11,508	+18.4
Arson	5,484	4,892	−10.8	1,318	1,172	−11.1

SOURCE: Crime in the United States 2012 (CIUS), 2015.

NOTE: 11,437 agencies reporting; 2015 estimated population 229,446,072; 2014 estimated population 228,153,502.

activity (for example, in cases involving intoxication). In addition, the new definition removes the requirement of force. As a result of these changes, the category of rape will now capture a greater diversity of sexual assaults. This new definition is more in line with the variety of laws related to rape and sexual assault that exist for each state. With this change in how these sexually based offenses are counted, it is not currently possible to compare data on the number of these cases prior to 2012. Over time, these changes will help present a more accurate picture of the prevalence of rape and sexual assault in society.

Third, the reporting of the crimes to the UCR is incomplete, because only the most serious crime is reported in cases where multiple crimes are committed during a single criminal event. These findings skew the understanding of the prevalence of crime, because several different offenses may occur within the context of a single crime incident. For example, a crime involving physical battery, rape, and murder is reported to the UCR by the most serious crime, murder. As a result, the understanding of the prevalence of physical battery and rape is incomplete.

Fourth, the reporting of these data is organized annually, which can alter our understanding of crime as police agencies respond to cases. For example, a homicide that is committed in one calendar year may not be solved with an arrest and conviction until the following calendar year. This might initially be read as an "unsolved crime" in the first year but as an arrest in the subsequent year.

Finally, the participation by agencies in reporting to the UCR has fluctuated over time. While there are no federal laws requiring agencies to report their crime data, many states today have laws that direct law enforcement agencies to comply with UCR data collection. For example, notice that 11,437 agencies reported data in 2014 and 2015, but only 9,581 agencies reported their arrest data in both 2006 and 2015. However, this means that the analyzers of crime trends over time need to take into consideration the number of agencies involved in the reporting of crime data. Failure to do so could result in a flawed analysis of crime patterns over time.

These flaws of UCR data can have significant implications for members of society about the understanding of crime data. Most of us get our information about crime from news headlines or other media reports about crime. These 30-second clips about crime rates do little to explain the intricate nature of UCR data definitions and collection practices. Indeed, when the UCR was first assigned to the FBI, early scholars commented, "In light of the somewhat questionable source of the data, the Department of Justice might do more harm than good by issuing the Reports" (Robison, 1966, p. 1033).

In an effort to develop a better understanding of the extent of offending, the **National Incident-Based Reporting System (NIBRS)** was implemented in 1988. Rather than compile monthly summary reports on crime data in their jurisdictions, agencies now forward data to the FBI for every crime incident. The NIBRS catalog involves data on 22 offense categories and includes 46 specific crimes known as Group A offenses. Data on 11 lesser offenses (Group B offenses) are also collected. In addition to an increased diversity in the types of crimes that data are collected on, the NIBRS abolished the hierarchy rule that was part of the UCR. This means that cases that involve more than one specific offense will now count all the different offenses that are reported and not just the most serious event. In addition, NIBRS data are collected on both completed and attempted crimes.

Overall, NIBRS allows for a more comprehensive understanding of crime in terms of the types of crimes that we collect information about and the data collected on these offenses. In 2015, NIBRS data noted that 63.3% of offenders were male, 25.7% were female (while gender was unknown in 11.0% of cases). NIBRS also tells us that half of victims in these crimes were women (50.9%). The majority of victims knew the perpetrator(s) (52.3%), and an additional 24.8% of victims were related to the offender (NIBRS, 2016a). Figure 1.3 and Table 1.3 shows the NIBRS arrest data for men and women in 2015. Comparing these two sources of data, we find similar results in the number

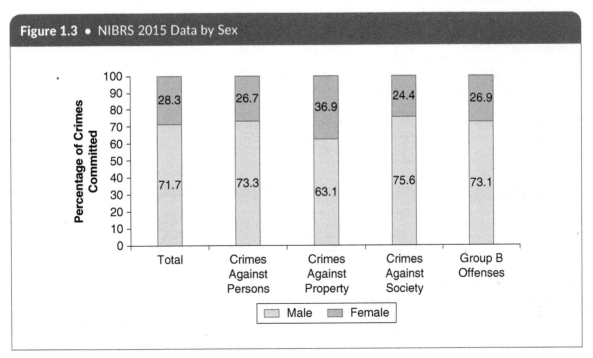

Figure 1.3 ● NIBRS 2015 Data by Sex

SOURCE: NIBRS (2016b)

Table 1.3 ● NIBRS 2015 Data by Sex

	Male	%	Female	%
Total	2,208,567	71.7%	873,042	28.3%
Crimes Against Persons	**323,371**	**73.3%**	**117,955**	**26.7%**
Assault Offenses	302,144	72.2%	116,390	27.8%
Homicide Offenses	2,380	87.1%	353	12.9%
Human Trafficking Offenses	6	75.0%	2	25.0%
Kidnapping/Abduction	5,469	89.2%	663	10.8%
Sex Offenses	11,877	96.5%	427	3.5%
Sex Offenses, Nonforcible	1,495	92.6%	120	7.4%
Crimes Against Property	**359,557**	**63.1%**	**210,006**	**36.9%**
Arson	1,719	80.1%	426	19.9%
Bribery	124	70.1%	53	29.9%
Burglary/Breaking & Entering	39,801	84.2%	7,459	15.8%
Counterfeiting/Forgery	9,107	63.0%	5,354	37.0%
Destruction/Damage/Vandalism	43,708	78.4%	12,024	21.6%
Embezzlement	2,797	45.3%	3,380	54.7%
Extortion/Blackmail	171	73.7%	61	26.3%
Fraud Offenses	20,248	61.6%	12,615	38.4%
Larceny/Theft Offenses	196,601	55.4%	158,008	44.6%
Motor Vehicle Theft	12,768	78.7%	3,461	21.3%
Robbery	15,933	85.4%	2,720	14.6%
Stolen Property Offenses	16,580	78.9%	4,445	21.1%
Crimes Against Society	**358,854**	**75.6%**	**115,805**	**24.4%**
Drug/Narcotic Offenses	324,869	75.0%	108,555	25.0%
Gambling Offenses	432	82.0%	95	18.0%
Pornography/Obscene Material	1,639	84.7%	295	15.3%
Prostitution Offenses	3,869	47.9%	4,211	52.1%
Weapon Law Violations	28,045	91.4%	2,649	8.6%

	Male	%	Female	%
Total	2,208,567	71.7%	873,042	28.3%
Group B Offenses	**1,166,785**	**73.1%**	**429,276**	**26.9%**
Bad Checks	3,717	48.4%	3,969	51.6%
Curfew/Loitering/Vagrancy Violations	9,567	71.3%	3,851	28.7%
Disorderly Conduct	82,781	71.7%	32,656	28.3%
Driving Under the Influence	228,773	74.5%	78,204	25.5%
Drunkenness	80,625	79.5%	20,851	20.5%
Family Offenses, Nonviolent	20,212	71.3%	8,134	28.7%
Liquor Law Violations	66,333	70.8%	27,358	29.2%
Peeping Tom	289	92.9%	22	7.1%
Trespass of Real Property	58,830	77.9%	16,689	22.1%
All Other Offenses	615,658	72.2%	237,542	27.8%

SOURCE: NIBRS (2016b)

of arrests for women and men. While UCR data shows that women made up 27.1% of all arrests in 2015, NIBRS data note that 28.3% of all arrests involved women. Similarities are also noted when we can compare like-defined categories. For example., women make up 11.7% of all homicide arrests in the UCR. In NIBRS, they make up 12.9% of arrests. In cases of larceny-theft, UCR data notes that women are 43.3% of all arrests. In NIBRS, women are 44.6% of arrests.

However, the transition of agencies to the NIBRS has been slow. Currently, the data obtained represents 36.1% of the reported crime and 58.1% of all police agencies in the United States. While the NIBRS is an improvement over the UCR, this system still carries over a fatal flaw from the UCR in that both are limited to reported crimes. In spite of this, it is hoped that the improvements in official crime data collection will allow an increased understanding of the extent of female offending patterns. NIBRS is slated to be fully implemented with all agencies reporting to it by January 1, 2021.

In contrast to the limitations of the UCR and NIBRS datasets, the **National Crime Victimization Survey (NCVS)** represents the largest victimization study conducted in the United States. National-level victimization data were first collected in 1971 and 1972 as part of the Quarterly Household Survey conducted by the Census Bureau. In 1972, these efforts evolved into the National Crime Survey (NCS), which was designed to supplement the data from UCR and provide data on crime from the victims' perspective. The NCS was transferred to the Bureau of Justice Statistics in 1979, where the bureau began to evaluate the survey instrument and the data collection process. Following an extensive redesign process, the NCS was renamed the National Crime Victimization Survey in 1991.

The greatest achievement of the NCVS lies in its attempt to fill the gap between reported and unreported crime, often described as the **dark figure of crime**. The NCVS gathers additional data about crimes committed and gives criminologists a greater understanding of the types of crimes committed and characteristics of the victims. In 2015, the NCVS interviewed 163,880 individuals aged 12 and older in 95,760 households. Based on these survey findings, the Bureau of Justice Statistics makes generalizations to the population regarding the prevalence of victimization in the United States (Truman & Morgan, 2016).

Table 1.4 • NCVS Crime Rates by Sex: 2002, 2010, and 2015										
	Violent Crime					Serious Violent Crime*				
	Rates			Percent Change		Rates			Percent Change	
	2002	2010	2015	2002–2015	2010–2015	2002	2010	2015	2002–2015	2010–2015
Total	32.1	19.3	18.6	−42.2	−3.6	10.1	6.6	6.8	−32.7	+3.0
Sex:										
Male	33.5	20.1	15.9	−52.5	−20.9	10.4	6.4	5.4	−48.1	−15.6
Female	30.7	18.5	21.1	−31.3	+14.1	9.5	6.8	8.1	+14.7	+19.1

SOURCE: Truman & Morgan (2016).

*Includes rape or sexual assault, robbery, and aggravated assault

In addition to reporting the numbers of criminal victimizations, the NCVS presents data on the rates of crime. You may ask yourself, "What is a crime rate?" A crime rate compares the number of occurrences of a particular crime to the size of the total population. The NCVS presents its findings in relation to the number of instances of the crime per 1,000 people. Crime rates make it easy to understand trends in criminal activity and victimization over time, regardless of changes to the population.

According to the National Crime Victimization Survey, the rate of violent victimization of women in 2002 was 30.7 per 1,000 people. By 2015, the crime rate had fallen to 21.1. Serious violent victimization also saw a significant decrease from 9.5 (2002) to 6.7 (2011), though in 2015 the rate had rebounded to 8.1 per 1,000 people.[2] Table 1.3 highlights the rates of crime for 2015 for violent and serious violent victimization. While NCVS data highlight these decreases, these patterns are not necessarily reflected in the UCR/NIBRS data, because many victims do not report these crimes to the police. With only 46.5% of victims reporting violent crime and 34.6% of victims reporting property crime, the NCVS provides valuable insight about the dark figure of crime that is missing in official crime statistics. This dark figure of crime varies by offense. For example, while 61.9% of cases of aggravated assault were reported, victims reported only 41.7% of simple assault cases. Similar patterns are observed in cases involving property crimes. While 69% of cases of motor vehicle theft were reported, other thefts were only reported 28.6% of the time (Truman & Morgan, 2016).

Just as the UCR/NIBRS is not the only data source on offending, the NCVS is not the only national-level data source on victimization. A number of different studies investigate victims of crime and how the justice system responds to their victimization. One example of this type of survey is the **National Violence Against Women Survey (NVAWS)**. The NVAWS consisted of a random sample of 8,000 women over the age of 18. The NVAWS was first administered between November 1995 and May 1996 and represented one of the first comprehensive data assessments of violence against women for the crimes of intimate partner abuse, stalking, and sexual assault. Another example is the **National Intimate Partner and Sexual Violence Survey (NISVS)**, which is conducted by the Centers for Disease Control and Prevention and the National Center for Injury Prevention and Control. In 2010, the NISVS included data from 16,507 interviews. The NISVS reports victimization from a variety of crimes, including sexual assault, intimate partner abuse, and stalking. These findings are then used to create estimates about the extent of crime throughout the United States. Figure 1.4 highlights the lifetime prevalence of rape by race and ethnicity based

---

[2]Includes rape, sexual assault, robbery, and aggravated assault

on data from the NISVS. These results demonstrate that 1 in 5 White (18.8%) and Black (22%) women and 1 in 7 (14.6%) Hispanic women in the United States have been raped at some point in their lifetime. By breaking up these data based on race and ethnicity, we can highlight how the issue of rape is even more dramatic within the American Indian/Alaska Native population, where 1 in 4 (26.9%) women experience rape in their lifetime. Unfortunately, we do not know much about how race and ethnicity impact rates of male rape from these data, only to say that less than 1 in 50 (2%) White men are impacted by the crime of rape in their lifetime (Black et al., 2011). Figure 1.5 presents the findings from this study for the crime of sexual assault. Here, we can see that not only are these crimes much more prevalent in general but also that we are able to see differences for both men and women by race/ethnicity. Studies such as these provide valuable data in understanding the experiences of victims (both men and women) that may not be reflected by the NCVS or UCR data.

While the UCR, NIBRS, and NCVS are examples of official data sources in the United States, international crime surveys can shed light on the nature of crime and victimization in other countries. The Australian Bureau of Statistics (ABS) collects data on arrested individuals throughout Australia. Unlike the UCR, which collects data on a calendar year basis, the ABS data cycle runs from July 1 to June 30. In its 2015–16 cycle, there were 422,067 individuals aged 10 and older processed by the police for eight different offenses (homicide, assault, sexual assault, robbery, kidnapping, unlawful entry with intent, motor vehicle theft, and other theft; Australian Bureau of Statistics, 2017). Another example of an official source of crime statistics is the annual report produced by the Bundeskriminalamt (Federal Criminal Police Office of Germany). The Bundeskriminalamt (BKA) statistics include data for all crimes handled by the police. In 2015, of the 6,330,649 crimes reported to the police, 5,927,908 were considered "cleared" or solved. Violent crime represents only 2.9% of crime in Germany. The largest crime category is theft and represents 39.2% of all criminal offenses. Men are much more likely to be considered a suspect by the police in these criminal activities—out of 2,369,036 suspects, only 24.8% are women. Men are also more likely to be victims (59.6%) (BKA, 2015). Australia's and Germany's crime statistical agencies are just two examples of official international data sources on criminal offending at the country level. Because of the differences in laws and reporting

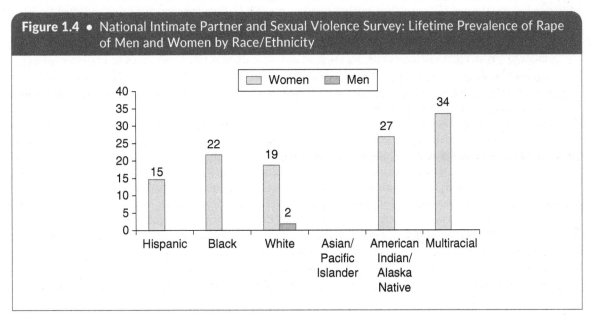

Figure 1.4 • National Intimate Partner and Sexual Violence Survey: Lifetime Prevalence of Rape of Men and Women by Race/Ethnicity

SOURCE: Black et al. (2011).

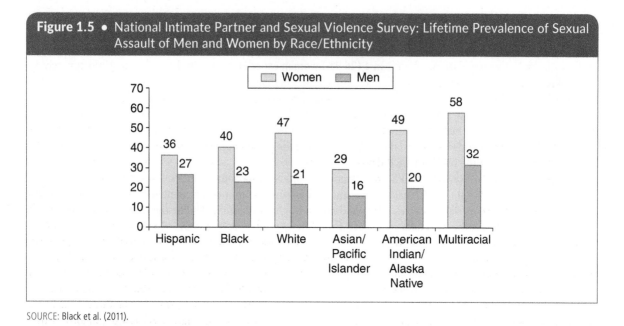

Figure 1.5 • National Intimate Partner and Sexual Violence Survey: Lifetime Prevalence of Sexual Assault of Men and Women by Race/Ethnicity

SOURCE: Black et al. (2011).

practices, it is difficult to compare such statistics at a global level. However, there have been attempts to collect basic information on recorded crime across several jurisdictions. The United Nations Survey of Crime Trends and Operations of Criminal Justice Systems (UN-CTS) compiles crime data from a variety of different sources, including the World Health Organization, Eurostat, and national police organizations from individual countries (to name a few). Their data indicate that there were 378,776 global victims of homicide reported to the police in 2012, or a crime rate of 10 per 100,000 (United Nations Office on Drugs and Crime, 2013). Data are currently being collected for 2016, and the questionnaire is distributed to member nations in six different languages: Arabic, Chinese, English, French, Russian, and Spanish (UNODC, 2017).

Similar to the NCVS, the Crime Survey for England and Wales (CSEW) is administered to a random sample of households and is designed to develop estimates about the rate of crime and victimization in England and Wales. The Crime Survey for England and Wales first began as part of the British Crime Survey in 1984 and included data from Scotland and Northern Ireland. Today, these jurisdictions carry out their own victimization survey, though the design and intent of these data collections are similar. In 2015–2016, approximately 35,000 adults and 3,000 children age 10–15 participated in the CSEW. Like the NCVS, the CSEW attempts to shed light on the dark figure of crime by capturing victimizations that may not be reported to the police. In 2013, the Crime Survey for England and Wales estimated that there were approximately 6.2 million incidents of victimization. Approximately three quarters of these crimes (4.7 million) were reported to the police (Office for National Statistics, 2017).

Finally, there are data sources that are collected as part of criminological research. These data typically focus on a particular crime within a particular region. The data can be either quantitative or qualitative (or both) and represent either a snapshot in time or follow a group of individuals over a range of time (longitudinal studies). While the findings of these studies are often not generalizable to the masses, they provide valuable insight about victimization and offending. Throughout this text, you'll be exposed to a number of these studies, within both the chapters and the highlighted readings.

In summary, official crime statistics offer only one perspective on the extent of crime in society. While the UCR and NCVS data and other international data sources provide a wealth of statistics about crime, their results are limited. Through the use of these official data programs, combined with self-report studies and victimization surveys, scholars can investigate issues of gender and crime in a variety of different ways. While each source of data has its strengths and weaknesses in terms of the types of data that are collected and the methods that are utilized, together, they provide a wealth of information that is invaluable in understanding the complex nature of gender and crime.

The Contributions of Feminist Methodology to Research on Women, Gender, and Crime

One of the criticisms of traditional mainstream criminology (and a central theme of feminist criminology) is that traditional perspectives on crime fail to recognize the intricate details of what it means to be a woman in society. The feminist movement has had a significant effect on how we understand women and their relationships with crime. As a result, the methods by which we conduct research on gender have also evolved. While many scholars who do research on gender engage in quantitative methods of research and analysis, this is not the only approach, particularly when dealing with sensitive issues. Here, the influence of feminism can alter the ways in which we conduct research, evaluate data, and make conclusions based on the findings yielded from the research experience. By incorporating a feminist perspective into the research environment, scholars are able to present a deeper understanding of the realities of women's lives by placing women and women's issues at the center of the research process.

The concept of giving women a voice, particularly in situations where they have been historically silenced, is a strong influence on **feminist research methods**. Many of the research studies in this book draw on feminist research methods. From the conceptualization of the research question to a discussion of which methods of data collection will be utilized and how the data will be analyzed, feminist methods engage in practices that are contrary to the traditional research paradigms. While the scientific method focuses on objectivity and the collection of data is detached from the human condition, the use of feminist methods requires a paradigm shift from what is traditionally known as research. While many of the researchers who first engaged in research through a feminist lens were women, feminist methodology does not dictate that the gender of the research participant or researcher be a woman. Rather, the philosophy of this method refers to the types of data a researcher is seeking and the process by which data are obtained (Westervelt & Cook, 2007). Feminist methods are largely qualitative in nature and allow for emotions and values to be present as part of the research process. While some feminist methodologists have criticized the process by which data are often quantified, because it does not allow for the intricate nature and quality of women's lives to be easily documented, others argue that quantitative data have a role to play within a feminist context. Regardless of the approach, the influence of feminism enables researchers to collect data from a subject that is theoretically important for their research versus data that are easily categorized (Hessy-Biber, 2004; Reinharz, 1992).

There is no single method of research that is identified as the *feminist method*. Rather, the concept of feminist methodology refers to *the process by which data are gathered* and *the relationship between the researcher and the subject*. This process involves five basic principles: (1) acknowledging the influence of gender in society as a whole (and inclusive of the research process); (2) challenging the traditional relationship between the researcher and the subject and its link to scientific research and the validity of findings; (3) engaging in consciousness raising about the realities of women's lives as part of the methodological process; (4) empowering women within a patriarchal society through their participation in research; and (5) an awareness by the researcher of the ethical costs of the research process and a need to protect their subjects (Cook & Fonow, 1986).

For many researchers who study women in the criminal justice system, the use of feminist methodologies is particularly beneficial. Not only does it enable researchers to explore in depth the issues that women face as victims and offenders, but it also provides the opportunity for the researchers to delve into their topics in a way that traditional methods fail to explore, such as the context of women's lives and their experiences in offending and victimization. For example, a simple survey question might inquire about whether an incarcerated woman has ever been victimized. We know that scholarship on incarcerated women has consistently documented the relationship between early-life victimization and participation in crime in adolescent and adult life. Yet traditional methods may underestimate the extent and nature of the victimization because the women may not understand the question or identify their experiences in this way. Feminist methodologies allow not only for the exploration of these issues at a deeper level but also for scholars to develop an understanding of the multifaceted effects of these experiences.

While many feminist researchers largely employ qualitative tactics, it is important to note that the use of feminist methods does not exclude the use of quantitative methods. In fact, quantitative methods can yield valuable data on the experiences of women (Westmarland, 2001). For example, survey data can yield information on the presence of gender discrimination, such as the sexual harassment among women in policing. In addition, the use of quantitative data and statistics is often useful for legislators when developing policies. Reinharz (1992) provides the example of the use of statistics in the development of sexual harassment policies whereby quantitative data "encouraged the establishment of sexual harassment committees in universities and . . . eventually provided legal redress for individuals" (p. 80). Indeed, researchers who study issues of women and crime can benefit from the lessons of feminist methodologies in their use of both quantitative and qualitative methods.

While feminist methods can provide valuable resources for the study of women and crime, feminist methods are not limited to issues of gender. Rather, feminist methodologies employ tools that are applicable across criminological topics.

By recognizing from the outset the class, racial, and gendered structures of oppression that may be at work in women's lives, this method gives voice to the larger structural processes that shape the experiences that often go unseen and unheard by others. Thus, this method provides a framework for building trust with those participants who may be unsure about the research process and creates opportunities for understanding individuals and groups who may very well be inaccessible when approached in any other way (Westervelt & Cook, 2007, p. 35).

Conclusion

The feminist movement has had a significant effect on the experience of women in the criminal justice system—from victims to offenders to workers. Today, the efforts of the pioneers of feminist criminology have led to an increased understanding of what leads a woman to engage in crime and the effects of her life experiences on her offending patterns, as well as the challenges in her return to the community. In addition, the victim experience has changed for many women in that their voices are beginning to be heard by a system that either blamed them for their victimization or ignored them entirely in years past. The feminist movement has also shed light on what it means to be a woman working within the criminal justice system and the challenges that she faces every day as a woman in this field. While women have experienced significant progress over the last century, there are still many challenges that they continue to face as offenders, victims, and workers within the world of criminal justice.

/// SUMMARY

- The terms *sex* and *gender* are often used interchangeably, but they have different implications for research on women and crime.

- Women are significantly more likely to be victimized by someone they know and are overrepresented in crimes such as sexual assault and intimate partner violence.

- Feminist criminologists have identified a significant link between victimization and offending.

- Many criminal justice occupations are male dominated and reflect gendered assumptions about women and work within these realms.

- Data from the Uniform Crime Reports (UCR) and National Incident-Based Reporting System (NIBRS) often fail to identify much of female victimization, because crimes of rape, sexual assault, and intimate partner abuse go largely underreported.

- Victimization studies, such as the National Crime Victimization Survey (NCVS), help illuminate the dark figure of crime by collecting data on crimes that are not reported to police.

- Self-report studies, such as the National Intimate Partner and Sexual Violence Survey (NISVS), provide estimates of the prevalence of rape, sexual assault, intimate partner abuse, and stalking in the United States.

- Feminist research methods give women a voice in the research process and influence how data on gender are collected.

/// KEY TERMS

Dark figure of crime 13

Feminism 2

Feminist criminology 3

Feminist research methods 17

Gender gap 5

Gendered justice 1

National Crime Victimization Survey (NCVS) 13

National Incident-Based Reporting System (NIBRS) 11

National Intimate Partner and Sexual Violence Survey (NISVS) 14

National Violence Against Women Survey (NVAWS) 14

Uniform Crime Reports (UCR) 7

/// DISCUSSION QUESTIONS

1. What impact has feminism had on the study of women and crime?

2. Discuss how the Uniform Crime Reports (UCR) and the National Incident-Based Reporting System (NIBRS) represent the measure of female offending and victimization in society.

3. How do datasets, such as the National Crime Victimization Survey (NCVS), the National Violence Against Women Survey (NVAWS), and National Intimate Partner and Sexual Violence Survey (NISVS), investigate issues of violence against women?

4. How do feminist research methods inform studies on women and crime?

/// WEB RESOURCES

Centers for Disease Control and Prevention: http://www.cdc.gov

Crime in the United States 2015: https://ucr.fbi.gov/crime-in-the-u.s/2015/crime-in-the-u.s.-2015

National Crime Victimization Survey: http://www.icpsr.umich.edu/icpsrweb/NACJD/NCVS/

National Incident-Based Reporting System: http://www.icpsr.umich.edu/icpsrweb/NACJD/NIBRS/

Uniform Crime Reports: http://www.fbi.gov/about-us/cjis/ucr/ucr

United Nations Survey of Crime Trends and Operations of Criminal Justice Systems: https://www.unodc.org/unodc/en/data-and-analysis/statistics/data.html

---

Visit **study.sagepub.com/mallicoat3e** to access additional study tools, including eFlashcards, web quizzes, web resources, video resources, and SAGE journal articles.

How to Read a Research Article

As a student of criminology and criminal justice, you may have learned about the types of research that scholars engage in. In many cases, researchers publish the findings of their studies as articles in academic journals. In this section, you will learn how to read these types of articles and how to understand what researchers are saying about issues related to criminology and criminal justice.

Several different types of articles are published in academic journals. As a student of criminology and criminal justice, you may at some point be given an assignment as part of your class that asks you to combine the findings of several articles. This is an example of a literature review. In some cases, a journal may publish a literature review, which is designed to provide a consolidated review of the research on a particular issue related to crime and justice. Articles can also be theoretical in nature. In these cases, the author is using the literature to advance a new idea or perspective. You will find several examples of these types of articles throughout this text.

In addition to theoretical articles or articles that review the existing literature in the field, journal articles publish pieces that contain original research. These articles are very different from a theoretical article or a review of the literature. These types of article focus on examining a hypothesis (or set of hypotheses) through an examination of information (or data) the researcher has collected. Generally speaking, a research article that is published in an academic journal includes five basic elements: (1) an introduction, (2) a review of the literature related to the current study, (3) the methods used by the researcher to conduct the study, (4) the findings or results of the research, and (5) a discussion of the results and/or conclusion.

Research in the social sciences generally comes in two basic forms: quantitative research and qualitative research. Quantitative research often involves surveys of groups of people or an examination of some previously collected data, and the results are reported using numbers and statistics. Qualitative research can involve interviews, focus groups, and case studies and relies on words and quotes to tell a story. In this book, you will find examples of both of these types of research studies.

In the introduction section of the article, the author will typically describe the nature of the study and present a hypothesis. A hypothesis frames the intent of the research study. In many cases, the author will state the hypothesis directly. For example, a research study in criminology or criminal justice might pose the following hypothesis: As the number of arrests increases, the length of the prison sentence will increase. Here, the author is investigating whether a relationship exists between a defendant's prior criminal record and sentence length. Similar to a hypothesis is the research question. Whereas a hypothesis follows an "if X happens, then Y will occur" format, research questions provide a path of inquiry for the research study. For example, a research question in criminology might ask, "What are the effects of a criminal record on the likelihood of incarceration?" While the presentation of a hypothesis and the presentation of a research question differ from each other, their intent is the same as each sets out a direction for the research study and may reference the expected results of the study. It is then left up to the researcher(s) and their data findings to determine whether they prove or disprove their hypothesis or if the results of their study provide an answer to their research question.

The next section of the article is the literature review. In this section, the author provides a review of the previous research conducted on this issue and the results of these studies. The purpose of the literature review is to set the stage for the current research and provide the foundation for why the current study is important to the field of criminology and criminal justice. Some articles will separate the literature review into its own section, while others will include this summary within the introductory section. Using the example from our earlier sample hypothesis, a literature review will consider what other scholars have said about the relationship between criminal history and incarceration and how their findings relate to the current research study. It may also point out how the current study differs from the research that has previously been conducted.

In the methods section, the researcher presents the type of data that will be used in the current study. As mentioned earlier, research can be either quantitative or qualitative (and some studies may have both types of data within the same research project). In the methods section, the researcher will discuss who the participants of the study were; how the data were collected (interview, survey, observation, etc.); when, where, and how long the study took place; and how the data were processed. Each of these stages represents a key part of the research experience, and it is important for researchers to carefully document and report on this process.

The results section details the findings of the study. In quantitative studies, the researchers use statistics (often accompanied by tables, charts, or graphs) to explain whether the results of the study support or reject the hypothesis/research question. There are several different types of statistics and analysis that might be used. These can generally be divided into three categories: (1) descriptive, (2) bivariate, and (3) multivariate. Descriptive statistics are generally used to describe the demographics of the sample, such as the average age of the respondents, their racial/ethnic identity, or their sex/gender. Bivariate statistics are used to compare two different variables. In this book, you may find examples where survey responses are compared between males and females. You should note which of these relationships are significant, meaning that the effect is not likely to have occurred by chance but instead reflects an important difference or result in the data. Most research places statistical significance at the .05 level. Finally, multivariate statistics, such as regression analyses, are used to look for differences in one variable while controlling for the effect of other variables. In qualitative studies, the researchers look for themes in the narrative data. Whereas quantitative studies rely on numbers, the qualitative studies in this text use words to describe the stories related to women and crime.

The research article concludes with a discussion and summary of the findings. The findings are often discussed within the context of the hypothesis or research question and relate the findings of this research study to related research in the field. Often, scholars will highlight their findings in light of the methods used in the study or the limitations of the study. The section concludes with recommendations for future research or may discuss the policy implications of the research findings.

Now that you've learned a bit about the different types of articles and the different components of a research article, let us apply these concepts to one of the articles here in your book. Depending on the type of article, some of these concepts may not apply to your analysis. This article appears in the second section of this book.

Women From Different Ethnic Groups and Their Experiences Within Victimization and Seeking Help

1. What type of article is this? Is it a theoretical article, a review of the existing literature, or an article that contains original research?

   - This article contains original research.

2. What is the thesis or main idea of this article?

   - The main idea of this article looks the prevalence of victimization for women of different racial and ethnic backgrounds and the differences by which these groups sought help managing this experience.

3. If this is a research article, what is the hypothesis or research question?

- There are three research questions in this article: (1) What is the prevalence of abuse for four different categories (child physical abuse, child sexual abuse, adult physical abuse, adult sexual abuse) among women with different racial and ethnic identities (Caucasian, African American and Latina)? (2) Do these women disclose their victimization, and if so, whom do they disclose to? (3) What types of services do women seek out to manage their victimization experience?

4. How does the previous literature answer these issues?

- The authors discuss the theoretical context around how and why women engage in help seeking and whether there are differences based on ethnicity.

5. What is the sample used in this study? How were the data for this research collected?

- This study involves data from three different populations: a state prison, several domestic violence and sexual assault organizations, and four general areas in the community. Recruitment flyers were posted in both English and Spanish in order to gather a diverse sample. Study participants were required to be at least 18 years old to participate and received a $25 cash incentive for their participation in the study (except for those participants who were from the state prison).

6. Is this a quantitative or qualitative study? If it is a quantitative study, what types of statistics are used? If it is a qualitative study, how are the data organized?

- In looking at the results section, you can determine that this is a quantitative study through its use of numbers and statistics. Data were collected via a 1-hour face-to-face interview. Data were tested using ANOVA and chi-square analyses to see whether there were any significant differences between the three racial/ethnic groups. Regression analysis was also used to see which variables were significant predictors in the use of tangible and professional services and support.

7. What are the results, and how do(es) the author(s) present the results?

- The authors present the data in five different tables. The first table looks at the descriptive data by race/ethnicity, the type of victimization that was experienced, whether they disclosed the abuse and whom they disclosed to. Overall, the sample experienced 2.48 different types of abuse. Caucasian women experienced the highest number of abuse types, followed by Latina women and African American women. The second table reports the tangible types of social service and support that women engaged in following their victimization, by race/ethnicity. Results note that African American women engaged in the greatest number of support options (3.50), compared to White women (2.97) and Latina women (2.38). Table 3 reports the types of professional social science and support that the women used. Here, white women used significantly greater number of supports (5.26) compared to African American women (4.50) and Latina women (3.59). The fourth table presents regression analysis for the use of tangible services and support. This analysis found that previously receiving welfare support and the number of experiences with abuse was significantly associated with seeking out tangible support for the victimization. The fifth table replicates this model for the use of professional services and support. In this model, the number of experiences with abuse, whether they disclosed physical IPV to formal supports, age and being recruited from an agency (compared to prison or the community) all significantly increased the use of professional services and support.

These models tell us that as the frequency of abuse increases, so does the likelihood of seeking help for victimization. While there were differences by race/ethnicity between individual variables, these differences disappear in predicting the type of services used.

8. Do you believe the author(s) provided a persuasive argument? Why or why not?

- While the assessment of whether the authors provided a persuasive argument is ultimately up to the reader, the data in this study do provide an interesting look at how women from different racial and ethnic groups seek help on both the frequency and type of victimization, as well as the types of help seeking that they engage in.

9. Who is the intended audience of this article?

- In thinking about the intended audience of the article, it may be useful to ask yourself, "Who will benefit from reading this article?" This article appeared in an academic journal, which is typically read by students, professors, scholars, and justice officials. Here, the information in the article can not only add to the classroom experience for students and professors who study this issue but also can ultimately influence practitioners who provide these resources to their communities.

10. What does the article add to your knowledge of the subject?

- The answer to this question will vary for each student, because it asks students to reflect about what they learned from this research and how it relates to their previous experience with the topic. An example from this article might be the understanding that while women of different racial and ethnic groups experience different rates and types of victimization, these results are not necessarily significant in predicting whether they will seek help or the types of help that they will utilize.

11. What are the implications for criminal justice policy that can be derived from this article?

- While this article does not necessarily influence criminal justice policy, the results from this study can have an impact on both the types of resources that are offered to women who experience victimization and how these offerings might alter based on cultural differences.

Now that you've seen these concepts applied to an article, continue this practice as you go through each reading in your text. Some articles will be easier to understand while others will be more challenging. You can refer back to this example if you need help with additional articles in the book.

READING /// 1

As you learned in the section, feminist criminology challenged not only the male-dominated views of criminality but also provided a new perspective for understanding the offending behaviors of women. Here, Drs. Chesney-Lind and Morash argue that while feminist criminology has made a number of valuable contributions to the discipline, the field needs to expand beyond its traditional boundaries in order to move toward a global understanding of gender and crime.

Transformative Feminist Criminology
A Critical Re-thinking of a Discipline

Meda Chesney-Lind and Merry Morash

Introduction

Early theories to explain delinquency, crime, and victimization were actually limited to theorizing male deviance, male criminality, and male victimization with a specific focus of showcasing the utility of the positivist paradigm to the study of the distributions and causes of these phenomena. Thus, the founders of criminology almost completely overlooked women's crime, and they ignored, minimized, and trivialized female victimization (Hughes, 2005). When they did consider women, they considered them in relation to men, and discussions of these relations rarely if ever included details of the horrific violence that many women suffered at the hands of those men (or blamed the woman for the assaults).

Based on the assumption that aspects of the social world could be precisely measured and clearly demonstrably linked as causes and effects, positivist methodology came to dominate criminology by the mid-twentieth century (see Deegan, 1990). This perspective emphasized the researcher as objective and detached from both the data collection process and the use of the findings. No consideration was given to the effect of field researchers on study participants or the potential that social phenomenon are given their meaning by individuals, and these meanings are as important as precisely measured "realities." Even those criminologists that used more qualitative data, such as Thrasher (1927) and Cohen (1955), failed to understand how their own gender colored their view of the world, which meant they completely ignored and/or sexualized girls and talked almost exclusively to boys and young men about gangs and delinquency.

Feminist criminology directed attention toward gender as a key force that shapes crime and social control, toward research methods that recognize power differentials between the researcher and the researched, and gave relatively powerless people voice to express their standpoints, and toward action-oriented research to reveal and promote justice.

SOURCE: Chesney-Lind, M., & Morash, M. (2013). Transformative feminist criminology: A critical re-thinking of a discipline. *Journal of Critical Criminology*, *21*(3): 287–304. © Springer Science+Business Media Dordrecht 2013. Reprinted with permission.

Feminist Theory's Unique Focus

To recognize the unique contributions of feminist criminological theory, we first consider what is "missing" in other paradigms, and we present key feminist work that has filled these gaps (Sprague, 2005). Specifically, inconsistent with the longstanding inattention to girls and women caught up in the justice system, research on the early history of US courts showed that concern for girls' immoral conduct fueled the so-called "child-saving movement" which established a separate system of justice for youth and that ended up incarcerating large numbers of girls for sexual offenses for many decades into the twentieth century (Chesney-Lind, 1977; Odem, 1995; Schlossman & Wallach, 1978). Another historical analysis (Rafter, 1990, p. 149–152) revealed that while reformatories housed white women deemed amenable to being "saved" through grooming for work as domestics, particularly in the South after the Civil War, the criminal justice system treated and punished imprisoned African American women as if they were men, requiring them to work alongside men in chain gangs, even subjected them to whipping, like men.

The recognition of women's and girls' variation in experiences based on race, gender, and other differences has become another cornerstone of feminist criminology. Feminist criminologists were also the first to recognize that many girls moved deep into the justice system after they ran away from a sexually abusive parent, were arrested for running or for "survival crime," and were then criminalized by the system (Chesney-Lind, 1989). This discovery stimulated much research on girls' and women's unique pathways into illegal activity and institutions of control (e.g., Belknap & Holsinger, 1998; Davis, 2007; Holsinger, 2000; Van Voorhis, Wright, Salisbury, & Bauman, 2010) and on the high prevalence of victimization among women offenders (e.g., Browne, Miller, & Maguin, 1999; Moe 2004; Richie, 1996).

The inclusion of women and girls in criminological research was catalyzed by the second wave of the feminist movement in the late 60s and early 70s.[1] As might be expected, feminist criminologists of this period brought the insights of feminist theories unrelated to crime and social control into their groundbreaking work; indeed, inter-disciplinarity is another earmark of feminist work. Contemporary criminologists who work from a feminist perspective continue to borrow heavily from the disciplines of women's studies, gender studies, and feminist scholarship in other social sciences and fields of study. Often their keenest insights come when they transgress criminology; that is, they focus on concepts apart from crime, victimization, and justice system; these imported concepts shed light on the operation of gender as it pertains to the core interests of criminology (Cain, 1990).

All the disciplines that contain feminist theory have different strands that vary in several ways: degrees of theoretical attention to intersectionality (i.e., combinations of gender with race, class, ethnicity, and other status markers that affect social life and individuals); preference for particular research methods; integration with constructionist, conflict, or other theoretical paradigms. The best known of the early theoretical influences on criminology were the notions of *radical feminist theory, liberal feminist theory,* and *socialist feminist theory. Radical feminism* stresses that patriarchal gender arrangements lead to men's efforts to control women's sexuality (and their reproductive capacity) often through violence and abuse (e.g., rape and wife battering). Men dominate over women throughout society, and meaningful change requires obliterating gender differences in power and opportunities (Brownmiller, 1975; Millet, 1970). *Liberal feminism* suggests that gender oppression would be reduced or eliminated by altering the way that girls and boys are socialized and by reforming laws and their implementation, for example, by eliminating bias in the sentencing of women and men and between racial groups (Bickle & Peterson, 1991). *Socialist feminism* made an important contribution to understanding that not just gender but also class results in oppression, so for example, countries where women receive little education and hold low occupational status experience high levels of sexual violence against women and produce women's tremendous fear of crime (Yodanis, 2004; also see Martin, Vieraitis, & Britto, 2006; Whaley, 2001). According to socialist feminists, since gender oppression takes on alternative forms and intensity

---

[1]The women's movement has traditionally been divided into two historic "waves," despite the fact that work on the status of women can be dated well before the first of these events, and continued in a rather clear form after the first "wave" passed. Generally, however, the first "wave" is recognized as starting with the Seneca Falls Convention in 1848, and the second "wave" is dated to the publication of Betty Friedan's influential book, *The Feminine Mystique* in 1963.

depending on social class, reforms require change in the economic system (e.g., a shift toward socialism) not just in the sex/gender system.

New schools of thought continue to appear on the feminist theoretical landscape and they, too, are of clear relevance to criminology. Each school has challenged both mainstream criminology and other feminist theory to more fully account for the complexity of how gender is connected to crime and justice. Despite different strands of feminist theory, there are important key concepts and both theoretical and epistemological assumptions that cut across the variants of feminist theory. The centrality of patriarchy and "feminine" and "masculine" identities, intersectionality that recognizes the combined effects of gender and other status markers, agency even of the oppressed, and feminist epistemology and research methods are persistent characteristics of feminist social science, including feminist criminology.

Patriarchy Matters

While the dictionary defines feminism as simply "the theory of the political, economic, and social equality of the sexes" (Merriam-Webster, 2009), the terrain has been made much more complicated in the years that followed that 1895 definition. The *sex/gender system* (also referred to as the *gender organization* and *gender arrangements*) stands as a central concept in feminist theory. The sex/gender system exists globally and in countries, cultures, regions, communities, organizations, families, and other groups. It affects individuals by impacting their identities, imposing gendered expectations, and prohibiting and sanctioning "gender inappropriate" behavior. Patriarchal sex/gender systems are characterized by males' exercise of power and control to oppress women (Hondagneu-Sotelo, 1994). The degree and the form of patriarchy vary by place and time and even for subgroups (e.g., social class, racial, ethnic, and age groups) sharing the same geography and period (Lerner, 1986a, b; Lown, 1983; Pateman, 1988, 1989). According to the ideology of extreme patriarchy, women's orientation should be totally restricted to the home with no participation in education or the workforce (Stankuniene & Maslauskaite, 2008). Slightly less extreme forms of patriarchy allow women to participate in the workforce but husbands and, depending on the culture, other relatives control women's earnings.

The sex/gender system typically functions as a system of social stratification, where both men and women and the tasks they perform are valued differently—with men's assumed qualities and the work they do valued more highly (Conway, Pizzamiglio, & Mount, 1996; Fiske, Cuddy, Glick, Xu, 2002; Gerber, 2009). To illustrate, many citizens and some police associate effective policing with characteristics assumed to be traits for men, especially traits surrounding "aggression, violence, danger, risk taking, and courageousness" (Franklin, 2005, p. 6; also Heidensohn, 1992; Hunt, 1984; Prokos & Padavic, 2002). In highly gendered (Acker, 1990) police organizations, women are stereotyped and channeled into restricted types of police work and support networks, are treated with hostility, and are rejected by other officers just on the basis of their gender (Martin & Jurik, 2007). Practices of exclusion from informal work cultures, gender segregation, differential assignments, sexual harassment, and marginalization of women with family responsibilities also characterize correctional organizations and the settings where legal professionals work (Martin & Jurik, 2007, p. 2).

The feminist conceptualization of the sex-gender system contrasts sharply with representation of a person's biological sex category as an individual-level variable—an approach that is frequently found in traditional criminological discussions of gender. In feminist theory, gender is not a variable nor is it an unchanging personal trait. A person's gender is constructed through actions and interactions to produce a form of "masculinity" or "femininity" that either reproduces or challenges common expectations for gender- appropriate behaviors (West & Zimmerman, 1987; also see West & Fenstermaker, 1995). The sex/gender system at the macro (structural) level affects individuals by affording them access to influence and resources depending on their sex and gender. Thus, to begin to fully explain key phenomenon, such as the gender gap in crime, as well as the seemingly perplexing responses of the criminal justice system to girls and women as both victims and offenders, we must *theorize* gender in terms of individual level identity and interactions embedded in a broader macro-level system of gender arrangements.

Feminist criminologists (e.g., Hunnicutt, 2009; Ogle & Batton, 2009) struggle to keep attention focused on how different forms of patriarchy influence crime, victimization, the justice system, and workers in that system. Importantly, they document inequities and suffering introduced by patriarchal arrangements to protest and change them.

Masculinities and Femininities

In criminology, one important explanation that has traditionally been "missing" from conversations about crime is that boys and men have always committed the most crime, especially of a violent type or in the "crimes of the powerful" category (Daly, 1989; Schwartz, Steffensmeier, & Feldmeyer, 2009; Steffensmeier, Schwartz, Zhong, & Ackerman, 2005). For decades criminologists by and large ignored the gender gap (or dropped girls and women from the analysis as many early longitudinal studies did), which had the effect of normalizing high levels of male violence. Although certainly not the only explanation for men's and boys' high levels of illegal behavior, theories about gender identities are one approach that holds promise in explaining the gender difference. Although feminist theory, by definition, is grounded in women's experience, some critical male scholars (DeKeseredy, 2011; Messerschmidt, 1993; Schwartz & DeKeseredy, 1997; Schwartz & DeKeseredy, this issue) have increasingly adopted feminist perspectives in their own research on men and male behavior as well as women, and they have explored the link of masculinities to crime. Also, feminist criminologists have made major advances by showing the connection of pressure to conform to particular aspects of manhood and male involvements in crime (Anderson & Umberson, 2001; Bowker, 1997; Bui & Morash, 2008).

The feminist perspective calls attention to gender (and thus masculinity) as something that is enacted in the context of patriarchal privilege, class privilege, and racism. The power of this perspective is clearly evident in work by Danner and Carmody (2001) who document how the media accounts of school shootings completely miss the role of gender in these crimes that so horrified the nation. Surveying newspaper coverage of shootings at multiple districts, Danner and Carmody noted that while the media was obsessed with the stories, all the stories "rounded up all the usual suspects"—general culture of violence, violent media, gangs, the access to guns, youth culture, and so forth—with virtually no realization that *all*

the perpetrators were male and the victims were predominantly female.

What about girls? Here the discussion focuses on how girls, particularly girls involved in crime, negotiate feminine norms that tend to reward obedience to authority, particularly male authority, passivity, and nurturance. Consider girls who are gang members. Despite the stereotype of gangs as hyper masculine, girls are present in gangs, and present in very significant numbers (one estimate is that that girls are roughly a third of gang members) (Snyder & Sickmund, 2006). Exactly how do these girls negotiate what some might imagine as a quintessentially male space? Are they simply embracing a "bad girl femininity" as an "aggressive, tough, crazy and violent" gang member? Laidler and Hunt (2001) do an outstanding job of documenting how African American, Latina, and Asian American girls negotiate not only dangerous neighborhoods and risky peer groups (since most girls are in mixed-sex gangs) but also engage in very complicated cultural notions of femininity. Contrary to the construction of gang girls as "a bad ass" (p. 675), they note that girls place a very high value on both "respect" and "respectability." They alternately challenge and embrace notions of traditional femininity through interactions with others in a range of settings but always return to behaviors that involve "defending one's reputation as respectable" (p. 676).

Irwin and Chesney-Lind (2008) build on the insight that girls' and women's crime, even violent crime, is not well understood or explained by simply assuming that girls are mimicking their male counterparts and taking up a form of dangerous masculinity (the "bad ass" perspective). Long dominant in criminology, these theories of "violence" assume that female violence can be explained by the same factors that have long been studied to explain male violence, since these "bad" women are seeking equality with men in the area of violence (and acting just like men). Irwin and Chesney-Lind also identify other approaches to female violence that stress its roots in female victimization in patriarchal society and the role of deteriorated neighborhoods in producing a female version of the "code of the streets" tough femininity, particularly for urban girls of color. Building on these more recent constructions, they conclude that one must examine how the multiple systems of oppression (based on class, race, ethnicity, and gender) interact in complex but co-equal ways to produce contexts where girls' violence makes sense (often as a survival mechanism) rather than understanding gender as something one "does" or doesn't do while negotiating more robust systems of race and class oppression (see Chesney-Lind & Jones, 2010).

Intersectionality

African American scholar and activist bell hooks's book, *Ain't I a Woman* (1981), highlighted and forever invalidated the sole focus on gender. Hooks argued against white feminists who felt that women were denied access to politics because they were stereotyped as frail and delicate. She pointed out that women like her had a history that fully contradicted this imagery, in part because of the hard labor and the severe living conditions imposed on slaves. The challenges of understanding the realities of the lives of women who differ in their combinations of age, color, class, ethnicity, sexual orientation, and other characteristics pervade feminist criminology, and are addressed in attempts to take these intersections into account in understanding individual identity, group and local context, and social structure.

Black feminist criminology makes its contribution by emphasizing race-related structural oppression, the influence of Black community and culture, intimate and familial relations affected by race, and the nature of women's identities as Black, female, of a particular class, and so on (Potter, 2006). In this tradition, Jones (2010) explored and explained the lives of Black girls who confront violence on a daily basis in their communities. Providing an example of feminist theory that attends to identity, context, race, and gender, Jones rejects placing the justice system at the center of the girls' lives and assuming that justice system labeling is a meaningful descriptor for the girls. Instead, she builds theory to show how the girls manage expectations for being "good girls" in communities and schools that are marked by conflict and require an offensive posture and even the use of violence for self-protection.

Agency

Theorists and researchers sometimes ignore women's agency and focus only on their compliance with patriarchal constraints (Gallagher, 2007; Macleod, 1991). Feminist

criminologists instead emphasize agency—an assertion of identity and attempts to steer one's life—even under extreme conditions (Lerner, 1986a, b, p. 239). Although in a context characterized by a constant threat of male and female violence, the girls that Jones (Jones, 2010) studied were active and agentic in navigating between "good" and "ghetto" messages about Black femininity. Similarly, Bosworth and Carrabine (2001) detailed how women in prison, who certainly suffered from a profound loss of freedom, found a variety of ways to resist, to cope with, and to survive the carceral conditions. As a final example, Morash and Haarr (2012) discovered that many women police resisted reproducing traditional female-male stereotypes and hierarchies that devalue traits commonly associated with women. Instead they fashioned complex positive occupational identities that in many cases were not tied to their sex category, but when they were, that associated women's positive attributes with excellent job performance.

Feminist Methodology and Epistemology

Although all sorts of research methods have been used to develop and improve feminist theory (Reinharz, 1992; Sprague, 2005), feminist criminologists have contributed some unique insights on "how we know" about social life and have challenged positivist science norms that render the researcher invisible and study participants powerless. Feminist approaches to research are suited to revealing human agency and the constructed nature of gender identity and structure. The recognition of these features of social life extends to the research process.

Specifically, feminist researchers believe that the subjects of research can contribute crucial information on their experiences, that their understandings are important, and that these experiences must be considered in the context of patriarchy to be understood. They recognize the need to consider the power differentials between the researched and the researcher, and how these differentials affect the production of knowledge (Ramazanoglu, 1989). Burman, Batchelor, and Brown (2001) put these principles into practice in their study of Scottish teenaged girls' views and experiences of violence. They faced many dilemmas in their ethnographic work that over time involved 800 girls. For instance, sometimes discussions of violence led to girls being violent toward each other, raising ethical issues about the appropriateness of group discussion and how the researcher should intervene. Also, researchers were strongly affected by girls' accounts of being bullied, sexually assaulted, or in other ways victimized, in some cases because the researchers had similar experiences during their own childhoods. Researchers struggled, too, with girls' descriptions of hitting or slapping each other as "fun" and "not violence."

The importance of feminist criminology's contribution to research methodology is striking in the literature on violence against women. Depending on whether they use positivist measurement and sampling approaches, researchers have drawn conflicting conclusions: either that men and women are equivalently violent in intimate partner relationships, or that men are markedly more violent and destructive than women. Feminist criminologists emphasize that adequate measurement requires adequate theoretical conceptualization of violence and its context and it must include aspects of male violence (such as stalking and sexual assault that women rarely commit) (DeKeseredy, 2011; Dobash, Dobash, Wilson, & Daly, 1992; Melton &d Belknap, 2003; Miller, 2005).

A valid measure of abuse must differentiate the types of intimate partner violence identified by Johnson and Ferraro (2000): *intimate terrorism,* which is violence used as one of many tactics in a general pattern of extreme effort to control an intimate partner through the combination of physical and emotional abuse; *violent resistance* in self-defense, often just once; *mutual violence* in which domestic partners use controlling and manipulative violence against each other; and *situational couple violence,* which "results from situations or arguments between partners that escalate on occasion into physical violence" (Kelly & Johnson, 2008, p. 485). Shelter and domestic violence advocacy program samples consist primarily of victims of intimate terrorism, but random samples drawn for surveys have high representation of situational violence victims. To bring this point home, we point out that intimate terrorism victims are often prohibited from leaving home, answering the phone, or reading the mail—so they are highly unlikely to take part in any sort of research, unless they are in shelters. By accurately measuring the type of violence and by recognizing the biases introduced by different sampling approaches, research demonstrates that in heterosexual couples, males most

often perpetrate the extremely damaging form of abuse, intimate terrorism, and that misogynist attitudes and gender traditionalism contribute to this form of abusive behavior (Johnson, 2006, 2011).

A central tenet of feminist methodologies is that research methods must be up to the task of producing knowledge that informs and promotes positive social change. As a case in point, guided by feminist theory and methodological approaches, Dobash and Dobash (2004) collected qualitative and quantitative data from a sample of couples. Their findings justified public policies that emphasize men's violence against women as well as cautions against the practice of dual arrests, in which police take couples into custody together. If they had studied a random sample of couples with methods to "count" incidents, Dobash and Dobash might have made recommendations for family therapy to address situational couple violence, thereby ignoring the imbalance of power and danger to the victim when intimate terrorism or violent resistance occurs. To challenge damaging policies and advance those that protect the less powerful, feminist criminologists often collaborate with and carefully listen to the people they study. Additionally, they collaborate with advocates to ensure that theoretical discoveries are translated into program and policy action (Haviland, Frye, & Rajah, 2008).

Challenges for Future Theorizing and Research

As feminist criminology enters the new century, it must embrace two important and exciting challenges: First, in an era of unparalleled inequality, we must find new and powerful ways to continue paying attention to the powerful and the oppressors. We must forcefully present the globalization of the world's issues and the increasing need to see violations of girls and women as human rights issues.

Consistent with the overarching critical criminology paradigm, feminist criminologists have directed attention to a serious limitation of much social science theory, which is its failure to explain the privilege and behavior of powerful people and its complementary concentration on understanding people who lack power (Sprague, 2005, p. 11–12). Given the connection of limited power with female status, feminist criminologists in particular need to be quite careful about "studying down"—that is, focusing exclusively on the powerless—which can result in pathologizing crime victims, or girls and women in conflict with the law, rather than showing how oppressive gender arrangements lead to victimization and harsh punishment. Understanding structures of power and context are crucial.

Globalization brings new challenges to feminist criminologists. Take the attempted assassination of Malala Yousufzai, the 14-year-old Pakistani girl shot in the head by the Taliban for speaking out about girls' rights to an education in October, 2012. Shortly after—in December, 2012—in India there was the terrible gang rape and resulting murder of a 23-year-old medical student, which provoked worldwide outrage, and ultimately a global women's protest that went viral because of the internet (see onebillionrising.org for images). So, if we were asked to chart out the pressing issues for feminist criminology, we would point to the following possibilities.

Malala Yousufzai's courage causes us to see the importance of girls' studies, not just women's studies, because today's girls will be tomorrow's women. The tragic and brutal death in India tells us about tolerance of girls' and women's victimization. As a horrific example, after she was repeatedly raped over a 90-minute period on a public bus she rode with a male friend, who also was severely beaten and left suffering, the couple was dumped on the road. The police who finally showed up argued for two hours about which of them would have to take the seriously beaten couple to the hospital (Pokharel & Rana, 2013). Both incidents blur the boundaries between victimization, crime, and profound human rights violations. They also put in stark focus the explicit failure of certain "courts" and "police" to protect women. Indeed, in some parts of Pakistan, the establishment of Sharia courts actually jail girls and women seeking help for abuse (such as the arrest of women for adultery if they report a rape) and often forcibly return them to their abusers from whom they are trying to escape (Asian Human Rights Commission, 2010; Hadi & Chesney-Lind, 2013).

These incidents are not isolated or unusual in the countries where they occurred or in many countries throughout the world. They are just two examples of a multitude of organized group efforts, in some cases sponsored or tolerated by the State, to enforce extreme patriarchy. The attack on girls' education is not atypical.

Around the world, students, teachers and schools are attacked at an alarming rate. This war against education, in which educating girls is often a motivating factor, gets very little attention or media coverage. But in at least 31 countries education has been the target of intentional attacks for political, ideological, sectarian, religious, military or other reasons. (Winthrop, 2012, p. 2)

In one year, largely motivated by beliefs that girls should not go to school, Pakistan experienced 152 bombings that destroyed schools, and Afghanistan had 35 schools burned; similar patterns occur in parts of Latin America, Europe, Africa, and the Middle East (Winthrop, 2012). Lack of education and resulting dependence on others place girls and women at risk for continued exposure to violence. If they leave or are expelled from their natal or marital families—and expulsion is another form of violence—they may turn to prostitution or illegal acts to survive and keep their children alive, and they often must live in dangerous places that expose them to victimization and the need to defend themselves, sometimes violently. The connection of girls and women being victims and being caught up as offenders in the courts and correctional programs and institutions is strong, and it is many times a causal connection.

Just as globalization alerts us to violence against women throughout the world, it directs attention to U.S. policies that bring women into prisons outside of the United States. Not only did the U.S. "war on drugs" develop into a "war against women" who in increasing proportions came to make up non-violent prison populations charged with drug-related offenses (Chesney-Lind, 1977; Johnson, 2006). Also, businesses that run and supply prisons, U.S. government entities, and U.S. politicians have promoted arrest, prosecution, and incarceration of women worldwide (Richie, 2012; Sudbury, 2002). U.S. pressure to criminalize people involved in the international drug trade and in prostitution had the unanticipated effect of promoting incarceration of women whose only means of survival, economically or in face of pressures from criminal men, is to carry drugs or prostitute themselves (Kempadoo, 2005).

One aspect of globalization is the movement of people across borders. There are an estimated 214 million international migrants worldwide, and 49 percent of them are women (http:// www.iom.int/jahia/Jahia/about-migration/facts-and-figures/lang/en). Migrant women are at high risk for sexual exploitation and violence by intimate partners (Piper, 2003). Hoping to improve their lives, women who join men as "picture brides" may barely know the men they marry, if they know them at all. They often find themselves vulnerable to abuse because they are isolated in a new country, unable to speak the local language, and unfamiliar with the justice system and sources of help. Alternatively, women may be lured to foreign countries to take jobs where they are exploited or forced to work in the sex trades. These and other circumstances create new patterns of girls' and women's victimization and new challenges for justice system response.

Although we advocate theoretical and research attention to conditions for women internationally, it is important to recognize that in the United States, which Hausmann, Tyson, and Zahida (2012) scores as providing equivalent education to females and males, inequality in economic participation and opportunity place women at risk for being unable to leave abusive relationships, move out of dangerous neighborhoods, or resist earning money through illegal means. Dramatic cuts in welfare support that began in 1996 leave increasing numbers of women (and their children) either without income or in low-paying jobs that do not provide medical or other benefits (Peterson, Zong, & Jones-DeWeever, 2002). The so-called feminization of poverty (formation of female headed households, fathers' failure to support children, and segregation of women in low-paying traditionally female occupations) leads to women's increased involvement in consumer-based crimes, such as shoplifting and welfare fraud (Chesney-Lind & Pasko, 2011; Steffensmeier & Streifel, 1992).

Theory as a tool to fuel the disassembly and replacement of destructive processes in the name of crime control and prevention is long over-due both in the United States and in all the countries that are tempted to emulate the tolerance of violence against women and the penal regimes that the United States has become so reliant on. Does the new century offer any hopeful signs for such a conversion in theory? The very fact that progressive and critical criminology, and particularly feminist criminology, has survived three decades of furious backlash politics gives us reason for hope. Beyond that, there is the vitality of our field. To do feminist criminology, this article has posited, does not necessarily mean that one is restricted to what was once the standard trilogy of our field: women as offenders, victims, and workers in the criminal justice system. Instead, the whole of the field of criminology can fruitfully be rethought from a feminist perspective. Finally, there is a growing body of international research, particularly in the area of the victimization of women, that allows us to hope that feminist criminology will become globally relevant in the decades to come. As it does so, the field will do more than simply "document and count" women's victimizations; instead, it will begin to act across "national" boundaries to name the problem and to reframe it in ways that make clear the centrality of the human rights of girls and women and also to find ways to take action on behalf of victimized and criminalized women.

Future Directions for Theory and Research

Feminist criminologists, along with other critical theorists, must increasingly embrace the insights of critical studies, particularly the role of the media in the construction and framing of the narratives that shape and define the "crime problem" (and the implicit solutions to same). The corporate media, whether print or television, turn to crime stories, along with celebrity gossip and scandals, as reliable front-page staples for a variety of reasons. This mix provides a sensationalistic and profitable filler for newspapers and television stations with shrinking newsrooms and diminished appetites to engage in serious investigative journalism (Hamilton, 1998; McManus, 1994).

Postmodern feminism directs attention to the "construction of truth" in such cultural outlets as the media, which can play a very critical role in the public's perception of the crime "problem." It is this emphasis on culture and the production of knowledge rather than on structure that is an earmark of postmodernism (Milovanovic, this issue). Websdale (1996), for example, documented how the media portrayal of sexual assault and abuse as perpetrated by strangers supported the passage of a Washington state law permitting "indefinite civil commitment" of sexual predators but excluded husbands and fathers assaulting wives and children as potential perpetrators. The law, supported by newspaper reports, creates a discourse that sex crimes rather than routine are "dreadful but rare" events that require tough sanctions rather than a confrontation with patriarchal families (Websdale & Alvarez, 1998 p. 65). In an earlier piece, Websdale and Alvarez documented how the corporate media traditionally discusses the murder of women by intimate partners by using an approach they call "forensic journalism." Here, the reader is given vivid and dramatic details of the event and is ultimately told "more and more about less and less." In essence, the readers are left with salacious details but little actual information that might prevent future such occurrences (Websdale & Alvarez, 1998).

Regarding offenders, we know that media exposure to crime stories does, in fact, have an impact: Heavier viewers of local television news are more likely to fear crime and criminal victimization (Romer, Jamieson, & Aday, 2003, p. 101). This is attributed to "pervasive coverage of violent crime stories," which also tends to increase fear of African Americans and other minorities who are disproportionately featured in crime stories (Romer, Jamieson, & DeCoteau, 1998). Research has shown that ideas about crime and criminals are based, in large part, on the stories that individuals learn about from the media (Antunes & Hurley, 1977; Chermak, 1994; Chiricos & Eschholz, 2002). A broader question, though, is the degree to which crime journalism influences punitive crime policies such as "the war on drugs" and "mass incarceration (see Brennan, Chesney-Lind, Vandenberg, & Wulf-Ludden, in press)."

We also know that the race of women offenders dramatically affects the way the media treat them. In a study of drug stories appearing on the front pages of 17 national newspapers, it was found that the stories about minority women who committed street-drug offenses were considerably more negative than the stories about white women who committed such offenses. The chief difference was the emphasis that journalists tended to place on an offender's degree of guilt, harm to another person, and reform potential. As an example, stories about white women drug offenders often included pictures of their families on a couch and discussions of a new drug program, while women of color were often portrayed as hopelessly drug addicted, and getting re-arrested and re-committed as a result (Brennan, Chesney-Lind, Vandenberg, & Wulf-Ludden, in press).

In an era of around-the-clock news coverage as well as the use of crime as entertainment, the media often misrepresents the majority of women who break the law and hides the circumstances of women who act with violence. Women who act violently are portrayed in the news as "irrational" and even "demonic," especially if they act against children (Grabe, Trager, Lear, & Rauch, 2006). By paying much more attention to violence by women than by men, the media suggests (incorrectly) that women are well represented among violent offenders (Naylor, 2001; Schlesinger, Tumber, & Murdock, 1991). Documentaries, televised news, and talk shows portray imprisoned women as violent and sex-crazed (Cecil, 2007), and "crack moms" are blamed for damage to unborn children (Humphries, 1999). Especially racial and ethnic minority women are described as abnormal and individually flawed (Mann & Zatz, 1996). Evidence that women are not and never have been as violent or criminal as men contradicts both media images and official punitive responses. The potential for such portrayals to influence responses to women offenders deserves more attention, because arrest statistics but not victim surveys show a narrowing in the gender gap for assaults (Schwartz, Steffensmeier, & Feldmeyer, 2009), and arrests of women for drunk driving are out of proportion to behavioral indicators (Schwartz & Rookey, 2008).

Conclusion

Beyond the idea of the increasing role of globalism and of the media—including video footage that we can now carry with us in our pockets—we would contend, there is a continuing need to better theorize feminist notions of patriarchy and systematically explore how patriarchal privilege is enforced though routine criminal justice practices. Borrowing from work of feminist political scientists such as Walby (1990), which early on identified that liberal notions of "public" and "private" greatly disadvantaged women, we must expand our thinking about the links between the observed patterns of women's victimization, women's offending, and women's experience with the criminal justice system within the context of patriarchy. The question of how masculinities or some other forces create the gender gap in criminality also begs for an answer.

We must also think about how feminist theorizing assists us in building a less violent and more just world, including systems of crime control that take us out of the penal regimes of the past century. Feminist criminologists have challenged the masculinist bias in their field, and they continue to do so today. As an example, both of us firmly believe that the assumption that fields grow and develop out of male styles of interaction and argument, or what might be called "mental combat," is a flawed way to think about intellectual work. We instead think that what builds knowledge is open conversation, real respect, and real listening. Given the growing significance of crime policy and the criminal justice system in an era of "governing through crime" (Simon, 2007) and mass incarceration of women in many parts of the world (Carlen, 2002; Carlen & Toombs, 2006; Lee, 2007; Mauer, 1999), the feminist perspective on crime in modern society remains all the more vital. Feminist criminologists have proposed alternatives to the expensive and damaging status quo. For example, drawing on Gilligan's (1982) understanding of the importance of care in girls' and women's moral thinking, Daly and Stubbs (2006) suggest that restorative justice may track with the feminist values of care and valuation of relationships as an alternative to the current emphasis on justice. Such notions of reconciliation, truth telling, and social responses to law violating that heal rather than punish and incapacitate will not only better reduce crime but also humanize the current dehumanizing systems of punitive courts and institutions, jails, and prisons that can oppress and destroy not only those held within them but those who are employed to serve as guards and wardens.

Theory as a tool to fuel the disassembly and replacement of destructive processes in the name of crime control and prevention is long over-due both in the United States and in all the countries that are tempted to emulate the penal regimes the United States has become so reliant on.

Does the new century offer any hopeful signs for such a conversion in theory? One can only hope that the right-wing control over the political process, which established crime as a code word for race in national politics, is finally winding down (and losing power in the United States). One would wish that this were a product of moral outrage, but it is also explained by demographics. Simply put, the desire to ever expand the racist, sexist, and homophobic rhetoric has run into a numbers problem. Once you seek to criminalize huge swaths of *all* minority groups in the United States while also seeking to dramatically contract on women's access to safe and legal birth control, you have alienated enough large constituencies to no longer hold national public office (Hadi & Chesney-Lind, 2013; Livingston, 2013).

In considering the future, we are cautiously optimistic that a feminist approach to the crime problem might be heard. Regardless of the odds, though, our work is informed by the expectation that we act as feminists to improve the social world in which we have found ourselves. This means, of course, that we again face the query: What constitutes feminism and being a feminist? Here, we'd like to conclude with first wave author and activist Rebecca West's wry, and as it turns out, timeless observation:

> I myself have never been able to find out what feminism is; I only know that people call me a feminist whenever I express sentiments that differentiate me from a doormat or a prostitute (West & Marcus, 1982)

In this article, we hope we have established that being called a feminist is not an insult or a signal that one cannot do good, scholarly or scientifically valid work (Faludi, 1989; Sprague, 2005). Instead, engaging in feminism and feminist theory offers all criminology incredible intellectual vitality and a recommitment to go beyond the collecting and disseminating of knowledge to seeking a just, equitable, and healthy world for all.

/// DISCUSSION QUESTIONS

1. What is intersectionality and what contributions does it make to feminist criminology?

2. How can feminist criminology help scholars understand the nature of male offending?

3. What challenges does feminist criminology face in the 21st century?

References

Acker, J. (1990). Hierarchies, jobs, bodies: A theory of gendered organizations. *Gender and Society, 4*(2), 139–158.

Anderson, K. L., & Umberson, D. (2001). Gendering violence: Masculinity and power in men's accounts of domestic violence. *Gender and Society, 15*(3), 358–380.

Antunes, G. E., & Hurley, P. A. (1977). The representation of criminal events in Houston's two daily newspapers. *Journalism Quarterly, 54*(4), 756–760.

Artz, S. (1998). *Sex, power and the violent school.* Toronto: Trifolium Books.

Asian Human Rights Commission. (2010, December 23). *Pakistan: Sharia Court launches major challenge to protection of women.* Retrieved from http://www.humanrights.asia/news/ahrc-news/AHRC-STM- 268-2010.

Belknap, J., & Holsinger, K. (1998). An overview of delinquent girls: How theory and practice have failed and the need for innovative changes. In R. T. Zaplin (Ed.), *Female crime and delinquency: Critical perspectives and effective interventions.* Gaithersberg, MD: Aspen.

Bickle, G. S., & Peterson, R. D. (1991). The impact of gender-based family roles on criminal sentencing. *Social Problems, 38*(3), 372.

Bosworth, M., & Carrabine, E. (2001). Reassessing resistance: Race, gender, and sexuality in prison. *Punishment and Society: The International Journal of Penology, 3*(4), 501–515.

Bowker, L. (1997). *Masculinity and violence.* Thousand Oaks: Sage.

Brennan, P., Chesney-Lind, M., Vandenberg, A., & Wulf-Ludden, T. (In Press). The saved and the damned: Racial and ethnic differences in media constructions of female drug offenders. *Journal of Criminal Justice and Popular Culture.*

Brownmiller, S. (1975). *Against our will: Men, women, and rape.* New York: Simon and Schuster.

Brown, L., Chesney-Lind, M., & Stein, N. (2007). Patriarchy matters: Toward a gendered theory of teen violence and victimization. *Violence Against Women, 13*(12), 1249–1273.

Browne, A., Miller, B., & Maguin, E. (1999). Prevalence and severity of lifetime physical and sexual victimization among incarcerated women. *International Journal of Law and Psychiatry, 22*(3–4), 301–322.

Bui, H., & Morash, M. (2008). Immigration, masculinity, and intimate partner violence from the standpoint of domestic violence service providers and Vietnamese-origin women. *Feminist Criminology, 3*(3), 191–215.

Burman, M. J., Batchelor, S. A., & Brown, J. A. (2001). Researching girls and violence: Facing the dilemmas of fieldwork. *British Journal of Criminology, 41,* 443–459.

Cain, M. (1990). Towards transgression: New directions in feminist criminology. *International Journal of the Sociology of Law, 18*(1), 1–18.

Campbell, R., Adams, A. E., & Wasco, S. M. (2009). Training interviewers for research on sexual violence: A qualitative study of rape survivors' recommendations for interview practice. *Violence Against Women, 15*(5), 595–617.

Carlen, P. (2002). Controlling measures: The repackaging of common sense opposition to women's imprisonment in England and Canada. *Criminal Justice, 2*(2), 155–172.

Carlen, P., & Tombs, J. (2006). Reconfigurations of penalty: The ongoing case of the women's imprisonment and reintegration industries. *Theoretical Criminology, 10*(3), 337–360.

Cecil, D. K. (2007). Looking beyond the caged heat: Media images of women in prison. *Feminist Criminology, 2*(4), 304–326.

Chaudhuri, S., Morash, M., & Yingling, J. (In Press). Marriage migration, patriarchal bargains, and wife abuse: A study of South Asian women. *Violence Against Women.*

Chermak, S. (1994). Body count news: How crime is presented in the news media. *Justice Quarterly, 11*(4), 561–582.

Chesney-Lind, M. (1977). Judicial paternalism and the female status offender: Training women to know their place. *Crime and Delinquency, 23*(2), 121–130.

Chesney-Lind, M. (1989). Girls' crime and woman's place: Toward a feminist model of female delinquency. *Crime and Delinquency, 35*(1), 5.

Chesney-Lind, M. (2006). Patriarchy, crime and justice: Feminist criminology in an era of backlash. *Feminist Criminology, 1*(1), 6–26.

Chesney-Lind, M., & Morash, M. (Eds.). (2011). *Feminist theories of crime. Volume in theoretical criminology series.* Surrey, UK: Ashgate Publishing Limited.

Chesney-Lind, M., & Pasko, L. (2011). *The female offender* (3rd ed.). Thousand Oaks: Sage.

Chiricos, T., & Eschholz, S. (2002). The racial and ethnic typification of crime and the criminal typification of race and ethnicity in local television news. *Journal of Research in Crime and Delinquency, 39*(4), 400–420.

Cohen, A. K. (1955). *Delinquent boys.* Glencoe, IL: The Free Press.

Conway, M., Pizzamiglio, M. T., & Mount, L. (1996). Status, communality, and agency: Implications for stereotypes of gender and other groups. *Journal of Personality and Social Psychology, 71*(1), 25–38.

Daly, K. (1989). Gender and varieties of white-collar crime. *Criminology, 27*(4), 769–797.

Daly, K., & Stubbs, J. (2006). Feminist engagement with restorative justice. *Theoretical Criminology, 10,* 9–28.

Danner, M. J. E., & Carmody, D. (2001). Missing gender in cases of infamous school violence: Investigating research and media explanations. *Justice Quarterly, 18*(1), 87–114.

Davis, C. P. (2007). At-risk girls and delinquency. *Crime and Delinquency, 53*(3), 408–435.

Deegan, M. J. (1990). *Jane Addams and the men of the Chicago school.* New Brunswick: Transaction Books.

DeKeseredy, W. (2011). *Violence against women: Myths, facts, and controversies.* Toronto, ON, Canada: University of Toronto Press.

Dobash, R. P., & Dobash, R. E. (2004). Women's violence to men in intimate relationships: Working on a puzzle. *British Journal of Criminology, 44,* 324–349.

Dobash, R. P., Dobash, R. E., Wilson, M., & Daly, M. (1992). The myth of sexual symmetry in marital violence. *Social Problems, 39*(1), 71–91.

Faludi, S. (1989). *Backlash: The undeclared war against American women*. New York: Crown.

Fiske, S. T., Cuddy, A. J. C., Glick, P., & Xu, J. (2002). A model of (often mixed) stereotype content: Competence and warmth respectively follow from perceived status and competition. *Journal of Personality and Social Psychology, 82*(6), 878–902.

Flavin, J. (2001). Feminism for the mainstream criminologist. *Journal of Criminal, 29*(4), 271–285.

Franklin, C. A. (2005). Male peer support and the police culture: Understanding the resistance and opposition of women in policing. *Women & Criminal Justice, 16*, 1–25.

Gallagher, S. K. (2007). Agency, resources, and identity: Lower-income women's experiences in Damascus. *Gender and Society, 21*(2), 227–249.

Gerber, G. L. (2009). Status and the gender stereotyped personality traits: Toward an integration. *Sex Roles, 61*(5/6), 297–316.

Gilligan, C. (1982). *In a different voice: Psychological theory and women's development*. Cambridge, MA: Harvard University Press.

Grabe, M. E., Trager, K. D., Lear, M., & Rauch, J. (2006). Gender and crime news: A case study test of the chivalry hypothesis. *Mass Communication & Society, 9*, 137–163.

Hadi, S. T., & Chesney-Lind, M. (2013). Silence and the criminalization of victimization: On the need for an international feminist criminology. In B. Heather, & B. Arrigo (Eds.), *Routledge handbook on international crime and justice studies*. New York: Routledge.

Hamilton, J. T. (1998). *Channeling violence: The economic market for violent television programming*. NJ: Princeton University Press.

Hausmann, R., Tyson, L. D., & Zahida, S. (2012). *The global gender gap report 2012*. Geneva, Switzerland.

Haviland, M., Frye, V., & Rajah, V. (2008). Harnessing the power of advocacy research collaborations: Lessons from the field. *Feminist Criminology, 3*(4), 247–275.

Heidensohn, F. (1992). *Women in control?: The role of women in law enforcement*. Oxford: Clarendon Press.

Holsinger, K. (2000). Feminist perspectives on female offending: Examining real girls' lives. *Women and Criminal Justice, 12*(1), 23–51.

Hondagneu-Sotelo, P. (1994). *Gendered transitions: Mexican experiences of immigration*. Berkeley: University of California Press.

Hughes, L. A. (2005). The representation of females in criminological research. *Women and Criminal Justice, 16*(1/2), 1–28.

Humphries, D. (1999). *Crack mothers: Pregnancy, drugs, and the media*. Columbus: Ohio State University Press.

Hunt, J. (1984). The development of rapport through the negotiation of gender in field work among police. *Human Organization, 43*, 283–296.

Hunnicutt, G. (2009). Varieties of patriarchy and violence against women: Resurrecting 'patriarchy' as a theoretical tool. *Violence Against Women, 15*(5), 553–573.

Irwin, K., & Chesney-Lind, M. (2008). Girls violence: Beyond dangerous masculinity. *Sociology Compass, 2/3*, 837–855.

Johnson, M. P. (2006). Apples and oranges in child custody disputes: Intimate terrorism vs. situational couple violence. *Journal of Child Custody, 2*(4), 43–52.

Johnson, M. P. (2011). Gender and types of intimate partner violence: A response to an anti-feminist literature review. *Aggression and Violent Behavior, 16*, 289–296.

Johnson, M. P., & Ferraro, K. J. (2000). Research on domestic violence in the 1990s: Making distinctions. *Journal of Marriage and the Family, 62*, 948–963.

Jones, N. (2010). *Between good and ghetto: African American girls and inner-city violence*. New Brunswick, NJ: Rutgers University Press.

Kelly, J. B., & Johnson, M. P. (2008). Differentiation among types of intimate partner violence: Research update and implications for interventions. *Family Court Review, 46*(3), 476–499.

Kelly, P., & Morgan-Kidd, J. (2001). Social influences on the sexual behaviors of adolescent girls in at-risk circumstances. *Journal of Obstetric, Gynecologic, and Neonatal Nursing, 30*(5), 481–489.

Kempadoo, K. (Ed.). (2005). *Trafficking and prostitution reconsidered: New perspectives on migration, sex work, and human rights*. Boulder, CO: Paradigm Publishers.

Laidler, K.-J., & Hunt, G. (2001). Accomplishing femininity among the girls in the gang. *British Journal of Criminology, 41*, 656–678.

Lee, M. (2007). Women's imprisonment as a mechanism of migration control in Hong Kong. *British Journal of Criminology, 47*(6), 847–860.

Lerner, E. (1986a). Immigrant and working-class involvement in the New York City woman suffrage movement, 1905–1917. In J. Friedlander (Ed.), *Women in culture and politics: A century of change* (pp. 223–236). Bloomington: Indiana University Press.

Lerner, G. (1986b). *The creation of patriarchy*. New York: Oxford.

Livingston, J. (2013). Demographics and the future of the GOP. *Sociological Images*. Retrieved from http://thesocietypages.org/socimages/2013/03/19/demographics-and-the-future-of-the-gop/

Lown, J. (1983). Not so much a factory, more a form of patriarchy: Gender and class during industrialization. In E. Gamarnikow, D. Morgan, J. Purvis, & D. Taylorson (Eds.), *Gender, class and work* (pp. 28–35). London: Heinemann.

MacLeod, A. (1991). *Accommodating protest: Working women, the new veiling, and change in Cairo*. New York: Columbia University Press.

Mann, C. R., & Zatz, M. S. (1996). *Images of color, images of crime*. Los Angeles: Roxbury Press.

Martin, S. E., & Jurik, N. C. (2007). *Doing justice, doing gender*. Thousand Oaks, CA: Sage.

Martin, K., Vieraitis, L. M., & Britto, S. (2006). Gender equality and women's absolute status - A test of the feminist models of rape. *Violence Against Women, 12*(4), 321–339.

Mauer, M. (1999). *Race to incarcerate*. New York: The New Press.

McManus, J. H. (1994). *Market driven journalism: Let the citizen beware.* Thousand Oaks, CA: Sage.

Melton, H. C., & Belknap, J. (2003). He hits, she hits: Assessing gender differences and similarities in officially reported intimate partner violence. *Criminal Justice and Behavior, 30*(3), 328–348.

Merriam-Webster (2009). Dictionary. http://www.merriamwebster.com/dictionary/feminist.

Messerschmidt, J. W. (1993). *Masculinities and crime: Critique and reconceptualization of theory.* Lanham, MD: Rowman and Littlefield.

Millet, K. (1970). *Sexual politics.* Garden City, New York: Doubleday.

Miller, S. (2005). *Victims as offenders: The paradox of women's violence in relationships (critical issues in crime and society).* New Brunswick: Rutgers University Press.

Moe, A. M. (2004). Blurring the boundaries: Women's criminality in the context of abuse. *Women's Studies Quarterly, 32*(3–4), 116–138.

Morash, M. (2006). *Understanding gender, crime, and justice.* Thousand Oaks, CA: Sage.

Morash, M. (2010). *Women on probation and parole: A feminist critique of community programs and services.* Boston, MA: Northeastern University Press.

Morash, M., & Haarr, R. N. (2012). Doing, redoing, and undoing gender: Variation in gender identities of women working as police officers. *Feminist Criminology, 7,* 3–23.

Naylor, B. (2001). Reporting violence in the British print media: Gendered stories. *Howard Journal of Criminal Justice, 40,* 180–194.

Odem, M. E. (1995). *Delinquent daughters: Protecting and policing adolescent female sexuality in the United States, 1885–1920.* Chappell Hill: The University of North Carolina Press.

Ogle, R. S., & Batton, C. (2009). Revisiting patriarchy: Its conceptualization and operationalization in criminology. *Critical Criminology, 17*(3), 159–182.

Pateman, C. (1988). *The sexual contract.* CA: Stanford University Press.

Pateman, C. (1989). *The disorder of women: Democracy, feminism, and political theory.* CA: Stanford University Press.

Peterson, J., Zong, X., & Jones-DeWeever, A. (2002). *Life after welfare reform: Low-income single parent families, pre- and post-TANF* (IWPR Publication no. D446). Washington, DC: Institute for Women's Policy Research.

Piper, N. (2003). Feminization of labor migration as violence against women: International, regional, and local nongovernmental organization responses in Asia. *Violence Against Women, 9*(6), 723–745.

Pokharel, K., & Rana, P. (2013, March 29). Friend of India rape victim criticizes police. *Wall Street Journal.* Retrieved from http://online.wsj.com/article/SB10001424127887323337450457822138 1250081390.html

Potter, H. (2006). An argument for black feminist criminology: Understanding African American women's experiences with intimate partner abuse using an integrated approach. *Feminist Criminology, 1,*106–124.

Prokos, A., & Padavic, I. (2002). "There oughta be a law against bitches": Masculinity lessons in police academy training. *Gender, Work & Organization, 9,* 439–459.

Rafter, N. H. (1990). *Partial justice: Women, prisons, and social control.* New Brunswick, NJ: Transaction.

Ramazanoglu, C. (1989). Improving on sociology: The problems of taking a feminist standpoint. *Sociology, 23,* 427–442.

Reinharz, S. (1992). *Feminist methods in social research.* Oxford: Oxford University Press.

Richie, B. E. (1996). *Compelled to crime: The gender entrapment of battered black women.* New York: Routledge.

Richie, B. E. (2012). *Arrested justice: Black women, violence, and America's prison nation.* New York: New York University Press.

Romer, D., Jamieson, K. H., & Aday, S. (2003). Television news and the cultivation of fear of crime. *Journal of Communication, 53*(1), 88–104.

Romer, D., Jamieson, K. H., & DeCoteau, N. (1998). The treatment of persons of color in local television news: Ethnic blame discourse or realistic group conflict. *Communications Research, 25*(3), 286–305.

Schlesinger, P., Tumber, H., & Murdock, G. (1991). The media politics of crime and criminal justice. *British Journal of Sociology, 42,* 397–420.

Schlossman, S., & Wallach, S. (1978). The crime of precocious sexuality: Female juvenile delinquency in the progressive era. *Harvard Educational Review, 48*(1), 65–93.

Schwartz, M. D., & DeKesseredy, W. S. (1997). *Sexual assault on the college campus: The role of male peer support.* Thousand Oaks, CA: Sage.

Schwartz, J., & Rookey, B. D. (2008). The narrowing gender in arrests: Assessing competing explanations using self-report, traffic fatality, and official data on drunk driving, 1980–2004. *Criminology, 46,* 637–671.

Schwartz, J., Steffensmeier, D. J., & Feldmeyer, B. (2009). Assessing trends in women's violence via data triangulation: Arrests, convictions, incarcerations, and victim reports. *Social Problems, 56,* 494–525.

Simon, J. (2007). *Governing through crime.* Oxford: Oxford University Press.

Snyder, H. N., & Sickmund, M. (2006). *Juvenile offenders and victims: 2006 national report.* Washington, DC: Office of Juvenile Justice and Delinquency Prevention.

Sprague, J. (2005). *Feminist methods for critical researchers: Bridging differences.* Walnut Creek, CA: Altamira Press.

Stankuniene, V., & Maslauskaite, E. (2008). Family transformations in the post-communist countries: Attitudes toward changes and the ideational shift. In C. Hohn, D. Avramov, & I. E. Kotowska (Eds.), *People, population change and policies: Lessons from the population policy acceptance study* (pp. 113–140). The Hague, The Netherlands: Springer.

Steffensmeier, D., & Streifel, C. (1992). Time series analysis of the female percentage of arrests for property crimes, 1960–1985: A test of alternative explanations. *Justice Quarterly, 9*(1), 77–104.

Steffensmeier, D., Schwartz, J., Zhong, H., & Ackerman, J. (2005). An assessment of recent trends in girls' violence using diverse longitudinal sources: Is the gender gap closing? *Criminology, 43*(2), 355–405.

Sudbury, J. (2002). Celling black bodies: Black women in the global prison industrial complex. *Feminist Review, 70,* 57–74.

Thrasher, F. M. (1927). *The gang: A study of 1,313 gangs in Chicago.* Chicago: University of Chicago Press.

Van Voorhis, P., Wright, E. M., Salisbury, E., & Bauman, A. (2010). Women's risk factors and their contributions to existing risk/needs assessment: The current status of a gender-responsive supplement. *Criminal Justice and Behavior, 37*(3), 261–288.

Wahab, S. (2003). Creating knowledge collaboratively with female sex workers: Insights from a qualitative, feminist, and participatory study. *Qualitative Inquiry, 9*(4), 625–642.

Walby, S. (1990). *Theorizing Patriarchy.* Oxford: UK.

Websdale, N. S. (1996). Predators: The social construction of "stranger danger" in Washington State as a form of patriarchal ideology. *Women and Criminal Justice, 7*(2), 43–68.

Websdale, N., & Alvarez, A. (1998). Forensic journalism patriarchal ideology: The newspaper construction of homicide-suicide. *Popular Culture, Crime and Justice, 126,* 128–130.

West, C., & Fenstermaker, S. (1995). Doing difference. *Gender and Society, 9*(1), 8–37.

West, R., & Marcus, J. (1982). The Young Rebecca: Writings of Rebecca West, 1911–17. In: J. Marcus (Ed.), London: Macmillan in association with Virago Press.

West, C., & Zimmerman, D. H. (1987). Doing gender. *Gender and Society, 1*(2), 125–151.

Whaley, R. B. (2001). The paradoxical relationship between gender inequality and rape. *Gender and Society, 15*(4), 531–555.

Winthrop, R. (2012). Malala's attack and the fight for girls' education mark international day of the girl child. Brookings Up Front. Retrieved from http://www.brookings.edu/blogs/upfront/posts/2012/10/12-international girl-day-winthrop.

Yodanis, C. L. (2004). Gender inequality, violence against women, and fear: A cross-national test of the feminist theory of violence against women. *Journal of Interpersonal Violence, 19*(6), 655–675.

READING /// 2

In Section I, you learned about how feminist research methods can provide an alternative perspective when researching issues of gender and crime. In this chapter, Dr. Jody Miller discusses how her research on issues of gender and female offending has benefited by placing gender at the center of her research methodology. Through the use of this process, Dr. Miller demonstrates how qualitative research (and in particular, in-depth interviews) can yield a meaningful understanding of how issues of crime and victimization are a gendered experience.

Grounding the Analysis of Gender and Crime
Accomplishing and Interpreting Qualitative Interview Research

Jody Miller

Introduction

As a feminist scholar and sociological criminologist, a primary question guiding my research concerns the impact of gender stratification, gendered practices, and gender ideologies on criminal offending. I seek to challenge and complicate binary assumptions about women and men and in doing so carefully attend to the complex ways in which gender—as one of the most basic organizing structures within and across societies—configures

SOURCE: Miller, J. (2012). Grounding the analysis of gender and crime: Accomplishing and interpreting qualitative interview research. In D. Gadd, S. Karstedt, & S. F. Messner (Eds.), *The SAGE handbook of criminological research methods* (pp. 49–62). Thousand Oaks, CA: Sage.

individuals' life experiences in ways that lead them to crime and that influences their motivations for offending, strategies for accomplishing it, and the situations and contexts in which this offending takes place. My method of choice for doing this research is the analysis of qualitative in-depth interview data.

In this article, I address the following questions: What makes in-depth interviewing a particularly useful methodological approach for feminist criminology? How is research that utilizes interview data put to use for understanding the relationships between gender, inequality, and crime? Finally, how do those of us who analyze in-depth interviews in our research go about doing so; what's the actual process by which we turn our data into meaningful theoretical contributions? I draw from three of my research projects—on young women's participation in gangs, women's and men's accomplishment of robbery, and young men's sexual violence against young women—to describe why qualitative interviews are my data of choice, and how I use inductive analytic techniques to produce my research findings.

Feminist Criminology and Qualitative Interview Accounts

Sociologist Christine Williams (2000: 9) describes academic feminism as "a general approach to understanding the status of women in society." Notwithstanding the range of theoretical and methodological approaches brought to bear on the question, she observes that "all feminist social scientists share the goals of understanding the sources of inequality and advocating changes to empower women" (ibid.). Thus, what differentiates *feminist* criminology from other criminological analyses that consider women and crime is the conceptual understanding of gender that guides our research: a concern with understanding *gender* is as much a starting point in feminist criminological analyses as is the concern with understanding *crime* (Daly, 1998).

Early treatises on feminist methodology, particularly the use of in-depth interview techniques, were situated in women's standpoint theory (Oakley, 1981). These were grounded in feminist goals of "giving voice" to women and their experiences, which had historically been silenced (see DeVault, 1999; Smith, 1987). This remains an

important goal of feminist scholars, though with critical understandings of its challenges. Initially, there was a relatively uncritical assumption that when women interviewed women, their shared experiences *as women* would result in identification, rapport, and consequently, the authentic revelation of "women's experiences." These rather romanticized assumptions have since been problematized, however. Most scholars now recognize, for example, that no research can provide authentic access to individuals' experiences or unmediated access to "truth," and this includes the accounts produced in the context of interviews (see Miller & Glassner, 2004; Silverman, 2006). Moreover, feminist scholars now recognize that women do not simply share experiences *as women.* Instead, many facets of difference come into play when we attempt to understand women's and men's lives, including race, ethnicity, cultural identity, nation, class, and age, as well as individual life trajectories and experiences (Presser, 2005; Song & Parker, 1995; Veroff & DiStefano, 2002).

Given this multifaceted understanding of the research process and its goals, many feminist scholars identify unique contributions that qualitative interview approaches can make in theorizing about gender and crime. This results both from how feminist scholars conceptualize gender and from our insistence that examining the meaning and nature of gender relations and inequalities are a critical component of understanding and theorizing about crime and criminality. To begin with, feminist scholarship challenges the premise that gender is simply an individual-level independent variable. Instead, our research starts with the understanding that the social world is systematically shaped by relations of sex and gender, and these operate at all levels of society, including individual, interactional, organizational, and structural (see Connell, 2002; Risman, 2004). As Daly and Chesney-Lind (1988: 504) sum up, "[G]ender and gender relations order social life and social institutions in fundamental ways."

As a consequence, feminist scholars recognize that gender operates both within the practices and organization of social life, as well as within "the discursive fields by which women [and men] are constructed or construct themselves" (Daly & Maher, 1998: 4). Taken for granted ideologies about gender are profoundly embedded in social life and often include commonsense notions of fundamental difference between women and men, coupled with the perception of maleness as the normative standard. These deeply engrained assumptions are regularly found in academic research and theory; the policies, practices, and operation of organizations and institutions; and in the interpretive frameworks women and men bring to their daily lives. Moreover, it is through the enactment of these gendered meanings that the most persistent, yet often invisible, facets of gender inequality are reproduced.

Perhaps most pronounced is the tendency to reproduce conventional understandings of gender *difference* (see Miller, 2002). Such interpretive frameworks—particularly cultural emphases on a psychologically based "character dichotomy" between women and men (Connell, 2002: 40) often guide the understandings of those we investigate and can also seep into researchers' conceptualizations. Thus, feminist scholars grapple with what Daly and Maher (1998: 1) refer to as an *intellectual double shift*: the dual challenge of examining the impact of gender and gender inequality in "real" life, while simultaneously deconstructing the intertwined ideologies about gender that guide social practices (see Connell, 2002). Indeed, illuminating the relationship between ideological features of gender and gendered practice is a key facet of feminist scholarship.

In addition, feminist conceptualizations of gender often require us to move beyond what broad, global explanations provide. While our starting point is the recognition that social life is patterned by gender, we also recognize—and empirical evidence demonstrates—that this gender order (Connell, 2002) is complex and shifting. For this reason, a key feature of feminist scholarship is the development of what Daly (1998) refers to as "middle range" theorizing—developing theoretical understandings that seek primarily to explain how broader structural forces are realized within particular organizational, situational, and interactional contexts.

So, what does the analysis of qualitative in-depth interviews have to offer in our attempts to attend to these complexities and challenges? From my point of view, the strength of such interviews lies in what they are: reflective accounts of social life offered from the points of view of research participants. As such, they provide two intertwined kinds of data: descriptive evidence of the nature of the phenomena under investigation—including the contexts and situations in which it emerges—as well as insights into the cultural frames that people use to make sense of their experiences (Miller & Glassner, 2004). Both are especially useful for feminist theorizing about gender and crime, particularly in the context of the intellectual double shift I noted previously.

In general, qualitative research is oriented toward the creation of contextual understandings of social worlds, emphasizing complexities in the meanings and social processes that operate within them. Interview data, in which people describe and explain their behaviors and experiences, help us identify and understand social processes and patterns at the interactional and situational levels, as well as the meanings people attribute to their experiences and behaviors (see Charmaz, 2006; Spradley, 1979; but compare Silverman, 2006). In criminology, this includes, for example, examining in situ motivations for behaviors such as offending or desistance (Maruna, 2001); social processes associated with crime, criminally involved groups, or the streets (Maher, 1997); situational analyses of crime events (Mullins & Wright, 2003; Wright & Decker, 1997), as well as life history analyses that examine pathways into and out of offending (Giordano, 2010). As such, qualitative in-depth interviews can provide us with ground level understandings of crime and criminal behavior.

In addition, because in-depth interviews are *accounts*, they hold promise for examining the social world from the points of view of research participants and for exploring how meanings are constructed together, including in the interview itself (see Miller, 2010). When analyzed not just as a source of information about the *who, what, when, where*, and *how* of criminal offending but also as a "linguistic device employed whenever an action is subjected to valuative inquiry" (Scott & Lyman, 1968: 46), the narrative accounts within in-depth interviews provide insight into "culturally embedded normative explanations [of events and behaviors, because they] represent ways in which people organize views of themselves, of others, and of their social worlds" (Orbuch, 1997: 455).

Given feminist scholars' concerns with how language and discourse "reflect and help constitute" gendered meaning systems (Cameron, 1998: 946), the analysis of in-depth interviews thus offers an especially useful tool for feminist scholars in simultaneously examining both social patterns and social meanings associated with gender, inequality, and crime. Recognizing interview accounts as evidence of both the nature of the phenomenon under investigation and the cultural frameworks that individuals use to interpret their experiences means that, in one's analysis, juxtaposing these facets of accounts—even or especially when they appear incongruous—can be useful for developing theoretical insight. Qualitative interview data are thus particularly well suited for addressing the goals of feminist criminologists for understanding how gender and gender inequality shape the experiences of those involved in crime.

Analyzing Qualitative Interview Data

Most qualitative researchers use some version of grounded theory techniques in their data analysis. Charmaz (2006: 2–3) provides the following explanation of what this entails:

> Stated simply, grounded theory methods consist of systematic, yet flexible guidelines for collecting and analyzing qualitative data to construct theories grounded in the data themselves. The guidelines offer a set of general principles and heuristic devices rather than formulaic rules. . . . Thus, data form the foundation of our theory and our analysis of these data generates the concepts we construct.

One of the most important principles of grounded theory analyses is that preliminary data analysis begins at the start of the project. Initial analyses of both what people say and how they say it open up new avenues of inquiry and also generate preliminary hypotheses to be further explored during ongoing data collection and analysis. This is accomplished through close and continuous reading of the data, during which the researcher codes the data and begins documenting preliminary analytic observations and hypotheses, which are then compared with and analyzed in light of additional data collected. Coding, as Charmaz explains, is a process by which "we attach labels to segments of data that depict what each segment is about. Coding distills data, sorts them, and gives us a handle for making comparisons with other segments of data" (ibid., 3).

The particular analysis strategy a qualitative interview researcher uses may vary for any given project. What they share in common, however, is recognition of the importance of beginning initial data coding by using grounded, open coding strategies.

This process helps avoid the application of preconceived concepts, assists in generating new ideas, and keeps the researcher thoroughly grounded in the data (Charmaz, 2006). Initial coding can take a variety of forms, including reading the interview text word by word, line by line, and incident by incident. The more closely we read the data, the more readily we can move beyond taken for granted or preconceived ideas we bring to our research, and the more likely we are to discover emergent concepts and patterns in the data.

An important part of the process is paying specific attention to interview participants' unique language and speech patterns (Spradley, 1979). Charmaz (2006: 55) refers to these as *in vivo* codes—terms or phrases that provide telling insights into social worlds or processes. In my recent work, *Getting Played* (2008), for example, the insider term *play* and its iterations became central to my analysis, and it was even the basis of the book's title. While analyzing interviews with urban African American youth about interactions between young women and young men and their relation to gendered violence, I was struck by the common and varied ways in which the term *play* entered into youths' accounts. Treating this as an in vivo code, I carefully examined its usage to identify the actions it represented and the implicit meanings *play* attached to them. This led me to an analysis of the variety of ways that play claims are used to minimize the significance of behavioral patterns that are harmful to girls. To illustrate, Reading Box 2.1 provides a partial excerpt of my analysis of play claims associated with sexual harassment.

In vivo codes can also be phrases that condense and distill significant analytic concepts. During her interview for *Getting Played*, one of the young women described offering the following advice to her sister for avoiding sexual violence: "Protect yourself, respect yourself. 'Cause if you don't, guys won't." Read in passing, it could easily be seen as simple advice. But my line-by-line coding flagged it as a phrase worth further examination. I made note of it in an analytic memo and then paid close attention to how youths talked about protection and respect. Ultimately,

Reading Box 2.1   Contested Play Claims: Humor or Disrespected?

[Y]oung men often downplayed the seriousness of sexual harassment by couching it in terms of "play." Antwoin said, "[Y]eah, I grabbed a girl bootie a couple of times . . . we was playing." Such touching, he said, was best understood as "like playing around. Sometimes the boys'll be messing with the girls and they'll just grab they bootie or something." . . . Similarly, asked why he and his friends touched on girls, Curtis said, "I don't know, just to have fun. Just playing."

"Just playing," however, was a characterization young women roundly rejected. Instead, to quote Nicole, girls found boys' sexually harassing behaviors to be "too much playing." . . . Katie complained, "[M]ost of the time boys and girls get into it because boys, they play too much. . . . Like they try to touch you and stuff, or try to talk about you, or put you down in front of they friends to made them feel better. . . . Just talk about you or something like in front of they friends so they can laugh."

Katie's comments tapped into an important feature of boys' play claim: The primary audience for this "play" was other young men. As Anishika argued young men's "humour" was for the benefit of their friends, and at the expense of the young woman:

> They just tryin' to be like person and that person. They already know, they know what's right. They know right from wrong. But when it's a lot of 'em, they think that stuff is cute, calling girls B's [bitches] and rats and all that stuff. They think that stuff cute, and some of these girls think that stuff cute. But it's not cute.

In fact, [young men's accounts] are indicative of the role male peers played in facilitating young men's behaviors. Thus, Frank [explained], "some people, when they see [you touch on a girl], they'll laugh or they give you some props. They give you like a little five of something like that. That's what the dudes do." . . . Thus, a number of girls said boys simply used play claims as an excuse for their behavior, and described explicitly rejecting these claims. For example, angry after a young man made sexual comments about her, Destiny said he responded to her anger by saying, "you ain't even gotta get that serious. I was just playin' wit' you." She replied, "I don't care. I don't want you playin' with me like that, stop playin' with me like that." And Nicole explained, "sometimes boys make it like, act like it's funny. But it's not. 'Cause you touchin' a girl and she don't wanna be touched. So, don't touch me, period. Don't even think about touchin' me."

Indeed, despite young men's routine use of play claims, their own accounts belied the notion that their behaviors were simply intended as harmless fun. For example, several young men said part of the fun in taunting girls was getting an angry response. . . . Moreover, several young men described treating girls in a derogatory way specifically to demarcate their (male) space and make it clear to the girl that she wasn't welcome. . . . [O]ne additional factor belies young men's characterizations of their behavior as "just play". Asked when harassing behaviors took place or whether they were directed at particular girls, a number of young men described targeting young women they deemed to be "stuck up," unwilling to show sexual or romantic interest, or otherwise unimpressed with the boy. . . . Curtis said, "[W]e'll see a girl in like a short skirt or short shorts, and we be kind of talking to her, and she don't, she ain't giving nobody no play. So, we just get to playing with her, touching on her butt and all that."

SOURCE: From Miller, 2008, p. 82–87.

my analysis revealed that it succinctly crystallized youths' understandings of the causes of sexual violence and girls' risk-management strategies in the face of limited interpersonal and institutional support (see Miller, 2008: 143–149).

Beyond the importance of open and in vivo coding, qualitative researchers employ a variety of specific coding and analysis strategies, depending on the research question at hand. Charmaz (2006) recommends that grounded theory research should code for *action* within the data, using gerund codes to preserve social processes. Lofland and Lofland (1984) encourage scholars to identify *topics* for analysis by combining particular units of analysis (e.g., practices, episodes, encounters, or relationships) with their aspects (e.g., cognitive, emotional, or hierarchical). Once identified, the researcher rigorously examines the data for instances that are topically relevant. Spradley (1979) utilizes domain analysis, by using semantic relationships to ask structured questions from the data (e.g., X is a kind of Y; X is a way to do Y). Each of these strategies allow us to approach the data in a systematic way, with the goal of moving from initial coding to systematic theoretical analyses.

Good qualitative research emerges from the thoroughness and rigor of the inductive analysis. In the process, *emergent* hypotheses are identified in the course of analysis as patterns begin to emerge. These hypotheses are then tested, refined, or rejected using the project data. A variety of strategies have been devised to ensure the rigor of the analytic induction process. Most important is the use of constant comparative methods, which are strengthened through the use of tabulations to identify the strength of patterns (see Silverman, 2006: 296–301, for a concise description of these strategies) and to aid in the identification of and analysis of deviant cases. As Charmaz (2006: 54) describes,

> You use "*constant comparative method*" . . . to establish analytic distinctions and thus make comparisons at each level of analytic work. . . . For example, compare interview statements and incidents within the same interview and compare statements and incidents in different interviews.

This allows you to test and refine emergent hypotheses against the data. It is also the case that qualitative researchers tend to reject the position that any research can tap into "pure" objective data, regardless of the methodological approach of the researcher. Thus, consideration of the researcher's place in the research process—from formulating research questions, to data collection, to analysis—is necessary. To illustrate these analytic strategies—focusing specifically on the utility of qualitative interview research for studying gender and crime—I now turn to a more detailed description of several of my research projects.

Up It Up: Studying Gender Stratification and the Accomplishment of Robbery

Early in my career, I was afforded the opportunity to utilize my colleagues' in-depth interview data with armed robbers (Wright & Decker, 1997) to examine the impact of gender on the enactment of robbery (Miller, 1998). My analysis of these data helps illustrate several key features of qualitative analysis techniques. I approached the data with two guiding questions: How do women, as compared to men, account for their motivations to commit robbery? And how do women, as compared to men, describe the process by which they accomplish robbery? The use of comparative samples—in this case, female and male robbers—is a particularly useful approach when doing qualitative research, because it allows for some specification of similarities and variations in social processes and meaning systems across groups or settings.

In this particular investigation, I coded the data with these two specific research questions in mind. First, I looked for evidence in the data for how robbers described their motivations to commit robbery and compared accounts both within and across gender. Next, I coded incident by incident, examining how women and men in the sample described accomplishing the robberies they committed. My identification within the data of both similarities and differences across gender led me to theorize about the impact of gender stratification in offender networks on women's participation in crime. This is an example of the type of middle range theorizing described previously—my research findings pointed me in the direction of stratification as the best fit for explaining the patterns I identified, and it offered an incisive analytic framework for explaining the structures and processes I uncovered.

Specifically, I found congruence across gender in interview participants' accounts of their *motivations* for committing robberies. For both women and men, the incentives to commit robbery were primarily economic—to get money, jewelry, and other status-conferring goods, but [they] also included elements of thrill seeking, attempting to overcome boredom, and revenge. However, women's and men's accounts of *how* they went about committing robberies were strikingly different. And within gender comparisons of incident accounts, [they] were equally illuminating.

Specifically, men's descriptions of their commission of robbery were markedly similar to one another. Their accounts were variations around a single theme: using physical violence and/or a gun placed on or at close proximity to the victim in a confrontational manner. The key, one explained, was to make sure the victim knew "that we ain't playing." Another described confronting his victims by placing the gun at the back of their head, where "they feel it," while saying, "Give it up, motherfucker, don't move or I'll blow your brains out." Explaining the positioning of the gun, he noted, "When you feel that steel against your head . . . [it] carries a lot of weight." Closely examining each man's accounts of strategies for committing robberies, as well as their descriptions of particular incidents, revealed that they accomplished robberies in noticeably uniform ways.

In contrast, women's accounts were notable both for the greater variation in the strategies they described using to accomplish robberies and for their absence of accounts that paralleled those provided by men, except under very specific circumstances: when they committed robberies in partnership with male accomplices. In short, though men described routinely using firearms to commit robberies and placing them on or in close proximity to the back of the victim's head, women's strategies for committing robberies varied according to the gender of their victim, and the presence or absence of co-offenders. They described three predominant ways in which they committed robberies: targeting female victims in physically confrontational robberies that did not involve firearms, targeting male victims by appearing sexually available, and participating with male co-offenders during street robberies of men.

Insights about the role of gender stratification in the commission of robbery emerged particularly prominently when I examined women's accounts of robbing men.

These incidents nearly always involved firearms but rarely involved physical contact. Notably, the rationale women provided for this strategy was especially telling. As one explained,

> [I]f we waste time touching men there is a possibility that they can get the gun off of us, while we wasting time touching them they could do anything. So, we just keep the gun straight on them. No touching, no moving, just straight gun at you.

The circumstances surrounding the enactment of female-on-male robberies were unique as well. The key, in each case, was that the woman pretended to be sexually interested in her male victim. When his guard dropped, this provided a safe opportunity for the robbery to occur.

Moreover, women specifically described playing on the stereotypes men held about women in order to accomplish these robberies—including the assumptions that women would not be armed, would not attempt to rob them, and could be taken advantage of sexually. For example, one woman explained,

> [T]hey don't suspect that a girl gonna try to get 'em. You know what I'm saying? So, it's kind of easier 'cause they like, she looks innocent, she ain't gonna do this, but that's how I get 'em. They put they guard down to a woman. . . . Most of the time, when girls get high they think they can take advantage of us so they always, let's go to a hotel or my crib or something.

Another said, "[T]hey easy to get, we know what they after—sex."

This and other evidence of the role that gender ideologies played in the enactment of robberies pointed explicitly to the importance of gendered organizational features of the street environment as an important explanatory factor. Most notable was the incongruity between the similarities in women's and men's motives for committing robbery and the dramatic differences in their strategies for accomplishing robbery. As such, the research highlighted the gender hierarchy present on the streets: while some women were able to carve out a niche for themselves in this setting, they were participating in a male-dominated environment, and their robbery strategies reflected an understanding of this. The differences in the way women, as compared to men, accomplished robberies were not a result of differences in their goals or needs. Instead, they reflected practical choices women made in the context of a gender stratified environment—one in which, on the whole, men were perceived as strong and women as weak. In this particular project, it was not just the availability of in-depth interview data that resulted in the analysis briefly described here but also specifically the *comparative* nature of the data. My ability to juxtapose women's and men's accounts facilitated the identification of commonalities and differences across gender and thus allowed me to build an analytic framework to make sense of them.

Running Trains: Gaining Insight Through Attention to the Interview as a Joint Accomplishment

Earlier in the chapter, I noted that qualitative researchers tend to reject the position that research can uncover pure objective data. In the context of in-depth interviewing, an important part of this is recognizing that the interview itself is a particular kind of interaction, in which both participants—the interviewer and the interviewee—are constructing narrative versions of the social world. The accounts produced in the context of interviews are, as noted earlier, "linguistic device[s] employed whenever an action is subjected to valuative inquiry" (Scott & Lyman, 1968: 46). We saw this in gang girls' claims of being one of the guys. It is also the case that our social positioning vis-à-vis those we interview affects the interview exchange. Attention to these interactional dynamics within the interview exchange offers an important site for social inquiry (Grenz, 2005; Miller, 2010; Presser, 2005). This is not about trying to control for interviewer effects per se; instead, "what matters is to understand how and where the stories [we collect] are produced, which sort of stories they are, and how we can put them to honest and intelligent use in theorizing about social life" (Miller & Glassner, 2004: 138).

Earlier, I argued that in-depth interview research utilizing comparative *samples* is particularly useful for theory building. Here, I provide an illustration of how comparative analysis of the data collected by different *interviewers* also provides an important opportunity for

theorizing about social life. I draw from one particular set of data from my recent project on violence against young women in urban African American neighborhoods (Miller, 2008)—young men's accounts of *running trains* on girls: a sexual encounter that involved two or more young men engaging in penetrative sexual acts with a single young woman. Specifically, this example shows that paying attention to how interviewers' social positioning matters in the interview context can reveal a great deal about how individuals construct particular sorts of accounts of their offending and about the contexts and meanings of this behavior.

Running trains was an all too common phenomenon in the data, with nearly half of the boys interviewed admitting that they had done so. Though researchers routinely classify such incidents as gang rape, and the young women interviewed described their experiences in this way as well, the young men in the study defined girls' participation in trains as consensual. Thus, it was particularly important in the project to examine how young men understood running trains and especially how they came to perceive these behaviors as consensual. In this case, interviews conducted by two different research assistants—one a White European man (Dennis), the other an African American woman who grew up in the same community as the research participants (Toya)—revealed two sets of findings about boys' constructions of running trains. These offered distinct types of accounts of the behavior, each of which revealed different dimensions of the meaning and enactment of running trains. Reading Box 2.3 provides excerpts from several of Dennis's and Toya's interviews with young men.

Comparing these two sets of accounts suggests a variety of ways in which Dennis's and Toya's social positions of similarity and difference with these African American adolescent boys shaped the ways in which they spoke about their participation in running trains. Moreover, the interviewers themselves took different approaches toward the interview exchanges, which are tied to their interviewing techniques, the kinds of information they were most interested in obtaining, and their own positionality vis-à-vis the interviewees.

An especially striking feature of the accounts provided in young men's interviews with Dennis was the adamancy with which boys claimed that girls were willing, even eager participants. Moreover, their descriptions

Reading Box 2.2 Young Men's Accounts of Running Trains

Interview Excerpts with Dennis

Lamont: I mean, one be in front, one be in back. You know sometimes, you know like, say, you getting in her ass and she might be sucking the other dude dick. Then you probably get her, you probably get her to suck your dick while he get her in the ass. Or he probably, either I'll watch, and so she sucking your dick, or while you fuck her in the ass. It, I mean, it's a lot of ways you can do it.

Frank: There's this one girl, she a real, real freak. . . . She wanted me and my friend to run a train on her . . . . [Beforehand], we was at the park, hopping and talking about it and everything. I was like, "man, dawg, I ain't hitting her from the back." Like, "she gonna mess up my dick." . . . He like, "Oh, I got her from the back dude." So we went up there . . . [and] she like, "which one you all hitting me from the back?" [I'm] like, "there he go, right there. I got the front." She's like, "okay." And then he took off her clothes, pulled his pants down. I didn't, just unzipped mine 'cause I was getting head. She got to slurping me. I'm like, my partner back there 'cause we was in the dark so I ain't see nuttin.' He was back, I just heared her [making noises]. I'm like, "damn girl, what's wrong with you?" [More noises] [I'm like], "you hitting her from the back?" He's like, "yeah, I'm hitting it."

Interview Excerpt with Toya

Terence: It was some girl that my friend had knew for a minute, and he, I guess he just came to her and asked her, "is you gon' do everybody?" or whatever and she said "yeah." So he went first and then, I think my other partna went, then I went, then it was like two other dudes behind me. . . . It was at [my friend's] crib.

Toya: Were you all like there for a get together or party or something?

Terence: It was specifically for that for real, 'cause he had already let us know that she was gon' do that, so.

Toya: So it was five boys and just her?

Terence: Yeah.

....

Toya: And so he asked her first, and then he told you all to come over that day?

Terence: We had already came over. 'Cause I guess he knew she was already gon' say yeah or whatever. We was already there when she got there.

Toya: Did you know the girl?

Terence: Naw, I ain't know her, know her like for real know her. But I knew her name or whatever. I had seen her before. That was it though.

....

Toya: So when you all got there, she was in the room already?

Terence: Naw, when we got there, she hadn't even got there yet. And when she came, she went in the room with my friend, the one she had already knew. And then after they was in there for a minute, he came out and let us know that she was 'gon, you know, run a train or whatever. So after that, we just went one by one.

were particularly graphic, focusing specific attention on the details of their sexual performances. Dennis was responded to by the young men as a naïve White male academic who knows little about street life (see also Miller, 2008: 232–234). His foreignness, as evidenced by his Dutch accent, further heightened the young men's perceptions of him as different. Thus, they appear to tell their stories in ways that simultaneously play on what they do have in common—maleness (and thus a perceived shared understanding of women as sexual objects)—and position themselves as particularly successful in their sexual prowess, an exaggerated feature of hegemonic masculinity in distressed urban neighborhoods in the United States (Anderson, 1999) that marks their difference from Dennis.

Notice that these accounts emphasized their sexual performance. In fact, research on gang rape suggests that group processes play a central role. The enactment of such violence increases solidarity and cohesion among groups of young men, and the victim has symbolic status and is treated as an object (Franklin, 2004; Sanday, 1990). Just as performance played a central role in young men's accounts of these incidents, their accounts were themselves a particular sort of masculine performance in the context of their interview exchange with a young, White male researcher far removed from their world on the streets (see also Presser, 2005).

In contrast, when young men were interviewed about their participation in running trains by Toya—the African American female interviewer—two different features emerged. First, they were much less sexually graphic in their accounts. Second, due in part to Toya's interview style and the specific concerns about consent she brought to the interview exchange, her conversations with young men about running trains challenged their attempts to construct the events as consensual. The interview excerpt with Terence in Box 2.3 reveals, for example, that the young woman in this incident arrived at the house of a boy [who] she knew and may have been interested in; waiting on her arrival were four additional young men whom she did not know or know well. And they had come specifically for the purpose of running a train on her. Because Terence's friend said "she was down for it," he either did not consider or discounted the question of whether the young woman may have felt threatened or had not freely consented. Instead, he took his turn and left.

Similar inconsistencies were revealed in Tyrell's—see above account, again precisely because of Toya's particular style of probing and concern with issues of consent:

This girl was just like, I ain't even know her, but like I knew her 'cause I had went to work [where she did] last year. . . . Then my boy, when he started working there, he already had knew her, 'cause he said he had went to a party with her last year. And he was gonna have sex with her then, but . . . [her] grandmamma came home or something, so they ain't get to do it. So one day he was just like, we was all sitting watching this movie [at work] and it was real dark or whatever. And she had come in there or whatever, and he was just talking to her, and he was like, "Let's all go 'head and run a train on you." She was like, "What?" And she started like, "You better go on." Then, like, [he said], "For real, let's go over to my house." And then, you know what I'm saying, she was like, "Naw."

Tyrell explained that later that day, he and his friend were leaving work and saw the girl "walking over there to the bus stop." His friend invited the girl over to his house, and she agreed to go. Tyrell admitted, "I think she liked him," and this was the reason she came over. However, because they had previously introduced the idea of running a train on her, Tyrell and his friend appear to have decided that her consent to go to his house was consent to have a train run on her. The discussion continued:

Toya: "Do you think she really wanted to do it?"
Tyrell: "I can't really say. 'Cause at first she was like laughing and stuff, like, 'Don't!' But we didn't pressure her. I didn't say nothing to her for the rest of the [work] day. I probably talked to her, but I say nothing about like that. And then she just came with us, so I mean, she had to want to."

Thus, in his account, Tyrell maintained his interpretation that the incident was consensual, offering evidence that the fact that he and his friend did not mention running a train on the girl again during the day they spent at work together meant they had not "pressured" her. He did not appear to consider an alternative interpretation—that their silence on the issue allowed the girl to interpret the earlier comments as innocuous. Instead, he insisted that "she knew" (see also King, 2003; Willan and Pollard, 2003).

Further, Tyrell's account of the young woman's behavior afterward—which, again, emerged as a result of Toya's continued questioning, also belied his insistence that she had engaged willingly. He explained that "she missed like a week of work after that." And while he believed the girl liked his friend before the incident, he said, "I know she didn't like him after that. . . . She don't even talk to him at all. Every time they see each other they'll argue." In addition, Tyrell said, "She go to my cousin's school now, and she be talking all stuff like, 'I hate your cousin!' But I don't care, I mean I don't even care. She shouldn't have did that."

Given this evidence, Toya asked whether he thought she felt bad about it, the conversation continued:

Tyrell: "I can't even say. I don't even know her like that. I really can't say. She do that kinda stuff all the time."

Toya: "She does?"

Tyrell: "No. I'm just saying. I don't know. If she don't she probably did feel bad, but if she do she probably wouldn't feel bad. . . . But if she didn't really wanna do it, she shouldn't have did it."

Notice how Tyrell slipped easily into noting that "she do that kinda stuff all the time," but when pressed, [he] conceded that he had no basis on which to draw such a conclusion.

In part, accounts like Terence's and Tyrell's emerged because they responded to Toya as a young African American woman who had an understanding of life in their neighborhoods. She was marked by similarities where Dennis was marked by difference, except when it came to gender. Young men thus did not portray running trains as graphic sexual exploits that demonstrated their manhood.

And the commonalities Toya shared with them allowed her to probe for factual details without evoking a defensive response that closed down communication within the interview.

These differences could be read as support for the position that social distance between researcher and research participant results in suspicion and lack of trust, which affects the process of disclosure (DeVault, 1999; Taylor, Gilligan, & Sullivan, 1995). My reading is somewhat different. While the role that social similarities and differences played in producing these disparate accounts of the same phenomenon is notable, both sets of interviews revealed important insights about the nature and meanings of running trains. Dennis's interviews demonstrated their function as masculine performance. In fact, young men's acts of *telling* Dennis about the events were themselves masculine performances, constructed in response to *whom* they were doing the telling. In contrast, Toya's interviews revealed important evidence of the processes by which young men construct their interpretations of girls' consent and reveal the various ways in which they do so by discounting the points of view of their female victims (see King, 2003).

This example suggests that it is both necessary and useful to pay close attention to how the interview context shapes accounts. Doing so can reveal multifaceted features of behaviors and their meanings, as they emerge in disparate accounts. Moreover, it reveals the benefits for data analysis that can emerge by utilizing diverse research teams, particularly when using this diversity itself as a means of furthering the analysis (see Miller, 2010).

Conclusion

A primary concern of feminist scholars in criminology is to examine, understand, and ameliorate the gender inequalities that shape crime, victimization, and justice practices. In this chapter, my goals were to describe why the use of in-depth interviews is an especially valuable methodological approach for conducting research on these issues and to explain how research that utilizes interview data puts them to use for understanding the relationships between gender, inequality, and crime.

What I find most useful with interview data is the simultaneous access these provide to both social processes—the *who, what, when, where,* and *how* of crime—and the cultural frames that individuals use to make sense of these activities and their social worlds. This makes interview accounts particularly useful for addressing the intellectual double shift I noted earlier: the dual challenge of examining the impact of gender and gender inequality in real life, while simultaneously deconstructing the intertwined ideologies about gender that guide social practices, including the strong tendency to view gender through an individualistic and binary lens.

Drawing on my own research, I have shown some of the ways in which the analysis of interview data can illuminate the impact of gender stratification, gendered practices, and gender ideologies on criminal offending. Key to the success of doing so is ensuring the rigor of one's inductive analyses. This includes, for example, working to ensure that initial data coding begins early in the process and remains open, and further into the project, utilizing

techniques such as constant comparative methods and deviant case analyses to strengthen the internal validity of one's findings. Finally, I have illustrated how attention to the social locations of interview participants—researchers and those researched alike—offer important opportunities to advance our understandings.

As a feminist scholar, the relevance of qualitative interview research for studying gender is specific to my particular theoretical goal of "illuminat[ing] gender as central to our understanding of social life" (Lewis, 2007: 274). Nonetheless, my discussion in this chapter has import for a broader criminological audience. It illustrates the unique contributions that qualitative interview research can provide in theorizing about crime and justice by offering a vital window through which to better understand the life, worlds, and experiences of those we study and the social processes and patterns in which they are embedded.

/// DISCUSSION QUESTIONS

1. How can feminist research methods provide insight on the role of gender for victims and offenders?

2. How can different coding strategies reveal important issues for feminist research?

Notes

1. Thus, again note that the title of the book—*One of the Guys*—made direct use of an in vivo code that became central to my analysis.

2. *Wreck* was a slang term used by young women to refer to girls who were seen as sexually promiscuous.

Additional Readings

Anderson, E. (1999). *Code of the street.* New York: W.W. Norton.

Cameron, D. (1998). Gender, language, and discourse: A review essay. *Signs, 23*: 945–973.

Charmaz, K. (2006). *Constructing grounded theory: A practical guide through qualitative analysis.* Thousand Oaks, CA: Sage.

Connell, R. W. (2002). *Gender.* Cambridge, UK: Polity Press.

Daly, K. (1998). Gender, crime, and criminology. In M. Tonry (Ed.), *The handbook of crime and justice* (pp. 85–108). UK: Oxford University Press.

Daly, K., & Chesney-Lind, M. (1988). Feminism and criminology. *Justice Quarterly, 5*(4): 497–538.

Daly, K., & Maher, L. (1998). Crossroads and intersections: Building from feminist critique. In K. Daly & L. Maher (Eds.), *Criminology at the crossroads: Feminist readings in crime and justice* (pp. 1–17). UK: Oxford University Press.

DeVault, M. L. (1999). *Liberating method: Feminism and social research.* Philadelphia: Temple University Press.

Franklin, K. (2004). Enacting masculinity: Antigay violence and group rape as participatory theater. *Sexuality Research & Social Policy, 1*(2): 25–40.

Giordano, P. (2010). *Legacies of crime: A follow-up of the children of highly delinquent girls and boys.* UK: Cambridge University Press.

Grenz, S. (2005). Intersections of sex and power in research on prostitution: A female researcher interviewing male heterosexual clients. *Signs, 30*: 2092–2113.

Joe, K. A., & Chesney-Lind, M. (1995). "Just every mother's angel": An analysis of gender and ethnic variations in youth gang membership. *Gender & Society, 9*(4): 408–430.

Kandiyoti, D. (1988). Bargaining with patriarchy. *Gender & Society, 2*(3): 274–290.

Kanter, R. M. (1977). Some effects of proportions of group life: Skewed sex ratios and responses to token women. *American Journal of Sociology, 82*(5): 965–990.

King, N. (2003). Knowing women: Straight men and sexual certainty. *Gender & Society, 17*(6): 861–877.

Lauderback, D., Hansen, J., & Waldorf, D. (1992). "Sisters are doin' it for themselves'": A Black female gang in San Francisco. *The Gang Journal, 1*(1): 57–70.

Lewis, L. (2007). Epistemic authority and the gender lens. *The Sociological Review, 55*(2): 273–292.

Lofland, J., & Lofland, L. H. (1984). *Analyzing social settings: A guide to qualitative observation and analysis.* Belmont, CA: Wadsworth.

Maher, L. (1997). *Sexed work: Gender, race and resistance in a Brooklyn drug market.* Oxford, UK: Clarendon Press.

Maruna, S. (2001). *Making good.* Washington, DC: American Psychological Association.

Miller, J. (1998). Up it up: Gender and the accomplishment of street robbery. *Criminology, 36*(1): 37–66.

Miller, J. (2001). *One of the guys: Girls, gangs and gender.* New York: Oxford University Press.

Miller, J. (2002). The strengths and limits of "doing gender" for understanding street crime. *Theoretical Criminology, 6*(4): 433–460.

Miller, J. (2008). *Getting played: African American girls, urban inequality, and gendered violence.* New York: New York University Press.

Miller, J. (2010). The impact of gender when studying "Offenders on offending." In W. Bernasco & M. Tonry (Eds.), *Offenders on offending: Learning about crime from criminals* (pp. 161–183). London, UK: Willan Press.

Miller, J., & Glassner, B. (2004). The "inside" and the "outside": Finding realities in interviews. In D. Silverman (Ed.), *Qualitative Research* (2nd ed., pp. 125–139). London, UK: Sage.

Mullins, C. W., & Wright, R. (2003). Gender, social networks, and residential burglary. *Criminology, 41*(3): 813–840.

Oakley, A. (1981). Interviewing women: A contradiction in terms. In H. Roberts (Ed.), *Doing feminist research* (pp. 30–61). London, UK: Routledge and Kegan Paul.

Orbuch, T. L. (1997). People's accounts count: The sociology of accounts. *Annual Review of Sociology, 23*(1): 455–478.

Presser, L. (2005). Negotiating power and narrative in research: Implications for feminist methodology. *Signs, 30:* 2067–2090.

Risman, B. J. (2004). Gender as social structure: Theory wrestling with activism. *Gender & Society, 18*(4): 429–450.

Sanday, P. R. (1990). *Fraternity gang rape: Sex, brotherhood, and privilege on campus.* New York: New York University Press.

Scott, M. B., & Lyman, S. M. (1968). Accounts. *American Sociological Review, 33:* 46–62.

Silverman, D. (2006). *Interpreting qualitative data: Methods for analyzing talk, text, and interaction.* Thousand Oaks, CA: Sage.

Smith, D. E. (1987). *The everyday world as problematic: A feminist sociology.* Boston, MA: Northeastern University Press.

Song, M., & Parker, D. (1995). Commonality, difference and the dynamics of disclosure in in-depth interviewing. *Sociology, 29*(2): 241–256.

Spradley, J. (1979). *The ethnographic interview.* New York: Holt.

Taylor, J. M., Gilligan, C., & Sullivan, A. M. (1995). *Between voice and silence: Women and girls, race and relationship.* Cambridge, MA: Harvard University Press.

Veroff, J., & DiStefano, A. (2002). Researching across difference: A reprise. *American Behavioral Scientist, 45*(8): 1297–1307.

Willan, V. J., & Pollard, P. (2003). Likelihood of acquaintance rape as a function of males' sexual expectations, disappointment, and adherence to rape-conducive attitudes. *Journal of Social and Personal Relationships, 20*(5): 637–661.

Williams, C. L. (2000). Preface. *The Annals of the American Academy of Political and Social Science, 571:* 8–13.

Wright, R., & Decker, S. H. (1997). *Armed robbers in action: Stickups and street culture.* Boston, MA: Northeastern University Press.

Theories of Victimization

Section Highlights

- Victims and the criminal justice system
- Gender and fear of victimization
- Theories on victimization

T his section is divided into three topics. The section begins with a review of the victim experience in the criminal justice system. This section highlights the experience of help seeking by victims and the practice of victim blaming. The section then turns to a discussion of victimization and focuses on how fear about victimization is a gendered experience. The section concludes with a discussion of victimization and how theories seek to understand the victim experience and place it within the larger context of the criminal justice system and society in general.

Victims and the Criminal Justice System

Why do victims seek out the criminal justice system? Do they desire justice? What does *justice* mean for victims of crime? Is it retribution? Reparation? Something else? Victims play an important role in the criminal justice process—indeed, without a victim, many cases would fail to progress through the system at all. However, many victims who seek out the criminal justice system for support following their victimization are often sadly disappointed in their experiences. In many cases, human victims of crime are reduced to a tool of the justice system or a piece of evidence in a criminal case. As a result, many of these victims express frustration over a system that seems to do little to represent their needs and concerns; victims can even be further traumatized based on their experiences in dealing with the criminal justice system.

As a result of increased pressures to support the needs of victims throughout the criminal justice process, many prosecutors' offices began to establish victim-assistance programs during the mid-1970s to provide support to victims as their cases moved through the criminal justice process. In some jurisdictions, nonprofit agencies for particular crimes, such as domestic violence and rape crisis, also began to provide support for victims during this time

(Perona, Bottoms, & Sorenson, 2006; U.S. Department of Justice, 1998). Community agencies such as rape crisis centers developed in response to the perceived need for sexual assault prevention efforts, a desire for increased community awareness, and a wish to ameliorate the pain that the victims of crime often experience (Parsons & Bergin, 2010). In response to a backlash against the rights of criminal defendants as guaranteed by the U.S. Constitution, citizens and legislatures increased their efforts toward establishing rights for victims in the criminal justice process.

In an effort to increase the rights of victims in the criminal justice system, several pieces of federal legislation have passed. These policies increase the voice of victims throughout the process, training for officials who deal with victims, and funding programs that provide therapeutic resources for victims. Some of these focus on victims of a specific crime. For example, the Violence Against Women Act provides support for criminal justice researchers studying issues related to intimate partner violence. You'll learn more about this important piece of legislation in Section III. Other examples of federal legislation provide protections for all crime victims, such as the Crime Victims' Rights Act of 2004. While attempts to pass an amendment to the U.S. Constitution on victims' rights have been unsuccessful, each of the 50 states includes references to the rights of victims in criminal cases. Table 2.1 illustrates some of the **core rights of victims** that are included in many state laws and constitutions.

Much of what we know about victims comes from official crime datasets or research studies on samples of victimized populations. A comparison between official crime data (arrest rates) and victimization data indicates that many victims do not report their crime to law enforcement, which affects society's understanding regarding the realities of crime. According to the Bureau of Justice's National Crime Victimization Survey, only about half of all victims surveyed report their victimization to law enforcement (Hart & Rennison, 2003). Victims of serious violent crime are generally more likely to report these crimes compared to property offenses. Robbery was the most likely crime reported (66%), followed by aggravated assault (57%). While women are generally more likely to report crimes to law enforcement than men, cases of personal violence are significantly underreported among female victims (Patterson & Campbell, 2010). For example, the NCVS indicates that only 42% of rapes and sexual assaults are reported, and the Chicago Women's Health Risk Study showed that only 43% of women who experience violent acts from a current or former intimate partner contacted the police (Davies, Block, & Campbell, 2007). Certainly, the relationship between the victim and offender is a strong predictor in reporting rates, because women who are victimized by someone known to them are less likely to report than women who are victimized by a stranger (Resnick, Acierno, Holmes, Dammeyer, & Kilpatrick, 2000).

Table 2.1 • Core Rights of Victims
The core rights for victims of crime include

- the right to attend criminal justice proceedings;
- the right to apply for compensation;
- the right to be heard and participate in criminal justice proceedings;
- the right to be informed of proceedings and events in the criminal justice process, of legal rights and remedies, and of available services;
- the right to protection from intimidation and harassment;
- the right to restitution from the offender;
- the right to prompt return of personal property seized as evidence;
- the right to a speedy trial; and
- the right to enforcement of these rights.

SOURCE: From VictimLaw (n.d.).

There are many reasons why victims might choose not to report their victimization to the police. Some victims feel embarrassed by the crime. Still others may decide not to report a crime to the police out of the belief that nothing could be done. In many cases, people do not report their crime because they believe that the crime was not serious enough to make a big deal over it, while others believe it is a personal matter.

However, a failure to report does not mean that victims do not seek out assistance for issues related to their victimization experience. Several studies on sexual assault and intimate partner violence indicate that victims often seek help from personal resources outside of law enforcement, such as family and friends, and many seek assistance through formal mental health services following a victimization experience

▲ **Photo 2.1** Much of the victimization that women experience involves offenders known to them. In many cases, their relationship with an offender leads many victims to not report the crime to the police.

(Kaukinen, 2004). While many victims may be reluctant to engage in formal help seeking, research suggests that victims who receive positive support from informal social networks, such as friends and family, are subsequently more likely to seek out formal services, such as law enforcement and therapeutic resources. In these cases, informal networks act as a support system for seeking professional help and for making an official crime report (Davies et al., 2007; Starzynski, Ullman, Townsend, Long, & Long, 2007).

The literature on barriers to help seeking indicates that fears of retaliation can affect a victim's decision to make a report to the police. This is particularly true for victims of intimate partner violence where research indicates that violence can indeed increase following police intervention in intimate partner violence (Dugan, Nagin, & Rosenfeld, 2003). The presence of children in domestic violence situations also affects reporting rates as many victims may incorrectly believe that they will lose their children as a result of intervention from social service agents.

Spotlight on Victim Rights in Mexico

While there are laws protecting crime victims for each state and U.S federal level, such is not the case in many other regions of the world. Victimization is often a stigmatizing experience, leading many crime victims to suffer in silence. This is further compounded by the fact that in many countries, crime victims do not have any legal rights and agencies to support the needs of victims are limited.

Consider the case involving hundreds, if not thousands of victims of femicide along the Ciudad-Juarez and Chihuahua borders. Since the mid-1990s, young women have been murdered in and around these border towns, which have become synonymous with high levels of violence and narcotics trafficking. Their bodies are discovered days, weeks, and months following their disappearance and are typically abandoned in vacant lots in Juarez and the surrounding areas; some women are never found. Many of these cases involve significant acts of sexual torture, including rape and the slashing of the breasts and genitals of the female victims (Newton, 2003). Many

(Continued)

(Continued)

of these women had traveled to these border towns from their villages in search of work in the maquiladoras—factories that assemble or manufacture products, which are then returned to the United States duty free under the North American Free Trade Agreement.

In describing the murders of these women, several commentaries have pointed toward a clash between the traditional roles for women, a machista (chauvinistic) culture, and the rise of women's independence as an explanation for the violence. According to a 2003 report by the Inter-American Commission on Human Rights (IACHR), the crimes against women in Ciudad Juarez have received international attention because of the extreme levels of violence in the murders and the belief that these killings may have been the result of a serial killer. However, their research indicates that these cases of femicide are not the result of a single serial killer but are part of a larger social issue related to a pattern of gender-based discrimination where the violence against women is not considered to be a serious issue. Given the relationship with gender in these cases, any official response to address these crimes must consider the larger social context of crimes against women and the accessibility of justice for women in these cases.

While the Mexican government created a victims services fund designed to provide monetary compensation to the families of the women and girls who have been murdered in Juarez, the program is poorly organized, and few families have been able to access the funds (Calderon Gamboa, 2007). Meanwhile, nonprofit organizations such as *Justicia para Nuestras Hijas* (Justice for our Daughters) work to combat the myths and victim blaming surrounding these cases through public education. They also provide legal assistance and therapeutic support services for victims of crime. The organizing also works to document these cases of femicide and lobby for support and legal change to the government (Villagran, n.d).

The grassroots movement for victims in Mexico has continued to grow. While groups are united in an effort to end violence in their communities, provide support for victims, and call attention to a failing justice system, there are significant debates within these efforts on how to accomplish these goals. In January 2013, the Mexican government passed the General Law of Victims. However, the law was heavily criticized, and many groups did not feel that the law went far enough to meet the needs of victims. The law was revised in May 2013 and incorporated a number of provisions for victims, including a national registry of victims, a governmental victim services agency, and a victim assistance fund (Villagran, n.d.). At the same time, the judicial system is working through several reforms to their process. In the words of Ernesto Canales, the cofounder of RENACE, "what is needed is an integral reform of the system . . . we cannot think that by augmenting the rights of victims and leaving the current system in place we'll be protecting (victims)" (Villagran, n.d., p. 138). While progress has been made in these areas, there is still significant work to be done.

Victim Blaming

Reporting practices and help-seeking behaviors by victims are also influenced by the potential of **victim blaming**. Victim blaming is the practice whereby the responsibility of the crime is diffused from the offender and blame is shifted to the victim.

Why do we blame the victim? The process of victim blaming is linked to a belief in a just world. The concept of a just world posits that society has a need to believe that people deserve whatever comes to them—bad things happen to bad people, and good things happen to good people (Lerner, 1980). Under these assumptions, if a bad thing happens to someone, then that person must be at fault for the victimization because of who he or she is and what he or she does. A just world outlook gives a sense of peace to many individuals. Imagining a world where crime victims must have done something foolish, dangerous, or careless allows members of society to distinguish themselves from this identity of victimhood—"I would never do that, so therefore I must be safe from harm"—and allows individuals to shield themselves from feelings of vulnerability and powerlessness when it comes to potential acts of victimization. There are several negative consequences stemming from this condition: (1) Victim blaming assumes that people are able to change the environment in which they live, (2) victim blaming assumes that only "innocent" victims are true victims, and (3) victim blaming creates a false sense of security about the risks of crime.

Given the nature of victimization patterns in society, few meet the criteria of a culturally ideal victim. This process of victim blaming allows society to diffuse the responsibility of crime between the victim and the offender. For example, the battered woman is asked, "Why do you stay?"; the rape victim is asked, "What were you wearing?"; the assault victim is asked, "Why didn't you fight back?"; the burglary victim is asked, "Why didn't you lock the door?"; and the woman who puts herself in harm's way is asked, "What were you thinking?" Each of these scenarios shifts the blame away from the perpetrator and assigns responsibility to the victim. Victim blaming enables people to make sense of the victimization. In many cases, the process of victim blaming allows people to separate themselves from those who have been victimized—"I would never have put myself in that situation"—and this belief allows people to feel safe in the world.

How does the **just world hypothesis** work, and what are the implications for this application in the criminal justice system? Consider the crime of sexual assault. Under the just world hypothesis, victim blaming occurs in subtle ways in typical cases and may be more obvious in high-profile cases. For example, in the accusations against Kobe Bryant, extensive news reports questioned why the victim entered the hotel room with Mr. Bryant. There was also significant speculation about the victim's sexual activity prior to and following the alleged act with Mr. Bryant. Under the just world hypothesis, the victim begins to assume responsibility for this alleged assault in the eyes of the public. This can impact future reporting trends, because victims may be less likely to report their own victimizations after observing what happened to the victim in the Bryant case. A belief in the just world hypothesis also leads to an increased support of rape myths. For example, college males who view newspaper articles in support of myths about rape were less likely to view nonconsensual sexual acts as criminal compared to females in general or males who read neutral news accounts of sexual assault (Franiuk Seefelt, Cepress, & Vandello, 2008).

Given that women tend to be disproportionately represented in many forms of victimization, such as rape, sexual assault, and intimate partner violence, victim blaming can be disproportionately gendered and directed toward women (Eigenberg & Garland, 2008). Research on victim blaming finds that men are more likely to blame female victims in cases of rape and sexual assault (Kohsin Wang & Rowley). Victim blaming is also more prevalence among older individuals and those with lower levels of education or lower socioeconomic status (Gracia & Tomas, 2014). Victim characteristics can also impact how much blame is attributed to the victim. For example, victims who violate traditional gender roles or who are intoxicated are more likely to experience victim blaming (Grubb & Turner, 2012). Attributions of responsibility are often levied against victims who do not physically fight back against their attacker (Spears & Spohn, 1996).

The presence of victim blaming has also been linked to the low reporting rates of crime. Here, victims reach out to law enforcement, community agencies, and family or peer networks in search of support and assistance and are often met with blame and refusals to help. These experiences have a negative effect on the recovery of crime victims. The media can also perpetuate victim blaming, particularly in cases involving celebrities. For example, during the alleged sexual assault by Kobe Bryant in 2003 the media used the term *accuser* in this particular case, whereas most accounts of sexual assault generally use the term *victim* (Franiuk et al., 2008). Another example is the high profile assault of Janay Rice by her husband, Baltimore Ravens running back Ray Rice. In September 2014, a video of Mrs. Rice surfaced where she was beaten unconscious by Mr. Rice. The NFL initially suspended Rice for two games for his behavior, and the Ravens later terminated his contract. In addition to articles expressing outrage over the incident, there were also several articles that questioned what Janay did to provoke her then-fiance (now husband). Still others asserted that Ray Rice might also be a victim. At a press conference on the incident, Janay stated that she regretted "the role that she played in that night" (Weymouth, 2014; Giris, 2014; Marcotte, 2014). In addition to the effects of victim blaming for these specific individuals, such high profile cases involving victim blaming can impact reporting rates. "I talked to specific survivors (of sexual assault) that said, 'I don't want to report this because I saw what happened in the Kobe Bryant case'" (Lopez, 2007, para. 8).

Victim blaming is not limited to high-profile cases that make news headlines. Victims are often blamed by those closest to them, such as friends and family, who suggest that the victim "should have known better." Victim blaming can even be internalized whereby victims engage in self-doubt and feel shame for allowing themselves to become a victim (Kohsuro, Wang & Rowley, 2007). Victim blaming can also inhibit how victims recover from their trauma (Campbell, Ahrens, Sefl, Wasco & Barnes, 2001).

Victim blaming can also come from formal sources. The concept of **secondary victimization** refers to the practice whereby victims of crime feel traumatized as a result of not only their victimization experience but also by the official criminal justice system response to their victimization. For those cases that progress beyond the law enforcement investigative process, few have charges filed by prosecutors, and only rarely is a conviction secured. Indeed, the "ideal" case for the criminal justice system is one that represents stereotypical notions of what rape looks like rather than the realities of this crime. The practice of victim blaming through **rape myth acceptance** is an example of secondary victimization. Given the nature of the criminal justice process, the acceptance of rape myths by jurors can ultimately affect the decision-making process. Victim blaming can also occur by police and related justice professionals in cases of intimate partner violence, particularly in cases where a victim returns to her abuser (DeJong, Burgess-Proctor & Elis, 2008). The experience of secondary victimization can have significant consequences for reporting, because research indicates that victims would not have reported the crime if they had known what was in store for them (Logan, Evans, Stevenson, & Jordan, 2005).

Fear of Victimization

The majority of Americans have limited direct experience with the criminal justice system. Most are left with images of crime that are generated by the portrayal of victims and offenders in mass media outlets (Dowler, 2003). These images present a distorted view of the criminal justice system, with a generalized understanding that "if it bleeds, it leads." This leads to the overexaggeration of violent crime in society (Maguire, 1988; Potter & Kappeler, 2006; Surette, 2003). Research indicates that as individuals increase their consumption of local and national television news, their fears about crime increase, regardless of actual crime rates, gender, or a personal history of victimization (Chiricos, Padgett, & Gertz, 2000). In addition to the portrayal of crime within the news, stories of crime, criminals, and criminal justice have been a major staple of television entertainment programming. These images, too, present a distorted view of the reality of crime, because they generally present crime as graphic, random, and violent incidents (Gerbner & Gross, 1980).

Consider the following scenario:

Imagine yourself walking across a parking lot toward your car. It's late and the parking lot is poorly lit. You are alone. Standing near your car is a man who is watching you. Are you afraid?

When this scenario is presented to groups, we find that men and women respond to this situation differently. When asked who is afraid, it is primarily women who raise their hands. Rarely, do men respond to this situation with emotions of fear. Research also notes that girls are more likely than boys to indicate fears about victimization in situations that involve things such as poorly lit parking lots and sidewalks, overgrown shrubbery, and groups loitering in public spaces (Fisher & May, 2009). This simple illustration demonstrates the **fear of victimization** that women experience in their daily lives. As De Groof (2008) explains, "Fear of crime is, in other words, partly a result of feelings of personal discomfort and uncertainty, which are projected onto the threat of crime and victimization" (p. 281).

Why are girls more fearful in these types of situations? Much of this can be attributed to how girls are socialized differently than their male peers. From a young age, girls are often taught about fear, because parents are more likely to demonstrate concern for the safety of their daughters, compared to their sons (De Groof, 2008). This fear results in a relative lack of freedom for girls, in addition to an increase in the parental supervision of girls. These practices, which are designed to protect young women, can significantly affect their confidence levels in regarding the world around them. The worry that parents fear for their daughters continues as they transition from adolescence to adulthood (De Vaus & Wise, 1996). Additionally, this sense of fear can be transferred from the parent to the young female adult as a result of the gendered socialization that she has experienced throughout her life.

Gender also plays a role in feelings of vulnerability, which can translate to fears about victimization. Research indicates that the fear of crime for women is not necessarily related to the actual levels of crime that they personally experience. Overall, women are less likely to be victimized than men, yet they report overall higher levels of fear of crime than their male counterparts (Fattah & Sacco, 1989). These high levels of overall fear of victimization may be perpetuated by a specific fear of crime for women—rape and sexual assault. Indeed, rape is the crime that generates the highest levels of fear for women. These levels of fear are somewhat validated by crime statistics, because women make up the majority of victims for sexually based crimes (Warr, 1984, 1985). However, research indicates that this fear of sexual victimization extends beyond fear of rape to fear of all crimes, not just crimes of a sexual nature. The "shadow of sexual assault" thesis suggests that women experience a greater fear of crime in general, because they believe that any crime could ultimately become a sexually based victimization (Fisher & Sloan, 2003). Yet even when women engage in measures to keep themselves safe, their fear of sexual assault appears to increase rather than decrease (Lane, Gover, & Dahod, 2009). This sense of vulnerability is portrayed by "movie of the week" outlets that showcase storylines of women being victimized by a strange man who lurks in dark alleys and behind bushes (Jones-Brown, 2007; Skolnick, 1966). Unfortunately, these popular culture references toward criminal victimization generally (and rape and sexual assault specifically) paint a false picture of the realities of crime and victimization. Most women are victimized not by strangers, as these films would indicate, but instead by people known to them (Black et al., 2011). Indeed, research indicates that many women fail to see *acquaintance rape* as something that could impact them personally (Pryor & Hughes, 2013). While the fear of sexual assault is a common theme in the literature, some scholars indicate that fears about crime can involve acts other than sexual assault. Cook and Fox (2012) found that fear of physical harm is a stronger predictor of fear about crime for women over the fear of sexual assault. Snedker (2012) found similar evidence, because the majority of women in her study expressed fears over being robbed, not raped.

While there is a significant body of research on how demographics such as gender can impact fear about crime, research is just beginning to look at how multiple marginalities can influence these fears. In a survey of hate crime victimization among the LGBT community, researchers noted that one-third (33.6%) of the study's participants had been victimized as a result of their sexuality. Indeed, LGBT individuals are likely to experience multiple victimizations over the course of their lifetime (Burks et al., 2015). Unlike research using samples of heterosexual men and women (which tend to find that women experience greater fears about crime than men), research by Otis (2007) found that LGBT men and women tend to have similar fears about crime and victimization. One explanation for this may be that gay men experience forms of marginalization and vulnerability similar to those of heterosexual women, particularly when it comes to fears about physical, emotional and sexually based violence. Meanwhile women who identify as lesbian may find these fears enhanced not just by their gender but through their sexual identity as well. Fear about crime among the LGBT population is also linked to prior experiences of victimization. Such fear is likely not only a reflection of their own personal victim experiences but also related to the awareness of hate crimes against LGBT individuals in their community (Tiby, 2001).

The fear of crime and victimization has several negative consequences. Women who are fearful of crime, particularly violent or sexual crimes, are more likely to isolate themselves from society in general. This fear reflects not only the concern of potential victimization but also a threat regarding the potential loss of control that a victim experiences as a result of being victimized. Fear of crime can also be damaging toward one's feelings of self-worth and self-esteem. Here, potential victims experience feelings of vulnerability and increased anxiety.

The effects of fears of victimization are also reflected in societal actions (Clear & Frost, 2007). For example, public transit agencies may increase security measures, such as the presence of personnel, the use of video cameras in stations, and improving service reliability (Yavuz & Welch, 2010). Fear also impacts policy practices within the criminal justice system. Agents of criminal justice can respond to a community's fear of crime by increasing police patrols, while district attorneys pursue tough-on-crime stances in their prosecution of criminal cases. Politicians respond to community concerns about violent crime by creating and implementing tough-on-crime legislation, such as habitual sentencing laws such as "three strikes," and targeting perceived crimes of danger, such as the war on drugs. While the public's concern about crime may be very real, it can also be inflamed by inaccurate data on crime rates or a misunderstanding about the community supervision of offenders and recidivism rates. Unfortunately, "public policy is influenced more by media misinformation and sensationalized high profile cases than by careful or thoughtful analysis" (Frost & Phillips, 2011, p. 88).

Theories on Victimization

In an effort to understand the victim experience, social science researchers began to investigate the characteristics of crime victims and the response by society to these victims. While criminology focuses predominantly on the study of crime as a social phenomenon and the nature of offenders, the field of victimology places the victim at the center of the discussion. Early perspectives on victimology focused on how victims, either knowingly or unconsciously, can be at fault for their victimization, based on their personal life events and decision-making processes.

One of the early scholars in this field, Benjamin Mendelsohn (1956), developed a typology of victimization that distinguished different types of victims based on the relative responsibility of the victims in their own victimization. Embedded in between his typology is the degree to which victims have the power to make decisions that can alter their likelihood of victimization. As a result of his work, the study of victimology began to emerge as its own distinct field of study.

Mendelsohn's theory of victimology is based on six categories of victims. The first category is the innocent victim. This distinction is unique in Mendelsohn's typology, because it is the only classification that does not have any responsibility for the crime attributed to the victim. As the name suggests, an innocent victim is someone who is victimized by a random and unprecipitated crime, such as a school shooting. Unlike the other categories in Mendelsohn's typology, the innocent victim is one with no responsibility in his victimization. In contrast, the other five categories assign a degree of blame or responsibility to the victim. Mendelsohn's second category is the victim with minor guilt. In this case, victimization occurs as a result of one's carelessness or ignorance. The victim with minor guilt is someone who, if she had given better thought or care to her safety, would not have been a victim of a crime. For instance, someone who was in the wrong place at the wrong time or one who places herself in dangerous areas where she is at risk for potential victimization is characterized as a victim with minor guilt. An example of this is a case of a victim who is walking alone down the street in a high-crime area and is robbed. Mendelsohn's third category is a victim who is equally as guilty as the offender. This victim is someone who shares the responsibility of the crime with the offender by deliberately placing himself or herself in harm's way. An example of this classification is the individual who seeks out the services of a sex worker, only to contract a sexually transmitted infection as a result of the interaction. The fourth category represents the case in which the victim is deemed "more guilty" than the offender. This is a "victim" who is provoked by others to engage in criminal activity. An example of this category is one who kills a current or former intimate partner following a history of abuse. The fifth category is a victim who is solely responsible for the harm that comes to him or her. These individuals are considered to be the "most guilty" of victims as they engaged in an act that was likely to lead to injury on their part. Examples of the most guilty victim

Table 2.2 ● Mendelsohn's Categories of Victims		
Category	**Definition**	**Example**
Innocent victim	No responsibility for the crime attributed to victim	Institutionalized victims, the mentally ill, children, or those who are attacked while unconscious
Victim with minor guilt	Victim precipitates crime with carelessness/ignorance	Victim lost in the "wrong part of town"
Voluntary victim	Victim and offender equally responsible for crime	Victim pays prostitute for sex; then prostitute robs victim ("rolling Johns")
Victim who is more guilty than the offender	Victim who provokes or induces another to commit crime	Burning bed syndrome: victim is killed by the domestic partner he abused for years
Victim who alone is guilty	Victim who is solely responsible for his or her own victimization	An attacker who is killed in self-defense; suicide bomber killed by detonation of explosives
Imaginary victim	Victim mistakenly believes he or she has been victimized	Mentally ill person who reports imagined victimization as real event

SOURCE: Adapted from Sengstock (1976).

include a suicide bomber who engages in an act that results in his or her death or when a would-be attacker is killed by another in an act of self-defense. Mendelsohn's final category is the imaginary victim. This is an individual who, as a result of some mental disease or defect, believes that he or she has been victimized by someone or something, when in reality this person has not been victimized.

While Mendelsohn focused on the influence of guilt and responsibility of victims, **Hans von Hentig's** (1948) typology of victims looked at how personal factors, such as biological, psychological, and social factors, influence risk factors for victimization. The categories in von Hentig's typology of victims include the young, the female, the old, the mentally defective and deranged, immigrants, minorities, dull normals, the depressed, the acquisitive, the wanton, the lonesome or heartbroken, the tormentor, and the blocked, exempted, or fighting.

While the application of von Hentig's theory helped develop an understanding of victims in general, his typology includes only a single category for females. However, experiences of female victimization can fit within each of von Hentig's other categories. For instance, young girls who run away from home are easy targets for pimps who "save" girls from the dangers of the streets and "protect" them from harm. The youth of these girls places them at a higher risk for violence and prostitution activities under the guise of protection. While von Hentig's category of mentally defective was designed to capture the vulnerability of the mentally ill victim, he also referenced the intoxicated individual within this context. Under this category, women who engage in either consensual acts of intoxication or who are subjected to substances unknown to them can be at risk for alcohol- or drug-facilitated sexual assault. Likewise, consider von Hentig's category of immigrants and the way in which immigration status can also play a key role for women victims. Many abusers use a woman's illegal immigration status as a threat to ensure compliance. In these cases, women may be forced to endure violence in their lives or are induced into sexual slavery out of fear of deportation. Von Hentig also discusses how race and ethnicity can affect the victim experience, and significant research has demonstrated how these factors affect the criminal justice system at every stage.

Spotlight on Gender and Kidnapping

Over the past decade, several stories of women who were kidnapped and held captive for decades hit the national news. One of these cases involved three women who were held in a dilapidated home in Cleveland, OH. On May 6, 2013, three women were rescued from a home in Cleveland, Ohio. Amanda Berry, Georgina "Gina" DeJesus, and Michelle Knight had been held captive by Ariel Castro, a 52-year-old man who had emigrated to the United States as a child from Puerto Rico. Each of the women had accepted a ride from Castro, who then abducted them and forced them into his basement where he kept the girls physically restrained. Michelle Knight was his first victim and was 21 years old when she was taken on August 22, 2002. His next victim, Amanda Berry, disappeared on April 21, 2003, just before her 17th birthday. Finally, Gina DeJesus was abducted on April 2, 2004. She was only 14. All three girls endured significant physical and sexual assaults throughout their captivity. Michelle Knight reported that she suffered several miscarriages, and Amanda Berry gave birth to a daughter fathered by Castro, born on Christmas Day 2006 (BBC, 2013). After a decade in hell, the women were rescued after garnering the attention of a neighbor who helped them escape (Steer, 2013).

While the prosecutors originally considered charging Castro with aggravated murder (in the cases of the forced miscarriages of Knight), he ultimately pled guilty to 937 counts of kidnapping, rape, and other crimes such as child endangerment and gross sexual imposition (Krouse, 2013; Mahoney, 2013; Sheeran, 2013). In speaking at his sentencing hearing, Michelle Knight told Castro, "I spent 11 years in hell, where your hell is just beginning" (DeLuca, 2013). However, Castro served very little of his sentence before he hung himself by a bedsheet in his cell. Some might argue that Castro's suicide cheated the justice system—"This man couldn't take, for even a month, a small portion of what he had dished out for more than a decade" (Mungin & Alsup, 2013).

▲ **Photo 2.2** Amanda Berry reads her victim impact statement during the sentencing hearing for Ariel Castro. Castro was convicted on several counts of kidnapping and rape against Berry and her two co-victims.

Another story with similar circumstances was that of Jaycee Dugard. Dugard was kidnapped by husband and wife Phillip and Nancy Garrido when she was just 11 years old and was held for eighteen years. Dugard was abducted walking home from a school bus stop in South Lake Tahoe. Phillip Garrido was a convicted sex offender who was on parole at the time of Jaycee's abduction. Much of her captivity was spent in makeshift tents or a shed that was located behind Garrido's home. Even though parole agents visited the home sixty times, they never checked the sheds in the yard. Meanwhile, Phillip Garrido sexually assaulted Jaycee on a regular basis, and she gave birth to two daughters during this time. The children were homeschooled, and ultimately Phillip and Nancy allowed Jaycee and her daughters to have contact with the public, under the guise that Jaycee was their sister, not their mother. Jaycee was even allowed to work for the Garridos' printing business, yet she was forbidden to tell anyone about her true identity. On August 24, 2009, Garrido traveled to U.C. Berkeley with the girls to seek permission to hold a special event on campus related to his ministry. The incident was referred to both the local police as well as Garrido's parole officer. While Dugard initially maintained her false identity, she ultimately told investigators who she was.

Phillip Garrido and his wife ultimately pled guilty to kidnapping and rape. On June 2, 2011, Phillip was sentenced to 431 years to life, and Nancy received 36 years to life. While Jaycee Dugard filed a suit against the U.S. government for failing to effectively monitor Garrido when he was a federal parolee, her suit was dismissed. Meanwhile, the state of California approved a settlement of $20 million. She has since written two books about her experience (Dooley, Scott, Ng, & Effron, 2016; Egelko, 2016; Salonga, 2016).

Routine Activities Theory

While early theories of victimization provided a foundation for understanding the victim experience, modern victimization theories expand from these concepts to investigate the role of society in victimization and to address how personal choices affect the victim experience. One of the most influential perspectives in modern victimology is Cohen and Felson's (1979) **routine activities theory**. Routine activities theory suggests that the likelihood of a criminal act (and in turn, the likelihood of victimization) occurs with the convergence of three essential components: (1) someone who is interested in pursuing a criminal action (offender), (2) a potential victim (target) "available" to be victimized, and (3) the absence of someone or something (guardian) that would deter the offender from making contact with the available victim. The name of the theory is derived from a belief that victims and guardians exist within the normal, everyday patterns of life. Cohen and Felson posit that lifestyle changes during the second half of the 20th century created additional opportunities for the victim and offender to come into contact with each other as a result of changes to daily routines and activities. Cohen and Felson's theory was created to discuss the risk of victimization in property crimes. Here, if individuals were at work or out enjoying events in the community, they were less likely to be at home to guard their property against potential victimization, and burglary was more likely to result.

Routine activities theory has been used to understand a variety of different forms of crime, particularly related to demographic differences in victimization. For example, research on routine activities theory demonstrates that minority women are more likely to experience risk of victimization when riding public transportation, and neighborhood factors can affect the odds of women's victimization (Like-Haislip & Miofsky, 2011). Gender can also mediate the types of victimization risk. While men are more likely to experience increased risks of violent victimization because they go out at night, women have an increased risk of theft based on increased shopping activities (Bunch, Clay-Warner, & Lei, 2012).

Routine activities theory has also been used to look at cybercrimes. Research by Navarro and Jasinski (2013) indicates that girls are at a greater risk for cyber-bullying than boys, even though boys engage in similar risky online behaviors. Among adolescents, the use of digital media such as social networking and texting can place youth at risk of cyber dating abuse. For example, youth who engage in sexting with their boy/girlfriend are more likely to be involved in an abusive dating relationship. The risk of victimization increases with the amount of time that they spend online (Van Ouytsel, Ponnet & Walrave, 2016).

Routine activities theory has been criticized by feminist criminologists, who disagree with the theory's original premise that men are more vulnerable to the risks of victimization than women. Indeed, the guardians that Cohen and Felson suggest protect victims from crime may instead be the ones most likely to victimize women, particularly in cases of intimate partner abuse and sexual assault. For example, research by Schwartz, DeKeseredy, Tait, and Alvi (2001) indicates that women who engage in recreational substance use (such as alcohol or drugs) are considered to be a suitable target by men who are motivated to engage in certain offending patterns. Attempts by administrators to increase safety on college campuses by implementing protections, such as escort patrols, lighted paths, and emergency beacons (modern-day guardians), may have little effect on sexual assault rates on campus, given that many of these incidents take place behind closed doors in college dormitories and student apartments. In addition, the concept of self-protective factors (or self-guardians) may not be able to ward off a potential attacker, given that the overwhelming majority of sexual assaults on college campuses are perpetrated by someone known to the victim (Mustaine & Tewksbury, 2002). In addition, perceptions of being a "good" girl can also lead women to believe they are at a reduced risk for victimization. "I'm not running around in tiny little dresses anymore" (Snedker, 2012, p. 86). Another woman expressed a similar sentiment of recognizing potential risks of victimization based on her patterns of behavior: "I'm not going to do anything stupid. If I'm coming home really late drunk and I'm by myself, I might be more of a target" (Snedker, 2012, p. 89). This scenario highlights the perception that a shift in routine activities can reduce the risk of victimization. Unfortunately, this adds to the myth that girls who dress provocatively or consume alcohol somehow deserve to be sexually assaulted, which shifts the blame to the victim and not the perpetrator.

Like routine activities theory, **lifestyle theory** seeks to relate the patterns of one's everyday activities to the potential for victimization. While routine activities theory was initially designed to explain victimization from property crimes, lifestyle theory was developed to explore the risks of victimization from personal crimes. Research by Hindelang, Gottfredson, and Garafalo (1978) suggests that people who engage in risky lifestyle choices place themselves at risk for victimization. Based on one's lifestyle, one may increase the risk for criminal opportunity and victimization through both an increased exposure to criminal activity and an increased exposure to motivated offenders. However, crime is not the only lifestyle that can place people at risk for victimization, because nonviolent deviant behaviors, mental health status, and substance use can place people at potential victimization. Gender also plays a role in how these factors influence victimization risk. For example, males who engage in binge drinking have an increased risk of victimization while females who abuse prescription drugs experience significantly higher odds of victimization (Zaykowski & Gunter, 2013).

Given the similarities between the foundations of lifestyle theory and routine activities theory, many researchers today combine the tenets of these two perspectives to investigate victimization risks in general. These perspectives have been used to explain the risks of sexual assault of women on college campuses. For example, young women in the university setting who engage in risky lifestyle decision-making processes (such as the use of alcohol) and have routine activity patterns (such as living alone or frequenting establishments such as bars and clubs where men are present and alcohol is readily available) are at an increased risk for sexual victimization. In addition, women who are at risk for a single incident remain at risk for recurrent victimizations if their behavior patterns remain the same (Fisher, Daigle, & Cullen, 2010).

Feminist Pathways Perspective

Feminist pathways perspective research draws on the historical context of women's and girls' lives to relate how events (and traumas) affect their likelihood to engage in crime. Researchers have identified a cycle of violence for female offenders that often begins with their own victimization and results with their involvement in offending behavior. While the pathways perspective is discussed at length in Section VI, the topic deserves a brief introduction as we conclude our discussion on theories of victimization.

The feminist pathways approach may provide some of the best understanding about female offending. Research on women's and girls' pathways to offending provide substantial evidence for the link between victimization and offending, because incarcerated girls are three to four times more likely to have been abused compared to their male counterparts (Belknap & Holsinger, 2006). A review of case files of delinquent girls in California indicates that 92% of delinquent girls in California reported having been subjected to at least one form of abuse, including emotional (88%), physical (81%), or sexual (56%) abuse (Acoca & Dedel, 1998b). Particularly for young female offenders, a history of abuse leads to a propensity to engage in certain types of delinquency, such as running away and school failures. The effects of sexual assault are also related to drug and alcohol addiction and mental health traumas, such as posttraumatic stress disorder and a negative self-identity (Raphael, 2005). In a **cycle of victimization and offending**, young girls often run away from home in an attempt to escape from an abusive situation. In many cases, girls were forced to return home by public agencies, such as the police, courts, and social services—agencies designed to "help" victims of abuse. Unfortunately, in their attempt to escape from an abusive situation, girls often fall into criminal behaviors as a mechanism of survival.

Indeed, there are several ways to think about the victimization of women and girls. As you move through the next three sections in this text, consider how each of these theoretical perspectives impact the victim experience for women and how the criminal justice system responds to these cases. How would you improve the experience of women as victims? What police recommendations would you recommend to agents of criminal justice? Finally, what remedies exist to limit the victimization of women, and what can you as a member of society do to affect change in this realm?

/// SUMMARY

- Not all victims report their crimes to the police but may seek out support from other sources.
- Victim-assistance programs have emerged as a key response to the secondary victimization often experienced by victims who come forward to the criminal justice system.
- Victim blaming has been linked to low reporting rates.
- Women experience higher rates of fear of crime than males.
- Gendered socialization and vulnerability to specific crime types such as rape may explain the gendered fear of crime.
- Mendelsohn's typology of victimization distinguishes different categories of victims based on the responsibility of the victim and the degree to which victims have the power to make decisions that can alter their likelihood of victimization.
- Von Hentig's typology of victimization focuses on how personal factors, such as biological, social, and psychological characteristics, influence risk factors for victimization.
- The just world hypothesis, which holds that people get what they deserve, is a form of victim blaming.
- Routine activities theory and lifestyle theory have been used to investigate the risk of sexual assault of women.
- The pathways perspective suggests a cycle of criminal justice involvement for women whereby early victimization is sometimes a precursor to later criminal offending.

/// KEY TERMS

Core rights of victims 52

Cycle of victimization and
    offending 62

Fear of victimization 56

Feminist pathways perspective 62

Just world hypothesis 55

Lifestyle theory 62

Mendelsohn, Benjamin 58

Rape myth acceptance 56

Routine activities theory 61

Secondary victimization 56

Victim blaming 54

von Hentig, Hans 59

/// DISCUSSION QUESTIONS

1. How do early theories of victimization distinguish between different types of victims? How might the criminal justice system use these typologies in making decisions about which cases to pursue?

2. What types of help-seeking behaviors do female crime victims engage in? How are these practices related to the reporting of crimes to law enforcement?

3. What effects does the practice of victim blaming have for future potential crime victims and the criminal justice system?

4. In what ways do media outlets support or dispel rape myths and victim blaming? How is this related to help-seeking behavior, official reporting, and revictimization?

5. How is fear of crime a gendered experience? What factors contribute to the differences in male versus female fear of crime? Do official crime statistics support or dispel the basis for these fear differences?

6. How might feminist criminologists critique modern-day victimization theories, such as routine activities theory and lifestyle theory?

7. How have historical theories on female offending failed to understand the nature of female offending?

8. What contributions has feminist criminology made in understanding the relationship between gender and offending?

/// WEB RESOURCES

Bureau of Justice Statistics: http://bjs.ojp.usdoj.gov

The National Center for Victims of Crime: http://www.ncvc.org

Office for Victims of Crime: https://www.ovc.gov

Feminist Criminology: http://fcx.sagepub.com

 Visit **study.sagepub.com/mallicoat3e** to access additional study tools, including eFlashcards, web quizzes, web resources, video resources, and SAGE journal articles.

READING /// 3

In the chapter, you learned that many of the fears of crime are gendered. Women experience different levels of fear about crime than men do. This reading highlights how gender impacts how someone experiences fear about being victimized on a college campus for certain types of crimes but that no differences exist between males and females for other types of crimes. In addition, the authors expose what factors lead to increased levels of fear for both men and women.

College Students' Crime-Related Fears on Campus
Are Fear-Provoking Cues Gendered?

Bonnie S. Fisher and David May

The notion that gender plays a central role in determining crime-related fear levels is so tightly woven into thinking about fear that it is by and large no longer subject to question. Decades of empirical scrutiny by sociologists, victimologists, psychologists, planners, and geographers have established that there are gender-based differences in fear levels across crime types and in certain types of environments, such as public places (Day, 1994; Fisher & Sloan, 2003; Klodawsky & Lundy, 1994; Lane & Meeker, 2003; May, 2001a; Nasar & Fisher, 1993; Reid & Konrad, 2004).

Despite these widely accepted gendered findings, much of the crime-related research has focused almost exclusively on why women are fearful (Madriz, 1997; Pain, 1997; Starkweather, 2007). A small, but growing, number of researchers have turned their attention to men as victims of fear and why they are fearful (Brownlow, 2005; Day, Stump, & Carreon, 2003). Only recently, a few comparative research pieces have been published that identify and explain which factors, if any, differentiate crime-related fear between women and men (Lane & Meeker, 2003; May, 2001b; May & Dunaway, 2000; May, Vartanian, & Virgo, 2002; Reid & Konrad, 2004; Schafer, Huebner, & Bynum, 2006; Smith & Torstenson, 1997; Wallace & May, 2005).

Despite researchers' efforts and explanations, gaps in understanding the relationship between fear-provoking cues and subsequent fear of crime are evident. The current research takes several important steps in a long overdue effort to close the gaps about what is known about which, if any, fear-provoking cues differ across gender and which ones, if any, influence males' and females' fear of specific types of crime. We employ survey data from a large sample of undergraduate students at a 4-year public university to address three research questions about the possible gendered nature of cues and crime-related fear that have not been previously addressed. First, are fear-provoking cues gendered? Simply stated, do males and females evaluate cues known to provoke fear of crime the same way or differently? Second, which of these

SOURCE: Fisher, B. S., & May, D. (2009). College students' crime-related fears on campus: Are fear-provoking cues gendered? *Journal of Contemporary Criminal Justice, 25*(3), 300–321.

AUTHORS' NOTE: This study was supported by a research grant awarded to Professor David May from the College of Justice and Safety Research Committee at Eastern Kentucky University in 2007. The opinions expressed in this article do not represent those of Eastern Kentucky University; they are the authors' opinions.

cues, if any, predict males' and females' fear of specific types of crimes? That is, are fear-provoking cues offense specific? For example, do certain fear-provoking cues predict fear of theft but not fear of violent crime? Third, do these cues equally predict specific crime-related fear across males and females? Simply put, do fear-provoking cues equally predict the same types of fear for males and females alike? Addressing these questions is among the first attempts to enhance our understanding about whether the relationship between fear-provoking cues and crime-related fears is a gendered one among college students while on campus.

Cognitive Mapping and Fear-Provoking Cues

From an evolutionary perspective, individuals use a cognitive map as an efficient mechanism for managing spatial and temporal information about the physical and social nature of their environment to guide behavioral decisions (Kitchin, 1996). Cognitive maps are important to individuals' safety; they protect people from harm. Environmental psychologists have suggested that these maps give individuals "a selective advantage in a difficult and dangerous world that is necessary for survival" (Kitchin, 1994, p. 2). Sighted individuals scan their immediate environment for cues of danger, physical threat, or harm that would make themselves, others, or their property vulnerable to attack. Merry (1981, pp. 11–12) described this process when she explained,

> [C]ues are structured into spatial, temporal, and personal cognitive maps that define places, times, and categories of persons who are likely to be safe or dangerous. The decision that a situation is (is not) dangerous depends on the intersection of these maps. To understand fear of crime, it is much less useful to ask how afraid an individual feels than it is to explore the content of his or her cognitive maps and the frequency with which he or she encounters situations these maps define as dangerous.

Ultimately, these cognitive maps shape an individual's sense of potential criminal victimization, and it is from these maps that individuals draw inferences about

their fear levels. Van der Wurff, Van Staalduinen, and Stringer (1989, p. 145) noted that as individuals venture into a specific place, they immediately heed the "criminalizability" of that space.

Given the gendered focus of this article, the nexus between cognitive maps and crime-related fear gives rise to an issue directed at possible differences between males and females in their perceptions of fear-provoking cues. At the core of this issue are three quite simple, yet unanswered, questions: (a) Do males and females differ with respect to their assessment of fear-provoking cues? (b) Do the same or different fear-provoking cues predict fear of different types of crimes, namely, property and violent ones? (c) Are these fear-provoking cues the same for males and females? The answers to these questions, however, are not so obvious.

Fear-Provoking Cues

There is ample evidence cutting across a variety of academic disciplines that supports a significant association between specific features of the immediate physical environment and crime-related fear (Brownlow, 2005; Fisher & Nasar, 1992; Merry, 1981; Nasar & Fisher, 1993; Warr, 1990, 2000). However, the findings from fear-provoking cues research suggest that there is not one cue that influences fear but rather a constellation of cues that include specific features of the physical environment from the presence of others to the visibility of police officers whose duty is to provide surveillance and protection.

Are the Cues That Predict Crime-Related Fear Gendered?

As we have discussed, cognitive maps are helpful in understanding how sighted individuals assess their fear of crime level. The growing body of research on fear-provoking cues also provides insights into what cues influence individuals' fear of crime. Bringing these bodies of research together raises issues as to whether the cues that predict crime-related fear are gendered. For example, does poor lighting influence fear of crime for both males and females, or does poor lighting influence only females' fear of crime? Does police presence predict males and females being fearful or predict only males being fearful?

It is somewhat surprising that researchers have largely neglected the integration of these bodies of research to examine if the relationship between cues and crime-related fear are similar or different across males and females. In part, the lack of attention may lie in the fact that researchers' focus has primarily highlighted females' experiences of crime-related fear (Madriz, 1997; Pain, 1997; Starkweather, 2007; for exception see Brownlow, 2005; Day et al., 2003; Lane & Meeker, 2003; May, 2001b; May & Dunaway, 2000).

Among the very few published studies to offer some guidance into addressing our gendered-based questions about the fear-provoking cues relationship is Brownlow's (2005) study of fear among young men and women in Philadelphia's Cobb Creek Park. From the focus group discussions with these youth and their rating of slides from the park, he concluded that "clear differences distinguish how the young men and women of the study negotiated their fears in public spaces" (p. 589). He reported that unlike their female counterparts, males do not judge an environment as safe based on the presence or absence of environmental cues. Brownlow found that males judge an environment based on their sense and perceptions of their negotiation of an environment, namely, whether they see themselves as being able to flee a risky or uncertain situation. Males consider their youth, physical strength, and speed to be a key in managing dangerous situations. These results suggest that environmental cues to crime-related fear differ across sexes. His conclusions provide starting points to unpacking the gendered nature, if it exists, of cues predicting students' crime-related fear while on campus.

Lighting and Gender

Previous research has reported that lighting affects sighted individuals' ability to see a potentially dangerous environment. Research has also shown that lighting is a significant correlate and predictor of fear of crime, in part, because poor lighting does not offer adequate illumination to observe environmental cues to danger such as being physically attacked or having property stolen. Poor lighting in certain areas such as parking garages that have a perceptional tendency to be isolated may have more pronounced effects on predicting fear than poor lighting in more public spaces, such as sidewalks. Regardless of the exact place of the lighting, poor lighting on campus might have different effects on whether males and females are fearful. In line with Brownlow's conclusions, we would expect that poor lighting might influence whether females' are fearful but not whether male counterparts are fearful. Research has shown that most females are physically and sexually vulnerable to attack and are physically challenged to thwart off such an attack. Most males, however, would have physical strength and ability to thwart off such an attack, but in line with Brownlow's work, if they cannot see how to escape when confronted, this situation might make them fearful. So poor lighting might equally influence both sexes' fearfulness.

Foliage and Gender

Researchers have shown that foliage influences individuals' fear of crime because it provides refuge or hiding places for a predator who can surprise attack a victim or even walk from inside or behind the greenery. On one hand, foliage, such as overgrown shrubbery, might have a positive effect on fear for women because of their sexual and physical vulnerability and physical inability to thwart an attack. Overgrown foliage on campus might not influence males' fear because of their physical confidence to thwart attack but could also present an element of confrontation that might heighten their fear. Hence, the effect of foliage on crime-related fear may be the same for males and females.

Youth Loitering and Gender

The presence of others, especially youth, congregating or loitering has been shown to heighten fear of victimization. Researchers attribute the elevated fear in these types of situations to individuals' perceiving a breakdown in social control, suggesting that if confronted by these youth, the infraction would go unchallenged by others. Much research has shown that this cue results in a lack of a sense of social control in that others may not effectively respond to the situation at hand (Skogan, 1990; Warr, 2000). For males, this might be especially so in light of research that shows that for many men, the public places and situations that challenged their gender identity, in particular their masculinity, generated fear (Day et al., 2003). Supportive of Day et al.'s (2003) results are those reported by Brownlow (2005), who reported that males felt less safety and security in situations where they lack the ability to flee a risky or uncertain situation. Groups loitering around campus may well predict males' fear but not females' fear. Another plausible speculation is that both sexes might sense a lack of social control in this situation in that others may not effectively respond to the situation at hand or that they would be unable to escape attack since they are outnumbered. The fear that confrontation would increase risk of being victimized might loom equally for both sexes.

Police Visibility and Gender

The relationship between police visibility and fear of crime for the sexes is less clear. The relationship appears to be contingent on the type of activities the police are engaged in during the time they are visible. As such, it is quite possible that the impact of police visibility on fear of crime will vary by gender as well. Increased visibility of police might reduce fear of crime among women because of their vulnerabilities discussed above yet may have no effect on male fear because they lack those same vulnerabilities.

Drawing from the research examining cognitive mapping, fear-provoking cues, and fear of crime, it is plausible that fear-provoking cues have different effects on whether or not males and females are fearful of being victimized. But it may be equally likely that there are no cues that significantly predict whether males and females are fearful, and hence, there are no fear-provoking cue differences predicting fear across the sexes. Because we are not certain whether cues that predict crime-related fear are gendered or not, we turn to our empirical analyses to explore this overlooked relationship.

Method

Data Collection

In March 2008, we asked for and received a list of all the general education courses offered during the current spring term on campus at a large public institution in the South. We randomly selected 25 of those courses and e-mailed each professor who was listed as the instructor for the course, requesting permission to administer the survey at one of his or her class meetings.

At the mutually agreed on time, a research team member visited the classroom and read a protocol that (a) described the process through which their course was selected, (b) asked the students for their cooperation, (c) assured them that their responses were voluntary and anonymous, (d) asked for their assistance with the data collection effort, and (e) advised them that if they had already completed the survey, to inform the research team member. The surveys were then distributed to the students, who took approximately 10 minutes to complete them.

Across the 24 participating courses, there were 904 students enrolled on February 17, 2008, the day the sample was randomly selected. None of the classes that we visited had the same number of students in attendance as were enrolled for that course; as such, data from students not attending were not obtained. In addition, a small number of students (approximately 2% of those contacted) were registered for more than one of the 24 classes we visited and thus completed the survey only in the first course we visited. Furthermore, eight students either declined to participate or submitted a blank survey at the end of the data collection period. Finally, one student indicated that [he was] a graduate student; this person was subsequently deleted prior to data analysis to ensure that only undergraduate students had participated in the study. Our final sample consisted of 607 students, resulting in a response rate of 67.1%.

Dependent Variables

The dependent variable is fear of criminal victimization while on campus. We included a number of questions that asked the student about being afraid of being a victim of different types of crime while on campus. Students were asked to indicate their level of agreement on a 4-point Likert-type scale with the following statements:

> While on campus at (name of school):
>
> I am afraid of being attacked by someone with a weapon.
>
> I am afraid of having my money or possessions taken from me.
>
> I am afraid of being beaten up.
>
> I am afraid of being sexually assaulted.

For the purpose of this study, the first item will serve as an indicator of fear of aggravated assault, followed by fear of larceny-theft, fear of simple assault, and fear of sexual assault.

In the original instrument, students were asked to indicate the relative strength with which they agreed with the above statements (e.g., *strongly agree, somewhat agree, somewhat disagree, strongly disagree*). With the exception of one variable (fear of larceny-theft, where 7% strongly agreed), less than 5% of the respondents strongly agreed that they were fearful of that situation. As such, we created a dichotomous measure of each of the four types of fear, with those who strongly agreed or agreed that they were *fearful* coded as 1 and those who *strongly disagreed* or *disagreed* coded as 0.

Independent Variables

The survey data allowed us a unique opportunity to examine the relationship between different fear-provoking cues and types of fear of victimization because included in the survey were five cue-specific fear-of-crime measures. Students were asked to indicate their level of agreement on a 4-point Likert-type scale with the following:

Since the beginning of this school year, I have been fearful of crime victimization on campus because of . . .

poorly lit parking lots

poorly lit sidewalks and common areas

overgrown or excess shrubbery

groups congregating or loitering

visibility of public safety officials

In the original question, students were asked to indicate the relative strength with which they agreed with the above statements (e.g., *strongly agree, somewhat agree, somewhat disagree, strongly disagree*). Due to the skewed nature of the distribution of each variable, we created a dichotomous variable from each of the five cue-specific fear-of-crime measures, with those who *strongly agreed* or *agreed* that they were fearful coded as 1 and those who *strongly disagreed* or *disagreed* were coded as 0.

Each of these cue-specific variables measures a different factor that past research has found to be associated with high levels of fear of crime. The two poor-lighting variables measure students' ability to see if a threatening or dangerous situation is in view (e.g., to observe if predator is close). The overgrown or excess shrubbery variable captures the notion of possible hiding places for would-be offenders. Groups congregating or loitering is an indication of some level of social incivility that could create an impression about the concentration of possible motivated offenders. Visibility of public safety officials is a measure of police presence that provides formal guardianship.

Control Variables

Two sets of control variables were used in our analyses. First, due to their association with fear of criminal victimization reported in the past research, we also included measures of age, student's current academic classification (freshman, sophomore, junior, and senior), course load status (full- or part-time student), and residence status (on or off-campus). Summary statistics for the control variables are presented in Reading Table 3.1.

The results presented in Reading Table 3.1 show that over half (55.9%) of the sample were females. Almost two in three were freshmen or sophomores (66.1%), freshmen being the largest academic group across all categories (37.1%). Most were full-time students (96.4%) and were between the ages of 18 and 24 (86.9%), with the mean age of the sample being nearly 21 (20.88) years of age. Approximately half of the respondents lived on campus (52.6%).

Given that the emphasis of this research is on gender differences in fear of criminal victimization, we examined how the distribution on the aforementioned variables varied by sex. These results, presented in Reading Table 3.1, demonstrate that the distribution of student classification ($p = .002$) and residence status ($p = .078$) were significantly different between females and males.

Second, given previous research, the importance of perceived risk of victimization as a significant predictor of fear of crime cannot be overlooked in any analysis. In light of the consistent positive effect of perceived risk on fear of crime, we included perceived risk as a control variable. Perceived risk of victimization was defined as the chance that a specific type of crime would happen to the student while on campus during the coming year. Students were asked to rate their perceived risk of specific types of crime on a 10-point scale from 1 meaning that *it is not at all likely to happen* to 10 meaning *it is very likely to happen.*

Perceived risk of four specific types of crimes was used as control variables: larceny-theft and aggravated, simple, and sexual assault. Each specific type risk was used as a control variable for the specific type of fear. For example, perceived risk of larceny-theft was used as a control variable only for predicting fear of larceny-theft.

Reading Table 3.1 • Sample Characteristics (N = 607)				
	Total	**Sex**		
Characteristic	**Sample % (*n*)**	**Females % (*n*)**	**Males % (*n*)**	**_p_ Value**
Sex				
Female	55.9 (335)			
Male	44.1 (264)			
Current academic classification				
Freshman	37.1 (221)	43.8 (145)	28.8 (76)	.002
Sophomore	29.0 (173)	26.3 (87)	32.6 (86)	
Junior	20.1 (120)	16.3 (54)	24.6 (65)	
Senior	13.8 (82)	13.6 (45)	14.0 (37)	
Type of student				
Traditional[a]	87.1 (520)	88.9 (296)	84.8 (223)	.145
Nontraditional/exchange	12.9 (77)	11.1 (37)	15.2 (40)	
Current course load				
Full time	96.4 (563)	96.0 (313)	96.9 (249)	.145
Part time	3.6 (21)	4.0 (13)	3.1 (8)	
Residence status				
On campus[b]	52.6 (314)	56.0 (187)	48.5 (127)	.078
Off campus	47.4 (283)	44.0 (147)	51.5 (135)	
	M (SD)	M (SD)	M (SD)	
Age in years	20.88 (4.53)	20.75 (4.90)	21.06 (3.98)	.418
Perceived risk				
Larceny-theft	4.58 (2.76)	4.86 (2.84)	4.22 (2.58)	.005
Aggravated assault	2.52 (1.90)	2.81 (1.98)	2.13 (1.67)	.000
Simple assault	2.86 (2.03)	3.29 (2.12)	2.26 (1.67)	.000
Sexual assault	2.44 (2.10)	3.13 (2.24)	1.55 (1.48)	.000

[a]Traditional students are those who are between the ages of 18 and 24 years old. Nontraditional students are those 25 years and older. Less than 1% (0.5%, *n* = 3) of the sample are exchange students.

[b]On campus includes on-campus dormitories (50.9%, *n* = 304) and on-campus apartments and family housing (1.7%, *n* = 10).

Much of the past research has shown that females, in particular college women, have higher perceived risk of different types of victimization from males (Fisher & Sloan, 2003; see May, 2001a, for review; for exception, see Lane and Meeker, 2003). As shown in Reading Table 3.1, our student sample follows this previously reported college student risk pattern reported by Fisher and Sloan (2003): Females reported being more at risk of victimization than males. In other words, females' perceived risk mean for each type of crime was significantly higher than the respective males' mean.

Results

Are Fears of Criminal Victimization-Provoking Cues Gendered?

The first step in examining whether fear-provoking cues are gendered was to explore the proportion of females and males who reported that a specific cue provoked their fear of victimization while on campus. As presented in Reading Table 3.2, at first glance it appears that fear-provoking cues might be gendered. There are statistically significant differences in the proportion of female students who agreed that specific cues provoked fear of crime victimization while on campus when compared to their male counterparts. For example, 65% of females reported that poorly lit parking lots provoked their on-campus fear of victimization compared to 34% of males, a 30 percentage point difference. About a third of females (32%) reported that overgrown or excessive shrubbery provoked their fear, whereas 19% of males reported feeling fear, a 13 percentage point difference.

These results, however, may be a bit misleading since research has consistently shown that females in general are more fearful than males, and our sample also shows this pattern as female students are more fearful than males for each of our four crime-related fears (larceny-theft, aggravated assault, simple assault, and sexual assault).

Another way to examine these fear-provoking cues results is to look at the ordering of the cues between females and males by rank ordering females' and males' proportion from largest proportion agreeing that the cue provoked them to be fearful of victimization while on campus to smallest proportion who agreed. From this lens, the rank ordering can be seen as an indicator of the relative magnitude of the order of fear-provoking cues between females and males from largest to smallest percentage agreeing. As can be seen in Reading Table 3.2, the Spearman's rank order correlation of their ranking is quite strong, but it is not statistically significant ($p = .19$). There appears to be no significant difference between females and males in the rank ordering of the fear-provoking cues, suggesting that these cues do not vary by gender in their ranking and, therefore, might not be gendered.

Are the Cues That Predict Crime-Related Fear Gendered?

The second step of our analyses examined which cues, if any, predict crime-related fear for females and males and which cues, if any, are different across female and male students. Findings from Reading Table 3.3 indicate that different fear-provoking cues are evident for females and males. Across fear of larceny-theft, aggravated assault, simple assault, and sexual assault, the visibility of public safety officials increased females' fearfulness. Overgrown or excessive shrubbery also increased women's fearfulness of larceny-theft and aggravated and sexual assault. Poor lighting on sidewalks and common areas also increased their fear of larceny-theft and aggravated assault. Groups loitering only increased females' fear of simple assault. Poorly lit parking lots did not predict fearfulness of any type of crime for females. For males, only two cues were significant predictors of fearfulness. Overgrown or excessive shrubbery increased their fear of aggravated assault. Groups congregating or loitering increased their fearfulness of larceny-theft.

Turning to possible gendered effects of cues on crime-related fear, the results from the equality of coefficients test indicate that none of the cues had significantly different effects across females and males. None of the fear-provoking cues had a stronger effect for either sex compared to the other, thus, suggesting that fear-provoking cues are not gendered.

Discussion

Among the major goals of this exploratory study was to begin to close the gaps about what is known about fear-provoking cues among females and males and to examine if these cues were gendered. To these ends, the

Reading Table 3.2 • Type of Fear-Provoking Cue by Sex of Respondent

	Proportion Agreeing Cue Provoked Them to Be Fearful of Victimization While on Campus				
	Females	Males	Proportions Test	Rank Order	
Type of Cue	% (n)	% (n)	z Score (p Value)	Females	Males
Poorly lit parking lots	64.5 (213)	34.0 (88)	7.37 (.000)	1	2
Poorly lit sidewalks and common areas	62.1 (205)	30.4 (79)	7.66 (.000)	2	3
Groups congregating or loitering	53.0 (175)	37.2 (97)	3.84 (.0001)	3	1
Visibility of public safety officials	35.0 (114)	22.7 (58)	3.24 (.0001)	4	4
Overgrown or excessive shrubbery	32.1 (105)	18.9 (49)	3.63 (.0003)	5	5

Spearman's rank order correlation = .70, p = .19.

results reported are among the first steps to unpacking the relationship among different fear-provoking cues and crime-related offense specific fear among females and males and provide informative findings for future research.

The wide range in proportions (19%–65%) of both females and males who indicated that specific cues provoked them to be fearful of criminal victimization while on campus gives credence to the past research findings that individuals see and distinguish cues in their immediate environment as fear generating. Interestingly, despite the relative difference in these proportions between females and males, there was not a statistically significant relationship between the rank orders of these proportions, suggesting that fear-provoking cues, at least in at the bivariate level, are not gendered. In addition, when considering the multivariate results, there were no significant differences across gender in the impact of the cues on either fear of larceny-theft, aggravated assault, or simple assault. As such, it appears that the fear-provoking cues under study are not gendered as Brownlow's research suggests.

There are a number of plausible explanations why our results suggest that fear-provoking cues are not gendered. With the exception of the limited number of lighting and foliage studies, most of the fear-provoking cues research has not been done within a university setting. The unique nature of the university setting, especially being relatively safe and secure, may contribute to the lack

of associations found in our study. It might be that the unique setting of a campus, relatively open to all yet populated with young studious adults, faculty, and staff on a daily basis, might influence the type of persons who loiter around the grounds. Many college students may find comfort (and therefore be less fearful) in seeing members of the college community congregating on campus.

Another explanation for the lack of "gendered findings" revolves around the fact that the questions used to measure fear-specific cues were not as detailed as they could have been. As discussed earlier, these questions did not incorporate the element of time of day, which may have reduced the impact of the fear-specific cue on the fear of the respondent. For example, it is possible that groups congregating or loitering and visibility of public safety officials at night might have different impact on fear of crime among females (or, conversely, males) from these cues during the day. Future research should carefully word these measures to distinguish between daytime and nighttime cues to further explore this effect.

Despite the fact that female students are more fearful than their male counterparts for each offense-specific fear, the relative safety and security of the university setting may also reduce the impact of gender on these relationships, as neither male or female students were generally fearful on campus. With the exception of fear of larceny-theft, where two in five respondents (40.0%) agreed that they were fearful of victimization on

Reading Table 3.3 • Fear of Type of Crime Logit Models Results

Independent Variable: Specific Fear-Provoking Cue	Larceny-Theft			Aggravated Assault			Simple Assault			Sexual Assault
	Females	Males	Equality of Coefficient Test z Score	Females	Males	Equality of Coefficient Test z Score	Females	Males	Equality of Coefficient Test z Score	Females
	b (SE)	b (SE)		b (SE)	b (SE)		b (SE)	b (SE)		b (SE)
Poorly lit parking lots	.12 (.37)	.13 (.53)	−.02	.20 (.44)	.71 (1.01)	−.46	.83 (.56)	.47 (.91)	.34	.49 (.42)
Poorly lit sidewalks and common areas	.86 (.36)**	.47 (.56)	.59	1.03 (.44)***	1.28 (1.02)	−.23	−.05 (.48)	1.32 (.93)	−1.31	.58 (.15)
Overgrown or excessive shrubbery	.64 (.33)**	.32 (.44)	.58	.61 (.35)*	1.86 (.70)***	−1.60	.58 (.39)	.55 (.63)	.04	.70 (.35)**
Groups congregating or loitering	.43 (.29)	.99 (.40)***	−1.13	.27 (.33)	.99 (.83)	−.81	.84 (.39)**	.84 (.70)	.00	.42 (.33)
Visibility of public safety officials	.54 (.31)*	.06 (.47)	.85	.59 (.33)*	.51 (.75)	.10	.61 (.37)*	−.15 (.82)	.84	.95 (.34)***
Constant	−3.14 (1.09)***	−1.71 (1.50)		−4.80 (1.21)****	−4.22 (2.90)		−5.0 (1.38)****	−3.73 (2.07)*		−4.33 (1.17)***
Model chi-square (df)	88.62 (10)	51.75 (10)		76.52 (10)	48.29 (10)		38.11 (10)	34.30 (10)		129.67 (10)
Significance	.000	.000		.000	.000		.000	.000		.000

NOTE: The respective perceived risk, age, and current residence status; academic classification; and course load were used as control variables.

$*p < .1$, $**p < .05$, $***p < .01$, $****p < .001$.

campus, the levels of fear among these respondents were relatively low (18.4% agreed that they were at least somewhat fearful of aggravated assault, and only 12.2% agreed that they were fearful of simple assault). In light of these findings, future research should attempt to replicate and build from our current study in nonuniversity settings, such as residential communities or even computer-generated settings that vary characteristics by known fear-generating cues, to determine if the relative safety and security of the university setting masks any impact that fear-provoking cues might have on fear of criminal victimization. Equally important to future research is examining whether this relationship is gendered. The past fear-provoking research provides ample evidence to suggest that there is quite a strong association between fear-provoking cues and fear of crime, but the question about this relationship conditioned on gender remains ripe for inquiry.

Despite the lack of gender differences in the association between fear-provoking cues and offense-specific fear, the reported results inform the research community about gender differences in fear of crime on a number of dimensions. First, the multivariate results offer some support for the "shadow of powerlessness" that has been used to explain differences in fear of crime among adolescent males (May, 2001b).

As May (2001b) suggests, males who feel that they have less power in a situation are likely to be more fearful of that situation. Both Day et al.'s (2003) and Brownlow's (2005) research are supportive of May's shadow of powerlessness suggestion. Their research jointly suggests that males are fearful in environments in which they experience a loss of control because, for some males, their masculine gender identity (e.g., aggression, physical strength) is challenged. For males, there were only two significant associations between fear-provoking cues and fear of crime found in the current study. For males, fear of crime because of groups congregating or loitering had a statistically significant association with fear of larceny-theft and fear of crime because of overgrown or excessive shrubbery had a statistically significant association with fear of aggravated assault. In both of these situations, this relationship might be explained by the challenges to their gender identity [that] some males feel in these types of environments.

Males may feel that their odds of resisting larceny-theft are reduced in a group setting where they are surrounded by a number of young adult males and females (the demographic most likely to loiter and congregate on a university campus); as such, the powerlessness they feel to overcome these odds may be responsible for the significant association between fear caused by groups loitering and fear of larceny-theft. These feelings of powerlessness may also explain male fear of aggravated assault in this sample as well. Although males may think that they can evade a person who wants to commit aggravated assault against them in a poorly lit parking lot or sidewalk or when public safety officials are not present, they may think they are less likely to be able to evade an assailant who confronts them in an area with overgrown shrubbery. As such, those males most fearful because of the overgrown shrubbery cue are significantly more fearful of aggravated assault than their male counterparts who are not as fearful because of that cue. This evidence of the impact of the shadow of powerlessness related to gender identify suggests that this line of thinking is a potentially rich area of exploration for the continued research into the possible gendered relationship between fear-provoking cues and offense-specific fear.

A second interesting gender-specific finding concerns the relationship between the visibility of police and crime-related fear for females. Females (but not males) who were most fearful of crime because of the visibility of public safety officials were significantly more likely than their counterparts to be fearful of every crime under consideration. Given that over 90% of both male and female respondents felt that the university public safety officials were either somewhat or very visible, this finding would appear to indicate that the visibility of police increases fear of crime for females but not for males. Nevertheless, analysis of a follow-up question reveals that this may not be the case. For males, one in three (38.1%) respondents agreed that they would "feel safer if public safety officials were more visible than they currently are"; two in three (67.9%) females agreed with that statement. As such, the presence of police may be more relevant for decreasing fear of crime among females than males. Given that this finding has not been uncovered in any study of which we are aware, this provides another particularly rich area of research that could inform the study of fear of crime.

In much the same way that the shadow of powerlessness may partially explain fear of victimization among the males in this sample, there is some evidence to suggest that the shadow of sexual assault (see May, 2001a, for review; Fisher & Sloan, 2003) may partially explain fear of victimization among the female students in this sample as well. Females who were most fearful because of overgrown or excessive shrubbery and visibility of public safety officials (but none of the other specific fear-provoking cues) were significantly more likely to be fearful of sexual assault than their counterparts were. This finding would suggest that certain cues, in this case, overgrown shrubbery and low police visibility, are relevant to increasing women's fear of sexual assault. This result can also be seen through the lens of several studies that have found that women are primarily fearful of being sexually assaulted, especially in public places at night because they are afraid of being attacked by a stranger (see Fisher & Sloan, 2003; Merry, 1981; Pain, 2001; Valentine, 1990). Again, this line of thinking provides another rich area of exploration in the area of gendered fear-provoking cues and fear of crime, in particular fear of sexual assault.

Although we have uncovered a number of interesting findings, this study is not without limitations. First, and most importantly, future researchers should develop measures of fear-provoking cues that incorporate richer descriptions of a specific cue. For example, although our survey question asked students about fear of groups congregating or loitering, the question was not specific about the demographic or nonstudent status composition of the group, the location, the activity of the group who was loitering, or the time of day the group was loitering. Anecdotal evidence suggests that those groups loitering on the campus under study here were mostly male college students loitering outside of one or more dormitories on campus who routinely verbally harass other students (particularly female students). The one measure included in the survey used to collect group loitering information did not allow us to fully examine these relationships which Warr's (2000) work suggests influences fear of crime. In addition, as alluded to above, the measure of visibility of public safety officials could be improved by . . . including even more types of police visibility (e.g., foot patrol, bicycle patrol, face-to-face interaction) to better unpack the police presence and crime-related fear relationship, especially to see if this relationship is gendered. The day–night distinction with respect to fear-provoking cues and fear of crime is also another measurement issue that was not fully addressed in the current research. It could well be that certain fear-provoking cues, for example poor lighting, only influence certain offense-specific fears during the nighttime but not during daylight. We could not address such issues in our work but leave this issue to future researchers to address.

Whether fear-provoking cues are gendered is clearly an issue deserving more scholarly attention. The current study is an important first exploration for informing an agenda for future researchers to examine the possible gendered nature of fear-provoking cues.

Like we have done in the current research, we would encourage future researchers to draw from the variety of disciplines that has examined different aspects of crime-related fear and integrate their theoretical approaches and findings to more fully comprehend which, if any, fear-provoking cues are gendered and their effects on offense-specific fears. Hopefully, in the next decade, a better understanding of the possible gendered relationship between fear-provoking cues and crime-related fear will mature and provide practical means to address fear-provoking cues and thereby reduce crime-related fears among both females and males.

/// DISCUSSION QUESTIONS

1. How is the fear of victimization similar for men and women? How is it different?

2. Is a fear of crime related to specific offenses? Does this fear vary by gender?

3. How can university administrators use the findings of this study to increase safety on college campuses?

References

Brownlow, A. (2005). A geography of men's fear. *Geoforum, 36*, 581–592.

Day, K. (1994). Conceptualizing women's fear of sexual assault on campus. *Environment and Behavior, 26*, 742–767.

Day, K., Stump, C., & Carreon, D. (2003). Confrontation and loss of control: Masculinity and men's fear of public spaces. *Journal of Environmental Psychology, 23*, 311–322.

Fisher, B. S., & Nasar, J. L. (1992). Fear of crime in relation to three exterior site features: Prospect, refuge, and escape. *Environment and Behavior, 24*, 35–65.

Fisher, B. S., & Sloan, J. J. (2003). Unraveling the fear of sexual victimization among college women: Is the "shadow of sexual assault" hypothesis supported? *Justice Quarterly, 20*, 633–659.

Kitchin, R. M. (1994). Cognitive maps: What are they and why study them? *Journal of Environmental Psychology, 14*, 1–19.

Kitchin, R. M. (1996). Are there sex differences in geographic knowledge and understanding? *Geographical Journal, 162*, 273–286.

Klodawsky, F., & Lundy, C. (1994). Women's safety in the university environment. *Journal of Architectural and Planning, 11*, 128–331.

Lane, J., & Meeker, J. W. (2003). Women's and men's fear of gang crimes: Sexual and nonsexual assault as perceptually contemporaneous offenses. *Justice Quarterly, 20*, 337–371.

Madriz, E. (1997). *Nothing bad happens to good girls.* Berkeley: University of California Press.

May, D. C. (2001a). *Adolescent fear of crime, perceptions of risk, and defensive behaviors: An alternative explanation of violent delinquency.* Lewiston, NY: Edwin Mellen Press.

May, D. C. (2001b). The effect of fear of sexual victimization on adolescent fear of crime. *Sociological Spectrum, 21*, 141–174.

May, D. C., & Dunaway, R. G. (2000). Predictors of adolescent fear of crime. *Sociological Spectrum, 20*, 149–168.

May, D. C., Vartanian, L. R., & Virgo, K. (2002). The impact of parental attachment and supervision on fear of crime among adolescent males. *Adolescence, 37*, 267–287.

Merry, S. E. (1981). *Urban danger: Life in a neighborhood of strangers.* Philadelphia: Temple University Press.

Nasar, J. L., & Fisher, B. S. (1993). "Hot spots" of fear and crime: A multi-method investigation. *Journal of Environmental Psychology, 13*, 187–206.

Pain, R. (1997). Social geographies of women's fear of crime. *Transactions of the Institute of British Geographies, New Series, 22*, 231–244.

Pain, R. (2001). Gender, race, age and fear in the city. *Urban Studies, 38*, 899–913.

Reid, L. W., & Konrad, M. (2004). The gender gap in fear: Assessing the interactive effects of gender and perceived risk on fear of crime. *Sociological Spectrum, 24*, 399–425.

Schafer, J. A., Huebner, B. M., & Bynum, T. S. (2006). Fear of crime and criminal victimization gender-based contrasts. *Journal of Criminal Justice, 34*(3), 285–301.

Skogan, W. G. (1990). *Disorder and decline: Crime and the spiral of decay in American neighborhoods.* New York: Free Press.

Smith, W. R., & Torstenson, M. (1997). Gender differences in risk perception and neutralizing fear of crime. *British Journal of Criminology, 37*, 608–634.

Starkweather, S. (2007). Gender, perceptions of safety and strategic responses among Ohio university students. *Gender, Place, and Culture, 14*, 355–370.

Valentine, G. (1990). Women's fear and the design of public space. *Built Environment, 16*, 279–287.

Van der Wurff, A., Van Staalduinen, L., & Stringer, P. (1989). Fear of crime in residential environments: Testing a social psychological model. *Journal of Social Psychology, 129*, 141–160.

Wallace, L. H., & May, D. C. (2005). The impact of relationship with parents and commitment to school on adolescent fear of crime at school. *Adolescence, 40*, 458–474.

Warr, M. (1990). Dangerous situations: Social context and fear of victimization. *Social Forces, 68*, 891–907.

Warr, M. (2000). Fear of crime in the United States: Avenues for research and policy. In D. Duffee (Ed.), *Measurement and analysis of crime and justice: Crime justice* (Vol. 4, pp. 451–490). Washington, DC: Department of Justice.

For women who experience abuse in childhood or adulthood, the assumptions are that surviving includes seeking help. This article explores the prevalence of victimization in the lives of Caucasian, African American, and Latina women, if and to whom they disclosed their victimization, and where they turned for services and support.

Women From Different Ethnic Groups and Their Experiences With Victimization and Seeking Help

Judy L. Postmus

For the millions of women[1] who experience abuse in childhood or adulthood, the assumptions are that surviving and lessening its impact include disclosing the abuse and reaching out for help from informal and formal supports (Coker et al., 2002; Hyman, Forte, Du Mont, Romans, & Cohen, 2006; Thompson et al., 2000). Yet, we still have a limited understanding of where abuse survivors turn for support, especially those survivors from different ethnic backgrounds. As such, the purpose of this article is to address these limitations by presenting a study that explores the prevalence of childhood and adulthood violence in the lives of Caucasian, African American, and Latina women, if and to whom they disclosed their victimization, and where they turned to for services and support.

Victimization, Disclosure, and Help-Seeking Experiences

Studies are mixed when it comes to identifying prevalence rates of child or adult victimization among African American and Latina women. When compared with Caucasian populations, some studies have identified higher rates of childhood abuse, sexual assault, or intimate partner violence (IPV) among non-Caucasian ethnic populations (Rennison & Welchans, 2000; Sorenson, 1996), whereas others have shown lower (Neff, Holamon, & Schluter,

1995; Sorenson & Siegel, 1992) or similar rates (Tjaden & Thoennes, 1998, 2006; Wyatt, 1990a). Regardless of ethnicity, rape and IPV survivors experience similar types of sexually violent acts, suffer physical injuries, and experience immediate and long-term emotional, psychological, and physical reactions (Sokoloff & Dupont, 2005; Wyatt, 1992). Most researchers, however, agree that there is limited information available to understand the experiences of victimization among women and girls of color (Fontes, Cruz, & Tabachnick, 2001; Wyatt, 1990a).

Telling someone is often the first step to getting help to survive the abuse and lessen its impact (Coker et al., 2002; Thompson et al., 2000); however, some victims seek help for unrelated problems (e.g., financial, physical health, mental health) and never disclose their abuse (Henning & Klesges, 2002; Macy, Nurius, Kernic, & Holt, 2005). We also know that not all abuse survivors turn to organizations designed to serve survivors; instead, survivors may turn to informal supports such as family and friends (Coker, Derrick, Lumpkin, Aldrich, & Oldendick, 2000) and then eventually to formal supports (Hutchison & Hirschel, 1998; Macy et al., 2005).

The research is also limited on the disclosure patterns of victims of child maltreatment or adult victimization. Regarding childhood sexual abuse, most studies agree that, regardless of ethnicity, most women rarely disclose their

SOURCE: Postmus, J. L. (2015). Women from different ethnic groups and their experiences with victimization and seeking help. *Violence Against Women* 21(3): 376–393.

abuse to anyone (Henning & Klesges, 2002; Romero, Wyatt, Loeb, Carmona, & Solis, 1999; Wyatt, Loeb, Solis, & Carmona, 1999); however, other studies found that most of their sample of college students disclosed their experiences of child sexual abuse (Arroyo, Simpson, & Aragon, 1997; Ullman, Starzynski, Long, Mason, & Long, 2008). Of those who disclose, African Americans are more likely to tell a family member, whereas Caucasians are more likely to tell someone else (e.g., friends, other family members, authority figures; Wyatt, 1990b; Wyatt et al., 1999). In contrast, Smith et al. (2000) found no differences in disclosure patterns of child sexual abuse among women from different ethnic backgrounds. Even less is known about the disclosure patterns related to childhood sexual abuse among Latinas, attributed to the widespread under-reporting and fear of reporting to authorities (Lowe, Pavkov, Casanova, & Wetchler, 2005; Wyatt, 1990a). One study of child sexual abuse among Latina women found that most (60%) did not disclose the abuse to anyone; in addition, those women who were less acculturated were also less likely to disclose the abuse (Romero et al., 1999). A more recent study found that Latinas were hesitant to disclose to formal sources, with only 20% seeking any type of formal help; most Latinas in the same study (58%) disclosed to informal sources such as parents, family, friends, or neighbors (Cuevas & Sabina, 2010).

Factors such as the political treatment of ethnic and immigrant groups, patriarchal family structures, values placed on sexual chastity before marriage and faithfulness afterward, the fear of racism, differing views on what constitutes child abuse, sexual assault or IPV, and the need to keep family matters private may create seemingly insurmountable barriers for survivors from African American, Latina, or Asian cultures to disclose their victimization experiences and seek help (Kasturirangan, Krishnan, & Riger, 2004; Lee & Law, 2001; Low & Organista, 2000; Wyatt, 1992; Yoshioka, Gilbert, El-Bassel, & Baig-Amin, 2003). Women of color may also be reluctant to disclose abuse for fear of bringing shame to their families and communities or reinforcing stereotypes (Gillum, 2002; Kasturirangan et al., 2004). Indeed, in the mental health field, researchers have shown that racial differences exist when seeking help, usually because of the stigma associated with mental health services (Ayalon & Young, 2005; Barksdale & Molock, 2008).

Researchers studying victimization have also tried to learn what factors predict use of services by relying on sociodemographic factors such as ethnicity, age, education, and poverty (Henning & Klesges, 2002; Hutchison & Hirschel, 1998; West, Kaufman Kantor, & Jasinski, 1998). Other factors include the severity and frequency of physical violence, relationship to the abuser (marriage status, cohabiting, or dating), and whether children are present (Henning & Klesges, 2002; Hutchison & Hirschel, 1998). Unfortunately, these results contradict each other, leaving gaps in our understanding of predicting when and where abuse survivors seek help. In more recent studies, factors that predicted seeking help include ethnicity (Caucasian), severity, older age, higher socioeconomic status, being married, and the presence of children (Henning & Klesges, 2002; Hyman, Forte, Du Mont, Romans, & Cohen, 2009; Kaukinen, 2002). Regardless of the factors that predict service usage, most abuse survivors do not seek help (Henning & Klesges, 2002).

In sum, we know that abused women turn to many formal and informal networks to get emotional, physical, and financial support to survive. What we do not know are the details of where women of color access social supports and interventions after their victimization. Hence, this article affords us the opportunity to expand our understanding as to where physically and sexually abused women from different cultural groups turn for help. Several research questions frame our study and include the following:

Research Question 1: What is the prevalence of four types of abuse (child physical or sexual abuse and adult physical or sexual violence) among different racial or ethnic groups (Caucasian, African American, and Latina) of women?

Research Question 2: Do these victimized women disclose their abuse experiences and, if so, to whom?

Research Question 3: What type of services or support do these women seek as a result of their victimization experiences?

Method

Data for this research were collected as part of a study which sought to identify risk and protective factors related to women's histories of physical and sexual victimization and the consequences of such victimization experiences (Postmus & Severson, 2006). This exploratory study, conducted in a Midwestern state, was cross-sectional with data collection occurring during face-to-face interviews with adult women. For this article, the focus is specifically on the victimization, disclosure, and help-seeking experiences of women of color, representing three ethnic groups: Caucasian women, African American women, and Latinas.

Sample

Women were recruited from three types of settings including a state prison, several domestic violence or sexual assault organizations, and four communities in a Midwestern state. To qualify for this study, participants had to be female and over the age of 18 years; no other criteria were included. Using convenience and adaptive sampling procedures (Campbell, Sefl, Wasco, & Ahrens, 2004), formal and informal locations in the community (e.g., service sites, day care centers, laundromats, grocery stores) where women are likely to frequent or gather were purposively chosen. To obtain a diverse sample, locations were carefully chosen where women of color may gather such as social service agencies with a large Latina clientele or beauty salons that cater to African American women. Flyers, printed in English and Spanish describing the study, were posted. The flyer included information about the criteria to participate (i.e., female and over the age of 18) and intent of the study (i.e., to ask about women's abilities and confidence to cope and manage mental health and well-being as well as the types of supports and services received as the result of abuse). If interested, women then contacted the research team to learn more about the specifics of the study. A convenient time and location were mutually chosen for the 1-hour, face-to-face interview; each interview was conducted in English or Spanish by trained graduate and undergraduate students hired from two different universities in the state. The interviewers were trained to be sensitive to how participants responded to difficult questions; each participant was given information on services available in the community should the participant need emotional or mental health support from the questions asked. Each woman from the community received a cash incentive of US$25 for her participation in the study; the prison system did not allow cash or in-kind incentives to be provided to participants.

For this analysis, the sample is divided into three groups—Caucasian women, African American women, and Latinas—based on narrow definitions and self-selection into these groups. Women who identified themselves as Native American ($n = 12$), Asian or Pacific Islander ($n = 6$), or Other ($n = 10$) are excluded from this analysis because their sample size is too small. The remaining sample of 387 women includes 233 Caucasian women, 105 African American women, and 49 Latinas. The average age of these three groups ranged from age 34 (African Americans) to age 36 (Caucasians and Latinas). There were significant differences in educational attainment, with Caucasian women having the highest educational level, followed by African American women, and then Latinas. More than half of each of the sample group received welfare (77% of African Americans, 70% of Caucasians, and 57% of Latinas); however, these differences are not significant. Finally, Latinas are significantly more likely to have been recruited from the communities; there were no significant differences between those women recruited from agencies or from prison.

Measures

The interview questions were developed from a combination of existing and modified standardized instruments and included topics such as child maltreatment, intimate partner violence (IPV), experiences of sexual victimization, and experiences with disclosure and supportive services.

Child maltreatment. Physical and sexual abuse during childhood is measured using the two summary questions from the Childhood Maltreatment Interview Schedule developed by Briere (1992). While there are no known studies on overall reliability or validity, the use of this measure in pilot studies suggests predictive and construct validity (Briere, 1992). The questions include, "To the best of your knowledge, before age 17, were you ever sexually abused ($1 = yes$, $0 = no$) . . . physically abused?" None of the questions ask the respondents to indicate if a single or multiple perpetrators were involved.

Intimate partner violence. Intimate partner violence, including physical and psychological abuse from an intimate partner, is measured using the Abusive Behavior Inventory (ABI) developed by Shepard and Campbell (1992). This inventory is a reliable measure with alpha coefficients ranging from .70 to .92 and has good criterion-related and construct validity (Shepard & Campbell, 1992). Physical IPV is the mean score of the 10 items on the ABI having to do with physical forms of abuse. The alpha coefficient in this study for Physical IPV is .92. The ABI includes 20 other items, measuring emotional or psychological abuse; however, it was decided to use the Physical IPV score, a statistically based decision to show greater variance between the sample groups.

Rape. Sexual assault in adulthood by an intimate partner, family member, or stranger is measured using the Sexual Experiences Survey (SES) developed by Koss and Oros (1982). For this analysis, the rape summary score of four questions was dichotomized. The remaining items from the SES (sexual coercion and attempted rape) were excluded to show greater variance between sample groups. The alpha coefficient for internal consistency in this study is .90, indicating high internal consistency in this sample.

Disclosure and response to disclosure. Questions about disclosing one's victimization were adapted from a previous study (McNutt, Carlson, Persaud, & Postmus, 2002). There are no known studies on the overall reliability or validity of the questions; however, many of these questions are adapted from a study conducted with adult women in the community who have experienced several different forms of physical and sexual abuse as children or adults (McNutt, Carlson, Rose, & Robinson, 2002). If the women answered yes to any of the four types of abuse (child physical abuse, child sexual abuse, IPV, or sexual assault), they were then asked a series of questions about the disclosure of the experience: Did they tell anyone? Who did they tell? Those to whom women disclosed their victimization were separated into the two categories of informal (parents, family, friends) and formal (social worker, religious leader, teacher, law enforcement).

Services and support received. Services and support include any formal or informal support received from agencies or family and friends. Support is measured using revised questions from the National Comorbidity Survey, implemented in 1992 as a nationally representative survey that assesses the prevalence and correlates of the *Diagnostic and statistical manual of mental disorders* (3rd ed., rev.; *DSM-III-R*; American Psychiatric Association, 1987) diagnoses (National Comorbidity Survey [NCS], 1992). There are no known studies on the overall reliability or validity; however,

many of these questions are adapted from a study conducted with adult women in the community who have experienced several different forms of physical and sexual abuse as children or adults (McNutt, Carlson, Persaud, et al., 2002). For analysis in this study, each support item was rated as 0 (*no, did not receive this support or service*) or 1 (*did receive this support or service*). The 24 possible social services and support were divided into two groups: tangible or professional services and supports. Tangible supports and services are those in which concrete, financial, or informal support was given. Examples include welfare, food bank, subsidized housing, and day care. Services and supports provided by a professional, paraprofessional, or trained helper are listed as professional services and include as examples professional counseling, medication, medical provider, legal services, domestic violence shelter, and rape crisis center.

Data Analysis

Significant differences across the three groups were tested using ANOVAs for continuous variables (e.g., number of supports received) and chi-square analyses for categorical variables (e.g., type of supports received). All tests for significance were two-tailed, $p < .05$. Logistic regression models were run to predict whether race-ethnicity, controlling for all other factors, is associated with the use of tangible or professional services among IPV survivors. The independent variables used in the regression included age, education, welfare receipt, having children, recruited from prison, recruited from sexual assault or domestic violence agencies, disclosed physical IPV to informal sources, disclosed physical IPV to formal sources, number of abuse experiences, and race.

Results

Patterns of Abuse and Disclosure

All women in this study reported high rates of the four types of victimization, with Caucasian women reporting the highest rates (see Table 1). However, physical IPV was the only type of victimization to significantly differ between the racial-ethnic groups with 95% of Caucasians more likely to experience this type of abuse when compared with 91% of African Americans and 74% of Latinas. Most of this sample (95%) experienced at least one type of abuse with more than 50% experiencing three to four types. The mean number of abuse types also differed by race-ethnicity, with

Caucasian women reporting significantly more types of abuse experiences ($M = 2.64$) compared with African American women ($M = 2.29$) and Latinas ($M = 2.12$).

Rates of disclosure were also high, ranging from lows of 55% among Latinas disclosing childhood physical abuse and 62% of African Americans and 68% of Caucasians disclosing childhood sexual abuse. The higher levels of disclosure include physical IPV (85% of Caucasians and 72% of African Americans) and rape (77% of Latinas). A statistically significantly greater percentage of Caucasian women (85%) disclosed physical IPV victimization compared with African Americans (72%) or Latinas (64%).

Table 1 also shows to whom the women disclosed their abuse. Regardless of racial-ethnic group, rates of disclosure to family and friends were higher than rates of disclosure to formal or professional support sources. Family and friends were the most frequent disclosure source for all women who experienced adult victimization (physical IPV or rape); however, their rates of disclosure to formal sources were also high. The only significant racial-ethnic difference occurred for physical IPV experiences, with significantly

more Caucasian than either African American or Latina women disclosing to a formal source such as social workers, police, or other professionals.

A different racial-ethnic pattern was observed with regard to the use of tangible supports or services (see Table 2), with significantly more African American women than Caucasian women or Latinas reporting use of these services. For example, among African American women, 40% used job training, 32% subsidized housing, and 15% vocational rehabilitation.

There were also significant differences between ethnic groups and the reported use of professional services and supports (see Table 3). Significantly more Caucasian women reported use of professional services compared with African American women and Latinas. Specifically, proportionately more Caucasian women used professional counseling (74%), medication (62%), support groups (56%), medical providers or legal services (55%), and psychotropic medication (52%) than the other two groups; proportionately more African American women used domestic violence (48%) or homeless shelters (35%).

Table 1 • Victimization and Disclosure by Ethnicity

	Caucasian (n = 233)		African American (n = 105)		Latina (n = 49)		Total (n = 387)		
	N	%	N	%	N	%	N	%	p
Childhood physical abuse Experienced victimization	113	48.5	38	36.2	22	44.9	173	44.7	
Disclosed victimization	79	69.9	26	68.4	12	54.5	117	67.6	
To whom? Informal (parent, family, friend)	59	74.7	19	73.1	12	100	90	76.9	
Formal (professional)	45	57.0	15	57.7	5	41.7	65	55.6	
Child sexual abuse Experienced victimization	116	49.8	40	38.1	20	40.8	176	45.5	
Disclosed victimization	77	67.5	24	61.5	13	65.0	114	65.9	
To whom? Informal (parent, family, friend)	62	80.5	21	91.3	10	76.9	93	82.3	
Formal (professional)	42	54.5	10	43.5	6	46.2	58	51.3	

(Continued)

Table 1 • (Continued)									
	Caucasian (n = 233)		African American (n = 105)		Latina (n = 49)		Total (n = 387)		
	N	%	N	%	N	%	N	%	p
Physical intimate partner violence Experienced victimization	222	95.3	95	90.5	36	73.5	353	91.2	***
Disclosed victimization	188	84.7	68	71.6	23	63.9	279	79.0	**
To whom? Informal (parent, family, friend)	162	86.2	62	91.2	22	95.7	246	88.2	
Formal (professional)	163	86.7	50	73.5	17	73.9	230	82.4	*
Rape Experienced victimization	164	70.4	67	63.8	26	53.1	257	66.4	
Disclosed victimization	125	76.2	45	67.2	20	76.9	190	73.9	
To whom? Informal (parent, family, friend)	102	81.6	35	77.8	16	80.0	153	80.5	
Formal (professional)	96	76.8	29	64.4	14	70.0	139	73.2	
Number of types of abuse experienced									
0	2	0.9	6	5.7	10	20.4	18	4.7	
1	41	17.6	29	27.6	9	18.4	79	20.4	
2	60	25.8	24	22.9	7	14.3	91	23.5	***
3	66	28.3	21	20.0	11	22.4	98	25.3	
4	64	27.5	25	23.8	12	24.5	101	26.1	
	M	SD	M	SD	M	SD	M	SD	F
Average number of abuse types experienced	2.64	1.09	2.29	1.26	2.12	1.49	2.48	1.21	**

$*p < .05.$ $**p < .01.$ $***p < .001.$

Predictors of Service Use

Based on results from the bivariate analyses, with IPV as the only type of violence for which statistically significant ethnic differences were found, separate multiple regressions were run to estimate predictors of tangible supports and professional services with analyses limited to women who had experienced this type of victimization (see Tables 4 and 5). Previous welfare receipt and number of abuse experiences were positively and significantly associated with the use of tangible support; the race-ethnicity

variable was not significant. The adjusted R^2 for this model for predicting use of tangible supports was .2—that is, 20% of the variance was explained by the model. The variables significantly associated with the use of professional services or supports included age, recruited from sexual assault or domestic violence agencies, disclosure of physical IPV to formal supports, and number of abuse experiences. Again, the race-ethnicity variable was not significant in predicting the use of professional services. The R^2 for this model was .27—that is, 27% of the variance was explained by this model.

Table 2 • Ethnicity and Tangible Social Services and Supports Used After Victimization (N = 369)

Support used	Caucasian (n = 231) N	Caucasian %	African American (n = 99) N	African American %	Latina (n = 39) N	Latina %	p
Emotional support	187	81.3	72	72.7	30	76.9	
Welfare	113	48.9	41	41.4	22	66.4	
Food bank	98	42.4	45	45.9	10	25.6	
Educational	60	26.0	30	30.3	9	23.1	
Job training	45	19.5	40	40.4	7	17.9	***
Subsidized housing	42	18.2	32	32.3	2	5.1	**
Daycare	35	15.2	18	18.2	5	12.8	
Unemployment	37	16.0	16	16.2	6	15.4	
Vocational rehabilitation	20	8.7	15	15.3	0	0.0	*
Reproductive services	18	7.8	9	9.1	4	10.3	
Worker's compensation	11	4.8	9	9.1	2	5.1	
Internet support	14	6.1	2	2.0	1	2.6	
Mean number of supports**		2.97		3.50		2.38	**

Table 3 • Ethnicity and Professional Social Services and Supports Used After Victimization (N = 369)

Support used	Caucasian (n = 231)		African American (n = 99)		Latina (n = 39)		p
	N	%	N	%	N	%	
Professional counseling	170	73.6	53	53.5	21	53.8	***
Medication	142	61.5	44	44.4	21	53.8	*
Support group	130	56.3	45	45.5	14	35.9	*
Medical provider	128	55.4	47	47.5	12	30.8	*
Legal services	127	55.0	33	33.3	16	41.0	**
Psychotropic medication	119	51.5	35	35.4	15	38.5	*
Religious counseling	96	41.6	44	44.4	17	43.6	
Domestic violence shelter	97	42.0	47	47.5	4	10.3	***
Hospital stay for emotional problems	76	32.9	30	30.3	8	23.1	
Homeless shelter	34	14.7	35	35.4	2	5.1	***
Rape crisis center	51	22.1	18	18.2	5	12.7	
Child protection services	45	19.5	14	14.1	4	10.3	
Mean number of supports	5.26		4.50			3.59	**

Table 4 • Regression Associating Use of Tangible Services and Support

Variables	Unstandardized coefficients		p
	B	SE	
Age	.01	.01	
Education	.01	.06	
Receipt of welfare	2.02	.33	***
Children	−.03	.39	
Recruited from prison	−.32	.36	
Recruited from agencies	.27	.36	
Disclosed physical IPV to informal support	−.39	.41	
Disclosed physical IPV to formal supports	.37	.34	
Number of type of abuse experienced	.26	.12	*
African American dummy variable[1]	.54	.30	
Latina dummy variable[1]	−.27	.47	

NOTE: 1. Dummy variable represent a subgroup of the sample.

Discussion

The information from this diverse group of women provides more detailed understanding of racial-ethnic differences in their experiences with victimization, disclosure patterns, and use of tangible and professional supports and services. These women experienced high rates of victimization of all types of violence with rates exceeding those reported in national studies based on survey data (Tjaden & Thoennes, 1998, 2006). Other researchers have found similarly high rates when using trained and empathic interviewers conducting face-to-face interviews (Russell & Bolen, 2000), methods used in this study. Given the sample design and recruitment strategies, the results from this study are not generalizable to the population of women, but they do allow racial-ethnic comparisons that are not possible in studies based on samples that do not oversample minority groups. The rates of all types of victimization were high, with Caucasians reporting the highest rate of all three ethnic groups and significantly higher rates of physical IPV. This finding continues to add to the literature that has yet to conclusively determine whether violence is more prominent in certain cultural groups (Tjaden & Thoennes, 1998).

Those who disclosed their victimization to someone usually disclosed to family or friends, a finding that is similar to other research (Coker et al., 2000; Macy et al., 2005). A unique contribution of this study is the result that more Caucasian women disclosed to social workers, law enforcement, teachers, and other professionals. Conversely, fewer Latinas and African American women disclosed to formal sources, a result consistent with other studies that report barriers faced by minority women who seek professional services (Ayalon & Young, 2005; Barksdale & Molock, 2008).

The women from this study also provided insight into the type of services and support used based on their racial or ethnic differences. More Caucasian women turned to traditional, therapeutic sources such as professional counseling, medication, or emotional support compared with African American women who tended to use tangible supports such as welfare, food banks, housing,

Table 5 • Regression Associating Use of Professional Services and Support

Variables	Unstandardized coefficients		
	B	SE	p
Age	.00	.00	**
Education	.00	.01	
Receipt of welfare	.04	.03	
Children	.06	.04	
Recruited from prison	.01	.04	
Recruited from agencies	.08	.04	*
Disclosed physical IPV to informal support	−.01	.04	
Disclosed physical IPV to formal supports	.13	.03	***
Number of type of abuse experienced	.08	.01	***
African American dummy variable	−.00	.03	
Latina dummy variable	−.04	.05	

NOTE: IPV = intimate partner violence. *$p < .05$. **$p < .01$. ***$p < .001$.

and job training. However, when controlling for a number of variables, the race-ethnicity factor is no longer significant when predicting which type of services and support are used.

Finally, results of multivariate models predicting service use showed that as the number of abuse types increased, the likelihood of help seeking also increased. The results also indicted that women in this sample who had received services from a sexual assault or domestic violence organization in the past 12 months and those who disclosed their physical IPV experiences to formal or professional supports were more likely to use professional services. These relationships indicate the important role that professionals, working in organizations specifically designed for survivors as well as those who may not be involved with such organizations, have a role in connecting survivors to professional services and support. Finally, those who had received welfare were more likely to use tangible services, a finding that is not surprising given that many of the tangible services include the use of welfare, food stamps, and other public assistance.

There are some limitations to this study that warrant attention. Given the sample design and recruitment strategies, the results from this study are not generalizable to the population of women, but they do allow racial-ethnic comparisons because of the purposive sampling of minority women. Second, the study relies on retrospective data, asking women to describe their victimization histories along with how they disclosed or sought help for those experiences. Their victimization experiences could also have been based on one or more perpetrators. In addition, the analyses did not include women's experiences with psychological or economic IPV, nor did it include women's experiences with sexual coercion or attempted rape; the decision to exclude these experiences relied solely on the lack of variance, because almost all of the women experienced some form of these types of violence. Researchers have yet to identify whether one form of violence has a greater impact than another; hence, the results should be viewed with an understanding of the specific type of victimization experienced. Regardless, the information provided by these women gives us a better understanding of their own responses and helps us shape practices and identify future research needs.

Implications

The results from this study have implications for both future research and practice. First, more research is needed to uncover specific cultural influences on how abuse is defined, decisions made, and the reactions given from the supports they used. Such research should use culturally competent methods involving collaborative and empowering approaches to engaging those from marginalized communities (Sokoloff & Dupont, 2005). In addition, researchers themselves should be culturally competent and sensitive to the unique needs of survivors, providing emotional and mental health referrals when needed.

Research is also needed to understand the individual and organizational contexts that influence frontline workers who respond to victims and whether they are able to respond in a culturally sensitive manner. Should disclosure and seeking help be encouraged for abuse survivors, those responding must not retraumatize or victimize the survivors through racist or inappropriate reactions (Campbell & Raja, 1999; Raj, Silverman, Wingood, & Diclemente, 1999; Ullman et al., 2008). To get to such nuanced information, more qualitative methods to further develop theories and learn more about different cultures and subcultures are needed.

The implications for social workers and other mental health professionals start with the importance of understanding and identifying all types of victimizations with their client populations. More education is needed in graduate programs to fully prepare students to work with survivors. Such work should include information on reaching out to underserved populations and knowing how to screen, assess, and appropriately and sensitively respond to survivors from all ethnic and racial groups. Unfortunately, social work and mental health professionals receive limited training or education on how to respond to someone who discloses abuse (Danis & Lockhart, 2003; Postmus, McMahon, Warrener, & Macri, 2011). How one responds to a victim is critical for ensuring that the victim continues down the path toward surviving and not become fearful of getting help from others. More training and education are needed for social workers and other professionals to avoid revictimizing women and, instead, to provide helpful information and support (Campbell & Raja, 1999; Danis & Lockhart, 2003; Ullman et al., 2008). Finally, social workers need to collaborate with other first responders—whether from formal or informal sources—to inform them of best practices, including how to respond to survivors.

In addition to appropriately responding to survivors, social workers and other mental health professionals should use a culturally competent approach (Bent-Goodley, 2005; Sokoloff & Dupont, 2005). Such an approach includes being sensitive to the importance of community and family influences to survivors from culturally diverse backgrounds as well as the importance of spirituality in the lives of some survivors. In addition, professionals should actively combine knowledge with social action, encouraging survivors to partner with them in challenging childhood and adulthood violence in their communities. Indeed, by placing survivors in the center of any advocacy effort, professionals will be more effective in creating an environment that encourages culturally diverse survivors to disclose their experiences and partner with them to end abuse.

/// DISCUSSION QUESTIONS

1. How do race and ethnicity impact their reporting experiences of women who have been victimized?

2. Are there any racial or ethnic differences in the types of services or support that women seek as a result of their victimization experiences?

3. What sorts of challenges exist in the assessment of cultural differences in victimization?

Note

1. This article specifically talks about violence against women, because women are disproportionately victimized, and men are typically perpetrators of physical, sexual, and other forms of violence. Consequently, we will refer to victims as female and perpetrators as male. This in no way diminishes the experiences of male victims nor absolves females of violence they might inflict on males or other females.

References

American Psychiatric Association. (1987). *Diagnostic and Statistical Manual of Mental Disorders* (3rd ed., rev.). Washington, DC: Author.

Arroyo, J. A., Simpson, T. L., & Aragon, A. S. (1997). Childhood sexual abuse among Hispanic and non-Hispanic White college women. *Hispanic Journal of Behavioral Sciences, 19,* 57–68.

Ayalon, L., & Young, M. A. (2005). Racial group differences in help-seeking behaviors. *Journal of Social Psychology, 145,* 391–403.

Barksdale, C. L., & Molock, S. D. (2008). Perceived norms and mental health help seeking among African American college students. *Journal of Behavioral Health Services & Research, 36,* 285–299.

Bent-Goodley, T. B. (2005). An African-centered approach to domestic violence. *Families in Society, 86,* 477–483.

Briere, J. (1992). *Child abuse trauma: Theory and treatment of the lasting effects.* Newbury Park, CA: Sage.

Brown, J. (1997). Working toward freedom from violence. *Violence Against Women, 3,* 5–26.

Campbell, R., & Raja, S. (1999). Secondary victimization of rape victims: Insights from mental health professionals who treat survivors of violence. *Violence and Victims, 14,* 261–275.

Campbell, R., Sefl, T., Wasco, S. M., & Ahrens, C. E. (2004). Doing community research within a community: Creating safe space for rape survivors. *American Journal of Community Psychology, 33,* 253–261.

Coker, A. L., Derrick, C., Lumpkin, J. L., Aldrich, T. E., & Oldendick, R. (2000). Help-seeking for intimate partner violence and forced sex in South Carolina. *American Journal of Preventive Medicine, 19,* 316–320.

Coker, A. L., Smith, P. H., Thompson, M. P., McKeown, R. E., Bethea, L., & Davis, K. E. (2002). Social support protects against the negative effects of partner violence on mental health. *Journal of Women's Health and Gender-Based Medicine, 11,* 465–476.

Cuevas, C. A., & Sabina, C. (2010). *The experience of sexual victimization and help-seeking among Latino women.* Washington, DC: U.S. Department of Justice, Office of Justice Programs, National Criminal Justice Reference Service.

Danis, F., & Lockhart, L. (2003). Domestic violence and social work education: What do we know, what do we need to know?

(Guest editorial). *Journal of Social Work Education, 39,* 215–224.

Fontes, L. A., Cruz, M., & Tabachnick, J. (2001). Views of child sexual abuse in two cultural communities: An exploratory study among African Americans and Latinos. *Child Maltreatment, 6,* 103–117.

Gillum, T. L. (2002). Exploring the link between stereotypic images and intimate partner violence in the African American community. *Violence Against Women, 8,* 64–86.

Henning, K. R., & Klesges, L. M. (2002). Utilization of counseling and supportive services by female victims of domestic abuse. *Violence and Victims, 17,* 623–636.

Hutchison, I. W., & Hirschel, J. D. (1998). Abused women: Help-seeking strategies and police utilization. *Violence Against Women, 4,* 436–456.

Hyman, I., Forte, T., Du Mont, J., Romans, S., & Cohen, M. M. (2006). Help-seeking rates for intimate partner violence (IPV) among Canadian immigrant women. *Health Care for Women International, 27,* 682–694.

Hyman, I., Forte, T., Du Mont, J., Romans, S., & Cohen, M. M. (2009). Help-seeking behavior for intimate partner violence among racial minority women in Canada. *Women's Health Issues, 19,* 101–108.

Kasturirangan, A., Krishnan, S., & Riger, S. (2004). The impact of culture and minority status on women's experience of domestic violence. *Trauma, Violence, & Abuse, 5,* 318–332.

Kaukinen, C. (2002). The help-seeking of women violent crime victims: Findings from the Canadian Violence Against Women Survey. *International Journal of Sociology and Social Policy, 22,* 5–44.

Koss, M. P., & Oros, C. J. (1982). Sexual experiences survey: A research instrument investigating sexual aggression and victimization. *Journal of Consulting and Clinical Psychology, 50,* 455–457.

Lee, M. Y., & Law, P. F. M. (2001). Perception of sexual violence against women in Asian American communities. *Journal of Ethnic & Cultural Diversity in Social Work, 10,* 3–25.

Liang, B., Goodman, L., Tummala-Narra, P., & Weintraub, S. (2005). A theoretical framework for understanding help-seeking processes among survivors of intimate partner violence. *American Journal of Community Psychology, 36,* 71–84.

Low, G., & Organista, K. C. (2000). Latinas and sexual assault: Towards culturally sensitive assessment and intervention. *Journal of Multicultural Social Work, 8,* 131–157.

Lowe, W., Pavkov, T. W., Casanova, G. M., & Wetchler, J. L. (2005). Do American ethnic cultures differ in their definitions of child sexual abuse? *American Journal of Family Therapy, 33,* 147–166.

Macy, R. J., Nurius, P. S., Kernic, M. A., & Holt, V. L. (2005). Battered women's profiles associated with service help-seeking efforts: Illuminating opportunities for intervention. *Social Work Research, 29,* 137–150.

McNutt, L. A., Carlson, B., Persaud, M., & Postmus, J. L. (2002). Cumulative abuse experiences, physical health, and health practices. *Annals of Epidemiology, 12,* 123–130.

McNutt, L. A., Carlson, B., Rose, I., & Robinson, D. (2002). Partner violence intervention in the busy primary care environment. *American Journal of Preventive Medicine, 22,* 84–91.

National Comorbidity Survey. (1992). Retrieved from www.hcp.med.harvard.edu/ncs

Neff, J. A., Holamon, B., & Schluter, T. D. (1995). Spousal violence among Anglos, Blacks, and Mexican Americans: The role of demographic variables, psychosocial predictors, and alcohol consumption. *Journal of Family Violence, 10,* 1–22.

Postmus, J. L., McMahon, S., Warrener, C., & Macri, L. (2011). Factors that influence attitudes, beliefs, and behaviors of students toward survivors of violence. *Journal of Social Work Education, 47,* 303–319.

Postmus, J. L., & Severson, M. E. (2006). *Violence and victimization: Exploring women's histories of survival.* Washington, DC: U.S. Department of Justice, Office of Justice Programs, National Crime Justice Reference Service.

Prochaska, J., DiClemente, C. C., & Norcross, J. C. (1992). In search of how people change: Applications to addictive behaviors. *American Psychologist, 47,* 1102–1114.

Raj, A., Silverman, J. G., Wingood, G. M., & Diclemente, R. J. (1999). Prevalence and correlates of relationship abuse among a community-based sample of low-income African American women. *Violence Against Women, 5,* 272–291.

Rennison, C. M., & Welchans, S. (2000). *Intimate partner violence.* Washington, DC: U.S. Department of Justice, Office of Justice Programs, Bureau of Justice Statistics.

Romero, G. J., Wyatt, G. E., Loeb, T. B., Carmona, J. V., & Solis, B. M. (1999). The prevalence and circumstances of child sexual abuse among Latina women. *Hispanic Journal of Behavioral Sciences, 21,* 351–365.

Russell, D. E. H., & Bolen, R. M. (2000). *The epidemic of rape and child sexual abuse in the United States.* Thousand Oaks, CA: Sage.

Shepard, M., & Campbell, J. A. (1992). The Abusive Behavior Inventory: A measure of psychological and physical abuse. *Journal of Interpersonal Violence, 7,* 291–305.

Smith, D. W., Letourneau, E. J., Saunders, B. E., Kilpatrick, D. G., Resnick, H. S., & Best, C. L. (2000). Delay in disclosure of childhood rape: Results from a national survey. *Child Abuse & Neglect, 24,* 273–287.

Sokoloff, N. J., & Dupont, I. (2005). Domestic violence at the intersections of race, class, and gender. *Violence Against Women, 11,* 38–64.

Sorenson, S. B. (1996). Violence against women: Examining ethnic differences and commonalities. *Evaluation Review, 20,* 123–145.

Sorenson, S. B., & Siegel, J. M. (1992). Gender, ethnicity, and sexual assault: Findings from a Los Angeles study. *Journal of Social Issues, 48,* 93–104.

Thompson, M. P., Kaslow, N. J., Kingree, J. B., Rashid, A., Puett, R., Jacobs, D., & Matthews, A. (2000). Partner violence, social support, and distress among inner-city African American women. *American Journal of Community Psychology, 28,* 127–143.

Tjaden, P., & Thoennes, N. (1998). *Prevalence, incidence, and consequences of violence against women: Findings from the National Violence Against Women Survey.* Washington, DC: U.S. Department of Justice, National Institute of Justice and Centers for Disease Control and Prevention.

Tjaden, P., & Thoennes, N. (2006). *Extent, nature, and consequences of rape victimization: Findings from the National Violence Against Women Survey.* Washington, DC: U.S. Department of Justice, National Institute of Justice and Centers for Disease Control and Prevention.

Ullman, S. E., Starzynski, L. L., Long, S. M., Mason, G. E., & Long, L. M. (2008). Exploring the relationships of women's sexual assault disclosure, social reactions, and problem drinking. *Journal of Interpersonal Violence, 23,* 1235–1257.

West, C. M., Kaufman Kantor, G., & Jasinski, J. L. (1998). Sociodemographic predictors and cultural barriers to help-seeking behavior by Latina and Anglo American battered women. *Violence and Victims, 13,* 361–375.

Wyatt, G. E. (1990a). The aftermath of child sexual abuse of African-American and White American women: The victim's experience. *Journal of Family Violence, 5,* 61–82.

Wyatt, G. E. (1990b). Sexual abuse of ethnic minority children: Identifying dimensions of victimization. *Professional Psychology, 21,* 338–343.

Wyatt, G. E. (1992). The sociocultural context of African American and White American women's rape. *Journal of Social Issues, 48,* 77–91.

Wyatt, G. E., Loeb, T. B., Solis, B., & Carmona, J. V. (1999). The prevalence and circumstances of child sexual abuse: Change across a decade. *Child Abuse & Neglect, 23,* 45–60.

Yoshioka, M. R., Gilbert, L., El-Bassel, N., & Baig-Amin, M. (2003). Social support and disclosure of abuse: Comparing South Asian, African American, and Hispanic battered women. *Journal of Family Violence, 18,* 171–180.

Women, Gender, and Victimization
Rape and Sexual Assault

SECTION

Section Highlights

- Historical perspectives on the sexual victimization of women
- Contemporary paradigms for sexual victimization
- Rape myths and rape myth acceptance
- Categories of sexual assault
- Criminal justice treatment and processing of female sexual assault victims

Historical Perspectives on Rape and Sexual Assault

Rape is one of the oldest crimes in society and has existed in every historical and contemporary society around the world. Laws prohibiting the act of rape, or intercourse under force, threat, or without the consent of the individual, have existed for almost four thousand years. One of the first laws prohibiting the crime of rape can be found in the Code of Hammurabi from Babylon. Ancient Greek, Roman, and Judaic societies also criminalized the act of rape under various circumstances. Some laws distinguished between the rape of a married versus an unmarried woman, and the punishments for these crimes varied based on the status of the victim (Ewoldt, Monson, & Langhinrichsen-Rohling, 2000). Others viewed rape not as a violent sexual offense but as a property crime (Burgess-Jackson, 1999). If the victim was an unmarried woman, the rape tainted her status and value for potential marriage. As a result, many fathers negotiated to have their daughters marry their rapists (Dodderidge, 1632). Even cases of forcible **sexual assault** (where the victim is compelled to engage in sexually based acts other than intercourse) brought shame to the victim, because the acknowledgment of a rape was an admission of sexual activity. In many cases of forcible sexual assault, women were blamed for tempting offenders into immoral behaviors. During criminal rape trials, a woman's sexual history was often put on display in an attempt to discredit her in front of a jury. By portraying female victims of sexual assault as complicit in the behavior, the responsibility of an offender's actions was mitigated. Such a practice represented a double standard because the courts did not request similar information about a man's sexual history, because it would be considered prejudicial in the eyes of the jury (Odem, 1995).

Until the 20th century, early American statutes on rape limited the definition to a narrow view of sexual assault. Consider the following definition of rape that was included in the Model Penal Code in 1955:

Section 213.1: Rape and Related Offenses

1. Rape. A male who has sexual intercourse with a female not his wife is guilty of rape if

    a. he compels her to submit by force or by threat of imminent death, serious bodily injury, extreme pain or kidnapping, to be inflicted on anyone; or

    b. he has substantially impaired her power to appraise or control her conduct by administering or employing without her knowledge drugs, intoxicants or other means for the purpose of preventing resistance; or

    c. the female is unconscious; or

    d. the female is less than 10 years old.

© Scott Houston/Corbis

▲ **Photo 3.1** In response to a Toronto police officer's comment that "women should avoid dressing like sluts in order not to be victimized," over 3,000 people gathered at Queen's Park in Toronto on in 2012 to protest the rape myth that women ask to be sexually assaulted based on their appearance. Since then, "Slut Walks" have been organized around the world to raise awareness about the danger of rape myths and their effects on victims.

What is wrong with this definition? First, it reduces the definition of rape to the act of intercourse, and it excludes other acts of sexual assault, such as oral sex, sodomy, or penetration by a foreign object. Second, it limits the victim-offender relationship to a male perpetrator and a female victim. While women make up the majority of victims, such a definition excludes cases of **same-sex sexual assault**, such as a female sexually assaulting another female or a male-on-male assault, or cases where the victim is a male (and the offender is female). Third, this definition requires that force, or the threat of force, must be used in order for an act to qualify as rape, and it focuses on violence and brutality as proof of the crime. Fourth, this definition creates a marital status exemption such that men cannot be prosecuted for raping their wives. Finally, the definition fails to acknowledge attempted rapes as a crime and the traumatic effects of these "near misses" of victimization. However, we do see some positive influences from the Model Penal Code that has influenced present-day laws on rape and sexual assault. First, the Model Penal Code acknowledges that the absence of consent for sexual intercourse (including in cases involving intoxication or unconsciousness) constitutes rape. Second, the definition (while limited) acknowledges that sexual acts involving children are a crime.

While contemporary definitions of rape vary from state to state, many present-day laws include similar provisions. Today, most laws broadly define sexual victimization as sexual behaviors that are unwanted and harmful to the victim. Most emphasize the use of force or coercion that is displayed by the offender rather than focusing on the response or conduct of the victim. This is not to say that the actions of the victim (such as her attire or behaviors) are not chastised by defense counsel or members of the jury, but the law itself does not require victims to demonstrate physical levels of resistance.

Another development in contemporary rape laws involves the abolishment of the marital-rape exemption clause. Historical acceptance of the marital-rape exception is rooted in biblical passages, which state that "a man should fulfill his duty as a husband and a woman should fulfill her duty as a wife, and each should satisfy the other's needs. A wife is not the master of her own body, but her husband is" (I Corinthians 7, 3–5). Today, every state has laws on the books that generally identify rape within the context of marriage as a criminal act. In an effort to resolve some of the limitations with the word *rape*, the term *sexual assault* is often used to identify forms of sexual victimization that are not included under the traditionally narrow definition of rape. These laws have expanded the definitions of sexual assault beyond penile-vaginal penetration and include sodomy, forced oral copulation, and unwanted fondling and touching of a sexual nature. Cases of child sexual assault are treated differently in many jurisdictions, and age of consent laws have led to the development of statutory rape laws. Finally, sex offender registration laws, such as Megan's Law and Jessica's Law, require the community receive notification of sexual offenders and the placing of residential, community, and supervision restrictions on offenders.

Defining Sexual Victimization

What behaviors are included within the definitions of rape and sexual assault? The answer to this question depends on the source. Historically, the Uniform Crime Reports considered only cases of forcible rape. Such a definition excluded the majority of cases of rape and sexual assault. In addition, this practice by the UCR did not account for cases of attempted rape/sexual assault. Although the Federal Bureau of Investigation (2012a, c) changed their data collection practice in 2012 to include both completed and attempted cases of rape and sexual assault, the National Crime Victimization Survey (NCVS) defines rape as the "forced sexual intercourse. . . (including) vaginal, oral, or anal penetration by offender(s)."[1] The NCVS collects data not only on penile penetration but also includes cases of penetration with a foreign object. At the same time, states vary significantly on their own definitions of these crimes. Some states limit rape to penile-vaginal penetration and use sexual assault as a catch-all category of other crimes, while other states use multiple statutes to distinguish between different forms of sexual assault. While some of these statutes are very specific, others combine multiple forms of assault under a single penal code definition.

The limited clarity on the legal definitions of rape and sexual assault, coupled with the personification of these crimes in popular culture and the media, can have a significant effect on victims. In many cases, people who experience acts that are consistent with a legal definition of rape or sexual assault may not label their experience as such. As a result, they do not see themselves as such and therefore do not report these crimes to the police, nor do they seek out therapeutic resources. In many of these cases, women who experience these acts do not define themselves as victims because their experience differs from their personal definitions of what rape and sexual assault look like. For example, the crime of sexual assault is perpetuated throughout fiction novels and made for television movies as a stranger who attacks a victim in his home or on a dark sidewalk at night. Despite the high degree to which such events are manifested within popular culture, real life cases of this nature are relatively rare. Indeed, findings from the NCVS data demonstrate that cases of stranger rape with female victims account for only 22% of all sexual assaults (Planty, Langton, Krebs, Berzofsky, & Smiley-McDonald, 2013). Such findings highlight that the majority of rapes and sexual assault are perpetuated by people who are known to the victim.

---

[1]See definitions at http://www.bjs.gov/index.cfm?ty=tda.

The lack of an understanding of a definition of rape and sexual assault affects offenders, as well. Many people who admit to engaging in behaviors that meet the legal criteria for rape or sexual assault generally do not define their own actions as criminal. One of the most frequently cited studies on rape and sexual assault surveyed 2,971 college men regarding self-reported conduct that met the legal definitions of rape, attempted rape, sexual coercion, and unwanted sexual contact. Based on these reports, the results indicated that 1,525 acts of sexual assault had occurred, including 187 acts of rape. Of those whose acts met the legal definition of rape, 84% of the "perpetrators" believed that their acts did not constitute rape (Warshaw, 1994).

Prevalence of Rape and Sexual Assault

Despite the acknowledgment that rape and sexual assault are two of the most underreported types of crimes, the known data indicate that these crimes pervade our society. According to the Rape, Abuse and Incest National Network (RAINN), a rape, attempted rape, or sexual assault occurs approximately once every 2 minutes. According to the National Crime Victimization Survey, there were 431,840 victims of rape and sexual assault in 2015. When we think about how common these crimes are, this data translates to 1.6 victims per 1,000 individuals age 12 or older (Truman & Morgan, 2016). While the U.S. Department of Justice (2003) found that 40% of victims report their crime to the police, other research has placed this number significantly lower, at 16% for adult women (Kilpatrick, Resnick, Ruggiero, Conoscenti, & McCauley, 2007). Given the stigmatizing nature of this crime, it is not surprising that rape, attempted rape, and sexual assault are some of the most underreported crimes, making it difficult to determine the extent of this problem. While researchers attempt to estimate the prevalence of sexual assault, they are faced with their own set of challenges, including differences in defining sexual assault, the emphasis on different sample populations (adolescents, college-aged adults, adults, etc.), or different forms of data (arrest data vs. self-report surveys). Regardless of these issues and the data it yields, it appears that sexual assault affects most individuals in some way (either personally or through someone they know) at some point in their lifetime.

Prevalence studies report a wide range of data on the pervasiveness of rape and sexual assault in the United States. A national study on rape published in 2007 indicated that 18% of women in America have experienced rape at some point in their lifetime, with an additional 3% of women experiencing an attempted rape. A comparison of these findings to the Violence Against Women survey in 1996 indicates that little change has occurred in the prevalence of this crime over time (15% of all women). Indeed, these results demonstrate an increase in the number of rape cases, which is contrary to the belief that rape has declined significantly in recent times. Findings from studies such as these have led researchers, rape-crisis organizations, and policy makers to posit that one in four American women will be victimized by rape or sexual assault (or an attempt) within their lifetime.

Rape Myths

Rape myths are defined as "attitudes and beliefs that are generally false but are widely and persistently held, and that serve to deny and justify male sexual aggression against women" (Lonsway & Fitzgerald, 1994, p. 134). Table 3.1 highlights some of the most commonly perpetuated myths about rape.

The acceptance of rape myths by society is a contributing factor in the practice of victim blaming. First, the presence of rape myths allows society to shift the blame of rape from the offender to the victim. By doing so, we can avoid confronting the realities of rape and sexual assault in society. This denial serves as a vicious cycle: As we fail to acknowledge the severity of rape and sexual assault, which leads to victims not reporting their crime to authorities, this results in greater acceptance that the crime is not taken seriously by society as a whole. Second, the presence of rape myths lends support to the notion of a just world hypothesis, which suggests that only good things happen to good people and bad things happen to those who deserve it. Rape myths, such as "she asked for it," serve to perpetuate the notion of the just world in action (Lonsway & Fitzgerald, 1994).

Offenders often use rape myths to excuse or justify their actions. Excuses occur when offenders admit that their behavior was wrong but blame their actions on external circumstances outside of their control. In these instances, offenders deny responsibility for their actions. Statements such as "I was drunk" or "I don't know what came over me" are examples of excuses. In comparison, justifications occur when offenders admit responsibility for their actions but argue that their behavior was acceptable under the circumstances. Examples of justifications include "She asked for it" or "Nothing really happened." Miscommunication appears to play a significant role for men, as well, who ask, "When does no mean no, or when does no mean yes?" By suggesting that men "misunderstand" their victim's refusal for sexual activity, the responsibility of rape is transferred from the offender back to the victim.

Some victims accept these excuses or justifications for their assault that minimize or deny the responsibility of their offender. In cases where the male offender "got carried away," female victims often accept the actions of the offender as a natural consequence of male sexuality. In these cases, victims feel that they deserve their victimization as a result of their own actions. Many victims argue that "they should have known better" or that "they didn't try hard enough to stop it." In these cases, victims believe that they put themselves at risk as a result of their own decision-making process.

The prevalence and acceptance of rape myths in society does a significant disservice to both victims and society in general in terms of understanding the realities of rape. These myths permit us to believe that stranger rape is "real" rape, whereas **acquaintance rape,** by persons known to the victim, is interpreted as less serious, less significant, and less harmful because the offender is known to the victim. Rape myths perpetuate the belief that women should be more fearful of the **symbolic assailant**—the stranger who lurks in the alley or hides in the bushes and

---

Table 3.1 ● Rape Myths

- A woman who gets raped usually deserves it, especially if she has agreed to go to a man's house or park with him.
- If a woman agrees to allow a man to pay for dinner, then it means she owes him sex.
- Acquaintance rape is committed by men who are easy to identify as rapists.
- Only women can be raped or sexually assaulted by men.
- Women who do not fight back have not been raped.
- Once a man reaches a certain point of arousal, sex is inevitable, and he cannot help forcing himself on a woman.
- Most women lie about acquaintance rape because they have regrets after consensual sex.
- Women who say "No" really mean "Yes."
- Certain behaviors such as drinking or dressing in a sexually appealing way make rape a woman's responsibility.
- If she had sex with me before, she has consented to have sex with me again.
- A man cannot rape his wife.
- Only bad women get raped.
- Women secretly enjoy being raped.

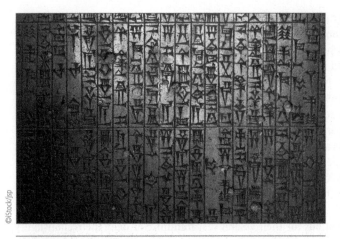

©iStock/jsp

▲ **Photo 3.2** The Code of Hammurabi is one of the oldest legal artifacts in the world and dates back to 1772 BC. It includes punishments for 282 different crimes, including rape. Today it is housed at the Louvre Museum in Paris, France.

surprises the victim. Rape myths suggest that in order for a woman to be raped, she needs to fight back against her attacker and leave the scene with bruises and injuries related to her efforts to thwart the assault. Rape myths also suggest that real rape victims always report their attackers and have evidence collected and that an offender is identified who is then arrested, prosecuted, and sentenced to the fullest extent under the law. Alas, this rarely occurs within our criminal justice system. Instead, the majority of cases involve victims who know their offender, and victims who do not report these cases to the police. Even when such cases are reported, the prosecution of an offender can be a difficult task. Here, the consequence of pervasive rape myths in society serves to limit the public's understanding about the realities of rape, which in turn can limit the victim's opportunity for justice.

Acquaintance Versus Stranger Assault

As illustrated above, cases of stranger rape are not the most common type of sexual assault. Young women are socialized to be wary of walking alone at night, to be afraid that a scary man will jump out of the bushes and attack them. Unfortunately, many prevention efforts that advise women on what they can do to keep themselves safe from sexual assault often focus on these situations of stranger danger. While these tools are certainly valuable in enhancing women's safety, they fail to acknowledge the reality of sexual assault. Acquaintance rape accounts for 90% of all rapes of college women (Sampson, 2003). Additionally, 60% of all rape and sexual assault incidents occur either at the victim's home or at the home of a friend, neighbor, or relative (Greenfeld, 1997). Cases of acquaintance rape and sexual assault tend to entail lower levels of physical force by the offender and involve less resistance by the victim compared to cases of stranger rape (Littleton, Breitkopf, & Berenson, 2008). Alas, each of these realities is missing from the stereotypical scripts about rape and sexual assault.

It is difficult to assess how many sexual assault victims disclose their victimization to police. Research conducted by Millar, Stermac, and Addison (2002) documented that 61% of acquaintance rapes are not reported to the police. In comparison, Rickert, Wiemann, and Vaughan (2005) found that only one of 86 study participants made a report to law enforcement authorities, and an additional four victims sought services from a mental health professional. While these findings demonstrate a dramatic range of reporting rates, it is safe to conclude that acquaintance rape is significantly underreported. Society tends to discount the validity of acquaintance rape, suggesting that it is a lesser criminal act than stranger rape (i.e., real rape). Yet research demonstrates that victims of acquaintance rape suffer significant mental health trauma as a result of their victimization. This trauma is often exacerbated by the fact that many victims of acquaintance rape tend to blame themselves for their own victimization. In many cases, these victims are less likely to seek assistance from rape crisis or counseling services.

Spotlight on Rape Culture

In August 2012, Steubenville was thrust into the national spotlight after a 16-year-old girl was sexually assaulted by several of her peers. What made this case particularly noteworthy is that her assault was videotaped and her assailants posted the video on social media sites, such as YouTube and Twitter. In the photos and videos, two Steubenville High football team members, Trent Mays and Ma'lik Richmond (both 16 at the time of the offense), are shown carrying the victim by her hands and feet because she was so intoxicated that she was unable to walk. Video also documents the accused penetrating the victim's vagina with their fingers and flashing her breasts to the camera (Abad-Santos, 2013).

Many blamed the victim (who was so intoxicated that she did not know she had been violated until she saw the photos and videos online) and called her a "train whore." Even one of the football coaches joined in on the blam-

▲ **Photo 3.3** Santa Clara County Superior Court Judge Aaron Persky drew significant criticism for his decision to sentence former Stanford University student Brock Turner to only six months in jail for sexually assaulting an unconscious woman. Prosecutors had requested that Turner be sentenced to six years. Turner was released after serving three months of his sentence.

ing, stating, "What else are you going to tell your parents when you come home drunk like that and after a night like that? She had to make up something. Now people are trying to blow up our football program because of it" (Abad-Santos, 2013). During the trial, the defense counsel introduced testimony that tried to paint the victim as culpable in her own attack by calling two former friends who testified that the victim not only had a history of drinking in excess but also told contradictory stories about the events of the evening (Welsh-Huggins, 2013a).

The judge found that the victim was so intoxicated that she lacked the cognitive ability to consent to sexual activity (Oppel, 2013). Both Mays and Richmond were found guilty in juvenile court and sentenced to one year in the state juvenile correctional facility. Mays received an additional one-year sentence for the crime of distributing nude images of a minor (Ng, 2013). In her report of the verdict, CNN reporter Poppy Harlow critiqued the court's decision, stating that it had been "incredibly difficult [to watch] as these two young men—who had such promising futures, star football players, very good students—literally watched as they believed their life fell apart" (Harlow, 2013). Richmond was released from custody after serving nine months of his sentence (Fox News, 2014). Mays served two years in a youth facility (Jablonski, 2015).

Alas, cases such as Steubenville are more common than we think. In 2015, three high school football players from Dietrich, Idaho, sexually assaulted a mentally disabled teammate by inserting a coat hanger into his rectum at the school locker room following a football practice. The victim's family argued that the attack occurred after months of racist abuse and bullying. The judge in the case was quoted as saying "this is not a rape case . . . this is not a sex case. This started out as penetration with a foreign object. . . . Whatever happened in that locker room was not sexual. It wasn't appropriate. There's nothing in this record that supports anything close to the sexual allegation against this young man" (LaGanga, 2017). School officials waited for several days before reporting the event to

(Continued)

(Continued)

the local authorities and instead conducted their own investigation and collected evidence from the locker room. Evidence also suggests that they recorded conversations with the victim in an effort to discredit him. Ultimately, the offenders went unpunished for the crime. One of the offenders was 18 years old at the time of the event, yet was sentenced to just probation for his crime, which was pled down to felony injury to a child (Boone, 2017), and adult felony charges were dropped against at least one of the juveniles involved in the case (KBOI news staff, 2016). The light sentence brought criticism to the judge and drew comparisons to the case of Brock Turner. Turner was sentenced to six months for assaulting an unconscious woman at a Stanford University fraternity party. Turner blamed the events of the evening on the culture of drinking that pervades university life. Under state sentencing recommendations, he could have faced fourteen years in prison, though prosecutors only asked for six years. In handing down his sentence, Judge Persky expressed concern that a harsher sentence could have a "severe impact" on the offender (Koren, 2016). Turner's father also defended his son's actions and advocated that his son should receive probation, stating "that is a steep price to pay for 20 minutes of action out of his 20 plus years of life" (Miller, 2016).

Following his release, Turner will be required to register as a sex offender for life. In December 2017, Turner's attorney filed an appeal for a new trial and requested that the registration requirement be removed.

Cases such as Steubenville, Dietrich, and Brock Turner highlight the role that rape culture continues to play in our society. These forms of violence contribute to a culture of rape whereby offender actions are minimized and blame for these events is often diverted.

Drug-Facilitated/Incapacitated Sexual Assault

A **drug-facilitated rape** is defined as an unwanted sexual act following the deliberate intoxication of a victim. In comparison, an **incapacitated rape** is an unwanted sexual act that occurs after a victim voluntarily consumes drugs or alcohol. In both cases, the victim is too intoxicated by drugs and/or alcohol to be aware of her behavior, and she is therefore unable to consent. Kilpatrick et al. (2007) found that 5% of women experience drug-facilitated or incapacitated rape.

Recent research has discussed a rise in incapacitated rapes through the involuntary drugging of victims. The terms *date rape drug* and *drug-facilitated sexual assault* have been used to identify how the involuntary consumption of substances have been used in sexual assault cases. Table 3.2 provides a description of the different types of substances that are commonly used in cases of drug-facilitated sexual assault. In many cases, these substances are generally colorless, odorless, and/or tasteless when dissolved in a drink and result in a rapid intoxication that renders a potential rape victim unconscious and unable to recall events that occurred while she was intoxicated. One research study identified that less than 2% of sexual assault incidents were directly attributed to the deliberate covert drugging of the victim (Scott-Ham & Burton, 2005). However, these findings document reported cases of sexual assault, and it is reasonable to conclude that many cases of drug-facilitated sexual assault go unreported, because victims may be reluctant to report a crime for which they have little recollection.

With the exception of alcohol, the majority of the substances that are used in cases of drug-facilitated sexual assault (such as GHB, or gamma-hydroxybutyrate, ketamine, and Rohypnol) are labeled as controlled substances, and the possession of these drugs is considered a federal offense under the Controlled Substances Act of 1970. In addition, the Drug-Induced Rape Prevention and Punishment Act of 1996 provides penalties for up to 20 years for the involuntary drugging of an individual in cases of violence (National Drug Intelligence Center, n.d.). Many states have enacted laws that provide specific sanctions in cases of drug-facilitated sexual assault. For example, Colorado Penal Code § 18–3–402(4d) distinguishes cases of drug-facilitated sexual assault as one where "the actor has substantially impaired the victim's power to appraise or control the victim's conduct by employing, without the victim's

Table 3.2 • Substances Commonly Used in Drug-Facilitated Sexual Assaults

GHB (Gamma-Hydrozybutyric acid)

- GHB comes in a few forms—a liquid that contains no odor or color, a white powder, and a pill. GHB has not been approved by the FDA since 1990, so it is considered illegal to possess or sell. GHB can take effect in as little as 15 minutes and can last for 3 to 4 hours. GHB is considered a Schedule 1 drug under the Controlled Substances Act. GHB leaves the body within 10 to 12 hours, making it very difficult to detect.

Ketamine

- Ketamine is an anesthetic that is generally used to sedate animals in a veterinarian's office. Ketamine can be particularly dangerous when used in combination with other drugs and alcohol. It is very fast acting and can cause individuals to feel as if they are dissociated from their body and be unaware of their circumstances. It can cause memory loss, affecting the ability of a victim to recall details of the assault.

Rohypnol (Flunitrazepam)

- Rohypnol is a dissolvable pill of various sizes and colors (round, white, oval, green-gray). Rohypnol is not approved for medical use in the United States, and much of the supply comes from Mexico. However, the manufacturer of this drug recently changed the chemistry of the pill such that if it is inserted into a clear liquid, it will change the color of the drink to a bright blue color, allowing for potential victims to increase the chance that they could identify whether their drink has been altered. Rohypnol effects can be noticeable within 30 minutes of being ingested; the individual appears overly intoxicated, and the drug affects their balance, stability, and speech patterns. Like many other substances, Rohypnol leaves the body in a rapid fashion, generally between 36 and 72 hours of ingestion.

Alcohol

- Alcohol is one of the most common "date rape" drugs. Not only do victims willingly consume alcohol, it is (generally, based on the age of the individual) legal and easily obtained. The consumption of alcohol impairs judgment, lowers inhibition, and affects a victim's ability to recognize potentially dangerous situations.

Spotlight on the Invisible War: Rape in the Military

As a prestigious military academy, the Air Force Academy in Colorado Springs, CO, receives high rankings for its training of pilots (as well as its football team). However, 2003 brought a new level of attention to the Academy, as allegations of sexual abuse among the ranks were made public. Not only did victims suggest that rape and sexual assault occurred within the student body on a regular basis, victims suggested that military officials knew of the abuse but did little to stop the systematic assault of female cadets by their male counterparts. Women who came forward with allegations were often punished by their superiors, leading many victims to remain silent about the abuse they endured. While six cadets came forward as part of the allegations, a survey of female graduates that same year suggested that the issue of rape, sexual assault, and sexual harassment is much more prevalent that these few cases. Over 88% of the female graduates participated in the survey, and 12% of women acknowledged that they experienced completed or attempted rape at some point during their college career. An additional 70% of women referenced cases of sexual harassment, including pressure to engage in sexual behaviors (Schemo, 2003). While the most common form of victimization involved sexual harassment, female cadets were significantly more likely to indicate that they had experienced

(Continued)

(Continued)

forms of unwanted sexual touching, sexual coercion, or rape. In addition, women were almost four times more likely to experience multiple acts of victimization compared to men (Snyder, Fisher, Scherer, & Daigle, 2012). Table 3.3 highlights some of the findings from this study.

Table 3.3 • Sexual Victimization at Military Academies

Type of Victimization	All Victims (%)	Males (%)	Females (%)
Unwanted sexual attention	22.65	10.79	41.24
Sexual harassment	55.73	38.40	82.89
Unwanted sexual contact	15.85	8.96	26.65
Sexual coercion	7.99	4.39	13.64
Rape	3.45	2.41	5.07
Total victimization	58.90	41.85	85.57
Multiple victimizations	25.00	12.23	45.04

SOURCE: Snyder, Fisher, Scherer, & Daigle (2012).

In response to these events, a Sexual Assault Prevention and Response (SAPR) team was developed in June 2005 and provides two victim advocates as well as a 24/7 hotline. When a sexual assault is reported, victims have the choice of filing a restricted or unrestricted report. While a restricted report allows victims to receive counseling and other services from the sexual assault response team, these reports remain confidential and no charges are filed. In an unrestricted case, the Air Force Office of Special Investigations is able to assess whether criminal charges will be filed against the perpetrator (Branum, 2013). In addition, SAPR delivers approximately 11 hours of training over the cadet's four-year educational experience on rape and sexual assault prevention. Similar programs are in place at all the military academies. In addition, each campus has added a special victims legal counsel to help individuals whose cases are handled through the military justice system.

The most recent data from the 2015–2016 academic year notes that while the overall number of cases has decreased, the number of reports at West Point and the Naval Academy have increased. At West Point, there were 26 reported cases of sexual assault, compared to 17 cases in the previous year. Similarly, there were 28 cases reported at the Naval Academy, compared to 25 in 2014–2015. Meanwhile, the number of reported incidents at the Air Force Academy dropped significantly. In 2014–2015 there were 49 reported cases. This year, there were 32 reported cases. In addition, more victims are choosing to have their cases handled by the military justice system (Cooper, 2017; Department of Defense, 2017).

Unfortunately, cases of rape and sexual assault are not limited to the military academies. In an effort to bring attention to the issue of rape in the military, filmmakers Kirby Dick and Amy Ziering presented their film *The Invisible War* at the Sundance Movie Festival in 2012. Drawing from real stories from military personnel, the film portrays the victimization of these soldiers and the response, or lack thereof, by military officials. Their story paints a grim picture about sexual violence in the military as they suggest that 20% of all active duty women are sexually victimized. Other scholars have indicated that 34% of active duty women (and 6% of men) suffer

[2]Data is collected for the fiscal year.

harassment of a sexual nature (Lipari, Cook, Rock, & Matos, 2008). Official data from 2015[1] notes that 6,083 reported of sexual assault involving service members as either victims and/or subjects were reported. Most of these reports were unrestricted and may be reviewed by the military justice system. Since [the documentary's] release, the Invisible No More Campaign has generated new conversations about how to combat this issue. Following his review of the film, Secretary of Defense Leon Panetta ordered that all sexual assault investigations be altered to provide multiple avenues for victims to report cases of assault. Previous military policy dictated that the assault be reported to the victim's immediate supervisor. Panetta also directed each branch to develop a Special Victims Unit to respond to allegations of sexual assault.[3]

▲ **Photo 3.4** Ariana Klay was gang raped in 2009 by a fellow marine and his civilian friend. When she reported the rape to her commanding officer, he replied, "It's your fault for wearing running shorts and makeup." One of her perpetrators was given immunity in the case while the other was convicted of adultery and indecent language and was sentenced to only 45 days in military jail. Klay and others have fought for changes to the way sexual assault cases are handled in the military

Despite recent changes, rape in the military continues to be a problem. In 2012, Air Force Staff Sergeant Luis Walker was convicted on twenty-eight counts of rape, sexual assault, and aggravated sexual misconduct against ten victims and received 20 years for this crimes (Peterson, 2012). While this one case led to a successful outcome, there are many others where victims fail to secure meaningful justice. Meanwhile the culture of sexual violence continues within our military branches. Recently, a criminal investigation was opened into a secret Facebook group involving over 30,000 active and veteran men from the U.S. Marines where photos of female Marines are posted without their permission. Many of the photos involve either nude images or women in various states of undress and are accompanied by sexist and derogatory commentary (Phillips, 2017).

In an effort to create systemic changes on how sexual assault cases are handled by the military, members of the U.S. Senate have made attempts to change the Uniform Military Code of Justice. Senators Kirsten Gillibrand (D-NY) and Claire McCaskill (D-MO), who are both members of the Senate Armed Services Committee, have tackled this issue head on and have challenged military officials to increase their understanding about rape in the military. According to Gillibrand, "Not every single commander necessarily wants women in the force. Not every single commander believes what a sexual assault is. Not every single commander can distinguish between a slap on the ass and a rape because they merge all these crimes together" (*NY Daily News*, 2013, para. 11). In December 2013, Congress passed the Military Justice Improvement Act, which makes a number of significant reforms for how cases of sexual assault are handled within the military ranks. These include an end to the statute of limitations for rape and sexual assault cases, makes retaliation against victims a crime, and bars military commanders from overturning convictions on sexually based crimes. It also mandates a dishonorable discharge for those convicted of such crimes (O'Keefe, 2013).

---

[3]See http://www.notinvisible.org/the_movie for information about the film *The Invisible War*.

consent, any drug, intoxicant, or other means for the purpose of causing submissions." Here, state law provides an assessment of a victim's ability to consent to sexual relations and holds that the level of intoxication, combined with the resulting mental impairment of the individual, must affect the victim's ability to exercise reasonable judgment. Here, the law provides for an elevated punishment of these cases. While sexual assault is generally considered a class 4 felony (punishable by 2–6 years in prison), drug facilitated sexual assault is considered a class 3 felony and calls for a punishment range of 4–12 years. The mandatory parole in these cases also increases from 3 to 5 years.

While there has been increased attention to sexual assault due to involuntary intoxication, this is not the primary form of drug-facilitated sexual assault. Rather, cases where the victim is sexually assaulted following her voluntary intoxication of alcohol make up the majority of drug-facilitated sexual assaults. In a sample of rape cases of college-aged women, alcohol was involved in 79% of cases of nonforcible rape (Kilpatrick et al., 2007). The use of drugs and alcohol places women at a greater risk for sexual assault. Not only may women be less aware of the risk for sexual assault and labeled as a target for potential offenders due to a reduction of their inhibitions, but they may also be unable to resist their attackers due to their incapacitated state. Additionally, while voluntarily intoxicated individuals are legally incapable of giving consent for sexual activity (Beynon, McVeigh, McVeigh, Leavey, & Bellis, 2008), these victims are often held as the most responsible of all sexual assault victims, since they chose to use intoxicating substances recreationally. As a result, the actions of perpetrators in these cases are most likely to be excused or diminished (Girard & Senn, 2008).

Spousal Rape

Earlier in this section, you learned about how early laws on rape included a marital exception clause, which argues that women automatically consent to sex with their husbands as part of their marriage. Even once the legal rights of women began to increase, the relationship between a man and wife was viewed as a private manner, not one for public scrutiny. This belief system permitted the criminal justice system to maintain a "hands-off" policy when it came to **spousal rape**. As existing rape laws began to change throughout the 1970s and 1980s, increased attention was brought to the marital rape exception. In 1978, only five states defined marital rape as a crime. While all 50 states have either eliminated laws that permitted marital rape or had expressly included laws that prohibited this practice, several states still have exceptions in the law that limit how marital rape is defined. For example, in Oklahoma, the crime of spousal rape requires that there be the use of force (or threats of use of force) (O.S. §, 21 45 1111). In South Carolina, cases of sexual battery must be reported to law enforcement within thirty days of the offense (SC Code §16-3-615).

While U.S laws generally prohibit marital rape, it is still legal in many other countries around the world (Fus, 2006). While Nigerian criminal law has criminalized rape in general (and provides for a life sentence for offenders), the law does not acknowledge rape by a spouse as a crime. In fact, "Section 282 of the Penal Code expressly states that sexual intercourse by a man with his own wife is not rape" (Chika, 2011). India also provides legal immunity in cases of rape when the victim is their wife (Mandal, 2014). Meanwhile, other regions of the world (such as South Africa and Britain) have criminalized marital rape but provide for lenient sentencing structures for offenders (Rumney, 1999; S v Modise, 2007)

The majority of cases of marital rape involve cases of emotional coercion rather than physical force in the assault. Examples of emotional coercion include inferences that it is a *wife's duty* to engage in sex with her husband (referred to as social coercion) or the use of power by a husband to exert sexual favors from his wife (referred to as interpersonal coercion). A third form of emotional coercion involves cases where a wife engages in sex for fear of unknown threats or damages that may occur if she refuses. Many of these occurrences are related to cases of domestic violence, where the possibility of violence exists. Cases of marital rape by the use of physical force are referred to as battering rape. In cases of battering rape, the sexual assault is an extension of the physical and emotional violence that occurs within the context of the relationship (Martin, Taft, & Resick, 2007). The physical effects of marital rape are generally greater compared to cases of stranger and acquaintance rape.

Contrary to popular belief, marital rape is as prevalent as other forms of rape, but this victimization is generally hidden from public view. Results from randomized studies showed that 7% to 14% of women experienced completed or attempted rape within the context of marriage, cohabitating, or intimate relationship (Bennice & Resick,

2003). Community samples tend to yield significantly higher rates of marital rape; however, they tend to draw from shelters or therapeutic settings, which offer skewed results. These studies find that 10% to 34% of women studied experienced rape within the context of marriage (Martin et al., 2007).

One of the challenges in the reporting and punishment of marital rape is that the perception persists that marital rape is not *real* rape. Research notes that acts of sexual assault (such as oral sex without consent) are less likely to be viewed as a form of marital rape. However there is a gender difference in these perceptions, because women are more likely than men to view nonconsensual acts such as vaginal and anal penetration, as well as penetration with an object as marital rape. Marital rape is also viewed as the least serious form of rape, compared to rape by a stranger, acquaintance (Kirkwood & Cecil, 2001; Ferro, Cermele, & Saltzman, 2008). Martial rape is only viewed as a serious act when there is a history of violence in the relationship, and victims receive greater levels of blame if there is a history of infidelity in the relationship. Such perceptions not only impact how others view these situations but can also lead to self-blaming behaviors by the victim (Langhinrichsen-Rohling & Monson, 1998; Munge, Pomerantz, Pettibone, & Falconer, 2007).

Despite the criminalization of spousal rape, the cultural acceptance of marital rape still fails to identify these women as victims. By leaving these victims with the belief that their experiences are not considered real rape, these women are less likely to seek assistance for their victimization. Thus, marital rape remains a significant issue in the United States and around the world.

Campus Sexual Assault

When defining **campus sexual assault**, many assume that these incidents are limited to crimes that occur on a college campus. However the term is much broader and includes experiences of rape and sexual assault that occur during the collegiate experience. Rates of sexual assault appear to be higher on college campuses, where it is estimated that between 20% and 25% of women will experience a completed or attempted rape at some point during their collegiate career (Fisher, Cullen, & Turner, 2000). University life contains many variables that may increase the risk for sexual assault—campus environments that facilitate a "party" atmosphere, easy access to alcohol and drugs, increases in freedom, and limited supervision by older adults (Sampson, 2003). In this environment, the majority of sexual assaults against university women occurred between the evening and early morning hours during or after a party. Alcohol was involved in most of these cases where the victims knew their attackers. Victims are also more likely to be younger and less knowledgeable about the dangers of sexual assault and its relationship to the school/party experience. In addition, the more that students engage in substance use, the greater the risk for victimization because they are more likely to cross paths with a motivated offender (Hines, Armstrong, Reed, & Cameron, 2012).

Research notes that the risk of sexual assault among college-age individuals is highest during the first year of the university experience. During this year, one in six female students experience either an attempted or completed incapacitated or forcible sexual assault. In addition, women who have previously experienced sexual violence during adolescence are more likely to be revictimized in college (Carey, Durney, Shepardson & Carey, 2015).

The recent attention to campus sexual assault involves Title IX of the Education Amendments of 1972 and states that "no person in the United States shall, on the basis of sex, be excluded from participation in, be denied the benefits of, or be subjected to discrimination under any education program or activity receiving Federal financial assistance" (20 U.S.C. §1681). At the time of its implementation, it was primarily used to ensure that women have equal access to programs such as law school and medical school (which had historically used quota systems to limit access to women) or to provide support and access for women's programs within college athletics (which had been either missing or lacked adequate funding). Directives such as the 2011 Dear Colleague letter where the Department of Education stated that the provisions in Title IX, which prohibit discrimination and harassment on the basis of sex, were also applicable in cases of sexual violence, initiated many of the changes that we see today on campuses. This call to action, coupled by the creation of the White House Task Force to Protect Students from Sexual Assault, resulted in increased requirements for schools to both respond to current acts of harassment and take steps to prevent similar acts in the future (Office of Civil Rights, 2011). One of the challenges facing colleges has been that these mandates are generally unfunded. This means that campuses must find a

©iStock/lofiolo

▲ **Photo 3.5** Emma Sulkowicz, a visual arts major from Columbia University, carried a mattress everywhere on campus during her senior year as part of a performance demonstration and protest of the way that her allegations of sexual assault were managed by the university.

way to support these new or enhanced infrastructures. Perhaps the best way to describe these efforts is to expand the focus from a responsive framework (albeit one that many colleges and universities were doing a poor job at) to one that includes prevention efforts as well as an accountability factor. For example, campuses have created requirements for training employees, procedures for reporting cases, and processes for responding to complaints. In addition, campuses are required to adopt prevention curriculum for students as well as provide support systems and resources for victims. While faculty are often mandatory reporters of any known incidents (regardless of whether they occurred on or off campus), most campuses have options for both confidential and anonymous reporting. Victims also have the option to pursue their case through campus disciplinary structures and to report the case to local authorities for criminal processing.

What effect have these changes had on campus sexual assault? Research notes that despite a renewed focus on educating students about campus resources in this area, students remain unfamiliar with the resources that are available (Burgess-Proctor, Pickett, Parkhill, Hamill, Kirwan, & Kozak, 2016). Bystander education programs are

Spotlight on Statutory Rape

Statutory rape refers to sexual activity that is unlawful because it is prohibited by legal statute. Unlike other forms of violent sexual assault, statutory rape generally involves individuals who are legally unable to consent to sexual activity because of their age.

While statutory rape laws were initially introduced to protect adolescents from adults, particularly in cases where there was a dramatic age difference, these laws have also been used against adolescents and their peers. Some would consider these to be victimless crimes because individuals in these cases often do not define themselves as a victim. Rather, they see themselves as willing participants in sexual activity. It is purely the legal distinction of who can, and who cannot consent, that makes these acts a crime. There are two different types of statutory rape laws. The first category includes states where the age of consent is considered a minimum age and sex with anyone under that age is considered a crime. For example, the age of sexual consent in California is 18, and anyone with engages in intercourse with someone under the age of 18 is in violation of the state's statutory rape law. So two 17-year-olds that engage in intercourse would be considered to be breaking the law. In the second category are states that define an age range between the individuals. In these cases, it would be considered a crime if one of the individuals was of a minimum age and the other individual was older by a specified number of years under the statute. For example, in Missouri, someone who is at least 21 years old who has sexual intercourse with someone younger than 17 is considered to have committed second degree statutory rape. (§ 566.034 (1)). In comparison, Tennessee state law considers statutory rape a criminal act if (1) it involves sexual penetration; (2) the victim is at least 13 but younger than 18; and (3) the offender is at least four years older than the victim. In addition, Tennessee requires that offenders under the age of 18 be tried as juveniles (§ 39-13-506).

Several states have increased their prosecution of statutory rape cases in an effort to reduce teen pregnancy and the demand on welfare. During the 1990s, legislators targeted welfare reform as a major cause of action. In passing The Personal Responsibility and Work Opportunity Reconciliation Act (PRWORA), legislators noted a significant increase in the number of unwed teen mothers between 1976 and 1991 and indicated that these young single mothers were more likely to apply for welfare benefits. In responding to this issue, legislators noted that "an effective strategy to combat teenage pregnancy must address the issue of male responsibility, including statutory rape culpability" (H.R. 3734-7). Encouraged by this directive, states began to increase their prosecutions of statutory rape cases. One of the most significant examples of this practice comes from California, where then-Governor Pete Wilson allocated additional funding to form a vertical prosecution unit specifically for statutory rape cases. Vertical prosecution units (where prosecutors stay with a case from the beginning and specialize in a particular offense category) generally yield a higher conviction rate because victims are more likely to participate in the process (Donovan, 1996). However, California is not the only state involved in increasing the prosecutions of these crimes. In an effort to assist prosecutors, Mississippi recently passed a law that requires the collection of DNA from babies born to mothers under the age of 16 in case the evidence is needed in statutory rape criminal cases (Diep, 2013).

The increased prosecution of statutory rape cases leads to collateral consequences for offenders. In many states, the conviction of statutory rape requires that offenders must register as a sex offender, which can significantly limit their academic standing as well as their ability to secure employment. Unfortunately, the minimum age of consent laws and state registry requirements fail to distinguish between "two immature high school kids hooking up at a party [and] a pedophile molesting the toddler next door" (Downey, 2007, B1). One suggestion is for states to adopt age-gap provisions to their statutory rape laws. Meanwhile, other states have adopted Romeo and Juliet laws, which maintain the age-gap provision, but do not include the sexual registry requirement. In Florida, if a victim is at least 14 years old and consented to sexual activity with someone who is no more than four years older, the offender can petition to have the registration requirement removed (The Florida Senate, 2011). However, these Romeo and Juliet clauses are not without problems in their own right, because many states do not provide exceptions for cases of same-sex statutory rape. Here, it is important that LGBT youth be protected in the same ways under the law, and states should work to close these gaps (Higdon, 2008). Provisions such as this can help ensure that the focus of statutory rape prosecution returns to situations of coercion of a victim by an offender, not on youthful offenders engaging in consensual sexual activity.

also showing positive effects in changing attitudes about sexual assault (Banyard, Moynihan, & Plante, 2007) and increasing bystander effectiveness (Katz & Moore, 2013). In addition, there is significant variation between institutions of higher education in how allegations of sexual assault are managed. For example, while some campuses use an adversarial trial-like model where evidence is presented and witnesses provide testimony and are cross-examined, others have implemented a process that is more focused on information gathering (Konradi, 2016). Such processes typically adopt a preponderance of the evidence for their burden of proof standard. While significant progress has been made to address issues of campus sexual assault, there is still significant work to be done.

LGBTQ Sexual Violence

Much of the existing research on rape and sexual violence involves a male offender and a female victim. Many of the theories to explain rape involve the use of violence by men to exert power and control over women. This explanation is rooted in a heterosexist ideology. Indeed, our laws, which in many states identify the crime of rape as the unlawful penetration of a penis into a vagina, do not allow for us to legally identify these same-sex cases as rape (though most have additional statutes of sexual assault that would be inclusive of same-sex acts of sexual violation).

Historically, much of the discussion about same-sex rape was limited to male-on-male sexual assault, and many of these studies were conducted within an incarcerated setting. Over the past decade, the focus on same-sex victimization has increased. Research from the National Alcohol survey noted that women who identified as bisexual were almost three times as likely (14.9%) to report sexual abuse as adults compared to heterosexual women. Rates for women who identified as lesbian had lower rates of victimization than those who identified as bisexual (8.1%), but higher rates of violence compared to heterosexual adult women (Drabble, Trocki, Hughes, Korcha, & Lown, 2013). Racial differences in victimization are also prevalent among the LGBT population, with Latina and Asian American LGBT women experiencing higher rates of adult sexual violence than white women (Balsam, Molina, Blayney, Dilworth, Zimmerman, & Kaysen, 2015). In addition, women who identify as lesbian are more likely to be abused by a family member (Sigurvindottir & Ullman, 2015). Over the course of their lifetime, a significant portion of the LGBTQ population experiences some form of sexual victimization. The National Intimate Partner and Sexual Violence Survey estimates that 46% of lesbian women and 75% of bisexual women are sexually assaulted in their lifetime. Similar results are noted for gay men (40%) and men who identify as bisexual (47%) (Walters, Chen, & Breiding, 2013). While the data on the prevalence of victimization vary from study to study, these studies have one key theme in common; LGBTQ individuals experience sexual violence at significantly higher rates than heterosexual individuals.

Research on recovery for victims of sexual violence notes that women who identify as bisexual or lesbian report higher levels of psychological and social challenges as a result of their victimization. Dealing with symptoms of post-traumatic stress disorder was the most common psychosocial outcome for all victims, yet women who identified as bisexual or lesbian reported significantly higher levels of PTSD compared to heterosexual women. Bisexual and lesbian women also report higher levels of problem drinking, drug abuse, and depression, compared to heterosexual women. Black bisexual women also reported higher levels of problem drinking compared to white bisexual women. (Sigurvindottir & Ullman, 2015).

While the research on sexual violence among lesbian, gay, and bisexual communities is increasing, a significant gap remains in studying violence and trauma within the transgendered community. Transgendered individuals are more than twice as likely to experience rape or sexual assault than LGBQ individuals (Langenderfer-Magruder, Wells, Kattari, Whitfield, & Ramos (2016). The National Center for Transgendered Equality notes that nearly half (47%) of all transgendered individuals are sexually assaulted at some point in their lifetime. For many transgendered individuals, violence begins at a young age, with 13% of individuals reporting sexual violence in K–12 as a result of being transgendered. Such rates are particularly high for trans women (21%) and crossdressers (18%). Rates of violence significantly increase for individuals who engage in prostitution and other acts of sex work (72%), with nearly one in five engaging in sex work to obtain money, food, or shelter. Of those who are arrested for sex work and other criminal violations, nearly one quarter (22%) believed that their identity as transgender influenced the officer's decision to make an arrest (James, Herman, Rankin, Keisling, Mottet, & Anafi, 2016). The effects of this violence are significant because transgendered men and women are significantly more likely to attempt suicide, compared to transgendered individuals who do not have a history of sexual violence (Testa, Sciacca, Wang, Hendricks, Bradford, & Bongar, 2012).

Reporting rates for sexual violence among the LGBTQ population are low. Research by Langenderfer-Magruder, et al. (2016) notes that 23.2% of cisgender individuals (with cisgender females more likely to report than cisgender males) and 15% of transgendered victims report their victimization to the police. LGBTQ individuals who report same-sex sexual violence are often confronted with a system where agents of the criminal justice system may reflect homophobic views (Wang, 2011). Such perspectives can potentially silence victims and prevent them from seeking legal remedies and social services. In cases where individuals do report these crimes to law enforcement, many victims state that their cases are mishandled by authorities (Stotzer, 2014).

While federal law states that crimes against someone on the basis of their "actual or perceived gender-related characteristics" is illegal, few states have incorporated such language into their statutes (Human Rights Campaign Foundation, 2014). Advocacy services have also been slow in responding to the unique and multiple needs of this population (Turrell & Cornell-Swanson, 2005). Given the unique intersectionality between sexual identity and sexual violence, programs need to consider how programs need to be adapted to deal with these multiple marginalities. While the recent reauthoritization of the Violence Against Women Act includes provisions for the LGBTQ community, some community service providers express a fear that offering services to the lesbian, gay, bisexual, and transgender (LGBT) population could potentially restrict their donations from government or socially conservative individuals and organizations. These conflicts limit the opportunities to identify same-sex sexual assault as a social problem (Girshick, 2002).

Racial Differences in Sexual Assault

Research suggests that women of color have different experiences of sexual assault, compared to Caucasian women. These differences can be seen in prevalence rates, reporting behaviors, disclosure practices, help-seeking behaviors, and responses by the justice system. For example, research indicates that 18% of White women, compared to 19% of Black women, 34% of American Indian/Alaska Native women, and 24% of women who identify as mixed race report a rape or sexual assault during the course of their lifetime (Tjaden & Thoennes, 2006). Two important issues are raised with these statistics: (1) We already know that rape generally is underreported, so it is possible to assume that the true numbers of rape and sexual assault within different races and ethnicities may be significantly higher than these data indicate; and (2) given the unequal distribution of these statistics by race and ethnicity, compared to their representation in the general population, it is reasonable to conclude that women of color are victimized at a disproportionate rate compared to their White sisters. Despite these issues, the experience of rape and sexual assault within minority communities is significantly understudied in the scholarly research. Here, we ask the question: How do race and ethnicity affect the experience of rape and sexual assault and the response to these crimes by the criminal justice system?

While much of the literature on racial differences in rape and sexual assault focuses on the African American female experience, statistics by Tjaden and Thoennes (2006) highlight the extreme rates of rape within the American Indian and Alaska Native population (AIAN). These data are particularly troubling given that the AIAN population is a small minority in the population, making up only 1.5% of the U.S. population (U.S. Bureau of the Census, 2000). Research using the National Crime Victimization data indicates that compared to other racial and ethnic groups, AIAN women are most likely to experience rape within an intimate partner relationship, versus stranger or acquaintance relationships. Within this context, they were more likely to have a weapon used against them and to be physically assaulted as part of the attack. Alcohol and drugs also play a stronger role in the attacks of AIAN women, with more than two thirds of offenders under the influence of intoxicants, compared to only one third of offenders in cases involving White or Black victims. While AIAN victims are more likely to report these crimes to the police, the majority of these reports come from people on behalf of the victim (family, officials, others) rather than the victim herself (Bachman, Zaykowski, Lanier, Poteyva, & Kallmyer, 2010).

Data is also limited on the Asian American/Pacific Islander experience with sexual violence. While data notes that women from these communities report the lower rates of rape and sexual assault, they are also unlikely to believe that rape can occur within a relationship (NAWHO, 2002). Research also notes that Asian American men and women are more likely to engage in victim blaming in cases of rape and sexual assault (Lee, Pomeroy, Yoo, & Rheinboldt (2005). These findings likely influence the low reporting rates for Asian American victims, because they are the less likely to disclose their victimization (Shenoy, Neranartkomol, Ashok, Chaing, Lam, & Trieu, 2010). Many victims also fail to seek support to cope with their victimization, with a majority of victims citing feelings of share as a barrier in help seeking (Lee & Law, 2001). This is particularly important because it can have long-term consequences, such as increases in alcohol use as a way to cope with their victimization (Nguyen, Kaysen, Dillworth, Brajcich, & Larimer, 2010).

Research by Boykins et al. (2010) investigates the different experiences of sexual assault among Black and White women who sought emergency care following their attack. While no racial or ethnic differences were found between victims in terms of the location of the assault (home, car, outdoors) or whether the offender was known to the victim, Black women were significantly more likely to have a weapon used against them during the attack than White women (42% vs. 16.7%). The intoxication of the victim (and offender) also varied by race, because White women were more likely to be under the influence of alcohol (47.2% of White women reported being under the influence, compared to 23.8% of Black women), as were their perpetrators (47.2% of offenders against White women were under the influence, compared to 23.8% of offenders against Black women). In contrast, the use of illicit drugs prior to the assault was more common among Black victims compared to White victims (28.7% vs. 12.5%). However, there were no racial or ethnic differences in the reporting of the assault to police or of the offering or acceptance of counseling resources. Despite the importance of these findings, it is important to keep in mind that few victims seek out emergency services following their assault, which may skew the interpretation of these results.

Not only are women of color less likely to disclose sexual assault, but there are also a number of factors that vary by race and ethnicity that can affect the disclosure and recovery process. Research by Washington (2001) showed that less than half of the women interviewed had disclosed their victimization; when they did disclose, they did so to friends or family members within 24 hours of the assault. However, most of these women experienced incidents of victim blaming as a result of their disclosure. As a result of historical personal and cultural experiences with law enforcement, the majority of these women did not seek out the police to make an official report of their attack. In addition, many of the Black women talked about not reporting as a cultural expectation of keeping their business to themselves. They also mentioned not wanting to perpetuate additional racist views against members of the African American community, particularly if their assailant was also Black.

> We have this element in our community that it's the White man or the White race that causes most, if not all, of the problems we have in our communities. If we begin to point out the Black male for specific problems, we tend to get heat . . . and even from some women because we as women have been socialized as well. And it's "Don't bring the Black man down. . . . He's already going to jail, dying, rumored to be an endangered species; so why should we as Black women bring our wrath against him?" (Washington, 2001, p. 1269)

Cultural expectations also limited the help seeking for some African American victims. These women assumed the identity of the "strong Black woman," which in turn restricted many women from seeking out therapeutic resources because "only crazy people went to therapy" (Long & Ullman, 2013, p. 310). Rather than share their victimization, which could make them appear weak, victims would not disclose their assaults, even to close friends or family members. Alas, the lack of support often led to psychological challenges for many survivors. For these women, finding someone that they could trust and talk to about their victimization proved to be a healing experience (Long & Ullman, 2013).

Likewise, cultural expectations also can inhibit the official reporting practices of women within the Asian American and Pacific Islander population (AAPI). As in the African American community, there is a high level of distrust of public officials (often because of negative experiences either in the United States or in the cases of immigrant and refugee individuals, in their home country) as well as a cultural expectation to keep personal issues in the private sphere. Research has highlighted that many AAPI women fail to understand the definitions of rape and sexual assault, which limits the likelihood that such incidents will be reported (Bryant-Davis, Chung, & Tillman, 2009). Concerns over immigration status and language barriers also limit victim reporting. These same factors affect the use of therapeutic resources because AAPIs have the lowest utilization of mental health services of any racial or ethnic minority group (Abe-Kim et al., 2007).

Within the Hispanic community, Latina women have the highest rates of attempted sexual assault of all ethnic groups. Stereotypes of Latina women as passionate and sexual women can lead to victim blaming by the victim herself and therefore limits the likelihood that they will report (or that their reports will be taken seriously). Given these challenges, it is important for agencies in Hispanic/Latino communities to reach out to the population and dismantle some of the stereotypes and attitudes that can inhibit reporting and help-seeking behaviors (Bryant-Davis et al., 2009). Indeed, research indicates that Hispanic/Latina women are more likely to seek out informal resources (68.9%) versus make a report to the police (32.5%). Their utilization of informal resources included seeking medical attention (34.7%) and disclosing their victimization to a parent (26.6%). However, the rates of disclosure (both formally and informally) were significantly reduced if the victim had a history of childhood victimization (Sabina, Cuevas, & Schally, 2012).

Culture shapes the manner in which people represent themselves, make sense of their lives, and relate to others in the social world. Indeed, the experience of trauma is no different, and we find that women of color are less likely to engage in help-seeking behaviors from traditional models of assistance. While many women of color believe that agencies such as rape-crisis centers can provide valuable resources to victims of sexual assault, they may be hesitant to call on these organizations for fear that these organizations would be unable to understand their experiences as women of color. In addition, many victims may be unaware that such services are available, particularly given the potential language barriers (Sabina et al., 2012). Instead, victims may turn to sympathetic leaders and women within their own communities. To increase the accessibility of these services to women of color, victims and scholars argue that services need to be culturally sensitive and address the unique considerations that women of various racial and ethnic identities face as victims of sexual assault (Tillman, Bryant-Davis, Smith, & Marks, 2010).

The Role of Victims in Sexual Assault Cases

Many women do not identify themselves as victims. According to a national survey of college women, 48.8% of women who were victimized did not consider the incident to be rape. In many cases, victims may not understand the legal definition of rape. Others may be embarrassed and not want others to know. Finally, some women may not want to identify their attacker as a rapist (Fisher et al., 2000).

According to the National Crime Victimization Survey, 32.5% of victims of rape and sexual assault reported their victimization to the police (Truman & Morgan, 2016). Several factors increase the likelihood that a victim will report the crime to the police, including injury, concern over contracting HIV, and their identification of the crime as rape. Victims are less likely to report the crime if the offender is a friend or if they were intoxicated (Kilpatrick et al., 2007). For college-age women, less than 5% of completed and attempted rapes were reported to the police. While women do not report these crimes to law enforcement or school officials, they do not necessarily stay silent, because over two-thirds of victims confided in a friend about their attack. The decision by victims to not report their assault to the police stems from a belief that the incident was not harmful or important enough to report. For these women, it may be that they did not believe that they had been victims of a crime or did not want family members or others to know about the attack. Others had little faith in the criminal justice system, because they were concerned that the criminal justice system would not see the event as a serious incident or that there would be insufficient proof that a crime had occurred (Fisher et al., 2000).

Victims who do report their crimes often do so to prevent the crime from happening to others (Kilpatrick et al., 2007). Documented key findings from the National Violence Against Women Survey show that only 43% of reported rapes resulted in an arrest of the offender. Of those reported, only 37% of these cases were prosecuted. Fewer than half (46.2%) of those prosecuted were convicted, and 76% of those convicted were sentenced to jail or prison. Taking unreported rapes into consideration, this means that only 2.2% of all rapists are incarcerated. Of those who reported their rape, less than half of victims indicated that they were satisfied with the way their case was handled by the authorities (Tjaden & Thoennes, 2006).

In addition to the low levels of initial reports to the police, victims may also withdraw their participation as their case moves through the criminal justice system. This is particularly common in cases where the assault experience does not reflect stereotypical notions of what rape and sexual assault look like to the average individual. For example, a case involving an assault by a stranger where a weapon was used against the victim is a mythological view of what sexual violence looks like. These cases are most likely to involve participation by the victim. Cases where there are witnesses to the attack are also more likely to encourage victim participation in the criminal justice process, particularly in cases where the witness can corroborate a victim's story of the assault. At the same time, some victims may be discouraged by the criminal justice process and withdraw their participation, particularly when victims are aware of the low conviction rates (Alderden & Long, 2016).

In other cases, victims decide to report their assaults in an effort to increase community awareness and attention by the criminal justice system to crimes of sexual violence. These victims acknowledge that the small number of successes within the legal system in these types of cases may mean that traditional avenues of justice may not be available to them. In some cases, victims talk of wanting to protect future victims from their assailant, even if nothing came of their report personally. Here, the need to raise awareness in their community trumped their own needs for closure. In the words of one victim,

> I looked back and thought; well I'm not going to let one situation put me off from doing the right thing and going through. I know it would be a harrowing experience sitting there telling them what happened over and over again, but at the end of the day you know people need to be accountable for what they've done. And I thought I've, whether it goes to court or whether it doesn't I've done everything in my power you know to prevent something. (Taylor & Norma, 2012, p. 34)

Many victims make these reports knowing that people and officials may not respond favorably or that family members may reject them, particularly in cases where the offender is a close relative or family friend. These are significant hardships that influence many victims to not disclose their victimization to either officials or personal social networks. Despite these challenges, some victims believed that reporting the crime helped in their survival because it validated their victimization experience (Taylor & Norma, 2012).

Victims of rape and sexual assault have both immediate and long-term physical and emotional health needs. Over half of the victims of sexual assault experience symptoms of posttraumatic stress disorder (PTSD) at some point during their lifetime. Symptoms of PTSD can appear months or even years following the assault. The levels of emotional trauma that victims experience lead to significant mental health effects, such as depression, low self-esteem, anxiety, and fear for personal safety. Women with a history of sexual assault are more likely to have seriously considered attempting suicide and are more likely to engage in behaviors that put them at risk, including risky sexual behaviors with multiple partners, extreme weight loss measures, and substance abuse involving alcohol and illegal drugs (Gidycz, Orchowski, King, & Rich, 2008; Kaukinen & DeMaris, 2009). Women who are victimized by strangers may experience anxiety and fear about their surroundings, particularly if the assault occurred in a public setting. For women who were assaulted by a family member, acquaintance, or date, they may experience issues with trusting people.

Given the limits of the criminal justice system, how can we meet the needs of victims in rape and sexual assault cases? The current rape crisis movement developed in response to the perceived need for prevention, community awareness, and amelioration of victims' pain. However, even the best community services are limited, and there is a lack adequate resources to effectively combat all needs for victims of sexual assault. While attempts to help survivors of sexual assault involve friends, family members, community agencies, and criminal justice personnel, efforts in help seeking may actually enhance the trauma that victims experience because of lack of support, judgment, and blame by support networks. Additionally, victims may experience further trauma by being forced to relive their trauma as part of the official processing of the assault as a crime (Kaukinen & DeMaris, 2009). Because of these negative experiences in disclosure, many victims choose to keep their assault a secret.

Ultimately, cases of rape and sexual assault can be very difficult to prove in a court of law. Convictions are rare, and many cases are plea-bargained to a lesser charge, many of which carry little to no jail time. Alas, the acceptance of rape myths by police, prosecutors, judges, and juries limits the punishment of offenders in cases of sexual assault.

Figure 3.1 ● Punishment and Rape

39% of rapes are reported to the police

If a rape is reported, there is a 50.8% chance of an arrest

If an arrest is made, there is an 80% chance of prosecution

If there is a prosecution, there is a 58% chance of a conviction

If there is a felony conviction, there is a 69% chance the convict will spend time in jail

So even in the 39% of attacks that are reported to the police, there is only a 16.3% chance the rapist will end up in prison

Factoring in unreported rapes, only about 6% of rapists will ever spend a day in jail

15 of 16 walk free

Figure 3.1 highlights how each stage of the criminal justice system reduces the likelihood that offenders will be arrested, charged, and punished for these cases. The effects of these practices can further discourage victims from reporting these crimes, believing that little can be done by criminal justice officials.

Conclusion

Research on rape and sexual assault indicates a number of areas where the criminal justice system and other social institutions can improve prevention and intervention efforts. Given that adolescents and young adults have higher rates of acquaintance rape and sexual assault, much of these prevention efforts have been targeted toward college campuses. While college campuses have increased their educational activities aimed toward preventing rape on campuses in recent times, these efforts may still be inadequate given the number of assaults that occur on campuses around the nation each year. However, the age of victimization appears to be decreasing, indicating a need for education efforts focused on high school students.

Victims indicate that an increase in public education about acquaintance rape and increased services for counseling would encourage more victims to report their crimes (Kilpatrick et al., 2007). Programs focusing on rape and sexual assault prevention should provide accurate definitions of sexual assault behaviors, the use of realistic examples, discussions about alcohol use and sexual assault, and an understanding of what it means to consent to sexual activity. By tailoring education efforts toward combating myths about rape, these efforts can help reduce the levels of shame that victims may experience as a result of their victimization and encourage them to seek help following a sexual assault. Services need to be made available and known to students, in terms of both services and outreach on campus and information available online.

SUMMARY

- Rape is one of the most underreported crimes of victimization.
- The risk of rape and sexual assault appears to be higher on college campuses.
- The acceptance of rape myths by society contributes to the practice of victim blaming.
- Many victims of rape and sexual assault fail to identify their experiences as a criminal act.
- Excuses and justifications allow perpetrators of rape and sexual assault to deny or minimize levels of blame and injury toward their victims.
- The majority of rapes and sexual assaults involve individuals who are known to the victim prior to the assault.
- The term *date rape drugs* has been used to identify a group of drugs, such as GHB, Rohypnol, and ketamine, that have been used to facilitate a sexual assault.
- Victims of rape and sexual assault are at risk for long-term physical and emotional health concerns.

KEY TERMS

Acquaintance rape 95	Rape 97	Statutory rape 104
Campus sexual assault 103	Same-sex sexual assault 92	Stranger rape 93
Drug-facilitated rape 97	Sexual assault 91	Symbolic assailant 95
Incapacitated rape 97	Spousal rape 102	

DISCUSSION QUESTIONS

1. How has the definition of rape evolved over time?
2. Why do many victims of rape and sexual assault choose not to report their crimes to the police?
3. What impact do rape myths play in victim blaming and the denial of offender culpability?
4. Why do many victims of rape and sexual assault fail to identify themselves as victims of a crime?
5. Why are acquaintance rape cases not viewed as "real" rape?

6. What tactics do perpetrators use to coerce sex from their victims?

7. In what ways can prevention efforts be used to educate women and men about the realities of rape and sexual assault?

8. What are the short- and long-term effects of sexual assault? How might early sexual assault yield a pathway to later victimization or offending?

/// WEB RESOURCES

Bureau of Justice Statistics: http://bjs.ojp.usdoj.gov

The National Center for Victims of Crime: http://www.ncvc.org

National Clearinghouse on Marital and Date Rape: http://ncmdr.org/

NCVC Rape Shield Laws: http://www.ncvc.org/ncvc/main.aspx?dbID=DB_FAQ:RapeShieldLaws927

Office of Victims of Crime: http://www.ojp.usdoj.gov

RAINN—State resources for sexual assault: http://www.rainn.org/get-help/local-counseling-centers/state-sexual-assault-resources

Rape, Incest and Abuse National Network: http://www.rainn.org

Visit **study.sagepub.com/mallicoat3e** to access additional study tools, including eFlashcards, web quizzes, web resources, video resources, and SAGE journal articles.

READING /// 5

Rape myths are a powerful tool that can alter how victims, offenders, and peers of these two populations understand crimes of rape and sexual assault. In this research study, Dr. Hayes-Smith and Dr. Levett look at whether the sharing of information about available sexual resources on college campuses is impacted by students' beliefs in these myths about rape.

Student Perceptions of Sexual Assault Resources and Prevalence of Rape Myth Attitudes

Rebecca M. Hayes-Smith and Lora M. Levett

Ground-breaking legislation such as the Student Right-to-Know and Campus Security Act of 1990 (n.d.) requires colleges to publicly report statistics on crime and to educate students on campus about policies designed to prevent crime and secure the campus environment. Later amendments to this Act require the creation of specific policies designed to prevent and respond to sexual assault on campus (Jeanne Clery Disclosure of Campus Security Policy and Campus Crime Statistics Act, 1998, 2011). Now referred to as the Clery Act,[1] it provides guidelines on what information is supposed to be made widely available to students. According to the Act, college administrators should adequately educate students about crime and provide resources for students when crime occurs. Given the prevalence of sexual assault on college campuses, educating students about it and providing resources for victims of sexual assault is especially important. Recent studies, however, demonstrate that resources directed at victims/survivors of sexual assault on campus range in their content and availability to students (Hayes-Smith & Hayes-Smith, 2009; Karjane, Fisher, & Cullen, 2002). However, even in those cases in which adequate resources were available on campus, it was still not clear whether those resources or programming efforts actually reach or affect the student population.

It is no longer a contested issue among researchers and scholars that sexual assault on college campuses is a widespread phenomenon (Boeringer, 1999). One needs only to conduct a search using a library search engine or even Google® to find numerous studies focused on sexual assault issues at universities (e.g., Fisher, Cullen, & Turner, 2000; Karjane et al., 2002; Koss, Gidycz, & Wisniewski, 1987; Perkins, 1997). A groundbreaking study by Koss (Koss et al., 1987) measured the prevalence of sexual assault beyond official statistics. Even though the Koss study was met with a backlash regarding the prevalence of sexual assault (see Roiphe, 1993), this study is still commonly used to demonstrate that sexual assault is more widely spread on campus than official statistics may suggest. Research has moved beyond simply studying the prevalence of sexual assault on campus and has expanded to things such as the close association between sexual assault and alcohol (Abbey, 2002; Mohler-Kuo, Dowdall,

SOURCE: Hayes-Smith, R. M., & Levett, L. M. (2010). Student perceptions of sexual assault resources and prevalence of rape myth attitudes. *Feminist Criminology, 5*(4), 335–354.

Koss, & Wechsler, 2003; Ullman, Karabatsos, & Koss, 1999) or how common it is for a sexual assault victim to know the offender (Greenfield, 1997), how often women self-blame (Warshaw, 1988), and, important to this study, what colleges [or] universities are doing to remedy the problem (Karjane et al., 2002).

Availability and Adequacy of Sexual Assault Resources on Campus

With researchers and scholars acknowledging the high prevalence of sexual assault occurring among college women and with legislation like the Clery Act, university administrators have taken steps to create programs to educate and assist their student bodies. Recent studies examining the availability and adequacy of resources on college campuses, however, have shown that there appears to be no uniformity across schools on response to sexual assault and resource availability (Hayes-Smith & Hayes-Smith, 2009; Karjane et al., 2002). In one study, researchers found that most of the schools complied with the federal requirement to report crime but were not necessarily consistent with current laws stating how to keep these records (Karjane et al., 2002). Even basic resources such as information about how to file criminal charges were not uniform across schools. Less than half of the institutions reported providing new students with sexual assault educational materials.

Given that students may seek information on the Internet, a subsequent study examined the resources available to students online and found that some schools fared better at providing online resources than other schools (Hayes-Smith & Hayes-Smith, 2009). This content analysis of universities in the Midwest showed that a few schools provided large amounts of information, much of which was victim centered, such as using the term *survivor* and stating, "it is not your fault." Most schools, however, barely provided the basic information online such as sexual assault policies and crime statistics (Hayes-Smith & Hayes-Smith, 2009).

Both of these studies called for better and more information on sexual assault policies and resources for students on campus (Hayes-Smith & Hayes-Smith, 2009; Karjane et al., 2002). Suggestions included developing

models for sexual assault education beyond current federal mandates and included recommendations drawn from sexual assault research designed to reduce belief in rape myths. Thus, part of the goal of disseminating sexual assault resources on campus is to dispel belief in rape myths.

Sexual Assault Programming and Deprogramming

Researchers have noted the difficulty involved with creating programs that attempt to prevent and react to the problem of sexual assault (see Yeater & O'Donohue, 1999). Programs created to either respond to or prevent sexual violence are likely to take into account the correlation between rape myth acceptance and sexual aggression in men (Bohner et al., 1998; Hamilton & Yee, 1990; Lanier, 2001) and rape myth acceptance and victim blaming behaviors in women (Cowan, 2000). Thus, these programs should attempt to dispel rape myths.

Both males and females have shown evidence of adhering to rape myths, although men are more likely to endorse rape myths compared to women (Lonsway & Fitzgerald, 1994). For example, in a study conducted by Amnesty International (2005), men were more likely than women to attribute blame to a woman for her own sexual assault if her wardrobe was revealing. This is troubling for a few reasons. First, acceptance of rape myths in men has been associated with their self-reported likelihood [that] they would commit a sexual assault (although rape myths only partially explain the motivation behind men's violence against women; Bohner et al., 1998). One study showed a positive correlation between men's attitudes about rape myths and their inclination toward sexual assault in both written sexual assault scenarios in which men responded to a realistic date rape scenario and in individual items asking about sexual aggression (Bohner et al., 1998). Furthermore, making rape myth attitudes accessible (by measuring them prior to measuring rape proclivity) increased the likelihood that the men would report higher rape proclivity in a subsequent survey. In a related exploratory study testing the validity of a rape myth scale, Burgess (2007) also found that men's acceptance of rape myths was correlated with self-reported sexual aggression. A longitudinal study further supported this and did not find support for the notion of rationalization whereby men who rape will begin to adhere to rape myths as a justification mechanism (Lanier, 2001). This same study also found that reducing adherence to rape myths in males would likely be effective in lowering sexually aggressive behavior (Lanier, 2001). These studies show that men who believe in rape myths may be more likely than men who do not to engage in sexually coercive or aggressive behavior, and programs should address this issue. Alternatively, it is also possible that rape myths may function as a justification for violent behavior, although more research is needed to address this possibility.

Programs should attempt to reach both men and women (Yeater & O'Donohue, 1999). Women who are disproportionately likely to be victims of sexual assault and who show evidence of adhering to rape myths make it difficult to reverse the cycle of violence against college-aged women (Cowan, 2000). Specifically, women who believe in rape myths may be contributing to [both] blaming the victim in crimes of sexual assault and the continual de-emphasizing of sexual assault compared to other crimes in our society, [which are] termed "internalized oppression" (i.e., one's own group attributing blame to the victim; Cowan, 2000). Women who report feelings of hostility toward women or hold negative stereotypes about women are more likely than those who do not to victim blame in incidences of sexual assault and to trivialize the occurrence of violence toward women (Cowan, 2000). Ultimately, when a woman believes in rape myths or has negative attitudes toward women, this may exacerbate the problem of sexual assault, thus, increasing victim and self-blame. Thus, programs designed to educate women can attenuate this problem.

False beliefs about sexual assault may result in victims blaming themselves or not believing that a sexual assault actually occurred. Women who endorse rape myths are less likely to define sexual assault behavior as such, despite the fact that the behavior in question meets the legal definition (Fisher et al., 2000; Norris & Cubbins, 1992). In addition, if a victim's claims that a sexual assault occurred are rejected by others because others believe that the victim is at fault, it can reconfirm self-blaming feelings, increasing the likelihood of victims not reporting victimization or seeking help (Schwartz & Leggett, 1999; Warshaw, 1988). The use of alcohol has also been linked with the victim self-blame phenomenon, in which victims will blame themselves and in turn not report the sexual assault because they believe it is their fault due to their use of alcohol (Schwartz & Leggett, 1999). Koss et al. (1987) found that 74% of perpetrators and 55% of sexual assault victims had been drinking alcohol right before the incident. At least half of sexual assaults include alcohol consumption by both or either parties involved in the assault (see Abbey, 2002 for a complete review). Many women report that the reason they believe the sexual assault is their fault is because they consumed an alcoholic beverage and were too intoxicated to consent. Belief in these types of rape myths can keep women from reporting or seeking out necessary resources to help them recover (Schwartz & Leggett, 1999; Warshaw, 1988).

Another example of a rape myth that likely perpetuates victim-blaming behavior is that rape is committed primarily by strangers. This myth is particularly problematic given that evidence continues to show that the majority of sexual assault is committed by someone the victim knows (Greenfield, 1997). On a college campus, this myth is especially harmful given that students may not exercise appropriate caution around acquaintances in risky situations (such as spending time alone with a friend at a party) yet are cautious when walking alone at night.

Collectively, these studies illustrate the importance of having programs that attempt to educate about *and react* to the occurrence of sexual assault. However, even if we create advocacy programs to assist survivors of sexual assault and educate the general population about sexual assault, we may not be successful in accomplishing those goals if the programs are not reaching the intended audiences. This study attempts to examine whether sexual assault resources are reaching the students and, if resources are reaching students, whether students' attitudes about sexual assault change.

Presumably, students receive educational information about sexual assault and therefore the students should hold more accurate beliefs about sexual assault. That is, past advocates of these types of resources and programs have noted that the programs should educate students through dispelling inaccurate beliefs about sexual assault and ultimately produce attitudinal change consistent with the education proffered; indeed, this is part of the goal in having sexual assault resources available to students (Heppner, Humphrey, Hillenbrand-Gunn, & DeBord, 1995). Thus, in our study, we attempted to measure whether attitudes about sexual assault were changed as a result of receiving sexual assault resources. Theories of attitude change, such as the elaboration likelihood model of persuasion (ELM; Petty & Cacioppo, 1986), demonstrate how attitudes about sexual assault may be changed as a result of exposure to these resources (e.g., Gidycz et al., 2001; Heppner et al., 1995). Specifically, the ELM states that attitude change takes place through two processes: central and/or peripheral processing. If one processes a message centrally (such as a sexual assault education program), change is likely to take place if the target of change is motivated to listen to the message, has the ability to understand the message, and thinks thoughtfully about the content of the message. Processing a message centrally is more likely to result in a stable, long-term attitude change compared to processing a message peripherally (i.e., relying on heuristics like the message sender's expertise or attractiveness in being persuaded; Petty & Cacioppo, 1986). Thus, exposure to sexual assault resources should presumably produce stable attitude change about attitudes toward sexual assault (e.g., rape myths) if students are centrally engaged in learning about those resources. So in our study, . . . exposure to [higher level] resources should be associated with [attitude change toward] lower [quality] beliefs in rape myths if those resources are being properly received (although in this study, the exact causal nature of the relationship cannot be assessed). However, it is possible that beliefs about sexual assault (and rape myths) may be resistant to attitude change due to the continued presence of patriarchy throughout society and the backlash hypothesis (DeKeseredy, 1999).

The backlash hypothesis is concisely defined as a simultaneous surge of criticism onto women as advances are being made in women's favor (Faludi, 1991). For example, DeKeseredy (1999) showed that when research attempts to highlight the prevalence of violence against women, critics immediately emerge and criticize the research methodology, usually by attacking the lack of the male victims. He calls this the "but women do it too" argument, which belittles the importance of raising awareness about violence that is directed mainly toward women (DeKeseredy, 1999). This type of backlash, where the focus is taken off of women, can make it particularly difficult for sexual assault programs to reach female students, whereby they may think sexual assault is not going

to happen to them. If an individual does not believe that a topic (e.g., sexual assault) is relevant to him or her or is important, he or she is not as likely to pay attention to the messages about the topic, making the job of spreading information difficult (Kahlor & Morrison, 2007).

Study Overview

The present study examined whether students were receiving information regarding sexual assault resources at a university that provided several resources. We examined whether students knew of the available resources, believed they would use the information, and considered the information informative. We also asked students how they would recommend the information be disseminated to students. In addition, we explored whether knowledge about the availability of sexual assault resources was associated with lower belief in rape myths. Last, we examined gender differences in knowledge of sexual assault resources and acceptance of rape myths.

Method

Participants

Participants were 224 criminology undergraduate students from a large southeastern university. Students were 61% female and 38% male (2% did not report their sex). The majority of the students were White (60%), followed by Hispanic/Latino (20%), Black (10%), Asian (6%), and other (4%). The average age was 21 ($SD = 2$) ranging from 18 to 46. The largest percentage of students were 3rd years (37%) followed by 4th years (28%), 2nd years (23%), 1st years (8%), and a few 5th years (3%).

Measures

Knowledge of sexual assault resources. Students' knowledge of resources was first measured by asking if they had received information on sexual assault resources when they began their education at the university. If they answered "yes," they were asked the following "yes" or "no" questions: (a) Did it include information about the number of sexual assault incidents? and (b) Do you know where to get information about sexual assault on campus?

To measure more general knowledge of sexual assault resources on campus, students responded to several statements. In responding to each statement, students indicated their agreement on a 7-point Likert-type scale ranging from 1 (*strongly disagree*) to 7 (*strongly agree*). The scale assessing general knowledge of sexual assault resources on campus averaged the items indicated in Reading Table 5.1 ($\alpha = .77$, scale ranging from 1.00 to 6.25). Three additional items were not included in the final scale because they did not factor in with the above scale, but mean responses to these items are reported in the results section. These items are also included in Reading Table 5.1.

Students also were asked nine questions measuring their awareness of each of the nine resources available at the university or in the community. Students indicated with a "yes" or "no" response whether they had knowledge of each of the following campus resources: (a) sexual assault victim advocates, (b) an office of victim services, (c) sexual assault counselors, (d) a "safe place" for victims of sexual assault, (e) a "Take Back the Night" rally, (f) a sexual assault crisis hotline, (g) a women's resource center, (h) a policy on sexual assault, and (i) a facility to get a forensic medical exam. The total number of "yes" responses were summed to create a scale; students' scores on this scale ranged from 0.00 to 9.00.

Students also were asked a question regarding where they would seek information on sexual assault issues. They responded to the following question: "Which one of the following places would you be most likely to seek information on sexual assault issues?" Students chose one of 6 choices (i.e., phonebook, crisis hotline, police, Internet, the university's web site, and other).

Reading Table 5.1 ● Students' Mean Responses to Knowledge of Sexual Assault Resources Available on Campus

	Mean Response (SD)	Median (item range)	% Disagree	% Agree	% Neutral
Scaled Items					
I am familiar with the procedures of reporting incidents of sexual assault at [the university]	3.30 (1.51)	3.00 (1–6)	59.2%	29%	12%
I am knowledgeable about the role of Judicial Affairs in sexual assault cases at [the university]	3.10 (1.49)	3.00 (1–7)	66%	21%	13%
I am familiar with the services offered by an Office of Victims Services	3.02 (1.46)	3.00 (1–7)	68%	19%	14%
I know where to go to receive help if I or someone I know were sexually assaulted at [the university]	4.17 (1.61)	5.00 (1–7)	36%	7%	57%
Individual Items					
If you report a sexual assault at [the university], you do not have to file a police report with the police	3.65 (1.55)	4.00 (1–7)	33%	20%	47%
I know what happens at a "Take Back the Night" rally	2.53 (1.62)	2.00 (1–7)	73%	13%	14%
I know the number (or where to get it) to the Sexual Assault Crisis Hotline	3.60 (1.90)	4.00 (1–7)	49%	41%	10%

NOTE: Students responded on a scale ranging from 1 (*strongly disagree*) to 7 (*strongly agree*).

Quality of resources. Those students who responded that they received information about sexual assault from the university rated the quality of the information they received. Again, students responded to statements on 7-point Likert-type scales ranging from 1 (*strongly disagree*) to 7 (*strongly agree*). Higher ratings indicate a more positive evaluation of the resources. All items are included in Reading Table 5.2.

Distribution of sexual assault resources. Participants also responded to an open-ended question asking where and how they would like to see information about sexual assault disseminated on campus. This question was coded for common themes using two independent coders. Overall agreement rates were high (κ = .85, *p* < .01). One hundred ninety-eight students answered the open-ended question, and several students gave more than one suggestion.

Rape Myth Scale. The Rape Myth Scale was developed by Burt (1980; see also Burt, 2004) to examine acceptance of rape myths. The scale included 11 statements, and participants indicated agreement with those statements on 7-point Likert-type scales ranging from 1 (*strongly disagree*) to 7 (*strongly agree*). For example, one item reads, "A woman who goes to the home or apartment of a man on their first date implies that she is willing to have sex." The entire Rape Myth Scale was used in the survey (available in Burt, 2004). We also created three additional items to add to the scale because of the relationship between sexual assault and alcohol use and sexual assault and drugs (Mohler-Kuo et al., 2003; Ullman et al., 1999): (a) If the victim of sexual assault was drinking alcohol at the time of the incident, it is partially his or her fault that the sexual assault occurred. (b) If the victim of sexual assault willingly took drugs at the time of the incident, it is partially his or her fault that the sexual assault occurred. (c) Even if a victim of sexual assault was drunk at the time of the incident, the sexual assault is not his or her fault. When conducting factor and reliability analyses on the new scale, two items from the original Rape Myth Scale did not factor on the construct and reduced the reliability of the overall scale ("any female can get raped" and "one reason women falsely report rape is that they frequently have a need to call attention to themselves"). These two items were dropped because they did not factor. Given that we added items to Burt's Rape Myth Scale, we conducted an exploratory factor analysis with varimax rotation to examine the factor structure. Burt (1980) originally proposed a single factor structure; however, this factor structure has been debated in the field (see Lonsway & Fitzgerald, 1994). Some have shown that the items in the scale rotate onto 3

Reading Table 5.2 • Students' Mean Responses to Quality of Resources Available on Campus

Scaled Items	Mean Response (SD)	Median (item range)	% Disagree	% Agree	% Neutral
The sexual assault resources given to students at [the university] is not informative enough	4.02 (1.25)	4.00 (1–7)	18.6%	23.1%	58.2%
I do not know enough about the sexual assault resources at [the university] to use them in a sexual assault situation	4.70 (1.52)	5.00 (1–7)	21.5%	63.3%	15.2%
The sexual assault information was very straightforward and easy to understand	4.40 (1.01)	4.00 (1–7)	9.8%	32%	58.3%
I would probably use the sexual assault information given to me by [the university] if I encountered a sexual assault situation	5.37 (1.25)	6.00 (1–7)	15.8%	80.2%	12.2%

NOTE: Students responded on a scale ranging from 1 (*strongly disagree*) to 7 (*strongly agree*).

(Hall, Howard, & Boezio, 1986) or 4 (Briere, Malamuth, & Check, 1985) factors. Others, however, report that the scale retained its original single factor structure (Krahe, 1988; Margolin, Miller, & Moran, 1989). In our factor analysis, a single factor emerged. Items included in the scale had factor loadings between .52 and .78. Items with smaller factor loadings were eliminated from the scale. The three new items were included in the final scale and scores were added according to Burt (2004 α = .86; range: −36.00 to 13.00). Students were also randomly assigned to complete the Rape Myth Scale before or after the measures inquiring about sexual assault resources to test for social desirability of responses to rape myth items.

Results

Student Knowledge of Sexual Assault Resources

When students were asked if they had received sexual assault resources, only roughly half of the students (54%) reported receiving information, 13% reported they had not received any information, and 33% reported not remembering if they had received information. Of the students who reported receiving information, 30% reported that the information included reports of the number of sexual assault incidents, and 39% reported they knew where to get information about sexual assault at the university. A series of chi-square tests revealed male and female students did not differ in their responses to these items, $p > .05$.

For the scale and items measuring knowledge of resources, the means of responses to most items were below the scale average, indicating that overall, many respondents were not aware of many of the resources. For the overall scale, students averaged 3.39 ($SD = 1.17$). This indicates that the overall average of students' knowledge of resources was below the median response. To provide the best picture of the data, we included descriptions of participants' responses in Reading Table 5.1. We also divided participants' responses into categories indicating proportions of students who agreed, disagreed, and were neutral in response to the items on the scales provided. Male and female students did not significantly differ in their knowledge of resources for either the scale or the individual items.

As expected, students who had indicated receiving resource information significantly differed from those students who indicated not receiving resources on the knowledge of resource scale. Students who remembered receiving information about sexual assault resources were more likely to report more knowledge of resources compared to those students who did not report or did not remember receiving information.

Next, we examined knowledge of specific resources on campus. Students knew an average of 4.00 resources out of the 9 which were available. 58% of students knew between 0 and 4 of the resources, and 42% knew about 5 or more of the available resources. All resources were readily available on campus. The students' knowledge of specific resources scale did not significantly differ by gender. Again, students who had indicated receiving resource information significantly differed on how many specific resources they knew about. Students who reported receiving information on entering the university knew about more resources compared with students who reported they had not received resources or those who did not remember receiving resources.

To determine where students would seek out information on sexual assault, a percentage was calculated for all responses indicating the proportion of students who would seek information from each of the sources. Overall, 41% of the students reported they would refer to the police, 34% reported they would use the Internet, and 11% reported they would go to the university's web site.

We asked students who answered that they had received information on sexual assault if the information was helpful and useful. Again, to provide the best picture of the data, we included descriptions of participants' responses in Reading Table 5.2. After examining the item distributions, it appears that students would use the university's sexual assault resources but still do not know enough about them to indicate whether or not they are informative and/or helpful. Students' responses to these items did not significantly differ by gender.

Students suggested the following mechanisms for distributing sexual assault information: a full school course (21%) or incorporating the information into current classes (11%), informative publications on campus (18%), disseminating information during new student orientation (18%), using the Internet (either through the university's portal or through a separate web site; 14%), organizing a campus event (20%), using an online course similar to the university's currently required alcohol awareness course (10%), using resources outside the university, including media outlets, such as commercials and billboards (2%), and using the school newspaper (1%).

Student Belief in Rape Myths

The Rape Myth Scale was coded so that negative scores mean an overall lowered acceptance of rape myths. The items were summed to create the scale not including the two items that did not factor in as discussed above. Overall acceptance of rape myths was low indicating that overall, students were low in their belief of rape myths.

A one-way ANOVA testing for gender differences in beliefs in rape myths showed an effect of gender on beliefs in rape myths. Women were less likely than men to accept rape myths. The relationship between gender and students' acceptance of rape myths remained significant even when students' knowledge of resources (as measured by a *yes, no,* or *I don't remember* question) was entered into the model in a two-way ANOVA. Both the effects of knowledge of resources and the interaction between gender and knowledge of resources were not significant. That is, knowledge of resources was not related to a lower belief in rape myths.

Discussion

Although some students at this university reported receiving information about sexual assault resources, the majority of our sample did not. Arguably, this group of university students has had more exposure than the average student to the issue of sexual assault because they are criminology students. Only half of the students, however, reported that they had received information about sexual assault resources at the university (despite the fact that all students should have received the information). Two possibilities may explain why so many students reported not receiving information: The university may not be uniformly distributing the information, or students may not be paying attention or actively engaged when they receive the information.

With students reporting low knowledge of the resources available on campus (including general knowledge and knowledge of specific available resources) and

women in the sample not significantly differing from men in their knowledge of sexual assault resources, this reveals a problematic picture. Many (if not most) resources available at this campus are directed toward women because this university has a reactive response as opposed to a preventative response to the problem of sexual assault. Therefore, the resources intended to assist women in case of sexual assault may not be serving women to the best possible capacity. However, students who reported receiving resource information did report more knowledge of sexual assault resources than those who reported that they did not receive such information. The university may need to consider a new dissemination strategy to ensure that the students have knowledge of all the resources available to them and are actively engaged in learning from those resources.

Our main suggestion is that a new approach should be taken by using the Internet as a primary source of dissemination.

In our study, 24% of students indicated that disseminating the information about sexual assault and sexual assault resources through the Internet (either through a required online course or a web site) may be the best way to reach the student body. Even though with this sample many responded they would go to the police for resources—which could be due to the fact they are criminology students—some students also reported that they would turn to the Internet for information in a sexual assault situation, indicating support for the idea that the university should provide sound information for students online (Hayes-Smith & Hayes-Smith, 2009). Places like Facebook® and Twitter®, popular college networking sites, may be an ideal place to disseminate resource information. These sites allow its users to subscribe as a fan to pages and have ways to contact users of an entire network (which each university is a network) notifying them of upcoming events. Given the popularity of these sites, it might make sense for universities to use them in disseminating information about available services at the university, including sexual assault resources.

Indeed, theoretically, creating interactive, long-term Internet-based programs makes sense. That is, research on sexual assault prevention programs has demonstrated that participating in a long-term program designed to teach students about sexual assault issues (e.g., consent) produced the most stable change in students' attitudes

(Anderson & Whiston, 2005; Borges, Banyard, & Moynihan, 2008). The interactive nature of using the Internet may make students more actively engaged and motivated to process the information meaningfully, which according to the ELM is likely to result in central processing of the information (Heppner et al., 1995; Petty & Cacioppo, 1986). This type of processing is likely to result in attitude change that is stable over time and resistant to counter-persuasion arguments (Heppner et al., 1995).

The suggestion of using Internet networking sites is more complicated than it appears; when using these sites, there is more to it than simply creating a profile. As Hayes-Smith & Hayes-Smith (2009) found in their study, simply having a web site with information does not mean it is quality or easily accessible. To use networking sites, there would likely need to be a process in which some marketing strategies might prove helpful to gain proper visibility. For example, on the network site Facebook®, creating a profile that is not public requires users to request inclusion, and because it is not public, it only appears on specific searches versus general keyword searches. The private profile increases security but decreases visibility. Security is an important issue to consider with programs geared toward survivors of sexual assault but may be of less concern when considering the prevention programs, where visibility is more likely to be helpful than harmful. Of course, these are only speculations, and future research should address the effectiveness of networking sites regarding resource dissemination and awareness.

Another interesting student suggestion for disseminating sexual assault resources and educating students about sexual assault was the call for a required online course. This suggestion is particularly pertinent to the university in this study as they already have one required online course to educate students about alcohol. This course is required for all incoming students and may have prompted the students to come up with the idea of an online course for educating students about sexual assault issues and resources. The online course could be given to all freshman-level students prior to their being allowed to register for classes, and they would have to acquire a specific grade. It would be feasible for the university to add sexual assault information to the alcohol course given the established relationship between alcohol and sexual

assault (Koss et al., 1987; Mohler-Kuo et al., 2003). Past research suggests that if such programming is to be successful in changing students' attitudes about sexual assault, it would need to engage students and send a meaningful, relevant message likely to invoke stable attitude change (Anderson & Whiston, 2005).

The alternative explanation regarding resource dissemination is that students receive information about sexual assault resources, but they may not be reading or paying attention to these resources. As Kahlor and Morrison (2007) propose, it is possible that students receive information but do not find it relevant. In this study, the majority of students who reported receiving resources seemed unable to evaluate the helpfulness or quality of the resources; this supports the notion that they are not paying attention. In addition, simply knowing that resources on campus exist to help victims of sexual assault may not be enough; universities may need to make more concerted efforts to educate the student population about sexual assault. A more involved program would need to be created to raise visibility *and* awareness. Indeed, research has shown that making the information more personally relevant to students increases the likelihood they will pay attention to the message and therefore change relevant attitudes and behaviors (Grube, Mayton, & Ball-Rokeach, 1994).

Regardless of dissemination, knowledge of resources was not correlated with a reduced acceptance of rape myths by men *or* women, and so maybe universities should implement more sexual assault prevention programs. It is possible that attitudes about sexual assault are ingrained in our culture, that the current programming and resources are not successful in reducing acceptance of rape myths because the programming does not successfully combat the backlash that continues to occur against the programs (DeKeseredy, 1999). Proactive programming may be more successful in producing attitude change. Sexual assault prevention programs are more proactive and attempt to educate both men and women about the culture that surrounds the incidence of sexual assault, whereas the programs that are reactive are only geared toward women (the survivors) and are helpful after the fact but not prior to. Scholars have long since suggested the importance of focusing sexual assault programs on men (Karjane et al., 2002; Schwartz & Dekeseredy,

1997). It has been argued that men, especially those who are in college, tend to facilitate a culture surrounding male peer support that is conducive to sexual assault (Sanday, 2007; Schwartz & Dekeseredy, 1997). The fraternity culture oftentimes facilitates the male peer support and encourages the objectification of women (Sanday, 2007).

Research evaluating sexual assault prevention programming is generally supportive of the prevention technique in dispelling commonly held rape myths (Breitenbecher, 2000; Foubert, 2000; Lanier, 2001). There are programs that educate men about how to stop violence against women, such as the national program Men Can Stop Rape (www.mencanstoprape.org) or Men Against Violence (see Choate, 2003, for a description). These programs generally focus on the notion that men are the ones with the most power to stop the violence because they are the typical perpetrator in these types of crimes. Thus, these programs attempt to create a new culture by encouraging men to assert that they will not tolerate violence against women (Schwartz & Dekeseredy, 1997). Fraternity members who were subjected to the Men against Violence training reported positive experiences with the program and expressed that prior to the program they were unaware of many of the issues surrounding sexual assault, such as alcohol and consent (Choate, 2003). Research has shown that men and women may communicate consent in different ways (Hickman & Muehlenhard, 1999), so

such programs may help attenuate this gender gap and educate men about sexual assault issues (and therefore, may be successful in preventing sexual assault). These programs complement programs educating women about the availability of sexual assault resources.

Conclusion

Overall, this study shows that even if sexual assault resources are available at a university, it does not mean students are receiving, using, or learning from them. Our nonprobability sampling method makes it impossible to generalize these findings to the whole university. However, this sample provided a conservative test of whether students were receiving resources; that is, this study was conducted with a sample of students currently enrolled in criminology, law, and society classes (in which they may receive information about those resources). Arguably, this sample should have had higher knowledge of sexual assault resources compared to those of the average student. Future research may benefit from using a random sample. However, even with this conservative sample, we demonstrated that merely providing resources about sexual assault may not be able to accomplish purposes intended. That is, if students do not know about the resources available to them, how will they use them in a time of need?

/// DISCUSSION QUESTIONS

1. How much knowledge do students have about sexual assault resources on their college campus?

2. What can universities do to reduce students' acceptance of rape myths?

3. How might university administrators use the findings of this study to make changes to their programs on campus?

Note

1. The Jeanne Clery Disclosure of Campus Security Policy and Campus Crime Statistics Act (20 USC § 1092) requires all public and private institutions of higher education that receive federal aid to disclose campus crime reports and campus security policies. Schools are required to publish a crime report and policies regarding crime, for example, sexual assault. The manner in which the schools are to disclose this information is not explicitly specified in the report.

References

Abbey, A. (2002). Alcohol-related sexual assault: A common problem among college students [Supplement 14]. *Journal of Studies on Alcohol,* 118–128.

Amnesty International. (2005). *Sexual assault research summary report.* London, UK: ICM.

Anderson, L. A., & Whiston, S. C. (2005). Sexual assault education programs: A meta-analytic examination of their effectiveness. *Psychology of Women Quarterly, 29,* 374–388.

Boeringer, S. B. (1999). Association of rape-supportive attitudes with fraternal and athletic participation. *Violence Against Women, 5,* 81–90.

Bohner, G., Reinhard, M. A., Rutz, S., Sturm, S. Kerschbaum, B., & Effler, D. (1998). Rape myths as neutralizing cognitions: Evidence for a causal impact of anti-victim attitudes on men's self-reported likelihood of raping. *European Journal of Social Psychology, 28,* 257–268.

Borges, A. M., Banyard, V. L., & Moynihan, M. M. (2008). Clarifying consent: Primary prevention of sexual assault on campus. *Journal of Prevention and Intervention in the Community, 36,* 75–88.

Breitenbecher, K. H. (2000). Sexual assault on college campuses: Is an ounce of prevention enough? *Applied & Preventive Psychology, 9,* 23–52.

Briere, J., Malamuth, N. M., & Check, J. V. P. (1985). Sexuality and rape supportive beliefs. *International Journal of Women's Studies, 8,* 398–403.

Burgess, G. H. (2007). Assessment of rape-supportive attitudes and beliefs in college men: Development, reliability, and validity of the rape attitudes and beliefs scale. *Journal of Interpersonal Violence, 22,* 973–993.

Burt, M. R. (1980). Cultural myths and support for rape. *Journal of Personality and Social Psychology, 38,* 217–230.

Burt, M. R. (2004). Acceptance of rape myths. In L. Wrightsman, A. L. Batson, & V. A. Edkins (Eds.), *Measures of legal attitudes* (pp. 115–117). Belmont, CA: Thomson-Wadsworth.

Choate, L. (2003). Sexual assault prevention programs for college men: An exploratory evaluation of the Men Against Violence Model. *Journal of College Counseling, 6,* 166–176.

Cowan, G. (2000). Women's hostility toward women and rape and sexual harassment myths. *Violence Against Women, 6,* 238–246.

DeKeseredy, W. S. (1999). Tactics of the antifeminist backlash against Canadian national women abuse surveys. *Violence Against Women, 5,* 1258–1276.

Faludi, S. (1991). *Backlash: The undeclared war against American women.* New York: Crown.

Fisher, B., Cullen, F., & Turner, M. (2000). *The sexual victimization of college women: Findings from two national-level studies.* Washington, DC: National Institute of Justice and Bureau of Justice Statistics.

Foubert, J. D. (2000). The longitudinal effects of a rape-prevention program on fraternity men's attitudes, behavioral intent, and behavior. *Journal of American College Health, 48,* 158–163.

Gidycz, C. A., Lynn, S. T., Rich, C. L., Marioni, N. L., Loh, C., Blackwell, L. M., . . . Pashdag, J. (2001). The evaluation of a sexual assault risk reduction program: A multisite investigation. *Journal of Consulting and Clinical Psychology, 69*(6), 1073–1078.

Greenfeld, L. A. (1997, February). *Sex offenses and offenders: An analysis of data on rape and sexual assault* (Report No. NCJ-163392). Washington, DC: U.S. Department of Justice.

Grube, J. W., Mayton, D. M., & Ball-Rokeach, S. J. (1994). Inducing change in values, attitudes, and behaviors: Belief systems theory and the method of value self-confrontation. *Journal of Social Issues, 50,* 153–173.

Hall, E. R., Howard, J. A., & Boezio, S. L. (1986). Tolerance of rape: A sexist or antisocial attitude. *Psychology of Women Quarterly, 10,* 101–118.

Hamilton, M., & Yee, J. (1990). Rape knowledge and propensity to rape. *Journal of Research in Personality, 24,* 111–122.

Hayes-Smith, R. M., & Hayes-Smith, J. M. (2009). A website content analysis of women's resources and sexual assault literature on college campuses. *Critical Criminology, 17,* 109–123.

Heppner, M. J., Humphrey, C. F., Hillenbrand-Gunn, T. L., & DeBord, K. A. (1995). The differential effects of rape prevention programming on attitudes, behavior, and knowledge. *Journal of Counseling Psychology, 42,* 508–518.

Hickman, S. E., & Muehlenhard, C. L. (1999). "By the semi-mystical appearance of a condom": How young women and men communicate sexual consent in heterosexual situations. *Journal of Sex Research, 36,* 258–272.

Jeanne Clery Disclosure of Campus Security Policy and Campus Crime Statistics Act, 20 U.S.C § 1092(f), (1998 & 2011). The 2011 ed. retrieved from http://www.gpo.gov/fdsys/pkg/USCODE-2011-title20/html/USCODE-2011-title20-chap28-subchapIV-partF-sec1092.htm

Kahlor, L., & Morrison, D. (2007). Television viewing and rape myth acceptance among college women. *Sex Roles, 56,* 729–739.

Karjane, H. M., Fisher, B. S., & Cullen, F. T. (2002). *Campus sexual assault: How America's institutions of higher education respond* (Final Report, NIJ Grant #1999-WA-VX-0008). Newton, MA: Education Development Center.

Koss, M. P., Gidcyz, C. A., & Wisniewski, W. (1987). The scope of rape: Incidence and prevalence of sexual aggression and victimization in a national sample of higher education students. *Journal of Consulting and Clinical Psychology, 55,* 162–170.

Krahe, B. (1988). Victim and observer characteristics as determinants of responsibility attributions to victims of rape. *Journal of Applied Social Psychology, 18,* 50–58.

Lanier, C. A. (2001). Rape-accepting attitudes: Precursors to or consequences of forced sex. *Violence Against Women, 7,* 876–885.

Lonsway, K. A., & Fitzgerald, L. F. (1994). Rape myths: In review. *Psychology of Women Quarterly, 18,* 133–164.

Margolin, L., Miller, M., & Moran, P. B. (1989). When a kiss is not just a kiss: Relating violations of consent in kissing to rape myth acceptance. *Sex Roles, 20,* 231–243.

Mohler-Kuo, M., Dowdall, G. W., Koss, M., & Wechsler, H. (2003). Correlates of rape while intoxicated in a national sample of college women. *Journal of Studies on Alcohol, 64*, 37–45.

Norris, J., & Cubbins, L. A. (1992). Dating, drinking and rape: Effects of victim's and assailant's alcohol consumption on judgments of their behavior and traits. *Psychology of Women Quarterly, 16*, 179–191.

Perkins, C. A. (1997, September). *Age patterns of victims of serious violent crime* (Report No. NCJ-162031). Washington, DC: U.S. Department of Justice.

Petty, R. E., & Cacioppo, J. T. (1986). *Communication and persuasion: Central and peripheral routes to attitude change.* New York: Springer-Verlag.

Roiphe, K. (1993). *The morning after: Sex, fear and feminism.* Toronto, Ontario, Canada: Little Brown.

Sanday, P. R. (2007). *Fraternity gang rape: Sex, brotherhood, and privilege on campus.* New York: New York University Press.

Schwartz, M. D., & DeKeseredy, W. S. (1997). *Sexual assault on the college campus: The role of male peer support.* Thousand Oaks, CA: Sage.

Schwartz, M. D., & Leggett, M. S. (1999). Bad dates or emotional trauma? The aftermath of campus sexual assault. *Violence Against Women, 5*, 251–271.

Student Right-to-Know and Campus Security Act (1990). (n.d.). Retrieved from http://nces.ed.gov/ipeds/glossary/index.asp?id=625

Ullman, S., Karabatsos, G., & Koss, M. (1999). Alcohol and sexual assault in a national sample of college women. *Journal of Interpersonal Violence, 14*, 603–625.

Warshaw, R. (1988). *I never called it rape: The Ms. Report on recognizing, fighting, and surviving date and acquaintance rape.* New York: Harper & Row.

Yeater, E. A., & O'Donohue, W. (1999). Sexual assault prevention programs: Current issues, future directions, and the potential efficacy of interventions with women. *Clinical Psychology Review, 19*, 739–771.

READING /// 6

In the section, you learned about how alcohol is the most common drug that contributes to rapes and sexual assaults. Drug-facilitated rape victims are often viewed as blameless; however, the discussion changes when someone voluntarily becomes intoxicated and is ultimately sexually violated. This study by Clare Gunby, Anna Carline, and Caryl Beynon includes focus group research with students enrolled at a British university and uses a hypothetical vignette of a potential offender and victim of rape following their consumption of alcohol.

Regretting It After?

Focus Group Perspectives on Alcohol Consumption, Nonconsensual Sex, and False Allegations of Rape

Clare Gunby, Anna Carline, and Caryl Beynon

Introduction

It is well documented that young people, including students, are high consumers of alcohol (Kypri, Cronin, & Wright, 2005; YouGov, 2010) and that they frequently use alcohol to facilitate sexual encounters, including increasing their confidence to approach members of the opposite sex (Bellis et al., 2008; Sumnall, Beynon, Conchie, Riley, & Cole, 2007). Research also indicates that this association between alcohol and sexual outcomes serves to influence judgments around the consensual nature of alcohol-involved intercourse[1] (George & Stoner, 2000). Indeed, recent social network responses to the conviction of the Welsh footballer Ched Evans for the rape of an extremely

SOURCE: Gunby, C., Carline, A., & Beynon, C. (2012). Regretting it after? Focus group perspectives on alcohol consumption, nonconsensual sex and false allegations of rape. *Social & Legal Studies, 22*(1), 87–106.

intoxicated woman, including the public "tweeting" of the victim's name, highlight the profound impact that alcohol consumption can have on third parties' assessments of the legitimacy of alcohol-involved rapes (Bancroft, 2012).

Drawing upon the findings of an empirical research project with university students, this article provides a timely examination of young peoples' attitudes and understandings around alcohol consumption, nonconsensual sex, and the role of alcohol in the false allegation process. More specifically, the project examined how, and to what extent, perspectives around false rape allegations and voluntary intoxication intertwine. It also examined more broadly how alcohol-involved intercourse is perceived by students and, by implication, possible attitudinal difficulties that may arise in achieving convictions in alcohol-involved rape cases. To this end, four focus groups were conducted based on a real case in which sex took place between two very drunk acquaintances and consent was contested.

The analysis that follows provides critical insights into how complainant and defendant credibility and responsibility are constructed and explores what is deemed to constitute consent. This is an area where further research is required in order to develop understanding around attitudes that may impinge on the treatment of rape complainants who have been drinking (Stern Review, 2010) and to gain clarity on how the association between alcohol and sex may influence judgments around the consensual nature of intercourse and, by default, link to ideas and understandings around false rape allegations. The article also offers preliminary insights into perspectives that may be drawn upon by jurors in their deliberations of alcohol-involved rape cases.

The article is presented over four sections. To commence, an outline of the law of rape and the key issues and research which relate to this $A = r^2$ are presented. Second, the study methodology is detailed followed by a critical analysis of the research findings. The final section of the article provides conclusions and suggestions for further research.

The Law of Rape and Research Context

In England and Wales, rape law was reformed in 2003 among concerns regarding the low reporting and conviction rate for the offence (Home Office, 2002). Rape is now governed by Section 1 of the *Sexual Offences Act 2003* and involves the nonconsensual penile penetration of a person's mouth, vagina, or anus. As with the previous law, the absence of consent is pivotal: The prosecution must prove beyond a reasonable doubt that the complainant did not consent, and the jury must be satisfied that the accused did not hold a reasonable belief in consent. In making this latter assessment, the jury is to take into account "all the circumstances, including any steps [the defendant] has taken to ascertain whether [the complainant] consents" (Section 1(2)).

For the first time, the 2003 Act implemented a statutory definition of consent. Section 74 states, "a person consents if he agrees by choice, and has the freedom and capacity to make that choice." Further significant reforms were implemented by virtue of Sections 75 and 76, which contain a range of evidential and conclusive presumptions regarding the absence of consent. Under these provisions, if the prosecution proves the existence of certain factors, it will be presumed that the complainant did not consent and/or that the defendant did not hold a reasonable belief in consent. While the presumptions in Section 75 are evidential and can therefore be rebutted by the defendant, under Section 76, lack of consent and/or belief in consent is conclusively presumed. Consequently, the circumstances which fall into this latter section are more narrowly construed, relating to cases involving certain types of deception. In contrast, the presumptions in Section 75 are wider and considered to represent situations in which most people would agree that consent was unlikely to be present (Home Office, 2002: p. 16). They include the use, or threats, of violence along with cases of involuntary intoxication/drink spiking. For the purposes of the present analysis, cases that involve *voluntary* intoxication would only fall within Section 75 if the complainant was so drunk that she became unconscious (Section 75 (2)(d)).

In 2006, a government consultation asked whether Section 75 should be amended to include situations involving extreme voluntary intoxication (Office for Criminal Justice Reform, 2006). One third of respondents argued that presumption Section 75(2)(d) should be changed to include situations in which the complainant was "too affected by alcohol or drugs to give free agreement." Certain respondents referred to situations in which men may "seek to take advantage of the fact that women are drunk [voluntarily] and therefore have less capacity to resist pressure or coercion" (Office for Criminal Justice Reform, 2007: p. 6). These proposals, however, were abandoned due to the fear of "mischievous accusations" (Office for Criminal Justice Reform, 2006: p. 12), arguments that presuppose some linkage between intoxication and the potential for false rape allegations.

Voluntary intoxication short of the point of unconsciousness therefore falls under the general Section 74 definition of consent, where specific consideration is to be given to whether or not the complainant retained the capacity to consent. The complexities of capacity and intoxication are well documented in the case of *R v Bree* (2007). While initially convicted for rape following sex with a complainant who was voluntarily and exceptionally intoxicated, his conviction was quashed on appeal due to the trial judge's inadequate jury directions (see Cowan, 2008; Elvin, 2008; Gunby, Carline, & Beynon, 2010 for a critical analysis of Bree, 2007). The Court of Appeal held that the jury should have received assistance with the meaning of the term *capacity* when a complainant is affected by her own voluntarily induced intoxication and noted that "capacity to consent may evaporate well before a complainant becomes unconscious" (Bree, 2007: p. 167 [case]). However, little further guidance was provided as it was considered to be a "fact-specific" issue and not appropriate to create a "grid system" which would enable the point of incapability to be linked to "some prescribed level of alcohol consumption" (Bree, 2007: p. 167).

Rape Myths, False Allegations, and Intoxication

Despite the reforms to the law of rape in 2003, continued concerns regarding the criminal justice system's handling of rape cases, along with the frequently reported 6% conviction rate and high levels of case attrition (Kelly, Lovett, & Regan, 2005), prompted a review into how rape complaints were handled by public authorities in England and Wales. The review noted that *rape myths* continue to impact upon the criminal justice process (Sanders, 2012; Stern Review, 2010), including myths which presuppose many rape allegations are false (Ellison & Munro, 2010a; Kelly, 2010; Kelly et al., 2005). Such perspectives have historically influenced legal practice, including, for example, the extensive cross-examination of the complainant's sexual history and corroboration warnings (see Temkin, 2002). While many of these provisions have been abandoned, or restrictions around their use applied, beliefs around the frequency of false rape reports continue to influence legal and political thinking and to problematise women's accounts of rape (Kelly, 2010). Recent suggestions to provide anonymity for those accused of rape, for example, were premised partially on arguments that false allegations impact frequently in rape cases (Almandras, 2010).

Adherence to such perspectives, and their complex relationship to the police recorded no-crime code, has been documented among police officers (Kelly, 2010; Kelly et al., 2005) as well as among members of wider society. Burton, Kelly, Kitzinger, and Regan (1998) found that from a sample of 2,039 young people, 74% agreed that females often or sometimes "cry rape" when really they just have second thoughts. The London-based Opinion Matters (2010) survey identified one in five participants aged 18–50 years agreed that most claims of rape are probably not true, with men being more likely to endorse this perspective. More recent findings have documented that 47.7% of male students aged 18–24 years, compared to 33.6% of female, agreed with the statement that a significant proportion of rapes reported to the police were false allegations (Gunby, Carline, Bellis, & Beynon, 2012). While gender is not a definitive predictor of adherence to false rape allegation beliefs, studies that have found gender distinctions may partially be explained through reference to differences in sexual expectations among young men and women (see Beres, 2007; Gunby et al., 2012; Humphreys, 2007).

Ideas around the elevated nature of false rape allegations remain despite evidence that levels of false rape reporting are no different to (Rumney, 2006), or potentially lower than (Kelly, 2010), the levels of false complaints found across other crimes. Estimates suggest that between 2% and 8% of rape allegations are possibly false (see Kelly et al., 2005; Lonsway, Archambault, & Lisak, 2009). While further research is undoubtedly needed (Stern Review, 2010), ideas around the elevated frequency of false rape allegations appear to have a limited evidence base.

Running parallel are studies which highlight that third parties often hold a woman who was drinking prior to being raped partially accountable and are hesitant to convict the accused (Finch & Munro, 2005, 2007; Gunby et al., 2012). If parties are depicted as equally intoxicated prior to nonconsensual sex, there is an increased reluctance to hold a defendant criminally liable for rape, even when the complainant's degree of intoxication has rendered her incapable of giving consent (Finch & Munro, 2005). However, when a defendant is depicted as sober, or less intoxicated than the victim, participants are more likely to hold the defendant criminally liable (Finch & Munro, 2005). When evaluating whether a complainant is able to consent, participants have been found to focus on a victim's level of consciousness at the time, with a number believing that as long as she maintained consciousness, she retained the capacity to reason (Finch & Munro, 2005), attitudes which contrast with the legal position (Bree, 2007 [case]).

It is possible to hypothesize that hesitance around believing an intoxicated female's account of rape relates to assumptions around the accusation being false and the consequence of a sober retraction of consent (Cowan, 2008). If rape victims believe such assumptions are made, they may feed further into the culture of reluctance to report rape and seek support. Evidence illustrates that such fears are not unfounded with skeptical attitudes around alcohol-involved rape and false allegations impacting on the way cases are dealt with by police, prosecutors, judges, and juries (Stern Review, 2010).

Methodology

Design, Recruitment, and Materials

Four single sex focus groups were carried out with a total of 21 students (12 female and 9 male). Single sex groups were used in recognition that men and women often talk differently about rape (Beres, 2007; Gunby et al., 2012; Schneider, Mori, Lambert, & Wong, 2009) and to minimize participants feeling inhibited to discuss perspectives due to having opposite sex individuals present. Participants were full-time undergraduate or postgraduate students studying on psychology (seven participants), criminology (three participants), medicine (two participants), and teacher training (nine participants) courses at an East Midlands university in England. A student sample was selected due to the 18- to 24-year demographic being

increasingly at risk of experiencing nonconsensual sex (Abbey, Zawacki, Buck, Clinton, & McAuslan., 2004; Walby & Allen, 2004). In light of students and young people using alcohol to facilitate sexual encounters, and the normalization of heavy drinking among this group (Bellis et al., 2008; Kypri et al., 2005), students were considered an appropriate sample choice to enable informed debates to be generated which may be specifically pertinent to this demographic. The study vignette (see below description) was based around the behavior of two students, which further made the sample an appropriate choice in terms of asking participants to reflect on experiences they may be able to relate to.

Participants were recruited through nonprobability sampling techniques. Existing contacts at the given university were asked to disseminate information about the study to a subset of individuals. Six individuals volunteered to participate through this process and were asked to invite their peers to take part in the study. It is recognized that a nonrandom sampling approach, and the decision to include individuals within focus groups who were familiar with each other, may impact on the nature of discussions. However, Doherty and Anderson (2004) emphasize the potential for socially desirable responding (the tendency to give positive descriptions) when adopting discussion-based methods that examine controversial rape perspectives.

Ellison and Munro (2010a: p. 799) also acknowledge that individuals may be "well versed" in "socially appropriate" attitudes in relation to rape. Howarth (2002) argues that to enable controversial, sensitive, and distressing topics to be discussed openly and with confidence, group participants should be known to each other at some level. Due to the emotive nature of the research topic, desire to foster uninhibited conversation and potential for socially desirable responding—especially in the presence of unknown individuals—it was rationalized that the recruitment strategy suggested by Howarth (2002) was appropriate. A focus group method was chosen to encourage debate between participants and to allow for the emergence of rich data. This approach also significantly reduces the directive influence of the interviewer (Morgan, 1997) and better corresponds to the process of jury deliberation, thus, highlighting the complex and potentially contradictory ways in which attitudes inform deliberations.

Discussions were based around a vignette that modelled the facts reported in the Bree (2007) case. As discussed, this is recognized to epitomize the problems associated with having sex when parties are extremely drunk, thus, enhancing the study's ecological validity (Doherty & Anderson, 2004). The vignette described Benjamin and Michelle who were briefly acquainted, spending a night out, initially with another couple and then later alone. They were witnessed leaving a bar in the early hours of the morning and walking to Michelle's flat where she vomits due to the alcohol consumed. Sex takes place which Michelle reports to a friend, and later to the police, as being nonconsensual. Michelle argues that her recollection was "very patchy" (Bree, 2007: p. 161) despite recognition that she had not consented at the time. Benjamin maintains throughout his statement to the police that sex was consensual.

While the authors were not aware of other studies that have used this case as a specific vignette, it was selected due to the fact that it has been the catalyst for much debate in the United Kingdom (see Cowan, 2008; Elvin, 2008; Wallerstein, 2009). Study findings are therefore argued to be applicable to, and enhance, the wider international work which has examined the role of alcohol consumption on third parties' attitudes towards sex and its consensual nature (for example, Norris & Cubbins, 1992; Wall & Schuller, 2000).

A focus group guide was used to direct conversation and addressed the following topics:

Whether participants personally felt that Benjamin should be found guilty of rape and why;

If not guilty of rape, then of some other crime;

The factors that impacted on whether participants personally believed Michelle had been raped;

Whether participants' personal perspectives would have differed if only Michelle had been drinking.

Initially, focus group participants were blind to the outcome of the Bree (2007) case. Towards the end of each focus group, participants were told that Bree (2007) was found "not guilty," in order to encourage further reflections on why Benjamin may have been acquitted. In light of the fact that most focus group participants had themselves decided that Benjamin should be acquitted, telling them that this had been the outcome resulted in no further information being elicited. Once focus groups had finished, all participants were informed of the decisions of both the jury and the Court of Appeal in the case.

All participants were provided with written copies of the legal definition of rape, sexual assault, and the Section 74 consent definition to ensure they were aware of these definitions prior to commencing the focus group.

Analysis and Discussion

The following analysis focuses on three primary topics: "not quite rape," "false allegations of rape," and "voluntary intoxication and intercourse." Within each higher order theme, further subthemes were identified and examined in order to draw out key perspectives relating to intoxicated sexual intercourse and false allegations of rape.

Not Quite Rape

Participants were reluctant to label the vignette sex as rape and the subthemes that were developed to compose this topic included "physical injury evidence," which denoted the lack of injury within the case vignette. The subtheme "stereotype of rapist and rape" was also developed to capture arguments around the behaviour of Benjamin failing to conform to that of a stereotypical sex attacker.

Physical Injury Evidence. The majority of participants did not perceive the sex depicted in the vignette to be representative of rape and almost all participants argued that they would have personally acquitted Benjamin. Key to this decision was their inability to be sure beyond reasonable doubt that rape had occurred, with certain misconceptions influencing judgements. It was argued that rape is "difficult to prove" (Focus Group 1, Female 4; (FGl, F4)) and that there were no signs of "physical evidence" (FGl, Fl) indicating rape had taken place. Consistent with past research (Ellison & Munro, 2009, 2010a), multiple participants expected evidence of physical injury: "this is like such an unspeakable, horrible thing to happen to you, and I've no idea what it could possibly feel like. But I'd expect to see some scratches or bruises on her, or something" (FG2, M3).

Several participants focused on this lack of physical evidence and argued that had severe bruising, cuts, or broken bones been present, this would be indicative of rape and convince them of such. Corroborative evidence is typically absent in rape cases and a lack of physical injury undoubtedly makes an allegation harder to prove and the criminal burden of proof more difficult to reach. It was clear that for certain participants, such evidential concerns influenced their arguments regarding the need for physical injury. However, for a smaller subset it was evident that rape was viewed as synonymous with violence. For this latter group, there is perhaps a dissonance between the legal stance and lay expectation. That is, the law does not require evidence of injury in order for consent to be deemed absent (see *R v Heard*, 2007; *R v Olugboja*, 1981). Legally, the harms that arise from rape are viewed in relation to the sex that takes place without consent; the presence of injury simply acts to exacerbate the seriousness of the crime. Perspectives that assume rape involves injury may feed into ideas around false allegations of rape, where it may come to be assumed that if there is no evidence of violence, the allegation is potentially false.

Stereotype of Rapist and Rape. Participants emphasized that the defendant "offered to spend the night in her bed. So, obviously, he does not mean it in a conscious term to be rape" (FGl, F2) and had not "pinned her down and shagged her" (FGl, F4). Certain actions perpetrated by Benjamin prior to the sex, such as bringing Michelle a glass of water and helping to clean her up after having been sick, were perceived to demonstrate he was "obviously quite respectful of her" (FG3, F5). Participants were consequently reluctant to define the sex as involving activity that should be criminalized: ". . . there's a certain lack of morality on his part. He's . . . I think, taking advantage of someone is vastly different to um . . . it's vastly different to committing a sort of offence . . ." (FG4, Ml). Instead, it was argued that Benjamin had acted morally wrong, been "foolish" (FG4, M2), made "an error of judgement" (FG4, Ml), and although a possible "scumbag" (FG2, M4) for taking advantage, had not necessarily "done anything wrong in the eyes of the law" (FG2, M4).

Participants did not consequently feel that his behavior was sufficient to warrant a prison sentence, and further reasons for this perspective focused on the normalization of the sex depicted: "it must happen too often to send people to prison for doing that" (FGl, F4). Such normalization suggests that the sex portrayed has to some extent come to be unquestionably accepted as reflective of the reality of heavy drinking situations, unsurprising in light of the noted research which demonstrates alcohol is used by young people to facilitate their sexual encounters (Bellis et al., 2008; Sumnall et al., 2007).

While reluctant to describe the vignette sex as a crime, participants acknowledged it was "obviously an unpleasant experience" (FGl, F4) but more in line with a "really bad one-night stand" (FG1, Fl). Sex was conceptualized to have been the result of mixed messages, poor communication, and a reduction in inhibitions. While these arguments lend weight to research that suggests when parties are equally intoxicated, participants look for a "mid-point" between rape and consensual sex to describe that intercourse (Finch and Munro, 2005), the current study suggests that this mid-point behavior is far more aligned with consensual sex (Gunby et al., 2012). The implications that stem from these arguments are that if participants are reluctant to conceptualize the situation depicted in the vignette as one that could involve the commission of a crime initially, they start from an assumption that will doubt the veracity of the complainant's rape allegation. If the scenario is not what constitutes rape for them, then how can her complaint be conceptualized as true?

False Allegations of Rape

The topic of false allegations was spontaneously raised by participants in all four focus groups without direction from the investigator, arguably demonstrating the pervasive nature of the issue. The subthemes that emerged from this topic included participants' perceptions around the "motivations" that drive a false allegation, "their frequency," and the "ramifications of a false allegation."

Motivations for a False Allegation of Rape. Participants in three of the groups raised for debate whether Michelle "regretted it afterwards . . ." (FG2, M3) or questioned whether "she has consented in a way, but she doesn't like the fact that she's done it" (FG3, F4), thus, providing the backdrop for a false allegation to be made:

> . . . being used is a very schoolyard term to have used . . . it kind of shows that her initial reaction was that she'd been used; she hadn't been raped. And then later on, perhaps when she'd thought about it . . . I don't know, perhaps she altered events in her head, to say it's rape. (FG3, F3)

The possibility of a rape allegation being the consequence of events being "altered" to fit with a rape experience is an issue individuals are entitled to consider when assessing the legitimacy of a case. However, the fact Michelle did not initially label her experience as rape is used by several participants to question the validity of her account. This perhaps highlights a limited understanding around the factors that impact on the labelling process (see Bondurant, 2001; Kahn, Jackson, Kully, Badger, & Halvorsen, 2003). Such findings sit within a wider framework that indicates third parties often expect rape complainants to adhere to stereotypical victim scripts which include the display of emotion, immediately reporting to the police (Ellison & Munro, 2009; Temkin & Krahe, 2008), and as currently suggested, to categorically identify and label that experience as rape.

While a subset of participants argued that the vignette was unlikely to be a false report, protests were sometimes qualified: "I don't see what she would get out of crying rape. I mean, unless she's got a boyfriend or something" (FG2, M5). The existence of a relationship appeared to increase the potential for a false allegation, based on the premise that such extreme actions would enable the complainant to "cover-up" (FG4, M2) her indiscretion. False reports were also viewed as a method for seeking revenge, motivations identified in related literature (Ellison & Munro, 2010a; Kelly et al., 2005; Lonsway et al., 2009):

> But also, I look at it um if she's used the term been used, she could also be using this court case as a way to get back at him. If she feels, herself, that she's been used, she could be thinking oh this is my way to get back at him, to show him that I didn't want it to happen; that I feel used, so I'll get my revenge, I'll do payback more

than anything, rather than feeling like she's been raped. (FG3, F2)

Frequency of False Allegations of Rape. After the issue of false rape allegations had been raised by participants, they were asked whether they felt such reports were commonplace. Almost all participants argued they were likely to be infrequent due to there being "no real reward" (FG3, F5) and that women would not want to go through the intrusive physical examination that would stem from making a claim. While this perspective perhaps sits at odds with the frequency with which participants suggested the vignette could be an example of a false report, such a contradiction resonates with existent findings. Ellison and Munro (2010a) for example, identified that when individually questioned on abstract rape perspectives, participants' attitudes did not always mirror those which become apparent via the group process of deliberating a concrete case example. The social process of discussion, in conjunction with addressing issues of reasonable doubt and belief, resulted in a more complex interplay of factors being considered, which potentially triggered additional logics (including in the current instance, the possibility of an allegation being false). While this may be one explanation for the dissonance in perspectives identified via direct questioning and the more subtle deliberative process, it is also possible that participants were aware that directly agreeing that false reports were frequent could have been perceived unduly unsympathetic (Doherty & Anderson, 2004), with such suggestions consequently remaining unendorsed.

While directly arguing that false rape allegations were likely to be infrequent, participants nevertheless stated that "it's easy to say rape, which I do think happens" (FG1, F1). It may be the perceived ease with which a false allegation can be made which linked to assumptions around the vignette being an example of a false report. As noted, this philosophy has resonated within criminal law and impacted on rape legislation (Rumney, 2006). While Matthew Hale's (1736: p. 634) famed argument that rape is an accusation easily made, yet hard to be defended, no longer resonates as profusely within legal thinking, Ellison and Munro (2010a) argue that the sentiment is still propelled via media reports (Gavey & Gow, 2001; Kitzinger, 2009; Lilith Project, 2008). Lonsway et al. (2009) similarly argue that media accounts of false allegations, often made against popular cultural figures, contribute towards the overestimation of false allegations in everyday life and can serve to enhance assumptions around false allegations being commonplace, despite participants acknowledging to "not knowing anything about it really" (FG2, M3).

The Ramifications of False Allegations. Multiple participants across the groups argued that false reports can "ruin people's lives" (FGl, Fl) and the "rumours will carry on" (FGl, F6), even if the accusation is identified as false. In this sense, the wrongs of a false rape allegation were seen to relate to the impact of having the term *rapist* attributed to an individual. The repeated arguments that focused on men being wrongly and knowingly accused of rape, disproportionately outweighed the conversation held in relation to the harms of the rape offence to the complainant and wider society. Gavey (2005) has noted that an overriding focus around the "wrongness" of false rape allegations, above and beyond the harms of rape itself, is an established feature of Western society and an example of the way in which the traumas of rape are marginalized.

Concern for the defendant was also expressed in relation to rape accusations and decisions to convict generally. Reflecting Ellison and Munro's (2010b) findings, a participant argued, "I don't think his entire life and career should be marred by a conviction, based on this" (FG3, F2), a comment that demonstrates awareness around the ramifications of being found guilty of rape. The majority of participants argued that in such ambiguous circumstances, and with such long-term implications, the defendant should be given the "benefit of the doubt" (FG1, F5). While such verdicts may relate to the problems of being sure beyond reasonable doubt when deciding on guilt, it was clear that for certain participants, in evaluating whether rape had occurred, the focus hinged on the harms of having the rape label attributed to the defendant.

Related to this issue, certain participants argued that the ramifications of being accused of rape made it irresponsible to take a complaint to the police unless the victim was *sure* rape has occurred: "so, if you're not sure, then I think it's quite irresponsible to make that claim" (FG2, M2). Although this perspective was challenged, for a small number of participants, there was the expectation that when memory of events was hampered by alcohol, at a minimum, the complainant should seek legal advice on how to proceed rather than "cry rape" (FG2, M3) at the onset.

This argument again fails to recognize the impact of sexual offences where the associated trauma may inhibit the ability to take immediate coherent action. It perhaps also demonstrates a naivety over the workings of the criminal justice system and a complainant's ability to access such legal advice, outside of the official police reporting route. The comment rightfully suggests that certain individuals may be confused about the sex they have experienced and may benefit from contact with someone suitably trained who could advise, and help categories, what had been encountered without placing pressure to officially report the incident. It is possible that for certain individuals, the reporting process is a fact-finding endeavor. If at the police reporting stage, it is established that rape has not occurred, this may feed into notions of false allegations of rape, with the genuinely confused complainant being perceived to have made a hasty decision to report, which they subsequently retract, and which may come to be conceptualized as a retraction based upon a sober reevaluation of the facts.

Voluntary Intoxication and Intercourse

Participants offered more general perspectives on alcohol-involved intercourse, with these conversations implicating potential difficulties in achieving convictions in alcohol-involved rape cases, while also elaborating further on the extent to which such views intertwine with wider ideas around false allegations. The subthemes developed included the "impact of alcohol on inhibitions," Michelle's "capacity to consent," and the "dual impact of alcohol on defendant and complainant behaviour."

Impact of Alcohol on Inhibitions. A large proportion of participants argued that alcohol reduces inhibitions and increases the potential for engaging in behaviors that may later be regretted: "alcohol lowers your inhibitions and fuels you to do things that perhaps you shouldn't" (FG3, F6). It was argued that if sex takes place during a period of extreme drunkenness, rape may be the "first reaction when they wake up" (FG1, F3). It was rationalized that while sex may have been consensually engaged in at the time, it may be regretted the following day and relabeled as nonconsensual:

> ... has she not to some extent woken up and just regretted it, and kind of come to and suddenly thought oh God, what are people gonna think of me, what am I thinking of myself? So, it's kind of an afterthought as well. (FGl, F2)

It was clear that when participants talked about a complainant modifying the sex that took place to align it with a rape act, this was not always deemed a conscious or vindictive process but one that may also be more subtle:

> When you're drunk, you sometimes ... you know, you're not sure what happened or what was a dream. And when you've spoken to Naomi, when you've still been drunk, that might all mesh into what you remember as well. (FG2, M3)

False allegations were thus constructed as both the product of an overt decision to make a complaint for the purpose of covering up regretted sex as well as potentially being the product of more subtle processes which involved events being "altered" during the course of trying to account for, and rationalize, regretted intercourse. It was clear that it was this impact of alcohol on inhibitions and behavior specifically, which related to participants' assumptions that false reports were more likely when drinking—either through an intentional decision to make a false claim or via the impact of alcohol on cognition, recollection, and the restructuring of events the next morning. Indeed, this explanation was offered significantly more frequently than motivations that focused on making a false claim for the purpose of revenge or to protect an existent relationship. While certain participants argued that having drank alcohol prior to a rape is likely to decrease a complainant's likelihood of reporting the assault, due to fears around being perceived noncredible, the majority of participants argued that people are more likely to use alcohol "as their excuse" (FGl, F5) for engaging in uninhibited behaviors. These findings support larger scale quantitative data which indicate that

81.1% of students ($N = 869$) aged 18 to 24 years agreed that being drunk when having sex increases the likelihood of a false rape allegation being made (Gunby et al., 2012).

Capacity. Section 74 of the Sexual Offences Act 2003 makes clear that an individual must retain the capacity to consent in order for that consent to be valid. Participants emphasized the difficulties of evaluating the vignette case facts and being able to accurately gauge Michelle's level of alcohol intoxication and, by default, degree of capability. While a subset of participants focused on the complainant having been sick, and felt that this should have been a sufficient indicator to prevent the defendant from having sex with her, it was not deemed sufficient in isolation to convince participants that she lacked the capacity to consent entirely: "you can have a few drinks and be sick, and not even really be that drunk" (FG3, F3). Certain participants also drew upon Michelle's ability to effectively verbalize and walk without staggering to determine her capacity: "if you can walk, you know, quite well, you'd think that someone was okay" (FG3, F3).

While the law acknowledges that an individual may lose the capacity to consent before the point of unconsciousness, the study suggests that for certain participants, such extreme states of intoxication may only be deemed suitable markers (Finch and Munro, 2006). These comments are perhaps unsurprising in light of arguments around the capacity construct being unhelpful in illuminating the nuanced stages of intoxication. Under such circumstances, it is argued that lack of capacity will typically be judged through reference to an extreme point (Cowan, 2008; Elvin, 2008). Despite these comments, there was a consensus that alcohol impacts differently on people, making it difficult to establish the point at which an individual loses the capacity to consent:

> Alcohol affects different people differently, and there are different times alcohol will affect the same individual. You can have three beers and be absolutely fine on one night. You could have a beer and a cocktail another night and be blasted. (FG1, Fl)

Participants thus expressed their sympathy for the defendant at this point, arguing it would have been impossible "to judge it really" (FG4, M2) and that in the absence of "a breath test" (FG2, M5), it was unreasonable to assume he should be able to appreciate whether the complainant retained the capacity to consent.

The Dual Impact of Alcohol on Defendant and Complainant Behavior: Constructing Female Responsibility. When participants were asked who they personally felt should take responsibility for ensuring consent was clearly established in a sexual situation, all participants argued that responsibility should be shared, or, it was a man's moral duty to ensure his partner was fully consenting. However, if both parties were equally intoxicated, men were deemed able to forfeit such duties: "I think in a normal sexual situation, it would be shared. But when you're both drunk, I think it's just whoever's the most sober should make the decision" (FG3, F4).

The majority of participants argued that if through alcohol the complainant was left too intoxicated to retain the capacity to consent to intercourse, alcohol may have similarly impacted on the defendant's ability to identify whether his partner had the capacity, thus, "making you more likely to think that they'd [the partner] given reasonable consent" (FG2, M2). While intoxication is not a factor that can be taken into account when determining whether the defendant held a reasonable belief in consent *(DPP v Majewski,* 1977; *R v Heard,* 2007), it was clear participants did not recognize this or, if they did, still sympathized with the drunken defendant: "but if he's drunk to a certain extent that he does reasonably believe that B consents, then he hasn't done anything wrong, in the eyes of the law" (FG2, M6). It is realistic to assume that for certain individuals, extreme intoxication will incorrectly be viewed as a reasonable excuse for believing consent had been given.

When participants were asked whether they personally felt that Benjamin would have been found guilty of rape if only the complainant had been drinking, there was consensus across the groups that there would have been an increased likelihood. If sober, the defendant was perceived to be in a position where he could appreciate the complainant's degree of capacity and had "enough coherence to have the responsibility to make the judgement call" (FGl, F6): "If you're sober and you know that someone is drunk, then you know full well that your moral responsibility is not to take advantage of them. ... I dunno if it's a law thing ... you just wouldn't, would you?"

(FG2, M6). This argument implies that the law is not the motivator that drives appropriate sexual encounters, but rather, a sense of morality influences behavior. Moral responsibility, however, still appeared to be something that could be forfeited when parties were equivalently intoxicated, but not when there was a disparity in that intoxication. These findings support the research that has identified that third parties perceive it unfair to hold a defendant criminally liable for rape if each individual is equally intoxicated (Finch and Munro, 2005; Gunby et al., 2012) yet are more inclined to label sex as rape when a complainant is drinking independently (Norris and Cubbins, 1992), or the defendant is less intoxicated (Finch and Munro, 2005). While Finch and Munro (2005) argue that a less drunk or sober defendant is perceived to be in a position whereby he is able to ensure the complainant has the capacity to consent, the current study indicates that an intoxicated defendant is perceived to be in a disadvantageous position whereby he is unable to clearly gauge the complainant's level of intoxication and therefore her capacity. Being in such a position was seen to reduce the defendant's responsibility for ensuring consent was present.

A subset of participants focused on the complainant's lack of verbalized "no" in rationalizing why they were insufficiently convinced that rape had taken place: ". . . at no point has she said . . . or she can't recall saying no to sex" (FG4, Ml). The dissonance between the law, which does not require consent to be verbally expressed (*R v Heard,* 2007), and lay assumption is again apparent. Female participants specifically emphasized that sexual intentions must be effectively communicated:

> She needs to say no beforehand. There's no point in saying I didn't want to do it afterwards . . . that's just gonna confuse everyone. So, like yeah, it's up to the woman to say before it happens, yes or no in an obvious and clear way. (FG3, F3)

The implications of this argument are multiple. It feeds into ideas around the retraction of consent which underpin previous arguments around false allegations being made upon reevaluation of the sex that occurred, as well as suggesting that if a verbalized "no" is not given, this could be deemed indicative of the allegation being false. It also implies that in the absence of clear articulation, the defendant will be left without sufficient ability to negotiate, or read, the sexual situation. As previously noted, under Section 1(2) of the Sexual Offences Act 2003, juries are required to take into account any steps taken by the defendant to ascertain consent, which could include asking a partner whether they are happy for the sexual interaction to progress. Despite being provided with the legal definition of rape, and participants therefore being aware of this responsibility on defendants, a minority (of women) still deemed the female to be the party who should take control over clarifying sexual expectations. While research suggests that men are more likely to endorse attitudes which feed into beliefs relating to false allegations (Gunby et al., 2012; Opinion Matters, 2010), women have been found to more frequently assume that other women should take some degree of responsibility for nonconsensual sex (Finch & Munro, 2007; Opinion Matters, 2010). This includes taking responsibility for avoiding miscommunication and for effectively communicating nonconsent through overt verbal responses (Ellison & Munro, 2010a).

While emphasizing the need for sexual intentions to be clear, it was paradoxically noted that it could be a "passion killer" for the man to ask whether he could have sex with his partner. In this sense, consent was still viewed as more natural and appropriate if controlled by the woman. The articulation of such arguments reflect the traditional sexual scripts that suggest men are responsible for the initiation of sexual encounters and the active pursuit of sexual outcomes, care of their higher sex drive. Women by contrast are seen to set sexual parameters and provide "control" over the time and place of sex (Frith, 2009). It is interesting to note that women still drew upon these scripts of supposedly "normal" male and female sexuality to ground their arguments and which perhaps provided a basis for explaining why women's ability to verbally resist male sexual advances received such scrutiny.

Female participants also highlighted the importance of personal responsibility when drinking and recognizing the ramifications of extreme drunkenness: ". . . I think people do have responsibilities to look after themselves. And I think that the amount that she drank, and the fact that she went out with another couple, will really go against her in that sense" (FG3, F4). The disproportionate focus on women (as opposed to men) taking personal responsibility when drinking may relate to women being at enhanced risk of experiencing sexual offences initially (Kershaw, Nicholas, & Walker, 2008), hence, their perceived role in attempting to reduce that vulnerability. Women are often subject to awareness raising campaign literature that warns them against the dangers of extreme drinking, leaving friends unattended on evenings out, and accepting drinks from strangers (Neame, 2003), also potentially sensitizing women to such arguments. While it is acknowledged that campaign literature is increasingly incorporating messages that are directed at men, in attempts to reduce the prevalence of rape, such messages will take time to infiltrate into public consciousness and to temper those which have long focused on the modification of female behavior (Neame, 2003).

While all individuals should perhaps work towards recognizing potential vulnerabilities when drinking, and to equally recognize such vulnerabilities in others, it is noteworthy that there was no comparable discussion around men needing to consider how much alcohol they consumed on a night out, or the possible impacts of their intoxication on their ability to read consent-relevant cues. The overriding focus on the steps that women should take to avoid sexual offences resonates with findings that indicate when rape occurs, the spotlight resides firmly on the female's actions prior to the assault (Finch & Munro, 2005, 2007; Kelly et al., 2005; Temkin & Krahe, 2008).

Conclusion

A key aim of the research project was to investigate how perspectives towards false allegations and alcohol intoxication intertwine. By investigating such attitudes, it is possible to reflect on the perceived role of alcohol within the false reporting process, provide insights into the way lay individuals apportion responsibility, and illuminate stereotypes that may exist. Accordingly, the study falls within the recommendations of the Stern Review (2010) to provide additional research that can enhance understandings of false rape allegations, thus, enabling unfounded stereotypes to be challenged.

The study highlighted considerable consensus across participants' perspectives regarding alcohol-involved rape. When members of a drinking dyad are presented as equally intoxicated, there was a reduced willingness to label the depiction of nonconsensual sex as rape. While alcohol intoxication is not a defense to a sexual offence, it was evident that participants viewed comparable degrees of drunkenness as a factor that was sufficient to reasonably mitigate the defendant's responsibility for ascertaining consent. When nonconsensual sex took place between equally intoxicated individuals, that intercourse was collectively constructed to be the unpleasant, but somewhat understandable, outcome of extreme intoxication, raising clear concerns around the potential for alcohol-involved nonconsensual intercourse to be recategorized at trial as simply being constitutive of "bad sex."

The impact of alcohol on cognition and inhibitions was deemed central in encouraging individuals to partake in behaviors they would not if sober. The potential for sex to occur, care of a disinhibited state, and later be reformulated as nonconsensual (either intentionally or via more subtle processes) to account for that behavior underpinned the assumption that false rape reports are more likely when drinking. Throughout the discussions, it was evident that the focus remained on Michelle's actions

prior to the intercourse, including her failures for having not explicitly verbalized nonconsent and for placing herself in a vulnerable position. No equivalent arguments were made in relation to the steps Benjamin could have taken to ensure consent was present and how his extreme alcohol consumption may have increased his potential for misperceiving Michelle's sexual intentions. To this end, additional awareness raising is paramount to help articulate the legal stance on rape, [to articulate] the rape victim experience, to emphasize that intoxication is not a defense to a charge of rape, and to raise awareness around men also being instrumental in preventing nonconsensual experiences. Awareness raising should also focus specifically on attitudes held in relation to false allegations of rape and dissemination of the facts that can dispel such myths. It is acknowledged that further research is needed to help categorically clarify rates of false rape reporting and the factors associated with these allegations. Only then will the extent of the situation, and the contextual factors surrounding false reports, be fully understood.

//// DISCUSSION QUESTIONS

1. Did the students think that Benjamin should be found guilty of rape? Are there differences between male and female students in this assessment?

2. What role did voluntary intoxication play in evaluating the victim/offender status of Benjamin and Michelle?

3. How are false allegations of rape viewed in light of the intoxicated state of Benjamin and Michelle?

Note

1. Alcohol-involved intercourse is defined here as sex that takes place between parties when one or both have been drinking voluntarily and are extremely intoxicated.

Cases

Bree, 2 Crim. App. R. 13 [2007].

DPP v Majewski, AC 443 [1977].

R v Heard, EWCA Crim 2056 [2007].

R v Olugboja, 73 Cr. App. R. 344 [1981].

References

Abbey, A., Zawacki, T., Buck, P. O., Clinton, A. M., & McAuslan, P. (2004). Sexual assault and alcohol consumption: What do we know about their relationship and what types of research are still needed? *Aggression and Violent Behavior, 9*(3): 271–303.

Almandras, S. (2010). *Anonymity in rape cases.* London, England: House of Commons Library, Home Affairs.

Bancroft, A. (2012). Twitter reaction to Ched Evans case shows rape culture is alive and kicking. Retrieved from: http://www.guardian .co.uk/commentisfree/2012/apr/23/ched-evansrape-culture-twitter

Bellis, M. A., Hughes, K., Calafat, A., Juan, M., Ramon, A., Rodriguez, J. A., . . . Phillips-Howard, P. (2008). Sexual uses of alcohol and drugs and the associated health risks: A cross sectional study of young people in nine European cities. *BMC Public Health, 8:* 155–165.

Beres, M. A. (2007). Spontaneous sexual consent: An analysis of sexual consent literature. *Feminism and Psychology, 17*(1): 93–108.

Bondurant, B. (2001). University women's acknowledgement of rape: Individual, situational, and social factors. *Violence Against Women, 7*(3): 294–314.

Burton, S., Kelly, L., Kitzinger, J., & Regan, L. (1998). *Young people's attitudes towards violence, sex and relationships: A survey and focus group study.* Edinburgh, Scotland: Zero Tolerance Charitable Trust.

Cowan, S. (2008). The trouble with drink: Intoxication, (in)capacity, and the evaporation of consent to sex. *Akron Law Review, 41*(4): 899–922.

Doherty, K., & Anderson, I. (2004). Making sense of male rape: Constructions of gender, sexuality and experience of rape victims. *Journal of Community and Applied Social Psychology, 14*(2): 85–103.

Ellison, L., & Munro, V. (2009). Reacting to rape: Exploring mock jurors' assessments of complainant credibility. *British Journal of Criminology, 49*(2): 202–219.

Ellison, L., & Munro, V. (2010a). A stranger in the bushes, or an elephant in the room? Critical reflections upon received rape myth wisdom in the context of a mock jury study. *New Criminal Law Review, 13*(4): 781–801.

Ellison, L., & Munro, V. (2010b). Getting to (not) guilty: Examining juror's deliberative processes in, and beyond, the context of a mock rape trial. *Legal Studies, 30*(1): 74–97.

Elvin, J. (2008). Intoxication, capacity to consent, and the Sexual Offences Act 2003. *Kings Law Journal, 19*(1): 151–157.

Finch, E., & Munro, V. (2005). Juror stereotypes and blame attribution in rape cases involving intoxicants: Findings of a pilot study. *British Journal of Criminology, 45*(1): 25–38.

Finch, E., & Munro, V. (2006). Breaking boundaries? Sexual consent in the jury room. *Legal Studies, 26*(3): 303–320.

Finch, E., & Munro, V. (2007). The demon drink and the demonized woman: Socio-sexual stereotypes and responsibility attributions in rape trials involving intoxicants. *Social and Legal Studies, 16*(4): 591–614.

Frith, H. (2009). Sexual scripts, sexual refusals and rape. In M. Horvath & J. Brown (Eds.), *Rape: Challenging contemporary thinking* (p. 99–122). Devon, England: Willan.

Gavey, N. (2005). *Just sex? The cultural scaffolding of rape.* Sussex, England: Routledge.

Gavey, N., & Gow, V. (2001). "Cry wolf," cried the wolf: Constructing the issue of false rape allegations in New Zealand media texts. *Feminism and Psychology, 11*(3): 341–360.

George, W. H., & Stoner, S. A. (2000). Understanding acute alcohol effects on sexual behaviour. *Annual Review of Sex Research, 11:* 92–124.

Gunby, C., Carline, A., Bellis, M. A., & Beynon, C. (2012). Gender differences in alcohol-related non-consensual sex:

Cross-sectional analysis of a student population. *BMC Public Health, 12*(216): 1–12.

Gunby, C., Carline, A., & Beynon, C. (2010). Alcohol-related rape cases: Barristers' perspectives on the Sexual Offences Act 2003 and its impact on practice. *Journal of Criminal Law, 74:* 579–600.

Hale, M. (1736). *History of the pleas of the Crown.* London, England: Professional Books.

Home Office. (2002). *Protecting the public: Strengthening protection against sex offenders and reforming the law on sexual offences.* London, England: Home Office.

Howarth, C. (2002). Identity in whose eyes? The role of representations in identity construction. *Journal for the Theory of Behaviour, 32*(2): 145–162.

Humphreys, T. (2007). Perceptions of sexual consent: The impact of relationship history and gender. *Journal of Sex Research, 44*(4): 307–315.

Kahn, A., Jackson, J., Kully, C., Badger, K., & Halvorsen, J. (2003). Calling it rape: Differences in experiences of women who do or do not label their sexual assault as rape. *Psychology of Women Quarterly, 27*(3): 233–242.

Kelly, L. (2010). The (in)credible words of women: False allegations in European rape research. *Violence Against Women, 16*(12): 1345–1355.

Kelly, L., Lovett, J., & Regan, L. (2005). *A gap or a chasm? Attrition in reported rape cases. HORS 293.* London, England: Home Office.

Kershaw, C., Nicholas, S., & Walker, A. (2008). *Crime in England and Wales 2007/08: Findings from the British Crime Survey and police recorded crime.* London, England: Home Office.

Kitzinger, J. (2009). Rape in the media. In M. Horvath & J. Brown (Eds.), *Rape: Challenging contemporary thinking* (p. 74–98). Devon, England: Willan.

Kypri, K., Cronin, M., & Wright, C. S. (2005). Do university students drink more hazardously than their non-student peers? *Addiction, 100*(5): 1672–1677.

Lilith Project. (2008). *Just representation? Press reporting and the reality of rape.* London, England: Matrix Chambers.

Lonsway, K., Archambault, J., & Lisak, D. (2009). False reports: Moving beyond the issue to successfully investigate and prosecute non-stranger sexual assaults. *The Voice, 3*(1): 1–11.

Morgan, D. (1997). *Focus groups as qualitative research, qualitative research methods series.* Thousand Oaks, CA: Sage.

Neame, A. (2003). *Beyond drink spiking: Drug and alcohol facilitated sexual assault: Briefing number 2.* Melbourne, Australia: Australian Centre for the Study of Sexual Assault.

Norris, J., & Cubbins, L. (1992). Dating, drinking, and rape: Effects of victim's and assailant's alcohol consumption on judgments of their behaviour and traits. *Psychology of Women Quarterly, 16*(2): 179–191.

Office for Criminal Justice Reform. (2006). *Convicting rapists and protecting victims—Justice for victims of crime: A consultation paper.* London, England: Home Office.

Office for Criminal Justice Reform. (2007). *Convicting rapists and protecting victims—Justice for victims of rape: Responses to consultation.* London, England: Home Office.

Opinion Matters. (2010). Wake up to rape research summary report. Retrieved from: http://www.thehavens.co.uk/docs/Havens_Wake_Up_To_Rape_Report_Summary.pdf

Rumney, P. (2006). False allegations of rape. *Cambridge Law Journal, 65*(1): 128–158.

Sanders, A. (2012). Speech on the prosecution of rape and serious sexual offences by Alison Saunders, Chief Crown Prosecutor for London. Retrieved from: http://www.cps.gov.uk/news/articles/speech_on_the_prosecution_of_rape_and_serious_sexual_offences_by_alison_saunders_chief_crown_prosecutor_for_london/

Schneider, L., Mori, L., Lambert, P., & Wong, A. (2009). The role of gender and ethnicity in perceptions of rape and its after effects. *Sex Roles, 60*(5–6): 410–421.

Stern Review. (2010). *A report by Baroness Vivien Stern CBE of an independent review into how rape complaints are handled by public authorities in England and Wales.* London, England: Home Office.

Sumnall, H. R., Beynon, C. M., Conchie, S. M., Riley, S. C. E., & Cole, J. C. (2007). An investigation of the subjective experiences of sex after alcohol or drug intoxication. *Journal of Psychopharmacology, 21*(5): 525–537.

Temkin, J. (2002). *Rape and the legal process.* Oxford, England: Oxford University Press.

Temkin, J., & Krahe, B. (2008). *Sexual assault and the justice gap: A question of attitude.* Oxford, England: Hart.

Walby, S., & Allen, J. (2004). *Domestic violence, sexual assault and stalking: Findings from the British Crime Survey. Home Office Research Study 276.* London, England: Home Office.

Wall, A., & Schuller, R. (2000). Sexual assault and defendant/victim intoxication: Jurors perceptions of guilt. *Journal of Applied Social Psychology, 30*(2): 253–274.

Wallerstein, S. (2009). A drunken consent is still consent: Or is it? A critical analysis of the law on a drunken consent to sex following Bree. *Journal of Criminal Law, 73*: 318–344.

YouGov. (2010). Drunk and disorderly. Retrieved from: http://today.yougov.co.u/life/drunk-and-disorderly

Women, Gender, and Victimization
Intimate Partner Abuse and Stalking

Section Highlights

- Historical overview of intimate partner abuse (IPA)
- Contemporary issues in IPA
- Barriers to leaving abusive relationships
- The crime of stalking, its various forms, and its impact on women
- Legal remedies and policy implications for IPA and stalking

---

M uch of history has documented the presence of violence within relationships. Throughout history, women were considered the property of men. Wife beating was a legal and accepted form of discipline of women by their husbands. During ancient Roman times, men were allowed to beat their wives with "a rod or switch as long as its circumference is no greater than the girth of the base of the man's right thumb" (Stevenson & Love, 1999, table 1, 753 B.C.). The "rule of thumb" continued as a guiding principle of legalized wife beating throughout early European history and appeared in English common-law practices, which influenced the legal structures of the early settlers in America. While small movements against wife beating appear in the United States throughout the 18th and 19th century, it was not until 1871 that Alabama and Massachusetts became the first states to take away the legal right of men to beat their wives. However, significant resistance still existed in many states on the grounds that the government should not interfere in the family environment. In 1882, wife beating became a crime in the state of Maryland. While defining wife beating as a crime meant that the act would receive criminal consequences, the enforcement of the act as a crime was limited, and husbands rarely received any significant penalties for their actions.

The rise of the feminist movement in the late 1960s and early 1970s gave a foundation for the **battered women's movement**. Shelters and counseling programs began to appear throughout the United States during the 1970s; however, these efforts were small in scale, and the need for assistance significantly outweighed the availability of services. While police officers across the nation began to receive training about domestic violence calls for service, most departments had a nonarrest policy toward cases of domestic violence, because many officers saw their role as a peacemaker or interventionist rather than as an agent of criminal justice. In these cases, homicide rates continued to increase because of the murders of women at the hands of their intimate partners, and more officers were dying in the line of duty responding to domestic violence calls.

The grassroots battered women's movement of the 1970s led to systemic changes in how the police and courts handled cases of domestic violence. Many of these changes occurred in response to research findings by the **Minneapolis Domestic Violence Experiment** (MDVE). The MDVE illustrated that when an arrest was made in a misdemeanor domestic violence incident, recidivism rates were significantly lower compared to cases in which police simply "counseled" the aggressor (Sherman & Berk, 1984). Many departments ushered in new policies based on these findings. However, replication studies did not produce similar experiences and instead indicated that arresting the offender led to increases in violence.

Throughout the 1980s, state and nonprofit task forces assembled to discuss the issues of intimate partner abuse. By 1989, the United States had over 1,200 programs for battered women and provided shelter housing to over 300,000 women and children each year (Dobash & Dobash, 1992; Stevenson & Love, 1999). In 1994, Congress passed the **Violence Against Women Act** (VAWA) as part of the Federal Crime Victims Act. The VAWA provided funding for battered women's shelters and outreach education, as well as funding for domestic violence training for police and court personnel. It also provided the opportunity for victims to sue for civil damages as a result of violent acts perpetrated against them. In 1995, the Office on Violence Against Women (OVW) was created within the U.S. Department of Justice and today is charged with administering grant programs aimed at research and community programming toward eradicating intimate domestic and intimate partner abuse in our communities (Office on Violence Against Women [OVW], n.d.). Table 4.1 highlights the allocation of resources and the provision of services through the different reauthorizations of the Violence Against Women Act.

Defining and Identifying Intimate Partner Abuse

A number of different terms have been used to identify acts of violence against women. Many of these descriptions fall short in capturing the multifaceted nature of these abusive acts. The term *wife battering* fails to identify cases of violence outside of marriage, such as violent relationships between cohabiting individuals, dating violence, or even victims who were previously married to their batterer. Excluding these individuals from the official definition of *battered* often denies these victims any legal protections or services. The most common term used in recent history is *domestic violence*. However, this term combines the crime of woman battering with other contexts of abuse found within a home environment, such as the abuse of children or grandparents. Today, many scholars and community activists prefer the term **intimate partner abuse** (IPA) because it captures any form of abuse between individuals who currently have, or have previously had, an intimate relationship (Belknap, 2007). However, the use of these terms can vary significantly between different research studies, which can make it difficult to understand the extent of these victimizations. For example, the Centers for Disease Control and Prevention defines intimate partner abuse as "physical, sexual or psychological harm by a current or former partner or spouse" (Centers for Disease Control and Prevention [CDC], n.d., para. 1). Meanwhile, the National Violence Against Women survey extended the definition of intimate partner abuse to include cases of rape/sexual assault, physical assault, and stalking behaviors. Other agencies such as the Bureau of Justice Statistics (2006) include additional crimes within the discussion of IPA, such as homicides and robberies involving intimate partners (Catalano, 2012).

According to the National Crime Victimization Survey, an estimated 1.3 million women are physically victimized each year by a current or former intimate partner. In the majority of cases, men are the aggressor and women are

Table 4.1 • The Violence Against Women Act

1994	**Violent Crime Control and Law Enforcement Act of 1994** **Title IV—Violence Against Women** • Allocated $1.6 billion in grant funds (1994–2000) for investigation and prosecution of violent crimes against women, community services for victims, and the creation of domestic violence helplines • Created new laws that target violators of civil restraining orders and that make interstate domestic violence a federal crime • Allows offenders to use civil justice in cases that prosecutors decline to prosecute • Established the Office on Violence Against Women within the Department of Justice
2000	**Victims of Trafficking and Violence Protection Act of 2000** **Division B—Violence Against Women Act** • Allocated $3.33 billion in grant funds (2001–2005) • Enhanced federal laws for domestic violence and stalking • Added protections for immigrant victims • Added new programs for elderly and disabled victims • Included victims of dating violence into VAWA protections and services
2005	**Violence Against Women Act and Department of Justice Reauthorization Act of 2005** • Allocated $3.935 billion in grant funds (2007–2011) • Created repeat offender penalties • Added protections for trafficked victims • Provides housing resources for victims • Enhanced resources for American Indian and Alaska Native populations • Provides increased training for health care providers to recognize signs of domestic violence • Enhanced protections for illegal immigrant victims
2013	**Violence Against Women Act Reauthorization of 2013** • Allocated $3.378 billion in grant funds (2013–2018) • Continues funding for grants for research and services • Maintains and expands housing protections • Expands options for tribal courts to address domestic violence • Requires reporting procedures for dating violence on college campuses • Prohibits discrimination for LGBT victims in accessing services • Maintains and increases protections for immigrant victims

SOURCES: Seghetti, L. M., & Bjelopera, J. P. (2012). The Violence Against Women Act: Overview, legislation and federal funding. Congressional Research Service. Retrieved from http://www.fas.org/sgp/crs/misc/R42499.pdf.; National Coalition Against Domestic Violence. (2006). Comparison of VAWA 1994, VAWA 2000 and VAWA 2005 Reauthorization Bill. Retrieved from http://www.ncadv.org/files/VAWA_94_00_05.pdf; Office on Violence Against Women. (n.d.). VAWA 2013 summary: Changes to OVW-administered grant programs. Retrieved from http://www.ncdsv.org/images/OVW_VAWA+2013+summary+changes+to+OVW-administered+Grant+Programs.pdf

© Viviane Moos/CORBIS

▲ **Photo 4.1** Intimate partner violence is composed of a variety of different behaviors used by an offender to have power and control over their victim. These include physical, sexual, emotional, and psychological abuse.

the victim (85%)[1] (CDC, 2003). Alas, most crimes of intimate partner abuse are considered a misdemeanor offense, even for repeat offenders. In these cases, prosecutors charge offenders with the crime of simple assault (77.9% of cases), which carries with it a penalty of no more than one year in jail (Klein, 2004; Smith & Farole, 2009).

Much of the abuse within an intimate relationship occurs behind closed doors and is not visible to the community. This makes it difficult for researchers to measure the extent of these acts or for community agencies to provide outreach and services for victims. Many are reluctant to report cases of abuse to anyone (police, friends, or family members) due to the high levels of shame that they feel as a result of the abuse. Others believe that the police will be unable to help. This belief is not unfounded. Research indicates that in some cases, the police scolded victims for not following through on previous court cases. Other victims were either blamed for causing the violence or were told to fix the relationship with the offender (Fleury-Steiner, Bybee, Sullivan, Belknap, & Melton, 2006).

Most people think of physical battering/abuse as the major component of intimate partner abuse. However, abuse between intimates runs much deeper than physical violence. Perhaps one of the most common (and some would argue the most damaging in terms of long-term abuse and healing) is **emotional abuse**. Those who batter their partner emotionally may call them derogatory names, prevent them from working or attending school, or limit access to family members and friends. An abuser may control the finances and limit access and information regarding money, which in turn makes the victim dependent on the perpetrator. Emotional abuse is a way in which perpetrators seek to control their victims, whether it be in telling them what to wear, where to go, or what to do. They may act jealous or possessive of their partner. In many cases, emotional abuse turns violent toward the victim, child(ren), or pet(s). Following acts of physical or sexual violence, the emotional abuse continues when a batterer blames the victim for the violent behavior by suggesting that "she made him do it" or by telling the victim that "you deserve it." Research indicates that emotional abuse is more common with younger males, and females and women are more likely to experience social isolation and property damage within the context of emotional abuse compared to men (Karakurt & Silver, 2013). Emotional abuse is particularly damaging because it robs the victim of her self-esteem and self-confidence. In many cases, victims fail to identify that they are victims of intimate partner abuse if they do not experience physical violence. Yet the scars left by emotional abuse are significant and long lasting. Unfortunately, few laws characterize the acts of emotional abuse as a criminal offense.

Economic abuse is another tool in which perpetrators of intimate partner abuse try and control their partner. Economic abuse involves acts that damage the victim's ability to be self-sufficient. It can also serve as a way to make it difficult for a victim to leave their batterer. Economic abuse includes acts such as restricting access to the family's bank account or prohibiting individuals from having their own bank account. This also extends to both jeopardizing one's employment status or prohibiting them from working, which only makes the individual more dependent on the abuser. While much of the research has looked at economic abuse from a very narrow view (and accordingly, the available data posits that such

[1]Given that the majority of data find men as the perpetrator and women as the victim, this text generally uses the term *he* to refer to the abuser and the term *she* as the victim. The use of these terms is not meant to ignore male victims of violence or abuse within same-sex relationships but only to characterize the majority of cases of intimate partner abuse.

abuse is rare), recent studies have attempted to increase the measurements of this phenomenon. These findings acknowledge that economic abuse is just as common as physical and emotional abuse (Postmus, Plummer, & Stylianou, 2015).

For a small number of women, physical violence in an intimate relationship escalates to murder. For these women, death was the culmination of a relationship that had been violent over time, and in many cases, the violence occurred on a frequent basis. The presence of a weapon significantly increases the risk of homicide, because women who are threatened or assaulted with a gun or other weapon are 20 times more likely to be killed (Campbell et al., 2003). Three-fourths of intimate partner homicide victims had tried to leave their abusers, refuting the common question of "why doesn't she leave?" While many of these women had previously sought help and protection from their batterers' abuse, their efforts failed (Block, 2003).

Spotlight on IPA and the NFL

In chapter two, you learned about the case of Ray Rice, who was suspended from the NFL for a domestic incident involving his then fiancée, Janay Rice. However, this is not the only incident of intimate partner abuse involving a football star. In fact, there are several active players that have a history of domestic violence. Between 2000 and 2014, there were 83 domestic violence arrests involving 80 players. Given that there are a maximum of 53 players on each of the 32 teams, this means that approximately 20% of all players in the NFL have a history of domestic violence. Indeed, cases of this nature make up 55.4% of all arrests within the league (McCann, 2014).

Brandon Marshall, who most recently played for the New York Jets, has had nine reported incidents related to intimate partner abuse and has been arrested on three separate occasions. In 2007, he was arrested on suspicion of domestic violence against his then girlfriend (Rasheedah Watley) and was arrested in 2009 for disorderly conduct during a fight with his fiancée (Michi Nogami-Campbell). In 2011, Marshall was stabbed by Nogami-Campbell, who claimed that she was acting in self-defense. During that same year, Marshall was diagnosed with borderline personality disorder. His most recent incident was in 2012, when he was accused of striking a woman at a club in New York City. None of these incidents led to a criminal conviction, though he was suspended for one game by the NFL in 2008. Since then, he has made several public appearances related to domestic violence awareness and prevention to speak out about his actions and history with violence. As a free agent, he is being considered by teams such as the Baltimore Ravens, which has not drafted or signed anyone with a history of domestic violence since the events involving Ray Rice in 2014 (Hensley, 2017). In the first three months of 2017, there were two cases involving arrests of active players for intimate partner violence: Ethan Westbrooks and Rodney Astin. Westbrooks, who was most recently a defensive tackle with the LA Rams, was booked on suspicion of domestic violence stemming from an incident with the mother of his child. While the charges were ultimately dropped, Westbrooks remains a free agent (McAtee, 2017). A third incident involved Trent Richardson (last played for the Ravens in 2014). Richardson was arrested and charged with third-degree domestic violence in Alabama (Sports Illustrated, 2017).

In August 2014, NFL Commissioner Roger Goodell sent a letter to all team owners about a new disciplinary policy within the National Football League in cases of intimate partner abuse and sexually based offenses. Any player that is arrested and charged with one of these offenses must undergo a personal evaluation, which could include a requirement for counseling or other services. Players would also be suspended without pay for six games. Subsequent offenses would result in a banishment from the NFL, though a player could apply for reinstatement after one year (Pelissero, 2014). However, the policy appears to be applied unevenly. Since its introduction, the six-game policy has only been applied in two of the eighteen allegations of domestic violence. Former Detroit Lions offensive lineman Rodney Austin was found guilty on domestic violence charges following a fight with his girlfriend. While he was suspended by the league (and was released by the Lions), Exekiel Elliott (Dallas Cowboys) and Ra'Shede Hageman (Atlanta Falcons) were both allowed to continue to play during the 2016–2017 post-season despite pending investigations (Pilon, 2017).

The Cycle of Violence

The greatest tool of perpetrators of intimate partner abuse is their ability to have power and control over their victim. To explain how violence and abuse occur in an intimate relationship, Lenore Walker (1979) conceptualized the **cycle of violence**. The cycle of violence is made up of three distinct time frames (see Figure 4.1). The first is referred to as tension building, where a batterer increases control over a victim. As anger begins to build for the perpetrator, the victim tries to keep her partner calm. She also minimizes any problems in the relationship. During this time, the victim may feel as though she is walking on eggshells because the tension between her and her partner is high. It is during the second time frame, referred to as the abusive incident, where the major incident of battering occurs. During this period, the batterer is highly abusive, and engages in an act of violence toward the victim. Following the abusive incident, the perpetrator moves to stage three, which is often described as the honeymoon period. During this stage, the offender is apologetic to the victim for causing harm. He often is loving and attentive and promises to change his behavior. In this stage, the perpetrator is viewed as sincere and in many cases is forgiven by the victim. Unfortunately, the honeymoon phase does not last forever, and in many cases of intimate partner abuse, the cycle begins again, tensions increase, and additional acts of violence occur. Over time, the honeymoon stage may disappear entirely.

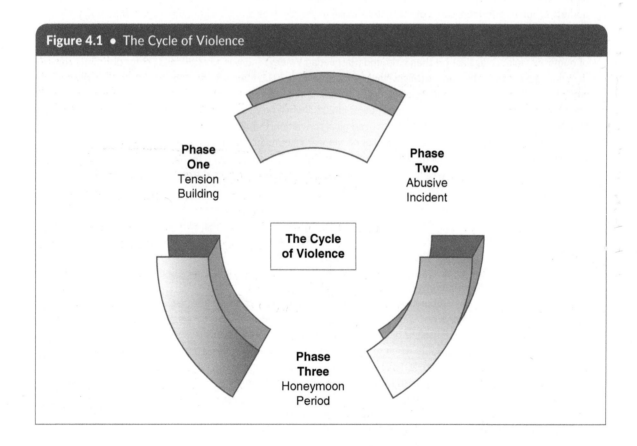

Figure 4.1 • The Cycle of Violence

Victims of Intimate Partner Abuse

Intimate partner abuse can impact victims of any sex, age, race, ethnicity, religion, nationality, and sexual orientation. Offenders who perpetuate these acts of violence are spouses, intimates (boyfriend/girlfriend, cohabiting partners), and ex-intimates. This section highlights some of the different relationship types and populations where IPA occurs. The section also includes a discussion of the challenges that victims face within intimate partner abuse.

Dating Violence

While initial laws on intimate partner abuse recognized only physical violence between married couples, recent laws have been changed to reflect the variety of relationship types where intimate partner abuse can occur. One such example is **dating violence**. Even though two people are unmarried and may or may not be living together, such relationships are not immune from violence. Prevalence rates of dating violence vary. According to the Centers for Disease Control and Prevention High School Youth Risk Behavior Survey, 11.7% of girls and 7.4% of boys have experienced physical violence within a dating relationship. Sexual violence in a dating relationship also impacts 15.6% of girls and 5.4% of boys (CDC, 2015). In contrast, research on dating violence on college campuses indicate that 32% of students report a history of dating violence in a previous relationship, and 21% of students indicate that they currently experience violence in their dating relationship (Sellers & Bromley, 1996). Similar results are noted from Copp, Giordano, Longmore, & Manning (2015) who found that 35% of youth had experienced some form of violence in either their current or most recent dating relationship. Teens, in particular, are at high risk for dating violence as a result of their inexperience in relationships and their heightened views of "romantic love," combined with a desire to be independent from their parents (Alabama Coalition Against Domestic Violence [ACADV], n.d.). Given the severity of this issue, it is concerning that few parents believe that dating violence is a significant issue for their children (Women's Health, 2004). The early onset of violence and abuse in a relationship continues for victims into adulthood, because adolescent victims often find themselves in a pattern of abusive relationships as adults (Silverman, Raj, Mucci, & Hathaway, 2001).

Children of Intimate Partner Abuse

Children are significantly affected by violence within the home environment, even if they are not the direct victims of the abuse. Research indicates that 68% to 87% of incidents involving intimate partner abuse occur while children are present (Raphael, 2000). One battered woman spoke of the effects this victimization has on children: "Our kids have problems dealing with us. When we argue and fight in front of them, when they see our husbands humiliating, beating, and cursing us, they will get affected. They will learn everything they see" (Sullivan, Senturia, Negash, Shiu-Thornton, & Giday, 2005, p. 928).

Children who reside in a home where violence is present tend to suffer from a variety of negative mental health outcomes, such as feelings of low self-worth, depression, and anxiety. Affected children often suffer in academic settings and have higher rates of aggressive behavior (Goddard & Bedi, 2010). Additionally, many children exposed to violence at a young age continue the cycle of violence into adulthood, because they often find themselves in violent relationships of their own. Research indicates that 30% of young boys who are exposed to acts of intimate partner abuse will engage in violence against an intimate partner later in life. In an effort to respond to families in need, many agencies that act as advocates for victims of intimate partner violence are connecting with child welfare agencies to provide a continuum of care for children and their families. However, it is important for agencies to make sure that they do not overemphasize this risk factor and label these children as potential offenders and victims, because it could lead to a self-fulfilling prophecy (Boyd, 2001).

LGBTQ and Intimate Partner Abuse

While the majority of intimate partner abuse involves a female victim and a male offender, data indicate that battering also occurs in same-sex relationships. The National Crime Victimization survey found that 3% of females who experienced IPA were victimized by another woman, while 16% of male victims were abused by their male counterpart (Catalano, 2007). However, these official statistics may not necessarily reflect the reality of this issue. Research on teen dating violence note that LGBTQ youth have significantly higher rates compared to heterosexual youth. Figure 4.2 highlights data for dating violence for LGBTQ and heterosexual youth. Is same-sex IPA a rare phenomenon (as official data may suggest), or is this issue more common yet hidden within this community? Like heterosexual victims of intimate partner abuse, many same-sex victims are reluctant to report their abuse. The decision to report same-sex IPA involves the same challenges as a heterosexual battering relationship. But these challenges are enhanced for LGBT victims because it exposes their sexual orientation to police, community organizations, peers, and family members (Irwin, 2008).

Research indicates that female victims of **same-sex intimate partner abuse** face many of the same risk factors for violence as heterosexual battering relationships. Figure 4.3 presents the power and control wheel for the LGBTQ community. While heterosexual IPA relationships face many of these same factors such as economic abuse, emotional abuse, and coercion, this figure adds factors such as heterosexism, external homophobia, and internalized homophobia as (further) influences on LGBTQ IPA relationships. For some victims, these additional factors can complicate their efforts to find support within the LGBTQ community. As one victim notes, "I think that people are very afraid to add to (the stigma of being queer) by saying . . . not only are we queer but we also have violence in our relationships and in our community" (Bornstein, Fawcett, Sullivan, Senturia, & Shiu-Thornton, 2006, p. 169). In addition, the connection that an IPA victim has to the LGBTQ community (or lack thereof) can also play a role in disclosure practices. For example, women who experienced abuse within the context of their first lesbian

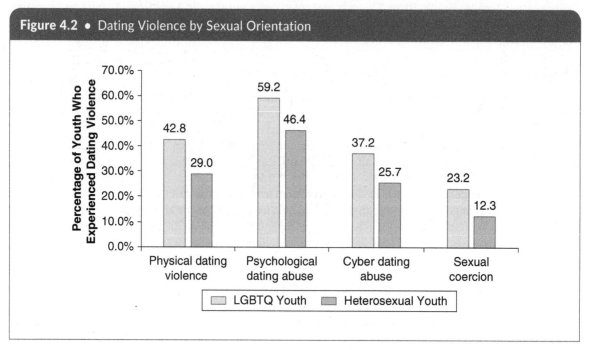

Figure 4.2 • Dating Violence by Sexual Orientation

SOURCE: Dank, M. Lachman, P., Zweig, J. M., & Yahner, J. (2014). Dating violence experiences of lesbian, gay, bisexual, and transgender youth. *Journal of Youth Adolescence, 43*: 846–857.

relationship tended to express fear about discrimination. Since many of these victims lacked a connection to the LGBTQ community, some wondered whether the abuse was a normal component of a lesbian relationship. This fear of being "outed" also led some victims to stay in the relationship for a longer period of time (Irwin, 2008). In comparison, women who had strong networks or attachments with the LGBTQ community were more likely to seek out help when their relationships turned violent (Hardesty, Oswald, Khaw, & Fonseca, 2011).

Given that LGBTQ victims of intimate partner abuse are in the minority, few programs and services exist to meet the unique needs of this population. In addition, resources that are often available to heterosexual victims of

Figure 4.3 • Lesbian/Gay Power and Control Wheel

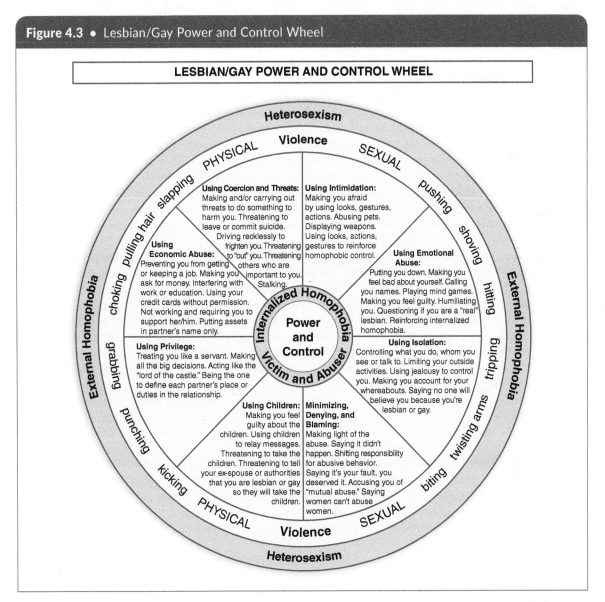

SOURCE: Developed by Roe & Jagodinsky, Texas Council on Family Violence. Adapted from the Power & Control and Equity Wheels developed by the Domestic Abuse Intervention Project.

IPA are expressly denied for the LGBTQ population. Three states have explicitly denied LGBT victims from seeking out a protective order in cases involving IPA (Montana, Louisiana, and South Carolina). Only one state (Hawaii) specifically includes language that allows LGBTQ individuals to seek out a **restraining order** against a current or former intimate. The remaining laws at the state level are silent on the issue because they neither permit nor exclude victims from seeking a restraining order. In these cases, the interpretation of the law is left up to the judiciary (American Bar Association Commission on Domestic Violence, 2008). Even service providers may view same-sex IPA incidents as less serious than cases of heterosexual IPA. This assumption can impact the level and type of services provided by an agency (Brown & Groscup, 2009). Effective programming needs to address the use of gender-role stereotypes when developing education and intervention efforts for the community. Agencies also need to develop "queer-specific" services to meet the needs for the LGBT community (Bornstein et al., 2006).

Effects of Race and Ethnicity on Intimate Partner Abuse

Issues of race and ethnicity add an additional lens through which one can view issues of intimate partner violence. While much of the early research on intimate partner violence focused exclusively on the relationships of gender inequality as a cause of abuse, the inclusion of race and ethnicity (and socioeconomic status) adds additional issues for consideration. For women of color, issues of gender inequality become secondary in the discussion of what it means to be a battered woman. Here, scholars acknowledge the role of cultural differences and structural inequality in understanding the experiences of IPV in ethnically diverse communities (Sokoloff, 2004). When investigating issues of violence among women of color, it is important that scholars not limit their discussions to race and ethnicity. Rather, research needs to reflect on the collision of a number of different factors, as "age, employment status, residence, poverty, social embeddedness, and isolation combine to explain higher rates of abuse within black communities—not race or culture per se" (Sokoloff, 2004, p. 141).

As a population, Black women are at an increased risk of being victimized in cases of intimate partner violence. Scholars are quick to point out that it is not race that affects whether one is more likely to be abused by a partner. Rather, economic and social marginalization can place women of color at an increased risk for victimization (West, 2004). Research by Potter (2007b) highlights how interracial abuse among Black women and men is related to feelings of being "devalued" by social stereotypes about "the Black man." Since men of color experience high levels of discrimination by society, many victims justify the violent acts that are perpetuated by their intimate partner. This can also impact the decision to seek assistance from the criminal justice system as some women of color may not want to further criminalize the men in their communities, because they are already disproportionately represented within the correctional system (Nash, 2006).

Understanding issues of intimate partner violence in the Asian community presents a number of challenges. First, it is difficult to determine how prevalent the issue is, because most surveys collect data on Asian or Asian-American/Pacific Islanders within a single category and do not highlight some of the unique differences between the different ethnic groups that fall under this label. Such studies, such as the National Violence Against Women Survey, note that the lifetime rate of violence for this combined group is much lower than for other groups (Tjaden & Thoennes, 2006). Yet others have noted that Chinese Americans have higher rates of intimate partner violence compared to Vietnamese or Filipino Americans (Cho, 2012a). In addition, there are unique cultural issues within Asian communities that can make identifying and reporting intimate partner abuse as an act of violence difficult. This can make delivering services to this community particularly challenging (Yoshihama, Ramakrishnan, Hammock, & Khaliq, 2012).

Women who experience IPA may be faced with a multitude of physical and psychological issues, and race and ethnicity can affect whether a victim will seek out support and resources from social service agencies, such as therapeutic and shelter resources. Here, research indicates that Black women were significantly more likely to use emergency hospital services, police assistance, and housing assistance, compared to White and Hispanic/Latina women. For example, 65.4% of Black IPA females indicated that they had used housing assistance during the past year, compared to only 26.9% of White IPA women and 7.7% of Hispanic/Latina IPA women (Lipsky, Caetano, Field, & Larkin, 2006). Meanwhile, Asian victims of IPA are less likely to use mental health services than Latinas (Cho, 2012b). Women of color also express a need for culturally relevant support in their communities. For example, traditional therapeutic communities may be ineffective for some victims of violence: "Black folks don't 'do' group. We 'do' church. . . . I will not sit there and [tell] all these White women my business. [Blacks] don't talk about our stuff [in public]—and especially to White folks" (Nash, 2006, p. 1437).

Unique Issues for Immigrant Victims of Intimate Partner Abuse

While intimate partner abuse is an issue for any community, the effects are particularly significant for immigrant communities. Research indicates that men in these communities often batter their partner as a way to regain control and power in their lives, particularly when their immigrant status has deprived them of this social standing. Battering becomes a way in which these men regain their sense of masculinity. For many, the education and training they may have received in their home countries does not easily transfer on their arrival to the United States. As Bui and Morash (2008) note, "Vietnamese immigrant men have lost power after immigrating to the United States. Many felt bad because they lack[ed] language and occupational skills and could not support their families" (p. 202).

Faced with their husband's inability to find a job to support the family, many immigrant women are faced with the need to work, which many immigrant men find to be in opposition to traditional cultural roles and a threat to their status within the family. This strain against traditional roles leads to violence. Many men blame the American culture for the gender clash occurring in their relationships. However, many women accept the violence as part of the relationship, because such behavior is considered normative for their culture. For example, violence is accepted behavior in Vietnamese traditional cultures, wherein men are seen as aggressive warriors and women are seen as passive and meek. Research on intimate partner violence within this community reveals high levels of verbal (75%), physical (63%), and sexual abuse (46%), with 37% experiencing both physical and sexual abuse (Bui & Morash, 2008). Within immigrant Asian communities, feelings of shame significantly impact the help-seeking behaviors. One woman characterizes these fears: "I do not share with others because if I share with someone, then that someone might tell another person who might happen to know my mother-in-law and so on. And the news will spread and it will bring bad name to my family" (Tonsing & Barn, 2016, p. 5)

For Ethiopian-immigrant women, the violent behavior of men is also accepted within the community, making it difficult for women to develop an understanding that battering is a crime and that they should seek out services. Help seeking is seen as a complaint by women, and in such cases, members of the community turn to support the perpetrator, not the victim (Sullivan et al., 2005). Intimate partner abuse is also discussed as a normal part of relationships for Russian-immigrant women. One woman stated that domestic violence "is part of the destiny, and you have to tolerate it" (Crandall, Senturia, Sullivan, & Shiu-Thornton, 2005, p. 945). These cultural expectations may inhibit women from seeking out assistance, because it would bring shame on the victim and her family, both immediate and extended. Strict gender-role expectations may lead women to believe that they do not have the right to disobey their partner, which legitimizes the abuse.

Many perpetrators use the fear of deportation to prevent victims from leaving an abusive relationship. Many Latina immigrant women are likely to remain in a battering relationship for a longer period of time due to fear surrounding their undocumented immigration status. In these cases, Latina immigrants are less likely to seek out help for intimate partner abuse compared to Latina nonimmigrants (Ingram, 2007). While the 2005 reauthorization of the Violence Against Women Act increased the protection of immigrant women who are victims of a crime (including domestic violence), it is unclear how many immigrant women are aware of these protections.

Perpetrators often build on a negative experience of law enforcement from their home country in an effort to create a sense of distrust of the U.S. legal system. For many Vietnamese women, a call to the police for help was a last resort and often done not to facilitate an arrest but rather to improve the relationship between the perpetrator and the victim by stopping the violence. Most victims did not want to have their partner arrested or prosecuted for domestic violence but rather they wanted to send a message that the abuse was wrong. Unfortunately, many were reluctant to seek police intervention because they feared the civil implications that a criminal record would bring, particularly in jurisdictions with mandatory arrest policies (Bui, 2007).

Language barriers may also affect victims' ability to seek help, because they may not be able to communicate with law enforcement and court personnel, particularly when resources for translators may be significantly limited (National Coalition Against Domestic Violence, n.d.). Lack of language skills, combined with a lack of understanding of the American legal system, also can prevent an immigrant/refugee woman from leaving her violent relationship. Not only may a victim not know what services are available; she may not understand how to navigate social systems, such as welfare and housing, and educational opportunities that are necessary in order to achieve economic independence from her batterer (Sullivan et al., 2005). In an effort to expand access to the courts in domestic violence cases, California amended its domestic violence laws in 2001 to ensure that legal documents in domestic violence cases would be made available in multiple languages. Today, paperwork to request a restraining order and other related documents is available in five different languages: English, Chinese, Spanish, Vietnamese, and Korean.[2]

Spotlight on Intimate Partner Abuse in India

Intimate partner abuse is a worldwide problem. Alas, issues such as patriarchy, power, and control know no geographical boundaries. In many countries, it is these values about women that exacerbate the abuse of women. Consider the case of India. As in many regions of the world, the marital relationship is considered private, and there are few laws against the abuse of women. Indeed, the cultural values reign supreme and essentially promote the power differential between men and women. It is some of these cultural indicators, such as the dowry and arranged marriages, that can encourage violence. For many families, the arranged marriage is an opportunity for the bride's family to increase their social status within the community because they "marry up" their daughters.

The inability to provide an adequate dowry then serves as a trigger for the abuse. For these women, the abuse begins almost as soon as the marriage begins (44% indicate that it began within a month of the marriage), and it is a regular occurrence. Seventy-nine percent of the women reported abuse within their marriage on a daily basis and another 15.6% once every two days. In many cases, the violence comes not only from her husband but also her in-laws. Women were not only physically beaten (100%) but were also threatened by knives and other weapons (47.8%). Psychological violence was also a common tactic because they were prohibited from contacting their families, friends, and even their own children (82.2%; Panchanadeswaran & Koverola, 2005).

Given the cultural context for these abusive relationships, women seek help from a variety of sources. For those women that do leave these abusive relationships, community legal aid and counseling shelters are the most helpful in exiting an abusive situation. The police are essentially useless in dealing with these incidents. Meanwhile, families are only moderately helpful because they are caught up within maintaining their image in the community:

> My parents and sister were very supportive and provided shelter from [sic] my daughter and me whenever we went. But after 3–4 days, my parents would always ask me to go back and try to reconcile with my husband. They were worried that if I stayed longer, he would not take me back . . . and the family honor will be affected, and I would be a stigma to the family and no one would marry my younger sister. (Panchanadeswaran & Koverola, 2005, p. 750)

---

[2]Each state has different policies on the availability of legal documents in languages other than English. Forms for the State of California are located at http:www.courtinfo.ca.gov.

Barriers to Leaving an Abusive Relationship

When hearing of cases of domestic violence, many members of the public ask, "Why doesn't she just leave?" Leaving a relationship where intimate partner abuse is present is a difficult and complex process. There are many issues that a victim must face. One of the greatest barriers to leaving a battering relationship is the financial limitations that victims face. Women who lack economic self-sufficiency are less likely to report intimate partner abuse and less likely to leave the relationship. The support from extended family and friends can play a critical role in a victim's ability to successfully depart from an abusive partner. However, these same individuals can increase the potential for victim blaming and a withdrawal of support and empathy if the victim returns to the relationship (Moe, 2007).

Inherent in the question of "why doesn't she just leave?" is the question of "why does she stay?" This question places the responsibility on the victim for staying with a violent partner rather than focusing on why her partner chooses to be violent. The reality is that many women do leave their batterers. The average battered woman leaves seven to eight times before she is successful in leaving for good (ACADV, n.d.). Violence does not always end when women report their crimes or leave their abuser. For some women, the levels of violence increase; women who were separated from their batterers reported higher rates of violence, compared to women who were married or divorced from their batterer (Catalano, 2007). These acts of violence can not only involve the initial victim but also can spread out, placing children, friends, and extended family members of the woman at risk. Concerns regarding these potential increases in violence may influence these women to remain in the relationship out of concern for their loved ones.

For some women, their children are the reason why they leave an abusive situation and seek help. For some women, the desire to provide their children with a happy childhood was their motivation to leave. For others, it was to demonstrate that abusive and violent behaviors are not normal parts of a healthy relationship. One woman states: "I wouldn't have left if it wasn't for her because I saw the damage that I was . . . she was . . . going through and when she told me she was scared, that really explained why I try not to be scared of her father" (Stephens & Melton, 2016, p. 7). At the same time, the desire to maintain the family unit can also delay help-seeking behaviors.

> I think they impact me a lot from the past because they love their dad and he is a good dad for them . . . I have always tried to keep my family together and it is really hard for them to be away from him. Like they cry for him and it hurts, you know, but I think this time, it's just getting too bad. I don't want them to end up seeing the violence. You know . . . I mean they can hear him call me names and stuff like that, you know, but they love their dad and so I think that['s] a lot of the reason why I just stayed (Stephens & Melton, 2016, p. 8).

Given that a significant portion of intimate partner abuse occurs in young adulthood, how do factors such as age and relationship status impact the decision to leave these relationships? It is interesting to note that the presence of physical violence did not impact the decision to stay in or leave a relationship for these youth. Rather, it was experiences with other negative relationship characteristics, such as emotional abuse or difficulties in communication that led to the ending of the relationship. The acceptance of the significant other by parents and peers also had an impact on this decision; those whose significant other was viewed favorably by their family and friends were more likely to stay, while negative perceptions were more likely to influence the decision to leave the relationship. Youth were also more likely to exit these relationships if they believed there was an opportunity to meet someone new.

In their search for support, some women may turn toward religious institutions for assistance in leaving a relationship characterized by intimate partner abuse. For many women, their faith gives them strength to leave (Wang, Horne, Levitt, & Klesges, 2009). Unfortunately, for some of these women, their spirituality may hinder their abilities to leave. Cultural scripts of some religious doctrines may encourage women to try to resolve the struggles of their relationship, because divorce and separation are not viewed as acceptable under the eyes of the church.

©Thinkstock/BananaStock

▲ **Photo 4.2** A domestic violence victim wears an alarm necklace that silently signals police in event of danger. Domestic violence agencies distribute the devices, called the A.W.A.R.E. alarm, which stands for Abused Women's Active Response Emergency.

Here, congregations encourage women to forgive the violence that their partners display (Potter, 2007a). Additionally, clergy may be ill equipped to deal with the issue of intimate partner abuse within their congregations because of a lack of understanding of the realities of the problem and limited training on service and support needs (Shannon-Lewy & Dull, 2005).

Many women struggle with their decision to leave an abusive relationship. Some women may still love their partner, despite the violence that exists within the relationship. Others may hope that their partner will change and believe the promises made by their loved one for a different life. In some multicultural communities, there is a greater pressure outside of the family unit to return to one's batterer. Members of these communities often place significant pressures on victims to reunite with their batterer (Sullivan

et al., 2005). For many women, they fear what their lives will be like without their partner. These fears may include how they will support themselves (and their children), the possibility that future relationships will have similar results, and even fear of loneliness. A key to successfully leaving an abusive relationship is the victim's belief that she will be better off without her batterer and have the confidence to make a new life free from violence.

Victim Experiences With Police and Corrections

As the criminal justice system becomes more involved in cases of intimate partner abuse, scholars have begun to ask questions about the victim experience with the criminal justice system. The findings of these studies vary. While some suggest that victims are satisfied by their experience with the police and courts in these cases, others highlight areas for significant improvement within the justice process.

The first step in asking for assistance often involves the police. The victim can either request the presence of the police or the police may be summoned on behalf of a victim, usually by a neighbor or other family member. Unlike cases where a third party reports the abuse, victims who initiate contact with the police are more likely to want to press charges against their assailant (Boivin & Leclerc, 2016). Research on this topic provides feedback on how victims feel about these interactions with the police. Women who felt that the officer listened to their concerns and provided information and referrals for help (such as shelters and other protective options) were the most satisfied with their experience with the police (Johnson, 2007). Gender of the responding officer also has an impact on victim satisfaction levels, because victims indicated that female officers were more receptive to their concerns overall and were not just focused on facilitating an arrest (Stalens & Finn, 2000). These positive experiences can encourage victims to seek out police assistance in the future should they need it (Johnson, 2007). There are also factors that can influence whether a case moves forward following a police report. If a perpetrator has a history of violent behavior, both the prosecutor and the victim are more likely to want to see the case move forward, whereas first-time offenders are more likely to have their charges dismissed or to be handled informally (Cerulli et al., 2015).

In contrast, women who do not feel that the justice system effectively responded to their concerns may be less likely to seek out help in the future. If an offender is let off with a "slap on the hand," victims may experience increased risks of violence in the future (Moe, 2007). Here, the criminal justice system did not serve as an effective deterrent for these offenders. This is also true in cases where the intimate partner abuse is limited to verbal abuse. Some women did not feel that the police took the issue of verbal violence seriously. At the same time, victims often minimized the severity of the verbal violence in order to discourage the police from making an arrest (Stewart, Langan & Hannem, 2013). Negative experiences with the police can also contribute to experiences with posttraumatic stress disorder for victims of IPV (Srinivas & DePrince, 2015). However, failing to achieve a desired outcome with the criminal courts does not necessarily dissuade victims from seeking out other avenues such as emergency departments or the civil court for remedies such as protection orders (Cerulli, et al., 2015).

Drawing from criticisms regarding the **discretionary arrest** policies of many police departments, mandatory arrest or pro-arrest policies began to surface in police departments across the nation during the 1980s and 1990s. **Mandatory arrest** policies refer to the legal duty of a police officer to make an arrest if the officer has reason to believe that domestic violence has occurred. The laws vary from state to state, but most state laws recognize both current and previous spouses or cohabitants as protected categories under the law, though not all states cover dating or prior dating relationships. Currently, 22 states have some form of mandatory arrest policy in place. In addition, the laws vary when a mandatory arrest can be made. For example, laws in Alaska and Missouri require that a report be made within 12 hours of the assault, whereas Mississippi and Nevada extend the time frame to 24 hours. Washington State and South Dakota represent some of the most narrowly defined time frames and require that the police make an arrest within 4 hours of the assault. Washington State law is also unique in that it limits cases to individuals who are 16 or older (Hirschel, 2008).

The movement toward mandatory arrest clarified roles for officers when dealing with domestic violence calls for service. It also removed the responsibility of arrest from the victim's decision and onto the shoulders of police personnel. For many women, they believed that a mandatory arrest policy would make officers understand that domestic violence is a serious issue and that it would legitimize their victimization. At the same time, the threat of arrest would serve as a deterrent for the offender. Here, women believed that an arrest would decrease levels of violence and send a message to the offender that battering is a crime and he would be punished. However, they acknowledged that the decrease in violence was only a temporary measure and that there existed a possibility of increased violence after an offender returned to the family home following an arrest or court proceedings (Barata & Schneider, 2004; Moe, 2007). Victims can feel disempowered by the mandatory arrest process, because it takes away their decision-making abilities. While mandatory arrest policies removed the victim's responsibility for instituting formal charges against an offender, there were some unintentional consequences. In many cases, a victim's call to the police for help resulted in her own arrest, leaving many victims feeling betrayed by the system that they sought help from (Burgess-Proctor, 2012). Other victims may be less likely to call for intervention knowing that their batterer (or themselves) would be arrested (Gormley, 2007; Miller & Peterson, 2007).

Dual arrests are more likely to occur when state laws or policies do not include a primary aggressor designation. As a result, officers are required to make a determination about who the "real" offender is. Even with a primary aggressor designation, officers may lack the training or experience to make a professional judgment about whom to arrest, resulting in both parties being arrested. These dual-arrest practices result in women being arrested for domestic violence with their partner. As a result, many women victims find themselves labeled as offenders of IPA by police and the courts for engaging in acts of self-defense (Miller, 2005). Dual-arrest policies also have negative consequences for the LGBT community. Research by Hirschel et al. (2007) found that in cases of intimate partner violence, same-sex couples were more likely to be involved in dual-arrest situations (female-to-female = 26.1% and male-to-male = 27.3%) compared to heterosexual couples (3.8%).

The increase in arrests has far-reaching implications for women, including the refusal of help by shelter services and challenges in child custody battles as a result of their "criminal" history (Miller & Meloy, 2006). In addition, gender differences in battering impact programming options for women who engage in acts of IPA. Here, scholars have noted that traditional batterer intervention programming (which is designed primarily for male offenders) may not be appropriate for women. Instead, therapeutic options should focus on the rationale and factors behind women who engage in IPA (Kernsmith, 2005).

In response to many mandatory arrest policies, many jurisdictions have instituted **no-drop policies**. Rather than force a victim to participate against her will, these jurisdictions developed evidence-based practices that would allow the prosecutor to present a case based on the evidence collected at the scene of the crime, regardless of any testimony by the victim (Gormley, 2007). Such policies were developed in response to a victim's lack of participation in the prosecution of her batterer. These policies may actually work against victims. When victims feel that their voice is not being heard by the criminal justice system, they may be less likely to report incidents of intimate partner abuse. While no-drop policies were designed to prevent victims from dismissing charges against their batterer, they instead led to disempowering victims.

When victims feel that the criminal justice system does not meet their needs in a case of intimate partner violence, they are less likely to seek assistance for subsequent victimizations. In many cases, victims felt that the event was not serious enough to report or expressed concerns that they would not be believed by the police. In addition, several victims were concerned about how contacting the police could lead to potential negative consequences for themselves or their families. Here, victims expressed concerns over the possibility of mandatory arrests or dual arrests (and the effects on children in the home), custody battles, and fear of how the offender would respond. Finally, even after multiple victimizations, some victims still express love and compassion for their abuser (Gover, Welton-Mitchell, Belknap, & Deprince, 2013).

Over time, many victims and advocates have expressed concern that the traditional criminal justice system may not be an effective tool to address the issues posed by intimate partner abuse. In response to these concerns, many jurisdictions have developed specialized courts that deal exclusively with cases of domestic violence. The professionals in these specialized courts (prosecutor, judges) often have specific training on issues such as the cycle of violence and the role of power and control within an intimate partner relationship. Research demonstrates that the use of specialized court practices can impact the level of satisfaction that victims experience as a result of their interactions with these environments. In their evaluation of a domestic violence court program in South Carolina, researchers Gover, Brank, and MacDonald (2007) found that a collaborative courtroom environment between the prosecutor, victim advocate, and judge had a significant effect on victim satisfaction levels. Unlike traditional criminal justice options that generally focus on punitive measures, this program emphasized the therapeutic options designed to treat the offender. As a result, the majority of victims and defendants believed that the outcome of their case was fair, positive, and respectful.

Programming Concerns for Victims of Intimate Partner Abuse

Not only are programs needed to address the needs of victims but it is also important to consider the value of battering prevention programs for men. Over the past three decades, batterer intervention programming has become one of the most popular options when sentencing offenders in cases of intimate partner abuse. Given the high correlation between substance use and intimate partner abuse, most programs also include substance abuse treatment as a part of their curriculum. The majority of these programs offer group therapy, which is popular not only for its cost-effectiveness but also because scholars suggest that the group environment can serve as an opportunity for program participants to support and mentor one another. One criticism of battering intervention programs is that they generally assume that all batterers are alike. This approach does not offer the opportunity for programs to tailor their curriculum to address the differences among men who abuse (Rosenbaum, 2009). In addition, victims of domestic violence voice their dissatisfaction with many of these types of programs, arguing that they are ineffective in dealing with the issues that the men face in their lives (Gillum, 2008).

Intimate partner abuse attacks every community, age, religion, race, class, and sexual identity. Programs that provide services for victims of battering must acknowledge the need for programming that is culturally diverse and reflect the unique issues within different racial and ethnic communities. The need for culturally relevant programming also extends to shelter programs for victims of domestic violence. In one program, participants noted the absence of women of color (particularly Black women) within the shelter administration and staff, even though the majority of the clientele was Black. Feeling culturally connected to program practitioners (as women of color and IPV survivors themselves) helped survivors understand what they were going through. As one woman notes, "Black womens understand other Black womens. Ain't no way a White woman understands what a Black women going through. . . . Because . . . we're different, we are totally different" (Gillum, 2009, p. 67). In addition, programs should be based within the targeted community to ensure participation from the community residents—if programs are difficult to access geographically, women are less likely to seek out services as a result of time, money (loss of work hours and cost of child care), and transportation limitations. Programs also need to be proactive and engage in prevention efforts with young women and men in the community (Bent-Goodley, 2004).

Culturally diverse programs are not enough to combat issues of violence between intimate partners. Rather, intervention efforts need to attack the systems that create social inequalities—racism, sexism, classism, and so on. In addition, the legal system and program providers need to understand how these issues are interrelated and not dominated by a single demographic factor (Sokoloff, 2004). Regardless of their individual effects on a single person, many of these interventions have the potential to fail at the macro level, as long as the social culture of accepting male violence against women remains (Schwartz & DeKeseredy, 2008).

Stalking and Intimate Partner Violence

According to the National Crime Victimization Survey, **stalking** is defined as "a course of conduct directed at a specific person that would cause a reasonable person to feel fear" (Baum, Catalano, Rand, & Rose, 2009, p. 1). Estimates by the Supplemental Victimization Survey (SVS) indicate that more than 5.9 million adults[3] experience behaviors defined as stalking[4] or **harassment**.[5] Table 4.2 illustrates the types and prevalence of stalking behaviors. In most cases, the acts that constitute stalking, such as sending letters or gifts, making phone calls, and showing up to visit, are not inherently criminal. These acts appear harmless to the ordinary citizen but can inspire significant fear and terror in victims of stalking.

Much of what the general public understands about stalking comes from Hollywood, where celebrities have long experienced acts of stalking. Consider the actions of John Hinckley Jr. who became infatuated with Jodie Foster when she first appeared as a child prostitute in the film *Taxi Driver*. Hinckley's obsession with Foster continued while she was a student at Yale, but he failed to gain her attention after numerous letters and phone calls. In 1981, Hinckley attempted to assassinate President Ronald Reagan in an effort to impress Foster. He was found not guilty by reason of insanity for his crimes and was committed to St. Elizabeth's Hospital for treatment. Another example of celebrity stalking is Madonna's stalker Robert Dewey Hoskins. He was convicted in 1996 for making threats against the star—he told the star that he wanted to "slice her throat from ear to ear" ("After Court Order," 1996, para. 6) and attempted to break into her house on two separate occasions. During one event, he successfully scaled the security wall of her home and was shot by one of her bodyguards. Other Hollywood victims of stalking include David Letterman, Sandra Bullock, Tyra Banks, and Lindsay Lohan, to name a few. Indeed, it seems that a number of Hollywood personalities have been stalked by an obsessed fan at some point

---

[3]The Supplemental Victimization Survey (SVS) includes only data on respondents aged 18 and older who participated in the National Crime Victimization Survey (NCVS) during January–June 2006. The data assess victimization incidents that occurred during the 12 months prior to the interview.

[4]According to these data, 3.4 million people are victims of stalking each year.

[5]Harassment is defined by the SVS as acts that are indicative of stalking behaviors but do not incite feelings of fear in the victim.

Table 4.3 • Prevalence of Stalking	
Experienced at least one unwanted contact per week	46.0%
Victims were stalked for 5 years or more	11.0%
Experienced forms of cyberstalking	26.1%
Received unwanted phone calls or messages	66.2%
Received unwanted letters and e-mail	30.6%
Had rumors spread about them	35.7%
Were followed or spied on	34.3%
Experienced fear of bodily harm	30.4%
Believed that the behavior would never stop	29.1%

during their careers. While noteworthy events of Hollywood stalkers brought significant attention to the crime of stalking, the attention was done in ways that reduced the social understanding of this crime to one that was limited to celebrities and the Hollywood circuit. Many of these cases involved perpetrators who suffered from mental disease or defect. This narrow definition had significant effects on the legitimization of this crime for ordinary victims of stalking.

Outside of the Hollywood context, a victim's relationship with her future stalker began in a very ordinary sense. Victims described these men as attentive, charming, and charismatic. But these endearing qualities soon disappeared, and their interactions became controlling, threatening, and violent. Many women blamed themselves for not recognizing the true colors of their stalker earlier. This pattern of self-blaming affected their ability to trust their own judgment and led these women to be hesitant about their decision-making abilities in future relationships as a result of their victimization.

As with many crimes, victims of stalking often do not report their victimization to police. According to SVS data, more than half of the individuals who were victims of stalking did not report their victimization. For many victims, their decision to not report these crimes stemmed from a fear of intensifying or escalating the stalking behaviors. Others dealt with their victimization in their own way, believing that their experience was a private and personal matter. Additionally, many believed that stalking was not a serious enough offense (or did not believe that a crime had occurred) to warrant intervention from the criminal justice system. Finally, some victims felt that nothing could be done to stop the behavior by their stalkers. For those individuals who did report their crimes, SVS data indicate that charges were filed in only 21% of these cases, further solidifying a belief for many victims that the criminal justice system was unable to effectively punish their stalkers in a court of law.

Victims engage in several different strategies in an effort to cope with their stalking victimization. Some victims attempted to solve the trauma through self-reflection and sought out therapeutic resources. Women also made significant changes to their behavior patterns. They might avoid community events out of a fear that their stalker would show up at the same function. Other women moved out of the area yet still expressed fear that their stalker would find them. Some victims tried to renegotiate the definitions of their relationship with their offender through bargaining, deception, or deterrence. Finally, some victims moved against their attackers by issuing warnings or pursuing a legal case against them (Cox & Speziale, 2009; Spitzberg & Cupach, 2003).

Spotlight on Stalking and College Campuses

In chapter three, you learned about Title IX and how recent attention on this legislation has led college campuses across the United States to revisit how they respond to cases of sexual assault, as well as implement prevention-based education for all students. Such efforts have also led to increased attention of cases of stalking on college campuses. In addition, the Jeanne Clery Act, which requires universities to annually publish their crime statistics, was recently amended to make stalking a mandatory reporting offense.

What is the prevalence of stalking on college campuses? It is the most common type of victimization among college-age individuals. Research by Myers, Nelson, & Forke (2016) notes that 16.0% of survey respondents from an urban university in Philadelphia reported experiencing stalking during their college experience, compared to 12.0% who reported sexual victimization, and 7.0% who reported physical victimization. Victims were more likely to be female (22.1%), and their perpetrators were more likely to be acquaintances or friends (41.1%). Intimate partners engaged in stalking in only 13.7% of cases. Other studies have noted that 27% of students experienced stalking while at campus (Spitzberg, 2016). While traditional research has identified a relationship between stalking and intimate partner abuse, research on college-age students note that the majority of stalking cases involve acquaintances or friends as offenders (Myers, Nelson & Forke, 2016).

College students often fail to understand the definition of stalking and often unlikely to label their experiences as stalking, even though they feel threatened or fearful as a result (Spitzberg, 2016). Research notes that many of the behaviors that constitute stalking are common occurrences within college-age relationships (Shorey, Cornelius, & Strauss, 2015). Similarly, behaviors that can be identified as cyberstalking are often rationalized among college-age students as a form of modern-day courtship and were not considered by the majority of the students to be of any particular significance, particularly in cases where the offender is known to the victim (Lee, 1998).

Recent changes to the Jeanne Clery Act (which requires that universities publish statistics about crime that occurs on or near campus) have included stalking as a reportable offense. In addition, the Dear Colleague letter on sexual violence has led universities to shift the way that they respond to cases of stalking under Title IX legislation. As you learned above, experiences of stalking can have negative mental health consequences. Within a university population, these challenges can present in a variety of ways, including issues with academic attendance and poor academic performance. Given the increasing presence of stalking behaviors on college campuses, colleges and universities are faced with expanding both their educational programming as well as their provision of services for victims (Myers, Nelson, & Forke, 2016).

Victims and Offenders of Stalking

Who are the victims of stalking? They are men and women, young and old, of every race, ethnicity, and socioeconomic status. Data indicate that there are certain groups that make up the majority of victims of stalking. A meta-analysis of 22 studies on stalking found that female victims made up 74.59% of stalking victims, while 82.15% of the perpetrators were male. In the majority of cases, the perpetrator was someone known to the victim, with 30.3% of all cases occurring as a result of a current or former intimate relationship. Only 9.7% of stalking cases involved someone who was a stranger to the victim (Spitzberg & Cupach, 2003).

While stalking is a crime in its own right, it is also a common experience for victims of intimate partner abuse. The degree to which victims are stalked is directly related to the levels of physical, emotional, and sexual abuse that they experienced with their intimate partner: The greater the abuse in the relationship, the higher the levels of

▲ **Photo 4.3** Many victims of stalking experience the constant fear or being followed and observed as they attempt to manage their daily lives. In this situation, the psychological terror that victims experience can be just as violent as any physical confrontation.

stalking can be. Several factors appear to influence whether a victim of domestic violence will be stalked. Women who are no longer in a relationship with their abuser are more likely to experience stalking compared to women currently involved in an IPA relationship. Additionally, domestic violence abusers who are more controlling and physically violent toward their victims are more likely to stalk them. Finally, abusers who use drugs and alcohol are more likely to stalk their partners. For those women who had moved on to new relationships, almost three fourths of them indicated that their new partner was harassed, threatened, or injured by their stalker (Melton, 2007).

Economics also impact the stalking experience for victims. Many victims find that they do not have the economic resources or abilities to move out of their communities to escape their stalker. Many of these women received governmental subsidies for housing—moving would mean giving up this assistance. This lack of mobility made it easier for their perpetrators to continue to stalk and harass their victims. In addition, the close-knit nature of many of these communities led to cases where a batterer's friends and family members were able to help the offender harass and intimidate their victim. Unfortunately, these cases of third-party stalking are not always recognized by the criminal justice system, or are not connected to the behaviors of the individual. As a result, many victims believe that an escape from the violence is impossible (Tamborra, 2012).

The experience of stalking has a significant effect on a woman's mental health. Women who experience significant levels of stalking over time are more likely to be at risk for depression and posttraumatic stress disorder. These rates of depression and posttraumatic stress disorder are significantly higher for women who blame themselves for the behaviors of their perpetrator (Kraaij, Arensman, Garnefski, & Kremers, 2007). Victims indicate feelings of powerlessness, depression, sleep disturbances, and high levels of anxiety (Pathe & Mullen, 1997). They are also likely to develop a chronic disease or other injury in response to the high levels of stress that victims of stalking experience (Davis, Coker, & Sanderson, 2002). It is clear that mental health services need to acknowledge how the experience of stalking affects the mental health status of victims and determine how to better provide services to this community.

Cyberstalking

The use of technology has changed the way in which many victims experience stalking. The use of devices such as e-mail, cell phones, and global-positioning systems (GPS) by offenders to track and monitor the lives of victims has had a significant effect on the experience of stalking. The term **cyberstalking** was created to address the use of technology as a tool in stalking. Of the 3.2 million identified victims of stalking identified by the SVS, one out of four individuals reported experiencing acts that are consistent with the definition of cyberstalking. Table 4.3 highlights examples of stalking aided by technology. As the use of technology continues to expand in our social world, so will its use to stalk, harass, and engage in acts of violence against individuals.

Like traditional methods of stalking, cyberstalking involves incidents that create fear in the lives of its victims. Just because cyberstalking does not involve physical contact does not mean that it is less damaging or harmful than physical stalking. Indeed, some might argue that the anonymity under which cyberstalkers can operate creates significant opportunities for offenders to control, dominate, and manipulate their victims, even from a distance, because there are no geographical limits for stalking within the domain of cyberspace. Indeed, someone can be stalked from just about anywhere in the world. For many victims of "traditional" stalking, cyberstalking presents a new avenue through which victims can be harassed, threatened, and intimidated. In cases of intimate partner abuse, technology and cyberstalking is a way in which abusers can continue to control and harass their victims from afar. "Some perpetrators text and phone repeatedly, creating dread and fear in the victim that the harassment will never end. Some women receive only one text or call daily or weekly, but this can be equally as terrifying in the context of their specific domestic-abuse history" (Woodlock, 2017, p. 586).

While cyberstalking is a relatively new phenomenon, research indicates that the prevalence of these behaviors is expanding at an astronomical rate. Youth and young adults appear to be particularly at risk for these forms of victimization, given their connections to the electronic world through the use of the Internet, blogs, text messaging, and social networking sites, such as Facebook. Consider that the simple act of tagging a friend in a photo on Facebook, Instagram, or other social media platform can provide valuable information to a stalker as it could inadvertently disclose their location (Dimond, Fiesler, & Bruckman, 2011). In addition, participation in activities such as sexting can increase the likelihood that one will be victimized online. Research indicates that 38% of study participants had either sent or received sexually explicit texts or photos. Participation in these activities increases the likelihood of cybervictimization (Reyns, Burek, Henson, & Fisher, 2013). In addition, stalkers can use information to publicly post information that is not only embarrassing but could jeopardize their relationships with friends, family and employers (Woodlock, 2017). Given the limited understanding of these crimes by victims (and the larger society), it is important that advocates and justice professionals have an understanding about the realities of these crimes in order to provide adequate support for victims.

Table 4.4 ● Experiences of Stalking via Mobile Technologies

Method	%
Used text messages, phone, and so on to call her names, harass her, or "put her down"	78
Used mobile technology to check her location	56
Made her feel afraid to not respond to a phone call or text because of what the caller might do (e.g., threaten suicide)	56
Checked her text messages without her permission	47
Threatened her via text, e-mail, and/or social media	44
Shared private photographs or videos of her without her permission	39
Posted negative information about her on social media	33
Tracked her via GPS (e.g., using applications such as Find My Friends)	17
Demanded her electronic password/s	17
Impersonated her in e-mails, text messages, and/or social media	14
Purchased a phone for her for the purpose of keeping track of her	8

SOURCE: Woodlock (2017).

Laws on Stalking

For the majority of the 20th century, stalking was not considered to be a crime. The first law criminalizing the act of stalking was created in 1990 by the state of California following the murder of actress Rebecca Schaeffer in 1989 by an obsessed fan. Schaeffer had risen to fame as an actress in the popular television show *My Sister Sam*. Robert Bardo had become obsessed with "Patti," the character played by Schaeffer on the show, and made several attempts to contact her on the set. He sent Schaeffer several letters and had built a shrine to her in his bedroom. Undeterred, he traveled cross-country, and he paid a private investigator $250 to obtain her home address. On making contact with Schaeffer at her residence, he shot her in the chest, killing her. Bardo was convicted of murder and sentenced to life in prison. Since the death of Rebecca Schaeffer and the creation of the first antistalking law in California, all 50 states, the District of Columbia, and the federal government have created criminal laws against stalking. In addition, the majority of state laws on stalking include details on stalking via electronic methods.

To prosecute someone for stalking, many state laws require victims to indicate that they experienced *fear* as a result of the offender's actions. Research indicates that women are more likely to experience fear as a result of being stalked compared to men (Davis et al., 2002). Using data from the National Violence Against Women Survey, Dietz and Martin (2007) found that nearly three fourths of women who were identified as victims of stalking behaviors indicated that they experienced fear as a result of the pursuit by their stalker. The levels of fear depended on the identity of the stalker (women indicated higher levels of fear when they were stalked by a current or former intimate or acquaintance) and how they stalked their victims (physical and communication stalking experiences generated higher levels of fear). Fear levels are also predicted by the severity and frequency of the contact (Reyns & Englebrecht, 2012). But what about women who experienced behaviors consistent with the definition of stalking but who did not feel fearful as a result of these interactions? Are these women not victims of stalking? In many states, they would not be considered victims, and the behaviors perpetrated against them would not be considered a crime.

The challenge with stalking is that many do not perceive stalking to be a significant event. Much of the research in this area is based on hypothetical scenarios, investigating what victims might do in these sorts of situations. From this research, we learn that the perceptions about stalking vary based on the gender of the victim and the offender and the type of relationship as well as the gender of the study participant. In addition, men are more likely to view stalking as a minor event and to engage in victim blaming toward stalking victims (Lambert, Smith, & Geistman, 2013). Victim blaming can be predicated by the type of relationship between the victim and the offender. Victims are the least blameworthy if the offender is a stranger but are considered culpable if the stalking results from a casual sexual relationship, such as a one-night stand. This can in turn impact perceptions of victim reporting—"When the victim reports this to the police, she will have to tell them everything, including how she had sex with him on the first night. This makes her look bad and she might be blamed for leading him on" (Cass & Mallicoat, 2014). If people do not perceive that victims will report these crimes to the police in hypothetical scenarios, we can assume that it is unlikely that they will reach out to the police should they face a similar victimization in their own lives.

Conclusion

Many victims of intimate partner violence and stalking did not report their victimization because they did not believe that what was happening to them was a criminal act, particularly in cases where there was no experience of physical violence. One victim noted that in assessing whether a relationship is healthy, women should look at themselves and any changes in their personal behaviors rather than obsessing on the actions of their stalker. "Think about how you were before this happened and how happy you were, and I think once ladies reminisce on that, I think that's where strength comes from" (Cox & Speziale, 2009, p. 12). Others advised that women should not stay silent on the issues of intimate partner abuse and stalking in order to protect their own safety, whether that meant filing a police report and obtaining a restraining order or letting friends, family, and coworkers know of their victimization. Here, victims acknowledge an increased need for community awareness about the nature of these victimizations and the resources available to them.

/// SUMMARY

- Intimate partner abuse is difficult to identify, because much of the abuse occurs behind closed doors and victims are reluctant to report cases of abuse.

- The Violence Against Women Act of 1994 provided funding for battered women shelters, outreach education, and training on domestic violence for police and court personnel.

- Children who are exposed to violence in the home are at risk for negative mental health outcomes and may continue the cycle of violence as adults.

- Gender-role stereotypes and homophobic views have a significant effect on identifying victims of same-sex IPA and giving them the assistance they need.

- Immigrant victims of domestic violence face a variety of unique issues such as cultural norms regarding violence, gender-role expectations, and a fear of deportation that affect their experience with battering.

- Walker's cycle of violence (1979) helps explain how perpetrators maintain control within a battering relationship.

- Women are confronted with a variety of barriers in their attempts to leave a relationship where intimate partner abuse is present.

- For many women, mandatory arrest policies have resulted in only a temporary decrease in the violence in their lives, with the potential of increased violence in the future.

- Stalking is defined as a "course of conduct directed at a specific person that would cause a reasonable person to feel fear."

- Cyberstalking involves the use of technology to track and monitor the lives of victims of stalking.

- Many victims do not report their experiences of being stalked to law enforcement, because they fear that a report will escalate the behavior, or they do not believe that stalking is a serious matter or that anything can be done to stop the stalking behavior.

- Stalking is often related to incidents of intimate partner abuse.

/// KEY TERMS

Battered women's movement 139

Cyberstalking 158

Cycle of violence 144

Dating violence 145

Discretionary arrest 153

Harassment 155

Intimate partner abuse 140

Mandatory arrest 153

Minneapolis Domestic
   Violence Experiment 140

No-drop policies 154

Restraining order 148

Same-sex intimate partner
   abuse 146

Stalking 155

Violence Against Women Act 140

/// DISCUSSION QUESTIONS

1. How have mandatory arrest and no-drop policies improved the lives of women involved in cases of intimate partner abuse? How have these policies negatively affected victims?

2. What unique issues do immigrant victims of intimate partner abuse face?

3. Describe the different forms of violence that can occur within an intimate partner abusive relationship.

4. Explain how the cycle of violence attempts to explain incidents of intimate partner battering.

5. What barriers exist for women in their attempts to leave a battering relationship?

6. How has the use of technology changed the way in which victims experience stalking? What challenges do these changes present for law enforcement and the criminal justice system in pursuing cases of cyberstalking?

7. How do victims cope with the experience of being stalked?

/// WEB RESOURCES

Bureau of Justice Statistics: http://bjs.ojp.usdoj.gov

National Coalition Against Domestic Violence: http://www.ncadv.org/

Office of Victims of Crime: http://www.ojp.usdoj.gov/

Office on Violence Against Women: http://www.ovw.usdoj.gov/

Stalking Resource Center: http://www.ncvc.org/src/Main.aspx

Stalking Victims Sanctuary: http://www.stalkingvictims.com

The National Center for Victims of Crime: http://www.ncvc.org

The National Domestic Violence Hotline: http://www.ndvh.org/

 Visit **study.sagepub.com/mallicoat3e** to access additional study tools, including eFlashcards, web quizzes, web resources, video resources, and SAGE journal articles.

READING /// 7

Many victims of intimate partner abuse only identify the effects of physical violence. Yet, behaviors that are controlling or coercive can also be a key component of abuse and is often unidentified by both victims and the criminal justice system. This article explores how these behaviors are both similar and distinct from one another.

"He Never Did Anything You Typically Think of as Abuse"

Experiences With Violence in Controlling and Non-Controlling Relationships in a Non-Agency Sample of Women

Alisa J. Velonis

For several decades, researchers and program advocates in the intimate partner violence (IPV) field have clashed over the theoretical and practical nature of relationship abuse. Feminist theorists argue that IPV is a function or byproduct of the patriarchal structure of society, that such violence is most often directed toward women by men, and that women's use of violence against male partners is principally reactive to men's violence against them (Gilfus, Trabold, O'Brien, & Fleck-Henderson, 2010). Increasingly, other experts disagree, pointing to studies that show women and men engage in violent behaviors against partners at equal rates and suggest that this phenomenon is a reflection of poor communication in our generally violent society (herein referred to as the *family conflict* perspective; Gilfus et al., 2010; Straus & Gelles, 1988). Whereas feminist-oriented research has emerged from decades of work with self-identified victims and perpetrators of IPV (from women's shelters, emergency rooms, and law enforcement settings; Anderson & Umberson, 2001; Dobash & Dobash, 2004; Hamberger & Guse, 2002; Melton & Belknap, 2003), evidence supporting the family conflict arguments comes chiefly from quantitative survey research conducted among large groups of men and women in generalizable samples (Archer, 2002; Dixon & Graham-Kevan, 2011; D. G. Dutton & Nicholls, 2005; Hines & Saudino, 2003; Straus, 2008). Finally, proponents of both viewpoints accuse the other of being driven by significant theoretical and methodological biases (Debbonaire & Todd, 2012; Dixon, Archer, & Graham-Kevan, 2012; D. G. Dutton, 2012; Johnson, 2011).

At their most basic levels, both perspectives address heterosexual relationship violence as a single phenomenon, even as they disagree about whether this violence is about male dominance or is simply about the use (or mutual use) of physical aggression to settle conflict. Attempting to bridge the philosophical gap between the camps, an increasing number of researchers and advocates have adopted a more complex understanding of IPV and gender. At the forefront of this movement, Johnson has argued for the existence of different types of IPV, some of which are clearly gendered in directionality and others that are not. *Situational partner violence* (violent incidents that are situation-specific and not part of an ongoing pattern of control), for example, is used as

SOURCE: Velonis, A. J. (2016). *"He never did anything you typically think of as abuse"*: Experiences with violence in controlling and non-controlling relationships in a non-agency sample of women. *Violence Against Women*, 22(9): 1031–1054.

frequently by women as by men, but *coercive controlling violence* or *intimate terrorism* (an ongoing pattern of abusive and coercive behaviors that includes violence) is predominantly directed at women by men, and *violent resistance* (violence used to resist or defend against a partner's use of controlling violence) is more likely used by women against men (Johnson, 2008). Participant samples from community agencies such as domestic violence programs, he argues, are likely to be biased in ways that lead to the identification of coercive controlling violence and violent resistance, whereas quantitative surveys administered to large, nonclinical samples find situational violence, in part because it is more common and in part because victims of terrorist violence may not participate in surveys (Johnson, 2008, 2011).

One result of this ongoing disagreement has been increased discussion about the relationship between gender, violence, and other controlling behaviors and whether all incidents of violence require similar responses (Anderson, 2009; Langhinrichsen-Rohling, 2010; Ross & Babcock, 2010; Stark, 2009; Tanha, Beck, Figueredo, & Raghavan, 2010). For example, if some events are rooted in a larger pattern of control and terror and others are situational, effective prevention and intervention strategies will likely need to reflect these distinctions (Johnson, 2006, 2008; Miller, 2006). Notably absent from the research are attempts to contextualize the violence identified in the quantitative literature by using the voices of the men and women who participated in these studies; this is particularly true of research participants drawn from community-based samples who reported experiencing violence and who did not receive intervention from social services or law enforcement.

This article addresses the findings related to the following research question: After identifying partner violence using a common quantitative measurement tool, will a closer examination of the context and experiences of incidents reported by women uncover qualitative differences based on the existence of additional coercive and controlling behaviors? Based on Johnson's proposed typologies, an in-depth look at the power dynamic within these relationships should distinguish those in which violence is situational in nature from others in which it is part of a larger pattern of coercion and control, although the community-based sampling frame should make finding the latter more difficult.

Given the continued disagreements over the nature of IPV and women's use of violence, this article contributes to the existing literature in three ways. First, as one of the few studies that qualitatively contextualizes incidents of partner violence reported within a nonagency sample, it partially addresses the criticism that the use of agency-based samples is a primary reason feminist research shows gender asymmetry. Second, the findings highlight how the existence of patterned coercive and controlling behaviors within relationships appears to substantially differentiate experiences with violence, suggesting that this dynamic is at least as important to identify as physical violence itself. Finally, the article discusses how these findings may apply to both feminist and family conflict arguments about gender and violence and ultimately why they are important for the development of effective prevention and intervention strategies.

Methods

The interviews described in this article were the second of a two-phased mixed-methods investigation into IPV and gender symmetry conducted on a large academic medical campus. In the initial (quantitative) phase, 398 individuals responded to an electronic request to employees and students at a large university medical setting using a list serve promoting research opportunities across the campus; although we estimate the original recruitment email was distributed to approximately 7,000 subscribers, because we cannot know if emails were received, read, or forwarded, we cannot generate a true response rate. Participants completed an online informed consent process, after which they were able to access a secure, electronically administered quantitative survey that included a complete version of the Revised Conflict Tactics Scales (CTS2; Straus, Hamby, & Warren, 2003). All participants who completed the final page of the survey were offered a $5 electronic gift certificate to a national coffee chain. Participants were not required to provide identifying information as part of this phase unless they accepted the gift certificate, in which case an active email address was needed. Finally, participants were asked to indicate if they were willing to be contacted by members of the study team as part of the follow-up phase of the research. Forty-eight individuals were considered withdrawals after failing to complete at least 10 survey questions, and another eight were dropped from the analysis when contact information suggested they did not reside in the state in which the study was being conducted, leaving a final sample size of 342 men and women who completed the quantitative survey (282 women, 53 men, 7 unknown; see Reading Table 1).

After completing the analysis of the quantitative data, 33 women who self-identified as having used and/or received physical violence or physical forms of sexual coercion and indicated an interest in future participation were identified. Although the initial research plan included conducting comparable interviews with men, in spite of having a male colleague contact and interview male participants, only two men (of the 21 who were eligible) agreed to participate in the interviews. Potential participants were identified from the eligible population using a stratified sampling frame that identified both typical and case-critical examples. Initial stratification was based on the receipt and/or use of physical violence, and further stratification was based on the severity of violence, the number and frequency of incidents, and demographic characteristics. Personal email invitations were sent to the potential participants, which resulted in 22 female interviews (67% positive response rate; see Reading Table 2).

Interviews were structured using a guide based on a priori themes identified in the literature and by domestic violence advocates. To take full advantage of the iterative process in-depth interviews offer, the guide served as a road map from which individual conversations digressed, allowing themes or stories to emerge that had not been anticipated. The guide for each interview was tailored according to participants' responses on the survey (e.g., "When you took the online survey, you indicated that you had slapped your partner within the previous year . . ."), and also allowed the interviewer to ask about additional arguments as well as decision making patterns and examples of conflict resolution. Interviews lasted approximately 1 hour and were digitally recorded. Participants were offered a $25 retail gift certificate in appreciation of their time.

Ethical and safety considerations were paramount, and both phases of this research were approved by the university's institutional review board. All participants had the option of completing the quantitative survey anonymously, and only participants who granted

Reading Table 1 • Demographics of Quantitative Phase Participants, by Gender (N = 342).

	n	Men[a]	Women[a]
Gender			
Men	53		
Women	282		
Missing	7		
Race/ethnicity			
Asian	20	2	18
Latino/a	25	7	18
White	275	42	229
Other	17	2	15
Missing	5	0	2
Education			
Less than college grad	46	5	39
College grad	148	26	121
Graduate school/ degree	144	22	121
Missing	4	0	1
Age			
≤25	79	17	62
26–35	151	23	127
36–45	52	5	45
46–55	34	5	29
56+	17	2	14
Missing	9	1	5

[a]Because 7 individuals did not report gender, these columns do not add up to 342.

permission to be contacted were eligible to participate in the interviews. Identifying information for the qualitative participants was kept secured at all times, and interviewees were assigned unique ID numbers and pseudonyms which were used in field notes and for analysis. Because the interviews were digitally recorded, participants were verbally cautioned about using first names when speaking about partners or others, and any names that were inadvertently recorded were altered or deleted during transcription. All interviews occurred in a semiprivate space (an office or conference room with a door) at a location of the participant's choosing; most were conducted on the campus where participants worked and/or attended classes, and one was conducted in a meeting room of a public library. Safety protocols were in place in the event that a participant showed up accompanied by someone else. At the conclusion of Phase 2, all identifying information, including email addresses, was purged from the data records.

Analysis

While not a primary focus of this article, we examined the quantitative results using regression analyses with the CTS2 question serving as the dependent variable and gender as the main independent variable. The qualitative analysis (discussed here) followed the general outline described by Creswell (2009, p. 185). An initial list of a priori themes and codes were identified based on the CTS2 scales and IPV literature.

Reading Table 2 • Demographics of Women Interview Participants (n = 22).	
	n
Age	
20–29	8
30–39	6
40–49	6
50–59	2
Race/ethnicity	
White	16
African American	1
Latina	3
Asian	2
Education	
Some college	5
College degree	10
Graduate school/degree	7

Interview transcripts and the author's field notes were coded over the course of the qualitative phase, and new in vivo codes were included as they emerged from the interviews. When appropriate, previously coded documents were reexamined. Using Miles and Huberman's (1994) technique of partially ordered matrices, experiences described by each participant were listed and examined by partner, controlling behaviors, use of violence, receipt of violence, and other variables. Many women described relationships with more than one partner, and whenever the level of detail allowed, each separate relationship was analyzed independently as well as part of each woman's complete story. By looking at relationships both across and within individuals, various themes and patterns emerged. Case studies were then constructed for all 22 participants, which told the story of each woman's relationship history (Creswell, 2009). Finally, each relationship was categorized as "controlling" or "not controlling" using Stark's definition (below) based on the emergence of identifiable patterns of controlling behaviors as well as women's own perceptions of their relationships.

Identifying Patterns of Control

The focus on identifying patterns of controlling and/or coercive behaviors reflects an understanding that the actions used to gain and maintain power rarely occur in isolation and that they are often culturally and contextually prescribed. Stark (2007) describes *coercion* as the use of force or threats to compel a particular response, and *control* as "structural forms of deprivation, exploitation, and command that compel obedience" by denying resources, dictating behaviors, and limiting options (pp. 228–229). Previous experiences, cultural expectations, socioeconomic status, and other micro- and macro-level influences give controlling and coercive behaviors their power, making them difficult to capture completely using a predetermined list of actions (e.g., "shouts or swears at victim"). Most intimate partners engage in minor, generally infrequent acts of manipulation or psychological attacks, but these do not comprise an ongoing or systematic attempt to gain dominance and authority over the other partner, which is at the crux of feminist characterizations of domestic violence. Using Stark's definition as a guide, we considered a relationship to have a unilateral controlling or coercive dynamic if the participant described either partner consistently using tactics that intimidate and/or dictate current or future actions of the other in ways that limited personal freedoms.

Results

Consistent with other research using the CTS/CTS2 with nonagency samples, few significant differences emerged between men's and women's experiences of violence in the quantitative phase of the study. Using this as the backdrop for the qualitative phase, the goal of the interviews was to contextualize the physical violence reported by participants on the quantitative survey, detect additional violent and/or coercive and controlling behaviors not captured by the quantitative survey, and identify patterns associated with the use and/or receipt of violence in relation to patterns of other controlling or coercive behaviors and gender.

The 22 women who were interviewed for this phase discussed a total of 30 separate relationships, over one third of which included some form of patterned controlling and/or coercive behaviors by at least one partner. Of the 11 relationships in which the controlling partner was male, all but one also involved at least one incident of male-to-female violence, and all but four included female-to-male violence. Only two women described their own patterned use of controlling behaviors, and for the remainder of the relationships, no patterned control was evident.

The stories and incidents described below illustrate thematic differences in how physical violence can be experienced or used when one partner engages in other controlling behaviors versus when the power dynamic between partners is equitable. Although Johnson's definition of intimate terrorism describes a severity of physical assaults and coercive behaviors that was rarely evidenced in this sample, the distinctions between controlling and noncontrolling relationships and the experiences of and responses to violence within them clearly emerge from the voices of these women. In addition to the narratives that follow, Reading Tables 3 and 4 provide supplementary illustrations of controlling and noncontrolling relationships. All names are pseudonyms, and

each story (below and in Reading Tables 3 and 4) reflects the actual experiences of a single participant.

Controlling Relationships

Kellsey met Kurt when she was 23. Three years older than she was, Kurt was initially "very romantic and wooing," and after dating for almost a year, they moved in together; that was when the relationship began its downhill slide. "We started fighting a lot," she recalled. "We had fought a little bit before then, but not like that. And it'd be like door-slamming fights and, you know, 'I'm leaving' type of fights." As time went on, Kurt grew more controlling. "[He] never did anything that you typically think of as abuse," she remarked. "For example,"

> I would be reading *Twilight* or *Harry Potter*, a book I was really into, and he would take it and hide it so that I couldn't read it and it was like a way of controlling me. And he wouldn't tell me where it was and we'd get in a fight about that because I would be like, "Stop it, I just want to read my book." And he'd be like "Ha, ha, ha, ha, you can't." And it was like a funny joke, but it wasn't funny, and it would go on to the point where I was angry, like, "Show me where my book is, that's not cool." It would just sort of escalate and until finally he'd take the book out, throw it, and be like, "Whatever. There's your book. Fine. Go read it if you want to. I just wanted to spend some time with you" or something like that.

Slowly, her universe became more isolated. "[He] didn't like me to have any sort of connection with the outside world, tried to disconnect me from family and friends." After becoming engaged, they fought over who would be invited to the wedding: Kellsey wanted to include her close family at the very least, but Kurt demanded the ceremony be completely private, with no guests except the officiant. After extensive arguments, Kellsey usually gave in, feeling she had no voice.

Although Kurt never hit or threw objects at Kellsey, he frequently told her that she looked or acted like a whore and played on her vulnerabilities. Once, he tossed her dog outside by the scruff of its neck after it had an

Reading Table 3 • Sample Cases of Relationships With Controlling Male Partners

Participant	Nonphysical controlling behaviors	Partner's use of violence	Participant's use of violence
Brenda (current boyfriend)	Independence and Isolation Insists on going with her to medical appointments. Becomes very upset if she does not spend days off with him. Harasses her when she goes out with friends. She lies to him about where she is and who she is with. She does not tell him if she takes a day off from work. She makes appointments close to work so he will not know. Reframes Reality Insists that being in a relationship means spending all time together. *"He's always saying that I just don't understand what relationships really are."* Ignores Needs Refused to take her home from a party, and refused to give her the car keys. *She walked several miles to get home through neighborhoods where gunshots were heard.*	Blocks her exit from a room when arguing. Grabs her if she tries to walk out. *Bruised her at least one time.* Shoved her when she blocked exit from room. Twisted arm behind her back because he wanted the television remote. *Left bruises*	Hit him in the arm after he grabbed her. Shoved him when he blocked the exit from a room.
Maya (estranged husband)	Uses Cultural and Gender Norms Against Her Divorce is not an option in her traditional culture; she said she is grateful he never beat her the way other husbands do. Controlled all aspects of family life and decision making *After being denied his own visa, applied on her behalf to U.S. graduate schools and insisted she accept (against her wishes), hoping that he would be able to enter the United States with her (this did not happen, and she is now separated from her children).* Financial Control Spends his salary on luxuries for himself, saving little for the family. *She described him as flying into a rage if she complained.* Uses Fear and Intimidation Continues to physically and verbally terrorize children into submission. At least once, he threw his dinner (possibly at her) when it was not satisfactory.	Physically punishes children if they disobey or displease him. Grabbed or threw her when she intervened as he was hitting children (at least once).	Threw cell phone at him. Slapped him after he committed a very egregious action against her (she refused to provide details about the event).

Participant	Nonphysical controlling behaviors	Partner's use of violence	Participant's use of violence
Regana (ex-boyfriend)	**Independence and Isolation** Convinced her to move away from family and friends and into small trailer. *Once they moved to live with his family across the country, then to a remote town where he had secured a job.* Insisted she quit job after moving to a small town. *He claimed he did not trust her to work shifts with men because she had previously dated colleagues (including him).* **Reframed Reality and Eroded Self-Confidence** Called her stupid, slut, whore, and more until she agreed with him. *Made her verbally admit to these characteristics, then said, "Well, even though you are all those things, I'm still going to give you another chance."* Convinced her that all of the relationship problems were her fault. *Insisted she see a psychologist to solve their mutual problems.* *Told her she did not know what an "adult" relationship looked like.* Punished her for events that happened prior to their relationship.	Blocked her exit from rooms when arguing. Threw clothing at her.	Shoved him when he blocked her exist. "Roughhoused" with him.
Connie (ex- boyfriend)	**Reframed Reality and Eroded Self-Confidence** Lied about the nature of his relationship with his ex-girlfriend; when presented with evidence of deceit, tried to convince her she did not understand. Criticized her constantly then insisted she misconstrued his words. *"So he would curse, use curse words at me—'you're such a bitch' or 'you're such a' whatever. Then he would say, 'Well, I didn't say you're such a bitch. I said you're being a bitch.' I'm like, 'No, that's not what you said.' . . . He would always assume or say that I just didn't get him . . . 'I'm trying to make you understand. What do I have to do to make you understand?' So he would start yelling."* **Independence and Isolation** Sabotaged plans involving her friends or family. Harassed her constantly if she went out with girlfriends. Became mistrustful when a meeting with her boss ran late.	Grabbed her during an argument and may have shoved her into a baker's rack (she gave conflicting reports). *She believed he was about to hit her.*	N/A

(Continued)

Reading Table 3 ● (Continued)

Participant	Nonphysical controlling behaviors	Partner's use of violence	Participant's use of violence
Rochelle (current husband)	Uses Fear and Intimidation Becomes verbally aggressive and abusive when upset. Flew into a rage when she refused to finish a gardening project immediately. He nearly slapped her, and she believes he would have hit her if she had not moved. She locked herself in a bathroom with a phone in case she needed to call 911. Verbally exploded when she used his thermos for their daughter's lunch, pouring the contents into the sink while yelling and tussling with her. She often removes their daughter from the house when he is upset.	She believed he would have hit her if she had not moved.	While tussling over the thermos, she wrapped her foot around a kitchen chair and pulled it into his chin.
	Reframes Reality Manipulates situations so that she becomes the villain. *Tells her she is not respectful of his feelings; if they end up in divorce court it will be her fault, etc.* Barrages her with a litany of her mistakes and weaknesses. *"I would try to brainstorm and come up with a solution, and it's like, before we'd even resolved that one, he would move on to issue number two, to issue number three, to issue number four, and—honestly, I counted one time, just to show him, it was nine issues in 14 minutes. And, um, by the eighth or ninth issue, none of which are getting resolved, but you know all of them were like 'let me lob this cantaloupe at you.'"* Uses Physical Strength to Control Environment *Intentionally moved furniture in a way she disliked, knowing she was physically unable to move it back.*	She feels threatened and manipulated into engaging in sex: *"[When] I will say something like 'tonight is not good' or 'today is not good, I have to be up tomorrow morning at 4:30' or whatever, he'll say, 'well, I don't matter to you, and when this [marriage] all falls apart, you just remember, you're the one who said this.'"*	

[a]Regana had advanced training in martial arts and both she and her boyfriend knew she could hurt him badly. This may or may not have served as a deterrent to his behavior, and she stated that she was careful not to hurt him.

Reading Table 4 ● Examples of Dynamics in Noncontrolling Relationship With Physical Violence			
Participant	**Participant use of violence**	**Partner's use of violence**	**Nonviolent dynamics**
Mary (husband)	"Punched" husband on the arm at the end of a joke.	While arguing, husband was gesturing wildly with arms and hit a vase, sending it across the room at her. She insists this was not intentional.	She and husband discussed aggression and violence, including the use of "mock" or playful aggression.
Ellen (ex- boyfriend)		While at a bar with people who had previously slighted him, her boyfriend got drunk and belligerent. She tried to get him out of the bar, and he shoved her. In the instant she thought he was going to hit her.	In hindsight, she has no idea why she thought he would hit her. The two had discussed power because he was older, and the dynamic appeared very equitable. The relationship ended shortly after.
Katrina (husband)	Struck her husband when he made a loud and annoying noise. He grabbed her hands, and calmly told her "no" and "never do that again."		She was clearly ashamed of her action, and it never happened again.
Jackie (husband)	When they were moving, she walked into the kitchen and found him reading old newspapers rather than packing the dishes. He ignored her request to return to work, and she threw a spoon to get him to "wake up."		That was the closest thing to violence she described; she said that the answers on the quantitative survey that indicated violence were errors.
Joanie (husband)	Joanie described several incidents when she hit or threw things at her husband when they were fighting.		She describes them as both having hot tempers and a passionate relationship. She gave several examples of power-sharing and good negotiation skills.
Wendy (ex- boyfriend)		Boyfriend grabbed her arm to stop her from walking off during an argument.	When she was at college in a different state, he tried to tell her to change clothes before a dance because she had a short skirt. Later, he tried using guilt to convince her to not take a summer internship. Neither attempt was successful, and she ended the relationship.

accident in the house. Some of the worst incidents were when he would physically dominate, but not actually harm, her:

> And there were a couple of times where, like one time he held me down, like he would like to tickle me, but to the point where it was uncomfortable. Like I did not like it and I'd be like, "Okay, stop, stop, stop." and it would escalate. . . . [He] liked to hold me down—I have this thing where when I was a kid, my friend and I used to play this game where . . . she would like kind of hold this blanket on you and see how long you could stay under the blanket or something. And I've kind of been traumatized since that and so I told him that I don't like to be held down or under a blanket too much and he would take advantage of that. He'd be like, "Ha, ha, ha. Isn't this so funny? I can make you freak out."

She learned quickly that the best way to get him to stop was to cry, prompting him to give her a disgusted look and tell her she was "weak."

Occasionally, Kellsey would respond with force of her own. She said that when they argued, one of them would often try to leave the house and the other would grab his/her arm or block them from going. Kellsey recalled one time when Kurt pushed her against a wall and blocked her way out of a room. "I did feel threatened. He was yelling, calling me names, and blocking the door." She asked him to move, he refused, and she pushed him.

> And it was definitely a light push, it wasn't like push you down the stairs to really hurt you. It was just like "I just need you to move right now. You're in my way and you won't let me out."

Kellsey eventually left Kurt, but only after several years of enduring his physically and emotionally controlling behaviors. Kellsey's story illustrates many of the nuances that make IPV difficult to conceptualize and harder still to measure. Kurt never brutalized her, never punched her or left bruises or did any of the things that television and cinema portray as "domestic violence." Looking only at her responses on the CTS2, it would be

easy to assume that the aggression was "mutual"; she indicated they both engaged in minor and severe acts of violence, as defined by the survey. What is not readily apparent without further examination of the context surrounding the actions is how Kurt used Kellsey's vulnerabilities to manipulate and control her.

Out of the 22 women interviewed, exactly half described at least one relationship with a male partner who used an identifiable pattern of controlling behaviors and two engaged in similar behaviors against a male partner. As exemplified by Kellsey, the level and severity of physical aggression between the partners was often minimal, but the nonviolent dynamic clearly resembled Stark's description of control. Participants recalled receiving frequent and harassing telephone calls or text messages whenever they spent time with friends; being verbally degraded, chastised, and blamed for problems in the relationship; and having to lie to partners about medical appointments, past relationships, or social events to avoid conflict. Some said their partners tried to reframe reality by twisting their words or lying, and one participant described how her husband used their South Asian cultural norms and values to ensure her obedience.

Receiving physical violence from a controlling partner. Women with controlling partners were more likely to describe repeated and serious incidents of physical violence than women with noncontrolling partners. Raelynne, now in her 30s, recounted three incidents from her early 20s when her ex-boyfriend assaulted her.

> The first time we got in a fight, that was physical, I was like four months pregnant and he pushed me down the stairs because I had busted him cheating on me and I put all of his stuff out on the porch.

She described the second time as "just" a slap, but the third time was the most serious. They were living apart, and she remembered nagging and calling him names:

> And he was a lot taller than I was and he came over and he was like yelling at me and I remember I said, "Will you step back, because you're spitting in my face?" And he totally just went and spit in my face! So I remember looking

down and working up the spit in my mouth and knowing that if I did it, something was going down, but I did it. And that was the last thing I remember.

She woke up in an ambulance, having no idea what had just happened. He was arrested, and eventually she moved from the state with their son.

Most participants with controlling partners did not describe the severity of violence that Raelynne experienced, but for many, the violence was a physical (and obvious) manifestation of the control. Rochelle described how she usually locked herself in a bathroom to get away from her husband's frequent verbal explosions, but it was only when he nearly hit her that she felt truly frightened. On that occasion, she grabbed the telephone as she fled, thinking that she may need to call 911 if he chased her through the house. Likewise, while Brenda didn't fear being injured by her boyfriend, she was bothered by his tendency to physically grab her:

> He wouldn't harm anyone just to harm them, but he gets frustrated and if you're not going to sit there and listen, he gets really frustrated and he wants to control the situation by controlling me physically, and you can't do that.

Perpetrating violence against a controlling partner. A majority of the women who were involved with controlling men admitted to using violent behaviors as well, but unlike the physical aggression their partners used, the violent behaviors women used *against* controlling partners more often presented as a response to a loss of control rather than as an offensive move. One of the most common scenarios involved pushing or hitting a partner when he blocked an exit or grabbed their arm to prevent them from leaving. One time, Brenda's boyfriend grabbed her with such force that he left bruises, and she responded,

> . . . we had said all we could say and nothing we said was going to change it anymore and I didn't want to talk anymore. I wanted to walk away. I wanted to go outside and go for a walk. I wanted to walk the dog to get away and he wasn't having that, and he grabbed me to the point one time

where he left bruises. I'm like, "Why are you doing this?" . . . [Then] one time I hit back.

For two women, the only violence they described was their own, yet this occurred in the shadow of ongoing verbal abuse and manipulation. When Rochelle shoved a chair into her husband's shin, it was after he exploded because she used his thermos for their daughter's lunch:

> [He] came down and he said, "That's my thermos, and you can't use it," and I said, "It's not your thermos, it's the family's thermos," . . . and he said, "No, she can't have it, she can't have it." So he starts dumping the stuff out, you know, I had prepared a lunch and he starts dumping it out, and, um, I said, "You would actually dump out your daughter's lunch." . . . I was screaming at him, I was *really* upset, and, um, and he starts yelling back, "It's mine! And you didn't ask" if I could use it, you know.

Eventually, they were both standing by the sink, grabbing for the thermos:

> . . . [He's] dumping out her lunch and I'm trying to grab it away, and, and, um, and then there was a chair that was kind of close to where we were having this tussle, and I grabbed it with my leg and I pushed it into his leg, and, and, he's like, "What? Are you going to throw the chair at me?" and it's like, "You know, I'm not really throwing the chair at you," but it was a pretty ugly moment.

Taken out of the larger context of the relationship, Rochelle's actions could be interpreted as situational and as a single incident that escalated out of control; she demonstrated no apparent fear for her safety, nor were her actions in response to a direct assault on her personal space or agency. However, over the course of their relationship, she had been the target of at least one attempted physical assault and numerous verbal attacks and spiteful actions, and although his aggression had eased with treatment for depression, he continued to use sexually manipulative tactics. In this light, his explosion over the thermos was part of a pattern of bullying and controlling behaviors, and her actions (which may or may not be condonable) take on a very different meaning than had they occurred during a one-off argument.

From a legal perspective, very few examples of women's violence could be labeled as "self-defense," yet most framed their behaviors in the context of the tactics used against them: He was blocking my way, so I grabbed him; he was calling me worthless, so I shoved him. Kellsey was the only participant who used the term self-defense to describe her behaviors, and although she later admitted that may not have been the right term, she insisted it was "something similar to that."

Despite not feeling frightened for their personal safety on an ongoing basis, all of the women with controlling partners described how their partners manipulated their vulnerabilities using guilt and harassment, attacked their self-esteem, reframed their perceptions of reality, isolated them from others, and occasionally dominated them physically. In most of the situations in which this group of women used violence, some type of controlling tactics had been employed against them immediately preceding their actions, and the violence they exhibited had the effect of leveling the playing field and reclaiming personal power that had been lost. When Megan eventually shoved her boyfriend, it was after months of denigrating comments, and she described his reaction as stunned: "It threw him off. I, like, it shocked him 'cause I actually defended myself."

Coercive and controlling women. Out of 22 interviews, Karen and Marisol were the only two women who described themselves as clearly being the primary perpetrator of controlling violence, and thus are the only voices of this kind in this study. For both women, violence was the go-to response when they felt threatened by their partners' independence. Marisol described several incidents in which she pushed, shoved, hit, and threw objects at her husband when she was afraid he would leave:

> Because all of a sudden, if he, if he threatened to leave the room, which again for me was a threat. For him it was just "I just need to separate myself from this. We need to deescalate this." But all of a sudden this abandonment thing would kick in for me, and it was like "No, no you're not leaving."

Both women had been diagnosed with and were receiving pharmacological treatment for conditions such as depression and bipolar disorder, and both reported histories of child sexual abuse. Regardless of whether their destructive behaviors were psychological, sociological, or related to a combination of factors, the pattern of physically and psychologically controlling behaviors both women used was clearly intended to dominate and control their partners and did not look the same as what occurred in noncontrolling relationships.

Noncontrolling Relationships

Lorraine, a professional woman in her 50s, has been married to Harry for 11 years. For most of her adult life, Lorraine has struggled with both posttraumatic stress disorder and clinical depression, which manifests as an internalized, passive–aggressive anger. Harry, already rather stoic and unaffectionate, has a tendency to respond to her depression by withdrawing emotionally, making her feel even worse. He demanded order and quiet in his home, often raising his voice when the children became rambunctious. She interpreted his reproaches as attacks on her fitness as a parent, but in hindsight, acknowledged that her own mental state likely colored her perceptions.

Early in the marriage, Lorraine discovered a stash of pornography in Harry's possession. Feeling a great deal of anger, she confronted Harry, and even after he apologized and promised to get rid of the offensive material, she admitted that she might have grabbed him. "The second time it happened," however, "was when I really got mad. And that's when I shoved him. And I hit him too."

> [We] were both standing up. Yeah. And he's a lot bigger and taller than I am, so it's pretty amazing that I could shove him that hard. In fact, I shoved him hard enough into the wall that he broke a painting that, a glass, you know. . . . It shocked me that I did that.

This was their worst fight, and the only time either of them has ever used violence. Although they continued to struggle with different worldviews and have engaged in occasional passive–aggressive behaviors, she did not think that either of them intentionally tries to be hurtful to the other. They have worked through disagreements over financial responsibilities and gender roles, and although she still senses resentment on his part, she has successfully negotiated more equity in cooking and decision making.

Unlike the majority of women's experiences with controlling partners, Lorraine's story illustrates how an imperfect relationship can nonetheless include shared decision making and mutual respect, even during times of contention. Women involved with noncontrolling partners described numerous ups and downs, but most felt positive about the overall power dynamic in the relationship. Physical aggression was usually seen as an anomaly rather than as part of an ongoing pattern of behaviors, and most women recounted numerous examples of successful negotiation, joint decision making, and intentional conversations about the use of power and violence within the relationship. Although women with controlling partners all had similar experiences on occasion, these were often overshadowed by the day-to-day struggles for control.

The incidents of violence in noncontrolling relationships clearly resembled Johnson's definition of "situational" partner violence (regardless of who was the aggressor): one-off events, most often minor in severity, and contained within a particular situational context, such as when Ellen's intoxicated boyfriend pushed her away when she tried to coax him out of a bar after he had too much to drink. Descriptions of "losing it" were common, and although similar accounts could be heard in the stories from controlling relationships, the lack of historical intimidation and coercive tactics in noncontrolling relationships gives these actions a different meaning and weight. When a controlling partner uses violence, it becomes part of a larger ongoing pattern of controlling behaviors; in a noncontrolling relationship, a shove or slap may have no meaning beyond the moment. Joanie characterized her marriage as one of equal power and passionate tempers, and shared her perception of fights with her husband:

> I try to match his anger. I'm never afraid, oh my gosh, because I've hit [my husband] and [am] like, "Oh, you make me so mad." And he doesn't hit back.... Sometimes I wish he would so I could hit back harder, because that's when I'm in the throes of like "Let's brawl! I am mad at you!"

Joanie's unapologetic attitude illustrates the ease with which many women dismiss situational violence, especially their own. In several cases, women had a hard time even considering a situation as "violent" because the event was so minor and normalized; for example, Jackie threw a kitchen spoon at her husband to get his attention, not to harm him. In contrast, none of the women with controlling partners expressed doubt about whether their partner's physical aggression was, in fact, violence.

Discussion

Is the Problem Violence or Control?

In traditional conceptualizations of IPV, controlling behaviors are considered secondary to physical violence; it is the threat of being beaten or killed that gives power to the coercive and controlling acts. In the experiences of many of these women, however, physical violence was merely one of many controlling tools used against them. Furthermore, a number of participants described using and receiving physical violence when there was no clear sign of other controlling or coercive behaviors. Rather than labeling the action of violence as controlling or situational, it may be useful to think about the dynamic within *relationships* as controlling or not controlling and recognize that both types of relationships can include violent behaviors, but the motivation and experiences of that violence may be different. Thus, rather than considering IPV as a single phenomenon, we may need to shift our thinking and see it as a series of closely-related outcomes that sometimes look alike but have different etiologies (Emery, 2011).

Until recently, public health research has taken a similar approach to IPV as with other common threats to health: identify an outcome of concern (violence and/or injury); examine individual and population-based etiologies that appear to contribute to the problem (risk factors); and develop research-driven strategies to reduce these causes or risks. But if IPV is not a single phenomenon but rather multiple issues that present with similar indicators but have different roots, we can hardly expect strategies based on a singular understanding to be effective. Indeed, the evaluation literature on perpetrator treatment programs and dating violence prevention programs show very mixed reports of success (Babcock, Green, &

Robie, 2004; Fellmeth, Heffernan, Nurse, Habibula, & Dethi, 2013; Stover, Meadows, & Kaufman, 2009). Presently, most batterer treatment programs are "one size fits all" interventions using a combination of feminist theory and cognitive behavioral group therapy. But strategies focused on identifying and changing patterns of abuse and control may have little relevance to someone whose single act of aggression is situational and anomalous.

What arises most clearly from these interviews is support for Johnson's assertion that at least two different phenomena are at play: violence in controlling relationships (or what he refers to as intimate terrorism or coercive controlling violence) and violence in noncontrolling relationships (which he characterizes as situational). Although Johnson's description of intimate terrorism connotes a level of violence and coercion that is more severe and limiting than what most participants with controlling partners in this study revealed, this may be reflective of the demographics of this sample: As well-educated women with support and options, the participants possessed the resources to leave these relationships or negotiate for change. In some situations, we may be seeing "pre-intimate terrorism" that could have escalated into a more physically threatening situation had the participants not had the resources to initiate change.

Another conceptualization of coercive control that may be applicable comes from Dutton and Goodman (2005). Building on previous work by French and Raven (French & Raven, 1959), they proposed a model of coercive IPV composed of several primary elements, including the social-ecological context of the relationships, stage-setting by the perpetrator, coercion involving a demand and consequences for noncompliance, surveillance, the victim's vulnerabilities, and her response to the coercive behaviors. While elements of these components can be seen in the stories of women with controlling partners, behaviors that set the stage for further coercion by exploiting vulnerabilities and wearing down resistance were by far the most common. Women were harassed until they quit a job or stopped seeing friends and family, accused of not loving their partner if they read a book or went to an appointment, and told they were weak, stupid, slutty, worthless, and lucky that anyone loved them. In Maya's case, culture became an element of control. Her husband forced her to accept a post-doctoral position in

the United States and leave her children in India because he believed it would allow him to immigrate, too, and she felt unable to refuse or to divorce him. In the end, he was not allowed entry into the country, but had her story (and that of many others) ended differently, the primarily nonphysical coercion could well have been an antecedent to other, more violent behaviors.

Feminism and Family Conflict

If the quantitative data were taken alone and at face value, this sample could be viewed as illustrating gender symmetry with respect to violence, consistent with similar surveys conducted in nonagency samples. However, when examined in conjunction with the interviews, this conclusion becomes incomplete. Rather than supporting or refuting either perspective in this debate, these findings lend credibility to arguments that context and control need to be considered before any determination is made regarding gender and IPV (Johnson, 2006; Stark, 2010).

Clearly, without comparable data from men, these findings cannot definitively support feminist or family conflict theories regarding gender symmetry. Among these 22 women, however, roughly half described at least one male partner systematically controlling numerous aspects of their lives. A feminist interpretation of this might argue that this finding illustrates how societal gender imbalances in power continue to translate into gender imbalances in intimate relationships, even among women who are highly educated, employed, and living in Western communities. Although most of the women with controlling partners did not present as traditional "battered women," they nonetheless described how partners used manipulation and exploitation to compel obedience. In the case of these participants, their own violence rarely occurred outside of having been physically or psychologically assaulted, and while their actions were not strictly defensive in nature, neither were they overtly offensive.

One way to view these women's violence against controlling partners is as a reactive response to ongoing attacks on self-worth and autonomy: These actions *reclaim* lost control. Although this motivation appears more obvious when that loss is immediate (such as being blocked from the exit of a room), the ongoing nature of coercive control creates an environment where the victim is constantly at a loss. Hautzinger (2007) refers to a pattern of *contestation* rather than *domination* in her exploration of violence in the lives of women in rural Brazil. As gender roles changed in the larger community, each partner struggled for power within the relationship. Men resorted to violence because it was the accepted masculine reaction, and rather than experience victimization, women asserted their own power in response (Hautzinger, 2007).

Although these findings may support *some* of the feminist beliefs about IPV, they do not support the argument that all—or even most—of women's violence against men is a response to male violence or control. Half of the relationships involving female-to-male incidents of physical violence occurred outside of a male-controlled dynamic, and there were clear illustrations of women throwing objects at or hitting male partners because they were angry. In some instances, participants recalled these events with little shame or guilt, despite the fact that their actions had the potential to seriously injure their partner and fit legal definitions of assault.

Thus, while this study is unable to directly address the question of gender symmetry, these preliminary findings suggest that neither perspective is likely to be completely accurate. Further research needs to address the following limitations to fill the gaps we still have related to gender and violence, including how men characterize women's violent behaviors toward them as well as their own behaviors toward their partners.

Limitations

As with all investigations, this project has several limitations. Given the study's overall goal of improving our understanding of gender and IPV, the most critical flaw is the lack of men's perspectives. This absence was not for lack of trying; as described earlier, we attempted to interview men using the same inclusion criteria as well as male interviewers, but were unsuccessful at generating sufficient participation. Without men's voices, it is impossible to draw the same level of conclusions about women's use of violence and controlling behaviors as were presented for men. Women described the behaviors of their partners in great detail, and although they were candid about their own use of physical violence and psychologically manipulative behaviors, without hearing about experiences from a similar group of men, the conclusions we can draw

about the symmetry of patterns of controlling and coercive behaviors are preliminary, at best. Likewise, although participants described both using and receiving violence with the same partner, these data allowed only limited discussion of the nature of bidirectional or "mutual" violence. The struggle we had recruiting men points to a need to improve our approaches to involving men in IPV research, an issue that will be critical for future research efforts but cannot be adequately addressed here.

Second, the participants were overwhelmingly well-educated, employed, and White, and the norms and expectations related to gender and violence may be different for these women than for those from other backgrounds. The resources available to this population increase the likelihood that participants were able to leave or manage violent partners in ways that are not available to other women, explaining why, despite high levels of controlling behaviors, few women experienced the levels of physical and sexual violence generally associated with "domestic violence" or "intimate terrorism." Other limitations include those generally associated with interview-based research: a self-selected sampling frame, the potential for interviewer bias, and (possibly most significant to this study) bias resulting from reliance on self-reported data. Although the latter could still have influenced the overall findings, if we had been able to include men's perspectives, much of this bias could have "evened out."

Conclusion

This examination represents one step toward improving our understanding of relationship violence, control, and the potentially dynamic role gender plays. Based on in-depth interviews with 22 women who had previously reported using and/or receiving violence in a heterosexual relationship, the experiences of these women suggest that when the context of violent incidents is more closely examined, meaningful differences emerged between relationships with a strongly controlling partner and those with a relative egalitarian power structure. Although the lack of equivalent data from men limits our ability to draw clear conclusions about the role that gender may play in the use of those controlling behaviors, the fact that half of the women in this sample reported experiences with a male partner who engaged in these behaviors (while only two women described their own patterns of control) suggests that before accepting arguments rejecting or in favor of gender symmetry in IPV, equivalent research with men is needed.

In addition, we need to consider the nature of "mutual" violence between partners and examine the role that other social, cultural, and community-level factors that often intersect with gender play in influencing controlling behaviors. If the motivations for using violence differ between controlling and non-controlling relationships, how do they differ, why do they differ, for whom do they differ, and what do these answers mean for the development of more effective intervention and prevention programs? Finally, if partner violence is a manifestation of two or more etiologically distinct phenomena, more work needs to be done to understand these differences, and develop tailored and effective identification approaches within both clinical and research settings.

//// DISCUSSION QUESTIONS

1. How are coercive and controlling behaviors used within the relationship?

2. How does violence occur within the context of these relationships?

3. Why do you think that we generally ignore these sorts of behaviors within the context of intimate partner abuse?

References

Anderson, K. L. (2009). Gendering coercive control. *Violence Against Women, 15*, 1444–1457.

Anderson, K. L., & Umberson, D. (2001). Gendering violence: Masculinity and power in men's accounts of domestic violence. *Gender & Society, 15*, 358–380.

Archer, J. (2002). Sex differences in physically aggressive acts between heterosexual partners: A meta-analytic review. *Aggression and Violent Behavior, 7*, 313–351.

Babcock, J. C., Green, C. E., & Robie, C. (2004). Does batterers' treatment work? A meta-analytic review of domestic violence treatment. *Clinical Psychology Review, 23*, 1023–1053.

Creswell, J. W. (2009). *Research design: Qualitative, quantitative, and mixed methods approaches.* Thousand Oaks, CA: Sage.

Debbonaire, T., & Todd, J. (2012). Respect response to Dixon et al. (2012) "Perpetrator programmes for partner violence: Are they based on ideology or evidence?" *Legal and Criminological Psychology, 17*, 216–224.

Dixon, L., Archer, J., & Graham-Kevan, N. (2012). Perpetrator programmes for partner violence: Are they based on ideology or evidence? *Legal and Criminological Psychology, 17*, 196–215.

Dixon, L., & Graham-Kevan, N. (2011). Understanding the nature and etiology of intimate partner violence and implications for practice and policy. *Clinical Psychology Review, 31*, 1145–1155.

Dobash, R., & Dobash, R. (2004). Women's violence to men in intimate relationships: Working on a puzzle. *British Journal of Criminology, 44*, 324–349.

Dutton, D. G. (2012). The case against the role of gender in intimate partner violence. *Aggression and Violent Behavior, 17*, 99–104.

Dutton, D. G., & Nicholls, T. L. (2005). The gender paradigm in domestic violence research and theory: Part 1—The conflict of theory and data. *Aggression and Violent Behavior, 10*, 680–714.

Dutton, M. A., & Goodman, L. (2005). Coercion in intimate partner violence: Toward a new conceptualization. *Sex Roles, 52*, 743–756.

Emery, C. R. (2011). Disorder or deviant order? Re-theorizing domestic violence in terms of order, power, and legitimacy. *Aggression and Violent Behavior, 16*, 525–540.

Fellmeth, G., Heffernan, C., Nurse, J., Habibula, S., & Dethi, D. (2013). Educational and skills-based interventions for preventing relationship and dating violence in adolescents and young adults. *Cochrane Database of Systematic Reviews, 6*. Retrieved from http://onlinelibrary.wiley.com.proxy.cc.uic.edu/doi/10.1002/14651858.CD004534.pub3/epdf/standard

French, J., & Raven, B. (1959). The bases of social power. In D. Cartwright (Ed.), *Studies in social power* (p. 150–167). Oxford, UK: University of Michigan.

Gilfus, M. E., Trabold, N., O'Brien, P., & Fleck-Henderson, A. (2010). Gender and intimate partner violence: Evaluating the evidence. *Journal of Social Work Education, 46*, 245–263.

Hamberger, L., & Guse, C. (2002). Men's and women's use of intimate partner violence in clinical samples. *Violence Against Women, 8*, 1301–1311.

Hautzinger, S. (2007). *Violence in the city of women: Police and batterers in Bahia, Brazil.* Berkeley: University of California Press.

Hines, D. A., & Saudino, K. J. (2003). Gender differences in psychological, physical, and sexual aggression among college students using the revised Conflict Tactics Scales. *Violence and Victims, 18*, 197–217.

Johnson, M. P. (2006). Conflict and control: Gender symmetry and asymmetry in domestic violence. *Violence Against Women, 12,* 1003–1018.

Johnson, M. P. (2008). *A typology of domestic violence: Intimate terrorism, violent resistance, and situational couple violence.* Boston, MA: Northeastern University Press.

Johnson, M. P. (2011). Gender and types of intimate partner violence: A response to an antifeminist literature review. *Aggression and Violent Behavior, 16,* 289–296.

Langhinrichsen-Rohling, J. (2010). Controversies involving gender and intimate partner violence in the United States. *Sex Roles, 62,* 179–193.

Melton, H., & Belknap, J. (2003). He hits, she hits: Assessing gender differences and similarities in officially reported intimate partner violence. *Criminal Justice and Behavior, 30,* 328–348.

Miles, M. B., & Huberman, A. M. (1994). *Qualitative data analysis: An expanded sourcebook* (2nd ed.). Thousand Oaks, CA: Sage.

Miller, J. (2006). A specification of the types of intimate partner violence experienced by women in the general population. *Violence Against Women, 12,* 1105–1131.

Ross, J. M., & Babcock, J. C. (2010). Gender and intimate partner violence in the United States: Confronting the controversies. *Sex Roles, 62,* 194–200.

Stark, E. (2007). *Coercive control: How men entrap women in personal life.* New York: Oxford University Press.

Stark, E. (2009). Rethinking coercive control. *Violence Against Women, 15,* 1509–1525.

Stark, E. (2010). Do violent acts equal abuse? Resolving the gender parity/asymmetry dilemma. *Sex Roles, 62,* 201–211.

Stover, C. S., Meadows, A. L., & Kaufman, J. (2009). Interventions for intimate partner violence: Review and implications for evidence-based practice. *Professional Psychology: Research and Practice, 40,* 223–233.

Straus, M. A. (2008). Dominance and symmetry in partner violence by male and female university students in 32 nations. *Children and Youth Services Review, 30,* 252–275.

Straus, M. A., & Gelles, R. J. (1988). Violence in American families: How much is there and why does it occur? In E. W. Nunnally, C. S. Chilman, & F. M. Cox (Eds.), *Troubled relationships* (pp. 141–162). Newbury Park, CA: Sage.

Straus, M. A., Hamby, S., & Warren, W. L. (2003). *The Conflict Tactics Scales handbook.* Los Angeles, CA: Western Psychological Services.

Tanha, M., Beck, C. J. A., Figueredo, A. J., & Raghavan, C. (2010). Sex differences in intimate partner violence and the use of coercive control as a motivational factor for intimate partner violence. *Journal of Interpersonal Violence, 25,* 1836–1854.

READING /// 8

In this section, you learned about how intimate partner abuse can also occur in dating relationships. This article by Katie M. Edwards, Christina M. Dardis, and Christine A. Gidycz uses both quantitative and qualitative data to look at the issue of dating violence. In particular, this study highlights some of the reasons why women may or may not choose to disclose these victimizations and how these experiences could be used to inform intervention efforts for college campuses and local communities.

Women's Disclosure of Dating Violence
A Mixed Methodological Study

Katie M. Edwards, Christina M. Dardis, and Christine A. Gidycz

The majority of women will be the victim of dating violence during their lifetime (Edwards, Desai, Gidycz, & Van Wynsberghe, 2009). A burgeoning body of research documents the deleterious consequences of dating violence to victims and society (Lewis & Fremouw, 2001). Less research, however, has focused on women's disclosure of dating violence, especially research utilizing mixed methodologies and samples of

SOURCE: Edwards, Katie M., Dardis, Christina M. and Gidycz, Christine A. (2012). Women's Disclosure of Dating Violence: A Mixed Methodological Study. *Feminism & Psychology* 22(4): 507–517.

non-treatment seeking college women in abusive dating relationships. Using a feminist lens, the purpose of the current study was to explore this gap in the literature. In particular, the present study represents a follow-up to Mahlstedt and Keeny's (1993) mixed methodological study about U.S. college women's disclosure of dating violence.

Mahlstedt and Keeny (1993) found that 92% of abused women disclosed the abuse to at least one source and that these women were much more likely to disclose abuse to informal support services than formal support services. Specifically, they found that although only 9% of abused women disclosed dating violence to police, 80% disclosed dating violence to a friend. Other common informal support sources to whom women disclosed were relatives, including mothers (43%), sisters (47%), brothers (33%), and fathers (15%). These rates of disclosure are similar to rates of sexual assault disclosure found in more recent studies with college (Orchowski & Gidycz, forthcoming) and community (Ullman, 1996, 2010) samples.

Mahlstedt and Keeny (1993) also documented that women endorse barriers to disclosure such as embarrassment about the abuse, believing that the abuse is a private matter, fear for their own safety, or concerns about social reactions. Orchowski and Gidycz (forthcoming) found that women who endorse lower levels of self-blame were more likely to disclose sexual violence than individuals who endorse higher levels of self-blame. The data from these studies are consistent with Ahrens (2006) and Ullman's (2010) assertions that violence against women serves to reinforce women's powerlessness in a patriarchal society and that silence (or nondisclosure) symbolizes this powerlessness.

In addition to assessing rates of disclosure and reasons for nondisclosure, Mahlstedt and Keeny (1993) assessed social reactions to abused women's disclosure. These researchers found that the most commonly reported responses to disclosure were that confidants "listened," "gave helpful advice," and were "angry with the assailant." The least frequent responses were "trivialized it," "saw me as a failure," and "made decisions for me." Responses that

women reported as the most helpful included "understanding," "advice-giving," "listening," and "interrupting victim blame." Mahlstedt and Keeny reported that excessive advice giving (e.g., to leave the abuser) was often interpreted by women as an insinuation of victim blame, and [these] were considered by women to be the most unhelpful responses. These results underscore the differences in social reactions that women receive to their disclosure of dating violence within the context of a patriarchal culture.

Although the Mahlstedt and Keeney (1993) study contributes to our knowledge of disclosure of dating violence, there remains a dearth of research assessing reasons for nondisclosure and the responses from confidants that college-aged women who disclose dating violence perceive as the most and least helpful. Also, there have been considerable efforts in our society (e.g., media awareness campaigns, dating violence prevention, and intervention programming) to raise awareness about dating violence over the past years (Gidycz et al., 2011), which may have contributed to changes in disclosure processes (Ullman, personal communication, January 6, 2011). In order to build upon the results of earlier research, we attempted to answer the following questions utilizing quantitative data: To whom do women disclose dating violence? What are the correlates of women's disclosure of dating violence? Utilizing qualitative data, we attempted to answer the following questions: For women who disclosed, who was the most helpful and why? Who was the least helpful and why? For women who did not disclose, what were their reasons for doing so? Of note, we agree with other researchers (e.g., Ahrens, 2006; Ullman, 2010) that social reactions to interpersonal violence emanate from broader social norms and attitudes related to violence against women and gendered power relations. Although we did not directly assess these social norms and attitudes in our study, we assert that these invariably affect social reactions to disclosure and survivors' perceptions of helpfulness and unhelpfulness of specific responses. We thus use a critical feminist lens when interpreting and discussing our results.

SOURCE: Edwards, K. M., Dardis, C. M., & Gidycz, C. A. (2012). Women's disclosure of dating violence: A mixed methodological study. *Feminism & Psychology, 22*(4), 507–517.

Method

Participants

Participants included 44 women who reported at least one incident of sexual, physical, or psychological abuse in their current heterosexual relationship, as measured by the Conflict Tactics Scale-Revised (CTS2; Straus, Hamby, Boney-McCoy, & Sugarman, 1996) and obtained from a larger screening sample ($N = 107$). The 44 women were predominantly young (mean age = 19.30, $SD = 1.36$) and white (82%).

Results

To Whom Do Women Disclose Dating Violence?

Approximately 75% ($n = 33$) of the sample disclosed dating violence to at least one source. As demonstrated in Reading Table 8.1, the most common disclosure sources were informal supports, specifically friends.

What Are the Correlates of Women's Disclosure of Dating Violence?

Three t-tests and a chi-square test were conducted to determine the correlates of women's disclosure of dating violence. Results from the t-tests (see Reading Table 8.2) suggested that, compared to nondisclosers, disclosers reported higher levels of stress associated with the experience and higher levels of partner blame. Results from the chi-square test (see Reading Table 8.3) suggested that disclosers were more likely to think about ending the relationship than nondisclosers.

For Women Who Disclosed, Who Was the Most Helpful and Why?

Content analyses showed that 56% of disclosers perceived their friends as the most helpful, with the remainder stating family members were most helpful. The most common reasons that disclosers stated people were helpful were that confidants offered good advice (36%), provided the opportunity to vent/talk about it (28%), and provided

Reading Table 8.1 • Rates of Disclosure

Source	Percentage Who Disclosed to Source
Female friend	73%
Male friend	25%
Sister	25%
Brother	2%
Mother	23%
Father	7%
Counselor	5%
Medical doctor	0%
Law enforcement	0%
Priest/minister	0%

NOTE: Percentages exceed 100% because many participants disclosed to multiple sources.

Reading Table 8.2 • Means (and standard deviations) for Variables of Interest

	Disclosers	Nondisclosers
Partner blame	3.15 (1.03)	2.45 (1.36)
Self-blame	1.67 (1.19)	1.36 (1.43)
Stress of situation	2.85 (1.03)	1.91 (1.58)

Reading Table 8.3 • Rates of Disclosure as a Function of Thoughts About Ending the Relationship

	Thoughts About Ending Relationship	
	Yes	No
Disclosers	58%	42%
Nondisclosers	18%	82%

comfort and other emotional support (20%). Additional helpful responses were that confidants related to the experience (16%), provided rationalization for the partners' behavior (12%), and provided a neutral perspective (8%). See Reading Table 8.4 for quotes depicting the reasons disclosers stated individuals were helpful.

For Women Who Disclosed, Who Was the Least Helpful and Why?

Content analyses showed that 49% of disclosers felt that friends were the least helpful, with the remainder stating their partner (20%), family member (19%), or counselor (13%) were the least helpful. Reasons that disclosers stated people were unhelpful were because others told them to break up with their partner (33%), provided "bad advice" (27%), did not understand (27%), and joked about the experience (20%). See Reading Table 8.5 for quotes depicting the reasons disclosers stated people were least helpful.

For Women Who Did Not Disclose, What Were Their Reasons?

The most common reason for nondisclosure was that the incident was "no big deal" (80%). Additional reasons included concerns that no one would understand (10%) and concerns about anticipated confidants' reactions (20%). See Reading Table 8.6 for quotes depicting the reasons participants did not disclose.

Reading Table 8.4 ● Quotes Depicting Most Helpful Responses	
Category	**Example Quotes**
Offered advice	"My friends told me they never see me and talked about [how] they hated him and my mom hated him so I knew he was no good."
	"My sister because I tell her everything and she gives me good advice."
	"[Friends] gave me a lot of guidance."
	"My friends told me not to talk to him for a couple of days so we can both cool down."
	"My sister and parents always give good advice."
Vent/talk about it	"Just talking it out to some of my girlfriends calmed me down."
	"My best friend just let me talk about it."
	"I talked to my roommate about it."
Emotional support	"They comforted me."
	"Friends [were] very supportive."
	"[My best friend] was very comforting."
Related	"I thought my best friend was helpful because she had it happen to her."
	"My friends were the most helpful because they have been there."
Rationalized behavior	"His friends were the most helpful because they informed me that this was how he always acted when he drank."
	"Male friends. They explained that he needed to cool off."
Neutral perspective	"[My friends] didn't justify the action, but allowed me a different perspective."
	"My best friend because she knows me so well and knows my boyfriend pretty well so she could give me an informed and helpful opinion."

Discussion

The purpose of this study was to assess college women's disclosure of dating violence utilizing a mixed methodological design. Similar to Mahlstedt and Keeny's (1993) study, many women were able to break their silence and disclose dating violence. Almost all women who disclosed did so to an informal support, most commonly female friends. Additionally, quantitative results demonstrated that there was a relationship between several factors—stress associated with abuse, partner blame, and thoughts about ending the relationship—and the disclosure of dating violence. However, given the retrospective nature of this study, the temporal sequencing of these variables is unclear . . . [for] the temporal sequencing of these variables (i.e., if a certain thought or emotion led to disclosure, or if the act of disclosing and the responses of others led to a certain thought or emotion).

Qualitative content analyses suggested that women's minimization of the abuse was the most commonly mentioned reason for nondisclosure. In fact, 80% of nondisclosers chose not to discuss the experience with anyone because it was "no big deal." This finding may be reflective of larger social ideologies that legitimize and normalize violence against women, often leading victims to internalize these norms and beliefs (Baly, 2010; Wood, 2001). Additional reported reasons for nondisclosure included fear that no one would understand, feelings of embarrassment, or believing that the experience was a private matter, all of which are consistent with Mahlstedt and Keeny's (1993) research and consistent with patriarchal social structures that influence micro-level disclosure processes. For those women who disclosed dating violence to others, responses from confidants varied in their perceived helpfulness. Perhaps due to the fact that 98% of women in this sample who disclosed did so to

Reading Table 8.5 • Quotes Depicting Least Helpful Responses

Category	Example Quotes
Encouraged relationship dissolution	"Female friends just said 'so dump him.'"
	"They aren't a fan of my boyfriend so they automatically wanted me to leave him."
	"My brother. He wants us to break up."
	"My mom wanted me to end the relationship."
	"[My friends] didn't understand why I wouldn't just leave him."
"Bad advice"	"Some friends said not to do anything which was worthless."
	"They couldn't give an informed opinion."
	"Telling me to call his mom."
	"My father because he didn't think it was appropriate to be dating at the age of 15–16."
Did not understand	"My counselor didn't know how to respond."
	"[My mom] didn't understand."
	"[My friends] didn't understand why I would be so upset."
	"They don't understand our relationship."
Joked	"Male friends because they jokingly asked why I wouldn't [give into sexual pressure]."
	"Male friends just laugh it off."

Reading Table 8.6 ● Quotes Depicting Reasons for Nondisclosure

Category	Example Quotes
"No big deal"	"It was not a big deal to me! Stuff happens; you get into fights, not a big deal."
	"It wasn't that big of a deal."
	"It was not a big deal—my boyfriend [and I] talked about it afterward."
	"The incident was no big deal. I just wanted to have sex but he wanted me to perform oral."
	"It was nothing out of the ordinary for two teenagers. I forgave him b/c he was sorry and we moved on, I did not need to discuss it with others—it was minuscule."
	"I felt like it was a normal dating thing and that it was unnecessary to tell anyone. Afterwards, I felt like he really didn't mean it to come out that way so I just forgot about it."
Would not understand	"I didn't feel anyone would understand the situation since they weren't there."
Concern about reactions	"Because I was embarrassed and it was my business I didn't want anyone else to know."
	"I think it's not a good thing to talk to the people who really care about me. I don't want to let them worry about me, especially my family."

friends, friends were perceived as both the most helpful (56%) and least helpful confidants (49%). Indeed, consistent with Mahlstedt and Keeny, women often disclosed to multiple friends, some of whom were helpful and some of whom were unhelpful.

Interestingly, we found that, whereas some individuals reported a particular response (such as telling one to leave) was helpful, others found the same response unhelpful. This finding is consistent with the transtheoretical model of change (Prochaska & DiClemente, 1984) and other research with abused women (e.g., Enander, 2011), such that for women who are in contemplation or preparation stages of leaving, advice such as being told to leave may be perceived as helpful (and consonant with one's own beliefs), whereas for precontemplative individuals, being told to leave would be dissonant with one's own beliefs about her relationship. This finding may also be related to patriarchal cultural factors and social discourses that maintain some women in abusive relationships and affect how women understand their role in relationships and their subjectivity as women. This notion

is related to feminist research suggesting that some women internalize oppressive social norms regarding gender ideologies and hold more accepting attitudes of violence against women (Baly, 2010; Wood, 2001), which undoubtedly affects the extent to which women find certain social responses to their disclosures of dating violence helpful or unhelpful.

Several limitations of the current study and suggestions for future research are noted. First, the sample size was small and the participant demographics of our sample were homogenous (i.e., white, heterosexual women). This limited our ability to assess differences in perceived helpfulness and unhelpfulness among the varying types of supports (e.g., informal vs. formal supports) and different abuse types (e.g., physical, sexual, and psychological). Additionally, the retrospective nature of this study did not allow us to assess the temporal sequencing of the correlates of dating violence or how disclosure of dating violence relates to women's long-term adjustment and relationship stability—questions that could be followed up using longitudinal mixed methodologies with larger, more diverse samples. Additionally, it is unclear from the qualitative data what constituted participants' perceptions of "good" and "bad" advice, as well why some participants viewed responses as helpful and others viewed the same responses as unhelpful. Accordingly, future research could attempt to understand participants' perceptions of various types of advice using more rigorous and in-depth qualitative methodologies (e.g., interviews) and assess readiness to change, empowerment, and cultural variables as possible explanations for variability in what women view as helpful and unhelpful.

Despite these limitations, the findings from the current study offer implications for dating violence programming and social awareness efforts. Given the large percentage of women who minimized the abuse, there is a need for psychoeducation and public awareness campaigns to educate people about dating violence. Further, these data underscore the importance of educating others—especially college students since they are the most likely source of their friends' disclosures—on how to

respond to the disclosure of dating violence. Although dating violence prevention programs often provide suggestions on how to help a friend in an abusive relationship (Black & Weisz, 2008; Foshee et al., 1998; Senn, 2011), findings from the current study underscore the complexity in what women deem as helpful and unhelpful responses to their disclosures of dating violence. Indeed, some of the responses that women reported as helpful (e.g., minimize the abuse) are responses that program developers and facilitators discourage and consider harmful. Clearly, this is a critical area for more mixed methodological and participatory action research that must include dialogue between researchers, clinicians, program developers, survivors of dating violence, and their formal and informal supports. Furthermore, programming efforts alone will not lead to widespread change in reactions to disclosure because these interpersonal reactions are situated in larger patriarchal social and institutional contexts that legitimize violence against women, and these too must be addressed.

/// DISCUSSION QUESTIONS

1. What do the quantitative results of this study tell us about dating violence and the disclosure practices of women?

2. What do the qualitative results of this study tell us about dating violence and the disclosure practices of women?

3. What did victims find were the most helpful resources in their disclosure? The least helpful?

References

Ahrens, C. E. (2006). Being silenced: The impact of negative social reactions on the disclosure of rape. *American Journal of Community Psychology, 38:* 263–274.

Baly, A. R. (2010). Leaving abusive relationships: Constructions of self and situation by abused women. *Journal of Interpersonal Violence, 25:* 2297–2315.

Black, B. M., & Weisz, A. M. (2008). Effective interventions with dating violence and domestic violence. In: Franklin, C., Harris, M. B., & Allen-Meares, P. (Eds.), *The school practitioner's concise companion to preventing violence and conflict* (pp. 127–139). New York: Oxford University Press.

Edwards, K. M., Desai, A. D., Gidycz, C. A., & Van Wynsberghe, A. (2009). College women's aggression in relationships: The role of childhood and adolescent victimization. *Psychology of Women Quarterly, 33:* 255–265.

Enander, V. (2011). Leaving Jekyll and Hyde: Emotion work in the context of intimate partner violence. *Feminism and Psychology, 21:* 29–48.

Foshee, V. A., Bauman, K. E., Arriaga, X. B., Helms, R. W., Koch, G. G., & Linder, G. F. (1998). An evaluation of Safe Dates, an adolescent dating violence prevention program. *American Journal of Public Health, 8:* 45–50.

Gidycz, C. A., Orchowski, L. M., & Edwards, K. M. (2011). Sexual violence: Primary prevention. In J. White, M. Koss, & A. Kazdin (Eds.), *Violence against women and children vol. 2: Navigating solutions.* Washington, DC: American Psychological Association, 159–179.

Lewis, S. F., & Fremouw, W. (2001). Dating violence: A critical review of the literature. *Clinical Psychology Review, 21:* 105–127.

Mahlstedt, D., & Keeny, L. (1993). Female survivors of dating violence and their social networks. *Feminism and Psychology, 3:* 319–333.

Orchowski, L. M., & Gidycz, C. A. (forthcoming). Psychological consequences associated with positive and negative responses to disclosure of sexual assault among college women: A prospective study. *Violence Against Women.*

Prochaska, J., & DiClemente, C. (1984). *The transtheoretical approach: Crossing traditional boundaries of therapy.* Homewood, IL: Dow Jones-Irwin.

Senn, C. Y. (2011). An imperfect feminist journey: Reflections on the process to develop an effective sexual assault resistance programme for university women. *Feminism and Psychology, 21:* 121–137.

Straus, M. A., Hamby, S. L., Boney-McCoy, S., & Sugarman, D. B. (1996). The revised Conflict Tactics Scales (CTS2): Development and preliminary psychometric data. *Journal of Family Issues, 17:* 283–316.

Ullman, S. E. (1996). Social reactions, coping strategies, and self-blame attributions in adjustment to sexual assault. *Psychology of Women Quarterly, 20:* 505–526.

Ullman, S. E. (2010). *Talking about sexual assault: Society's response to survivors.* Washington, DC: American Psychological Association.

Wood, J. T. (2001). The normalization of violence in heterosexual romantic relationships: Women's narratives of love and violence. *Journal of Social and Personal Relationships, 18:* 239–261.

International Issues in Gender-Based Violence

Within a global environment, millions of women personally experience violence or live representations of savagery and brutality that can last for decades. You've already learned about the issues of intimate partner abuse and rape/sexual assault in Sections III and IV. However, these are not the only acts of violence that women around the world endure. Some of the most common forms of violence against women include human trafficking, femicide, genital mutilation, and murder in the name of honor. Each of these crimes are related to the status of women within their communities, and suggestions for change are rooted within a shift of gendered normative values and the treatment of women in these societies. Within this section, you will learn about the nature of these crimes, the implications for women in these regions, and how criminal justice policies address these issues within an international context.

As you read through the experiences of the women and their victimizations, it is important to consider how the cultural context of their lives affects their victimization experience. The effects of culture are significant, because it can alter not only how these crimes are viewed by agents of social control (police, legal systems) but also how the community interprets these experiences. These definitions play a significant role in determining how these crimes are reported (or if reports are made), as well as any response that may arise from these offenses. It can be dangerous to apply a White, middle-class lens or an "Americanized identity" to these issues; what we might do as individuals may not necessarily reflect the social norms and values of other cultures.

Human Trafficking

Rathana was born to a very poor family in Cambodia. When Rathana was 11 years old, her mother sold her to a woman in a neighboring province who sold ice in a small shop. Rathana worked for this woman and her husband for several months. She was beaten almost every day, and the shop owner never gave her much to eat. One day, a man came to the shop and bought Rathana from the ice seller. He then took her to a faraway province. When they arrived at his home, he showed Rathana a pornographic movie and then forced her to act out the movie by raping her. The man kept Rathana for more than 8 months, raping her sometimes two or three times a day. One day, the man got sick and went to a hospital. He brought Rathana with him and raped her in the hospital bathroom. Another patient reported what was happening to the police. Rathana was rescued from this man and sent to live in a shelter for trafficking survivors.

Salima was recruited in Kenya to work as a maid in Saudi Arabia. She was promised enough money to support herself and her two children. But when she arrived in Jeddah, she was forced to work 22 hours a day, cleaning 16 rooms daily for several months. She was never let out of the house and was given food only when her employers had leftovers. When there were no leftovers, Salima turned to dog food for sustenance. She suffered verbal and sexual abuse from her employers and their children. One day while Salima was hanging clothes on the line, her employer pushed her out the window, telling her, "You are better off dead." Salina plunged into a swimming pool three floors down and was rescued by police. After a week in the hospital, she returned to Kenya with broken legs and hands.

Katya, a student athlete in an Eastern European capital city, dreamed of learning English and visiting the United States. Her opportunity came in the form of a student visa program, through which international students can work temporarily in the United States. But when she got to America, rather than being taken to a job at a beach resort, the people who met her put her on a bus to Detroit, Michigan. They took her passport away and forced her and her friends to dance in strip clubs for the traffickers' profit. They controlled the girls' movement and travel, kept keys to the girls' apartment, and listened in on phone calls the girls made to their parents. After a year of enslavement, Katya and her friend were able to reach federal authorities with the help of a patron of the strip club in whom they had confided. Due to their bravery, six other victims were identified and rescued. Katya now has immigration status under the U.S. trafficking law. (U.S. Department of State, 2011)

Each of these scenarios represents a common story for many victims of human trafficking. These examples reflect a life experience where women victims of trafficking have been manipulated, abused, and exploited. These are but a few examples of the crimes that make up the category of human trafficking.

Human trafficking is the second largest criminal activity and the fastest growing criminal enterprise in the world. Estimates by the United Nations (2008) suggest that approximately 2.5 million people from 127 countries are victims of trafficking. Due to the nature of these crimes, it is difficult to determine a precise number of human trafficking victims worldwide. According to data provided by the U.S. State Department, between 600,000 and 820,000 men, women, and children are trafficked across international borders every year. These numbers do not include the thousands, and potentially millions, of individuals who are trafficked within the boundaries of their homelands (U.S. Department of State, 2013).

Trafficking can involve cases within the borders of one's country as well as transport across international boundaries. Thailand is a well-known location for the sexual trafficking of women and girls who migrate from other Southeast Asian countries, such as Cambodia, Laos, Myanmar (Burma), and Vietnam, as well as other Asian countries, such as China and Hong Kong. Others find their way to Thailand from the United Kingdom, South Africa,

Czech Republic, Australia, and the United States (Rafferty, 2007). However, examples of trafficking are not limited to countries from the Southeast Asian region. The trafficking of women and children is an international phenomenon and can be found in many regions around the world, even in the United States.

Within the discussion of human trafficking, it is sex trafficking that receives the greatest amount of attention. Between January 2007 and September 2008, there were 1,229 documented incidents[1] of human trafficking in the United States. An astounding 83% of these cases were defined as alleged incidents of sex trafficking (such as forced prostitution and other sex crimes), of which 32% of these cases involved child sex trafficking and 62% involved adults (Kyckelhahn, Beck, & Cohen, 2009). According to the U.S. Trafficking Victims Protection Act (TVPA), which was passed by Congress in 2000, sex trafficking occurs when

> a commercial act is induced by force, fraud or coercion, or in which the person induced to perform such an act has not attained 18 years of age; or the recruitment, harboring, transportation provision, or obtaining a person for labor or services through the use of force, fraud or coercion [is] for the purpose of subjection to involuntary servitude, peonage, debt bondage, or slavery. (U.S. Department of State, 2011, p. 8)

Trafficked victims may find themselves working in a variety of settings, including brothels, strip clubs, and sex clubs. They also appear in pornographic films, live Internet sex chats, and on the streets where they solicit money in exchange for sexual services. Traffickers use several methods to manipulate women and girls into the sex trade and prey on their poor economic standing and desires for improving their financial status. These enticements include offers of employment, marriage, and travel. Each of these opportunities is a shield to trap women into sexual slavery. In some cases, women may be kidnapped or abducted, although these tactics are rare compared to the majority of cases, which involve lies, deceit, and trickery to collect its victims (Simkhada, 2008). In some cases, young children are recruited by "family friends" or community members or may even be intentionally sold into servitude by their own parents. According to Rafferty (2007)

> Traffickers use a number of coercive methods and psychological manipulations to maintain control over their victims and deprive them of their free will, to render them subservient and dependent by destroying their sense of self and connection to others, and to make their escape virtually impossible by destroying their physical and psychological defenses. The emotional and physical trauma, as well as the degradation associated with being subjected to humiliation and violence, treatment as a commodity, and unrelenting abuse and fear, presents a grave risk to the physical, psychological and social-emotional development of trafficking victims. (p. 410)

Victims are dependent on their traffickers for food, shelter, clothing, and safety. They may be trafficked to a region where they do not speak the language, which limits opportunities to seek assistance. They may be concerned for the safety of their family members, because many traffickers use threats against loved ones to ensure cooperation (Rafferty, 2007). Girls who are imprisoned in a brothel are often beaten and threatened in order to obtain compliance. They are reminded of their "debts" that they are forced to work off through the sale of their bodies. Most girls have little contact with the world outside the brothel and are unable to see or communicate with the family members that are left behind.

While some girls are able to escape the brothel life on their own, most require the intervention of police or social workers. Girls receive services from "rehabilitation centers," which provide health and social welfare assistance to victims of trafficking. The intent of these agencies is to return girls to their homes; however, many of these girls

---

[1]The Human Trafficking Reporting System (HTRS) is part of the Department of Justice and tracks incidents of suspected human trafficking for which an investigation, arrest, prosecution, or incarceration occurred as a result of a charge related to human trafficking.

indicate they experience significant challenges on return to their communities. Many of these girls are not looked on as victims but rather as damaged goods when they return home. As such, they are shunned and stigmatized not only by society at large but also by their family members (Simkhada, 2008). As a result, many victims keep their trafficking experiences a secret, which can complicate outreach and recovery efforts. Particularly in cases where women leave home for a job, they may be chastised for not sending money back to the family or feel anguish over having left their children. Even when victims did disclose their experiences to family members, they were not believed. In some cases, the husbands accused their wives of marital infidelity and did not understand that the women were victimized. In others, the stigma of trafficking and the fear of others knowing of their experience led many victims to stay silent about their victimization (Brunovskis & Surtees, 2012).

Despite being aware of trafficking as a social issue, many jurisdictions have failed to effectively address the problem in their communities. Much of the intervention efforts against trafficking involve nongovernmental organizations (NGOs), national and international antitrafficking agencies, and local grassroots organizations. While several countries have adopted legislation that criminalizes the sale and exploitation of human beings, many have yet to enact antitrafficking laws. In some cases, countries may have laws on the books but have limited resources or priorities for enforcing such laws. Still other countries punish the victims of these crimes, often charging them with crimes such as prostitution when they seek out assistance from the police. While grassroots and antitrafficking organizations have developed policies and practices designed to punish traffickers and provide assistance to the victims, few of these recommendations have been implemented effectively or on a worldwide scale.

Labor Trafficking

While sex trafficking is the most common discussed form of trafficking, there are other acts of trafficking. **Labor trafficking** is defined as "the recruitment, harboring, transportation, provision, or obtainingof a person for labor or services, through the use of force, fraud, or coercion for the purpose of subjection to involuntary servitude, peonage, debt bondage, or slavery" (Victims of Trafficking and Violence Protection Act of 2000). While men are more likely to be the victims of labor trafficking, women make up approximately one-third of the victims in these cases. Certain types of labor trafficking, such as domestic servitude, are more likely to have female victims (UNODC, 2016). Forced labor can also involve immigrants and migrant workers that are in need of employment. Research on a migrant community in Southern California found that 30% of the undocumented workers were victims of labor trafficking. More than half of these individuals had experienced exploitation and abuse by their employers. In contrast, studies on forced labor in international settings notes that temporary migration programs, such as guest worker programs, often place individuals at risk for exploitation (Belanger, 2014). While victims of labor trafficking are subjected to threats to their physical safety and restrictions on their access to friends and family, female victims of labor trafficking are also at risk for sexual harassment and assault. (Abdul, Joarder & Miller, 2014; Zhang, Spiller, Finch, & Qin, 2014) Estimates indicate that forced labor generates more than $30 billion dollars annually (International Labour Organization, 2005).

Often embedded in cases of forced labor trafficking is debt bondage. **Debt bondage** requires victims to pay off a debt through labor. Debt may be inherited as a result of the actions of other family members or may be acquired in response for employment, transportation, and housing or board (U.S Department of Health & Human Services, 2011). In some cases, the costs of these debts are so high that it is impossible for the victim to ever depart the situation. While men, women, and children are all at risk for being victimized, women are disproportionately presented in these cases (U.S. Department of State, 2012).

Cases of labor trafficking are far less likely to be identified by local law enforcement. In many instances, cases of forced labor trafficking are hidden within legal forms of employment (Barrick, Lattimore, Pitts, & Zhang, 2014). In addition, agencies have limited training on how to identify cases of labor trafficking and lack the adequate resources to be able to pursue cases of labor trafficking. These jurisdictions also tend to lack services that are targeted for victims of trafficking (Farrell, Owens & McDevitt, 2014).

Responses to Human Trafficking

There are a number of items of national legislation and international policies that outline efforts to address human trafficking worldwide. While there is no uniform standard across jurisdictions, these generally include three basic themes involving the prosecution of traffickers, protection of victims, and prevention of human trafficking.

In the United States, legislation known as the **Trafficking Victims Protection Act of 2000** (TVPA)[2] is designed to punish traffickers, protect victims, and facilitate prevention efforts in the community to fight against human trafficking. Enacted by Congress in 2000, the law provides that traffickers can be sent to prison for up to 20 years for each victim. In 2008, the Department of Justice obtained 77 convictions in 40 cases of human trafficking, with an average sentence of 112 months (9.3 years). Over two-thirds of these cases involved acts of sex trafficking. At the state level, 42 states currently have antitrafficking legislation in their jurisdictions and are active in identifying offenders and victims of these crimes (U.S. Department of State, 2008).

While the TVPA includes protection and assistance for victims, these provisions are limited. For example, victims of trafficking are eligible for a **T-visa**, which provides a temporary visa. However, there are only 5,000 T-visas available (regardless of the numbers of demand for these visas), and issuance of this type of visa is limited to "severe forms of trafficking (such as) involving force, fraud or coercion or any trafficking involving a minor" (Haynes, 2004, p. 241). In addition, applications for permanent residency are conditional on a victim's participation as a potential witness in a trafficking prosecution. In the 2 years following the implementation of the T-visa program, only 23 visas had been granted, a far cry from the demand given that over 50,000 people are trafficked into the United States alone each year (Oxman-Martinez & Hanley, 2003).

In an effort to track antitrafficking campaigns on a global level, the U.S. Department of State assesses the efficacy of policies and practices. Each country is organized into one of three tiers, and the United States uses these rankings in making funding decisions for countries in need. Countries need to demonstrate that they are working to prosecute the offenders of trafficking and protect the victims. "If governments fail to meet this minimum standard, or do not make strides to do so, they will be classified as a Tier 3 country. Under those circumstances, the United States will only provide humanitarian and trade-related assistance" (Wooditch, 2011, pp. 475–476). Table 5.1 illustrates data on the global enforcement of trafficking under the Trafficking Victims Protection Reauthorization Act of 2003. While well intentioned, the *Trafficking in Persons (TIP) Report* has been criticized, there have been few policy recommendations that have been implemented as a result of its findings. Research indicates that over the past decade, antitrafficking efforts have remained stable despite the introduction of the tier ranking system. While countries may have made efforts in combating human trafficking, it may not be enough to impact their tier ranking. In addition, the tier system has not always led to decision making in terms of the grant allocation process as it was initially intended to do (Wooditch, 2011).

In 2000, the United Nations proposed the *Protocol to Prevent, Suppress and Punish Trafficking in Persons, especially Women and Children*. While the intent of this multinational legal agreement was to join together international entities to identify and respond to victims and offenders of human trafficking, efforts have been slow to action. For example, the protocol applies to only those countries that have agreed to comply. While 147 countries have joined, several have raised concerns or objections to the process by which conflicts would be resolved (for example, via a third-party arbitration). So while many applaud the United Nations for attempting to tackle the issue of human trafficking, these efforts have been largely unsuccessful.

Similar to the TVPA in the United States, and as suggested by Cho, Dreher, and Neumayer (2011), the European Union policies on trafficking prioritize the prosecution of offenders over the needs of victims, and visas are granted only for the purposes of pursuing charges against the traffickers. In addition, there is no encouragement or pressure by the EU for states to develop programs to address the needs of trafficked victims (Haynes, 2004). While the push

---

[2]Reauthorized by Congress in December 2008.

Table 5.1 • Global Law Enforcement on Trafficking

Year	Prosecutions	Convictions	Victims Identified
2008	5,212	2,983	30,961
2009	5,606	4,166	49,105
2010	6,017	3,619	33,113
2011	7,206	4,239	41,210
2012	7,705	4,746	46,570
2013	9,460	5,446	44,758
2014	10,051	4,443	44,462
2015	18,930	6,609	77,823

SOURCE: U.S. Department of State (2017).

to *jail the offender* of these crimes appears positive, the reality is that few prosecutions have succeeded in achieving this task. Even in cases where prosecutions are "successful" and traffickers are held accountable for their crimes, their convictions result in short sentences and small fines, the effect of which does little to deter individuals from participating in these offenses in the future.

Despite the laws that have increased the punishments for traffickers, research notes that most cases within the United States are reactive and focus on the prosecution of offenders rather than proactive strategies that could help identify traffickers and their victims (Farrell, Owens & McDevitt, 2014). While local law enforcement could serve a valuable role, most officers lack the training in order to identify both offenders and victims in these cases (Farrell, McDevitt, & Fahy, 2010]).

In contrast to the prosecution-oriented approach, several international organizations have developed models to fight trafficking that focus on the needs of the victim. These approaches focus on the security and safety of the victims, allow them to regain control over their lives, and empower them to make positive choices for their future while receiving housing and employment assistance. While this approach provides valuable resources for victims, it does little to control and stop the practice of trafficking from continuing.

Promising Solutions to End Human Trafficking

Given the limitations of the **jail the offender and protect the victim models**, research by Haynes (2004) provides several policy recommendations that would combine the best aspects of these two approaches. These recommendations include the following:

1. *Protect, do not prosecute the victim:* As indicated earlier, many victims find themselves charged with prostitution and other crimes in their attempts to seek help. Not only does this process punish the victim, but it also inhibits additional victims from coming forward out of fear that they too might be subjected to criminal punishments. Antitrafficking legislation needs to ensure that victims will not be prosecuted for the actions in which they engaged as a part of their trafficked status. In addition, victims need to be provided with shelter and care to meet their immediate needs following an escape from their trafficker.

2. *Develop community awareness and educational public service campaigns:* Many victims of trafficking do not know where to turn for help. An effective media campaign could provide victims with information on how to recognize if they are in an exploitative situation, avenues for assistance such as shelters and safety options, and long-term planning support, such as information on immigration. Media campaigns can also help educate the general public on the ways in which traffickers entice their victims and provide information on reporting potential victims to local agencies. Recent examples of prevention efforts in fighting trafficking have included raising public awareness through billboard campaigns, the development of a national hotline to report possible human trafficking cases, and public service announcements in several languages, including English, Spanish, Russian, Korean, and Arabic, to name a few (U.S. Department of State, 2009). These efforts help increase public knowledge about the realities of human trafficking within the community.

3. *Address the social and economic reasons for vulnerability to trafficking:* The road to trafficking begins with poverty. Economic instability creates vulnerability for women as they migrate from their communities in search of a better life. For many, the migration from their homes to the city places them at risk for traffickers, who seek out these women and promise them employment opportunities only to hold them against their will for the purposes of forced labor and slavery. Certainly, the road to eradicating poverty around the world is an insurmountable task, but an increased understanding of how and why women leave could inform educational campaigns, which could relay information about the risks and dangers of trafficking and provide viable options for legitimate employment and immigration.

4. *Prosecute traffickers and those who aid and abet traffickers:* Unfortunately, in many of these jurisdictions, law enforcement and legal agents are subjected to bribery and corruption, which limits the assistance that victims of trafficking may receive. "Police are known to tip off club workers suspected of harboring trafficked women in order to give owners time to hide women or supply false working papers (and) are also known to accept bribes, supply false papers or to turn a blind eye to the presence of undocumented foreigners" (Haynes, 2004, p. 257). To effectively address this issue, police and courts need to eliminate corruption from their ranks. In addition, agents of justice need to pursue cases in earnest and address the flaws that exist within the system in order to effectively identify, pursue, and punish the offenders of these crimes.

5. *Create immigration solutions for trafficked persons:* An effective immigration policy for victims of trafficking serves two purposes: Not only does it provide victims with legal residency rights and protections, but it also helps pursue criminal prosecutions against traffickers, especially since the few effective prosecutions have relied heavily on victim cooperation and testimony. At its most fundamental position, victims who are unable to obtain even temporary visas will be unable to legally remain in the country and assist the courts in bringing perpetrators to justice. In addition, victims who are offered immigration visas contingent on their participation in a prosecution run the risk of jeopardizing potential convictions, because defense attorneys may argue that the promise of residency could encourage an "alleged" victim to perjure his or her testimony. Finally, the limited opportunities to obtain permanent visa status amount to winning the immigration lottery in many cases, because these opportunities are few and far between and often involve complex applications and long waiting periods.

6. *Implement the laws:* At the end of the day, policy recommendations and legislation do little good if such laws are not vigorously pursued and enforced against individuals and groups participating in the trafficking of humans. In addition, such convictions need to carry stern and significant financial and incarceration punishments if they hope to be an effective tool in solving the problem of trafficking.

While efforts to prioritize the implementation of antitrafficking laws may slow the progress of eliminating these crimes against humanity, the best efforts toward prevention focus on eliminating the need for people to migrate in search of opportunities to improve their economic condition. An ecological perspective suggests that the cause of trafficking lies within issues such as poverty, economic inequality, dysfunction within the family, gender inequality, discrimination, and the demand for victims for prostitution and cheap labor. At its heart, human trafficking "is a crime that deprives people of their human rights and freedoms, increases global health risks, fuels growing networks of organized crime and can sustain levels of poverty and impede development in certain areas" (U.S. Department of State, 2009, p. 5). Until these large-scale systemic issues are addressed, the presence of trafficking will endure within our global society.

Spotlight on Witch Burnings in Papua New Guinea

Between 1692 and 1693, 200 people were accused and 19 were executed in Salem, Massachusetts, for practicing witchcraft. The paranoia of this region stemmed from a similar craze between the 12th and 15th century in Europe where people believed that the devil could empower individuals to bring harm on his behalf. While the people of Salem ultimately admitted that these trials were conducted in error and provided compensation to the families of the wrongfully convicted, these witch trials mark a unique point of history for colonial America (Blumberg, 2007).

While the Salem witch trials are a part of history, the beliefs of witchcraft remain alive in a number of global regions. One area that has recently been drawing attention is Papua New Guinea, which is located in the South Pacific north of Australia. As a country of over 800 different cultures and languages, one of the unifying factors between them is a belief in black magic (Mintz, 2013).

Consider the following case: Kepari Leniata was burned alive in February 2013 after she was accused of being a witch. She was tortured, bound, and soaked with gasoline and set afire among the community trash (Pollak, 2013). She was blamed for engaging in sorcery and causing the death of a young boy in the village. Rather than accept that the child may have died from illness or natural causes, it is not uncommon for villagers to look to the supernatural to explain death (Bennett-Smith, 2013). "Black magic is often suspected when misfortune strikes, especially after the unexplained death of a young man, because it is said that they have a long life ahead of time and it has been cut short" (Alpert, 2013, para. 4). Leniata's death is not the only case of witch burning in recent times because two women narrowly escaped a similar fate, and in June 2013, a local schoolteacher was beheaded for being a witch (Chasmar, 2013). The punishment for sorcery is generally a public display in an effort to deter others from using magic (OXFAM, 2010). Women are most often the victims of accusations of sorcery, and it is often men who make such accusations. While the most egregious punishment for sorcery is death, people who have been accused of these crimes can also lose their land and homes and be banished from the community (OXFAM, n.d.). The legal system in Papua New Guinea provides little help in preventing acts of witch burning and other tortures of those accused of sorcery. While there are laws that prohibit sorcery, they do little to deter the practice. The 1971 Sorcery Act punishes those who engage in sorcery with a two-year incarceration sentence, a rather insignificant punishment. In addition, people who commit murder can use sorcery as a mitigating factor. Here, murder is justified in the eyes of the offender as an act of greater good of the community. The United Nations has called for an end to witch burning, because "these reports raise grave concern that accusations of sorcery are used to justify arbitrary and inhumane acts of violence" ("UN: 'Sorcery' murders must end," 2013, para. 8). The Papua New Guinea government recently overturned the Sorcery Act and has called for the expansion of the death penalty for offenders of these crimes. Despite this strong stance by governmental officials, it is unknown what effect, if any, this change will have on the practice of witch burning (UN News Centre, 2013).

Rape as a War Crime

In Chapter 3, you learned about the research on rape and sexual assault. Rape as a crime is an act of power and control. From World War II and the Holocaust to the acts of violence in Uganda, Bosnia-Herzegovnia, and the Democratic Republic of Congo, acts of sexual violence have been perpetuated against civilian women and children. In times of war, acts of sexual assault become a weapon by those who are either in power or seek to be in power. In 2008, the United Nations officially declared rape as a weapon of war. In cases of rape as a war crime, it is not about an individual being targeted and attacked but rather a systematic perpetuation of sexual assault against entire communities.

The case of the Democratic Republic of Congo is one of the most significant events of rape in the context of war in recent history, Located in Central Africa, the country has been involved in civil and continental wars since the mid-90's. These conflicts have led to the rise of armed groups, as well as agents of the government, engaging in violence against each other and citizens of the country (Human Rights Watch, 2017a). Recent conflicts have involved the murders of men, women, and children of the Kamuina Nsapu militia by members of the Congolese army, as well as the murder of two UN experts (Human Rights Watch, 2017b, 2017c).

The extent of sexual violence in this region has led to a characterization of the DRC as the rape capital of the world. Reports indicate that sexual violence is often a public event and is used to incite fear in communities and their residents. Women and children are disproportionately victimized in these cases. While data on these events are difficult to obtain, research suggests that approximately 1.8 million Congolese women experienced rape during the two decades of conflict in the Democratic Republic of Congo (Peterman, Palermo & Bredenkamp, 2011). Other estimates report that almost 40% of all women are survivors of sexual assault (Johnson, Scott & Rughita et al., 2010). Victims are often unlikely to report their victimization and suffer in silence. Their suffering includes both physical and psychological trauma from these violent events. Ten to twelve percent of victims contract HIV as a result of being raped (Nanivazo, 2012).

In response to these crimes, the United Nations Security Council has officially noted "sexual violence as a tactic of war, which exacerbates situations of armed conflicts and impedes the restoration of peace and security" (Nanivazo, 2012). Due to pervasive corruption throughout the Congolese government, judicial system of the DRC has historically been unable to effectively respond and punish offenders. However, recent progress has led to several military tribunals and restitution for victims (United Nations, 2015).

Female Genital Mutilation

Female **genital mutilation** (FGM; also known as female cutting or circumcision) includes a number of practices whereby young girls are subjected to the vandalism or removal of their genitalia. The purpose of this process is to both protect the purity of girls' virginity while at the same time eliminating the potential for sexual pleasure. These procedures are far from safe because the tools are rarely sanitized and anesthesia is not used. In addition, the people performing these procedures do not have any sort of medical training. Yirga, Kassa, Gebremichael, and Aro (2012) list the four types of female genital mutilation:

> [T]ype 1, partial or total removal of the clitoris and/or the prepuce (clitoridectomy); type 2, partial or total removal of the clitoris and labia minora, with or without excision of the labia majora (excision); type 3, narrowing of the vaginal orifice with creation of a covering seal by cutting and appositioning the labia minora and/or the labia majora, with or without excision of the clitoris (infibulation); and type 4, all other harmful procedures to the female genitalia for nonmedical purposes, such as pricking, piercing, incising, scraping, and cauterization. (p. 46)

While there has been significant outrage at an international level, genital mutilation remains a significant issue. Estimates indicate that 100–140 million women across Africa are genitally mutilated every year. This means that the majority of women in these countries have endured this experience. For example, 94% of women in Sierra Leone and 79% in Gambia have been circumcised. Many women who undergo this process experience significant infection and are at risk for sterilization, complications during pregnancy, and sexual and menstrual difficulties. In addition to these physical challenges, victims experience high levels of psychological trauma (Foundation for Women's Health Research and Development, 2012).

Genital mutilation is a cultural normative practice, and it is viewed as an expression of womanhood. Females who have not undergone a circumcision process are often viewed as lower status and less desirable, which impacts their value in marriage. In addition, the failure to be circumcised carries significant examples of urban legend and fear: "A girl that is not circumcised cannot have children because the clitoris is still there. When the baby's head touches the clitoris at birth, the baby will die" (Anuforo, Oyedele, & Pacquiao 2004, p. 108). Other myths suggest that uncircumcised women are unclean, that circumcision aids in childbirth, and the vagina is more visually appealing without it (Akintunde, 2010). It is also believed that circumcision helps maintain sexual purity and prevents promiscuity. For many of these tribal communities, they express hope that the practice of female circumcision will continue and resent the belief by Westerners that the practice is abusive. However, migration and modernization may help encourage these communities to abandon the practice. For example, women who immigrate to the United States are more likely to believe that female cutting practices should end. However, change is not just an American ideal, because some research indicates that women's attitudes about FGM are changing, which could lead to shifts in the practice. Here, experiences such as education and employment influence such changes. For example, women who attend college or who are employed outside of the home are significantly less likely to circumcise their daughters. (Boyle, McMorris, & Gomez, 2002). For those that believe that the practice should continue, they suggest some practical changes that would allow the cultural values of FGM to remain. Here, some suggest that the procedure be performed in a medical environment with trained practitioners who could respond to any complications that might arise (Anuforo et al., 2004).

While social change may be possible within the communities that practice female genital mutilation, few laws have been passed to outlaw the practice. However, several groups have engaged in advocacy work within these communities. The World Health Organization conducts extensive research and public awareness campaigns in hopes of educating African women about the detrimental effects of genital mutilation (World Health Organization, 2012). However, these practices are not limited to the African countries and other regions of the world where the practice is commonly accepted. For example, the United Kingdom has been a major source for immigrants and refugees from these regions. Even though people are physically removed from their countries of origin, their cultures and practices follow them. As a result, nations such as Great Britain need to engage in outreach with these communities that reside within their borders (Learner, 2012).

Honor-Based Violence

The category of **honor-based violence** (HBV) includes practices such as honor killings, bride burnings, customary killings, and dowry deaths. Each of these crimes involves the murder of a woman by a male family member, usually a father, brother, or male cousin. These women are killed in response to a belief that the women have offended a family's honor and have brought shame to the family unit. The notion of honor is one of the most important cultural values for members of these communities. "Honor is the reason for our living now . . . without honor life has no meaning. . . . It is okay if you don't have money, but you must have dignity" (Kardam, 2005, p. 16).

At the heart of the practice of honor-based violence is a double standard rooted in patriarchy, which dictates that women should be modest, meek, pure, and innocent. Women are expected to follow the rules of their fathers and, later, their husbands. In some cases, honor killings have been carried out in cases of adultery, or even perceived infidelity. Consider the recent case of a 15-year-old girl who died after an acid attack in her home in Kashmir, Pakistan. Her crime was that she was talking to a boy outside of her family home. Unfortunately, this case, nor the response by her family members, is not uncommon. On their arrest, her parents justified their actions because their daughter had brought shame to their family's honor (Burke, 2012). Hina Jilani, a lawyer and human rights activist, suggests that, in some cultures, the "right to life of women . . . is conditional on their obeying social norms and traditions" (Amnesty International, 1999, para. 2). Women are viewed as a piece of property that holds value. Her value is based on her purity, which can be tainted by acts that many Western cultures would consider to be normal, everyday occurrences, such as requesting a love song on the radio or strolling through the park (Arin, 2001). For many women, their crime is that they wanted to become "Westernized" or participate in modern-day activities, such as wearing jeans, listening to music, and developing friendships. For other women, their shame is rooted in a sexual double standard where a woman is expected to maintain her purity for her husband. To taint the purity of a woman is to taint her honor and, thereby, the honor of her family. The concept of honor controls every part of a woman's identity. As Kardam (2005) explains, "When honor is constructed through a woman's body, it entails her daily life activities, education, work, marriage, the importance of virginity (and) faithfulness" (p. 61).

Women who are accused of bringing negative attention and dishonor are rarely afforded the opportunity to defend their actions (Mayell, 2002). Even women who have been victimized through rape and sexual assault are at risk of death via an honor killing, because their victimization is considered shameful for the family. In many cases, the simple perception of impropriety is enough to warrant an honor killing. Amnesty International (1999) explains the central role of *perception* in honor in Pakistan:

> The distinction between a woman being guilty and a woman being alleged to be guilty of illicit sex is irrelevant. What impacts the man's honour is the public perception, the belief of her infidelity. It is this which blackens honour and for which she is killed. To talk of "alleged kari" or "alleged siahkari" makes no sense in this system nor does your demand that a woman should be heard. It is not the truth that honour is about but public perception of honour. (p. 12)

The practice of honor and customary killings are typically carried out with a high degree of violence. Women are subjected to acts of torture, and their deaths are often slow and violent. They may be shot, stabbed, strangled, electrocuted, set on fire, or run over by a vehicle. In fact, doing so is expected in certain cases, because "a man's ability to protect his honour is judged by his family and neighbors. He must publicly demonstrate his power to safeguard his honour by killing those who damaged it and thereby restore it" (Amnesty International, 1999, p. 12). One would assume that the women in these countries would silently shame these acts of violence. Contrary to this belief, however, research indicates that the women in the family support these acts of violence against their daughters and sisters as part of the shared community understanding about honor (Mayell, 2002).

▲ **Photo 5.1** Supporters of Tehrik-e-Minhaj ul Quran, an Islamic Organization protest against "honor killings" of women in Lahore, Pakistan. Hundreds of women die each year in these honor attacks, which are generally committed by male relatives (husband, father, brother, etc.) for bringing shame on the family.

© epa/Corbis

While the United Nations (2000, 2010) estimates more than 5,000 honor killings each year around the world, researchers and activists indicate that the true numbers of these crimes are significantly greater. Estimates indicate that tens of thousands of women are killed each year in the practice of honor-based violence. Yet many of these crimes go unreported, making it difficult to develop an understanding of the true extent of the issue. According to research by Chesler (2010), the majority (95%) of the victims of honor killings are young women (mean age = 23). In 42% of cases, there were multiple perpetrators involved in the killing, a characteristic that distinguishes these types of crimes from the types of single-perpetrator femicide that are most commonly reported in Western countries. Over half of these women were tortured to death and were killed by methods such as stoning, burning, beheading, strangulation, or stabbing/bludgeoning. Nearly half (42%) of these cases involved acts of infidelity or alleged "sexual impropriety," while the remaining 58% of women were murdered for being "too Western" and defying the expectations that are set through cultural and religious normative values. Yet men are never criticized for their acceptance of Western culture. Women in such cultures "are expected to bear the burden of upholding these ancient and allegedly religious customs of gender apartheid" (Chesler, 2010, pp. 3–11).

While much of the practice of honor killings occurs outside of the United States (and other Westernized jurisdictions), we do see occasional incidents of honor killings in these regions. These cases are exclusively linked to an immigrant culture or community where honor killings are a more accepted practice. Despite laws that prohibit murder, the perpetrators in these crimes generally maintain that their actions were culturally justified. Perhaps one of the most recent cases of honor violence within the Western world involves the January 2012 conviction of the Shafia family in Ontario, Canada. Mohammad Shafia, his wife Tooba Yahya, and their son Hamen were found guilty of first-degree murder in the deaths of their children/sisters Zainab (age 19), Sahar (age 17), and Geeti (age 13) as well as Rona, Mohammad's first wife from his polygamous marriage. The four women were found in a submerged car staged to look like an accident. Prosecutors argued that the daughters were killed for dishonoring the family. While the Sharia family members all maintained their innocence and have publicly stated their intent to appeal their conviction, evidence in the case included wiretapped conversations, which included Mohammad stating, "There can be no betrayal, no treachery, no violation more than this . . . even if they hoist me up onto the gallows . . . nothing is more dear to me than my honor" ("Canada Honor Killing Trial," 2012, para. 25).

Even if justice officials do become involved in these cases, perpetrators are rarely identified and even more rarely punished to any extent. When human rights organizations and activists identify these incidents as honor-based violence, family members of the victim are quick to dismiss the deaths of their sisters and daughters as "accidents." In Turkish communities, if a woman has fractured the honor of her family, the male members of her family meet to decide her fate. In the case of "customary killings," the task of carrying out the murder is often given to the youngest male member of the family. Typically, these boys are under the age of criminal responsibility, which further reduces the likelihood that any punishments will be handed down in the name of the victim (Arin, 2001).

In their quest to improve the lives of women who may be victims of the practice of honor killings, Amnesty International (1999) outlines three general areas for reform:

1. *Legal Measures.* The current legal system in many of these countries does little to protect victims from potential violence under the normative structures that condone the practice of honor killings. Women have few, if any, legal rights that protect them from these harms. Legal reforms must address the status of women and provide them with opportunities for equal protection under the law. In cases where women survive an attempted honor killing, they need access to remedies that address the damages they experience. In addition, the perpetrators of these crimes are rarely subjected to punishment for their actions. Indeed, the first step toward reform includes recognizing that violence against women is a crime, and such abuses need to be enforced by the legal communities. International law also needs to recognize these crimes and enforce sanctions against governments that fail to act against these offenders. However, it is unclear how effective these legal measures will be for individual communities. In their discussions of what can be done to stop the practice of honor killings, Turkish activists did not feel that increasing the punishments for honor-based violence

would serve as an effective deterrent, particularly in regions where the practice is more common and accepted within the community, because "punishments would not change the social necessity to kill and that to spend long years in jail can be seen as less important than lifelong loss of honor" (Kardam, 2005, p. 51).

2. *Preventive Measures.* Education and public awareness is the first step toward reducing honor-based violence toward women. These practices are rooted in culture and history. Attempts to change these deeply held attitudes will require time and resources aimed at opening communication on these beliefs. This is no easy task given the normative cultural values that perpetuate these crimes. One of the first tasks may be to adopt sensitivity-training programming for judicial and legal personnel so that they may be able to respond to these acts of violence in an impartial manner. In addition, it is important to develop a sense of the extent of the problem in order to provide effective remedies. Here, an enhanced understanding of data on these crimes will help shed light on the pervasiveness of honor-based violence as a first step toward addressing this problem.

3. *Protective Measures.* Given the limited options for women seeking to escape honor-based violence, additional resources for victim services need to be made available. These include shelters, resources for women fleeing violence, legal aid to represent victims of crime, provisions for the protection of children, and training to increase the economic self-sustainability for women. In addition, the agencies that offer refuge for these women need to be protected from instances of backlash and harassment.

While these suggestions offer opportunities for change, many agents working in the regions most affected by honor-based killings indicate feelings of hopelessness that such changes are even possible. Certainly, the road toward reform is a long one, because it is rooted in cultural traditions that present significant challenges for change. "When an honor killing . . . starts to disturb everybody . . . and when nobody wants to carry this shame anymore, then finding solutions will become easier" (Kardam, 2005, p. 66). Indeed, the first step in reform involves creating the belief that success is possible.

Spotlight on Malala Yousafzai

Pakistan has one of the largest populations of children that do not attend school, two-thirds of whom are girls. Spending on education represents only 2.3% of the gross national product (GNP), and over 49 million adults are illiterate (Torre, 2013). Girls were prohibited from attending school under Taliban rule, and over 170 schools were destroyed between 2007 and 2009 (Brumfield & Simpson, 2013).

Malala Yousafzai was born on July 12, 1997, in Pakistan. As a young girl, Malala became interested in politics and education and became an outspoken advocate for girls' education in her country. At 11 years old, she gave her first speech titled "How dare the Taliban take away my basic right to education," and at 12 she began blogging for the BBC about life under Taliban rule (Kuriakose, 2013). Her public profile began to rise through her speeches and writings, and her efforts were applauded by several international organizations. In 2012, she began to develop a foundation to help young girls receive an education. However, she was considered a threat to the Taliban, and on October 9, 2012, she was shot while riding on a bus home from school (Walsh, 2012). The Taliban argued that she was targeted not for promoting education but for using propaganda against the Taliban. "Taliban are not opposed to girls education, but they could not support anti-Islamic agendas and Westernized education systems" (Brumfield & Simpson, 2013, para. 11). For this crime, they have stated that

(Continued)

(Continued)

▲ **Photo 5.2** Malala Yousafzai was shot by the Taliban when she was only 15 years old for speaking out about girls' rights to education. She is a worldwide advocate on the issue and won the Nobel Peace Prize in 2014.

she will continue to remain a target. While a *fatwa* was issued against the Taliban gunman, he remains at large.

Yousafzai was seriously wounded in the attack as the gunman's bullet fired through her head, neck, and shoulder. She was transported to the United Kingdom for treatment where she went through several surgeries, one of which replaced a piece of her skull with a titanium plate. Amazingly, she did not suffer any neurological damage (Brumfield & Simpson, 2013). Since then, she has resided in Birmingham, England, because it is too dangerous for her to return to Pakistan. However, the violence has not silenced Malala. She continues to speak out about the importance of education for girls and created the Malala fund to raise support for educational projects for girls worldwide. She has received a number of international awards and was nominated for the Nobel Peace Prize. Six months after the shooting, Malala returned to school in the United Kingdom, a day she described as the most important day of her life (Quinn, 2013). One year following her attack, Malala released her biography *I Am Malala* (Farid, 2014).

Conclusion

While this chapter covers some of the victimizations that women face around the world, it is by no means an exhaustive discussion. Many of these crimes occur due to the status of women in society and gender-role expectations of women. Alas, the needs for victims in these cases are high, and the nature of these crimes can challenge the accessibility and delivery of services. Ultimately, reform for these victims is linked to changing the gendered cultures of our global society.

//// SUMMARY

- Human trafficking involves the exploitation of individuals for the purposes of forced labor or involuntary servitude, debt bondage, and sexual exploitation. The majority of these cases involve sexual exploitation and abuse, and human trafficking disproportionately affects women.

- Traffickers prey on women from poor communities and appeal to their interests in improving their economic standing as a method of enticing them into exploitative and manipulative work environments.

- International efforts to combat human trafficking have focused on "3Ps": prosecution (of traffickers), protection (of victims), and prevention (of trafficking cases), but there has been little international progress in reducing the prevalence of human trafficking worldwide.

- Recommendations for best practices against trafficking involve improved victim services, increased public awareness about trafficking, and implementation and enforcement of stricter laws against the practice.

- Honor-based violence involves the murder of women for violating gendered cultural norms. Most incidents of honor-based violence are committed by a male family member, such as a father, husband, brother, or cousin.

- Offenders of honor-based violence are rarely punished, because the killings are an accepted practice within the communities.

- Efforts toward reducing or eliminating honor-based violence include legal reform, education and public awareness, and additional resources for victim services.

- Female genital mutilation is a cultural practice throughout much of Africa. Much of the Western world views these practices as acts of violence toward women.

- Rape has been used as a crime of torture against civilians during times of war.

//// KEY TERMS

Debt bondage 190

Femicide 187

Genital mutilation 195

Honor-based violence 196

Human trafficking 188

Jail the offender and protect the
    victim models 192

Labor trafficking 190

Trafficking Victims Protection
    Act of 2000 191

T-visa 191

//// DISCUSSION QUESTIONS

1. How is the concept of shame created in cultures where honor-based violence is prevalent?

2. To what extent are offenders in honor-based violence cases punished? What measures need to be implemented to protect women from these crimes?

3. How do women enter and exit the experience of sexual trafficking?

4. Compare and contrast the jail the offender and the protect the victim models of trafficking enforcement. What are the best practices that can be implemented from these two models to address the needs of trafficking victims?

5. What suggestions have been made to work within the communities that support genital mutilation?

6. What challenges exist in responding to cases of rape during times of war?

//// WEB RESOURCES

Desert Flower Foundation: http://www.desertflowerfoundation.org/en/

Forward UK: http://www.forwarduk.org.uk/key-issues

HumanTrafficking.org: http://www.humantrafficking.org

Not for Sale: http://www.notforsalecampaign.org/about/slavery/

Polaris Project: http://www.polarisproject.org/

Stop Honour Killings: http://www.stophonourkillings.com/

Trafficking in Persons Report: https://www.state.gov/j/tip/rls/tiprpt/2016/

United Nations, Sexual Violence in Conflict: http://www.un.org/sexualviolenceinconflict/

Visit **study.sagepub.com/mallicoat3e** to access additional study tools, including eFlashcards, web quizzes, web resources, video resources, and SAGE journal articles.

READING /// 9

While much has been written about victims of human trafficking, little is noted about the perpetrators of these acts. This article looks at why people become involved in trafficking, their operations and earnings, and how the criminal justice system responds to these cases.

Human Trafficking and Moral Panic in Cambodia

Chenda Keo, Theirry Bouhours,
Roderic Broadhurst, and Brigitte Bouhours

Cambodia was one of the first countries to enact a law on human trafficking in 1996. This law, one of the harshest in the country, punished trafficking as severely as premeditated murder. Although there had been some concern about human trafficking within Cambodia, a global campaign, led by the United States, had been waging a "war on human trafficking" that required action on the part of the Cambodian government to ensure the continuation of development aid to the country. Human trafficking, or "modern day slavery," was described by the U.S. Department of State (USDS) and the United Nations Office on Drugs and Crime (UNODC) as a transnational enterprise controlled by organized crime, which enslaved 12.3 million people, generated $32 billion in profit for human traffickers, was the third most profitable business for organized crime, and posed a serious threat to national and global security (UNODC, 2008; USDS, 2009). Such unverified, high estimates suggested the presence of a "moral panic" about human trafficking and have subsequently been found to be unreliable or inflated in terms of the number of individuals involved and the profits earned by trafficking (UNODC, 2012).[1]

Apart from some NGO reports and a few studies of trafficked persons, virtually nothing is known about the individuals involved in human trafficking in Cambodia, and some evidence suggests that the experiences of individuals involved in Cambodian trafficking stand in contrast to prevalent claims about the abusive and criminal characteristics of human trafficking. In 2006, one of this article's authors interviewed nine boys and eight girls under 18 years of age, all of whom had been "trafficked" to work in Thailand and subsequently reintegrated into their family or community in Cambodia (Keo, 2006). None saw themselves as "victims." They had willingly followed their recruiters to Thailand to earn an income and support their impoverished family. They considered themselves "good children" because of their ability to work and share the burden of supporting their family. Most had been "trafficked" by family members, relatives, or neighbors, and a few by strangers. Few had suffered physical abuse and most of them had been treated well. From their accounts, human trafficking did not sound like a risky activity, and traffickers did not seem to make big profits.

Since the late 1990s, the authors have been engaged in a longitudinal study of the trends and patterns of criminal activity in Cambodia, which included victimization surveys. We have found scant evidence that trafficking is a major problem or that it involves organized crime, and our

SOURCE: Keo, C., Bouhours, T., Broadhurst, R., & Bouhours, B. (2014). Human trafficking and moral panic in Cambodia. *The ANNALS of the American Academy of Political and Social Science*, 653(1), 202-224.

results are consistent with those of another study (Steinfatt, 2011). This article presents some of the results of our research in Cambodia, which as far as we know is the first to draw on in-depth interviews with alleged offenders.[2] We examine not only traffickers' characteristics and the methods they use but also the way in which human trafficking, especially as a customary practice, has been problematized and criminalized. This study illustrates how trafficking has been officially constructed and the resulting negative consequences in Cambodia. We argue that the hegemonic agenda of the West—in terms of security, morality (especially prostitution), and human rights—triggered a security and moral panic about trafficking worldwide. Pressured by foreign and local NGOs and the need for foreign aid, Cambodia adopted a repressive law that defined human trafficking ineptly and in effect targeted consensual commercial sex activities. In the hands of a dysfunctional criminal justice system, harsh laws have not deterred potential traffickers but produced serious unintended consequences that have turned law enforcement into an instrument for corruption and injustice, and against the powerless.

The Global Moral Panic Around Human Trafficking

Following an independent and critical review of nearly one thousand publications on human trafficking, we reached the same conclusions as have a growing number of researchers (e.g., Davies, 2009; Zhang, 2009). The literature is replete with unsubstantiated, extraordinary estimates of the extent and profitability of the phenomenon, as well as unsupported claims about its control by organized crime syndicates. The striking statistics, estimates, and claims are recycled and augmented, report after report, by uncritical authors who routinely conflate human trafficking with human smuggling and prostitution. Weitzer (2007) has shown that an unusual alliance of moral entrepreneurs, including ideologically motivated radical feminists committed to the abolition of prostitution, played a leading role in promoting the global human trafficking panic. Others have compared it to the moral panic about white slavery during the nineteenth and early twentieth centuries (Doezema, 2000; Sandy, 2007). Cohen defined a *moral panic* as follows:

> A condition, episode, person, or group of persons emerges to become defined as a threat to societal values and interests; its nature is presented in a stylized and stereotypical fashion by the mass media; the moral barricades are manned by editors, bishops, politicians, and other right-thinking people; socially accredited experts pronounce their diagnosis and solutions. . . . Sometimes the panic passes over and is forgotten . . . at other times it has more serious and long-lasting repercussions and might produce such changes as those in legal and social policy or even in the way the society conceives itself. (Cohen, 1973, p. 2)

We found only two studies that focused on human traffickers, as distinct from trafficked persons and their rescuers. Levenkron (2007) examined the court dossiers of 325 Israeli traffickers and their accomplices who were convicted between 1990 and 2007. Nair (2004) conducted interviews with 160 active sex traffickers of women and children in India, in addition to 561 trafficked persons.[3] Nearly half (47 percent) of the trafficked persons reported that their traffickers were female. In contrast, Levenkron found that only 10.5 percent of the Israeli traffickers were female. This gender difference raises interesting questions about women's involvement in trafficking activities and their treatment by the criminal justice system in different nations. Both studies found that most offenders had engaged in trafficking in an attempt to escape poverty and alleviate dire financial situations. Neither study supported claims about the high profitability and involvement of organized crime in human trafficking. On the contrary, they showed that human trafficking was generally perpetrated by individuals or small, loosely organized criminal networks. This finding was corroborated by Brown (2007), who conducted in-depth interviews with 515 Cambodian sex workers. Many of the female traffickers had themselves been previously trafficked as sex workers.

The Cambodian Context

Cambodia is among the poorest countries in the world, ranked 138th out of 186 countries on the 2012 Human Development Index. In 2004, it was estimated that 35 percent of Cambodians were living below the poverty line set by the World Bank at $0.45 per person per day. More than half of the population is either illiterate or never completed primary school, and a lack of education among females is common (National Institute of Statistics, 2009). Good governance is inhibited by a highly centralized administrative structure, corruption, nepotism, cronyism, lack of transparency, and incompetent officials (Kato et al., 2000).

The policing system is tarnished by allegations of malpractice, corruption, and favoritism. Torture, forced confessions, and illegal arrests and detentions have been frequently reported by the media and human rights NGOs (Asian Legal Resource Centre, 2001). Recruitments, appointments, and operations are politicized and influenced by cronyism. There is a general lack of professionalism within the police force, and many units are understaffed. The reputation of the judiciary is equally compromised by allegations of capture by the executive and corruption. The working environment in the courts is generally subpar. Chronic understaffing and a lack of judges and courtrooms result in large case overload often dealt with by swift and unfair rulings. In addition, judges may experience intimidation and their personal safety is not guaranteed (Broadhurst & Keo, 2011; Khiev, 2004).

The Origin of the 1996 Law

Following the arrival in 1992 of the United Nations Transitional Authority in Cambodia (UNTAC), which coincided with both a boom in the local sex industry and the proliferation of foreign (mostly Western) NGOs, Cambodia joined the battle against trafficking to protect children and women from this crime. From only twenty-five in the 1980s, the total number of NGOs in the country had grown to more than two thousand by 2008 (Ek & Sok, 2008). Since controlling human trafficking involves multiple approaches and discourses, antitrafficking programs were embedded within various sectors of NGO activity with an estimated two hundred institutions working on the problem in Cambodia and employing some five thousand people (Delauney, 2007). To sustain this level of NGO activity, significant donor funding was necessary.

Trafficking is criminalized in Article 3 of a hastily enacted 1996 statute: the Law on Suppression of the Kidnapping, Trafficking, and Exploitation of Human Beings:

> Any person who lures a human being, male or female, minor or adult of whichever nationality by ways of enticing or by any other means, promising to offer any money or jewelry, with or without the person's consent, by ways of forcing, threatening, or using of hypnotic drugs, in order to kidnap him/her for sale or prostitution, shall be subjected to imprisonment from ten to fifteen years. The perpetrator shall be punished to imprisonment from fifteen to twenty years if such victim is a minor of less than 15 years old. Those who are accomplices, traffickers/sellers, buyers, shall be subject to the same punishment term as the perpetrator(s); shall also be considered as accomplices, those who provide money or means for committing offences.[4]

The law did not define "trafficking" but amalgamated selling, procuring, and recruiting people for prostitution, irrespective of whether the individual was coerced or was moved across or within national borders; neither did the law define the terms "victim," "accomplice," and "buyer." The unqualified term "accomplice" meant that a wide range of people—including a brothel's security guards, cleaners, cooks, and law enforcement or military personnel providing protection to brothels—could be subjected to the same punishment as a procurer or trafficker (Perrin et al., 2001).

The 1996 law was enacted with little understanding of trafficking and was, de facto, a law against the organization of commercial prostitution. Because consent was irrelevant by law ("with or without the person's consent") virtually all sex workers could be declared victims and those helping or managing sex work, human traffickers. Yet Keo (2010) has shown that the majority of women and girls who had been "trafficked" between 2007 and 2009 in Cambodia were destitute, aware that they were being recruited into commercial sex work, and willing to do such work. For example, in 2009, twenty-seven NGOs reported eighty-five cases of trafficking involving 109 victims. Roughly half the victims were from broken or economically unstable families. Most (95 percent) were recruited voluntarily, 76 percent had agreed to engage in prostitution at the time of recruitment, and 31 percent of them had previously worked in the sex industry (Keo, 2010).

In 2000, the Ministry of Interior created the Department of Anti-Trafficking and Juvenile Protection Police with financial and technical support from various NGOs.

In 2007, the government established a national taskforce to work in cooperation with a myriad of government and nongovernment antitrafficking agencies. A U.S.-based NGO, Asia Foundation, received some $3 million from USAID to conduct a countertrafficking program in Cambodia, and is believed to have been behind the establishment of the national task force. With the help of an international consultant, the Ministry of Justice drafted a new antitrafficking law, which was passed on January 18, 2008, after pressure from the Bush administration.

The 2008 law on the Suppression of Human Trafficking and Sexual Exploitation did not address the inconsistencies of the 1996 law but rather cast an even wider net encompassing child and adult prostitution, pornography, indecency against minors, the management of prostitution, and the nebulous concept of human trafficking. Implicitly, the law conveyed the message that the "prostitution institution" was intrinsic to human trafficking; although it did not expressly prohibit voluntary prostitution, it created conditions that made lawful prostitution virtually impossible (Keo, 2009). Terms such as "exploitation" and "organized group," which are crucial when one has to interpret and enforce the law, were left to the interpretation of criminal justice officials. When the Cambodian Center for Human Rights (2010) monitored trafficking trials, it concluded that "it is clear that the application of the law has been inconsistent at best and incorrect at worst. . . . It casts doubt on the judiciary's understanding of LHTSE [the antitrafficking law]."

Prostitution and Trafficking in Cambodia

Estimates of the number of prostitutes working in Cambodia are inconsistent. In 2000, the Cambodia Human Development Report echoed the estimate made by the NGO Human Rights Vigilance of Cambodia (HRVC), which claimed that 80,000–100,000 prostitutes worked in Cambodia (cited in Steinfatt, 2011). A 2003 survey by UNICEF suggested that there were 55,000 sex workers in Cambodia. However, after careful scrutiny and through direct observations and triangulation of different sources, Steinfatt (2011) showed that these figures were fallacious. He put the number of sex workers operating in sex establishments in 2002 at 20,829, of which 2,488 may have been trafficked. He estimated that in 2003 there were 18,256 direct prostitutes[5] in Cambodia, with 2,000

regarded as trafficked (Steinfatt, 2011). Steinfatt's estimates of the sex worker population were about five times lower than the HRVC estimate in 2000. More recent figures—essentially corroborating Steinfatt's—put the number of sex workers in Cambodia at 17,000, with 75 percent of them working outside brothels as independent or indirect sex workers (Home and Community Care Program, 2008).

Official trafficking statistics in Cambodia are equally inconsistent and unreliable. In 2003, only seventeen instances of trafficking were recorded by the police, and in 2008, the number was 108. It is difficult to assess the accuracy of these figures. For example, official statistics from 2005 to 2009 recorded no human trafficking events, but the 2008 *Annual Report of the National Police* reported 77 and 108 events in 2007 and 2008, respectively (National Police Commissariat, 2009). From 2003 to 2009, the Cambodian police cleared 23,604 criminal events; of these, 379 (1.6 percent) involved human trafficking, and 585 alleged traffickers were arrested (1.7 percent of all arrested offenders). In 2006, Police Commissioner Hok Longdy remarked, "we cracked down on 614 cases of sex trading offences, arrested 670 ringleaders (67 female), all of whom were referred to the court, and we rescued 789 females. Among these offenders, 92 were charged" (National Police Commissariat, 2007, p. 3). These figures do not match official statistics, but, as is often also the case, the commissioner did not clearly differentiate between offences relating to prostitution and those relating to human trafficking.

In 2007 and 2008, the Cambodian League for the Promotion and Defense of Human Rights (LICADHO) conducted prison surveys with large samples representing 56 percent of the total prison population in Cambodia. In 2007, 3.5 percent of inmates were incarcerated for human trafficking and among them 80 percent were female (LICADHO, 2008). In 2008, 3.8 percent of inmates in the sample were incarcerated for human trafficking, and among them 77 percent were female (LICADHO, 2009). In both years, among the twenty-five reported types of crime, human trafficking was the crime for which the largest number of females were incarcerated. LICADHO (2008) documented many complaints from women who said they had been wrongly imprisoned or had received a long sentence for failing to pay a bribe; LICADHO also noted that the majority of female prisoners did not have access to legal advice or representation.

Methods

We investigated five major themes about traffickers in Cambodia: who are they, why they became involved in human trafficking, how they operate, their earnings, and how the Cambodian criminal justice system responds to their activities. We used a multimethod and multisource research design and drew on police and prison records and interviews with 466 individuals, including police, prison, and court officers; NGO workers; villagers and migrants; and ninety-one incarcerated traffickers.[6] In Cambodia, court records are not available to the public and researchers, so we could not replicate Levenkron's (2007) study or triangulate with their court dossiers the information provided in the interviews by the incarcerated traffickers. For some of our traffickers, we were able to check their accounts by talking to village heads/commune officials and in some cases complainants or the police officers involved. Our sample included the five provincial prisons of Banteay Meanchey, Battambang,

Koh Kong, Kompong Cham, and Svay Rieng; and the Correctional Centers in Phnom Penh (CC1 and CC2) and Kompong Cham (CC3). These prisons contained 55 percent of the total prison population in 2008 and were situated in areas often mentioned either as sources or destinations for internal and cross-border trafficking (Brown, 2007; Derks, Henke, & Ly, 2006). A comparison with prison statistics between 1997 and 2007 suggested that our sample was representative of the population of incarcerated traffickers.

Our sample of ninety-one interviewees represented 45.7 percent of all incarcerated traffickers held in the eight prisons at the time. Although 71.4 percent of these imprisoned traffickers were female, our sample included only 53.8 percent ($n = 49$) female traffickers. We oversampled male traffickers ($n = 42$) for two important reasons. First, a review of the literature indicated that female offenders were rarely involved in organized crime; therefore, it may not have been possible to detect participation in organized crime with only a small sample of male

Table 1 • Demographic Profile of Incarcerated Traffickers		Female ($n = 49$)	Male ($n = 42$)	Total ($N = 91$)
Age (years)	Mean age at interview	37.7*	32.3	38.5
Ethnicity (%)	Khmer	79.6	83.3	81.3
	Non-Khmer (Vietnamese or Thai)	20.4	16.7	18.7
Marital status (%)	Single	10.2*	33.3	52.7
	Married	51.0	54.8	20.9
	Divorced/widowed	38.8*	11.9	26.4
Education (%)	No schooling	30.6	31.0	30.8
	Primary: 1–6 years	69.4*	38.1	54.9
	Secondary: 7–12 years	0	26.1	12.1
	Postsecondary	0	4.8	2.2
Socioeconomic status (%)	Poor or very poor	83.7	76.2	80.3
	Average[a]	16.3	23.8	19.7

a. Average is defined as an income above the poverty line, set at $0.45 per person per day by the World Bank in 2004.

*$p < .05$

interviewees. Second, the Israeli study suggested that male traffickers had a greater likelihood of conviction (89.5 percent) than females (10.5 percent), because their involvement was perceived as more serious than that of female traffickers.

Profile of Incarcerated Traffickers

The majority of the ninety-one incarcerated individuals were Cambodians. Tables 1 and 2 present the characteristics of the sample in terms of demographics and offense and show distinct patterns between male and female traffickers. The average age was 38.5 years, but female traffickers were generally older than male traffickers. Men were significantly more likely to be single than women; however, a larger share of women than men were divorced or widowed. Among those who were or had been married, 80 percent had children, and 18 percent had large families of five to eight children. Although most of the participants had only very limited education, women had significantly fewer years of schooling than men, and none had education beyond primary school.

The offending pattern was also gendered: women were more likely to have been charged with or convicted of human trafficking than men (54 percent were women,

46 percent men), a larger proportion of whom had been charged with or convicted of procuring for prostitution (see Table 2). Seventy participants had been sentenced for human trafficking; twenty-one of them (fifteen women and six men) admitted to their offense during our interview or their narratives matched the broad definition of their offense because they had engaged in some form of deception or coercion. We refer to them as *confirmed traffickers*. However, forty-nine participants did not admit that they had committed the offense and their accounts suggest that they had not been convicted beyond a reasonable doubt. At best, they appear to have been doubtfully, and at worst wrongly, convicted. There was little or no evidence in their narratives linking their activities to human trafficking, as defined by Article 3 of the 1996 law. We refer to them as the *doubtfully convicted.* The thirteen participants convicted of procuring for prostitution either admitted to their offense or their narratives supported their conviction. Just over half the participants had been convicted for victimizing adults (55.4 percent), around one-quarter (27.7 percent) for victimizing children, and the remainder for both children and adults. The doubtfully convicted were significantly more likely to have adult (alleged) victims (71.4 percent) than the two other groups.

Table 2 • Offense Profile of Incarcerated Traffickers (in percent)

Offense charged or convicted[a]	Female (*n* = 49)	Male (*n* = 42)	Total (*N* = 91)
Human trafficking	89.8	50.0	71.4
Abduction for sale or sale into prostitution	6.1	16.7	11.0
Procuring for prostitution	4.1	33.3	17.6
Redefined status of convicted participants[b]	**Female (*n* = 43)**	**Male (*n* = 40)**	**Total (*N* = 83)**
Confirmed traffickers	34.9*	15.0	25.3
Doubtfully convicted	58.1	60.0	59.0
Procuring for prostitution	7.0	25.0*	15.7

a. Includes attempted offenses.

b. The status of convicted participants was redefined based on whether or not they admitted to their offense during the interview and whether their account matched the definition of the offense for which they had been convicted.

*$p < .05$

The prison terms of the eighty-three convicted participants ranged from two to 27 years and averaged 12.1 years. We assessed which factors impacted the length of the prison term imposed. Apart from age, socioeconomic status, and involvement of a child as the victim, all the independent variables had a statistically significant relationship with length of sentence. Women received significantly longer average prison terms than men (13.5 years and 10.6 years, respectively) as did participants who had been sentenced for human trafficking compared with those sentenced for procuring for prostitution (12.7 and 9 years, respectively). In addition, non-Cambodians, those who were married or divorced, had little education, and had worked as sex workers themselves received significantly longer sentences than other groups. The length of sentence was not entirely arbitrary, since traffickers were more severely punished than procurers for prostitution. However, other factors were also predictors—such as the offender's sex, education, ethnicity, and occupation—suggesting discriminatory practices by the criminal justice system against women and socioeconomically disadvantaged persons. Women were significantly more likely than men to be destitute.[7] Bribing police officers or judges was a way of avoiding arrest or reducing one's sentence, but the most destitute defendants were the ones least able to pay a bribe.

Findings

Below we outline what we learned from our participants and illustrate the findings with case studies. Of the twenty-one participants categorized as confirmed traffickers, eleven claimed that they had no prior knowledge that their conduct constituted human trafficking. Nine were aware that their activity was unlawful, but they either had assumed that the punishment was not severe or had no idea about its seriousness. Only one was fully cognizant of the severity of his offence. For seventeen of them, it was the first time that they had attempted to traffic someone, but four had successfully trafficked people more than once in the past. Six confirmed traffickers had trafficked adult women for prostitution. The others (four men, eleven women) had abducted a child whom they intended to sell, or coaxed a child into sex work or some other form of labor.

Why People Became Involved in Trafficking

Our participants' accounts and their lifestyle prior to being jailed showed that they were poor and their illegal activities were not particularly lucrative. However, even if an illegitimate opportunity such as human trafficking was not very lucrative, it was still more lucrative than legitimate work. In addition, many Cambodians, and particularly those in our sample, cannot even access these legitimate opportunities because of their lack of education and skills. This was the case with Krouch,[8] a 22-year-old male who could not find legitimate employment and started working as a *spruiker*. Spruikers are generally independent male agents who are not paid a fixed salary but a small commission depending on the number of customers they manage to introduce to the brothel. On average, they manage to make $75 per month, but competition among spruikers in red-light districts is fierce. Krouch reported:

> I am an orphan and migrated from Vietnam with three friends. Once in Cambodia, my friends got jobs as builders, but I could not find a job. A brothel owner asked me to become a spruiker at his Svay Park brothel. He told me that it was not illegal. It was easy, but competitive. I just hung around the street, approached men, and told them that the brothel had lots of beautiful girls and they were not expensive. I got 25¢ for each customer I introduced to the brothel, and each night I earned about $3. After three years on the job, I was arrested in a raid. The brothel owner was never arrested. (Krouch was sentenced to 10 years' imprisonment for procuring for prostitution.)

The data suggest that respondents' involvement in trafficking was strongly influenced by both push and pull factors, that is, a lack of legitimate opportunities and the presence of illegitimate opportunities that enabled them to survive. We have seen that poor and uneducated women are overrepresented in the statistics of incarcerated traffickers. Apart from basic interpersonal skills, no particular knowledge and abilities are necessary to participate in trafficking. Traffickers and trafficked persons form overlapping populations that comprise many impoverished women with familial responsibilities. Human trafficking appears to offer an illegitimate opportunity to earn money for poor and uneducated women of the developing world, who become both victims and perpetrators, in a social phenomenon that has been called the "feminization of the global circuits of survival" (Sassen, 2002, p. 258).

When Kadas, a 22-year-old Vietnamese sex worker, paid $20 to have herself smuggled into Cambodia, she hoped that she would earn enough money to support her family. In Phnom Penh, she worked in a bar catering to westerners, and provided sexual services on negotiation. She formed a close sexual relationship with an American customer, Sam, but continued to be a bartender. Sam helped her pay her rent and had asked her to find young girls for him. Through her social network, she managed to procure several underaged girls for Sam. Kadas generally brought the girls and their parents to meet Sam so they could make a deal with him directly. Sam gave Kadas $20 every time she taught a girl some sexual skills to pleasure him. In 2006, Kadas and Sam were arrested, and she was sentenced to 27 years in prison. Kadas reported that she was unaware that introducing willing girls with the consent of their parents to have sex with a foreigner and teaching them sexual skills was a serious crime. These activities were common practices at the bar where she worked.

How do Traffickers Operate?

Despite numerous claims in the literature that trafficked women are often recruited forcefully, our interviews supported Nair's (2004) and Surtees's (2008) findings: They argued that "forced recruitment" was relatively uncommon. Twelve confirmed traffickers, particularly female offenders in sex trafficking cases, had used seduction or deceptive inducement to recruit people. The trafficked persons were lured to follow the traffickers because the latter had created expectations of a better life in a new place. Participants who had previously managed brothels reported that brothel owners generally refrained from involving children or coercing women into prostitution. Most of them were prosecuted not because they coerced women into prostitution, but because under Article 5 of the 1996 law, operating a brothel is considered a criminal act. Choumpou, a

43-year-old man sentenced to seven years in prison for procuring a woman for prostitution declared:

> The police have more tolerance for brothels not involved in forced prostitution. Some NGOs keep a close eye on brothels. Brothel owners, therefore, avoid forced and child prostitution. Besides, there is no need to use coercion because there are plenty of women ready to work as sex workers.

A prosecutor who had worked on many sex trafficking cases told us that most of these cases turned out to be cases of procuring for prostitution, not sex trafficking. He echoed Choumpou's claim that brothel operators did not need to traffic anyone, because many women were "willing to prostitute themselves for a myriad of reasons."

None of the incarcerated traffickers abducted women or forced them into prostitution, but in some cases, they needed to persuade them, for example, using feigned love. Speu and his friend Pnaov used to steal and rob to feed their drug habit. They told another friend, Lvear, that they wanted to sell Speu's girlfriend, Orng, to buy drugs. Lvear had experience in trafficking women and told Speu and Pnaov to take her to Sihanouk Ville where he knew a brothel owner. Speu and Pnaov enticed Orng to participate in their criminal activities by saying that they loved her very much but they needed money to buy guns for their robberies. She could help them by working in a brothel for a while. Once they had made a few robberies, they would be able to get her out of the brothel and take care of her. Orng complied, going with Speu, Pnaov, and Lvear to Sihanouk Ville. They were attempting to pawn Orng at a brothel for $120,[9] when an NGO that had been investigating Lvear's activities reported them to the police. The three men were arrested, and Orng was rescued. Police officers asked Speu for $1,200 for their release. He did not have the money, so the three men were incarcerated. Pnaov was released because his family managed to strike a deal with the court, but Speu and Lvear were sentenced to 10 and 11 years, respectively, for sex trafficking.

Abduction was used only with young children to be sold into adoption. Seven participants (including five women) abducted small children who were too young to be persuaded to follow them. One case involved Romdoul,

38, who moved from Prey Veng province to work in Phnom Penh, leaving her three children with her mother. Romdoul had quit her job and left her husband when she discovered that he was having an affair with a coworker. Cheakmeas, a 58-year-old female job broker got Romdoul a job in a shop, where she was earning $35 a month. Some weeks later, Romdoul decided to return home and look after her children. Cheakmeas knew a couple who was offering $200 to adopt a child. Romdoul abducted her friend's one-year-old daughter and gave the girl to Cheakmeas, who then took her to the couple. The girl's mother reported the two women to the police. Romdoul and Cheakmeas were sentenced to 15 years' imprisonment.

Twenty-five of the ninety-one incarcerated participants had been arrested for their alleged involvement in cross-border trafficking. However, the majority of the incidents reported by our participants occurred within Cambodia, and complex and costly means of transportation were not necessary. Champei, a 61-year-old woman, told us:

> I managed to convince two girls to work in a karaoke parlor in Koh Kong. We traveled in a shared taxi from Phnom Penh to Koh Kong. Because the girls were willing to go with me, the taxi driver was not suspicious. We acted as if we were ordinary passengers. (Champei was serving 10 years' imprisonment for trafficking.)

Although much emphasis is given to sex trafficking, not all our respondents were prosecuted for activities relating to prostitution. Two male participants had been involved in labor trafficking. Karot was convicted of trafficking two children to work in plantations in Thailand. He had brought groups of illegal Cambodian laborers into Thailand before. As a group leader, he was responsible for subcontracting assignments with plantation owners to perform specific jobs such as cutting trees or removing grass. He would come to the plantation with a team of workers who did the jobs, negotiate a lump sum payment with the owner, and pay his workers as he wished. He himself labored to increase his income, which averaged $10 a day. By Cambodian living standards, this was a good income. However, he was arrested and could not afford the $1,500 demanded by the police for his freedom. He was sentenced to 10 years in prison for labor trafficking.

Smuggling people across borders so they could work outside Cambodia was frequent. Kabas, 41, a widow with a second-grade education, supporting eight children, had spent $87 to be smuggled to Bangkok to work in a restaurant. She could speak Thai and soon knew the routes to Thailand, and could commute easily and cheaply between the two countries with no need for smugglers. She got acquainted with some Cambodian and Thai border police and started smuggling people. Within a few years, she managed to smuggle thirty elderly women to work as beggars in Bangkok. Deducting transportation costs, she made $12.50 per smugglee. She was eventually arrested and convicted to eight years in prison for human trafficking and smuggling. She said: "People think smugglers make heaps of money, but in fact they do not. They have to share the proceeds with border patrollers of both sides. Had I $3,000 for a bribe, I would not be spending time behind bars."

The organization of traffickers was simple: Among the twenty-one confirmed traffickers, fifteen operated alone, five were linked to three independent and small-scale social networks, and only one claimed to be a former member of a large Cambodian organized crime syndicate. In a few cases several individuals had been convicted for their connection to a single trafficking incident. Their accounts did not suggest that they belonged to a criminal organization but rather that they merely happened to be acquainted. For example, a trafficker who abducted and sold a child may have had no prior relationship with the buyer, but both seller and buyer were then arrested and convicted of trafficking. Confirmed traffickers were mostly recruiters or procurers for others such as owners of brothels and karaoke parlors, child adopters, and child molesters to whom they were minimally connected. Only two confirmed traffickers continued to exploit the trafficked persons after they had arrived at the destination. What is important to note is that eleven confirmed traffickers had prior relationships with the trafficked persons: they were family members, relatives, friends, acquaintances, lovers, or neighbors.

For example, Somaly, a 54-year-old widow, was a sole operator who was accused of trafficking her granddaughter and her granddaughter's friend. Somaly's granddaughter, Sopham, had been disowned by her parents. Sopham and two female friends, including Rodeng who was 16, asked Somaly to help the three of them find a job. Somaly recommended them to a garment factory where she was employed at the time. However, after nine days, the three girls were fired. Unable to help them with a new job, Somaly persuaded them to work in a brothel fronting as a coining house[10] that was run by Rolous (another female participant), who gave Somaly a $100 commission. A month later, Rodeng's sister found out that Rodeng was working at the coining house and called the police who arrested Rolous and Somaly. Rolous was sentenced to 18 years in prison for human trafficking and procuring for prostitution, and Somaly to 14 years. This case did not involve coercion or transportation of the person to a different location, but it is legally a case of human trafficking because money had been exchanged, and whether the "trafficked" person consented to enter into sex work was irrelevant under the 1996 law.

Each of the three networks we uncovered consisted of three to six individuals who had formed an informal alliance without clearly defined roles and responsibilities or a hierarchy. These networks were family or friend-based, weak, amateurish, and had no clearly formulated plan. They were based on the temporary partnership of a few individuals looking for ways to make quick money and who came up with the idea of abducting a child, or procuring or trafficking a woman into prostitution. Seng and her husband belonged to such a network. In 2006, Seng (a bartender who occasionally prostituted herself), her husband, and a street-seller procured two young girls for a U.S. national. The street-seller introduced the daughters of her friend to Seng for a small commission. Seng's husband transported the girls to the house of the American. All four were apprehended: Seng and the street-seller were convicted of child trafficking; Seng's husband, of being an accomplice; and the American national, of child molestation.

The characteristics of the networks described by our participants did not match the features of criminal organizations described by the UNODC (2002): they were small, independent, poorly resourced, and loosely organized networks. They were involved in only occasional operations with no long-term goals or established leadership, similar to the Chinese human smuggler rings studied by Zhang and Chin (2002). One of the twenty-one confirmed traffickers, Lvear (see above) claimed to be a former member of a large organized crime syndicate. He described a Mafia-like syndicate characterized by a clear power structure. However, human trafficking was not part of its activities, which primarily involved drug production and distribution, robbery, fencing of stolen motor vehicles, production of pornographic films, and death squad operations. He believed that the syndicate was under the control of a few senior Cambodian military officials and benefited from sophisticated links with police and other crime syndicates in Thailand and Malaysia.

He had already served seven of his 11-year term in prison for attempting to sell a woman into a brothel. His story about the syndicate was not always credible, some of it sounded exaggerated, most of his accounts could not be verified, and the little that could did not match his claims. Finally, his trafficking activities had little connection with the syndicate, but were side operations for his personal benefit. Lvear's story is important because he claimed to have been a member of a criminal organization. The interviewer therefore thoroughly questioned what Lvear was telling him and went to a village in Kampong Cham province, where Lvear said that, in 1998, he had trafficked three women to be sold in Sihanoukville. The interviewer talked to local people and authorities about the case, but no one had ever heard of such incidents. This story and that of other respondents led us to conclude that the general social, economic, cultural, and criminal justice conditions in Cambodia allow for a simple modus operandi by traffickers that made the involvement of organized crime unnecessary and also improbable given the limited financial returns.

Traffickers' Earnings

None of the participants reported that they had earned much money from their illegal activities. Eight participants (including three females) had been operating brothels and were prosecuted for prostitution-related activities, but their businesses did not seem very lucrative. They rented the premises, which doubled as a brothel and their own residence. They were aware that operating brothels was illegal, but they reported that corrupt local authorities, police, and the gendarmes turned a blind eye as long as brothel operators were prepared to pay bribes to them. Rent seeking by corrupt officials cost them between $5 and $50 a month. In fact, thirteen participants, many sentenced for procuring for prostitution, said that some junior police officers were actively involved in the operation of sex establishments and protection rackets.[11] The brothels they operated housed no more than five to ten women, and the cost of sex services ranged from $2.50 to $5, which they shared with the sex workers. In the most profitable scenario, involving ten women serving ten clients a day, and charging $5 per client, the brothel operator could make $250 per day, from which all operating costs needed to be deducted. Most operators were unlikely to earn even half this optimistic income, as Roeung, a 28-year-old female brothel operator, sentenced to six years in prison for procuring for prostitution, complained:

> People think brothel owners make a lot of money, but they have no idea of our difficulties. We risk prosecution. We are harassed by police and local authorities, especially when we fail to pay the bribes in time. Our earnings are spent on bribery, rent, food for our girls, utilities, and more. Often the girls borrow money from us, and some run away without repaying the loan. Some even report to the police that they have been trafficked so they can default on the loan.

The Criminal Justice System's Response

The treatment by the criminal justice system of the forty-nine participants that we categorized as doubtfully convicted suggests, at best, negligence by the criminal justice system, and at worst, corruption. For the confirmed traffickers, the leading cause of arrest was a complaint to the police by the family of the alleged victim, but for the doubtfully convicted, it was direct "investigations" by the police. Overall, our participants' accounts suggest that they had been the subjects of attempted extortion by unscrupulous individuals and corrupt criminal justice system officials, as well as victims of incompetent law enforcement. We do not claim that all these participants were innocent. The reliability of the accounts of the doubtfully convicted can be questioned on the grounds that convicted traffickers may lie rather than admit guilt. However, some of them confessed to us that they had committed other offences, such as drug trafficking, procuring for prostitution, and human smuggling, but they

denied being involved in human trafficking. In addition, other data lend credence to the accounts of these individuals. For instance, fifty-five prison officers, six antitrafficking policemen, and fourteen court officials were also interviewed and their narratives confirmed the accounts of the ninety-one incarcerated participants that the 1996 law had little deterrent effect and produced harmful unintended consequences.

Most of the interviewed Anti-Trafficking and Juvenile Protection Office officers confessed that they and their colleagues had very limited knowledge of human trafficking. Some had only attended a one-day training workshop on the subject. They blamed their poor performance on a lack of resources, training, and focus. Instead of spending time investigating potential trafficking incidents, they were told to cooperate with NGOs in raising public awareness about the dangers of illegal migration, prostitution, and human trafficking.

The court officials, like the police officers and the convicted traffickers, had limited knowledge of what constituted human trafficking. According to the NGOs we contacted, few Cambodian judges know enough about human trafficking to deliver a sound and fair judgment. One NGO lawyer concluded about the cases she had worked on:

> Most offenders were unaware that they had committed offences qualified as human trafficking. A majority of law enforcement officers also did not have a good knowledge of the 1996 law, which they had never read. Their actions are based on what they have been told, heard, or what has been sensationalized. The dramatization of trafficking issues in Cambodia, created by a big group of powerful NGOs and UN agencies, seems to play a major part in the incorrect enforcement of the law.

Corruption was a major factor in the unfair application of the law, and legal ambiguities could also be used as opportunities for abuse of power.[12] About half the convicted participants reported that if they had been able to pay the bribe requested by the police or the judiciary, they would not have been convicted or would have received a more lenient sentence. Accusations of extortion attempts by judicial officials, as documented in our case studies, were numerous.[13] Corrupt practices are so common in the judiciary that the judges and prosecutors we talked to did not even pretend they did not engage in them. Rather they down-played their role by blaming the system in which they operated and the corruption of officials. In the words of a prosecutor:

> Compared to government officials, courts and prosecutors have a modest living standard. We don't make as much money as they do. We deal mostly with the poor. Even if we only ask for a small bribe, the poor complain loudly, making it sound like a big thing. Government officials deal with the rich. Even if they take a lot more, the rich are still happy and keep quiet.

We spoke to a number of NGOs in Cambodia and they all confirmed that many judges handed down guilty rulings despite a lack of compelling evidence against an accused, especially if the latter could not afford to pay a bribe. We interviewed a judge who confirmed these allegations: "Even when evidence is slim, in the absence of financial reward, many judges I know tend to convict a person accused of trafficking. This is partly to avoid being seen as corrupt if they had acquitted the accused. As for me, I normally exonerate the accused if there is not enough evidence."

Failed attempts at extortion against poor individuals, sometimes by acquaintances or friends, resulted in some of our respondents being accused and eventually convicted of trafficking. These accounts reveal one of the typical mechanisms of the perversion of justice when the law becomes an instrument of victimization. They also document how unscrupulous individuals in collusion with corrupt police exploited the sensationalized issue of human trafficking to falsely accuse other people of being traffickers and extort money from them. Three of the participants, all from different prisons, told stories in which they appeared to have been doubtfully convicted because they had had love affairs that others objected to; in Cambodian culture such affairs bring shame to the family. To imprison and punish the violator, the aggrieved family can bribe the police or the judge who can now, in addition to rape charges,[14] also use the antitrafficking law.

The story of Bopha and her father illustrates how false accusations, incompetence, and corruption in all likelihood resulted in a miscarriage of justice. This case is particularly interesting because, exceptionally, we were able to review the court dossier, which was provided by sources we cannot reveal. Bopha was sentenced to three years' imprisonment and Cheak, her father, to 10 years for attempting to traffic two of her girlfriends, Malis and Kabas. Cheak was a moto taxi driver and the only income earner in the family that included his sick wife and three children. Bopha dropped out of school in third grade because of dire poverty and to nurse her mother who eventually died at home from a brain tumor. After his wife's death, Cheak built a small wooden house on land donated by villagers. He wanted Bopha to live with a relative in a provincial town. When Bopha told Malis and Kabas that she was leaving the village, the two girls said they would like to go with her.

The next day, Cheak took Bopha to town, and on their way, they met Malis and Kabas who asked for a lift, claiming that they had permission from their parents to go and work as fruit sellers. Soon they were stopped by the local police, who, following a complaint from the girls' parents, arrested Bopha and Cheak. The girls' parents wanted $500 in exchange for not pressing charges against Cheak and Bopha. Cheak did not have such a sum of money and offered to sell his motorcycle, but the girls' parents refused to wait and lodged a formal complaint.

Three legal aid NGOs got involved in the case. One represented Malis and Kabas against Cheak and Bopha's NGO lawyers. According to Cheak's lawyer, at some stage Malis's and Kabas's parents said that they regretted having lodged a complaint and that the accused were innocent. Another lawyer told us that a week before the hearing, hundreds of villagers, including Malis's and Kabas's parents, made a request to the court, endorsed by the local authorities, for the release of Cheak and Bopha, but the hearing continued. Cheak reported that before handing down his verdict, the judge asked him and Bopha to wait outside the courtroom. There, a court official, prosecutor, or clerk, requested $500 from Cheak to have them both exonerated by the judge. Cheak again offered to sell his motorcycle to get the money. When Cheak and Bopha went back into the courtroom, they were convicted of attempting to traffic Malis and Kabas, and the motorcycle was confiscated as a criminal implement.

According to the lawyers representing Malis and Kabas, the evidence against Cheak and Bopha was: (1) Cheak had been caught red-handed carrying Malis and Kabas on his motorbike, and (2) Malis and Kabas testified that they had been enticed by Bopha to come to town to sell fruit in the street. Cheak's lawyer remarked that after the trial, the judge had told him: "It does not sound fair for the defendants, but I don't have a choice. I have to convict them to avoid criticism." Cheak did not appeal the decision because like many poor Cambodians he is a fatalist: "It was my destiny to go to jail," he said. However, in actuality, he did not have the $5 required for an appeal application, and he also feared that the Appeal Court might increase his sentence.

The court dossier showed that after Cheak and Bopha's arrest, Malis and Kabas told the police that they had come voluntarily to town with Bopha. However, the two girls had been placed into an NGO shelter for children who are victims of violence, abuse, or human trafficking. According to the lawyers, the girls then changed their testimony, alleging that they had been enticed by Bopha to go to sell fruit in the streets. The lawyers suspected that Malis and Kabas might have indeed been enticed not by Bopha, but by their desire to be regarded as victims of child trafficking because they would then meet the NGO's criteria for support, such as free education, accommodation, and food.

Our last case study also exemplifies how poor individuals may become the victims of false accusations and end up in court, where they are unable to meet demands for money by court officials, and are convicted. We include this story because the participant ultimately was acquitted, making him the most auspicious person among our sample of doubtfully convicted. Kuy was a poor fisherman. In 2004, he had an argument with his wife and beat her rather badly. Kroch, his brother-in-law, was very angry with Kuy for beating his sister and brought him to the court office. He asked the court to allow his sister to divorce Kuy; Kuy agreed to the divorce but requested custody of two of his four children. His wife wanted full custody of all four children. Rather than allowing a divorce, the judge ordered Kuy to be detained on the charge of attempting to sell his children. During

his hearing, which lasted less than an hour in the absence of legal representation, Kuy was sentenced to 15 years in prison for attempted child trafficking. He told the interviewer: "I spent most of the time on the water, fishing. I had little contact with others. I knew where to sell fish, but certainly not where to sell my two sons." In 2008, he was assisted by an NGO to appeal the provincial court's decision. During our fieldwork in Cambodia in late 2009, we found out from a prison officer that the appeal court had already acquitted Kuy.

The Trafficking Panic in Cambodia

The findings in this study do not support popular claims about the high prevalence, profitability, or role of organized crime in human trafficking in Cambodia. Our research indicates that the majority of incarcerated traffickers in Cambodia are destitute women who, pushed by a lack of legitimate opportunities and pulled by the presence of illegitimate opportunities, engage in unsophisticated criminal activities for very modest gains. Over half of them are probably the victims of miscarriages of justice because the law enforcement response has become open to corruption and injustice rather than a measure that enhances the protection of human rights.

Problems such as predatory crime, drug use, prostitution, and illegal migration, though, do share an important characteristic: They are likely to provoke popular anxiety and moral indignation. The level of anxiety and outrage is often disproportionate to the prevalence of these problems. The popular perception is that the problem is worsening despite evidence to the contrary. These anxiety-provoking problems are often dramatized and sensationalized in newspaper articles, movies, and TV shows that select the most fear-provoking and extraordinary cases for popular consumption. A significant consequence is the diversion of attention and resources from other pressing social issues (Talbot, 1999; Weitzer, 2011). The findings of evidence-based studies should reduce misrepresentations and misperceptions; yet despite the evidence, these distortions can reach prodigious proportions. When such a situation arises, a moral panic is in full sway.

Talbot (1999) listed four recurring characteristics of moral panics: (1) wildly inflated statistics that are circulated and reported without any skepticism or correction; (2) the rejection of credible counterevidence; (3) unreliable research; and (4) indiscriminate merging of various crimes to make the problem look much more serious than it is. Drawing from Cohen (1973) and Talbot, we can distinguish four features of the human trafficking moral panic: (1) the elements delineated by Talbot and generally presented in highly emotional language and discourses; (2) the vested interests outlined by Cohen, which include moral entrepreneurs, journalists, politicians, rescuers, and other professionals; (3) the scope of the panic ranging from the local to the national and international levels; and (4) the negative consequences such as bad legislation, misuse of resources, demonization of certain groups, and criminalization of innocent people. Our study of traffickers in Cambodia illustrates these four characteristics.

In the early 1990s, the end of the Cold War and the globalization of economic activities drove people from the developing world to developed nations through new global channels of migration, and led the western world in an intensified campaign against illegal migrants and those who facilitated them—the smugglers. During the same period, governments and elements of civil society in the developed world "discovered" a related but even more alarming threat to humanity and global order: human trafficking. Moral entrepreneurs with various agendas coalesced their concerns about illicit migration, indentured work, prostitution, and child protection in an accelerating panic about human trafficking. Foreign NGOs and aid donors, the United States in particular, influenced the design and adoption of the Cambodian law on trafficking. This law was poorly written, ambiguous, and confounded trafficking, smuggling, illegal migration, and prostitution; it cast a wide net over many ill-defined "deviant" behaviors. Cambodia was just emerging from 30 years of armed conflict and still grappling with high levels of violence, and poverty and social inequality were widespread. The criminal justice system was weak and corrupt; police and judiciary were poorly trained and paid and known to systematically engage in rent seeking and extortion. This anomic period in Cambodia was embedded in a larger transformation brought about by globalization, and itself a generator of anomic conditions. The new rules of this transnational, globalized game created both legitimate

and illegitimate opportunities in new "global circuits of survival" (Sassen, 2002). Through these circuits, women from developing countries such as Cambodia increasingly moved abroad to try to make a living, and became exposed to the risk of being exploited and abused, but also to being criminalized.

Given the many known shortcomings of the Cambodian criminal justice system, the adoption of such a law becomes problematic. We have seen how the aims of well-meaning antitrafficking NGOs could be seriously perverted in the environment under such a law. Was the hegemonic agenda too irresistible or pressing and the moral and security panics too strong for their supporters to contemplate the disastrous effects of their "good work" on the powerless of the subordinate world?

Eliminating systemic corruption in the Cambodian criminal justice system requires serious structural changes, only achievable in the long term. In the short term, legal reforms could reduce opportunities for corrupt behaviors and injustice. For example, voluntary prostitution could be legalized but regulated through an indigenous democratic policy involving all stakeholders.

It is practically impossible to enforce the 2008 antitrafficking law in ways that respect and protect the rights of suspects and victims. One option worth considering (and possibly applicable to other countries) is to repeal the law on human trafficking and instead use the existing criminal laws (about abduction, deprivation of liberty, forced labor/prostitution, and so on), which already prohibit and punish all the types of victimization covered by the human trafficking concept.

Finally, efforts to professionalize law enforcement and judicial officials should be made so as to strengthen the criminal justice system. Due to the complex nature of the human trafficking phenomenon, it is crucial that specialized anti-trafficking and juvenile protection police take the lead in dealing with human trafficking cases. In each municipality/province, at least two prosecutors and judges should be adequately trained on and entrusted with human trafficking related cases. Countertrafficking efforts should also put increased focus on economic development among the most at-risk populations to reduce their vulnerability to become traffickers and trafficked victims. Ultimately, what is required in Cambodia to address human trafficking is not more law and punishment but more legitimate opportunities to survive.

/// DISCUSSION QUESTIONS

1. Why do people engage in human trafficking?

2. How does the criminal justice system respond to these cases and how does that impact the behaviors of the perpetrators of these acts?

3. What sorts of myths and misconceptions exist about human trafficking in Cambodia?

Notes

1. For example, the 2012 report ventures that the estimate is in the "billions."

2. Further details of this project on sex trafficking in Cambodia can be found in Keo (2013).

3. Levenkron did not specify which definition of trafficking was used; Nair adopted the UN definition.

4. Law on Suppression of the Kidnapping, Trafficking, and Exploitation of Human Beings, 1996, available from http://www.wcwonline.org/pdf/lawcompilation/Cambodia_Law%20on%20Kidnapping,%20 Trafficking%20and%20Exploitation%20Pe.pdf.

5. "Direct sex worker" refers to those working in brothels or other prostitution settings. "Indirect sex worker" refers to those working in settings that are not places of prostitution.

6. We define a "human trafficker" as any person charged or convicted under Article 3 of the 1996 antitrafficking law.

7. There was little variance in the socioeconomic status (SES) scale (all participants were poor) but "level of education" can be regarded as a proxy for SES, and women were less educated than men.

8. We use fictional names in all the cases described here.

9. Although Cambodia's official currency is the riel, U.S. dollars are routinely used. For comparison, at the time of the study the average daily wage of a worker was around $2.50 with no other benefit.

10. A traditional form of medicinal massage common in Cambodia.

11. USDS (2009) reported that a number of police and government officials extorted money or accepted bribes from brothel operators, and that courts acquitted traffickers in return for bribes. Former Phnom Penh Police Commissioner, Heng Pov, who was in office between 2004 and 2006, is currently serving a 92-year prison term for a number of crimes, including murder, extortion, and kidnapping (Chrann, 2009).

12. In 2007, the municipal court acquitted Meng Say, who in 2006 had been suspended for extorting money from South Korean nationals. Three other police officers involved in the case were sentenced to between five and seven years in prison for corruption in trafficking incidents (USDS, 2009; Prak, 2006).

13. In December 2010, a provincial prosecutor was arrested by the Anti-Corruption Unit of Cambodia for abuse of power, corruption, and extortion (Southeast Asia Weekly, December 6, 2010).

14. There have been reports in the local media about rape in Cambodia that suggest that sometimes consenting girls claim rape to avoid the wrath of their parents and community. Other cases involve premarital sexual relationships that lead to monetary compensation or forced marriage.

References

Asian Legal Resource Centre. (2001). Police abuses in Cambodia. Written submission to the UN Commission on Human Rights, 57th Session. retrieved from www.humanrights.asia/ Broadhurst, R., & Keo, C. (2011). Cambodia: A criminal justice system in transition. In C. Smith, S. Zhang, & R. Barbaret (Eds.), *International handbook of criminology* (p. 338–348). New York, NY: Routledge.

Brown, E. (2007). *The ties that bind: Migration and trafficking of women and girls for sexual exploitation in Cambodia*. Phnom Penh: International Organization for Migration (IOM).

Cambodian Center for Human Rights (CCHR). (2010). *Human trafficking trials in Cambodia: A report by the Cambodian Center for Human Rights*. Phnom Penh: CCHR.

Chrann, C. (2009, June 12). Heng Pov: Judges to rule on top cop appeal. *Phnom Penh Post*.

Cohen, S. (1973). *Folk devils and moral panics*. St. Albans, UK: Paladin-Granada.

Davies, N. (2009, October 19). Prostitution and trafficking: The anatomy of a moral panic. *The Guardian*.

Delauney, G. (2007, April 6). Trafficking crackdown in Cambodia. *BBC News Phnom Penh*. Retrieved from news.bbc.co.uk/2/hi/asia-pacific/6532181.stm

Derks, A., Henke, R, & Ly, V. (2006). *Review of a decade of research on trafficking in persons in Cambodia*. Phnom Penh: Asia Foundation.

Doezema, J. (2000). Loose women or lost women? The re-emergence of the myth of white slavery in contemporary discourses of trafficking in women. *Gender Issues, 18* (1): 23–50.

Ek, C., & Sok, H. (2008). *Aid effectiveness in Cambodia.* Working Paper #7. Washington, DC: Wolfensohn Center for Development.

Home and Community Care Program (HACC). (2008). *Reflection on the implementation of the Law on Suppression of Human Trafficking and Sexual Exploitation.* Phnom Penh: HACC.

Kato, T., Kaplan, J., Chan, S., & Real, S. (2000). *Cambodia: Enhancing governance for sustainable development.* Working Paper #14. Phnom Penh: Cambodian Development Resource Institute.

Keo, C. (2006). *Life after reintegration: The situation of child trafficking survivors.* Phnom Penh: IOM-Cambodia.

Keo, C. (2009). *Hard life for a legal work: The 2008 anti-trafficking law and sex work.* Phnom Penh: Cambodian Alliance for Combating HIV/AIDS (CACHA).

Keo, C. (2010). *NGO joint statistics project: Database report on trafficking and rape in Cambodia 2009.* Phnom Penh: ECPAT-Cambodia.

Keo, C. (2013). *Moral panic and human trafficking in Cambodia: The road to hell is paved with good intentions.* London: Routledge.

Khiev, S. (2004). *What makes Australia's judicial system first grade? Why not in Cambodia?* Phnom Penh: Center for Democratic Institution.

Levenkron, N. (2007). *"Another delivery from Tashkent": Profile of the Israeli trafficker.* Tel Aviv: Hotline for Migrant Workers. Retrieved from www.ungift.org/

League for the Promotion and Defense of Human Rights (LICADHO). (2008). *Prison conditions in Cambodia, 2007: The story of a mother and child.* Phnom Penh: LICADHO.

League for the Promotion and Defense of Human Rights (LICADHO). (2009). *Prison conditions in 2008: Women in prison.* Phnom Penh: LICADHO.

Nair, P.M. (2004). *A report on trafficking in women and children in India, 2002–2003.* New Delhi: National Human Rights Commission.

National Institute of Statistics. (2009). *General population census of Cambodia 2008: National report on final census.* Phnom Penh, Cambodia: Ministry of Planning, Royal Government of Cambodia.

National Police Commissariat (NPC). (2007). *2006 national police report.* Phnom Penh: NPC, Cambodian Ministry of Interior.

National Police Commissariat (NPC). (2009). *2008 national police report.* Phnom Penh: NPC, Cambodian Ministry of Interior.

Perrin, B., Majumdar, S., Gafuik, N., & Andrews, S. (2001). *The future of Southeast Asia: Challenges of child sex slavery and trafficking in Cambodia.* Phnom Penh: Future Group.

Prak, C. T. (2006, March 23). Anti-trafficking official missing after suspension. *Cambodia Daily.*

Sandy, L. (2007). Just choice: Representations of choice and coercion in sex work in Cambodia. *Australian Journal of Anthropology, 18* (2): 194–206.

Sassen, S. (2002). Women's burden: Counter-geographies of globalization and the feminization of survival. *Nordic Journal of International Law, 71*:255–274.

Steinfatt, T. (2011). Sex trafficking in Cambodia: Fabricated numbers versus empirical evidence. *Crime, Law, and Social Change, 56*:443–462.

Surtees, R. (2008). Traffickers and trafficking in Southern and Eastern Europe: Considering the other side of human trafficking. *European Journal of Criminology, 5*:39–68.

Talbot, M. (1999, March 15). Against innocence: The truth about child abuse and the truth about children. *New Republic.* Retrieved from www.ipce.info/library_2/pdf/talbot_99.pdf United Nations Office on Drugs and Crime (UNODC). (2002). *Results of a pilot survey of forty selected* organized criminal groups in sixteen countries. New York, NY: UNODC. Retrieved from www.unodc.org/pdf/crime/publications/Pilot_survey.pdf

United Nations Office on Drugs and Crime (UNODC). (2008). *Human trafficking: An overview.* New York, NY: UNODC.

United Nations Office on Drugs and Crime (UNODC). (2012). *Global report on trafficking in persons 2012.* New York, NY: UNODC.

U.S. Department of State (USDS). (2009). *Trafficking in persons report, 2009.* Washington, DC: Department of State.

Weitzer, R. (2007). The social construction of sex trafficking: Ideology and institutionalization of a moral crusade. *Politics and Society, 35*:447–475.

Weitzer, R. (2011). Sex trafficking and the sex industry: The need for evidence-based theory and legislation. *Journal of Criminal Law and Criminology, 101*:1337–1370.

Zhang, S. (2009). Beyond the "Natasha" story: A review and critique of current research on sex trafficking. *Global Crime, 10*:178–195.

Zhang, S., & Chin, K. L. (2002). Enter the dragon: Inside Chinese human smuggling organizations. *Criminology, 40*(4): 737–768.

READING /// 10

War rape is a unique experience, both from other types of war-trauma experiences and other forms of rape and sexual assault. This article discusses the experiences of women who faced rape during the Bosnian war.

Victim and Survivor
Narrated Social Identities of Women Who Experienced Rape During the War in Bosnia-Herzegovina

Inger Skjelsbaek

Introduction

The war in Bosnia-Herzegovina (hereafter, Bosnia) from 1992 to 1995 was marked by the systematic use of rape and sexual violence. While rape in war is by no means a new phenomenon, the international and domestic attention received by this particular aspect of the Bosnian war was extraordinary. This led to a degree of openness about a phenomenon that has historically been hidden and ridden with shame. Because it is openly recognized that systematic use of rape took place in Bosnia, and because numerous victims of these crimes are willing to talk about their ordeals, the Bosnian conflict thus opened up a new possibility for research on this particular form of violence.

It is commonly believed that, when utilized in ethnic conflicts, as in the Bosnian case, sexual violence is employed as a weapon of demoralization against entire societies (Coneth-Morgan, 2004: 22). The demoralization is characterized by a violent invasion of the interior of the victim's body, which thereby constitutes an attack upon the intimate self and dignity of the individual human being (Goldstein, 2001: 362–363). How this attack impacts on its victims and their relationships is however, unanswered. The narratives presented in this text represent one attempt at unfolding the impact sexual violence has had on five Bosnian women.

Sexual Violence During the Bosnian War of 1992–1995

It was *Newsday* journalist Roy Gutman who reported the first instances of rape and what appeared to be systematic sexual violence against women in Bosnia to the international public. His accounts tell of mass rapes seemingly carried out under orders in a systematic campaign of ethnic cleansing (Gutman, 1993: 64–76, 144–149, 157–167). United Nations (UN) Security Resolution 820 from 17 April 1993 also underscores the systematic use of rape by stating that its use has been 'massive, organized and systematic' (S/RES/820/A6). We will never know just how many women (and men) suffered from this particular form of violence, however. Indeed, a range of different estimates have been given by numerous organizations and agencies.[1] Furthermore, alongside attempts to document the crimes, the estimation of numbers has been used and misused for political purposes (see discussions in Nikolic-Ristanovic, 2000; Thomas & Ralph, 1994: 93). Meznaric (1994: 92) summarizes what we can assert with confidence in the following manner:

One could say that there is agreement in the sources concerning several important points: (1) mass rape had at least several thousand

SOURCE: Skjelsbaek, I. (2006). Victim and survivor: Narrated social identities of women who experienced rape during the war in Bosnia-Herzegovina. *Feminism & Psychology*, 16(4), 373–403.

victims; (2) there have been many rapes of young girls between the ages of seven and fourteen; (3) rape is often committed in the presence of the victim's parents/children and generally the rape victim is raped by several assailants.

There exists a rich literature of oral testimonies given by victims of these crimes that confirms Meznaric's summary (see, for instance, CID, 2002; Helsinki Watch, 1993; Stiglmayer, 1994; Vranic, 1996). The majority of these testimonies come from women who were raped within the first months of the war, when their villages, most of them situated in the rural border areas, were attacked in early April 1992. The Helsinki Watch Report from 1993, documenting war crimes in Bosnia-Herzegovina (Helsinki Watch, 1993), lists the different ways in which rapes were carried out in the various regions of Bosnia. This list includes rape in separate rape camps, in concentration camps, in people's homes and in facilities made to appear as brothels. The ways in which these acts were carried out were limited only by the imagination of the perpetrators.[2] Here, it is important to note that the documentary record shows that rape was used as a war strategy by all sides in the conflict. This is pointed out in the Helsinki Watch Report (Helsinki Watch, 1993), which lists the use of rape by all warring parties in the conflict. It is also emphasized in other publications, such as Nizich (1994); Stiglmayer (1994); UN Economic and Social Council (1993, 1994). However, most commentators are careful to point out that the majority of these crimes were committed by Serb (ir) regular forces against the Muslim population of Bosnia (see, for instance, Nizich, 1994: 25; Stephens, 1993: 13).

Research literature on these crimes emphasizes that sexual violence was carried out in order to humiliate, or destroy, the *identity* of the victim, and that this was the way in which the violence constituted a weapon of war (see, for instance, Allen, 1996; Gutman,1993; Nikolic-Ristanovic, 2000; Stiglmayer, 1994). In her contested book *Rape Warfare*, Allen (1996: xiii) argues that for the perpetrators it was the female victims' ability to bear children that was most important. Allen characterizes this intention as genocidal because, she argues, the aim of the perpetrators was to create more babies with the perpetrator's ethnicity and through this to destroy and erase the ethnic, religious, and national identities of their female victims. Whether or not one chooses to define such acts as genocidal, the issue of forced

impregnation stands as a disturbing example of how the identities of victims were violated and misused. In a special report on recognizing forced impregnation as a war crime, Goldstein (1993: 4) argues that "the assault should be punishable as attempted forced impregnation even if it does not result in pregnancy, so long as the intent to impregnate can be established." Inherent in this argument is the notion that the female body constitutes yet another battlefield where ethnic conflict can be fought,[3] where a woman's sexual identity—in conjunction with her political and religious national identity—is the main target for the actions being carried out.

Although there is a clear need to expand the legal framework to include rape and forced impregnation as war crimes, there is an equally strong need to broaden the scholarly knowledge and understanding of war rape. Not only is there relatively limited (although increasing) research on this form of war violence, there are few, if any, empirically based studies. In addition, argues Hydén on the scholarly literature of battered women, there is a risk of confining abused women to their sufferings and thereby constructing a homogenous and monolithic conceptualization of female victimhood (Hydén, 2005: 172). The literature on sexual violence in war outlined above clearly runs this risk. Hydén (2005: 173) argues that in each story of oppression and suffering there runs a parallel history of opposition. The aim of this article, therefore, is both to generate empirical knowledge about war rape by analysing lived experiences as narrated by five protagonists, and also to show how they employ different strategies for war-rape survival and identity construction. Before doing so, however, a few words on this particular form of analysis are in order.

Narrative Theory and Analysis

Narrative analyses have gained increasing momentum within social science research in general, and particularly within social constructionist psychology.[4] While, in terms of content, this form of analysis is similar to discourse analysis—that is, the study of the relationship between ideas and ideals in our social worlds and how they are represented and manifest on different levels—narrative analysis is more stringent in form and more narrowly focused on the storied nature of the *self*. Sarbin (1986) argues that the narrative form has an ontological status in that it offers a way of being: We are the stories we tell and that are told by others. Along with Bruner (1985, 1990), Gergen (1994), and Polkinghorne (1988), Sarbin shows that we are, indeed, born into a storied world. Epistemologically, the self is seen not as an individual's personal or private structure but as a form of relational discourse about the self-performed and framed through language available in the public sphere (Gergen, 2001: 247). Human beings impose structures on experiences and events in such a way that when we recount life experiences as major achievements, disappointments and turning points, we do not normally tell random tales of discrete points in time. On the contrary, argues Gergen (1994, 2001), the stories are put together in a narrative structure, which typically has a beginning, a middle and an end. Within this structure, it is the main plot that brings the elements of the story together. Indeed, Polkinghorne (1995: 5) goes so far as to define a narrative as a way of combining elements into an emplotted story.

According to Gergen (1994: 207), the major function of the narrative is to unite the past with the present and signify future trajectories for the self. In addition, says Murray (2003: 113), the narrative serves as an organized interpretation of a sequence of events in which we attribute agency to the characters in the narrative and infer causal links between the events. The ways in which the narrators attribute agency is through positioning themselves and others within the plot. Davies and Harré (2001: 264) argue that positioning can be seen as a discursive process "whereby selves are located in conversation as observably and subjectively coherent participants in jointly produced story lines."

Gergen (1994, 2001: 253–254) has identified three different narratives of the self,[5] and says that they are established according to the following order: a valued endpoint is established; events are selected and ordered in accordance with how relevant they are for the endpoint; identity is presented as stable; causal linkages are made between events; and, finally, narratives are framed by demarcation signs. Within these processes, the narrator creates stories about himself- or herself in cooperation with, and in relation to, others. It is these relationships that provide us with our ideologies of self and reinforce and/or contrast our stories. Gergen (1994: 208) argues that "constructions of the self-require a supporting cast", and it is within this network of relationships that identities are formed, altered and maintained.

As we can see from the last quote, within Gergen's terminology *self* and *identity* are used interchangeably, and both

terms denote processes of social construction. In the following, however, I will use the term social construction to refer to the same processes that Gergen has outlined. The reason for this choice of terminology is that I wish to underscore that the locus of analysis is more how the protagonists position and narrate their identities in a *social* context, and less their personal identity (which would have required a different kind of methodology). The object of this study is twofold: first, to analyze the ways in which the five women construct their social identities through their narratives; second, to assess the impact the war rapes have had on their social identity construction. In these processes it is the intersectionality, such as the mutual saturation and toning among social categories (Søndergaard, 2005: 192), between victimhood, survival, ethnic and gendered identities that are the core focus.

Because the war rapes happened under extraordinary violent and potentially fatal circumstances, it has been important to find an analytical format that makes it possible to analyze the war rapes separately from other horrific events that happened to these women during the war. By structuring the analysis as a narrative and analyzing the interviews with the victims as narratives, we come closer to an understanding of how the war rapes have affected the victims in unique ways. In this scenario, it is the war rapes that serve as the valued endpoint, and other events and accounts are selected and ordered as they are seen as relevant to these experiences.

Method

Setting out to learn about the postwar identities of women subject to the war rapes in Bosnia was difficult. There were practical issues to resolve, such as identifying interview subjects, arranging meeting points and finding suitable interpreters. In addition, there were ethical and psychological concerns: Would my research hurt the interviewees? What kinds of questions could I ask or not ask them? How would I react to their stories? What would I do if an interviewee needed psychological help during or after an interview? In order to address these concerns, I adhered to the following principles: (1) The interviews had to be based on voluntary participation, and an interviewee could at any point during an interview decline to answer my questions; (2) the interviewees had to be recruited through an organization, so that there was a network of people available for them if necessary;[6] (3) in preparing the questions to ask and how to behave and not behave around severely traumatized women, I interviewed a number of therapists in Bosnia and abroad who had worked with traumatized women, and I studied numerous publications containing oral testimonies from traumatized women in Bosnia.[7]

The narrative analysis that follows is based on seven interviews with five different women. Names have been changed and details withheld to protect the anonymity of the interviewees. Three of these women—"Azra," "Ceca," and "Danira"—were aged 44 at the time of the interviews (autumn 2001/early spring 2002) and were married and had children before the war. They had remained married to their husbands after the war. "Berina" was 24 at the time of the interview; she is a widow and has one child. "Emila" was 25 at the time of the interview and has no children. These women all identify themselves as Bosniak. While it is a well-established fact that Serb and Croat women were also victims of similar forms of sexual violence during the war, this study draws its empirical findings from interviews with Bosniak women. There are pragmatic reasons for this choice. Though many of the local organizations I contacted aim to be multiethnic, there are simply more Bosniak women members of such organizations than members from other nationalities. It was therefore easier to get in touch with Bosniak women who were willing to talk than to contact similar women from other nationalities. Further, the study does not aim to compare the impact of sexual violence in a cross-national perspective, but rather focuses on implications for notions of the *self* as victim and survivor. The interviewees are therefore not primarily regarded as ethnic/national subjects. Each of the interviews lasted about 1.5 hours, and they were all structured along thematic lines.[8] However, the interview format was sufficiently open to permit a great deal of flexibility and changes of topic and focus according to the wishes of the interviewees.

All interviews were carried out with an interpreter. I used two different interpreters, both women. This was a deliberate choice. One had extensive experience with the theme of my research, because she also worked as a project leader at a psychosocial centre for traumatized women. The other had extensive experience with interviews with raped women during the war, when she had worked for the International Committee of the Red Cross (ICRC). Both interpreters were briefed about my research before the interviews took place. I also instructed them not to carry out

simultaneous translation, as this would interfere with the trains of thought of both myself and the interviewees. The interpretation therefore took the form of summaries. As a result, the transcribed text on which the analysis is based is essentially a construction based on three voices: the interviewer, the interviewee, and the interpreter. The interviews were psychologically draining for all involved: interpreters, interviewees, and myself. Both I and the interpreters cried at several points during the interviews. One of the interpreters told me it was particularly hard to hear the rape stories in the aftermath of war, because it made her realize that she lives among perpetrators and victims of such crimes, and that it was within such a world that her children were growing up. She even contemplated leaving Bosnia after working for me.

The interpreters became very involved in the interview situation. When things grew difficult and painful, they both stepped in and comforted the interviewees, as did I with my very limited language skills. As a result, the interpreters in this study played a much more active role in the social interaction between researcher and interviewee than might be considered appropriate in mainstream textbooks on interview methodologies. However, given the gravity of the themes discussed, I regarded their behavior as both appropriate and ethical. When confronted with ordeals like those the interviewees had gone through, it is only human to show how deeply you are touched by their stories—whether you are a researcher or an interpreter.

In order to establish a common point of reference, it was important to ask the interviewees to talk about their rape experiences. However, this was naturally a very delicate endeavour. Both the interviewees and I knew that the reason I wanted to talk to them was because of their war-rape experiences, but at the same time it seemed highly inappropriate to begin the interviews with questions about those particular events. It had been made clear to the interviewees that they should not feel obliged to recount details of their ordeals, yet some sort of acknowledgement of their experiences had to be established in the interview situation in order to be able to link the traumatic events they had experienced to their accounts of post-conflict life. I therefore began each interview with factual questions on such issues as the interviewee's age, educational background, where they had lived before the war, and what their family situation had been like. Gradually, the interviews would move toward the rape issue through questions about their current *relationships* (does your husband/mother know what happened to you during the war?), their *material* life conditions in the past (would you mind telling me what happened to you when your village was destroyed/your house was burned?), possible *bodily* pains (do you sometimes have difficulties sleeping/remembering things?). It was hoped that this would establish a degree of rapport between the interpreter, the interviewee and myself, which in turn would make the interviewee feel more comfortable talking about her traumas. Nevertheless, despite my careful preparations, the ways in which the rape issue was disclosed was surprising and very different in each case, as will be shown below.

Analysis

According to Ricoeur (cited in White, 1987: 51):

> Every narrative combines two dimensions in various proportions, one chronological and one non-chronological. The first may be called the episodic dimension, which characterizes the story made out of events. The second is the configurational dimension, according to which the plot construes significant wholes out of scattered events.

The stories to be told over the following pages are characterized by the same chronological outline, which takes the following format:

Beginning: Accounts of pre-war life. This was characterized by material and social security, multi-ethnic coexistence and peace. It is a story of a harmonic life and comes close to a paradise account compared to interviewees' accounts of their current life situations.

Middle: Accounts of war rapes. A major part of the stories is centred on the outbreak of war and the sudden and extreme violence the interviewees experienced. Their accounts of war rapes are told along with other stories of extreme life-changing events, such as loss of homes, family and friends.

End: Accounts of post-conflict life. An equally major part of the stories focuses on the aftermath of war: how and where the interviewees live, their family relationships, poverty and uncertain future prospects.

Within this main chronological structure, two different plots emerge—namely, that of being an *ethnic survivor* versus *gendered victim*. The ways in which these plots come out depend on how the protagonists position themselves within their stories. The different ways of positioning do not simply result from an arbitrary decision on the part of the narrators, but rather depend on the actual and anticipated actions and behaviors of the other characters in their stories. In addition, it is important to point out that the interviewees do not simply position themselves as either ethnic survivor or gendered victim. As Hydén (2005: 178) points out, it is common for interviewees to talk from conflicting, parallel and opposing subject positions within the same story. The plot structures I identify in the following analysis suggest that the interviewees emphasize one structure over the other, but they should not be considered as mutually exclusive plots. Furthermore, as Murray (2003: 116) argues, narrative accounts are not told in a vacuum, but are shaped and encouraged by specific contexts. In other words, there is a layer outside the story—that is, the sociopolitical *context* in which it is told—which influences what, how and why elements within the story are seen as important and relevant. Within this line of thought, the narrator is regarded as a complex psychosocial subject who is an active agent in a social world, and it is through the narrative analysis that we can understand both narrators and their worlds (Murray, 2003: 116).

Narratives of Ethnicity and Survival

Ethnicity is by far the most dominant discourse informing the literature on the Bosnian conflict. At the start of the war, a common perception among U.S. politicians—U.S. president Bill Clinton in particular—was that the reason for the conflict was the age-old hatred between the different ethnic groups in the region, and therefore that international intervention would be futile (Holbrooke, 1999: 22). Witnessing the Bosnian nightmare unfold eventually forced the international community to reconsider its passivity. However, even when the international community did finally intervene,[9] its belief that the root cause of the conflict was ethnic hatred remained unchanged. The mere division of Bosnia into a Serb Republic and a Croat/Muslim federation after the Dayton Peace Agreement, brokered in December 1995, clearly attests to this.

Domestically, however, the picture is more complex. While ethnic hostilities became stronger throughout the conflict years, accounts of pre-war life in Bosnia were characterized by multiethnic coexistence. Bringa's (1995) study, for instance, describes an ethnically heterogeneous village in central Bosnia in the pre-war years, where it was precisely mutual respect for ethnic and religious differences that characterized the inhabitants' very way of life. Indeed, most of the informants in my study provide a "paradise" account of the pre-war years, in which multiethnicity is a core factor. The outbreak of war—along with the ethnic hatred that came with it—is consequently seen as a sudden and completely unexpected break with the kind of life and ethnic tolerance they had become accustomed to during the Yugoslav years, which were characterized by "brotherhood and unity," in the words of Tito's infamous slogan.

While it is clear that "something" must have caused the outbreak of the conflict, and we can strive to identify what that "something" consists of, it is clear that *through* the conflict ethnic differences came to define friend and foe, compatriots and enemies, perpetrators and victims. War rapes were also defined and understood along these lines: Ethnic difference between perpetrator and victim made the rapes political. We assume that the intent of such acts was to destroy and/or severely harm the identity of the victim and those affiliated to her, but we know very little about whether it actually did so—or indeed how this destruction took form. Ultimately, we do not know how it is to be a victim of ethnically based war rape, nor what this ethnic label might do to the individual victim's understanding of self in the aftermath. The stories recounted by Danira and Azra are examples of narratives in which the ethnic dimensions of the conflict are central, and their stories will provide insights on the subject matter.

The first narrative is that of Danira, who was 44 at the time of the interview. She had been separated from one son and her husband during the war, because both had been in the army. Together with one daughter and another son, she spent a year as a refugee in a western European country and was reunited with the other members of her family in Bosnia in 1995. Danira does not elaborate much on her pre-war life. She indicates that she was a housewife, that her husband had a good job, and that her father-in-law had given them some land where they had built a house. She characterizes her pre-war life

as very happy, where she had a good life with her husband and children. Danira is the most upfront about the war rapes of all the interviewees. In fact, the interview starts with Danira entering the room, pulling up her sweater and showing me marks of torture stemming from when she was held in detention and raped. Before I had even managed to ask her what had happened, she had told me the elementary facts: where she was imprisoned and how many times she believed she was raped. There was no time to "ease in," and my interpreter started translating immediately:

Danira: I will tell you everything and you can ask me. Here you can see what they did to me. They put cigarettes here [points to her body] and they bit me here [points to her body]. [She then recounts details of where she came from, where she was imprisoned, and what happened to her fellow villagers.] Since I left the concentration camp I take sedatives.

I: Do you want to tell me what happened to you in the concentration camp?

Danira: How would you like to start? From the beginning or only the most important details? Do you want to hear about the attack on the village or only about the concentration camp?

I: We can start with what you feel is most important.

Danira: They attacked us at 05:00 [she adds the date], and all of us went to a shelter in the forest and we spent seven days there. Around half the village was there. They surrounded us and shot from everywhere and two men were killed. After that, they took us to some barracks and from the first day they raped us. They asked about my husband and my brother and what kinds of weapons they had. I said that they had weapons but they [the enemy] took them away from them, and then they said I should take my clothes off. I asked them to kill me. I was not supposed to have my menstruation, but I immediately started bleeding all over my pants and clothes and then they said a bad word for a

Muslim woman, that I was dirty. After that they let me go, but that was just before the real hell started. The youngest woman who was there was only 14 years old. There were about 60 or 90 people there. I cannot tell exactly because there were not only people from my village.

I: Did it happen many times?

Danira: It must have happened over 100 times that I was raped. They raped me everywhere, in burnt-out houses and in different rooms in the concentration camp. Once I asked them to kill me, because I could not go back to my kids after this, but they did not do this. Every day there were different men, and usually they came in groups and they would take out some women and rape them and bring them back, and after that a new group came.

Azra has an equally horrific story to tell. Azra was also married and had three children before the war. She was separated from her husband during the war years, but has since been reunited with her entire family. She is somewhat shy and timid, but still firm and upfront about the fact that she was raped. Before the war, Azra was a factory worker and her husband was a construction worker. She does not elaborate much on her pre-war life. In the first interview (I interviewed her twice), she discloses her rape experiences in connection with an explanation about her contact with people from the International War Crimes Tribunal (ICTY). She also talks extensively about how she wants to see the men who raped her get punished:

I: You told me that you have been in contact with the people from the ICTY in The Hague. Can you tell me how they came in contact with you?

Azra: It was in [she says the name of the place] in 1995, where the police—the federal police— asked me if I wanted to tell them what happened to me. They knew that I was injured and that I survived the war rapes. You know, what they [the perpetrators] did to me is something wrong. They committed a crime against me, and what they did I will never forget. I want them to

be punished for that. They could have killed me, and I do not know why they did not. Maybe it was God's will or destiny—I do not know—but I want them to be responsible for what they did to me, because those things that happened to me are criminal things. They are crimes against humanity.

I: Can you identify the people who did this to you?

Azra: Yes. I know them because they were my neighbors.

It is during the second interview that she provides details about how and where the rapes happened. The perpetrators were her young neighbors, and she points to the fact that they had only been boys when she got married. In other words, these perpetrators had gone from being the young boys next door to becoming soldiers and her enemies. We started the interview by recounting what she had talked about in the first interview. When we reached the rape theme, she described the following sequence:

Azra: These boys they were my neighbors. I remember them as young boys when I got married. One day he [the rapist] came to my house during the war and asked me to show him all the rooms in the house, and my son was playing in the garden when all of a sudden he took a knife and put it under my neck and asked me if I wanted to do it there by my own will or not, and at that point I knew exactly what would happen. He beat me so I could not breathe, and he kicked me in my stomach. I lost consciousness, and when I regained consciousness he raped me and there was blood all over. When he saw what happened, he just left me alone. He went out and asked the two soldiers that were in front of the house if they wanted to come up and rape me too.

I: And did they?

Azra: No.

I: Was this man in uniform or civilian clothes?

Azra: He was in uniform.

Later in the second interview she makes the following comment:

> He [the rapist] said "halalite"—in our jargon, that I would forgive him before God for raping me. But I will never forgive and I will never forget.

They came back to her house twice more before she escaped and fled barefoot into the forest, leaving her children, who had witnessed what happened to their mother, with another neighbor. Despite the fact that she elaborates somewhat more on the rapes in the second interview, the accounts by Azra of what happened to her during the war are strikingly similar in both interviews. In the second interview, she expanded on core themes (such as her relationship to her family members, her current living situation and her thoughts about the future). Nevertheless, the story she told was more or less the same on both occasions. This might be indicative of the fact that she has told her story many times to various members of the international community, local authorities and health workers. It appears as though her account has taken on a stringent form of its own, which she adheres to in a variety of different settings.

At first sight, the ethnic dimensions of these two narratives may not appear to be central. Indeed, stories about other women or the interviewees' husbands, children and current living conditions are given much more room in these two women's accounts. Nevertheless, ethnicity is present in the stories—and at crucial points. Careful reading reveals that, when describing the war rapes as they took place, both protagonists make reference to their Muslim identities. Danira lets us know that her perpetrators "said a bad word for a Muslim woman" when raping her, while Azra explains that her rapists said "halalite," an Islamic term for forgiveness. In other words, at the valued endpoint in their narratives—that is, the turning point in their stories about whom they have become—they position themselves as Muslim—that is, Bosniak women. My interpretation, therefore, is that the ethnic identity of the women is not openly discussed in

their stories because it serves as the basic premise for their entire narrative. This interpretation can be substantiated by looking at how the ethnic identity is manifest at different levels of their accounts.

Before looking at these different levels, however, it is important to look at how Danira and Azra describe their post-war situation. How do they look upon themselves and their relationships in the aftermath of war? There is one crucial element in their stories of the aftermath of war that unites Danira and Azra, that sets their stories apart from the other three interviewees—namely, the fact that they have disclosed to their husbands that they were raped. Danira chose to acknowledge it to her husband the first time they met, and he was supportive:

> Danira: My husband is very supportive. When we met for the first time, he said to me, "Do not tell me. I know everything." He knew when they took me to the concentration camp what would happen to me, and if he had not been so supportive I would have committed suicide. I know two women who do not talk about what happened to them because they are ashamed, and they have not told their husbands. They do not even want to talk to each other or to other women because they are so ashamed!

I: Do you feel shame?

> Danira: I am not ashamed. It did not happen from my will, and everybody knows it. It was like having a knife under your cheek and a gun to your head.

Also, Azra expresses a great deal of appreciation for the support she received from her husband after the war. But, she admits that she hesitated telling him what happened:

> Azra: If I had met my husband immediately after what had happened to me, I could not have stayed married to him probably. I felt disgust at males in general. But it was such a long period of time before our reunion, and during that time I sort of calmed down and stayed married to my husband. When we had the first coffee we had together [after the war] I told him. I wanted to

tell him instead of somebody else telling him, and then we would have had misunderstandings. I said that this is what happened, so it is your decision if we can continue to live together. If you want to live with me, we can; if not, then you go on with your life and I go on with my life. He has never made any bad comment about what happened to me, because he is aware that women who were much older survived the same experience.

I: If I ask you whether you feel like a victim or a survivor, how would you answer?

Azra: If I survived 1992, I can survive anything! I feel like a survivor, but the situation in Bosnia now is very uncertain. You know it is very confusing [she cries]. You can survive something— yes, definitely I survived and therefore I am a survivor—but I live my life from a distance, without really knowing where I am going with my life. The environment and the life conditions here are so strange, they are so hard [she cries even more]. You know, I know that I survived, but I do not know why. I can only thank God that I did, but what am I going to do with the fact that I am alive? The life conditions here are so hard and so strange.

I: Do you think it is harder to talk about rape during the war compared to other crimes that people experienced?

Azra: I think so, but it is a new situation now because before nobody talked about these crimes, and now in The Hague [i.e. the ICTY] they talk about it as a very specific crime. It is like killing really, in my opinion. You know, I think sometimes that it would have been better for me if they had killed me instead of raping me.

However, she does not talk about what happened to her daughter and son who witnessed her traumas:

My daughter does not like to think about that even now. She does not like to talk about it, because she does not want to remember.

The quotes above show that, on a personal level, Danira explains that she does not feel shame for what happened to her. The rapes did not happen of her own will, she says, and "everybody knows it." She qualifies this further by stating that it was like "having a knife under your cheek and a gun to your head." Azra describes the rapes as criminal acts and even as crimes against humanity. The latter characterization places her rape experiences alongside other breaches of the Geneva Conventions— that is, the laws of war—and underlines the political nature of the acts. Agger and Jensen (1993: 687) have characterized rape in war as sexual torture, and they argue that "the essential part of sexual torture's traumatic and identity damaging effect is the feeling of being an accomplice in an ambiguous situation that contains both aggressive and libinal elements of a confusing nature." This description, however, does not fit the narratives of Danira and Azra. They do not regard the war-rape situation as ambiguous, nor do they see themselves as accomplices to the relevant acts. One plausible explanation for this clear-cut perception of nonresponsibility (and I do not suggest that this might be wrong) may be that they are certain they were raped during the war because of their Bosniak identity. Zarkov (1997) argues that, in writings on the Bosnian conflict, the perpetrator is more often than not cast as a Serb male, while the identity of the victim is more often than not that of a Bosniak female. Danira and Azra are most likely aware of this dominant understanding of the conflict, and they therefore have an interpretive repertoire available to them through which they can position themselves as ethnic victims. In addition, their victimization places their suffering alongside that of all other Bosniak victims in the war, both male and female. This "side-effect" impinges on male–female relations in ways contrary to what the perpetrators might have anticipated.

On the interpersonal level, the most important element within the stories of Danira and Azra is how supportive their husbands have been after they chose to tell them that they had been raped during the war. Azra lets us know that this was a difficult choice to make, because she was aware that her husband might leave her. Danira also tells us that she was aware of such a possibility, because she knew of other women's stories where the women had chosen to tell and the husband had left the wife. Again, the stories of Danira and Azra contradict prevalent assumptions about the status of raped women.

It is commonly thought that raped women in traditional patriarchal families will be stigmatized by their families and thereby further penalized by husbands and/or male family members. Male honour and women's sexuality are seen as interconnected, and an affront to the woman's body is also an affront to male members of her family. Based on this logic, and in the context of the Bosnian conflict, the argument has frequently been made that the woman subject to war rape was targeted because the abuse carried out against her would, by default, also be an attack on the men within the same ethnic/ religious/political groups she was seen to represent (Allen, 1996; Brownmiller, 1994: 181; Card, 1996; MacKinnon, 1994; Seifert, 1994: 65). Indeed, the notion that rape can constitute a weapon of war is, in part, based on this line of thinking. However, the stories of Danira and Azra show us that when the victim positions herself as an ethnic subject, this also creates a possibility for a new-found solidarity between men and women of the same ethnic belonging, a solidarity that can supersede traditional patriarchal relationships within the family. The husbands of Danira and Azra did not reject them, but rather supported them. When they were reunited after the war, they met on equal grounds as fellow ethnic survivors of horrific ordeals. The impact of war rapes within patriarchal family structures may therefore be quite different from what one might expect.

On a societal level, the stories told by Azra and Danira show us that when ethnicity is the dominant discourse forming our—and their—understanding of the conflict, other interpretations of rapes are placed in the background. This comes out very clearly in the case of Azra. She describes what happened to her as war rape, and the organization of which she is a member (and which helped me get in touch with her) presented her to me as a war-rape victim. Unlike the other women in this study, she knew her perpetrators well because they were her neighbors. We also know that she was raped in her own home. Under different circumstances, one might have considered these acts to be the result of criminal, aggressive, and abusive behavior by the two men in question. In the context of war, however, the acts are perceived and defined as political acts where it is the ethnicity of the male perpetrator which is decisive. The fact that the perpetrators wore uniforms also reinforces this political interpretation. For Danira, who was taken to special

facilities, kept imprisoned and repeatedly raped by groups of men in uniform (who occasionally had Serbian and Montenegrin accents), the situation is more clear-cut. There was little doubt in her mind that she was raped as part of a war strategy in which her ethnic/national/religious identity was the main target. Since Danira does not feel personal shame, she has taken it upon herself to speak up, and one of the ways in which she does this is by volunteering to testify before the ICTY. Once again, her family is a source of support, and this is how she experienced her first trip to The Hague:

> I said yes immediately, and my husband was very supportive. He did not try to stop me, and he was only worried about how my health would be when I had gone through all that. But, I took some medicine. I needed that, and I felt better afterwards [. . .] If they convict more I will go again if they can get the people who raped and tortured me.

In the Bosnian setting, regarding rape in war as a war crime has led to an increased focus on violence against women in general. Azra explains that the way in which rape is perceived has changed in Bosnia. She says that "it is a new situation now because before nobody talked about these crimes, and now in The Hague [i.e., the ICTY] they talk about it as a very specific crime." This change has made it easier for these two women to talk, and has made both women eager to travel to The Hague to testify before the ICTY.

By bringing ethnic dimensions to the forefront of their narratives—or rather setting them as a basic premise—Danira and Azra tell stories in which the main plot is that of being a *survivor*. Gergen might have argued that their stories are examples of stable/progressive self-narratives with a limited degree of upward mobility. The two protagonists downplay the stigma normally attached to rape victims, and they emphasize that they are first and foremost survivors. It is clear that the support of their husbands contributes to maintaining this understanding. As survivors, the women have taken it upon themselves to testify voluntarily before the ICTY and thereby show that their rape experiences have rendered them neither passive nor silent. Their bodies have been part of the battlefield, but their female identities have not been destroyed. They are still mothers of their children, wives to their husbands and caretakers within their families. All these tasks are performed with difficulty, but nevertheless maintained. The fact that their husbands and children know what happened to them has not changed this. Positioning oneself as an ethnic victim of war violence therefore makes possible the construction of a survivor identity in the post-conflict aftermath.

It is important to underscore, however, that this interpretation does not suggest that Danira and Azra only see themselves as survivors. The rapes they endured happened in the midst of extraordinary violent circumstances and they also very much situate themselves as victims of war in their accounts. The theme of constant suffering is central in both Danira's and Azra's stories. For Danira, her current living conditions are a constant source of worry. Her daughter has a medical condition for which they need to purchase medication and visit the hospital on a regular basis. This is a challenge given their meagre income. Yet she acknowledges that she is not starving and that, compared to others, they are doing OK. All the same, life is strenuous:

> Life today is really hard for me. My husband started working recently, but before that he was only getting 50 DM because he is an invalid and that is what they get for that. Now he works for a company that cleans the city, and his salary is 260 DM. But we live in a Serb house and I expect that we have to move anytime. But, we are not starving; we have bread and milk, but nothing special.

Occasionally she gets together with other women from her village who were in the concentration camp with her. She describes how they immediately start talking about what happened to them: They simply cannot stop talking about the suffering they went through. Despite the openness she feels in these settings, she knows that there are women among them who have experienced war rapes that will talk neither with other women nor with their families and husbands about what happened to them. This is because they are ashamed, explains Danira.

Most of the interview with Azra centres on her current life and worries. She is concerned with the future of her children and the uncertainty of their living situation:

> We do not pay rent because we live in a deserted house, but the owner applied to get back and get the house, and I will probably be ordered to move from the house. But where shall I move? I do not know what to do, because I cannot go back to my village and I do not have the money to pay the rent here in Sarajevo. It is too expensive. The food is expensive. To send your children to school is expensive. And . . . I mean everything is very expensive when you do not have money.

The ways in which Danira's and Azra's accounts are different from the other stories will become apparent when comparing the next three stories.

Narratives of Gender and Victimization

While it is clear that the women who suffered war rapes in Bosnia were targeted on the basis of their ethnicity, it is also clear that they were targeted with this particular form of violence by men because they were *women*. In other words, it was the combination of their gender identity and their ethnic identity that made them "eligible" for war rape.

The war zone, in general, is a place of increased gender polarization. Men are called to fight and/or be killed, whereas women, in the words of Enloe (1983: 46), are set to keep the home fires burning. Through this division of labor, women come to represent stability, future prospects and peace. The image of women taking care of the home and family while men are called to fight serves to legitimize the war as such: He is fighting to protect his family and to secure the (peaceful) future for his children. The Bosnian conflict was no exception to this norm: "In general . . . gender roles have become more polarized by nationalism and war," says Benderly (1997: 60) in her description of the Bosnian conflict. Rape against women in the war zone can therefore be regarded as an attack on current, and future, family formations: In other words, rape can be seen as an attack on the mere legitimization of the male fight because it demonstrates the man's inability to protect his family and home.

How, then, do the victims of war rape regard their experiences from a gendered perspective? In other words, which self-narratives are made possible when gender aspects serve as the core theme in their accounts? The first narrative comes from Ceca who was married and had children before the war. She was separated from her entire family, but was reunited with them all after the war. She is very timid, and she tells me that she has taken tranquillizers before the interview. Ceca says very little about her pre-war life. She simply states where she lived, where she and her husband come from, and what kind of house they had. Ceca is the only one in this sample who admits to having become pregnant from the rapes, and she starts the interview by talking about her physical and psychological pains. She explains that she does not have a job because it is psychologically very difficult, and says that she cannot do basic work at home. She tells of how she suffers from insomnia and has nightmares when she sleeps. She also has occasional stomach pains. The way she starts talking specifically about having been raped is through a description of her youngest son (born after the war) and the negative feelings she has towards him. She is afraid that, because he is a man, he can commit the same crimes she has experienced:

> Ceca: Sometimes I think that since he is a man he can do the things that others have done to me. I never told my husband that I have been raped and that my daughter was as well. He does not know what happened to us, and I find excuses all the time to avoid having sex. I also worry about my daughter.
>
> I: Do you and your daughter ever talk about this together?
>
> Ceca: I tried, but my daughter does not want to. She refuses to talk to me about this and has asked me to keep it a secret. She does not want anyone to know about it, and when I suggested that she could join this organization she did not want to. She said it would bring back memories . . .
>
> I: Were you raped many times?
>
> Ceca: I was raped more than a hundred times, I think. I was so destroyed I had to have an operation.
>
> I: Were you in a camp?
>
> Ceca: Yes.

> I: Were there many other women there?
>
> Ceca: About 150, I think.
>
> I: And they were all raped?
>
> Ceca: I do not know. I stayed there for two and a half months, and they came and took women and some never came back. They were killed.
>
> I: And your daughter was in the same camp?
>
> Ceca: Yes. We were together the whole time.
>
> I: You told me that after the rapes you fled and were hiding in different places. Did you tell anyone then what had happened to you during that time?
>
> Ceca: I only told my mother. She helped me get an abortion. It was not a proper abortion. I took medicines and different teas—I mean different grasses—and one night I went to the toilet and felt that I lost the baby. I could not bear to have a baby whose father I didn't know, a baby made during those circumstances.

Emila was in her early teens when the war broke out. She had had no sexual experiences prior to the war rapes. Emila talks quietly and jumps from theme to theme. She excuses herself for being inconsistent, but she has suffered from insomnia for long periods of time and has problems focusing on one issue at a time. She lost many of her immediate and extended family members. In the aftermath of war, she acts as a parent for a younger sibling because her mother is incapable of taking care of the young child. Her father is dead. We start the interview by talking about her pre-war life. She explains that she was one of seven siblings living in the same house along with their grandmother and parents. Her father worked in a shop and her mother was at home, and she characterizes her life as "normal." It takes a long time before we start talking about the rape issue. Halfway into the interview, she starts talking about what happened to her in order to explain why she has trouble working and going to school to get an education:

> I used to work in a shop for 200 DM per month, but now I clean people's houses during the

weekend. But the memories of the war are always there, and it is hard to work, but I just have to do something to live.

The interpreter tells me that Emila is ashamed that she has that kind of work, and we take a break in the interview, during which the interpreter assures Emila that cleaning people's houses is a decent job:

I: Do you, or anyone in your family, receive any form of pension from the government?

Emila: My mother gets some money after my brother who died, and she is also trying to get some money from my father. But there are many problems, because they were civilian victims of war.

She goes on to describe details about what happened to her family members during the war.

I: Can you tell me what happened to you during the war?

Emila: At the very beginning I was locked up at home, and after that I was taken to the secondary school in [she says the name of the place]. Would you like me to start from the very beginning?

She goes on to provide details of the first attack on her village; how she became separated from her family; how she saw family members, relatives and neighbors killed; and how she was taken to a house where she was kept prisoner:

I: How long were you imprisoned?

Emila: Altogether, one month. First, we were together in a house, and they moved us to a concentration camp. Everybody who tortured me I knew. It was only during the weekends that they came from Serbia, but on the other days it was the local guys.

I: What did they do to you in the concentration camp?

Emila: They raped me. Sometimes they were old and sometimes they were young, and it happened more than 50 times. I was only 16 years old, and every day I asked them to kill me, because I did not know anything about my family and all this was happening.

I: Can I ask you a difficult question, which you only need to answer if you want to? Did you have any sexual experiences before the rapes?

Emila: No, that was the first. I was raised in that kind of family.

Berina was the youngest interviewee in the group. She was only a year younger than Emila, but was already married and had a baby when the war broke out. Berina is very withdrawn in her way of communicating. She has a child who was born during the early stages of the war, and the father of her child was killed during the same period of time. Before we start the first interview, Berina laughs and tells me she has taken tranquilizers before meeting me. Before the war, Berina was in elementary school. She became pregnant at the age of 14. She was married to the child's father, but did not live with him for very long because the war started. Berina needs a lot of time before she talks about being raped. I interviewed her twice, and during the first interview she only hinted at what happened to her and acknowledged being raped only in passing while describing a series of events during the first weeks of the war. She said that she could tell me what happened to her during the war, but she did not wish to tell "all the details." She answered all questions with no more than one or two sentences and was very shy and timid:

The enemy came and then they took my husband and my father to prison, and we still do not know anything about them, and they were chasing us all the time. First in our apartment, and then we moved from that apartment and into another house. Then they would find us and chase us there too. At night, they would take us away to be raped, and then one night I escaped during the night through the woods.

In the second interview, however, she talks more freely, but is still very short and matter-of-fact in her various descriptions of what happened to her during the war. She does not use the word "rape" herself, but says that her perpetrators 'tortured' her. It was only when I asked her specifically if she was raped that she acknowledged it:

> Berina: They came and they took me to the prison. But it was not really a prison. It was more like they locked us up at home. In the beginning, they were coming to our apartment and they tortured us, and then they came to take us to another house.
>
> I: Did they rape you in that house?
>
> Berina: Yes.

She starts crying and does not elaborate on details about the rapes, but changes her focus and talks about how she escaped from her apartment, fled and hid in the forest until she was found by a Serb woman, who took her in and let her live with her for one year.

In the above narratives, the stories about the war rapes are told to explain difficulties and complications the women experience in their everyday lives. In other words, the war rapes have damaged these three women in ways that affect how they view themselves and their relationships. The ways in which their female bodies were made part of the battlefield have altered their female identities and gendered relationships. This destruction is narrated on different levels.

On the personal level, the war rapes are narrated as having destroyed the core of their female identities: their sexual and procreative abilities. They talk about how the war rapes have damaged them by describing bodily pains, and they thereby position themselves as (female) biological subjects within their stories. Ceca lets us know that she suffers from insomnia, takes tranquillizers and sometimes cannot do basic work at home. She goes on to say that she has problems with men in general, and that when a man approaches her she "immediately has pains in her stomach." The mass rapes she experienced damaged her to such an extent that she had to have a gynaecological operation after the war. In addition, she is the only woman in this study who admits to having become pregnant as a result of the rapes, but she had an abortion carried out with nonprofessional assistance. Since the war, she has given birth to a son and, as shown in the first quotes from her interview, it was her feelings about this son that triggered her accounts of being raped. Throughout the entire

interview, her victimization is narrated through accounts of her body. For Emila, the war rapes were her first sexual experiences. She says that simply the sight of men in uniform can be a trauma trigger, and can cause her physical discomfort when she is premenstrual. Berina is not as explicit as Ceca and Emila, but she indicates that she has had to take tranquillizers before talking to me about her war experiences, thereby suggesting that being reminded of her war trauma triggers bodily pains. Experiencing bodily pains in the aftermath of severe trauma is not unusual. Post-traumatic stress disorder (PTSD), for which these women have received therapeutic treatment, is characterized by a combination of generalized anxiety symptoms, specific fears, and an elevated level of arousal: Their bodies are always on the alert for danger (Herman, 1997: 36). What makes the stories of Ceca, Emila, and Berina special cases of PTSD[10] is that their trauma triggers are so clearly *gendered*, through sexual contact, the birth of a son, seeing men in uniform, and so forth.

On an interpersonal level, the narratives of victimized female bodies become stories of dysfunctional womanhood manifest in the women's social relationships with immediate family members. Ceca considers herself a bad mother to her son who was born after the war. It is as though her son came out of a different body from the body her children born before the war came out of. Her post-war body is presented as foul, as are her feelings towards her son. In addition, Ceca has chosen not to let her husband know about the war rapes, because this is "something stronger" than her other war experiences. The war rapes have changed the way she looks at herself as a woman, and she fears that it might affect the way her husband looks at her as a wife:

> I told him everything except for being raped. That is somehow stronger, and I cannot tell him. I suffer a lot because of the sexual side of our marriage. But what can I do? I do not have the feelings, positive feelings towards that, and all the time I find excuses to avoid having sex.

Her feelings for her youngest son and her daughter are central in the interview. She says that she is often aggressive towards her youngest son, and that she has many negative feelings towards him. Her daughter was also raped, and she wants to talk to her about this but her daughter refuses to do so. This is a great concern for Ceca. For Emila and Berina, their war-raped bodies affect the relationships they have to their respective mothers. Both have chosen not to disclose to their mothers the fact that they were raped in order to protect their mothers. In the aftermath of war, Emila has only shared her war-rape experiences with her sister (who also was raped). Her mother does not know about the rapes. Emila has decided to keep it that way because her mother was also raped and lost many of her children, as well as her parents:

> My sister knows, because she was also raped. My mother was raped as well, but I cannot tell her because I had a sister who was killed and burnt together with my grandparents. Also, I was separated from her for six years, so I cannot tell her.

Emila still suffers from physical pains linked to the war-rape trauma:

> Sometimes, just before I have my period, I have pains and phobias. I cannot see people in uniform. I do not even like the SFOR people.

Emila is very concerned about her living situation and her family's economic instability. She feels that her material living conditions are victimizing her once more:

> The authorities are deaf and blind to what has happened [there] when they force us to leave the house we live in now and move back to our houses that have completely burned. [. . .] I understand that everyone has a right to property and everything else, but I cannot understand why I and all the people who experienced all the things I experienced still have to suffer. I suffered a lot and I am still suffering. [. . .] Nobody gave us any form of compensation. I live a life, but it is not really a life. With all these struggles, it is not easy to live.

She sees no justice in the ICTY either:

> I was not pleased with the verdicts for those who committed sexual crimes and abuse. They would get 10 to 15 years in prison, and they

would use that time to complete their studies and go to school or other things like that, while behind them are the women who were tortured. I do not think that justice in my sense of the word will be done.

Future prospects for marriage are also a great concern and source of sorrow for Emila:

> I will never get married . . . I cannot trust anybody, and even if someone is just inviting me to have a coffee somewhere I think that maybe he is going to take me somewhere [. . .] Sometimes I have an impression that everybody knows . . . even though I know that is not possible.

The underlying argument is that letting their mothers know about the rapes would be yet another trauma for them. Emila argues that her mother has suffered enough. Berina makes the same argument, but adds that she also feels shame about the rapes and is unsure how her mother would react if she knew. Today, Berina lives with her child, her mother and a brother. The fact that she has been raped is a secret she has shared only with her sister. She does not want to let her mother know what happened to her:

> I would rather tell everybody else than my mother, because she was hurt enough. I also have shame and fear for how she would cope with knowing. Basically, I do not want to hurt my mother more [she is crying].

She fears that her child might ask about her war experiences, and she does not want her to find out either:

> My worst fear is that she [the child] will ask me. I do not think that I will tell, because my worst fear is that she will go through the same. Therefore, I do not want to let her know what happened to me.

She wants to remarry but fears that this will be difficult because the family of her child's father might not approve. In addition, she has difficulties with relationships with men:

> I had a nice sexual relationship with my husband, and I had a boyfriend after the war. But, I

did not feel anything [in the sexual relationship with the new boyfriend]. I had no feelings at all.

Although it is not stated explicitly in the interviews, one might assume that Berina and Emila know that their mothers would worry about their daughters' virginity, and thus their eligibility for marriage later in life. Emila has said that she was a virgin before being raped, and that she was raised in "that kind of family"—that is, a traditional patriarchal family. Assuming that women's sexuality is linked to family honor, telling their mothers about the rapes would potentially victimize the mothers further through association with their daughters, and Berina and Emila therefore keep silent. If we take Gilligan's (1982) work on motherhood and the ethics of care as a point of departure, it is possible to interpret the decisions by Emila and Berina to keep their war-rape stories secret as a way of letting their mothers maintain a status of "good motherhood." According to Gilligan, a woman's moral career is influenced by ethics of care and responsibility for others. Motherhood is the manifestation of this process, because it enables the woman to demonstrate care and responsibility through her connection with others, most notably her children. The war-raped bodies of Emila and Berina, therefore, come to represent failed motherhood through the mothers' "failure" to protect their own children. Emila and Berina position themselves as good children by keeping their war-rape experiences hidden from their mothers.

They do this, however, as a way of protecting their mothers, and consequently it is Emila and Berina who are "mothering" their mothers.

On a societal level, these three protagonists position themselves as "damaged goods" within a patriarchal culture. This perception comes out most clearly in the story of Emila when she talks about her future prospects for marriage. She thinks that she will never get married, because she has an "impression that everybody knows." What she fears that "everybody" knows is that she is not an untouched woman, she is not a virgin. Because she was "raised in that kind of family"—that is, a traditional patriarchal family—we can assume that she was taught to believe that her virginity was key in her eligibility for marriage. For Ceca, who was already married before the war rapes, her decision not to tell her husband what happened to her is another manifestation of "damaged goods"

positioning. Assuming that the relationship between Ceca and her husband is based on patriarchal values, the violations against her body might be seen as violations of her husband's "property." Her sexuality—and her body—is her husband's possession. Perhaps this is one of the reasons why she had another baby after the war: as a way of giving something back to her husband after those who raped her had taken something—*her* body—away from him. Berina wants to become reestablished with a new man (i.e., a new husband and ideally someone who can be a good father for her child). However, this might prove to be difficult, because she is a single mother. In addition, she lets us know that she has attempted—but found it very difficult—to start a new sexual relationship.

By bringing stories of their bodies and their gendered relationships to the forefront of their narratives, the three protagonists construct stories in which the main plot is that of being a *victim*. They position themselves as stigmatized bodily subjects, and this affects their social relationships (as mothers, daughters and girlfriends/wives) as well as their future prospects (eligibility for marriage). The victim plot structure creates a stable/regressive narrative characterized by a downward development, and the core theme in this story is a violated, and damaged, gender identity.

Concluding Discussion

In concluding the analysis above, we need to consider *what* the rape stories have told us about rape in war; *how* the context in which the stories are told has affected the storytelling itself; and, finally, *why* narrative analysis has proven to be a particularly viable venue for understanding the impact of rape in war.

First, the five protagonists have taught us that rape in war has an impact upon and violates the social identity of its victims in at least two distinct ways. Because rape in war targets both the *ethnic* and *gendered* identity of its victims, this dual identity violation creates a possibility for dual identity construction in the aftermath. Through their accounts, the five women have created two distinctly different narrative plots, within which their primary positioning within the stories varies. As ethnic victims, the elements of their stories create a *survivor* plot characterized by absence of guilt, support from family members and active engagement in getting their perpetrators convicted. As female victims, however, the elements of their stories create a *victim* plot characterized by feelings of guilt and shame, hiding their stories from immediate family members, and bodily pains and immobility. These observations show (1) that the victims have power to redefine their social identities in the post-conflict sociopolitical space; (2) that their ability to do so, however, depends on the material, social, and political reality in which they find themselves in the post-conflict setting, as well as the ways in which their "supporting cast" plays its part; and, finally, (3) that positioning oneself mainly as a victim versus survivor (or the other way around) has different impacts on intrapersonal, interpersonal and societal relations.

Second, it is important to consider the context in which the stories are told, in order to better understand the motivations of the protagonists in telling their stories. This contextual setting is multifaceted. First, it is important to recognize that asking questions about wartime rape in Bosnia as a foreign, western European and female researcher is in itself a political task. What the interviewees tell me during the interviews is based on an elaborate understanding of the political power relationships that exist between us. As a western European researcher, I am positioned as *international*, and the international presence in Bosnia is so overwhelming that Bose (2002: 6) argues that this constitutes yet another conflict line, in addition to the conflicts that exist between the three main ethnic groups. The international community in Bosnia, furthermore, is an important source of income for the local population, but the taste of the economic benefits thus provided is bitter-sweet. The international presence is of such a nature that it has deprived many Bosnians of a sense of ownership over their own economic, democratic and political development.[11] Asking questions about the war as a western European researcher therefore means asking from a position as a power-holder. This comes out clearly in the opposition between *us* and *them*. Although I am a woman and could be part of a female *us*, I am more often cast as an international *them*.[12] As a result, it is highly likely that the stories the interviewees told me were based on an understanding of what they think the international community—that is, the power-holders—ought to know about the ordeals they went through. Members of the organization through which I came in contact with the women in this study told me that many of the raped women felt so forgotten by the world outside that they were very happy to receive a researcher who was interested in their lives now that the cameras and journalists had moved on to other parts of the world. Second, the protagonists are aware that their war-rape stories can be narrated within different genres. In other words, how the stories are to be told is not a given. As we saw in the interviews, two of the interviewees (Danira and Emila) asked how I would like to have the story told: "from the beginning" or, alternatively, "only the most important details." All the women in this study had previously told their stories to different people (aid workers, representatives for the ICTY, and therapists), and in all these contexts their stories are told to serve different functions. By asking me how I would like to have the story told, they are simultaneously asking me what the function of their story will be for me. In other words, the power relationships between the researcher and the interviewee force both of us to find ways of telling the story—that is, genres—that make them intelligible to us both. The researcher defines the function of the story, and the interviewee adjusts the narration of her experiences accordingly. Finally, it is clear that the political and economic power hierarchy that exists between "internationals" and local Bosnians has created a climate in which having a war story to tell can be regarded as a potential commodity. On my field trips to Bosnia, I heard numerous horror stories describing how international journalists had capitalized on the misery of raped women. Drakulic (1994: 178) describes international journalists coming off the plane at the airport in Zagreb, going to the nearest refugee settlement in which Bosnian refugees were sheltered, and asking the following infamous question: "Anyone here been raped and speaks English?" Having a rape story to tell also means having experiences for sale. Journalists, researchers and nongovernmental organization (NGO) workers are all potential "buyers" of these stories. The journalist may be able to write an intriguing story; the researcher (like myself) will have data to analyse in order to generate knowledge production; and NGO workers might use the stories to apply for funding to initiate different kinds of activities. This mutual dependency between the one who has a story to tell and the one who can "use" it is not necessarily unethical, but in trying to "buy" stories to help the women involved, the "buyer" walks a fine line in terms of personal benefit. For the women who have stories to tell, however, there is also a potential for empowerment through talking: talking to the ICTY might get perpetrators convicted; talking to therapists might facilitate recovery; and talking to international academics and journalists might bring attention and understanding to a wider audience.

Finally, the narrative analysis has brought an empirically based understanding of the diverse impact that Bosnian war rapes had in the local context. The many commentaries and academic publications on the war-rape tragedy in Bosnia have argued almost with one voice that raped Bosniak women would be stigmatized and ostracized by their families. This analysis has shown that, yes, that did happen—and presumably also to a large extent—but it does not represent the complete picture. The experiences of Ceca and Azra must also have a place in our understanding of the impact of war rapes. In other words, we must not base our understanding only on the findings that confirm our assumptions, but must also be open to findings that might contradict and challenge our initial convictions. This analysis has shown that, to understand the diverse impact of war rape, one must look for local findings. The local findings in this study have shown that the five women intersect multiple social categories in their positioning of their war-rape experiences and in their social identity construction processes. These intersectionalities have different strengths and outcomes as diverse plots (ethnic and survivor versus gendered and victimized) in their respective narratives. Assuming that war rape has universal effects on women because of universal hierarchical relationships between men and women will not help us to see the complete picture and does not help us see the diverse strategies women employ in living with war rape in its aftermath.

Notes

1. At the end of 1992, the Bosnian government released a figure stating that the number of women who had been raped was about 14,000 (Olujic, 1998: 40). Later the same year (in December), the European Community set the number of women of Muslim ethnicity who had been raped by Bosnian Serb soldiers at around 20,000 (Drakulic, 1993: 270; Meznaric, 1994: 92; Olujic, 1998: 40; Nikolic-Ristanovic, 2000: 43; Wing and Merchan, 1993: 11, note 54). The Bosnian Ministry of the Interior set the number at around 50,000 (Olujic, 1998: 40;

Nikolic-Ristanovic, 2000: 43; Wing and Merchan, 1993: 11, note 54). In a report by the Institute for War and Peace Reporting (IWPR) (Becirbasic and Secic, 2002), it is stated that the European Union (EU) Commission estimated the number of victims at 50,000. At a conference entitled "Violation of the Human Rights of Women in Bosnia and Herzegovina During the War 1992–1995," held in Sarajevo on 10–11 March 1999, the President of the Organizational Committee, Mirsad Tokaca, stated that the Commission for Gathering Facts on War Crimes in Bosnia and Herzegovina set the number of raped women at 20,000 (Tokaca, 1999). Drakulic (1993) reports that the Sarajevo State Commission for Investigation of War Crimes estimates that the number up until October 1992 was 50,000, and she adds that these numbers are highly controversial. Meznaric (1994: 92) writes that the report of the Coordinative Group of Women's Organizations of Bosnia and Herzegovina estimates that between 20,000 and 50,000 women were raped.

2. In an interview in Sarajevo on 13 June 2002 with representatives of the Association of Former Prison Camp Inmates of Bosnia-Herzegovina, I was told that 40 new torture methods had been discovered in Bosnia.

3. Again, there is considerable uncertainty in the estimates of the numbers of children conceived through war rapes. Drakulic (1994: 180) quotes an estimate from the Bosnian Ministry of Works and Social Affairs that 35,000 women were impregnated through rape and released only when abortion was impossible. Salzman (1998: 363) quotes the same source and confirms the estimate of 35,000 women—primarily Muslim, but also Croat—who became pregnant. He points out, however, that, according to the way in which medical studies estimate the number of cases of intercourse that result in pregnancy (one single act of intercourse results in pregnancy between 1 percent and 4 percent of the time), this would lead to the conclusion that about 3,500,000 acts of rape took place in Bosnia. Salzman concludes that this repeals the shortcomings to obtaining reliable information on the number of rapes and pregnancies. In a population of about 4,000,000, it is simply impossible that as many as 3,500,000 were raped. In general, it is extremely difficult to find approximations of the number of children conceived through such acts owing to the fact that many mothers will not say what happened, many had legal and illegal abortions, and many children were adopted after birth. Further, single-parent female-headed households are not uncommon in post-conflict Bosnia, and mothers who have had, and kept, children conceived through rape do not necessarily stand out in their local communities. This might make it easier for them to conceal the origin of their child.

4. This can be regarded as a sub-field within the larger domain of discourse analysis within social science, in that the locus of the analysis is the individual and discourses of the self. Contrary to the predominant theories within mainstream

psychology, in which the self is seen as having a true nature waiting to be discovered and described (see outline and discussion of the traditional approaches in Potter and Wetherell 1987: 95–110), the social constructionist approach takes the position that selves are formed, framed and understood within language. Indeed, the main question becomes how we *talk* about selves and use language to define what it means to be a person (see outline and discussion of this in Burr, 1995: 95–158). This way of thinking is inherently social psychological, because the ways in which we talk about ourselves are highly dependent on the discourses available to us in our social settings. Social constructionist psychology rests on the assumption that sense-making is produced collaboratively in the course of social interaction between people (see Wilkinson, 2003: 187).

5. The stability narrative is one that "links events so that the individual's trajectory remains essentially unchanged in relations to a goal or outcome" (Gergen, 2001: 253). The progressive narrative links events together over time so that the movement is incremental, while the regressive does the opposite, by creating a narrative with a downward movement. Further, Gergen (2001: 257) argues that self-narratives are immersed within processes of ongoing interchange, and it is these processes that construct the basis for the future. The sustainability of a self-narrative (whether progressive or regressive) depends on the willingness of others to play out certain parts of the relationship. Gergen (2001: 258) defines this as a *network of reciprocating identities* and adds that "the moment any participant chooses to renege, he or she threatens the array of interdependent constructions."

6. Most of the interviewees were recruited through a psychosocial centre. This meant that most had been through a minimum of psychological treatment, and it was their therapists who initially contacted them and asked if they would volunteer for the interviews.

7. A complete list of the texts that I went through can be found in Skjelsbæk (1999).

8. The themes covered were: present life situation of the interviewees (work, family, housing/living situation); their lives before the war (work, family, housing/living situation); with whom they have shared or revealed their war experiences, and with whom they can seek comfort and trust; what sort of help they have received in the aftermath (psychological, economic and medical); how they would characterize themselves—victim and/or survivor; thoughts about the future.

9. The NATO Stabilization Force (SFOR) in Bosnia-Herzegovina came into place at 20 December 1996. The SFOR operation replaced the Implementation Force (IFOR) that had been deployed the previous year as an immediate result of the General Framework Agreement for Peace (GFAP). Whereas the role of IFOR was to implement the peace, the role of SFOR was to stabilize it. A UN Protection Force (UNPROFOR) had preceded IFOR and was present in Bosnia during the war—that is, from 1992 onwards. IFOR was deployed following UN Security Council Resolution 1031 in December 1995. In December 1996, the Security Council authorized member states to set up a multinational stabilization force to succeed IFOR. The main task of SFOR was to oversee the parts of the 11 annexes to the GFAP that address military issues. Since December 2004, the EU has assumed responsibility for peacekeeping operations through EUFOR, and the SFOR mission, in its original form, has ended.

10. Hydén (2005: 172) warns against inscribing abused women into the PTSD diagnosis because this reduces the violated woman to her sufferings. This is also a central theme and concern in other feminist critiques of the PTSD diagnoses (e.g., Shaw & Proctor, 2005).

11. The parliamentary election of October 2002—the first election the Bosnian authorities organized without the immediate supervision of the Office of the High Representative (OHR) and the Organization for Security and Co-operation in Europe (OSCE)—showed that efforts to "educate" the Bosnia population in democratic values and tolerance had not provided the results hoped for by the international community. Not only was voter turnout extremely low (less than 55 percent), but those who did show up voted for nationalist candidates. In a critical article, Knaus and Martin (2003: 60) criticize the OHR—and High Representative Paddy Ashdown in particular for demonstrating the "unlimited authority of an international mission to overrule all of the democratic institutions of a sovereign member state of the United Nations."

12. One woman explained to me that, despite the very frequent use of rape during the conflict, it was first when the SFOR soldiers came to the region that the spreading of venereal diseases became a problem. She explained it thus: "It was not *our* men, but *your* men who brought the problem to us."

References

Agger, I., & Jensen, S. B. (1993). The psychosexual trauma of torture, in J. P. Wilson & B. Raphael (Eds.), *International handbook of traumatic stress* (p. 685–701). New York: Plenum.

Allen, B. (1996). *Rape warfare: The hidden genocide in Bosnia-Herzegovina and Croatia*. Minneapolis: University of Minnesota Press.

Becirbasic, B., & Secic, D. (2002, October). Invisible casualties of war. Retrieved from http:www.iwpr.net/index.pl?archive/bcr3_200211_383_4_eng.txt

Benderly, J. (1997). Rape, feminism, and nationalism in the war in Yugoslav successor states, in L. A. West (Ed.), *Feminist nationalism* (p. 59–72). London: Routledge.

Bose, S. (2002). *Bosnia after Dayton: Nationalist partition and international intervention.* New York: Oxford University Press.

Bringa, T. (1995). *Being Muslim the Bosnian way.* NJ: Princeton University Press.

Brownmiller, S. (1994). Making female bodies the battlefield. In A. Stiglmayer (Ed.), *Mass rape: The war against women in Bosnia-Herzegovina* (p. 180–182). London: University of Nebraska Press.

Bruner, J. (1985). *Actual minds, possible worlds.* Cambridge, MA: Harvard University Press.

Bruner, J. (1990). *Acts of meaning.* Cambridge, MA: Harvard University Press.

Burr, V. (1995). *An introduction to social constructionism.* London: Routledge.

Card, C. (1996). Rape as a weapon of war. *Hypatia, 11*(4): 5–18.

CID. (2002). *I begged them to kill me: Crime against the women of Bosnia-Herzegovina.* Sarajevo: Center for Investigation and Documentation of the Association of Former Prison Camp Inmates of Bosnia-Herzegovina (CID).

Coneth-Morgan, E. (2004). *Collective political violence: An introduction to the theories and cases of violence conflicts.* New York: Routledge.

Davies, B., & Harré, R. (2001). Positioning: The discursive production of selves, In M. Wetherell, S, Taylor, & S. Yates (Eds.), *Discourse theory and practice: A reader* (p. 261–271). London: Sage.

Drakulic, S. (1993, March 1). Women hide behind a wall of silence. *The Nation*, 268–272.

Drakulic, S. (1994). The rape of women in Bosnia. In M. Davies (Ed.), *Women and peace* (p. 176–181). London: Zed.

Enloe, C. (1983). *Does khaki become you?* London: Pluto Press.

Gergen, K. (1994). *Realities and relationship: Soundings in social construction.* Cambridge, MA: Harvard University Press.

Gergen, K. (2001). Self-narration in social life. In M. Wetherell, S. Taylor, & S. Yates (Eds.), *Discourse theory and practice: A reader* (p. 247–260). London: Sage.

Gilligan, C. (1982). *In a different voice: Psychological theory and women's development.* Cambridge, MA: Harvard University Press.

Goldstein, A. T. (1993). *Recognizing forced impregnation as a war crime under international law: A special report of the International Program.* New York: Center for Reproductive Law & Policy.

Goldstein, J. S. (2001). *War and gender.* Cambridge: Cambridge University Press.

Gutman, R. (1993). *A witness to genocide.* New York: Macmillan.

Helsinki Watch. (1993). *War crimes in Bosnia-Herzegovina, vols. I and II.* USA: Human Rights Watch. Retrieved from http://www.iwpr.net/index.pl?archive/ bcr/bcr_20011015_1_ir_eng.txt

Herman, J. L. (1997[1992]). *Trauma and recovery: From domestic abuse to political terror.* Cornwall: Pandora.

Holbrooke, R. (1999). *To end a war.* New York: Modern Library.

Hydén, M. (2005). "I must have been an idiot to let it go on": Agency and Positioning in battered women's narratives of leaving. *Feminism and Psychology, 15*(2): 171–90.

Knaus, G., & Martin, F. (2003). Travails of the European Raj. *Journal of Democracy, 14*(3): 60–74.

MacKinnon, C. A. (1994). Turning rape into pornography: Postmodern genocide. In A. Stiglmayer (Ed.), *Mass rape: The war against women in Bosnia-Herzegovina* (p. 73–81). London: University of Nebraska Press.

Meznaric, S. (1994). Gender as an ethno-marker: Rape, war and identity in the former Yugoslavia. In V. M. Moghadam (Ed.), *Identity politics and women: Cultural reassertion and feminism in international perspective* (p. 76–97). Boulder, CO: Westview.

Murray, M. (2003). Narrative psychology. In J. A. Smith (Ed.), *Qualitative psychology: A practical guide to research methods* (p. 111–131)-. London: Sage.

Nikolic-Ristanovic, V. (2000). Sexual violence. In V. Nikolic-Ristanovic (Ed.), *Women, violence and war: Wartime victimization of refugees in the Balkans* (p. 41–77). Budapest: Central European Press.

Nizich, I. (1994). Violations of the rules of war by Bosnian Croat and Muslim forces in Bosnia-Herzegovina. *Hastings Women's Law Journal, 5*(1): 25–52.

Olujic, M. B. (1998). Embodiment of terror: Gendered violence in peacetime and wartime in Croatia and Bosnia-Herzegovina. *Medical Anthropology Quarterly, 12*(1): 31–50.

Polkinghorne, D. E. (1988). *Narrative knowing and the human sciences.* Albany, NY: State University of New York Press.

Polkinghorne, D. E. (1995). Narrative configuration in qualitative analysis. *International Journal of Qualitative Studies in Education, 8*(1): 5–23.

Potter, J. & Wetherell, M. (1987). *Discourse and social psychology: Beyond attitudes and behaviour.* London: Sage.

Salzman, T. A. (1998). Rape camps as a means of ethnic cleansing: Religious, cultural and ethical responses to rape victims in the former Yugoslavia. *Human Rights Quarterly, 20*(2): 348–378.

Sarbin, T. S. (1986). The narrative as a root metaphor for psychology. In T. S. Sarbin (Ed.), *Narrative psychology: The storied nature of human conduct* (p. 3–21). New York: Praeger.

Seifert, R. (1994). War and rape: A preliminary analysis. In A. Stiglmayer (Ed.), *Mass rape: The war against women in Bosnia-Herzegovina* (p 54–72). London: University of Nebraska Press.

Shaw, C. & Proctor, G. (2005). Women at the margins: A critique of the diagnosis of borderline personality disorder. *Feminism and Psychology, 15*(4): 483–490.

Skjelsbæk, I. (1999). *Sexual violence in times of war: An annotated bibliography.* PRIO Report 4/1999. Oslo: International Peace Research Institute, Oslo (PRIO).

Søndergaard, D. M. (2005). Making sense of gender, age, power and disciplinary position: Intersecting discourses in the academy. *Feminism & Psychology, 15* (2): 189–208.

Stephens, B. (1993). Women and the atrocities of war. *Human Rights, 20*(3): 12–15.

Stiglmayer, A. (1994). The rapes in Bosnia-Herzegovina. In A. Stiglmayer (Ed.), *Mass rape: The war against women in Bosnia-Herzegovina* (p. 82–169). Lincoln, NE and London: University of Nebraska Press.

Thomas, D. Q., & Ralph, R. E. (1994). Rape in war: Challenging the tradition of impunity. *Sais Review, 14*(1): 81–99.

Tokaca, M. (Ed.). (1999). *The sin of silence: The risk of speech*, collection of reports from the international conference on Violation of the Human Rights of Women in Bosnia and Herzegovina During the War 1992–1995, Sarajevo, 10–11 March. Bosnia and Herzegovina: The Commission for Gathering Facts on War Crimes in Bosnia and Herzegovina.

UN Economic & Social Council. (1993). Situation of human rights in the territory of the former Yugoslavia (report submitted by Mr Tadeusz Mazowiecki, Special Rapporteur of the Commission on Human Rights, 10 February, E/CN.4/1993/50).

UN Economic & Social Council. (1994). Situation of human rights in the territory of the former Yugoslavia (report submitted by Mr Tadeusz Mazowiecki, Special Rapporteur of the Commission on Human Rights, 21 February, E/CN.4/1994/110).

Vranic, Seada (1996) Breaking *The Wall of Silence: The Voices of Raped Bosnia*. Zagreb: Anti Barbarus.

White, H. (1987). *The content of the form: Narrative discourse and historical representation*. Baltimore, MD: Johns Hopkins University Press.

Wilkinson, S. (2003). Focus groups. In J. A. Smith (Ed.), *Qualitative psychology: A practical guide to research methods* (p. 184–204). London: Sage.

Wing, K. A., & Merchan, S. (1993). Rape, ethnicity and culture: Spirit inquiry from Bosnia to Black America. *Columbia Human Rights Law Review, 25*(1): 1–48.

Zarkov, D. (1997). War rapes in Bosnia: On masculinity, femininity and power of the rape victim identity. *Tijdschrift voor Criminologie, 39*(2): 140–151.

Women, Gender, and Offending

This section is devoted to the theoretical explanations of female offending. The section begins with a review of the failures of mainstream criminology to provide adequate explanations for women who offend. This section first examines how traditional theories of crime failed to understand how female offenders differed from male offenders. While these original authors did little to acknowledge gender, scholars have since looked to whether modern-day applications of these perspectives can help explain female offending. The section then turns to a discussion of how feminist scholars have sought out new theories to represent the female offender and her social world. The section concludes with a discussion on feminist criminology and how the offending patterns of women are often intertwined with their experiences of victimization.

Theoretical Perspectives on Female Criminality

Theories on criminal behavior try to explain why offenders engage in crime. These theories of crime may focus on causes of crime from either macro or micro explanations for criminal behavior. Macro theories of crime explore the large-scale social explanations for crime, such as poverty and community disorganization. In contrast, micro theories of crime focus on individual differences between law-abiding and law-violating behaviors. Since the late 19th century, researchers have investigated the relationship between gender, crime, and punishment from macro as well as micro perspectives. As Belknap reflects, "Female lawbreakers historically (and to some degree today) have been viewed as abnormal and as worse than male lawbreakers—not only for breaking the law but also for stepping outside of prescribed gender roles of femininity and passivity" (2007, p. 34). Theories on the nature of female criminality have ranged from describing these offenders as aggressive and violent to women who are passive, helpless, and in need of protection. Consequently, theories on the etiology of female offending have reflected both of these

Figure 6.1 • Timeline on Theories of Female Offending

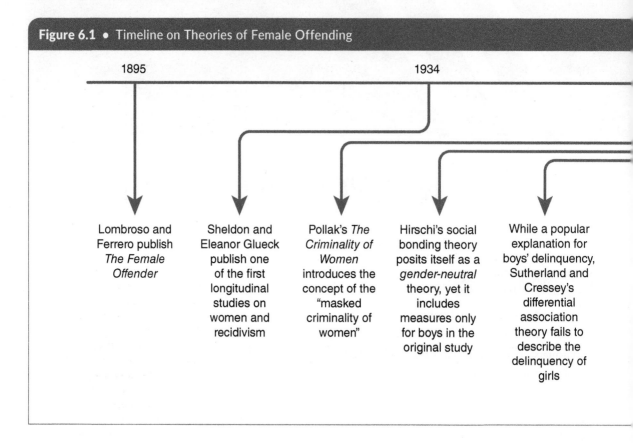

perspectives. While theories on female crime have grown significantly from the early perspectives, it is important to debate the tenets of these historical viewpoints, because they provide a foundation for a greater understanding of female offending (see Figure 6.1).

Historical Theories on Female Criminality

Cesare Lombroso and William Ferrero represent the first criminologists to attempt to investigate the nature of the female offender. Expanding on his earlier work, *The Criminal Man,* Lombroso joined with Ferrero in 1895 to publish *The Female Offender.* Lombroso's basic idea was that criminals are biological throwbacks to a primitive breed of man and can be recognized by various "atavistic" degenerative physical characteristics. To test this theory for female offenders, Lombroso and Ferrero went to women's prisons, where they measured body parts and noted physical differences of the incarcerated women. They attributed a number of unique features to the female criminal, including occipital irregularities, narrow foreheads, prominent cheekbones, and a "virile" type of face. Although they found that female offenders had fewer degenerative characteristics compared to male offenders, they explained these differences by suggesting that women, in general, are biologically more primitive and less evolved than men. They also suggested that the "evil tendencies" of female offenders "are more numerous and more varied than men's" (Lombroso & Ferrero, 1895, p. 151). Female criminals were believed to be more like men than women, in terms of both mental and physical qualities, suggesting that female offenders were more likely to experience suppressed

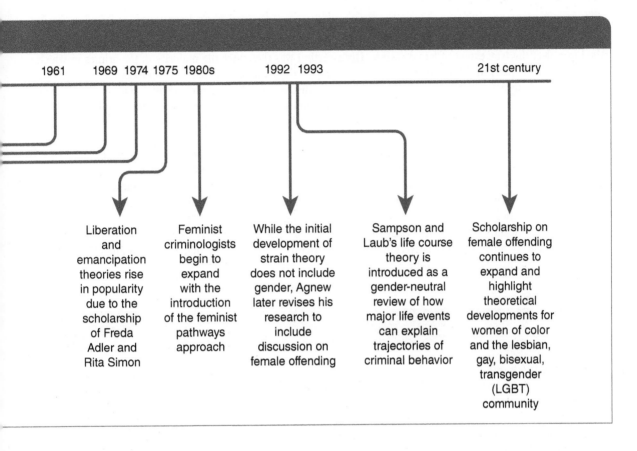

| 1961 | 1969 | 1974 | 1975 | 1980s | 1992 | 1993 | 21st century |

Liberation and emancipation theories rise in popularity due to the scholarship of Freda Adler and Rita Simon

Feminist criminologists begin to expand with the introduction of the feminist pathways approach

While the initial development of strain theory does not include gender, Agnew later revises his research to include discussion on female offending

Sampson and Laub's life course theory is introduced as a gender-neutral review of how major life events can explain trajectories of criminal behavior

Scholarship on female offending continues to expand and highlight theoretical developments for women of color and the lesbian, gay, bisexual, transgender (LGBT) community

"maternal instincts" and "ladylike" qualities. They were convinced that women who engaged in crime would be less sensitive to pain, less compassionate, generally jealous, and full of revenge—in short, criminal women possessed all the worst characteristics of the female gender while embodying the criminal tendencies of the male.

The methods and findings of Lombroso and Ferrero have been harshly criticized, mostly due to their small sample size and the lack of heterogeneity of their sample demographics. They also failed to control for additional environmental and structural variables that might explain criminal behavior regardless of gender. Finally, their key assumptions about women had no scientific basis. Their claim that the female offender was more ruthless and less merciful had more to do with the fact that she had violated sex-role and gender-role expectations than the nature of her actual offending behaviors.

The works of Sheldon and Eleanor Glueck represent some of the earliest longitudinal studies on crime and delinquency. In 1934, the Gluecks followed up their study of 500 incarcerated men with a similar study on the female offender, titled *Five Hundred Delinquent Women*. These researchers sought only to distinguish female offenders from male offenders, but this work was also one of the first studies on recidivism among this population. Although *Five Hundred Delinquent Women* was not as well known as their other works, it was similar in philosophy and methodology to their other publications. Most notably, the Gluecks looked at a variety of different factors to explain criminality, which was a dramatically different approach compared to other studies during this time period. For example, they were among some of the first researchers to investigate the role of the family on delinquency. In addition, the Gluecks drew from a multidisciplinary perspective, and they were influenced by a variety of disciplines such as biology, sociology, psychology, and anthropology.

More than a half century passed between the publication of Lombroso and Ferrero's *The Female Offender* and the publication of *The Criminality of Women* by **Otto Pollak** (1961). Pollak believed that criminal data sources failed to reflect the true extent of female crime. His assertion was that since the majority of the crimes in which women engage are petty in nature, many victims do not report these crimes, particularly when the victim is a male. Additionally, he suggested that many police officers exercise discretion when confronted with female crime and may issue only informal warnings in these cases. His data also indicated that women were more likely to be acquitted, compared to their male counterparts. Altogether, he concluded that the crimes of women are underreported, and when reported, these women benefit from preferential treatment by the systems of criminal justice. His discussion of the **masked criminality of women** suggested that women gain power by deceiving men through sexual playacting, faked sexual responses, and menstruation. This power allowed female criminality to go undetected by society. Likewise, Pollak believed that the traditional female roles of homemaker, caretaker, and domestic worker gave women an avenue to engage in crimes against vulnerable populations, such as children and the elderly.

While each of these works represented a new frontier in criminological theory, much of the assumptions about gender were significantly flawed. These early theories of female criminality placed a heavy reliance on stereotypes about the female offender as manipulative, cunning, and masculine—all identities that limited the analysis of female criminality to a narrow perception of the world.

Spotlight on the Manson Women

In the late 1960s, the charismatic Charles Manson lived with a few dozen followers on an abandoned ranch/movie lot near Topanga Canyon in L.A. County, engaging in free love and drug experimentation. He called these followers his "family." Among his more radical ideas, Manson believed a race war called Helter Skelter was coming, and he developed a plan to initiate this inevitable race war. He persuaded several of his followers to commit murder, thereby testing their loyalty and sparking Helter Skelter. Several members of his "family" followed his request, including the "Manson women": Susan Atkins, Leslie Van Houten, and Patricia Krenwinkel. Susan Atkins and Patricia Krenwinkel participated in the infamous murder of the pregnant actress Sharon Tate and her houseguests on August 8, 1969. Two days later, Van Houten joined as Atkins, Krenwinkel, and Watson stabbed a wealthy grocer, Leno LaBianca, and his wife, Rosemary. Leslie Van Houten, Susan Atkins, and Patricia Krenwinkel were convicted and sentenced to death for committing murder. Their death sentences were commuted in 1972 to life sentences with the possibility of parole when state and federal courts declared capital punishment unconstitutional.

To date, there have been many theories that have attempted to explain why Van Houten, Atkins, and Krenwinkel were led to engage in murder. Each of these women were users of LSD, a powerful hallucinogenic drug, during their time with Manson, which altered their mental functioning. Van Houten had experimented with LSD during her adolescence and rebelled against her conservative upbringing. To date they have each served over forty years for crimes that they committed during their 20s and while under the influence of drugs.

In addition, all three women also experienced strain in their family relationships, which led them to seek out new relationships for love and acceptance. For each of the women, Manson and his family fulfilled this need. Van Houten became pregnant at 16 and had an abortion, which increased the tensions between her and her mother. Strain theory can be applied to explain her substance abuse and early delinquency, because she experienced strain from the breakdown of the relationship to her mother (Atchison & Heide, 2011). Susan Atkins grew up in a supportive nuclear family, but her mother died of cancer when she was just fifteen. While she was a good student throughout childhood, her academic performance suffered following her mother's death. Her home environment also suffered and she ultimately moved out on her own. Patricia Krenwinkle's parents divorced when she was 17, and she had a history of being bullied significantly as a teen (Biography.com).

Following their conviction, the three were finally free of the influence of Manson. They have been model prisoners and have been involved in efforts to rehabiliate themselves. However, each of the women has been denied parole multiple times, despite their good behavior in prison and their efforts to rehabilitate themselves. Leslie Van Houten is very active in the Prison Pups program, which allows inmates to train service dogs for the disabled. In September 2017, Van Houten was recommended by the parole board for release for the 2nd time. It will be up to Governor Brown whether the board's recomendation will be affirmed.

▲ Photo 6.1 Susan Atkins, Patricia Krenwinkel, and Leslie Van Houten walk to their hearing in the murder case of Sharon Tate in 1970. The three women, known as the Manson Women, were sentenced to death, but their sentences were commuted to life in prison. While each of the women has faced numerous parole hearings, Krenwinkel and Van Houten remain incarcerated in California Institute for Women, Chino. Atkins died of cancer in 2009.

After being denied parole thirteen times, Patricia Krenwinkle's recent hearing focused on whether the board should consider her history of abuse by Manson. Under California law, parole commissioners can give greater weight to experiences of physical or emotional abuse if it impacted their offense. While Krenwinkle testified that Manson was abusive toward her, the board rejected her defense and denied her request for parole (Thompson, 2017). Today, Krenwinkle has served longer than any other female inmate in the state of California. Meanwhile, Susan Atkins was diagnosed with brain cancer in 2008. Her requests for compassionate medical release were denied, and the board stated that she remained a danger to society. She passed away on September 24, 2009, as an inmate in the California prison system. Charles Manson passed away in November 2017.

Traditional Theories of Crime and Gender

A number of criminological theories rose to fame during the mid- and late 20th century. The majority of these explanations focused exclusively on male criminality, with little consideration for women's lives. Many of these theorists excluded women from their research on the grounds that they represented such a small proportion of the offending population. Instead, some theorists simply made gross gendered stereotypes about women and girls.

Travis Hirschi's social bond theory (1969) is one example of an alleged gender-neutral theory of crime that failed to consider the lives of girls and women. While most theories up to this point focused on why offenders engage in crime, Hirschi's work was unique in that looked for explanations as to why people might desist from criminal behavior. His theory focused on four criteria, or *bonds,* that prevent people from acting on potential criminological impulses or desires. He identified these bonds as (1) **attachment**, (2) **commitment**, (3) **involvement**, and (4) **belief**. *Attachment* refers to the bond that people have with family, friends, and social institutions (such as government, education, and religion) that may serve as an informal control against criminality. Hirschi posited that people refrain from criminal behavior as a result of these attachments because they do not want to disappoint people in their lives. For example, youth who have positive attachments to parents or peers may limit their delinquent behavior

© Bettmann/Corbis

▲ **Photo 6.2** Throughout the 20th century, the number of arrests involving females has increased dramatically. Feminist criminologists highlight that many of the traditional theories of crime fail to address the unique needs of offending women. In addition, much of these data reflect changes in policies regarding societal perspectives of female offending versus a direct increase in the rates of offending by women.

because they do not want to disappoint these important relationships. The second concept, *commitment,* refers to the investment that an individual has to the normative values of society. In many ways, the concept of commitment embodies the spirit of rational choice perspectives. For example, if one is committed to obtaining a college degree, then a violation of the law might limit one's ability to achieve that goal. As a result, one might decide not to engage in the illegal behavior out of fear of jeopardizing one's future. *Involvement* refers to the level at which one might participate in conventional activities such as studying or playing sports. The idea behind involvement is that youth who are more involved in these sorts of activities are less likely to engage in delinquent activities. Finally, *belief* refers to a general acceptance of the rules of society—"the less a person believes he should obey the rules, the more likely he is to violate them" (Hirschi, 1969, p. 26).

For Hirschi, families serve as one of the strongest inhibitors of delinquency. Research shows that the attachment to the family unit varies by gender, because girls are more emotionally attached to their parents. It is this bond that serves to protect girls from delinquency (Heimer, 1996). Likewise, research by Huebner and Betts (2002) showed that a strong attachment bond to parents and other adults serves as a protective factor for girls. However, this attachment to the family may also be related to the increased focus of parents on their daughters. As a result, when girls engage in delinquent behavior, they can experience higher levels of shaming by their parents (Svensson, 2004).

While much has been said about the influence of social bond theory on delinquency, the majority of this scholarship has been restricted to the American criminal justice system. Research by Ozbay and Ozcan (2008) investigates whether **social bond theory** can be used to explain the context of male and female delinquency among Turkish youth. Like findings on American youth, their results indicate that social bonds have a stronger effect on the lives of female students. Within Turkish cultures, the family is an important institution, and girls are highly attached to the family unit. Much of this has to do with differential socialization between the sexes. In contrast, the attachment to school and teachers is a stronger influence in preventing delinquency for boys. While studies on American students indicate that an attachment to school can serve as a protective factor against delinquency for both boys and girls (Lowe, May, & Elrod, 2008), girls who are less attached to school are more likely to engage in nonviolent acts of delinquency (Daigle, Cullen, & Wright, 2007). Educational bonds can also help explain why girls are less likely to engage in alcohol and marijuana use compared to boys (Whaley, Hayes-Smith & Hayes-Smith, 2010).

While Hirschi's social bond theory is considered a macro-level perspective on criminal behavior, his general theory of crime (with Michael Gottfredson) is considered more of a micro-level theory. Gottfredson and Hirschi focus on self-control as the single explanatory factor for delinquent and criminal behavior. According to the general theory of crime, those individuals with high levels of social control will remain law abiding, while those with low social control will be more likely to engage in deviant and criminal activities. But the question remains: What influences an individual's self-control, and for the purposes of this discussion, what role does gender play in this process? Gottfredson and Hirschi posit that the development of self-control is rooted in the family. The more involved parents are in their children's lives, the more likely they are to be aware of challenges to the development of their children's self-control. This awareness then leads to action, and parents are more likely to correct these issues at a young age. As a result, Gottfredson and Hirschi's general theory of crime suggests that early intervention efforts are the only effective tool to deter individuals from crime. From their perspective, variables such as gender, race, and class are irrelevant, because everything comes down to self-control (Gottfredson & Hirschi, 1990).

Since the development of Gottfredson and Hirschi's general theory of crime, many researchers have looked at the role of gender in this process using constructs such as impulsivity, risk taking, and aggression as indicators of self-control. However, these findings demonstrate that the general theory of crime can explain the delinquency of boys but fails in its explanation for girls. For example, research by DeLisi et al. (2010) on delinquent youth housed in the California Youth Authority facility indicate that while self-control measures are effective in predicting behavioral violations for incarcerated males, the misconduct in girls is more likely to be explained by other variables such as age (younger girls are more likely to act out) and the presence of a psychiatric disorder. Similarly, research by Shekarkhar and Gibson (2011) noted that while low self-control did predict offending behaviors for Latino boys and girls in terms of violent offenses, it did not predict the behaviors of girls who engage in property offenses (which generally comprise much of female offending patterns). Even in those studies where self-control might explain the offending characteristics for girls, these effects are often eliminated when other variables such as opportunity or social learning theory are introduced (Burton, Cullen, Evans, Alarid, & Dunaway, 1998; LaGrange & Silverman, 1999). In addition, any gender differences in self-control tend to disappear over time (Jo & Bouffard, 2014).

Edwin Sutherland's (Sutherland, & Cressey 1974) **differential association theory** focuses on the influence of how relationships lead to crime, in particular, the influence of peer relationships on delinquent behavior. Differential association theory is influenced by social learning theory, which suggests that criminality is a learned behavior. Differential association theory posits that these learned behaviors are a result of peer associations. As youth spend time with people, these people then influence their knowledge, practices, and judgments on delinquent behavior. The more that people are exposed to these delinquent attitudes and behaviors, the more they are able to influence this person. Like many social theories of the 20th century, discussions of gender were absent in differential association theory.

Recent research has provided mixed results in the application of differential association theory for female offenders. In addition, race and ethnicity impact the effects of the peer relationship for girls' delinquency. Silverman and Caldwell (2008) find that peer attitudes have the greatest effect on youth behavior for Hispanic girls. Here, the *strength of the peer relationship* plays a key factor—if the peer group deems that delinquency is an acceptable behavior, the rates of violent delinquent behavior increase. In contrast, *time* plays the biggest role for White girls. As the proportion of time that is spent with the peer group increases, the greater the influence these peers have on violent delinquent behavior (Silverman & Caldwell, 2008). However, not all research demonstrates support for the applications of differential association theory to girls. Research by Daigle et al. (2007) and Lowe, May, and Elrod (2008) indicates that influences from delinquent peers does lead to an increase in delinquency for boys but that negative peer influence does not have an effect for girls. Here, it may be that while peer associations can impact delinquency, the effect is stronger for the delinquency of boys than girls (Piquero, Gover, MacDonald, & Piquero, 2005).

Another theory that has frequently been used to explain offending behaviors is *strain theory*. While several theorists have made contributions to the understanding of how an individual's aspirations collide with the goals of society, the works of Robert Agnew represent perhaps the most modern of these applications in terms of criminal behavior. While traditional theories of strain by scholars such as Merton (1938) and Cohen (1955) focused on the structural limitations of success, Agnew's (1992) general strain theory looks into individualized psychological sources as correlates of criminal behavior. Agnew highlights three potential sources of strain: (1) failure in achieving positive goals, (2) the loss of positive influences, and (3) the arrival of negative influences.

Agnew has continued to develop his general strain theory to consider how strain might impact the delinquency and at-risk behaviors for girls as well as boys. Research by Broidy and Agnew (1997) argues that general strain theory can be used to explain gender differences in crime. However, it is important to keep some key distinctions in mind when using a gendered approach to general strain theory. First, males and females have different sources of strain. For example, girls are more likely to experience strain as a result of violence in the home (physical, emotional, and sexual), which in turn leads to delinquent acts, such as running away and substance abuse. Second, boys and girls respond to strain differently. Here, Broidy and Agnew highlight that while strain can manifest as anger for both boys and girls, they exhibit this anger in different ways. For example, girls are more likely to internalize their feelings of anger, which can lead to issues of self-destructive behaviors and depression. In contrast, boys tend to exhibit anger in physical and emotional outbursts (Broidy & Agnew, 1997).

In addition to the work by Broidy & Agnew, other scholars have looked at how gender can impact how youth experience strain. Research notes that males and females tend to experience different types of strain, which in turn can impact the types of offending behaviors (Moon & Morash, 2017). While boys experience higher levels of traditional strain than girls (defined here as aspirations for higher educational success), girls are more likely to have negative life events and report higher levels of conflict with their parents. Yet these negative life events and higher levels of conflict increase the involvement in delinquency. Some research indicates that educational success becomes the vehicle for bringing out these issues (Daigle et al., 2007) while others identify specific experiences with strain (such as a history of physical abuse or living with someone who uses drugs and alcohol) as an indirect cause of daily substance abuse (Sharp, Peck, & Hartsfield, 2012). Meanwhile, research by Garcia and Lane (2012) identifies that a major source of strain among female delinquents is relationship strain. Strain within the family (such as with parents) can manifest in behaviors such as running away, substance abuse, or poor relationship choices. These poor relationship choices can also be their own source of strain, particularly when girls become involved with system-involved or older males. Peer relationships can also perpetuate strain, particularly in the cases of *frenemies*. Unlike other theories that discuss how deviant peers might encourage delinquency, Garcia and Lane find that girls may engage in delinquent acts (such as fights) out of anger toward other female peers or status offenses (such as truancy) in an effort to avoid being bullied. In cases of drug use, research notes that gender does impact the strain that youth experience, particularly in their likelihood to recidivate. For example, youth who live in single-parent homes are more likely to relapse in their drug use compared to youth who reside in a two-parent household, and that this behavior is more common for boys than girls (Grothoff, Kempf-Leonard, & Mullins, 2014).

While these classical theories of crime generally offered little evidence or explanation about female criminal activity at their inception, later research has investigated if and how these traditional theories of crime can understand the role of gender in offending. To date, these conclusions are mixed—while some provide evidence that these theories can make contributions to understanding female crime, others are more suited to explaining male criminality, as they were originally conceived. It is also important to consider how issues of intersectionality can impact these findings and future research should consider how issues such as race, ethnicity, and sexuality can also influence gender issues within these classical theories of offending.

Modern Theories of Female Offending Behaviors

The emergence of works by **Freda Adler** and **Rita Simon** in the 1970s marked a significant shift in the study of female criminality. The works of Adler and Simon were inspired by the emancipation of women that was occurring during the 1960s and 1970s in the United States and the effects of the second wave of the feminist movement. Both authors highlighted how the liberation of women would lead to an increased participation of women in criminal activities. While Adler (1975) suggested that women's rates of violent crime would increase, Simon (1975) hypothesized that women would commit a greater proportion of property crimes as a result of their liberation from traditional gender roles and restrictions. While both authors broke new ground in the discussion of female crime, their research has also been heavily criticized. Analysis on crime statistics between 1960 and 1975 indicates that while female crime rates for violent crimes skyrocketed during this time period, so did the rates of male violent crime. In addition, one must consider the reference point of these statistics. True, more women engaged in crime. However, given the low number of female offenders in general, small increases in the number of crimes can create a large percentage increase, which can be misinterpreted and overexaggerated. For example, if women are involved in 100 burglaries in one year and this number increases to 150 burglaries in the next year, this reflects a 50% increase from one year to the next. If, however, men participated in 1,000 burglaries in one year and in 1,250 during the next, this is only a 25% increase, even though the actual numerical increase is greater for men than women.

Another criticism of Adler and Simon's works focuses on their overreliance on the effects of the women's liberation movement. While it is true that the emancipation of women created increased opportunities and freedoms to engage in crime, this does not necessarily mean that women were more compelled to engage in crime. Changing policies in policing and the processing of female offenders may reflect an increase of women in the system as a result of changes in the response by the criminal justice system to crimes involving women.

In addition to Adler and Simon's focus on the emancipation of women as an explanation for increasing crime rates, theories shifted from a focus on individual pathology to one that referenced social processes and the greater social environment. One of the few theories during this time frame that incorporated gender as a major theme was **power control theory**, which assesses how patriarchy can influence gender-role socialization and, in turn, how this process impacts rates of delinquency. Developed by **John Hagan** (1989), power control theory starts with the premise that women and girls are socialized in different ways from men and boys. For example, under a patriarchal family structure, boys will be encouraged to be more aggressive, ambitious, and outgoing and benefit from increased freedom compared to girls. Power control theory suggests that these differences in power lead girls to have lower rates of crime because of reduced opportunities. In contrast, families that are structured in a more egalitarian or balanced manner will socialize their children in a similar fashion regardless of their sex. This in turn leads to fewer gender differences in delinquency. For example, women in South Korea that were raised within a more patriarchal family structure were likely to be law-abiding (regardless if they were high or low risk takers) while families with less patriarchal families were more likely to engage in criminal behaviors (Kim, Gerber, Henderson, & Kim, 2012).

One of the major weaknesses of Hagan's theory is that it focuses on the two-parent family structure; under a patriarchal structure one could assume that the father or male figurehead exerts the primary source of control in the family. As the number of children residing in divorced, separated, and noncohabitating homes continues to increase, it is important to consider how power control theory might apply in these settings. Research by Bates, Bader, and Mencken (2003) finds that single fathers tend to exert similar levels of parental control over their children compared to two-parent patriarchal families, while single mothers exert lower levels of parental control over children. In families with higher levels of parental control, girls are more likely to refrain from deviant behaviors because they view them as risky. Yet the single parent may be less likely to exert parental control over his child due to reduced opportunities to supervise the youth. As a result, this family structure may present an indirect, though important, effect on youth delinquency.

Another modern theory that has been used to investigate the causes of female offending is **Robert Sampson** and **John Laub's** (1993) **life course theory**. Life course theory suggests that the events of one's life (from birth to death) can provide insight as to why one might engage in crime and highlights the importance of adolescence as a crucial time in the development of youthful (and ultimately adult) offending behaviors. Here, ties to conventional adult activities such as family and work can serve as a protective factor in adulthood, even if the individual has engaged in delinquent acts during adolescence. While not specifically a feminist theory of crime, life course theory does allow for a gender-neutral review of how the different developmental milestones in one's life can explain criminal behavior.

Recent applications of life course theory have included discussions of gender in their analyses. Research by Thompson and Petrovic (2009) investigated how variables such as marriage, education, employment, and children can have gendered effects on an individual's illegal substance use. Their research indicates that these social bonds impact men and women differently. While Sampson and Laub suggested that marriage serves to inhibit criminal behavior in men, Thompson and Petrovic (2009) did not find a similar effect for women in terms of illicit drug use. Their findings indicate that marriage alone is not enough to reduce illicit drug use for women. Instead, it is the strength of the marriage that has an effect in reducing substance abuse for women. Adding to the discussion on life course theory and women, research by Estrada and Nilsson (2012) demonstrates that female offenders are more likely to come from childhoods that are traumatized by poverty. In addition, women who engage in chronic offending into adulthood are less likely to have consistent employment histories and be involved in healthy romantic relationships. Indeed, these instabilities may in fact lead women toward lifestyles that can encourage criminal behavior.

While life course theory can have value for understanding offending behaviors of girls and women, scholars suggest that life course theory needs to expand its understanding of what is considered a "significant life event." In particular, Belknap and Holsinger (2006) point to the effects of early childhood abuse traumas, mental health concerns, and sexual identity as a significant life event that can be used to understanding criminality.

These modern theories made significant improvements in understanding the relationship between gender and crime. Unlike traditional theorists, these modern theories placed gender as a significant focus in their theoretical development. However, critiques of these theories demonstrate that there is increased need for greater discussions about women and crime, particularly given the relationship between the context of their lives and their offending behaviors.

Spotlight on Men and Masculinity

The concept of masculinity refers to qualities that are typically associated with the male gender. These include characteristics such as dominance, control, aggression, and strength (or the opposite of weakness). Like feminist theory, theories of masculinity also focus on the role of patriarchy and hegemonic ideals. But in this case, masculinity plays upon these constructs to assess how men and boys "should" behave. These definitions are socially constructed, meaning that they are created by the cultural structures of society rather than the biological characteristics of an individual.

While many of the traditional theories of crime focused primarily on male crime, few of these theories looked at the role of gender and the construction of masculinity as it pertained to male-offending behaviors. And while many of the historical theories about female offending suggested that female criminality was best described by women who were less feminine and more masculine (and therefore, more like male offenders), early theories about male criminals were viewed as an abnormal subset of the population. Contemporary theories of crime began to allude to issues of masculinity through discussions of dominance and the physicality of offending behaviors.

The work of James Messerschmidt has been influential in understanding the relationship between masculinity and crime, particularly on issues of violence. His work builds upon the concept of hegemonic masculinity, which was first developed by Raewyn Connell (1987). Hegemonic masculinity explains how a culture of dominance creates social structures whereby men are placed in roles of power and dominance compared to the social culture of women. For Messerschmidt, hegemonic masculinity is measured by "work in the paid labor market, the subordination of women, heterosexism, and the uncontrollable sexuality of men...practices towards authority, competitive individualism, independence, aggressiveness, and the capacity for violence" (1993, p. 82). This notion of maleness was something for men to aspire to and idealize and crime was a normal expression of masculinity. "Crime, therefore, may be invoked as a practice through which masculinities (and men and women) are differentiated from one another. Moreover, crime is a resource that may be summoned when men lack other resources to accomplish gender." (Messerschmidt 1993 , p. 85). From here, it is not a far jump to understand how crimes, such as sexual assault and intimate partner violence, can be illustrations of hegemonic masculinity whereby men exhibit their power over women. As you learned in Sections III and IV of this text, crimes of sexual and intimate violence are most likely perpetuated against women by men and that such acts are best explained as an illustration of power and control. Theories of masculinity can also be used to understand acts of violence by men, in general, in their search for maleness. For example, most of the high-profile school shooting events throughout the 1990s and 2000s involved boys who used their acts of violence to retaliate against individuals who were viewed as popular or who had bullied them throughout their youth. The mass shooting at Columbine High School in 1999 is an example of this type of masculine violence whereby Eric Harris and Dylan Klebold carried out a planned attack against their high school, killing 12 students and a teacher before turning their guns on themselves. The case of masculinity and violence has also been used to describe acts of gang violence (Heber , 2017) and prison violence (Michalski, 2017).

Feminist Criminology

The emergence of feminist criminology builds on the themes of gender roles and socialization to explain patterns of female offending. Here, scholars begin with a discussion on the backgrounds of female offenders in an effort to assess who she is, where she comes from, and why she engages in crime. Feminist criminology reflects several key themes in its development. Frances Heidensohn (1985, p. 61) suggested that "feminist criminology began with the awareness that women were invisible in conventional studies in the discipline. . . . Feminist criminology began as a reaction . . . against an old established male chauvinism in the academic discipline." While some criminologists suggested that traditional theories of crime could account for explanations in female offending, others argued that in order to accurately theorize about the criminal actions of women, a new approach to the study of crime needed to be developed.

> Theoretical criminology was constructed by men, about men. It is simply not up to the analytical task of explaining female patterns of crime. . . . Thus, something quite different will be needed to explain women and crime. . . . Existing theories are frequently so inconsistent with female realities that specific explanations of female patterns of crime will probably have to precede the development of an all-inclusive theory. (Leonard, 1982, pp. xi–xii)

How can feminist thought influence the field of criminology? Daly and Chesney-Lind (1988) point out that feminist discussions about crime are not limited to "women's issues." They argue that it is important that any discussion of women's lives and criminality incorporates conversations on masculinity and patriarchy. Given the historical distortions and the casual assumptions that have been made about women's lives in relationship to their criminal behaviors, incorporating feminist perspectives can provide a richer understanding about not only the nature of female offending but also the role of how experiences with victimization of women shape this process. In addition, feminist perspectives highlight that feminist criminology is not a single identity but an opportunity to consider multiple influences when understanding issues of gender and crime.

The use of feminist theory, methodologies, and activism in discussions of criminology has led to a variety of new understandings about gender and crime. Perhaps one of the most influential perspectives to date on female offending is the feminist pathways approach. Feminist pathways research seeks to show how life events (and traumas) affect the likelihood to engage in crime. While the pathways approach has many similarities with other theories such as life course or cycle of violence perspectives, these theories do not explain women's criminality from a feminist perspective. In comparison, the feminist pathways approach begins with a feminist foundation (Belknap, 2007). Within the feminist pathways approach, researchers have identified a cycle of violence for female offenders that begins with their own victimization and results with their involvement in offending behavior. Belknap and Holsinger (1998) posit that one of the most significant contributions of feminist criminology is understanding the role of victimization in the histories of incarcerated women, because female offenders report substantially high occurrences of physical, emotional, and sexual abuse throughout their lifetimes. "While such an explanation does not fit all female offenders (and also fits some male offenders), the recognition of these risks appears to be essential for understanding the etiology of offending for many girls and women. Yet this link between victimization and offending has largely been invisible or deemed inconsequential by the powers that be in criminology theory building and by those responsible for responding to women's and girls' victimizations and offenses" (Belknap & Holsinger, 1998, p. 32).

Another example of research incorporating a feminist pathways perspective is Wesely's (2006) research on homeless women and exotic dancers. The levels of childhood abuse and victimization that the women in her study experienced were "located within a nexus of powerlessness, gender-specific sexualization and exploitation, economic vulnerability and destitution, and social alienation and exclusion" (Wesely, p. 309). These women grew up to believe that violence was an ordinary and normal experience, which in turn influenced their decision-making practices throughout their lives. For example, these women learned that sexuality is a tool to manipulate and gain control over others. As a result, many of the women chose to engage in sex work at a young age in an effort to escape the physical and sexual abuse they experienced by their parents and family members. Unfortunately, the decision to live and work on the streets placed them at risk for further violence. These "lived experiences contributed to a downward spiral in which the women were preoccupied with daily survival, beaten down, depressed, and unsuccessful at making choices or having opportunities that improved their life conditions" (Wesely, p. 314–315).

A third approach by Brennan, Breitenbach, Dieterich, Salisbury, and von Voorhis (2012) on feminist pathways identifies multiple pathways to crime. While abuse still plays a theme in some of these pathways, their work identifies eight different pathways within four unique themes. The first theme describes women who have lower experiences with victimization and abuse but whose major criminality revolves around their addiction. The first pathway in this theme contains women who are younger and are the parents of minor children, while the second pathway involves women who are older and do not have children. The second theme highlights the classic role of victimization and abuse within offending. Many of these women also experience emotional and physical abuse by a significant other. The first pathway within this theme involves younger single mothers who may suffer from depression. Many of their offenses involve drugs and dual arrests from intimate partner violence. The second pathway involves women who engage in higher rates of crime and who have greater issues with drugs and mental health. They are older and not involved in parenting. The third and fourth themes have a common foundation in that these women have been highly marginalized throughout their lives. They typically lived in high-crime areas with high rates of poverty. They suffered in school and often lack adequate vocational skills to provide sustenance for their lives. Within these similarities, there are also differences. The first theme involves lower rates of victimization and fewer mental health issues. Many of these women were involved in acts of drug trafficking. Within this theme, the first pathway highlights women who tend to be younger and single parents, while the second pathway describes cases where the women have higher rates of crime and noncompliance with the criminal justice system and are less dependent on a significant other. As in the case with other pathways, these women tend to be older and nonparenting. The final theme involves women who are antisocial and aggressive. They have limited abilities to develop a stable environment for their lives and are often homeless. These women are distinguished primarily by their mental health status. In contrast, the second pathway within this theme involves women who are considered actively psychotic and are at risk for suicide. These women have a significant history with violence and aggression.

Indeed, the feminist pathways approach may provide some of the best information on how women find themselves stuck in a cycle that begins with victimization and leads to offending. Research on women's and girls' pathways to offending provides substantial evidence for the link between victimization and offending, because incarcerated girls are three to four times more likely to be abused than their male counterparts. A review of case files of delinquent girls in California indicates that 92% of delinquent girls in California reported having been subjected to at least one form of abuse (emotional = 88%; physical = 81%; sexual = 56%; Acoca & Dedel, 1997).

For female offenders, research overwhelmingly indicates that a history of abuse leads to a propensity to engage in certain types of delinquency. However, the majority of research points to women committing such offenses as running away and school failure rather than acts of violence. The effects of sexual assault are also related to drug and alcohol addiction and mental health traumas, such as posttraumatic stress disorder and a negative self-identity (Raphael, 2004). In a cycle of victimization and offending, young girls often ran away from home in an attempt to escape from an abusive situation. In many cases, girls were forced to return home by public agencies, such as the police, courts, and social services—agencies designed to help victims of abuse. Girls who refused to remain in these abusive situations were often incarcerated and labeled as "out of parental control."

A review of case files of girls who had been committed to the California Youth Authority facilities during the 1960s showed that most girls were incarcerated for status offenses (a legal charge during that time frame). Many of these girls were committed to the Youth Authority for running away from home, where significant levels of alcoholism, mental illness, sexual abuse, violence, and other acts of crime were present. Unfortunately, in their attempt to escape from an abusive situation, girls often fell into criminal behaviors as a mechanism of survival. Running away from home placed girls at risk for crimes of survival, such as prostitution, where the level of violence they experienced was significant and included behaviors such as robbery, assault, and rape. These early offenses led these girls to spend significant portions of their adolescence behind bars. As adults, these same girls who had committed no crimes in the traditional sense later were convicted for a wide variety of criminal offenses, including serious felonies (Rosenbaum, 1989). Gilfus's (1992) work characterizes the pathway to delinquency as one of "blurred boundaries," because the categories of victim and offender are not separate and distinct. Rather, girls move between the categories throughout their lives, because their victimization does not stop once they become offenders. In addition to the victimization they experienced as a result of their survival strategies, many continued to be victimized by the system through its failure to provide adequate services for girls and women (Gaarder & Belknap, 2002).

Feminist criminologists have also worked at identifying how issues such as race, class, and sexuality impact criminality (and the system's response to these offending behaviors). From this inquiry, we learn that women of color experience multiple marginalized identities, which in turn impacts their trajectories of offending. Research by Potter (2006) suggests that combining Black feminist theory and critical race feminist theory with feminist criminology allows for an enhanced understanding of how Black women experience crime. This perspective of a *Black feminist criminology* identifies four themes that alter the experiences for Black women in the criminal justice system. First, many Black women experience structural oppression in society. Second, the Black community and culture feature unique characteristics as a result of their racialized experiences. Third, Black families differ in their intimate and familial relations. Finally, this perspective looks at the Black woman as an individual, unique in her own right (Potter, 2006). Together, these unique dimensions lead to a different experience for Black women within the criminal justice system that needs to be recognized within theoretical conversations on women and crime.

Developments in feminist research have addressed the significant relationship between victimization and offending. A history of abuse is not only highly correlated with the propensity to engage in criminal behaviors, but also it often dictates the types of behaviors in which young girls engage. Often, these behaviors are methods of surviving their abuse, yet the criminal nature of these behaviors brings these girls to the attention of the criminal justice system. The success of a feminist perspective is dependent on a theoretical structure that not only has to answer questions about crime and delinquency but also has to address issues such as sex-role expectations and patriarchal structures within society (Chesney-Lind, 2006). The inclusion of feminist criminology has important policy implications for the justice system in the 21st century. As Belknap and Holsinger (2006, p. 48–49) note,

> The ramifications of the traditionally male-centered approaches to understanding delinquency not only involve ignorance about what causes girls' delinquency but also threaten the appropriateness of systemic intervention with and treatment responses for girls.

As feminist criminology continues to provide both an understanding of the causes of female offending and explanations for the changes in the gender-gap of offending, it will also face its share of challenges. Both Chesney-Lind (2006) and Burgess-Proctor (2006) have suggested that the future of feminist criminology centers on expanding the discussions on the intersections between gender, race, and class. For example, recent research has posited that increases in the number of women that are incarcerated as a result of the war on drugs not only represents a war on women in general (Bloom, Owen, & Covington, 2004) but also has had specific and detrimental effects on women of color (Bush-Baskette, 1998, 1999). Feminist scholars also need to continue to pursue opportunities to link their research and activism, particularly given some of the recent trends in crime control policies that have both intentional and unintentional consequences for the lives of women, their families, and their communities.

/// SUMMARY

- Early biological studies of female criminality were based on gross assumptions of femininity and had limited scientific validity.

- Historical theories of crime saw women as doubly deviant—not only did women break the law but they also violated traditional gender-role assumptions.

- Applications of social bond theory illustrate that family bonds can reduce female delinquency, while educational bonds have a stronger effect for boys.

- Recent tests of differential association theory indicate that peer associations may have a stronger effect on male delinquency than female delinquency.

- Research on general strain theory illustrates that not only do girls experience different types of strain from boys but they also respond to experiences of strain differently.

- Life course theory examines how adverse life events impact criminality over time and can provide insight on both female and male offending patterns.

- Theories of female criminality during the 1960s and 1970s focused on the effects of the emancipation of women, gendered assumptions about female offending, and the differential socialization of girls and boys.

- The feminist pathways approach has identified a cycle for women and girls that begins with their own victimization and leads to their offending.

//// KEY TERMS

Adler, Freda 248

Attachment 245

Belief 245

Commitment 245

Differential association theory 247

Hagan, John 249

Hirschi, Travis 245

Involvement 245

Laub, John 249

Life course theory 249

Lombroso, Cesare, and William Ferrero 242

Masked criminality of women 244

Pollak, Otto 244

Power control theory 249

Sampson, Robert 249

Simon, Rita 248

Social bond theory 246

Sutherland, Edwin 247

//// DISCUSSION QUESTIONS

1. How have historical theories of female offending failed to understand the nature of female offending?

2. What has recent research on gender and traditional theories of crime illustrated about the nature of female offending?

3. What contributions has feminist criminology made in understanding the relationship between gender and offending?

//// WEB RESOURCES

Bureau of Justice Statistics: http://bjs.ojp.usdoj.gov

Feminist Criminology: http://fcx.sagepub.com

 Visit **study.sagepub.com/mallicoat3e** to access additional study tools, including eFlashcards, web quizzes, web resources, video resources, and SAGE journal articles.

READING /// 11

Throughout this section, you learned about how traditional and modern theories of crime failed to include women in their research. This article involves a case study of a young woman convicted of a drug offense. Dr. Bernard looks at the experiences of this woman's offending behaviors as an illustration of feminist criminology in action.

The Intersectional Alternative
Explaining Female Criminality

April Bernard

Introduction

Female criminality has been explained from a variety of feminist perspectives; marginalization from conventional institutions, disrupted family and personal relationships, and institutionalized racism, sexism, and economic disadvantage have all been explored as explanations for the involvement of women in crime (Broidy & Agnew, 1997; Chesney-Lind, 1986, 1997; Daly & Chesney-Lind, 1988; Owen, 1998; Ritchie, 2004). Marginalized women involved in crimes tend to be young, poor, non-white, high school dropouts, unmarried mothers, un/underemployed and educated, with a history of drug problems, family violence, and sexual abuse. The vulnerabilities that color the lives of marginalized women can be difficult to measure due to the overlapping influence, or intersectionality, of multiple forms of subjugation, such as ingrained racism, sexism, economic disadvantage, abuse, exploitation, and the historical undervaluation of women in society (Collins, 2000; Kelly, 1994).

The need for grounding theorizing about women's criminality in an understanding of intersecting identities that emerge from crosscutting systems of oppression has been emphasized in Black and multiracial feminist and criminology analyses (Baca Zinn & Thornton Dill, 1996;

Barak, 1998; Beale, 1995; Belknap, 2001; Britton, 2004; Brown, 2010; Burgess-Proctor, 2006; Collins, 2000; Daly & Stephens, 1995; Gordon, 1987; King, 1988; Potter, 2006; Ritchie, 1996; Wing, 2003). Collins describes this intersectionality as functioning within matrices of domination that represent amalgamations of micro- through macro-level power structures and interrelated systems of oppression. The historically and socially specific ways in which these power structures are constructed and systems of oppression are blended create different kinds of social realities, identities, and experiences. This analysis uses an intersectional approach to provide an explanation of women's criminality in that it seeks to be grounded in an intimate understanding of the multiplicative, overlapping, and cumulative effects of the simultaneous intersections of oppressions that affect women's decisions to engage in crime.

This article begins by challenging aspects of male-stream theorizing on crime that fail to capture the multiple forces that serve to construct gender realities (Carlen, 1985; Dekeseredy & Perry, 2006; Maidment, 2006). The significance of the intersectional approach is discussed as a viable alternative paradigm that recognizes the influence of multiple constraining factors on women's criminality. The concept of *doing identity* is then introduced to

SOURCE: Bernard, A. (2013). The intersectional alternative: Explaining female criminality. *Feminist Criminology, 8*(1), 3–19.

describe the unique attempts of individuals, particularly marginalized women, to navigate through power structures and multiple systems of oppression that shape their life experiences. A case study consisting of an exploration of factors contributing to one woman's decision to engage in criminal activity as a means of doing identity is presented. The importance of this intersectional model for feminist criminology is underscored through a discussion of implications and recommendations for theoretical praxis, policy, and programmatic provisions.

Alternative Theorizing: Strained or Constrained Realities

The primary tenet underlying this alternative approach is that counter to male-stream perspectives on crime, women's criminality may be best understood as an adverse response to a lack of legitimate means for women to demonstrate an authentic and efficacious identity that is unfettered by the constraining effects of intersecting systems of oppression. Although my critique seeks to offer an alternative to the male-streaming of mainstream criminal justice research in general, the intention is not to diminish the significance of any of these contributions.

This work should be understood as an attempt to encourage the extension of male-stream theorizing on crime by acknowledging the potential of the intersectional approach to encompass the complexities of the realities that are faced by marginalized women. In this vein, an analysis of Merton's strain theory using an alternative intersectional perspective is provided as one, but not the only, example of the limitations of male-stream theorizing in general on women's criminality. This application of an intersectional perspective on Merton's strain theory is one demonstration of the need for more in-depth analyses of the underlying causes and complexities that influence women's decisions to engage in crime that hopefully will encourage further intersectional analyses of this and other theories in the future.

According to Merton (1968), deviance is an adaptive response to a lack of legitimate means to achieve shared cultural goals. A commitment to the cultural goals and institutionalized means for success results in conformity, yet when access to the institutionalized means for success is strained or limited (typically due to differences in class), innovative attempts to achieve and retain shared cultural goals are forwarded. Deviance and crime increase in society when the option to conform is not accepted, and this innovation results in illegitimate means to achieve success.

Merton viewed the rejection of cultural goals and/or institutional means as an innovative or adaptive response that occurs within an anomic context in which incongruence between shared cultural goals and institutional means for success exists. Strain, frustration, and stress result where goals exceed means. The alternative intersectional paradigm suggests that women's criminality may be more an expression of constrained rather than strained realities. This alternative approach de-emphasizes individual frustrations and pathologies and instead stresses the ways in which power structures and systems of oppression work to circumscribe the life experiences of persons socially located at the intersections of multiple vulnerabilities.

The proposed alternative framework also suggests that although there may exist agreement on the general nature of the cultural goals that are shared among the population in a society (such as obtaining an education, a job, a house, and a car in Westernized capitalist societies) as described by Merton, the specifics of each individual's desired goals and opportunities may differ in regard to quality and quantity. The intersections that shape unique experiences of privilege/oppression in turn foster the development of multiple realities in which one person's specific goals and opportunities to obtain a particular type of house, number of cars, or quality of education may be very distinct in comparison to another's. Having an understanding of an individual's specific desired goals and opportunities is therefore suggested as taking precedence over having knowledge of shared cultural goals and institutionalized means for success in explaining decisions to engage in criminal activity.

This alternative framework also reconstructs Merton's concept of a class differential and suggests that the disparities that influence access to opportunities and life outcomes represent the cumulative impact of the intersections of multiple inequalities/privileges including (but not limited to) race, class, and gender on the life experiences of individuals. The differential advantage some have over others is less a reflection of their individual merit and propensity toward conformity than of differences in power.

The social, economic, and political place and space individuals hold within society relative to the legitimate means, resources, and opportunities for achieving some measure of success may be more or less constrained depending on the ways in which they affect and are affected by existing power structures and systems of oppression. Embedded within the concept of a matrix of domination is the recognition that to achieve the ideals of social justice and equality would require the reduction of the differential advantage of some over others through the restructuring of the domains of power (law, bureaucracy, culture, and relationships/interactions) and the dismantling and eradication of their interconnections that function to maintain (and are maintained by) ideologies and systems of oppression that foster multiple and overlapping inequalities, including, but not limited to, race, class, and gender.

What affects an individual's access to legitimate means for success is not just about social capital, social networks, or other class indicators, but encompasses the micro- through macro-level social, sexual, national, economic, political, and other socially inherited and ascribed histories, norms, and social spaces an individual represents and encounters (Collins, 2000; Harding, 2004). This intersectional approach claims that *social location*, or the combination of micro- through macro-level social identities and social roles and relationships, is a primary contributing factor to decisions about criminality. The decision to engage in crime is influenced by the unique combination of factors that represent a particular social location regardless of an individual or group's relationship to income-generating resources and assets or differences in class as postulated by Merton. Social location can be described as the cumulative impact of intersections of oppression/privilege and represents the intercorrelation of multiple factors and conditions that are unique to each individual that influence his or her experiences, opportunities, and choices.

The significance of Merton's concept of institutionalized means is minimized in this alternative framework due to its ambiguity and the pejorative implications for developing policies that respond to the variety of social and economic conditions affecting marginalized populations. From this alternative perspective, the belief in the existence of omnipresent functional, normal, stable, fixed, and solid social structures, institutions, communities, families,

opportunities, or *institutional means* (to which individuals can choose to conform, accept, or reject) requires rethinking to acknowledge the particular matrix of domination and systems of oppression and the fluidity of associated factors that characterize an individual's social and economic condition. The fluidity of relationships, norms, cultures, and institutions in global and modern societies has been identified as a key contributor to the growing sense of social isolation, decay, risk, and insecurity that depict the challenges of late modernity (Bauman, 2000; Beck, 1992). Instead of institutionalized means, emphasis in the proposed paradigm is placed on the acknowledgment of existing social contradictions (the limitations of capitalist ideology and the erosion of the American Dream), risk (the potential for victimization, exploitation, subjugation), and uncertainty (various forms of insecurity) within contemporary society that function to further disadvantage members of vulnerable populations.

This alternative theoretical framework challenges the assumption that the social contradictions, risk, and uncertainty that are evident in late modernity can be effectively managed through equal opportunity and antidiscrimination legislation, social control, and punitive reforms. The assumption that the impact of these factors on the ability of all individuals to cope with the challenge of navigating through the complexity of their vulnerabilities and inequalities toward achieving success can be mitigated through obedience to the law and conformity to dominant social norms is also challenged. This alternative framework acknowledges the relativity of deviance and rejects paradigms built upon the premise that deviance and conformity are dichotomous states rather than overlapping spheres of potential responses that can be differentially interpreted depending on the circumstances or context (Curra, 2000). What is deemed deviant in one community (fighting among youth, for example) may be viewed as good common sense in another.

Not all marginalized women resort to crime, and some affluent women seek illegitimate means to achieve their goals. Conformity in an intersectional context can be defined as individuals actively engaged in the process of constantly assessing and reassessing their goals and resigning themselves to accept those that can be achieved given their social location in relation to opportunities (means) amid multiple inequalities, risks, and uncertainty that exist in society. For marginalized women, if the consequences of conformity may require an acceptance of a life that is less than their goals prescribe, then crime may become an innovative response. What may distinguish the affluent female criminal from another of less wealth is that though both choose an illegitimate response to their circumstances, their opportunities and agency to commit crimes differ in regard to quality and consequences (Reiman, 2003).

When combined, the concepts of individual (rather than shared) goals for success, social location (as opposed to a class differential), and societal contradictions, insecurity, and risk (instead of institutionalized means) result in a differential means for "doing" identity (navigating through multiple inequalities to achieve a particular or individual-specific measure of success), which leads to an adaptive response that is more or less legitimate depending on the context. Doing identity can be described as a process of producing unique biographical solutions to systemic contradictions (Beck, 1992). This concept of doing identity is based on the work conducted by Carlen (1988) and Messerschmidt (1993) and their perspectives on crime for marginalized populations as an adaptive response to societal circumstances.

Pat Carlen (1988) addresses the issues of conformity, identity, and criminality among underclass women. Based on her study of 39 convicted women between the ages of 15 and 46, Carlen suggests that the cultural goals for success that govern the lives of women are influenced by two social compromises or deals related to gender and class. The *class deal* stipulates that women's conformity is motivated by the opportunity for them to earn their own wages and ultimately achieve financial success, or the "good life," as defined by the society, through their work in the public domain.

The *gender deal* is motivated by the promise of a happy and fulfilling family life that is to result from the woman's labor for and love of a man who is the primary breadwinner. The gender deal breaks down when women are unable to obtain or maintain successful relationships with a male breadwinner, are abused, and/or socially isolated, and the class deal is compromised when women are unable to achieve financial success through work. Carlen's thesis is that women resort to crime when the class and/or gender deals break down.

Although Carlen's thesis is convincing, the question remains whether class and gender are the only socially relevant aspects of women's existence upon which deals can be made and whether there are other aspects of women's identities or social locations that significantly factor into their responses to adversity and potential criminality. The following analysis will also seek to reveal additional factors as well as consider Carlen's description of the class and gender deals as significant factors that influence women's adaptive responses to risk and contradictions in society.

Messerschmidt (1993) provides a gendered approach to the development of criminological theory to describe the relationship between masculinity and crime. Messerschmidt suggests that to understand male behavior, including crime, one must begin by acknowledging the historical and social structural conditions that construct hegemonic masculine ideologies and social actions. He argues, "Hegemonic masculinity emphasizes practices toward authority, control, competitive individualism, independence, aggressiveness, and the capacity for violence" (p. 82). Crime, he observes, may be one way of "doing gender," or demonstrating one's masculinity, when legitimate means of demonstrating one's identity are stifled.

Messerschmidt's thesis is that crime as a means of doing gender becomes a form of social action or a practical response to structured opportunities and constraints in society that are related to class, race, and gender relationships. Although Messerschmidt's analysis does not involve women and emphasizes the construct of masculinity, I argue that it is not simply "doing masculinity" or "doing femininity" or "doing race" that is the issue but rather doing identity. How one navigates through multiple oppressions to achieve his or her desired goals and ultimately find space and place for self in contemporary capitalist society is a complex process of which an individual's sex, age, gender, sexual identity, race, nationality, class, level of education, and a host of other factors are significant components.

This alternative paradigm suggests that the issue of crime and women (and perhaps men) with multiple vulnerabilities can be explained based on an understanding of the process of doing identity or the process of becoming somebody (self-defined) while navigating through multiple social contradictions and inequalities. Becoming somebody requires individuals to draw upon complex and advanced decision-making capabilities that can be employed at life's perpetual crossroads to assess the vulnerabilities of their social location amid the solid and liquid aspects of their reality. Here at the crossroads, individuals are challenged with the task of identifying among the plethora of ends the ones that are reasonable and feasible given their social location, circumstances, and context (Bauman, 2000). Establishing priorities in a world that appears to be full of possibilities adds complexity to the challenge, and the uncertainty of life's comparative objectives is all the more perplexing to persons facing multiple vulnerabilities in the process of doing identity.

Method

The primary aim of the methodology was to utilize a feminist and interpretive approach to the data collection, interpretation, and analysis of the life stories and reflections of incarcerated women who have committed drug-related crimes (Denzin, 1989; Lynch, 1996; Oakley, 1981). Rather than seeking results that can be generalized to broader populations, the purpose of the methodology is to ground the findings in the standpoint of the women interviewed, and ultimately, to demystify and humanize their lived experiences and perspectives while providing a range of practical explanations of the choices and behavior of women involved in drug-related crimes. This preliminary analysis focuses on the life story of one young Afro-Caribbean woman who was incarcerated in 2010 due to a drug-related crime. This analysis begins with this single case of one woman as an intentional means of avoiding conundrums inherent in (a) positivists' research that tends to quantify experiences rather than validating nuances, difference, and the production of knowledge based on a single case, and (b) androcentric approaches that reinforce the "male-stream" nature of criminology that often omit or misrepresent the experiences of women due to an emphasis on male crime (Belknap, 2001). The intention of this article is not to ignore men or avoid the rigors of scientific study involving multiple cases (both will be considered in future analysis) but simply to begin with the experiences of women and, in this case, one woman as the unit of analysis. The single case that was selected for this analysis is of a Jamaican female in her early 20s serving 2 years for attempting to transport marijuana from Jamaica to St. Maarten with the hope of earning US$900. For the purpose of telling her story, the pseudonym Angelique will be used when referring to the respondent.

The use of a single case as the unit of analysis also provides an opportunity to explore the unique ways in which the conceptual categories that make up the theoretical framework fit the particular case and allows the researcher to assess whether the constructs need further refinement before being applied to a broader set of cases. This process is purposefully iterative in nature and intends to reveal and refine conceptual categories that can be used to further feminist theorizing on the topic of women (and perhaps men) and crime.

In writing this analysis, a difficult methodological consideration I had to make was whether or not to point to a specific theory as an example of male-stream criminological theorizing. I was initially uncomfortable with using Merton's strain theory directly as a means to demonstrate the significance of the intersectional approach for examining women's criminality, and I tried to avoid doing so by looking at *strain theories* in general, but the distractions were apparent. I then considered focusing on a single aspect of one strain theory, but that did not allow me to demonstrate the potential breadth and depth of the intersectional analytical approach. To more accurately describe Angelique's circumstances as *constrained* rather than *strained,* I felt strongly that I wanted to compare and contrast the intersectional approach with an existing theoretical framework as a means to develop salient alternative concepts in relation to the findings. With this as my motivation, I felt compelled to maintain a focus on Merton's strain theory, not as a critique of the significance of the theory, but as a means to encourage continued articulation and solidification of the intersectional approach as something distinct from, yet useful within, existing theoretical traditions. The following analysis briefly describes one woman's process of navigating through multiple oppressions within a high-risk context and incorporates the concepts of (a) individual goals for success; (b) social location; (c) social contradictions, risk, and uncertainty; and (d) adaptive responses that include legitimate (legally sanctioned by dominant culture) versus illegitimate (illegal, yet sanctioned by subculture) means to achieve desired success. Together these concepts will be used to describe a unique attempt at doing identity.

Findings: There Is No Safe Place

A safe space, prison is not, but a correction facility may be the only environment where the extent to which inequality, deprivation, and the randomness of uncertainty that affect the lives of marginalized women is to some degree leveled, controlled, or restricted. In prison, there exists no class or gender deal that requires work or marriage to be successful, social location within the dominant social structure has limited significance, and the cultural goals for success are redefined to fit a new (although typically temporary) reality. Angelique's story will be discussed without a particular beginning or ending, using the concepts from the theoretical framework as a guide to explaining her journey toward crime.

Goals

Angelique states that she had her aspirations set on achieving her dream of the good life, which for her meant "becoming somebody" and consisted of obtaining an education, a job, a house, and a future for her children:

> I wanted to better my life. I wanted to give my sons a future, a good life, an education—something I never get.
>
> I wanted to own a business—be a hair dresser and own a house. I had the dream. I went to cosmetology school and got a certificate. If my sister no die we would finish school together, save our money together and open a [beauty] parlor and buy a house together.

Angelique shared the socially sanctioned belief that all are entitled to seek an array of possibilities toward achieving the good life. She believed in the class deal that if she could only find a job and work hard that she could obtain financial prosperity. Her specific goals for success included becoming a hairdresser and working in collaboration with her sister to combine the resources necessary to start a business and buy a house. Although her goals seemed reasonable and feasible, Angelique's dream of owning a salon and a home was formally disrupted when her sister died. In time, her commitment to finding legitimate means to achieve her dream of becoming somebody

began to wane. She describes how she began to lose faith in her ability achieve her goals:

> When I started college my sister died [her sister was killed by a distant relative]. From that time my life went down. We went to the same school, we were very close. After she died I lived carefree.

Social Location

Unfortunately, Angelique's unique combination of social factors and conditions that influenced her reality included a history of sexual and physical abuse, family disruption, and marginalization from social, educational, and economic resources and support. Her environment was imbued with images that included men who distributed guns to young boys, young girls that danced at strip clubs, and adults and children struggling to survive by selling chicken on the roadside while others were selling drugs. She states, "In my area, people do what they can to survive." For Angelique, these were the only examples and opportunities that were available, and it was within this limited and restricted reality that Angelique sought to achieve success.

Angelique's reality contradicted her dream of becoming somebody. As a victim of ongoing abuse by her mother and her mother's boyfriend, Angelique found it difficult to reconcile to the fate she seemed to have inherited. Her attempts to try to find a solution to her circumstances were met with disdain; repeatedly, she was silenced or ignored:

> I lived with mother, my mother's boyfriend and six siblings in one bedroom house. My mother beat me all the while. I had to wash for she, her man, and my brothers and sisters. One time after she gave me lunch money, I put it down and her boyfriend took my lunch money and gone. So I asked someone in my yard (a neighbor) for lunch money and my mom chopped me with a knife.
>
> The worst of the abuse was at night. I slept on the ground and my mom, she boyfriend and my brother and sister slept in the bed. Him (the boyfriend) come down and abuse me every

night. Me tell her and she never believe me. She love him more than me. He come on the ground and force my foot open every night. The first time I was 9 and this continued until I was 12. I continued to tell my mother what happened. One time she threw hot porridge on me to burn me and I ran. Then I start to runaway.

Compiled upon [in addition to] her experience of being repeatedly silenced at home was her feeling of being socially excluded at school. Angelique describes the first time she contemplated suicide:

> I felt like I was not human. Me don't feel like me loved. I tried to commit suicide when I was 10. My mom abuse me, he abuse me. I felt left out at school. My friends had a good life, and me no have none. She was at work and I tried to do it, then I say why kill myself. I said I will reach my goal and show my mother I can be somebody.

Angelique was not a good student academically and often got into fights at school. She stated she often felt angry at school due to her inability to discuss the victimization she experienced at home. She responded to her feelings of being excluded in school by dropping out and seeking the type of wage-paying employment that was available to young undereducated women in her neighborhood:

> I dropped out of school at age 16 and started to dance at a strip club. I made $600 JA [Jamaican dollars] a night plus tips, and I danced every day. I was able to pay some of my school fees and got in contact with my father and he helped pay my fees for me to start college [to become a hair dresser]. I danced naked freelance to make money. I had to take care of my children.

Angelique's early introduction into adulthood was void of legitimate opportunities to demonstrate the identity she sought to achieve. The abuse she suffered, the death of her sister, and the social exclusion she faced at school were a harsh introduction into the reality of the combined effects of multiple oppressions that shaped her social location and their unique impact on her ability to achieve her goals.

Contradiction and Risk

As a young adult, the only guides through the maze of uncertainty available to Angelique were the local examples of success that she befriended and others to whom she was related. All of them were engaged in socially deviant behavior. Angelique's first child was born when she was 15, and she describes the child's father as worthless because, as she states, "him no want work, I don't want that life so I move out." Angelique's observation of the father of her first child suggests that she initially sought to conform to the gender deal, by seeking a male primary breadwinner to assist her in achieving her desired reality, yet he was unable to fulfill her expectations and hope of achieving her ideal of the good life; therefore, the relationship ended.

A subsequent boyfriend was a drug dealer. This boyfriend offered Angelique an alternative means to achieve the good life and an opportunity to achieve her dreams. Life with this boyfriend meant that Angelique would have to relinquish her desire to conform to the promises of the class deal through her notion of legitimate institutionalized means and adapt to an environment in which the rules that sanctioned behavior deviated from those of the dominant society. Angelique's new reality included the indulgence in drugs, and although this boyfriend could function as the primary breadwinner, his methods for achieving wealth required her to engage in crime:

> My friends set me up with a youth who was a bad man. They had money and things. They would drink, do drugs and gamble for fun. They would rob too. If they want me to carry a gun I say I would do it, for him. With my friends I felt happy, stress free. When I smoke, things just gone. They were kind of like a family. I prefer to be with them than my own. I always felt burdened when I came home [to my mother], but I never felt like that with them. I would rob, but mainly with my boyfriend.

For Angelique, her new family allowed her the freedom to combine the class and gender deals, albeit through illegitimate means, and to adopt an acceptable (if not desired) reality (identity). Unfortunately, this new reality did not free Angelique from risk, as the abuse she suffered from her mother was replaced by exploitation.

> [When I went to England to live with my boyfriend] I had to send money two times a week to my mother because she was taking care of my children. My mother cravin' [is greedy]. She wanted to carry it [drugs] up [from Jamaica to England]. I told her she was not ready, but she neva stop. She wanted to come to England. So we gave her ganja [marijuana] in a tin and some coke [cocaine]. She get catch [arrested] in Jamaica. I flew down and my boyfriend too. She was in jail and we had to put $100,000 [Jamaican dollars to post bond].

Adaptive Response

Disruption in Angelique's life continued as her boyfriend was also arrested after returning to England. With her primary source of income gone, Angelique adapted to this change by relying on her own income-earning abilities to obtain the means to maintain her mother's now abandoned children as well as her own. With the bulk of her experience, networks, and opportunities concentrated around her boyfriend's illegal endeavors, Angelique inherited his business and began to engage in the transportation of drugs:

> My boyfriend got 17 years. He got caught with drugs and guns in the house. I had to start to carry drugs to small islands in a suitcase. The drugs were built into the suitcase. I traveled every week carrying ganja from Jamaica [to England] and coke [from England] back to Jamaica, Grenada, St. Maarten and Panama. With 3–4 pounds of weed I could make $800 US and with 1 kilo of coke, $900 US for myself. My boss would send money to immigration to clear my way and collect the money, but I don't know his name.

Upon reflection, Angelique says she realizes that she could have made better choices. She stated that she could

have obviously continued to go to school to be a hairdresser and potential salon owner after her sister died, as an example, yet with an understanding of her social location and history of risks and contradictions, she may have had little faith that her conformity to the class deal would have resulted in the trappings of the good life she imagined. In Angelique's quest to become somebody, the lack of available legitimate examples, means, and opportunities to help augment her ability to navigate through the complexities of multiple subjugations, uncertainties, risks, and contradictions she encountered was compensated by adaptive responses characterized by increasing levels of deviance.

As an ex-offender, upon her release, Angelique may find her options for access to education and the formal labor market further restricted. When pressed to specify the choices she plans to make in the future upon her release from prison, as if acknowledging the high degree of uncertainty she will face given the addition of the label of *ex-offender* to the other vulnerabilities that characterize her social location, Angelique spoke with ambiguity and then with resolve:

> I want to get a job and go to [cosmetology] school in England, but me don't know what me may do [when I get out of prison]. I don't know my situation. I may go back into it [carrying drugs].

For Angelique, the American Dream has been replaced by a reality that reflects her limitations and the constraints, circumscription, and contradictions within society. For Angelique and other vulnerable men and women, the process of doing identity is wrought with constraints and barriers that place their reach just short of their aspirations. Angelique attempts to define herself, achieve her dreams, and possibly benefit from the class and gender deals ascribed for women in society, yet her attempts are met with a dearth of feasible and legitimate options that are compensated by illicit ones. A life of crime, for Angelique, becomes the practical solution to social and economic conditions that are ripe with uncertainty and contradictions.

Angelique's profile of vulnerabilities and inequalities fits those of other women who may turn to crime as a solution to life's limitations. She is young, poor, non-white, a high school dropout, an unmarried mother, and unemployed and has a history of family violence, sexual abuse, and some drug use. Throughout her life, the impact of the combination of these factors remained virtually ignored by all but one social institution (the prison) and the "family of friends" that she adopted as a refuge and escape from her own. Her new family provided her with an example of how to obtain the tokens and semblance of the good life that could be acquired through illegal means. Due to the random and incremental accumulation of loss and lack in addition to the deprived conditions she inherited, in time Angelique became removed from her vision of being somebody and achieving her goals through legitimate means and decided to join her new family in search of some remnant of a dream. Eventually, she ends up in prison, with little hope of finding alternative means to navigate through the inequalities and social contradictions that face her upon release.

One of the unanticipated findings this analysis revealed is the extent to which motherhood factors into women's decisions to commit crime or continue to pursue their dreams through legitimate means while confronting adversity. Angelique described how her children were the source of her motivation for achieving her goals and her sole inspiration in difficult times; here, she states how her children give her the will to live despite continued abuse and challenges:

> I tried to commit suicide again. A girl told me what to buy, and I tried to kill myself. I drink some, but not enough, and then I vomit, vomit, vomit. I got weak, and pale and my mother took me to the hospital. During the drive to the hospital my mother told me I was wicked. I spent weeks in the hospital. In the hospital I was thinking about my son. He so bad loves me, and I said I would never do that again. When I came out, I got involved with a youth [a young boy] and got pregnant again. My children give me the strength to move, they make me want to live.

For Angelique, like many mothers, her children function as a tremendous source of encouragement in the midst of uncertainty. Despite the option to forfeit parental responsibilities due to strained social and economic conditions, many mothers continue to try to care for their children. Perhaps this phenomenon of commitment despite uncertainty can be described as another deal that can be added to Carlen's class and gender deals. The mother deal can be found at the intersection between the class and gender deals where the belief that the good life (as defined in noneconomic and more affective terms) results from a mother's dedication to her children. Crime results when illegitimate options for mothers to meet the needs of their children as well as their own are more readily available than those that are legitimate. Tapping into this bond between some mothers and their children as a way to guide and nurture their progress toward the achievement of their goals through legitimate means may lead to innovative policy and programmatic responses to female criminality.

Conclusion: Policy Implications

Although Adler (1975) contends that women's liberation resulted in increasing levels of women's willful criminality, her thesis fails to explain the higher likelihood of young, poor, non-white, high school dropouts, unmarried mothers, un/underemployed or educated, with a history of drug problems, family violence, and sexual abuse, to be represented among incarcerated women. If a correlation between women's liberation and an increase in women's criminality exists, perhaps this is due to the increased vulnerability of marginalized women to being criminalized as a result of punitive polices that blame them for the same conditions that constrain their progress.

The State through its promotion of policy, norms, and ideology contributes to the illusion that the financial prosperity of the affluent is somehow justified due to their hard work, integrity, and good choices. The consequence of upholding this belief is that it supports the claim that a life of less for others is often attributed to their own individual pathologies, deficiencies, and lack of conformity; and therefore, should the less affluent become deviant, they should be removed from society and punished. To effectively remove the constraints that limit access to *legitimate* options for the vulnerable to achieve an equitable reality would mean breaking the illusion of justified position or class in society and creating a new ideology, norms, institutions (safe places), and social policies that have the notions of interdependency and collective responsibility at the core. Rather than advocating the need for a revolution to combat crime, Left Realists would recommend, and I agree, that the focus of policy and interventions must be on creating communities of care that rebuild neighborhoods and encourage social responsibility and community cohesion as strategies to mitigate against the relative depravation that affects the life outcomes of vulnerable individuals. Left Realist criminologists are critical of conservative policies that seek to build more prisons and lengthen sentences to deal with crime and are supportive of realistic solutions that fit within the existing social framework (Young, 1997). The increasing incarceration rate for women due to drug-related crimes suggests a need to revisit short-sighted legislative policies and to develop opportunities to prevent women's criminality through intervention at the micro (individual and family) and mezzo (groups and community) levels of society. One example of an innovative intervention that seeks to reduce social isolation and capitalizes on the potential bond between mothers and their children is the creation of women-centered kinship networks consisting of a community of fictive and biological mothers, aunts, grandmothers, and nonparents, some of whom may be education and social service providers who can function as sources of support, examples, guidance, and communal child care for young mothers who may be at risk of dropping out of school, engaging in crime, or other forms of deviance (Collins, 2000; Mullins, 1997; White, 1985).

Nonresponsive policies and programs have resulted from a lack of understanding of the complex influence of multiple forms of oppression on women's lives and have rendered many marginalized women virtually invisible (Belknap, 2001). Addressing the problem of women and crime requires society to be willing to confront its failures, including its core ideologies, institutions, norms, and policies that justify a war on marginalized women (and men) under the guise of a war on drugs (Chesney-Lind, 1991). The challenge is for theorizing on female criminality to complicate male-stream perspectives on women's criminality by including more empirical studies that seek to deconstruct one-dimensional and essentialist understandings of women's lives while intentionally exploring the interconnected, constraining, and multiple, yet unique, manifestations of power and oppression. The praxis of feminist criminology serves as a reminder that alternative theorizing, policy, and programmatic provisions in support of innovative interventions designed to nurture the development of each member of society are needed. An intersectional approach to feminist criminology functions to confront the collective culpability of all members of society in perpetuating oppressive ideologies and structures that favor the progress of the elite over those who, like Angelique, have limited means to escape the margins.

/// DISCUSSION QUESTIONS

1. How does feminist criminology explain the criminality of Angelique?

2. How does this approach differ from other theoretical standpoints? What might other theories of crime have to offer to this analysis?

3. What value do case studies provide when conducting research? What are the limitations to this method of analysis?

References

Adler, F. (1975). *Sisters in crime*. New York, NY: McGraw-Hill.

Baca Zinn, M., & Thornton Dill, B. (1996). Theorizing difference from multiracial feminism. *Feminist Studies, 22*(2), 321–331.

Barak, G. (1998). *Integrating criminologies*. Boston, MA: Allyn & Bacon.

Bauman, Z. (2000). *Liquid modernity*. Cambridge, UK: Polity.

Beale, F. (1995). Double jeopardy: To be Black and female. In B. Guy-Sheftall (Ed.), *Words of fire: An anthology of African-American feminist thought* (p. 146–155). New York, NY: New Press. (Original work published 1970)

Beck, U. (1992). *Risk society: Towards a new modernity*. New Delhi, India: Sage.

Belknap, J. (2001). *The invisible woman: Gender, crime and justice.* Belmont, CA: Wadsworth.

Britton, D. M. (2004). Feminism in criminology: Engendering the outlaw. In P. J. Schram & B. Koons-Witt (Eds.), *Gendered (in) justice: Theory and practice in feminist criminology* (p. 49–67). Long Grove, IL: Waveland.

Broidy, L., & Agnew, R. (1997). Gender and crime: A general strain theory perspective. *Journal of Research in Crime and Delinquency, 34*(3), 275–306.

Brown, G. (2010). *The intersectionality of race, gender, and reentry: Challenges for African- American women* (Issue Brief: 1–18). Washington, DC: American Constitution Society for Law and Policy.

Burgess-Proctor, A. (2006). Intersections of race, class, gender, and crime: Future directions for feminist criminology. *Feminist Criminology, 1*(1), 24–47.

Carlen, P. (1985). *Criminal woman.* Cambridge, UK: Polity.

Carlen, P. (1988). *Women, crime and poverty.* London, UK: Open University Press.

Chesney-Lind, M. (1986). Women and crime: The female offender. *Signs, 12*(1), 78–96.

Chesney-Lind, M. (1991). Patriarchy, prisons and jails: A critical look at trends in women's incarceration. *The Prison Journal, 51*(11), 51–67.

Chesney-Lind, M. (1997). *The female offender: Girls, women and crime.* Thousand Oaks, CA: Sage.

Collins, P. H. (2000). *Black feminist thought: Knowledge, consciousness, and the politics of empowerment* (2nd ed.). New York, NY: Routledge.

Curra, J. (2000). *The relativity of deviance.* Thousand Oaks, CA: Sage.

Daly, K., & Chesney-Lind, M. (1988). Feminism and criminology. *Justice Quarterly, 5*(4), 497–535.

Daly, K., & Stephens, D. J. (1995). The "dark figure" of criminology: Towards a Black and multi-ethnic feminist agenda for theory and research. In N. Hahn Rafter & F. Heidensohn (Eds.), *International feminist perspectives in criminology: Engendering a discipline* (p. 189–215). Philadelphia, PA: Open University Press.

Dekeseredy, W., & Perry, B. (2006). *Advancing critical criminology: Theory and application.* Lanham, MD: Lexington Books.

Denzin, N. K. (1989). *Interpretive interactionism.* Thousand Oaks, CA: Sage.

Gordon, V. V. (1987). *Black women, feminism and Black liberation: Which way?* Chicago, IL: Third World Press.

Harding, S. (Ed.). (2004). *The feminist standpoint theory reader.* London, UK: Routledge.

Kelly, M. (1994). *Critique and power: Recasting the Foucault/ Habermas debate.* Boston: MIT Press.

King, D. K. (1988). Multiple jeopardy, multiple consciousness: The context of Black feminist ideology. *Signs: Journal of Women in Culture and Society, 14*(1), 42–72.

Lynch, M. J. (1996). Class, race, gender and criminology: Structured choices and the life course. In D. Milovanovic & M. D. Schwartz (Eds.), *Race, gender, and class in criminology: The intersections* (p. 3–28). New York, NY: Garland.

Maidment, M. (2006). Transgressing boundaries: Feminist perspectives in criminology. In W. DeKeseredy & B. Perry (Eds.), *Advancing critical criminology: Theory and application* (p. 43–62). Lanham, MD: Lexington Books.

Merton, R. (1968). *Social theory and social structure* (enlarged edition). New York, NY: Free Press.

Messerschmidt, J. (1993). *Masculinities and crime: Critique and reconceptualization of theory.* Lantham, MD: Rowman and Littlefield.

Mullins, L. (1997). *On our own terms: Race, class and gender in the lives of African American women.* New York, NY: Routledge.

Oakley, A. (1981). Interviewing women: A contradiction in terms. In H. Roberts (Ed.), *Doing feminist research* (p. 30–62). London, UK: Routledge & Kegan Paul.

Owen, B. (1998). *"In the mix": Struggle and survival in a women's prison.* Albany, NY: SUNY Press.

Potter, H. (2006). An argument for Black feminist criminology: Understanding African American women's experiences with intimate partner abuse using an integrated approach. *Feminist Criminology, 1*(2), 106–124.

Reiman, J. (2003). *The rich get richer and the poor get prison: Ideology, class, and criminal justice* (7th ed.). Boston, MA: Allyn & Bacon.

Ritchie, B. E. (1996). *Compelled to crime: The gender entrapment of battered Black women.* New York, NY: Routledge.

Ritchie, B. E. (2004). Feminist ethnographies of women in prison. *Feminist Studies, 30*(2), 438–450.

White, D. (1985). *Ar'n't I a woman? Female slaves in the Plantation South.* New York, NY: Norton.

Wing, A. K. (Ed.). (2003). *Critical race feminism: A reader* (2nd ed.). New York: New York University Press.

Young, J. (1997). Left Realist criminology: Radical in its analysis, realist in its policy. In M. Maguire (Ed.), *The Oxford handbook of criminology* (p. 473–498). Oxford, UK: Oxford University Press.

READING /// 12

This reading looks at how original works of criminological theory failed to investigate issues of gender with theorizing about delinquency and criminology, and concludes with a discussion on the future opportunities for feminist criminology.

Has Criminology Awakened From Its "Androcentric Slumber"?

Kimberly J. Cook

The purpose of this article is to trace some of the foundations and impacts of feminist criminology within the field. Doing so is prompted by two factors: the 30th anniversary of the American Society of Criminology (ASC; www.asc41.com) Division on Women and Crime (DWC; http://ascdwc.com), and the 10th anniversary of our journal *Feminist Criminology*. Others have documented the history of the DWC (Rasche, 2014), and during the 2014 conference, many special sessions were devoted to our 30th anniversary. One of the crowning achievements of the DWC (so far) is our journal launched in 2006 with its focus on feminist research within criminology. I have been active in the ASC/DWC since 1989 and have served on many committees as an officer of the DWC since that time. Feminist criminology has been largely motivated by the acknowledgment that gendered analysis of crime is vitally important to the field, and that sexism influences social life in ways that are nuanced, complex, and enduring. We are also motivated to produce knowledge that can be used to inform policy and practice related to violence against women and girls, incarcerated women and girls, gendered injustices throughout society, and impacts related to broad social policies that contribute to the oppression of women and girls. In addition, more recently, feminist criminologists have been much more explicit about examining the specific complexities of sexism and racism as companions of social inequalities overall.

The feminist critique offered here emerges from an exploration of missed opportunities within criminology to analyze gender and crime, and a marriage-of-sorts between criminology's exploration of the impacts of socioeconomic oppressions and non-dualistic feminist epistemologies (Collins, 1991). This exploration claims in effect: "*Yes*, social class inequality is certainly important, *and* let's also expand our scope of concern to gender inequalities, racialized inequalities, and inequalities based on sexual orientation." Conventional quantitative criminology is deeply invested in large datasets that help to measure the impacts of theoretically framed independent variables on dependent variables while controlling for multiple other independent variables. Conventional approaches have much to offer and still have a long way to go when it comes to analyzing how gender, race, social class, and heteronormativity impact crime. Rather than ask if gender, race, class, or other social characteristics are more important, feminist criminologists have been saying "yes, and . . . " to these findings. *Yes*, it is important to study social class and crime *and* we need to expand our conceptualizations of crime to more fully so as to examine gender, race, socioeconomic class, heteronormativity, and their impacts on crime. This article offers a reflection on lost chances and an appreciation for the emergence of feminist intersectional criminology. It is also a plea for continuing to expand our analysis of these

SOURCE: Cook, K. J. (2016). Has criminology awakened from its "Androcentric Slumber"?. *Feminist Criminology, 11*(4), 334–353.

social dynamics in criminology. As the field evolves, the *yes/and* scholars push the research into new directions that interrogate and illuminate complex impacts on crime and crime control.

Criminological Theory on Gender and Crime: A History of Missed Opportunities

When Edwin Sutherland first defined criminology in 1924 as the study of law-making, law-breaking, and social reaction to it (Sutherland & Cressey, 1974), criminology was already established through the work of classical scholars mainly concerned with the techniques of control and punishment (Garland, 1990). Main arenas of concern included how to punish men to dissuade them from committing crime (deterrence theory from Beccaria and Bentham; Beirne, 1993). Early scholars focused almost exclusively on men as criminals and as inmates, and it was—and in some cases remains—taken for granted that men and boys were the objects of study in most generalizable criminological research. Yet this empirical pattern alone has rarely been interrogated. Problems of gendered and racialized patterns of criminal offending have been apparent from the start of the discipline but, until the emergence of feminist criminology, were rarely analyzed as conceptual subjects in and of themselves. Sutherland and Cressey (1974) offer their view on the "sex ratio" of criminal offending:

> . . . no other trait has as great a statistical importance as does sex in differentiating criminals from noncriminals. But no one feels that he [*sic*] has an explanation of criminality when he learns that the criminal is male . . . The variations in the sex ratio in crime are so great that it can be concluded that maleness is *not* significant in the causation of crime in itself but only as it indicates social position, supervision, and other social relations. Moreover, since boys and girls live in the same homes, in equal poverty, and with equally ignorant parents, and live in the same neighborhoods, which are equally lacking in facilities for organized recreation, these conditions of the social environment *cannot* be considered causes of delinquency . . .

Probably the most important difference is that girls are supervised more carefully and behave in accordance with anticriminal behavior patterns taught to them with greater care and consistency than in the case of boys. (p. 129–130, emphasis added)

Their explanation for this sex ratio difference is found in gendered familial supervision strategies of parents. And so, with the stroke of the pen, Sutherland and Cressey proclaim that the leading predictor of crime is inconsequential to understanding the causes of crime, and amputated gender from serious consideration by the scholarly community for decades to come.

They were more inclined to acknowledge that racial bias exists within the crime control apparatus in the United States:

> Numerous studies have shown that African Americans are more likely to be arrested, indicted, convicted, and committed to an institution than are whites who commit the same offenses, and many other studies have shown that blacks have a poorer chance than whites to receive probation, a suspended sentence, parole, commutation of a death sentence, or pardon. (Sutherland & Cressey, 1974, p. 133)

They continued with a review of research findings on racial bias as it relates to Black Americans, including reference to a study from which they concluded that in "urban Negro communities the problems of divergent mores, real or assumed, are most apparent at the police level" (Sutherland & Cressey, 1974, p. 134). They go on to examine official crime statistics relating to "White, Negro, Indian, Chinese, and Japanese" people who were arrested. And, finally, they offer cross-tabulations of arrest rates by race and gender. About these trends, Sutherland and Cressey (1974) argue that "they can be explained only by social interaction. The specific theory of social interaction which explains these racial ratios in crime has not been determined" (p. 140).

Taking those social interactions more seriously, for example, let us turn to the classic study *Delinquent Boys* by Albert Cohen (1955). As evidenced by its title, Cohen understood that he was examining delinquency among urban boys—not girls, not women—and, yet, he did not take issues of gender *qua* gender as serious contributing factors affecting the crime experiences of these boys. We can applaud his sensitivity to the social class issues associated with boys' delinquency (particularly the "middle-class measuring rod") and regret that criminology did not benefit as much from his intellect where masculinity is concerned. When gender rose to the level of his concern, he wrote,

> Social class status, we observed, is a status position shared by members of a family; that, in turn, is determined primarily by the lineage, wealth, personal qualities and, above all, the occupational achievement of the husband and father . . . The wife and children, by improper behavior, can seriously "reflect on the family" and thus deprive it of some of the status to which it might otherwise be entitled . . . Furthermore, it is the male who carries the largest share of the *moral responsibility* for his family's status. His wife and children may feel shame if the family's position falls because of the father's unemployment, business failure, or other occupational or financial reverses, but the "fault" is likely to be imputed to the father and the burden of guilt to rest most heavily on him . . . The woman has more to gain by "marrying up" and more to lose by "marrying down." (Cohen, 1955, p. 141)[1]

Cohen alludes to aspects of ethnic backgrounds as examples of "subcultures" but does not fully employ the concepts associated with racial inequality to examine boys' delinquency. Early in the book, Cohen (1955) writes that "the contrasting ways of Hindus, Chinese and Navahos are for the most part a matter of indoctrination into a different culture" (p. 12). It is within subcultures then that, according to Cohen (1955), "boys' gangs flourish most conspicuously in [] our larger American cities . . . " (p. 13). From there, he moves on to social class differences and his famous exploration of the "middle-class measuring rod":

> Systematic class-linked differences in the ability to achieve will relegate to the bottom of the status pyramid those children belonging to the

most disadvantaged classes, not by virtue of their position as such but by virtue of their lack of the requisite personal qualifications resulting from their class-linked handicaps. (Cohen, 1955, p. 86)

Cohen's contributions are classics in the field, and he deserves a great deal of credit for exploring the impacts of social inequalities on the problem of juvenile crime. It is from this platform that he created a perspective that later generations of scholars would continue to shape, particularly within the broader area of critical criminology. Still, while Cohen's focus was adolescent boys, gender and race as contributing social conditions in and of themselves were not central to his analysis, resulting in another missed opportunity. Similar points could be made regarding other classics in criminology (i.e., Shaw & McKay, 1942; Thomas & Znaniecki, 1918/1974), though it is beyond the capacity of this article to fully document this theme in those works.

Mainstream Contemporary Criminology

I focus now on two types of mainstream criminological theory as illustrated in the books *A General Theory of Crime* (Gottfredson & Hirschi, 1990) and *Lifecourse Theory* (Sampson & Laub, 1993). Both claim to offer generalizable explanations of criminal offending. My rationale for exploring these two stems from an empirical trend I have observed anecdotally and statistically over 22 years as a faculty member with experience in hiring (including 10 as a chair), and over 27 years attending ASC conferences, hundreds of dissertation titles, conference presentations, and papers have been written by scholars concerned with control and lifecourse theories. In this context, *A General Theory of Crime* is arguably influential indeed for empirical research, having inspired quantitative analyses frequently used in doctoral dissertations and published research. Furthermore, one could contend that this theoretical orientation has attracted funding central for doctoral training in criminology. Searching online produces over 177,000 scholarly articles and 57 books associated with *A General Theory of Crime*.[2] Second, I consider lifecourse theory as another important perspective within mainstream criminology that has provided rich analyses of crime causation over a lifetime. Here, a quick search online produces more than 600 scholarly articles and two books related to "lifecourse theory of crime." Both theoretical traditions document that men/boys are most actively engaged in criminal offending, but neither digs deeply into gender as an analytical frame. Another scholar may have chosen different traditions to explore for equally valid reasons.

In the preface to their book, Gottfredson and Hirschi (1990) pose the question "why are men, adolescents, and minorities more likely than their counterparts to commit criminal acts?" (p. xvi). Clearly this indicates that the examination presented incorporates gender and race, in addition to age, which has been this theory's most enduring contribution. They broaden the conception of crime beyond the legalistic definition to include "acts of force or fraud undertaken in pursuit of pleasure" (Gottfredson & Hirschi, 1990, p. 15). Operationalizing these forms of force and fraud revolves largely around the standard Uniform Crime Report's conception of conventional crime: burglary, robbery, homicide, rape, and embezzlement; it also includes white-collar crime and substance abuse–related crimes. Criminality arises as a consequence of "low self-control," and people with low self-control are more likely to be "versatile" in their criminality where "offenders commit a wide variety of criminal acts" instead of "specializing" in specific types of crimes (p. 91). According to Gottfredson and Hirschi, "ineffective child-rearing" is the main cause of low self-control and includes parental failures to monitor, recognize, and punish deviant behavior (p. 97). Ultimately, they argue that "single-parent families" are "among the most powerful predictors of crime rates" (p. 103). They point out that the single parent "(usually a woman)" (p. 104) is less able to monitor, recognize, and punish deviant behavior. Observing gendered patterns of criminal offending, they write that "men are always and everywhere more likely than women to commit criminal acts" (p. 143), and ultimately they imply that women, especially single mothers, are responsible for the problem while not excavating these patterns. As for race/ethnic patterns associated with criminal offending, Gottfredson and Hirschi (1990) dispute the "inequality thesis" (p. 152) and argue that race and crime is also a consequence of low self-control rather than merely a consequence of system bias or social discrimination; they contend this is a "fruitless" effort (p. 153).

Gottfredson and Hirschi perpetuate androcentric conceptions within criminology (Potter, 2015). Potter (2015) documents that Gottfredson and Hirschi "did not consider differential socioeconomic effects and cultural, racial, or religious dynamics" contributing to crime and therefore the analysis they present "appears to be based on . . . a colonialist, White, middle-class framework" (p. 92). Consequently, they dismiss volumes of criminological research documenting that gender is the leading predictor of crime (Braithwaite, 1989; Flavin, 2001). Like Sutherland and Cressy, and Cohen, again, they miss (or ignore) another important opportunity to advance our understanding of gender and crime.

Sampson and Laub (1993) present a highly regarded mainstream criminological exploration of crime; they use rich longitudinal data from the famous Glueck and Glueck studies of juvenile delinquency among males. A quick scan of the index indicates that issues of gender and crime do not factor into their main points as there are no entries for the following concepts: sex or sex ratio, gender, masculinity, males, females, or femininity. Similarly, race and ethnicity include merely three page references in the index. Sampson and Laub (1993) conduct extensive follow-up interviews with the Gluecks's original participants and document experiences of crime throughout their lives. Employing lessons from Hirschi's original social bond theory, particularly as it relates to the observed patterns associated with age and crime, Sampson and Laub are mainly interested in how crime continues to impact their lives, and advance the field by documenting long-term consequences. Their exploration of these mens' life histories offers a significant methodological contribution to the field that should not be overlooked. But, as one reads their analysis, it is obvious that the men are "gendered beings" even if the scholars themselves do not interrogate this meaning. For instance, in the case of Candil, Sampson and Laub document Candil's violent behavior toward his wife. They write that the

> source of the trouble appeared to be that the subject drank excessively, which led to much arguing in the home . . . He accused his wife of being a "tramp" when he married her . . . the marital relationship involved a fair share of bickering and arguing and was marked by

temporary separations, neglect, and assault. (Sampson & Laub, 1993, p. 208)

By claiming that the source of the violence was from excessive alcohol use, the authors missed an opportunity to explore the facets of masculinity that, by 1993, had been well documented in the research on violence against women (Dobash & Dobash, 1979; Martin, 1976; Pizzey, 1977), and after the "drunken-bum" theory of violence against women had been debunked (Kantor & Straus, 1987).

As for racial/ethnic patterns associated with their (White) subjects' experiences with crime, Sampson and Laub (1993) argue that

the Glueck data allow us to discuss crime in a "deracialized" and, we hope, depoliticized context . . . we believe that the causes of crime across the life course are not rooted in race[3] . . . but rather in structural disadvantage, weakened by informal social bonds to family, school, and work, and the disruption of social relations between individuals and institutions that provide social capital. (p. 254–255)

Still, one needs to bear in mind that at the time the Gluecks were collecting their data, ethnic differences among Whites included contours of structural disadvantage: Irish and Italian identities, for instance, were not considered "White" in the same way we conceive this today (Ignatiev, 1995). They venture into the policy/political realm in the next paragraph by acknowledging structural disadvantages:

imprisonment may have powerful negative effects on the prospects of future employment and job stability. In turn, low income, unemployment, and underemployment are themselves linked to heightened risks of family disruption. Through its negative effects on male employment, imprisonment may thus lead indirectly through family disruption to increase in future rates of crime and violence. The extremely high incarceration rate of young black males [] renders this scenario very real. (p. 255)

This early acknowledgment of gender/race/economic class disadvantage may be an indication that lifecourse theory helps criminology interrogate gender, race, class, and heteronormativity. But Sampson and Laub do not extend their analysis to such questions. Unfortunately, they continue to argue that their findings "can be applied to all individuals" (Potter, 2015, p. 105). Thus, while we can applaud the lessons of their analysis, particularly regarding structural disadvantages, it is regretable that these criminologists continued the historical story of missed opportunities to analyze gender and racial as well as class-based dynamics. One might expect that within critical criminology, the examination of gender and race would be more central. Let us turn to this question next.

Turning to Critical Criminology

Whereas lifecourse theory explicitly "deracialized" and "depoliticized" crime, critical criminology began to embrace, explain, and expand policy-oriented critiques of crime and its control. Still, the social realities of gender remained largely invisible to the visionaries in critical criminology; until the 21st century, androcentrism continued without in-depth study of power dynamics associated with gender. On the contrary, critical criminology proffered keen analyses of power dynamics: Its scholarship has been geared toward promoting progressive political agendas to combat social class and racialized inequalities (DeKeseredy, 2011). According to DeKeseredy (2011), "critical criminology is defined as a perspective that views the major sources of crime as the unequal class, race/ethnic, and gender relations that control our society" (p. 7). DeKeseredy (2011), citing Gelsthorpe and Morris (1988), acknowledges that early critical criminology was "gender-blind" (p. 27), and that androcentrism remains a problem within some of the critical criminological studies published.

Taking on the challenge of economic analyses, early critical criminologists theoretically established links between social class inequality and crime (Chambliss, 1975; Spitzer, 1975; Taylor, Walton, & Young, 1973). In doing so, they identified a major area of concern and began to explore the contours of racial inequality present in crime/justice issues. A key accomplishment of critical criminology included commitment to being proximal to the subjects whose lives they were documenting

(DeKeseredy, 2011). By prioritizing analyses of the exercise of unequal power, critical criminologists exposed vastly different worlds associated with street crime versus corporate crime (Chambliss, 1975; Christie, 1977, 1993; Friedrichs, 1996; Michalowski, 1985). They showed, among other studies, how political economy determines so much about crimes' definition and prosecution (Chambliss, 1975); how the state has the power to "steal" our experiences of crime and render us voiceless when pursuing redress (Christie, 1977); how a vast industry of crime control emerged in modern Western societies (Christie, 1993); how analogous social injury is to serious injury, and real people suffer real harms even when inflicted by the powerful through corporate violence (Michalowski, 1985); and how "trusted criminals" can be far more dangerous than stereotypical criminals (Friedrichs, 1996).

Moreover, critical criminologist Raymond Michalowski (1985) can be credited for writing a section of one chapter that examined gender and crimes of the powerless. He focused on women as offenders in property crimes, and tackles debates over "sex-roles" and crime using available research literature at the time. According to Michalowski, "while many women may be more psychologically prepared to participate in formerly 'masculine' property crimes as a result of sex-role changes, an equally important factor is the deteriorating economic position of women" (Michalowski, 1985, p. 304). He went on to offer additional points regarding socioeconomic patterns associated with women's involvement in property crimes. Feminist criminologists would react to such points by saying "*yes*, that's a good point" *and* "let's not overlook that men are gendered beings too, so let's extend the ideas of inequality to consider masculinity."

Roger Matthews and Jock Young (1992) directly tackled feminist critiques of criminology; they expressed support for more feminist research on gender and crime as well as consternation with then-current debates in the field. For instance, "there can be little doubt that the impact of feminists on criminological thinking has been one of the most productive and progressive inputs into the subject over the last decade or so" (p. 14). Matthews and Young moved on to summarize "two broad trajectories" of feminist criminology, the political and epistemological. The former includes classification of feminist theories as liberal, Marxist, radical, or socialist; the latter includes "postmodernist, standpoint feminist and empiricist"

criminology, to which they devote deeper consideration. They cite Maureen Cain as an example of standpoint feminist criminology and query "that people from the same standpoint do not speak with the same voice but often speak with competing and oppositional voices. How do we know which voices are authentic?" (Matthews & Young, 1992, p. 15). This desire to ascertain what is authentic, true, and accurate stems from quests for certain knowledge. The epistemological frame is based on the binary notion that if one truth is accurate, then the other is false: Allegedly, one perspective or experience is "true" and the other not. One of the most important lessons of feminist criminology, though, is that all voices are—or at least can be—authentic. Moreover, different voices reveal varying experiences with common problems, all of which are "real" to those experience myriad oppressions. Using Patricia Hill Collins (1991), I would suggest that in this sense, the work of Matthews and Young was insufficiently multidimensional and could have benefited from feminist insights using "both/and" rather than "either/or" frameworks of analysis and understanding. It is the "both/and" framework, more than "either/or" perspectives, that comes closer to approximating the lived experiences of ordinary people who have been crime victims and/or offenders.

Feminist Contributions and Clarifications

In 1988, Daly and Chesney-Lind (1988) explore the foundations and contours of feminist theory and its applicability to criminology; they argued "criminologists should begin to appreciate that their discipline and its questions are a product of White, economically privileged men's experiences" (p. 506). Observing that Canadian and British criminologists were documenting gendered patterns of crime, Daly and Chesney-Lind (1988) write that "their work signaled an awakening of criminology from its androcentric slumber" (p. 507). Five years later, Renzetti (1993) writes about similar needs for the discipline to take gender and race more seriously, and in frustration asked, "why should I have to make this case *again*?" (p. 232, emphasis in the original). Hannon and Dufour (1998) document androcentrism within criminological research. They were specifically interested in measuring if criminological research with men-only samples generalized their findings to "all" crimes (male-bias in generalizability), and if research with women-only samples also suggested their findings were generalizable to "all" crimes. Their findings showed, in part, that "male only studies typically overgeneralized their titles, and [] almost all female only studies specified the limits of generalizability in their titles" (p. 69). Other scholars have documented androcentrism within criminology as well (Baro & Eigenberg, 1993; Eigenberg & Baro, 1992). Britton (2000) bluntly states that "[g]iven men's overrepresentation as offenders and victims, the screaming silence in criminology around the connection between masculinity and crime has always been something of a paradox" (p. 73).

Jeanne Flavin (2001) invites mainstream criminologists to appreciate and embrace feminist insights within criminology as "[g]ender is the strongest predictor of criminal involvement: boys and men perpetrate more, and more serious crimes than do girls and women" (p. 273). She argued that gender and race biases within the field led to epistemological blind spots that do not appreciate the complex nuances of crime. She rightly points out that

> recognition of the importance of epistemology and the biases of scientific method lies at the core of transforming the discipline. Gaining a better understanding of gender and crime requires not only filling in gaps in knowledge but also challenging the assumptions upon which existing knowledge is based. (Flavin, 2001, p. 275)

In addition, Flavin (2001) argues that "feminism challenges criminology to reject androcentric thinking" and to be "thoughtful and relevant" (p. 281). When these concerns are overlooked or rejected, she insists, the discipline loses opportunities for sharper analysis on relevant social interactions that perpetuate crime and victimization; moreover, we lose opportunities to improve social policy and practice.

Within sociology as well as criminology, theories of "doing gender" and of intersectionality have also moved the study of gender and crime beyond the androcentric past. A paradigm shift occurred in feminist theory when West and Zimmerman (1987) published their now-famous article "Doing Gender." Renzetti (2013) documents this as the most widely cited article published in *Gender and Society* with its vivid description of a "fluid, dynamic

conceptualization of gender as accomplishment" (p. 51).[4] Later, West and Fenstermaker (1995) expand the concept beyond gender alone, positing that we do gender as much as we do ethnicity, race, and social class. Within criminology, this theoretical advance has contributed significant knowledge to understanding crime and victimization (Cook, 2006; Messerschmidt, 1993, 1997; Miller, 2002). Within criminology, a cornerstone of this approach has been Messerschmidt's (1997) argument that crime is "resource" for doing gender (specifically masculinity): men and boys use crime to demonstrate their masculinities. A critique of doing gender theory, though, is that it reinforces rather than challenges gendered binaries (Renzetti, 2013). It is a critique applied and presented by Jody Miller (2002), who writes that "recognizing gender as a *situated* action allows for recognition of agency, but does so in a way thoroughly grounded in the contexts of structural inequalities such as those of gender, sexuality, race, class and age" (p. 434). Jody Miller's (2001, 2002, 2008) work has advanced this theoretical insight into the realm of women and girls' criminal offending beyond a gendered binary. Renzetti (2013) suggests that this theoretical framework has helped to expose "a multitude of masculinities and femininities as well as the agency that social actors exercise in constructing these multiple identities" (p. 56).

An additional component to "doing gender" and/or "doing difference" is accountability—that is, being held accountable by others to gender, race, class, heteronormative scripts that are meant to guide behavior (Cook, 2006). While observing restorative justice diversionary conferences in Australia and New Zealand, I noted that the dynamics of accountability are heavily gendered, raced, and classed. In social life, people are expected to behave in ways that conform to gendered scripts and are held accountable for failing to do so. For example, Connell (cited by Cook, 2006) outlines the concept of gender projects, stating that "men and boys accomplish their gender projects by aspiring towards hegemonic masculine practice, whereas girls and women typically aspire towards emphasized feminine practice" (p. 108). In other words, through social life, we learn to "be a man" or "act like a lady" and when we fail, or refuse, we are held accountable for this failure or refusal. Furthermore,

> accountability . . . is the *process* of questioning someone's behavior and the *power* to command

an answer from that person ... [it is] a structural and cultural process of scrutiny juxtaposed to the obligation of the persons being scrutinized to explain their behaviours. (Cook, 2006, pp. 108-109)

Specifically,

[f]or theories of gender, difference and restorative justice, understanding and examining the dynamics of accountability illuminates how social structure is "accomplished." Class, gender and ethnicity are prisms of scrutiny ... where [] the socially constructed categories of difference are not eliminated, but instead are used as subtle devices of domination. (Cook, 2006, p. 120)

While the lessons learned from theories of doing difference are significant, there is room for their expansion within criminology. The framework can be applied more thoroughly to a variety of mainstream criminology's arenas of concern: How is "low self-control" impacted by the situated accomplishments of gender, race, social class, and heteronormative expectations? How can we document the situated lifecourse dynamics of doing difference and accountability in longitudinal research? Certainly, some good efforts are being made in this direction through narrative criminology (Presser & Sandberg, 2015).

Another illuminating advance within feminist criminology focuses on the intersection of gender, race, sexuality, and social class as they impact social patterns of crime offending and victimization (Burgess-Proctor, 2006; Chesney-Lind, 2006; Crenshaw, 1991; Potter, 2006, 2015). Crenshaw (1991) launches her analysis by pointing out that "[c]ontemporary feminist and antiracist discourses have failed to consider intersectional identities such as women of color" (p. 1242–1243). By documenting women of color's experiences with gendered violence, Crenshaw explodes the idea that all women experience violence similarly. She emphasizes that where

systems of race, gender, and class domination converge, as they do in the experiences of battered women of color, intervention strategies based solely on the experiences of women who do not share the same class or race backgrounds

will be of limited help to women who because of race and class face different obstacles. (Crenshaw, 1991, p. 1246)

Indeed Potter (2015) and others (Donnelly, Cook, Van Ausdale, & Foley, 2005; Donnelly, Cook, & Wilson, 1999; Potter, 2008; West, 1999) provide much more detail on this issue than can be covered here; suffice it to say that Crenshaw has had a profound and inspiring impact on feminist criminology.

In 2006, Amanda Burgess-Proctor declared "the future of feminist criminology lies in our willingness to embrace a theoretical framework that recognizes multiple, intersecting inequalities" (p. 28). She provides a rich history and detailed coverage of how criminology overall has benefited, and will continue to gain from feminist intersectional research. Because the interaction of power and privilege shape social life at the individual and institutional levels, it is incumbent on contemporary feminists to pursue this line of scholarly inquiry.

Like feminist theory and action writ large, feminist criminology has been the target of considerable backlash (Chesney-Lind, 2006), and our efforts to promote culturally and structurally relevant analyses of crime have generated some heated reactions. While documenting the media reaction to research on women and girls involved in criminal offending, Chesney-Lind (2006) points out that when "experts" are interviewed in the media, they usually offer individualistic analyses rather than criticizing structural inequalities. She provides an example from the *Boston Globe* about "BAD GIRLS" engaging in violence that had been exclusively the province of men, a journalistic story then supported by "experts" who say that girls/women are "calling the shots" (p. 12). In addition, Chesney-Lind (2006) highlights how the conventional criminological view that "women are as violent as men" has resulted in very real, and brutal, consequences in terms of higher rates of women being arrested and incarcerated. She concludes by calling for more progressive social action by feminist criminologists because "feminist criminology is uniquely positioned to do important work to challenge the current political backlash ... [and to] engage in exploration of the interface between systems of oppression based on gender, race, and class" (Chesney-Lind, 2006, p. 21). This is not a frivolous academic exercise; rather, the work we do has real "flesh and blood" consequences (Flavin, 2009), and feminist criminologists have long advocated for turning analyses and evidence into actions and agendas.

Potter (2006) brilliantly weaves together strands of contemporary feminist theory with critical race theory and produces Black Feminist Criminology that "extends beyond traditional feminist criminology so as to view African American women (and conceivably, other women of color) from their multiple marginalized and dominated positions in society, culture, community, and families" (p. 107). By explicitly examining the experiences of Black women who have been battered, Potter illuminates multiple structural inequalities that contaminate the lives of these women and affect their access to safety and security. As criminologists, this is exactly the sort of research and theorizing that ought to be central to, rather than marginalized within, our discipline. Such research also helps to identify needed reforms in our legal system so that as a society, we can move toward humane and comprehensive remedies for social inequalities caused by or productive of crime.

Finally, pushing criminology even further, Carrie Buist and Emily Lenning (2016) articulate "queer criminology" that "moves beyond the traditional deviance framework and shifts the spotlight from the rule breakers to the rule makers" (p. 4). Among the vital lessons they draw from queer criminology is that, given certain laws, structural barriers, cultural beliefs, and customs, some people's very existence is treated as criminal simply because of sexual/gender identity. As Buist and Lenning (2016) posit, "We cannot be complacent to the injustices and terrors that Queer people face around the world every single day based solely on their sexual orientation and/or gender identity" (p. 17). Here then, in contemporary feminist scholarship, is a good example of the "yes/and" approach that draws on criminological knowledge to document, analyze, and *resist* the systems of oppression that lesbian, gay, bisexual, and transgender (LGBT) people endure throughout the lives. Buist and Lenning rightly show needs within the field for further research that includes better data collection to ensure accurate information and analysis, better documentation of LGBT experiences with crime and the legal system, and thereafter improved policy reforms that acknowledge and understand queer realities. They argue that

by failing to recognize sexuality and gender identity as integral to one's experiences in the same manner in which we recognize the significance of race or social class, we reinforce the stereotype that being Queer is a deviant act as opposed to an inherent part of one's self and something that has bearing on experiences and outcomes in the criminal legal system. (p. 120)

In advocating for improved policy, Buist and Lenning focus on laws that criminalize consensual adult sexual behavior, limit or ban specific gendered expressions from public life, and improve treatment of hate crime victims and their cases. They also call for more sensitive and supportive care for queer prisoners, and for better treatment of LGBT employees in the legal system and throughout society. Last but not least, they urge criminologists to continue the legacy of action/activist oriented scholarship and quote Audre Lorde's conclusion that "there is no such thing as a single-issue struggle because we do not live single-issue lives" (cited in Buist & Lenning, 2016, p. 123). Exactly.

These critiques of the field offer conceptual roadmaps for learning about inequalities and crimes. By endorsing Cohen's early acknowledgment that social class differences matter, and by expanding that concern to sexism, racism, and heterosexism, we have a richer and more complete criminology awakening from a slumber that was both androcentric *and* biased in terms of race and sexualities.

Moving Forward

So where do we go from here? The path forward includes the need for much more research on the intersectionality of crime and crime control; more serious inclusion of gender, race, sexual orientation, and social class into mainstream criminology; and a discussion at the organizational level about how we collaborate in the field.

Potter (2015) argues that expanding intersectionality in the field can and ought to revolutionize criminology. She also provides an excellent list of recent criminological research that demonstrates the value of feminist intersectional approaches. I invite readers to speculate on what criminology might have looked like had Sutherland and Cressey emphasized instead of amputated gendered inequalities. Imagine if they had written this instead:

> The variations in the sex ratio in crime are so great that it can be concluded that maleness is *the most* significant *factor, along with racial, social class, and sexual orientation biases*, in the causation of crime *because* it indicates social position, supervision, and other social relations. Moreover, since boys and girls live in the same homes, in equal poverty, and with equally *oppressed/marginalized* parents, and live in the same neighborhoods, which are equally lacking in facilities for organized recreation, these conditions of the social environment *must* be considered causes of delinquency. (emphasis added)

We will never know how criminologists in previous eras would have reacted to this restatement. Perhaps they would have been ignored, or perhaps they would have inspired a different series of doctoral dissertations and developments in the field that took criminological research in a different direction decades earlier. Or perhaps later perspectives, like social control theory, would have taken these issues much more seriously. Imagine if the missed opportunities had been taken up at the time they were presented? They were not, however, necessitating that we take stock now and move forward from here.

Organizationally, within the ASC, much attention has been given to varying forms of social inequalities as they impact the study of crime. We have celebrated the 30th Anniversary of the DWC whose pioneers include Betsy Stanko, Nicole Hahn Rafter, Chris Rasche, CoraMae Richey Mann, Ruth Petersen, and many others. Scholars who are interested in gender and crime likely gravitate to the DWC. Scholars interested in globalization and crime may associate with the Division on International Criminology. Scholars interested in the political economy and crime may move toward the Division on Critical Criminology; scholars with interests in racial oppressions and crime may join and work within the Division on People of Color and Crime. These are just a few of the specialized structures within the field that exist organizationally to help build collaboration and share interests. At first blush, we might say these sections demonstrate our mutual commitment to multiple lenses of inquiry. At closer examination, though, one might conclude that such "divisions" are divisive and in fact create exclusionary silos rather than avenues for connection. My view is that it largely depends on how people use their membership in the Society and within/throughout the divisions. Many scholars are members of more than one division, which speaks to the larger claim that the avenues of collaboration and networking are fluid. Certainly within the DWC, we are deliberately and conscientiously welcoming to new scholars; when criticized for being too "White women" oriented, we have taken steps to remedy that condition. I am also aware that on campuses around the country, "women's studies" programs have mostly been re-named to "Women's and Gender Studies" to expand the scope of concern. Feminist criminology is not only about women anymore, nor is it only about gender. What we, as a Division, do about this (if anything) remains to be seen.[5] Combining our scholarly interest with policy advocacy renders feminist criminology relevant to the modern conundrum of crime; too many examples exist to possibly be able to cite them all. My own research has been profoundly shaped by feminist research methods, feminist theory, and has resulted in policy-relevant insights (Baumgartner, Westervelt, & Cook, 2014; Cook, 2006; Cook, Westervelt, & Maruna, 2014; Donnelly et al., 2005; Donnelly et al., 1999; Westervelt & Cook, 2010, 2012). We cannot simply publish our findings and let the policy chips fall where they may; feminist scholars have a long legacy of advocating social change analogously with the political edge that currently also marks critical criminology. Within the ASC, members of the DWC help support each other in our efforts to translate feminist theory into action with the annual "Feminist Theory in Action" workshop held on the Tuesday afternoon prior to the first sessions at the conference. This tradition was launched by Mona Danner (Old Dominion University) and Nancy Wonders (Northern Arizona University) in the 1990s. The workshop is a place to share activist ideas, policy goals, research challenges, and constructive solutions to oppressive social problems related to criminology. In recent years, thanks in part to the success of this journal and to the generosity of Professor Larry Siegel, we have been able to support excellent graduate student work focused on gender and crime; this deliberate cultivation of feminist scholarship is vital to the on-going awakening from traditionally androcentric criminology.

After reading Lauren Silver's recent book (2015), I would like to see feminist criminologists work on developing what I call "survivor criminology"; similar to "convict criminology," this would cultivate more trauma-informed research. Feminist criminologists, to varying individual degrees, are committed to conducting research that helps to push the policy arena farther along toward human rights without apologizing for the portion of feminist work that is politically relevant as well as empirically researched. Arguably, many of us in feminist criminology are already "survivors"[6] and thus already engage in "survivor criminology." After all, our lives are deeply influenced by the same sexism, racism, classism, and homophobia that has influenced the field in which we work; to ignore that our personal experiences are also political would require us to amputate a significant part of our analytical capacity, a specious separation that I am not willing, like many other feminists, to endure.

Understanding the complexity of gender in the everyday lived realities of crime experiences within various settings is as complicated as it is essential: Jody Miller (2001, 2002, 2008), Lauren Silver (2015), Joanne Belknap (2014), Hillary Potter (2006, 2015), Amanda Burgess-Proctor (2006), Walter DeKeseredy (2011), James Ptacek (1999, 2016), Carrie Buist and Emily Lenning (2016) all show that crime is gendered, racialized, classed, and heteronormative. In spite of the slow uptake in mainstream criminology, scholars who do intersectional analyses of gender, race, class, and sexualities have made indelible contributions to our understandings of crime and its control. We have woken up from the androcentric slumber, and we have staked a claim that these broad social inequalities impact crime in substantial ways. Mainstream criminology may still be napping amid its androcentric history, but many of us are awake and paying careful attention.

Conclusion

Scholarly research is a dynamic social process that is not free from bias, assumptions, interests, and judgment calls on the road to illuminating the social world. Good science, though, requires that such assumptions are revealed, acknowledged, and taken into consideration as the field evolves. Like other disciplines, criminology exists within a complex social environment where criminologists recycle biases, assumptions, interests, and judgments. According to Kournay (2009), "science is a patriarchal institution, and [] the masculinist personal and social and political and economic interests and values [] influence or virtually determine its outcomes" (p. 212). Feminist standpoint theory encourages scholars to articulate and reveal these dynamics, particularly as they impact our research and interests. Citing Longino, Kourney (2009) adds that

> scientists' interests and values can and do determine which questions they investigate and which they ignore, . . . [] can and do influence the observational or experimental data they select to study and the way they interpret those data, and so on. (p. 212)

The broader scientific community in any discipline, then, is obliged to critique and remedy the knowledge that derives from assumptions and interests. It remains the case that the vast majority of leading criminologists have been White males, and that a "white racial frame" (Potter, 2015, pp. 3-4) has also often emerged within criminology insofar as many criminologists have ignored or removed gender from serious theoretical and empirical consideration. Evidence of social inequalities and their impact on crime rates emerged early on with Cohen, thereafter becoming a foundation of critical criminology. Over decades, though, increasing numbers of scholars have become interested in multidimensional "yes/and" approaches to understanding crime and social inequalities—from their investigation of class and racial dynamics, to recently much greater attention given to gender dynamics by feminist criminologists. By now, contemporary scholarship regularly attends to both sexism and heterosexism within and outside criminology per se. We have learned to say "*yes*, they all matter," realizing that a more inclusive criminology has far more to offer and illuminate in the future than was possible in the relatively gender-blind criminological past.

/// DISCUSSION QUESTIONS

1. How have control and lifecourse theories been used to understand issues of gender in offending?

2. What are some of the current failures of feminist criminology and how do scholars need to address these issues?

Notes

1. Interestingly, in an endnote, Cohen references an unpublished doctoral dissertation by George H. Grosser (Harvard University) titled "Juvenile Delinquency and Contemporary American Sex Roles" completed in 1952 as "the most thorough discussion in the literature of sex differences in delinquency" (p. 193). To my knowledge, this dissertation or its findings have not been published in criminological journals and is not referenced in criminology text books. It does lead me to wonder why Grosser's study has not been more widely cited given Cohen's high praise of it.

2. In contrast, comparable numbers for other theories are as follows: social learning theory (57,000), learning theory (61,000), differential association theory (29,000), and social disorganization theory (6,000).

3. Or, presumably, gender.

4. An online search produced over 323,000 scholarly articles and 169 books for "doing gender."

5. Perhaps a new name, such as the Division on Feminist Criminology (DFC), would respond to this issue. Such a name change, of course, would require an extensive discussion within the Division to ensure inclusiveness and honoring of our history. Such a conversation would be slow and possibly difficult, nor is the change being advocated here. My point is to raise a possible point for further discussion.

6. Like others whose names will not be cited out of respect for their privacy, I am a survivor of domestic and sexual violence.

References

Baro, A., & Eigenberg, H. (1993). Images of gender: A content analysis of photographs in introductory criminology and criminal justice textbooks. *Women & Criminal Justice, 5,* 3–36.

Baumgartner, F., Westervelt, S. D., & Cook, K. J. (2014). Public policy responses to wrongful convictions. In A. Redlich, J. Acker, R. Norris, & C. Bonventre (Eds.), *Examining wrongful convictions: Stepping back, moving forward* (p. 251–266). Durham, NC: Carolina Academic Press.

Beirne, P. (1993). *Inventing criminology: Essays on the rise of "Homo Criminalis."* Albany: State University of New York Press.

Belknap, J. (2014). *The invisible woman: Gender, crime, and justice* (4th ed.). New York, NY: Cengage Learning.

Braithwaite, J. (1989). *Crime, shame, and reintegration.* Cambridge, UK: Cambridge University Press.

Britton, D. (2000). Feminism in criminology: Engendering the outlaw. *Annals of the American Academy of Social Sciences, 571,* 57–76.

Buist, C., & Lenning, E. (2016). *Queer criminology.* New York, NY: Routledge.

Burgess-Proctor, A. (2006). Intersections of race, class, gender, and crime: Future directions for feminist criminology. *Feminist Criminology, 1,* 27–47.

Chambliss, W. (1975). Toward a political economy of crime. *Theory and Society, 2,* 149–170.

Chesney-Lind, M. (2006). Patriarchy, crime, and justice: Feminist criminology in an era of backlash. *Feminist Criminology, 1,* 6–26.

Christie, N. (1977). Conflicts as property. *British Journal of Criminology, 17,* 1–15.

Christie, N. (1993). *Crime control as industry: Towards gulags, western style.* New York, NY: Routledge.

Cohen, A. (1955). *Delinquent boys: The culture of the gang.* New York, NY: The Free Press.

Collins, P. H. (1991). *Black feminist thought: Knowledge, consciousness, and the politics of empowerment.* New York, NY: Routledge.

Cook, K. J. (2006). Doing difference and accountability in restorative justice conferences. *Theoretical Criminology, 10,* 107–124.

Cook, K. J., Westervelt, S., & Maruna, S. (2014). The problem of fit: Parolees, exonerees, and prisoner reentry. In A. Redlich, J. Acker, R. Norris, & C. Bonventre (Eds.), *Examining wrongful convictions: Stepping back, moving forward* (p. 237–250). Durham, NC: Carolina Academic Press.

Crenshaw, K. (1991). Mapping the margins: Intersectionality, identity politics, and violence against women of color. *Stanford Law Review, 43,* 1241–1299.

Daly, K., & Chesney-Lind, M. (1988). Feminism and criminology. *Justice Quarterly, 5,* 497–538.

DeKeseredy, W. (2011). *Contemporary critical criminology.* New York, NY: Routledge.

Dobash, R., & Dobash, R. E. (1979). *Violence against wives: A case against the patriarchy.* New York, NY: The Free Press.

Donnelly, D., Cook, K. J., Van Ausdale, D., & Foley, L. (2005). White privilege, color blindness, and services to battered women. *Violence Against Women, 11,* 6–37.

Donnelly, D., Cook, K. J., & Wilson, L. (1999). Provision and exclusion: The dual face of services to battered women in three deep south states. *Violence Against Women, 5,* 710–741.

Eigenberg, H., & Baro, A. (1992). Women and the publication process: A content analysis of criminal justice journals. *Journal of Criminal Justice Education, 3,* 293–314.

Flavin, J. (2001). Feminism for the mainstream criminologist: An invitation. *Journal of Criminal Justice, 29,* 271–285.

Flavin, J. (2009). *Our bodies, our crimes: The policing of women's reproduction in America.* New York: New York University Press.

Friedrichs, D. O. (1996). *Trusted criminals: White collar crime in contemporary society.* New York, NY: Wadsworth.

Garland, D. (1990). *Punishment and modern society: A study in social theory.* Chicago, IL: University of Chicago Press.

Gottfredson, M. R., & Hirschi, T. (1990). *A general theory of crime.* Stanford, CA: Stanford University Press.

Hannon, L., & Dufour, L. R. (1998). Still just the study of men and crime? A content analysis. *Sex Roles, 38,* 63–71.

Ignatiev, N. (1995). *How the Irish became White.* New York, NY: Routledge.

Kantor, G. K., & Straus, M. (1987). The "drunken bum" theory of wife beating. *Social Problems, 34,* 213–230.

Kournay, J. A. (2009). The place of standpoint theory in feminist science studies. *Hypatia, 24,* 209–218.

Martin, D. (1976). *Battered wives.* San Francisco, CA: Glide Publications.

Matthews, R., & Young, J. (1992). Reflections on realism. In J. Young & R. Matthews (Eds.), *Rethinking criminology: The realist debate.* (p. 1–23). Newbury Park, CA: SAGE.

Messerschmidt, J. (1993). *Masculinities and crime.* Lanham, MD: Rowman & Littlefield.

Messerschmidt, J. (1997). *Crime as structured action: Gender, race, class, and crime in the making.* Thousand Oaks, CA: SAGE.

Michalowski, R. (1985). *Order, law, and crime: An introduction to criminology.* New York, NY: Random House.

Miller, J. (2001). *One of the guys: Girls, gangs, and gender.* New York, NY: Oxford University Press.

Miller, J. (2002). The strengths and limits of "doing gender" for understanding street crime. *Theoretical Criminology, 6,* 433–460.

Miller, J. (2008). *Getting played: African American girls, urban inequality, and gendered violence.* New York: New York University Press.

Pizzey, E. (1977). *Scream quietly or the neighbor's will hear.* Short Hills, NJ: Enslow.

Potter, H. (2006). An argument for black feminist criminology: Understanding African American women's experiences with intimate partner abuse using an integrated approach. *Feminist Criminology, 1,* 106–124.

Potter, H. (2008). *Battle cries: Black women and intimate partner abuse.* New York: New York University Press.

Potter, H. (2015). *Intersectionality and criminology: Disrupting and revolutionizing studies of crime.* New York, NY: Routlege.

Presser, L., & Sandberg, S. (Eds.). (2015). *Narrative criminology: Understanding stories of crime.* New York: New York University Press.

Ptacek, J. (1999). *Battered women in the courtroom: The power of judicial responses.* Boston, MA: Northeastern University Press.

Ptacek, J. (2016). Rape and the continuum of sexual abuse in intimate relationships: Interviews with U.S. women from different social classes. In K. Yllö, & G. Torres (Eds.), *Marital rape: Consent, marriage, and social change in global context.* (p. 123–138). New York, NY: Oxford University Press.

Rasche, C. (2014). The ASC division on women and crime from 30 years out. *Feminist Criminology, 9,* 253–269.

Renzetti, C. (1993). On the margins of the malestream (or, they still don't get it, do they?): Feminist analysis in criminal justice education. *Journal of Criminal Justice Education, 4,* 219–234.

Renzetti, C. (2013). *Feminist criminology.* New York, NY: Routledge.

Sampson, R. J., & Laub, J. H. (1993). *Crime in the making: Pathways and turning points through life.* Cambridge, MA: Harvard University Press.

Shaw, C. R., & McKay, H. D. (1942). *Juvenile delinquency and urban areas: A study of rates of delinquency in relation to differential characteristics of local communities in American cities.* Chicago, IL: University of Chicago Press.

Silver, L. (2015). *System kids: Adolescent mothers and the politics of regulation.* Chapel Hill: University of North Carolina Press.

Spitzer, S. (1975). Toward a Marxian theory of deviance. *Social Problems, 22,* 638–651.

Sutherland, E. H., & Cressey, D. R. (1974). *Criminology* (9th ed.). New York, NY: J. B. Lippincott.

Taylor, I., Walton, P., & Young, J. (1973). *The new criminology: For a social theory of deviance.* London, England: Routledge.

Thomas, W. I., & Znaniecki, F. (1974). *The Polish peasant in Europe and America.* New York, NY: Octagon Books. (Original work published 1918)

West, C., & Fenstermaker, S. (1995). Doing difference. *Gender & Society, 9,* 8–37.

West, C., & Zimmerman, D. (1987). Doing gender. *Gender & Society, 1,* 125–151.

West, T. (1999). *Wounds of the spirit: Black women, violence, and resistance ethics.* New York: New York University Press.

Westervelt, S. D., & Cook, K. J. (2010). Framing innocents: The wrongly convicted as victims of state harm. *Crime, Law, and Social Change, 53,* 259–275.

Westervelt, S. D., & Cook, K. J. (2012). *Life after death row: Exonerees search for community and identity.* New Brunswick, NJ: Rutgers University Press.

Girls, Gender, and Juvenile Delinquency

Section Highlights

- The rise of the juvenile court
- The "double standard" for girls in the juvenile justice system
- The new *violent* girl
- Contemporary risk factors associated with girls and delinquency
- Gender-specific needs of young female offenders

While the majority of this book focuses on the needs of women and girls generally, this section highlights some of the specific issues facing girls within the juvenile justice system. Beginning with a discussion on the rise of the juvenile courts, this section highlights the historical and contemporary standards for young women in society and how the changing definitions of delinquency have disproportionately and negatively affected young girls. These practices have manifested into today's standards of addressing cases of female delinquents. This section concludes with a discussion of reforms designed to respond to the unique needs of girls within the juvenile justice system.

The Rise of the Juvenile Court and the Sexual Double Standard

The understanding of adolescence within the justice system is a relatively new phenomenon. Originally, the development of the term *juvenile delinquent* reflected the idea that youth were "malleable" and could be shaped into law-abiding citizens (Bernard, 1992). A key factor in this process was the doctrine of *parens patriae. Parens patriae* began in the English Chancery Courts during the 15th century and evolved into the practice whereby the state could assume custody of children for cases where the child had no parents or the parents were deemed unfit care providers. As time passed, parens patriae became the government's justification for regulating adolescents and their behaviors under the mantra in the best interests of the child (Sutton, 1988).

Prior to the development of the juvenile court, the majority of cases of youth offending were handled on an informal basis. However, the dramatic population growth, combined with the rise of industrialization, made it increasingly difficult for families and communities to control wayward youth. The doctrine of parens patriae led to the development of a separate system within the justice system designed to oversee the rehabilitation of youth who were deemed out of control.

Developed in 1825, the New York House of Refuge was one of the first reformatories for juvenile delinquents and was designed to keep youth offenders separate from the adult population. Unlike adults, youths were not sentenced to terms proportionate to their offenses in these early juvenile institutions. Instead, juveniles were committed to institutions for long periods of time, often until their 21st birthday. The doctrine of parens patriae was often used to discriminate against children of the poor, because these youth had not necessarily committed a criminal offense. Rather, youth were more likely to be described as "coming from an unfit home" or displaying "incorrigible behaviors" (Bernard, 1992). The practices at the House of Refuge during the 19th century were based less on controlling criminal behaviors and more on preventing future pauperism, which the reformers believed led to delinquency and crime (Sutton, 1988). Rather than address the conditions facing poor parents and children, reformers chose to respond to what they viewed as the "peculiar weaknesses of the children's moral natures" and "weak and criminal parents" (Bernard, 1992, p. 76).

The Progressive Era of the late 19th and early 20th century in the United States led to the child-saving movement, which comprised middle- and upper-class White citizens who "regarded their cause as a matter of conscience and morality (and) viewed themselves as altruists and humanitarians dedicated to rescuing those who were less fortunately placed in the social order" (Platt, 1969, p. 3). The efforts of the child-savers movement led to the creation of the first juvenile court in Chicago in 1899. The jurisdiction of the juvenile court presided over three youth populations: (1) children who committed adult criminal offenses, (2) children who committed status offenses, and (3) children who were abused or neglected by their parents (Chesney-Lind & Shelden, 2004).

Parens patriae significantly affected the treatment of girls who were identified as delinquent. During the late 19th and early 20th centuries, moral reformers embarked on an **age-of-consent campaign**, which was designed to protect young women from *vicious men* who preyed on the innocence of girls. Prior to the age-of-consent campaign, the legal age of sexual consent in 1885 ranged between 10 and 12 for most states. As a result of the efforts by moral reformers, all states raised the age of consent to 16 or 18 by 1920. While their attempt to guard the chastity of young women from exploitation was rooted in a desire to protect girls, these practices also denied young women an avenue for healthy sexual expression and identity. The laws that resulted from this movement were often used to punish young women's displays of sexuality by placing them in detention centers or reformatories for moral violations with the intent to incarcerate them throughout their adolescence. These actions held women to a high standard of sexual purity, while the sexual nature of men was dismissed by society as normal and pardonable behavior. In addition, the reformers developed their policies based on a White, middle-class ideal of purity and modesty; anyone who did not conform to these ideals was viewed as out of control and in need of intervention by the juvenile court (Chesney-Lind & Shelden, 2004). This exclusive focus by moral reformers on the sexual exploitation of White, working-class women led to the racist implication that only the virtues of White women needed to be saved. While reformers in the Black community were equally interested in the moral education of young women and men, they were unsupportive of the campaign to impose criminal sanctions on offenders for sexual crimes, because they were concerned that such laws would unfairly target men of color (Odem, 1995).

Age-of-consent campaigners viewed the delinquent acts of young women as inherently more dangerous than the acts of their male counterparts. Because of the emphasis on sexual purity as the pathway toward healthy adulthood and stability for the future, the juvenile reformatory became a place to shift the focus away from their sexual desire and train young girls for marriage. Unfortunately, this increased focus on the use of the reformatory for moral offenses allowed for the practice of net widening to occur, and more offenders were placed under the supervision of the juvenile courts. **Net widening** refers to the practice whereby programs such as diversion were developed to inhibit the introduction of youth into the juvenile justice system. However, these practices often expanded the reach to offenses and populations that previously were outside the reach of the juvenile justice system. The effects of this practice actually increased the number of offenders under the general reach of the system, whether informally or formally.

Beyond the age-of-consent campaign, the control of girls' sexuality extended to all girls involved in the juvenile court, regardless of offense. A review of juvenile court cases between 1929 and 1964 found that girls who were arrested for status offenses were forced to have gynecological exams to determine whether or not they had engaged in sexual intercourse and if they had contracted any sexually transmitted diseases. Not only were these girls more likely to be sent to juvenile detention than their male counterparts, but they also spent three times as long in detention for their "crimes" (Chesney-Lind, 1973). Indeed, throughout the early 20th century, the focus on female sexuality and sexually transmitted infections (STI) reached epic proportions, and any woman who was suspected to be infected with a STI was arrested, examined, and quarantined (Odem, 1995).

In addition to being placed in detention centers for engaging in consensual sex, young women were often blamed for "tempting defendants into immoral behavior" (Odem, 1995, p. 68) in cases where they were victims of forcible sexual assault. Other historical accounts confirm how sexual victimization cases were often treated by the juvenile court in the same manner as consensual sex cases—in both situations the girl was labeled as delinquent for having sex (Shelden, 1981). These girls were doubly victimized, first by the assault and second by the system. During these court hearings, a woman's sexual history was put on display in an attempt to discredit her in front of a jury, yet the courts did not request similar information about a man's sexual history because it would "unfairly prejudice the jury against him" (Odem, 1995, p. 70). These historical accounts emphasized that any nonmarital sexual experience, even forcible rape, typically resulted in girls being treated as offenders.

The trend of using sexuality as a form of delinquent behavior for female offenders continued throughout the 20th and into the 21st century. The court system has become a mechanism through which control of female sexuality is enforced. Males enjoy a sense of sexual freedom that is denied to girls. In regard to male sexuality, the only concern generally raised by the court is centered on abusive and predatory behaviors toward others, particularly younger children. Here, probation officer narratives indicate that court officials think about sexuality in different ways for male and female juvenile offenders. For boys, no reference is made regarding noncriminalized sexual behaviors. Yet for girls, the risk of victimization becomes a way to deny female sexual agency. Here, probation officers would comment in official court reports about violations of moral rules regarding sexuality and displays of sexual behavior. In many cases, these officers expressed concern for the levels of sexual activity in which the girls were engaging. In many cases, such professional concerns are used as grounds for identifying these girls as "out of control" and therefore in need of services by the juvenile court (Mallicoat, 2007).

The Nature and Extent of Female Delinquency

Girls are the fastest growing population within the juvenile justice system. Not only have the number of arrests involving girls increased but the volume of cases in the juvenile court involving girls has also expanded at a dramatic rate. Despite the increased attention on females by the agents of the juvenile justice system and the public in general, it is important to remember that girls continue to represent a small proportion of all delinquency cases, because boys' offending continues to dominate the juvenile justice system.

As discussed in Section I, the Uniform Crime Reports (UCR) reflects the arrest data from across the nation. This resource also includes information on juvenile offenders. Given that law enforcement officials represent the most common method through which juvenile offenders enter the system, arrest data provide a first look at the official processing of juvenile cases. Here, we can assess the number of crimes reported to law enforcement involving youth offenders, the most serious charge within these arrests, and the disposition by police in these cases. You have also learned that the UCR data is not without its flaws. Given that juveniles are often involved in acts that are not serious and nonviolent in nature, these practices of crime reporting and how the data are compiled can have a significant effect on the understanding of **juvenile delinquency** by society. Despite these flaws, the UCR remains the best resource for investigating arrest rates for crime (Snyder & Sickmund, 2006).

UCR data on juvenile offenders indicate that in 1980, girls represented 20% of juvenile arrests. By 2003, girls' participation in crimes increased to 27%. Today, juvenile girls make up 29% of the arrests of individuals under the age of 18. Data from 1980 to 2003 show the female proportion of violent crime index offenses increased from 10% to 18%, while property offenses increased from 19% to 32%. These shifts in girls' arrests have certainly increased the attention of parents, juvenile court officials, and scholars (Knoll & Sickmund, 2010; Snyder & Sickmund, 2006). However, it appears that the majority of this increase occurred during the late 1980s to early 1990s when the rise of "tough on crime" philosophies spilled over into the juvenile arena. Figure 7.1 illustrates data on the juvenile arrests and the percentages of males and females involved in crimes for 2003 and 2012. Even though the percentage of female arrests within the juvenile population has increased over the past decade, the actual number of arrests has fallen in every crime category.

Despite the fact that females continue to represent a smaller proportion of the offending population compared to males and that the overall number of arrests has decreased significantly, the hype of the female delinquent continues to dominate discussions about juvenile delinquency. The increased attention on female delinquency by law enforcement has, in turn, affected the handling of these cases by the juvenile courts. In 2007, the U.S. juvenile

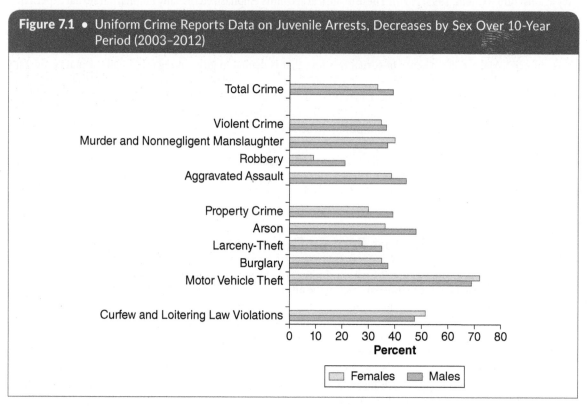

Figure 7.1 • Uniform Crime Reports Data on Juvenile Arrests, Decreases by Sex Over 10-Year Period (2003–2012)

SOURCE: Crime in the United States 2012 (2012).

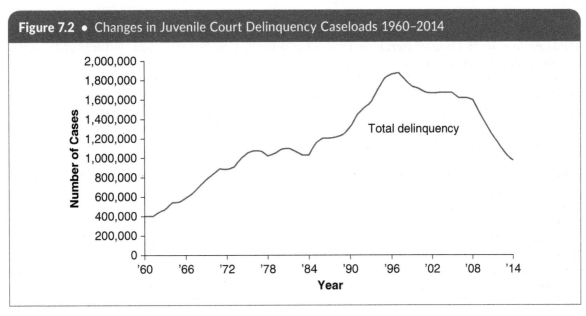

Figure 7.2 • Changes in Juvenile Court Delinquency Caseloads 1960–2014

SOURCE: Hockenberry & Puzzanchera (2017).

courts were dealing with an estimated 1.7 million cases each year. Since the early 1990s, girls have represented a growing proportion of cases in the juvenile courts. In 1991, girls made up 19% of delinquency cases, 26% in 2002, 27% in 2007, and 28% in 2009. Youth of color also continue to represent a disproportionate number of youth in the juvenile court. This is particularly noteworthy given that the percentage of arrests has decreased significantly in recent years (Knoll & Sickmund, 2010, 2012; Snyder & Sickmund, 2006, Hockenberry & Puzzanchera, 2017) (Figure 7.2). However, these trends may be stabilizing as the proportion of girls in the juvenile court has stabilized since 2005.

The dramatic increase of girls in delinquency caseloads during the 1990s and 2000s led many scholars to investigate the causes of these changes. Were girls engaging in higher levels of delinquent behavior or were there changes to the way in which we responded to these cases? Research by Steffensmeier, Schwartz, Zhong, and Ackerman (2005) showed the increase in arrests and **formal processing** of juvenile cases has disproportionately

Table 7.1 • Juvenile Court Cases Involving Girls, 2005 and 2014

Most Serious Offense	2005	2014
Person	30%	28%
Property	34%	37%
Drugs	10%	8%
Public Order	26%	27%

SOURCE: Hockenberry & Puzzanchera (2017).

impacted girls through the practice of up charging by prosecutors and a decrease in tolerance for girls who "act out." Meanwhile, boys benefit from a greater acceptance of these "unacceptable" behaviors (Carr, Hudson, Hanks, & Hunt, 2008). Given the increase in the number of female cases that are handled by the juvenile court, it is no surprise that punishments also increased for girls during this time frame. While boys are more likely to be detained for their cases (22% of cases, compared to 17% of girls' cases), girls who are denied release generally spend significantly greater amounts of time in detention compared to boys (Belknap, Dunn, & Holsinger, 1997; Snyder & Sickmund, 2006). Girls of color were disproportionately affected by the shift to formal processing of delinquency cases, because Black and Hispanic girls are more likely to receive detention, whereas White girls are more likely to be referred to a residential treatment facility (Miller, 1994). In addition, girls are subjected to longer periods of supervision, a practice that appears to increase the delinquency in girls due to excessive and aggressive monitoring techniques (Carr et al., 2008). Finally, the number of residential placements or sentences to formal probation terms had also increased for girls.

Over the past decade, the proportion of girls who are referred to the juvenile court has remained stable. In 2014, girls accounted for 28% of the overall juvenile caseload, which was the same as 2005. While some offense categories saw small increases by gender, other categories remained the same or saw decreases. Table 7.2 highlights the differences by gender for each offense type for 2005 and 2014. Looking at this data, we find that the proportion of girls involved in crimes against persons and drugs cases increased over the past decade and decreased for property crimes and public order offenses. However, these patterns were also reflected in the delinquency cases for boys.

Table 7.2 ● Changes in Juvenile Court Cases by Gender, 2005 and 2014

Most Serious Offense	Boys 2005	Boys 2014	% Changes	Girls 2005	Girls 2014	% Changes
Person	25%	25%	+1%	28%	30%	+2%
Property	37%	34%	−3%	37%	34%	−3%
Drugs	8%	10%	+2%	12%	15%	+3%
Public Order	26%	26%	0%	27%	26%	−1%

SOURCE: Hockenberry & Puzzanchera (2017).

While there were efforts to reduce the use of detention in the juvenile court during the early 21st century, recent trends note that the percentage of cases for both boys and girls has increased slightly for both boys and girls over the past five years. In 2009, 22% of boys were detained compared to 24% in 2014. Similarly, 15% of girls were detailed in 2009 compared to 17% in 2014. The likelihood of having cases processed formally also increased slightly for both boys and girls. However, these gains did not translate into an increase in the proportion of cases that were adjudicated delinquent because both boys and girls saw a decrease over the past five years. In 2009, 61% of cases involving males and 56% of cases involving females were adjudicated delinquent. Within five years, these proportions fell to 55% of boys' cases and 49% of girls' cases (Hockenberry &Puzzanchera, 2017).

Spotlight on the Sexual Abuse of Girls in Confinement

While the historical discussions on facilities for delinquent girls and offending women have indicated that females experienced high levels of physical and sexual abuse by both guards and other inmates, it is assumed that such experiences are ancient history and are not relevant to modern-day discussions about girls in custody. Unfortunately, these abuses still continue at many juvenile institutions.

The Survey of Youth in Residential Placement was administered to over 7,000 youth in custody during Spring 2003. The results from this survey indicate that 4% of youth in custody experienced sexual victimization. Half of these youth identified staff members as the offenders in these cases (Sedlak, McPherson, & Basena, 2013). Fast-forward to several years later, and it appears that the abuse of youth in custody has increased. The National Survey of Youth in Custody surveyed 9,198 adjudicated youth housed in juvenile facilities across the United States between June 2008 and April 2009 (Beck, Harrison, & Guerino, 2010). Like previous studies, the NSYC finds that the majority of these assaults are perpetuated by staff (10.3%); 41.7% of these involved use of force by the staff member, and the remaining 58.3% were "consensual" (even though state law would disagree with this definition of consensual given the context of the relationship). Juvenile males were more likely to be victims of staff sexual abuse, and their offenders were typically female staff members. In comparison, juvenile females were more likely to experience acts of abuse from other inmates (9.1% of girls compared to 2.0% of boys). LGBT youth experienced some of the highest levels of victimization (12.1%). In particular, transgendered girls are at extreme risk for victimization (Just Detention International [JDI], 2009). In many cases, staff members not only fail to protect transgendered youth in custody but often join in on the abuse (Fellner, 2010). While surveys such as these yield valuable information about the nature of abuse within juvenile facilities, the data are collected anonymously. This makes it difficult for facility and state officials to follow up on these cases of abuse. In addition, few of these assaults are ever reported to officials. In many cases, victims fear that reporting these crimes will increase the likelihood for future victimization (Human Rights Watch, 2006). While these research findings demonstrate that sexual assault within juvenile confinement facilities is a significant issue, failure to report these cases on even anonymous surveys such as the[se] may skew the findings, and the actual extent of this problem may be even higher.

While the National Prison Rape Elimination Commissions have made a number of recommendations to reduce the extent of abuse within confinement facilities, many of these reforms are costly and out of reach. Public officials have also argued that conducting annual reviews of abuse within juvenile facilities would be too costly. However, allowing such abuse to continue is also an expensive burden, because the emotional experience of victimization impacts youth long after they have departed the facility. In addition, the failure to respond to systemic abuse within the prisons places facilities at risk for lawsuits by youth and their families. In 2007, Alabama paid $12.7 million settlement in response to a class action lawsuit by 48 girls that served time at a state youth correctional facility. The core of their complaint centered on allegations of significant abuse involving over 15 staff members.[1] While international standards prohibit the supervision of female offenders by male staff (a policy that could reduce the cases of abuse of female youth by male guards), many facilities continue to allow cross-gender supervision, continuing to place these girls at potential risk (Human Rights Watch, 2006).

---

[1]For a state-by-state review of systematic maltreatment within juvenile facilities, go to http://www.aecf.org/OurWork/ JuvenileJustice/~/media/Pubs/Topics/Juvenile%20Justice/Detention%20Reform/NoPlaceForKids/SystemicorRecurring MaltreatmentinJuvenileCorrectionsFacilities.pdf

©CanStock/monkeybusiness

▲ **Photo 7.1** Recent years have seen an increase in the reporting of cases involving "violent girls". Are girls really becoming more violent, or have parents, schools, and police changed the way in which they respond to incidents of girls who are deemed to be "out of control"?

The "Violent" Girl

Over the past two decades, media reports have alluded to the rise of the violent juvenile offender. This portrayal of "bad girls" by the media has been linked to data that reflected a significant increase in the number of arrests for crimes of violence involving girls. Based on these findings, researchers ask, Are girls really becoming more violent? Or is there something else to blame for these increases? Have parents, schools, and police changed the way in which they respond to incidents of girls who are deemed to be out of control?

While official crime rates appear to demonstrate that the rate of violent offenses by juvenile girls is increasing, these data reflect only increases in the number of arrests, which is a reflection of the response by the police. Meanwhile, self-report studies do not support this claim and indicate that the levels of violence have actually decreased for both boys and girls. For example, results from the Youth Risk Behavior Survey indicate that between 1991 and 2001, acts of violence by girls decreased 30.5% while boys' violence decreased by 14.1% (Centers for Disease Control and Prevention, 1992–2002).

A review of recent trends in female juvenile cases indicates an overrepresentation of incidents of family-based violence (Brown, Chesney-Lind, & Stein, 2007). The rise in these cases reflects a shift in the way in which families and officials respond to these cases. Consider that adolescence often corresponds with a new discovery of freedom, which often collides with parents' desire to maintain some control and authority over their children. In some cases, parents may turn to the police and the juvenile court for help. Juvenile authorities may talk to or threaten the youth or use fear as a tool to gain compliance from the youth (Davis, 2007). Once upon a time, the police treated these interventions as a social service rather than a criminal matter. But this practice is shifting, and cases of domestic dispute and minor assault against family members are now handled as formal acts of delinquency by the police and court system (Brown et al., 2007; Feld, 2009).

Many parents seek out the police because they do not know what else to do and believe that once their kids are involved in the juvenile justice system, they will have greater opportunities for resources such as individual and family therapy (Sharpe, 2009). Once the formal processing of these cases places these girls under the supervision of probation, any subsequent power struggles between the parent and child may then become the grounds for a technical violation of probation. As a result, the court becomes a new and powerful method for enforcing parental authority. Parents in turn can hold a high level of power in the eyes of the court when it comes to the disposition of their child's case. Indeed, it is not uncommon during juvenile court proceedings for a judge to consult with a parent in judicial decisions. If a parent agrees that a child can come home (under the order of obeying house rules), the court may be more likely to return the youth home. If, however, a parent does not want physical custody of the child, a judge may decide to institutionalize the youth (Davis, 2007).

Family-based cases are not the only type of offense that has increased in recent years. Juvenile courts have also seen a marked increase in the number of cases of school-based violence. Once upon a time, outbursts and minor assaults were handled within the school's administration using punishments such as detention and suspension. As a result of zero-tolerance policies, these cases are now dealt with by local police agencies. Given that girls are more likely to engage in acts of violence against family members or peers (whereas boys are more likely to commit acts of violence against distant acquaintances or strangers), such policies may unfairly target girls (Feld, 2009).

Girls that engage in violence often have a history of violence in their own lives. This is an important characteristic to consider because many girls who act out may simply be reacting to the social and personal conditions of their lives. Research by Tasca, Zatz, and Rodriguez (2012) indicates that girls who engage in violence come from home environments that are significantly impoverished. In some cases, there is a history of parental drug abuse. Many of the girls experience sexual abuse and are exposed to violent acts, such as intimate partner abuse, within the home environment. For these girls, home is not a safe place but is one where violence reigns.

Technical Violations: The New Status Offense

Like the historical and contemporary control of female sexuality, status offenses are another realm where doctrines such as parens patriae allow for the juvenile court to intervene in the lives of adolescents. **Status offenses** are acts that are illegal only if committed by juveniles. Examples of status offenses include the underage consumption of alcohol, running away from home, truancy, and curfew violations. While the juvenile court was founded with the idea of dealing with both delinquency and status offenses, today's courts have attempted to differentiate between the two offense categories because of constitutional challenges on status offenses (Bernard, 1992). One of the elements of the **Juvenile Justice and Delinquency Prevention (JJDP) Act of 1974** called for the decriminalization of status offenders in any state that received federal funds. Prior to its enactment, young women were much more likely to be incarcerated for status offenses compared to their male counterparts (Chesney-Lind & Shelden, 2004). While the institutionalization of sexually wayward girls officially ended with the JJDP act of 1974, funds were not made available to provide resources to address the needs of girls. "Status offenders are not a unique or discrete category of juveniles, and they share many of the same characteristics and behavioral versatility as other delinquent offenders" (Feld, 2009, p. 245). Given that status offense charges were frequently used as the basis for incarcerating girls, many assumed that the presence of girls in the juvenile justice system would decrease following the decriminalization of status offenses. However, this decline did not last long. While youth can no longer be incarcerated specifically for status offenses, we still see cases where youth appear before the juvenile court for these cases. Data from an urban county in Arizona indicate that race and gender have an effect on whether youth will be adjudicated for status offenses, such as curfew violations, running away from home, using alcohol and/or tobacco, and truancy. While White girls were the least likely to be adjudicated delinquent for a status offense, Native American boys were the most likely to be adjudicated, followed by girls of color (African American and Hispanic; Freiburger & Burke, 2011).

In addition, researchers contend that the practice of institutionalizing girls who are deemed out of control continues today (Acoca & Dedel, 1998a; Chesney-Lind & Shelden, 2004). The modern-day practice of institutionalizing girls for status offenses is known as **bootstrapping.** The process of bootstrapping involves cases where a girl is currently on probation or parole for a criminal offense and then is prosecuted formally for a probation violation as a result of committing a status offense, such as running away from home or truancy (Owen & Bloom, 1998). While provisions of the **Reauthorization of the Juvenile Justice and Delinquency Prevention (JJDP) Act (1992)** attempted to make the practice of bootstrapping more difficult for courts, evidence indicates that the practice continues in an inequitable fashion against girls. Research by Feld (2009) suggests that acts that were once treated as status offenses are now processed as minor acts of delinquency due to the expansion of the discretionary powers available to schools, police, and juvenile justice officials. The replacement of status offenses by probation violations has allowed justice officials to recommit girls to these residential facilities. While a commitment to a state institution or detention center for these types of status offenses is prohibited by the original authorization of the JJDP Act in 1974, it appears that the juvenile justice system has found a new method to "incarcerate" young girls deemed out of control by the courts (Carr et al., 2008).

Risk Factors for Female Delinquency

Earlier chapters of this text have highlighted the historical failures of criminology to address the unique causes of women and girls' offending. The theoretical inattention to these issues has significantly affected the identification and delivery of services for women and girls. It is a failure for policymakers and practitioners to assume that, just because girls typically engage in nonviolent or nonserious acts of crime and delinquency, their needs are insignificant (Chesney-Lind & Shelden, 2004). Indeed, a historical review of the juvenile justice system finds that programs and facilities are ill equipped to deal with the needs of girls. While boys and girls can exhibit many of the same risk factors for delinquency, such as family dysfunction, school failures, peer relationships, and substance abuse, the effects of these risk factors may resonate more strongly for girls than they do for boys (Moffitt, Caspi, Rutter, & Silva, 2001). In addition, research indicates that girls possess significantly higher risk factors toward delinquency than boys. For example, boys are more likely to increase their underage alcohol consumption due to peer pressure, while this doesn't have an effect for girls, who are more likely to binge drink as a result of personal victimization experiences and feelings of peer approval (Whaley, Hayes & Smith, 2014). It is interesting to note that while White girls tend to exhibit significantly higher levels of risk for certain categories (such as substance abuse), youth of color, particularly African American youth, are significantly overrepresented in the juvenile court (Gavazzi, Yarcheck, & Lim, 2005). Given these failures of the juvenile courts, it is important to understand the **risk factors for female delinquency** in an effort to develop recommendations for best practices for adolescent delinquent and at-risk girls. For juvenile girls, the most significant risk factors for delinquency include a poor family relationship, a history of abuse, poor school performance, negative peer relationships, and issues with substance abuse. In addition, these risk factors are significantly interrelated.

Family

The influence of the family unit is one of the most commonly cited references in the study of delinquency. The family represents the primary mechanism for the internalization and socialization of social norms and values (Hirschi, 1969), and social control theorists have illustrated that a positive attachment to the family acts as a key tool in the prevention of delinquency. Yet research indicates that girls may have stronger attachments to the family compared to boys, which can serve as a protective factor against delinquency. However, families can serve as a protective factor only when they exist in a positive, prosocial environment. Research indicates that girls benefit from positive communication, structure, and support in the family environment (Bloom, Owen, Deschenes, & Rosenbaum, 2002b). Just as the family unit can protect girls from delinquency, it can also lead girls into delinquency at a young age. Youth may turn to delinquency to enhance their self-esteem or to overcome feelings of rejection by their families (Matsueda, 1992). Research has indicated that delinquent girls have lower bonds with their family compared to nondelinquent girls (Bourduin & Ronis, (2012). In addition, these negative family issues constitute a greater problem for girls than boys (Shepherd, Luebbers, & Dolan, 2013). Family fragmentation because of divorce, family criminality, and foster care placements, in addition to family violence and negative family attachment, has been identified as family risk factors for female delinquents. Girls with blended families (stepparent) are more likely to engage in high rates of delinquency and alcohol use, compared to girls that reside with both birth parents. Girls who live with just one parent are also more likely to engage in frequent alcohol use (Vanassche, Sodermans, Matthijs, & Swicegood, 2014). Families with high levels of conflict and poor communication skills, combined with parents who struggle with their own personal issues, place girls at risk for delinquency (Bloom et al., 2002b). Family factors can also serve to encourage relapse and recidivism because girls are more likely to be at risk for continuing behaviors in families where either the parent is involved in the justice system or uses drugs or alcohol (van der Put et al., 2014). In addition, once a girl becomes immersed in the juvenile justice system, her delinquency can serve to increase the detachment between her and her family (Girls Incorporated, 1996). Indeed, incarcerated girls are less likely to

receive support from their parents compared to boys. This has significant implications in two ways. First, girls are more likely to experience depression, and the lack of family support can contribute to their mental health status. Second, many intervention programs within the juvenile court rely on parental involvement. Measures of success in these programs could be compromised if girls feel less supported by their parents (Johnson et al., 2011).

Abuse

Sexual, physical, and emotional abuse has long been documented as significant risk factors for female offenders. The impact of abuse is intensified when it occurs within the family. Such abuse can be detrimental to the positive development of the adolescent female and can result in behaviors such as running away, trust issues, emotional maladjustment, and future sexual risk behaviors. This is not meant to suggest that violence and victimization are not present in the lives of male delinquents, only that it is more common for girls. Research by Belknap and Holsinger (2006) shows that 58.9% of girls (versus 18.5% of boys) indicated they had been sexually abused by either a family member or other individual in their life. While sexual abuse is the most studied form of abuse for girls, other forms of maltreatment can have a significant effect on the development of girls. Girls experience higher rates of physical abuse than their male counterparts (62.9% of girls compared to 42.8% of boys). Research suggests that girls who are abused may have lower (strength) bonds to protective factors, such as parents and school, that could serve to inhibit their involvement in delinquency (Bourduin & Ronis, 2012).

Experiences of childhood abuse are often the tip of the iceberg for the issues that affect preteen and adolescent females. In many cases, acts such as running away from home reflect an attempt to escape from a violent or abusive home environment. Unfortunately, in their attempt to escape from an abusive situation, girls often fall into criminal behaviors as a mechanism of survival. Widom (1989) found that childhood victimization increases the risk that a youth will run away from home and that childhood victimization and running away increase the likelihood of engaging in delinquent behaviors. A history of sexual abuse also affects the future risk for victimization, because girls who are sexually abused during their childhood are significantly more likely to find themselves in a domestically violent relationship in the future (McCartan & Gunnison, 2010).

Peers

The presence of delinquent peers presents the greatest risk for youth to engage in their own acts of delinquency. While much of the research suggests that girls are more likely to associate with other girls (and girls are less likely to be delinquent than boys), research by Miller, Loeber, and Hipwell (2009) indicates that girls generally have at least one friend involved in delinquent behaviors. While girls in this study indicated that they associated with peers of both genders, it is not the gender of the peers that can predict delinquency. Rather, it is the number of delinquent peers that determines whether a youth engages in problem behaviors. Here, the effects of peer pressure and the desire for acceptance often lead youth into delinquency, particularly if the majority of the group is involved in law-violating behaviors.

Several factors can affect one's association with delinquent peers. First, scholars indicate the shift toward unsupervised *free time* among youth as a potential gateway to delinquency, because youth who are involved in after-school structured activities are less likely to engage in delinquency (Mahoney, Cairns, & Farmer, 2003). However, girls tend to spend less time with their delinquent peers compared to boys and experience less peer pressure as a result (Weerman & Hoeve, 2012). Research indicates that negative peer relationships have a stronger effect for African American girls than boys, while boys' delinquency is more likely to be limited by parental monitoring (O'Donnell, Richards, Pearce, & Romero, 2012). Given the slashing of school-based and community programs because of budgetary funds, there are fewer opportunities to provide a safe and positive outlet for youth in the hours between the end of the school day for youth and the end of the work day for parents. Second, age can also affect the delinquent peer relationship. For girls, peer associations with older adolescents of the opposite sex have an impact on their likelihood to engage in delinquent acts if the older male is involved in crime-related behaviors (Stattin & Magnusson,

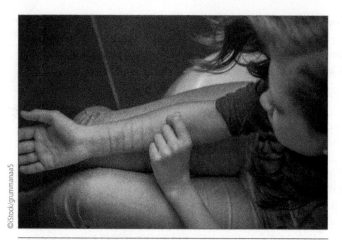

▲ **Photo 7.2** Many girls with experiences of childhood sexual abuse engage in a variety of self-injurious behaviors, including addiction and cutting.

1990). Finally, negative family attachment also affects the presence of delinquent peers, because girls whose parents are less involved in their daily lives and activities are more likely to engage in problem behaviors (such as substance abuse) with delinquent peers (Svensson, 2003).

School

School failures have also been identified as an indicator of concern for youth at risk. Truancy can be an indication of school failures, such as suspension, expulsion, or being held back. In research by Acoca and Dedel (1998a), 85% of incarcerated girls in their study compared their experience in school to a war zone, where issues such as racism, sexual harassment, peer violence, and disinterested school personnel increased the likelihood of dropping out. For girls, success at school is tied to feelings of self-worth: The more students feel attached to the school environment and the learning process and develop a connection to their teachers, the less likely they are to be at risk for delinquency (Crosnoe, Erickson, & Dornbusch, 2002). Additionally, the slashing of prosocial extracurricular activities has also negatively affected girls. Here, activities that involve creativity, build relationships, and enhance personal safety help build **resiliency** in young women and guard against delinquent behaviors (Acoca & Dedel, 1998a). Finally, the involvement of a parent in the daughter's school progress can help build resiliency for girls (Bloom et al., 2002b).

Substance Abuse

Several risks have been identified for adolescent females' involvement in alcohol and drug use: early experimentation and use, parental use of drugs and alcohol, histories of victimization, poor school and family attachments, numerous social opportunities for use, poor self-concept, difficulties in coping with life events, and involvement with other problem behaviors (Bloom et al., 2002b). Substance abuse affects female delinquency in two ways. First, girls who experience substance abuse in their families may turn to behaviors such as running away to escape the violence that occurs in the home as a result of parental drug and alcohol use. Engagement in substance abuse can also be facilitated by their parents.

> Jenna did OxyContin with her mom the first time. That's how Jenna's mom found out that Jenna was doing it and snorting it because they sniffed it when they did it together, It was weird because her mom patted her on the back for snorting it. Like most kids get patted on the back by their moms for playing sports or something, and Jenna's mom patted her on the back for snorting pills. It made Jenna feel like a badass, kinda cool. (Dehart & Moran, 2015, p. 303).

Second, girls themselves may engage in substance abuse as a mechanism of self-medication to escape from abuse histories (Chesney-Lind & Shelden 2004). In addition, research indicates that the use of substances can be a gendered experience. While boys tend to limit their drug use to marijuana, girls experiment with and abuse a variety of substances, including methamphetamines, cocaine, acid, crack, and huffing chemicals. Not only did their poly-drug use indicate significant addiction issues, but their substance abuse also altered their decision-making abilities, influenced their criminal behaviors, and placed them at risk for danger (Mallicoat, 2007). While substance abuse increases the risk for delinquency for girls, the absence of substance abuse serves as a protective factor against delinquency (McKnight & Loper, 2002).

Finally, girls may use illicit substances as an escape from the violence that they have observed in their communities. Often this trauma is a precursor for offending, because it is present long before girls begin to engage in at-risk or delinquent behavior. From viewing murders in their neighborhood to, such events have a damaging impact on the development of youth. In a study of 100 girls involved in the juvenile justice system, 90% had witnessed violence, ranging from witnessing a violent attack with a weapon (55%) to having a close friend or family member who was murdered (46%). Over a third of girls (35%) had witnessed a murder, One girl described an event where she observed a man and woman arguing. "He took a gun out of his back pocket. . . . There was brain everywhere. That image . . . it was terrifying" (DeHart & Moran, 2015, p. 303). Here, violence prevention programs in school and community-based programs could assist in healing these wounds rather than waiting for aggressive and self-harming behaviors to escalate to the point of requiring attention from the juvenile justice system.

Mental Health

Youth in custody experience high rates of trauma throughout the course of their lives. Girls experience higher rates of emotional trauma than boys. (See Hennessey, Ford, Mahoney, Ko, & Siegfried, 2004, for a review of the literature.) For many youth, these traumas place them at risk for posttraumatic stress disorder (Shufelt & Cocozza, 2006) and suicidal ideation. Girls are also more likely to engage in self-injurious behaviors (Shepherd, Luebbers, & Dolan, 2013). This is particularly important for girls under custody because 45% of girls in detention indicated that they had attempted suicide at some point in their lives (Belknap & Holsinger, 2006). Girls are also more likely to suffer from anxiety-related disorders, which typically stem from early childhood experiences with abuse and victimization. In many instances, these anxiety-related disorders are co-occurring with substance abuse and addiction, which can create unique challenges for programming and treatment (Shufelt & Cocozza, 2006). It is important for the juvenile justice system to note and respond to these issues. Unfortunately, many detention facilities are ill equipped to deal with the mental health needs of youth in custody, and these girls end up falling through the cracks. A failure by the system to effectively recognize the mental health needs of delinquent girls not only places these youth at risk for future harm but also places them at risk for increased involvement with the system (Hennessey et al., 2004).

Meeting the Unique Needs of Delinquent Girls

While girls may make up a minority of offenders in the juvenile justice system, their needs should not be absent from juvenile justice policies. As indicated earlier, girls have a number of different and interrelated issues that historically have been ignored by the system. The 1992 Reauthorization of the Juvenile Justice and Delinquency Prevention Act acknowledged the need to provide gender-specific services to address the unique needs of female offenders. Over the past two decades, research has highlighted the factors that may affect a young woman's road to delinquency, and the reauthorization of the JJDP mandates that states incorporate this understanding into the assessment tools and programming options for girls.

What should **gender-specific programming** for girls look like? Programs must be able to address the wide variety of needs of the delinquent girl; given that many of the risk factors for delinquency involve a web of interrelated issues, programs need to be able to address this tangled web of needs rather than attempt to deal with issues on an individual and isolated basis. Research identifies that a history of victimization is the most significant issue facing at-risk and delinquent girls. According to Belknap & Holsinger (2006), 55.8% of girls believe that their experiences with abuse throughout their childhood had an effect on their offending behaviors. The prevalent nature of a victimization history in adolescent females raises this issue to one of central importance in gender-specific programming. Not only do programs need to provide counseling services for both boys and girls that focus on the trauma in their lives, but placement services for youth need to be expanded as well. Given that many girls run away from home to escape an abusive environment, punishment in detention is not an appropriate place for girls. Because early childhood victimization often leads to risky sexual behaviors with the conclusion of teenage pregnancy and parenthood, education should be offered to these girls as a preventive measure for pregnancy and sexually transmitted diseases. However, it is important to remember that not even gender responsive programming is a one-size-fits-all girls model. For girls that have gender-sensitive risk factors such as a history of trauma or physical/mental health needs, gender-responsive programming is helpful in preventing recidivism. However, for girls that do not have a abuse history, such programs can actually lead to higher risks for recidivism (Day, Zahn, & Tichavsky, 2015).

Spotlight on Arts Programming and At-Risk Youth

Once upon a time, schools offered arts programming as part of a child's education. Courses in the visual arts and music were as much a part of the curriculum as math and science. However, budget cuts and an emphasis on standardized testing has led to the minimization or cancelation of arts-related programming. The loss of the arts has had a significant effect on the academic successes of our youth population. Research from the National Education Longitudinal Study of 1988 tells us that children who have a rich experience with the arts demonstrate greater achievements in science and writing and a higher GPA compared to those with a lower engagement in the arts. In addition, these youth were more likely to attend college (71% compared to 48%) and receive an associate's (24% compared to 10%) or bachelor's degree (18% compared to 6%). In addition, the effect of art-related education is stronger for those kids with a lower socioeconomic status background. (Catterall, Dumais, & Hampden-Thompson, 2012).

Arts education programming has been shown to have a positive impact on the lives of at-risk youth. In their evaluation of three arts education programs, the YouthARTS development project has identified that participation in these programs not only provided youth with a positive outlet to express their emotions and to develop their communication skills but also had an impact on recidivism rates for juvenile participants. Not only did the youth in the program receive fewer juvenile court referrals, but their offenses were [also] less serious for those that did engage in delinquency (Americans for the Arts, 2000). Arts-related programming has also had a significant impact on youth in custody. Youth that participated in a visual arts program while in juvenile detention demonstrated significantly lower rates of misbehavior (63%), which increased the time that staff could use for positive interactions, versus disciplinary actions (Ezell & Levy, 2003).

But what about girls? Few of the arts education programs in practice utilize gender-responsive practices. The Share Art Program in Flint, Michigan, began as a coed program with youth incarcerated at the Genesee Valley Regional Center. The program focuses on visual art and spoken-word poetry as ways that the youth can express themselves and make sense of their lives, which are often very chaotic. As a short-term detention facility, youth serve there an average of 21 days, which gives program providers a limited time with most of the youth. In an effort to meet the unique needs of the girls in the facility, the Share Art Program adapted their program design to reflect gender-responsive practices. The female-only environment provided the opportunity for the girls to have a safe space to share their emotions through their art, and as they developed their writing, the girls began to feel more confident about their abilities. Through their poetry, the girls began to explore their histories, life experiences, and their visions for the future. Many of the girls commented that the program not only increased their self-confidence but also provided them with a skill set to work through their emotions and decision-making processes. In addition, the girls learned how to work with others and build a support network. Finally, the staff of the program also served as important role models for the girls. By creating a space where the girls could focus on the risk and resiliency factors in their lives, the program was able to effectively serve the needs for this female population and provided a valuable resource for the community (Rosenbaum & Spivack, 2013).

As in the case of the needs of high-risk pregnancies, juvenile justice facilities are often ill equipped to deal with the physical and mental health needs of incarcerated females (Tille & Rose, 2007). The emotional needs of developing teenagers, combined with the increase in the prevalence of mental health disorders of incarcerated females, makes this an important component for gender-specific programming for female populations. Physical and mental health complaints by youth need to be interpreted by staff and facilities as a need, not as a complaining or manipulating behavior. Additionally, such interventions must be established on an ongoing basis for continual care, versus limited to an episodic basis (Acoca & Dedel, 1998a).

When designing programs for youth, it is important to consider the variety of different backgrounds and cultures that delinquent girls come from, because this impacts not only their pathways to offending but also affects how they will respond to interventions. Research has indicated that race and ethnicity impact the pathways of girls to the juvenile justice system. While White females experience higher levels of physical and sexual abuse and substance abuse compared to African American girls, the abuse of girls of color remains high. Seventy percent of Black girls indicate a history of physical abuse, and 46% have been sexually abused in their lifetime (compared to 90% of White girls who are physically abused and 62% who are sexually abused; Holsinger & Holsinger, 2005). Other research shows that factors such as lack of parental monitoring, antisocial attitudes, school commitment, and peer pressure can be used to explain delinquency among girls in the Hmong community (Ciong & Huang, 2011).

These factors can alter the way in which girls respond to these experiences. White girls are more likely to engage in self-injurious behaviors compared to girls of color. Here, it appears that White girls are more likely to respond to the abuse experience through internally harming behaviors, whereas girls of color are more likely to engage in outward displays of violence (Holsinger & Holsinger, 2005). The greatest long-term successes come from programs that provide support, not just for the individual girl but for her extended family as well. Unfortunately, many family members resist being involved in programming, because they fail to accept responsibility for the role that they may have played in the development of their daughter's delinquency (Bloom, Owen, Deschenes, & Rosenbaum, 2002a). This lack of involvement raises significant concerns for the family environment of these girls. Although more than one half of girls reported that they do not get along with their parents (51%) and the view that their relationship with their parents contributed to their delinquency (59%), 66% of the girls stated that they would return to live with their parents following their release from custody. This is particularly concerning given that 58% of the girls surveyed reported experiencing some form of violence in the home. It is impossible to develop programs for incarcerated females without reevaluating policies that contribute to the destruction of the family. Gender-specific programming for adolescent females needs to focus on rebuilding the family unit and developing positive role modeling. Here, programs such as family counseling and family substance abuse treatment models can positively affect troubled families.

Spotlight on Girls' Voices

As you learned in earlier sections of this text, listening to the stories of women and girls is one of the key strengths of feminist research methods. From this type of research, we learn that girls have a lot to share about their lives [and] their experiences with the juvenile justice and criminal justice systems and have ideas about what they need to improve their lives. Research tells us that girls benefit from a structured environment and that tools such as effective discipline, expectations for behavior, and guidance can provide valuable support for girls (Garcia & Lane 2010). Many of the girls in these research studies discuss the power that a positive role model has for their lives. Strong female staff within the juvenile justice system (and related

(Continued)

(Continued)

ancillary organizations) can serve as mentors for girls and provide valuable mentorship support and guidance for girls (Bright, Ward, & Negi 2011). As one female who had spent time in a juvenile facility indicated about the power of a positive mentor, "we depend on that support and that bond with somebody that we can talk to and trust and confide in" (Bright, Ward, & Negi, p. 2011, p. 38). While girls echo the need for therapeutic resources to address drug addiction and victimization histories, they also believe that developing independent life skills and reentry programming is essential in preventing recidivism as a girl transitions into adulthood (Garcia & Lane, 2010). Beyond discussions about the types of programming and the role of mentors in their lives, this research provides a vivid picture of the environments that these girls come from—and ultimately will return to.

The economic marginality that surrounds the lives of girls impacts their future outlooks for success. For many of the girls, what they see within their own families and communities is all they know. To hope and aspire for a better life simply seems like a dream that is out of reach. As a result, many young girls submit themselves to a life filled with violence:

> I came from the ghetto. And people didn't go to college. They barely made it out of high school, if they made it out of high school. So it's not normal for us to think, you know it's just not something that crosses our minds. (Garcia & Lane, 2010, p. 237)

Regardless of the successes that girls may experience within the juvenile justice system, the reality is that these girls will most likely return to the chaotic environments of their families and communities. While some girls fight to maintain the positive changes in their lives by working toward goals for their future, others reference that this will be an uphill battle based on the environments in which they reside:

> It was just harsh, hard. You had to be a rough kid. . . . It was a place that should have been condemned a long time ago. Every day people getting shot. You stand on the sidewalk, you know, somebody running by with a gun, kids getting ran over, people sneaking in people's windows, raping people. (Bright, Ward, & Negi, 2011, p. 40)

For other girls, returning to the juvenile system represents perhaps the safest place for them. Given the economic marginality, violence, and chaos that encompass their lives, it is no surprise that a structured orderly environment that provides food, clothing, and shelter is viewed as a favorable option, even if it means being incarcerated. For families that are involved in abusive and criminal behaviors, a return home for the youth can also mean a return to the behaviors that led them to the juvenile court in the first place.

> Here I am back on the streets and if I do this again and get into trouble then I'm just gonna go back to a place where they are gonna feed me and I don't have to worry about somebody beatin' me there; I don't have to worry about somebody molestin' me there, you know? (Garcia & Lane, 2010, p. 235)

> I think if they would have kept me in longer, I think I probably would have been better off than what I am now. When I first got out . . . I was doing good here. . . . Then I got out of the little program and stuff, came back over here [living at home], and everybody was still doing the same thing they was doing, and I fell right back into the habit (Morash, Stevens, & Yingling, 2014).

Although traditional research on female offenders has focused on the risk factors that lead to negative behaviors, recent research has shifted to include resiliency or protective factors to fight against the risks of delinquent behavior. These factors include intelligence; brilliance; courage; creativity; tenacity; compassion; humor; insightfulness; social competence; problem-solving abilities; autonomy; potential with leadership; engagement in family, community, and religious activities; and a sense of purpose and belief in the future. While these resiliency factors typically develop within the context of the family, the support for such a curriculum needs to come from somewhere else, since many delinquent girls often come from families in crisis (Acoca & Dedel, 1998a). Research notes that participating in programs that are gender responsive and focus on building resiliency are not only effective in increasing coping skills for life challenges and improving participants abilities to develop long range goals but engagement in at-risk behaviors and psychological distress also decrease (Javdani & Allen, 2016).

While the intent to provide gender-specific services indicated a potential to address the unique needs of girls, not all scholars are convinced that girls will be able to receive the treatment and programs that are so desperately needed. While many states embarked on data-heavy assessments reflecting the needs of girls, few of these adventures have translated into effective programmatic changes (Chesney-Lind & Shelden, 2004). Funding remains the most significant barrier in providing effective services for girls. Even when gender-specific programming options exist, the need for these services can outweigh the available options. The limited number of placements, combined with long waiting lists for such services, often makes treatment options unavailable for most girls (Bloom et al., 2002a). However, several individual and community factors also affect program delivery, including lack of information or difficulties in accessing services, resistance toward programming by girls and their families, and distrust of service providers. In addition, racial, economic, and cultural issues can affect whether communities will seek out assistance and the degree to which these services will reflect culturally relevant issues (Bloom et al., 2002b). To develop effective and available programming, the system needs to place the allocation of resources as a priority in identifying and addressing the needs of girls in the juvenile justice system.

/// SUMMARY

- Arrest data and self-report data present contradictory images on the nature and prevalence of female violence.

- While arrests for violent offenses involving girls have increased, self-report data among girls indicate a decrease in the levels of violence.

- Police and the courts have altered the way in which they respond to cases of female delinquency, particularly in cases of family or school violence.

- Many incidents of family violence stem from symbolic struggles for adolescent freedom between girls and their parents.

- For juvenile girls, the most significant risk factors for delinquency include a poor family relationship, a history of abuse, poor school performance, negative peer relationships, and issues with substance abuse.

- Issues of emotional and mental health are a high area of need for delinquent girls.

- Effective gender-specific programming needs to provide long-term programming for girls and their social support network that addresses the causes of delinquency in girls' lives.

- Programming that includes resiliency or protective factors plays a significant role in gender-specific programming.

- Programs face significant barriers in implementing services for girls.

/// KEY TERMS

Age-of-consent campaign 280

Bootstrapping 287

Formal processing 283

Gender-specific programming 291

Juvenile delinquency 282

Juvenile Justice and Delinquency Prevention (JJDP) Act of 1974 287

Net widening 280

Parens patriae 279

Reauthorization of the Juvenile Justice and Delinquency

Prevention (JJDP) Act (1992) 287

Resiliency 290

Risk factors for female delinquency 288

Status offenses 287

/// DISCUSSION QUESTIONS

1. How did the age-of-consent campaign punish girls and deny healthy expressions of sexuality? What effects of this movement remain today?

2. How have girls continued to be punished for status offenses, despite the enactment of the JJDP Act of 1974?

3. What risk factors for delinquency exist for girls?

4. How has the treatment of girls by the juvenile justice system altered society's understanding of violence among girls?

5. What should gender-specific programming look like? What challenges do states face in implementing these programs?

/// WEB RESOURCES

Girls Study Group: http://girlsstudygroup.rti.org/

National Center for Juvenile Justice: http://www.ncjj.org

Office of Juvenile Justice and Delinquency Prevention: http://www.ojjdp.gov

 Visit **study.sagepub.com/mallicoat3e** to access additional study tools, including eFlashcards, web quizzes, web resources, video resources, and SAGE journal articles.

READING /// 13

As you've learned, girls have unique needs that have often been ignored by the justice system. Over the past several decades, the focus on gender-specific programming has sought to address these unique needs. But are these programs effective? This article explores that question by using juvenile justice staff members to explore the challenges of implementing these programs.

Assessing the Status of Gender-Specific Programs Through the Lens of Juvenile Justice Staff

Jessica P. Hodge, Kristi Holsinger, & Kristen Maziarka

Prior to the 1970s, criminological theories and criminal justice practices ignored girls involved in the justice system. Criminological theories failed to explain girls' delinquency by either neglecting girls entirely, explaining their behavior in sexist ways, or attempting to fit them into theories developed for boys (Belknap & Holsinger, 1998; Holsinger, 2000). Similarly, in juvenile justice system practices, girls were either disregarded or placed in programs that had been designed for boys or designed to return them to their stereotyped gender role. Because of the small number of girls relative to boys within the system, girls were often treated as an afterthought and not considered a priority among policymakers and practitioners. When federal, state, or local governments acknowledged girls' needs for equal attention, a gender-neutral approach was considered an appropriate response; this equal treatment often meant that girls were dealt with in the same manner as boys and their distinct needs were overlooked.

After being ignored for years, girls are no longer invisible within juvenile justice systems. One reason is because of their growing proportion of system involvement relative to boys. Although relying on statistics fails to account for how changes in social control mechanisms (e.g., the policies and procedures of schools and law enforcement

officials) have contributed to rising arrest rates (Goodkind, 2005; Schwartz & Rookey, 2008; Steffensmeier, Schwartz, Zhong, & Ackerman, 2005), reports show that girls are getting into trouble and becoming involved in juvenile justice systems at higher rates than in previous years. According to one report, juvenile courts handled more than 400,000 cases involving girls in 2007, more than twice the number of cases compared to 1985 (Knoll & Sickmund, 2010). In addition, great strides have been made over the past few decades as many feminist scholars have brought gender issues to the attention of mainstream criminology and have attempted to better understand girls' unique pathways to delinquency (Bailey & McCloskey, 2005; Belknap, 1996; Burgess-Proctor, 2006; Campbell, 1981; Chesney-Lind, 1989; Chesney-Lind & Shelden, 1992; Daly & Chesney-Lind, 1988; Holsinger, 2000; Holsinger & Holsinger, 2005; Naffine, 1996). Girls' needs have also come to the attention of criminal justice practitioners as federally funded research has continued to highlight girls' unique needs and experiences (Belknap & Holsinger, 1998, 2006; Peters, 1998). Instead of utilizing a gender-neutral approach, which meant just placing girls into programs originally created for boys, many jurisdictions have developed programs and policies that attempt to address the specific needs of system-involved girls (Foley, 2008; Peters, 1998).

SOURCE: Hodge, J. P., Holsinger, K., & Maziarka, K. (2015). Assessing the status of gender-specific programs through the lens of juvenile justice staff. *Women & Criminal Justice, 25*(3), 184–200. Copyright © 2015 Routledge. Reprinted with permission from Taylor & Francis.

With the implementation of gender-specific programs and policies throughout juvenile justice systems over the past several years, research needs to examine whether such programs and policies are meeting their intended goals. Although a program evaluation is beyond the scope of this study, the present research provides insight into whether the implementation of gender-specific policies is being accomplished in one county juvenile court system that has made a concerted effort to do this. Using in-depth interviews with juvenile justice staff, this study explores the obstacles and successes of one court's efforts to incorporate gender-responsive programming and policies.

Gender-Specific Programming

The movement toward gender-responsive programming and policies for system-involved girls gained momentum during the 1990s. As the number of girls involved with the juvenile justice system increased, there was a growing concern regarding the lack of appropriate services for females. In response to this concern, in 1992, Congress amended the Juvenile Justice and Delinquency Prevention Act of 1974 to require states to provide an analysis of gender-specific needs and to put forth a plan to address these needs in order to receive funding under the Act (Bloom, Owen, Deschenes, & Rosenbaum, 2002; Maniglia & Temple, 1998). At the same time, Congress created a program under Title II of the Juvenile Justice and Delinquency Prevention Act that provided funds that specifically challenged states to develop and implement policies that addressed gender bias in placement and treatment and to establish programs that addressed the needs of system-involved girls (Kempf-Leonard & Sample, 2000; Maniglia & Temple, 1998).

The enduring demand for gender-responsive programs and policies has been the result of a proliferation of empirical evidence that demonstrates the different pathways to delinquency and the varying needs of system-involved girls and boys. The term *gender specific,* although relevant for both girls and boys, primarily references programs intended for system-involved girls (Foley, 2008; Goodkind, 2005). Although studies show that there are similar correlates for delinquency between boys and girls, such as socioeconomic status, difficulties in school, and disruption in family backgrounds, research continues to show that there are distinct gender differences in pathways to crime and that there are varied reasons why females and males participate in delinquent behaviors (Bloom & Covington, 2001). For instance, data demonstrate that there is a strong link between victimization, trauma, and girls' delinquency (Belknap & Holsinger, 2006; Bloom & Covington, 2001; Bloom et al., 2002; Chesney-Lind, 1999; Chesney-Lind & Sheldon, 2004; Dembo, Williams, Wothke, Schmeidler, & Brown, 1992). In their study of more than 400 institutionalized youth, Belknap and Holsinger (2006) found that girls experienced significantly greater amounts of abuse than boys, including verbal, physical, and sexual abuse. Dembo et al. (1992) discovered in their study of girls in detention that childhood abuse and neglect played a significant role in their involvement in the juvenile justice system.

Research also shows that girls often experience greater mental health issues than boys (Acoca, 1999; Hubbard & Matthews, 2008; McCabe, Lansing, Garland, & Hough, 2002; Sedlak & McPherson, 2010; Zahn et al., 2010). In their study of more than 600 adjudicated youth in San Diego County, McCabe and colleagues (2002) found that girls had higher rates of clinical diagnoses than boys. This included diagnoses of major depression, posttraumatic stress disorder, separation anxiety, and disruptive disorders. A loss of self-esteem can also contribute to girls' delinquency. Psychologists consider the loss of self-esteem to be part of the growing up process for females because of "the negative messages young women receive from society about their bodies, their minds, and their worth," which often results in dramatic changes for girls in their self-images and their behavior (Maniglia & Temple, 1998, p. 16).

The manner in which girls' behaviors are dealt with by the juvenile justice system often perpetuates further involvement in delinquency. Studies demonstrate how girls' delinquency is often the result of the abuse and victimization they experience; girls run away from home and/or use drugs as a means of coping with and surviving the traumatic events in their lives (Bloom & Covington, 2001; Goodkind, 2005; Zahn et al., 2010). Behaviors that originated because of negative life events then become the reason for girls' involvement in the juvenile justice system. Moreover, studies show that girls often receive harsher penalties for less serious crimes and that this treatment is due to a lack of alternatives available for girls within juvenile justice systems (Beger & Hoffman, 1998, Potter, 1999 as cited in Hubbard & Matthews, 2008).

As a result of the differing pathways to delinquency, girls have distinct needs that must be addressed in order to prevent further involvement in crime. Gender-specific policies and programs are a response to these unique needs. Morgan and Patton (2002) explained how gender-specific programming:

> intentionally allows gender to affect and guide services in areas such as site selection, staff selection, program development, content, and material to create an environment that reflects an understanding of the realities of girls' lives, and is responsive to the issues and needs of the girls and young women being served. (p. 58)

More specifically, Covington and Bloom (2006) provided six guiding principles for a gender-responsive approach (pp. 3–5):

1. Acknowledge that gender makes a difference.

2. Create an environment based on safety, respect, and dignity.

3. Develop policies, practices, and programs that are relational and promote health connections to children, family, significant others, and the community.

4. Address substance abuse, trauma, and mental health issues through comprehensive, integrated, and culturally relevant services and appropriate supervision.

5. Provide women with opportunities to improve their socioeconomic conditions.

6. Establish a system of community supervision and reentry with comprehensive, collaborative services.

In sum, gender-specific programs provide opportunities and programs that focus on the specific needs of girls as established by research. This is not to say that

existing theoretical explanations are without merit when it comes to girls or that existing best practices in correctional intervention should be eliminated. It is necessary to acknowledge, however, that gender-specific research and approaches have not been meaningfully integrated with existing theoretical work or with the principles of effective correctional intervention (Hubbard & Matthews, 2008). Although the rationale driving the gender-responsive approach is evidence based, scant research has examined whether the implementations of such programs are being accomplished as originally intended, and even less research exists to determine whether these programs are effective at reducing recidivism.

In Bloom et al.'s (2002) evaluation of one state's efforts to address gender-specific programming, the authors found that there was still much work to be done in order to meet the needs of system-involved girls. Respondents in their survey indicated that they needed more information about working with girls, particularly the identification of best practices and models for gender-responsive programs. Bloom and colleagues discovered that funding for gender-specific programs was "critically inadequate" and that this affected the quality and quantity of appropriate services (p. 50). Holsinger, Like, and Hodge (2009) found in their study of one county juvenile court that there remained a number of issues related to services for girls despite the court's ostensive efforts to be gender-responsive. Holsinger and colleagues explained how the "officers felt that girls had needs that were not being addressed in any concrete way by the court" (p. 10). Specifically, there was a lack of programming that addressed critical needs of girls, such as self-esteem, healthy relationships, abuse, and trauma counseling. Another area that needed to be addressed, according to Holsinger et al., involved staff sensitivity to working with girls. This issue is further explored in the following section.

Staff Perspectives: Working With Girls

Bloom and Covington (2001) asserted that there is "a paucity of research on the attitudes and experiences of professionals who work with girls" (p. 5); however, the few studies that have explored the perspectives of juvenile justice staff have generated similar conclusions. One such conclusion is that girls are considered to be more difficult to work with than boys (Baines & Alder, 1996; Belknap, Holsinger, & Dunn, 1997; Bond-Maupin, Maupin, & Leisenring, 2002; Gaarder, Rodriguez, & Zatz, 2004). For instance, Baines and Alder (1996) revealed in their study that youth workers often described boys as "easier" to work with because boys were not as "complex" and their needs were easier to meet (p. 481). The youth workers also claimed that girls harbored resentment for longer periods than boys and that they had to be more careful about what they said or did when working with the girls.

In Gaarder et al.'s (2004) study of juvenile probation officers, the officers described the girls as needy, whiny, manipulative, and promiscuous. During interviews, officers made comments about the girls such as "They play the system real well. Girls play the system better than the boys do. They're manipulative" and "They're more like criers. Girls will do that. They'll break down and you'll be in the sympathy thing for awhile you know, but then you realize what they're doing" (p. 556). Gaarder et al. also found that some of the probation officers did not see the need for gender-specific programs; these officers felt that all of the juveniles had similar needs and that they should be treated the same, regardless of gender. Even when there was agreement that gender-specific programming was a good idea, the majority of the probation officers could not identify a program that was specifically developed for girls.

Holsinger et al. (2009) reached similar conclusions. Staff members described girls as "emotional" and "overwhelming" and felt that girls needed more time and one-on-one nurturing than boys (p. 11). As a result, Holsinger et al. discussed the need for training that would increase staff members' sensitivity to working with girls and increase staff support for gender-specific programs and policies. Without this training, girls' needs would not be adequately addressed, nor would girls develop relationships with staff that were needed to facilitate behavioral changes. As Baines and Alder (1996) explained,

> The negativity and lack of enthusiasm displayed by a number of workers toward work with young women does not bode well for the quality of service available to marginalized young women within a system where contact with a

> sympathetic and understanding worker may be crucial in the process of moving in from the margins. (p. 483)

Despite the proliferation of scholarship discussing the importance of gender-specific programming and policies for system-involved girls, there remains a dearth of methodologically rigorous research examining the implementation of such programs and policies. Research has failed to explore whether the push for gender-responsive programming has been successful, and, as discussed previously, scant research has explored this area through the lens of juvenile justice staff. This study used a qualitative approach to further this line of inquiry.

Data and Methods

Data for this project derived from 21 in-depth interviews conducted with juvenile justice staff during the summer of 2012. The staff members were all employees of a midwestern county family court system located within the United States. The county, with a population of approximately 800,000 people, is generally considered an urban area and consistently maintains the highest total crime index in the state (State Highway Patrol Statistical Analysis Center, 2014[1]). The county's population is primarily White (70.5%) and Black (24.1%). The percentage of people living below the poverty level is high (17% as of 2012), with a median household income of approximately $47,000 (U.S. Census Bureau, 2014). The county family court holds jurisdiction over a wide range of domestic relations and juvenile issues, including juvenile delinquency, child dependency, and child custody matters. In delinquency cases, youths age 16 and younger are generally considered juveniles within this family court.

This particular family court has taken concerted steps to incorporate gender-responsive policies and programs for system-involved girls, which allowed us to assess whether a county that has taken such measures has in fact accomplished a gender-responsive approach. Specifically, the family court has engaged in research projects to learn more about this population from both the girls' and staff members' viewpoints (see, e.g., Holsinger et al., 2009). It has also initiated gender-specific trainings for staff members that were developed and facilitated by one

... Through the Lens of Juvenile Justice Staff

of the authors; such trainings have been held in 2009 and again in 2010. In these trainings, staff ... about the distinction between gender differences and ... differences, the risk factors associated with girls' delinquency, the key components of the gender-responsive approach, and how to become an advocate of gender-specific programming. Moreover, since 2011, the family court has implemented the Savvy Sisters model. Savvy Sisters is a program premised on the Girls Matter curriculum developed through the National Council on Crime and Delinquency and is considered a practical application of the core concepts of the gender-responsive approach (Ravoira et al., n.d.).[2] The Savvy Sisters curriculum is divided into topics such as safety, communication, relationships, sex, spirituality, and career and vocation choices. The objectives of the program include increasing protective factors and reducing risk factors associated with girls' delinquency and providing opportunities for girls to learn how to make informed, positive choices for a safe, healthy, and productive future (Ravoira et al., n.d.).

A purposive sampling strategy was used because we were interested in learning from staff who worked directly with system-involved girls and, theoretically, would be the most informed about the gender-responsive approach taken with the girls in their care. In other words, this recruitment strategy allowed us to target individuals who could speak directly to the issues of interest (Hennink, Hutter, & Bailey, 2011). The staff members involved in this study worked either at the one residential facility within the county that houses incarcerated girls or as gender-specific juvenile probation officers who only have girls on their caseloads. The residential facility can house approximately 50 juveniles, and the residents are there for an average of 6 months. Although the facility has the capacity to hold up to 13 girls at one time, only eight female residents were there at the time of this study. The juvenile probation officers have, on average, approximately 20 female clients in their caseload.

Participants were recruited for this study in two ways. The researchers attended staff meetings at the facility for each of the three shifts in which the purpose of the study was explained. The voluntary nature of participation and the ability to schedule interviews during staff members' regularly scheduled work hours was emphasized. Recruitment of the two juvenile probation officers who worked specifically with girls was initiated via e-mail

... the same information shared with facility staff. ...ws were conducted on site, either at the resi... expla...or at the probation office in a private space voluntary...iewees could speak freely about their participation, ...experiences. Consent forms were conducted by the ...d methods and procedures, the sion of each particip...ation, rights to discontinue order to further ensure c...iality. The interviews were participants with a pseudonym ...rs, and with the permission ... recorder was used. In All of the interviews were transcribe... we provided the to help with clarity and readability, on octim... their identities. text either by eliminating unnecessary filler w... however, using punctuation. The interviews ranged from 40 min... edited just over an hour, with an average length of approximately 50 min.

We used an interview guide with open-ended questions that encouraged participants to speak openly and directly about their experiences working with system-involved girls. The participants were asked questions about the challenges they faced working with girls, what they liked about working with girls, whether they felt the girls' needs were being met, and what services they felt were still needed for the girls. The participants were also asked whether they felt they received adequate training in order to be successful in their respective positions. These questions served as categories of interest during data analysis. Working directly from verbatim transcripts of each interview, we analyzed the data by hand using an open coding method, a strategy consistent with grounded theory (Charmaz, 2006). Each researcher coded the transcripts separately in order to identify relevant and common themes and to ensure interrater reliability. Quotes were used to illustrate and offer depth to the themes that surfaced.

Sample Description

The sample included 21 juvenile court staff members: 19 worked at the residential facility and two worked as gender-specific juvenile probation officers. This represented a participation rate of 84%. All of the participants currently worked with girls in their respective positions, but many of them also had experience working with system-involved boys. The 19 participants employed at the of the authors; such trainings have been held twice, once in 2009 and again in 2010. In these trainings, staff learned about the distinction between gender differences and sex differences, the risk factors associated with girls' delinquency, the key components of the gender-responsive approach, and how to become an advocate of gender-specific programming. Moreover, since 2011, the family court has implemented the Savvy Sisters model. Savvy Sisters is a program premised on the Girls Matter curriculum developed through the National Council on Crime and Delinquency and is considered a practical application of the core concepts of the gender-responsive approach (Ravoira et al., n.d.).[2] The Savvy Sisters curriculum is divided into topics such as safety, communication, relationships, sex, spirituality, and career and vocation choices. The objectives of the program include increasing protective factors and reducing risk factors associated with girls' delinquency and providing opportunities for girls to learn how to make informed, positive choices for a safe, healthy, and productive future (Ravoira et al., n.d.).

A purposive sampling strategy was used because we were interested in learning from staff who worked directly with system-involved girls and, theoretically, would be the most informed about the gender-responsive approach taken with the girls in their care. In other words, this recruitment strategy allowed us to target individuals who could speak directly to the issues of interest (Hennink, Hutter, & Bailey, 2011). The staff members involved in this study worked either at the one residential facility within the county that houses incarcerated girls or as gender-specific juvenile probation officers who only have girls on their caseloads. The residential facility can house approximately 50 juveniles, and the residents are there for an average of 6 months. Although the facility has the capacity to hold up to 13 girls at one time, only eight female residents were there at the time of this study. The juvenile probation officers have, on average, approximately 20 female clients in their caseload.

Participants were recruited for this study in two ways. The researchers attended staff meetings at the facility for each of the three shifts in which the purpose of the study was explained. The voluntary nature of participation and the ability to schedule interviews during staff members' regularly scheduled work hours was emphasized. Recruitment of the two juvenile probation officers who worked specifically with girls was initiated via e-mail

conveying the same information shared with facility staff. All interviews were conducted on site, either at the residential facility or at the probation office in a private space so that the interviewees could speak freely about their perceptions and experiences. Consent forms were explained that outlined methods and procedures, the voluntary nature of participation, rights to discontinue participation, and confidentiality. The interviews were conducted by the first two authors, and with the permission of each participant, a digital recorder was used. In order to further ensure confidentiality, we provided the participants with a pseudonym to protect their identities. All of the interviews were transcribed verbatim; however, to help with clarity and readability, on occasion we edited text either by eliminating unnecessary filler words or by using punctuation. The interviews ranged from 40 min to just over an hour, with an average length of approximately 50 min.

We used an interview guide with open-ended questions that encouraged participants to speak openly and directly about their experiences working with system-involved girls. The participants were asked questions about the challenges they faced working with girls, what they liked about working with girls, whether they felt the girls' needs were being met, and what services they felt were still needed for the girls. The participants were also asked whether they felt they received adequate training in order to be successful in their respective positions. These questions served as categories of interest during data analysis. Working directly from verbatim transcripts of each interview, we analyzed the data by hand using an open coding method, a strategy consistent with grounded theory (Charmaz, 2006). Each researcher coded the transcripts separately in order to identify relevant and common themes and to ensure interrater reliability. Quotes were used to illustrate and offer depth to the themes that surfaced.

Sample Description

The sample included 21 juvenile court staff members: 19 worked at the residential facility and two worked as gender-specific juvenile probation officers. This represented a participation rate of 84%. All of the participants currently worked with girls in their respective positions, but many of them also had experience working with system-involved boys. The 19 participants employed at the residential facility included youth workers, facility and shift supervisors, case managers, and counselors.[3] The professional experiences of the sample varied, but the majority of the sample had worked in some capacity with system-involved girls for several years. The number of years of related professional experience ranged from only 6 months to more than 30 years.

Both of the gender-specific juvenile probation officers were female; one identified as African American and one identified as White. Of the 19 residential staff members, 14 were female and five were male. Eleven of the residential staff members identified as African American and eight of the residential staff members identified as White.

Findings

Three dominant themes emerged among interviews with the juvenile court staff. The first aligned with previous studies involving the perceptions of staff members who work with girls on a regular basis: The majority of the participants expressed frustration and described girls as more difficult than boys. The second theme spoke to the lack of appropriate programs available for system-involved girls: All of the participants expressed concerns and could easily identify key areas in which the girls' needs were not being addressed. The third theme illustrated a basic misconception among staff regarding the intent and goals of a gender-specific approach. Although this county's family court had taken steps to become more responsive to girls' needs, our participants' responses confirmed that there was still much work to be done.

Challenges Working With Girls

Consistent with findings of Baines and Alder (1996), Belknap et al. (1997), Bond-Maupin et al. (2002), and Gaarder et al. (2004), the juvenile justice staff in this study expressed many challenges when working with girls. Girls were considered to be more needy, manipulative, and dramatic than the boys. Girls were also thought to be more catty than boys, and staff expressed frustration with the "rollercoaster of emotions" that girls often demonstrated. The following responses convey these messages: "I don't want to say very needy but they always have an issue over small stuff" (male, residential staff) and "You

never really know who's really getting along because they can have a fistfight and then 2 hours later they're like, doing each other's hair and you're like, okay" (female, residential staff). One of the residential staff members with experience working with both boys and girls commented on how the staff members who work with girls have "a lot harder job than the staff working with boys." She explained that this was because the girls were "much more needy, much more emotional, [and had] many more health problems, at least in their mind." This same staff person went on to say,

> Girls are smart, you know, so you can't get caught up in their little trick bags and their little manipulations, because I mean overall, I've always seen them as smarter than the boys. So you have to be careful as staff.

Another challenge was that girls were thought to harbor resentment or maintain anger for longer periods than the boys. One of the male residential staff members stated, " . . . Working with the girls has been different. I mean, they're, uh, totally different, it's night and day from the boys. Girls, they seem to keep a grudge no matter what." One of the female probation officers commented on how the girls "always hear the negative, and never the positive . . . they feed off their own negative energy and others' negative energy." However, one of the female staff members offered a different perspective. Although recognizing that girls "don't let things go until it's resolved," she asserted that this was a positive thing because ". . . it gives them an opportunity to express who they are, their feelings, you know, their femininity."

Despite the challenges expressed by the staff members, all of the participants said they enjoyed working with girls. This was true even though many staff members also expressed frustration with the lack of court services or appropriate resources for the girls.

Girls' Needs: The Missing Pieces

Although this family court had made efforts toward being gender responsive, it was discovered through the interviews that many components of this approach were still missing. Research consistently demonstrates how girls' delinquency is linked to the trauma and victimization they experience in their lives (Belknap & Holsinger, 2006; Bloom & Covington, 2001; Bloom et al., 2002; Chesney-Lind, 1999; Dembo et al., 1992). Thus, in order to effectively address girls' delinquency, programs must adequately address girls' trauma, and as many of the participants in this study explained, this need was not being addressed. Several of the staff members discussed how the amount of trauma that the girls experienced affected their behaviors and their progress while in the facility. For example, one of the male residential staff members reflected on his experiences working with girls:

A lot of girls come in with more things, much more trauma than I've ever seen before. I mean, beforehand, you'd definitely have the parent, the girls that came in, their dads weren't involved in the family. Um, occasional abuse in the family. A neglect case. But now, we're seeing more. Girls come in with sexual assaults, ah, rape cases. Different things like this. Tremendous amount of abuse. And it's just like, it seems like in the past 3 to 4 years, it's been one massive trend and I think kids are coming in with traumatic trauma. And it's, ah, very different. It's changing. You have to learn how to work with them very differently because of the trauma.

One of the female residential staff members also expressed her concerns about the girls not receiving enough trauma counseling:

. . . When it comes to the girls, they're going through a lot of trauma and stuff like that. Yeah, they get counseling and stuff here for it, but it seems like it's never really that in depth and a lot of them need way more than they're being offered . . .

Not only was the lack of trauma counseling for the girls viewed as a critical gap in available services, but a consistent theme among the participants was also the need for staff training to learn how to address the girls' traumatic histories. Many of the participants expressed concern that they were not able to adequately deal with these issues when brought up by the girls. The following comments convey this message:

. . . It seems like a lot of [the girls] have experienced a lot of trauma, especially early on in their lives and it's sometimes hard to deal with that and especially when they are opening up to you and talking to you about it, it's sometimes hard to like, okay what do I say, what do I do . . . (Female, residential staff)

. . . [When] you really look at of all the kids we got, 98% of the kids I gather here has had some type of trauma in their life, and so being able to, ah, understand and maybe be able to pick that out, you know, um, allows you to be able to deal with a kid. (Male, residential staff)

. . . Some of the staff have psych degrees, I have a psych degree but I'm not a counselor. I'm still in school, you know, just because I have my bachelor's, I've got a long way to go to be anything, you know, truly helpful and you just never know, some staff here don't have any degree and, and you know, it's just, they're just doing what they can . . . (Female, residential staff)

The lack of trauma counseling and the lack of staff training on this topic is alarming. Research consistently demonstrates how critical it is to address the traumatic experiences of system-involved girls (see, e.g., Ford, Chapman, Hawke, & Albert, 2007; Lyman & Spinney, 2009). Although boys may also experience trauma, sexual and physical abuse victimization is more common among girls than boys (Ford et al., 2007; Greene, Peters, & Associates, 1998; National Council on Crime and Delinquency, 2010). Boys may report witnessing more violent acts than girls; however, girls report experiencing more violence (Ford et al., 2007). For instance, according to Sedlak and Broadhurst (1996), girls are 3 times more likely than boys to have been sexually abused. Consequently, research also indicates that the rate of posttraumatic stress disorder among incarcerated female delinquents not only is higher than that in the gender population but surpasses the incidence of posttraumatic stress disorder among incarcerated male delinquents as well (Cauffman, Feldman, Waterman, & Steiner, 1998). Because addressing trauma is a cornerstone of the gender-responsive approach, it is troubling that staff not only felt ill equipped to work with the girls but felt that the girls were not obtaining the necessary counseling to work through these traumatic experiences.

Another area in which staff members felt that girls' needs were not being addressed related to sex and relationship education. Although staff members acknowledged that current gender-specific programming touched on these issues, they felt like the programs were not fully addressing the girls' needs. For example, one of the gender-specific juvenile probation officers spoke about how the majority of her caseload either was pregnant or thought that they were pregnant at any given time. She discussed the need for more specific education for the girls regarding the consequences of having sex, including sexually transmitted diseases and pregnancy. Many staff members also expressed the need to educate the girls on topics such as budgeting finances, cooking, and other life skills, skills that could help the girls support themselves. It is notable that Garcia and Lane (2009) discovered that this was one of the program areas most desired among girls in the focus groups they conducted. Holsinger (2003) revealed similar findings in her survey of system-involved girls in Ohio: Out of 17 potential programs, the most wanted programs related to job/career skills and independent living skills. As in the current study, however, very few of these skills were being taught to the girls.

The literature confirms that girls need opportunities to create positive changes in their lives and within their community (Sharp & Simon, 2004), and many staff members spoke about this issue as well. Staff members discussed how the girls needed more opportunities to "broaden their horizons" or to do service work within the community so that they could learn about life "outside of their own neighborhood." One of the female residential staff members suggested that the girls could volunteer at local hospitals or even tour the local airport:

> . . . Take them to places that they've never gone before. Like an airport. We have an airport not too far from here. . . . Let them go . . . let them tour so it can, you know, broaden their horizon and not only that, allow them to think bigger than where they're at and where they've come from. And because sometimes, just, I would like

to, you know, dress 'em up and take 'em out to like a formal dinner just to let them know that there's just more than . . . there's life past 27th street.

The community outreach could also provide an opportunity to educate the girls on what resources were available for them once they left the facility. For instance, another female residential staff member suggested that the girls volunteer at a food pantry or a domestic violence shelter so that they would be aware of these resources if they were needed.

Finally, as previously mentioned, another major component of gender-specific programs is to establish a system of community supervision and reentry with comprehensive, collaborative services (Covington & Bloom, 2006). Several of the staff members at the residential facility discussed how this component was missing and felt that there needed to be "a bridge" for girls leaving the facility that was in addition to the probation services offered. This bridge was discussed as including better follow-up with the girls once they left the facility, to providing better education about the resources available to them in the community, to having a place or "safe space" for the girls to go that was not part of their disposition or probation (i.e., a place where they could speak freely about their activities with someone without getting into trouble). Many participants felt that this bridge was a critical gap missing in the services provided to girls.

As shown, staff members were able to clearly articulate practical ideas for programs and activities that would benefit the girls—such as community outreach, life skills training, more effective aftercare—and many of these suggestions were consistent with the ideals of gender-specific services. Furthermore, several of the long-term staff members spoke about activities that they used to do with girls that had allowed for greater access to opportunities in the community, but these programs had been eliminated because of either funding cuts or increased concerns about the liability of youth leaving the facility. Because of the staff members' awareness of girls' needs, it was surprising that many of them continued to hold negative and sexist images, or at the very least gender-stereotypical ideas, about women and girls. This issue is further explored in the next section.

Gender-Specific Policies and Programs: Getting Lost in Translation

This particular juvenile court, as stated before, had taken steps to implement gender-specific policies and incorporate gender-responsive programs for the girls in the residential facility and on probation. Specifically, over the past few years, the juvenile court had hired more women to work directly with girls, which included the development of gender-specific probation officer positions. Also, as previously explained, the court had implemented programming for the girls in the residential facility and on probation that has been designated as gender-responsive curricula.

Despite these efforts, it was apparent through the participants' responses that more work still needed to be done in order to implement these types of policies and programs effectively and appropriately. Several of the participants discussed participating in gender-specific trainings as either probation officers or residential staff members, yet when the staff members were asked about what sorts of programs or policies had been implemented in order to be gender-responsive, their responses demonstrated how there was still a lack of understanding as to what this entailed. For example, there was a common misconception that "gender specific" translated to "girly stuff" and reinforcing traditional gender roles. Several of the participants discussed how the policies were gender-responsive because the girls were allowed to feel "like a young lady," as they now could have things such as makeup and perfume. One of the male residential staff members explained it this way:

> When I first started back in [year omitted] we treated [the boys and girls] the same. We started the gender specific initiative, and I see the trend of, we still hold them accountable for their actions and stuff, we still treat them rules-wise like the boys, but we still, we give them, I'd say, girl stuff. We allow them to have the makeup, the fingernail polish, the ability to do their hair. To do the things, they've got the sink where they can wash it, they can do their hair and stuff like this.

Another residential member who was female noted,

> I think [the gender-specific program] is a good program. I also think that the policies that kind of helps allow them to be young ladies, that teach them to be young ladies [are good]. . . . but you know to be a lady or to teach a lady to be a lady you have to let them experience those things, makeup maybe, perfume, doing their nails, the things that [go] with the qualities of a woman or a lady.

Several staff recommended trainings for the girls on how to apply makeup and suggested classes on cooking, home economics, sewing, and "first aid for nursing." Some staff mentioned how the girls could dress up and learn proper etiquette in preparation for dating scenarios with boys. One staff member longingly recalled a time in which a woman with a modeling school taught the girls how to model and then brought them to a local mall to walk the runway.

These comments hearken back to a period in corrections that emphasized teaching girls how to best fulfill a stereotypical gender role that narrowly defined who women and girls were allowed to be. These comments unexpectedly came from older and younger staff alike and were in stark contrast to the comments discussed earlier regarding the lack of programs teaching girls relevant job and survival skills to support independent living.

Perhaps one of the reasons for the lack of understanding regarding gender-specific policies is due to the lack of education or training surrounding these issues. Although the participants commented on how they had received gender-specific training, many of them spoke to how they could use more opportunities to learn about these types of issues: " . . . sometimes you can just get so wrapped up in the work, and I think always learning something new and gaining more knowledge about working with the gender population is always a great thing" (female, gender-specific probation officer). The demands of the job also hindered the proper implementation of the gender-specific programs. For instance, one of the gender-specific probation officers explained that because of high staff turnover and escalating responsibilities, the probation officers could not focus on the girls and the gender-specific aspects of the program; instead, they were focused more on administrative duties and making sure that the girls were compliant with court orders.

Discussion

The family court involved in this study had implemented a program labeled as *gender-responsive curricula* and required staff members to attend gender-specific trainings in the past. Despite these efforts, doubts remained as to whether the implementations of the gender-specific policies and programs were being done effectively. This begged the question: Why is it so difficult to implement the gender-responsive approach?

A quick and easy place to point blame is the lack of funding for such programs. Previous research has shown that funding gender-specific programs is problematic for many jurisdictions (Belknap et al., 1997; Bloom et al., 2002). Although federal grants have been made available for such purposes, resources are dwindling because of budget constraints occurring across the country. Indeed, participants in this study spoke to how they had seen programs cut because funding was no longer available, even though the girls seemed to benefit from the programs. Moreover, as one of the gender-specific probation officers in this study mentioned, increased caseloads make it difficult for these staff members to focus on the gender-responsive components.

Not having enough funds or resources is an obstacle to adequately implementing gender-responsive programs. The provision of fewer funds for girls' services because there are smaller numbers of system-involved girls than boys, or because girls are considered less dangerous, is sexist and detrimental not only to the girls but to the larger society as well. Moreover, when there are not as many alternatives available for system-involved girls as there are for boys, girls are often required to participate in programs that do not fit their specific needs (Holsinger et al., 2009). This practice limits the effectiveness of such programs and decreases the chances of successful rehabilitation and reduced recidivism.

Another potential obstacle for the implementation of gender-specific programs and policies is the lack of support that these types of programs garner from direct line staff and/or court administrators. Gaarder et al. (2004) found in their study that juvenile probation officers rejected the need for gender-specific programming; they asserted that treatment options should be based on individual characteristics rather than gender. However, in the current study, the problem of staff buying into the gender-responsive approach did not appear to be the issue. Even though there was a lack of understanding of what gender-responsive programs and policies looked like, many of the participants maintained that these types of programs were warranted.

On the one hand, the staff members' responses may have been filtered because of their prior participation in gender-specific trainings offered by one of the authors. It is certainly plausible that staff members claimed to support the gender-specific approach because they were familiar with the researcher's background and prior involvement with the family court. The participants' candor when speaking about the challenges associated with working with girls, however, alleviated some concerns about the authenticity of their responses. If they were merely pretending to buy in to the gender-specific approach, it seems logical that the staff would have also filtered their responses in other capacities as well. Moreover, the most recent training conducted by the researcher was held in 2010, almost 2 years prior to data collection for this project. Although several staff members recalled having participated in these trainings, others had been hired afterward, and thus seemingly were not familiar with or influenced by the author's connection to the gender-specific curriculum.

On the other hand, like critics of gender-specific programs claim, perhaps these types of programs are difficult to implement because the goals of the programs, as well as the design and implementation, are not clearly conveyed to staff, nor are the efforts integrated into existing intervention efforts. According to Kempf-Leonard and Sample (2000), "Most recommendations [for gender-specific programs] fail to explain why the program elements for girls are any different from elements appropriate for boys" (p. 118). The authors argued, for instance, that both boys and girls experience victimization and trauma, yet because gender is only one element when considering how these experiences affect them, treatment should be based on a variety of individual factors. Kempf-Leonard and Sample asserted that "it is difficult to understand how good *female-specific* services differ from good *youth* services" (p. 118, emphasis in the original). They suggested that the lack of a clear explanation as to what is needed to design and operate effective gender-specific services has hindered the justification for and the implementation of such programs.

Goodkind (2005) offered a different critique of the gender-responsive approach. She argued that this approach is faulty in design for a number of reasons, one reason being gender essentialism. Goodkind took issue with the fact that much of the literature regarding gender-specific services neglects the diversity within genders. Because these services often ignore how gender intersects with other identities, such as race, ethnicity, class, and sexuality, the programs are inherently flawed and ineffective. Goodkind also took issue with the fact that these services focus on treating the individual rather than the structural and institutional changes that are needed. Moreover, as Goodkind explained,

> I was troubled by the findings of our evaluation, which indicated that despite the good intentions of the staff, the gender-specific treatment at one facility was serving to reinforce oppressive gender expectations, thus perpetuating the juvenile justice system's history of policing sexuality and maintaining gender conformity. (p. 56)

This concern is similar to what was discovered in the current study. Although the staff claimed that gender-responsive programs and policies were warranted, they continued to reinforce gender expectations by associating "gender specific" with "girly stuff." Girls were expected to present themselves in a manner that emphasized traditional notions of femininity; this included defining their femininity through their relational expectations (e.g., learning how to interact in dating scenarios with boys) or through the use of makeup and perfume. The continued reliance on these gendered norms and stereotypes fails to address the girls' unique pathways to delinquency and only serves to maintain girls' subordination within society as they are "socialized for, and restricted to, limited aspirations, options, roles, and rewards" (Schur, 1984, p. 11). An illustration of this occurred earlier in the negative assessment of "smart" girls. Rather than perceiving intelligence as a positive quality, staff viewed the smart girls as undesirable or difficult to work with. Because the girls

were not conforming to traditional notions of femininity—such as nurturance, warmth, and submissiveness—they were instead perceived as "manipulative" by staff and thus susceptible to negative sanctions.

Indeed, the issue of gender essentialism is important to recognize when developing and implementing programs for girls in juvenile justice systems and when training staff who work with girls. Not all girls share a single female experience: The life experience of a girl who identifies as White and gay is markedly different from that of a girl who identifies as African American and straight. Gender-specific programs need to acknowledge these differences so that girls utilizing these services do not feel further alienated by a system that does not understand and recognize how their identities intersect to shape their lived experiences (Brubaker & Fox, 2010). Moreover, staff need to be trained in this capacity so as not to further gendered stereotypes, thus negatively affecting how girls respond to such programs. The goals of the approach are undermined by allowing girls to wear fingernail polish and labeling this as *gender responsive* (Holsinger et al., 2009).

A lack of rigorous evaluation studies has also been an obstacle in the full implementation of the gender-responsive approach (Foley, 2008; Sherman, 2012; Zahn, Day, Mihalic, & Tichavsky, 2009). For instance, Foley (2008) discovered in her review of the literature that gender-specific programs did have a significant impact on a range of outcomes, such as substance use, school attendance, self-esteem, and peer relations, but the evaluation designs were problematic and limited the strength of the conclusions. The absence of thorough evaluation studies could mean that what is now considered best practice is not in fact the most effective use of programming resources. This void could translate to frustration and apathy among staff due to the lack of guidance or positive outcomes with programs and policies currently in use, which in turn would affect girls' investment in the provided services. Indeed, this negative cycle may be what is creating barriers for staff in the current study. Perhaps because of a lack of regular training on how to appropriately and consistently facilitate the specific programming, or perhaps because of the lack of rigorous evaluation regarding the program's fidelity, the gender-specific approach is not fully understood or valued by staff.

Conclusion

This study demonstrates that there are still problems with the implementation of gender-specific programming. Not only do staff members continue to express negative comments regarding the girls they work with on a regular basis, but there continues to be a lack of understanding regarding the gender-responsive approach and a lack of appropriate programs that address girls' critical needs. These findings are particularly worrisome due to the fact that this specific juvenile court had made concerted steps over the years toward implementing gender-responsive policies and programs.

The findings from this research must be interpreted within the limitations of the study's methodology. Although there are many advantages to using in-depth interviews with a small sample, including the ability to delve into the complexities of a particular topic, the findings are limited in their generalizability as a result. Gender differences were noted, but unfortunately the sample size was not large enough to analyze how staff race or years of experience shaped staff members' perspectives. Future research could address these issues by conducting similar studies with larger samples or in other jurisdictions for comparison purposes. Furthermore, one of the key features of the gender-responsive approach is gathering input from girls who are actually processed through the system (Holsinger et al., 2009). It is important for girls to be able to voice their own concerns and priorities when it relates to their treatment. Future research should address this by incorporating girls' perspectives on whether the gender-responsive approach is being implemented as needed. This approach would be in line with evaluating the program's fidelity as well.

Despite these limitations, this study underlines the need to continue to explore the implementation of gender-responsive policies and programs. As more girls become involved in juvenile justice systems, it is essential that their needs be evaluated and that programs labeled as *gender specific* appropriately address these needs. However, not only should there be rigorous evaluations of programs using this label, but researchers should continue to assess whether staff are effectively implementing best practices. Gender-responsive policies and programs can only be as effective as the staff responsible for implementing them. Finally, steps must be taken not only to recognize but also to fully appreciate the diversity of experiences within genders. Race, ethnicity, class, and sexuality play a significant role in shaping girls' experiences, both outside of and within juvenile justice systems.

⫶⫶⫶ DISCUSSION QUESTIONS

1. According to the staff interviewed in this study, what are some of the challenges that the face when working with delinquent girls?

2. What are some of the issues that gender specific programs need to spend more time on?

What challenges exist at a structural level in implementing gender specific programming?

Notes

1. The specific state is omitted from the citation in order to protect the identity of the participants.

2. The National Girls Institute has labeled the Savvy Sisters model as *gender-responsive curricula*. The National Girls Institute is a research-based clearinghouse designed to advance and improve girls' issues and programs. The Institute is a federally funded partnership between the National Council on Crime and Delinquency and the Office of Juvenile Justice and Delinquency Prevention. For more information, visit http://www.nationalgirlsinstitute.org/

3. To protect the identity of the participants, we do not identify the specific positions for quotes; rather, any quotes highlighted in the Findings section only identify the participants as working within the residential facility.

REFERENCES

Acoca, L. (1999). Investing in girls: A 21st century strategy. *Juvenile Justice, 6*(1), 3–13.

Bailey, J., & McCloskey, L. (2005). Pathways to adolescent substance use among sexually abused girls. *Journal of Abnormal Child Psychology, 33,* 39–54.

Baines, M., & Alder, C. (1996). Are girls more difficult to work with? Youth workers' perspectives in juvenile justice and related areas. *Crime & Delinquency, 42,* 467–485.

Belknap, J. (1996). *The invisible woman: Gender, crime, and justice.* Cincinnati, OH: Wadsworth.

Belknap, J., & Holsinger, K. (1998). An overview of delinquent girls: How theory and practice have failed and the need for innovative changes. In R. T. Zaplin (Ed.), *Female crime and delinquency: Critical perspectives and effective interventions* (p. 31–59). Gaithersburg, MD: Aspen.

Belknap, J., & Holsinger, K. (2006). The gendered nature of risk factors for delinquency. *Feminist Criminology, 1*(1), 48–71.

Belknap, J., Holsinger, K., & Dunn, M. (1997). Understanding incarcerated girls: The results of a focus group study. *The Prison Journal, 77,* 381–404.

Beger, R. R., & Hoffman, H. (1998). Role of gender of detention disposition of juvenile violators. *Journal of Crime and Justice, 21,* 173–188.

Bloom, B. E., & Covington, S. S. (2001, November). *Effective gender-responsive interventions in juvenile justice: Addressing the lives of delinquent girls.* Paper presented at the annual meeting of the American Society of Criminology, Atlanta, GA.

Bloom, B., Owen, B., Deschenes, E. P., & Rosenbaum, J. (2002). Moving toward justice for female juvenile offenders in the new millennium: Modeling gender-specific policies and programs. *Journal of Contemporary Criminal Justice, 18*(1), 37–56.

Bond-Maupin, L., Maupin, J. R., & Leisenring, A. (2002). Girls' delinquency and the justice implications of intake workers' perspectives. *Women & Criminal Justice, 13*(2/3), 51–77.

Brubaker, S. J., & Fox, K. C. (2010). Urban African American girls at risk: An exploratory study of service needs and provision. *Youth Violence and Juvenile Justice, 8*(3), 250–265.

Burgess-Proctor, A. (2006). Intersections of race, class, gender, and crime: Future directions for feminist criminology. *Feminist Criminology, 1* (1), 27–47.

Campbell, A. (1981). *Girl delinquents.* New York, NY: St. Martin's Press.

Cauffman, E., Feldman, S. S., Waterman, J., & Steiner, H. (1998). Posttraumatic stress disorder among female juvenile offenders. *Journal of the American Academy of Child and Adolescent Psychiatry, 37,* 1209–1216.

Charmaz, K. (2006). *Constructing grounded theory.* Thousand Oaks, CA: Sage.

Chesney-Lind, M. (1989). Girls' crime and woman's place: Toward a feminist model of female delinquency. *Crime & Delinquency, 35*(1), 5–29.

Chesney-Lind, M. (1999). Challenging girls' invisibility in juvenile court. *Annals of the American Academy of Political and Social Science, 564,* 185–202.

Chesney-Lind, M., & Shelden, R. G. (1992). *Girls, delinquency, and juvenile justice.* Pacific Grove, CA: Brooks/Cole.

Chesney-Lind, M., & Sheldon, R. (2004). *Girls, delinquency, and juvenile justice.* Belmont, CA: Wadsworth.

Covington, S. S., & Bloom, B. E. (2006). Gender-responsive treatment and services in correctional settings. *Women and Therapy, 29*(3/4), 9–33. Retrieved from http://stephaniecovington.com/assets/files/FINALC.pdf

Daly, K., & Chesney-Lind, M. (1988). Feminism and criminology. *Justice Quarterly, 5,* 497–535.

Dembo, R., Williams, L., Wothke, W., Schmeidler, J., & Brown, C. H. (1992). The role of family factors, physical abuse, and sexual victimization experiences in high-risk youths' alcohol and other drug use and delinquency: A longitudinal model. *Violence and Victims, 7,* 245–266.

Foley, A. (2008). The current state of gender-specific delinquency programming. *Journal of Criminal Justice, 36,* 262–269.

Ford, J. D., Chapman, J. F., Hawke, J., & Albert, D. (2007, June). *Trauma among youth in the juvenile justice system: Critical issues and new directions.* Delmar, NY: National Center for Mental Health and Juvenile Justice.

Gaarder, E., Rodriguez, N., & Zatz, M. S. (2004). Criers, liars, and manipulators: Probation officers' views of girls. *Justice Quarterly, 21,* 548–578.

Garcia, C. A., & Lane, J. (2009). What a girl wants, what a girl needs: Findings from a gender-specific focus group study. *Crime & Delinquency, 59,* 536–561. doi:10.1177/0011128709331790

Goodkind, S. (2005). Gender-specific services in the juvenile justice system: A critical examination. *Affilia, 20*(1), 52–70.

Greene, Peters, & Associates. (1998, October). *Guiding principles for promising female programming: An inventory of best practices.* Washington, DC: Office of Juvenile Justice and Delinquency Prevention.

Hennink, M., Hutter, I., & Bailey, A. (2011). *Qualitative research methods.* Thousand Oaks, CA: Sage.

Holsinger, K. (2000). Feminist perspectives on female offending. *Women & Criminal Justice, 12*(1), 23–51.

Holsinger, K. (2003). Services for girls: What they need—what they get. *Women, Girls, & Criminal Justice, 4*(4), 49–64.

Holsinger, K., & Holsinger, A. (2005). Differential pathways to violence and self-injurious behavior: African American and White girls in the juvenile justice system. *Journal of Research in Crime & Delinquency, 42,* 211–242.

Holsinger, K., Like, T. Z., & Hodge, J. P. (2009). Gender-specific programs: Where we are and where we need to go. *Women, Girls, & Criminal Justice, 11*(1), 1–16.

Hubbard, D. J., & Matthews, B. (2007). Reconciling the differences between the "gender responsive" and the "what works" literatures to improve services for girls. *Crime & Delinquency, 54*(2), 225–258.

Kempf-Leonard, K., & Sample, L. L. (2000). Disparity based on sex: Is gender-specific treatment warranted? *Justice Quarterly, 17*(1), 89–128.

Knoll, C, & Sickmund, M. (2010). *Delinquency cases in juvenile court, 2007.* Washington, DC: Office of Juvenile Justice and Delinquency Prevention.

Lyman, L., & Spinney, E. (2009). *Girls and boys have unique needs: Report on high risk girls and gender-specific programming.* Roxbury, MA: The girls' Initiative.

Maniglia, R., & Temple, A. K. (1998). *Female juvenile offenders: A status of the states report.* Washington, DC: Office of Juvenile Justice and Delinquency Prevention.

McCabe, K. M., Lansing, A. E., Garland, A., & Hough, R. (2002). Gender differences in psychopathology, functional impairment, and familial risk factors among adjudicated delinquents. *Journal of the American Academy of Child and Adolescent Psychiatry, 41,* 860–867.

Morgan, M., & Patton, P. (2002). Gender-responsive programming in the justice system—Oregon's guidelines for effective programming for girls. *Federal Probation, 66*(2), 57–65.

Naffine, N. (1996). *Feminism and criminology.* Philadelphia, PA: Temple University Press.

National Council on Crime and Delinquency, Center for Girls and Young Women. (2010). *Understanding trauma through a gender lens.* Oakland, CA: National Council on Crime and Delinquency.

Peters, R. S. (1998). *Guiding principles for promising female programming.* Washington, DC: Office of Juvenile Justice and Delinquency Prevention.

Potter, C. C. (1999). Violence and aggression in girls. In J. M. Jenson & M. O. Howard (Eds.), *Youth violence: Current research and recent practice innovations* (p. 113–138). Washington, DC: NASW Press.

Ravoira, L., Rose, B., Miller, T., Tracey, M., Rinehart, L., Patino-Lydia, V., & Graziano, J. (n.d.). *Savvy Sister: Model programming.* Oakland, CA: National Council on Crime and Delinquency, Center for Girls and Young Women.

Schur, E. (1984). *Labeling women deviant: Gender, stigma, and social control.* New York, NY: Random House.

Sedlak, A. J., & Broadhurst, D. D. (1996). *Third national incidence study of child abuse and neglect.* Washington, DC: U.S. Department of Health and Human Services.

Schwartz, J., & Rookey, B. D. (2008). The narrowing gender gap in arrests: Assessing competing explanations using self-report, traffic fatality, and official data on drunk driving, 1980–2004. *Criminology, 46,* 637–670.

Sedlak, A. J., & McPherson, K. S. (2010). *Youth's needs and services: Findings from the survey of youth in residential placement.* Washington, DC: Office of Juvenile Justice and Delinquency Prevention.

Sharp, C., & Simon, J. (2004). *Girls in the juvenile justice system: The need for more gender-responsive services.* Retrieved from the Child Welfare League of America website: www.cwla .org

Sherman, F. T. (2012). Justice for girls: Are we making progress? *UCLA Law Review, 59,* 1584–1628.

State Highway Patrol Statistical Analysis Center. (2014). *[State omitted] Uniform Crime Reporting Program, offense report—Part 1 crimes.*

Steffensmeier, S., Schwartz, J., Zhong, H., & Ackerman, J. (2005). An assessment of recent trends in girls' violence using diverse longitudinal sources: Is the gender gap closing? *Criminology, 43,* 355–1–05.

U.S. Census Bureau. (2014). *State and county quickfacts.* Retrieved from http://www.census.gov/en.html

Zahn, M. A., Agnew, R., Fishbein, D., Miller, S., Winn, D., Dakoff, G., . . . Chesney-Lind, M. (2010). *Girls study group: Understanding and responding to girls delinquency.* Washington, DC: Office of Juvenile Justice and Delinquency Prevention.

Zahn, M. A., Day, J. C., Mihalic, S. F., & Tichavsky, L. (2009). Determining what works for girls in the juvenile justice system: A summary of evaluation evidence. *Crime & Delinquency, 55*(2), 266–293.

READING /// 14

In this chapter, you learned about how many of the girls involved in the juvenile justice system experience high rates of trauma and victimization in their childhoods. This article reviews both the existing literature as well as the current trends and practices within justice-related agencies. The article concludes with recommendations on how to improve services and treatment for LGBTQ girls in the juvenile justice system.

Trauma Among Lesbians and Bisexual Girls in the Juvenile Justice System

Juliette Noel Graziano and Eric F. Wagner

A large research literature has found that experiencing trauma related to sexual or physical abuse is linked to a host of negative psychological, behavioral, and health-related outcomes among adolescents and adults (Breslau, Davis, Andreski, & Peterson, 1991; Briere & Runtz, 1993; Dembo, Williams, & Schmeidler, 1993; Giaconia et al., 2000; Mullen, Martin, Anderson, Romans, & Herbison, 1996; Neumann, Houskamp, Pollock, & Briere, 1996; Ritter, Stewart, Bernet, Coe, & Brown, 2002; Widom, 1995). While there seems to be a particularly strong relationship between trauma, operationalized as either post-traumatic stress disorder (PTSD) or subsyndromal symptoms of traumatic stress, and delinquency, especially among girls, this topic has only recently received attention (Simkins & Katz, 2002; Smith, Leve, & Chamberlain, 2006; Widom, 1995). Criminological theories have historically focused on men rather than on women, and little attention has been devoted to gender-specific variables that may predict and explain female offending. To this end, feminist researchers argue that there are important gender differences regarding pathways into the justice system, including a particularly strong linkage between girls' experiences of trauma related to physical or sexual abuse and subsequent offending behavior (Bloom, Owen, & Covington, 2005). Since characteristic female responses to such types of trauma (e.g., running away from home, acting out, aggression, etc.)

are often viewed as symptoms of conduct disorder or problematic antisocial behavior, and thus are criminalized, traumatized girls become entangled in the justice system without adequate attention to gender-specific needs such as trauma-focused treatment (Chesney-Lind & Shelden, 2004; Simkins & Katz, 2004).

Sexual abuse, physical abuse, traumatic stress, and PTSD are much more likely to be reported by youth with juvenile justice system involvement than by youth without justice system involvement (Acoca & Dedel, 1998; Cauffman, Feldman, Waterman, & Steiner, 1998). While the prevalence of traumatic stress and PTSD among juvenile justice populations (primarily male) has been estimated to be at least 8 times greater than found in adolescent community samples (Wolpaw & Ford, 2004), research shows that the prevalence of trauma-related stress and diagnoses among female juvenile justice populations is *more than 200 times* the national average (Smith et al., 2006). Moreover, histories of physical and sexual abuse are significantly more prevalent among juvenile offender girls than among juvenile offender boys (McCabe, Lansing, Garland, & Hough, 2002). Since trauma-related stress, PTSD, physical abuse, and sexual abuse are especially associated with delinquency for girls, research concerning risk factors for abuse (and subsequent trauma) and delinquency among girls is a priority.

SOURCE: Graziano, J. N., & Wagner, E. F. (2011). Trauma among lesbians and bisexual girls in the juvenile justice system. *Traumatology, 17*(2), 45–55.

An adolescent subpopulation at particularly high risk for experiencing trauma are lesbian, gay, bisexual, transgender, queer, and/or questioning (LGBTQ) youth. While it is well documented that LGBTQ youth experience significantly higher rates of trauma and sexual orientation violence than do their heterosexual counterparts (Rivers & D'Augelli, 2001; Saewyc et al., 2006; Savin-Williams, 1994), the interconnectedness of trauma, delinquency, and sexual-minority status among teenage girls has not been well studied. There has been a general increase in research concerning the health and well-being of LGBTQ youth; however, there remains a dearth of research specifically focused on PTSD rates. D'Augelli, Grossman, and Starks (2006) did include a measure of PTSD in their study of LGBTQ adolescents and found that 9% of the lesbians, gay, and bisexual youth met criteria for a PTSD diagnosis. Three times the number of girls reported PTSD compared to boys, and PTSD was also significantly associated with gender atypical behavior and physical sexual orientation violence. This is in line with previous studies that show in community samples girls are 2 times more likely than boys to develop PTSD after being exposed to trauma (Breslau et al., 1998). Juvenile offender girls as a group report high rates of trauma, and LGBTQ youth may be at particular risk for experiencing sexual orientation violence, gender atypicality trauma, family rejection, stigmatization, and peer victimization (Berlan, Corliss, Field, Goodman, & Austin, 2010; Birkett, Espelage, & Koenig, 2009; Davis, Saltzburg, & Locke, 2009; Kosciw, Greytak, & Diaz, 2009). Since sexual-minority youth are at an elevated risk for trauma and girls are more prone to meet criteria for PTSD than are boys, the link between trauma and delinquency among lesbians and bisexual girls warrants investigation.

Delinquency during adolescence can have serious long-term negative consequences for physical and mental health and places girls at risk of future arrests, reduced educational and employment opportunities, domestic violence, and dysfunctional parenting (Bardone et al., 1998; Bushway & Reuter, 2002; Clingempeel, Britt, & Henggeler, 2008; Dembo et al., 2000; Giordano, Milhollin, Cernkovich, Pugh, & Rudolph, 1999; Piquero, Daigle, Gibson, Leeper, & Tibbetts, 2007; Serbin, Peters, McAffer, & Schwartzman, 1991; Sweeten, 2006). Given (a) the lack of research focused on sexual-minority women in the justice system and (b) the pronounced trauma-related treatment need among juvenile offending girls, this review will focus on recent trauma

research involving juvenile justice system–involved lesbians and bisexual girls. The goals of our review are to identify strengths and weaknesses of current approaches to female juvenile offenders and provide guidance for how services for juvenile offending girls may be improved.

Background

Definitions of Trauma and PTSD

Current definitions of what constitutes trauma and the necessary and sufficient criteria for a diagnosis of PTSD differ regarding the initial stressor needed for a PTSD diagnosis, symptom onset, and duration among those diagnosed with PTSD and the functional impact of PTSD. According to the *Diagnostic and Statistical Manual of Mental Disorders Fourth Edition* (*DSM–IV*; American Psychiatric Association [APA], 1994), a stressor signifies a traumatic event when the person has "experienced, witnessed, or was confronted with an event or events that involved actual or threatened death or serious injury, or a threat to the physical integrity of self or others" (p. 427). In addition, the response of the person includes "intense fear, helplessness, or horror" (p. 428). The *DSM–IV* notes that the response in children may differ and "be expressed instead by disorganized or agitated behavior" (p. 428). In addition, the person must exhibit a variety of symptoms, for a specified duration, with compromised functioning. According to the World Health Organization's (WHO) International Classification of Diseases (ICD–10), PTSD is a response to a stressful event or situation "of an exceptionally threatening or catastrophic nature, which is likely to cause pervasive distress in almost anyone" (WHO, 2007, Section F43.1). Predisposing factors, typical symptoms, and the onset time frame are outlined, and the diagnosis requires evidence of symptom arousal within 6 months of the event.

Abram et al. (2004) argued that the definition of trauma by the *DSM–IV* is somewhat ambiguous, and there are scant reliability and validity studies of PTSD measures based on the *DSM–IV* criteria. They argue that there remains a lack of consistent measures of trauma, and the most utilized instruments measure different types of trauma. For example, violent victimization, sexual victimization, and/or family victimization may be measured differently or not at all, depending on the specific assessment instrument. This state of affairs ultimately reduces reliability and validity and muddies the waters regarding what is the most appropriate way to conceptualize trauma and its impact. PTSD clinical researchers argue in favor of a "consensually understood and empirically validated framework to define and measure traumatic events" (p. 408). That said, such a framework would include narrowing the focus and specifically naming the different types of trauma being investigated for research endeavors that explore trauma and its impact. While important advances have been made regarding the diagnosis of trauma and its impact, notable discrepancies remain (Peters, Slade, & Andrews, 1999), which could have serious implications for populations that have suffered from trauma, such as not meeting criteria for receiving services.

Types of Trauma

Trauma is a risk factor for delinquency and a host of other emotional, physical, and health-risk problems (Chesney-Lind 1989; Gover, 2004; Jaffee, Caspi, Moffitt, & Taylor, 2004; Perez, 2000; Robertson, Baird-Thomas, St. Lawrence, & Pack, 2005; Simkins & Katz, 2002; Smith et al., 2006; Zierler et al., 1991). There are numerous forms of trauma, which include interpersonal violence (sexual abuse, physical abuse, and domestic violence) and/or the witnessing of interpersonal violence. In addition, neglect, the loss of a loved one, serious accidents, terrorism, natural disasters, and wars and other forms of political violence are often traumatic for the individual experiencing them.

Natural disasters, political violence, the loss of a loved one, and serious accidents can be extremely traumatic. However, there is no reason to believe lesbian and bisexual girls are disproportionately affected by such trauma. In contrast, the association between child abuse and victimization and delinquency has been well established, and, in fact, as Steiner, Garcia, and Matthews (1997) found among violent youth in California who met criteria for PTSD, "none of them reported the recent natural disasters in California, which some of them lived through and most of them heard about and saw on television (Loma Prieta earthquakes, Oakland firestorm, Rodney King riots)" as traumatic events (p. 361). Instead, they reported interpersonal violence in the family, including abuse, injury, and murder. Since interpersonal violence seems to be the type of trauma most strongly and directly linked to juvenile offending, this review will focus on the trauma that ensues after

interpersonal violence (i.e., physical abuse, sexual abuse, and sexual orientation violence). Moreover, in addition to reporting higher rates of sexual abuse and physical punishment, girls also report experiencing violence, in comparison to boys who more frequently report witnessing violence (Abram et al., 2004; Ford, Chapman, Hawke, & Albert, 2007; Hennessey, Ford, Mahoney, Ko, & Siegfried, 2004).

Trauma and PTSD Among Lesbians and Bisexual Girls Involved in the Justice System

Prevalence of Trauma and PTSD

We conducted an exhaustive literature search and found not a single publication that addresses the prevalence of trauma and PTSD among girls who are both (a) juvenile justice system–involved and (b) lesbian or bisexual. While the empirical literature has documented higher rates of trauma and PTSD among juvenile justice system–involved girls (compared to girls not involved in the juvenile justice system) as well as higher rates of trauma and PTSD among lesbian or bisexual girls (compared to heterosexual girls), the combination has not been examined. Since girls who are both juvenile offenders and lesbian or bisexual exhibit two risk factors known to be positively associated with trauma and PTSD, it may be that the combination of these two risk factors compound risk additively or multiplicatively. However, the absence of empirical research on this topic leaves unknown the issue of how juvenile offending and lesbianism or bisexuality may interact in regard to risk for trauma and PTSD.

While at this time it is unknown how many lesbians and bisexual girls are involved in the juvenile justice system, a handful of studies have included a measure of sexual orientation and can provide some insight. For example, Belknap and Holsinger (2006) studied 444 female and male incarcerated youth and found that sexual identity was an important variable in offending behavior. Twenty-two percent of incarcerated youth self-identified as bisexual, and 5% self-identified as lesbian/gay. Girls, however, were 6 times as likely to identify as bisexual than boys and 3 times as likely to identify as homosexual compared to boys. The authors acknowledge they could not discern "whether boys are less likely to report gay or bisexual identities or if it is an identity that places girls, but not boys, at increased risk of marginalization and delinquency" (p. 55). In a study that included more than 2,000 youth in detention facilities conducted by Ceres Policy Institute found that 13% of the youth in their sample were LGBTQ, where 11% of the boys and 23% of the girls were "not straight" (Irvine, 2009). In a study that focused on girls only, Schaffner (1999) interviewed and reviewed files of more than 100 justice system–involved young women and reported that between one-fifth and one-third of the sample were bisexual or lesbian. The consensus among researchers and clinicians working in juvenile offending is that minority sexual orientation is especially overrepresented among female delinquents. This lack of specific information regarding the prevalence of lesbians and bisexual girls severely limits our understanding of their specific risk factors and needs.

Research has documented the prevalence of and specific issues related to abuse, trauma, and PTSD among justice system–involved girls as well as community samples of lesbians and bisexual girls. In addition, qualitative research has started to focus on the experiences of LGBTQ in the juvenile justice system, and collectively, these sources can provide insight regarding the trauma-related treatment needs of lesbians and bisexual girls in the justice system.

Trauma Among Justice System–Involved Girls

Prevalence of Abuse, Trauma, and PTSD

Estimates of the prevalence of abuse, trauma, and PTSD vary depending on the types of abuse or trauma under review; instruments used to detect abuse, trauma, or PTSD; and the segment of the justice population investigated (Teplin, Abran, McClelland, Dulcan, & Mericle, 2002), though in general, offending youth typically report much higher rates of physical and sexual abuse, trauma, and PTSD than do youth not involved in the juvenile justice system (Abram et al., 2004). Having been abused places youth at increased risk for violent behavior and arrests, and among juvenile justice system populations is associated with an earlier age of first offense and a greater number of total offenses (Smith et al., 2006; Widom & Maxfield, 2001).

These associations appear to be particularly strong among justice system–involved girls. Belknap and Holsinger (2006), Brosky and Lally (2004), and Dembo, Williams, Wothke, Schmeidler, and Brown (1992) all documented significantly higher rates of sexual and physical abuse

among delinquent girls than among delinquent boys, which range from 28% to 60% of girls reporting sexual abuse and 38% to 75% reporting physical abuse. Cauffman et al. (1998), Ford et al. (2007), and Mueser and Taub (2008) all documented significantly higher rates of PTSD among justice system–involved girls than among justice system–involved boys, with more than 40% of girls reporting PTSD. According to Cauffman, these rates are 50% higher than the rate typically reported by male juvenile delinquents. Studies focused exclusively on juvenile offending girls have confirmed that they are especially likely to report physical abuse, sexual abuse, and trauma related to abuse experiences (Acoca & Dedel, 1998; Simkins & Katz, 2002). Moreover, abuse appears to be a stronger predictor of offending behavior for women than for men, with female abused youth 7 times more likely to be arrested than their nonabused, same-sex counterparts (Makarios, 2007).

It should be noted that epidemiological research has found differences between childhood sexual and physical abuse in the areas of age, race/ethnicity, gender, and relationship between perpetrator and victim, which has important clinical implications (Jason, Williams, Burton, & Rochat, 1982). Likewise, type of abuse may be linked to different behaviors and outcomes. For example, in studies that compared sexual and physical abuse, somatic complaints and anxiety disorders were more prevalent among sexually abused children (Green, Russo, Navratil, & Loeber, 1999), and research consistently documents that sexual abuse may be more related to high-risk sexual behaviors (Buzi et al., 2003; Fergusson, Horwood, & Lynsky, 1997; Robertson, Baird-Thomas, & Stein, 2008). Sexually abused girls in the justice system, in particular, report poorer mental health, such as more suicide attempts and more negative feelings about life, than their female counterparts that do not report sexual abuse (Goodkind, Ng, & Sarri, 2006).

Any type of abuse though, particularly sexual and physical abuse, places youth at risk for both internalizing and externalizing behaviors such as violent and nonviolent delinquency and aggression (Gore-Felton, Koopman, McGarvey, Hernandez, & Canterbury, 2001; Herrera & McClosky, 2003). Moreover, experiencing both forms of abuse have been shown to have even worse outcomes and problem behaviors, and this co-occurrence is more common in clinical versus community samples (Chandy, Blum, & Resnick, 1996; Green et al., 1999). However, it is important to note that while experiencing abuse does increase the risk for a variety of adolescent problem behaviors, most sexually and/or physically abused children do not engage in delinquent behavior as teens.

While the majority of studies examining gender differences in trauma exposure and PTSD have found higher rates among juvenile offending girls than among juvenile offending boys, not all studies have supported gender differences in trauma exposure among teenage offenders. For example, Abram et al. (2004) examined the prevalence estimates of exposure to trauma and 12-month rates of PTSD among youth involved in the justice system and found significantly more number of boys had experienced at least one traumatic event than girls had (93% of boys compared to 84% for girls). Interestingly, while girls reported fewer traumatic experiences, they were just as likely as boys to meet PTSD diagnoses. Wasserman, McReynolds, Ko, Katz, and Carpenter (2005) and McCabe et al. (2002) also found no significant gender differences among justice system–involved youth in rates of PTSD, though those researchers suggest possible methodological issues such as low statistical power, sample selection limitations, and the reliability of measures and diagnostic criteria may have been responsible for their nonsignificant findings.

Trauma Among Lesbians and Bisexual Girls

As previously stated, there have been no empirical studies focusing on trauma among justice system–involved lesbians and bisexual girls, though numerous studies have shown that both sexual and physical victimization is especially prevalent among community samples of lesbians and bisexual girls compared to their heterosexual peers. (Austin et al., 2008; Balsam, Rothblum, & Beauchaine, 2005). For example, Saewyc et al. (2006) in a multisample study found that lesbians and bisexual girls reported the highest rates of sexual abuse and physical abuse by family members. Austin et al. conducted a study of women's past abuse victimization experiences and found lesbians reported higher rates of physical and sexual abuse than heterosexual women. Compared to heterosexual women, bisexual women were more likely to report physical abuse beginning in adolescence. Lesbians were also more likely to report physical abuse in adolescence compared to heterosexual women. Balsma et al. conducted a study, which compared LGB adults

with their adult siblings. LGB siblings reported higher rates of childhood sexual abuse, psychological [abuse], and physical abuse by parents or caretakers, as well as partner victimization and sexual assault. Saewyc et al. also found high rates of sexual abuse reported by gay and bisexual boys, which were close to the rates of bisexual girls and lesbians. In conclusion, a growing body of literature supports that lesbians and bisexual girls experience higher rates of sexual and physical abuse than even heterosexual female counterparts.

Lesbians and bisexual girls may also be at increased risk for other potentially harmful behaviors and traumatic experiences. Like bisexual and gay boys, lesbians and bisexual girls may experience high rates of parental rejection and violence. For example, D'Augelli (1998) found that it was more common for lesbians to be threatened with physical violence and actually attacked, most often by their mothers, when they disclosed their sexual orientation to parents. Other studies document strained family relationships and parental rejection (Salzburg, 1996; Savin-Williams & Ream, 2003; Williams, Connolly, Pepler, & Craig, 2005), school violence (Bontempo & D'Augelli, 2002; Hansen, 2007; Kosciw, Diaz, & Greytak, 2008), substance use (Garofalo, Wolf, Kessel, Palfrey, & Durant, 1998; Marshal et al., 2008; Marshal, Friedman, Stall, & Thompson, 2009), suicide risk (Kitts, 2005; Remafedi, French, Story, Resnick, & Blum, 1998; Russell & Joyner, 2001; Silenzio, Peña, Duberstein, Cerel, & Knox, 2007), and high-risk sexual behaviors (Garofalo et al., 1998; Saewyc et al., 2006; Wright & Perry, 2006).

LGBTQ Youth in the Justice System

Unique Considerations Related to Families and Schools

The developmental period of adolescence is marked by a number of additional challenges for LGBTQ youth, which affect their overall well-being. In particular, unique issues related to family and school problems have a significant effect on LGBTQ youth. While family dysfunction and poor academic performance are established risk factors for all youth, particularly girls (Acoca & Dedel, 2000; Henggeler, Edwards, & Borduin, 1987), an extensive study by Majd, Marksamer, & Reyes (2009) outlines how family rejection and school harassment lead to negative outcomes for LGBTQ youth. In their survey of more than 400 justice and legal professions, 90% identified a lack of parental support as a serious problem for LGBTQ youth. Specifically, family rejection often underlies many of the offenses with which LGBTQ are charged, including ungovernability or incorrigibility, runaway, homelessness, survival crimes (i.e., shoplifting and prostitution), substance use, and domestic disputes (Equity Project, 2007, 2008; Feinstein, Greenblatt, Hass, Kohn, & Rana, 2001; Ray, 2006). Irvine in Majd et al. [*Hidden Injustice* (2009)] found LGBTQ youth in detention were twice as likely to have been removed from the home due to someone hurting them and more than twice as likely to be detained for running away from home or placement when compared to their heterosexual peers. The findings speak directly to some of the unique challenges faced by LGBTQ youth.

School harassment, which is associated with multiple negative academic outcomes, also plagues LGBTQ youth (Harris Interactive & GLSEN, 2005; Henning-Stout, James, & McIntosh, 2000; Murdock & Bolch, 2005; Rivers, 2000). GLSEN's 2007 School Climate Survey results revealed that 86% of LGBTQ youth had been verbally harassed, 44% had been physically harassed, and 61% felt unsafe in school due to their sexual orientation (Kosciw, Diaz, & Greytak, 2008). Such types of trauma are directly associated with poor academic performance and truancy (Kosciw et al., 2008). Judges typically interpret such bad behavior at school as the result of antisocial tendencies, best managed by punishment, rather than of PTSD, best managed by treatment.

Current Practices and Policy

Current Trends

Historically, girls have typically entered the justice system because of status offenses. Odem and Schlossman (1991) found that in 1920, 93% of the girls brought into the system were charged with status offenses, of whom 65% were charged with immoral sexual activity. In 1950, there was an increase in the number of Black girls entering the system. By the 1980s, girls were entering the justice system for more serious crimes as opposed to primarily status

offenses. Schaffner (2006) argued, "The data reflect a shift away from a criminalization of girls' sexual misconduct toward a focus on girls' violent crimes" (p. 39). Stahl (2008) reported that in 2004, girls composed only 44% of the total petitioned status offenses.

According to the *Juvenile Offenders and Victims: 2006 National Report,* since 1994, there has been a general decline in juvenile violence, though the proportion of girls' violent crimes has increased, particularly for assault (Snyder & Sickmund, 2006). For example, the Violent Crime Index rose 103% for girls between 1981 and 1997, compared to 27% for boys during the same time frame (Acoca, 1999). The trend has continued where the juvenile arrest rate for simple assault increased 19% for girls as opposed to 4% decrease for boys between the years 1997 and 2006 (Snyder, 2005, 2008). Regarding aggravated assault, there was a 24% decrease for boys compared to a 10% decrease for girls during the same period (Snyder, 2005, 2008).

Chesney-Lind and Eliason (2006) argued that recent trends in societal perceptions and media portrayals of the potential for violence among lesbians may have serious negative consequences for sexual-minority and ethnic/racial-minority women. Majd, Marksamer, and Reyes (2009) found that many of the juvenile justice professionals they interviewed lamented that LGBTQ youth are viewed as mentally ill and sexual predators. One respondent remarked, "The whole case was about sensationalizing lesbians . . . [The prosecution] played it like she was a deranged lunatic lesbian" (p. 52). The second trend may result in more harsh treatment by the justice system for women who are perceived as lesbians. According to the authors, these trends affect all girls and women since they serve as a warning of the consequences of countering dominant gender ideals.

In general, gender transgressions in any form challenge traditional views regarding "acceptable" female behaviors. Lesbian and bisexual delinquent girls often enter justice systems that are ill prepared to address their sexuality in affirming ways that often further traumatizes them due to homophobic environments and practices. The ways in which sexism and heterosexism interact may place lesbians and bisexual girls at high risk for justice system involvement as well as for receiving treatment inappropriate and inadequate for meeting their clinical needs.

Current Practices

Given the preceding, there is a need to examine both the factors that place lesbians and bisexual girls at risk of justice system involvement as well as their unique experiences once they have entered the justice system. The lack of research on LGBTQ youth in the justice system is remarkable since sexual-minority status appears to be a risk factor for juvenile justice system involvement, and LGBTQ youth appear to have particularly negative experiences in the juvenile justice system (Urban Justice Center, 2001).

Majd et al. (2009) documented how at every stage of contact and processing, competent treatment of and services for LGBTQ youth are lacking. They outline practices that serve as barriers to fair treatment when LGBTQ have contact with police and court officials as well as unjust practices within the system. For example, they found that LGBTQ youth have remained a hidden population, where approximately 20% of the juvenile justice professionals interviewed stated that they had not worked with LGBTQ youth in the past 2 years, though they may in fact be an overrepresented group. A combination of different factors contribute to the invisibility of sexual-minority youth. Juvenile justice professionals may lack awareness regarding sexual orientation, and/or youth may choose not to disclose information about their sexual orientation. One interviewee estimated that 75% of the lesbian and bisexual court-ordered girls with whom she works typically do not feel comfortable sharing sexual orientation information initially due to safety concerns.

Misconceptions on the part of professionals serving justice system–involved youth persist, such as the belief that youth are too young to know whether they are LGBTQ, sexual orientation can be changed through treatment, and/or LGBTQ identity is pathological. These misconceptions regarding sexual orientation among key decision makers, juvenile justice professionals, and service providers in turn influence LGBTQ youth contact with system officials. Majd et al. (2009) documented how LGBTQ youth are targeted and abused by police, lack appropriate sentencing options, are overcharged with sex offenses, and undergo inappropriate treatment such as sex offender treatment and reparative therapy. For example, several interviewees indicated that it is more common for LGBTQ youth to be prosecuted for consensual sex that is

age appropriate. In addition, interviewees recounted cases where youth were ordered to receive counseling to address or change their sexual orientation. The sum effect is that LGBTQ sexual identity is targeted, criminalized, and ultimately punished. To illustrate, a case was cited where a judge ordered a young lesbian to be placed in a private hospital for 2 weeks because of her sexual orientation.

Once LGBTQ youth enter the justice system, they are often met with a lack of programs and services. Few placements [facility officials] are willing to accept LGBTQ youth, either because they are not competent to do so or cite safety concerns as a major issue (Majd et al., 2009). In general, competent individual mental health and family counselors are scarce (Majd et al., 2009). LGBTQ youth report a host of problems such as abuse inside institutions from peers and staff and discriminatory policies and practices.

LGBTQ youth safety inside juvenile justice programs is a major concern. Unfortunately, there have been high rates of physical, sexual, and emotional abuse of LGBTQ youth reported while in custody (Krisberg, 2009; Majd et al., 2009). Sexual-minority youth are targeted by both peers and staff, and in one study, 80% of survey participants stated that safety was a serious problem for sexual-minority youth, and more than 50% of detention staff reported that they know of situations where LGBTQ youth were mistreated because of their sexual orientation (Majd et al., 2009). More specifically, LGBTQ "often experience rejection, harassment, and discrimination at the hands of their peers, as well as their caretakers and professionals charged with their care" (Estrada & Marksamer, 2006, p. 171–194), a fact well recognized by juvenile justice officials: "I wonder . . . about how their life is now and how much this traumatized them. . . . It would be hard anyway (to be locked up). But (to be) locked up and verbally abused and told this was a bad sick thing—" (Curtain, 2002, p. 291).

In addition to threats to safety, LGBT youth report services and policies unresponsive to their treatment needs and staff unprepared for treating LGBT youth (Urban Justice Center, 2001). Other discriminatory practices include isolating or segregating youth, utilizing overly harshly discipline, and harassment. While many delinquent youth may feel that they are not receiving the treatment and services they need, the justice system and other out-of-home systems "routinely subject LGBTQ youth to differential treatment, deny them appropriate services, and fail to protect them from violence and harassment" (Estrada & Marksamer, 2006, p. 171–194).

Examples of just how bad it can get inside the system include "the presence of male security personnel, being strapped to beds, forced medication, seclusion, precautions which force disrobing, forced physical exams, and invasive body searches," all of which are almost certainly revictimizing for girls who have suffered from abuse (Ford et al., 2007). Even more common practices that employ physical confrontation, isolation, and restraint may retraumatize girls who suffer from PTSD (Hennessey et al., 2004). In general, the environment is marked by staff insensitivity and loss of privacy, which can increase negative feelings for LGBTQ girls and lead to self-harm (Hennessey et al., 2004). Simply spoken, the conditions faced by LGBTQ juvenile offender girls are uniquely grim and greatly reduce the effectiveness of current treatment and rehabilitation efforts.

Recommendations

Given the preceding, our first recommendation is that much more research should be conducted with juvenile offending LGBTQ youth, focusing on their unique experiences and treatment needs, particularly in regard to trauma. Many juvenile justice agencies do not collect information about sexual orientation, which limits our understanding of how many delinquent youth identify as LGBTQ. Needs assessments should at least include general information about intimate relationships and the role they play in the youth's life. To this end, the National Council on Crime and Delinquency (NCCD) has developed an assessment for girls, called JAIS (Juvenile Assessment and Intervention System), which captures information about sexual orientation in the context of relationships. Juvenile offending girls are not asked directly about their sexual orientation, but instead whether they have a significant/ special partner, which gives them the choice to disclose whether they have same-gender relationships. JAIS's inclusion of lesbian and bisexual orientations as possible realities in the lives of offending girls marks the importance of being attentive to sexual identity. Needs assessments should also include general information about trauma experienced prior to and during juvenile justice system

involvement, with particular attention to sexual orientation violence. Finally, research is sorely needed that examines girls' risk factors for and trajectories of juvenile offending and how these may differ as a function of sexual orientation; such research would help elucidate the unique prevention and intervention needs of LGBTQ youth.

Our second recommendation is that more and better training and education regarding LGBTQ issues among delinquent youth should be provided to juvenile justice professionals. The Model Standards Project's (MSP) work for LGBTQ youth in the juvenile justice system has been cited as a possible resource (Estrada & Marksamer, 2006; Schaffner, 2006). MSP is a national project aimed at establishing a model and disseminating information regarding professional standards for working with LGBTQ youth. The overarching goal of the MSP is to "develop a practice tool to highlight the needs of LGBT youth in out-of-home care and improve services and outcomes" (Wilber, Reyes, & Marksamer, 2006, p. 135). MSP makes several recommendations for how to improve treatment services for LGBTQ youth, including (a) creating an inclusive organization culture, (b) recruiting and supporting competent caregivers and staff, (c) promoting healthy adolescent development, (d) respecting privacy and confidentiality, (e) providing appropriate placements, and (f) providing sensitive support services. Adults working with juvenile offending youth need to understand that while minority sexual orientation does not directly lead to criminality, the negative experiences associated with minority sexual status complicate and exacerbate juvenile offending trajectories.

Our final recommendation is that more and better training and education regarding trauma among delinquent youth, and how this may vary by sexual orientation, should be provided to juvenile justice professionals. In the past decade, juvenile justice systems have placed more emphasis on trauma and its impact on the juvenile offending population. Ford et al. (2007) reviewed recent advances in trauma-related treatment that include (a) trauma screening and assessment, and (b) treatment and rehabilitation of traumatic stress disorders. They emphasize the need for screening and assessments since behaviors that occur in response to trauma resemble delinquent behaviors. Several instruments have been developed to measure trauma and symptoms resulting from traumatic events. Though interventions that target trauma, some of which were designed and evaluated specifically with women, have been implemented, in general, there remains a lack of trauma-informed care for youth involved in the justice system.

Covington and Bloom (2003) argued that services need to be trauma-informed in order to be effective for women. They propose that trauma-informed treatment (a) take the trauma into account; (b) avoid triggering trauma reactions and/or traumatizing the individual; (c) adjust the behavior of counselors, other staff, and the organization to support the individual's coping capacity; and (d) allow survivors to manage their trauma symptoms successfully so that they are able to access, retain, and benefit from the services (Harris & Fallot, 2001). These recommendations are particularly relevant for sexual-minority youth since their specific traumatic experiences should be considered and retraumatizing triggers be avoided. The limited literature in this area suggests that the behavior of staff is an issue in serious need of adjustment in order to be supportive to all youth regardless of sexual orientation. Finally, sexual-minority youth should have access to trauma-related treatment in order to be able to manage their symptoms.

Conclusion

Lesbians and bisexual girls are overrepresented among, and at elevated risk for becoming, juvenile offenders. Lesbians and bisexual girls are at particularly pronounced risk for experiencing trauma, and trauma appears to increase the risk for juvenile justice system involvement. The justice system is ill equipped to deal with sexual-minority girls and underequipped for addressing issues related to trauma. Moreover, it appears they often inflict further trauma through policies and procedures completely at odds with the needs of LGBTQ juvenile offender girls. Specialized efforts are needed to ensure the protection, safety, and appropriate treatment of all youth, including sexual-minority girls involved in the justice system. Recommended actions include (a) more research with juvenile offending LGBTQ youth focusing on their unique experiences and treatment needs, particularly in regard to trauma; (b) more and better training and education regarding LGBTQ issues among delinquent youth for juvenile justice professionals; and (c) more and better training and education regarding trauma among delinquent youth and how this may vary by sexual orientation, for juvenile justice professionals.

/// DISCUSSION QUESTIONS

1. What sort of issues do LGBTQ youth experience related to trauma?

2. How should the juvenile justice system respond to the needs of these youth?

3. How can training of staff improve the treatment of LGBTQ youth in custody?

References

Abram, K. M., Teplin, L. A., Charles, D. R., Longworth, S., McClelland, G., & Dulcan, M. (2004). Posttraumatic stress disorder and trauma in youth in juvenile detention. *Archives of General Psychiatry, 61*, 403–410.

Acoca, L. (1999). Investing in girls: A 21st century strategy. *Juvenile Justice, 6*(1), 3–13.

Acoca, L., & Dedel, K. (1998). *No place to hide: Understanding and meeting the needs of girls in the California juvenile justice system.* Oakland, CA: National Council on Crime and Delinquency.

Acoca, L., & Dedel, K. (2000). *Educate or incarcerate: Girls in the Florida and Duval County juvenile justice systems.* Oakland, CA: National Council on Crime and Delinquency.

American Psychiatric Association. (1994). *Diagnostic and statistical manual of mental disorders* (4th ed.). Washington, DC: Author.

Austin, S., Jun, H., Jackson, B., Spiegelman, D., Rich-Edwards, J., Corliss, H., & Wright, R. J. (2008). Disparities in child abuse victimization in lesbian, bisexual, and heterosexual women in the Nurses' Health Study II. *Journal of Women's Health, 17*, 597–606.

Balsam, K. F., Rothblum, E., & Beauchaine, T. P. (2005). Victimization over the life span: Comparison of lesbian, gay, bisexual and heterosexual siblings. *Journal of Consulting and Clinical Psychology, 73*, 477–487.

Bardone, A. M., Moffitt, T. E., Caspi, A., Dickson, N., Stanton, W. R., & Silva, P. A. (1998). Adult physical health outcomes of adolescent girls with conduct disorder, depression, and anxiety.

Journal of the American Academy of Child & Adolescent Psychiatry, 37, 594–601.

Belknap, J., & Holsinger, K. (2006). The gendered nature of risk factors for delinquency. *Feminist Criminology, 1,* 48–71.

Berlan, E. D., Corliss, H. L., Field, A. E., Goodman, E., & Austin, S. B. (2010). Sexual orientation and bullying among adolescents in the growing up today study. *Journal of Adolescent Health, 46,* 366–371.

Birkett, M., Espelage, D. L., & Koenig, B. (2009). LGB and questioning students in schools: The moderating effects of homophobic bullying and school climate on negative outcomes. *Journal of Youth Adolescence, 38,* 989–1000.

Bloom, B., Owen, B., & Covington, S. (2005). *Gender-responsive strategies for women offenders: A summary of research, practice, and guiding principles for women offenders* (NIC Accession No. 020418). Washington, DC: National Institute of Corrections.

Bontempo, D., & D'Augelli, A. (2002). Effects of at-school victimization and sexual orientation on lesbian, gay, or bisexual youths' health risk behaviors. *Journal of Adolescent Health, 30,* 364–374.

Breslau, N., Davis, G. C., Andreski, P., & Peterson, E. (1991). Traumatic events and posttraumatic stress disorder in an urban population of young adults. *Archives of General Psychiatry, 48,* 216–222.

Breslau, N., Kessler, R. C., Chilcoat, H. D., Schultz, L. R., Davis, G. C., & Andreski, P. (1998). Trauma and posttraumatic stress disorder in the community: The 1996 Detroit Area Survey of Trauma. *Archives of General Psychiatry, 55,* 626–632.

Briere, J., & Runtz, M. (1993). Child sexual abuse: Long-term sequelae and implications for psychological assessment. *Journal of Interpersonal Violence, 8,* 312–330.

Brosky, B. A., & Lally, S. J. (2004). Prevalence of trauma, PTSD, and dissociation in court-referred adolescents. *Journal of Interpersonal Violence, 19,* 801–814.

Bushway, S., & Reuter, P. (2002). Labor markets and crime risk factors. In L. Sherman, D. Farrington, B. Welsh, & D. MacKenzie (Eds.), *Evidence-based crime prevention* (p. 198–240). New York: Rutledge.

Buzi, R. S., Tortolero, S. R., Roberts, R. E., Ross, M. W., Addy, R. C., & Markham, C. M. (2003). The impact of a history of sexual abuse on high-risk sexual behaviors among females attending alternative schools. *Adolescence, 38,* 595–605.

Cauffman, E., Feldman, S. S., Waterman, J., & Steiner, H. (1998). Posttraumatic stress disorder among female juvenile offenders. *Journal of the American Academy of Child & Adolescent Psychiatry, 37,* 1209–1216.

Chandy, J. M., Blum, R. W., & Resnick, M. D. (1996). Gender-specific outcomes for sexually abused adolescents. *Child Abuse & Neglect, 20,* 1219–1231.

Chesney-Lind, M. (1989). Girls' crime and woman's place: Toward a feminist model of female delinquency. *Crime & Delinquency, 35,* 5–29.

Chesney-Lind, M., & Eliason, M. (2006). From invisible to incorrigible: The demonization of marginalized women and girls. *Crime, Media, Culture, 2,* 29–47.

Chesney-Lind, M., & Shelden, R. G. (2004). *Girls, delinquency, and juvenile justice.* Belmont, CA: Wadsworth.

Clingempeel, W. G., Britt, S. C., & Henggeler, S. W. (2008). Beyond treatment effects: Comorbid psychopathologies and long-term outcomes among substance-abusing delinquents. *American Journal of Orthopsychiatry, 78*(1), 29–36.

Covington, S., & Bloom, B. (2003). Gendered justice: Women in the criminal justice system. In B. Bloom (Ed.), *Gendered justice: Addressing female offenders.* Durham, NC: Carolina Academic Press.

Curtain, M. (2002). Lesbian and bisexual girls in the juvenile justice system. *Child and Adolescent Social Work Journal, 19,* 285–301.

D'Augelli, A. R. (1998). Developmental implications of victimization of lesbian, gay, and bisexual youths. In G. M. Herek (Ed.), *Psychological perspectives on lesbian and gay issues. Vol. 4: Stigma and sexual orientation: Understanding prejudice against lesbians gay men, and bisexuals* (p. 187–210). Thousand Oaks, CA: Sage.

D'Augelli, A. R., Grossman, A. H., & Starks, M. T. (2006). Childhood gender atypicality, victimization, and PTSD among lesbian, gay, and bisexual youth. *Journal of Interpersonal Violence, 21,* 1462–1482.

Davis, T., Saltzburg, S., & Locke, C. R. (2009). Supporting the emotional and psychological well-being of sexual minority youth: Youth ideas for action. *Children and Youth Services Review, 31,* 1030–1041.

Dembo, R., Williams, L., & Schmeidler, J. (1993). Gender differences in mental health service needs among youths entering a juvenile detention center. *Journal of Prison and Jail Health, 12,* 73–10.

Dembo, R., Williams, L., Wothke, W., Schmeidler, J., & Brown, C. H. (1992). The role of family factors, physical abuse, and sexual victimization experiences in high-risk youths' alcohol/other drug use and delinquency. *Violence and Victims, 7,* 245–266.

Dembo, R., Wothke, W., Shemwell, M., Pacheco, K., Seeberger, W., Rollie, M., . . . Schmeidler, J., (2000). A structural model of the influence of family problems and child abuse factors on serious delinquency among youths processed at a juvenile assessment center. *Journal of Child and Adolescent Substance Abuse, 10,* 17–31.

Estrada, R., & Marksamer, J. (2006). The legal rights of LGBT youth in state custody: What child welfare and juvenile justice professionals need to know. *Child Welfare, 85*(2), 171–194.

Feinstein, R., Greenblatt, A., Hass, L., Kohn, S., & Rana, J. (2001). *Justice for all? A report on lesbian, gay, bisexual and transgendered youth in the New York juvenile justice system.* New York: Urban Justice Center.

Fergusson, D. M., Horwood, J., & Lynsky, M. T. (1997). Childhood sexual abuse, adolescent sexual behaviors and sexual revictimization. *Child Abuse & Neglect, 21,* 789–803.

Ford, J. D., Chapman, J. F., Hawke, J., & Albert, D. (2007). *Trauma among youth in the juvenile justice system: Critical issues and new directions.* Washington, DC: National Center for Mental Health and Juvenile Justice Research Brief, Department of Health and Human Services.

Garofalo, R., Wolf, R., Kessel, S., Palfrey, J., & Durant, R. H. (1998). The association between health-risk behaviors and sexual orientation among a school-based sample of adolescents. *Pediatrics, 101,* 895–902.

Giaconia, R. M., Reinherz, H. Z., Hauf, A. C., Paradis, A. D., Wasserman, M. S., & Langhammer, D. M. (2000). Comorbidity of substance use and post-traumatic stress disorders in a community sample of adolescents. *American Journal of Orthopsychiatry, 70,* 253–262.

Giordano, P. C., Milhollin, Y. J., Cernkovich, S. A., Pugh, M. D., & Rudolph, J. L. (1999). Delinquency, identity, and women's involvement in relationship violence. *Criminology, 37,* 17–39.

Goodkind, S., Ng, I., & Sarri, R. C. (2006). The impact of sexual abuse in the lives of young women involved or at risk of involvement with the juvenile justice system. *Violence Against Women, 12,* 456–477.

Gore-Felton, C., Koopman, C., McGarvey, E., Hernandez, N., & Canterbury, R. J. (2001). Relationships of sexual, physical, and emotional abuse to emotional and behavioral problems among incarcerated adolescents. *Journal of Child Sexual Abuse, 10,* 73–88.

Gover, A. R. (2004). Childhood sexual abuse, gender, and depression among incarcerated youth. *International Journal of Offender Therapy and Comparative Criminology, 48,* 683–696.

Green, S. M., Russo, M. F., Navratil, J. L., & Loeber, R. (1999). Sexual and physical abuse among adolescent girls with disruptive behavior problems. *Journal of Child and Family Studies, 8,* 151–168.

Hansen, A. L. (2007). School-based support for GLBT students: A review of three levels of research. *Psychology in the Schools, 44*(8), 839–848.

Harris, M., & Fallot, R. D. (Eds.). (2001). *Using trauma theory to design service systems. New directions for mental health services series.* San Francisco: Jossey-Bass.

Harris Interactive, & GLSEN. (2005). *From teasing to torment: School climate in America. A survey of students and teachers.* New York: GLSEN.

Hennessey, M., Ford, J., Mahoney, K., Ko, S., & Siegfried, C. (2004). *Trauma among girls in the juvenile justice system.* Los Angeles, CA: National Child Traumatic Stress Network.

Henning-Stout, M., James, S., & McIntosh, S. (2000). Reducing harassment of lesbian, gay, bisexual, transgender and questioning youth in schools. *School Psychology Review, 29,* 180–191.

Henggeler, S. W., Edwards, J., & Borduin, C. M. (1987). The family relations of female juvenile delinquents. *Journal of Abnormal Child Psychology, 15,* 199–210.

Herrera, V. P., & McCloskey, L. A. (2003). Sexual abuse, family violence and female delinquency: Findings from a longitudinal study. *Violence and Victims, 18*(3), 311–334.

Irvine, A. (2009, April 20). The inappropriate use of secure detention for lesbian, gay, bisexual, transgender, and queer youth, presented at the Columbia University Gender on the Frontiers Symposium. In K. Majd, J. Marksamer, & C. Reyes. *Hidden injustice: Lesbian, gay, bisexual, and transgender youth in juvenile courts.* San Francisco: The Equity Project.

Jaffee, S. R., Caspi, A., Moffitt, T. E., & Taylor, A. (2004). Physical maltreatment victim to antisocial child: Evidence of an environmentally mediated process. *Journal of Abnormal Psychology, 113,* 44–55.

Jason, J., Williams, S. L., Burton, A., & Rochat, R. (1982). Epidemiologic differences between sexual and physical child abuse. *The Journal of the American Medical Association, 247,* 3344–3348.

Kitts, R. L. (2005). Gay adolescents and suicide: Understanding the association. *Adolescence, 40,* 621–628.

Kosciw, J. G., Diaz, E. M., & Greytak, E. A. (2008). *2007 National School Climate Survey: The experiences of lesbian, gay, bisexual and transgender youth in our nation's schools.* New York: GLSEN.

Kosciw, J. G., Greytak, E. A., & Diaz, E. M. (2009). Who, what, where, when and why: Demographic and ecological factors contributing to hostile school climate for lesbian, gay, bisexual and transgender youth. *Journal of Youth and Adolescence, 38,* 976–988.

Krisberg, B. (2009). *Special report: Breaking the cycle of abuse in juvenile facilities.* Oakland, CA: National Council on Crime and Delinquency.

Majd, K., Marksamer, J., & Reyes, C. (2009). *Hidden injustice: Lesbian, gay, bisexual, and transgender youth in juvenile courts.* San Francisco: The Equity Project.

Makarios, M. D. (2007). Race, abuse, and female criminal violence. *Feminist Criminology, 2,* 100–116.

Marshal, M. P., Friedman, M. S., Stall, R., King, K. M., Miles, J., Gold, M. A., . . . Morse, J. Q. (2008). Sexual orientation and adolescent substance use: A meta-analysis and methodological review. *Addiction, 103,* 546–556.

Marshal, M. P., Friedman, M. S., Stall, R., & Thompson, A. (2009). Individual trajectories of substance use in lesbian, gay, and bisexual youth and heterosexual youth. *Addiction, 104,* 974–981.

McCabe, K. M., Lansing, A. E., Garland, A., & Hough, R. (2002). Gender differences in psychopathology: Functional impairment, and familial risk factors among adjudicated delinquents. *Journal of the American Academy of Child and Adolescent Psychiatry, 41,* 860–868.

Mueser, K. T., & Taub, J. (2008). Trauma and PTSD among adolescents with severe emotional disorders involved in multiple service systems. *Psychiatric Services, 59,* 627–634.

Mullen, P. E., Martin, J. L., Anderson, J. C., Romans, S. E., & Herbison, G. P. (1996). The long-term impact of the physical, emotional, and sexual term impact of the physical, emotional, and sexual abuse of children: A community study. *Child Abuse & Neglect, 20,* 7–22.

Murdock, T. B., & Bolch, M. B. (2005). Risk and protective factors for poor school adjustment in lesbian, gay, and bisexual (LGB) high school youth: Variable and person-centered analyses. *Psychology in the Schools, 42,* 159–172.

Neumann, D. A., Houskamp, B. M., Pollock, V. E., & Briere, J. (1996). The long-term sequelae of childhood sexual abuse in women: A meta-analytic review. *Child Maltreatment, 1,* 6–16.

Odem, M., & Schlossman, S. (1991). Guardians of virtue: The juvenile court and female delinquency in the early 20th century Los Angeles. *Crime & Delinquency, 37,* 186–203.

Perez, D. M. (2000). The relationship between physical abuse, sexual victimization, and adolescent illicit drug use. *Journal of Drug Issues, 30,* 641–662.

Peters, L., Slade, T., & Andrews, G. (1999). A comparison of ICD10 and *DSM–IV* criteria for posttraumatic stress disorder. *Journal of Traumatic Stress, 12,* 335–343.

Piquero, A. R., Daigle, L. E., Gibson, C., Leeper, N., & Tibbetts, S. G. (2007). Are life-course-persistent offenders at risk for adverse health outcomes? *Journal of Research in Crime & Delinquency, 44,* 185–207.

Ray, N. (2006). *Lesbian, gay, bisexual and transgender youth: An epidemic of homelessness.* New York: National Gay and Lesbian Task Force Policy Institute and the National Coalition for the Homeless.

Remafedi, G., French, S., Story, M., Resnick, M., & Blum, R. (1998). The relationship between suicide risk and sexual orientation: Results of a population-based study. *American Journal of Public Health, 88,* 57–60.

Ritter, J., Stewart, M., Bernet, C., Coe, M., & Brown, S. A. (2002). Effects of childhood exposure to familial alcoholism and family violence on adolescent substance use, conduct problems, and self-esteem. *Journal of Trauma Stress, 15,* 113–22.

Rivers, I. (2000). Social exclusion, absenteeism, and sexual minority youth. *Support for Learning, 15,* 13–18.

Rivers, I., & D'Augelli, A. R. (2001). The victimization of lesbian, gay, and bisexual youths: Implications for intervention. In A. R. D'Augelli & C. J. Patterson (Eds.), *Lesbian, gay, and bisexual identities and youths: Psychological perspectives* (p. 199–223). New York: Oxford University Press.

Robertson, A. A., Baird-Thomas, C., St. Lawrence, J. S., & Pack, R. (2005). Predictors of infection with chlamydia or gonorrhea in incarcerated adolescents. *Sexually Transmitted Diseases, 32,* 115–122.

Robertson, A. A., Baird-Thomas, C., & Stein, J. A. (2008). Child victimization and parental monitoring as mediators of youth problem behaviors. *Criminal Justice and Behavior, 35,* 755–771.

Russell, S. T., & Joyner, K. (2001). Adolescent sexual orientation and suicide risk: Evidence from a national study. *American Journal of Public Health, 91,* 1276–1281.

Saewyc, E. M., Skay, C. L., Pettingell, S. L., Reis, E. A., Bearinger, L., Resnick, M., . . . Combs, L. (2006). Hazards of stigma: The sexual and physical abuse of gay, lesbian, and bisexual adolescents in the United States and Canada. *Child Welfare, 85,* 195–213.

Salzburg, S. (1996). Family therapy and the disclosure of adolescent homosexuality. *Journal of Family Psychotherapy, 7,* 1–18.

Savin-Williams, R. C. (1994). Verbal and physical abuse as stressors in the lives of lesbian, gay male, and bisexual youths: Associations with school problems, running away, substance abuse, prostitution, prostitution, and suicide. *Journal of Consulting and Clinical Psychology, 62,* 261–269.

Savin-Williams, R. C., & Ream, G. L. (2003). Sex variations in the disclosure to parents of same-sex attractions. *Journal of Family Psychology, 17,* 429–438.

Schaffner, L. (1999). Violence and female delinquency: Gender transgressions and gender invisibility. *Berkeley Women's Law Journal, 14,* 40–65.

Schaffner, L. (2006). *Girls in trouble with the law.* New Brunswick, NJ: Rutgers University Press.

Serbin, L., Peters, P. L., McAffer, V. J., & Schwartzman, A. E. (1991). Childhood aggression and withdrawal as predictors of adolescent pregnancy, early parenthood, and environmental risk for the next generation. *Canadian Journal of Behavioral Science, 23,* 318–331.

Silenzio, V., Peña, J., Duberstein, P., Cerel, J., & Knox, K. (2007). Sexual orientation and risk factors for suicidal ideation and suicide attempts among adolescents and young adults. *American Journal of Public Health, 97,* 2017–2019.

Simkins, S., & Katz, S. (2002). Criminalizing abused girls. *Violence Against Women, 8,* 1474–1499.

Smith, D. K., Leve, L. D., & Chamberlain, P. (2006). Adolescent girls' offending and health-risking sexual behavior: The predictive role of trauma. *Child Treatment, 11,* 346–353.

Snyder, H. (2005). *Juvenile arrests, 2003.* Washington, DC: U.S. Department of Justice.

Snyder, H. (2008). *Juvenile arrests 2005.* Washington, DC: U.S. Department of Justice.

Snyder, H. N., & Sickmund, M. (2006). *Juvenile offenders and victims: 2006 National Report.* Washington, DC: U.S. Department of Justice.

Stahl, A. (2008). *Petitioned status offense cases in juvenile courts, 2004* (OJJDP Fact Sheet, February 2008, #02). Washington, DC: U.S. Department of Justice.

Steiner, H., Garcia, I., & Matthews, Z. (1997). Posttraumatic stress disorder in incarcerated juvenile delinquents. *Journal of the American Academy of Child and Adolescent Psychiatry, 36,* 357–365.

Sweeten, G. (2006). Who will graduate? Disruption of high school education by arrest and court involvement. *Justice Quarterly, 23,* 462–480.

Teplin, L., Abran, K., McClelland, G., Dulcan, M., & Mericle, A. (2002). Psychiatric disorders in youth in juvenile detention. *Archives of General Psychiatry, 59,* 1133–1143.

Urban Justice Center. (2001). *Justice for all? A report on lesbian, gay, bisexual and transgendered youth in the New York juvenile justice system.* New York: Author.

Wasserman, G., McReynolds, L., Ko, S., Katz, L., & Carpenter, J. (2005). Gender differences in psychiatric disorders at juvenile probation intake. *American Journal of Public Health, 95,* 131–137.

Widom, C. S. (1995). *Victims of childhood sexual abuse—Later criminal consequences* (National Institute of Justice: Research in Brief). Washington, DC: U.S. Department of Justice.

Widom, C. S., & Maxfield, M. G. (2001). *An update on the "Cycle of Violence"* (National Institute of Justice: Research in Brief). Washington, DC: U.S. Department of Justice.

Wilber, S., Reyes, C., & Marksamer, J. (2006). The Model Standards Project: Creating inclusive systems for LGBT youth in out-of-home care. *Child Welfare Journal, 85,* 133–149.

Williams, T., Connolly, J., Pepler, D., & Craig, W. (2005). Peer victimization, social support, and psychosocial adjustment of sexual minority adolescents. *Journal of Youth and Adolescence, 34,* 471–482.

Wolpaw, J. W., & Ford, J. D. (2004). *Assessing exposure to psychological trauma and post-traumatic stress in the juvenile justice population.* Los Angeles: National Child and Traumatic Stress Network. Retrieved from http://www.NCTSNet.org

World Health Organization. (2007). *International statistical classification of diseases and related health problems* (10th rev., Chapter 5: Mental and Behavioural Disorders, F00-F99; Neurotic, Stress-Related and Somatoform Disorders, F40-F48). Retrieved from http://apps.who.int/classifications/apps/icd/icd100nline/

Wright, E. R., & Perry, B. L. (2006). Sexual identity distress, social support, and the health of gay, lesbian, and bisexual youth. *Journal of Homosexuality, 51,* 81–109.

Zierler, S., Feingold, L., Laufer, D., Velentgas, P., Kantrowitz-Gordon, I., & Mayer, K. (1991). Adult survivors of childhood sexual abuse and subsequent risk for HIV infection. *American Journal of Public Health, 81,* 572–575.

Female Offenders and Their Crimes

Women engage in every type of criminal activity. Much like their male counterparts, females are involved in a variety of different types of crime. While female crimes of violence are highly sensationalized by the media, these crimes are rare occurrences. Instead, the majority of female offending is made up of crimes that are nonviolent in nature or are considered victimless crimes, such as drug abuse and sexually based offenses.

Males have always engaged in greater numbers of criminal acts. However, women are becoming more involved in crime and the criminal justice system. Research over the past several decades has focused on the narrowing of the gender gap, which refers to the differences in male and female offending for different types of offenses. But what does this really mean? Are women becoming more violent than they were in the past, as media reports have suggested? Is the rise in women's incarceration a result of more women engaging in serious criminal acts? What contributes to these changes? How do we investigate these questions?

In Section I, you learned about the changes in male and female crime participation over a 1-year and 10-year period, using arrest data from the Uniform Crime Reports. Using these same data, we can investigate the gender gap in offending. Figure 8.1 and Table 8.1 compares the percentage of males and females in different offense types. These data illustrate that the proportion of violent crime cases is far greater for males than females. In contrast, the proportion of property crimes is greater for females than males, because property crimes make up 84.6% of all female arrests, compared to 69.3% of male arrests. While these data illustrate that the gender gap may be narrowing in terms of gender proportions of crime, it is important to note that the number of male arrests is

Figure 8.1 • 2015 UCR Arrest Data

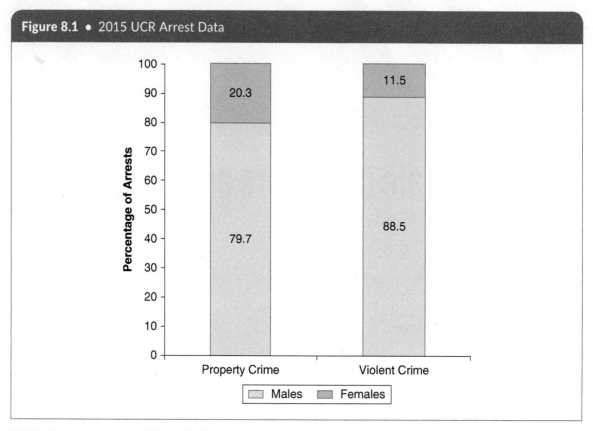

SOURCE: Crime in the United States 2015. https://ucr.fbi.gov/crime-in-the-u.s/2015/crime-in-the-u.s.-2015/tables/table-42.

twice that of the number of arrests of women for index crimes and almost three times greater than the number of arrests for all crimes.

Arrest trends over time also demonstrate an overall decrease in violent crimes for both men and women, but they show an increase in property crimes for women. Table 8.2 demonstrates the 5- and 10-year trends in male and female arrests from 2006 to 2015. For example, between 2011 and 2015, women's arrests in property-related crimes decreased 6.5%, yet between 2006 and 2015, arrests for women in this category increased 25.9%. This leads us to conclude that arrests of women for property crimes dramatically increased between 2006 and 2011, and then marked a significant downturn between 2011 and 2015. In addition, much of this variability comes from changes in the number of arrests for larceny-theft crimes. Despite these fluctuations, it is important to remember that women remain a small proportion of the total number of arrests.

While data from the Uniform Crime Report provide valuable insight into the current state of female offending, research by Steffensmeier and Allan (1996) examines the proportion of male and female arrests for three separate snapshots of time during the 20th century: 1960, 1975, and 1990. Their findings indicate that females make up 15% (or less) of arrestees for most types of major crimes (such as crimes against persons and major property crimes) across all time periods. For minor property offenses, the greatest increases are noted between 1960 and 1975 arrest data. Here, the female percentage of arrests increased from 17% in 1960 to 30% in both 1975 and 1990. The only

Table 8.1 ● 2015 UCR Arrest Data: Males Versus Females

	Number of Offenders		Percentage of Offense Type Within Gender (%)	
	Males	Females	Males	Females
Violent crime	309,253	78,829	79.7%	20.3%
Homicide	7,549	984	88.5%	11.5%
Rape	16,990	514	97.1%	2.9%
Robbery	62,721	10,509	85.6%	14.4%
Aggravated assault	221,993	66,822	76.9%	23.1%
Property crime	699,250	434,069	61.7%	38.3%
Burglary	135,064	31,545	81.1%	18.9%
Larceny-theft	511,557	388,520	56.8%	43.2%
Motor vehicle theft	47,169	12,662	78.8%	21.2%
Arson	5,460	1,342	80.3%	19.7%

SOURCE: Crime in the United States 2015. https://ucr.fbi.gov/crime-in-the.s/2015/crime-in-the-u.s.-2015/tables/table-42.

NOTE: Total male arrests for index crimes = 1,008,503; total female arrests for index crimes = 512,898. Arrests for index crimes make up 16.6% of male arrests and 22.9% of female arrests.

exception where women make up the majority of arrests is for the crime of prostitution (where women make up between two-thirds and three-fourths of all arrests across all three time periods).

In contrast to Steffensmeier and Allan's research, which relied on UCR data, Rennison (2009) compared offending data from the National Crime Victimization Survey (NCVS) for the 9 years between 1992 and 2001. Her work indicates that there have been negligible differences in the gender gap between male and female offending behaviors during this time frame. By using the data from the NCVS, we see a different view of men's and women's offending behaviors because it includes the dark figure of crime—that is, those crimes that were not reported to the police, as well as the crimes where the police were notified of the crime. These findings note that any differences in the gender gap result not from the increases of female offending but rather from the decreases in male offending rates for particular offenses, which fell at a greater rate than the decrease in female offending rates.

While women participate in many different types of crimes, this section highlights five general categories of crime, all which involve gendered assumptions about crime and offending. The first category focuses on a topic that is at the heart of the dramatic rise of female participation in the criminal justice system: drug addiction. The second category investigates the role of women in property crime. The third category focuses on prostitution and sex work. While this is a crime that is often identified as a victimless crime, a review of women who engage in sexually based offenses often face high levels of victimization in their lives. The fourth category looks at the role of women within gang organizations. The section concludes with a look at women who engage in acts of murder.

Table 8.2 • 5- and 10-Year Arrest Trends 2006–2015: UCR Arrest Data: Males Versus Females				
	Percent Change Within Gender Between 2011 and 2015		Percent Change Within Gender Between 2006 and 2015	
	Males	Females	Males	Females
Violent crime	−6.1	−1.8	−17.8	−3.8
Homicide	+0.8	−1.8	−13.2	−9.1
Rape	−	−	−	−
Robbery	−13.1	+2.7	−23.8	−0.4
Aggravated assault	−5.5	−3.0	−17.3	−4.6
Property crime	−11.1	−6.5	−10.8	+20.2
Burglary	−29.2	−13.4	−30.9	−8.1
Larceny-theft	−6.3	−6.7	+1.6	+25.9
Motor vehicle theft	+9.2	+34.9	−38.9	−23.3
Arson	−24.2	−12.3	−47.0	−35.3

SOURCES: Crime in the United States 2015. https://ucr.fbi.gov/crime-in-the-u.s/2015/crime-in-the-u.s.-2015/tables/table-33 and https://ucr.fbi.gov/crime-in-the-u.s/2015/crime-in-the-u.s.-2015/tables/table-35

Women and Drugs

Throughout the majority of the 20th century, women were not identified as the typical addict or drug abuser. In many cases, the use of prescription and illegal substances by women (particularly White women) was normalized, often as a response to the pressures of gender-role expectations. For example, cocaine and opiates were legally sold in pharmacies and were frequently prescribed by doctors for a variety of ailments. Historically speaking, "women's addiction [was] constructed as the product of individual women's inability to cope with changing versions of normative femininity" (Campbell, 2000, p. 30). Examples of this can be found in advertisements depicting women and antianxiety medications in an effort to calm the frenzied housewife who is overwhelmed with her duties as a wife and mother. In the modern era, drug use was once again promoted as desirable (for White women) with the image of the heroin chic fashionista of the 1990s, personified by supermodel Kate Moss.

Without question, the war on drugs has had a significant impact on women with illicit drug addictions. In the last few decades, female incarceration rates grew 108%, but raw numbers grew eightfold (Harrison & Beck, 2006). These increases can be attributed almost exclusively to the female drug offender (or attributed to the rise in other offenses because of her drug use). This disproportionality continues to increase. In 2012, female drug offenders account for 25% of the state prison population, whereas in male prisons, these crimes make up only 16% of all offenders (Carson & Golinelli, 2013). This is a significant increase compared to 2008 data, where only 9% of drug offenders were women (Guerino, Harrison, & Sabol, 2011).

An endless number of pathways to lead the onset of drug addiction and offending. However, research consistently identifies similar pathways of drug use for women, regardless of race, ethnicity, or drug of choice. Whether the discussion focuses on women addicted to crack cocaine in lower income communities or middle-class women who abuse alcohol or prescription drugs, substance use becomes a method of coping with their lives (Inciardi, Lockwood, & Pottiger, 1993). These primary pathways include exposure to alcohol and drugs at a young age, early childhood victimization and trauma, mental health challenges, and economic challenges (Bloom, Owen, & Covington, 2003).

For some women, their experiences with addiction begin at an early age. These girls are often exposed to drug use within their home environment. A family environment can influence the pathway to addiction in terms of an increased availability of these illicit drugs as well as an environment that is accepting of substance use. In some cases, substance abuse becomes a part of the family culture and a way in which children can spend time with their parents and siblings (Carbone-Lopez, Gatewood Owens, & Miller, 2012). On the other hand, lack of parental supervision may lead to substance use for girls (Bowles, DeHart, & Webb, 2012). Early experimentation with substance abuse can also lead to a longer term of addiction (Dennis, Scott, Funk, & Foss, 2005).

Another pathway to addiction is represented through the issues that result from victimization and trauma, particularly during early childhood. Women who experience violence and abuse during their formative years are more likely to abuse alcohol and other drugs compared to women without a history of abuse. Here, research estimates that 48% to 90% of addicted women have endured physical or sexual victimization during their childhood (SAMHSA, 2009). Left untreated, drugs become a way to escape from the pain of childhood abuse and trauma (Carbone-Lopez et al., 2012). The presence of mental health issues can also serve as a pathway to addiction. Mental illness and substance use go hand in hand because 72% of men and women with severe mental disorders have a co-occurring substance abuse problem (Baillargeon, Binswanger, Penn, Williams, & Murray, 2009). Additionally, research indicates that women have higher rates of mental illness compared to men (James & Glaze, 2006). If effective mental health treatment (including psychotropic medication) is unavailable, many may choose to self-medicate with illicit substances, which can lead to issues with addiction (Harris & Edlund, 2005). Finally, women may engage in substance abuse as part of their romantic relationship with a significant other. In many cases, their experimentation quickly translates into addiction and continues even once the relationship ends (Ryder & Brisgone, 2013).

Addiction limits the abilities for many women to develop a self-sustaining life. In addition to placing them at risk for homelessness, violence, and incarceration in an effort to fund their drug use, addiction has collateral consequences, particularly for her minor children. Indeed, the images of the pregnant addicted mother and crack babies of the 80s and 90s represented the greatest form of evil found in the drug-abusing woman. Many women with addiction issues often fail to recognize that they are pregnant until late in their pregnancy where their substance use and lack of prenatal care can place their child at significant risk for health and developmental issues. However, for some women, the realization that they are expecting may encourage them to seek out treatment and give them a reason to change their lives (Silva, Pires, Guerreiro & Cardoso, 2012). However, relapse issues can threaten this newfound

©iStock/microgen

▲ **Photo 8.1** Research highlights that women and men vary in their drug use, in terms of both their drug of choice and their motivations for use. Here, a woman is shown using drugs intravenously.

journey toward stability and have lasting effects both for her life as well for her children. Relapse, incarceration, and time in a treatment facility mean that mothers are separated from their children. Even in cases where these mothers were physically present, their addiction meant that they were often emotionally unavailable for their children. Over time, an intergenerational pattern emerges, and these daughters turn to the same addictions that their mothers endure.

Regardless of their pathway to addiction, increases in number of women using drugs and the marginalization of addicts fed the war on drugs. As the behaviors of addicted women shifted toward criminal activity in an effort to support their drug habit, the perception that drug addiction is *dangerous* spread among the general public. Drug use became something to fear by members of society. The shift of addiction from a public health issue to a criminal justice issue fueled the fear about the link of drug use and crime.

The heightened frenzy over the dangerousness of drugs has fueled the war on drugs into an epidemic. The war on drugs and its effects on the criminal justice system have been documented extensively, and the introduction of mandatory minimum sentencing represented a major change in the processing of drug offenders. While these sentencing structures were applied equally to male and female defendants, the role of women's participation in drug offenses often differs substantially from male involvement in drug-related crimes. With the elimination of judicial discretion, judges were unable to assess the role that women played in these offenses (Merolla, 2008). As a result, women now received long sentences of incarceration where they had once been granted probation and other forms of community supervision. The effect of this shift was dramatic. Between 1986 and 1991, the incarceration rates of women for drug-related offenses increased 433%, compared to a 283% increase for males (Bush-Baskette, 2000). Drug-convicted women make up 72% of the incarcerated population at the federal level (Greenfeld & Snell, 2000). Most of these cases involve women as users of illegal substances. Even in the small proportion of cases where women are involved in the sale of drugs, they rarely participate in mid- or high-level management in the illegal drug market, often because of sexism within the drug economy (Maher, 2004b). For those women who are able to break through the glass ceiling of the drug trade, they are often characterized by justice officials as either more like their male counterparts (much as early criminologists did in describing female criminality) or worse than their male counterparts for violating gender norms about drug dealing. However, for most of the women who enter the drug trade, it is their relationship with an intimate partner that explains their criminality in terms of both drug use and manufacturing. Not only were women introduced to new, serious substances (such as heroin and opioids) through their relationships (Ventura-Miller, Miller & Barnes, 2016), but courts viewed these women as less culpable in their offending as they were "under the influence" of these criminal men (Mann, Menih, & Smith, 2014).

While recent changes in federal drug sentencing laws have reduced the disparities in sentencing, the damage has already been done. The effects of these laws created a new system of criminal justice where the courts are overloaded with drug possession and distribution cases, and the growth of the prison economy has reached epic proportions. Yet these efforts appear to have done little to stem the use and sale of such controlled substances. At the same time, there is recent chatter by government leaders, such as Attorney General Jefferson Sessions that there should be a return to the war on drugs. Under his leadership, he has instructed federal prosecutors to pursue harsh punishments for drug-related crimes, even low-level offenses. In justifying this change in policy, Sessions has cited an perceived increase in crime rates over the past year, arguing that such increases may be a sign of a new trend (Ford, 2017). This marks a dramatic shift from policy changes that were enacted under President Obama. Indeed, the overall rates of crimes other than drug-related cases have changed little during the last 40 years. The effects of these policies have produced significant consequences for families and communities, particularly given the increase in the incarceration rates of women. Sections X and XI explore in depth the consequences in the incarceration of women, for both themselves and their families, as well as their communities. It is these consequences that have led some scholars to suggest that the war on drugs has in effect become a war on women (Chesney-Lind, 1997).

Property Crime

The category of property crime is relatively broad and encompasses a number of different offenses. Generally speaking, property crime refers to the illegal acquisition of money, goods, or valuables, but without the use of force or fear to obtain the property. While the Uniform Crime Report includes arson, burglary, larceny-theft, and motor vehicle theft as Part 1 offenses under the category of property crime, the National Crime Victimization Survey (NCVS) includes only burglary, motor vehicle theft, and theft (larceny) in its definition. As a more inclusive representation of crime, the National Incident Based Reporting System incorporates many more types of property offenses into its definition, such as arson, bribery, burglary, vandalism, embezzlement, blackmail, fraud, larceny-theft, motor vehicle theft, stolen property offenses, and bad checks.

According to the Bureau of Justice Statistics, the rate of property crime victimization within U.S. households (property crime per 1,000 households) has steadily declined since 1993. Today's rate is roughly one-third of the 1993 victimization rate (110.7 victimizations per 1,000 households in 2015, compared to 320 in 1993) (Truman & Morgan 2016). While females are more likely to be involved in property offenses compared to other types of crimes, males still commit the overwhelming majority of these crimes. Men committed 62% of property crimes in 2010, while women were responsible for about 38% of these offenses.

Earlier in this section, you learned about how women's lives are shaped by addiction. Addiction can also shape women's participation in crimes, particularly for property offenses, because women may engage in these crimes to either support their drug habit or commit crime while under the influence. Indeed, drugs are the most common factor among females who engage in property crimes. Research by Johnson (2004) finds that 52% of property offenders engage in crime to get money so that they can buy drugs. In comparison, only 15% of violent offenders stated that their crime was directly related to obtaining drugs for personal use.

—) Another factor in female property offending is economic survival. Given that only 40% of incarcerated women were employed prior to their arrest, it appears that many women engage in these crimes in order to provide for themselves and their families. Research does note that welfare reform during the 1990s did lead to a small reduction of female involvement in serious property crimes (Corman, Dave, & Reichman, 2014). However, to suggest that poverty and unemployment lead people to engage in property-based offending is a narrow view of the issue. Certainly, addiction can play a role for some offenders. Here, the decision to engage in crime helps not only to fund their substance abuse but also to provide support to maintain a household. This is particularly poignant given that many individuals who suffer from addiction are unable to hold down functional employment.

The image of women in property crimes varies dramatically. On one hand, shoplifting is typically described as a "pink-collar" crime. While shoplifting may be an act that some undertake to support other areas of criminality, such as drug use, others use shoplifting as their primary occupation and sell their goods to buying customers. These women view themselves as professionals, and their ability to shoplift is a skill. Much like the drug dealer, the shoplifter develops a list of clients who will purchase their goods from her. Her attire is based on what types of stores she will steal from so that she blends in with the rest

▲ Photo 8.2 The majority of crimes involving women are property offenses and include crimes such as burglary and theft. Here, a woman engages in shoplifting from a store.

© Can Stock Photo Inc./diego_cervo

of the legitimate shoppers and goes undetected by security personnel (Caputo & King, 2011). Another example involves women and the crime of robbery. Some scholars highlight how women engage in robbery as solo offenders; how women choose to engage in crime is gendered in that they typically do not engage in overt acts of violence and select other women as their victims (Miller, 1998a). Meanwhile, other cases show women who use their femininity to draw in their victims as part of a larger mixed-gender group (Contreras, 2009). In each of these cases, women use their gender in their favor.

Spotlight on Women and Bank Robbery

Historically, male offenders have dominated the crime of bank robbery. Even in cases where women have been involved in these crimes, they were either coconspirators with a male or were reduced to a minor role. Consider the example of Bonnie Elizabeth Parker (1910–1934) who was romantically involved with Clyde Chestnut Barrow (1909–1934). Barrow and his gang committed over a dozen bank robberies during the Great Depression. Urban legend suggested that Bonnie was an equal participant in these crimes. However, evidence suggests that Bonnie never actually killed a single victim.

While the days of Bonnie and Clyde are long gone and men remain the most likely offender of these crimes, times are changing. Women are becoming more involved in these crimes. In the last decade, the number of bank robberies committed by women has shifted. While there were more females involved in bank robberies in 2003, there were more of these offenses in general. According to the Uniform Crime Reports, women made up 524 of the 9,714 offenders involved in these crimes. This means that women made up 5.5% of all bank robbery offenders in 2003. In 2011, they made up 429 of the offenders for these crimes. However, the overall number of offenders in these cases fell by 37% to 6,088 (Federal Bureau of Investigation [FBI], 2003, 2011).

Perhaps one of the most famous cases of bank robbery involved Patricia Hearst. Hearst was the 19-year-old socialite granddaughter of newspaper publishing mogul William Randolph Hearst. In 1974, Patty Hearst was kidnapped by members of the Symbionese Liberation Army, a domestic terrorist group. The SLA manipulated Hearst to join their criminal actions. During her 18 months under SLA captivity, she participated in three bank robberies and several other criminal activities. Despite her defense that she had been brainwashed by her captors, Hearst was sentenced to 7 years in prison for her part in the robbery. Her sentence was commuted after 2 years by then President Jimmy Carter, and she was pardoned by President Clinton (Cable News Network [CNN], 2001).

A recent example of a female bank robber is Lee Grace Dougherty. In August 2011, Lee Grace, with her brother Ryan and stepbrother Dylan, robbed a local bank in Georgia. While all three had previously been involved with the criminal justice system, Lee Grace drew the attention of the media both for her status as a woman and for her online statements that "I like causing mayhem with my siblings." She was sentenced to 35 years in prison for her involvement in the bank robbery and faces additional time for her subsequent offenses as part of their multistate crime spree (Coffman, 2012; Gast, 2011; MacIntosh, 2011).

Prostitution

Hollywood images of prostitution depict a lifestyle that is rarely found in the real world. Movies such as *Pretty Woman, Leaving Las Vegas,* and *Taxi Driver* paint a picture of the young, beautiful prostitute who is saved from her life on the streets. In reality, there are few Prince Charmings available to rescue these women. The reality that awaits most of these women is one filled with violence, abuse, and addiction—deep scars that are challenging to overcome.

Prostitution involves the act of selling or trading sex for money. Prostitution can take a variety of forms, including escort services, massage parlors, or work in brothels, bars, and truck stops. However, street-level prostitution is perhaps the most visible form of sex work. According to the Uniform Crime Reports, police agencies arrested 36,931 offenders for the crime of prostitution in 2012. Two-thirds of such offenders were female (see FBI, 2011, 2012b). Most of these offenders are workers of the trade and not the traffickers or customers associated with these crimes.

For those women who engage in street-level prostitution, money may not be the only commodity available in exchange for their bodies, because they also trade sex for drugs or other tangibles such as food, clothing, and shelter. In addition, women in this arena experience the high levels of risk for violence and victimization.

The journey into prostitution is not a solitary road. Rather, it involves a variety of individual, contextual, and environmental factors. A history of abuse is one of the most commonly referenced risk factors for prostitution, and research by Dalla (2000) indicates that drug addiction almost always paves the way for work in prostitution. However, poverty also plays a role. In Section V, you learned about the issue of forced prostitution and human trafficking, yet many women choose to enter **street prostitution** and brothel work out of financial need (Karandikar, Gezinski, & Meshelemiah, 2013).

One of the most common pathways for women in prostitution is the experience of early childhood sexual victimization. Although there is no direct link that indicates that the experience of incest is predictive of selling one's body, research indicates that there is a strong correlation between the two (Nokomis Foundation, 2002), and one prostitution recovery program indicates that 87% of their participants experienced abuse throughout their early childhood, often at the hands of a family member. For these women, incest became the way in which they learned about their sexuality as a commodity that could be sold and traded, and some suggest this process of bargaining became a way in which these victims could once again feel powerful about their lives (Mallicoat, 2006). In Section VII, you learned about how young girls who have been abused within the home often run away to escape the ongoing violence and victimization. Once on the streets, they are at risk for even more violence. Many of these girls turn to prostitution to support their basic survival needs, such as food and shelter. They also enter prostitution as a way to regain some agency and control of their sexuality, compared to their abusive history where others held the power and control—"because from my childhood, I had been molested. And then as time went on, I was still getting molested, so I got tired. And I said well, if a man is going to take it from me, why not sell myself" (Cobbina & Oselin, 2011). For other girls who enter prostitution during adolescence, the decision to enter prostitution is one that is normalized where prostitution is practiced within the family/community and is viewed as an economic opportunity.

Women in prostitution experience high levels of violence during their careers. On the streets, they witness and experience violence on a daily basis. More than 90% of these women are brutally victimized (Romero-Daza, Weeks, & Singer, 2003). They are robbed, raped, and assaulted by their customers and pimps alike (Raphael & Shapiro, 2004). Violence can also occur at the hands of an intimate partner or pimp (DeHart, Lynch, Belknap, Dass-Brailsford, & Green, 2014). Many do not report these incidents out of fear that they will be arrested for engaging in prostitution, coupled with a belief that the police will do little to respond to these crimes. Indeed, women often return to the streets immediately following their victimization. This temporary intervention is viewed as a delay in work rather than an opportunity to search for an exit strategy. One woman characterized her experience as normal—"society and law enforcement consider a prostitute getting raped or beat as something she deserves. It goes along with your lifestyle. There's nothing that you can do" (Dalla, Xia, & Kennedy, 2003, p. 1380–1381).

Female sex workers also witness significant acts of violence perpetuated against their peers, an experience that often leads to significant mental health issues. Drug use becomes a way to cope with the violence in their daily lives. As the pressure to make money increases in order to sustain their substance abuse addiction or to provide a roof over their head at night, women may place themselves in increasingly risky situations with their customers (Norton-Hawk, 2004). In an effort to protect against potential harms, women rely on their intuition to avoid

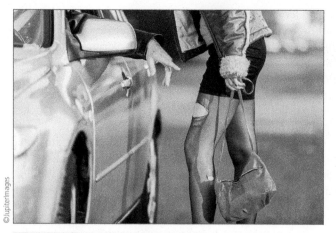

▲ **Photo 8.3** While street prostitution comprises a small proportion of sex work, it is one of the most visible forms. It is also one of the most dangerous forms of sex work. Many women who work the streets risk significant victimization from their clients. Unfortunately, many victims do not report these crimes to the police out of concerns that their cases will not be treated seriously by the justice system.

potentially violent situations. Many girls indicate that they will not leave a designated area with a client and generally refuse to get into a car with a client. Others carry a weapon, such as a knife. Despite the risks, some women reference the thrill and power they experience when they are able to survive a violent incident (Dalla, Xia, & Kennedy, 2003). Many women are surprised when they reflect on the levels of violence that they experienced on the streets. Some may dissociate themselves from the realities of this journey and believe that the experience was not as traumatic as they originally believed. However, the battle scars from their time on the streets provide the evidence for the trauma they endured, both physically and mentally.

The role of substance abuse is central to the discussion of risk for prostituting women. About 70% of women in prostitution have issues with drug addiction. Some women begin their substance use prior to their entry in prostitution to cope with the pain associated with past or current sexual violence in their lives. They then resort to prostitution to fund their drug habits (Raphael, 2004). For others, entry into substance abuse comes later in an effort to self-medicate against the fear, stress, and low self-esteem resulting from the selling of sex (Nixon, Tutty, Downe, Gorkoff, & Ursel, 2002). As their time on the streets increases, so does their substance abuse (Cobbina & Oselin, 2011). Indeed, the relationship between drug use and prostitution may be a self-perpetuating cycle in which they feed off one another. A sample of women in jail for prostitution had significantly higher rates of drug use compared to women arrested for non-prostitution-related offenses (Yacoubian, Urbach, Larsen, Johnson, & Peters, 2000).

In recent years, media accounts have focused significant attention on the use of crack cocaine by street prostitutes. Research has linked the presence of crack to an increased number of individuals working on the street, which in turn decreases the price that women receive for their services. Addiction to drugs such as crack has created an economy where money is no longer traded for sex. Rather, sexual acts become a commodity to be exchanged for drugs. The levels of violence associated with the practice of selling sex increases in this drug-fueled economy (Maher, 1996).

While drug addiction presents a significant health concern for women in prostitution, additional issues exist for women in terms of long-term physical health. Women engaged in sex work are at risk for issues related to HIV, hepatitis, and other chronic health concerns, including dental, vision, neurological, respiratory, and gynecological problems (Farley & Barkin, 1998). Finally, the death rate of women in prostitution is an astonishingly 40 times higher than the death rate of the overall population (Nokomis Foundation, 2002).

Mental health concerns are also a significant issue for women engaged in the sex trade. Cases of **posttraumatic stress disorder (PTSD)** are directly related to the levels of violence that women experience on the streets, and an estimated two thirds of prostituted women experience symptoms of PTSD (Schoot & Goswami, 2001). Prostitutes suffering from PTSD may be unable to accurately assess the levels of threat and violence that surround their lives, which in turn places them at increased risk for ongoing physical and sexual victimization (Valera, Sawyer, & Schiraldi, 2000).

The Legalization Debate

The question of whether prostitution should be considered a criminal activity is one of considerable debate. In Nevada, legal prostitution is limited to counties with a population under 400,000, excluding high-traffic areas, such as Reno and Las Vegas, from offering legalized brothels.[1] The laws within Nevada focus almost exclusively on the minimization of risk and reduction of violence for women in prostitution. Since 1986, Nevada has required that prostitutes who work in brothels must submit to weekly exams to assess for any sexually transmitted infections or the presence of HIV. Brothels also implement a variety of regulations to ensure the safety and security of the facility and the women who work there, such as audio monitoring and call buttons in the rooms. Most brothels limit services outside of the brothel environment to control any potentially negative behaviors of clients. Research indicates that women who work in brothel settings feel safe and rarely experience acts of violence while working as prostitutes. Indeed, such safety mechanisms led women to believe that brothel sex work is by far the safest environment in which to engage in prostitution, compared to the violence and danger that street prostitutes regularly experience (Brents & Hausbeck, 2005).

In the Netherlands, the legalization of brothels in 2000 created a new way to govern the sex trade. While the act of prostitution has been legalized since the early 20th century, it was the brothel environment (popularized by the red light district and "window" shopping in the city of Amsterdam and other cities) that was illegal. At the time of brothel legalization, the practice of prostitution in the Netherlands was not an uncommon phenomenon, and estimates suggest that over 6,000 women per day were working in prostitution-related activities (Wagennar, 2006). The effects of the legislation lifted the formal prohibition of the brothel, even though many municipalities tolerated their presence, and agents of social control, such as law enforcement and the courts, largely refrained from prosecuting cases. By creating a system whereby brothels had to be licensed, authorities were able to gain control over the industry by mandating public health and safety screenings for sex workers. As part of the decriminalization of prostitution, the state created the opportunity for brothel owners to have a legal site of business. Labor laws regarding the working conditions for prostitutes were put into effect. In addition, it created a tax base in which revenue could be generated (Pakes, 2005). The goals of decriminalization allowed for the Dutch government to improve the lives of women in prostitution by creating safe working conditions, creating a system of monitoring of the sex trade, and regulating illegal activities that might be associated with the selling of sexuality, such as street crimes associated with prostitution, the exploitation of juveniles, or the trafficking of women into the sex industry (Wagenaar, 2006).

By creating a sustainable economy of prostitution, some critics suggest not only that the needs of the customer are met but also that these regions create an economic strategy for women, particularly women within challenged economic situations. However, creating a system of legislation is no guarantee that laws will be followed; even with the legalization of prostitution in New South Wales, Australia, the majority of brothels fail to register their businesses and pay little attention to the regulatory rules for operation. In addition, illegal sexual practices have continued to flourish; the Netherlands is identified as a leading destination for pedophiles and child pornographers, many of which operate under the belief that the promotion of legalized prostitution has created opportunities for illegal prostitution in these regions, as well (Raymond, 2004).

Other legislation focuses on the criminalization of the demand for sexual services. In addressing the issue of prostitution in Sweden, legislatures have focused on making the purchasing of sex from women a criminal act. The belief here is that criminalizing the male demand for sex may significantly decrease the supply of women who engage in these acts. By criminalizing the "johns," Sweden has taken a stand against a practice that the country feels constitutes an act of violence against women (Raymond, 2004). In the passing of these laws, the parliament indicated, "[I]t is not reasonable to punish the person who sells a sexual service. In the majority of cases . . . this person is a weaker partner who is exploited" (Ministry of Labour, Sweden, 1998, p. 4).

In the United States, even in an environment where both the purchaser and seller of sex can be subjected to criminal prosecution, the data indicate that women are significantly more likely to face sanctions for selling sex, compared to men who seek to purchase it (Farley & Kelly, 2000). Although the focus on demand is an important characteristic in the selling of sex, it is not the only variable. Indeed, larger issues such as economics, globalization, poverty, and inequality all contribute to a system where women fall victim to the practices of sexual exploitation.

Farley and Kelly (2000) suggest that even with the legalization of the brothel environment, prostitution remains a significant way in which women are brutalized and harmed. The social stigma of women who engage in the selling of sex does not decrease simply because the act of prostitution becomes legal. Indeed, the restriction of brothels to specific regions only further isolates women from mainstream society and magnifies the stigma they may experience (Farley, 2004). In cases of victimization, women employed in sex work continue to experience significant levels of victim blaming when they are victimized, even if prostitution is decriminalized. The system of public health, which is promoted as a way to keep both the prostitute and her client safe, fails to meet some of the most critical needs of women in this arena, because these efforts toward promoting safety are limited exclusively to physical health, and little to no attention is paid to the mental health needs of women engaged in prostitution (Farley, 2004).

Research indicates that women involved in street prostitution often want to leave the lifestyle, but they express concern over how their multiple needs (including housing, employment, and drug treatment) may limit their abilities to do so. There are few programs that provide adequate levels of services to address the multiple needs of women during this transition. A review of one prostitution recovery program found that affordable safe housing is the greatest immediate need for women in their transition from the streets (Mallicoat, 2011). Homelessness puts women at risk for relapse: "Without reliable housing, it is challenging to escape the cycle of prostituting" (Yahne, Miller, Irvin-Vitela, & Tonigan, 2002, p. 52).

In addition, women must possess necessary skills and have access to support in order to facilitate this process. Women exiting the streets indicate a variety of therapeutic needs, including life skills, addiction recovery programming, and mental health services designed to address the traumas they experienced. An exit strategy needs to acknowledge the barriers to success and continuing struggles that women will experience as a result of these traumas.

Gender and Violence

True-crime documentaries and fictionalized television dramas give the perception that the rates of female offending, particularly in cases involving violence, have increased dramatically in recent years. Yet rates of crime for women in these types of cases have actually decreased. This discussion about women and violent crimes investigates three different categories of female offenders. The first topic highlights the role of women in gangs. The second topic looks at general crimes of female violence, including murder. The section concludes with a specific type of female homicide with women who kill their children.

Girls and Gangs

While girls have traditionally made up a small proportion of gang members, there was significant media attention on the rise of gang girls throughout the late 20th century. Surveys conducted by law enforcement agencies in the 1990s estimated that between 8% and 11% of gang members were female (Moore & Terrett, 1998). However, not all law enforcement jurisdictions include girls in their counts of gang members, a practice that can skew data about the number of girls involved in gangs (Curry, Ball, & Fox, 1994). Whereas the National Youth Gang Center suggests that these rates have remained consistent and reflect little change in rates of female gang participation (2009), other data tell a different story. Self-report studies during this same time frame reflect a higher percentage of female gang participation compared to law enforcement data and suggest that 38% of the self-identified gang members between the ages of 13 and 15 were female (Esbensen, Deschenes, & Winfree, 1999). Recent self-report data indicate that girls represent between 31% and 45% of gang members (Esbensen & Carson, 2012).

Who are female gang members? Much of the early literature on girls and gangs looked at female gang members as secondary to issues surrounding male gangs. Classic studies by Campbell (1984) and Moore (1991) illustrated that girls entered the gang lifestyle as a result of a brother or boyfriend's affiliation. Girls in the gang were often distinguished from their male counterparts by their sexuality. This sexualization manifested in several ways: (1) as a girlfriend to a male gang member, (2) as one who engages in sex with male gang members, and (3) as one who uses her sexuality in order to avoid detection by rival gang members and law enforcement (Campbell, 1995). Modern research builds on this early work, suggesting that female gangs are not only increasing their membership ranks but also expanding their function and role as an independent entity separate from the male gang. Girls in the gang are no longer the sexual toy of the male gang but have become active participants in crimes of drugs and violence.

The lives of girls in gangs tell a story filled with violence, poverty, racism, disenfranchisement, and limited resources. They come from families who struggle to make ends meet in economically depressed areas. In these communities, opportunities for positive, prosocial activities are significantly limited, and the pressure to join a gang runs rampant. Many of the girls have limited achievements in the classroom, and their educational experience has little to do with books or teachers. Instead, they share stories of disorder, threats, and crime (Molidor, 1996). The majority of their parents never married, and the presence of intimate partner abuse within the home was not uncommon. Many of the girls had a parent or other family members who were involved in the criminal justice system and were either currently incarcerated or had been incarcerated during some part of their lives.

For some girls, membership in a gang is a family affair, with parents, siblings, and extended family members involved in the gang lifestyle. Research by Miller (2000) indicates that 79% of girls who were gang involved had a family member who was a gang member, and 60% of the girls had multiple family members in gangs. For these girls, gang affiliation comes at an early age. During the childhood and preteen years, their gang activities may consist of limited acts of delinquency and drug experimentation. During junior high, girls exhibit several risk factors for delinquency, including risky sexual behavior, school failures, and truancy. By the time these girls become teenagers, they are committed to the gang and criminal activity and participate in a range of delinquent acts, including property crimes, weapons offenses, and violent crimes against persons. The later adolescent years (ages 15–18) represent the most intense years of gang activity (Eghigian & Kirby, 2006).

While the gang is a way of life for some girls, many others find their way to the gang in search of a new family. Many girls involved in gangs have histories of extensive physical and sexual abuse by family members during early childhood. Many of the girls run away from the family residence in an attempt to escape the violence and abuse in their lives. In an attempt to survive on the streets, the gang becomes an attractive option for meeting one's immediate and long-term needs such as shelter, food, and protection. Not only does the gang provide refuge from these abusive home environments, but it provides as well a sense of family that was lacking in their families of origin (Joe & Chesney-Lind, 1995). Research by Miller (2000) indicates that it is not so much a specific risk factor that propels girls into the gang but rather the relationship among several life situation factors, such as a neighborhood exposure to gangs, a family involvement in the lifestyle, and the presence of problems in the family, that illustrates the trajectory of girls into the gang lifestyle.

The literature on female gangs indicates that the lifestyle, structure, and characteristics of female gangs and their members are as diverse as male gangs. Some girls hang out with gangs in search of a social life and peer relationships, but they typically do not consider themselves as members of the gang. The structure of the girl gang ranges from being a mixed-gender gang to functioning as an independent unit. For girls involved in mixed-gender gangs, their role ranged from being an affiliate of the male gang unit to even, in some cases, having a "separate but equal" relationship to their male counterparts (Schalet, Hunt, & Joe-Laidler, 2003).

The initiation process for girls varies from being "jumped" in or **walking the line**, whereby the girls were subjected to assault by their fellow gang members, to being "sexed" in or **pulling a train**, an experience that involved having sex with multiple individuals, often the male gang members. However, not all these initiation rites came with a high degree of status within the gang, because those girls who were sexed in general experienced lower levels of respect by fellow gang members (Miller, 2000). Girls who had been "sexed into the gang" were subjected to continued victimization from within the gang. Although not all girls were admitted to the gang in this manner, this image negatively affected all the girls.

> The fact that there was such an option as "sexing in" served to keep girls disempowered, because they always faced the question of how they got in and of whether they were "true" members. In addition, it contributed to a milieu in which young women's sexuality was seen as exploitable. (Miller, 1998a, p. 444)

Recent media attention has targeted the gang girl and [thus created] the perception that violence by these girls is increasing. Yet data indicate that female gang members participate in criminal acts at rates similar to male gang members (Esbensen & Carson, 2012). Research by Fleisher and Krienert (2004) indicated that among girls who described themselves as active members of a gang, almost all (94%) had engaged in a violent crime during the previous 6 months, and two-thirds (67%) had sold drugs during the past 2 months. More than half (55%) had participated in property crimes, such as graffiti or destruction to property, while two-thirds (67%) engaged in economic crimes, such as prostitution, burglary, robbery, or theft, in the previous 6 months. Here, violence is more than just engaging in criminal offenses. Indeed, the participation in a delinquent lifestyle that is associated with gang membership places girls at risk for significant victimization. Girls who are "independent" of a male gang hierarchy tend to experience high levels of violence as a result of selling drugs and their interactions on the streets with other girls. These independent girls are aware of the potential risk they face and take a number of precautionary measures to enhance their safety, such as possessing a weapon, staying off the streets at night, and traveling in groups. While the close relationship with the male gang can often serve as a protective factor, it can also place the girls at risk of rape and sexual assault by their "homeboys" (Hunt & Joe-Laidler, 2001). In addition, girls whose gang membership is connected to a male gang unit tend to experience higher levels of violence on the streets compared to girls who operate in independent cliques. These girls are at a higher risk of victimization due to the levels of violence that they are exposed to from assaults and drive-by shootings that involve the male gang members. Indeed, many of these crimes (and potential risks of victimization) would not be present if they were not involved in the gang lifestyle (Miller, 1998b).

The exit from the gang lifestyle for girls can occur in several ways. For most girls, this exit coincides with the end of adolescence. They may withdraw from the lifestyle, often as a result of pregnancy and the need to care for their young children. For others, their exit is facilitated by an entry into legitimate employment or advanced education. Others will be removed from their gangs as a result of incarceration in a juvenile or adult correctional facility. While some may choose to be "jumped out," most will simply diminish their involvement over time rather than be perceived as betraying or deliberately going against their gang peers (Campbell, 1995). The few women who choose to remain in the gang have several pathways from which to choose. They may continue their gang participation as active members and expand their criminal résumé. Their relationships with male gang members may continue with their choice of marriage partners, which allows them to continue their affiliation in either a direct or indirect role (Eghigian & Kirby, 2006).

Gender and Violent Crime

Despite public perceptions, females make up a small proportion of violent offenders. While violent crime perpetuated by women does occur, it is rare. As you learned earlier in this chapter, men engage in far more acts of violence than females. For example, women's participation in the crime of homicide accounts for less than half of the arrests of men. And as with the rates of male violence, women's participation in these crimes has decreased, with homicide offending rates for females declining from 3.1 offenders per 100,000 in 1980 to 1.6 offenders per 100,000 in 2008 (Cooper & Smith, 2011). Women are more likely to kill someone known to them, compared to a stranger. Research by Kellermann & Mercy (1992) indicates that while 60% of female offenders knew their victims, only 20% of male murders had known victims. Generally speaking, women generally kill their spouses, significant others, or their children (Cooper & Smith, 2011).

Spotlight on Women and Self-Defense

Much of the fascination about women who kill comes from the perception of these offenders either as cold and calculating murderers or cases where women just "snap." But what about those cases of women who kill in self-defense? How do we make sense of these crimes of violence?

Consider the case of Marissa Alexander. During a confrontation with her husband in August 2010, Marissa fired a bullet into the wall to scare her husband. Alexander had a history of abuse with her partner and this incident occurred nine days after she had given birth to their daughter (Hauser, 2017). She testified that she felt threatened and luckily no one was hurt in the incident. Even though Alexander drew on Florida's Stand Your Ground Law, the jury convicted her of aggravated assault with a deadly weapon, and she was sentenced to 20 years in prison. Her actions triggered a mandatory minimum gun law, which increases the sentence in certain felonies if a gun is brandished or fired. Even lawmakers in the state argued that the intent of the law was not to punish cases like Alexander's but was designed to increase sentences for those who brandished or used a firearm during the commission of a crime such as robbery or assault (Stacy, 2012). Her initial conviction was overturned on appeal for errors by the trial judge in the instructions to the jury, While awaiting a retrial, he accepted a plea deal that allowed her to serve 3 years in prison and 2 years on house arrest. She was released from house arrest in January 2017 and has developed a nonprofit to be an advocate for victims of intimate partner abuse and criminal justice policy reform (Hauser, 2017).

Another case of self-defense that has drawn recent attention involves Sara Kruzan. In 1995, Kruzan was only 16 years old when she was convicted of first-degree murder and sentenced to life without the possibility of parole. She had no juvenile record and had been an honor student as a young child. The victim was her pimp, a 31-year-old man named G. G. Howard, who had begun grooming Sara when she was only 11 years old and had been sexually trafficking her for the past 4 years (Sharma, 2013). Even though her age made it possible for the case to be tried in juvenile court (where the maximum sentence would have resulted in her incarceration until age 25), prosecutors transferred her case to criminal court, where she was tried as an adult. In January 2011, new legislation was enacted that allowed for the reconsideration of juvenile cases where life sentences were handed down. Following the new law, then-Governor Schwarzenegger granted clemency to Kruzan and commuted her [life without parole] LWOP sentence to 25 years with the possibility of parole. Additional legislation signed into law by Governor Jerry Brown required parole boards to give special consideration in parole decisions involving juvenile offenders who were tried as adults and who had served at least 15 years of their sentences. After serving 19 years, Kruzan was paroled in part due to these new policies (St. John, 2013).

In both of these cases, public attention played a significant role in raising awareness about these cases. Sara Kruzan was featured in social action campaigns by Abolish Slavery and Human Rights Watch and drew the attention of lawmakers who were seeking changes in how juvenile cases were handled. Kruzan has become the face for thousands of youth who are serving sentences for crimes they committed as juveniles (De Atley, 2013). Similarly, Alexander's case involved a ground of activists and organizations who joined together in a campaign titled Free Marissa Now, to which organized grassroot activities such as educational events on domestic violence, social media campaigns and petitions to state officials on her case. Since her release, the group has continued to be an advocate for other women who have been incarcerated in cases of domestic and gender-based violence (free marissanow.org).

Much of the fascination about female violent crime stems from how these crimes are portrayed by popular culture. The cable television show *Snapped* (Oxygen network) focuses on true-crime cases of women who kill and their motivations for crime. Movie story lines have included both fictional and "ripped from the headlines" examples of women who stalk, torture, and murder their victims. The 1987 film *Fatal Attraction* tells the story of

Alex (portrayed by Glenn Close), who obsesses over her married lover Dan (played by Michael Douglas). Alex engages in all sorts of crimes toward Dan, including pouring acid on his car and killing the family rabbit (Maslin, 1987). The Broadway show (and film adaption) *Chicago* tells the story of Velma Kelly and Roxie Hart, who are arrested for the murders of their paramours. The backdrop for this story came from several true-crime cases from the 1920s where women were tried and ultimately acquitted for killing their husbands or lovers. These cases were sensationalized in local newspapers, and these women became celebrities throughout their trials (Perry, 2010). Even popular song lyrics draw attention (and justify) the actions of women who damage the side panel, vandalize its interior, and slash the tires of their cheating boyfriend's car (*Before He Cheats*).

Beyond the Hollywood portrayals of violence by women, the public is fascinated by the real-world examples of women who kill. Consider the case of Pamela Smart. Twenty-two years old and married after a quick courtship, she and her husband Gregory Smart had been having significant problems in their marriage, and they began to spend time apart. Pamela began spending time outside of her job at Winnacunnet High School with several students. She ultimately began an intimate relationship with one of these youth, William "Billy" Flynn. On May 1, 1990, Smart arrived at her home in Derry, New Hampshire, after the workday to find her husband Gregory dead of a bullet wound to the head. The case immediately aroused the suspicions of the local police. While the crime scene appeared to be staged to look like a robbery gone bad, Gregory Smart had been killed execution style. While Pam had an alibi at the time of the murder, police began to suspect that she was involved in her husband's murder. An anonymous call to the police suggested that Pam had orchestrated the killing. Billy Flynn and two of his friends were arrested for murder. Although the police believed they had the individuals who were responsible for carrying out the murder, they conducted audio surveillance on Pam Smart, where she admitted details of planning the murder of her husband with Flynn (Rideout, 2007). Billy Flynn testified against Smart that she persuaded him to murder her husband so that they could be together (Dinan, 2005). While Flynn was sentenced to 40 years to life, Pamela Smart received a sentence of life without the possibility of parole.

The trial of Pamela Smart gained national attention, and it was the first to be televised on the cable television channel Court TV (Rideout, 2007). By the time the trial began, there were over 400 various articles written about the case in local and national newspapers. By the end of the trial, this number approached 1,200. These articles portrayed Flynn as "hot for teacher" and Smart as seducing her young student (even though Smart was an administrator for the school district and not a teacher). They also described Smart's cold demeanor during the trial, labeling her as the *Ice Princess* (Lyons, 2006). This real-life case became iconized by the movie *To Die For* starring Nicole Kidman and Joaquin Phoenix.

A more contemporary example of the media's fascination with a female murder trial is the case of Casey Anthony, who was tried for the 2008 murder of her 2-year-old daughter Caylee in Orange County, Florida. The police began to suspect Anthony after several discrepancies in her story regarding her daughter's disappearance. Anthony had alleged that Caylee was kidnapped by her nanny (Zenaida Fernandez-Gonzalez), who, it was later determined, never existed. In addition, Anthony had not reported her daughter missing, which further raised the suspicions of her family and the police. Caylee's decomposed body was found in a wooded area on December 11, 2008 (Casey Anthony, 2014).

Casey Anthony's trial began in June 2011 with significant media attention. In portraying Anthony as responsible for her daughter's death, the state linked [the death to] a search on Casey's computer for chloroform. Remnants of this toxic chemical were found in the trunk of Anthony's car, coupled with the smell of decomposing waste. Anthony was also described as an out of control party animal that did not want to be a mother. However, there was no evidence that directly linked Anthony to the murder of her daughter (Alvarez, 2011). Following her acquittal in July 2011, Anthony's attorneys vilified the press for its role in creating a sensationalized image of Casey to the public that assumed her guilt. However, newspapers were not the only ones to blame for these behaviors. Like Pamela Smart's trial, the trial of Casey Anthony was televised. Twenty years later, however, there are many other sources of information that dominate the public perceptions of crime. These included a live video feed online of the trial, numerous Facebook pages in the names of Casey and her daughter, and even a Twitter account managed by the Ninth Judicial Circuit Court of Florida (Cloud, 2011). This level of intimate accessibility allowed the public to feel as if it were a part of the trial experience and had a personal investment in its outcome. Indeed, the public outcry over Anthony's acquittal was significant. "Because many American murder cases, such as the Casey Anthony trial, are shown on television, they sometimes appear to the public as if they were reality television shows. There is great disappointment, therefore, when the result is a verdict of not guilty" (Dershowitz, 2011, para 8). Not surprisingly, the public's fascination with women who engage in crimes of violence appears to have increased with the times because there are now multiple sources through which one can satisfy their desires for this dramatized portrayal of crime and justice.

These themes were once again displayed in the case of Jodi Arias. Over the course of her four-month trial, every moment of the trial was broadcast on cable television. In addition, there was no shortage of "legal experts" waiting to give their opinion on the events of the day, the evidence presented, or the demeanor of the defendant. Arias was charged and ultimately convicted for the murder of her boyfriend, Travis Alexander. Alexander was found in his shower where he had been stabbed 27 times, his throat had been slit, and he had been shot in the head (Sholchet, 2013). One of the particularly sensationalized parts of the trial involved Arias 'own testimony, which lasted 18 days. Under Arizona law, members of the jury are allowed to submit questions to the accused should they choose to take the stand in their own defense. "Some of the questions seemed to serve no other purpose but to mock Arias and illustrate the jurors' annoyance with her claims" (Fagel, 2013). While she was convicted of first-degree murder, the same jury was unable to come to a verdict on whether Arias should be given the death penalty. She is currently serving life in prison without the possibility of parole (Kiefer, 2015).

Spotlight on the Case of Michelle Carter

"You better not be bull sh*ting me and saying you're gonna do this and then purposely get caught."

"Like, are you gonna do it then? Keep being all talk and no action and everyday go throu saying how badly you wanna kill yourself? Or are you gonna try to get better?"

"You're just making it harder on yourself by pushing it off and you say you'll do it but u never do. Its always gonna be that way if u don't take action"

These are just a few of the texts that 17-year-old Michelle Carter sent to her boyfriend Conrad Roy III over a four-week period in 2014. Roy ultimately committed suicide in July 14 by outfitting his truck with tubing connected to his tailpipe so that he could inhale the carbon monoxide (LeBlanc, 2017). Carter was found guilty of involuntary manslaughter and faces up to 20 years in prison. What makes the case particularly interesting to legal scholars is that Carter was not physically present when Roy ultimately took his life. Instead, she was held criminally responsible for encouraging Roy to carry out his suicide. The case hinged both on these text messages, as well as evidence that Carter may have been on the phone with Roy at the time of his death, encouraging him to follow through with the action. Prosecutors contended that Carter was on the phone with Roy and told him to "get back in the truck" when he stepped out of the truck. The call was not recorded and only came to the attention of authorities when Carter told a friend several weeks later via text that she was on the phone with Roy—"his death is my fault, like honestly I could have stopped him. I was on the phone with him and he got out of the car because it was working and he got scared" (Seelye & Bidgood, 2017).

What makes the case particularly interesting is that while Carter's behavior is certainly offensive, is it criminal? Suicide is an act of free will by an individual and typically lacks the legal causation that is required for most offenses. Defense experts also testified that Carter was "involuntarily intoxicated" by her use of antidepressants that were legally prescribed to her (Sanchez & Lance, 2017). Her conviction will likely be appealed, and many experts have suggested that her conviction could be overturned because her actions did not directly cause Roy's death. Massachusetts is one of 10 states that does not have any laws that criminalize assisted suicide, though it is possible that the state's legislature may introduce new policy as a result of this case (Suerth, 2017).

Mothers Who Kill Their Children

While the crime of **filicide** is a rare occurrence, it raises significant attention in the media. The case of Andrea Yates is one of the most identifiable cases of filicide in the 21st century. After her husband left for work on June 20, 2001, Yates proceeded to drown each of her five children one at a time in the bathtub of the family home. Her case illustrates several factors that are common to incidents of maternal filicide. Yates had a history of mental health issues, including bipolar disorder, and she had been hospitalized in the past for major depression. She was the primary caretaker for her children and was responsible for homeschooling the older children. She and her husband were devout evangelical Methodists. Yates indicated that she felt inadequate as a mother and wife, believed that her children were spiritually damaged, and stated that she was directed by the voice of Satan to kill her children (Spinelli, 2004).

The case involving the children of Andrea Yates is just one tragic example of a mother engaging in filicide, or the killing of her children. There are several different categories of filicide. **Neonaticide** refers to an act of homicide during the first 24 hours after birth, compared to cases of **infanticide**, which includes acts whereby a parent kills his or her child within the first year of life. Here, the age of the child distinguishes these cases from general acts of filicide, which include the homicide of children older than 1 year of age by their parent. While the practice of filicide does not exclude the murder of a child by its father, mothers make up the majority of offenders in cases of infanticide and neonaticide.

What leads a woman to kill her child? There are several different explanations for this behavior. Research by Resnick (1970) distinguishes five different categories of infanticide. The first category represents cases where the infant was killed for **altruistic** reasons. In these incidents, the mother believes that it is in the best interests of the child to be dead and that the mother is doing a good thing by killing the child. Here, the mother believes (whether real or imagined) that the child is suffering in some way and that the child's pain should end. Based on Resnick's (1970) typology, Yates would be identified as a mother who kills her children out of altruistic reasons. A review of Yates's case indicates two themes common to altruistic filicide. The first theme reflects the pressure that exists in society for women to be good mothers. For Yates, this pressure was influenced by her religious fundamentalism, which placed the importance of the spiritual life of her children under her responsibility. The pressure to be a perfect mother was exacerbated by her history of mental illness. The second theme reflected the pressure of bearing the sole responsibility to care for the children. Here, Yates expressed feeling overwhelmed by the demands of their children's personal, academic, and spiritual needs, in addition to the responsibilities of caring for the family home. She also lacked any support from outside of the family, which further contributed to her feelings of being overburdened (West & Lichtenstein, 2006).

The second category in Resnick's typology refers to the killing of a child by an acutely psychotic woman. These cases are closely linked with explanations of postpartum psychosis where the mother suffers from a severe case of mental illness and may be unaware of her action or be unable to appreciate the wrongfulness of her behaviors. Examples of this type of filicide may involve a woman who hears voices that tell her that she needs to harm her child. The third category represents the killing of an unwanted infant. In many cases, these are cases of neonaticide. Research indicates that there are similar characteristics within the cases of mothers who kill their children within their first day of life. These women tend to be unmarried, under the age of 25, and generally tend to conceal their pregnancy from friends and family. Some women may acknowledge that they are pregnant, but their lack of actions toward preparing for the birth of the child indicate that they may be in denial that they may soon give birth. Others fail to acknowledge that they are pregnant and explain away the symptoms of pregnancy (Miller, 2003). They typically give birth without medical intervention and generally do not receive any form of prenatal care. The majority of these women do not suffer from any form of mental illness, which would help explain the death of their children. Instead, most of the cases of homicide of the infant are simply a result of an unwanted pregnancy. In these instances, the children are typically killed by strangulation, drowning, or suffocation (Meyer & Oberman, 2001). The fourth category involves the "accidental" death of a child following incidents of significant child abuse and maltreatment.

Often, the death of a child occurs after a long period of abuse. The fifth category represents cases where the death of a child is used as an act of ultimate revenge against another. In many cases, these vengeful acts are against the spouse and father of the child (Resnick, 1970).

Mothers who kill their children present a significant challenge to the cultural ideals of femininity and motherhood. Society dictates that mothers should love and care for their children, behave in a loving and nurturing manner, and not cause them harm or place their lives in danger. In many cases, the presence of a psychological disorder makes it easier for society to understand that a mother could hurt her child. Information on postpartum syndromes is used at a variety of different stages of the criminal justice process. Evidence of psychosis may be used to determine whether a defendant is legally competent to participate in the criminal proceedings against her. However, this stage is temporary, because the woman would be placed in a treatment facility until such a time that she is competent to stand trial. Given that postpartum syndromes are generally limited to a short period of time (compared to other forms of psychiatric diagnoses), these court proceedings would be delayed only temporarily.

More often, information about postpartum syndromes is used as evidence to exclude the culpability of the woman during a trial proceeding. In some states, this evidence forms the basis of a verdict of "not guilty by reason of insanity." Here, the courts assess whether the defendant knew that what she was doing at the time of the crime was wrong. "The insanity defense enables female violence to coexist comfortably with traditional notions of femininity. It also promotes empathy toward violent women, whose aberrance becomes a result of external factors rather than conscious choice" (Stangle, 2008, p. 709). In cases where an insanity defense is either not available or is unsuccessful, evidence of postpartum syndromes can be used to argue for the diminished capacity of the offender.

A third option allows for courts to find someone guilty but mentally ill (GBMI). Here, the defendant is found guilty of the crime, but the court may mitigate the criminal sentence to acknowledge the woman's mental health status. For many offenders, this distinction can allow them to serve a portion of their sentence in a treatment hospital or related facility (Proano-Raps & Meyer, 2003). While Andrea Yates was convicted of murder and sentenced to 40 years to life by the state of Texas in 2002, her conviction was later overturned. In her second trial, she was found not guilty by reason of insanity and was committed to a state mental health facility for treatment.

/// SUMMARY

- Women engage in every category of crime, yet their rates of offending are significantly lower than male offending practices.

- Regardless of race, ethnicity, or class, women have similar pathways to addiction: depression, abuse, and social and economic pressures.

- For many women, entry into addiction is rooted in early trauma: Drugs are used for escape, and prostitution and property crimes are then committed for survival.

- The war on drugs has led to increased incarceration rates for both men and women but has had particularly damaging effects for women.

- Women in prostitution face significant mental and physical health issues as a result of their time on the streets. These issues lead to significant challenges as they try to exit prostitution and make a new life off the streets.

- Women are most likely to commit property-based offenses.

- Sexuality can be a component of the gang life for some girls, but it is not necessarily the experience for all girls involved in gangs.

- Although female perpetrated homicide is rare, it is generally sensationalized in the media when it occurs.

- There are several different reasons why mothers may kill their children, but not all involve issues of mental illness.

KEY TERMS

Altruistic 342

Filicide 342

Infanticide 342

Neonaticide 342

Posttraumatic stress
  disorder (PTSD) 334

Pulling a train 337

Street prostitution 333

Walking the line 337

DISCUSSION QUESTIONS

1.   Why is the media obsessed with the image of the female offender? What implications does this have on understanding the realities of female offending?

2.   What does research say about the gender gap in offending?

3.   How have drug addiction and the war on drugs become a gendered experience?

4.   How are drugs, property crimes, and prostitution connected for many female offenders on the streets?

5.   What are the risk factors for prostitution? How do these issues affect a woman's ability to exit the streets?

6.   Why are jurisdictions reluctant to legalize or decriminalize prostitution?

7.   Why do women engage in property offenses?

8.   How do girls use their gender within the gang context?

9.   Discuss the types of violent crimes in which women most typically engage.

10.   What role does mental illness play in cases of women who kill their children?

WEB RESOURCES

Children of the Night: http://www.childrenofthenight.org

National Gang Center: http://www.nationalgangcenter.gov/

Prostitutes Education Network: http://www.bayswan.org

Prostitution Research and Education: http://www.prostitutionresearch.com

SAMHSA Center for Substance Abuse Treatment: http://www.samhsa.gov/about/csat.aspx

SAMHSA National Center for Trauma-Informed Care: http://www.samhsa.gov/nctic/

The Sentencing Project: http://www.sentencingproject.org

Women and Gender in the Drug War: http://www.drugpolicy.org/communities/women

 Visit **study.sagepub.com/mallicoat3e** to access additional study tools, including eFlashcards, web quizzes, web resources, video resources, and SAGE journal articles.

READING /// 15

In the section, you learned how issues with drug use and addiction can contribute to women's criminality. In this article by Drs. Ryder and Brisgone, you'll hear from two groups: women who experienced addiction during the crack cocaine era and girls who grew up with parents addicted to crack during this time frame.

Cracked Perspectives
Reflections of Women and Girls in the Aftermath of the Crack Cocaine Era

Judith A. Ryder and Regina E. Brisgone

In 1983, a new, cheap version of cocaine was disproportionately introduced into poor African American neighborhoods across the United States, where its use quickly expanded. Within only a few years, crack cocaine was entrenched in inner-city New York where it remained popular throughout the 1990s (Johnson, Dunlap, & Tourigny, 2000).[1] In the early years of that decade, however, both national surveys of arrestees and ethnographic neighborhood studies confirmed a significant transition: Inner-city youths preferred marijuana to crack and other hard drugs (Curtis, 1998; Furst, Johnson, Dunlap, & Curtis, 1999; Hamid, 1992). The transition was hailed with cautious optimism and speculation that because the younger generation was not using crack or heroin, youths may not "suffer the severe health and legal problems associated with those [hard] drugs" (Golub, Johnson, Dunlap, & Sifaneck, 2004, p. 362). The current project augments these findings by analyzing in-depth interviews with two generations of females who lived through this devastating period. We confirm the lack of crack use among female youths but find excessive alcohol and marijuana use. In addition, our analysis reveals disrupted emotional attachments between women and their children and concurrent traumatic experiences among the girls. We explore how this potent combination may have contributed to girls' involvement in serious delinquency.

Research on drug use in the Crack Era and the so-called Marijuana/Blunt Era that followed (Johnson, Golub, & Dunlap, 2000) is based primarily on studies of men and boys and generally uses epidemiological methods that may be insufficient for flagging the vulnerabilities of drug-involved females (Maher, 2002). As a result, little is known about how the Crack Era affected the lives of drug-using women and girls. The current project brings a gendered perspective to the generational drug research by analyzing commonalities and differences in female drug involvement. We extend prior research by exploring the ways in which drug involvement shaped family relationships and contributed to the weakening of emotional bonds between mothers and children during a turbulent

SOURCE: Ryder, J. A., & Brisgone, R. E. (2013). Cracked perspectives: Reflections of women and girls in the aftermath of the crack cocaine era. *Feminist Criminology*, 8(1), 40–62.

NOTE: The authors disclosed receipt of the following financial support for the research, authorship, and/or publication of this article: The original research was partially funded by two separate federal grants, NIDA Grant No. F31 DA006065, and NIDA Grant No. R01 DA08679.

social and economic period. We do not make causal claims, but our work is informed by the psychological construct of attachment (Bowlby, 1988) that allows for a developmental understanding of the effects of the Crack Era on the health and legal problems of a younger generation. Our analysis of the narratives of females born into two distinct drug eras is a pooled case comparison, a method situated in a tradition of cross-study comparative analysis. West and Oldfather (1995) liken pooled case comparison to "the overlaying of one transparency on another" (p. 454) in an effort to understand both groups more fully while maintaining the primacy of each group's voice. Finally, we propose recommendations for improving treatment services to better address the needs of drug-using women and girls.

Women and Children in the Crack Era

We examine female drug use within a broad historical context, using the concept of *drug eras,* a term that reflects the fluctuations of disease epidemics but with an emphasis on the cultural aspects of the phenomenon. The term describes a point in a historical period when a substance is introduced, adopted, and "institutionalized within certain segments of the population" (Johnson, Golub, & Dunlap, 2000, p. 21). The drug era model uses aggregated (mostly male) arrest data to delineate generational cohorts based on date of birth. The model marks a distinct historical break between the drug-use patterns of those born between 1955 and 1969 (Cocaine Crack Era) and those born since 1970 (Marijuana/Blunts Era; Johnson, Golub, & Dunlap, 2000).

When crack cocaine hit the streets of America in the 1980s, inner-city communities were already suffering from the prior decade's economic dislocations and widespread unemployment (Small & Newman, 2001; Wilson, 1996). With manufacturing jobs gone and large numbers of men out of work, the number of female head-of-households dramatically increased, and more women became sole caregivers of dependent children (Sampson, 1987; Wilson, 1987). At the same time, women were drawn to crack cocaine in unprecedented numbers, a trend attributed to the drug's low cost and social perceptions of smoking (as opposed to injecting) as a less intrusive

method of drug use and more in keeping with established gender norms (Sterk, 1999).

Despite an increase in the number of female primary breadwinners and the number of women using crack, little research investigates this intersection or the effect of crack-era drug dependency on parent–child relationships or includes children's perspectives. Maher and Hudson (2007) conducted an important metasynthesis of the qualitative literature on women *working* in the illegal drug economy but did not include women's own drug use and identified only two themes pertaining to family relationships and children: the importance of kinship structures (Adler, 1985; Denton, 2001; Waldorf, Reinarman, & Murphy, 1991) and women's ability to structure their drug dealer role around parental responsibilities (Dunlap & Johnson, 1996; Morgan & Joe, 1996; Sterk, 1999). Other research specific to female drug use details how, as women's crack dependency increased, their lives became more transient and chaotic, pressuring the women to seek the aid of social networks (Brisgone, 2008; Wilson & Tolson, 1990). By the 1980s, however, kin networks that traditionally had supported impoverished families were economically and emotionally worn down by long-term unemployment, punitive criminal justice policies, and the ravages of HIV/AIDS (Miller-Cribbs & Farber, 2008). Thus, children of crack-using mothers were often left without supportive adults to care for them, and some were placed in the care and custody of the state, solidifying the disruption in the parent–child relationship.

Hardesty and Black's (1999) study of Latina addicts in recovery is one of only a few to explore drug dependency and parent–child relationships. Women discussed the significant effort they employed to maintain their self-image as "good" mothers in the context of Puerto Rican culture, even as their drug activities became all engrossing. In another study, recovering heroin addicts reflected on the consequences of parental drug use, including parents' inability to "be there" to meet children's material and emotional needs, family violence, and family dissolution (McKeganey, Barnard, & McIntosh, 2002).

Distinct from the few studies that analyze parental perspectives on drug use is an ethnographic study of mother–daughter pairs from two crack-user households in New York City's Central Harlem (Dunlap, Stürzenhofecker, Sanabria, & Johnson, 2004). The paired study exposes disruptions in parent–child emotional bonds and suggests that mothers' crack use contributed to the inter-generational cycle of "child abuse, neglect, and abandonment of parental responsibilities" (Dunlap, Golub, & Johnson, 2006, p. 133). Although children born to the Crack Generation did not use the drug, they continued to face major deficits arising from their childhoods. These analyses stop short, however, of exploring how disruptions in the parent–child relationship, and other traumatic events, may have contributed to children's later involvement in delinquency and violence.

The Role of Disrupted Attachments

A primary purpose of the current project is to explore the dynamics underlying parent–child relationships among drug-using women and girls. In particular, we sought to understand how the disruption of emotional attachments between these dyads might contribute to girls' problem behaviors. Many criminological theories stress the importance of social bonds and relationships and some, such as developmental life-course theories, explicitly examine the complexities and messiness of *lives in social context*. However, such theories are primarily supported by research on boys and men and thus are likely to miss gendered behaviors and situations.[2] Life events such as sexual abuse and assault, which feminist scholarship has demonstrated to be much more extensive in the lives of female offenders than among male offenders, are rarely examined despite the potential to negatively redirect victims' life trajectories. The feminist pathway perspective stresses the importance of social bonds and relationships and specifically connects girls' traumatic experiences, such as sexual abuse, with substance abuse and arrests for violent offending (Daly, 1992; Gaarder & Belknap, 2002; Schaffner, 2007; Siegel & Williams, 2003). Both developmental life course and the feminist pathway perspective help, but are not sufficient, to explain how childhood events and experiences might contribute to a young woman adopting delinquent behaviors herself.

In an effort to understand the processes underlying the health and legal problems of a generation of girls growing up during the Crack Era, we place the narratives of women and girls within a developmental framework and employ the psychological construct of attachment. As conceptualized by John Bowlby and others (1973/1969, 1988; Ainsworth, Blehar, Waters, & Wall, 1978), attachment is considered an innate human need. This counters the use of the term in the criminological literature, particularly control theories, that consider attachment the result of proper socialization (e.g., Gottfredson & Hirschi, 1990). Bowlby's attachment theory proposes that children need more than food and shelter; they require security: "a quality of care . . . sufficiently responsive to the child's needs to alleviate anxiety and engender a feeling of being understood" (Ansbro, 2008, p. 234). Attachment behavior is designed to care for and protect the young by forming an affective bond between children and significant others. Furthermore, the role of the caregiver in nurturing and supporting the child's emotional bonds is critical to healthy development across the life span (Cernkovich & Giordano, 1987; Fonagy, 2004; Sroufe & Fleeson, 1986).

When a primary caregiver abandons, neglects, or abuses a child, attachment bonds are weakened. With attachment needs thus unmet, the child becomes emotionally vulnerable and will exhibit a predictable pattern of protest and despair and—without the intervention of loving and attuned adults—detachment (Ainsworth, 1972; Bowlby, 1973/1969; Margolin & John, 1997). This need for connection influences the course of the child's later development, with much research demonstrating that detachment in childhood is associated with long-term negative outcomes (Hayslett-McCall & Bernard, 2002). The detached child may psychically wall off her needs, even as her yearning for connection continues, or she may still cling to those who have caused the trauma because her terror of being abandoned exceeds her terror of the abuser. She also may seek connection to others through violence, sexual activity, or substance abuse and be comforted by an abusive attachment because it is familiar and similar to the original love object (Robinson, 2011; Ryder, 2007; Shengold, 1999; Smith & Thornberry, 1995). Although such behaviors are maladaptive and potentially destructive, a trauma-saturated child may not see the distinction (Herman, 1997).

Narrative Reflections

The current project encompasses two small groups of drug-using females. We begin with the adult women who were crack and heroin users and (most of them) primary caregivers of children. We add to this the perspective of adolescent girls, a rare dimension even in qualitative studies centered entirely on females (Lopez, Katsulis, & Robillard, 2009, cited in McKeganey et al., 2002). The project evolved from the authors' informal discussions about our separate National Institute on Drug Abuse (NIDA)-funded studies and how, in theory, the adult women could be mothers of the teenaged girls.[3] With some common focus areas and similar methodology, each study includes rich data on drug involvement and the importance of family relationships. Both studies posed questions about family functioning, community characteristics, traumatic events, and illegal activities including drug use and trafficking. The adult cohort also answered questions about prostitution activity and periods in jail and drug treatment. Brisgone interviewed the women between 1998 and 2001 as part of an ethnographic study of heavy drug users involved in prostitution. Interviews were conducted in various settings (e.g., streets, HIV outreach offices, and county jail). In her study, Ryder completed face-to-face, semistructured interviews with girls who had been remanded to custody for a violent offense. Interviews were conducted in 1996 in four state-run, juvenile residential facilities.

The two samples, or "cohorts," are primarily females of color, of low socioeconomic status, and from the New York City metropolitan area. They differ from one another, however, in ways predicted by larger, mostly male, studies of the Crack Era and subsequent Marijuana/Blunts Era. In addition to variation in drug choice, of particular interest is the age differential. Each of our two data fits sets squarely within the generational categories established in earlier, mostly quantitative studies (Johnson, Golub, & Dunlap, 2000). Both adults and juveniles told of extensive drug involvement and strained family relationships, and, although their perspectives sometimes overlapped, they just as frequently diverged. The spaces where the two groups differed revealed a poignant yearning for connection. As we continued to discuss our work and findings, we dubbed these differing viewpoints the "what I'd tell my daughter, what my mom should have known" model, and considered the dynamics of an imaginary dialogue between the generations. Findings from the separate projects caused us to think about how the female narratives might enhance existing knowledge about the effects of the Crack Era.

Selected demographics are presented in Reading Table 15.1. Each cohort falls within previously established generational drug eras, based on year of birth (Johnson, Golub, & Dunlap, 2000). The women of the Crack Era were born from 1958 through 1971; at the height of the era in 1989, their median age was 23 years. The postcrack cohort was born from 1980 through 1983, placing them a decade into the so-called Marijuana/Blunts Era. In 1989 when the Crack Era peaked, the girls' median age was only 8 years. More than three-fourths of the adult females were Black, and approximately one-fifth was Hispanic; three-fourths of the girls self-identified as Black or Hispanic. Most of the women had at least one child ($n = 51$); the median number of children per woman was two, with a range of one to nine children. Three of the girls had one child. Forty-six women were arrested on prostitution charges, and nearly a fourth (24%) had also been charged with drug sales. The girls were adjudicated and remanded to custody for assault (79%) or robbery (21%).

In presenting portions of the narratives, we examine these complicated relationships first from one side of the mirror and then from the other. On one side sit adult women who discuss how much, how often, and what drugs they used during their adult years and how they perceived the impact of their actions on family relationships, particularly those with their dependent children. On the other side, adolescent girls look back a short distance to review the years growing up in crack-affected families, linked to histories of traumatic loss and victimization.

Drug Involvement

The adult cohort (Crack Era) is characterized by pervasive drug use in an era of historically high female drug use, a traditional outlook regarding dependence on men, and participation in a street drug network perceived as menacing and ruthless. The women began their drug careers with crack or heroin and were abusing the drugs, on average, 4 years before they began prostituting. The narratives of the juvenile cohort (Marijuana/Blunt Era) indicate excessive use of marijuana and alcohol, typically initiated with family members; participation in drug sales; and involvement with street violence. Drug Involvement describes drug initiation, drug use, and drug-related activities.

Reading Table 15.1 • Selected Demographics of the Two Cohorts

	Adult Women (*N* = 58)	Juvenile Girls (*N* = 24)
Period of birth	1958–1971	1980–1983
Median age at height of Crack Era (1989)	23 years	8 years
Age (Range [Median])	26–40 years (32 years)	13–16 years (15 years)
Race/ethnicity		
Black	78%	58%
Hispanic/Latina	19%	17%
Biracial/multiracial	–	17%
White	3%	8%
Any children	88%	12.5%
Used regularly (at least 3–4 times a week)	Cocaine 19%	Marijuana 71%
	Heroin 12%	Alcohol 33%
	Both cocaine and heroin 69%	Both marijuana and alcohol 33%

Women's Drug Initiation

The women generally initiated or progressed into hard drug use with intimate partners in the context of family life. Irraida, a poly-drug user, was a new wife and mother when she started using drugs with her husband.

> He would do everything for me. He took care of me and my drug habit. . . . I was 18 [when] I had met him. . . . I had no idea about drugs. He introduced me to it. . . . That's how I started using. He didn't force me to do it, and he told me what it was like. . . . Most likely I never would've done it if I hadn't met him.

Using drugs with male partners was considered romantic and protective, something all the women desired. Women previously in such relationships looked back longingly and were always on the outlook to re-create them. Shawnice spoke of this yearning: "I didn't ever have to come outside [to prostitute]. He would bring me my dope. I could smoke all the cocaine I could. . . . That's

what I want to go back to." Many who started with cocaine before trying heroin did not realize their addiction until it was too late: "I liked the warm feeling [of heroin]. . . . I didn't want to get high every day, but I did. . . . Then the girl told me I had a habit. Habit? Habit? What habit!" Women generally moved swiftly from initiation to drug dependence as their habit came to match that of their older, heavy drug-using male partners.

Girl's Drug Initiation

For most girls, drug use began at home. Nearly 80% said that someone in the household drank alcohol or used drugs, and mothers were most commonly mentioned.[4] Other users in the household included mothers' partners, relatives, and siblings. The girls' median initial age for trying tobacco and alcohol was 10 years old; the median initial age for trying marijuana was 12 years old. None of the girls considered initiation a significant event but rather viewed it as a natural progression. Sixteen-year-old Natalie described how she started using marijuana with relatives:

I was used to people around me smoking and like my family being out in the room, catch a contact, so I just started smoking it. . . . I felt like I was already smoking it because I was already in the room where my aunt and uncle were smoking away.

Joanne began smoking marijuana with her mother and siblings "because I guess, if you watch somebody use it for long enough you are gonna want to try it and see how it is." Raised by her grandfather and father, Michelle recalled drinking small glasses of rum "for a chest cold, it broke the cold up." She was about 7 years old when her father gave her beer, but, she noted, "he didn't give it to me for colds, he just gave it to me to drink." Her father also introduced her to marijuana, and she continued to drink and smoke regularly on her own: "I was hooked on it some. . . . I was just high almost every day."

Women's Drug Use

Overall, the women were dependent on cocaine and physically addicted to heroin with its debilitating withdrawals. Cocaine was generally smoked and heroin sniffed, but nearly a third of the women injected at least some of the time. Women used from 2 to 10 packets (bags) of heroin a day; cocaine use ranged from less than one to more than 10 vials daily. Cocaine and poly-drug users followed a pattern of binging and resting.

Poly-drug users relied on heroin to level out their mood after a cocaine binge and used cocaine to sharpen their concentration on the street. Said Boobie, "It's like a . . . roller-coaster all the time." Christina explained further,

> With a crack hit, five minutes later you're running and chasing that feeling, that high. If you do a lot of coke, you're going to need the dope because the dope eats the coke. If you do a lot of crack, your heart gets all jiggery and you need a lot of dope so you can calm down.

Baby, a poly-drug user and mother of a teenage daughter, was on the streets for a decade. She described how her drug use eliminated most structure and routine: "People like you, you live around a calendar. Me, I get up,

and I don't know what I'm going to do. I'm not on a clock. . . . I use drugs and then I forget. . . . Time flies when you're in a drug haze." Although women did abstain when forced (i.e., in jail), most relapsed unless they broke from the drug scene entirely.

Girls' Drug Use

In stark contrast to the women's cohort, none of the girls reported ever having tried crack, but two tried cocaine in powder form. Jennifer claimed, "The older people smoke crack, it's not . . . you don't see no younger kids that smoke crack." Furthermore, the girls had contempt for those who did use the drug. As one girl declared, "Crack heads are crazy. They'll do anything." Although all girls renounced crack, four had tried hallucinogens, and three had tried PCP [phencyclidine, i.e., angel dust]. None reported trying heroin or injecting any drug. A third of the girls drank alcohol on a regular basis (at least 3 to 4 days a week), and nearly three-fourths smoked marijuana regularly during the year prior to incarceration. Often, marijuana was smoked as a blunt, wrapped inside a cigar shell. Indicative of the extent of their use, a third of the girls regularly used *both* marijuana and alcohol. At home, in school, in the streets, regardless of the context, "everybody was doing, every teenager used marijuana and alcohol. That was like normal."

Girls incorporated drug use into most of their activities. For example, alcohol and marijuana were a regular part of holidays and personal celebrations, such as birthdays, as well as upsetting or traumatic experiences, of which there were many. One 14-year-old described her response to the fatal shooting of her boyfriend.

> We all got ripped at the funeral. I mean that was the first time I ever really got so drunk I could hardly even walk, I was so high I couldn't even see straight. That was the first time. . . . I was already ripped and stuff, I was gone, I was like in another world.

Elena described how after being initiated into her female gang, members used copious amounts of marijuana and alcohol to commemorate "stepping up" through the ranks: "If you succeed when we did something violent you have to smoke at least 25 blunts so you could move up. We didn't do nothing else. Well, oh yeah, we used to drink." The amounts of alcohol and marijuana reported by individual girls may be exaggerated, as some present themselves in a particular "pose," but overall, the amounts are indicative of heavy usage (Majors & Billson, 1993).

Women's Drug-Related Activities

Progression into hard drug use with men led women to a variety of drug-related criminal activities, including check fraud and drug sales, but particularly prostitution. In general, the women were inexperienced and had little heart for street crime. "I don't like robbin' and stealin'. I'm too chicken," Irraida confessed. The few who did deal drugs found that as users they were poor handlers of both the drugs and money; many reported an arrest and/or jail time for drug sales. Sam, a former dealer on the run, explained, "I had to keep away from people who wanted to hurt me. . . . Being on drugs and being in these places put you in danger, and I'm a very scary person" (a local colloquialism for easily frightened). Women dealers also noted the hierarchical, gender-stratified nature of the market and the low-level, exploitive work opportunities. Tina dealt heroin with a younger man but believed such relationships oppressed women:

> They [men] very rarely let women sell drugs. It's because of male chauvinism. A robber try a woman quicker than a man. It's dominance. I learned this back in college. Main thing: They don't want women to get the power. Dealing is dangerous too. They want you to do 80% of the work.

Desiree believed male dealers took advantage of women who then suffered the consequences: "I think they [male drug managers] think we're going to get it easier if we get caught. They just don't know. If we get caught, just like them, we're going to do that time." Because women sold on the streets, they were more visible to police and more vulnerable to arrest than were men.

The women's initiation to hard drug use fostered a relationship between intimacy and drugs and set a path toward street prostitution. Forty percent of the women began to prostitute when intimate partners were no longer available to provide their drugs because of a romantic breakup, incarceration, death, or the loss of the partner's means of obtaining drugs. Sugartoo, for example, started prostituting at age 32 when her boyfriend, a drug dealer, died during a gang fight in jail: "I'm a good person. I just started doing it [prostitution] since my old man passed. . . . It took me a long time to get used to it. I don't like nothing about this running." Prostitution was a pragmatic response to women's relative inexperience in rough drug-using street scenes, combined with their urgent need for drugs. As Toni stated, "After [my kids'] father took off, I wanted men for only one thing. I'd call up a john. I'd use men for my drug addiction. I'd get out there, take care of business, and get what I needed." Pumpkin was adamant that she would never solicit except for her drug habit: "Of course not! I have an income—I work the [prostitution] stroll just for drugs." Another woman explained, "If I didn't have a habit I'd probably be working at something else. But I got a habit so the stroll is it." All of the women reported street prostitution as their *main hustle* for drugs, and half of them said prostitution was their *exclusive* hustle for drugs.

Although most of the women rejected drug dealing and predatory crimes because of the perceived dangers, prostitution greatly increased their vulnerability to street violence. The women were prey to robbers, rapists, and murderers. They reported multiple victimizations, especially when, because they were intoxicated or desperate for drugs, they solicited indiscriminately.

Girls' Drug-Related Activities

The girls' early familiarity with drug use facilitated access to people and opportunities in the illegal drug trade. Drug sales, drug use, and crime quickly became closely intertwined with daily activities. For example, Kathy and her friends "used to get together and go to the movies sometimes but mainly it was selling drugs and robberies." Despite their disdain for crack users, the girls were very much involved in the sale of the popular street drug. More than two-thirds had participated in some aspect of drug trafficking beginning at the median age of 12; with the exception of one girl, all were still active in the business during the year prior to custody. Generally, girls partnered with other girls or boyfriends and worked low-level jobs in small organizations under the auspices of male suppliers. Several managed to amass a fairly large amount of cash. The economic benefits were a major enticement and, at least initially, mitigated safety concerns. One girl used her drug proceeds to rent a city ice-skating rink for the evening for all her friends. Royale, who desperately wanted a pair of sneakers she could not afford, told how she increased her purchasing power when she began selling crack:

> . . . my cousin gave me some drugs to sell and he said this will get you it quick. And I did and I liked it because I got money real quick. Instead of buying my sneakers I bought my own stuff [drugs] and doubled my money and got more than one pair of sneakers!

Another girl explained that she began selling drugs as a way of obtaining household money for her alcohol- and drug-using mother.

Transactions were conducted primarily in public locales, where, despite the high risk of arrest, many believed police were less likely to stop a girl. Young and generally optimistic, girls indicated that if stopped, "All I gotta do is, like, 'no, sorry, but I'm a female, you can't do that.' You know, then, they couldn't search me." The girls did complain that "guys used to try to gyp me and stuff," and many admitted that they had been shot at, physically threatened, and sexually assaulted. Thus, despite some success on their own, most girls eventually came to rely on older males for protection precisely because of their gender and age. This arrangement, however, put them at great disadvantage and exposed them to additional emotional, physical, and sexual harm.

Even with male "protectors," the work required girls to negotiate volatile and violent situations. As part of their tutelage, they learned to use force against others. Violence (for themselves and their clients) was the cost of not adhering to established business norms and conventions. In one instance, a girl said she "beat this crack head up so bad because she wouldn't pay us and she was sending people that we never seen before to our house. . . ." Another young seller told of a nonpaying female customer who put "my life in jeopardy" when her earnings were short. Her male manager verbally threatened her, then gave her a gun and told her she had "better handle your business." The seller and her cousin shot the customer in the head. Minimizing the killing, the girl claimed, "You couldn't do nothing. She was a crackhead anyway."

Family Relationships

The two cohorts each suffered from disruptions in their familial relationships. The women espoused conventional aspirations for family life but in their current circumstances failed to live up to them. Their erratic lifestyle and parenting practices created emotional distance between them and their families, especially their children. They believed traditional kinship networks could sufficiently provide for their children, yet this resource had worn thin. From the perspective of girls passed between and among the tattered network of caregivers, adults generated more harm than the interviewed mothers were able or willing to disclose. The girls tell of traumatic losses and emotional detachment, as well as physical and sexual violence—much of which was associated with maternal substance abuse and the lack of intervening, supportive caregivers. This section on Family Relationships describes family composition and structure and emotional connections.

Women's Family Composition and Structure

Though most women in the study were currently not married and not with their dependent children, more than one third reported that they either had been raised in a two-parent family or had raised their own children as part of a stable couple. They described families of origin with "stable enough" finances and parenting and portrayed their mothers as the glue that kept the family together and the ones who upheld mainstream values in difficult circumstances. Lena, for example, credits her mother with raising her two sons and keeping her from getting worse: "It's mainly because I have a mother who's there for me. Without her, God knows where I'd be." When the women were in their worst drug-using phases, they avoided family out of shame and to avoid conflicts that would prevent them from returning home in better times. Women were well aware of how far they had fallen from their own and their family's expectations and, like Sugartoo, remained concerned with others' perceptions: "I'm from an all-right family. I pray to God I never get caught out there soliciting. I'm afraid to [get caught] because of my family."

Most women had at least one child and maintained a committed relationship with the child's father—at least initially—but few were legally married. Of the 51 mothers, 22% were regular drug users when their first child was born. They relied on their family of origin to help raise the children when drug use and criminality forced them to relinquish parental roles. Circumstances forced the majority of the women to disperse their children among relatives so that many siblings were separated and frequently moved. Three fourths had surrendered custody of their children; nine women had ceded custody of at least one child to state child welfare authorities. The women described a pattern of drifting back and forth from their estranged families, and shifting alliances with men as their troubles waxed and waned. They were intermittently homeless or worse, bouncing from home to drug houses to abandoned warehouses as they pursued drugs and engaged in prostitution.

Girls' Family Composition and Structure

Girls depicted home as a shifting configuration of caregivers and locations. At some time in their lives, 71% of the girls had lived with adults other than a parent, residing in both kin and nonrelative foster care, residential treatment centers, and group homes. Locations changed when mothers went to jail or drug treatment, or families were evicted or forced to leave unsafe conditions. The household composition also changed when a mother's new husband or boyfriend arrived or girls ran away, deciding to stay with fathers, extended family, or friends. Mother–daughter separations could be brief stints or last for months—or even years—when mothers could or would not care for their daughters, and the children often were placed in foster care. Paula's description is typical of the cohort's residential instability.

> I was back and forth because I was in—it depends—I would be in foster care, then I would be in group homes, then I would go AWOL, go to my house, . . . I don't know where my house—me saying my house—that meant I would go to my father's house. . . . Other times I

would go to my boyfriend's house or my sister-in-law's house.

Women's Emotional Connections

Most of the women did not have custody of their children and in interviews avoided revealing the details of that loss. Only two mentioned neglect or child abuse and revealed that the events triggered their drug abuse. Dinah said the state took her children because "their father molested them" and added that she had tried to hide and protect the children from him. Sunshine, a poly-drug user, was defensive: "I was falsely accused of child abuse." She added that the courts took custody of her children and gave them to her ex-husband. "I started drugs when my children were taken from me." Prostitution kept women on the streets all hours of the day and night, further disrupting relationships with their children. The lifestyle upset domestic routines and left little time or emotion for family. Too often, the women say, they promised to quit drugs and resume their parental role—only to fail—repeatedly dashing their children's hopes. Gina expressed her regret over relapsing and disappointing her children.

> I was so ashamed. . . . I have beautiful children who I talk to all the time. . . . How many times are they going to put up with the same bullshit again? My kids know about my drug addiction. I don't want to lose them and I'm tired of losing me.

Lena echoed these sentiments: "I want to do something for their lives. They want a mommy who gets up with them in the morning and goes to bed at night. They're tired of their grandmother taking care of them."

Most women said they tried to visit their children regularly but also realized the need to stay away when they were heavily involved in drugs. They contributed financially when they could, handing over government checks or making family members official recipients of the aid for children, and using their illegal earnings for gifts and special occasions. Desiree, whose three young children stayed with her mother, said,

> I try to see them every week. Now and then I see them more. I'll go with them to the park. On

their birthdays I chip in and buy them a cake. If they're going on a school trip, I give them what they need.

Despite their love and attempts to bond with their children, the women recognized their inability to offset previously disrupted attachments and physical absences, and they worried about how their behavior affected the children's life chances. Doreen had been gone for a year when, during a brief visit home, she was devastated to see her teenage daughter's strong bond with the aunt who raised her.

Sometimes I feel like I made a mistake over there. Sometimes I know I did something right. I took my daughter over to my sister when she was 12 years old. Now she's 18 years old. . . . She calls me mommy, but she goes over and hugs my sister. It upsets me. She goes right over to her and talks with her like a mother.

Doreen's decision to leave her daughter was an act of love and protection.

Her schoolwork was suffering. She was staying up worrying about me. That's why I took her to my sister's house. I took her over there because I loved her. I didn't want nothing to happen to her. . . . I don't want her to go through what I have gone through.

Girls' Emotional Connections

The girls described physical and sexual violence in their homes and the numerous losses that strained relationships with their mothers and others entrusted with their well-being (Ryder, 2007). By the median age of only 10, three-fourths had been physically abused, and 29% had been sexually abused by a family member; more than half had witnessed family physical abuse, and 13% had witnessed family sexual abuse. Girls told of seeing their mothers regularly attacked and beaten by male partners: "He tried to hit her and then I came out you know, I was screaming on him . . . he tried to hit her, he tried to beat her up." They also talked about the violence their mothers and others inflicted on them. One girl described her

mother as "very abusive when she was drunk . . . yelling, throwing things. When she was high, she used to take the hangers and beat me with it."

The physical absence and psychological unavailability of mothers further disrupted girls' emotional attachments. Sometimes, a mother's whereabouts were unknown to her daughter. Paula's parents separated when she was an infant, and shortly thereafter, her mother left her with an aunt. Paula said, "I don't know where she went, then she came back and got me later,"—when the girl was 3 years old. For the most part, however, girls reported that when their mothers were physically absent, it was because they were on the streets, incarcerated, or residing in a mental health or substance abuse facility. Fourteen-year-old Gina had only sporadic contact with her mother, having lived with relatives or in institutional settings most of her life. The girl explained that her mother "used to have a problem with drugs and alcohol and so she gave me to my grandmother." Another girl, Gayle, said her father died before she was born, and her mother was repeatedly incarcerated for selling drugs. Gayle described theirs as "a close relationship," but mother and daughter visited only intermittently: "If I would see her we would talk. We didn't see each other that often. She'll come see me like every six months."

Even when physically present, many mothers were incapable or unwilling to nurture girls' basic emotional needs. The dynamics of substance abuse were a primary contributor to such psychological unavailability. For example, Elena stated, "My mother's like antisocial. She don't like speaking to nobody. She just keeps her problems in. . . . I don't know, it was just the crack just really getting to her." Royale complained that her drug-using mother provided physical necessities but that an emotional void existed between them: "I ate regularly, lived in a regular house, like my mother would cook us dinner . . . it was OK, we, never, we didn't hardly talk 'cause my mother was on drugs so my brother had to take care of us." Joanne similarly confided that her mother's regular drug use and involvement with other users affected the mother–daughter relationship. Late night parties and constant visitors to the home kept the girl up and the mother estranged: ". . . when I got older it bothered me because it started to take more of the relationship out of all of us."

All the girls indicated that their victimizations and losses were exacerbated by the fact that they felt little parental attachment, and nearly a third said there was no one with whom they felt safe and secure. Most never told any of the people they lived with when something was bothering them. Instead, the girls learned to rely on themselves. Fourteen-year-old Jill acknowledged that despite the fact that her mother was present "to protect me and stuff, [I] . . . never felt safe with her. Maybe because we didn't have a good relationship." The lack of emotionally attuned adults to help girls integrate traumatic experiences into their lives and fulfill their attachment needs is a likely contributor to their subsequent use of drugs and involvement in violent activities.

Discussion

In the early 1990s, crack cocaine use began to decline, even in the hardest hit, low-income, minority neighborhoods of New York City (Hamid, 1992). In a related trend, marijuana use was on the rise among individuals born since 1970. Some researchers believe this shift enhanced youths' prospects and limited health and legal risks because marijuana-blunt use tended to promote "conduct norms of controlled alcohol intake" and the sanctioning of "threatening or violent behavior" (Johnson, Golub, & Dunlap, 2000, p. 187). Based primarily on epidemiological studies of male drug patterns, the optimistic projections do not necessarily apply to behaviors and experiences of females. Our study provides the space to hear the stories of women and girls whose lives were shaped by the crack and marijuana drug eras and so posits a more nuanced, gendered perspective on drug involvement and family relationships. The women speak of a desire to explain the reality of their troubled lives and how, contrary to sensationalistic rhetoric about crack-using mothers, they loved and tried to care for their children (see Humphries, 1999; Logan, 1999; Reeves & Campbell, 1994). The girls, however, describe a host of traumatic experiences and describe their caregivers as emotionally and often physically absent. They wanted adults to understand that their mothers' problems, including those associated with illicit drug use, diminished their own chances to live a healthy and productive life. A mother's attempt to shield her daughter from a drug-centered life, for example, may be experienced by the daughter as abandonment and the disruption, or even severance, of primary attachment bonds. The combined narratives reflect a new perspective

on the Crack Era and its aftermath by locating drug-related activities of females within the context of disrupted personal and family relationships.

The Gendered Nature of Drug Use

Growing up in families of the poor and working poor, the women had mainstream aspirations of employment and a family life. This vision dissipated, however, after the women became intimately involved with male partners who helped initiate their long careers with crack and heroin. When legitimate work disappeared, personal relationships ended, and supply sources were lost, the women faced a crisis. In a panic of loss and drug cravings, the women chose prostitution to continue to finance their habits. As their drug use escalated and their economic and social stability deteriorated, the women became increasingly estranged from family life. Despite their inability to demonstrate their love for their children in a consistent and meaningful way, the women spoke repeatedly of wanting to "put things right." They struggled to love and protect their offspring as best they could, which sometimes meant leaving children with relatives or friends and acknowledging that at times it was best to stay away. The experience of losing a child, particularly in cases when children were placed with state authorities, presented an enormous challenge to the women's sense of self as a loving parent. The women served their own needs, but they also recognized that involvement with drugs and prostitution contributed to their diminished, or total abandonment of, parental responsibilities (Dunlap et al., 2004).

The girls' drug use patterns diverged from those of the adult women, as did their perceptions of adult caregivers' behaviors. This group of girls reported heavy, regular use of marijuana and alcohol. Typically, girls' drug use began when they were young children as a normal extension of family life, wherein adults regularly drank alcohol and smoked marijuana and crack cocaine. The girls' drug involvement quickly escalated and expanded into peer networks until heavy usage was fully integrated into routine activities and events. Family life, in addition to providing a setting for drug use, was violent and dangerous, where girls were subjected to multiple and repetitive traumatic events, including physical and sexual abuse, loss of caregivers, and frequent relocations. Girls characterized their caregivers as emotionally detached and physically absent. Angered and shamed by their sense of loss and abandonment, girls engaged in physical violence, as well as crack cocaine sales where, under the "protection" of older male dealers, their experiences of victimization within the home were often replicated.

Although others have described the Marijuana Generation—the children of Crack Era parents—as "being reared in severely distressed households" (Johnson, Golub, & Dunlap, 2000, p. 185), little research has investigated any further. In contrast to earlier, more hopeful predictions based on male data, the limited qualitative research on women and girls suggests that escalating drug abuse and imprisonment among adults of the Crack Era may have contributed to the subsequent problems of the next generation of girls (Males, 2010, p. 28). Our analysis of narrative data from two generations of females goes deeper to expose the underlying dynamics and suggests a developmental understanding of the younger generation's problems.

Both cohorts refer to the fragility of family relationships and, to varying degrees and from different perspectives, each reference loss, abandonment, neglect, and violence. Considered within the framework of attachment theory, such experiences weaken the bond between mothers and children. Despite the women's desire to care for their children, crack and heroin use interfered with their ability to do so, creating situations detrimental to strong mother–child bonds and to girls' emotional development. Adults' behaviors left the girls in this study feeling alone and seemingly unloved. Without other adults to support and protect them, girls struggled on their own to cope with the effects of trauma (Margolin & John, 1997). Lacking a sense of attachment or safety, the girls sought connections through the maladaptive means of substance abuse and violence.

Implications and Recommendations

Bonds between the drug-using females of the Crack and Marijuana Eras were disrupted, but there is also evidence of a yearning to repair the emotional connection. Any policy designed to intervene in women's recovery from drug dependency must first take into account that many women are also mothers and the head of household.

Women's role as caregivers of the young deserves the implementation of empathic strategies that balance treatment services with parenting. Furthermore, if policy makers and practitioners seek to interrupt the intergenerational transmission of drug-related problems, they must acknowledge and address the primacy of early attachment bonds and find ways to support mother–child relationships and strengthen family cohesiveness. Appropriate services for recovering women with children must be delivered in the context of total family needs. Women in substance abuse treatment want "more of a family-focused lens that treats the connection and bond of the family with ongoing nurturance, consideration, and respect" (Smith, 2006, p. 456). Policies that strengthen family cohesiveness have long-term societal benefits, unlike, for example, lengthy prison sentences for drug offenses that attenuate family ties and lower children's life chances.

Drug-using mothers and daughters each have their own set of treatment concerns relative to their age and situation, but both also need structured time together to develop or repair emotional bonds. Treatment programs might arrange for mother–child visits that work toward reconnection and reunification. Joint programming between adult and child services may also be possible, necessitating, perhaps, new protocols that enable agencies to share client information. Without improvements in the flow of information between adult-focused agencies and child welfare services, recovery and reconnection may be compromised (McKeganey et al., 2002). Finally, outreach and support for law-abiding and willing family members' participation in treatment and recovery efforts can be extremely helpful in mending mother–daughter relationships and strengthening family unity across generations.

Despite the decrease in the number of crack users nationally, the effects of crack involvement, particularly for those embedded pockets of the urban poor, have carried over into the new millennium. The associated emotional, social, and economic problems continue to plague a younger generation, and yet few holistic and female-oriented drug treatment programs and policies are available to confront this challenge (Sterk, Elifson, & Theall, 2000). As much as we may want to believe that the era is over, "the Age of Crack persists, characterized by whole urban communities demoralized by poor health, violence, poverty, child neglect, and family decay"

(Allen, 2003, p. 205). Programs and policies oriented toward changing individual drug use must be accompanied by a parallel commitment to bring down the structural impediments of concentrated poverty, harsh criminal justice sanctions, and widespread sexism and racism. The need for structural transformation, however, must not excuse delays in the implementation of supportive treatment services for women and girls. Neither the mothers nor the daughters of the Crack Era have fared well, and to ignore their stories is to watch the repetition of destructive patterns in future generations, regardless of the next "drug of choice."

/// DISCUSSION QUESTIONS

1. How did women's drug use influence their criminality? How did this differ from girls' drug use and offending?

2. How did women's drug use impact their family relationships? What effect did drug use have on the lives of girls and their relationships with their families?

3. How should treatment providers respond to the needs of women and girls involved in substance abuse?

Notes

1. Much of this research is based on Drug Use Forecasting surveys that report the number of arrestees who test positive for drugs. Arrestees volunteer to be tested, and results cannot be generalized. City prevalence rates also vary greatly.

2. As Farrington (2003) states, "Generally, DLC [Developmental Life Course] findings and theories apply to offending by lower class urban males in Western industrialized societies in the past 80 years or so" (p. 223). Two exceptions to the all-male study are Moffitt, Caspi, Rutter, and Silva (2001) and Silverthorn and Frick (1999).

3. "Combining Drug Treatment and Law Enforcement for Drug-Addicted Offenders," NIDA Grant No. F31 DA006065; "Learning About Violence and Drug Use among Adolescents (LAVIDA)," NIDA Grant No. R01 DA08679.

4. Nearly two thirds of the girls lived mostly with their mothers for at least part of their lives.

References

Adler, P. A. (1985). *Wheeling and dealing: An ethnography of an upper-level drug dealing and smuggling community.* New York, NY: Columbia University Press.

Ainsworth, M. (1972). Attachment and dependency. In J. L. Gerwitz (Ed.), *Attachment and dependency* (pp. 97–137). Washington, DC: Winston.

Ainsworth, M., Blehar, M., Waters, E., & Wall, S. (1978). *Patterns of attachment. A psychological study of the strange situation.* Hillsdale, NJ: Erlbaum.

Allen, A. (2003). Against drug use. In A. K. Wing (Ed.), *Critical race feminism: A reader* (2nd ed., pp. 197–208). New York, NY: New York University Press.

Ansbro, M. (2008). Using attachment theory with offenders. *Probation Journal, 55*(3), 231–244.

Bowlby, J. (1973). *Attachment and loss* (Vols. 1–2). New York, NY: Basic Books. (Original work published 1969)

Bowlby, J. (1988). *A secure base.* New York, NY: Basic Books.

Brisgone, R. (2008). *Varieties of behavior across and within persons of drug-using street prostitutes: A qualitative longitudinal study* (Doctoral dissertation). Rutgers, The State University of New Jersey, New Brunswick. Available from ProQuest database. (UMI No. 332692)

Cernkovich, S., & Giordano, P. (1987). Family relationships and delinquency. *Criminology, 25,* 295–321.

Curtis, R. (1998). The improbable transformation of inner-city neighborhoods: Crime, violence, and drugs in the 1990s. *Journal of Criminal Law and Criminology, 88,* 1233–1266.

Daly, K. (1992). Women's pathways to felony court: Feminist theories of lawbreaking and problems of representation. *Southern California Review of Law and Women's Studies, 2*(11), 11–51.

Denton, B. (2001). *Dealing: Women in the drug economy.* Sydney, Australia: University of New South Wales Press.

Dunlap, E., Golub, A., & Johnson, B. (2006). The severely distressed African-American family in the Crack Era: Empowerment is not enough. *Journal of Sociology and Social Welfare, 33*(1), 115–139.

Dunlap, E., & Johnson, B. (1996). Family and human resources in the development of a female crack-seller career: Case study of a hidden population. *Journal of Drug Issues, 26*(1), 175–198.

Dunlap, E., Stürzenhofecker, G., Sanabria, H., & Johnson, B. (2004). Mothers and daughters: The intergenerational reproduction of violence and drug use in home and street life. *Journal of Ethnicity in Substance Abuse, 3*(2), 1–23.

Farrington, D. (2003). Developmental and life-course criminology: Key theoretical and empirical issues. *Criminology, 41,* 221–255.

Fonagy, P. (2004). Psychodynamic therapy with children. In H. Steiner (Ed.), *Handbook of mental health interventions in children and adolescents: An integrated developmental approach* (pp. 621–658). New York, NY: Jossey-Bass.

Furst, T., Johnson, B., Dunlap, E., & Curtis, R. (1999). The stigmatized image of the "crack-head": A sociocultural exploration of a barrier to cocaine smoking among a cohort of youth in New York City. *Deviant Behavior, 20*(2), 153–181.

Gaarder, E., & Belknap, J. (2002). Tenuous borders: Girls transferred to adult court. *Criminology, 40,* 481–517.

Golub, A., Johnson, B., Dunlap, E., & Sifaneck, S. (2004). Projecting and monitoring the life course of the marijuana/blunts generation. *Journal of Drug Issues, 34,* 361–388.

Gottfredson, M., & Hirschi, T. (1990). *A general theory of crime.* Stanford, CA: Stanford University Press.

Hamid, A. (1992). The developmental cycle of a drug epidemic: The cocaine smoking epidemic of 1981–1991. *Journal of Psychoactive Drugs, 24,* 337–348.

Hardesty, M., & Black, T. (1999). Mothering through addiction: A survival strategy among Puerto Rican addicts. *Qualitative Health Research, 9,* 602–619.

Hayslett-McCall, K., & Bernard, T. (2002). Attachment, masculinity, and self-control: A theory of male crime rates. *Theoretical Criminology, 6*(1), 5–33.

Herman, J. (1997). *Trauma and recovery.* New York, NY: Basic Books.

Humphries, D. (1999). *Crack mothers: Pregnancy, drugs, and the media.* Columbus: Ohio State University Press.

Johnson, B., Dunlap, E., & Tourigny, S. (2000). Crack distribution and abuse in New York. In M. Natarajan & M. Hough (Eds.), *Illegal drug markets: From research to prevention policy* (pp. 19–57). Monsey, NY: Criminal Justice Press.

Johnson, B., Golub, A., & Dunlap, E. (2000). The rise and decline of hard drugs, drug markets and violence in New York City. In A. Blumstein & J. Wallman (Eds.), *The crime drop in America* (pp. 164–206). New York, NY: Cambridge University Press.

Logan, E. (1999). The wrong race, committing crime, doing drugs, and maladjusted for mother-hood: The nation's fury over "crack babies." *Social Justice, 26*(1), 115–138.

Lopez, V., Katsulis, Y., & Robillard, A. (2009, April). Drug use with parents as a relational strategy for incarcerated female adolescents. *Family relations, 58,* 135–147.

Maher, L. (2002). Don't leave us this way: Ethnography and injecting drug use in the age of AIDS. *International Journal of Drug Policy, 13,* 311–325.

Maher, L., & Hudson, S. (2007). Women in the drug economy: A metasynthesis of the qualitative literature. *Journal of Drug Issues, 37,* 805–826.

Majors, R., & Billson, J. (1993). *Cool pose: The dilemmas of Black manhood in America.* New York, NY: Lexington Books.

Males, M. (2010). Have girls gone wild? In M. Chesney-Lind & N. Jones (Eds.), *Fighting for girls: New perspectives on gender and violence* (pp. 13–32). Albany, NY: SUNY Press.

Margolin, G., & John, R. (1997). Children's exposure to marital aggression: Direct and mediated effects. In G. K. Kantor & J. Jasinski (Eds.), *Out of the darkness: Contemporary research perspectives on family violence* (pp. 90–104). Thousand Oaks, CA: Sage.

McKeganey, N., Barnard, M., & McIntosh, J. (2002). Paying the price for their parents' addiction: Meeting the needs of the children of drug-using parents. *Drugs: Education, prevention and policy, 9,* 233–246.

Miller-Cribbs, J. E., & Farber, N. B. (2008). Kin networks and poverty among African-Americans: Past and present. *Social Work, 53*(1), 43–51.

Moffitt, T., Caspi, A., Rutter, M., & Silva, P. (2001). *Sex differences in antisocial behavior: Conduct disorder, delinquency and violence in the Dunedin Longitudinal Study.* Cambridge, UK: Cambridge University Press.

Morgan, P., & Joe, K. (1996). Citizens and outlaws: The private lives and public lifestyles of women in the illicit drug economy. *Journal of Drug Issues, 26*(1), 125–142.

Reeves, J., & Campbell, R. (1994). *Cracked coverage: Television news, the anti-cocaine crusade, and the Reagan legacy.* Durham, NC: Duke University Press.

Robinson, R. (2011). "Just leave me alone! I'm so afraid to be alone": Helpful lessons from attachment and object relations theory. In R. Immarigeon (Ed.), *Women and girls in the criminal justice system* (pp. 1–6). Kingston, NJ: Civic Research Institute.

Ryder, J. (2007). "I wasn't really bonded with my family": Attachment, loss and violence among adolescent female offenders. *Critical Criminology. An International Journal, 15*(1), 19–40.

Sampson, R. J. (1987). Urban Black violence: The effect of male joblessness and family disruption. *American Journal of Sociology, 93,* 348–382.

Schaffner, L. (2007). Violence against girls provokes girls' violence: From private injury to public harm. *Violence Against Women, 13,* 1229–1248.

Shengold, L. (1999). *Soul murder revisited: Thoughts about therapy, hate, love, and memory.* New Haven, CT: Yale University Press.

Siegel, J., & Williams, L. (2003). The relationship between child sexual abuse and female delinquency and crime: A prospective study. *Journal of Research in Crime and Delinquency, 40*(1), 71–94.

Silverthorn, P., & Frick, P. (1999). Developmental pathways to antisocial behavior: The delayed-onset pathway in girls. *Development and Psychopathology, 11*(1), 101–126.

Small, M., & Newman, K. (2001). Urban poverty after *The truly disadvantaged:* The rediscovery of the family, the neighborhood, and culture. *Annual Review of Sociology, 27,* 23–45.

Smith, C., & Thornberry, T. (1995). The relationship between childhood maltreatment and adolescent involvement in delinquency. *Criminology, 33,* 451–477.

Smith, N. (2006). Empowering the "unfit" mother: Increasing empathy, redefining the label. *Affilia, 21,* 448–457.

Sroufe, L., & Fleeson, J. (1986). Attachment and the construction of relationships. In W. Hartup & Z. Rubin (Eds.), *Relationships and development* (pp. 51–72). Mahwah, NJ: Erlbaum.

Sterk, C. (1999). *Fast lives: Women who use cocaine.* Philadelphia, PA: Temple University Press.

Sterk, C., Elifson, K., & Theall, K. (2000). Women and drug treatment experiences: A generational comparison of mothers and daughters. *Journal of Drug Issues, 30,* 839–862.

Waldorf, D., Reinarman, C., & Murphy, S. (1991). *Cocaine changes: The experience of using and quitting.* Philadelphia, PA: Temple University Press.

West, J., & Oldfather, P. (1995). Pooled case comparison: An introduction for cross-case study. *Qualitative Inquiry, 1,* 452–464.

Wilson, M., & Tolson, T. (1990). Familial support in the Black community. *Journal of Clinical Child and Adolescent Psychology, 19,* 347–355.

Wilson, W. (1987). *The truly disadvantaged: The inner city, the underclass, and public policy.* Chicago, IL: University of Chicago Press.

Wilson, W. (1996). *When work disappears: The world of the new urban poor.* New York, NY: Knopf.

READING /// 16

As you learned, women often turn to prostitution as a way to support a drug habit, in response to abuse in their lives, or to create options for economic support. In this article by Corey Shdaimah and Chrystanthi Leon, you'll learn how women use their experience in prostitution as a way to assert power and control over their lives

"First and Foremost They're Survivors"
Selective Manipulation, Resilience, and Assertion Among Prostitute Women

Corey S. Shdaimah and Chrysanthi Leon

Abstract

Based on qualitative data from three sites (N = 76), we describe prostitute women's agency and problematize dominant assumptions. Prostitute women exhibit creative, resilient, and rational conduct. Rejecting victimhood, our respondents demonstrate moral reasoning, make choices, work systems that dominate their lives, and assert power and control when they can. Their resistance, while serving a symbolic function, also expresses their system savvy and self-advocacy that produce measurable benefits. We distinguish between "being manipulative" and contextspecific ethical conduct intended to further their survival.

Prostitute Women as Survivors

Much of the literature on women engaged in prostitution, particularly at the street level, highlights their victimization on the job as well as an association between prostitution and childhood abuse and other forms of trauma (Caputo, 2009; Wiechelt & Shdaimah, 2011; Wilson & Widom, 2008, 2010). In addition to the empirical work

SOURCE: Shdaimah, C. S. & Leon, C. (2015). "First and foremost, they're survivors": Selective manipulation, resilience, and assertion among prostitute women. *Feminist Criminology* 10(4): 326–347.

that documents widespread trauma and victimization, when prostitution is discussed in political and academic contexts, there is often a deliberate mobilization of victim narratives (Anderson, 2008; Dowty, 2013).

The construction of women as victims has been critiqued as unrepresentative of the broad range of sex work (Sanders, O'Neill, & Pitcher, 2009; Weitzer, 2005). Constructing women as victims can be an important strategy for building empathy for female offenders (Shdaimah & Leon, in press). Such strategic choices are made by organizations seeking resources and by individuals explaining their lives by referencing an acceptable narrative (O'Brien, 2013). Empirical data from our respective studies of women in prostitution, however, demand that such strategies are balanced with narratives that recognize positive aspects of their experiences and the strengths and skills that they use to survive in an often difficult and highly marginalized work setting.

Although victimization is increasingly acknowledged and mobilized, a growing number of books and articles focus on the rational choice of street-based prostitution as an exercise of agency in the face of limited options. Rosen and Venkatesh (2008) found that 50 of 75 residents in a Chicago public housing building chose sex work from a repertoire of low-wage work to meet immediate economic needs. According to Rosen and Venkatesh, "[S]ex work offers just enough money and flexibility to make the job worthwhile, and just enough autonomy and professional satisfaction to make it more attractive than other options" (p. 418). Shdaimah and Wiechelt's (2012) study at a drop-in center found that women displayed courage and resourcefulness, engaging in street-based sex work to meet survival needs and escape abusive relationships. Elizabeth Bernstein (2007) documented the careers of women in a variety of other forms of sex work. Her sample included aspiring academics and middle-class mothers who engage in prostitution and other forms of sex work to support themselves, their families, and their education. These scholars deny neither the circumscribed nature of many women's choices nor the prevalence of their victimization, but they also recognize that self-determination, resilience, and strength provide a fuller picture. In this article, we examine manifestations of these characteristics from our own research with women engaged in survival prostitution[1] in Baltimore, Philadelphia, and another urban Northeastern location, referred to here as Peterson County.[2] Catherine Heathcliff,[3] the probation officer

whose quote serves as the title to this article, notes that the ability to survive often brutal circumstances should be acknowledged and respected in any discussions with or about street-level prostitute women, "First and foremost they're survivors."

Women's criminal conduct, particularly of a sexual nature, is viewed and assessed by the criminal justice system through a gendered lens (Anderson, 2008; Corrigan & Shdaimah, 2012; Wyse, 2013). Thus, ascriptions of agency and strength, where they exist, are often portrayed in highly judgmental and negative terms. One study found that probation officers viewed juvenile female offenders as "criers, liars, and manipulators" (Gaarder, Rodriguez, & Zaatz, 2004). Although lying and manipulation certainly point to levels of agency among women and girls, it paints their actions as devious and underhanded, rather than as reasonable survival mechanisms. It also fails to account for moral reasoning that informs women's albeit limited choices. Our study shows women's agency within limited circumstances, what Kathy Abrams (1995) describes as "partial agency" (p. 306), both while they are engaged in survival prostitution and when they are moving through the criminal justice system. We focus on how a particular group of highly stigmatized women may be viewed from alternative perspectives that highlight their strengths and agency as rational actors.[4] In this article, we use lenses of gender and class as our samples comprise almost exclusively women in poverty. Although our current data do not allow for an intersectional analysis of race, we recognize that racialized judgments form an important context for the gender and class analysis.[5] In this article, we present data that problematize the dominant assumptions about women involved in survival prostitution.

Method

Data in this article are drawn from two primarily qualitative studies that discuss criminal justice–affiliated prostitution diversion programs. All programs share the same basic goals: specialized therapeutic programming for criminal defendants to lessen criminal justice sanctions and address the factors that motivate women to engage in prostitution. Shdaimah (2010) looked at two court-affiliated criminal justice programs in Baltimore and Philadelphia. Baltimore's 90-day Specialized Prostitution Diversion (SPD) program[6] is pre-plea. The charges of successful participants are null processed while unsuccessful participants return to court to plead with no adverse legal consequences for failure. Philadelphia's Project Dawn Court (PDC) is a four-phase program that runs for a minimum of 1 year; program breaches entail sanctions and a restart of the participant's program phase. Entrance into the program requires a no-contest plea, which is held in abeyance. Successful participants' charges are dismissed with prejudice; if participants fail, their no-contest pleas are accepted, which triggers sentencing. Although these two programs differ significantly, participants in both meet with program staff on a regular basis and follow a program designed to offer encouragement, treatment, and heightened supervision. Participants in both programs must comply with program staff directives, which often include regular drug testing, and compliance with the additional obligations of any programs that they attend.[7] Leon draws from data collected to investigate the scope and the context of survival prostitution in Peterson County, to inform the creation of a diversion program similar to the existing programs described by Shdaimah.[8] One of the advantages of this data set is that it included both women who were involved in court-mandated programs and women who were not involved in such programs. The congruence of findings across the studies indicates that women's responses were not influenced by their status of being court-involved at the time of the study.

Both authors conducted extensive observations at relevant sites, including courts, probation offices, and prisons, as well as focus groups and interviews with 76 current and former prostitute women at the three sites.[9] Both authors also interviewed program staff and criminal justice professionals, although data from these interviews are not reported here. Although sampling was not representative, samples were reflective of the respective study populations in terms of race and age.[10] Recruiting continued until saturation was achieved in both authors' studies.[11] Table 1 provides a breakdown of the numbers of respondents in each program and the demographics.[12]

Across the samples, interviews and focus groups sought the perspectives of women on their motivation for engaging in and desisting from[13] prostitution and descriptions of their experiences with the criminal justice system. In the context of these discussions, many women described survival methods and resilience that became the basis for this article. We also observed interactions among the women and between women and program staff that corroborated these stories. All interviews and focus groups were audio-recorded and transcribed verbatim.[14] Transcriptions and notes from observations were analyzed and coded by the authors separately, in the context of their respective studies. Both authors independently engaged in inductive coding that allowed themes emphasized by the women to come to the forefront (see Fereday & Muir-Cochrane, 2008, on hybrid deductive and inductive coding). In these original inductive analyses of both data sets, shared themes related to rational action, resilience, and strength emerged. After recognizing the similarity of each other's findings, the authors then collaborated to conduct a secondary analysis of the data sets through these lenses (Sands, 2004), which led to the development of new codes through discussion and consensus. In the following section, we present our findings organized by these themes. First, we show a context for women's decision making of survival (for self and others) combined with hard-headed realism. Women's portrayals of agency and decision making were consistent across our samples and across data collection methods (observations, focus groups, and interviews). They were also corroborated by criminal justice personnel in interviews, focus groups, and observations, although we do not draw on these data for the current study beyond Catherine Heathcliff's characterization in the title. We then discuss their responses along the themes of system savvy, selective manipulation and morality, resilience and self-advocacy, and assertion of control.

Findings

A Backdrop of Survival and Realism

Like other women engaged in survival prostitution, our respondents' choices are shaped by their experiences. They are also shaped by other factors, such as their socioeconomic circumstances, education, and networks of support. In our studies of women currently and formerly engaged in survival prostitution, we found a nuanced picture of moral and rational choice-making in an extremely circumscribed universe of options. Women faced limited economic and social opportunities, and prostitution provided a means to sustain themselves. Our respondents were also influenced by their family and relational ties in ways that made prostitution a logical choice. Sometimes, this was through coercive relationships, in which women were pressured to engage in prostitution by parents or partners. On other occasions, it was

Table 1 • Study Respondents Demographics

	Philadelphia's Project Dawn Court	Baltimore's SPD program	Peterson County	Total
Number of respondents	19	12	37	68
Age range, years	28–45	18–50	18–72	
Race/ethnicity[a,b]				
African American/ Black	6	5	16	27 (out of 55 respondents)
White/Caucasian	11	3	6	20 (out of 55 respondents)
Hispanic/Latina	1	0	4	5 (out of 55 respondents)
Triracial/mixed	1	2	0	3 (out of 55 respondents)

NOTE. SPD = Specialized Prostitution Diversion.

[a]As explained in the text, 11 of the Peterson County and 2 of Baltimore's SPD respondents did not provide demographic information and therefore the racial/ethnic breakdown is for the 55 respondents for whom we have this information.

[b]These are the terms that our respondents used to describe themselves.

a chosen means to help support family members, including sick relatives and children.

Sexual victimization experiences were common in both samples. For example, in Leon's sample, respondents had experienced an average of five of the eight major traumas described in the Treatment Entry Questionnaire (TEQ). The vast majority of this group (86%, 18/21[15]) reported sexual assault, and nearly one-third of those (29%, 6/21) reported that the sexual assault took place during their sex work (most often unpaid sex forced or coerced by clients or authority figures such as a police officer and a public defender). For some of our respondents, backgrounds of victimization—especially sexual abuse—eroded boundaries surrounding sex as a transaction. Some had experiences that they now view as sexual abuse, but at the time did not characterize them that way often because they were too young or because they had no other frame of reference. Tootles, a 43-year-old African American[16] participant in Philadelphia's PDC, described sexual abuse that started at an early age:

[When I was seven, my family's landlord] told me he'll give me a dollar if I have sex with him orally, and I said okay. I didn't know any better 'cause I remember my uncle touching my breast or whatever. And I continued to let him do it because it felt good and I never felt good before; I always was sad, a sad child.

Later, Tootles's stepfather molested her and, in giving her money, attempted to make her a partner in her own abuse just as her family's landlord had done when she was seven:

And I tried to tell my mom what happened; she didn't believe me. So then again I thought it was normal for him to do that. So I continued to let it happen [until I was 19]. And at the time of when I was 12 years old I thought that if a man wanted to sleep with me, he had to pay me like my stepfather did. And I began to be promiscuous with a lot of people and I got into the lifestyle of prostitution.

Tootles's experiences in which her molesters gave her payment set up an association of sex with money that she later described as problematic both in setting her on a path of prostitution and in contaminating her relationships with men.

For others, selling sex appears as one of the only available economic means to ensure survival. According to Clara, an African American woman in her 50s from Peterson County, her own survival and others' needs were often overlapping and mutually reinforcing:

> Last year, I lost my job to take care of my husband and my aunt, both hospice patients. I collected unemployment, they only gave me $165 a week. I went to apply for food stamps, they gave me $16. Now, my husband gets an income, my aunt gets an income but my mortgage is $1,500. Now, if I had not been in this recovery process, I could have very well said, I know what I need to do to make some money.

Clara described these tough choices to explain the economic basis of decisions to prostitute. Although her commitment to recovery prevented prostitution in this instance, her choices in the past were informed by her need for housing, her care responsibilities to others, and her lack of clear alternatives that would allow her to shoulder these burdens. In a focus group about programming for prostitute women, she highlighted the inadequacy of current social safety nets as a reason to encourage empathy for women currently involved in prostitution and to support interventions that meet economic needs, such as housing, hygiene, mental and other medical health needs, and food.

The women we spoke with about prostitution describe themselves as agents who make conscious choices even in limited circumstances. This is true even for those who described their engagement in prostitution as initiated through desperation combined with lack of appropriate behavior models, such as Tootles. Brandi, a White woman in her 40s from Peterson County, described these in negative and oppositional terms: "at a certain age I wouldn't have listened to the people around me, I was hard-headed and wouldn't take advice . . . but I had free will and made the choice to end." In this example, Brandi is describing how important it has been to her to make independent choices, in this case to curtail drug use. Like several of our respondents, Brandi implies that while independence and hard-headedness were part of her survival at an early stage, and that accepting help has been crucial to her recent recovery, her own choice and

self-determination have been constant features of her life. Thus, the flipside of hard-headed stubbornness is a strong will to survive, cited by many of our respondents as necessary to cope with life on the streets. Many prostitute women, following the probation officer quoted in our title, describe themselves as realistic hard-headed survivors.

When a strong will is coupled with a clear, pragmatic reading of their circumstances, some women like 50-year-old Pink, a White participant in Baltimore's SPD, use their stubbornness to reach difficult goals:

> I have to do [the SPD]. And I know this. I am hell-bent and determined to make this thing work. 'Cause I have a family that loves me, and me being out there—I may end up losing—[emotional] . . . and I don't want to go to jail. And I don't want to go to jail. I've been there *so* many times. I have 17 prior convictions, and I don't want to go back to jail.
>
> Interviewer: Right. Exactly. Well, this will be it for you? Right?
>
> Pink: Yeah. This is *it* for me. This is the last—this is it—this is the last straw. It's hard. [But] this is all I have left to save my life is this [emotional, crying].

Pink shows herself, like many women, to be simultaneously stubborn and vulnerable. She is painfully aware of the consequences of program failure, and hopes that she will be able to marshal her strength to avoid them.

In the following sections, we draw on our data to expand upon the narratives women construct about themselves that emphasize agency. Although it could be argued that these are merely rationalizations that women use to feel better about their lives, narrative constructions are constitutive: The more they tell their stories in a particular light, the more they embody those stories (Engel & Munger, 2003; McCann, 1996). Similar to the women described by Leverentz (2014) in her study of re-entry, "the women's interpretations of their lives and their relationships represent a cognitive schema through which women account for who they are and the choices they have made" (p. 6). Choosing to describe past actions in a light that emphasizes free will, as Brandi does, exemplifies how women mobilize to navigate court-ordered programs and addiction. Accounts of self-determination are not just rhetorical: Prostitute women in our samples use their knowledge and resources to make decisions about their involvement in prostitution and to navigate their interactions with criminal justice personnel. Although we categorize these accounts under separate headings, many of the aspects of agency and careful consideration that we describe in the following sections reflect shared threads— we do not mean to present them as mutually exclusive but as shades of difference.

System Savvy

Despite expressions of agency, once involved in court and therapeutic programs, we found that women's level of understanding and free will were compromised by perceived or actual coercion. Like Clara, the 50-something African American woman from Peterson County quoted above, many of the women entered their respective programs due to a dire need for services, or a desperate fear of getting or staying incarcerated.[17] As she explains,

> It goes back to anybody who is a survivor, if you threaten me, if that's going to get me off the street, I'll say whatever you want me to say. In the back of my mind, I'm still not ready. But since you offered that to keep my ass out of jail, I'll do that.

Compliance with a program can be a strategic choice that is not the same as acceptance of the values or goals of the program. Such calculations mean that prostitute women often do *not* enter free of coercion. Rather, they work within a framework of constrained choices, asserting agency wherever possible.

Women across our samples often insisted that their participation in rehabilitation and success (as well as failure) resulted from their choices, regardless of coercive conditions. Sara, a 44-year-old White woman in Philadelphia's PDC, explained,

> As you know, we're already all of us, are court mandated to [comply with the program]. [pause]. You have a handful of girls that are really, really wanting to do this thing. That really

don't want to ever go back to that lifestyle again. So they're really *into* it. And if they see the advantages that are being given to them, they will take full advantage of it.

> Then you have your girls that are court mandated— and are only doing it because they have to do it. And then they go right back out again after they—there's a couple girls that graduated from it and I know they're right back out on the street already. They just waited for that day. To come. So that they wouldn't be on probation anymore or none of that. And now they're starting that vicious cycle all over again. So I really believe that your whole body, mind and soul has got to want this. And not for the courts. You gotta want it for you. If you don't want it for you you're not getting it.

Echoing a refrain consistent among those who have succeeded in court programs, Sara explains that mandated treatment cannot produce change. Full involvement in treatment programs requires buy-in and hard work from participants. Elsewhere we have described how some of the criminal justice professionals and women in our respective samples actually view the coercive aspect of court-based therapeutic programs as one of their advantages (Leon & Shdaimah, 2012). In the context of coercion, respondents still saw themselves as making use of their ability to play the system and make use of their limited choices to achieve "less bad" outcomes.

Although respondents did not always have correct information about specific program obligations or the ability to navigate the terms of their engagement, many prostitute women displayed an overall system savvy and used it when they had the opportunity to do so. In a focus group with women in drug treatment who had backgrounds in prostitution, Tricia, a 42-year-old White woman, explained a tactical insight: In Peterson County, drug charges are preferable to prostitution charges, and whenever possible, women should try to go for drug charges if given the choice:

> Actually it's in your favor if you get drug or other charges [since you have the options of other programs] but they see "prostitute" and

it means you're the bottom of the barrel, homeless, working the street, they take that all into consideration when they take you to bond, sentencing.

She further explained that she had weighed the value of fighting charges over acceding to them to be able to get back out on the streets as quickly as possible:

> They told me when I first got popped, you got two choices, you can fight this and win, or you can pay the fine and keep on truckin. Now I knew I had work to do, so I paid the fine and keep on truckin.

Tricia shows that women make (and disseminate) strategic choices based on system information. Many of the women have long histories of prostitution and criminal justice contact; the overwhelming majority also struggle with addiction and may have a history of drug-related charges as well. These histories provide experience that is mined to predict possible outcomes and select the best options to suit their objectives.

Brown Sugar, a 36-year-old tri-racial Baltimore SPD participant, was also keenly aware of the consequences of various criminal charges, including what are often called "collateral consequences." Brown Sugar's calculus differs from Tricia's, likely due to the divergent legal landscapes:[18]

> A prostitution charge [in Maryland] is only a misdemeanor . . . If you doing drugs, it's better for you to take the prostitution charge than to take that drug charge. Because when you got a felony on your case, you can't get housing. You can't get no public assistance. You got a felony, you're not gonna get nothing. You [got] to sign your kids over somebody else so they can get *public assistance*.

Brown Sugar drew a line when a friend tried to persuade her to sell drugs. Her refusal stemmed from a fear of what would happen if she got caught. They were also part of her worldview; Brown Sugar believes that those who take risks should be willing to live with the possible consequences:

> [a] young lady I thought was my friend, she came to me "you know we can get some money. . . . Let's fuck with some drugs . . ." [I said:] "No, boo. Me, I'm not dealing anybody drugs. I don't give a fuck where they come [from], I'm not doing it." You get more time for selling cocaine than you do for prostitution. And my main model is if you can't do the time, don't do the crime. . . . So now I've cut her off. I told her, "I can't hang with you no more because now you are trying to lead me down another path. I'm already on a path that I'm trying to fall off of."

Brown Sugar and Tricia are not victims being blindly led down a path—they are conscious actors making decisions about their practical and moral boundaries. These choices are limited, to be sure, but it would be wrong to assume that they do not exist.

Selective Manipulation and Morality

Many of the women in our samples described themselves as champion manipulators, most often regarding their interactions around addiction and the criminal justice system. We find that prostitute women employ techniques of manipulation selectively and consciously. At times, women described situations where they manipulated with relish, enjoying their skill and triumphing in challenging situations. Other times, women spoke regretfully, indicating that they sometimes were so good at manipulating that they ended up manipulating (and hurting) themselves. Approximately one third of Leon's respondents were women interviewed in one of several Peterson County drug treatment programs, who reflected upon their past experiences with court processes and program requirements. Coleen, age 36, African American, speaking for many of these women, explained that when placed in a coercive program, every revelation counts and must be carefully managed: "Pick and choose like [what you tell the court] like you pick and choose your friends. Pick and choose who you are going to be completely honest with." The first author's respondents similarly described pragmatic dealings with supervisory staff. CeeJay, a 26-year-old African American woman in Baltimore's SPD, told us that she makes conscious choices in her interactions with criminal justice personnel. For example, she explained, "I only lie when it's beneficial to me. Not harmful to me." CeeJay later explained that she wanted to finish the program honestly:

> Actually I wanted to come back into the program because I wanted to finish something that I started . . . the right way. Not the evil and conniving and the [laughs] wheeling and dealing out of it way [laughs].

Like Coleen, CeeJay demonstrates her own ability to assess when to comply with program demands. She also portrays these choices as part of her moral compass. We do not suggest that honesty with program staff is always the moral choice, but rather that prostitute women engage in moral reasoning about when, how, and whether to engage in prostitution.

Nearly all the women in our sample rejected the stigma attached to prostitution. As with Brown Sugar and Tricia, many declared their own normative boundaries in opposition to stigmatized portrayals of prostitution. For many women, prostitution stood in contrast to stealing or what they viewed as other clearly immoral behaviors. Ava, a 43-year-old White PDC participant, explained prostitution as a moral choice relative to other options, even though society often stigmatizes it:

> It's such a stigma, prostitution; you know "she did that?!" But to me, stealing from my 75-year-old mother who's on social security is worse than that [starting to cry]. To me, that was the lesser of all evils. Not to harm another person. I realized that I harmed others of course in other ways and . . . society. I'm sure kids walking by seeing me; you know that wasn't the greatest thing to do. And I didn't feel good about doing it but rather than . . . ripping off my family or doing a home invasion or something like that. I didn't rob the men I was doing it with.

Although she recognized the pain and worry she had caused them, Ava also indicated in the interview that *because* she had not stolen from her family, they were always there for her,

> And a lot of women I've spoken with out there . . . told me the same thing. "I'd rather hurt myself. I'm not stealing, taking my baby's diapers money. I'm not doing that. I'm not selling my food stamps that my kids need." You know? So, I guess it is—was an ethical thing for me. And I didn't want to involve my family and the people that love me in my addiction.[19]

Ava's explanation reinforces her ability to draw boundaries between her illegal prostitution and the options she rejected as immoral, such as home invasion, stealing her mother's social security, or otherwise implicating her family in her addiction.

Resistance and Self-Advocacy

Prostitute women in our sample often challenged the decisions of criminal justice personnel and demonstrated keen awareness of fairness and justice. Although some might view their challenges to authority as oppositional, the prostitute women we spoke with offered a different interpretation. Their interpretation framed resistance as legitimate self-advocacy. Sharon, a 44-year-old African American participant in Philadelphia's PDC, explained how she resisted and prevailed against what she thought was an unfair sanction:[20]

> If you wanna blame me for being a prostitute or being this and that or a crackhead or whatever like that, and then sanction me or wanna throw the book at me for this, that, and the third, then I think your ducks should be in a row. Don't just fling me along. And I really felt that that was something that [Project Dawn] didn't do—that they were responsible for this woman [at the recovery house], and I felt like they should of screened these people better, and not just allow anybody to be in these positions to do this.

Sharon saw it as the program's responsibility to provide her with the tools that she needed to succeed and not to place her in a position that led to temptation and failure. As the program required her to go to a poorly run recovery program, PDC staff (and not she) should be held responsible for the consequences. Sharon described how she prevailed over her probation officer who did not ultimately sanction her for this program breach.

Leon's respondents, when asked specifically about the features of existing programs, also insisted that proposed intervention programs should substantially address the needs of clients in addition to placing demands for compliance upon them. Three quarters of these respondents' comments included a critique of well-intentioned but poorly organized and resourced government agencies, outreach, and service providers, who were rarely able to meet immediate needs. Many also required travel (without providing transportation) to multiple sites to meet subsistence, health, and welfare needs (Leon, Silverman, & Ralston, 2011; see also Leon & Shdaimah, 2012).

Court observations also provided examples of self-advocacy. Leon followed the case of Jennifer, a White woman aged 19 at entrance, over nearly 2 years, from induction into a court-based intervention program to community placement for residential treatment. Jennifer repeatedly sought revisions to the program rules through her relationship with the judge who presided over her conditional probation. When brought before the judge during regular supervision sessions, Jennifer used her time in court to successfully argue for modifications to her treatment plan that allowed her access to exercise equipment, the right to grow out her nails (in opposition to her probation officer's previous conditions) and family visits. In this instance, Jennifer's record of compliance with program rules earned her the respect of the court, which she recognized and used to her advantage. Despite the significance of her efficacy, it must also be remembered that Jennifer's achievements were limited: At times, she sought changes in her housing, employment, and medications and in these instances was always overruled.

Self-advocacy and court responses take place within the performative realm of the court (Portillo, Rudes, Viglione, & Nelson, 2013). Court performances shape and instruct participants on what criminal justice professionals consider responsible advocacy. The following, recorded during observations of Philadelphia's PDC, illustrates the high stakes nature of self-advocacy:

> Erin[21] is brought in from lock up. She was taken into custody because she had tested positive for PCP. . . . Erin says that she did not use PCP . . . during the exchange there is eye-rolling

and comments such as "come on" from the women in the court, who clearly do not believe Erin and watch the exchange closely. The DA says "two times someone testing positive is an indication. But I'm going to ask Erin a question. Were you using something else?" Erin: "No." DA: "Are you lying to me?" And Erin says she didn't do anything. The DA then says "I'm no chemist." The Judge notes "it's one of the few instances we've had where someone comes in adamant that she's not using."

At the next PDC meeting,

> The judge [says to Erin] "We were all thrilled to see that the full test came back and that you didn't use and we were really proud of you that you didn't cave in [even though] we came down hard on you. It is still probation policy [to lock up immediately on PCP detection] . . . because of the danger to yourself and others." The judge intimates that they might review the policy, but because of the potential danger it will not likely be changed. The DA turns to Erin: "I am proud of you for believing in yourself enough and having enough courage to stand up to me and Her Honor and it takes guts and that's what this court is about." From around the courtroom, there are shouts of "good job" and "you go girl."

It is important to note that Erin's resistance was well-received and successful within the context of PDC, where the criminal justice personnel encourage dialogue and women's agency. Erin knew that she was risking stiffer sanctions should her retests show positive drug use. Leon similarly observed women question electronic monitoring system data, insisting they had not actually broken curfew, in some cases causing further review of the data and at least one vindication.

When criminal justice personnel take women's challenges seriously and answer with respect, this reinforces the sense that strong self-advocacy in the right circumstances can be beneficial. Although we celebrate these successful moments of resistance, they must be viewed in the wider context, outside the specialized programs that are oriented toward therapeutic rather than wholly punitive assessments of offenders and their claims. Both authors have observed numerous instances in which offenders are not given the benefit of the doubt, and resistance is viewed disfavorably, confirming the dominant view of offenders as liars and manipulators. Our data suggest that women in our sample, such as CeeJay, gauge whether and how to resist in particular situations.

Rather than blanket opposition, the most successful women in our sample also reflect savvy about when to challenge and when resistance will not be effective, for example, when their status as a "known prostitute" would undermine any attempt to dispute criminal charges.[22] In addition to the common calculation as to whether they could succeed in contesting current cases against them, they also recognized when they would be unable to obtain "victim" status in the eyes of the law. In one of our studies, women in a focus group realized during the conversation that many of them had been raped by the same government official. During that focus group, and in individual follow-ups as well as a subsequent group including almost all of the same women, they repeatedly insisted that formal reporting would only lead to "payback," specifically, beatings and further assaults from government officials. They also agreed that their particularly degraded status meant their assaults did not "matter" to anyone else. Although an extreme example, this sense of when the stigma attached to them would overshadow legitimate grievances was common across our respondents.

It is well-documented in the literature that reports of sexual assault by women known or suspected to be engaged in prostitution are often discounted (e.g., Corrigan, 2013). However, Shdaimah documents several incidences when PDC and SPD staff, including prosecutors, probation officers, and judges, took women's claims of assault very seriously and helped them to follow through with charges. These incidents involved different women and a variety of situations including domestic assault, sexual assault of the women, sexual assault of one participant's daughter, and rape by a police officer. It may be that prostitute women's claims are taken more seriously in the context of programs such as the PDC and SPD, which recognize them as victimized offenders who are trying to make changes in their lives (Corrigan & Shdaimah, 2012).

Assertions of Control

As we note in our review of the literature, women engaged in street-level prostitution are known to have more traumatic experiences than most people. Although sharing stories of victimization, and reporting shockingly high rates of trauma, women across our samples also reported the importance of their own assertions of self and of taking full advantage of opportunities to seize control in relationships. Often, women described this control against the backdrop of sexual exploitation. In these instances, explaining involvement in sex work as an independent choice, rather than as an experience of abuse, provided a sense of power to women that they preferred to the passive portrayal of victim. These assertions of agency should be understood against the backdrop of women's limited choices, both in particular encounters and relationships and in their socioeconomic circumstances. This was especially evident during one of Leon's focus groups, during which several women discussed how they had asserted themselves "on the job." Amid sharing memories of attempted rapes by johns, and the need to carry weapons for self-defense, they described not fear, but active wariness made possible by the knowledge that they had significant power over johns.

Interviewer: You had control over the situation?

ALL: Yes!

Tanya: It was something [johns] wanted, so it made me feel like I had control over the whole situation, I could talk to him any kind of way 'cause he wants me, I'm the boss. . . . My scariest moment was when I got in a car and I had a sense it wasn't right, I was taken all the way up behind Denny's and because I didn't want to give it up for free, I got put out on a dark road.

[Two chime in to say they carried weapons]

This exchange among the women reflects the extremely constrained, exploitative, and dangerous working conditions that characterized their prostitution. But within the danger and constraint, all reflect back on their experiences and highlight their own assertions of power and control, even if, in retrospect, those instances of felt power came at high risk and high price (Oselin & Cobbina, forthcoming).

Earlier, we discussed Brandi's reflection on the strong will to survive, shared by many respondents, which emphasized that decisions to accept help or make changes often ran aground of the hard-headed survivalism that helped them adapt to life on the streets. Amy, a 29-year-old White woman in Philadelphia's PDC, explained how survival mechanisms in the context of street-based prostitution can be maladaptive in encounters with the criminal justice system. On one hand, lawyers, judges, and probation officers might not recognize women's manipulation or aggressive behavior as survival strategies. Prostitute women may also fail to recognize when strategies that have proved helpful in one context might not serve them well in another context:

You have to be of a certain mental capacity when you're on the street . . . because you go through a lot on the street. Not just weather. I mean I was out there in the rain, the snow, you know, 2 feet of snow I was out there coping, out there trying to get a date. And in heat, 90-degree weather, 100-degree weather . . . [and] you have to be strong to be able to handle the people on the street. . . . You don't know if the next person, if the next car you get into if you're gonna get outta that car, if that guy's gonna rape you, if he's gonna put a gun to your head, if he's gonna put a knife to your throat. . . . [W]hen you come into court and you have that whole façade. . . . "Ha ha," like I'm strong and nobody's gonna tear me down, you have to humble yourself when you come into a courtroom setting and you have to kind of bring yourself down to the level where like, you have to come back to being a normal person. You have to allow people to put their hand out and help you. You have to allow people to express their opinion and. . . it's really hard because you're a survivor and you're used to being out there and taking care of yourself.

In more common examples, criminal justice personnel were often cognizant that heated verbal and physical responses to discomfort or challenge may be adaptive behavior for many of the women in our sample on the streets. Using empathy, therapeutic techniques, and coercion, they instruct women that such behavior is unacceptable in other settings such as court, treatment programs, and places of employment. The punishment and reward structure for forms of advocacy influence many of our respondents. Resilient women in our sample respond to these lessons and modulate their reactions to suit their audience to their benefit and, in Erin's case, potentially to the benefit of others. Women who are unwilling or unable to do so have been labeled resistant, immature, and in some cases, they have been deemed not ready to take advantage of the diversion programs. Although criminal justice personnel and other program participants largely see this latter group as a failure, at least two in the first author's sample interpreted their own such actions as successful acts of defiance and resistance.

Discussion

The prevailing criminal justice narrative views women in the justice system through two primary lenses: as deviant offenders or as victims. These views are often held simultaneously, but separately (e.g., Gaarder, Rodriguez, & Zaatz, 2004), allowing professionals to express sympathy for women's experiences and circumstances while also generally viewing them as culpable. The prostitute women we interviewed start from a position of deviance, but, depending on their actions, behaviors, context, and factors, they can at times move to the position of victim in the eyes of criminal justice professionals (Corrigan & Shdaimah, 2012). They are sex workers, and in many cases, have been violent. Their deviance, thus, is in reference not only to the legal system but also to social expectations for women, who are not supposed to be violent or engage in too much sex (Horn, 2003; Lombroso, & Ferrero, 2004). Prevailing views hold that women should sacrifice rather than harm and even supposedly gender-sensitive policies often reinforce norms of women as essentially relational (Hannah-Moffat, 2010). Therefore, when women's involvement in prostitution can be understood as exploitation or sacrifice, the victim lens provides an alternative to the uncomfortable portrayal of deviance. As we described here and in other work, our respondents sometimes explained their entry into prostitution through coercion out of economic necessity (Leon & Shdaimah, 2012; Shdaimah & Wiechelt, 2012).

Separate from the judgment-laden determinations of deviance or victimhood, prostitute women's choices are also rational. Other scholars have similarly called for such recognition (Rosen & Venkatesh, 2008; Shdaimah & Wiechelt, 2012). Although the women in our samples, like the women in Rosen and Venkatesh's and Shdaimah and Wiechelt's research, are engaged in street-level prostitution and may have few options, all are characterized by the rationality of their choices and by their need for savvy and street smarts in the face of criminalized work. Miller (2002) suggests adopting aspects of rational choice theory, which posits that acts are based on a calculus of self-interest. As our data make clear, for women in rehabilitative programming who try to surmount the powerful stigma that accompanies prostitution, the alternative lens of victim for viewing themselves and their choices is unsatisfactory.[23] Rather than accepting the passivity that accompanies victim identities (Bumiller, 1987; Lamb, 1996; Shdaimah & Leon, in press), prostitute women in our sample demonstrate skills and moral reasoning that include the ability to make choices, work the systems that dominate their lives, and assert power and control when they can. In contrast to the expectations of the governmental and hybrid programs that surveil, punish, and assist them, they describe creative, resilient, and rational conduct. This is consistent with Carissa Showden's (2011) exposition of women's agency across domains (domestic violence, assisted reproduction, and sex work) as existing not at the polar ends of a continuum between victims and "heroic individuals" who somehow liberate themselves. Instead, she sees agency as situation specific, exercised within material and structural constraints as "a form of resistance in that it opens up or reorders one's life circumstances in some positive way for the individual who is acting" (p. xi)[24]

Although Miller cautions against rational choice theory as an all-compassing paradigm, it provides a tool to recognize the agency of individuals and the choices that they make to engage in criminal activities. In addition, in Anderson's (2008) collection of empirical studies of women involved in drug worlds, each author's work demonstrates that while women in constrained circumstances may lack "power over," they frequently express "power to," understood as relational and connected to both empowerment (the ability and competence to influence and achieve desired outcomes) and agency (action; Anderson, 2008, p. 16). Across the studies Anderson (2008) reviews, she identifies five types of agency, of which two are clearly evident in our sample: survival/instrumental agency and symbolic resistance.

We found many examples of prostitute women that demonstrate "power to." We further found that although prostitute women in our sample have been victimized, these women are survivors who may engage in what we call selective manipulation in line with Anderson's view of instrumental agency. The women in our study work within a structure of limited opportunities, forced to be criminal, but then judged, punished, and further limited by broader society and most of the criminal justice personnel with whom they interact. Like the girls in Miller's (2002) study of street crime, our respondents are aware of societal roles and norms (gendered and otherwise), as well as societal expectations. They make calculated decisions to engage in particular criminal behaviors even as they also make decisions to eschew others. The women in our sample displayed symbolic resistance, as they fought stigma. This resistance is also an expression of system savvy and self-advocacy that produces measurable benefits. The cynical standpoint that women will take advantage and connive, articulated by criminal justice professionals cited in the literature and by some women and program staff in our studies, may accurately reflect particular interactions. But this cynicism should not be generalized to a characterological assumption, which does not account for the way prostitution itself is a gendered crime. As Ava explained, she and other women recognize their bodies as one of the few means to acquire shelter, money, or drugs without hurting others. Women also use gendered norms around victimization to their advantage, both to avoid punishment and to elicit sympathy.

Is selective manipulation worth celebrating? Anderson (2008) argues that rather than viewing women offenders as villains, we should appreciate women's capacities. Joe Soss (2002) has differentiated between external efficacy, or the ability to make systems responsive, and internal efficacy, which is the ability to navigate or work systems to one's benefit. Prostitute women in our sample, like the women in the focus group who do not believe that police or prosecutors would be responsive to their accounts of sexual assault, "learn" that they have little likelihood of success within systems. However, nearly all of our respondents considered themselves skilled at working these to meet their needs. In their exercise of agency and strategic manipulation, women express high levels of internal efficacy and gain a modicum of control in what are often otherwise chaotic lives.

Like Brandi and Ava, women make moral choices, sometimes to break the law, to support themselves and their families. Some even further identify bureaucracies and policies that create these choices as immoral or unfair, as did Sharon and Erin when successfully protesting their treatment by criminal justice personnel. James Scott (1985) coined the term *weapons of the weak* to describe how marginalized people create opportunities for resistance and agency even in the most limited circumstances. These choices echo what other scholars have found about how women learn to manipulate and navigate government and nonprofit agencies that often exercise control over their lives, such as Jill McCorkel's (2013) work showing how incarcerated women use strategies of resistance and compliance for both practical and symbolic purposes in a prison treatment program. In the civil legal context, resistance strategies have been documented by Kaaryn Gustafson (2012) in her study of welfare beneficiaries' decision making around lawbreaking.

Gaarder et al. (2004) point out a contrast between the way probation officers viewed adolescent female offenders as manipulative in character, whereas the authors' independent review of the case files provided evidence that the girls' manipulation was a survival tactic. Our work benefits from hearing directly from the women currently and formerly engaged in prostitution, and we find a similar distinction between the character trait of "being manipulative" and context-specific conduct intended to further their survival. Similar to the way we use the term "prostitute women" rather than "prostitutes," the women we spoke with largely thought of themselves as generally ethical people who used prostitution and worked the system as best they could to support often insidious addiction and meet basic needs.

Our findings destabilize current practices of sorting women into more and less deserving groups. According to Kathy Ferguson (1984), coping skills that women learn to comply with bureaucratic imperatives further subjugate them and stifle resistance in ways that may be harder to detect and, thus, harder to combat. Feminist research, which is rooted in people's lived experiences, questions existing societal discourses that privilege some people and marginalize others. Prostitute women's lived experiences of resistance through manipulation, contestation, and assertions of agency shine a critical eye on the gendered structures that shape social and economic opportunities. Prevalent criminal justice approaches that often pathologize women as either manipulative offenders or victims provide a limited menu of options by which women's behaviors and actions are interpreted and assessed to classify and process them within the criminal justice system (Corrigan & Shdaimah, 2012). A more realistic reflection of women's experiences is an approach that recognizes women's strengths and resilience (Van Wormer, 1999) in the face of limited opportunities and marginalization. This has implications for programming and policy that would consider the intersection of women's choices and motivations, as well as the structural factors that impact their decisions to engage in or desist from prostitution (Oselin, 2010). A rational choice approach also challenges neo-liberal practices that often responsibilize individuals while obscuring systemic and criminogenic practices that impact the choices of women as well as the range of discretion exercised by criminal justice personnel. Listening to the voices of women serves as an antidote to the dominant pathology and powerlessness narrative (Anderson, 2008) and may lead to better programming, better policy, and better scholarship.

Declaration of Conflicting Interests

The author(s) declared no potential conflicts of interest with respect to the research, authorship, and/or publication of this article.

Funding

The author(s) disclosed receipt of the following financial support for the research, authorship, and/or publication of this article: Leon's study was supported by the Office of Women's Health. As per instructions of Leon's Institutional Review Board (IRB) to maintain confidentiality regarding her study site, we do not provide the number or other identifying details of the grant.

//// DISCUSSION QUESTIONS

1. How do the life histories of women inform their pathway to prostitution?

2. Discuss the role that treatment and programming played in the lives of these women.

3. How did the women engage in advocacy to meet their needs?

Notes

1. By survival prostitution, we mean that the women in our respective samples indicate that they engage(d) in prostitution largely to meet survival needs such as food, shelter, or drugs due to addiction. These likely differ from women who may engage in prostitution as a career choice or a means to empowerment. We use the term "women engaged in prostitution" or "prostitute women" rather than the broader term *sex worker* as the women in our samples largely do not identify with that term or focus on the employment aspects that sex work connotes. We also avoid the passive "prostituted women" and the term *prostitute*, as women in our sample do not see prostitution as an identity but rather something that they do to survive.

2. The Institutional Review Board (IRB) overseeing research at this site required that the site not be identified.

3. Names of study participants are pseudonyms to protect confidentiality. Respondents in the first author's study chose their pseudonyms and pseudonyms in the second author's study were assigned.

4. Elsewhere we address the way women use narratives of mutual assistance and morality to counter stigmatized identity (Shdaimah & Leon, in press), but that is not our focus in this article.

5. Judgments of desert clearly rely on racialized perceptions as well (Chesney-Lind, 2006; Mauer & Huling, 1995). Theoretical and empirical studies of intersectionality demonstrate that "discrimination and disadvantage are not just additive; categories may intersect to produce unique forms of disadvantage" (Best, Edelman, Krieger, & Eliason, 2011, p. 993). These unique forms of disadvantage are likely produced in part by the "discrete stereotypes for various intersectional categories" (Best et al., 2011, p. 994) that experimental psychologists have documented in the population.

6. The program has been expanded to include people charged for other offenses but with prostitution records or prostitution-related offenses, and thus the name has been changed to the Specialized Early Resolution Program. The content of the program remains the same and we retain the original appellation to retain consistency across publications and because data were collected before the name was changed.

7. For detailed descriptions of the Specialized Prostitution Diversion (SPD), Project Dawn Court (PDC), and other court-affiliated prostitution diversion programs around the country, see Mueller (2012).

8. For further details and a comparison of the three programs studied, see Leon and Shdaimah (2012). For information on Baltimore's SPD, see Shdaimah (2010).

9. Neither author's sample was designed to test differences between racial groups or to draw conclusions about racialized experiences. As we acknowledge above, racialized constructions are likely an important facet of the treatment prostitute women experience, and this merits its own sustained investigation.

10. Shdaimah's sample reflected race and age of the PDC and SPD programs; Leon's sample reflected race and age of the subgroup of incarcerated women in the state who report past involvement in some form of prostitution (71 of the 216 women surveyed)—these women were the intended participants in the diversion program under development.

11. Leon and her research assistants recruited participants to share their general views on prostitution in three ways: at neighborhood association meetings, by approaching people awaiting violation of probation hearings at Superior Court, and at three treatment programs that serve women involved in street prostitution. After completing a general interview about the perceived issues surrounding prostitution, individuals who volunteered their own experience with sex work (37/49) were invited to complete a health needs interview (26/37). Shdaimah and her research assistant approached respondents who were present during court observations and asked them to participate in the study. Some respondents referred others on their own initiative, and still others self-referred. Respondents participated in a series of interviews as they moved through their respective program and after termination or completion.

12. We did not see differences in strategies or skills with respondents of different ages, although older respondents were more likely to discuss mentoring others and younger respondents more likely to discuss being mentored, as would be natural. Therefore, we do not have any data that would suggest that our findings are informed by age.

13. To be clear, our study is not about desistance per se or any other facet of sex work or prostitution, but rather about the decisions that women make along a continuum of involvement in prostitution at any stage in their lifetime.

14. Emotions, affect, and actions are included in the transcriptions in brackets.

15. Only 21 of the 37 provided answers to these questions; however, comments from all 37 in Peterson County highlighted the prevalence of severe trauma in their lives, for example, 3 of the remaining 16 who did not fill out a Treatment Entry Questionnaire (TEQ) described watching the death of a loved one; most of the 16 commented during focus groups on the frequent occurrence of sexual assault on the job.

16. Not all of the respondents provided their age and racial or ethnic identity. Where we have this information, we include it in the first mention of the study participant. This information was only collected systematically in the interviews conducted by Shdaimah and Leon but not in focus groups or observations.

17. On this phenomenon among Baltimore SPD participants, see Shdaimah and Bailey-Kloch (2014).

18. Many scholars have noted the disproportionate impact of drug policy and implementation on racial and ethnic minorities (e.g., Alexander, 2010). As noted in our "Method" section, we do not have data available that would allow us to assess whether there were differences based on race in types of charges and arrest rates nor, if there were such differences, whether women in our sample considered them in their calculations.

19. In this quote, Ava alludes to herself as a good mother. Many of the women in our sample also talked about good and bad mothering. This discourse deserves its own treatment and is also part of a larger discourse of morality among prostitute women that we discuss elsewhere (Shdaimah & Leon, in press).

20. Project Dawn includes graduated sanctions, from an essay through jury box to incarceration. In addition to each sanction, as indicated in the program description, participants must re-start whichever phase they are in at the time of the breach.

21. Erin did not participate in the interview study, so we do not have demographic data. We believe Erin is a White woman in her early 30s.

22. Because of the sensitive nature of our data, we do not indicate from which study these incidents are drawn.

23. Feminist legal theorist Kathryn Abrams accounts for the development of what she calls "dominance feminism." She is careful to distinguish challenges to dominance feminism, which overdo their critique of "victim identity," citing popular critics like Roiphe and Paglia who complain that victim narratives do not map well onto women's lives and experiences. In contrast, academic critics are more likely to appreciate the partial agency that women assert under structural constraints (Abrams, 1995).

24. For Showden, agency also "contributes to a broader understanding of the conditions that both limit action and construct what kind of action makes sense in different circumstances" (p. xi). Thus, agency also has the potential for creating and informing political change, something that we do not explore in this article.

References

Abrams, K. (1995). Sex wars redux: Agency and coercion in feminist legal theory. *Columbia Law Review, 95*, 304–376.

Alexander, M. (2010). *The new Jim Crow: Mass incarceration in the age of colorblindness.* New York, NY: The New Press.

Anderson, T. L. (2008). *Neither villain nor victim: Empowerment and agency among women substance abusers.* New Brunswick, NJ: Rutgers University Press.

Bernstein, E. (2007). *Temporarily yours: Intimacy, authenticity, and the commerce of sex.* Chicago, IL: Chicago University Press.

Best, R. K., Edelman, L. B., Krieger, L. H., & Eliason, S. R. (2011). Multiple disadvantages: An empirical test of intersectionality theory in EEO litigation. *Law & Society Review, 45*, 991–1025.

Bumiller, K. (1987). Victims in the shadow of the law. *Signs: Journal of Women in Culture and Society, 12*, 421–439.

Caputo, G. A. (2009). Early life trauma among women shoplifters and sex workers. *Journal of Child & Adolescent Trauma, 2*, 15–27.

Chesney-Lind, M. (2006). Patriarchy, crime, and justice: Feminist criminology in an era of backlash. *Feminist Criminology, 1*, 6–26.

Corrigan, R. (2013). *Up against a wall: Rape reform and the failure of success.* New York: New York University Press.

Corrigan, R., & Shdaimah, C. S. (2012, January 4). *"These are people with secrets": Victimization, objectification, and criminal justice strategies.* Feminist Legal Theory Pre-Conference, Association of American Law Schools, George Washington University Law School, Washington, DC.

Dowty, D. (2013). *In new strategy playing out in Syracuse, prostitutes are victims and pimps are sex traffickers* [Syracuse Post-Standard] Retrieved from http://www.syracuse.com/news/index.ssf/2013/11/in_new_strategy_tested_in_syracuse_prostitutes_are_victims_ and_pimps_are_sex_tra.html.

Engel, D. M., & Munger, F. W. (2003). *Rights of inclusion: Law and identity in the life stories of Americans with disabilities.* Chicago, IL: University of Chicago Press.

Fereday, J., & Muir-Cochrane, E. (2008). Demonstrating rigor using thematic analysis: A hybrid approach of inductive and deductive coding and theme development. *International Journal of Qualitative Methods, 5*, 80–92.

Ferguson, K. (1984). *The feminist case against bureaucracy.* Philadelphia, PA: Temple University Press.

Gaarder, M., Rodriguez, N., & Zaatz, M. S. (2004). Criers, liars, and manipulators: Probation officers' views of girls. *Justice Quarterly, 21*, 547–578.

Gustafson, K. (2012). *Cheating welfare: Public assistance and the criminalization of poverty*. New York: New York University Press.

Hannah-Moffat, K. (2010). Sacrosanct or flawed: Risk, accountability and gender-responsive penal politics. *Current Issues in Criminal Justice, 22*, 193–216.

Horn, D. G. (2003). *The criminal body: Lombroso and the anatomy of deviance*. New York, NY: Routledge.

Lamb, S. (1996). *The trouble with blame: Victims, perpetrators, and responsibility*. Cambridge, MA: Harvard University Press.

Leon, C. S., & Shdaimah, C. S. (2012). JUSTifying scrutiny: State power in prostitution diversion programs. *Journal of Poverty, 16*, 250–273.

Leon, C. S., Silverman, B., & Ralston, K. (2011). *Delaware community health needs assessment* (Report to the U.S. Office of Women's Health). Delaware Coalition for a Healthier Community.

Leverentz, A. (2014). *The ex-prisoner's dilemma: How women negotiate competing narratives of reentry and desistance*. New Brunswick, NJ: Rutgers University Press.

Lombroso, C., & Ferrero, G. (2004). *Criminal woman, the prostitute, and the normal woman* (M. Gibson, Trans.). Durham, NC: Duke University Press.

Mauer, M., & Huling, T. (1995). *Young Black Americans and the criminal justice system: Five years later*. Washington, DC: The Sentencing Project. Retrieved from http://www.sentencing project.org/doc/publications/rd_youngblack_5yrslater.pdf

McCann, M. (1996). Causal versus constitutive explanations (or, on the difficulty of being so positive...). *Law & Social Inquiry, 21*, 457–482.

McCorkel, J. A. (2013). *Breaking women: Gender, race, and the new politics of imprisonment*. New York: New York University Press.

Miller, J. (2002). Reconciling feminism and rational choice theory: Women's agency in street crime. In A. R. Piquero & S. G. Tibbets (Eds.), *Rational choice and criminal behavior: Recent research and future challenges* (pp. 219–240). New York, NY: Routledge.

Mueller, D. (2012). *Treatment courts and court-affiliated diversion projects for prostitution in the United States*. Chicago, IL: Chicago Coalition for the Homeless. Retrieved from http://www .issuelab.org/resource/treatment_courts_and_court_affiliated_ diversion_projects_for_prostitution_in_the_united_states

O'Brien, E. (2013). Ideal victims in human trafficking awareness campaigns. In K. Carrington, M. Ball, E. O'Brien, & J. M. Tauri (Eds.), *Crime, justice and social democracy: International perspectives* (pp. 315–326). Basingstoke, UK: Palgrave Macmillan.

Oselin, S. (2010). Weighing the consequences of a deviant career: Factors leading to an exit from prostitution. *Sociological Perspectives, 53*, 527–550. Retrieved from http://dx.doi .org/10.1525/sop.2010.53.4.527

Oselin, S.S., & Cobbina, J. (forthcoming). "I got you": Street prostitutes' perceptions of protective strategies against violence. In K. Hail-Jares, C. Shdaimah, & C. Leon, *New perspectives on street-based sex work*. New York: Columbia University Press.

Portillo, S., Rudes, D. S., Viglione, J., & Nelson, M. (2013). Frontstage stars and backstage producers: The role of judges in problem-solving courts. *Victims & Offenders, 8*(1), 1–22.

Rosen, E., & Venkatesh, S. A. (2008). A "perversion" of choice: Sex work offers *just enough* in Chicago's urban ghetto. *Journal of Contemporary Ethnography, 37*, 417–441.

Sanders, T., O'Neill, M., & Pitcher, J. (2009). *Prostitution: Sex work, policy & politics*. Thousand Oaks, CA: Sage.

Sands, R. G. (2004). Narrative analysis: A feminist approach. In D. K. Padgett (Ed.), *The qualitative research experience* (pp. 48–62). Thousand Oaks, CA: Sage.

Scott, J. (1985). *Weapons of the weak: Everyday forms of peasant resistance*. New Haven, CT: Yale University Press

Shdaimah, C. S. (2010). Taking a stand in a not-so-perfect world: What's a critical supporter to do? *University of Maryland Law Journal of Race, Religion, Gender and Class, 10*, 89–111.

Shdaimah, C.S., & Bailey-Kloch, M. (2014). "Can you help me with that instead of putting me in jail?": Participant perspectives on Baltimore City's Specialized Prostitution Diversion Program. *Justice System Journal*. DOI: 10.1080/0098261X.2013.869154

Shdaimah, C. S., & Leon, C. S. (in press). Relationships among stigmatized women engaged in street level prostitution: Coping with stigma and stigma management. *Studies in Law, Politics, and Society*.

Shdaimah, C. S., & Wiechelt, S. A. (2012). Crime and compassion: Women in prostitution at the intersection of criminality and victimization. *International Review of Victimology 19*(1), 23–35.

Showden, C. (2011). *Choices women make: Agency in domestic violence, assisted reproduction, and sex work*. Minneapolis: University of Minnesota Press.

Soss, J. (2002). *Unwanted claims the politics of participation in the U.S. welfare system*. Ann Arbor: University of Michigan Press.

Van Wormer, K. (1999). The strengths perspective: A paradigm for correctional counseling. *Federal Probation, 63*, 51–58.

Weitzer, R. (2005). Flawed theory and method in studies of prostitution. *Violence Against Women, 11*, 934–949.

Wiechelt, S. A., & Shdaimah, C. S. (2011). Trauma and substance abuse among women in prostitution: Implications for a specialized diversion program. *Journal of Forensic Social Work, 1*, 159–184.

Wilson, H. W., & Widom, C. S. (2008). An examination of risky sexual behavior and HIV in victims of child abuse and neglect: A 30-year follow-up. *Health Psychology, 27*, 149–158.

Wilson, H. W., & Widom, C. S. (2010). The role of youth problem behaviors in the path from child abuse and neglect to prostitution: A prospective examination. *Journal of Research on Adolescence, 20*, 210–236.

Wyse, J. J. B. (2013). Rehabilitating criminal selves: Gendered strategies in community corrections. *Gender & Society, 27*, 231–255.

Processing and Sentencing
of Female Offenders

Section Highlights

- Processing and sentencing of female offenders
- Treatment of female offenders
- Role of patriarchy, chivalry, and paternalism in processing and sentencing

A s you learned in Section I, the gender gap in crime has remained consistent since 1990. For most crime types, the increase in female arrests reflects not an increase in offending rates of women but rather a shift in policies to arrest and process cases within the criminal justice system that historically had been treated on an informal basis (Rennison, 2009; Steffensmeier & Allan, 1996; Steffensmeier, Zhong, Ackerman, Schwartz, & Agha, 2006). This section highlights the different ways in which gender bias occurs in the processing and sentencing of female offenders.

How might we explain the presence of gender bias in the processing of female offenders? Research highlights that women and girls can be treated differently from their male counterparts by agents of social control, such as police, prosecutors, and judges, as a result of their gender. Gender bias can occur in two different ways: (1) Women can receive lenient treatment as a result of their gender, or (2) women may be treated more harshly as a result of their gender. These two competing perspectives are known as the chivalry hypothesis and the evil woman hypothesis. The chivalry hypothesis suggests that women receive preferential treatment by the justice system. As one of the first scholars on this issue, Otto Pollak (1950) noted that agents of the criminal justice system are reluctant to criminalize women, even though their behaviors may be just as criminal as their male counterparts. However, this leniency can be costly, because it reinforces a system whereby women are denied an equal status with men in society (Belknap, 2007). While most research indicates the presence of chivalrous practices toward women, the potential for sex discrimination against women exists when they are treated more harshly than their male counterparts, even when charged with the same offense. Here, the evil woman hypothesis suggests that women are punished not only for violating the law but also for breaking the socialized norms of gender-role expectations (Nagel & Hagan, 1983).

Research throughout the past 40 years is inconclusive about whether or not girls receive chivalrous treatment. While the majority of studies indicate that girls do receive leniency in the criminal justice system, the presence of chivalry is dependent on several factors. This section focuses on five general themes in assessing the effects of chivalry on the processing and treatment of female offenders: (1) the stage of the criminal system, (2) the race and ethnicity of the offender, (3) the effects of the war on drugs for female offenders, (4) the effect of legal and extralegal characteristics, and (5) the effects of sentencing guidelines on judicial decision making. This section concludes with a discussion of some of the international sentencing practices of women.

Stages of the Criminal Justice System

Chivalry can occur at different stages of the criminal justice system. Much of the research on whether women benefit from chivalrous treatment looks at only one stage of the criminal justice process. This single snapshot approach makes it difficult to assess the potential effects of chivalrous treatment for each case, region, or time frame. In addition, it can be difficult to determine how the effects of chivalry at one stage of the criminal justice process may impact subsequent decisions as a case moves throughout the system.

Much of our data about crime begins at the arrest stage, since this is generally the first involvement that an offender will have with the criminal justice system. However, the experience of chivalrous treatment can actually begin prior to an arrest. Police officers exercise discretion as part of their everyday duties. As a result, offenders may experience chivalrous treatment as a result of their gender. For example, police use discretion in determining when to engage in stop-and-frisk tactics. Brunson and Miller (2006) noted that African American boys receive greater levels of attention by police officers compared to girls of the same race, yet this may also be dictated by offense type. For example, the girls in this study indicated that their involvement with the police was typically related to incidents of truancy, curfew violations, and other low-level offenses. In contrast, the police generally made contact with the boys over higher criminal offenses, such as drug possession or distribution.

> The police will mess with the males quicker than the females. If it's a group of girls standing across the street and it's a group of dudes standing across the street, [the police] fina [getting ready to] shine they lights on the dudes and they ain't fina mess with the girls. (Brunson & Miller, 2006, p. 539)

Contrary to popular belief, women do not always experience chivalrous treatment. In an early study on gender, chivalry, and arrest practices, Visher (1983) found that it was not just gender that affected whether chivalrous treatment was extended but that variables such as age, race, and behavior also had a strong effect on whether police exercised their discretion in favor of the women. For example, older Caucasian women benefited the most from chivalrous treatment by the police. In comparison, younger women and women of color were significantly more likely to be arrested, even in cases involving similar offenses.

In Section VII you learned about how some of the changes in police practices and school policies have altered how the juvenile justice system has responded to cases of delinquency. We have also seen a ripple effect in the arrests of women as a result of the introduction of mandatory arrest policies in intimate partner abuse cases. Policies such as these have altered how police deal with cases of simple assault, and girls are disproportionately impacted by these changes. Here, the message has been that girls who act outside of traditional normative expectations for behavior are treated more harshly by police (Strom, Warner, Tichavsky, & Zahn, 2010).

Research also indicates that women are more likely to be treated leniently than men by prosecutors who determine the charges that will be filed against an offender and whether charge-reduction strategies will be employed in order to secure a guilty plea. Charge-reduction strategies involve a guilty plea by an offender in exchange for a lesser charge and a reduction in sentence. Some research indicates that women are less likely to have charges filed against them or are more likely to receive charge reductions, compared to their male counterparts (Albonetti, 1986; Saulters-Tubbs, 1993). Research by Spohn, Gruhl, and Welch (1987) found that women of all ethnic groups were more likely, compared to men of all ethnic groups, to benefit from a charge reduction. Given the shift toward determinant sentencing structures and the reduction of judicial discretion, the power of the prosecutor in this practice increases. While research by Wooldredge and Griffin (2005) indicated an increase in the practice of charge reductions under state sentencing guidelines in Ohio, their results indicated that women did not benefit from this practice any more or less than male offenders. While seriousness of crime and criminal history remain the best predictors of receiving a charge reduction, research is inconclusive on the issue of the effect of gender on this process.

At the pretrial stage, the courts are concerned with two primary factors: (1) whether an individual will engage in additional criminal activity if they are not detained prior to trial, and (2) whether they will show up for their court appearances. Most of these decisions are made primarily on an offender's criminal history. Given that women generally have lower criminal histories than men, it is not surprising that women are often treated more leniently during the pretrial stage. Several factors can influence the presence of chivalrous treatment for women at this stage. Offense type affects this process, because female offenders who were charged with property-based offenses were less likely to receive pretrial detention compared to males with similar offenses (Ball & Bostaph, 2009). Generally speaking, females are typically viewed as less dangerous than their male counterparts, making them less likely to be detained during the pretrial process (Leiber, Brubacker, & Fox, 2009). Women are more likely to have significant ties to the community, such as family and childrearing duties, which make it less likely that they will fail to appear for future court proceedings (Steffensmeier, Kramer, & Streifel, 1993). Offense type also plays a role because women who are charged with drug or property crimes are less likely to be detained prior to trial compared to women who engage in crimes against persons (Freiburger & Hilinski, 2010). This gender bias appears throughout the pretrial process, for women are 30% less likely than men to be detained prior to trial and also receive lower bail amounts than men (and therefore run less risk of being forced to remain in custody because of an inability to make bail) (Pinchevski & Steiner, 2016). However, not all women are treated in the same way. For example, women with who are arrested on higher level crimes and with more serious criminal histories are less likely to be released on their own recognizance and are more likely to be denied bail. Such effects are stronger for women than similarly situated men, proving that judges may punish women (i.e., evil women) who engage in serious crimes more harshly than their male counterparts (Pinchevski & Steiner, 2016). At the same time, women who appear before the court on less serious offenses are often granted greater leniency than their male counterparts (Tillyer, Hartley, & Ward, 2015). The decision to detain someone during the pretrial stage can also have consequences later in the process because women who are detained prior to trial receive longer incarceration sentences compared to those who do not receive pretrial detention (Sacks & Ackerman, 2014).

A related body of work that suggests that an offender's needs can also predict whether an individual will be successful. There is limited research on how gender and gender-specific needs impact this process. In a study by Gehring and VanVoorhis (2014), issues with substance abuse, mental health, housing instability, a history of abuse and failure to secure employment were also associated with a defendant's failure to appear as well as the likelihood that the offender would engage in additional criminal activity. These findings suggest that using criminal history as the sole predictor of success may not only fail to understand the unique needs of both male and female offenders but could simultaneously set up for failure individuals who have high needs but limited criminal histories. At the same time, there are variables that impact both men and women in similar ways. Research by Zettler and Morris (2015) notes that economic issues can be one of the greatest risks for failure during the pretrial stage. One of the primary causes of failure to appear because of indigence can be transportation issues that prevent offenders from appearing in court or attending pretrial supervision meetings.

Gender also has a significant impact on how cases are disposed of by the courts. In Florida, a felony conviction carries a number of consequences beyond the criminal justice system. Felons lose many of their civil rights as well as professional certifications required for certain occupations, and the restoration of these rights is not an automatic process following the completion of their sentence and requires a lengthy application process. One way of avoiding this process is to avoid a formal conviction and instead be sentenced by the judge to probation. Under state law, the adjudication of offenders is delayed, and if they successfully complete the terms and conditions of their probation, they are not considered a convicted felon (although the case remains a part of their criminal record). Women are more likely to benefit from these withheld adjudications than men. This practice continues even in violent offenses, such as assault, and in some cases, women were more likely to benefit from a withheld adjudication for crimes that are dominated by male offenders, such as drug manufacturing (Ryon, 2013).

The appearance of preferential or chivalrous treatment in the early stages of criminal justice processing also affects how women and girls will be treated in later stages. Females who already receive favorable treatment by prosecutors continue to receive such chivalrous treatment as their case progresses. The majority of research indicates that women are more likely to receive chivalrous treatment at sentencing. At this stage of the criminal justice process, women are less likely to be viewed as dangerous (Freiburger & Hilinski, 2010) and are less likely to recidivate (Daly, 1994). Indeed, women are viewed as better candidates for probation supervision compared to male offenders (Freiburger & Hilinski, 2010). Research on the decision to incarcerate reflects that women are less likely to be sent to jail or prison for their crimes, compared to men (Spohn & Beichner, 2000). Offense type also affects the relationship between gender and sentencing, because women are less likely to receive prison sentences for property and drug cases than their male counterparts. In those cases where women are incarcerated for these crimes, their sentences are significantly shorter compared to the sentence length for male property and drug offenders. Here, the disparity in sentencing can be attributed to the levels of discretion exercised by judges in making sentencing decisions (Rodriguez, Curry, & Lee, 2006). Overall, judges are more likely to sentence women to lesser sentences than male offenders (Goulette, Wooldredge, Frank, & Travis, 2015; Ward, Hartley and Tillyer, 2016). Even in cases where **sentencing guidelines** are used, such as in the federal system, the odds of a substantial assistance departure are significantly greater for women (Ortiz & Spohn, 2014; Spohn & Belenko, 2013). Even in cases where offenders are already involved in the criminal justice system and have received a new charge, women are more likely to receive a substantial assistance departure either to prevent women from having to serve long terms of incarceration or to divert women already under probation supervision from having to go to prison (Ortiz & Spohn, 2014). Although there is a consistent pattern of the preferential treatment in sentencing, not all crime types in all jurisdictions report this experience. While several studies on drug offenders find that women receive preferential treatment by the courts in terms of the decision to incarcerate and the length of the sentence, research by Koeppel (2012) finds that there are no differences in the sentencing practices between male and female property offenders in rural areas.

Race Effects and the Processing of Female Offenders

Historically, African American women have been punished more harshly than White women. This punishment reflected not only a racial bias but also a pattern consistent with their levels of offending, because women of color engaged in higher levels of crimes than White women. In many cases, the types of offenses committed by women of color had more in common with male offenders. Over time, research indicated that the offending patterns of White women shifted such that women, regardless of race or ethnic status, engaged in similar levels of offending.

Significant bodies of research address concerns over the differential processing of male offenders on the basis of race and ethnicity. Here, research consistently agrees that men of color are overrepresented at every stage of the criminal justice system. Given these findings, what effect does discrimination have for female offenders? Several scholars have suggested that chivalry is selective and is more likely to advantage White females over women of color. For example, African American women are less likely to post bail compared to white women (Pinchevsky & Steiner,

2016). This may be an effect of how bail is set by the courts, because minority women receive higher bail amounts than White women (Goulette et al., 2015).

When it comes to sending women to prison, research indicates that the rates of incarceration for White women have increased by 47% between 2000 and 2009; during the same period, incarceration rates for Black women declined 31%. However, women of color still dominate the statistics given their proportion in the population. The rate of incarceration for Black women is 142 per 100,000 (compared to 50 per 100,000 for White women; Mauer, 2013). Not only are women of color more likely to be sent to prison, but their incarceration sentences tend to be significantly longer than the sentences given to white women (Goulette, et al., 2015). Given these findings, some researchers have questions on whether discriminatory views about women offenders, and particularly women of color, may negatively influence prosecutorial and judicial decision-making processes (Gilbert, 2001). Even though women of color may be deemed as more "salvageable" than men of color (Spohn & Brennan, 2011), the potential effect of racial bias can be significant considering the significant powers of prosecutors in making charge decisions, offering plea agreements and charge reductions, and making sentence recommendations, as well as on judges who hand down sentences.

You have already learned that gender can impact the decision to hold someone in custody prior to trial. But how does race play into this process? Whereas interactions between gender and race can give the impression that women of color are treated more harshly by the criminal justice system, research findings indicate that the bias may be one of economics rather than race. Katz and Spohn (1995) found that White women are more likely to be released from custody during the pretrial stages, compared to Black women, as a result of the ability to fulfill demands for bail. When defendants cannot make bail, there may be incentives to accept a plea deal that would limit the time spent in custody. Yet this "freedom" comes at a cost, because the label of an *ex-felon* can affect them and limit their opportunities for the rest of their lives. This relationship between race/ethnicity, **legal factors,** and **extralegal factors** can also impact sentencing outcomes. For example, research by Brennan (2006) demonstrated that misdemeanor cases involving female defendants were more likely to be sentenced to incarceration if the offender had a prior criminal history. Here, race serves as an intermediating effect because the Black women in this study had greater criminal histories compared to White and Hispanic women. In addition, women of color were less likely to have strong positive ties to their community. This is a factor that also increased the likelihood of incarceration in these cases.

Research also finds that skin tone can influence the length of a prison sentence for women of color. Black women who are described as "light skinned" received shorter sentences by 12%, compared to offenders that were described as "darker" skinned (Viglione, Hannon, & DeFina, 2011). Similar findings are also demonstrated in research on men of color, whereas darker Black males were more likely to receive harsher punishments by the criminal justice system compared to lighter skinned Black males (Gyimah-Brempong & Price, 2006).

However, not all research demonstrates that girls and women of color suffer from harsher treatment by the courts. Some scholars find evidence that girls and women of color have benefited from chivalrous treatment. Here, scholars suggest that the preferential treatment of African American girls by judges is seen as an attempt to remedy the biased decision making of criminal justice actors during earlier stages of the criminal justice process that may have led to harsher attention (lack of pretrial release and bail options, less likely to receive charge reductions; Leiber et al., 2009). Race can have an effect on the sentencing practices for both adult and juvenile offenders. In one study on sentencing outcomes for juveniles, Guevara, Herz, and Spohn (2008) indicated that race effects did not always mean that girls of color were treated more harshly than White girls. Their results indicate that White females were more likely to receive an out-of-home placement. While many would suggest that an out-of-home placement is a more significant sanction, their research indicates that juvenile court officials may be engaging in "child saving" tactics in an effort to rehabilitate young offenders. In another study involving juvenile court practices, race did not impact the decision to detain youth in detention, because girls of all races and ethnicities were more likely to receive leniency in this decision compared to boys (Maggard, Higgins, & Chappell, 2013).

It is important to note that while research on race, ethnicity, and processing can demonstrate valuable results for women of color in the criminal justice system, these results are significantly limited. Much of the research investigating race and gender effects involves a comparison between White and Black women. It has been only within the last few decades that scholars have extended the discussion to the ethnicity and included data on Hispanic/Latina females. Few studies investigate how race can impact the processing for other racial and ethnic groups, such as Asian American, Native Americans, or Pacific Islanders. In addition, while recent implementations of the U.S. Census have utilized the category of "one race or more" to acknowledge that many women of color identify as bi- or multiracial, few studies on the processing of female offenders included this variable in their research. One explanation for this stems from the different sources of data that are used by scholars, such as official data statistics like the Uniform Crime Reports. These sources are limited in how they collect data about race and ethnicity. In many cases, these assessments about race come not from how the offender self-identifies, but from the perceptions of police officers on the streets, court officials, and correctional personnel.

The War on Drugs and Its Effects for Women

The heightened frenzy about the *dangerousness* of drugs has fueled the war on drugs into an epidemic. The war on drugs first appeared as an issue of public policy in 1971, when President Richard Nixon called for a national drug policy in response to the rise of drug-related juvenile violence. Over the next decade, controlled substances, such as cocaine, were illegally smuggled into the United States by drug kingpins and cartels throughout Mexico and South America (National Public Radio, n.d.).

Since the 1980s and the passage of the Anti-Drug Abuse Act, the incarceration rates for both men and women have skyrocketed. Figure 9.1 demonstrates how these new laws impacted the arrest rates for women. Using 1972 data as a baseline, the passage of the first drug bill by President Ronald Reagan led the arrest rates for drug cases to skyrocket (Merolla, 2008). Yet the majority of persons imprisoned on these charges are not the dangerous traffickers who bring drugs into neighborhoods and place families and children at risk. Rather, it is the drug user who is at the greatest risk for arrest and imprisonment. In response to the social fears about crack cocaine in the inner city, lawmakers developed tough-on-crime sentencing structures designed to increase the punishments for crack cocaine. Sentencing disparities between powder and crack created a system whereby drug users were treated the same as mid-level dealers. In 1995, the U.S. Sentencing Commission released a report highlighting the racial effects of the crack and powder cocaine sentencing practices and advised Congress to make changes to the mandatory sentencing practices to reduce the discrepancies. Their suggestions fell on deaf ears among congressional members who did nothing to change these laws. For the next 15 years, cases of crack and powder cocaine perpetuated a 100:1 sentencing ratio, whereby offenders in possession of 5 grams of crack were treated the same as dealers in possession of 500 grams of powder cocaine. In 2010, President Obama signed the Fair Sentencing Act, which reduced the disparity between crack and powder cocaine sentences to a ratio of 18:1. Under this revised law, offenders receive a 5-year mandatory minimum sentence for possessing 28 grams of crack (compared to 5 grams under the old law) and a 10-year sentence for possessing more than 280 grams of crack cocaine.

Prior to the war on drugs and mandatory sentencing structures, most nonviolent drug conviction sentences were handled within community correction divisions. Offenders typically received community service, drug treatment, and probation supervision. The introduction of mandatory minimum sentencing represented a major change in the processing of drug offenders. While these sentencing structures are applied equally to male and female defendants, the extent of women's participation often differs substantially from male involvement in drug-related crimes. With the elimination of judicial discretion, judges were unable to assess the role that women played in these offenses. The result was a shift from community supervision to sentences of incarceration, regardless of the extent of women's participation in criminal drug-related activities (Merolla, 2008).

While the focus by the federal government on drugs shifted criminal justice practices during the mid and late-1980s, it was not until the 1990s that state governments began to alter their policies and practices related to drug

Figure 9.1 • Female Arrests for All Crimes Versus Drug Arrests, 1972–2004

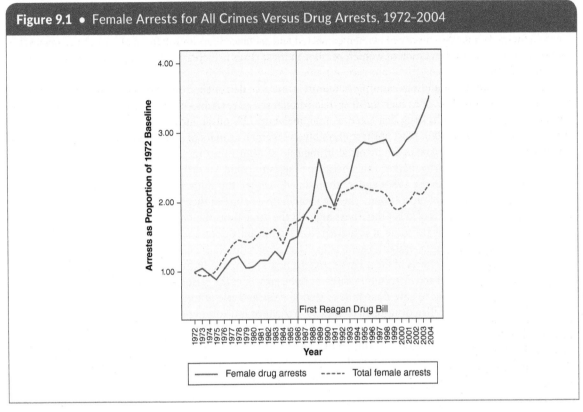

SOURCE: Merolla (2008).

crimes. In Florida, the legislature introduced the Criminal Punishment Code (CPC) in 1994. This new law called for increases not only for drug crimes but for many other crime categories as well. Here, the influence of the war on drugs reflected a shift toward a more punitive and retributive stance by criminal justice agencies. Not only did these changes have a significant effect for women in general, but these practices were also particularly detrimental for women of color. In particular, these changes increased the number of racial disparities in sentencing, an ironic consequence given that the focus of the mandatory minimum sentencing practices at the federal level were intended to reduce such disparities by race and ethnicity. For example, prior to the implementation of the CPC in Florida, sentences were 27% higher for Black women and 24% greater for Hispanic/Latina women, compared to those sentences given to White women. By 2003, these disparities had increased to 38% longer sentences for women of color compared to White women.

While much of the attention about the war on drugs has focused on the crack and powder cocaine debate (and the resulting disparities in sentencing between these two substances), these substances no longer reflect the drug of choice trends that currently exist for women. Crack cocaine has been replaced by methamphetamines, to the point where meth has been labeled as the "pink collar crack" (Campbell, 2000). As with changes that occurred to drug laws about crack and powder cocaine in the 1980s and 90s, recent history has seen changes to the laws on methamphetamine production and use that have not only increased likelihood of incarceration but also increased the sentence length for these crimes. As a result, the number of women sentenced for a meth-related drug conviction increased from 10.3% in 1996 to 23.0% in 2006 (Bush-Baskette, 2010). The length of sentences increased 300% as well during this time frame. While the majority of women convicted and sentenced for meth-related offenses were once White (99.5% in 1996), the representation of women of color in these cases is increasing (27% in 2006; Bush-Baskette, & Smith, 2012).

The shift to incarceration from community supervision had a detrimental effect on women. Between 1986 and 1991, the incarceration rates of women for drug-related offenses increased 433%, compared to a 283% increase for males (Bush-Baskette, 2000). Drug-convicted women make up 72% of the incarcerated population at the federal level (Greenfeld & Snell, 2000). Most of these cases involve women as users of illegal substances. Even in the small proportion of cases where women are involved in the sale of drugs, they rarely participate in mid- or high-level management in the illegal drug market, often because of sexism within the drug economy (Maher, 2004a). In addition, the presence of crack in the 1980s and meth in the 90s shifted the culture of the street economy, particularly for women involved in acts of prostitution. The highly addictive nature of these substances led more women to the streets in an effort to find a way to get their next high. At the same time, the flood of women in search of sex work created an economy whereby the value of sexual services significantly decreased.

While recent changes in federal drug sentencing laws have reduced the disparities in sentencing, the damage has already been done. The effects of these laws created a new system of criminal justice where the courts are overloaded with drug possession and distribution cases, and the growth of the prison economy has reached epic proportions. Yet these efforts appear to have done little to stem the use and sale of such controlled substances. Indeed, the overall rates of crimes other than drug-related cases have changed little during the last 40 years. The effects of these policies has produced significant consequences for families and communities, particularly given the increase in the incarceration rates of women. Section X explores in depth the consequences in the incarceration of women, both for herself and her family, as well as her community. These consequences have led some scholars to suggest that the war on drugs has in effect become a war on women (Chesney-Lind, 1997).

The Effects of Extralegal Factors on Sentencing Women

The assessment of whether women benefit from chivalrous treatment by the criminal justice system is not as simple as comparing the sentences granted to men and women in general. Many factors must be considered, including the severity of the offense, the criminal record of the offender, the levels of injury experienced by the victim, and the culpability, or blameworthiness, of the offender. For example, women generally have a less extensive criminal history than males and are less likely to engage in violent offenses or play a major role in criminal offenses.

In assessing whether women receive chivalrous treatment, it is important to control for these legal and extralegal variables. Research indicates that legal variables do affect the decision-making process for both males and females, albeit in different ways. As you learned earlier in this section, the effects of gender vary with each stage of the criminal justice system. For example, offense type and criminal history influence whether a defendant will be detained during the pretrial stages or receive charge reductions and leniency in sentencing. Type of offense also plays a role in whether chivalry will be extended because women who are charged with a drug offense are more likely to be denied bail and less likely to be granted ROR compared to their male counterparts (Pinchevsky & Steiner, 2016).

Not only do legal factors, such as criminal history and offense severity, appear to affect the pretrial decision process for women, but extralegal factors, such as the type of attorney, affect as well the likelihood of pretrial release for women. Women who were able to hire a private attorney were 2.5 times more likely to make bail, compared to those women who relied on the services of a public defender. Clearly, the ability to hire (and financially afford) a private attorney is linked to the ability to satisfy the financial demands of bail set by the court. In comparison, women who were represented by a public defender were twice as likely to be detained at the pretrial stage (Ball & Bostaph, 2009). Ties to the community (such as family life) can also serve as an extralegal factor that can mediate sentencing practices. For example, motherhood mitigates the likelihood of a prison sentence, because women with dependent children are less likely to be incarcerated compared to women who do not have children. In these cases, judges appear to consider the social costs of imprisoning mothers and the effects of incarceration on children, particularly in cases of nonviolent or drug offenses (Spohn & Beichner, 2000). Research indicates that variables such as single parenthood and pregnancy have been used by judges to justify a departure from strict sentencing guidelines and offer a reduced sentence (Raeder, 1995). Here, it is not gender specifically that accounts for mitigation but rather concern for the family (as non-"familied" women do not receive similar instances of leniency in sentencing). These departures have been confirmed by the courts in cases such as *U.S. v. Johnson,* 964 F.2d 124 (2d Cir. 1992). Indeed, such departures are not reserved exclusively for women but can also benefit male defendants who are the primary caregiver for minor children (see *U.S. v. Cabell,* 890 F. Supp. 13, 19 [D.D.C. 1995], which granted a departure from the sentencing guidelines for a male offender who was the primary caregiver for the children of his deceased sister).

The Effects of Sentencing Guidelines on Judicial Decision Making

Throughout most of history, judges have had discretion in handing out sentences to offenders. In most cases, judges were free to impose just about any type of sentence, from probation to incarceration. Essentially, the only guidance for decision making came from the judge's own value system and beliefs in justice. This created a process whereby there was no consistency in sentencing, and offenders received dramatically different sentences for the same offenses, whereby the outcome depended on which judge heard their case. While this practice allowed for individualized justice based on the needs of offenders and their potential for rehabilitation, it also left the door open for the potential of bias based on the age, race, ethnicity, and gender of the offender.

During the 1970s, the faith in rehabilitation for corrections began to wane and was replaced with the theory of "just deserts," a retributive philosophy that aimed to increase the punishment of offenders for their crimes against society. In an effort to reform sentencing practices and reduce the levels of discretion within the judiciary, many jurisdictions developed sentencing guidelines to create systems by which offenders would receive similar sentences for similar crimes. At the heart of this campaign was an attempt to regulate sentencing practices and eliminate racial, gender, and class-based discrimination in courts. As part of the Sentencing Reform Act of 1984, the U.S. Sentencing Commission was tasked with crafting sentencing guidelines at the federal level. Since their implementation in November 1987, these guidelines have been criticized for being too rigid and unnecessarily harsh. In many cases, these criticisms reflect a growing concern that judges are now unable to consider the unique circumstances of the crime or characteristics of the offender. Indeed, the only standardized factors that are to be considered under the federal sentencing guidelines are the offense committed, the presence of aggravating or mitigating circumstances, and the criminal history of the offender.

Prior to sentencing reform at the federal level, the majority of female offenders were sentenced to community-based programs, such as probation. Under federal sentencing guidelines, not only are the numbers of incarcerated women expanding, but the length of time that they will spend in custody is increasing as well.

Research by Koons-Witt (2006) investigates the effects of gender in sentencing in Minnesota. Minnesota first implemented sentencing guidelines in 1980. As in the case of federal sentencing guidelines, Minnesota founded its guidelines on a retributive philosophy focused on punishment for the offender. The guidelines were designed to be neutral on race, gender, class, and social factors. However, the courts can consider aggravating and mitigating factors, such as the offender's role in the crime, if they make a decision outside of the sentencing guidelines. Koons-Witt investigated the influence of gender at three distinct points in time: prior to the adoption of sentencing guidelines in Minnesota, following their introduction (early implementation 1981–1984), and in 1994, 14 years after the sentencing guidelines were implemented (late implementation). Her research indicated that female offenders were more likely to be older than their male counterparts and have a greater number of dependent children. In contrast, men were faced with more serious crimes, were more likely to be under community supervision at the time of the current offense, and had more significant criminal histories. Prior to the implementation of sentencing guidelines, gender did not appear to have an effect on sentencing guidelines. This finding contradicted the findings of other research, which illustrated that judges did treat female offenders in a chivalrous fashion. The one exception for Koons-Witt's findings was that sentences were reduced for women who had dependent children. Following the early implementation of sentencing guidelines (1981–1984), several legal outcomes increased the potential for incarceration regardless of gender. These legal factors include prior criminal history and pretrial detention. This pattern was repeated during the late implementation time period (1994). However, the influence of extralegal factors reappeared during this time period, whereby women with dependent children were more likely to receive community correctional sentences compared to women who did not have children. In these cases, Koons-Witt suggests that the courts may be using the presence of dependent children as a mitigating factor in their decision to depart from the sentencing guidelines, producing an indirect effect for the preferential treatment of women.

Not all states deal with directive sentencing in the same way. While Minnesota's sentencing guidelines are similar in design to the federal sentencing guidelines, Pennsylvania's sentencing guidelines are not limited to just a retributive focus but also reference tenets of rehabilitation, deterrence, and incapacitation that allow for additional opportunities for judges to exercise their discretion. Pennsylvania first developed its sentencing guidelines in 1982 but suspended the practice and reinstated the practice with new provisions in 1988. Research by Blackwell, Holleran, and Finn (2008) investigated the effects of gender and sentencing during these three time periods (when the sentencing guidelines were in effect [1986–1987 and 1988–1990] and during the suspension [1987–1988]). Their findings demonstrated that Pennsylvania's sentencing guidelines did not reduce the sentencing disparities by sex. However, it is possible that the higher levels of judicial discretion within Pennsylvania's sentencing guidelines may also contribute to this effect.

Like Minnesota and Pennsylvania, Ohio utilizes a guided sentencing structure. Felony crimes are organized into five basic categories. Unlike other state sentencing schemes, Ohio's law allows for increased opportunities for judicial discretion because each category has a wide range of options for sentencing (in terms of sentence length). Unlike other states, which demonstrated increases in the number of offenders sent to prison as well as the sentence length, Ohio documented decreases in both of these categories following its implementation of sentencing guidelines. These decreases were observed for both women and men and in the majority of offense categories (with drug cases as the exception). Racial disparities were also reduced for Black female offenders (Griffin & Wooldredge, 2006).

In contrast to the states that have either implemented or later disbanded sentencing guidelines, South Carolina considered the adoption of sentencing guidelines but ultimately failed to implement a practice. Over the two decades when the state debated whether to adopt such a schema, the state's sentencing commissions collected extensive data from the judicial, corrections, and probation/parole departments on all criminal offenses where the minimum punishment was a $500 fine or greater than 90 days in jail. Research by Koons-Witt, Sevigny, Burrow, and Hester (2012) examines these data to determine how factors such as gender, race, age, and offense type affect sentencing outcomes in a region that did not adopt structured guidelines. Their findings indicate that women benefited from chivalrous treatment by the court, because they were less likely to be incarcerated. When women were sent to prison, they received shorter sentences compared to male offenders. However, this benefit is selective, because it is extended only for White women and not for women of color.

Some critics of gender-neutral sentencing argue that directed sentencing structures such as the federal sentencing guidelines have affected women in a negative fashion. These sentence structures assume that men and women have an equal position in society and that, therefore, the unique needs of women do not need to be considered when making sentencing decisions. Whereas the intent behind the creation of sentencing guidelines and mandatory minimums was to standardize sentencing practices so that offenders with similar legal variables received similar sentences, the effect has been an increased length of incarceration sentences for both men and women. Given the inability of judicial officials to consider extralegal factors in making sentencing decisions, these efforts to equalize sentencing practices have significantly affected women.

International Perspectives on the Processing of Female Offenders

While women in the United States have seen significant progress toward equality over the past century, research on gender and criminal justice processing indicate that women still experience gender bias. Here, women either positively benefit from chivalrous treatment or are penalized in part by their gender and receive harsher punishments. Given these experiences throughout the United States, how do women fare in criminal justice systems in other regions of the world, particularly in countries with significant paternalistic views toward women?

China is one example where the paternalistic treatment of women is integrated within the cultural viewpoint. Women are considered as subordinate members of society. As a result, the legal system may treat women with "kid gloves." This need to protect women can potentially lead to reductions in punishment. As women's participation in criminal activity increases, the legal system is faced with how to respond to these cases. In China, there has been a documented increase in the number of women involved in drug possession and trafficking cases. Research by Liang, Lu, and Taylor (2009) indicates that female drug traffickers received significantly lower punishments than their male counterparts. In addition, women benefit from chivalrous treatments, even in cases where their offenses and criminal history were similar to

▲ **Photo 9.1** Amanda Knox reacts after hearing the verdict during her appeal in Perugia on October 3, 2011. The Court of Cassation (Italy's highest court) cleared 24-year-old American Knox and her former boyfriend Raffaele Sollecito of the 2007 murder of British student Meredith Kercher and ordered they be freed after nearly four years in prison. One of the many motives presented by prosecutors argued that Kercher was murdered as part of an orgy gone wrong with Knox and Sollecito. Stories of Knox's sexuality were frequently used in headlines about the case.

male drug traffickers. The most important variable in these cases was the woman's behavior before the court—if the offender was remorseful about her actions and showed respect to the court, she received a more lenient sentence. However, chivalry was extended only to lower-level offenders. In cases where the woman was facing a potential death sentence, the desire for equality between men and women overpowered any influence of patriarchy. The offender's demeanor is an important variable for South Taiwanese women as well. If a female defendant demonstrates a submissive and apologetic demeanor toward the judge, she benefits from leniency in her punishment. To a certain extent, the demeanor of the defendant is just as important as the offense type or the criminal history of the offender (Hsu & Wu, 2011).

Women in South Korea also benefit from chivalry in sentencing. Female offenders are less likely to be sent to prison and have received significantly shorter sentences compared to male offenders. In addition, offenders who had a prior criminal history and were detained at the pretrial stage received significantly harsher punishments. This practice echoes many of the findings with women in the American justice system. Drug of choice also has a significant impact on sentence outcomes. While cases involving methamphetamines received harsher punishments compared to marijuana cases (a likely response given stricter legal directives), female offenders were more likely to experience chivalrous treatment in terms of the length of sentence that is handed down, because male offenders received a longer sentence of incarceration than women.

However, chivalry may not be extended to all women. Research on sentencing practices in Australia looks at whether indigenous women receive preferential treatment by the courts. The term *indigenous* refers to a minority group that typifies the early inhabitants of a region. For example, we would identify *Native Americans* as an indigenous group in the United States. In Australia, a person who identifies as indigenous is of either aboriginal or Torres Strait Islander origin. Research by Bond & Jeffries (2012) finds that women of indigenous status do receive preferential treatment by justice officials. In these cases, justice officials appear to consider how unique extralegal variables within these communities (such as the presence of trauma in early childhood and the marginalization of their cultural identity) may have a significant effect on their offending behaviors. These findings suggest that judicial officials weigh the risk that indigenous offenders pose to the community in comparison to the potential consequences that incarcerating indigenous persons for a significant period of time can have for these communities (Bond & Jeffries, 2009, 2012).

Unlike these examples where chivalry can benefit women in certain cases, women in Finland do not benefit from preferential treatment by justice officials. Whereas in many of the jurisdictions where chivalry can have an impact, Finland is much more progressive in policies and practices, and there are greater levels of gender equality between men and women throughout the workplace and home. For example, Finnish family-leave policies are more generous than those in the United States, which has created increased opportunities for mothers to participate in the labor force. Women are also more likely to be active in the political realm in Finland compared to women in the United States. These examples of gender equality have also translated to the criminal justice system, where women and men are considered equal under the law. Gender appears to have no significant effect on sentencing decisions, controlling for legal variables (such as criminal history and crime severity) and social factors (such as employment and family status; Kruttschnitt & Savolainen, 2009).

Conclusion

This chapter reviewed how and when preferential treatment is extended to female offenders. Whether chivalry exists within the criminal justice system is not an easy question to answer, because it is dependent on the stage of the criminal justice system, the intersections of race and ethnicity, legal and extralegal factors, and the implementation of determinate sentencing structures. Even in cases where research suggests that chivalrous treatment serves women through shorter sentences and an increased likelihood to sentence offenders to community-based sanctions over incarceration, not all scholars see this preferential treatment as a positive asset for women. For many, the presence of chivalry is also linked to these gender-role expectations whereby "preferential or punitive treatment is meted out based on the degree to which court actors perceive a female defendant as fitting the stereotype of either a good or bad woman" (Griffin & Wooldredge, 2006, p. 896). Not only does the potential for women to be punished for breaking gender role expectations exist (i.e., the evil woman hypothesis) but there exists as well a double-edged sword in fighting for special treatment models. Gender equality does not necessarily mean "sameness." Rather, this perspective suggests that women possess cultural and biological differences that should be considered in determining the effects of "justice." However, there is a potential danger in treating women differently as a result of these cultural and biological indicators. Given that the law affords reductions in sentencing based on mental capacity and age (juvenile offenders), to extend this treatment toward women can suggest that women "cannot be expected to conform their behavior to the norms of the law . . . thus when women are granted special treatment, they are reduced to the moral status of infants" (Nagel & Johnson, 2004, p. 208).

SUMMARY

- Generally speaking, women are more likely to be released during pretrial stages, receive charge reductions, and receive a jail or probation supervision sentence.

- When women are incarcerated, they typically receive shorter sentences compared to men.

- Research on race and gender is mixed, with some studies indicating that women of color are treated more harshly than Whites, and other researchers finding that women of color are treated in a more lenient fashion.

- Legal factors, such as criminal history and offense type, affect the processing of women.

- Extralegal factors, such as the type of attorney and family status, can affect the likelihood of pretrial release for women.

- Sentencing guidelines have significantly increased the number of women serving time in U.S. prisons.

KEY TERMS

Chivalry 375

Evil woman hypothesis 375

Extralegal factors 379

Legal factors 379

Sentencing guidelines 378

DISCUSSION QUESTIONS

1. Why is it important to study the processing of female offenders at each stage of the criminal justice system, versus just during the final disposition?

2. How do prosecutors and judges use their discretion to give preferential or chivalrous treatment toward women?

3. Which legal and extralegal factors appear to have the greatest impact on the processing of females? Which variables indicate preferential treatment of women in unexpected ways?

4. How do women in foreign countries benefit from chivalrous treatment?

> online resources Visit **study.sagepub.com/mallicoat3e** to access additional study tools, including eFlashcards, web quizzes, web resources, video resources, and SAGE journal articles.

READING /// 17

As you learned in the section introduction, gender can affect the sentencing decisions of females, often resulting in preferential treatment of female offenders. However, the majority of research on the issue of chivalry is conducted at the sentencing stage, after women may have already benefited from chivalrous treatment throughout the justice process. This reading explores whether women receive preferential treatment during the pretrial stage. The authors explore whether gender and race affect the decision to use preventive detention for offenders.

The Impact of Race, Gender, and Age on the Pretrial Decision

Tina L. Freiburger and Carly M. Hilinski

The majority of sentencing literature has examined the final sentencing decision (i.e., the in/out decision) and the sentence length. Few studies have examined earlier decision-making points in the judicial system, such as the pretrial release outcome. Because of this, advancements in final sentencing literature have not extended to pretrial release research. Most notably, the examination of race, gender, and age interactions has not been examined in the pretrial release research. Using the focal concerns perspective, the current research addresses this gap by examining how race, gender, and age affect defendants' odds of pretrial detention.

Instead of focusing solely on race or gender, current sentencing research has carefully examined how courtroom experiences vary across different race and gender combinations. The development of the focal concerns perspective by Steffensmeier et al. (Steffensmeier, 1980; Steffensmeier, Kramer, & Streifel, 1993; Steffensmeier, Ulmer, & Kramer, 1998) has greatly contributed to this line of sentencing research. The focal concerns perspective comprises the three focal concerns

of blameworthiness, dangerousness, and practical constraints. Blameworthiness is largely determined by the legal factors of offense severity and prior record. Dangerousness is determined by variables such as offense type (e.g., personal, property, or drug), use of a weapon, and education and employment status of the defendant. Practical constraints consist of factors that influence a defendant's ability to serve a period of incarceration, including organizational factors such as jail space and case flow as well as individual factors such as familial responsibilities (e.g., child care duties and marital status).

According to focal concerns theory, it is through these three focal concerns that judges make their sentencing decisions. However, when judges make sentencing decisions, they must often do so with limited information and with limited time and do not have access to all of the information included in each of the three focal concerns. Thus, the demographic characteristics of an offender are often used to shape the three focal concerns. Certain demographic combinations, specifically age, gender, and

SOURCE: Freiburger, T. L., & Hilinski, C. M. (2010). The impact of race, gender, and age on the pretrial decision. *Criminal Justice Review, 35*(3), 318–334.

race, are especially influential, as judges tend to view younger minority males as more dangerous and more blameworthy, leading to harsher sentences for these individuals (e.g., Spohn & Beichner, 2000; Steffensmeier & Demuth, 2006; Steffensmeier, Kramer et al., 1993; Steffensmeier, Ulmer et al., 1998).

Current research examining these interactions has supported the focal concerns perspective. Specifically, this research has found that both Black and White females are treated more leniently than males (e.g., Freiburger & Hilinski, 2009; Steffensmeier & Demuth, 2006) and that Black males are sentenced more harshly than White males (e.g., Albonetti, 1997; Steffensmeier & Demuth, 2006; Steffensmeier, Ulmer et al., 1998). Research specifically focusing on the treatment of females, however, has been more mixed, with some studies finding that Black females are treated more leniently than White females (e.g., Bickle & Peterson, 1991; Spohn & Beichner, 2000; Steffensmeier & Demuth, 2006) whereas others have found the opposite (Crawford, 2000; Steffensmeier, Ulmer et al., 1998).

Prior sentencing studies also have found that age has varying impacts on the sentences of males and females and Black and White defendants (Steffensmeier, Ulmer et al., 1998). The results here also are mixed, with several studies finding that young Black men are treated most harshly (Spohn & Holleran, 2000; Steffensmeier, Ulmer et al., 1998) and others finding that middle-aged Black men are treated most harshly (Freiburger & Hilinski, 2009; Harrington & Spohn, 2007). Despite the numerous studies examining the impact of race, gender, and age on sentencing decisions, no studies have been conducted that examined the impact of gender, race, and age interactions on early court decisions. The current research fills this gap by examining how these three factors interact to affect the pretrial release decision.

Literature Review

The pretrial release decision is a crucial point in the judicial system. A common finding in the final sentencing research is that the pretrial release status of a defendant is significantly correlated with their [the individual's] likelihood of incarceration; offenders who are detained have a greater chance of receiving a sentence of incarceration (see Freiburger & Hilinski, 2009; Spohn & Beichner, 2000;

Steffensmeier & Demuth, 2006). There is also less scrutiny on the pretrial release decision, which allows judges a great deal of discretion. This has led some researchers to argue that it might actually be subject to more bias in judicial decision making (Hagan, 1974; Steffensmeier, 1980). Pretrial detention can further negatively affect defendants' final sentences by hindering their ability to participate in the preparation of their defense (Foote, 1954). Despite these findings illustrating the importance and significance of the pretrial decision, few studies have been conducted to examine the factors that affect this decision.

Race and Pretrial Release

The majority of research examining the effects of race on pretrial release decisions has found that White defendants receive greater leniency at this stage than Black defendants (Demuth, 2003; Katz & Spohn, 1995). Demuth (2003) and Katz and Spohn (1995) found that Black defendants were less likely to be released than White defendants. Although these studies failed to find a significant relationship between race and bail amount for both White and Black defendants, Demuth found that Black defendants were less likely to make bail. Furthermore, Demuth found that Black defendants were significantly more likely to be ordered to detention (denied bail). No race difference was found, however, for Black and White defendants' odds of receiving a nonfinancial release (release on recognizance [ROR]) rather than bail.

Other studies examining slightly different outcome measures have produced evidence to suggest White defendants are granted greater leniency in pretrial release. Patterson and Lynch (1991) found that non-White defendants were less likely than White defendants to receive bail amounts that were lower than the amount recommended by bail guidelines. However, they also found that White and non-White defendants were equally likely to receive bail amounts that were more than the amount recommended by bail guidelines. Albonetti (1989) did not find a direct race effect, though she did find that White defendants were less likely to be detained if they had higher levels of educational attainment and a higher income. White defendants' outcomes, however, were more negatively affected by increases in the severity of the offense.

Gender and Pretrial Release

Few studies have been conducted that examine the effect of gender on pretrial release and outcome. Overall, the studies that have examined this relationship have found that females were treated more leniently than male defendants. Daly (1987b) and Kruttschnitt and Green (1984) found that females were less likely to be detained prior to trial. Additional studies have found that females were more likely to be granted a nonfinancial release (Nagel, 1983) and be assigned lower bail amounts (Kruttschnitt, 1984). Unfortunately, no recent studies were located that focused solely on the effect of gender on pretrial release.

Race-Gender-Age Effects and Pretrial Release

Only one study has examined the interactions of race/ethnicity and gender. Demuth and Steffensmeier (2004) analyzed data from felony defendants in 75 of the most populous counties in state courts for the years 1990, 1992, 1994, and 1996. Their results indicated that race and gender significantly affected whether defendants were released prior to trial. More specifically, females were more likely to be released than males, and White defendants were more likely to be released than Black and Hispanic defendants. Although females experienced leniency at every decision point (they were less likely to be detained due to failure to make bail or ordered to detention, more likely to secure nonfinancial release, and receive lower bail), the findings for race were more mixed across the different decision points. Blacks were more likely to be detained than White defendants, but Black and White defendants were equally likely to be ordered to detention (not granted bail) and be given a nonfinancial release. Demuth and Steffensmeier (2004) also found that there was no difference in the amount of bail assigned to Black and White offenders. It appeared, therefore, that the race effect was due to Black defendants' failure to post bail.

When race and gender interactions were examined, female defendants were less likely to be detained than their male counterparts across all racial and ethnic groups. The gender gap, however, was the smallest for White defendants (followed by Black defendants and Hispanic defendants).

According to categorical gender/race variables, the results further indicated that White women were the least likely to be detained, followed by Black women, Hispanic women, White men, Black men, and Hispanic men.

We were not able to locate any studies that examined the interactions of race, gender, and age on pretrial release; however, prior sentencing studies have examined the interacting effects of these factors on the final sentencing decisions. The findings of these studies are mixed. Steffensmeier, Ulmer et al. (1998) found that young offenders were more likely to be sentenced to incarceration, with young Black males being treated the most harshly. In their examination of sentencing decisions in Chicago, Miami, and Kansas City, Spohn and Holleran (2000) found that offenders aged 20–29 received the harshest sentences. When age and race were examined, they found that young and middle-aged Black males were more likely to be incarcerated than middle-aged White defendants. In Kansas City, young Black and White males had higher odds of incarceration than middle-aged White males.

Harrington and Spohn (2007) found that Black males in the middle age (30–39) category were less likely than White males of all age groups to be sentenced to probation versus jail. When the decision to sentence an offender to prison instead of jail was examined, however, the opposite was found. White males of all ages were more likely than middle-aged Black men to receive a prison sentence. Freiburger and Hilinski (2009) found that being young benefited White males but resulted in harsher sentences for Black males. Older Black males were only granted leniency in the decision to incarcerate in jail rather than prison. For Black females, age was not a significant predictor of sentencing. Young White women, however, were treated more leniently in the decision to sentence to probation or jail.

Previous studies that have examined the influence of race and gender on pretrial release decisions have failed to consider factors that are likely to influence release decisions. When judges make pretrial release decisions, they are typically concerned with the level of risk the offender poses to the community and the likelihood that the offender will return to court for future appearances (Goldkamp & Gottfredson, 1979). Although prior record and offense severity are important factors that judges consider in this stage, other factors such as marital status, education, community ties, and employment also are used to assess these concerns (Goldkamp & Gottfredson, 1979; Nagel, 1983; Petee, 1994; Walker, 1993). In addition, the focal concerns perspective notes these factors as influential to the focal concern of dangerousness (Steffensmeier, Ulmer et al., 1998). The only previous study that examined race and gender interactions (Demuth & Steffenmeiser, 2004) did not assess the impact of these important factors. Additionally, no studies have examined the interactions of race, gender, and age on the pretrial release decision despite the fact that judges are differently influenced by these various combinations. Thus, the current study builds on the previous research by examining the effect of race, gender, and age interactions on pretrial release outcomes while considering other factors (e.g., income, education, and marital status) that have been linked to the pretrial release decision and the focal concerns perspective.

Methods

The current study examined the effects of race, gender, and age on the pretrial detention outcomes of felony offenders in an urban county in Michigan. The data analyzed contain information collected from presentence investigation reports completed for all offenders convicted of a personal, drug, property, or public order offense in the county during 2006. The original data set contained 3,316 offenders. We removed defendants who were Hispanic or of another ethnicity ($N = 73$) from the data set because a meaningful analysis was not possible with such a small number of cases; cases that were missing important information pertaining to offense severity level and prior record level ($N = 608$) also were removed from the data set because it was necessary to include these variables in sentencing research.[1] Thus, the final data set contained 2,635 cases.

Dependent Variable

The dependent variable in the current study was a dichotomized measure of the actual pretrial outcome, with 0 representing "defendants released prior to sentencing" and 1 representing those "detained prior to

sentencing." Coding for this variable, and all independent variables, is included in Reading Table 17.1. Although we agree with prior research that argues that the pretrial release is best assessed through the examination of both the judicial decision and the actual outcome (see arguments by Demuth, 2003 and Demuth & Steffensmeier, 2004), the current data only allow for the assessment of the actual pretrial outcome (whether the defendant was detained or released). This is considered a limitation of the current study; however, the pretrial outcome is the most telling of the decision points. It signifies the actual experience of the defendant by considering the consequences of pretrial detention (e.g., reduced ability to prepare defense and severed social ties due to incarceration). Despite this limitation, the ability to assess race, gender, and age interactions while including other facts relevant to pretrial release contributes substantially to the current literature.

Independent Variables

Several legal variables shown to be relevant in sentencing decisions were included in the analysis. The Michigan Statutory Sentencing Guideline's 6-point offense severity measure was used to control for the seriousness of the crime.[2] The state guideline's 7-point measure of prior record also was used.[3] The analysis also controlled for offense type through four separate dummy variables (property, drug, personal, and public order offense), with personal crimes left out as the reference category. A dummy variable also was included for current criminal justice supervision. Those who were on probation, parole, or incarcerated at the time of the bail decision were considered under criminal justice supervision and were coded as 1.[4]

The main extralegal variables of interest (gender, race, and age) also were included in the analysis. Gender was included and coded as 0 for female and 1 for male and race was coded as 0 for White and 1 for Black. Because age was found to have a curvilinear effect on pretrial detention, it was entered into the models as three categorical variables. As in prior research (Freiburger & Hilinski, 2009; Harrington & Spohn, 2007), the three age categories created were 15–29, 30–39, and 40+ years, with 30–39 being left out of the analysis as the reference variable.

Several other variables that measured defendants' stability in the community also were included in the models. These variables were important in assessing the focal concerns perspective as these factors have been theorized by Steffensmeier and colleagues (Steffensmeier, 1980; Steffensmeier, Kramer et al., 1993; Steffensmeier, Ulmer et al., 1998) to affect judges' perceptions of dangerousness. None of the defendants in the sample had a college education; therefore, education was entered as a dichotomous variable of high school education or General Education Diploma (GED) coded as 1 or no high school education

coded 0. Marital status also was included as a dummy variable; those who were not married were coded as 0 and those who were married were coded as 1. A direct employment measure was not available; however, two income variables were recorded in the presentence investigation (PSI) reports and were included in the analysis. The first assessed whether the defendant had an income of $75 or more a month (0 = no income above $75 and 1 = income above $75). The second variable indicated whether the defendant had assets of $1,500 or more (0 = no assets totaling $1,500 and 1 = assets totaling $1,500 or more).

Reading Table 17.1 • Description of Variables

Independent Variable	Description
Individual characteristics	
Age	Separate dummy variables for ages 15–29, 30–39, and 40+; age 30–39 is the reference category
Race	Black = 1, White = 0
Gender	Male = 1, Female = 0
Marital status	Married = 1, Not married = 0
High school (HS)	HS diploma/GED = 1, No HS diploma/GED = 0
Income over $75/month	Income over $75/month = 1, income less than $75/month = 0
Assets over $1,500	Assets over $1,500 = 1, assets < $1,500 = 0
Case characteristics	
Prior record variable (PRV)	7-category scale (1 = least serious, 7 = most serious)
Offense variable (OV)	6-category scale (1 = least serious, 6 = most serious)
Type of conviction charge	Separate dummy variables for property offense, public order offense, personal offense, and drug offense; personal offense is the reference category
CJS supervision	CJS supervision (probation, parole, incarceration) = 1, No CJS supervision = 0
Dependent variable	
Pretrial detention	Detention = 1, Release = 0

NOTE: CJS = Criminal Justice System supervision.

a. None of the cases in the current data set had a prior record score of 7.

Results

The individual and case characteristics of the offenders included in the current research are presented in Reading Table 17.2. The majority of both male and female offenders were 15–29 years of age. Both male and female offenders were more likely to be White, unmarried, and without a high school diploma. Further examination of the descriptive statistics reveals that over half of the females had a monthly income over $75 but less than 40% of the males earned more than $75 per month. Across both males and females, only about 15% had assets that were worth $1,500 or more. Case characteristics reveal that male offenders were charged most often with a personal offense, but female offenders were most often charged with a property offense. Males were also more likely to be under some form of criminal justice supervision at the time of the current offense. Finally, both men and women were more likely to be released prior to trial.

We estimated the effect of race, gender, and age on pretrial release, using logistic regression models. First the effects of race, gender, and age were examined separately. The models were then split by gender and race; z scores also were calculated to determine whether the independent variables had a significantly different effect on the pretrial outcome for male and female and Black and White defendants. The final models contain categorical variables for gender and race and categorical variables for race, gender, and age combinations.

The logistic regression coefficients for pretrial detention are presented in Reading Table 17.3. Four models are presented. The first model presented displays the effects of age, race, and gender without the inclusion of any other independent variables. In this model, gender, race, and both age variables are significant. The variable for gender indicates males have a significantly greater likelihood of being detained than females. Black defendants had a significantly greater likelihood of detention than White defendants. The age variables show that young defendants and older defendants were less likely to be detained than offenders 30–39. Model 2 shows the coefficients after the income variables are controlled. Although the gender and age variables remain significant, race is no longer significant. When the legal variables are added in Model 3, the gender, age, and income variables remain significant. Race, however, is not significant. Therefore, it appears that the initial effect of race was due in part to differences in the financial capabilities of Black and White defendants.

The full model also is presented in Reading Table 17.3 and contains all of the independent variables. As shown in the table, males were significantly more likely to remain detained than females; however, the coefficient for race was not significant. Young defendants and older defendants were less likely to be detained than defendants in the middle age category. Completing high school or obtaining a GED further resulted in a lower likelihood of being detained. Both income variables also were significant, indicating that defendants with an income over $75 a month and assets exceeding $1,500 were less likely to be detained.

In an attempt to garner a better understanding of the differences in the detention status of male and female defendants, we estimated split models to determine whether the same factors influenced the pretrial status of both groups. The results of this analysis are presented in Reading Table 17.4. Examination of the female model shows that race was significant in the pretrial status for females with Black female defendants having reduced odds of being detained compared to White females. Race did not, however, significantly affect the pretrial release status of males. The z score for race also was significant, indicating that the effect of race was significantly stronger for females than males. The coefficients for age indicate that young males were significantly less likely to be detained than males aged 30–39. Neither the age coefficient for females nor the z score for females was significant. Thus, the impact of age was not significantly different for males and females.

Further examination of the split models indicates that males and females ($b = .716, p < .01$) had an increased odds of detention with each increase in prior record severity. The z score reveals that prior record did not have a significantly greater impact on the pretrial release of males than females; however, it came very close to reaching significance. Severity of offense, conversely, was significant for males but not for females. The z score reveals that the difference was significant for males and females, with offense severity more strongly affecting males' pretrial detention status. Committing a property crime (compared to committing a personal crime) resulted in a decreased likelihood of being detained for females but not for males. The z score was significant, indicating that the differing effect was significant. The coefficient for drug offense was significant for both males and females. The z score also was significant, suggesting that committing a drug offense had a stronger impact for females than for males.

Reading Table 17.2 • Descriptive Statistics

	Total (n = 2635)		Males (n = 2187)		Females (n = 448)	
	n	Percentage	n	Percentage	n	Percentage
Individual characteristics						
Age						
15–29	1,397	53.0	1,184	54.1	213	47.5
30–39	597	22.7	480	21.9	117	26.1
40+	641	24.3	523	23.9	118	26.3
Race						
White	1,421	53.9	1,139	52.1	282	62.9
Black	1,214	46.1	1,048	47.9	166	37.1
Gender						
Male	2,187	83.0	–	–	–	–
Female	448	17.0	–	–	–	–
Marital status						
Married	289	11.0	237	10.8	52	11.6
Not married	2,346	89.0	1,950	89.2	396	88.4
High school (HS)						
HS diploma/GED	1,277	48.5	1,070	48.8	207	46.2
No HS diploma/GED	1,358	51.5	1,117	51.1	241	53.8
Income over $75/month						
Yes	1,081	41.0	835	38.2	246	54.9
No	1,554	59.0	1,352	61.8	202	45.1
Assets over $1500						
Yes	382	14.5	314	14.4	68	15.2
No	2,253	85.5	1,873	85.6	380	84.8

	Total (n = 2635)		Males (n = 2187)		Females (n = 448)	
	n	Percentage	n	Percentage	n	Percentage
Case characteristics						
Prior record						
1	431	16.4	322	14.7	109	24.3
2	369	14.0	278	12.7	91	20.3
3	571	21.7	469	21.4	102	22.8
4	613	23.3	525	24.0	88	19.6
5	370	14.0	323	14.8	47	10.5
6	281	10.7	270	12.3	11	2.5
Offense severity						
1	1,323	50.2	1,081	49.4	242	54.0
2	812	30.8	672	30.7	140	31.3
3	298	11.3	245	11.2	53	11.8
4	98	3.7	88	4.0	10	2.2
5	70	2.7	69	3.2	1	0.2
6	34	1.3	32	1.5	2	0.4
Conviction charge						
Property offense	805	30.6	580	26.5	225	50.2
Public order offense	190	7.2	140	6.4	50	11.2
Personal offense	963	36.5	871	39.8	92	20.5
Drug offense	677	25.7	596	27.3	81	18.1
CJS supervision						
Supervision	912	34.6	774	64.6	138	30.8
No supervision	1,723	65.4	1,413	35.4	310	69.2
Pretrial detention						
Detained	960	36.4	866	39.6	94	21.0
Not detained	1,675	63.6	1,321	60.4	354	79.0

Reading Table 17.3 • Logistic Regression Estimates

Variable	Model 1			Model 2			Model 3			Full Model		
	B	SE	Exp(B)	B	SE	Exp (B)	B	SE	Exp (B)	B	SE	Exp (B)
Offender characteristics												
Age 15–29	−.467**	.102	.627	−.664**	.110	.515	−.341**	.122	.711	−.422**	.125	.656
Age 40+	−.371**	.119	.690	−.254*	.128	.776	−.259*	.139	.772	−.253**	.139	.776
Race (Black = 1)	.253**	.083	1.288	.010	.089	1.010	−.172	.102	.842	−.184	.102	.832
Gender (male = 1)	.909**	.125	2.482	.832**	.132	2.297	.533**	.146	1.705	.565**	.147	1.760
Marital status										−.270	.175	.764
High school										−.287**	.099	.750
Income over $75				−1.292**	.097	.275	−1.087**	.104	.337	−1.072**	.104	.342
Assets over $1,500				−1.255**	.164	.285	−1.056**	.176	.348	−.970**	.179	.379
Case characteristics												
Prior record							.456**	.039	1.578	.461**	.039	1.585
Offense severity							.194**	.048	1.214	.202**	.049	1.224
Property offense							−.542**	.126	.582	−.531**	.126	.588
Public order offense							−.276	.201	.758	−.266	.202	.588
Drug offense							−.530**	.134	.589	−.527**	.135	.590
CJS supervision							.733**	.103	2.082	.745**	.104	2.107
Constant	−1.116***	.138	.328	−.258*	.151	.773	−2.127**	.246	.119	−2.007**	.249	.134
Nagelkerke R²	.046			.193			.344			.348		
Cox and Snell R²	.034			.141			.251			.254		

SIGNIFICANCE: * $p < .05$; ** $p < .01$.

Reading Table 17.4 • Female and Male Split Models

Variable	Females			Males			z Score
	B	SE	Exp (B)	B	SE	Exp (B)	
Offender characteristics							
Age 15–29	−.072	.358	.931	−.461**	.135	.631	1.02
Age 40+	−.198	.377	.820	−.243	.151	.784	0.11
Race (Black = 1)	−.979**	.331	.376	−.090	.110	.913	2.55*
Marital status	−.854	.576	.426	−.191	.187	.826	1.09
High school	.137	.302	1.146	−.310**	.106	.733	1.40
Income over $75	−.898**	.296	.407	−1.072**	.112	.342	0.55
Assets over $1500	−.737	.589	.479	−.981**	.190	.375	0.39
Case characteristics							
Prior record	.716**	.139	2.047	.435**	.041	1.545	1.94
Offense severity	−.234	.206	.791	.234**	.051	1.264	2.21*
Property offense	1.531**	.392	.216	−.379	.135	.685	2.78*
Public order offense	−.223	.485	.800	−.553*	.237	.576	0.61
Drug offense	−1.556**	.512	.211	−.452**	.140	.636	2.08*
CJS supervision	.955*	.313	2.598	.723**	.111	2.061	0.70
Constant	−1.811*	.728	.163	−1.465	.241	.231	
Nagelkerke R^2	.423			.308			
Cox and Snell R^2	.272			.229			

$*p < .05; **p < .01.$

Discussion

The current study attempted to further the understanding of the effects of race, gender, and age on pretrial release outcomes. Given the logic of the focal concerns perspective (Steffensmeier, 1980; Steffensmeier, Kramer et al., 1993; Steffensmeier, Ulmer et al., 1998), it is not surprising that gender and age directly affect pretrial outcomes as females and young defendants are often viewed as less blameworthy and dangerous. The findings for race, however, were more complex. A strong race effect was found prior to entering the economic variables into the model, with Black defendants less likely to be released pretrial than Whites. Once these variables were included, however, race was no longer significant. In fact, the sign of the coefficient changed, suggesting Whites were actually more likely to be detained. Therefore, it appears that Black defendants are more likely to be detained because they do not have the financial means necessary to secure release. This indicates that Black disadvantage in the court system may not be as simple as racial bias but instead stems from inequality and general disadvantage in society. This is especially noteworthy because prior studies on pretrial releases have not included these variables (e.g., Demuth & Steffensmeier, 2004).

The effect of race was significant, however, in regard to the sentences of men and women separately. Consistent with prior research conducted by Demuth and Steffensmeier (2004), the results indicated that the gender gap was the smallest for White defendants. Even so, White females were not most likely to be released pretrial. Instead, Black females were the least likely to be detained. This finding held across Black females of every age group. The odds of release for White women, however, were not significantly different [from] that of White and Black males. Although Black females were less likely to be detained than White females, the age/race/gender analysis showed that this finding was only applicable to White females aged 30–39. Younger and older White females were not significantly more likely to be detained than their Black female counterparts. When compared to males (both Black and White), however, Black females of all age groups were the least likely to be detained.

Although these findings seem inconsistent with the focal concerns perspective, it is possible that this inconsistency is actually due to the absence of practical constraint factors. Steffensmeier and colleagues (Steffensmeier, 1980; Steffensmeier, Kramer et al., 1993; Steffensmeier, Ulmer et al., 1998) suggest that defendants whose incarceration poses a greater practical constraint (e.g., leaving behind dependent children that will require care, need correctional facilities that are not available) will be granted leniency. It is possible, therefore, that the inclusion of family responsibility variables might account for the increased odds of Black females being released. Daly (1987a) suggests that judges are concerned with the social costs of incarcerating defendants who perform vital familial responsibilities. This is especially pertinent, given that more Black women in the criminal justice system are often single parents to dependent children (U.S. Bureau of the Census [*2000 Census*], 2003). Furthermore, prior research on the effect of gender on pretrial release has shown that the inclusion of these controls reduces the gender gap (Daly, 1987b; Kruttschnitt & Green, 1984). Unfortunately, the data used for the

current study had a great deal of missing data for the measure of dependent children, making it impossible to assess this possibility.

The gender split models also show that judges give less consideration to legal factors for females than for men. This might indicate that judges find males with more serious offenses as posing a greater risk to society. Therefore, it is possible that legal factors play less of a role in shaping the focal concerns associated with early court decisions for women as [*sic*] they do for men. This finding indicates a need for additional studies that closely examine the different factors that affect males' and females' sentencing decisions. It is possible that judges' focal concerns for males and females are influenced by different factors. The inconsistencies across research studies also cause questions of the ability to generalize these findings and signify a need for future research that examines the impact of race, gender, and age on sentencing decisions in other jurisdictions.

Overall, the current study has made an important contribution to the literature examining the factors affecting the pretrial decision. Most notably, it is the only study to date that has examined the effect of race, gender, and age interactions on the pretrial release outcome of defendants while also considering extralegal factors, including income, educational attainment, and marital status. The current study is limited, however, in its examination of only one jurisdiction. Although this is not uncommon in the sentencing literature, it does pose a limitation as findings may vary across location. This study also is limited in its ability to measure the focal concern of practical constraint. It is likely that individual practical constraints (e.g., familial responsibility) as well as organizational constraints (e.g., available jail space) could have an effect on pretrial detention. Additionally, these constraints may have varying effects by race, gender, and age of the defendant.

Future research should assess the impacts of race after controlling for economic factors on a more comprehensive set of dependent variables (e.g., ROR or bail, bail amount, ability to make bail). This is especially important given the finding that the race effect was eliminated once economic variables were included in the analysis. In addition, Demuth (2003) found that Black defendants were less likely to post bail than White defendants. If a more comprehensive dependent variable is assessed, it can be determined whether the Black disadvantage is due to a difference in bail amounts. In other words, are Black defendants receiving higher bail amounts or are Blacks simply more often than Whites in situations where they cannot afford to pay bail? The ability to examine a dependent variable of this nature would greatly contribute to the understanding of the effect of race on the pretrial release.

//// DISCUSSION QUESTIONS

1. What impact does gender have on the decision to release an offender during the pretrial stage?

2. What impact does race have on the decision to release an offender during the pretrial stage?

3. What impact do race and gender have on the decision to release an offender during the pretrial stage?

Notes

1. Significance tests performed to determine whether any differences existed between the cases excluded from the data set due to missing data and the cases included in the final analysis indicated that there were some significant differences between the two groups (presented below). Two age groups, ages 15–29 and 40+, were significantly different across the two groups; race also was significantly different across the two groups. An examination of the remaining independent variables reveals that cases excluded due to missing information were less likely to have a high school diploma or GED, less likely to have a monthly income of $75 or more, and less likely to have assets of more than $1,500. They were also less likely to be under criminal justice system supervision at the time of their arrest and more likely to be detained prior to trial. Although the missing data pose a limitation to the research, it is not unique to this study; most sentencing literature is limited in the amount of usable data. For instance, Harrington and Spohn (2007) were only able to use 59% of the cases in their original data set, and Freiburger and Hilinski (2009) were only able to use 62.4% of the cases in their original data set. In the current study, nearly 80% of the cases in the original data set were able to be included in the final analysis.

2. Michigan Statutory Sentencing Guidelines assigns an offense variable (OV) to each offense. There are 19 possible offense variables that can be scored, including aggravated use of a weapon, physical or psychological injury to the victim, victim asportation or captivity, and criminal sexual penetration; the sentencing guidelines stipulate which variables will be scored based on the crime group of the current offense (e.g., crimes against a person, crimes against property, and crimes involving a controlled substance). Based on the crime group, each relevant variable is scored and then combined to create a total offense variable that ranges from 1 (least serious) to 6 (most serious;

Michigan Judicial Institute, 2007). This offense variable (coded 1–6) was included in each model to control for the severity of the offense.

3. The prior record variable is a composite score based on factors such as prior adult felony and misdemeanor convictions, prior juvenile felony and misdemeanor adjudications, and the offender's relationship with the criminal justice system at the time of the current offense (i.e., whether the offender is a probationer or parolee). For each of the seven prior record variables, a numerical score is assigned. The sum of these seven scores determines the offender's prior record level, which ranges from A (least serious) to F (most serious; Michigan Judicial Institute, 2007). This variable was recoded and included in the models (coded 1–6) to control for prior record.

4. Although it is likely that those who are incarcerated are more likely to be detained pretrial than those on probation or parole, only seven offenders in the sample were actually incarcerated in jail or in prison. Due to the small number, it was impossible to meaningfully assess this difference; therefore, they were combined with those on probation and parole.

References

Albonetti, C. A. (1989). Bail and judicial discretion in the District of Columbia. *Sociology and Social Research, 74,* 40–47.

Albonetti, C. A. (1997). Sentencing under the federal sentencing guidelines: Effects of defendant characteristics, guilty pleas and departures on sentencing outcomes for drug offenses, 1991–1992. *Law and Society Review, 31,* 789–822.

Bickle, G. S., & Peterson, R. D. (1991). The impact on gender-based family roles on criminal sentencing. *Social Problems, 38,* 372–394.

Crawford, C. (2000). Gender, race, and habitual offender sentencing in Florida. *Criminology, 38,* 263–280.

Daly, K. (1987a). Structure and practice of familial-based justice in a criminal court. *Law & Society Review, 21,* 267–290.

Daly, K. (1987b). Discrimination in the criminal courts: Family, gender, and the problem of equal treatment. *Social Forces, 66,* 152–175.

Demuth, S. (2003). Racial and ethnic differences in pretrial release decisions and outcomes: A comparison of Hispanic, Black, and White felony arrestees. *Criminology, 41,* 873–907.

Demuth, S., & Steffensmeier, D. (2004). The impact of gender and race-ethnicity in the pretrial release process. *Social Problems, 51,* 222–242.

Foote, C. (1954). *Compelling appearance in court: Administration of bail in Philadelphia.* Philadelphia, PA: Temple University Press.

Freiburger, T. L., & Hilinski, C. M. (2009, February 24). An examination of the interactions of race and gender on sentencing decisions using a trichotomous dependent variable. *Crime & Delinquency.* doi:10.1177/ 0011128708330178

Goldkamp, J. S., & Gottfredson, M. R. (1979). Bail decision making and pretrial detention: Surfacing judicial policy. *Law and Human Behavior, 3,* 227–249.

Hagan, J. (1974). Extra-legal attributes and criminal sentencing: An assessment of a sociological viewpoint. *Law and Society Review, 8,* 337–383.

Harrington, M. P., & Spohn, C. (2007). Defining sentence type: Further evidence against use of the total incarceration variable. *Journal of Research in Crime and Delinquency, 44,* 36–63.

Katz, C., & Spohn, C. (1995). The effect of race and gender on bail outcomes: Test of an interactive model. *American Journal of Criminal Justice, 19,* 161–184.

Kruttschnitt, C. (1984). Sex and criminal court dispositions: An unresolved controversy. *Journal of Research in Crime and Delinquency, 12*(3), 213–232.

Kruttschnitt, C., & Green, D. E. (1984). The sex-sanctioning issue: Is it history? *American Sociology Review, 49,* 541–551.

Michigan Judicial Institute. (2007). *Sentencing guidelines manual.* Retrieved from http://courts.michigan.gov/mji/resources/ sentencing-guide lines/sg.htm–srdanaly

Nagel, I. (1983). The legal/extra-legal controversy: Judicial decision in pretrial release. *Law and Society Review, 17,* 481–515.

Patterson, E., & Lynch, M. (1991). The biases of bail: Race effects on bail decisions. In M. J. Lynch & E. Britt Patterson (Eds.), *Race and criminal justice.* New York, NY: Harrow and Heston.

Petee, T. A. (1994). Recommended for release on recognizance: Factors affecting pretrial release recommendations. *Journal of Social Psychology, 134,* 375–382.

Spohn, C., & Beichner, D. (2000). Is preferential treatment of felony offenders a thing of the past? A multisite study of gender, race, and imprisonment. *Criminal Justice Policy Review, 11,* 149–184.

Spohn, C., & Holleran, D. (2000). The imprisonment penalty paid by young unemployed black and Hispanic male offenders. *Criminology, 38,* 281–306.

Steffensmeier, D. (1980). Assessing the impact of the women's movement on sex-based differences in the handling of adult criminal defendants. *Crime & Delinquency, 26,* 344–358.

Steffensmeier, D., & Demuth, S. (2006). Does gender modify the effects of race ethnicity on criminal sanctions? Sentences for male and female, White, Black, and Hispanic defendants. *Journal of Quantitative Criminology, 22,* 241–261.

Steffensmeier, D., Kramer, J., & Streifel, C. (1993). Gender and imprisonment decisions. *Criminology, 31,* 411–446.

Steffensmeier, D., Ulmer, J., & Kramer, J. (1998). The interaction of race, gender, and age in criminal sentencing: The punishment cost of being young, black, and male. *Criminology, 36,* 763–797.

U.S. Bureau of the Census. (2003). *2000 census of the population.* Washington, DC: U.S. Government Printing Office. Retrieved from http://www.factfinder.census.gov

Walker, S. (1993). *Taming the system: The control of discretion in criminal justice, 1950–1990.* New York, NY: Oxford University Press.

READING /// 18

Throughout this text, you have learned about the gender gap between male and female criminality. This section discussed some of the ways in which women are processed through the criminal justice system. This article uses federal data to assess the role that gender plays in sentencing practices and whether legal and extralegal variables impact male and female sentence outcomes.

Gender and Sentencing in the Federal Courts
Are Women Treated More Leniently?

Jill K. Doerner and Stephen Demuth

Federal sentencing guidelines are designed to encourage the uniform and proportional treatment of defendants based on legally relevant factors. A main goal of the guidelines is to produce fair and honest outcomes that minimize unwarranted disparities based on defendants' social characteristics. A large body of disparity research has developed over time and, not surprisingly given America's sordid racial history, the overwhelming majority of studies focus on racial and ethnic differences in sentencing outcomes (Demuth, 2002; Demuth & Steffensmeier, 2004; Spohn, 2000; Steffensmeier & Demuth, 2006). What has not been a strong focus of past research is an arguably more common, yet apparently less controversial, form of disparity based on gender.

Like a defendant's race, gender is considered to be an extralegal factor in decision making at the sentencing stage. However, there are at least three factors that might explain both the persistence of gender disparities in sentencing despite guidelines designed to curtail them and a diminished concern for studying and remedying these disparate outcomes. First, unlike claims of racism in the application of laws and sanctions, there is no general presumption that women, the disadvantaged minority group, have historically been subjected to a consistent pattern of discrimination resulting in unwarranted harsher punishments (Nagel & Hagan, 1983). Second, in the context of

societal and court concerns about crime and public safety and given the known greater propensity for crime among men, women are viewed as better recidivism risks and more deserving of leniency than men (Spohn, 2002). Third, a major difference in the social lives of men and women is the level of responsibility in caring for family, or more specifically for their dependent children (Bickle & Peterson, 1991; Daly, 1987a, 1987b, 1989). This practical consideration might make the court reluctant to sentence women as harshly as men.

In sum, there is a tension in the guidelines between the goal of a gender-neutral implementation of the law emphasizing uniform treatment based on offense severity and criminal history and the realization that important differences exist between the lives of men and women that might create a need or desire for differential treatment (for a similar argument about race, see Tonry, 1996). In fact, the guidelines recognize this dilemma and provide limited ways for judges and prosecutors to take gender into account. For example, the guidelines allow for some discretion through the use of departures, which enable factors such as family ties and responsibilities to be considered. But, overall, unexplained gender disparities persist despite policy changes designed to minimize them. This suggests that reformers may have had unrealistic

SOURCE: Doerner, J. K., & Demuth, S. (2012). Gender and sentencing in the federal courts: Are women treated more leniently? *Criminal Justice Policy Review* *10*(10), 1–28.

expectations about the ability of guidelines to structure outcomes as intended (Spohn, 2000).

For all these reasons, an underdeveloped body of scholarship exists that addresses the topic of gender differences in sentencing. Much of this research is dated, having been published in the 1970s and 1980s using smaller state data sets or single city samples. Another shortcoming of many past studies is a lack of robust controls for legal case characteristics, such as offense seriousness and criminal history. Most importantly, past research tends to examine only whether sex differences exist at the sentencing stage and typically does not explore empirically how gender influences outcomes (for a review, see Chiricos & Crawford, 1995; Daly & Bordt, 1995). Researchers who examine gender and court processing tend to treat gender as a fixed attribute of individuals; however, work by Daly (1986, 1989, 1994) and Kruttschnitt (1984) explores how gender and patterned roles associated with gender can influence court decisions. That male defendants tend to commit more serious offenses and have more extensive criminal records than female defendants helps explain why men tend to receive harsher sentences than women (Bickle & Peterson, 1991; Daly, 1989, 1994; Daly & Bordt, 1995; Doerner & Demuth, 2010; Spohn, 2000, 2002; Steffensmeier, Kramer, & Streifel, 1993; Steffensmeier, Kramer, & Ulmer, 1995, 1998). But legal factors alone do not appear to fully explain the gender gap, and few studies have attempted to account for the remaining, often sizable, differences in sentence outcomes between men and women.

In the present study, we use data from the United States Sentencing Commission (USSC) to more fully explore the gender gap in federal sentencing and examine the various ways in which gender continues to influence outcomes even within a system of formal rules designed to minimize the impact of extralegal factors. We contribute to the gender and sentencing literature in several important ways. First, we use data that have rich and detailed measures of legal case characteristics. A concern in prior research was that weak or incomplete measures of offense seriousness and criminal history failed to adequately capture the real differences in offending between men and women and made the gender gap in sentencing outcomes look larger than it actually was. With more robust measures, we reduce the likelihood of finding a gender gap that is simply an artifact of model misspecification.

Second, we examine a series of nested regression models to determine not just if a gender gap in incarceration

and sentence length outcomes exists, but why. We begin by looking at the gender gap before accounting for differences in legal characteristics between men and women. Next, we control for legal differences to see how much gender differences in sentencing are explained by legal factors. Lastly, and most importantly, we examine the gender gap after adding controls for extralegal characteristics that are associated both with gender and sentencing outcomes: education, marital status, and the number of dependents for which the defendant is responsible. Much prior research tends to add all legal and extralegal variables to the model at the same time, making it difficult to compare the gender gap before and after controlling for legal factors. And central to our earlier criticism of existing gender-sentencing work is that most prior studies examine gender as a fixed attribute and do not attempt to address what aspects of gender influence sentencing. Building upon the research of Daly (1986, 1989, 1994) and Kruttschnitt (1984), we explore several gender-related possibilities.

Third, in addition to examining the main effect of gender, we examine whether legal and extralegal factors have different effects on sentencing outcomes for men and women. Most prior studies focus on the main effect of gender and do not consider the possibility that sentencing could be a gendered process. Prior research by Daly (1987a, 1987b, 1989) has shown that court personnel assumed gender divisions in the work and family responsibilities of familied defendants, and this resulted in differential outcomes during the sanctioning process. These court officials also viewed caretaking labor, most often provided by women, as more difficult to replace. In addition, Koons-Witt (2002) found that the interaction between gender and number of dependents was a significant predictor of incarceration decisions, with women with dependent children significantly more likely to be sentenced to sanctions within the community. Thus, we explore whether there are differences between men and women with respect to legal and extralegal factors.

Gender and Sentencing Literature

The treatment of women in the courts has not been static in the United States (Farrell, 2004). Historically, female offenders were less likely to be arrested and often sentenced more leniently than similarly situated male offenders. However, such judicial discretion has often been a double-edged sword for women. Rafter (1990) and colleagues (with Stanko, 1982) documented a dual system of punishment for female offenders during the middle of the 19th century. Women deemed "feminine" or "trainable" by the court were most often sent to reformatories, while women viewed as "bad" or "masculine" were subject to incarceration in penal institutions, often alongside male prisoners (Butler, 1997). Gendered sentencing laws at the turn of the 20th century still allowed judges to send women to prison for minor public order offenses (e.g., alcohol-related offenses, DUI, and prostitution) for which men were rarely even arrested (Rafter, 1990; Temin, 1980). Indeed, until the 1970s, state sentencing laws allowed judges to sentence women differently [from] men because female offenders were perceived to be more amenable to rehabilitation and would benefit from longer indeterminate sentences (Pollock-Byrne, 1990).

Currently, a fairly persistent finding in the sentencing literature is that female defendants are treated more leniently than male defendants (Bickle & Peterson, 1991; Daly & Bordt, 1995; Doerner & Demuth, 2010; Griffin & Wooldredge, 2006; Spohn, 2002; Steffensmeier et al., 1993); however, one study reported no gender differences (Kruttschnitt & Green, 1984). Doerner and Demuth (2010) showed that female defendants were significantly less likely to receive incarceration sentences than male defendants. The odds of incarceration for female defendants were approximately 42% lower than the odds of incarceration for male defendants. Griffin and Wooldredge (2006) found that female defendants in general were less likely than men to be sent to prison both before and after the sentencing reform efforts in Ohio and that the magnitude of this effect did not change significantly over time (.51 to .43 for men, and .38 to .34 for women). Spohn (2002) reported that the odds of receiving a prison sentence were 2.5 times greater for male offenders than for female offenders after controlling for legally relevant factors. Steffensmeier and Motivans (2000) found that female defendants were sentenced less harshly than male defendants—on average they were about 14% less likely to be incarcerated and received prison sentences about 7 months shorter. Similarly, previous research by Steffensmeier et al. (1993) indicated that gender, [and] net of other factors, had a small effect on the likelihood of imprisonment, with female defendants less likely to receive an incarcerative sentence than male defendants.

Even so, they found that gender had a negligible effect on sentence length outcomes.

According to Gruhl, Welch, and Spohn (1984), female defendants were treated more leniently than male defendants, based on a simple breakdown with no controls. Even though they plead[ed] guilty and were convicted at about the same rates as males, females were more likely to have their cases dismissed and were less likely to be incarcerated. When the authors controlled for legal and extralegal factors, significant gender differences remained for dismissal and incarceration, even though the difference between males and females was reduced somewhat.

In terms of gender, women are thought to be less dangerous, less blameworthy, less likely to recidivate, and more likely to be deterred than men (Spohn, 2002). Therefore, the more lenient sentences that are imposed on them might reflect the fact that judges believe them to possess these qualities more than men. According to Belknap (2001), studies consistently show that females generally commit fewer crimes than males but also tend to commit offenses that are less serious and violent in nature. However, [despite] net of case severity, charge severity, type of offense, prior record, and other defendant characteristics, male and female defendants were still treated differently on the basis of their ties to and responsibilities for others. Kruttschnitt (1984) found that controlling for gender-related statuses (i.e., being a wife or mother) mediated the length of probation sentences. In addition, she concluded that women were more likely than men to remain free, both prior to adjudication and after conviction, and that the determinants of these two decisions varied significantly with the offender's gender. Therefore, her analysis provided some insight into why females receive preferential treatment by criminal courtroom personnel.

Familial Responsibility Literature

It has long been observed that female defendants who are married or who have children receive greater leniency from the courts than their male or unmarried and childless female counterparts (Bickle & Peterson, 1991; Daly, 1987a, 1987b, 1989; Eaton, 1987; Farrington & Morris, 1983; Kruttschnitt & Green, 1984; Kruttschnitt & McCarthy, 1985; Simon, 1975). Early explanations of how and why gender-based family roles were important in judicial decision making focused on the impracticality of harsh sanctions for female offenders compared to their male counterparts (Bernstein, Cardascia, & Ross, 1979; Simon, 1975). More specifically, Simon (1975) reported that officials' accounts of gender differentials in sentencing in both New York (1963–1971) and California (1945–1972) emphasized that women have families, both husbands and children, to care for, and sending women to prison would seriously disrupt the family unit.

Kruttschnitt (1982a, 1984), along with her colleagues (with Green, 1984; with McCarthy, 1985) examined gender differentials in sanctioning, specifically pretrial release and sentencing outcomes, using data from Minnesota. In addition to gender, these analyses included either a composite measure of informal social control or one or more sex-based family role factors, including family/household composition, number of children, employment status, and sources of support. Overall, the findings from this research indicated that gender-based disparities were affected but not eliminated by including family role factors and that when composite measures of informal control were considered, there was little support for the claim that familial social control was a sex-specific determinant of criminal sanctioning.

In a more recent study of imprisonment decisions in Minnesota, Koons-Witt (2002) found that gender alone did not have a significant influence on sentence outcomes prior to the use of sentencing guidelines, but results indicated a significant interaction between gender and the presence of dependent children. The presence of dependent children for women significantly reduced their likelihood of going to prison. She also found that the interaction between gender and number of dependent children was a significant predictor of the incarceration decisions after sentencing guidelines were enacted. In this instance, women with dependent children were significantly more likely to be sentenced to a community sanction than were women without dependent children.

In her 1989 study, Daly found that a defendant's work–family relations affected the sentencing of both men and women. Furthermore, she reported that what defendants did for families, in terms of providing economic support or care for dependents, mattered to judges. Familied men and women (those with dependent children) were less likely to be detained pretrial, and they were less likely to receive the harsher types of nonjail sentences than childless men and women. In addition, the mitigating effect of being familied was stronger for women than men (Daly, 1987a). Furthermore, having dependents, whether in a marital context or

not, was generally the more determining feature of whether defendants receive lenient treatment. For men, being married without dependent children conferred no advantage at the pretrial release or the two sentencing decisions but having dependent children did. Married women, and especially those with dependent children, were accorded greater leniency at the pretrial release decision. In addition, at the sentencing stage, women with dependents received the most lenient sentences.

What appears to matter most for court personnel is whether defendants have day-to-day responsibilities for the welfare of others; such care or economic support can occur with or without a marital tie, and the specific form of care and economic support can vary by gender. In addition, the greater leniency accorded familied women than familied men stems from contemporary gender divisions in work and family life, specifically that women are more likely to care for others. The mitigating effects of family were found in both the pretrial release and nonjail sentencing decisions. Thus, familied defendants may be accorded leniency even when decisions do not center on a defendant's loss of liberty (Daly, 1987a).

Daly (1987b) found that court officials consistently drew on the categories of work and family in explaining why some defendants deserved leniency. One theme present was that defendants who provide economic support or care for others deserve more lenient treatment than those without such responsibilities. Leniency toward the familied defendants was therefore justified on the grounds that these defendants were more stable and have more to lose by getting into trouble again. Court personnel assume gender divisions in the work and family responsibilities of familied men and women.

These differences, combined with the family profiles of defendants, foster discrepancies in the treatment of familied men and familied women. In addition, officials often justified treating familied defendants more leniently because of the social costs of removing them and jeopardizing the family unit. Sex differentials in outcomes stem from the perceived differential responsibilities of females versus males. Officials viewed it as more costly or impractical to jail women with families than men with families because breadwinning support, usually provided by males, was more readily replaced than caretaking labor (Daly, 1987b).

Overall, research has shown that legal factors play a large role in the sentencing outcomes of male and female defendants, but even after controlling for characteristics like criminal history and offense severity, unexplained differences still persist. As a result, our understanding of why women are sentenced more leniently than men remains limited. In addition, research on familial responsibility indicates that having dependents (more specifically, dependent children) creates leniency at sentencing, especially for women. The present study sets out to explore how legal and extralegal factors play a role in the sentencing of male and female defendants, using data from the United States Sentencing Commission. We pay particular attention to whether characteristics such as education, marital status, and the presence of dependents help to explain the remaining gap in sentencing outcomes, as previous research in this area has discovered, after controlling for legally relevant variables outlined under the federal sentencing guidelines.

Theoretical Framework and Research Expectations

As previous research has shown, sentencing outcomes continue to be influenced by a host of extralegal factors, even with sentencing guidelines in place (Doerner & Demuth, 2010; Steffensmeier & Demuth, 2000; Steffensmeier et al., 1998; Ulmer, 1995). The focal concerns perspective developed by Steffensmeier (1980) serves as a framework for understanding why extralegal factors, such as gender, race/ethnicity, and age, might influence sentencing decisions, despite the implementation of formal guideline systems. The theory outlines three focal concerns that are important to judges and other criminal justice actors in reaching sentencing decisions: blameworthiness, protection of the community, and practical constraints and consequences. Grounded in research on organizational decision making, inequality and stratification, and criminal stereotyping, Steffensmeier and colleagues (with Kramer & Streifel, 1993; with Kramer & Ulmer, 1998) argue that defendant status characteristics may influence sentencing decisions insofar as stereotypes and behavioral expectations linked to these characteristics relate to the focal concerns of legal agents.

Blameworthiness follows the principle that sentences should depend on the offender's culpability and the degree of injury caused. The primary factors influencing perceptions of blameworthiness are legal factors, such as the seriousness of the offense, the defendant's criminal history or

prior victimization at the hands of others, and the defendant's role in the offense (Steffensmeier et al., 1998). Albonetti (1997) suggests that court officials attempt to achieve rational outcomes in the face of incomplete knowledge by relying on stereotypes that differentially link defendant groups to recidivism. Research by Daly (1994) indicates that judges, at least to some extent, share common beliefs portrayed by the media and are influenced by them in their sentencing decisions. In other words, when decisions have to be made quickly, judicial professionals may rely on limited resources to reach an outcome in the time available.

Protection of the community typically focuses on the need to incapacitate the offender or to deter future crime. Albonetti (1991) argues that sentencing is an arena of bounded rationality, in which court actors, particularly judges, confront the goal of protecting the public and preventing recidivism in the context of high uncertainty about offenders' future behavior. Judges' assessments of offenders' future behavior is often based on attributions predicated primarily on the nature of the offense and the offender's criminal history. However, these decisions may also be influenced by extralegal characteristics of the offender, such as gender, race/ethnicity, age, and socioeconomic status (SES). As mentioned previously, criminal justice professionals may give in to stereotypical notions as a means of making decisions more quickly, especially in the face of pressure from the media, victims' families, and members of the community.

Practical constraints and consequences relate to how sentencing decisions impact the functioning of the criminal justice system as well as the circumstances of individual defendants [and] their families and communities. Organizational concerns include maintaining working relationships among courtroom actors, ensuring the stable flow of cases, and being sensitive to local and state correctional crowding and resources (Dixon, 1995; Flemming, Nardulli, & Eisenstein, 1992; Steffensmeier et al., 1993, 1998; Ulmer, 1995; Ulmer & Kramer, 1996). Individual concerns include the offender's ability to do time, health conditions, special needs, the cost to the correctional system, and disruption to children and family (Daly, 1987a; Hogarth, 1971; Steffensmeier, 1980; Steffensmeier et al., 1995).

Expectations

Guided by the focal concerns perspective and the findings of past research on the effect of gender on sentencing outcomes, we develop several hypotheses for the present study to answer two research questions. First, can the gender gap in sentencing be explained by accounting for differences in legal and extralegal factors? Second, do legal and extralegal factors have the same impact for male and female defendants? Drawing on prior research, we expect to find that, on average, female defendants will receive more lenient sentences than male defendants (H1), and that this finding will hold true even after controlling for relevant legal and contextual factors (H2). In addition, we expect that defendants who have more education, more marital stability, and dependents will be afforded greater leniency than defendants who have less education, are single, or have no dependents (H3). Furthermore, we hypothesize that legal and extralegal factors will exert similar effects on sentencing outcomes for both male and female defendants (H4).

Data and Method

In the present study, we use data from three years (2001–2003) of the Monitoring of Federal Criminal Sentences program compiled by the USSC. The data include all cases received by the USSC that had sentencing dates between October 1, 2000, and September 30, 2003, and were assessed as constitutional (total = 194,521 cases). Data from the three years were combined to create one large data set, thus providing larger case sizes for both male and female defendant groups. These data are especially appropriate as they contain some of the richest and most detailed information available on cases at the sentencing stage. Many of the single-city or state-level data sets used in prior studies have lacked the large number of legal control variables found in the federal guidelines data. Having these variables available enabled a more adequate elimination of alternative explanations for extralegal effects on sentencing outcomes (e.g., Demuth & Steffensmeier, 2004; Spohn & Holleran, 2000). Furthermore, the federal sentencing guidelines provide a more rigid and conservative test of the impact of extralegal factors on sentencing outcomes.

For this analysis, we eliminate several defendant groups from the sample. First, noncitizens are deleted from the analysis. Federal sentencing of noncitizen defendants often differs greatly from sentencing of citizen defendants in many ways and, as a result, makes comparisons of sentencing outcomes between them difficult

(Demuth, 2002). For instance, a large proportion of noncitizen cases involve immigration violations. Furthermore, because noncitizens can be deported, the sentencing process for noncitizens is often qualitatively different (the goal being to send the defendant back to his or her country of origin and not to punish) from that of U.S. citizens. Finally, case information provided for noncitizens may be incomplete and this will most likely result in an underestimation of prior criminal history.

Second, defendants under the age of 18 are excluded from the analysis because their cases are substantively and legally different due to their juvenile status. Third, defendants who receive upward departures are deleted from the analysis as they comprised [*sic*] only 0.8% of departure cases and made comparisons across departure type very difficult. Fourth, using listwise deletion, all cases with missing information for all variables used in the analysis are deleted. Analyses were run predeletion and postdeletion of missing information and the elimination of these cases did not significantly change the overall results. The final analytic sample for the present study is 109,181.

Dependent Variables

The sentencing outcome is the result of a two-stage decision-making process: The decision to incarcerate and, once incarceration is selected, the sentence length decision (for discussion, see Spohn, 2002). In the present study, we use logistic regression to model the incarceration decision. The in/out decision variable is coded dichotomously, with 1 indicating a prison sentence and 0 indicating a nonincarceration sentence (e.g., probation, community service). The sentence length decision is modeled using ordinary least squares (OLS) regression and includes only those defendants who receive a prison sentence. Sentence length is a continuous variable representing the logged length of the prison sentence in months. Logging sentence length helps to normalize the distribution, and taking the antilog of the coefficient in the logged sentence length model provides a useful proportional interpretation. Sentence length is capped at 470 months. Any sentence length beyond that duration is considered to be life in prison.[1]

Extralegal Variables

Defendant gender is a dummy variable coded 1 if the defendant is female and 0 if the defendant is male. Race/

ethnicity is coded as four dummy variables: White non-Hispanic, Black non-Hispanic, Hispanic of any race, and Other.[2] Defendant age is a continuous variable representing the age of the defendant at the time of sentencing and ranges from 18 to 100. In this case, defendant age has been grouped in logical ranges consistent with Steffensmeier et al. (1998) and is coded as a series of dummy variables (18 to 20, 21 to 29, 30 to 39, 40 to 49, 50 to 59, and 60 and over).

Education level is coded as three dummy variables: less than high school, high school, and more than high school, with those who graduated high school as the reference category. Marital status is coded as six dummy variables: single, married, cohabiting, divorced, widowed, and separated. Those defendants who are single serve as the reference category. Number of dependents[3] is a continuous variable indicating responsibility of support by the defendant of their dependents. For the purposes of this study, number of dependents has been recoded into a dichotomous variable indicating that defendants either have no dependents or have one or more dependents.[4] Many studies have shown that female defendants that are married or have dependents receive greater leniency from the courts than their male or unmarried and childless female counterparts (Bickle & Peterson, 1991; Daly, 1987a, 1987b, 1989; Eaton, 1987; Farrington & Morris, 1983; Kruttschnitt & Green, 1984; Kruttschnitt & McCarthy, 1985; Simon, 1975). Having dependents, whether in a marital context or not, is generally the more determining feature of whether defendants receive lenient treatment. However, while the majority of prior research uses the terms "child or children," the present study uses "dependent" as the data do not specify what type of dependent the defendant is responsible for.

Legal Variables

Under the federal guidelines, federal judges retain discretion for sentencing individuals within the range determined by the offense level and criminal history of the offender. Sentence ranges are determined using a grid that takes these two variables into account, one on each axis. However, it has been argued (see Engen & Gainey, 2000) that a variable representing the presumptive guideline sentence, where criminal history and offense severity are combined into a single measure, is a more appropriate strategy and actually explains more of the variation in sentencing outcomes. This analytic strategy is also used by the USSC (2004). Therefore, we include a variable representing the guideline minimum sentence, in months. We also include a measure of criminal history, which ranges from 1 to 6 and indicates the final criminal history category of the defendant, as assigned by the court. According to Ulmer (2000), measures of offense severity and prior record have important main, curvilinear, and interactive influences on in/out and sentence length that cannot be reduced to the effect of presumptive sentence measures. This suggests that it is statistically and substantively important to include offense severity and prior record even if one is including a presumptive sentence measure. However, Ulmer also points out that including all three legally prescribed variables results in problematic multicollinearity in the OLS models of sentence length. As a result, an offense severity score variable is not included in the analysis because it is highly collinear with the guideline minimum sentence variable.

Case disposition is a dichotomous variable, which indicates whether the offender's case is settled by plea agreement or trial. It is coded 1 for trial and 0 for guilty plea. We also include a measure of multiple counts. A dummy variable is coded 0 for cases involving a single count and 1 for cases that involve multiple counts. The defendant's offense type (see Appendix for a complete breakdown of categories) is coded as four dummy variables: violent (i.e., murder, manslaughter, sexual abuse), drug (i.e., trafficking, simple possession), white-collar (i.e., fraud, embezzlement, bribery), and other (includes all other offenses in the federal data). Defendants committing other types of offenses serve as the reference group. The variable departure indicates the defendant's departure status. Departure status is dummy-coded into 3 categories: no departure (the reference), downward departure, and substantial assistance departure. Upward departure cases were deleted from the sample as they made up only 0.8% of the sample and deleting them does not significantly change the findings. The federal sentencing statutes include provisions that permit judges to depart either above or below the sentence prescribed by the guidelines. Judges may award these sentencing departures based on a legitimate reason if they feel the defendant does not deserve the sentence stated under the prescribed guidelines. Overall, however, the overwhelming direction of departures is downward.

The narrow range of factors that judges may consider when sentencing either above or below the prescribed guideline range makes the federal sentencing guidelines much more rigid than similar state structured sentencing systems (Farrell, 2004). Consequently, federal courts are prohibited from departing from the guidelines based on the race, gender, religion, or class of an individual defendant. However, the Sentencing Commission has deferred to the courts to interpret how extensively judges may use offender characteristics to justify departures from the guideline range.

Several control variables are also included in the models. Since multiple years of data were used in the present study, a dummy variable for each of the three years was constructed. Prior studies have indicated that judicial circuit, as well as other court contextual variables, may be important influences on sentencing outcomes (Peterson & Hagan, 1984; Steffensmeier & Demuth, 2000). One cause of disparities is that not all states or judicial circuits have implemented guidelines systems. The variable judicial circuit indicates the judicial circuit in which the defendant was sentenced. Judicial circuits are broken down into 11 categories, which were then made into dummy variables.

Results

In the present study, we analyze the data and present the results in several stages. In the first section, we present descriptive statistics for all variables used in the models (Reading Table 18.1). Second, we use logistic and OLS regression (including only those defendants who receive a prison sentence) to examine the independent effects of gender on incarceration and sentence length decisions (Reading Table 18.2) in three separate models. Third, we partition the full model by gender, examining the differential influence of legal and extralegal variables on sentencing outcomes of male and female defendants (Reading Table 18.3). It is important to note that the data set we use in the present study is not a sample. It includes the entire population of defendants sentenced in the federal courts during the period. Statistical tests of significance are not particularly meaningful in that there is no sampling error and no need to make inferences (Berk, 2010; Raftery, 1995). In our discussion of results, we focus mostly on the size and direction of coefficients, but nonetheless include indicators of significance ($p < .05$) in the tables.

Descriptive Statistics

Overall, men make up 83% of the sample. In terms of race, we found similar percentages in each racial category for both men and women. The plurality of defendants in the sample is White, approximately 44%, while 34% are Black and 18% are Hispanic. In terms of age, the largest portion of the sample fell in the 21 to 29 age range, followed closely by the 30 to 39 age range.

Looking at sentencing outcomes, a smaller percentage of women are incarcerated than men, with 85% of men receiving a prison sentence while only 62% of females in the sample are incarcerated. The sentence length gap for incarcerated defendants is also quite substantial between male and female defendants; male defendants receive sentence lengths of roughly 70 months, while female defendants are sentenced to approximately 34 months of incarceration. The average sentence length for the total sample falls close to that for male defendants (approximately 65 months).

These large differences in sentencing outcomes may be explained by both legal and extralegal factors. In terms of legal characteristics, male defendants have higher criminal histories, and they also receive higher recommended minimum guideline sentences than do female defendants due to the greater severity of the offenses committed by men. In addition, a higher percentage of male defendants are sentenced on multiple counts. Furthermore, a smaller percentage of female defendants go to trial. However, men and women receive sentencing departures at similar rates. A higher percentage of males commit violent, drug, and other offenses, while a higher percentage of females commit white-collar offenses.

Looking at extralegal factors that might be related to gender, a slightly higher percentage of female defendants have one or more dependents. More specifically, about 62% of female defendants have at least one dependent, compared to 59% for male defendants. Also, male defendants are more likely to be single than female defendants (46% vs. 40%), but female defendants are more likely to be divorced (14% vs. 11%) or separated (8% vs. 5%) than male defendants. Furthermore, a higher percentage of female defendants, roughly 6% more, have more than a high school education compared to their male defendant counterparts.

Reading Table 18.1 • Descriptive Statistics by Gender

Independent variables	Overall		Males		Females	
	N	Percentage	N	Percentage	N	Percentage
Gender						
Male	90,297	82.70	90,297	100	–	–
Female	18,884	17.30	–	–	18,884	100
Race						
White	48,003	43.97	39,568	43.82	8,435	44.67
Black	37,541	34.38	31,408	34.78	6,133	32.48
Hispanic	19,348	17.72	15,988	17.71	3,360	17.79
Other	4,289	3.93	3,333	3.69	956	5.06
Age						
18–20	5,427	4.97	4,516	5.00	911	4.82
21–29	37,777	34.60	31,455	34.84	6,322	33.48
30–39	32,702	29.95	26,950	29.85	5,752	30.46
40–49	20,305	18.60	16,427	18.19	3,878	20.54
50–59	9,537	8.74	8,000	8.86	1,537	8.14
60 & over	3,433	3.14	2,949	3.27	484	2.56
Legal variables						
Multiple counts	23,142	21.20	20,274	22.45	2,868	15.19
Trial	4,536	4.15	4,062	4.50	474	2.51
Prior criminal history (points)	2.40	–	2.57	–	1.60	–
Guideline minimum sentence (months)	58.92	–	65.11	–	29.33	–
Offense type						
Violent	6,092	5.58	5,609	6.21	483	2.56
Drug	48,688	44.59	41,626	46.10	7,062	37.40

(Continued)

Reading Table 18.1 • (Continued)

Independent variables	Overall		Males		Females	
	N	Percentage	N	Percentage	N	Percentage
White-collar	23,259	21.30	16,371	18.13	6,888	36.48
Other	31,142	28.52	26,691	29.56	4,451	23.57
Departures						
No departure	72,938	66.80	60,816	67.35	12,122	64.19
Downward departure	12,866	11.78	10,289	11.39	2,577	13.65
Substantial assistance departure	23,377	21.41	19,192	21.25	4,185	22.16
Education						
Less than high school	38,587	35.34	32,794	36.32	5,793	30.68
High school	40,484	37.08	33,544	37.15	6,940	36.75
More than high school	30,110	27.58	23,959	26.53	6,151	32.57
Marital status						
Single	48,909	44.80	41,349	45.79	7,560	40.03
Married	30,588	28.02	25,448	28.18	5,140	27.22
Cohabit	10,702	9.80	9,087	10.06	1,615	8.55
Divorced	12,529	11.48	9,817	10.87	2,712	14.36
Widowed	626	0.57	315	0.35	311	1.65
Separated	5,827	5.34	4,281	4.74	1,546	8.19
Number of dependents						
No dependents	44,677	40.92	37,411	41.43	7,266	38.48
One or more dependents	64,504	59.08	52,886	58.57	11,618	61.52
Dependent Variables						
Incarcerated	88,647	81.19	76,979	85.25	11,668	61.79
Sentence length (months)[a]	65.12	–	69.80	–	34.25	–
N	109,181		90,297		18,884	

[a] Sentence length is for those who received an incarceration sentence.

Independent Effects of Gender

Reading Table 18.2 shows the main effects of gender in three nested models.[5] Model 1 controls only for basic defendant demographics including gender, race, and age. Overall, female defendants have odds of incarceration roughly 74% lower than similarly situated male defendants. Hispanic defendants have the highest odds of incarceration, while White defendants have the lowest, and Black defendants fall in the middle. The odds of incarceration follow an upside-down U-shaped pattern with increasing age. Defendants aged 21 to 39 have odds of incarceration roughly 40% to 50% higher than defendants aged 18 to 20. After age 50, the likelihood of

Reading Table 18.2 • Main Effects Model						
	Model 1		**Model 2**		**Model 3**	
Variable	In/out	Ln(Length)	In/out	Ln(Length)	In/out	Ln(Length)
Gender						
Male[a]	–	–	–	–	–	–
Female	0.26*	−0.70*	0.61*	−0.25*	0.61*	−0.25*
Race						
White[a]	–	–	–	–	–	–
Black	1.65*	0.40*	0.96	0.04*	0.95	0.03*
Hispanic	1.80*	0.13*	1.40*	−0.03*	1.34*	−0.03*
Age						
18–20[a]	–	–	–	–	–	–
21–29	1.48*	0.26*	1.00	0.05*	1.08	0.06*
30–39	1.42*	0.32*	0.88*	0.04*	0.98	0.05*
40–49	1.05	0.20*	0.84*	0.04*	0.94	0.05*
50–59	0.73*	0.08*	0.74*	0.06*	0.82*	0.07*
60 & over	0.48*	−0.06*	0.54*	0.02	0.59*	0.03
Legal variables						
Multiple counts			1.64*	0.29*	1.65*	0.29*
Trial			1.68*	0.10*	1.71*	0.10*
Prior criminal history			1.66*	0.06*	1.62*	0.06*
Guideline minimum sentence			1.12*	0.01*	1.12*	0.01*

(Continued)

Reading Table 18.2 ● (Continued)

Variable	Model 1 In/out	Model 1 Ln(Length)	Model 2 In/out	Model 2 Ln(Length)	Model 3 In/out	Model 3 Ln(Length)
Offense type						
Violent			1.80*	0.39*	1.77*	0.39*
Drug			1.41*	0.26*	1.37*	0.26*
White-collar			1.18*	−0.41*	1.23*	−0.41*
Other[a]			−	−	−	−
Departures						
No Departure[a]			−	−	−	−
Downward departure			0.27*	−0.41*	0.27*	−0.41*
Substantial assistance departure			0.12*	−0.44*	0.12*	−0.44*
Education						
Less than high school					1.35*	0.02*
High school[a]					−	−
More than high school					0.99	−0.01*
Marital status						
Single[a]					−	−
Married					0.92*	−0.01*
Cohabiting					1.07	0.00
Divorced					1.15*	0.01
Widowed					0.67*	0.02
Separated					1.07	0.00
Number of dependents						
No dependents[a]					−	−
One or more dependents					0.92*	0.00
Max-resealed R^2	0.13	−	0.59		0.59	−
Adjusted R^2	−	0.12	−	0.67	−	0.63
N	109,181	88,647	109,181	88,647	109,181	88,647

NOTE: Controls for circuit and year are included in all models.

[a]Represents the reference category.

*$p < .05$.

receiving an incarceration sentence drops substantially, with defendants aged 60 and over having odds of incarceration roughly half that of the youngest defendants.

For the sentence length decision, female defendants receive sentences that are about 50% ($\exp[b]$) shorter than similarly situated male defendants. Black defendants receive the longest sentence lengths, approximately 50% longer than White defendants. Hispanic defendants fall in the middle when it comes to sentence length outcomes. Overall, sentence lengths increase until age 30 to 39 then decrease thereafter, with defendants aged 60 and over receiving sentences similar to those received by defendants aged 18 to 20.

Model 2 builds on the baseline variables by adding legal factors indicating number of counts, trial or guilty plea, prior criminal history, guideline minimum sentence (which accounts for offense severity), offense type, and receipt of departure. As expected, the legal factors are strongly related to whether a defendant receives a prison sentence or probation. Defendants with longer criminal histories are more likely to be sentenced to prison than defendants with shorter criminal records. In addition, defendants that are sentenced for multiple offense counts have odds of incarceration that are 64% higher than defendants sentenced on only a single count. Furthermore, defendants that go to trial are more likely to be sentenced to an incarceration term than defendants that plead guilty (odds ratio = 1.68). Defendants who commit violent offenses have the highest odds of incarceration, roughly 80% higher than defendants in the other offense category. Defendants committing drug and white-collar offenses are also more likely to be incarcerated (41% and 18%, respectively) than the reference group. Finally, defendants receiving a sentencing departure are less likely to receive an incarceration sentence than defendants who do not receive a sentencing departure. Looking at gender, net of legal factors, the odds of incarceration for females are 39% lower than the odds of incarceration for males. This represents a substantial reduction in the gender gap as compared to the findings presented in Model 1 where the odds of incarceration for women are 74% lower for women than men.

Similar findings emerge for sentence length in Model 2. After controlling for legal factors, female defendants receive sentences approximately 23% shorter than those received by male defendants. As with the in/out decision, defendants with longer criminal histories and

those who go to trial receive slightly longer sentences. Those defendants with multiple counts receive sentences approximately 34% longer than those sentenced for only a single count. In addition, defendants who commit violent or drug offenses receive significantly longer sentences (48% and 30% longer, respectively) than those defendants in the reference group. However, defendants who commit white-collar offenses, or receive a sentencing departure, are given significantly shorter sentence length outcomes than their respective reference categories. Notably, by including legal variables in the model, the male–female gap in sentence length is reduced from a 50% difference to a 23% difference.

Model 3 represents the full model and includes three groups of variables indicating educational attainment, marital status, and number of dependents. These extralegal variables were added separately because they can be considered gendered in nature. The odds ratio for female defendants remains the same as in Model 2, indicating that female defendants have odds of incarceration approximately 39% lower than male defendants with similar characteristics. Defendants with less than a high school education are more likely to be incarcerated than those with a high school education. Furthermore, defendants that are divorced have higher odds of incarceration than defendants that are single, while married and widowed defendants are less likely to be incarcerated. In addition, defendants that have one or more dependents are significantly less likely to be incarcerated than defendants who have no dependents. In terms of the sentence length decision, female defendants receive the same sentence length outcome as they did in Model 2, even after the addition of educational attainment, marital status, and number of dependents. Overall, there remains a moderately large gender gap that cannot be explained by legal and extralegal factors.

Main Effects Models by Gender

In Reading Table 18.3, we present the results separately for the male and female defendants in the sample. This is done to determine whether legal and extralegal factors differentially influence the sentencing outcomes of male and female defendants.

In terms of race, incarceration outcomes appear to be influenced differently for men and women. Hispanic male and female defendants have the highest odds of incarceration with defendants roughly 44% and 13% more likely to be incarcerated than their respective White counterparts. On the other hand, Black female defendants have the lowest odds of incarceration compared to White females. We use z-tests of difference of means to compare coefficients between models. Z-tests of difference indicate that the having prior criminal history plays a stronger role for female defendants than male defendants. This also holds true for female defendants who commit drug and white-collar offenses. Defendants, male and female, have lower odds of incarceration if they receive a sentencing departure, but the magnitude of the effect appears to be similar for both gender groups who receive substantial assistance departures. In addition, being less educated hurts male defendants more than women. More specifically, male defendants completing less than a high school education are 46% more likely to be incarcerated than those male defendants with a high school education.

Reading Table 18.3 • Main Effects Model—Males Versus Females

Variable	Males		Females	
	In/out	Ln(Length)	In/out	Ln(Length)
Race				
White[a]	–	–	–	–
Black	1.02[b]	0.05*[b]	0.81*[b]	−0.04*[b]
Hispanic	1.44*[b]	−0.03*	1.13*[b]	0.00
Age				
18–20[a]	–	–	–	–
21–29	1.19*[b]	0.06*	0.85[b]	0.04
30–39	1.03	0.05*	0.88	0.08*
40–49	1.00	0.03*[b]	0.80*	0.15*[b]
50–59	0.90[b]	0.04*[b]	0.65*[b]	0.23*[b]
60 & over	0.66*[b]	0.01[b]	0.46*[b]	0.18*[b]
Legal variables				
Multiple counts	1.60*	0.29*	1.84*	0.27*
Trial	1.74*	0.09*[b]	1.69*	0.21*[b]
Prior criminal history	1.59*[b]	0.06*[b]	1.70*[b]	0.09*[b]
Guideline minimum sentence	1.12*	0.01*[b]	1.12*	0.01*[b]
Offense type				
Violent	1.78*	0.37*[b]	1.56*	0.65*[b]
Drug	1.27*[b]	0.23*[b]	1.76*[b]	0.42*[b]

Variable	Males		Females	
	In/out	Ln(Length)	In/out	Ln(Length)
White-collar	1.07*b	−0.40*b	1.75*b	−0.24*b
Other[a]	−	−	−	−
Departures				
No Departure[a]	−	−	−	−
Downward departure	0.25*b	−0.40*b	0.31*b	−0.47*b
Substantial assistance departure	0.13*	−0.45*	0.12*	−0.44*
Education				
Less than high school	1.46*b	0.01b	1.13*b	0.05*b
High school[a]	−	−	−	−
More than high school	1.02	−0.02*b	0.95	0.05*b
Marital status				
Single[a]	−	−	−	−
Married	0.90*	−0.01	0.95	−0.03
Cohabiting	1.06	0.00	1.07	0.00
Divorced	1.10*	0.02	1.23*	−0.03
Widowed	0.78	−0.06	0.57*	0.05
Separated	1.06	0.00	1.09	−0.03
Number of dependents				
No dependents[a]	−	−	−	−
One or more dependents	0.95	0.01	0.89*	0.02
Max-resealed R^2	0.58	−	0.55	−
Adjusted R^2	−	0.67	−	0.58
N	90,297	76,979	18,884	11,668

NOTE: Controls for circuit and year are included in all models.

[a]Represents the reference category.

[b]Coefficients are different between male and female defendants at $p < .05$ level (two-tailed z-test).

*$p < .05$.

In terms of sentence length outcomes, the results for male and female defendants are somewhat different. Black male defendants receive the longest sentence terms, roughly 5% longer than similarly situated White defendants. On the other hand, Black female defendants receive the shortest sentence length outcomes, approximately 4% shorter than their White female counterparts. Defendants, both male and female, who go to trial and those with prior criminal history receive longer sentence lengths overall. Defendants receiving sentencing departures are given significantly shorter sentences than defendants who do not receive a sentencing departure; however, this appears to play a slightly larger role for female defendants who receive downward sentencing departures. Having anything but [or less than] a high school education appears to play a stronger role for females than males, with female defendants receiving sentences 5% longer than female defendants that finish high school.

Overall, when it comes to the incarceration decision, several things were found to weigh differently for male and female defendants. Racial differences were found among defendant groups, with Hispanic males and females most likely to be incarcerated and Black females least likely to be incarcerated. In terms of legal variables, having prior criminal history plays a stronger role for women than men. For the extralegal measures, having less education negatively affects the sentencing outcomes of men. Looking at sentence length outcomes, racial differences were found. Black male defendants receive the longest sentence lengths, while Black female defendants receive the shortest. Educational differences were also found. Having anything but [or less than] a high school education leads to negative effects for female defendants (longer sentences).

Discussion and Conclusions

The current study had several major goals. First, we wanted to perform a rigorous analysis of the possible causes of gender disparities in sentencing outcomes. Gender disparities are quite common and usually discouraged or prohibited by statute yet receive relatively little attention in the literature. Furthermore, many past studies have used older data, small localized samples, or have not had sufficiently robust legal measures with which to provide adequate statistical control. In the current study, we

used some of the richest and most detailed data available to examine how differences in the legal and extralegal case characteristics of men and women contribute to the gender gap in sentencing.

Second, beyond explanations based on differences in legal case characteristics, we wanted to gain a better understanding of how gender impacts sentencing outcomes through other extralegal factors related to both gender and sentencing. Past studies typically examine gender as a fixed attribute and do not consider how gendered roles might impact court decisions. In the current study, we drew on research from the areas of criminology, criminal justice, and family sociology to examine whether differences in marriage, education, and the presence of dependents helped to account for the gender gap. We also looked to see if there were gender differences in the impact of extralegal and legal factors on sentencing outcomes.

Finally, and more broadly, the current study set out to address the limitations of the criminal justice system after the implementation of fixed sentencing reforms, like formal guidelines, designed to reduce unwarranted extralegal disparities. Central to the guidelines is the notion that defendant characteristics, such as gender, should not be considered during the sentencing process. However, even with these guidelines in place, gender disparities persist, calling into question the effectiveness of their implementation. In the current study, we examined possible mechanisms by which gender may influence the sentencing process in spite of guidelines.

Consistent with prior sentencing research, we found that legal factors play an important role in determining sentencing outcomes. Overall, regardless of gender, defendants with more extensive criminal histories and those who committed more serious offenses were more likely to receive harsher sentences than defendants with less serious criminal pasts and current convictions. However, the findings of the current research also showed that gender appears to have a significant effect on sentencing outcomes, after accounting for legal and extralegal factors. Female defendants were less likely to receive an incarceration sentence than male defendants and also received shorter sentence length terms.

Several important findings emerged from the analysis in relation to our research questions and hypotheses. As expected in our first hypothesis, female defendants received more lenient sentence outcomes than their similarly situated male counterparts. Second, legal factors accounted for a considerable portion of the gender gap in sentencing. However, even after accounting for these legal factors, a sizable gender gap remained in that male defendants continued to be sentenced more harshly than their female counterparts, as proposed in our second hypothesis. Third, although education level, marital status, and number of dependents appeared to influence sentencing outcomes in some instances, they did not help to minimize the gender gap in sentencing outcomes. Thus, our third hypothesis was supported in the expected direction in that [those] defendants who have more marital stability and dependents received more lenient sentence outcomes, but there were no significant advantages for defendants with more than a high school education. One reason as to why this group of variables may not be helping to narrow the sentencing gap between male and female defendants is that judges on the federal level, compared to the state level, are more insulated from community pressures and political forces and less able to exercise their discretion than their state or local counterparts. Overall, the gender gap in sentencing outcomes cannot be fully explained by accounting for legal and extralegal factors.

Finally, contrary to our expectations in hypothesis four, when each gender group was examined separately we found that some legal and extralegal factors did influence sentencing differently for male and female defendants. In terms of legal variables, prior criminal history played a more important role in receiving an incarceration sentence for female than male defendants. In terms of extralegal variables, having less than a high school education negatively influenced the incarceration decision of male defendants (raising their odds of incarceration). However, when it came to sentence length outcomes, having less than, or more than, a high school education increased sentence lengths for female defendants. Race also influenced male and female defendants differently. For the incarceration decision, Hispanic male and female defendants had the highest odds of being sent to prison, while Black females had the lowest odds of incarceration. For the sentence length decision, Black males received the longest sentence length terms and Black female defendants received the shortest terms. Overall, legal and extralegal factors were found to have differential impacts on male and female defendants.

The results of the current study are consistent with the focal concerns perspective (Steffensmeier, 1980; Steffensmeier et al., 1993, 1998) that argues that legal decision making is organized around concerns of blameworthiness, protection of the community, and practical constraints and consequences. Overall, the primary influences of sentencing decisions are legal factors (e.g., prior criminal history, offense seriousness); however, we also found that extralegal characteristics play an important role in some defendants' outcomes. The findings support the idea that judges attribute meaning to past and present behavior of defendants, as well as stereotypes associated with various gender or racial/ethnic groups. These extralegal sources of sentencing disparity indicate that these stereotypes may be very influential and that inequalities in the application of the law and subsequent court proceedings may be taking place, despite the existence of sentencing guidelines designed to avoid such unequal treatment.

One limitation of this study was that socioeconomic status (SES) information was not available in the data set (Monitoring of Federal Criminal Sentences) and thus could not be included in the current analysis. It is not unusual for measures of SES to be missing from sentencing research. In prior years of federal data, a variable representing defendant income was available; however, over 50% of defendants listed their incomes as US$0, making it difficult to analyze the true effects of this variable and how it might interact with gender (see Steffensmeier & Demuth, 2000). Future research should explore the extent to which gender disparities are truly a function of gender perceptions versus economic constraints that limit the ability of defendants to resist legal sanctions and acquire appropriate counsel.

Another limitation of the current study is that the variable indicating number of dependents does not differentiate between the types of dependents. In other words, it is unclear as to whether the defendant is claiming responsibility for their dependent children, their spouse or significant other, some other family member, or a combination of all of the above. Much of the prior research cited in the current study specifically explores the effect of children on sentencing outcomes, regardless of the defendant's marital context (Bickle & Peterson, 1991; Daly, 1987a, 1987b; 1989; Eaton, 1987; Farrington & Morris, 1983; Kruttschnitt & Green, 1984; Kruttschnitt & McCarthy, 1985; Simon, 1975). However, in this context, the definition leaves much room for interpretation. This is especially true given the very different worlds of parenting across various racial/ethnic groups, including instances of multiple partner fertility, mixed family households, extended family care, and responsibilities for aged dependents. Therefore, future research would benefit from an analysis broken down by marital status, specifically targeting single defendants, to determine if significant differences are present when children are the only dependent [variable] examined. Furthermore, future research should strengthen our understanding of

different family forms, especially across racial/ethnic groups and same-sex partnerships.

In conclusion, the topic of differential treatment at sentencing will continue to be an important topic, given the Supreme Court decisions (*Blakely v. Washington; U.S. v. Booker; U.S. v. Fanfan*) which changed the sentencing guidelines from mandatory to voluntary. While the full implication of these changes are still to come, they will likely result in significant changes in sentencing outcomes and, more specifically, the role that judges and other members of the courtroom work group play in those sentencing decisions.

Appendix

Breakdown of Offense Types by Category

Coding No.	Offense Type Name	Overall Number	Overall Percentage	Males Number	Males Percentage	Females Number	Females Percentage
	Violent	6,092	5.58	5,609	6.21	483	2.56
1	Murder	145	0.13	128	0.14	17	0.09
2	Manslaughter	125	0.11	98	0.11	27	0.14
3	Kidnapping/hostage	65	0.06	58	0.06	7	0.04
4	Sexual abuse	585	0.54	566	0.63	19	0.10
5	Assault	1,032	0.95	920	1.02	112	0.59
6	Bank robbery/other robbery	4,140	3.79	3,839	4.25	301	1.59
	Drug	48,688	44.59	41,626	46.10	7,062	37.40
10	Drugs: Trafficking	46,606	42.69	39,992	44.29	6,614	35.02
11	Drugs: Communication facilities	923	0.85	721	0.80	202	1.07
12	Drugs: Simple possession	1,159	1.06	913	1.01	246	1.30
	White-collar	23,259	21.30	16,371	18.13	6,888	36.48
18	Fraud	14,837	13.59	10,535	11.67	4,302	22.78

Coding No.	Offense Type	Overall		Males		Females	
	Name	Number	Percentage	Number	Percentage	Number	Percentage
19	Embezzlement	1,913	1.75	775	0.86	1,138	6.03
20	Forgery/counterfeiting	3,159	2.89	2,353	2.61	806	4.27
21	Bribery	375	0.34	329	0.36	46	0.24
22	Tax offenses	1,333	1.22	1,093	1.21	240	1.27
23	Money laundering	1,642	1.50	1,286	1.42	356	1.89
	Other Offenses	31,142	28.52	26,691	29.56	4,451	23.57
9	Arson	176	0.16	162	0.18	14	0.07
13	Firearms: Use/possession	13,339	12.22	12,832	14.21	507	2.68
15	Burglary/breaking & entering	118	0.11	111	0.12	7	0.04
16	Auto theft	370	0.34	352	0.39	18	0.10
17	Larceny	5,125	4.69	3,205	3.55	1,920	10.17
24	Racketeering/extortion	1,627	1.49	1,492	1.65	135	0.71
25	Gambling/lottery	271	0.25	246	0.27	25	0.13
26	Civil rights offenses	211	0.19	201	0.22	10	0.05
27	Immigration	3,299	3.02	2,597	2.88	702	3.72
28	Pornography/prostitution	1,714	1.57	1,689	1.87	25	0.13
29	Offenses in prison	741	0.68	638	0.71	103	0.55
30	Administration of justice-related	1,982	1.82	1,324	1.47	658	3.48
31	Environmental, game, fish, and wildlife offenses	312	0.29	297	0.33	15	0.08
32	National defense offenses	16	0.01	12	0.01	4	0.02
33	Antitrust violations	39	0.04	38	0.04	1	0.01
34	Food and drug offenses	171	0.16	151	0.17	20	0.11
35	Traffic violations and other offenses	1,631	1.49	1,344	1.49	287	1.52
	Overall totals	109,181		90,297		18,884	

/// DISCUSSION QUESTIONS

1. Do female defendants receive more lenient sentences than male defendants?

2. How does the consideration of legal and contextual factors impact sentencing practices for female defendants? For male defendants?

3. How do extralegal factors impact the sentencing decisions for female defendants? For male defendants?

Notes

1. Many sentencing studies model the sentence length decision including a correction term for selection bias stemming from the decision to incarcerate (Berk, 1983). This involves controlling for the "hazard" of incarceration (estimated in the in/out model) in the sentence length model. The hazard variable represents for each observation, the instantaneous probability of being excluded from the sample conditional upon being in the pool at risk. However, Stolzenberg and Relles (1997) and Bushway, Johnson, and Slocum (2007) find that this correction term can often introduce more bias into the sentence length model than it eliminates due to high levels of colinearity between the correction term and other predictors of sentence length. This is especially likely when the predictors of incarceration are very similar to the predictors of sentencing length as in the present study. Also, Stolzenberg and Relles (1997) argue that a correction term is often unnecessary when there is a low level of selection. In the current data, because only 19% of defendants avoid incarceration, it is unlikely that a selection bias will strongly influence the sentence length findings. For these reasons, we do not include a correction term for selection bias in the sentence length model.

2. Defendants in the "Other" racial category have been included in the analysis models but were not included in the regression tables as they are not the focus of this study and only constitute a small percentage of the sample (3.9%).

3. The "number of dependents" variable may not accurately represent a defendant's potential family responsibilities because the Sentencing Commission has not differentiated among types of dependents (e.g., children, spouses, significant others, aged parents, or extended family members, etc.).

4. Initial analyses were conducted using a full range of categories for this variable, but it was found that no differences existed between higher levels of dependents.

5. All models in the analysis control for judicial circuit and year. Model fit for the full in/out model as indicated by the area under the ROC curve (0.931) is very good. For the full sentence length model, an examination of variance inflation factor scores indicates that all variables are well below 10, which is typically considered to be an acceptable cutoff.

References

Albonetti, C. (1991). An integration of theories to explain judicial discretion. *Social Problems, 38,* 247–266.

Albonetti, C. (1997). Sentencing under the federal sentencing guidelines: Effects of defendant characteristics, guilty pleas, and departures on sentence outcomes for drug offenders, 1991–1992. *Law & Society Review, 31,* 789–822.

Belknap, J. (2001). *The invisible woman: Gender, crime, and criminal justice.* Belmont, CA: Wadsworth.

Berk, R. A. (1983). An introduction to sample selection bias in sociological data. *American Sociological Review, 48,* 386–398.

Berk, R. A. (2010). What you can and can't properly do with regression. *Journal of Quantitative Criminology, 26,* 481–487.

Bernstein, I., Cardascia, J., & Ross, C. (1979). Defendant's sex and criminal court decisions. In R. Alvarez & K. G. Lutterman (Eds.), *Discrimination in organizations* (pp. 329–354). San Francisco, CA: Jossey-Bass.

Bickle, G., & Peterson, R. (1991). The impact of gender-based family roles on criminal sentencing. *Social Problems, 38,* 372–394.

Bushway, S., Johnson, B., & Slocum, L. (2007). Is the magic still there? The use of the Heckman two-step correction for selection bias in criminology. *Journal of Quantitative Criminology, 23*(2), 151–178.

Butler, A. (1997). *Gendered justice in the American West: Women prisoners in men's penitentiaries.* Champaign, IL: University of Illinois Press.

Chiricos, T., & Crawford, C. (1995). Race and imprisonment: A contextual assessment of the evidence. In D. F. Hawkins (Ed.), *Ethnicity, race, and crime: Perspectives across time and place* (pp. 281–309). Albany: State University of New York Press.

Daly, K. (1986, November). *Gender in the adjudication process: Are judges really paternalistic toward women?* Revised paper presented at the American Society of Criminology Annual Meeting, San Diego, CA.

Daly, K. (1987a). Discrimination in the criminal courts: Family, gender, and problems of equal treatment. *Social Forces, 66,* 152–175.

Daly, K. (1987b). Structure and practice of familial-based justice in a criminal court. *Law and Society Review, 21,* 267–290.

Daly, K. (1989). Rethinking judicial paternalism: Gender, work-family relations, and sentencing. *Gender and Society, 3*(1), 9–36.

Daly, K. (1994). *Gender, crime, and punishment.* New Haven, CT: Yale University Press.

Daly, K., & Bordt, R. (1995). Sex effects and sentencing: An analysis of the statistical literature. *Justice Quarterly, 12,* 141–175.

Demuth, S. (2002). The effects of citizenship status on sentencing outcomes in drug cases. *Federal Sentencing Reporter, 14,* 271–275.

Demuth, S., & Steffensmeier, D. (2004). Ethnicity effects on sentence outcomes in large urban courts: Comparisons among White, Black, and Hispanic defendants. *Social Science Quarterly, 85,* 994–1011.

Dixon, J. (1995). The organization context of criminal sentencing. *American Journal of Sociology, 100,* 1157–1198.

Doerner, J., & Demuth, S. (2010). The independent and joint effects of race/ethnicity, gender, and age on sentencing outcomes in U.S. federal courts. *Justice Quarterly, 27*(1), 1–27.

Eaton, M. (1987). The question of bail: Magistrates' responses to applications for bail on behalf of men and women. In P. Carlen & A. Worrall (Eds.), *Gender, crime, and justice* (pp. 95–107). Philadelphia, PA: Open University Press.

Engen, R., & Gainey, R. (2000). Modeling the effects of legally relevant and extralegal factors under sentencing guidelines: The rules have changed. *Criminology, 38,* 1207–1229.

Farrell, A. (2004). Measuring judicial and prosecutorial discretion: Sex and race disparities in departures from the federal sentencing guidelines. *Justice Research and Policy, 6*(2), 45–78.

Farrington, D., & Morris, A. (1983). Sex, sentencing, and reconviction. *Journal of British Criminology, 21,* 229–249.

Flemming, R., Nardulli, P., & Eisenstein, J. (1992). *The craft of justice: Work and politics in criminal court communities.* Philadelphia: University of Pennsylvania Press.

Griffin, T., & Wooldredge, J. (2006). Sex-based disparities in felony dispositions before versus after sentencing reform in Ohio. *Criminology, 44*(4), 893–923.

Gruhl, J., Welch, S., & Spohn, C. (1984). Women as criminal defendants: A test for paternalism. *Western Political Quarterly, 37,* 456–467.

Hogarth, J. (1971). *Sentencing as a human process.* Toronto, ON: University of Toronto Press.

Koons-Witt, B. (2002). Decision to incarcerate before and after the introduction of sentencing guidelines. *Criminology, 40,* 297–327.

Kruttschnitt, C. (1982a). Women, crime, and dependency: An application of the theory of law. *Criminology, 19,* 495–513.

Kruttschnitt, C. (1984). Sex and criminal court dispositions: The unresolved controversy. *Journal of Research in Crime and Delinquency, 21,* 23–32.

Kruttschnitt, C., & Green, D. (1984). The sex sanctioning issue: Is it history? *American Sociological Review, 49,* 541–551.

Kruttschnitt, C., & McCarthy, D. (1985). Familial social control and pretrial sanctions: Does sex really matter? *Criminal Law and Criminology, 76,* 151–175.

Nagel, I., & Hagan, J. (1983). Gender and crime: Offense patterns and criminal court sanctions. In M. Tonry & N. Morris (Eds.), *Crime and justice: An annual review of research* (Vol. 4, pp. 91–144). Chicago, IL: University of Chicago Press.

Peterson, R., & Hagan, J. (1984). Changing conceptions of race: Towards an account of anomalous findings of sentencing research. *American Sociological Review, 49,* 56–70.

Pollock-Byrne, J. (1990). *Women, prison, and crime.* Pacific Grove, CA: Brooks/Cole.

Rafter, N. (1990). *Partial justice: Women, prison, and social control.* Piscataway, NJ: Transaction.

Rafter, N., & Stanko, E. (1982). *Judge lawyer victim thief: Women, gender roles, and criminal justice.* Boston, MA: Northeastern University Press.

Raftery, A. (1995). Bayesian model selection in social research. *Sociological Methodology, 25,* 111–163.

Simon, R. (1975). *Women and crime.* Lexington, MA: Lexington Books.

Spohn, C. (2000). Thirty years of sentencing reform: The quest for a racially neutral sentencing process. *Criminal justice 2000* (Vol. 3, pp. 427–501). Washington, DC: National Institute of Justice.

Spohn, C. (2002). *How do judges decide? The search for fairness and justice in punishment.* Thousand Oaks, CA: Sage.

Spohn, C., & Holleran, D. (2000). The imprisonment penalty paid by young unemployed Black and Hispanic male offenders. *Criminology, 38,* 281–306.

Steffensmeier, D. (1980). Assessing the impact of the women's movement on sex-based differences in the handling of adult criminal defendants. *Crime and Delinquency, 23,* 344–356.

Steffensmeier, D., & Demuth, S. (2000). Ethnicity and sentencing outcomes in U.S. federal courts: Who is punished more harshly? *American Sociological Review, 65,* 705–729.

Steffensmeier, D., & Demuth, S. (2006). Does gender modify the effects of race-ethnicity on criminal sanctioning? Sentences for male and female White, Black, and Hispanic defendants. *Journal of Quantitative Criminology, 22,* 241–261.

Steffensmeier, D., Kramer, J., & Streifel, C. (1993). Gender and imprisonment decisions. *Criminology, 31,* 411–446.

Steffensmeier, D., Kramer, J., & Ulmer, J. (1995). Age differences in sentencing. *Criminal Justice Quarterly, 12,* 701–719.

Steffensmeier, D., Kramer, J., & Ulmer, J. (1998). The interaction of race, gender, and age in criminal sentencing: The punishment cost of being young, Black, and male. *Criminology, 36,* 763–797.

Steffensmeier, D., & Motivans, M. (2000). Older men and older women in the arms of criminal law: Offending patterns and sentencing outcomes. *Journal of Gerontology, 55,* 141–151.

Stolzenberg, R., & Relles, D. (1997). Tools for intuition about sample selection bias and its correction. *American Sociological Review, 62,* 494–507.

Temin, P. (1980). Regulation and the choice of prescription drugs. *American Economic Review, 70,* 301–305.

Tonry, M. (1996). *Sentencing matters.* New York, NY: Oxford University Press.

Ulmer, J. (1995). The organization and consequences of social pasts in criminal courts. *Sociological Quarterly, 36,* 587–605.

Ulmer, J. (2000). The rules have changed—So proceed with caution: A comment on Engen and Gainey's method for modeling sentencing outcomes under guidelines. *Criminology, 38,* 1231–1243.

Ulmer, J., & Kramer, J. (1996). Court communities under sentencing guidelines: Dilemmas of formal rationality and sentencing disparity. *Criminology, 34,* 383–408.

U.S. Sentencing Commission (USSC). (2001, 2002, 2003). *Monitoring of Federal Criminal Sentences* [Computer files]. ICPSR versions. Washington, DC: U.S. Sentencing Commission (Producer), 2001, 2002, 2003. Ann Arbor, MI: Inter-University Consortium for Political and Social Research (distributor).

U.S. Sentencing Commission (USSC). (2004). *Fifteen years of guidelines sentencing: An assessment of how well the federal criminal justice system is achieving the goals of sentencing reform.* Washington, DC: U.S. Sentencing Commission.

The Supervision of Women
Community Corrections, Rehabilitation, and Reentry

Section Highlights

- Gender-responsive treatment and programming for women in the criminal justice system
- Supervision of women in the community
- Reentry challenges for women

This section focuses on issues related to the supervision of women within the community corrections setting. This section highlights how the differential pathways of female offending affect the unique needs of women and presents a review of the tenets of gender-responsive programming. The chapter then turns to a discussion on how the needs of women can impact their successes and failures on probation. Within this context, this section also looks at the role of risk assessment tools and how they are used to make decisions about the supervision of women. The section concludes with a discussion on the challenges that female offenders face as they return to their communities following their incarceration.

Gender-Responsive Programming for Women

The needs of women have been significantly neglected by the criminal justice system throughout history. In an effort to remedy the disparities in treatment, several court cases began to challenge the delivery of services for female offenders. Most of these decisions began with the practices in women's prisons; however, their rulings have had implications for women in community correctional settings and programs as well. The case of *Barefield v. Leach* (1974) was particularly important for women because it set the standard by which the courts could measure whether women received a lower standard of treatment than men. While *Barefield* was heard in the District Court of New Mexico and could not be applied outside of the state, it was one of the first of its kind to address this issue. Later cases such as *Glover v. Johnson* (1979) from the District Court of Michigan, held that the state must provide the

423

same opportunities for education, rehabilitation, and vocational training for females as provided for male offenders. Later cases such as *Cooper v. Morin* (1979) from the Court of Appeals of the State of New York held that the equal protection clause prevents prison administrators from justifying the disparate treatment of women on the grounds that providing such services for women is inconvenient. Ultimately, the courts have held to a general precedent that "males and females must be treated equally unless there is a substantial reason which requires a distinction be made" (*Canterino v. Wilson*, 1982)

While these cases began to establish a conversation on the accessibility of programming for women, they generally focused on the issue of parity between male and female prisoners. At the time, women constituted only about 5% of the total number of incarcerated offenders. During the 1970s, prison advocates worked toward providing women with the same opportunities for programming and treatment as men. Their efforts were relatively successful in that many gender-based policies were abolished, and new policies were put into place mandating that men and women be treated similarly (Zaitzow & Thomas, 2003). However, feminist criminologists soon discovered that parity and equality for female offenders does not necessarily mean that women benefit from the same treatment as men (Bloom, Owen, & Covington, 2003, 2004). Indeed, research has documented that programs designed for men fail the needs of women (Belknap, 2007).

These findings led to the emergence of a new philosophy of parity for women—**gender-responsive programming**. Gender-responsive or gender-specific programming first emerged in response to the dramatic increase in the number of girls that were appearing before the juvenile court. However, few jurisdictions were prepared to address the needs of this new population. As you learned in Section VII, the 1992 reauthorization of the Juvenile Justice and Delinquency Prevention Act mandated that states assess the needs of girls and develop gender-specific options to address the unique needs of female offenders. Following the efforts of the juvenile court, the criminal justice system has engaged in similar conversations regarding the adult female offending population. In an effort to respond to the needs of women and girls, scholars and practitioners were left to determine what it means to be gender responsive in our correctional environments. Research by Bloom et al. (2003, 2004) highlights how six key principles can change the way in which programs and institutions design and manage programs, develop policies, train staff, and supervise offenders. These six principles are (1) gender, (2) environment, (3) relationships, (4) services and supervision, (5) socioeconomic status, and (6) community. Together, these six principles provide guidance for the effective management of female offenders.

The first principle of gender discusses the importance for criminal justice systems and agents to recognize the role that gender plays in the offending of women and the unique treatment needs of women. As you learned earlier in this book, the pathways of women to crime are dramatically different from the pathways of men. Even though they may be incarcerated for similar crimes, their lives related to these offenses are dramatically different. As a result, men and women respond to treatment in different ways and have different issues to face within the context of rehabilitation. To offer the same program to men and women may not adequately address the unique needs for both populations. Given that the majority of programs have been developed about male criminality and are used for male offenders, these programs often fail the unique needs of women.

The second principle of environment focuses on the need for officials to create a place where staff and inmates engage in practices of mutual respect and dignity. Given that many women involved in the criminal justice system come from a background of violence and abuse, it is critical that women feel safe and supported in their journey toward rehabilitation and recovery. Historically, the criminal justice system has emphasized a model of power and control, a model that limits the ability for nurturing, trust, and compassion. Rehabilitative programs for women need to create an environment that is a safe place where women can share the intimate details of their lives (Covington, 1999).

The third principle of relationships refers to developing an understanding of why women commit crimes; the context of their lives prior to, during, and following incarceration; and the relationships that women build while they are incarcerated. In addition, the majority of incarcerated women attempt to sustain their relationships with family members outside the prison walls, particularly with their minor children. Given that the majority of incarcerated women present a low safety risk to the community, women should be placed in settings that are minimally restrictive, offer opportunities for programs and services, and are located within reasonable proximity to their families and minor children. The concept of relationships also involves how program providers interact with and relate to their clients. Group participants need to feel supported by their treatment providers, and the providers need to be able to empower women to make positive choices about their lives (Covington, 1999).

The fourth principle identifies the need for gender-responsive programming to address the traumas that women have experienced throughout the context of their lives. As indicated throughout this text, the cycle of offending for women often begins with the experience of victimization. In addition, these victim experiences continue throughout their lives and often inform their criminal actions. Historically, treatment providers for substance abuse issues, trauma, and mental health issues have dealt with offenders on an individualized basis. Gender-responsive approaches highlight the need for program providers and institutions to address these issues as co-occurring disorders. Here, providers need to be cross-trained in these three issues in order to develop and implement effective programming options for women. In addition, community correctional settings need to acknowledge how these issues translate into challenges and barriers to success in the **reentry** process. This awareness can help support women in their return to the community.

The fifth principle focuses on the socioeconomic status of the majority of women in prison. Most women in prison turn to criminal activity as a survival mechanism. Earlier in this volume, you learned that women in the system lack adequate educational and vocational resources to develop a sustainable life for themselves and their families and struggle with poverty, homelessness, and limited public assistance resources, particularly for drug-convicted offenders. To enhance the possibilities of success following their incarceration, women need to have access to opportunities to break the cycle of abuse and create positive options for their future. Without these skills and opportunities, many women will fall back into the criminal lifestyle out of economic necessity. Given that many women will reunite with their children following their release, these opportunities will help women make a better life not only for themselves but for their children as well.

The sixth principle of community focuses on the need to develop collaborative relationships among providers in order to assist women in their transition toward independent living. Bloom et al. (2003) call for the need to develop wraparound services for women. **Wraparound services** refer to "a holistic and culturally sensitive plan for each woman that draws on a coordinated range of services within her community" (p. 82). Examples of these services include public and mental health systems, addiction recovery, welfare, emergency shelter organizations, and educational and vocational services. Certainly, wraparound services require a high degree of coordination between agencies and program providers. Given the multiple challenges that women face throughout their reentry process, the development of comprehensive services will help support women toward a successful transition. In addition, by having one case manager to address multiple issues, agencies can be more effective in meeting the needs of and supervising women in the community while reducing the levels of bureaucracy and "red tape" in the delivery of resources.

Table 10.1 illustrates how the principles of gender, environment, relationships, services and supervision, socioeconomic status, and community can be utilized when developing gender-responsive policies and programming. These suggestions can assist institutional administrators and program providers in developing policies and procedures that represent the realities of women's lives and reflect ways that rehabilitation efforts can be most effective for women. Within each of these topical considerations, correctional agencies should be reminded that the majority of female offenders are nonviolent in nature, are more likely to be at risk for personal injury versus harmful toward others, and are in need of services.

Table 10.1 • Questions to Ask in Developing a Systemic Approach for Women Offenders

Operational Practices

- Are the specifics of women's behavior and circumstances addressed in written planning, policy, programs, and operational practices? For example, are policies regarding classification, property, programs, and services appropriate to the actual behavior and composition of the female population?
- Does the staff reflect the offender population in terms of gender, race/ethnicity, sexual orientation, language (bilingual), ex-offender, and recovery status? Are female role models and mentors employed to reflect the racial/ethnic and cultural backgrounds of the clients?
- Does staff training prepare workers for the importance of relationships in the lives of women offenders? Does the training provide information on the nature of women's relational context, boundaries and limit setting, communication, and child-related issues? Are staff prepared to relate to women offenders in an empathetic and professional manner?
- Are staff training in appropriate gender communication skills and in recognizing and dealing with the effects of trauma and PTSD?

Services

- Is training on women offenders provided? Is this training available in initial academy or orientation sessions? Is the training provided on an ongoing basis? Is this training mandatory for executive-level staff?
- Does the organization see women's issues as a priority? Are women's issues important enough to warrant an agency-level position to manage women's services?
- Do resource allocation, staffing, training, and budgeting consider the facts of managing women offenders?

Review of Standard Procedures

- Do classifications and other assessments consider gender in classification instruments, assessment tools, and individualized treatment plans? Has the existing classification system been validated on a sample of women? Does the database system allow for separate analysis of female characteristics?
- Is information about women offenders collected, coded, monitored, and analyzed in the agency?
- Are protocols established for reporting and investigating claims of staff misconduct, with protection from retaliation ensured? Are the concepts of privacy and personal safety incorporated in daily operations and architectural design, where applicable?
- How does policy address the issue of cross-gender strip searches and pat downs?
- Does the policy include the concept of zero tolerance for inappropriate language, touching, and other inappropriate behavior and staff sexual misconduct?

Children and Families

- How do existing programs support connections between the female offender and her children and family? How are these connections undermined by current practice? In institutional environments, what provisions are made for visiting and for other opportunities for contact with children and family?
- Are there programs and services that enhance female offenders' parenting skills and their ability to support their children following release? In community supervision settings and community treatment programs, are parenting responsibilities acknowledged through education? Through child care?

Community

- Are criminal justice services delivered in a manner that builds community trust, confidence, and partnerships?
- Do classification systems and housing configurations allow community custody placements? Are transitional programs in place that help women build long-term community support networks?
- Are professionals, providers, and community volunteer positions used to facilitate community connections? Are they used to develop partnerships between correctional agencies and community providers?

SOURCE: Bloom, Owen, & Covington (2003).

The Supervision of Women in the Community

Community-based supervision is the most common form of intervention utilized by the criminal justice system. Within community supervision, the most popular option is **probation**. When offenders are sentenced to probation, they are allowed to remain in the community rather than serve out their sentence in jail or prison. In addition, a sentence to probation allows for offenders to access programs and services that focus on rehabilitation. Offenders on probation must follow specific terms and conditions that allow them to remain in the community. These can include a curfew, participation in therapeutic programs such as anger management counseling and drug treatment, or maintaining a job or enrollment in school. Offenders may also be required to pay fines to the court, restitution to the victim, or to complete community service hours. If an offender fails to follow the directives as ordered by the court and her probation officer, she runs the risk of losing her privilege to remain in the community.

In 2015, 4,650,900 adults were supervised in the community through probation services. According to the Bureau of Justice Statistics, 25% of these probationers were female. This is a slight increase from 2005 where 23% of the probation population were women (Kaeble & Bonczar, 2015). Probation has traditionally been an option offered for many female offenders because it allowed them to remain in the community. This is particularly important given that many women are often the primary caregivers for young children.

The central tenet of probation is about reducing risk to the community. When offenders are sentenced to serve out their sentence under community supervision, how can we be sure that they will be successful? How can we be sure that they are not a danger to themselves or others? In evaluating the risks and needs of women on probation, many agencies use assessment instruments to gauge the risk that an offender presents to the public. At the same time, these tools can help identify what the needs of the offender are, which can help probation officers provide services and supervision for these offenders. However, these *gender-neutral* assessments may not adequately identify the needs of female offenders (Davidson, 2011). In addition, the needs of women are often misrepresented as risks, which can lead to increased punitive punishments by probation officers.

One of the most common assessment tools used in community corrections is the **Level of Service Inventory-Revised (LSI-R)**. While the LSI-R has been validated within the male offender population, research on the LSI-R for female offenders has been mixed. In some cases, the LSI-R fails to identify the gender-specific needs of women. In others, the LSI-R has led to the over-classification of women. Even when the LSI-R is effective in identifying the risks of recidivism, this tool may not be able to assess the context of these risks. Finally, the LSI-R fails to identify some of the most significant needs of women with their abuse histories, health issues, and motherhood issues (Davidson 2011).

Table 10.2 ● Characteristics of Women in Community Corrections

	Under Community Supervision	In Jail
White	62%	36%
African American	27%	44%
Hispanic	10%	15%
Median age	32	31
High school/GED	60%	55%
Single	42%	48%
Unemployed	–	60%
Mother of minor children	72%	70%

▲ **Photo 10.1** Women walk along a corridor at the Los Angeles County women's jail in Lynwood, California, April 26, 2013. The Second Chance Women's Re-entry Court is one of the first in the U.S. to focus on women, and offers a cost-saving alternative to prison for women who plead guilty to nonviolent crimes and volunteer for treatment. Of the 297 women who have been through the court since 2007, 100 have graduated, and only 35 have been returned to state prison.

Given some of these limitations of the LSI-R and other assessment tools, scholars have worked to develop gender-responsive tools to provide a better reflection of the needs of female offenders. The first instrument is shorter in length and is designed to supplement existing assessments that are not gender specific, while the second instrument is designed to replace existing measures and be used as a stand-alone tool in evaluating risk and identifying needs for female offenders. The philosophy behind these new tools is to allow for community correctional agencies to record the high needs that many female offenders may have without increasing their risk levels. (Salisbury, Van Voorhis, Wright, & Bauman, 2009). Another example is the Dynamic Risk Assessment for Offender Reentry (DRAOR), which has been used by Community Probation Services throughout New Zealand and has also been adapted in some U.S. jurisdictions. While this tool was developed for use of male populations, research notes that it can be effective in predicting the risk of recidivism for women (Yesberg, Scanlan, Hanby, Serin, & Polaschek, 2015). These tools allow community correctional agencies to be advocates for female-only and smaller caseloads as well as partner with other agencies and providers in the community to develop wraparound services that will help increase the success levels of women on probation (Van Voorhis, Salisbury, Wright, & Bauman, 2008).

The failure by community-based services to develop and implement gender-responsive programs that meet the needs of offenders is connected to recidivism rates. One example of an effective gender-responsive program for female probationers is the *Moving On* program. The curriculum is designed to help women build tools for resiliency in their personal lives and develop ways to generate support and resources within their communities. Here, the focus of the program is to increase women's self-awareness of their challenges and triggers that might lead to recidivism. Assessments of the *Moving On* program have demonstrated its efficacy, because these women had lower rates of recidivism (in terms of new offenses) compared to those women under traditional probation supervision. While the women from the *Moving On* program were more likely to receive a technical violation of probation, these violations occurred in cases where the women failed to complete the program. These findings conclude that the completion of a gender-responsive program can be an effective tool in reducing the recidivism rates of women on probation (Gehring, Van Voorhis, & Bell, 2010).

Once on probation, gender has an effect on how offenders experience probation, because probation officers view male and female offenders differently, which alters their supervision style. Research by Wyse (2013) indicates that probation officers are more likely to focus on the rules of probation with male probationers. Here, the emphasis was placed on whether the men were employed and desisting from criminal behavior. In these cases, the relationship between the offender and the officer was very formal. In contrast, the relationship between the probation officer and female clients was more intimate and emotional in nature. In many cases, this allowed offenders to develop trust with their probation officers, and offenders seek out their help in finding referrals for treatment and support (Hall, Golder, Conley, & Sawning, 2013). Officers frequently encouraged their clients to find ways to increase their self-esteem. Women were also encouraged to build self-reliance and stay away from romantic relationships in general. Indeed, officers spend far greater time policing these relationships for women, while this is rarely mentioned for male offenders (Wyse, 2013).

Women on Parole

The term **parole** invokes a variety of meanings. On one hand, an offender in prison can be up for parole and have her file reviewed by a board of officials to determine whether she should be released back into the community. At the same time, parole also refers to the supervision of offenders following their release from prison. In 2011, of the 853,900 people who were supervised on parole, 11% of the parole population were women (Maruschak & Parks, 2012). Given that women make up such a small proportion of the offenders placed on parole, it has been challenging to provide appropriate gender-responsive programming and services for this population. While parole supervision was once intended to help offenders successfully transition back to the community, the role of parole officers has shifted. Because of the high caseloads that many parole offices face, the opportunities to provide an individualized case to these offenders are limited. Instead, the majority of their time is spent monitoring offenders, waiting to respond if and when an offender violates the conditions of their release. One woman shares the struggles in meeting these demands, expressing fear and the unknown of her new life and her ability to be successful in her reentry process:

> I start my day running to drop my urine [drug testing]. Then I go see my children, show up for my training program, look for a job, go to a meeting [Alcoholics Anonymous], and show up at my part-time job. I have to take the bus everywhere, sometimes eight buses for 4 hours a day. I don't have the proper outer clothes, I don't have the money to buy lunch along the way, and everyone who works with me keeps me waiting so that I am late to my next appointment. If I fail any one of these things I am revoked. I am so tired that I sometimes fall asleep on my way home from work at 2:00 a.m. and that's dangerous given where I live. And then the next day I have to start over again. I don't mind being busy and working hard . . . that's part of my recovery. But this is a situation that is setting me up to fail. I just can't keep up and I don't know where to start. (Ritchie, 2001, p. 381)

Reentry Issues for Incarcerated Women

The needs of incarcerated women returning to their communities are high. While much of the research on reentry issues has focused on whether offenders will reoffend and return to prison (recidivism), recent scholars have shifted the focus on reentry to discussions of how to successfully transition offenders back into their communities. This process can be quite traumatic, and for women, a number of issues emerge in creating a successful reentry experience.

Consider the basic needs of a woman who has just left prison. She needs housing, clothing, and food. She may be eager to reestablish relationships with friends, family members, and her children. In addition, she has obligations as part of her release—appointments with her parole officer and treatment requirements. In addition, the majority of women find themselves returning to the same communities in which they lived prior to their incarceration, where they face the same problems of poverty, addiction, and dysfunction. Finding safe and affordable housing is challenging, and for many women, the only options place them at risk for relapse and recidivism (Hall et al., 2013). Figure 10.1 highlights the types of short and long-term housing that women utilize in their exit from prison. Research by the Urban Institute notes that women often sacrifice their safety in exchange for housing: Within the first year of their release, 19% of female ex-offenders in Texas were residing with someone who abused drugs and 22% of women were living with someone who was abusing alcohol (LaVigne, Brooks, & Shollenberger, 2009).

Women are also less likely to have participated in any vocational training programs while behind bars (LaVigne, Brooks, & Shollenberger, 2009). For those few women who were able to receive some therapeutic treatment in prison, most acknowledge that these prison-based intervention programs provided few, if any, legitimate coping skills to deal with the realities of the life stressors that awaited them on their release. Many women also hope to reunite with their children. While a return to motherhood may be a powerful motivation to get their lives back on track, the reality of returning as the authority figure in a family is compromised by a number of factors. These include the separation from her children during incarceration, the loss of her children to other family members or social services, and a lack of confidence to effectively raise her children (Brown & Bloom, 2009). On top of all these struggles, offenders face a new identity on their release from prison—the *ex-offender* status. This identity can place significant challenges for offenders and threaten their ability to be successful on release. Consider the number of employment opportunities that require applicants to disclose whether they have ever been arrested for a crime. In many cases, this automatically excludes the applicant from consideration. For women, the inability to find suitable employment has a significant effect, particularly if she is trying to create a stable home environment to regain custody of her

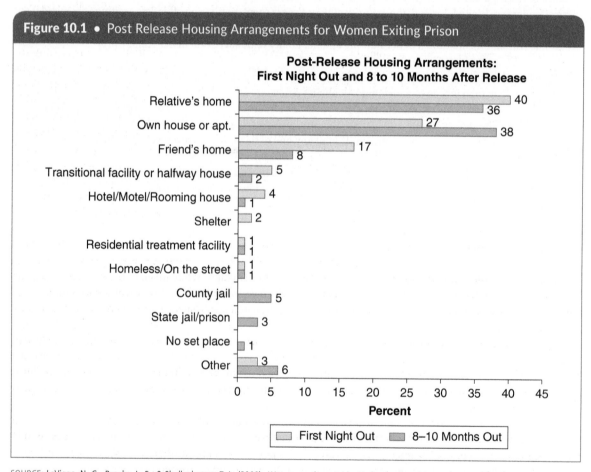

Figure 10.1 • Post Release Housing Arrangements for Women Exiting Prison

SOURCE: LaVigne, N. G., Brooks, L. E., & Shollenberger, T. L. (2009). *Women on the outside: Understanding the experiences of female prisoners returning to Houston*, Texas. Urban Institute Justice Policy Center. Retrieved at http://www.urban.org/sites/default/files/publication/30401/411902-Women-on-the-Outside-Understanding-the-Experiences-of-Female-Prisoners-Returning-to-Houston-Texas.PDF

children. Many women also reference how their lack of education or training makes it difficult to secure legal and stable employment (Hall et al., 2013). A recent campaign to *ban the box* has many states and companies changing the way they handle ex-convicts' applications for employment. In Minnesota, recent legislation makes it illegal for state employers to ask about an offender's criminal history on a job application. As one of the largest retailers, Target has reformed its hiring policies such that questions about any criminal history are not raised until an applicant has been granted an interview (Strachan, 2013).

In addition to the challenges of returning home from prison, many women continue to battle the demons that led them to criminal activity in the first place. As you learned in Section VIII, drug addiction is one of the primary reasons why women are involved in criminal activity and ultimately sent to prison. Given the limited availability of treatment options both behind bars and within the community, issues of addiction can lead to recidivism, particularly for women of color (Huebner, DeJong, & Cobbina, 2010). Drug addiction has a multiplying effect in the lives of women—not only can addiction threaten a woman's status on parole, but it impacts as well her ability to maintain stable employment, secure housing, and reunify with her children.

Without community-based resources, many women will return to the addictions and lifestyles in which they engaged prior to their incarceration. In addition, women have limited access to physical and mental health care, often because of a lack of community resources, an inability to pay, or lack of knowledge about where to go to obtain assistance. Sixty-seven percent of women who exit prison have been diagnosed with some sort of chronic health condition, such as asthma, high blood pressure, or an infectious disease. In addition, more than half of the women suffer from mental health issues (LaVigne, Brooks, & Shollenberger, 2009). Given the status of mental and physical health needs of incarcerated women, the management (or lack thereof) of chronic health problems can impede a woman's successful reentry process (Ritchie, 2001). Unfortunately, mental health services within the community overemphasize the use of prescription psychotropic medications. Coupled with the limited availability of therapeutic interventions, these health interventions resemble more of a Band-Aid than a comprehensive stable approach for women (Kitty, 2012). This lack of therapeutic support has a significant impact particularly for women with children because both the women and their children could benefit from these resources (Snyder, 2009). Figure 10.2 highlights the types of services that women say would be the most beneficial in aiding their reentry process. The three most desired resources include job training programs, educational programs, and housing programs. Findings such as this highlight the role of basic sustainability when exiting prison (LaVigne, Brooks, & Shollenberger, 2009).

Reentry can also be challenging depending on the offense that brought women to prison in the first place. You've learned in this section about the challenges of reentry for women who continue to struggle with addiction. But what about women who are convicted of one of the most stigmatizing crimes: sexual offenses? What issues do they face? Like other offenders, women convicted of a sexually based offense express concerns about finding housing and a job. In particular, they acknowledged that their offenses come with special terms and conditions of their release such as community notification and residency restrictions. In particular, women were concerned about how this might affect their relationships with their children: Would they be allowed to see them participate in activities such as sports if they were held at their children's school or at a local park? Another concern was the stigma that comes with the all-encompassing label of sex offender, regardless of the nature of their specific offense. Indeed, this label can complicate what is already a difficult transition to the community (Tewksbury, Connor, Cheeseman & Rivera, 2012).

While women may turn to public assistance to help support their reentry transition, many come to find that these resources are either unavailable or are significantly limited. The **Welfare Reform Act of 1996** imposed not only time limits on the aid that women can receive, but it has also significantly affected the road to success by denying services and resources for women with a criminal record, particularly in cases of women convicted on a felony drug-related charge (Hirsch, 2001). Section 115 of the welfare reform act calls for a lifetime ban on benefits such as Temporary Assistance for Needy Families (TANF) and food stamps to offenders convicted in the state or federal

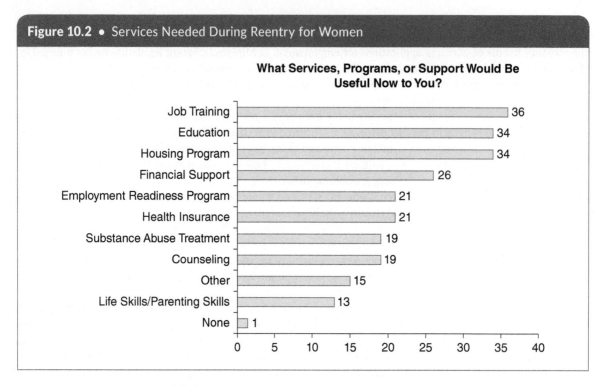

Figure 10.2 ● Services Needed During Reentry for Women

What Services, Programs, or Support Would Be Useful Now to You?

Service	Value
Job Training	36
Education	34
Housing Program	34
Financial Support	26
Employment Readiness Program	21
Health Insurance	21
Substance Abuse Treatment	19
Counseling	19
Other	15
Life Skills/Parenting Skills	13
None	1

SOURCE: LaVigne, N. G., Brooks, L. E., & Shollenberger, T. L. (2009). *Women on the outside: Understanding the experiences of female prisoners returning to Houston, Texas.* Urban Institute Justice Policy Center. Retrieved at http://www.urban.org/sites/default/files/publication/30401/411902-Women-on-the-Outside-Understanding-the-Experiences-of-Female-Prisoners-Returning-to-Houston-Texas.PDF

courts for a felony drug offense. In addition, women convicted of a drug offense are barred from living in public housing developments and, in some areas, a criminal record can limit the availability of Section 8 housing options[1] (Jacobs, 2000). Drug charges are the only offense type subjected to this ban—even convicted murderers can apply for and receive governmental benefits following their release (Sentencing Project, 2006). Indeed, the limits of this ban jeopardize the very efforts toward sustainable and safe housing, education, and drug treatment that are needed in order for women to successfully transition from prison.

How many women are affected by the lifetime bans on assistance? Research by the Sentencing Project indicates that, as of 2011, more than 180,000 women have been affected by the lifetime TANF welfare ban (Sentencing Project, 2015). They also estimate that the denial of benefits places more than 135,000 children at risk for future contact with the criminal justice system because of economic struggles. The ban also disproportionately affects women of color. Since its enactment in 1996, 39 states have rescinded the lifetime ban on resources, either in its entirety or in part. However, 11 states have retained this ban on assistance, placing family reunification efforts between women and their children in jeopardy (Legal Action Center, 2011: Sentencing Project, 2006). In Georgia, a state that has a full ban for both TANF and SNAP benefits for individuals convicted on a drug offense, some legislators have questioned whether such a ban is an effective policy. Georgia State Representative Rich Golick has supported lifting the ban: "You had individuals who were coming out of the system convicted of a violent crime who had the eligibility to apply

---

[1]Section 8 housing provides governmental subsidies for housing in nonpublic housing developments. Here, private landlords are paid the difference between the amount of rent that a tenant can afford, based on his or her available income, and the fair market value of the residence.

Table 10.3 • State Drug Conviction Policies on Cash Assistance (TANF) and Food Stamps (SNAP)

TANF			SNAP		
Full Ban	**Modified Ban**	**No Ban**	**Full Ban**	**Modified Ban**	**No Ban**
Alaska	Arkansas	Kansas	Alaska	Arkansas	Delaware
Alabama	Arizona	Maine	Alabama	Arizona	Iowa
Delaware	California	Michigan	Georgia	California	Kansas
Georgia	Colorado	New Hampshire	Missouri	Colorado	Maine
Illinois	Connecticut	New Jersey	Mississippi	Connecticut	Michigan
Missouri	Florida	New Mexico	South Carolina	Florida	New Hampshire
Mississippi	Hawaii	New York	Texas	Hawaii	New Jersey
Nebraska	Iowa	Ohio	West Virginia	Iowa	New Mexico
South Carolina	Idaho	Oklahoma	Wyoming	Idaho	New York
South Dakota	Indiana	Pennsylvania		Illinois	Ohio
Texas	Kentucky	Rhode Island		Indiana	Oklahoma
West Virginia	Louisiana	Vermont		Kentucky	Pennsylvania
	Massachusetts	Wyoming		Louisiana	Rhode Island
	Maryland			Massachusetts	South Dakota
	Minnesota			Maryland	Vermont
	Montana			Minnesota	Wyoming
	North Carolina			Montana	
	North Dakota			North Carolina	
	Nevada			North Dakota	
	Oregon			Nevada	
	Tennessee			Oregon	
	Utah			Tennessee	
	Virginia			Utah	
	Washington			Virginia	
	Wisconsin			Wisconsin	
12	**25**	**13**	**9**	**25**	**16**

SOURCE: The Sentencing Project (2015, updated). sentencing project.org/wp-content/uploads/2015/12/A-lifetime-of-punishment.pdf. Reprinted with permission from The Sentencing Project.

for food stamps, whereas someone who went in on a drug charge, including possession, didn't have that ability. You're increasing the changes that they may reoffend because they don't have the ability to make ends meet. Doesn't this go against what we're trying to achieve as they reenter society" (Wiltz, 2016).

Even women without a drug conviction still face significant issues in obtaining public assistance. Federal welfare law prohibits states from providing assistance under programs such as TANF (Temporary Assistance for Needy Families), SSI (Supplementary Security Income), housing assistance, or food stamps in cases where a woman has violated a condition of her probation or parole. In many cases, this violation can be as simple as failing to report for a meeting with a probation officer when she has a sick child. In addition, TANF carries a 5-year lifetime limit for assistance. This lifetime limit applies to all women, not just those under the criminal justice system. In addition, the delay to receive these services ranges from 45 days to several months, a delay that significantly affects the ability of women to put a roof over their children's heads, clothes on their bodies, and food in their bellies (Jacobs, 2000). Ultimately, these reforms are a reflection of budgetary decisions that often result in the slashing of social service and government aid programs, while the budgets for criminal justice agendas, such as incarceration, remain supported by state and governmental officials. These limits affect not only the women who are in the greatest need of services but their children as well, who will suffer physically, mentally, and emotionally from these economic struggles (Danner, 2003).

Despite the social stigma that comes with receiving welfare benefits, women in one study indicated that the receipt of welfare benefits represented progress toward a successful recovery and independence from reliance on friends, family, or a significant other for assistance. A failure to receive benefits could send them into a downward spiral toward homelessness, abusive relationships, and relapse.

> We still need welfare until we are strong enough to get on our feet. Trying to stay clean, trying to be responsible parents and take care of our families. We need welfare right now. If we lose it, we might be back out there selling drugs. We're trying to change our lives. Trying to stop doing wrong things. Some of us need help. Welfare helps us stay in touch with society. Trying to do what's right for us. (Hirsch, 2001, p. 278)

Throughout the reentry process, women also struggle with gaining access to addiction-based services. Without these referrals by probation and parole, most women are denied access to treatment due to the limited availability of services or an inability to pay for such resources on their own. Here, women are actually at risk for recidivism, because their needs continue to be unmet. In addition, many of these programs fail to work within the context of their lives. For example, the majority of inpatient drug treatment programs do not provide the option for women to reside and care for their children. These programs promote sobriety first and rarely create the opportunity for family reunification until women have successfully transitioned from treatment, have obtained a job, and can provide a sustainable environment for themselves. For many women, the desire to reunite with their children is their primary focus, and the inability for women to maintain connection with their children can threaten their path toward sobriety (Jacobs, 2000).

Clearly, women who make the transition from prison or jail back to their communities must achieve stability in their lives. With multiple demands on them (compliance with the terms and conditions of their release; dealing with long-term issues such as addiction, mental health, and physical health concerns; and the need for food, clothing, and shelter), this transition is anything but easy. Here, the influence of a positive mentor can provide significant support for women as they navigate this journey.

> While it is true a woman in reentry has many tangible needs (housing, employment, family reunification, formal education), attention to intangible needs (empowerment, a sense of belonging, someone to talk to) can promote personal growth through positive reinforcement of progress, encouragement and support in the face of defeat and temptation, and a place to feel like a regular person. (Women's Prison Association [WPA], 2008, p. 3)

Several key pieces of legislation have focused on the need for support and mentorship throughout the reentry process and have provided federal funding to support these networks. For example, the Ready4Work initiative (U.S. Department of Labor, 2008), the Prisoner Reentry Initiative (Bush, 2004), and the Second Chance Act (2007) all acknowledged the challenges that ex-offenders face when they exit the prison environment. These initiatives help support community organizations that provide comprehensive services for ex-offenders, including case management, mentoring, and other transitional services (WPA, 2008). Given the struggles that women face as part of their journey back from incarceration, it is clear that these initiatives can provide valuable resources to assist with the reentry process.

Spotlight on Life After Parole

What is it like to experience freedom after spending over 25 years in prison? For women like Brenda Clubine and Glenda Virgil, it's a new life compared to what they experienced prior to entering prison. Both women endured significant abuse by their intimate partner. And both women were incarcerated in the California Institution for Women for killing their abusers.

Brenda Clubine was sentenced to 17 years to life in 1983 for the murder of her husband, Robert Clubine. During their seven month marriage, she had endured significant beatings and multiple trips to the emergency room. One night, she struck him over the head with an empty wine bottle and he died from blunt force trauma (Hastings, 1993). Glenda Virgil killed her boyfriend with a shotgun when he charged at her with a shovel, threatening to kill her. Like Clubine, Virgil was abused physically and sexually throughout their four-year relationship. She was sentenced in 1987 to 15 years to life (CBSLA.com, 2013). Neither woman was allowed to present evidence of their abuse histories during their trials.

Behind the walls of the California prison, Clubine founded a group called Convicted Women Against Abuse, where she met women like herself, women like Glenda Virgil. Their stories, as well as the stories of other women like them, were featured in a 2008 documentary called "Sin by Silence." In addition to building a community of abused women behind bars and providing support to each other, the group has been active in trying to change legislation related to abused victims in the criminal courts. During the early 1990s the group was involved in allowing the Battered Women's Syndrome to be used in clemency cases. Their efforts led to the release of several women in the group (Hillard, 2012).

After serving 26 years behind bars, Clubine was released from prison in 2008. Since her release from prison, she has continued her advocacy efforts. In 2012, Governor Brown signed into law new legislation that allowed victims of domestic violence to petition for new sentencing and parole hearings. During these hearings, inmates are now allowed to present evidence of their abuse and its relationship to their crimes (CISION, 2012). It was under this new law that Glenda Virgil was granted parole after two and a half decades in prison (Ma, 2013). At the time of her release, she had been diagnosed with stage 4 cancer. She passed away in 2017.

Recidivism and Female Offenders

Whether it is probation, prison, or parole, the goal of the corrections is to reduce and prevent recidivism. But does it? Recidivism can be a difficult thing for scholars to measure. What "counts" as recidivism? Is it being arrested or convicted for a new criminal offense? Is it a technical violation of probation or parole? What is the time limit that we use to determine recidivism? One year following release? Five? Ten?

While women are slightly more likely to be successful on parole than their male counterparts, the failure for women is still high with 47.1% of women returning to prison within one year of release (compared to 59.2% of men returned to prison during the same time period) (Blackburn, Pfeffer, & Harris, 2016). Research by Mears, Cochran, and Bales (2012) indicates that prison can produce a criminogenic effect for women. This means that prison can actually encourage offenders to engage in crime rather than prevent it, at least in terms of particular offenses. While time in prison is more likely to increase property and drug crimes for male offenders, incarceration for women increases their recidivism for property offenses. In addition, prison produces the strongest effect for recidivism, compared to probation. Women who returned to prison during that first year were more likely to have mental health issues that were either untreated or undertreated, a factor that played a significant role in their recidivism (Blackburn, Pfeffer, & Harris, 2016). Women are also more likely to fail on parole due to a technical violation and fail at a faster rate compared to men (Huebner & Pleggenkuhle, 2015). Younger women are also more likely to recidivate (McCoy & Miller, 2013). However, protective factors did serve to inhibit recidivism for women. While romantic and familial relationships increased recidivism risk for male offenders, these relationships (when positive in nature) served to protect women from recidivism (Cobbina, Huebner, & Berg, 2012). These results indicate that the *most punitive* punishment may be the least effective in terms of rehabilitation and that reentry efforts need to consider these factors when providing support.

Building Resiliency for Women

With so much attention on the negative focus of women's lives and their relationships, there has been little discussion within the research about how women involved in the criminal justice system build strength and resiliency in their lives. In Section VII, you learned about how factors such as a positive mentor and support networks are important factors for delinquent girls, and the same holds true for incarcerated women. Research by Wright, DeHart, Koons-Witt, and Crittenden (2013) indicates that there are several relationships that can serve as buffers against criminal behavior, including positive family relationships, prosocial peer relationships, supportive significant others, and motherhood. In some cases, family members helped them escape from dangerous situations such as an intimate partner. "Normal" friends may inspire women to want normalcy in their lives. While much has been written about the power of a negative romantic relationship, a healthy relationship can also provide support throughout incarceration and provide a sense of stability on release. Finally, the presence of children may encourage women to turn away from a life of crime and focus on their roles as mothers. While these relationships presented positive opportunities, these women also had negative associations to battle, and it was these bad contexts and relationships that would overpower the positive opportunities in their lives. In the words of one woman,

> It all goes back to trying to please people that you care about. . . . It keeps you focused. If you care about your family and love them, you aren't going to put yourself in a position to have yourself taken away from them. (Wright et al., p. 81)

/// SUMMARY

- Probation allows women to receive correctional supervision while remaining in the community.
- On release, many women return to the communities in which they lived prior to their incarceration, where they face issues of addiction and dysfunction in their lives.
- Gender-responsive programming is designed to address the unique needs of female offenders.

/// KEY TERMS

Barefield v. Leach 423

Canterino v. Wilson 424

Cooper v. Morin 424

Gender-responsive
   programming 424

Glover v. Johnson 423

Level of Service InventoryRevised
   (LSI-R) 427

Parole 429

Probation 427

Reentry 425

Welfare Reform Act of 1996 431

Wraparound services 425

/// DISCUSSION QUESTIONS

1. If you were to design a program that reflected gender-responsive principles, what key features would you integrate into your curriculum?

2. What challenges do women face during their reentry process? How does the Welfare Reform Bill limit access to resources for some women following their incarceration?

3. How do traditional risk assessment instruments fail female offenders? What are the implications of these findings?

/// WEB RESOURCES

Hour Children: http://www.hourchildren.org

Our Place DC: http://www.ourplacedc.org

The Sentencing Project: http://www.sentencingproject.org

Women's Prison Association: http://www.wpaonline.org

 Visit **study.sagepub.com/mallicoat3e** to access additional study tools, including eFlashcards, web quizzes, web resources, video resources, and SAGE journal articles.

READING /// 19

Women who leave prison are faced with a number of challenges. This article focuses on three of these challenges: This reading highlights the way parole structures women's reintegration efforts post-incarceration. The women's experiences highlight how parole governance intersects, conflicts with, and complicates their efforts to return to their communities and transition out of the gaze of the penal state.

"It's Their World, So You've Just Got to Get Through"
Women's Experiences of Parole Governance

Tara D. Opsal

Introduction

Extensive research documents that leaving prison and returning to one's community is a challenging transition for most. Indeed, important scholarship identifies a variety of barriers that former prisoners face as they experience the reentry process and work to desist from crime including the challenges of finding housing and employment, reconnecting with family, and accessing health care and other social services (Mallik-Kane & Visher, 2008; Pager, 2003; Petersilia, 2003; Richie, 2001). Notably, individuals navigate these difficulties within a broader social context. For example, the stigma of a criminal record has tremendous impacts on the formerly incarcerated as do various policies and laws that institutionalize a variety of legal and cultural consequences of holding this discredited social identity (Travis, 2005). Feminist scholars have made central contributions to research on reentry and point out the way other identities such as gender and race converge to create additional or unique experiences post-incarceration. For example, women are more likely to experience a lack of familial resources, parental statuses, and trauma backgrounds that shape the resources they draw on as well as the obstacles they face post-incarceration (Huebner, DeJong, & Cobbina, 2010; La Vigne, Brooks, & Shollenberger, 2009; Morash, 2010; O'Brien, 2001).

More recently, researchers also examine how parole intersects with the reentry process. Some of this work focuses on understanding the factors that increase one's likelihood of returning to prison while under the supervision of parole (Lin et al., 2010; Steen & Opsal, 2007; Steiner, Travis, & Makarios, 2011) or how the state can respond in gender-responsive ways (Morash, 2010). More recently, a handful of scholars explored how the institution of parole extends the gaze of the penal state and regulates and governs a group of marginalized people returning to their communities (Pollack, 2007; Turnbull & Hannah-Moffat, 2009; Werth, 2012).

Research that focuses on reentry or parole paints a rich picture of the social conditions that the formerly incarcerated negotiate; however, it remains less clear how women on parole experience, respond to, and negotiate the governance of parole and its associated conditions that regulate their lives post-incarceration. The data in this article illuminate this gap. Drawing on longitudinal qualitative data with a group of women newly released from prison, this project illustrates the impact of parole conditions that focus on governing and regulating "risky subjects." I begin by briefly reviewing the literature that illuminates women's unique experiences with corrections and, more specifically, reentry. Then, I situate the experience of individuals on parole and explain how this

SOURCE: Opsal, T. (2015). "It's their world, so you've just got to get through": Women's experiences of parole governance. *Feminist Criminology, 10*(2), 188–207.

institution intersects the reentry process. Taken together, these bodies of research contextualize the findings I present later, which highlight how parole supervision intersects and complicates women's reintegrative efforts in ways that make it more difficult for them to achieve the very goals that parole wants them to attain. In this, it becomes clear how the institutionalized idea of the parolee as one in need of risk management functions to systematically disadvantage them.

Considering Women's Experiences With Reentry

Social scientists have increasingly pushed the experience of women to the forefront of criminological and sociological inquiries; thus, notable research on their experiences with corrections and reentry exists. This focus is particularly important given that U.S. "get tough on crime" policies—particularly those connected to the War on Drugs—have had significant impacts on women, the extent to which they experience incarceration and, thus, reentry (Chesney-Lind & Pasko, 2004); indeed, since 1980, the number of women held in state and federal facilities increased by well over 600% (Mauer, 2013). Broadly, this body of research tells an important story about the way the correctional system is gendered. Because gender structures the social world—and thus the criminal processing system—women often have different experiences than men before, during, and after incarceration.

Ample research, for example, indicates that women's experiences of victimization, substance abuse, and mental health issues—created and then perpetuated by tremendous structural inequities—are often central pathways into the criminal processing system (Daly, 1994; Richie, 1996). Prisons, however, seldom effectively address the needs of women they house; even rehabilitative or "gender-responsive programming" thought to be designed to meet women's unique needs and empower them on their own terms may end up doing the opposite (McCorkel, 2013). As a result, incarceration often ends up increasing women's experience of marginalization and social inequity, which affects their release and return to the community. Indeed, individuals must navigate intersecting and complex demands and circumstances post-incarceration (Richie, 2001).

For example, motherhood is a central aspect of many women's challenges as they navigate the correctional system, and as a result, significant research focuses on understanding this aspect of their prison and reentry experiences (Brown & Bloom, 2009; Michalsen, Flavin, & Krupat, 2010). Indeed, many women involved in the criminal processing system are mothers and are more likely to be primary caregivers before and after incarceration than men (Glaze & Maruschak, 2008). Despite evidence that indicates maintaining bonds between children and parents during incarceration can be beneficial for both parent and child, prison rules and policies do not usually facilitate the maintenance of these relationships (Glaze & Maruschak, 2008; Pollock, 2002). Women are often incarcerated in areas that are far from their home (Mumola, 2000); moreover, relationships with their children's caregivers can be complex and uncertain (Enos, 2001). Thus, physically seeing their children is an even rarer event than other forms of communication such as phone calls and letters (Michalsen et al., 2010). Taken together, these circumstances can amplify mother/child reunification concerns and problems as they leave prison, return to their communities, and try to reestablish relationships with their children (Brown & Bloom, 2009; Ferraro & Moe, 2003; Opsal, 2011).

Negotiating other familial relationships can also be complex for women during reentry. While economic and emotional support from families can be an important aspect of a successful return home (Cobbina, 2010; O'Brien, 2001), families of origins and (ex)partners are often sources of emotional, physical, or sexual abuse prior to incarceration for women. Thus, because avoiding or shedding these relationships might be necessary for women to successfully reintegrate into their communities (Leverentz, 2006), they may also be more vulnerable to social isolation or inadequate support structures.

Finally, women's involvement in the criminal processing system directly shapes their reentry experience because the "mark of a criminal record" is stigmatizing. Indeed, cultural ideas about individuals with a felony record as well as formal policies that restrict the rights and privileges of individuals with a record create immense reentry obstacles. For example, being encumbered by a felony record makes finding work (Mallik-Kane & Visher, 2008; Pager, 2003) and housing (Bergseth, Jens, Bergeron-Vigesaa, & McDonald, 2011; Travis, 2005) difficult; notably, the very things that having a criminal record limits access to are very often critical aspects of a successful reintegration.

Clearly, then, individuals face a variety of obstacles post-incarceration that can make a return to the community an onerous process. Moreover, feminist criminological scholarship, in particular, highlights the unique ways that gender and the correctional system can shape women's experiences. I continue to review this important body of research later in this article to contextualize the findings I present. Next, however, I consider the changing role of parole in corrections and the ways this institution intersects the reentry process.

Situating the Experience of the Risky Parolee

The institution of parole, as a form of post-release supervision, is charged with supervising individuals newly released from prison as they return to their communities. The state requires that individuals on parole abide by a set of conditions that regulate their behavior; while the central rule requires a crime-free reintegration into the community, all individuals on parole must also follow a host of technical conditions. In the present study, mandatory conditions of supervision for the women newly released into parole included weekly meetings with their assigned parole officer (PO), mobility restrictions (such as being unable to drive, change residences, and enter into particular establishments such as liquor stores), working or actively seeking employment, not associating with individuals with a record, and attending various forms of treatment. In addition, parole boards and officers assigned supplementary conditions or "targeted" forms of governance (Turnbull & Hannah-Moffat, 2009) to each woman depending on their conceptualization of her risk.

Critically interrogating the way that the institution of parole utilizes technical conditions, as well as understanding how individuals on parole experience them, as this research does, is important for a variety of reasons. For example, the conditions clearly proceed from, and therefore reproduce, hegemonic cultural ideas about good citizenship (Bosworth, 2007). These constructions are gendered and create consequences for women under the gaze of the penal state, especially if their gender

performances do not align with correctional discourse (Pollack, 2007). Relatedly, technical conditions often fail to acknowledge or align in many ways with the material conditions of women's lives. For example, given the disproportionate impact of mass incarceration policies and the reality of concentrated incarceration, the condition prohibiting association between individuals with records is not only impractical but also structurally problematic. In addition, conditions regulate behaviors that under normal circumstances (when a person is not under supervision) or when completed by the right person (not criminal, felon, parolee) are not understood as criminal. However, while serving time on parole, officers can use violations of these conditions as fodder to increase surveillance or reincarcerate. Notably, for many under the supervision of parole, technical violations have become a central route back to jail or prison as revocations make up just over 20% of all prison admissions (Lin, 2010).

These trends are related, in part, to a shifting philosophical orientation of parole. Historically, the foundational goals of parole were centered more heavily on treatment, rehabilitation, and reintegration (Simon, 1993). The orientation of today's state parole systems are divergent, complex, and often profess that they meet multiple (competing) goals including reintegration, supervision, and public safety. Moreover, parole officers' on-the-ground actions do not always reflect the discursive mission the state parole system sets forth (Lynch, 1998). Despite this, many of today's state parole systems provide reintegrative resources but are more focused on surveillance, control-oriented practices, and risk management strategies (Seiter & Kadela, 2003; Simon, 1993; Travis & Stacey, 2010). In the present study, whether it was the intention of the state or parole officers, the women overwhelmingly reported experiencing parole as a form of surveillance rather than as a reintegrative process; they explained that its purpose was to "catch people" or "keep an eye on them" and that it allowed the state to say to the community "this person is being monitored."[1]

Cultural technological advancements in addition to a neoliberal climate emphasizing individual responsibility have provided the fodder for parole to advance in this way. In practice, parole officers rely heavily on surveillance technologies such as electronic monitoring, Global Positioning System (GPS), and (especially) drug testing to monitor their caseloads (Petersilia, 2003). Notably, the growing use of this latter strategy has distinct impacts on women and women of color, in particular, because their drug use over the past three decades has been increasingly criminalized and brought under the purview of the state (Chesney-Lind & Pasko, 2004). Regardless of the focus of the condition, scholars have criticized them as being unrealistic, redundant, and impractical, thus, impeding a successful return home (Jacobson, 2005; Travis & Stacey, 2010).

While researchers surmise that parole complicates an already difficult reentry process, fewer projects illuminate precisely how these challenges directly manifest in the lives of people on parole (for notable exceptions, see Opsal, 2009; Pollack, 2007; Werth, 2012). This article highlights this process and illustrates how the institution shapes the reentry process because it conceptualizes the parolee as a risky subject who must be governed in risk-appropriate ways via technical conditions (Turnbull & Hannah-Moffat, 2009). In particular, I consider how the gaze of the state and the resultant conditions that regulate individual-level risks and choices parole deems as problematic interrupts the women's efforts to connect with roles, relationships, and institutions that could ease their return to the community.

Method

The findings presented in this article are based on a series of open-ended, semi-structured, qualitative interviews conducted with 43 women under the supervision of parole. I conducted first-round interviews with women as soon as possible after their release from prison; second-round interviews ($n = 30$) occurred approximately 3 months after the first. Consistent with grounded theory (Charmaz, 2009), I interviewed nine women a third time after they had been out of prison for at least 1 year to fine tune themes that emerged as central during data analysis.

To recruit for the study, I initially partnered with a women's prison from which nearly all women in Colorado release. They allowed me to enter the facility weekly and talk with women about to be released to the community. As the study progressed, I relied on other recruitment methods including local community organizations that provide resources to newly released individuals, as well as snowball sampling. Women were often exposed to a variety of recruitment materials before they contacted me.

These recruitment and sampling strategies produced a diverse sample in age, race, and ethnicity. Specifically, the age of participants ranged from 23 to 54 years (M and median = 37). Forty-four percent of the sample were White, 35% Black, and 16% Native American; in comparison with all women released to parole in the state during sample recruitment, Black women are overrepresented. All women in this sample were released to an urban center and were under the supervision of parole officers in four different offices distributed throughout the city.

The majority of women released into precarious economic circumstances. To meet their initial financial needs, most women relied on a combination of support from family, as well as government resources. The majority of women (77%), however, acknowledged that these sources were inadequate to meet their needs and set out to search for work on release. Two thirds of the women initially lived with family or in a privately-run reentry residential facility while a full one quarter released homeless. Thirty-one (72%) women reported they were mothers. While some reported their children were placed with the state's foster care system when they were incarcerated, other women called on extended family to provide temporary care for their children. However, on release from prison, no women had immediate custody.

Finally, I systematically coded and analyzed data in several stages using NVIVO software. Drawing on a grounded theory approach (Charmaz, 2009), I coded each interview using a line-by-line approach, looked for common patterns among the narratives, and developed broad analytic themes that characterized the data that I present in this article. The findings presented here draw on developing research on women, reentry, and parole as a form of governance. In particular, the findings I present next show various ways parole—as a form of governance—intersects and complicates women's reentry, desistance, and reintegration efforts.

Conflicting Demands, Disrupted Reentry

As new releases, all the women in this study expressed a strong desire not only to complete parole successfully but also to be different kinds of people "on the outs." About this, Deidra explained,

> I just don't want it any more. It's different than before. Before I wanted it. I was doin' it [not using] just 'cause of the courts, just 'cause of the system, whatever. But this time I'm doin' it [not using] because I want to do it. . . . I want to make it this time. I want to find out what life's really all about, 'cause I don't know.

These types of narrative projects assist people in creating new (pro-social) self-concepts, and although these narratives may be fractured (Werth, 2012) or disrupted (Opsal, 2011), they can be central to going straight (Maruna, 2001). Parole helps craft the bounds of these narratives because the institution provides explicit direction around what is respectable behavior; it also functions as the proving grounds for these emerging self-concepts given the costs associated with being understood by parole as noncompliant. In addition, however, the following data I present illustrate how the women experienced parole as a central obstacle to engaging in and manifesting the roles that are crucial to these narrative projects.

Becoming an Employee

Throughout the 20th century, employment has played a significant role for the institution of parole (Simon, 1993). Parole officers have consistently relied on labor as a normalizing institution, a source of social control, and as a sign of competent reintegration. As stated earlier, in the state wherein these women were under supervision, not seeking work is considered a violation of one's parole agreement. Thus, it is not surprising that the majority of participants in the present study reported understanding that being a successful parolee meant being an employee. Despite this, however, parole directly impeded the women's ability to work. About this, Alice explained,

> I don't want to lose what I've worked so hard gaining just because I have a—sometimes it's a balancing act and it scares me a little bit. I may wake up and [my boss] may try calling me into work and I'll call the color line and they'll tell me I have a UA and there's no one in here [at

work] to cover and then I'll look like I'm the irresponsible one. But who I am responsible to? I have two people that I am accountable to. . . so it kind of scares me.

As Alice describes, parole challenged her ability to fully commit to work and subsume an employee identity in instrumental ways. Other women, like Alice, explained how the conditions of parole got in the way of work. For example, on any given day that they were working, participants may also be expected to submit to a urinary analysis (UA), report to their parole officer for a check-in, report to their case manager, attend a counseling session, or participate in other group or individual programming. Moreover, parole stipulated that no new release could drive; thus, women had to negotiate these competing demands by walking, navigating public transportation, or relying on social networks.

As new releases, parole governance was particularly high and, thus, often particularly disruptive to work. However, women reported that some POs were willing to be flexible to mitigate the amount of conflict parole obligations had on their working commitments. Participants explained that some POs changed curfew hours, found alternate classes that fit with their schedules, and—after "proving" themselves—even cut back on the number of times a month they needed to drop UAs. Some POs, though, were not accommodating or open to these changes; furthermore, some women did not want to approach their POs with any kind of request because they preferred to "fly under the officer's radar" believing that any extra attention they called on themselves was bad attention.

Notably, then, rather than mitigating these competing demands through parole, women more commonly reported looking for work that fit around their parole schedule. Ashley found telemarketing work early in her job search and explained with enthusiasm,

> They're offender-friendly! They allow me time to go drop UAs if I need to. They allow me time to go see my parole officer. I don't know if he's the owner or the manager, he's an ex-offender. So, he totally understands what we're coming from and where we're coming from. . . and so it's cool because it allows me time to go see [my

parole officer] when I need to, it allows me time to go do my UAs when I need to. I'm off in time to go to group on Monday night.

While "felon friendly" is typically conceptualized in public policy conversations as jobs open to individuals with a record, for these women, the phrase took on a different meaning and referred to flexible jobs willing to take on employees negotiating competing demands from the criminal processing system. Likewise, "felon-friendly," in the present study, nearly always meant jobs characterized by low wages, sporadic hours, little or no upward mobility, and no benefits. As women attempted to mitigate the conflicting demands set forth in their parole conditions with their attempts to become workers, they simultaneously funneled themselves into low-wage labor. Clearly, individuals with records enter into low-wage labor for a multitude of reasons (Flowers, 2010). However, the women in this study "chose" this type of work because they viewed it as a way to meet parole expectations without conflict. Clearly, though, this strategy that enabled them to negotiate parole governance produced different problems for the women in this study because it contributed to their economic marginalization.

Occasionally, parole intersected women's working pursuits in other more directly harmful ways. For example, Linda found a job working the front desk of a motel near her home. She explained that she worked the graveyard shift, in a marginalized neighborhood that, for her, often meant navigating requests for rooms from people who could not pay. On rare occasion, these interactions would result in her contacting the police for assistance. Repeated police contact and interacting with "high-risk" individuals were red flags for her PO, and he asked her to try and find other work. When she did not, he increased his own surveillance of her by often stopping into her workplace. About this, she explained,

So, he came in [to work] on the night of the 12th and I just happened not to be working. My boss was working that night. And he started reaming my boss about, "She's having too much police contact. I don't like the hours she's working." So, I walked into work on Sunday and he's [my boss] like, "I need you to come into my office," so I went into his office, and he was like,

"I can't deal with that. I can't deal with your parole officer coming in here. I'm gonna have to let you go."

These experiences illustrate a number of important issues regarding parole governance, the way it complicates reentry, and its consequences for the women in this study. Clearly, parole governed the women's relationships to employment in ways that often did not facilitate their reentry into the public sphere; this is particularly problematic given that these women are *already* navigating a labor market from a disadvantaged position. Indeed, women enter a gendered labor market that shapes the opportunities and wages available to women and, especially, women of color. Furthermore, the stigma of a criminal record limits their job opportunities (Pager, 2003) as do legal restrictions. Indeed, participants looking for entry-level positions in pink-collar ghetto work such as child care, health care, and office work found that they were not eligible because of their record.

Furthermore, it is particularly problematic that parole adds extra layers of complexity to women's attempts to integrate into the labor market post-incarceration given that it is an established turning point for individuals returning to their communities. Because work is a pro-social institution (Sampson & Laub, 1993) that decreases economic marginalization (Holtfreter, Reisig, & Morash, 2004) and is a hook for change that shifts one's self-concept (Giordano, Cernkovich, & Rudolph, 2002; Maruna, 2001), even those who gain marginal employment opportunities are more likely to succeed post-incarceration than those with none (Uggen, 2000). Although historically a more robust finding for men, research also provides notable evidence that working is a central aspect of women's successful reintegration (Farrington, 2007; Flowers, 2010; Opsal, 2012; Uggen & Kruttschnitt, 1998).

Here, then, as Turnbull and Hannah-Moffat (2009) posit, "parole conditions are a technique of discipline and self-governance . . . that is simultaneously responsibilizing and de-responsibilizing" (p. 537); indeed, the paroled subject is understood as both an agent who must take responsibility for his or her own (pro-social) change and as culpable, risky, and in need of monitoring and direction. The consequence of this conceptualization for the women in this study was that the institution was simultaneously committed to their failure and success as employees. Although parole was committed to developing law-abiding citizens who work, this goal could not come at the sacrifice of the women's own governability.

On Mothering: Resuming the Role as a Risky Proposition

The vast majority—nearly three quarters—of the women in the present study were mothers and narrated a strong connection to this identity often pointing to their mother selves as a primary reason to go straight. Like employment, research indicates that parenting can be an important "hook for change" in the desistance and reentry process. In the case of women, while mothering from economic margins can certainly be an entry point into crime, an emerging body of literature indicates that being a mother can also serve as a source of motivation to stay away from drugs and crime and, under particular conditions, enhances the likelihood of desistance (Edin & Kefalas, 2011; Kreager, Matsueda, & Erosheva, 2010). Given this empirical reality alongside participants' strong identification as mothers, it is notable that very few women in the present study pursued full custody of their children on release; parole often shaped and constrained women's capacity to do so.

When the state sentenced Elana to prison, it also court-ordered her 11-year-old son to reside with her father; thus, on release, she was able to see him regularly but explained,

> Elena: It's just like, I want to be a loving, attentive [parent] like when he was a baby . . . it's just really hard to get back into that because I'm afraid that somethin's gonna go wrong . . . maybe I'll be locked back up again . . .
>
> Interviewer: Do you have that concern with parole?
>
> Elana: Yeah, I've always got—even though I know I'm doing the right thing, but it's always your word against theirs. If they say you're doing something, if something even remotely happens and they think you're guilty, what they do is, they lock you up [in jail] until you go back before parole . . . I mean I know that I'm doing good, but I don't know if any thing's gonna

happen. It's always in the back of your mind that something could happen at any time.

> Interviewer: Do you think that affects your relationship with your son?
>
> Elana: I think it does. I know he's worried, too, that I might go and I'm worried that I might leave him and disappoint him again. It's hard.

Women who knew their caregivers and had some form of contact with their children on release often spoke of maintaining physical or emotional distance from their children for some time. Many, like Elana, were motivated to do this out of fear they would desert and disappoint their children again. Such concerns, however, were less about their own individual-level culpability and more about the unpredictability of parole supervision and PO decision making. In other words, being understood as a compliant parolee by one's PO (and thus maintaining freedom on the outside) was not an objective reflection of one's behavior. As a result, being subject to continued state supervision made *fully* reconnecting with children a risky proposition for these mothers.

For other participants, parole supervision more directly shaped their capacity to reconnect with children and resume mothering responsibilities. Some women were unable to have contact with their children once they released to the outside because parole explicitly prohibited it or because a technical condition of their parole agreement somehow made contact with their kids illegal. Ronda's children, for example, moved to California to reside with Ronda's parents when she and her ex-husband were arrested and imprisoned for fraud. On release from prison, Ronda immediately requested a parole transfer to that state so she could both serve out her parole sentence and be reunited with her children. She explained that her PO told her, "No, you have to get established here, you're not going back to California." Ronda feared she would not have the economic resources or support system to relocate her kids from California. Although she planned on reuniting with them as soon as possible, in the short-term, parole prevented her from fully taking on the mother role. Daisy was also prohibited from having contact with her child when she released from prison because Daisy's son was with her ex-partner who had a felony record. Parole forbade her from having contact with either. About this, Daisy explained matter-of-factly, "I talk[ed] to him to see my son. I wasn't supposed to, but I did. That's my son. I haven't seen my son in two years, and I'm gonna see my son."

Like Daisy, a few other women explained they too violated technical conditions of their parole agreement to see their children. In his work on how individuals on parole "restructure rules," Werth (2012) explains that participants complied with "important rules" such as drug testing because they "were easily visible to parole agents, while the superfluous rules tended to be ones whose violations was less likely to be detected" (p. 340). In addition, though, the findings presented here indicate that for many women, being a mother was central to their self-concept. Thus, to enact that identity to some degree, they were willing to violate these less visible rules and prioritize being a mother. These kinds of choices also illustrate how technical conditions—and by extension, the gaze of the state—is gendered. Indeed, incarcerated women are more likely to have relationships with their children before and after serving time in prison than men (Mumola, 2000); in addition, men's prescribed gender role does not include intimate connection or caretaking of their children, whereas women's attempt to connect with their kids after being in prison can be viewed as an extension of their culturally expected gender roles. Thus, by forbidding and regulating their contact with children, parole puts these mothers in a lose–lose situation where, ultimately, they become more at risk of failing as both mothers and parolees.

Notably, Black mothers were significantly less likely to report experiencing problems balancing motherhood and parole than either White or Hispanic women. This can be explained, in part, because Black women in this study were more likely to be mothers to adult children and more likely to have experienced formal custodial revocation by the state prior to their incarceration. However, Hispanic and White women were much more likely to retain formal custody of their children while they were incarcerated; White mothers, in particular, were significantly more likely to report that their children remained in the care of kin networks. While informal kin networks of support are typically understood as stronger among families of Blacks and ethnic minorities (Hogan, Hao, & Parish, 1990), the state has simultaneously scrutinized

poor, Black, women's child-rearing practices to a higher degree (Mink, 2001; Roberts, 1999). Indeed, in the case of the present research, it appears that White and Hispanic women had to spend more time negotiating being parolees and mothers because their parental rights were more likely to be intact and unsevered by the state.

Robert Werth (2012) explains that parole represents a liminal position—somewhere in between incarcerated and free, and that individuals on parole must learn how to navigate and respond to this fractured position. The data here, in particular, illustrate how liminality functions in the lives of women post-incarceration as they negotiated parole governance alongside parenthood. The state, rather than viewing motherhood as an opportunity to motivate and facilitate reentry, viewed it—at best—as irrelevant or—at worst—as a risky site in need of regulation. As a result, participants were compelled to maintain physical or emotional distance from their children or violate the conditions of their parole agreement to enact the identity to some degree.

The Consequences of Regulating Women's Relationships

As presented so far, a central facet of parole governance is regulating the behavior of its clients. A central organizational effort to realize this goal entails the condition prohibiting association with persons the state deems as antisocial or contributing to the risky subject's criminality. In the case of the present study, this translated into anybody who had a criminal record. The parole agreements read:

> You shall not associate with anyone with a criminal history (including felonies, misdemeanors, municipal codes, or offenders in facilities or halfway houses), without prior permission from your Community Parole Officer (this also includes correspondence by phone, mail, or electronic messaging). You must submit the names and dates of birth of any person you would like to associate with to your Community Parole Officer. Not knowing that they have a criminal history is not an excuse. It is your responsibility to ask them, and to ask your Community Parole Officer for permission.

Based on assumptions of social bond theory, this type of targeted governance exists to discourage the development of relationships and circumstances that might inhibit ties to conventional relationships and institutions. However, as I illustrate throughout this section, this—and other conditions that restrict mobility—governs in a vacuum because it does not acknowledge the structural or material conditions that exist in the lives of many formerly incarcerated women.

Creating a System of Support

Relationships are often at the center of sociological research on crime, delinquency, desistance, and reentry. Most existing research on the role of support systems in the lives of the previously incarcerated focuses on the importance of family in providing material and economic resources to individuals on release from prison (La Vigne & Kachnowski, 2005; Visher & Travis, 2003). There is evidence, though, that women are more likely to navigate obstacles in garnering a network of support. For example, women have a more difficult time reconnecting with family post-incarceration (La Vigne et al., 2009; Leverentz, 2011; O'Brien, 2001), and opposite-sex romantic partnerships are less likely to create opportunities for desistance (Leverentz, 2006). In addition, Pollack (2007) posits that correctional risk discourses can be a site of control regulating women's relationships on the outside.

The women in the present study explained that familial and peer relationships played significant roles in their lives as they returned to their communities. Participants stated these kinds of relationships provided them with a sense of belonging, emotional support, and motivation to stay out of prison. Many, however, were frustrated that parole prohibited contact with individuals who were previously or currently under the supervision of the state. Alice explained,

> I know people that used to have the [criminal] life and now they're not in that life. And I would love to be able to talk to them and gain some insight. . . . I have more in common with them than the average person and when I see myself going through troubles that are related to feeling like crap when I come back from going on an apartment search and having them tell me,

"get the hell out of here" [because I am a felon and they won't rent to me]—no one really relates. They're like, "oh that's bad." But they're not like, "dude, I know that sucks. Don't worry about it, there's this little place [that rents to felons]"—they know about these things because they're felons.

Relatedly, women who lived in transitional housing that were strictly composed of individuals currently under the supervision of the state found dealing with association conditions particularly uncertain and frustrating. POs instructed these women that it was permissible to socialize *at the house* but that they could not "run around" with one another outside of the supervision of the transitional home.

Given the way the stigma of a criminal record shapes and constrains women's housing and employment opportunities (as well as their ability to form new or different social networks) alongside law and policy that endorse numerous invisible punishments, the women in the present study were often compelled to ignore this condition for the sake of their own survival on the outside. Indeed, many, like Alice expressed above, valued the perspective of individuals who were currently or had already navigated the reentry process because they were relatable, supportive, and sources of valuable logistical information. Thus, most participants explained their networks of support were made up mostly or entirely of people with a history of involvement in the criminal processing system.

A few women ($n = 6$), however, responded differently to this situation. Dina explained,

> Right now, I don't really talk to anybody because I don't want to get back involved with the wrong crowd, with the wrong kind of friends. So, I don't know. I feel—that's why I feel lonely and unsupported I guess.

For this group of women, then, parole conditions stipulating what appropriate relationships looked like meant that they established no bonds at all, thus isolating themselves from people, relationships, and sources of emotional support. The effect of this self-isolating behavior is particularly problematic in the case of women, given that research notes gender differences with regard to support networks and friendship. In particular, intimate, healthy, friendships are important sources of social and psychological well-being for women (Comas-Diaz & Weiner, 2013; Miller & Stiver, 1997). Relatedly, O'Brien (2001) explains that for the women in her study, emotionally supportive relationships were a "crucial ingredient" (p. 115) for them as they reconstructed their lives after prison. Considering these dynamics alongside research that indicates women draw on less familial support on release than men raises a number of concerns about social support inadequacy, the impact this has on women post-incarceration, and the way parole systematically exacerbates this concern as it focuses on mitigating women's risk factors by regulating their relationships.

Finding a Place to Call Home

Finally, finding safe and secure housing is central to a successful reentry; housing provides individuals with shelter as well as a secure foundation on which to build (O'Brien, 2001). In addition, residing in a stable home is often a requirement for women seeking to reunite with children post-incarceration. Unfortunately, finding housing can be difficult for individuals newly released from prison. Research indicates that although some who leave prison are uncertain what they will be able to call home, most individuals initially depend on their families to provide them a place to lay their heads but wind up shuttling between "family, friends, shelters, and the streets" (Travis, 2005, p. 219). Parole officials report that finding housing for parolees is "by far their biggest challenge"—even more difficult than finding a job (Petersilia, 2003, p. 120); economic marginalization, stigma, and public housing exclusions for individuals with felony records are all tremendous obstacles (Bergseth et al., 2011). The women in the present study experienced many of these same difficulties in their search for housing. However, parole rules that governed their relationships and movement created additional obstacles and structured their housing choices.

All the women in this study explained that residential planning began prior to their release. Case managers assisted them in creating "parole plans" that served as concrete planning tools where participants confirmed where they hoped to live, potential jobs, and resources they would utilize to facilitate their transition. Before release, POs typically visited proposed homes and

approved or denied requests. The women in this study had very few promising housing options at this stage. Participants who had no other options often requested to release to privately run transitional housing facilities; many, however, initially asked to live with family or friends. Parole officers denied the requests of one third ($n = 7$) of those women who requested to live with relatives or peers.

Daisy explained she was not allowed to live with her grandmother—one of her only surviving relatives in the state—because her uncle, who was serving time on parole, resided there. In addition to denying residential requests because somebody in the residence had previously had some form of contact with the criminal processing system, parole officers deemed residences unsuitable for other reasons. Lou Lou, for example, could not live with her niece because her husband was drunk when the parole officer visited the home, while Rae's parole officer denied her request to live with an 81-year-old friend who kept a gun in the home. While two of these women found other relatives to live with that parole found suitable, the remaining five women released directly from prison to the cities' central homeless shelter that contracted beds with the Department of Corrections.

Linda explained what she viewed as the irony of being displaced from a friend's or relative's house to this homeless shelter:

> You're getting out on parole and they're going to stick you in the middle of they call it, "crackville or methville" because you can walk out the door and there's people shooting heroin on the corner. That's not what you're going to need because most women are drug addicts that go to prison. They drop you off there and you walk out the door and that's the first thing you see.

Thus, POs understood space as problematic because of its potential to mobilize antisocial actions via relationships. More precisely, however, POs problematized these spaces because they were outside of the state's scrutiny. Indeed, after disallowing women to reside with "problematic" relatives or friends, POs typically helped women find a bed in a shelter in a space surrounded by public, criminal behavior but where the rules of the shelter and the supervision of the staff extended the structure and surveillance of the parole system. The same logic applied to women whose POs encouraged them to reside in transitional facilities. All these facilities were located in economically marginalized neighborhoods where, as I conducted field research, I often observed public buying and selling of drugs, prostitution, and gun fire. Yet, these spaces were constructed as suitable—whether or not the women themselves found them so—because the facilities provided state-approved structure, programming, and surveillance.

Conclusion

Over the past decade, researchers have increasingly turned their attention toward documenting and understanding post-incarceration reentry. Feminist scholars have made a central contribution to this body of work by exploring and bringing attention to the post-incarceration experiences of women (Morash, 2010; O'Brien, 2001; Richie, 2001). Researchers, however, have been less likely to examine how women experience parole supervision and its forms of targeted governance while on parole; this is the central goal of the present article. In particular, I shed light on the way parole governance intersects, conflicts with, and complicates the desistance, reentry, and reintegration efforts of women transitioning out of the gaze of the penal state.

The women's narratives provide considerable and poignant evidence that parole supervision did not—in important ways—facilitate women's reentry into roles that could have aided their reintegration into their communities. Specifically, while parole required that the women in this study work, or at least actively seek employment, parole conditions as well as PO enforcement of those conditions shaped the kind of work women looked for while colliding in more direct ways that occasionally cost women their jobs. The vast majority of the participants in this study were in economically perilous positions, and the extra burdens created by parole exacerbated their situations.

Similarly, parole governance limited the extent to which women reconnected with their children once they released from prison. For some, this meant limiting contact or maintaining emotional distance out of fear that being a parolee represented a liminal space that threatened their ability to be a mother; for other women, however, parole directly impeded their capacity as a parent making contact with their children somehow a violation of their parole agreement. Morash (2010) posits that

parole agencies occasionally exerted control over women in her study by punishing them when they suspected child endangerment. The present study builds on this idea and illustrates that parole used motherhood as a site of social control over some women. This parole-created conflict, in particular, was a significant source of stress for the women I interviewed.

Another theme the women in this study depicted centered on the problematic ways parole intersected their lives, particularly how the institution governed relationships. Because parole regulates in ways that assume parolees are not yet prepared for conventional self-governance (Turnbull & Hannah-Moffat, 2009), the institution prioritized limiting women's contact with associates understood as potentially criminogenic (and thus potential sources of risk for their clients). Limiting association is particularly complex for individuals releasing from prison because it ignores the structural reality of concentrated incarceration (Clear, 2009). Indeed, differential enforcement of drug and other "get tough" laws and policies helped create the socially, economically, and politically marginalized communities to which most of the women in this study released. Thus, the women explained that it was particularly difficult adhering to this form of governance given that the women's communities, social networks, families, and places of employment almost always contained individuals with whom they were not supposed to be associating. The women, however, also explained how this condition affected their ability to draw on their limited social capital, find housing, and form emotionally supportive bonds, all of which research indicates are central to a successful reentry process and, in addition, would have eased their efforts to return to their communities.

Pollack (2007) as well as Turnbull and Hannah-Moffat (2009) explain that the governing of relationships by parole is a gendered project because official explanations of women's offending have become wrapped up in relationships. In other words, criminal justice rhetoric and, in some cases, programming, has come to conceptualize women's risk factors as stemming from *their choices* to become involved with the wrong kinds of friends and intimate partners. As a result, parole (and other criminal justice programming) increasingly regulates women's relationships. The present project illustrates how women on parole experience the *consequences* of these policies and how they are gendered.

Ultimately, this analysis of parole governance—in the context of women's lives—demonstrates that women experience parole as layers of supervision that have a cumulative negative effect on their reentry. Although many, like those on parole in Werth's (2012) study, resisted total compliance and navigated governance in different ways, (re)incarceration always loomed as a possibility. Parole, then, not only "contradicts with the demands of everyday life" (Turnbull & Hannah-Moffat, 2009, p. 548) but can also systematically work against parole's goal of reintegration. In fact, although the institution desires to simultaneously manage public safety and reintegration, these women's experiences with parole indicates that it ultimately functions to create governable subjects.

What, then, would a more effective system of parole look like? Based on the findings discussed here, not only should parole encourage individuals to work or connect their clients to employment resources but POs should also make serious efforts to make sure that fulfilling parole and work obligations do not conflict with one another. Parole can achieve this, in part, by offering flexible ways to meet parole conditions or extending the hours parole offices are open. Moreover, while PO "field visits" to employment sites can be a useful way for them to understand how their clients are doing, POs must simultaneously recognize that their visits are disruptive to the workplace and often experienced as embarrassing or stigmatizing.

In addition, POs must see that women on parole are often mothers, and as a result, parenthood is an area of stress, concern, and focus during their reentry process. Parole officials would be wise to view motherhood as an opportunity rather than as a site of risk and control. As addressed earlier, some women use their mother identity as avenues to desist from crime. Thus, parole should facilitate women's reintegration into this role—when appropriate for child and mother—by, for example, connecting women to relevant social service or legal agencies or not forbidding contact. By not making changes in this sphere, parole will continue to create stress in mothers' lives as they navigate uncertain custodial relationships. This issue best highlights the way that parole—at least in the present study—fails to incorporate effective gender-responsive programming and pursues "reintegration" in an androcentric way. While gender-responsive programming may (re) regulate women under the supervision of parole in different but equally problematic ways (Pollack, 2007), women on parole also point out that this type of programming is positive and impactful (Morash, 2010). Thus, this article highlights the need for exploration of gender-responsive reentry and parole programming, the way women experience it, and how this type of state supervision affects and shapes their return to their communities.

Finally, parole authorities should reconsider the utility of the condition of association as it ignores the reality of concentrated incarceration. Moreover, the absence of a criminal record (and thus, the absence of this form of governance) certainly does not illuminate, with precision, "pro-social" others. Thus, to facilitate former prisoners' buildup of an effective social support system and to limit unnecessary revocations due to the enforcement of the condition, parole should minimize the extent to which they list it on a parole agreement.

In the end, then, parole must consider the lived structural and cultural realities of parolee subjects as well as the multiple identities they hold; indeed, parolees are also mothers, children, employees, and friends, and the institution would be wise to capitalize on individuals' attempts to inhabit these identities. These kinds of shifts would create an institution that complements women's existing efforts and desires to "go straight" rather than working against them.

//// DISCUSSION QUESTIONS

1. How did being on parole impact women's efforts to successfully reintegrate into the community?

2. How did women who were mothers negotiate their return to the lives of their children?

3. What are some of the consequences that women experience in their relationships as a result of their status on parole?

References

Bergseth, K. J., Jens, K. R., Bergeron-Vigesaa, L., & McDonald, T. D. (2011). Assessing the needs of women recently released from prison. *Women & Criminal Justice, 21*, 100–122.

Bosworth, M. (2007). Creating the responsible prisoner: Federal admission and orientation packs. *Punishment & Society, 3*, 501–515.

Brown, M., & Bloom, B. (2009). Reentry and renegotiating motherhood: Maternal identity and success on parole. *Crime & Delinquency, 55*, 313–336.

Charmaz, K. (2009). *Qualitative interviewing and grounded theory analysis*. London, England: SAGE.

Chesney-Lind, M., & Pasko, L. (2004). *The female offender: Girls, women, and crime*. Thousand Oaks, CA: SAGE.

Clear, T. (2009). *Imprisoning communities: How mass incarceration makes disadvantaged neighborhoods worse*. New York, NY: Oxford University Press.

Cobbina, J. (2010). Reintegration success and failure: Factors impacting reintegration among incarcerated and formerly incarcerated women. *Journal of Offender Rehabilitation, 49*, 210–232.

Comas-Diaz, L., & Weiner, M. B. (2013). Sisters of the heart: How women's friendships heal. *Women & Therapy, 36*, 1–10.

Daly, K. (1994). *Gender, crime, and punishment*. New Haven, CT: Yale University Press.

Edin, K., & Kefalas, M. (2011). *Promises I can keep: Why poor women put motherhood before marriage*: Berkeley, University of California Press.

Enos, S. (2001). *Mothering from the inside: Parenting in a women's prison*. Albany: State University New York Press.

Farrington, D. P. (2007). Advancing knowledge about desistance. *Journal of Contemporary Criminal Justice, 23*, 125–134.

Ferraro, K. J., & Moe, A. M. (2003). Mothering, crime, and incarceration. *Journal of Contemporary Ethnography, 32*, 9–40.

Flowers, S. M. (2010). *Employment and female offenders: An update of the empirical research*. Washington DC: National Institute of Corrections, U.S. Department of Justice.

Giordano, P. C., Cernkovich, S. A., & Rudolph, J. L. (2002). Gender, crime, and desistance: Toward a theory of cognitive transformation. *American Journal of Sociology, 107*, 990–1064.

Glaze, L. E., & Maruschak, L. (2008). *Parents in prison and their minor children*. Washington, DC: Bureau of Justice Statistics, U.S. Department of Justice.

Hogan, D. P., Hao, L. X., & Parish, W. L. (1990). Race, kin networks, and assistance to mother-headed families. *Social Forces, 68*, 797–812.

Holtfreter, K., Reisig, M. D., & Morash, M. (2004). Poverty, state capital, and recidivism among women offenders. *Criminology & Public Policy, 3*, 185–208.

Huebner, B. M., DeJong, C., & Cobbina, J. (2010). Women coming home: Long-term patterns of recidivism. *Justice Quarterly, 27*, 225–254.

Jacobson, M. (2005). *Downsizing prisons: How to reduce crime and end mass incarceration*. New York: New York University Press.

Kreager, D. A., Matsueda, R. L., & Erosheva, E. A. (2010). Motherhood and criminal desistance in disadvantaged neighborhoods. *Criminology, 48*, 221–258.

La Vigne, N. G., Brooks, L. E., & Shollenberger, T. L. (2009). *Women on the outside: Understanding the experiences of female prisoners returning to Houston*, Texas. Justice Policy Center, Urban Institute.

La Vigne, N. G., & Kachnowski, V. (2005). *Texas prisoners' experiences returning home*. Washington, DC: The Urban Institute.

Leverentz, A. (2006). The love of a good man? Romantic relationships as a source of support or hindrance for female ex-offenders. *Journal of Research in Crime & Delinquency, 43*, 459–488.

Leverentz, A. (2011). Being a good daughter and sister: Families of origin in the reentry of African American female ex-prisoners. *Feminist Criminology, 6*, 239–267.

Lin, J. (2010). Parole revocation in the era of mass incarceration. *Sociology Compass, 4*, 999–1010.

Lin, J., Grattet, R., & Petersilia, J. (2010). Back-end sentencing and reimprisonment: Individual, organizational, and community predictors of parole sanctioning decisions. *Criminology, 48*, 759–795.

Lynch, M. (1998). Waste managers? The new penology, crime fighting, and parole agent identity. *Law & Society Review, 32*, 839–870.

Mallik-Kane, K., & Visher, C. (2008). *Health and prisoner reentry: How physical, mental, and substance abuse conditions shape the process of reintegration*. Washington, DC: The Urban Institute.

Maruna, S. (2001). *Making good: How ex-convicts reform and rebuild their lives*. Washington, DC: American Psychological Association.

Mauer, M. (2013). *The changing racial dynamics of women's incarceration*. Washington, DC: The Sentencing Project.

McCorkel, J. (2013). *Breaking women: Gender, race, and the new politics of imprisonment*. New York: New York University Press.

Michalsen, V., Flavin, J., & Krupat, T. (2010). More than visiting hours: Maintaining ties between incarcerated mothers and their children. *Sociology Compass, 4*, 576–591.

Miller, J. B., & Stiver, I. P. (1997). *The healing connection: How women form relationships in therapy and in life*. Boston, MA: Beacon Press.

Mink, G. (2001). Violating women: Rights abuses in the welfare police state. *Annals of the American Academy of Political and Social Science, 577*, 79–93.

Morash, M. (2010). *Women on probation and parole: A feminist critique of community programs and services*. Boston, MA: Northeastern University Press.

Mumola, C. J. (2000). *Incarcerated parents and their children*. Washington, DC: U.S. Department of Justice, Bureau of Justice Statistics Special Report).

O'Brien, P. (2001). "Just like baking a cake": Women describe the necessary ingredients for successful reentry after incarceration. *Families in Society: The Journal of Contemporary Human Services, 82*, 287–295.

Opsal, T. (2009). Women on parole: Understanding the impact of surveillance. *Women & Criminal Justice, 19*, 306–328.

Opsal, T. (2011). Women disrupting a marginalized identity: Subverting the parolee identity through narrative. *Journal of Contemporary Ethnography, 40,* 135–167.

Opsal, T. (2012). 'Livin'on the straights': Identity, desistance, and work among women post-incarceration. *Sociological Inquiry, 82*(3), 378–403.

Pager, D. (2003). The mark of a criminal record. *American Journal of Sociology, 108,* 937–975.

Petersilia, J. (2003). *When prisoners come home: Parole and prisoner reentry.* Oxford, UK: Oxford University Press.

Pollack, S. (2007). "I'm just not good in relationships": Victimization discourses and the gendered regulation of criminalized women. *Feminist Criminology, 2,* 158–174.

Pollock, J. (2002). Parenting programs in women's prisons. *Women & Criminal Justice, 14*(1), 131–154.

Richie, B. (1996). *Compelled to crime: The gendered entrapment of battered Black women.* New York, NY: Routledge Press.

Richie, B. (2001). Challenges incarcerated women face as they return to their communities: Findings from life history interviews. *Crime & Delinquency, 47,* 368–389.

Roberts, D. (1999). *Killing the black body: Race, reproduction, and the meaning of liberty.* New York, NY: Vintage Books.

Sampson, R. J., & Laub, J. H. (1993). *Crime in the making: Pathways and turning points through life.* Cambridge, MA: Harvard University Press.

Seiter, R. P., & Kadela, K. R. (2003). Prisoner reentry: What works, what does not, and what is promising. *Crime & Delinquency, 49,* 360–388.

Simon, J. (1993). *Poor discipline: Parole and the social control of the underclass, 1890–1990.* Chicago, IL: University of Chicago Press.

Steen, S., & Opsal, T. (2007). "Punishment on the installment plan": Individual-level predictors of parole revocation in four states. *The Prison Journal, 87,* 344–366.

Steiner, B., Travis, L. F., & Makarios, M. D. (2011). Understanding parole officers' responses to sanctioning reform. *Crime & Delinquency, 57,* 222–246.

Travis, J. (2005). *But they all come back: Facing the challenges of prisoner reentry.* Washington, DC: The Urban Institute.

Travis, J., & Stacey, J. (2010). A half century of parole rules: Conditions of parole in the United States, 2008. *Journal of Criminal Justice, 38,* 604–608.

Turnbull, S., & Hannah-Moffat, K. (2009). Under these conditions: Gender, parole, and the governance of reintegration. *British Journal of Criminology, 49,* 532–551.

Uggen, C. (2000). Work as a turning point in the life course of criminals: A duration model of age, employment, and recidivism. *American Sociological Review, 65,* 529–546.

Uggen, C., & Kruttschnitt, C. (1998). Crime in the breaking: Gender differences in desistance. *Law & Society Review, 32,* 339–366.

Visher, C. A., & Travis, J. (2003). Transitions from prison to community: Understanding individual pathways. *Annual Review of Sociology, 29,* 89–113.

Werth, R. (2012). I do what I'm told, sort of: Reformed subjects, unruly citizens, and parole. *Theoretical Criminology, 16,* 329–346.

READING /// 20

As you learned in the section, women's reentry process is often dependent on how she negotiates the relationships in her life and the levels of support that she has in her community. This reading looks at relationships between female in-prison contact, post-release support, and recidivism and how familial relationships during incarceration can impact a successful reintegration for women.

Reentering Women
The Impact of Social Ties on Long-Term Recidivism

Kelle Barrick, Pamela K. Mattimore, and Christy A. Visher

Over the past decade, the United States experienced an unprecedented increase in the number of offenders leaving prison, as more than 700,000 inmates were released each year (Sabol & Couture, 2008; West, Sabol, & Greenman, 2010). Research suggests that as many as half of released prisoners will be

SOURCE: Barrick, K., Lattimore, P. K. & Visher, C. A. (2014). Reentering women: The impact of social ties on long-term recidivism. *The Prison Journal, 94*(3): 279–304.

reincarcerated within 3 years (Langan & Levin, 2002). Not surprisingly, a growing body of research has focused on examining means to improve outcomes of reentering offenders. Research on the effectiveness of various reentry strategies at reducing recidivism suggests that cognitive-behavioral approaches and programs that target criminogenic factors and individual needs and that focus on individual-level change may be most effective at reducing recidivism among adults and juveniles (Andrews & Bonta, 2003; Andrews et al., 1990; Aos et al., 2006; Fonagy & Kurtz, 2002; Lipsey, 1995; Lipsey & Cullen, 2007; MacKenzie, 2006). Other studies suggest that the neighborhood to which an offender returns may affect recidivism with those returning to areas of concentrated disadvantage and poverty faring worse than others (Huebner, DeJong, & Cobbina, 2010; Kubrin & Stewart, 2006).

Relatively little attention has been given to the relationship between inmate social ties and recidivism (see Bales & Mears, 2008, for a recent exception). This lack of research is somewhat surprising as most modern criminological theories anticipate that social ties should reduce criminal behavior (e.g., Hirschi's, 1969, social bond theory; Sampson & Laub's, 1993, age-graded theory of informal social control; and Agnew's, 2006, general strain theory). The limited body of research suggests that inmate social ties may reduce recidivism; however, the existing studies are limited in a number of ways. Frequently cited studies supporting the social ties–recidivism relationship often use dated samples and draw conclusions based on bivariate analyses (e.g., Glaser, 1964). Also, though more recent studies have used multivariate techniques, they have also narrowly defined social ties as in-prison visits within 12 months of release from prison (e.g., Bales & Mears, 2008). However, visitation is not the only form of in-prison contact and social ties may be sustained through a combination of visits, telephone calls, and mail correspondence (Tewksbury & DeMichele, 2005). Other studies have examined a broader spectrum of contact but focused on in-prison infractions rather than recidivism upon release (e.g., Jiang & Winfree, 2006). In addition, most research on family ties has focused on in-prison relationships and subsequent recidivism and ignored the social processes by which in-prison family relationships may affect recidivism, including the role of post-release family support in successful reintegration (Visher & Travis, 2003). Finally, much of this research either has relied on entirely male samples or does not report findings separately by sex (Visher & Travis, 2003; see Bales & Mears, 2008, for a recent exception). This gap is unfortunate given evidence that family relationships and social ties may be particularly important for female offenders (Bloom, Owen, & Covington, 2002; Jiang & Winfree, 2006; Kiser, 1991).

Although women represent less than 10% of the total inmate population, between 2000 and 2008, the average number of female prisoners grew faster (2.6% annually) than the average number of male prisoners (1.8% annually; West et al., 2010). This increasing rate, with an attendant increase in incarcerated women from 93,234 in 2000 to 113,462 in 2009, highlights the importance of understanding correlates of recidivism among women. Although research has demonstrated that a number of factors may be important in explaining recidivism among males and females (e.g., low levels of education and limited job opportunities), the issue of in-prison social ties may be more important to women. For example, research suggests that female prisoners are more likely to have parental responsibilities and may be more preoccupied with family relationships during prison than male counterparts (Kiser, 1991).

The current study seeks to fill a gap in the literature by examining the relationship among in-prison social ties (in-person visits, telephone calls, mail correspondence, and perceived family emotional support), post-release social support (perceived family emotional and instrumental support), and long-term recidivism outcomes among reentering women.

Reentering Women

Returning prisoners face multiple obstacles, including limited occupational and educational experience and training to prepare them for employment, drug and alcohol addictions, mental and physical health problems, strained family relations, and limited opportunities due to the stigma of a criminal record (Broner, Lattimore, & Steffey, 2010; Petersilia, 2003; Travis & Visher, 2005). Although research suggests male and female prisoners are similar in having relatively low educational attainment and poor employment histories (Robbins, Martin, & Surratt, 2009), women have unique life experiences and pathways to crime (Belknap, 2001) that may complicate successful reentry. For example, Bloom et al. (2002)

identified pathways that research suggests are particularly salient for women, including histories of personal abuse, mental illness and substance abuse, economic and social marginality, homelessness, and relationships. These circumstances that may have played a role in their initial criminal involvement are further compounded upon release. For example, when released from prison, women often have difficulty accessing substance abuse and mental health treatment, have unresolved issues related to prior victimization, have difficulty securing employment, and may need to rely on family members for financial support to avoid homelessness (Richie, 2001).

Family support may be particularly important in reentry success. Research has documented that the primary reentry concerns for female offenders are to successfully reunite with their children, maintain a suitable lifestyle, and sustain relationships with family and intimate partners (La Vigne, Brooks, & Shollenberger, 2008; O'Brien, 2001; Richie, 2001). In an analysis of female offenders returning to Houston, Texas (La Vigne et al., 2008), many women expected to have emotional and financial support from their families and relationships upon release. Maintaining contact with family and supportive others while incarcerated may play an important role in ensuring successful reunification upon release. Interviews with female inmates in one prison in Illinois revealed that familial visits were extremely important to female inmates, who interpreted the visits as evidence that their family members supported them (Kiser, 1991). However, women who did not receive visitors indicated that this absence was one of the most difficult aspects of serving time.

Prisoner Social Ties and Recidivism

Research has long suggested that social ties may influence criminal behavior and may be important to successful reentry. For example, Ohlin (1954) found that among prisoners released from Illinois prisons in the 1920s and 1930s, inmates who maintained an active interest in family (measured as frequency of family contacts) were more likely to be successful on parole than those classified as loners. A follow-up study examining prisoners released during the 1940s and 1950s reaffirmed these results

(Glaser, 1964). Similarly, in a study of 412 male parolees, Holt and Miller (1972) found that the number of visitors an inmate had during the last year of incarceration increased the likelihood of parole success (fewer parole violations and arrests). However, not all research has supported these findings. For example, Adams and Fischer (1976) found that neither the average number of visits nor letters received from family, friends, and others was associated with recidivism in their study of 120 released prisoners.

Although these studies provide an important foundation for examining the relationship between in-prison social ties and recidivism, they included only male prisoners, and the findings were based on bivariate analyses that did not control for other characteristics (e.g., criminal history). More recent studies have examined both perceived emotional support, including close family relationships, acceptance, and encouragement (e.g., Nelson, Deess, & Allan, 1999; Visher, Kachnowski, La Vigne, & Travis, 2004), and inmate mail, telephone, and in-person contact (Bales & Mears, 2008; Jiang & Winfree, 2006) with multivariate analytic techniques.

The limited research examining the impact of perceived emotional support suggests such support may aid successful reintegration. In 1999, Nelson and colleagues interviewed 49 offenders released from New York jails and prisons about 30 days post incarceration and found that family emotional support, such as acceptance and encouragement, affected success with regard to drug use, employment, and criminal activity. The reentering offenders indicated that family acceptance allowed them to plan for the future and develop pro-social relationships. However, not all social bonds were helpful; offenders who reunited with criminal and drug-using friends were more likely to fail. Similar findings were reported in a study of offenders returning to Baltimore. Visher et al. (2004) found that close family relationships and strong family support were associated with improvements in employment and substance use outcomes post release. However, they also noted the potential for family to have a negative influence on reentering offenders; more than half of the inmates had family members who had been convicted of a crime and more than 25% had at least three family members with a substance abuse problem.

A few recent studies have examined the impact of in-prison social contact on recidivism. Social contact has typically been defined as the occurrence or frequency of in-prison visitation, telephone calls, and mail correspondence. Overall, the results suggest a protective effect of in-prison contact. Using data from the 1997 State and Federal Correctional Facilities in the United States survey, Jiang and Winfree (2006) examined whether an inmate's level of social support was associated with the number of rule violations received while incarcerated. Three dichotomous (*yes/no*) variables were used to measure support from outside the prison: visits by children, telephone calls made to or received from children, and mail sent to or received from children. Both male and female inmates who received calls from their children had fewer rule violations. However, neither visitation nor mail contact with children had a significant effect on violations. These findings were limited to in-prison behavior rather than post-release recidivism and examined only contact with children not with other family members or friends.

Bales and Mears (2008) used data from the Florida Department of Corrections to examine whether in-prison visitation affected recidivism outcomes for 7,000 male and female inmates released in 2001 and 2002. The effect of visitation was examined separately by type of visitor (parent, spouse, significant other, child, relative, friend, or other person) on both the occurrence and timing of conviction for a new felony resulting in incarceration within 2 years following release. Findings suggest that the existence and frequency of visitation both reduce the occurrence and delay the onset of recidivism. Although visits from family and friends had positive outcomes, the effects were strongest for spousal visitation. Somewhat surprisingly, child visitation was associated with a higher likelihood of reconviction. Even though this was not hypothesized by the authors, it is consistent with prior research, which found that mothers visited by their minor children are more likely to receive prison infractions than mothers who do not receive such visits (Casey-Acevedo, Bakken, & Karle, 2004). Finally, in a study of over 200 male prisoners reentering Chicago, La Vigne, Naser, Brooks, and Castro (2005) found that inmates who maintained family contact had stronger post-release family relationships. More specifically, in-prison visits were found to be more important for relationships with partners and children, whereas phone and mail contact were more important for other members of the family. Although this study did not examine recidivism, the results highlight the important role

that in-prison family contact plays in successful reintegration. They also suggest that the relationship between in-prison social ties and recidivism may be mediated through post-release relationships.

The goal of the current study is to build on this literature by examining the relationship among in-prison social ties, including multiple forms of contact with family members and friends and perceived family emotional support, post-release social support, and long-term recidivism outcomes for women. Based on the limited literature, we anticipate finding (a) a positive relationship between in-prison family contact and post-release family support, and (b) a negative relationship between in-prison family contact and reincarceration that is at least partially mediated through post-release family support.

Data and Method

The data presented here were collected as part of the Multi-Site Evaluation of the Serious and Violent Offender Reentry Initiative (SVORI; e.g., Lattimore, Barrick, et al., 2011; Lattimore & Visher, 2009; Lattimore, Visher, & Steffey, 2011; Lindquist, Barrick, Lattimore, & Visher, 2009; Winterfield, Lattimore, Steffey, Brumbaugh, & Lindquist, 2006), a multi-site evaluation of state and local reentry initiatives. The data were collected as part of this evaluation through inmate surveys during interviews 30 days before release and 3, 9, and 15 months after release; data from state agencies and the National Criminal Information Center (NCIC) identified post-release recidivism. The sample includes 255 women from Iowa, Indiana, Ohio, Oklahoma, South Carolina, and Washington who either participated in SVORI programs or were members of control or comparison groups between 2004 and 2007.[1] The study participants were high-risk offenders who had extensive criminal and substance use histories, low levels of education and employment skills, and families and peers who were substance- and criminal justice system–involved.

Dependent Variables

Two measures of recidivism were included in the analyses. The occurrence of recidivism was defined as whether the offender was *reincarcerated* (1 = *yes*) within nearly 5 years of release from prison. The *time to reincarceration* was measured as the number of days from release to reincarceration (up to 2,282 days). For both measures, reincarceration included returns to prison for either a new offense or for a parole or probation revocation.

Independent Variables

Our primary independent variables included perceptions of family emotional support and in-prison contact with family members and others. *In-prison family emotional support* was measured with a scale of the following 10 items: "I feel close to my family," "I want my family to be involved in my life," "I consider myself a source of support for my family," "I fight a lot with my family," "I often feel like I disappoint my family," "I am criticized a lot by family," "I have someone in my family to talk to about myself or my problems," "I have someone in my family to turn to for suggestions about how to deal with a personal problem," "I have someone in my family who understands my problems," and "I have someone in my family to love me and make me feel wanted." Response options ranged from *strongly agree* (4) to *strongly disagree* (1). These 10 items were summed so that a high score indicates greater perceived family emotional support (negatively worded items were reverse-coded). *Post-release family emotional support* was measured using the same variables asked at the 3-, 9-, and 15-month post-release interviews. The scale was calculated at each wave, but to reduce attrition, the average of the three post-release scales was calculated. Of the 255 women in the sample, 193 had data to construct this scale.

Post-release family instrumental support was measured with a scale of the following items (asked at each of the three post-release interviews): "I have someone in my family who would provide help or advice on finding a place to live," "I have someone in my family who would provide help or advice on finding a job," "I have someone in my family who would provide support for dealing with a substance abuse problem," "I have someone in my family who would provide transportation to work or other appointments if needed," and "I have someone in my family who would provide me with financial support." Response options ranged from *strongly agree* (4) to *strongly disagree* (1). These five items were reverse-coded and summed so that a high score indicates greater perceived family instrumental support. Similar to family emotional support, the average of instrumental support across the three waves was calculated.

In-prison contact was measured by constructing two scales of the type and frequency of contact inmates reported: *family contact* and *non-family contact*. Each inmate was asked how frequently (*daily* = 4, *weekly* = 3, *monthly* = 2, *a few times* = 1, or *never* = 0) they talked on the phone, sent or received mail, or were visited by family members and others. The *family contact* scale was constructed by summing the frequency with which inmates reported contact with family members through phone calls, mail, or in-person visits. Similarly, the *non-family contact* scale was constructed by summing the analogous items for non-family members. In addition, to assess the relative importance of each contact type, six dichotomous indicators (1 = *had contact type*, 0 = *never had contact type*) were developed: *family phone contact, non-family phone contact, family mail contact, non-family mail contact, family visit,* and *non-family visit*.

Control Variables

The multivariate models control for a number of individual characteristics that research has suggested may predict recidivism. Demographic variables included race (*non-White* = 1), age, relationship status (*married or in a steady relationship prior to release* = 1), employment history (*employed during 6 months prior to incarceration* = 1), educational attainment (*high school graduate* = 1, if completed 12th grade or equivalent), and having *minor children* (1 = *yes*).

Because criminal history has been demonstrated to be one of the strongest predictors of recidivism, we included the *age at first arrest*, the *number of prior convictions*, whether the current incarceration was for a probation or parole violation (*probation/parole violation* = 1), the number of times in *juvenile detention*, a measure of risk[2] (*maximum risk* = 1, *medium or low risk* = 0), total number of prior *violence charges*, and the total number of prior *nonviolent charges* (property, drug, public order, other).

Because research on female offenders has suggested that certain factors may be particularly salient for predicting women's recidivism (Bloom et al., 2002), we included indicators for mental health (Global Severity Index score [GSI]), substance abuse (*prior AOD tx* = 1, if received alcohol or drug treatment prior to this incarceration), and *victimization prior to incarceration* (scale of frequency and severity of victimization prior to this incarceration).[3] In addition, recent research has suggested that the institutional context may also affect recidivism (Huebner, DeJong, & Cobbina, 2010), so we included controls for the frequency and severity of *victimization during this incarceration*, receipt of at least one disciplinary *infraction* (1 = *yes*) this incarceration, and placement in administrative *segregation* (1 = *yes*) this incarceration. In addition to these variables, we also controlled for site (IA, IN, OH, OK, WA). South Carolina was selected as the reference category because it had largest number of respondents.

Findings

Sample Description

A description of the 255 women included in the analyses is presented in Reading Table 1. Nearly half (44%) were

reincarcerated within 5 years of release. On average, the prisoners were 33 years old at the time of release and the majority was non-White. About half of the women had been married or in a steady relationship prior to release and nearly three quarters had minor children. More than half of the women had a high school diploma or equivalent and were employed during the 6 months prior to incarceration. The women presented relatively serious prior criminal histories. On average, the inmates were 20 years old at the time of their first arrest and had more than five prior convictions. While they only had about one prior charge for a violent offense, they had nearly 13 prior charges for non-violent offenses (e.g., property, drug, public order, and other).

With regard to in-prison social ties, mail was the most common type of contact respondents had with family (93%) and non-family (78%). The majority of respondents reported having telephone contact with family (81%) and

Reading Table 1 • Description of Sample, by Reincarceration Status

Variable	Description	Full sample (N = 255)		Reincarcerated (n = 113)		Not reincarcerated (n = 142)	
		M or %	SD	M or %	SD	M or %	SD
Reincarcerated	Reincarcerated within 5 years of release	0.4431	0.4977				
Time to reincarceration	Number of days from release to first reincarceration (among women who were reincarcerated)	1,357.12	714.1194				
In-prison family emotional support*	Scale of self-reported family emotional support (in-prison)	30.6145	6.0718	29.5089	6.4668	31.5182	5.5916
Family contact*	Scale of frequency of family contacts during incarceration (in- person visits, phone calls, and letters)	5.4157	2.7707	4.7168	2.7725	5.9718	2.6496
Non-family contact	Scale of frequency of non-family contacts during incarceration (in-person visits, phone calls, and letters)	3.5079	2.8503	3.4894	2.8476	3.531	2.8663

Variable	Description	Full sample (N = 255)		Reincarcerated (n = 113)		Not reincarcerated (n = 142)	
		M or %	SD	M or %	SD	M or %	SD
Family phone contact*	Had phone contact with family (1 = yes)	0.8107	0.3923	0.6667	0.4735	0.8652	0.3427
Non-family phone contact	Had phone contact with non-family (1 = yes)	0.5044	0.5007	0.5413	0.5006	0.4526	0.4996
Family mail contact	Had mail contact with family (1 = yes)	0.9326	0.2511	0.9115	0.2853	0.9362	0.2453
Non-family mail contact	Had mail contact with non-family (1 = yes)	0.7810	0.4142	0.7727	0.421	0.7482	0.4356
Family visit*	Had visit from family (1 = yes)	0.5666	0.4963	0.4595	0.5006	0.6214	0.4868
Non-family visit	Had visit from non-family (1 = yes)	0.3186	0.4666	0.3148	0.4666	0.365	0.4832
Post-release family emotional support*	Scale of self-reported family emotional support (post-release)	31.2901	5.3774	29.3889	5.2949	32.7759	4.9773
Post-release family instrumental support*	Scale of self-report family instrumental support (post-release)	15.7775	3.1801	15.1147	3.2265	16.2955	3.0578
Non-White	Non-White vs. White	0.5765	0.4951	0.5664	0.4978	0.5845	0.4946
Age	Age at release from prison for this incarceration	32.6314	7.2338	32.4779	6.9025	32.7535	7.509
Relationship status	Married or in a steady relationship prior to release	0.4940	0.5010	0.5405	0.5006	0.4571	0.4999
Employment history	Employed during 6 months prior to incarceration	0.5216	0.5005	0.5133	0.5021	0.5282	0.501
High school graduate	Completed 12th grade or GED/other high school equivalent	0.5843	0.4938	0.5664	0.4978	0.5986	0.4919
Minor children	Have child(ren) under age 18	0.7451	0.4367	0.7257	0.4482	0.7606	0.4283
Age at first arrest*	Age at first arrest	19.6964	6.5853	17.8257	5.5791	21.1739	6.9534

(Continued)

Reading Table 1 • (Continued)

Variable	Description	Full sample (N = 255)		Reincarcerated (n = 113)		Not reincarcerated (n = 142)	
		M or %	SD	M or %	SD	M or %	SD
Number of prior convictions*	Number of prior convictions	5.6025	5.7372	7.3084	6.8148	4.2701	4.3054
Probation/ parole violation	Current incarceration is for probation or parole violation	0.2235	0.4174	0.2301	0.4228	0.2183	0.4146
Juvenile detention*	Times in juvenile detention/lock-up	1.3936	3.3705	2.156	4.0235	0.8	2.6231
Maximum risk*	Pseudo LSI-R:SV risk classification = maximum	0.2706	0.4451	0.3982	0.4917	0.169	0.3761
Violence charges†	Total number of prior charges for a violent offense	1.2667	1.7044	1.3363	1.8449	1.2113	1.5882
Other charges*	Total number of prior charges for property, drug, and other offenses	12.9686	11.7278	15.3097	12.8973	11.1056	10.3805
GSI*	Global Severity Index	77.4745	30.1231	82.1239	33.1754	73.7746	27.0047
Prior AOD tx*	Received alcohol or other drug treatment at least once prior to this incarceration	0.5373	0.4996	0.6195	0.4877	0.4718	0.501
Victimization prior to incarceration†	Scale of frequency and severity of victimization prior to this incarceration	3.9647	2.7513	4.3186	3.0656	3.6831	2.4477
Reentry program	Enrolled in a prison reentry program	0.3608	0.4812	0.3628	0.483	0.3592	0.4815
Victimization during incarceration	Scale of frequency and severity of victimization during this incarceration	2.7333	1.3130	2.8496	1.5824	2.6408	1.0474
Infraction	Received disciplinary infraction this incarceration	0.4667	0.4999	0.4956	0.5022	0.4437	0.4986
Segregation	Placed in administrative segregation this incarceration	0.3098	0.4633	0.3451	0.4775	0.2817	0.4514

NOTE. GED = General Educational Development; LSI-R:SV = Level of Service Inventory–Revised: Screening Version.

†Reincarcerated and not reincarcerated groups are significantly different at $p < .10$. *Reincarcerated and not reincarcerated groups are significantly different at $p < .05$.

half spoke on the phone with non-family members. Just over half of the women indicated they were visited by family (57%), whereas less than one in three women was visited by someone who was not a family member (32%).

On average, women scored 31 on both in-prison and post-release family emotional support scales (range: 16–40). The mean post-release family instrumental support score was 16 (range: 5–20).

Bivariate Analyses

Prior to developing multivariate models, we ran *t* tests to assess any differences between the reincarcerated and not reincarcerated women (Reading Table 1). Not surprisingly, the reincarcerated women had more severe criminal histories. On average, those who were reincarcerated within 5 years of release were younger at the time of their first arrest, had more prior convictions, spent more time in juvenile detention, were more likely to be classified as high risk, and had a greater number of prior charges for non-violent offenses than those who were not reincarcerated. Supporting gendered pathways theories, the women who recidivated had worse mental health pre-release and were more likely to have been in substance abuse treatment prior to this incarceration than those who did not recidivate. Finally, the bivariate analyses support the notion that women with greater social ties are less likely to recidivate. Women who were not reincarcerated reported higher family emotional and instrumental support and more in-prison family contact than those who were reincarcerated. However, the level of non-family contact was not significantly different. Two bivariate ordinary least squares regression models were estimated to determine whether in-prison family contact is predictive of post-release family emotional support and post-release family instrumental support. In both models, in-prison family contact was significant (data not shown).

Multivariate Analyses

Next, a series of logistic regression models was estimated to assess the impact of in-prison and post-release social ties on the likelihood of reincarceration within 5 years of release (Reading Table 2).[4] Model 1 includes in-prison support measures and the full set of covariates. Post-release family emotional support and instrumental support are added in Models 2 and 3, respectively.[5]

In Model 1, having minor children was the only demographic characteristic associated with recidivism; women with children were less likely to be reincarcerated. Although a number of criminal history variables were significantly associated with reincarceration in the bivariate models, only risk level retained significance when other variables were included. Not surprisingly, women classified as high risk were more likely to be reincarcerated than those who were medium or low risk. Also, the number of prior convictions and non-violent prior charges approached significance. Consistent with our expectations, the multivariate analyses suggest that women with greater family ties are less likely to recidivate. Having greater family contact was associated with a reduced likelihood of being reincarcerated. However, family emotional support did not have a significant impact on the likelihood of reincarceration and non-family contact was associated with a marginally significant increase in the likelihood of reincarceration.

Post-release family emotional support was added to Model 2 and was significant. However, in-prison family contact remains significant, suggesting that its impact is not entirely mediated through improving family emotional support post release. Similar results were achieved for post-release instrumental support; both post-release instrumental support and in-prison family contact are significant predictors of reincarceration (Model 3). Furthermore, the size of the in-prison effect remains roughly the same across all three models.

Similar results were found in survival models assessing the time to reincarceration (Reading Table 3). In Model 1, none of the included demographic characteristics was associated with the timing of reincarceration. Women who were younger at first arrest recidivated more quickly than those who were older. Risk class and non-violent prior charges were associated with a marginally significant increase in the time to reincarceration. Again, support was found for the relationship between family ties and reincarceration. Women who reported having greater contact with their families were slower to recidivate than those with less contact. However, those who reported having greater non-family contact were reincarcerated more quickly than those with less contact. Analogous to the findings in the logistic models, post-release family emotional support and in-prison family contact were significant in Model 2, and both post-release instrumental support and in-prison family contact were significant in Model 3.

Reading Table 2 ● Logistic Regression Models of Reincarceration Within 5 Years of Release

Variable	Model 1 SE OR			Model 2 O			Model 3		
	Coefficient	SE	OR	Coefficient t	SE	OR	Coefficient	SE	OR
Intercept	0.3853	1.9283		5.0065	2.5233		2.3001	2.3228	
Post-release family emotional support				−0.2055*	0.056	0.814			
Post-release family instrumental support							−0.1586*	0.0717	0.853
In-prison family emotional support	0.0112	0.0336	1.011	0.0583	0.046	1.06	0.0213	0.0397	1.022
In-prison family contact	−0.3287*	0.0866	0.72	−0.3634*	0.1058	0.695	−0.3425*	0.0974	0.71
In-prison non-family contact	0.1134†	0.0663	1.12	0.1617*	0.0804	1.175	0.1582*	0.0769	1.171
Non-White	−0.2652	0.4118	0.767	−0.1054	0.5087	0.9	−0.0838	0.4823	0.92
Age	−0.0188	0.0312	0.981	0.0126	0.0391	1.013	−0.00265	0.0353	0.997
Partner	0.422	0.356	1.525	0.5593	0.4329	1.75	0.4949	0.4054	1.64
Employment history	−0.1246	0.3694	0.883	0.0683	0.4402	1.071	0.0874	0.4169	1.091
High school graduate	−0.0993	0.3657	0.906	0.1901	0.439	1.209	0.1367	0.4182	1.147
Minor children	−0.9881*	0.441	0.372	−1.0975*	0.5242	0.334	−0.9926*	0.4934	0.371
Age at first arrest	−0.0279	0.0358	0.973	−0.048	0.0415	0.953	−0.039	0.0396	0.962
Number of prior convictions	0.0687†	0.0399	1.071	0.0459	0.0462	1.047	0.0662	0.0457	1.068
Probation/parole violation	−0.1565	0.4382	0.855	−0.4832	0.5294	0.617	−0.4309	0.5141	0.65
Juvenile detention	−0.00889	0.0656	0.991	−0.0117	0.0951	0.988	0.0109	0.0944	1.011
Maximum risk	1.2082*	0.4502	3.347	1.0798	0.5532	2.944	1.3049*	0.5254	3.687
Violence charges	0.0152	0.115	1.015	−0.04	0.133	0.961	−0.0726	0.1284	0.93
Other charges	0.0345†	0.0177	1.035	0.0437*	0.0201	1.045	0.0346†	0.0192	1.035
GSI	−0.00426	0.00669	0.996	−0.0117	0.00842	0.988	−0.00747	0.00779	0.993
Prior AOD tx	0.484	0.3574	1.623	0.4931	0.4297	1.637	0.6334	0.414	1.884
Victimization prior to incarceration	0.0527	0.068	1.054	0.0824	0.0821	1.086	0.1042	0.0805	1.11

Variable	Model 1 SE OR			Model 2 O			Model 3		
	Coefficient	SE	OR	Coefficient t	SE	OR	Coefficient	SE	OR
Reentry program	0.1341	0.4486	1.143	−0.2267	0.522	0.797	−0.1627	0.499	0.85
Victimization during incarceration	0.0651	0.1587	1.067	0.1608	0.197	1.174	0.0343	0.1843	1.035
Infraction	−0.0901	0.4658	0.914	−0.1256	0.5501	0.882	−0.1156	0.5258	0.891
Segregation	0.7803	0.5478	2.182	0.6332	0.6511	1.884	0.7916	0.625	2.207
IA	1.836*	0.6701	6.271	2.3328*	0.8066	10.307	1.7188*	0.7388	5.578
IN	0.9901	0.6173	2.691	0.8125	0.6927	2.254	0.7216	0.6794	2.058
OH	0.4341	0.6628	1.544	0.1475	0.8761	1.159	0.4288	0.8338	1.535
OK	−0.1537	1.0159	0.857	−0.2456	1.3461	0.782	−0.4432	1.2424	0.642
WA	−1.3618	1.0113	0.256	−2.5237*	1.2309	0.08	−2.559*	1.2892	0.077

NOTE. GSI = Global Severity Index; AOD tx = alcohol or other drug treatment.

$\dagger p < .10$. $*p < .05$.

While most prior research has focused on in-prison visits, it is plausible that other forms of social contact may also impact recidivism. To examine whether one type of contact is more beneficial than others, we created six dichotomous variables indicating whether a prisoner reported any phone, mail, and in-person contact with family and non-family. Logistic models are presented in Reading Table 3. Consistent with the bivariate differences presented in Table 1, in all three models, family phone contact seems to have the biggest impact on both the occurrence and timing of reincarceration. Women who reported having phone contact with a family member during this incarceration were significantly less likely to be reincarcerated within 5 years post release than women who did not report family phone contact. Women who reported receiving a family visit were less likely to be reincarcerated than those who did not. Again, both post-release family emotional support (Model 2) and family instrumental support (Model 3) were associated with a reduced likelihood of reincarceration. Regarding non-family contact, phone contact was associated with a marginal increase in the likelihood of reincarceration;

however, mail contact and in-person visits were not associated with the likelihood of recidivism.

Discussion

Studying the impact of social support among prison inmates is important for a number of reasons, most notably the potential this support has to improve outcomes upon release. Although prior research has found some support for the social ties–recidivism relationship, no study of which we are aware has rigorously examined the relationship between in-prison family emotional support and contacts, post-release family emotional and instrumental support, and recidivism among reentering women. This research is particularly important in light of evidence that social ties may be particularly relevant for women. The results of this study provide evidence that maintaining family social ties while incarcerated is an important element in success upon release for female offenders.

In sum, more than half of the women reported having each type of contact with family members during this

Reading Table 3 • Logistic Regression Models of Reincarceration Within 5 Years of Release, by Contact Type

Variable	Coefficient	Model 1 SE	OR	Coefficient	Model 2 SE	OR	Coefficient	Model 3 SE	OR
Intercept	*0.2968*	*2.2274*		*5.9222**	*3.0166*		*3.6502*	*2.8238*	
Post-release family emotional support				−0.2068*	0.058	0.813			
Post-release family instrumental support							−0.192*	0.0795	0.825
In-prison family emotional support	−0.0102	0.0356	0.99	0.0387	0.0499	1.039	0.00525	0.0439	1.005
Family phone contact	−1.807*	0.5489	0.164	−1.5671*	0.6256	0.209	−1.8333*	0.6159	0.16
Non-family phone contact	0.8525†	0.4572	2.345	1.1349*	0.5469	3.111	1.133*	0.5361	3.105
Family mail contact	1.084	0.9644	2.956	−0.3252	1.3436	0.722	0.0663	1.2674	1.069
Non-family mail contact	0.085	0.5235	1.089	0.404	0.6242	1.498	0.3133	0.5986	1.368
Family visit	−0.7049†	0.4255	0.494	−0.9826†	0.5201	0.374	−0.9017†	0.4952	0.406
Non-family visit	−0.4522	0.4413	0.636	−0.6348	0.5231	0.53	−0.5308	0.5074	0.588
Non-White	−0.4713	0.4455	0.624	−0.28	0.5555	0.756	−0.3102	0.5333	0.733
Age	−0.0169	0.0323	0.983	0.0186	0.0412	1.019	−0.00184	0.0373	0.998
Partner	0.1417	0.3684	1.152	0.2178	0.4497	1.243	0.2632	0.4317	1.301
Employment history	−0.2739	0.3938	0.76	−0.0697	0.4703	0.933	−0.1328	0.4486	0.876
High school graduate	−0.1883	0.3907	0.828	0.1138	0.4595	1.121	0.0984	0.4445	1.103
Minor children	−0.9191*	0.4684	0.399	−1.1591*	0.554	0.314	−1.046*	0.5324	0.351
Age at first arrest	−0.0237	0.0385	0.977	−0.0417	0.0455	0.959	−0.0293	0.0433	0.971
Number of prior convictions	0.0833†	0.0432	1.087	0.0524	0.0517	1.054	0.0761	0.0505	1.079
Probation/parole violation	−0.4296	0.4732	0.651	−0.5579	0.5647	0.572	−0.5293	0.5504	0.589

Variable	Coefficient	Model 1 SE	OR	Coefficient	Model 2 SE	OR	Coefficient	Model 3 SE	OR
Juvenile detention	0.0211	0.0669	1.021	0.0572	0.1071	1.059	0.0666	0.1037	1.069
Maximum risk	1.2461*	0.4833	3.477	1.087†	0.5905	2.965	1.2946*	0.5715	3.649
Violence charges	−0.0783	0.1251	0.925	−0.1132	0.1443	0.893	−0.133	0.1412	0.875
Other charges	0.0382*	0.0188	1.039	0.0447*	0.0214	1.046	0.0384†	0.0206	1.039
GSI	−0.0038	0.00733	0.996	−0.0118	0.00888	0.988	−0.00875	0.00833	0.991
Prior AOD tx	0.0125	0.3865	1.013	0.1945	0.4606	1.215	0.3173	0.4436	1.373
Victimization prior to incarceration	0.0629	0.0715	1.065	0.0731	0.0867	1.076	0.0923	0.0862	1.097
Reentry program	0.6053	0.4747	1.832	0.1804	0.5565	1.198	0.2785	0.534	1.321
Victimization during incarceration	0.0381	0.1662	1.039	0.1341	0.2076	1.144	0.00743	0.1968	1.007
Infraction	0.1792	0.4876	1.196	0.1583	0.5905	1.172	0.1514	0.5644	1.164
Segregation	0.7637	0.5698	2.146	0.7613	0.6913	2.141	0.8962	0.662	2.45
IA	1.6361*	0.6895	5.135	1.8699*	0.8289	6.488	1.3317†	0.7678	3.788
IN	0.9776	0.6403	2.658	0.5225	0.7295	1.686	0.5348	0.7209	1.707
OH	0.5531	0.7266	1.739	0.2983	0.9554	1.348	0.4081	0.9047	1.504
OK	−0.0857	1.1215	0.918	−0.7098	1.5564	0.492	−0.8999	1.455	0.407
WA	−1.4989	1.0916	0.223	−3.4378*	1.4429	0.032	−3.4509*	1.4897	0.032

NOTE. GSI = Global Severity Index; AOD tx = alcohol or other drug treatment.

†$p < .10$. *$p < .05$.

incarceration, with mail and telephone contact being the most common. A relatively large proportion of the women also reported maintaining contact with individuals other than family. Overall, the results suggest that maintaining contact with family members is associated with higher levels of emotional and instrumental support post release and with a lower likelihood of recidivism. One notable finding is that in-prison family emotional support is not associated with either the occurrence or timing of reincarceration. This suggests that having family members actually demonstrate support by taking time to speak on the telephone or make an in-person visit is more important than the inmate's expressed perception of emotional support. Furthermore, when separately examining types of contact, familial telephone contact was most consistently associated with reductions in recidivism. This is consistent with research showing that telephone contact had the greatest impact on in-prison rule violations (Jiang & Winfree, 2006) and reaffirms the need to define social ties more broadly than visitation. In contrast to Bales and Mears (2008), who found that contact with friends was protective, non-family contact, particularly telephone calls, was associated with an increased likelihood of reincarceration.

The positive impact of family telephone contact is encouraging in light of numerous obstacles to in-prison visitation. For example, Hairston, Rollin, and Jo (2004) noted that the greater the distance between an inmate's home and the prison, the fewer visits an inmate receives. This is problematic since many inmates serve time in institutions far from their homes. Yet, obstacles remain even for maintaining telephone contact with families, including limited access to telephones (Katz, 1998) and the need to rely on family and friends accepting collect calls, which can be cost prohibitive (Hairston et al., 2004). More specifically, Hairston et al. (2004) noted that "rates at which families pay to receive collect phone calls from their imprisoned relatives are often as much as 200 times the going rates for phone calls made outside the institution" (p. 3). Rather than discouraging phone contact through imposing such high costs on inmates' families, efforts should be made to reduce challenges to maintaining familial relationships while incarcerated. Encouraging and facilitating contact with families may be a cost-effective way of producing positive effects on post-release behavior.

Limitations

Although this study provides an important contribution to the literature by examining social ties among reentering women, a few limitations should be noted. The most notable limitation in this research is the inability to differentiate between various types of family members (i.e., child, parent, and spouse). For example, there is some evidence that spousal visitation has a greater impact on recidivism (Bales & Mears, 2008) whereas contact with children may actually result in negative outcomes (Bales & Mears, 2008; Casey-Acevedo et al., 2004). However, information about the nature of the familial relationship with the inmate was not asked in this study and could not be assessed here. In addition, recent research has found that characteristics of the community to which an inmate is released (e.g., concentrated disadvantage) may also affect her ability to succeed (Huebner et al., 2010). Unfortunately, neighborhood-level data were not available for the reentering women in this sample. Finally, the women included in these analyses were not randomly sampled, had histories of serious crime and violence, and were released from institutions in only six states. It is thus possible that the results here may not generalize to less serious female offenders and those incarcerated in other states. However, there is no theoretical reason to expect findings to vary significantly across states.

Future Research

Additional research is needed to broaden our understanding of why the maintenance of some relationships is protective against recidivism whereas others may be criminogenic. It is possible that family relationships are beneficial because family members are more likely than friends to provide the prisoner both emotional and instrumental support upon release. Another possibility is that friends may be more likely than family members to be involved in criminal activity and substance use. Research that includes characteristics of individuals with whom inmates have contact, in addition to relationships, may help resolve some of these unanswered questions. Similarly, research that helps identify the mechanism by which social ties reduce recidivism is also needed. For example, it is plausible that in-prison family contact improves family reunification and increases the level of emotional and instrumental support a family provides upon release. However, it is also possible that strong family relationships are associated with improvements in other release outcomes, such as housing, employment, substance use, which mediate the relationship between family support and recidivism. Further research is needed to address these issues.

/// DISCUSSION QUESTIONS

1. What factors describe women who were more likely to be reincarcerated?

2. What factors described women who were less likely to be reincarcerated?

3. What impact did visits from a family member have on the integration of women following

References

Adams, D., & Fischer, J. (1976). The effects of prison residents' community contacts on recidivism rates. *Corrective and Social Psychiatry and Journal of Behavior Technology Methods and Therapy, 22*, 21–27.

Agnew, R. (2006). Foundation for a general strain theory of crime and delinquency. *Criminology, 30*, 47–88.

Andrews, D. A., & Bonta, J. (2003). *The psychology of criminal conduct* (4th ed.). Newark, NJ: Lexis/Nexis.

Andrews, D. A., Zinger, I., Hoge, R. D., Bonta, J., Gendreau, P., & Cullen, F. T. (1990). Does correctional treatment work? A clinically relevant and psychologically informed meta-analysis. *Criminology, 28*, 369–404.

Aos, S., Miller, M., & Drake, E. (2006). *Evidence-based public policy options to reduce future prison construction, criminal justice costs, and crime rates*. Report #06-10-1201. Olympia, Washington: Washington State Institute for Public Policy.

Bales, William D., & Daniel P. Mears. (2008). Inmate social ties and the transition to society: Does visitation reduce recidivism? *Journal of Research in Crime and Delinquency, 45*, 287–321.

Belknap, J. (2001). *The invisible women: Gender, crime, and justice.* Belmont, CA: Wadsworth.

Bloom, V., Owen, V., & Covington, S. (2002, November). *A theoretical basis for gender-responsive strategies in criminal justice.* Paper presented at the American Society of Criminology Annual Meeting, Chicago, IL.

Broner, N., Lattimore, P. K., & Steffey, D. M. (2010). Mental health needs and services receipt of reentering offenders: A multi-site study of men, women and male youth. In H. A. Dlugacz (Ed.), *Re-entry planning for offenders with mental disorders: Policy and practice* (pp. 12-1 through 12-41). Kingston, NJ: Civic Research Institute.

Casey-Acevedo, K., Bakken, T., & Karle, A. (2004). Children visiting mothers in prison: The effects on mothers' behavior and disciplinary adjustment. *Australian & New Zealand Journal of Criminology, 37*, 418–430.

Fonagy, P., & Kurtz, A. (2002). Disturbances of conduct. In P. Fonagy, M. Target, D. Cottrell, J. Phillips, & Z. Kurtz (Eds.), *What works for whom? A critical review of treatments for children and adolescents* (pp. 106–192). New York, NY: Guilford Press.

Glaser, D. (1964). *The effectiveness of a prison and parole system.* Indianapolis, IN: Bobbs-Merril.

Hairston, C. F., Rollin, J., & Jo, H. (2004). *Family connections during imprisonment and prisoners' community reentry* (Children, Families, and the Criminal Justice System Research Brief). Chicago: University of Illinois at Chicago.

Hirschi, T. (1969). *Causes of delinquency.* Berkeley and Los Angeles: University of California Press.

Holt, N., & Miller, D. (1972). *Explorations in inmate-family relationships.* Research Report No. 4. Sacramento: California Department of Corrections.

Huebner, B. M., DeJong, C., & Cobbina, J. (2010). Women coming home: Long-term patterns of recidivism. *Justice Quarterly, 27*, 225–254.

Jiang, S., & Winfree, L. T. (2006). Social support, gender, and inmate adjustment to prison life: Insights from a national sample. *The Prison Journal, 86*, 32–55.

Katz, P. C. (1998). Supporting families and children of mothers in jail: An integrated child welfare and criminal justice strategy. *Child Welfare, 77*, 495–511.

Kiser, G. C. (1991). Female inmates and their families. *Federal Probation, 55*, 56.

Kubrin, C. E., & Stewart, E. A. (2006). Predicting who reoffends: The neglected role of neighborhood context in recidivism studies. *Criminology, 44*, 165–197.

Langan, P. A., & Levin, D. J. (2002). *Recidivism of prisoners released in 1994* (Bureau of Justice Statistics Special Report No. NCJ 193427). Washington, DC: Bureau of Justice Statistics, Office of Justice Programs, U.S. Department of Justice.

Lattimore, P. K., & Visher, C. (2009, December). *Multi-site evaluation of SVORI: Summary and synthesis* (Prepared for the National Institute of Justice). Retrieved from http://www.urban.org/uploadedpdf/412075_evaluation_svori.pdf

Lattimore, P. K., Visher, C. A., & Steffey, D. M. (2011). Measuring gaps in reentry service delivery through program director and participant reports. *Justice Research and Policy, 13*, 77–100.

Laub, J. H., & Sampson, R. J. (1993). Turning points in the life course: Why change matters to the study of crime. *Criminology, 31*, 301–325.

La Vigne, N. G., Brooks, L. E., & Shollenberger, T. L. (2008). *Women on the outside: Understanding the experiences of female prisoners returning to Houston, Texas.* Washington, DC: Urban Institute.

La Vigne, N. G., Naser, R. L., Brooks, L. E., & Castro, J. L. (2005). Examining the effect of incarceration and in-prison family contact on prisoners' family relationships. *Journal of Contemporary Criminal Justice, 21*, 314–335.

Lindquist, C. H., Barrick, K., Lattimore, P. K., & Visher, C. (2009, December). *Prisoner reentry experiences of adult females: Characteristics, service receipt, and outcomes of participants in the SVORI multi-site evaluation* (Prepared for the National Institute of Justice). Retrieved from https://www.ncjrs.gov/pdffiles1/nij/grants/230420.pdf

Lipsey, M. W. (1995). What do we learn from 400 research studies on the effectiveness of treatment with juvenile delinquency? In J. McGuire (Ed.), *What works: Reducing reoffending.* West Sussex, England: John Wiley & Sons.

Lipsey, M. W., & Cullen, F. T. (2007). The effectiveness of correctional rehabilitation: A review of systematic reviews. *Annual Review of Law and Social Science, 3*, 297–320.

MacKenzie, D. L. (2006). *What works in corrections? Reducing the criminal activities of offenders and delinquents.* New York, NY: Cambridge University Press.

Nelson, M., Deess, P., & Allan, C. (1999). *The first month out: Post-incarceration experiences in New York City*. New York, NY: Vera Institute of Justice.

O'Brien, P. (2001). Just like baking a cake: Women describe the necessary ingredients for successful reentry after incarceration. *Families in Society: The Journal of Contemporary Human Services, 82*, 287–295.

Petersilia, J. (2003). *When prisoners come home: Parole and prisoner reentry*. New York, NY: Oxford University Press.

Richie, B. E. (2001). Challenges incarcerated women face as they return to their communities: Findings from life history interviews. *Crime & Delinquency, 47*, 368–389.

Robbins, C. A., Martin, S. S., & Surratt, H. L. (2009). Substance abuse treatment, anticipated maternal roles, and reentry success of drug-involved women prisoners. *Crime & Delinquency, 55*, 388–411.

Sabol, W. J., & Couture, H. (2008, June). *Prison inmates at midyear 2007* (Bureau of Justice Statistics Bulletin No. NCJ 221944). Washington, DC: Bureau of Justice Statistics, Office of Justice Programs, U.S. Department of Justice.

Tewksbury, R., & DeMichele, M. (2005). Going to prison: A prison visitation program. *The Prison Journal, 85*, 292–310.

Travis, J., & Visher, C. (Eds.). (2005). *Prisoner reentry and crime in America*. Cambridge, UK: Cambridge University Press.

Visher, C. A., Kachnowski, V., La Vigne, N., & Travis, J. (2004). *Baltimore prisoners' experiences returning home*. Washington, DC: Urban Institute.

Visher, C. A., & Travis, J. (2003). Transitions from prison to community: Understanding individual pathways. *Annual Review of Sociology, 29*, 89–113.

West, H. C., Sabol, W. J., & Greenman, S. J. (2010, December). *Prisoners in 2009* (Bureau of Justice Statistics No. NCJ 231675). Washington, DC: Bureau of Justice Statistics, Office of Justice Programs, U.S. Department of Justice.

Winterfield, L., Lattimore, P. K., Steffey, D. M., Brumbaugh, S., & Lindquist, C. (2006). The serious and violent offender reentry initiative: Measuring the effects of service delivery. *Western Criminology Review, 7*(2), 3–19.

Women, Gender, and Incarceration

Section Highlights

- Historical trends in the incarceration of women
- Contemporary issues in the incarceration of women

This section focuses on patterns and practices in the incarceration of women offenders. Ranging from historical examples of incarceration to modern-day policies, this section looks at the treatment and punishment of women in jails and prisons. This section also highlights how children become unintended victims in the incarceration of mothers. This section concludes with a discussion about the lives of women in prison and their survival strategies as they "do time."

Historical Context of Female Prisons

Prior to the development of the all-female institution, women were housed in a separate unit within the male prison. Generally speaking, the conditions for women in these units were horrendous and were characterized by an excessive use of solitary confinement and significant acts of physical and sexual abuse by both the male inmates and the male guards. Women in these facilities received few, if any, services (Freedman, 1981). At Auburn State Prison in New York, women were housed together in an attic space where they were unmonitored and received their meals from male inmates. In many cases, these men would stay longer than necessary to complete their job duties. To no surprise, there were many prison-related pregnancies that resulted from these interactions. The death of a pregnant woman named Rachel Welch in 1825 as a result of a beating by a male guard led to significant changes in the housing of incarcerated women. In 1839, the first facility for women opened its doors. The Mount Pleasant Prison Annex was located on the grounds of Sing Sing, a male penitentiary located in Ossining, New York. While Mount Pleasant had a female warden at the facility, the oversight of the prison remained in the control of the administrators of Sing Sing, who were male and had little understanding about the nature of female criminality. Despite the intent by administrators to eliminate the abuse of women within the prison setting, the women incarcerated at Mount Pleasant continued to experience high levels of corporal punishment and abuse at the hands of the male guards.

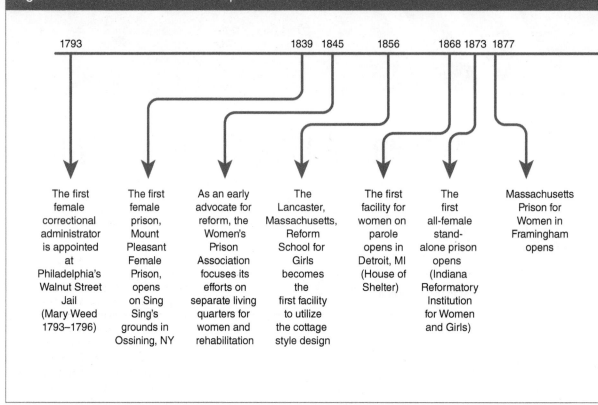

Figure 11.1 • Timeline on the Development of Women's Prisons

| 1793 | 1839 | 1845 | 1856 | 1868 1873 | 1877 |

The first female correctional administrator is appointed at Philadelphia's Walnut Street Jail (Mary Weed 1793–1796)

The first female prison, Mount Pleasant Female Prison, opens on Sing Sing's grounds in Ossining, NY

As an early advocate for reform, the Women's Prison Association focuses its efforts on separate living quarters for women and rehabilitation

The Lancaster, Massachusetts, Reform School for Girls becomes the first facility to utilize the cottage style design

The first facility for women on parole opens in Detroit, MI (House of Shelter)

The first all-female stand-alone prison opens (Indiana Reformatory Institution for Women and Girls)

Massachusetts Prison for Women in Framingham opens

SOURCES: Freedman, E. B. (1981). *Their Sisters' Keepers: Women's Prison Reform in America 1830–1930.* Ann Arbor: University of Michigan Press; Rafter, N. H. (1985). *Partial Justice: Women, Prisons and Social Control.* New Brunswick, CT: Transaction; Watterson, K. (1996). *Women in Prison: Inside the Concrete Womb.* Boston, MA: Northeastern University Press; Women's Prison Association (n.d., "History & Mission"). Retrieved from http://www.wpaonline.org/about/history

Conditions of squalor and high levels of abuse and neglect prompted moral reformers in England and the United States to work toward improving the conditions of incarcerated women. A key figure in this crusade in the United Kingdom was **Elizabeth Fry** (1780–1845). Her work with the Newgate Prison in London during the early 19th century served as the inspiration for the American women's prison reform movement. Fry argued that women offenders were capable of being reformed and that it was the responsibility of women in the community to assist those who had fallen victim to a lifestyle of crime. Like Fry, many of the reformers in America throughout the 1820s and 1830s came from upper- and middle-class communities with liberal religious backgrounds (Freedman, 1981). The efforts of these reformers led to significant changes in the incarceration of women, including the development of separate institutions for women. (See timeline in Figure 11.1.)

The Indiana Women's Prison (IWP) is identified as the first stand-alone female prison in the United States. It was also the first maximum-security prison for women. At the time of its opening in 1873, IWP housed 16 women (Schadee, 2003). By 1940, 23 states had facilities designed to exclusively house female inmates.

A review of facilities across the United States reveals two different models of institutions for women throughout the 20th century: custodial institutions and reformatories. In **custodial institutions**, women were simply ware-housed, and little programming or treatment was offered to inmates. Women in custodial institutions were typically

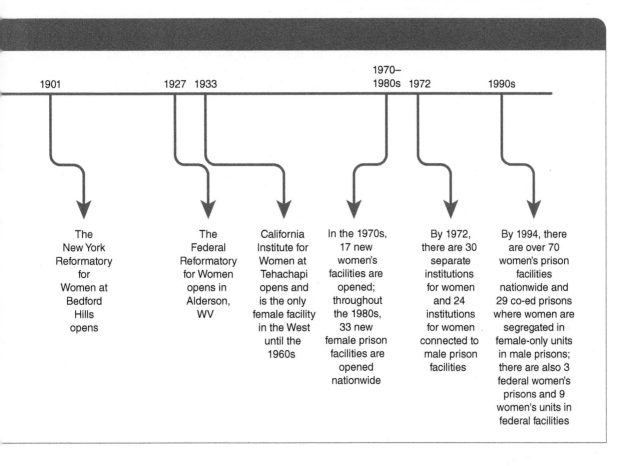

1901	1927	1933	1970–1980s	1972	1990s
The New York Reformatory for Women at Bedford Hills opens	The Federal Reformatory for Women opens in Alderson, WV	California Institute for Women at Tehachapi opens and is the only female facility in the West until the 1960s	In the 1970s, 17 new women's facilities are opened; throughout the 1980s, 33 new female prison facilities are opened nationwide	By 1972, there are 30 separate institutions for women and 24 institutions for women connected to male prison facilities	By 1994, there are over 70 women's prison facilities nationwide and 29 co-ed prisons where women are segregated in female-only units in male prisons; there are also 3 federal women's prisons and 9 women's units in federal facilities

convicted on felony and property-related crimes, with a third of women convicted of violent crimes. The custodial institution was more popular with southern states. In cases where a state had both a reformatory and a custodial institution, the distribution of inmates was made along racial lines—custodial institutions were more likely to house women of color who were determined to have little rehabilitative potential, while reformatories housed primarily White women (Freedman, 1981). Black women were also sent to work on state-owned penal plantations under conditions that mimicked the days of slavery in the South. Women of color generally had committed less serious offenses compared to White women, and yet they were incarcerated for longer periods of time. It was rare to see women of color convicted of moral offenses—since Black women were not held to the same standards of what was considered acceptable behavior for a lady, they were not deemed as in need of the rehabilitative tools that characterized the environments found at the reformatory (Rafter, 1985). Prison conditions for women at the custodial institution were characterized by unsanitary living environments with inadequate sewage and bathing systems, work conditions that were dominated by physical labor and corporal punishment, a lack of medical treatment for offenders, and the use of solitary confinement for women with mental health issues (Kurshan, 2000).

Unlike the custodial institution, which was similar in design and philosophy to most male prisons where inmates were simply housed while they did their time, the **reformatory** offered women opportunities for rehabilitation. This was a new concept in incarceration. Women were sent to the reformatory for an indeterminate period of time. In some cases, this meant that women were incarcerated for longer periods of time than their male counterparts, even for the same offenses. The philosophy of the reformatory focused on improving the moral character of women, and these facilities were mostly filled with White, working-class women who were sentenced for a variety of offenses, including "lewd and lascivious conduct, fornication, serial premarital pregnancies, adultery [and] venereal disease" (Anderson, 2006, pp. 203–204). Many of these offenses were not serious or violent crimes but rather were public order offenses, and women were punished under the premise that such behaviors were not ladylike.

Reformatories were meant to improve on the conditions that existed in many custodial institutions. For example, the reformatories were staffed with female guards. This was done in response to the historical treatment of women by male guards, which often involved sexual abuse. Reformatories were also the first to provide treatment for female offenders. However, these efforts have been criticized by feminist scholars because this treatment was based on curing women who had violated the socially proscribed norms of womanhood. As a result, the reformatory became a place that embodied an attempt by society to punish the wayward behaviors and autonomy of women and instill in them the appropriate morals and values of society (Kurshan, 2000).

One of the most successful reformatories during this time frame was the Massachusetts Correctional Institution (MCI) in Framington. Opened in 1877, Framington possessed a number of unique characteristics, including an all-female staff, an inmate nursery that allowed incarcerated women to remain with their infants while they served their sentence, and an on-site hospital to address the inmates' health care needs. Several activities were provided to give women opportunities to increase their self-esteem, gain an education, and develop a positive quality of life during their sentence. While MCI Framington is the oldest running prison still in use today, it bears little resemblance to its original mission and design; the modern-day institution bears the scars of the tough-on-crime movement. Today's version of the institution has lost some of the characteristics that made Framington a unique example of the reformatory movement and now mimics the structure and design of the male prisons located throughout the state (Rathbone, 2005).

During the 1960s, the California Institution for Women was also known for its efforts in rehabilitation. Like the early reformatories, women were sentenced to indeterminate terms of incarceration. Any decisions for parole considered not just her offense(s) but also her participation in various rehabilitative efforts during her incarceration. Most of these programs were very gendered and offered little opportunity for sustainable income once she exited prison. "Like the ideal mother, each WCS (women's correctional supervisor) also supervised prisoners' training in homemaking, deportment, dress and grooming, and was expected to participate in the moral regulation of prisoners, particularly as this related to their sexuality" (Gartner & Kruttschnitt, 2004, p. 279).

By the mid-1970s, the focus on sentencing had shifted away from rehabilitation and back to punishment as a punitive and retributive ideal. For example, the passage of California's Uniform Determinate Sentencing Act in 1976 meant that group and individualized counseling was no longer mandatory. Indeed, only a few options for rehabilitation were available and were typically run either by community volunteers or by the inmates themselves:

> Work, educational, vocational and volunteer programs were offered as a way for women to empower themselves, boost their self-esteem, and accept personal responsibility for their lives in order to change them. The prisoner was no longer expected to rely on clinical experts to design her route to rehabilitation but had become a rational actor. (Gartner & Kruttschnitt, 2004, pp. 282–283)

Today, most states have at least one facility dedicated to a growing population of female offenders. Unlike male prisons, which allow for different facilities based on the security level of the offender, the smaller incarcerated female population means that women's prisons house offenders of all security levels. In addition, these prison facilities are located in remote areas of the state, far from the cities where most of the women were arrested and where their families reside. The distance between an incarcerated woman and her family plays a significant role in the ways in which she copes with her incarceration and can affect her progress toward rehabilitation and a successful reintegration. In contrast, the sheer number of male facilities increases the probability that these men might reside in a facility closer to their home, which allows for an increased frequency in visitations by family members.

Contemporary Issues for Incarcerated Women

Since the 1980s, the number of women incarcerated in the United States has multiplied at a dramatic rate. As discussed in Section IX, sentencing policies, such as mandatory minimum sentences, and the war on drugs have had a dramatic effect on the numbers of women in prison. These structured sentencing formats, whose intent was to reduce the levels of sentencing disparities, have only led to the increases in the numbers of women in custody. At year-end 2015, there were 111,495 women incarcerated in prisons in the United States, a number that makes up 7% of the total incarcerated population. Compared to the previous year, this reflects a reduction of 1.4% fewer women in prison. The majority of this reduction is found in a significant decrease of the number of women in the federal prison system, which saw a 7.5% reduction in its female inmate population. However, several individual states also saw their numbers decrease, including California (largely because of the passage of Proposition 47), Indiana (where inmates with shorter sentences and goodtime credits were transferred to local jail facilities), Florida, and Oklahoma (Carson & Anderson, 2016). Table 11.1 illustrates a profile of women found in the criminal justice system today. Much of the rise in female criminality is the result of minor property crimes, which reflects the economic vulnerability that women experience in society, or cases involving drug-related crimes and the addiction issues facing women.

A review of 2016 census data notes that African Americans are 13.3% of the population, Hispanic/Latinos make up 17.8% and biracial individuals are 2.6%. However, the demographics of our state and federal prisons note that women of color are significantly overrepresented behind bars. Indeed, research indicates that Black women today are being incarcerated at a greater rate than both White females and Black males (Bush-Baskette, 1998). Figure 11.2 highlights the rates of incarceration of White, Black, and Hispanic women. Women of color have incarceration rates that are up to four times greater than the rates of White women (Carson & Anderson, 2016). While White women are typically incarcerated for property offenses, women of color are more likely to be incarcerated for violent and drug-related offenses (Guerino, Harrison, & Sabol, 2011). Poverty is also an important demographic of incarcerated women, because many women (48%) were unemployed at the time of their arrest, which affects their ability to provide a sustainable environment for themselves and their children. In addition, they tend to come from impoverished areas, which may help explain why women are typically involved in economically driven crimes, such as property, prostitution, and drug-related offenses. Women

Table 11.1 • Characteristics of Women in Prison	

Race/Ethnicity
  White
  African American
  Hispanic
	33%
	48%
	15%

Median age	33
High school/GED	56%
Single	47%
Unemployed	62%
Mother of minor children	65%

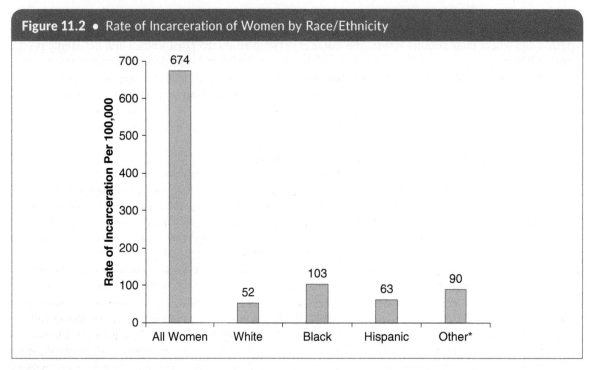

Figure 11.2 • Rate of Incarceration of Women by Race/Ethnicity

*Includes American Indians and Alaska Natives; Asians, Native Hawaiians, and other Pacific Islands; and persons of two or more races.

SOURCE: (Carson & Anderson, 2016).

also struggle with limited education and a lack of vocational training, which places them at risk for criminal behavior. The majority of women in state prisons across the United States have not completed high school and struggle with learning disabilities and literacy challenges. For example, 29% of women in custody in New York have less than a fifth-grade reading ability. Yet many prison facilities provide limited educational and vocational training, leaving women ill prepared to successfully transition to the community following their release. For example, of the 64% of women who enter prison without a high school diploma, only 16% receive their GED, and only 29% participate in any form of vocational training while they are incarcerated (Women's Prison Association [WPA], 2003, 2009a).

The rise in the female prison population means that many facilities are overcrowded, which creates a strain on basic resources within the facility and impacts the delivery of services of women. Overcrowding also can increase stress and anxiety levels leading to increases in negative mental health issues, such as depression, self-harm, and suicidal ideation. As a result, not only may women be unable to receive the treatment that they need, but also staff may be unable to recognize when women are at risk for negative mental health issues. Given the effects that overcrowding can have for female inmates, it is important that prisons be able to provide adequate resources to screen for potential self-harming behaviors and develop necessary therapeutic resources to address these issues (Clements-Nolle, Wolden, & Bargmann-Losche, 2009).

Spotlight on California Prison Realignment and Its Effect on Female Inmates

In 2011, the U.S. Supreme Court ruled that the current state of overcrowding and the resulting conditions of the state's prisons were a violation of the prisoners' Eighth Amendment protection against cruel and unusual punishment. As a result, the California Department of Corrections was required to substantially reduce the state's prison population. To bring the prison population to 137.5% of the institutional design capacity, the state needed to reduce its prison population by 40,000 prisoners (*Brown v. Plata*, 2011).

As part of the efforts to reduce the population in the state prison, correctional officials have shifted much of the correctional supervision of lower level offenders, parolees, and parole violators, to the local governments. In particular, the state legislature has altered how the state punishes felony crimes. Historically, felons were sent to the state prison and only misdemeanor offenders served their time in local jail facilities. The introduction of Assembly Bill 109 reclassified certain felonies (nonviolent, nonserious, and nonsexual offenses) to permit offenders to serve their time in county jails. Additional legislation allows offenders to receive good time credits based on time served as well as participation in specialized programming (Smude, 2012).

As a result of California's realignment plan, the state prison population has seen dramatic changes in 2011 and 2012, both in terms of its overall size and also in terms of the types of offenders that remain housed in these state prison facilities. While some decreases were noted in 2011,[1] the full effects of realignment are apparent with 2012 data. While there have been noted changes in the prison population for both male and female offenders, women have seen proportionally greater reductions. Table 11.2 highlights how the population of California's female population has shifted as a result of realignment. Not only has the number of women in prison decreased by 39% but the types of offenders are [also] more likely to be violent offenders. As a result of realignment practices, nonviolent and drug offenders are now no longer housed in state prison facilities. This represents a dramatic change in practices since the growth of women in prison during the late 20th and early 21st centuries. Table 11.3 highlights the types of sentences that women are now incarcerated on in California's state prisons. Both men (44.0%) and women (55.4%) are most likely to receive a determinate sentence. This means that once they have completed their specific sentence, they are released from custody. Similar to this category are second strikers, who have had one prior serious or violent felony in their criminal history. Their sentences are double the length of the specific offense term and they are released on the earliest possible date without having to appear before the parole board. 21.6% of incarcerated women are considered 2nd strikers. To be considered for parole, third strikers and lifers must appear before the parole board after they have served a specific number of years in custody. Approximately 19% of women in California prisons fall into this category (CDCR, 2013).

Each county has handled its realignment efforts differently. Some have utilized alternative-to-incarceration programs, such as drug treatment or probation. Meanwhile, other counties, such as Los Angeles County, have simply shifted their population from the prison yard to the county jail, where, due to limited programming or other opportunities to earn good time credits, women may actually serve longer sentences compared to what they would have spent in state prison (Ryon, 2013).

---

[1]The California Public Safety Realignment program was enacted on October 1, 2011. By end of year 2011, the program had been in effect for only 3 months. 2012 represents the first full year of the program.

Table 11.2 • Profile of Women in California's State Prisons

Offense	2010 (n = 9,759)	2012 (n = 5,992)	Percent Change
Violent Crime	40.9%	62.4%	+21.5
• **Murder**	14.7%	24.6%	+9.9
• **Manslaughter**	1.3%	2.0%	+0.7
• **Rape**	0.1%	0.2%	+0.1
• **Robbery**	9.9%	14.5%	+4.6
• **Aggravated or Simple Assault**	9.6%	13.4%	+3.8
Property Crime	33.3%	22.3%	−10.0
• **Burglary**	11.2%	10.9%	−0.3
• **Larceny-Theft**	9.9%	4.8%	−5.1
• **Motor Vehicle Theft**	3.3%	1.7%	−1.6
• **Fraud**	6.3%	3.0%	−3.3
Drug Offenses	21.1%	10.9%	−10.2

SOURCE: Carson & Golinelli (2013).

Table 11.3 • California's Prison Sentences by Gender (2013)

	Gender				Total	
	Female		Male			
	N	%	N	%	N	%
Total	5,982	100%	128,178	100%	134,160	100%
2nd Strike	1,294	21.6%	33,405	26.1%	34,699	25.9%
3rd Strike	64	1.1%	7,911	6.2%	34,699	25.9%
Determinate Sentence	3,317	55.3%	56,402	44%	59,719	44.5%
Lifer	1,072	17.9%	25,023	19.5%	26,095	19.5%
LWOP	186	3.1%	4,501	3.5%	4,687	3.5%
Death	20	0.3%	714	0.6%	734	0.5%

SOURCE: California Department of Corrections and Rehabilitation (CDCR) (2013). Prison Census Data as of June 30, 2013. Table 10 Prison Census Data, Total Institution Population. Offenders by Sentence Status and Gender. Retrieved at www.cdcr.ca.gov/Reports_Research/Offender_Information_Services_Branch/Annual/Census/CENSUSd1306.pdf

With all the challenges that women face within prison, how do they develop social support networks within the prison walls? Research by Severance (2005) finds that women rely on a variety of experiences to develop these internal support structures. For example, women who are from the same neighborhoods or did time together in jails may bond together. The dormitory style housing environment in prisons can also provide women the opportunity to develop these emotional connections. While being in close proximity can help establish relationships, it can also be challenging for some women to build trust within these environments, particularly given the lack of privacy and the high levels of gossip that exist within these correctional settings (Severance, 2005).

The level of attachment and trust can vary because inmates have different types of relationships within the prison walls. Research by Severance (2005) describes four different categories of relationships that are found within women's prisons: acquaintances, friends, family, and girlfriends. Acquaintances are superficial relationships that involve low levels of trust between inmates. Friends are more meaningful than acquaintances because they involve an increased level of trust. Unlike acquaintances, which are typically temporary relationships, friends have the potential to continue once the women have left prison. While family relationships, or **pseudo-families,** can also provide supportive networks, these relationships are not always positive experiences due to the lack of respect that can occur between family members. Finally, girlfriends can provide emotional and romantic support. What makes this type of relationship unique is that the majority of women in prison do not identify as homosexual.

▲ **Photo 11.1** A woman spends time with a family member during a no-contact visit. A no-contact visit means that the inmate cannot touch or hug her family and friends when they come to visit. For many women, the lack of physical contact with their loved ones can contribute to the stress and loneliness of incarceration.

These relationships are generally not for sexual purposes but rather are for emotional support and companionship. Intimate relationships can also serve to provide economic benefits, particularly in cases where one partner has more resources (i.e., money for canteen supplies) than the other. Here, sex becomes a commodity that can be exchanged. Unlike the "girlfriends" described by Severance (2005), these relationships are often engaged in by offenders with shorter sentences and are purely sexual (Einat & Chen, 2012).

Physical and Mental Health Needs of Incarcerated Women

Women in custody face a variety of physical and mental health issues. In many cases, the criminal justice system is ill equipped to deal with these issues. Incarcerated women are 3.7 times more likely to experience physical or sexual trauma in their lives compared to women in the general population (Grella, Lovinger, & Warda, 2013). Given the high rates of abuse and victimization that these women experience throughout their lives, it is not surprising that the incarcerated female population has a high demand for mental health services. Women in prison have significantly higher rates of mental illness than women in the general population. Official data indicate that 13% of women in federal facilities and 24% of women in state prisons have been diagnosed with a mental disorder (General Accounting Office, 1999).

The pains of imprisonment, including the separation from family and adapting to the prison environment, can exacerbate mental health conditions. In addition, many offenders with life sentences (45%) often experience suicidal ideation on receiving this sentence. The experience of prison can also exacerbate mental health conditions, such as depression, particularly given the life experiences of many female inmates. In addition, women with limited support from family on the outside experience suicidal ideation (Dye & Aday, 2013).

Unfortunately, the standard course of treatment in many facilities involves prescription psychotropic medications. Often these medications are prescribed in excess and often in lieu of counseling or other therapeutic interventions. For example, one study indicates that 21 of the 22 participants were given the prescription Seroquel,[2] which is used to treat bipolar disorder. Yet only one of the women was actually officially diagnosed with bipolar disorder. Although the manufacturer or Seroquel recommends that people who take this medication be reassessed at regular intervals, few of the women actually received such treatment while in prison. While some drugs were readily available, the same did not hold true for all psychotropic medications. In some cases, women noted that prison doctors would prescribe new drugs to the women rather than continue to offer prescriptions for drugs that had been effective in the past. "Prison doctors just do whatever they want—the opposite of what you were getting before you went in so that they can show you who's boss. It's just a way for them to show you how much control they have" (Kitty, 2012, p. 171). Not only can the failure to comply with a prescribed medication protocol be grounds for a disciplinary action while in prison, but such behaviors can also be used against an offender during a parole hearing.

Some women believe that their mental health status improves during incarceration because they were appropriately medicated, were no longer using illicit substances, and were engaged in therapeutic support programs. However, the majority of women believed that incarceration exacerbated their mental health issues and that a number of variables contributed to this. First, incarceration is a stressful experience, and stress can increase feelings of anxiety and insecurity. Second, the majority of resources for mental health were focused on crisis intervention and not therapeutic resources. In particular "lifers" felt that they were often placed at the end of the list and were denied services due to their sentence. Finally, many of the women felt degraded and abused by the staff, which added to their trauma (Harner & Riley, 2013).

Women also face a variety of physical health needs. Women in prison are more likely to be HIV positive than women in the community, presenting a unique challenge for the prison health care system. While women in the general U.S. population have an HIV infection rate of 0.3%, the rate of infection for women in state and federal facilities is 3.6%, a tenfold increase. In New York state, this statistic rises to an alarming 18%, a rate 60 times that of the national infection rate. These rates are significantly higher than the rates of HIV-positive incarcerated men. Why is HIV an issue for women in prison? Women who are HIV positive are more likely to have a history of sexual abuse, compared to women who are HIV negative (WPA, 2003). While the rates of HIV-positive women have declined since an all-time high in 1999, the rate of hepatitis C infections has increased dramatically within the incarcerated female population. Estimates indicate that between 20% and 50% of women in jails and prisons are affected by this disease. Hepatitis C is a disease that is transmitted via bodily fluids, such as blood, and can lead to liver damage if not diagnosed or treated. Offending women are at a high risk to contract hepatitis C given their involvement in sex and drug crimes. Few prison facilities routinely test for hepatitis C, and treatment can be expensive due to the high cost of prescriptions (Van Wormer & Bartollas, 2010).

While the physical health needs of women in prison are significant, there are often limited resources for treatment within the prison walls. The medical staff is generally overwhelmed with the high number of inmates that require medical care. In addition, many women expressed concerns about the environment in prison and felt that

---

[2]The manufacturer of Seroquel indicates that "Seroquel is an antipsychotic medication, useful as a mono-drug therapy or as an adjunct to the drugs lithium or divalproex for the treatment of schizophrenia and the acute manic and depressive episodes in bipolar disorder" (Kitty, 2012, p. 168).

it put them at risk for increased health issues in a number of ways, such as the physical conditions of the prison and housing that combine healthy inmates with inmates with chronic and communicable illnesses. Finally, the women expressed a desire for increased health education on issues such as prevention, diet, and exercise (Morgan, 2013).

Spotlight on the Financial Challenges Behind Bars

One of the myths about prison life is that everything is provided for inmates. "Three hots and a cot" is a term thrown about that notes that inmates have food and shelter. There have also been criticisms levied by the public over "free" medical care and education. However, a review of these sorts of programs notes that prison life is anything but free. Medical care is one of the top five greatest expenditures for correctional institutions, costs that are only expected to increase because tough on crime sentencing practices mean that inmates will have increased demands on prison medical systems as they age (The Pew Charitable Trusts and the John D. and Catherine T. MacArthur Foundation, 2014). A recent case of an female inmate who was dying of pancreatic cancer cost the State of California over $100,000 in overtime fees alone for guards to supervise her during the 36 days that she was hospitalized prior to her death (Henry, 2013). As state institutions look for ways to reduce costs, many have adopted health-care payment fees, which can range from $2 to $5. That may not sound like much compared to the $15–$20 that most insurance plans charge for the average individual, but consider the context. Inmate jobs pay very little: The Prison Policy Initiative notes that inmate wages can be as low as $0.13 per hour with the average prison job paying $0.93 per hour. Depending on the state, these wages are taxed at anywhere between 30–50%. One inmate who worked in the prison kitchen netted between $5.25 and $8.75 per week after administrative costs (Bozelko, 2017). Given this context, paying between $2.00 and $5.00 for a medical visit is a significant burden. In addition, women in prison are more likely to utilize prison health-care services at a higher rate than male inmates (Marshall, Simpson & Stevens, 2001). Research notes that many women end up negotiating between paying for a health visit and other expenses, such as phone cards or letter writing supplies in order to stay connected to family members. Phone calls can be prohibitively expensive; a 15 minute call can range from $5.15 to $10.00 (Harner, Wyant, & Da Silva, 2017).

The availability of funds in an inmate's commissary account can also be a status symbol behind bars. However, this could also be a difficult relationship to negotiate, both inside and out. Family members could deposit funds for their loved one. However, these funds often took a significant amount of time to be processed. In addition, such contributions were subjected to fees by the institution. In California, deposits to an inmate's commissary account are taxed at 50% to satisfy any restitution orders with an additional 10% administrative fee (CDCR, n.d.). Many inmates expressed feeling guilty for asking their family members to contribute to their accounts, knowing that it was a burden for them to do so. For others, having family members send money (or withhold money) became a symbol of their relationship: Inmates with strong relationships with family members were likely to have deposits made to their accounts while inmates who had deteriorating or poor relationships were less likely to receive such support (Smoyer, 2015).

Given the tenuous financial circumstances that many women find themselves in prior to arriving at prison, the costs of life behind bars can not only exacerbate preexisting physical and mental health conditions but also place additional strain on the relationships that are essential to recovery, rehabilitation, and reentry.

Considering the number of women that come to prison on drug-related charges, or whose criminal activity is related to their drug use, the demand for drug treatment in prison is high. Women are more likely to participate in prison-based drug treatment (Belenko & Houser, 2012), and those who participate have lower rates of recidivism

▲ **Photo 11.2** The rise of female incarceration has had significant impacts on the lives of their children, who are left to grow up without their mothers. Here, CYA inmate Angela Rodrigiez holds her daughter for the first time during a visit.

over the long term (Grella & Rodriguez, 2011). Many of the drug treatment programs in prison have been based on therapeutic community (TC) models. The TC model is designed to provide individuals with tools to help them live a drug-free lifestyle. However, TC programming may not adequately address some of the gender-specific needs of the female incarcerated population. Research by Messina, Grella, Cartier, and Torres (2010) found that women in the gender-specific drug treatment program were more likely to stay away from drugs for a longer period of time and were more successful on parole compared to those who participated in a TC treatment program. These findings indicate the importance of offering programs designed with the unique needs of women in mind.

While women inmates have a higher need for treatment (in terms of both prevalence and severity of conditions) than male inmates, the prison system is limited in its resources and abilities to address these issues. For example, most facilities are inadequately staffed or lack the diagnostic tools needed to address women's gynecological issues. Women also have higher rates of chronic illnesses than the male population (Anderson, 2006). However, the demands for these services significantly outweigh their availability, and the lack of accessible services ranks high on the list of inmate complaints regarding quality of life issues in prison (WPA, 2003).

Children of Incarcerated Mothers: The Unintended Victims

Children of **incarcerated mothers** (and fathers) deal with a variety of issues that stem from the loss of a parent, including grief, loss, sadness, detachment, and aggressive or at-risk behaviors for delinquency. Additionally, these children are at high risk for ending up in prison themselves as adults. The location of many prisons makes it difficult for many children to retain physical ties with their mother throughout her incarceration. While more than two-thirds of incarcerated mothers have children under the age of 18, only 9% of these women will ever get to be visited by their children while they are incarcerated (Van Wormer & Bartollas, 2010).

A small number of women enter prison already pregnant. Estimates indicate that approximately 6% of women in jail, 4% to 5% of women in state prisons, and 3% of women in federal prison are pregnant when they were arrested for their crimes (Glaze & Maruschak, 2008). While pregnancy is generally a happy time for most expectant mothers, these mothers-to-be face high levels of stress over how their incarceration might affect the lives of their children. One concern centers on the quality of prenatal care that she might experience behind bars. Here, women are concerned about how their physical health before and during their incarceration will impact their unborn child. Most of these women will give birth and return to prison within a few days without their new baby. This separation between mother and child can lead to mental health complications for the mother. In addition, they may be concerned over who will care for their child and fear they will miss out on the physical and emotional connections that mothers traditionally experience with a new baby (Wismont, 2000).

Giving birth while incarcerated can be a traumatizing experience. Consider the following scenario:

> A nurse in the labor room goes to attend to one of her patients who is in active labor and is ready to deliver her baby. The correctional officer removes the women's leg shackles and hand cuffs and immediately replaces them after the baby is born. (Ferszt, 2011, p. 254)

In 2012, 33 states had policies that permitted women to be shackled while they were in labor. Yet even those states that prohibit the practice demonstrate great variability of the law. Some prohibit the use of shackles only during the labor and delivery process. Rhode Island has one of the most comprehensive and liberal laws, in that it prohibits the use of restraints at any time during the second and third trimester, as well as during postpartum (World Law Direct, 2011). These laws state that prisoners needed to be restrained due to safety and security concerns. Several professional organizations, including the American Congress of Obstetricians and Gynecologists and the American Medical Association, have expressed concerns over these policies because they can lead to health risks to both the mother and her baby (Berg, 2011). For example, if a woman is shackled (meaning her legs are either restrained to each other or to the side of the bed), it can be difficult for hospital staff to assist a woman during a

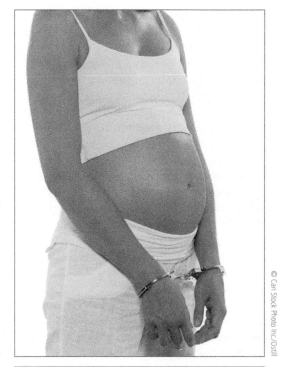

▲ **Photo 11.3** While many states have outlawed the practice of shackling women during childbirth, the use of restraints on pregnant women continues to present a number of health risks for both the mother and the child.

normal childbirth experience and can significantly complicate the delivery during an emergency situation. This has potentially disastrous effects for both the woman and her baby. "If the fetal heart beat slows, and an immediate Caesarian-section is required, the time lost to fumbling with shackle locks could cause brain damage and even death" (WPA, n.d., "Laws Banning," para. 4).

Over the past several years, a number of states have passed new laws that forbid the practice of shackling female inmates during delivery. For example, Florida recently abolished the use of shackling of any pregnant woman during labor and delivery, the first such law in a southern state (Lopez, 2012). California recently passed a law that prohibits the use of shackles (feet), handcuffs (hands), or belly chains during childbirth ("Shackling Pregnant Inmates", 2012). However, some jurisdictions have been slow to respond to new laws in their jurisdiction. While Illinois in 1999 outlawed shackling inmates during labor, the practice continued up until 2012 at places such as the Cook County Jail in Chicago. Eighty women filed a class action suit alleging that they were unnecessarily shackled during birth and recovery and were awarded 4.1 million dollars in damages in May 2012 (Mastony, 2012).

In an effort to both improve the emotional well-being of the mother and encourage attachment and bonding between a mother and her infant, nine states (New York, California, Illinois, Indiana, Ohio, Nebraska, South Dakota, Washington, and West Virginia) have integrated prison nurseries into their facilities, which allow women to remain with their infant children for at least part of their sentence (WPA, 2009b). The oldest prison nursery program is located at Bedford Hills Correctional Facility in New York. Founded in 1901, this program is the largest in the country and allows 29 mothers to reside with their infant children. Women who participate in these prison nursery programs take classes on infant development and participate in support groups with other mothers. Although most programs limit the time that a child can reside with his or her mother (generally 12–18 months), the Washington Correctional Center for Women is unique in that its prison nursery program allows children born to incarcerated women to remain with their mothers for up to 3 years (WPA, 2009b). Other states allow overnight visits with children, either in special family units on the prison grounds or in specialized cells within the facility. At Bedford Hills, older children can participate in programs at the facility with their mothers (Van Wormer & Bartollas, 2010). These programs help families repair and maintain ties between a mother and her child(ren) throughout her incarceration.

Prison nursery programs are not without their critics, because some suggest that prison is an inappropriate place for children. However, separating mothers and their children can also have detrimental effects, because children of incarcerated mothers are more likely to have educational challenges and limited emotional attachments. There is also a cycle of incarceration because children of imprisoned parents have an increased risk toward delinquent and criminal behaviors. Not only do these programs such as the mother-baby nurseries help end the cycle of incarceration for both the mother and child, but they also assist in the reduction of recidivism once a woman is released from custody (WPA, 2009b). Unfortunately, many prison administrators are unaware of the benefits that a prison nursery can supply. Additional concerns involve the costs of implementing such a program and a belief that prison was an inappropriate place for children (Campbell & Carlson, 2012).

While the concept of the prison nursery and programming for children of incarcerated mothers helps promote the bond between parent and child, what about those states where these types of programs are not available? What happens to these children? The majority of women in the criminal justice system are the primary custodial parents for their young children, and these women must determine who will care for their children while they are incarcerated. Some may have a husband or children's father to turn to for assistance, though many will seek out extended family members, including grandparents. Seventy-nine percent of children who have an incarcerated parent are raised by an extended family member (WPA, 2003). In cases where an extended family member is unable or unavailable to care for a woman's minor child(ren), social services will place them in foster care. When a woman faces a long term of incarceration, the Adoption and Safe Families Act of 1997 terminates the parental rights in cases where children have been in foster care for 15 months (out of the previous 22 months). Given the increases in strict sentencing practices, the effects of this law mean that the majority of incarcerated women will lose their children if a family member is unable to care for them while the mother serves her sentence (Belknap, 2007).

Given that many of these women will regain custody of their children following the completion of their sentence, it is important that they maintain a connection with their children during this time. This can be a challenging prospect. In many cases, prison facilities are far removed from where these children reside. The cost of traveling to visit a parent can be prohibitive, particularly for families that struggle with the day-to-day economics of raising a child. This means that the majority of women in custody do not receive regular physical visits from their children. While 35% of women correspond with their children via the telephone and 49% communicate via letters, this means that half of the children do not have a relationship with their mother during her incarceration. This can have a detrimental impact on the parent–child relationship. In cases where the women will return to an authoritative parental role following their release from prison, it is important for families to maintain a parent–child bond. Here, extended family members play a crucial role in maintaining the connection between incarcerated women and their children (Stringer & Barnes, 2012).

Given that the majority of women in prison are mothers and that many were the primary caregiver of minor children prior to their incarceration, facilities have begun to implement parenting programs designed to help inmates develop effective parenting skills. Not only can these programs help provide a better relationship between a mother and her child(ren), but it can also help prevent recidivism. As a result of this curriculum, these mothers increased their knowledge about childhood development, altered their attitudes about physical discipline, and developed an understanding about the needs and well-being of their children (Sandifer, 2008).

Spotlight on the Girl Scouts Beyond Bars Program

Funded by the National Institute of Justice, the first Girl Scouts Beyond Bars (GSBB) program was offered at the Maryland Correctional Institution for Women in November 1992 (Girl Scouts [GSA], 2008). As part of the program, mothers meet with their daughters twice a month on prison grounds to work on troop projects, such as math and science projects, as well as creative activities that focus on topics such as self-esteem, relationships, and teen development/pregnancy prevention. By 2008, there were over 37 programs nationwide. Research has shown that the Girl Scouts Behind Bars program has been effective in a number of ways. First, the program facilitates regular contact between mothers and their daughter(s), which allows the mothers to have an active role in childrearing. Spending quality time together also strengthens the mother-child bond even though she is incarcerated (Moses, 1995). Research indicates that the majority (85%) of girls who participated in these programs had a closer bond with their mom following their participation in the program (GSA, 2008). Second, the program benefits the children, because research documents that their behavior at home and educational involvement improve (Block & Potthast, 1998). Additionally, the girls learned a variety of prosocial behaviors, such as respect and leadership, and developed a positive attitude about their personal futures (GSA, 2008).

While there are significant benefits to be gained by participating in the Girl Scouts Beyond Bars program, they do require significant emotional and physical investments by its supporters. Similar to traditional Girl Scouts (GS) programs, GSBB programs are run primarily by volunteers. In traditional GS programs, parents serve as the troop leaders. GSBB programs require a commitment by the community and family members to help organize and lead these programs (Block, 1999). Despite these challenges, the Girl Scouts Beyond Bars represents a program with positive effects for both a mother and her daughter.

/// SUMMARY

- The first prison for women was opened in 1839 in response to the growing concerns of abuse of women in male prison facilities.

- The reformatory prison was designed to rehabilitate women from their immoral ways.

- The custodial institution offered very little in terms of rehabilitative programming for incarcerated women.

- Women of color are overrepresented in women's prisons.

- While in prison, women develop acquaintances, friendships, pseudo-families, and romantic relationships to provide emotional support.

- Women in custody face a variety of unique issues, many of which the prison is ill equipped to deal with.

- Some facilities have prison nursery programs, which allow mothers to remain with their infant children while incarcerated.

- Programs such as Girl Scouts Beyond Bars help provide the parent–child bond while mothers are incarcerated.

KEY TERMS

Custodial institutions 468

Incarcerated mothers 478

Reformatory 469

Fry, Elizabeth 468

Pseudo-families 475

 DISCUSSION QUESTIONS

1. If you were to build a women's prison that reflected gender-responsive principles, what key features would you integrate into your facility?

2. Discuss the profile for women who are incarcerated in our prison facilities. In what ways are incarcerated women different from incarcerated men?

3. What challenges do incarcerated women face? How does prison impact the children of these mothers?

WEB RESOURCES

Hour Children: http://www.hourchildren.org

Our Place DC: http://www.ourplacedc.org

The Sentencing Project: http://www.sentencingproject.org

Women's Prison Association: http://www.wpaonline.org

---

online
resources

Visit **study.sagepub.com/mallicoat3e** to access additional study tools, including eFlashcards, web quizzes, web resources, video resources, and SAGE journal articles.

READING /// 21

One of the challenges in building relationships while incarcerated is the lack of trust that can exist between inmates, which in turn can impact therapeutic communities that many rehabilitative programs are built upon. This article highlights the challenges of these relationships and the role they play in the rehabilitative process for women.

Social Relationships and Group Dynamics Inside a Community Correction Facility for Women

Andrea Cantora, Jeff Mellow, and Melinda D. Schlager

Group treatment is the most common method for engaging criminal justice populations in need of treatment (e.g., 12 steps and other mutual-help groups, cognitive-behavioral therapy, and therapeutic community [TC] models). Its popularity is based on a number of factors: (a) The cost of group treatment is usually less than individual-level therapy; (b) research indicates it is as effective as one-on-one treatment (McRoberts, Burlingame, & Hoag, 1998); and (c) it can provide a safe environment, which fosters mutual support, assistance, trust, and feedback from one's peer group (DeLeon, 1995). In the correctional rehabilitation field, cognitive-behavioral group approaches are the most effective strategy (Andrews & Bonta, 2010). For women offenders, gender-responsive strategies designed to address women-specific issues in a group setting are becoming increasingly popular (Gehring, Van Voorhis, & Bell, 2010; Messina, Grella, Cartier, & Torres, 2010; Wright, Van Voorhis, Salisbury, & Bauman, 2009).

Understanding what works best for specific populations is necessary for providing effective treatment and for producing successful outcomes. Part of understanding what works involves assessing intradynamics of a group treatment environment. Much of the research on treatment environment is highlighted in the substance abuse

and gender-responsive literature. Both literatures are discussed in this article, with a specific focus on therapeutic relationships and engagement within the group context. The literature on peer relationships within female prisons is also discussed to provide further context. The current study presented examines the specific context of a female community correction setting that incorporates group treatment. Resident relationships and perceptions of on-site and off-site group treatment are discussed.

The Nature of Women's Prison Relationships

The study of social relationships in female prisons has been examined since the 1960s. Themes from early studies provide a portrayal of women's prisons as homelike, supportive, and consisting of strong pseudo-kinship[1] relationships (Giallombardo, 1966; Ward & Kassebaum, 1965). Also common were intimate sexual relationships among inmates (Giallombardo, 1966; Jones, 1993; Owen, 1998; Propper, 1982; Ward & Kassebaum, 1965). Research from the past 15 years indicates similarities but also points to a shift in relationship dynamics among female inmates.

SOURCE: Cantora, A., Mellow, J., & Schlager, M. D. (2016). Social relationships and group dynamics inside a community correction facility for women. *International Journal of Offender Therapy and Comparative Criminology*, 60(9), 1016–1035.

Several qualitative studies examining women's social relationships find women in prison struggle to develop supportive relationships with others due to their inability to trust (Einat & Chen, 2012; Greer, 2000; Kruttschnitt, Gartner, & Miller, 2000; Severance, 2005). In Severance's (2005) study, participants described feeling uncomfortable talking openly with other inmates due to gossiping. Participants were also suspicious of other women after observing women stealing personal items. Regardless, some women developed friendships with others based on common backgrounds, work assignments, or living areas. Although some relationships did exist, Severance (2005) and Greer (2000) failed to find support for pseudo-kinships.

Einat and Chen (2012) further found that gossip increases the social conflict, weakens the settings' cohesive dynamics, creates inequality among women, isolates them, and may cause psychological harm. Although gossip was viewed as a negative social behavior, Einat and Chen found that gossiping relieves some of the pains of imprisonment. For example, they found that women gossip out of the desire to gain emotional support, reduce stress, improve social status, and obtain material benefits. Regardless of the negative or positive benefits of gossiping, women collectively viewed gossiping as an unacceptable behavior.

Both Kruttschnitt et al. (2000) and Greer (2000) suggested that the lack of cohesive relationships among women prisoners may be due to the changing physical environment of modern prisons (e.g., shift from therapeutic homelike cottage system to a controlled dormitory setting). Greer suggested that increased access to the outside world (e.g., visitation, television, and correspondence) and changes in gender roles (i.e., emphasis on individuality vs. social role) influence inside relationships. Greer further suggested that these shifts may explain the challenges of creating supportive relationships and instead contribute to the desire to socially withdraw.

Relational Focused Treatment

The literature on correctional treatment does not take into account the nature of women's relationships with those in the treatment setting. As illustrated in the above literature, peer relationships among women incarcerated are often hostile and untrusting, yet women are often required to participate in programs with their peers. For example, the current emphasis on providing gender-responsive treatment involves two core principles: creating a safe, respectful environment and creating programs that are relational and promote healthy connections to loved ones and the community (Bloom, Owen, & Covington, 2003). These principles are grounded in relational theory.

Relational theory is based on the relationship connections that women develop during their life course. Forming trusting interpersonal relationships is the core of the relational model (Covington, 1998; Gilligan, 1982; Miller, 1986). Bloom and Covington (1998) argued that "when a woman is disconnected from others, or involved in abusive relationships, she experiences disempowerment, confusion, diminished zest, vitality and self-worth . . ." (p. 12). As described by Covington (2003), the lives of women offenders often consist of "disconnected" and "growth hindering" relationships. Women offenders experience an overabundance of disconnections, including physical and emotional violations in their relationships with others. These disconnections prevent them from becoming self-sufficient and from developing positive self-esteem. Covington (2003) argued that it is the positive connections in women's lives that help them to grow and develop a sense of self-worth.

Research further suggests that women's positive relationships with family, friends, and children may reduce their desire to engage in criminal behavior (Wright, DeHart, Koons-Witt, & Crittenden, 2013). Other research finds that women are more likely to complete community-based programs if they are reunited with their children (Lichtenwalter, Garase, & Barker, 2010). Furthermore, research on programs that target women's psychological and physical well-being (including programs that address parenting issues and physical/sexual abuse) shows reductions in recidivism and substance abuse (Tripodi, Bledsoe, Klim, & Bender, 2011). Although the research is limited on the importance of relationships with program peers, the empirical literature discussed indicates that positive relationships play a crucial role in women's reentry success.

Recognizing that women prisoners often come from environments that are characterized as abusive, the gender-responsive literature recommends correctional programs create environments that are physically safe, psychologically secure, and where women can develop positive, supportive relationships with others (Bloom et al., 2003; Koons, Burrow, Morash, & Bynum, 1997). It is within the group setting that women from similar backgrounds can develop strong and empowered relationships. The literature further suggests that group treatment should involve women-only settings due to the idea that women may struggle to open up and disclose their personal experiences when men are in the room (Bloom & Covington, 2009). Drawing on the substance abuse literature, we can examine ways to strengthen the relationships among peers in treatment-oriented settings, and why these relationships are so vital to program success.

Therapeutic Engagement and Relationships

Two important components of a treatment setting, identified in the substance abuse literature, and relevant to the current study, are therapeutic relationships and engagement. According to Broome, Knight, Knight, Hiller, and Simpson (1997), therapeutic relationships entail both the development of supportive bonds between clients and staff, and peer-to-peer connections. Developing strong, supportive relationships with staff and peers is necessary for individual change to occur in a treatment setting (Melnick & DeLeon, 1999). Furthermore, developing strong relationships with staff and other clients increases treatment retention and reduces substance use (Simpson, 1997).

Treatment engagement involves individual needs, motivation, and program characteristics (e.g., treatment staff attributes, service accessibility, and therapeutic bonding; Simpson, 2001). Simpson further explains that level of treatment readiness determines therapeutic engagement. Welsh and McGrain (2008) defined therapeutic engagement as "a client's active involvement in and commitment to treatment" (p. 272). Research finds that clients with higher levels of therapeutic engagement are likely to remain in treatment (Joe, Simpson, & Broome, 1998; Simpson, 2001; Simpson, Joe, Rowan-Szal, & Greener, 1995), refrain from drug use, and recidivate less (DeLeon, Melnick, & Kressel, 1997; Simpson & Joe, 1993).

Therapeutic engagement and relationships are necessary for all types of treatment settings; however, these components are best understood within a TC context. DeLeon (1995) described the components of the TC model with an emphasis on addressing substance abuse, social, and psychological problems through a "community as method" approach. This method involves developing a peer network within the treatment setting where all activities are group-oriented. Other peer components include the use of peer role models as a social learning mechanism; peer encounter groups ("to heighten individual awareness of specific attitudes or behavioral patterns that should be modified"; DeLeon, 1995, p. 11); awareness training (learning how behavior and attitudes affect others in the environment); and emotional growth training (identifying, expressing, and managing feelings).

Welsh and McGrain (2008) studied the TC dimensions of peer support and counselor rapport as components predictive of therapeutic engagement. They found support for the "community as method" component of the TC model. For example, they measured peer support using items assessing peer relationships and perceptions of treatment group cohesiveness. They found positive peer support, counselor competence, and rapport to be strong predictors of therapeutic engagement. In another study that supports the "community as method" approach, Hiller, Knight, Leukefeld, and Simpson (2002) examined how motivation influences therapeutic engagement in correctional settings. They studied a TC program with a group of male and female probationers. One of the key measures was therapeutic engagement, which included items measuring personal involvement, personal progress, and psychological safety. Of interest to this research is the personal involvement measure, which asked questions about willingness to talk about feelings in the group, and the psychological safety measure assessing perceived level of trust for peers. High levels of psychological safety, and personal involvement, were related to motivation for treatment (i.e., treatment readiness and desire for help; Hiller et al., 2002).

Mosher and Philips's (2006) study on the dynamics of a prison TC program for women looked at the internal dynamics of the program. They found that unruly participants and those less amicable to treatment disrupt the culture of the program. Mosher and Philips found that by removing disruptive residents from the program, overall dynamics among residents and staff improved.

In summary, the research on therapeutic engagement and relationships lends support to the notion that psychologically supportive environments improve motivation, participation, and program outcomes. Prior research on substance abuse treatment with criminal justice populations suggests more research is needed to understand "during-treatment" aspects of a client's experience (Broome et al., 1997), including how peer support plays a role in increasing therapeutic engagement (Welsh & McGrain, 2008). Research on the social environment within female prisons sheds light on some of the challenges associated with creating a supportive environment with this population. To understand these relationships, the social context of a community correction setting is examined. Specifically, this qualitative study examines three core research questions:

Research Question 1: How do women get along with other residents in the halfway house?

Research Question 2: How do they perceive on-site group treatment groups?

Research Question 3: How do they perceive off-site group treatment programs?

The following sections provide details on the methodology used, a description of the study sample, and an overview of the halfway house program. The "Results" section introduces themes related to the core research questions. The article concludes with a discussion of findings, study limitations, and recommendations for improving group treatment for women in correctional settings.

Method

Data Collection

Permission to conduct research at the halfway house site was approved by the director of the facility and the Institutional Review Board at John Jay College of Criminal Justice. All women residing at the halfway house between June 2007 and November 2007 were eligible to participate in this study. The researcher selected to interview any resident present at the halfway house during the hours the researcher was on-site. To reach all potential participants, the researcher visited the halfway house during the day,

afternoon, and on many evenings. Caseworkers used a daily roster to determine which residents were on-site. Once several residents were identified, the caseworker, or other halfway house staff, would call them down one by one and send them to the location of the interview space. During the day, interviews often took place in a private classroom space where group treatment was held. During the evening, the interviews took place in the case manager's office after she left for the day. Both spaces had a door that was closed during the interview. When a resident entered the interview space, the researcher introduced the study and consent process. The researcher informed participants about the voluntary nature of the interview, and that confidentiality would be protected. After women agreed to participate, the researcher asked for further permission to audio record the interview.

Forty-three women were residing in the halfway house on the day of the first interview. Over a 6-month period, 35 women were conveniently selected to be interviewed; however, only 33 agreed to participate. Four of the 33 women refused to have the interview recorded. The in-depth qualitative interviews lasted between 45 min and two hr. Each interview was structured around a series of broad questions on women's pathway to prison, their experience at the New Jersey Department of Corrections (NJDOC), the transition to the halfway house, daily life at the house, addressing reentry needs (e.g., job searching, housing, family reunification, treatment for substance abuse and mental health, etc.), family and peer relationships, and expectations for reentry to the community. All recorded interviews were transcribed by the researcher. The researcher took detailed notes during the four interviews where participants refused to be recorded.

In addition, demographic, criminal history, and family history data on the sample population were collected from resident case files. Data from case files included Pre-Sentence Investigation Reports, the NJDOC Comprehensive Assessment Profile, a Correctional Facility Assessment, and the Level of Service Inventory–Revised (LSIR) conducted by halfway house staff. These documents were used to develop a profile for each participant.

Analysis

As the interviews covered a wide range of topics, the researcher identified subsections of the transcripts where respondents specifically spoke about on-site group treatment programs, off-site treatment, and interactions with residents. A process of initial coding then took place as a method of studying fragments of transcripts (Charmaz, 2006). As segments of transcripts were labeled, the researcher analyzed the meaning of the participants' words by writing analytical memos (Strauss & Corbin, 1998). Codes developed during initial coding were applied during the second analytical phase of focused coding. During this phase, the qualitative software program, ATLAS.ti, was used to aid in making connections between interviews and to search for additional themes related to women's perceptions of the halfway house experience. This phase allowed the researcher to further identify aspects of the data that may have been overlooked during initial coding and also allowed for greater comparison between participants (Charmaz, 2006). Last, to develop a sample profile, the researcher reviewed case files and analyzed the data using descriptive statistics related to demographic, criminal history, and family variables. Profiles were created to develop an overall sample profile of participant characteristics (see the following section). Profiles were also used to provide further context to women's experiences and perceptions of group treatment.

Sample

The average age of interviewees was 39. Women were primarily African American (52%), followed by 27% White and 21% Hispanic. More than half of the sample was unmarried (61%), and the majority had at least one child under the age of 18 (64%). Sixty-one percent of the participants had a high school diploma or general education development (GED), yet 55% were frequently unemployed prior incarceration. The majority of the sample had an extensive criminal history with 58% having three or more criminal convictions. Sixty-four percent of the sample had a history of substance use; however, only 49% had a current substance abuse problem. An indication of a mental health problem was less frequently identified. Twenty-four percent of the sample reported receiving previous mental health treatment. In addition, 46% experienced domestic violence and 30% were sexually abused in their childhood.

The Setting

The overall mission of the halfway house was to provide a range of interventions to reduce reoffending, enforce accountability, and promote public safety. Residents entered the halfway house with a range of needs, including substance abuse, mental health, physical and/or sexual abuse, and limited employment histories. The program is considered holistic in the sense that all needs are identified and treatment plans are developed to address individual needs.

The halfway house follows a gradual phase system that provides residents with privileges as they achieve certain goals and maintain good standing in the program. Program objectives include attending job readiness class, participating in mandatory on-site treatment groups, obtaining and maintaining employment or education, and following other goals outlined on individualized treatment plans. To help residents achieve their individual treatment goals, staff requires eligible residents to participate in an on-site substance abuse and gender-responsive treatment groups. In addition, residents receive individual life skills coaching, employment assistance, and case management services. Women in need of additional services, such as mental health, domestic violence counseling, and parenting, are referred to outside programs in the local area.

During the data collection period for this study, the halfway house offered a gender-responsive treatment group, an on-site substance abuse group, weekly on-site Alcoholics Anonymous meetings, and outside opportunities to attend Narcotics Anonymous (NA) groups or outpatient treatment. Fourteen participants were engaged in some type of drug treatment—including 8 enrolled in the mandatory on-site group. Nine different participants were enrolled in the mandatory on-site gender-responsive group. Participants in the gender-responsive group had no history of substance use or had a lengthy history of sobriety. The gender-responsive group focused on family issues, relationships, and problem-solving and communication skills. Women learned skills to cope with high-risk situations, how to build upon personal strengths, and were encouraged to develop healthy support networks and community resources. Observations of these groups, and participants' perceptions of them, are discussed in this article.

Results

Six major themes emerged during the analysis of interview transcripts and observational field notes. The six themes identified include (a) trust and avoidance, (b) negative treatment perceptions, (c) repetitive and irrelevant treatment, (d) positive treatment perceptions, (e) desire for outside treatment, and (f) benefits of outside treatment.

Trust and Avoidance

Participants in this study all came from the same correctional facility after serving varying terms of incarceration. Within the first few days of arriving at the halfway house, women described feeling a heightened sense of physical and psychological safety within the confines of the facility. The majority developed therapeutic connections with halfway house staff. Residents perceived staff as supportive, trustworthy, caring, and effective (see Cantora, Mellow, & Schlager, 2014). Relationships with residents, however, lacked cohesion and were generally nonsupportive. This section highlights the challenges women had trusting other residents.

The majority of residents have been living with other incarcerated women for long periods of time (for some, several years) and felt that the residents at halfway house were the "same" type of women from prison. According to one participant, "They still have their attitudes. Everybody's still got their guard up, you know, nobody trusts anybody. It's the same." Another participant stated, "I just tolerate most of them. I get along with some of them. You still have the same tension and craziness [as prison]. You'd think being here would alleviate some of it." The fact that women were in a less restrictive environment, with opportunities to prepare for reentry, did not seem to change the lack of trust or tension in the environment. For women who have been through the system multiple times dealing with other women was part of the experience.

Sometimes I get to a point where I can't stand being around women. One thing that I think is good about it for me [being around women for so long]—like I think it's easy for me to deal with because of my attitude. Rather than someone who has never been in prison—I think sometimes it really gets to me being around all these women and their attitudes, the hollering and screaming. I don't know I just deal with it. (Amy)

Another resident, Carol, described not wanting to develop relationships with other residents due to trust issues: "When I go home I had relationships with women and men, I can talk more. But a place like this no. You can't trust people here. Cause always someone has a motive." April also described her general mistrust of women as the reason for her unwillingness to discuss personal problems when other women are present. For April, disclosure meant the risk of someone gossiping about her. She described her anger as a major trigger and worried about being in a vulnerable situation that would test her anger.

"I don't like women, I don't be around women in the street and it was like me sitting there with all these women. I didn't want to (open up) 'cause women like to talk—they gossip. I just felt like opening up some of my personal issues with strangers—I have an anger problem, so for me to hear someone talking about something I might have said that is a trigger. Why should I subject myself to the arguments? I am very short tempered."

Participants described wanting to take care of their own lives and did not want to associate with others— "I just do what I need to do for me and I stay focused." Participants often described keeping to themselves and avoiding conflict with others. Avoidance by not speaking, or associating, with confrontational residents was a common response. As was the case with many residents, avoidance of others was the result of lack of trust and the desire to "just go home."

Avoiding residents was more challenging to do in the halfway house than in the prison setting. Participants had more privacy in prison because sleeping accommodations were limited to sharing with one other person, whereas in the halfway house, several women roomed together. As in prison, residents developed ways to avoid other women, including listening to music, reading, and watching television. This avoidance behavior is similar to what other researchers have found (Kruttschnitt et al., 2000; Owen, 1998).

When asking the following participant about recommendations for additional programming at halfway house, Linda suggested developing a program to help residents deal with the social aspect of the halfway house.

They should have more programs. There are a lot of attitudes and I think we need other groups. Some women are really mentally disturbed. Some are scared to get out and they should talk about their fears. There's not enough time to share with one another and ask about our day. They are always at each other's throats, they steal from each other, they are still doing the same stuff; women don't want to talk about it. We have Monday night government groups—but people shut down and don't want to talk about house problems, they feel like they are snitching.

Linda described the general lack of trust among residents. She suggested developing an open forum where women can talk about both personal issues and problems that occur within the house as a way to potentially eliminate the negative tension. Overall, findings from observations and interviews indicated that residents did not trust the majority of women in the house. Surprisingly, many participants were able to form relationships with one or two other residents (see Cantora et al., 2014). These relationships were often formed during their incarceration. Regardless of these connections, the majority described an environment that lacked cohesion and trust.

Negative Treatment Perceptions

During the time period this study was conducted, two mandatory treatment groups were offered inside the halfway house. Based on individual needs, women were enrolled in either the 3-month substance abuse or gender-responsive program. To understand how women perceived these groups, the researcher asked several questions about their participation. Women were asked to discuss what programs they participated in, how they perceived the curriculum, whether the group was helpful in addressing their needs, and how the group might be improved to better meet their needs. In addition to interviewing women about their group experience, the researcher observed both groups over the course of 3 months.

During observations of both mandatory on-site groups, several residents expressed boredom, many barely participated, and when participating did so at a superficial level—meaning their participation during group sessions did not appear genuine. Many women simply participated in the groups because they were mandated to do so. For example, two women in the substance abuse group were observed rolling their eyes when other residents shared their experiences, and they occasionally made negative statements out loud to the entire group. During interviews, both participants discussed aspects of

the group they disliked. They perceived the group as too "educational" and "boring," too overpowered by certain women who controlled group discussions, and interfered with their jobs. Debbie openly stated that she did not want to participate in treatment because she was not "looking for help." She also did not want to hear other women disclosing their "war stories."

No, I could care less, to be honest. I'm just doing it because I have to. I'm not looking for help. And none of us really want to hear it neither. Like everybody in there really just wants to get it over with, so none of us are really there for listening to anybody's war stories or anything like that, you know what I mean? It's just like just be quiet and answer the questions and get it over with. That's pretty much how we're doing it. (Debbie)

Debbie did not pursue treatment outside the halfway house, and instead was more interested in working and saving money for release. Kate, who had similar perceptions as Debbie, attended NA groups in the community.

I hate that class. I don't hate the class but there's just certain people in there irk me to death. I mean, just shut-up. I don't need to know about your friends, mothers, fathers, sisters, brothers. You know, it's the residents, two in particular. And it drives Ms. [instructor] crazy, too, and you can see it but she can't say just shut-up! You know what I mean, so—It's not very professional. I can but she can't. (Kate)

Another resident, Carol, who expressed boredom during group sessions was asked how she felt about group treatment. She struggled with her response to this question, shrugged her shoulders, rolled her eyes, and sarcastically responded:

It's good. It's fun. It's good to get out of here. I like walking from here to there.

It's new. I learn coping, life skills. I don't know. Everything I learn. I don't know . . . there are things that are helpful. (Carol)

Carol, a resident who served 15 years in prison, did not seek out outside treatment while at the halfway house. She explained that she enjoyed leaving the halfway house to attend the group. The group was held several doors down from the halfway house in a building that housed the program's administrative offices. Carol looked forward to the opportunity to get fresh air and have a quick cigarette.

Repetitive and Irrelevant Treatment

Several women in the on-site substance abuse group perceived the groups as repetitive of other programs they participated in prison or other community settings. A common response was, "I've heard this all before." Three women in the gender-responsive group identified specific components of the group that were unrelated to their needs— "I don't have that problem." For example, older participants, and those with strong family connections, perceived the family module as irrelevant to their lives. Although the curriculum was designed to address common issues experienced by women prisoners, not all women shared similar problems and/or experiences (e.g., family and relationship problems).

> It's not beneficial. I mean those things that they are talking about establishing I already do. I work, I have contact with my kids, even though they don't come and visit I keep contact with them all the time. I take care of my kids financially. I just paid for my son, I just paid for his college books and I sent my brother 300 dollars for him to buy school clothes and things. I am still being the productive parent I would be in the community, but I am doing it in here. (Stacy)

Jenny, a resident with a long history of substance abuse, completed a TC program while incarcerated. She expressed frustration with having to participate in another drug treatment program. Although she was dissatisfied with the on-site group treatment program, she attended NA groups in the community.

> It's alright [on-site drug treatment], it's . . . things that I have heard over and over and over again. But it's alright I am going to participate and I am

going to be there. And it's going to . . . ya know I don't know everything so there is always something to learn. And that's the attitude I have to keep. It's frustrating to write the same story over again. My story is not going to change. I've been writing my story since 2005, it's not going to change. (Jenny)

Monique, who also attended outside NA groups, shared a similar perception:

> You could never have enough knowledge. You know what I am saying. The other day we touch on a lot of good things. But basically, I've been through all this. I am just ready to go. I went through this over and over and over again. But still like I said, there still might be something to see that I can grab onto and keep it. So, the program is good. You know? I could have never experienced going to a program, never had the chance to you know experience what I did, it is what it is . . . it's a good program to have. And like I said you could never get enough knowledge, I mean there might be something I missed somewhere else that I can grab here. (Monique)

Both Jenny and Monique were positive in their comments about on-site drug treatment. Several women who have been through treatment programs prior to the halfway house viewed the halfway house substance abuse group as repetitive but acknowledged that there was "always something to learn." A maintenance program, such as Narcotics and Alcoholics Anonymous, may better fit their treatment needs.

Positive and Helpful Treatment

Several women discussed positive aspects of the on-site treatment groups. Marie, a 44-year-old woman with a lengthy criminal history, has participated in a variety of different drug treatment programs in the past. Marie highlights the positive aspects of the drug treatment group, including her ability to connect well with the group instructor and the size of the group. She also identifies the reasons others in the group may not enjoy it as she does.

I love it. It's not just like a group where you can talk. They teach you about each drug and what it does. It makes you aware of what you put in your body. Everybody has their own way of bringing it and Ms. M [instructor] is very awesome. She makes you want to do it. And it's a small group. Other groups are always so big . . . if you have something to say she'll let you, but for the most part most people just want to come in and get it done, because most of them work. It's the evening, you've had a hard day, or they're getting ready to work the night shift, or it's their only day off and it's being interrupted.

Another resident, 19-year-old Annie, described receiving positive feedback from others in the drug treatment group. Annie was the only participant who described her peers as "family." Annie's positive experience may be attributed to the fact that most of her peers were much older (average age 39), and her exposure to the adult system was relatively new. Although she felt comfortable talking in the group setting, she will not engage in the same type of dialog with her group members in the common living areas of the halfway house.

Feels like family—I've grown to love my group, I talk to the ladies only when in group not in room. It's my chance to open up and it took me a little while getting a lot of feedback from everyone. In the room upstairs I play around with the girls but will not sit down and talk to them like in group. (Annie)

Both Marie and Annie did not participate in off-site treatment groups. Another participant with positive views of the gender-responsive group struggled with the idea of opening up in the group setting. Ella discussed keeping her abusive relationship a secret from her family but recognized that talking about it might reduce some of her internal anger. She participated in the group but struggled to disclose her "secret."

We just went through abusive relationships now. It is touchy. Cause you are sitting in a group. And this is my secret—this is something I hold in. Family don't know, nobody knows. But I might let it out 'cause it has a lot to do with my anger. Just a lot that has to do with me. I talk a little bit [in group], but not too much. I was in a relationship for four years and I am not ready to open up to a group of people . . . it's just me.

At the time the interview was conducted, Ella was in the process of searching for a domestic violence group in the community. Most of the women interviewed were interested in, or already attending, outside treatment. Regardless of their outside treatment participation, or their desire to attend alternative programs, they were still required to attend the on-site groups. They understood that attending mandated on-site groups was part of the halfway house requirements. They attended, responded when addressed, and minimally participated. There was a variety of women in these groups—those who were clearly defiant by their under-the-breath comments and facial expressions, those who remained silent, and those who overpowered the group dialog. Although many participants identified negative aspects of the groups, as illustrated above, some participants were able to benefit from the content of the groups.

Desire for Outside Treatment

The relationship dynamics within the halfway house led to many women desiring treatment away from the house. This was true for women in need of substance abuse treatment, as well as women seeking mental health and victimization services. Stacy, for example, was proactive in the search for outside treatment and found a local women's group that provided both individual and group counseling. Her desire to receive treatment outside the halfway house came from years of harassment by other incarcerated women. Having worked in a profession that was not respected by other women in prison, Stacy sought treatment outside the halfway house.

I go to a women's group now that is in ___. I go once a month. I found that group myself. And I talk to the lady and she helps boost my self-esteem and we talk about different issues but, that is better because it is in a private setting and nobody there knows I am ___.[2]

This quote illustrates the connection between building self-esteem and forming a therapeutic alliance that allows women to feel comfortable talking about problems. Stacy was unable to open up in the on-site gender-responsive group because she perceived the social environment as threatening. Other residents also discussed wanting treatment outside of the halfway house because they found it difficult to disclose personal information in on-site groups. Participants, like Ella, discussed not being "ready" to disclose their past to others and expressed concern with other residents' ability to keep their personal stories within the group setting. The connection between wanting private treatment and not trusting other residents is illustrated in the following passage:

> I wanted something separate from here. To get away for the elements of here, of the girls and I didn't want anyone in my business. See we all . . . you have to know about people and girls. Not only here . . . they are catty. And at different times, they may be your friend today and tomorrow they might be biting your back. And once you're in therapy with people it's what is said in the room does not stay in the room. No, that doesn't work. They don't respect people like that. So, that is why I do not want you to be in therapy with me. That's why I want my own therapy. I want it private. (Phyllis)

Phyllis, a resident with an extensive history of abuse, drug use, and mental health problems, described wanting private therapy because she did not trust other residents. The researcher continued to ask Phyllis about attending treatment with women at the halfway house. To Phyllis, residents at the halfway house were emotionally harmful toward one another, which made opening up in the groups too risky. "It's all made out of hurt and emotions here. It's a cancer. Everyone is stepping on each other to get up. Let me step on you so I can get higher." Regardless of where the group was located, some women were unwilling to disclose their "secrets" in a public domain. Many women, however, voluntarily sought out individual and group treatment not affiliated with the halfway house.

Benefit of Outside Programs

One of the most prominent findings from asking women about participating in services outside the halfway house were the multiple benefits of going to non-halfway house programs. Women did not describe anything negative about the services and treatment they received outside the halfway house, and appeared to be more responsive to these services. The most common type of treatment attended off-site were coed 12-step groups (i.e., Narcotics and Alcoholics Anonymous). Women described attending these groups to learn about community resources, develop new pro-social associations, escape the halfway house environment, hear stories for motivation, and meet men for sexual gratification.

When asking participants about attending outside 12-step groups, several discussed a recent incident at an NA group held at a local church. Some participants responded that "something happened" but would not elaborate on why the meetings were canceled. Others overtly stated that residents were engaging in sexual activity with men at the meetings. "When I got here it seemed like they had this problem that all the girls going to meet the men. I don't know if you know, one of the girls had this sexual thing so they stopped that." Once the halfway house learned of the incident, they prohibited residents from attending meetings at the church. Residents did, however, continue to attend meetings at other locations throughout the community. Although correctional program administrators may perceive this incident as a negative consequence of sending women to outside treatment, there were many positive benefits discussed during the interviews.

Several participants discussed the value of networking with people in recovery. One resident, estranged from her family, discussed looking forward to returning to her hometown 12-step meetings where she would see her old peers. This group of peers was her only support system. Another participant, Kate, discussed using community NA meetings to meet new pro-social peers.

> I think meetings are helpful, because not only are they helpful but you're sharing yourself with people who are clean and you start to hang out so, you know, you start doing your thing. I'm not

going to go to meetings and then come down here and hang out with people at the transportation center.[3] I'm going to go to meetings and meet new people.

In addition to forming friendships, networking with other group members helped participants learn about community resources. Beth was able to secure transitional housing after informing her 12-step group members that she was searching for a place to live.

And I shared in group one day, there were like 80 people around but I don't care I need to get something off my chest. And you get feedback from people, sometimes you get a bunch of jerks, sometimes you get good feedback. So, I shared that . . . you know most people know I am from the facility around the corner and my time is getting short and I don't want to go back to where I came from, I want to stay in this town and keep my job. After group, she came to me and said "yo let me tell you about this program." (Beth)

When asking participants about the type of services or programs they would have liked to receive while residing at the halfway house, they frequently suggested more on-site and community 12-step groups. The fact that many participants with drug histories voluntarily attended these groups and requested the halfway house to provide more opportunities to attend 12-step groups implies that they "wanted" to participate in drug treatment. Whether their participation was to develop new pro-social relationships, learn about community resources, meet others for sexual gratification, hear stories for motivation, get feedback from people similar, or to just get away from the "chaos" of the halfway house, off-site groups were the most desired treatment.

Discussion

This study examined women's experiences at a community correction facility in New Jersey. Peer dynamics and engagement in on-site and off-site group treatment were discussed.

As has been found in other research (Einat & Chen, 2012; Greer, 2000; Severance, 2005), most participants struggled to trust other residents and avoided social interactions. The dynamics of resident relationships made it difficult for women to engage in on-site group treatment. The lack of group cohesion and the desire for private treatment were two of the main reasons participants wanted individual or group treatment in the community. Participants also described the on-site groups as not meeting their needs, too educational, boring, and unhelpful. There were a few, however, who perceived the groups as useful to addressing their needs. The fact that many women were unresponsive to on-site groups but participated in programs off-site suggests that residents were not unresponsive to group treatment in general, but rather that their unresponsiveness was attributed to the programs delivered inside the halfway house. Mandatory group treatment with women who have been incarcerated with each other for a long time—women perceived as "chaotic" and untrustworthy—was unappealing to most participants. As long as the treatment was away from the house, women were open to it and sought it out. Women desired to be in a setting where no one knew them, to meet new non-incarcerated people, and to have the opportunity to speak about problems without fear of disclosure.

Although the findings from this study are important in understanding women's experience in treatment settings, there are some limitations. Due to the small sample size and nature of data collection, this method does not allow for generalizing findings to other female community correction programs. The researcher also did not ask program staff or administrators about resident relationships or their perceptions of on-site group treatment. Another limitation of this study was the lack of off-site treatment group observations. Observing off-site NA groups attended by halfway house residents would have generated a comparison between on-site and off-site group treatment engagement. Gathering these data is something important to generating a global understanding of the context of community correction programs, and how women respond to different treatment environments (e.g., mandatory on-site vs. voluntary off-site). Regardless of these limitations, the study's findings support the notion that peer relationships play an important role in women's experiences inside community correction programs.

A major question remaining from the findings of this study is, "Would women be more amenable to on-site treatment if the dynamics among residents were more supportive?" Findings suggest that the internal dynamics affected residents' ability to trust others, which may have indirectly resulted in the desire for outside group programming with people outside their social and familial network. Evidence from the substance abuse literature suggests that peer support and "community as method" are factors that contribute to treatment motivation (Hiller et al., 2002; Welsh & McGrain, 2008). The gender-responsive literature also supports this finding by emphasizing the importance of creating therapeutic environments within correctional programs. Improving the social environment of female residential correctional programs to follow the principles of gender-responsive treatment, and TC models, is something program developers and administrators need to seriously consider. In community correction settings, where clients already know each other from their prison stay, pre-group skills training may be beneficial. Skills training where clients learn to trust their peers, and staff, to develop therapeutic relationships with them may improve the on-site group experience. Otherwise, clients with trust issues, and other interpersonal difficulties, will not benefit from this type of group setting and may pose a risk to the entire group process (MacNair & Corazzini, 1994).

However, considering the nature of the relationships among incarcerated women, creating such an environment in a community setting may be rather challenging. As illustrated in this study, and supported by the research on the nature of women's prison relationships, women have already come to "know" their peers while incarcerated. Shift in environment, regardless of therapeutic design, may not change how women perceive their peers, their ability to trust them, or where they desire to attend treatment. It is important for program administration to recognize conflict among clients before mandating them to on-site treatment groups. To understand, and measure, how women perceive the program setting, administrators should consider conducting an assessment of the social climate. This would include measuring women's level of trust, treatment readiness, interest in on-site treatment, and concerns about participating in groups with other residents. Identifying specific client concerns would allow administrators to determine the value and benefit of providing on-site groups and, if conducive, develop ways to improve the overall social climate within the setting.

In addition to the social climate of a treatment setting affecting participation, being required to partake in a group irrelevant to perceived needs will also create resistance. Correctional programs sometimes require clients to participate in "one-size-fits-all" treatment groups. As illustrated in this article, this approach to treatment is problematic. Participants in this study were mandated to attend treatment groups that did not always address their perceived needs. These women identified community programs that better fit their needs.

If the social climate is threatening to the group process, and/or the group is irrelevant to women's needs, then treatment alternatives may need to be considered. In this case, enhancing individual treatment opportunities and/or off-site group programs may be warranted. Although the benefit of providing on-site group treatment allows administrators to monitor client progress, deliver adequate treatment, and supervise clients, the presence of a negative social climate may not be worth these benefits. However, off-site treatment prevents program staff from monitoring client progress, treatment quality, and clients' whereabouts. These drawbacks may prevent many community correction programs from utilizing off-site treatment. However, as illustrated in this study, connecting clients to community service providers and non-incarcerated clients had multiple benefits. As a reentry strategy, outside treatment may actually be the smarter approach.

/// DISCUSSION QUESTIONS

1. What role did the mandatory treatment groups play in the rehabilitation of the women in this study? What sorts of suggestions did the residents make on how to improve these groups?

2. How did the relationships between the women at the facilitate, help, or impede their efforts in treatment?

3. How would programs outside of the facility serve a positive role for the women?

References

Andrews, D. A., & Bonta, J. (2010). *The psychology of criminal conduct* (5th ed.). Newark, NJ: LexisNexis.

Bloom, B., & Covington, S. (1998, November 11–14). *Gender-specific programming for female offenders: What is it and why it is important?* Paper presented at the 50th annual meeting of the American Society of Criminology, Washington, DC.

Bloom, B., & Covington, S. (2009). Addressing the mental health needs of women offenders. In R. Gido & L. Dalley (Eds.), *Women's mental health issues across the criminal justice system* (pp. 160–176). Saddle River, NJ: Prentice-Hall/Pearson.

Bloom, B., Owen, B., & Covington, S. (2003). *Gender-responsive strategies: Research, practice and guiding principles for women offenders.* Washington, DC: U.S. Department of Justice, National Institute of Corrections.

Broome, K. M., Knight, D. K., Knight, K., Hiller, M. L., & Simpson, D. D. (1997). Peer, family, and motivational influences on drug treatment process and recidivism for probationers. *Journal of Clinical Psychology, 53*, 387–397.

Cantora, A., Mellow, J., & Schlager, M. (2014). What about nonprogrammatic factors? Women's perceptions of staff and resident relationships in a community corrections setting. *Journal of Offender Rehabilitation, 53*, 1–22.

Charmaz, K. (2006). *Constructing grounded theory: A practical guide through qualitative analysis.* Thousand Oaks, CA: Sage.

Covington, S. (1998). The relational theory of women's psychological development: Implications for the criminal justice system. In R. Zaplin (Ed.), *Female crime & delinquency: Critical perspectives & effective interventions* (pp. 113–131). Gaithersburg, MD: Aspen.

Covington, S. S. (2003). A women's journey home: Challenges for female offenders. In J. Travis & M. Waul (Eds.), *Prisoners once removed* (pp.67–103). Washington, DC: Urban Institute.

DeLeon, G. (1995). Residential therapeutic communities in the mainstream: Diversity and issues. *Journal of Psychoactive Drugs, 27*, 3–15.

DeLeon, G., Melnick, G., & Kressel, D. (1997). Motivation and readiness for therapeutic community treatment among cocaine and other drug abusers. *American Journal of Drug and Alcohol Abuse, 23*, 169–189.

Einat, T., & Chen, G. (2012). Gossip in a maximum security female prison: An exploratory study. *Women & Criminal Justice, 22*, 108–134.

Gehring, K. S., Van Voorhis, P., & Bell, V. (2010). "What Works" for female probationers. An evaluation of the moving on program. *Women, Girls, & Criminal Justice, 11*(1), 6–10.

Giallombardo, R. (1966). *Society of women: A study of a women's prison.* New York, NY: Wiley.

Gilligan, C. (1982). *In a different voice.* Cambridge, MA: Harvard University Press.

Greer, K. (2000). The changing nature of interpersonal relationships in women's prisons. *The Prison Journal, 80*, 442–468.

Hiller, M. L., Knight, K., Leukefeld, C., & Simpson, D. D. (2002). Motivation as a predictor of therapeutic engagement in mandated residential substance abuse treatment. *Criminal Justice Behavior, 29*, 56–75.

Joe, G. W., Simpson, D. D., & Broome, K. M. (1998). Effects of readiness for drug abuse treatment on client retention and assessment of process. *Addiction, 93*, 1177–1190.

Jones, R. S. (1993). Coping with separation: Adaptive responses of women prisoners. *Women & Criminal Justice, 5*(1), 71–97.

Koons, B. A., Burrow, J. D., Morash, M., & Bynum, T. (1997). Expert and offender perceptions of program elements linked to successful outcomes for incarcerated women. *Crime & Delinquency, 43*, 512–532.

Kruttschnitt, C., Gartner, R., & Miller, A. (2000). Doing her own time? Women's responses to prison in the context of the old and the new penology. *Criminology, 38*, 681–718.

Lichtenwalter, S., Garase, M. L., & Barker, D. B. (2010). Evaluation of the house of healing: An alternative to female incarceration. *Journal of Sociology & Social Work, 37*(1), 75-94.

MacNair, R. R., & Corazzini, J. G. (1994). Client factors influencing group therapy dropout. *Psychotherapy, 31*, 352–362.

McRoberts, C., Burlingame, G. M., & Hoag, M. J. (1998). Comparative efficacy of individual and group psychotherapy: A meta-analytic perspective. *Group Dynamics: Theory, Research, and Practice, 2*, 101–117.

Melnick, G., & DeLeon, G. (1999). Clarifying the nature of therapeutic community treatment: The Survey of Essential Elements Questionnaire (SEEQ). *Journal of Substance Abuse Treatment, 16*, 307–313.

Messina, N., Grella, C., Cartier, J., & Torres, S. (2010). A randomized experimental study of gender-responsive substance abuse treatment for women in prison. *Journal of Substance Abuse Treatment, 38*, 97–107.

Miller, J. B. (1986). *Toward a new psychology of women.* Boston, MA: Beacon Press.

Mosher, C., & Philips, D. (2006). The dynamics of a prison-based therapeutic community for women offenders: Retention, completion, and outcomes. *The Prison Journal, 86*(6), 6–31.

Owen, B. (1998). *"In the mix": Struggle and survival in a women's prison.* Albany: State University of New York Press.

Propper, A. M. (1982). Make-believe families and homosexuality among imprisoned girls. *Criminology, 20*, 127–138.

Severance, T. A. (2005). "You know who you can go to": Cooperation and exchange between incarcerated women. *The Prison Journal, 85*, 343–367.

Simpson, D. D. (1997). *Patient engagement and duration of treatment* (Unpublished Paper funded by National Institute on Drug Abuse, Grant No. R01DA06162). Fort Worth: Institute of Behavioral Research, Texas Christian University.

Simpson, D. D. (2001). Modeling treatment process and outcomes. *Addiction, 96*, 207–211.

Simpson, D. D., & Joe, G. W. (1993). Motivation as a predictor of early dropout from drug abuse treatment. *Psychotherapy, 30*, 357–368.

Simpson, D. D., Joe, G. W., Rowan-Szal, G., & Greener, J. (1995). Client engagement and change during drug abuse treatment. *Journal of Substance Abuse, 7,* 117–134.

Strauss, A., & Corbin, J. (1998). *Basics of qualitative research: Techniques and procedures for developing grounded theory.* Thousand Oaks, CA: Sage.

Tripodi, S. J., Bledsoe, S. E., Klim, J. S., & Bender, K. (2011). Effects of correctional-based programs for female inmates: A systematic review. *Research on Social Work Practice, 21,* 15–31.

Ward, D. A., & Kassebaum, G. G. (1965). *Women's prison: Sex and social structure.* Chicago, IL: Aldine.

Welsh, W. N., & McGrain, P. N. (2008). Predictors of therapeutic engagement in prison-based drug treatment. *Drug and Alcohol Dependence, 96,* 271–280.

Wright, E. M., DeHart, D. D., Koons-Witt, B. A., & Crittenden, C. A. (2013). "Buffers" against crime? Exploring the roles and limitations of positive relationships among women in prison. *Punishment & Society, 15,* 71–95.

Wright, E. M., Van Voorhis, P., Salisbury, E., & Bauman, A. (2009). Gender-responsive prisons: Lessons from the NIC/UC gender-responsive classification project. *Women, Girls, & Criminal Justice, 10,* 81–96.

READING /// 22

The literature has consistently documented the high mental health needs of women in prison. In addition, we have learned that the prison experience may exacerbate the presence of mental health disorders. This research by Holly Harner and Suzanne Riley looks at the issue of mental health of female inmates from a mixed methods approach: a quantitative survey of inmates and qualitative focus groups involving a smaller subset of the population. Their results provide insights for three groups of inmates: (1) those who believe prison had a negative effect on their mental health status, (2) those who believe prison had a positive effect on their mental health status, and (3) those who believe prison did not have any effect on their mental health status.

The Impact of Incarceration on Women's Mental Health
Responses From Women in a Maximum-Security Prison

Holly M. Harner and Suzanne Riley

Incarcerated women are an extremely vulnerable and often "invisible" (Braithwaite, Treadwell, & Arriola, 2008, p. S173) population in the United States (Kim, 2003). Many women enter correctional institutions with complex mental health issues, including depression, anxiety, posttraumatic stress disorder (PTSD), and addiction (James & Glaze, 2006). Despite the rapid increase in the rate at which women in the United States are being incarcerated, there is often not a commensurate increase in available services and programs to support their

SOURCE: Harner, H. M., & Riley, S. (2013). The impact of incarceration on women's mental health: Responses from women in a maximum-security prison. *Qualitative Health Research, 23,* 26–42.

complex health needs (Young, 2000). Furthermore, treatment modalities supported by evidence in nonincarcerated populations do not necessarily transfer their efficacy to correctional populations (Covington, 1998). To identify mental health treatment modalities that effectively address incarcerated women's mental health needs, an important first step is to better understand the nature and context of incarcerated women's experiences of mental health in prison, as well as their perceptions of how incarceration affects their overall mental health. The purpose of our qualitative investigation, which was guided by the principles outlined in Harris and Fallot's (2001) trauma-informed systems framework, was to better understand women's perceptions of how their mental health was affected by incarceration in a maximum-security prison.

Evolution of the Study

The first author's previous clinical practice as a women's health nurse practitioner in a maximum-security women's prison and her mental-health-related research with women incarcerated in the same prison informed this investigation. The first author's prior investigations (Harner & Burgess, 2011; Harner, Hanlon, & Garfinkel, 2010; Harner, Hentz, & Evangelista, 2011) generated data identifying that many incarcerated women suffer from significant mental health issues—some of which are antecedents to incarceration and some of which are consequences of incarceration. Although the prison population has expanded, with a dramatic rise, especially, in the number of incarcerated women, a similar growth in available prison services, especially mental health services, has not been demonstrated in most institutions. One incarcerated woman commented, "The mental health care in here is busted." Indeed, because of the complex needs of this growing population, correctional mental health professionals often operate out of necessity from a "crisis oriented" model of care. The limitations imposed by this model are felt by incarcerated women, one of whom commented, "They just care if I want to kill myself or someone else" (Harner & Burgess, 2011, p. 473).

Review of the Literature

We examined existing literature related to incarceration and women's mental health. Nurse, Woodcock, and Ormsby (2003) examined, via focus groups, the impact of the prison environment and organization on the mental health of incarcerated men and women and correctional staff in either a medium-security prison (18 men) or a training/rehabilitation unit (13 women) in southern England. The most common factors contributing to poor mental health included (a) isolation and lack of mental stimulation, (b) drug misuse, (c) negative relationships with prison staff, (d) bullying of vulnerable prisoners, and (e) lack of family contact. These themes were often interrelated, because prisoners identified that being locked in cells for long periods of time with little or no mental stimuli adversely affected their mental health. This isolation generally led to drug use to try to cover up the monotony of incarceration. Women commented specifically about the lack of family contact and limited control over external events. One woman noted, "If you've got a relative out there who's ill, you can't do nothing about it, you can't, and that makes you feel ten times worse" (Nurse et al., 2003, p. 2). Prisoners identified a pattern of negative interactions with the prison staff. For example, when an inmate was treated badly by an officer, prisoners would then make the officer's life more difficult, which resulted in increased stress for the officer. Another woman commented, "They respond to us and then we respond to them" (p. 3).

Prison staff who participated in separate focus groups identified experiencing increased stress levels related to perceived lack of management support, a negative work environment, safety issues, and stress-related sickness (Nurse et al., 2003). A *circle of stress* functioned in the following manner: "[L]ow morale and staff shortages increase stress levels, which in turn increase staff sickness rates, reduce staffing levels, further lower the morale of remaining staff and lead to more stress and staff sickness" (p. 3). It is in this circle of stress that the interconnected nature of prisoner mental health and staff mental health becomes evident. Stress-related staff absences lead to staff shortages. Shortages lead to longer inmate lock-up time. Longer lock-up time increases inmate stress and frustration. Finally, inmates release their stress and frustration on prison staff.

Douglas, Plugge, and Fitzpatrick (2009) evaluated "women prisoners' perceptions of the impact of imprisonment on their health" (p. 749). Using both focus groups (6 focus groups; $n = 37$ participants) and individual interviews ($n = 12$), the investigators explored incarcerated women's "perceptions of 'health' and 'healthiness'; health problems of women in prison; personal health status prior to imprisonment; impact of imprisonment on health; experiences of prison healthcare services; and recommendations for service development" (p. 750) in two women's prisons in England. Participants described both short-term and long-term impact on health and well-being. Women reported "shock and fear" on entering prison. Concern and worry for children who were left in the care of others was also commonly identified. Women were fearful about what awaited them in prison (violence, intimidation, isolation), and were deeply disturbed when they witnessed other women's distress (detoxification, seizures, self- injury, and mental health problems). Disempowerment and "inconsistent application of prison rules" (p. 750) were also identified as stressful, frustrating, and anxiety producing. Women reported difficulty coping, which often resulted in depression and, for some, suicidality. As with the women who participated in the Nurse et al. (2003) investigation, women in this study were also affected by the behaviors of others. After witnessing a prison suicide, one participant commented,

> I was mad. I hated the officers, I hated the nurses, I hated—I just went mad, I wouldn't eat. . . . I didn't sleep well. All month, you know, I just kept seeing—and then I started hearing things like, I start hearing that my kids were crying, I started—I was in another world, you know. (Douglas et al., 2009, p. 751)

Women also described that poor hygiene, lack of cleanliness, limited access to physical activities, and nutritionally poor diets also negatively affected health (Douglas et al., 2009). The researchers identified that the aforementioned issues were not problematic for everyone in the study. Women who had a history of "chaotic drug misuse" found "an enforced respite from addiction and associated health neglect" (p. 751). The investigators commented, "For some women, prison offered an opportunity to get the help that they needed. Better nutrition, a stable routine and an opportunity to access healthcare and drug treatment services were important opportunities" (p. 751). Imprisonment also separated victims of domestic violence and sexual exploitation from their abusers. Similar findings were also described by participants in Bradley

and Davino's (2002) investigation on perceived levels of safety in prison.

Gaps in the Literature

Research supports that many women enter correctional institutions with complex mental health issues (James & Glaze, 2006). Despite their need, women often have limited access to appropriate resources that might be able to improve their mental health. Findings from two qualitative investigations conducted in England (Douglas et al., 2009; Nurse et al., 2003) suggest that incarcerated women's mental health in prison is closely linked to their experience of incarceration, including their interactions with health and correctional professionals and other inmates. To date, few investigations have specifically examined how women's mental health is affected by incarceration. With this study, we aimed to fill this gap.

Methods

We conducted this investigation in a maximum-security women's prison located in the United States. The prison housed approximately 1,600 women at the time of our investigation. We collected data in two stages via two methods: Stage One: the Prison Health Survey (PHS) and Stage Two: focus groups.

Findings

The first author distributed the PHS to 900 incarcerated women in Stage One. Almost half of the women ($n = 445$) returned a completed survey. The average age of respondents was 38 years (range 20 to 85). Most women were White (68%) and had been convicted for a drug-related crime (27%) or murder (19%; i.e., drug-related crimes and murder accounted for the top 2 offenses committed). Twelve focus groups, consisting of a total of 65 women, were conducted during Stage Two. The average age of respondents was 43 years (range 23 to 46). Most were White (62%), and most were convicted for murder (39%) and drug-related crimes (18%). Analysis of the data from both the PHS and the inmate focus groups revealed three broad categories: worse mental health status, better mental health status, and the same mental health status as a result of incarceration. We reviewed the broad categories as well as the subcategories identified from these data.

Worse Mental Health

Many women described that their mental health worsened while in prison. Several factors led to poor mental health, including fear, stress, being away from loved ones, limited access to mental health services, worry over physical health issues, and poor treatment by health and correctional professionals.

We Fear for Our Lives in Here. Women described experiencing fear for their own personal safety in prison: "You never know who you are put in a cell with. They could just kill you without even thinking about it. There are some crazy women in here." Although violent events between inmates in women's prisons occur less frequently than in men's prisons, a violent incident between two women occurred in the prison just prior to the start of our focus groups. This event was particularly fear inducing for many women and generated much discussion in the focus groups. One woman commented,

> You're put in rooms and you don't know what you're dealing with. Everything gets lost in the sauce—mental-health wise. It's tragic that it [the violent incident] happened, but the fact it doesn't happen more is amazing. It's frightening. Behind closed doors, you fend for yourself. You got to work things out amongst yourself.

Similarly, another woman stated,

> What happened the other night affected everybody. When things like this happen, it puts all the staff on high alert and we suffer. Stuff like this makes the staff stressed and it trickles down to us. They do rounds more and ask us a hundred thousand questions about everything. Women are scared for their lives. Women were even scared to ring the buzzer during the attack because they were scared that the crazy woman would retaliate against them when she got out of the hole [a high security housing unit for women who had broken a prison rule or who needed

> protective custody]. We fear for our lives in here. I feel safer in an open unit [versus a unit with traditional cells]. If something goes down [happens], there are plenty of people who hear you screaming. It's scary in here. I don't like telling my family horror stories.

The lack of "official" knowledge about the incident, coupled with the rampant (and often inaccurate) *rumor mill* amplified women's fears. One woman described this:

> We all saw the hospital helicopter in the parking lot. We saw it and knew something bad had happened. Girls in the kitchen heard about it from the officers talking about it. They said her throat was slit, [she was] stabbed, brain coming out of her nose. Brains on the walls. Drowned in the toilet. You never know what the real story is, though. There is so much talk in here. Everybody thought she was dead at one time. They need to help us and find out who is upset about it and let us talk about it.

During a later focus group, an inmate who had participated in an earlier focus group entered the day room and announced in a panicked tone to the room, "It happened again. Oh my God, it happened again. Someone just got stabbed in [name] unit." This woman, who had just returned from chapel (where she heard this information from another inmate), was clearly traumatized and fearful. We witnessed her frantic and fearful reaction being transferred to the other women in her housing unit. It was later determined that the event she was describing was actually a planned security training event conducted by the officers.

The Stress Is Tremendous. Women described persistent and high levels of stress in prison. Common sources of stress included their lack of control over their own lives and stress associated with common institutional issues and procedures. One woman wrote, "Before I came in, I was always feeling anxious and stressed. In here, the anxiety is heightened, and with the absolute lack of control over my life, the stress is tremendous." Another participant identified that her mental health was worse and that she was "stressed and worried" about not knowing when her final mandatory program would start, which had implications for when she would be released. For some, stress seemed related to the length of time the women had already been incarcerated, as well as their sentence length. One woman serving a life sentence for murder described being "overwhelmed and stressed" by the amount of time she received (i.e., was sentenced to).

Women, especially those with preexisting mental health issues, experienced stress related to common institutional security procedures, including strip searches, pat downs, and random urine drug screens. One woman, incarcerated for prostitution, recounted,

> I've been depressed since I was little. I've been homeless and a prostitute on the streets. I've been down in the dumps and my depression is getting worse. I don't have any help from home. . . . I can't stomach the meds [medications]. I force myself not to isolate. I got bipolar, low self-esteem, severe depression. The racing thoughts keep me awake. I'm so tired, but I can't sleep. I am so stressed. Every single day I'm stressed and scared in here. I got picked for a random drug test in here once, but I couldn't pee [urinate]. I kept trying but it wouldn't come out. They give you a few hours to pee, but I just couldn't go because I was so anxious and stressed. The officers knew I don't do drugs in here but they got to follow their rules. So I got sent to the hole for refusing to pee. Now I'm such a nervous wreck about it. I worry about getting tested again, so I hold my pee each morning until 11:00 a.m. [head] count. After I pee, I drink a lot of water, tea, and coffee so I can always go if they make me. Every day I have to do this, and this stress makes me crazy.

Routine pat downs and full-body strip searches were also stress inducing, especially for women who had suffered past abuse. In fact, several women who described past sexual abuse commented that they avoided seeing visitors, including their children, because they did not want to go through the "stress and humiliation" of full-body strip searches.

Being Away From My Family Is Killing Me. Women expressed how they ached to be with their children and mourned for the time they were losing with family because of their incarceration. Some women described feeling guilty for not being good mothers when they had the chance and longed to make up for past mistakes. Women frequently described separation from their children as one of the most difficult aspects of incarceration. One woman wrote, "My kids think I am dead. My ex [ex-husband] told them I was dead. I don't know where they are." Another woman commented, "It's been hell being taken away from my kid and family."

Being in prison was the first time that many women had ever been away from their children. They often did not know where their children were and, with limited contact, often feared for their health and safety. One 34-year-old woman sentenced for murder wrote, "I stay in constant fear of something happening to them. My oldest daughter has stomach cancer. She is 13. She was in a coma for two weeks." Another woman, incarcerated for 10 to 25 years for theft and larceny, wrote,

> The stress related to being away from my family is killing me. My son just turned 18 and I miss him as much as a young child. My husband got killed one month after I got locked up and my kids moved out West. I only see them once a year. I can only call once a week because a 15-minute call costs $10.63 and they take 20% out of each pay for fines and stuff. I don't have the money. If I could call three times a week I would be in a better state of mind. It frustrates me and stresses me out.

Although prison visiting hours were available on a fairly regular basis, many women had family members who lived long distances from the prison, making regular visits difficult, expensive, and often impossible. Women were dependent on friends and family members to bring their children for visitation, which had the potential to be problematic and confrontational. One woman said, "My ex won't let the kids come visit me in here." For security reasons, visitation was also highly regulated by the DOC [Department of Corrections]. A 26-year-old participant angrily described how her then 6-year-old son was no longer allowed to sit on her lap during family visitation:

My son, at age three, was diagnosed with cancer. He is now in remission and this happened during my incarceration. He's six years old now, and six-year-old kids cannot have physical contact with their mothers. These security procedures are designed for men. My son has been visiting for four years and now there is some arbitrary restriction that he can't sit on my lap during our visits because of sex offenders. This made my son so angry because he didn't understand it. I don't understand it. I'm here for drugs. This was the first time I ever saw him angry.

Although many mothers ached for visits from their children, one participant decided that visitation placed too much mental stress on her teenaged children and herself and elected to decline family visits:

Mentally I had my ups and downs, too. I still have my family support, but I elected not to have my visits. They have a life out there and I don't want me being in here to affect their life. I talk to my family once a week. They coped very hard with not being able to see me. It was hard for them in the beginning. When I was in county [county jail], I would have a visit, and after that I would go downhill after and so would they. I didn't think it was fair for any of us.

Several of the women in our study were pregnant when they entered prison. Universally, these women described that giving birth while incarcerated and then being required to release their newborns to a family member or social service agency immediately after delivery contributed to poor mental health. One woman commented,

After I delivered, I stayed one night in the infirmary but it was so bad I didn't want to stay. . . . I just had a baby. I was so depressed and upset, and wanted to be around people who actually cared about me, not people who just let me sit there. . . . Having such little time with my son was hard. I refused to let them take him out of my hospital room and got him for the night. The officers who came to pick me up were very nice and tried to give me extra time, saying I wasn't discharged when I really was. But probably because they only wanted to stay out of the prison. I didn't care. I was just thankful to have the extra time with him.

Another woman, who returned to prison for violating parole, described her postpartum experience and her desire to have her newborn return to prison with her following delivery:

There is no information [in prison] about taking care of yourself after the baby. There is the prenatal and postnatal group, which sucked. It was about nothing. Just people showing off their pictures. The only thing that helped me was using the phone a lot. My oldest daughter, she's twenty, is watching my daughter. But she is due in June and has her hands full. I think they should let you keep your baby here for the first year. It depends on the crime. But we have dogs in here, and they're okay with that. As long as they were in a separate unit and away from people with crimes against kids.

There's Nothing Here to Help Us. Women identified having few resources available to support their mental health needs. Frequently, women described putting their name "on the list" and waiting to be seen by a mental health professional. Given the vast mental health needs in the institution and the limited resources, placement on the list did not necessarily guarantee a definitive timeline for the receipt of services. Circumstances of the prison mental health system (high need, limited resources) necessitated that services were allocated to the most acute cases. This crisis-oriented system left women believing they had been abandoned by mental health providers and were in competition with their fellow inmates for resources. Access to mental health services was viewed as a zero-sum endeavor by many women. One participant, who described being physically and sexually abused by her father, commented,

I've had numerous flashbacks and had to deal with issues on my own. I am more emotional now than I ever was, and I have trouble sleeping. Where are the programs for women? Men's prisons have everything and we don't have anything. I wanted to be in the abuse program, but I was told that there were people who were worse off than me; that my abuse wasn't as bad as other people's.

A 28-year-old participant identified that prison mental health was often crisis oriented, focusing primarily on inmates who were homicidal or suicidal:

This place is set up for the worst-case scenario, but not for the everyday needs of women. By the grace of God, we are surviving. I didn't get the help I needed because I wasn't homicidal or suicidal. It is the squeaky wheel that gets the groups in here. I wrote to mental health and waited for six weeks to talk to someone. They just put you on the list to see your housing unit's counselor. I don't understand why they would just brush you off. If you're not on meds, they don't care. I tried to speak with the counselor on my unit and [the counselor] said, "Your browns [the color of the prison uniform] are the same color as everyone else's. I have too many files and not enough hours in the day. You have fifteen minutes. What would you like to talk about?" Now how therapeutic is that?

Echoing a common refrain, one woman identified that mental health treatment in prison largely consisted of medication management, with very limited talk therapy:

It's hard to find people to talk to, and if you do, they want to prescribe psych [psychiatric] drugs, which I don't think is the right thing to do all the time. They don't have enough people to help us here. Not enough groups here. The mental health department is overworked. You got the same amount of people when there were only six hundred to seven hundred people here. The population grew but the staff didn't. You try to get help, but they kick you out after fifteen minutes. A lot of things that go wrong in this prison wouldn't happen if things were taken care [of] to start with.

Medication did not always resolve women's mental health symptoms. Women described not getting the "right" psychiatric medication, which resulted in worsening mental health. One participant commented, "I don't get the proper psych meds. When they have prescribed it, it gets crushed and I vomit. Mentally, it helps only a little. But physically, it makes me worse." Another woman wrote, "The doctor took me off my medication and put me on something different altogether. So my mental health is worse. The medication he has me on don't work. I'm still depressed, anxiety, etc." Another participant wrote,

I experience anxiety daily but the prison offers no medication for this problem alone. My mental health is worse. I am not a sociable person like I was. I feel lonely, worried, paranoid, stressed and closed-off most of the time.

Women serving life sentences frequently commented that they were "at the bottom of most lists" because (as several women identified), "We aren't going anywhere. We're lifers." One woman said,

The mental health in this jail is horrible. Not enough emphasis is put on the head games we have to play with ourselves to get through every day. It's worse on lifers because we have our guards up for retaliation. It's like all of us are one person. I make it my business to keep my hands to myself, even if I want to bust somebody in the mouth. I deal with it on a regular basis. I'm in my forties but I feel like I am sixty-five. I got to play the old lady so I don't flip out like the young woman I am. . . . It drains you day after day, and it makes people lose their hope. Some people feel like they have to pull their damn hair out to get what they need around here. To get basic responses and treatment. The system needs a new page. A whole damn new manual when it comes to dealing with mental health. Especially when it comes to people dealing with life sentences.

Even access to resources for women serving life sentences did not always result in improved mental health. One woman, who had already served more than 20 years of her sentence, wrote, "Although there are people I can talk to about my mental health, due to the amount of time I have, sometimes I feel like suicide is my only option."

I'm Worried About My Health. Women's concerns for their physical health contributed to poor mental health. Some women entered prison with complex physical health problems, many of which, by their accounts, were not "taken seriously" by correctional medical professionals. Women described being misdiagnosed, given another inmate's medication (which several women referred to as "being overdosed"), and suffering from chronic, untreated pain, all of which intensified existing mental health issues. Although some women feared they would die in prison, others wished for death rather than continue to agonize in pain. One woman, sentenced to life in prison, suffered a back injury while on a prison work detail. After enduring "three years of pain," she was evaluated by an outside surgeon:

> He said that my disc had exploded. He said he couldn't fix it. I said to him, "Do you think that at the age [of] thirty-eight it's okay that my roommate wipes my ass?" My roommates did everything for me. My personality changed. It was so bad that I didn't even have to stand for count. I was a little devil because of the pain. My personality changed. I gained fifty pounds. I turned into a damn monster. I literally wanted to die because I hurt so bad. It takes a toll on you. I just laid it out for the doctor and he finally said, "I'll see you in the morning for surgery." . . . They think we are all the same and trying to game the system [manipulate the system for personal gain]. In one sense, I worked in the criminal justice system before I came here. I see it from both sides. I can play devil's advocate. But with health, there is no devil's advocate. Point blank. Period. They don't do [treat] us right.

Women also expressed frustration and distrust related to the institutional mandatory copayment ($5 for a visit; $5 for medication) required to see a physical health care provider (copayments were not required for mental health care). Copayments were financially crippling for many women because most had limited sources of income (the highest pay rate in prison for many women was less than 50 cents/hour). Women's frustration and distrust were compounded by both health and correctional professionals making comments such as, "You got it lucky. I wish my copay was only five dollars." One woman commented, "They are five-dollaring us to death in here."

Women acknowledged that medical professionals were overwhelmed by the growing prison population and women's increasing medical needs. One woman commented, "The doctors, a lot of time, their hands are tied. I don't think they have the things they need to do their jobs here. They are overworked and overtired." Women also identified that inmates "trying to game the system or get over on medical [manipulate the prison medical system for personal gain]" and "thinking that they are going to get everything fixed in a two-year bid [sentence]" resulted in medical professionals questioning the veracity of all women's medical complaints:

> They sort of shrug us off and think we are not qualified to make judgments of what we need or are lying about symptoms. But we know our bodies. They just get us in and out as quickly as possible, without actually diagnosing us properly.

Many women in our study had limited knowledge of common health issues. Lack of knowledge and lack of access to health-related resources (health literature or Internet access) left women powerless to understand medical and mental health conditions. This powerlessness contributed to their high levels of stress and worry, and left many feeling vulnerable during medical appointments. Women often did not fully understand their diagnoses or available treatment options (or treatment they had already received). For example, several women described being treated for cancer during their imprisonment, but often did not know what type of cancer they had, or their prognosis. For some women, especially those with histories of mental illness, being diagnosed with even common, non-life-threatening conditions was frightening and necessitated additional explanation by health providers. Without access to basic health literature, women relied on outside family members to investigate symptoms and diagnoses on the Internet and then mail them printed medical information. One former health care provider, then serving a sentence for assault, said,

> We have tons of books banned. . . . It would take an act of God to get a health-related book in this place. They have a PDR [*Physician's Desk Reference*], which, let's face it, isn't the easiest thing to read. It freaks everyone out. . . . Women come to me with questions about the PDR.

Women's limited knowledge and power, coupled with their frustration and lack of confidence in an overburdened prison health system, increased worry about real and perceived medical conditions. This worry and anxiety was compounded by their resentment and anger at being required to pay what to them was an exorbitant sum for medical care in which they had no choice of provider and no input as to treatment. As a result, some women intentionally avoided seeking care for their medical symptoms but then suffered from these symptoms, as well as having their anxiety grow about their etiology. Women's understanding that other inmates similarly avoided seeking medical care resulted in a generalized fear of being unnecessarily exposed to contagious infections, especially methicillin-resistant staph aureus.

It's Like We Aren't Even Human. Although women identified individual health and correctional professionals as "kind," "caring," and "fair," the institutional milieu as a whole was generally characterized as "disrespectful" and at times "degrading." Participants described being treated "like nothing" or "subhuman," and being "put down" and "disrespected" by medical and correctional professionals. One participant wrote, "Most staff treat us as if we are subhuman and assume we're all very stupid, addicted to drugs, or criminal masterminds." Being "yelled at" by correctional officers, especially male officers, resulted in increased anxiety and stress among inmates, particularly those with trauma histories:

> You get yelled at and you are stressed out and don't know what to do. There is nothing you can do. I just get paralyzed. I freeze. I think my mental health is worse because I'm always stressed and very depressed. I know that it's because I'm in prison. But how they treat you doesn't help your mental health, either.

Similarly, another woman wrote, "Officers have no respect in the manner they talk to inmates and/or handle certain situations. Some officers use their authority to go above and beyond what they are actually authorized to do." The power differential was obvious to the women, most of whom were unable to advocate for respectful treatment. One participant described feeling "degraded" while giving birth in prison:

> I had to have an officer stand right in front of me while I was having my baby. Now every time I see her, it makes me uncomfortable. She could have just moved to the side. But she just wanted to watch me deliver. That was so ignorant. Every time I was pushing, I had to look at her face. Tell me, where does "care, custody, and control" [i.e., the principle roles of many departments of correction] come into that? It was the most degrading experience ever.

Some women were scared to report disrespectful or abusive treatment because they feared receiving disciplinary reports or losing privileges:

> Even when the officers lash out, we can't say anything because then we get it worse from the officer. I have a very abusive boss. He calls us dumb and retarded. I can't say anything, though. I eat that [ignore it] because I want to go home to my kids. But some people can't handle that.

Women who "complained" about inappropriate treatment risked additional punishment. One woman described being removed from an institutional program after she reported inappropriate behavior by an officer:

> They degrade us here as a woman. They cuss at us. We are deprived and denied. The officers can say whatever they want and do whatever they want. We have no voice. It makes me cringe. There is an officer in the kitchen that does inappropriate searches. . . . I am afraid that if I say something I will be reprimanded. All the women try to go to another officer to be searched. Everybody knows about him. You get penalized if you complain. I was kicked out of a program

because I said something [about another offi-cer's actions]. They have our life in their hands.

Several inmates who had been incarcerated for lon-ger periods of time commented that, in general, correc-tional officers' attitudes had changed over the last decade. They attributed these changes to officers needing to manage a larger, younger, more drug-addicted and violent population entering prison. One woman serving a life sentence described how treatment by the officers changed during her 15 years in prison:

I know from experience that officers can be the liaison to get your sanity back. But not every staff member has the education to deal with us. They don't get the training they used to. They used to tell them, "Their punishment is to be in here. It is not your job to punish them." But they don't come in with that attitude anymore.

Participants also acknowledged the difficulties health and correctional professionals must face when working with such a "demanding" population. For the most part, women understood that some inmates who were "bad apples" made it more difficult for the rest of them. Women acting simple and stupid and women trying to game the system resulted in harsh and uniform consequences for everyone. One woman serving a life sentence wrote,

The majority of women here have continued/consistent poor character, poor decision-making ability, and low maturity levels. That makes it hard for the ones that are not like that. We are often treated as if we all act that way.

Improved Mental Health

A number of women described that their mental health had improved during their incarceration. In addition to numerous responses on the PHS similar to, "My mental health got better," some women commented that they were "less depressed" and "more positive in thoughts and feelings." They felt "more stable" and that their "mental health was more under control in prison." One woman commented, "I feel good about life." Women described feeling less "hopeless," "being aware of feelings," and

"having a real chance at life now." One woman com-mented that she "didn't think of death so much anymore." The structure available in prison was viewed as positive for some women, including one who expressed, "The structure here has taught me that sanity isn't necessarily boring." Finally, one participant summarized her feelings as, "I've been here seven years. It has been the best seven years. In here, you either get bitter or better. I got better, much better." Women identified several factors that led to improved mental health, including access to the right medication, being "clean" [not taking illegal drugs], hav-ing the opportunity to work on their "issues" with mental health providers, being away from violence, becoming closer to God, and allowing time to heal old wounds and adapt to the prison environment.

I'm Getting the Right Medication Now. Women iden-tified that access to psychotropic medication in prison improved their mental health. Some described currently being on a combination of the "right medications" that were properly treating their symptoms. One 32-year-old woman who suffered from schizoaffective disorder remarked that her medications were adjusted and she felt more "stable." Another participant who suffered from schizophrenia described that medication helped "get the voices under control." In addition to medication actually reducing mental health symptoms, the side effect profile of many of the prescribed psychotropic medications included somnolence or sleepiness. For many women, this was a welcome side effect because improved sleep resulted in a perceived improvement in mental health.

Although access to medication was important, actu-ally taking the medication as prescribed and not self-medicating were equally vital. One participant who had been incarcerated for more than 10 years for murder suffered from bipolar disorder. She identified that her symptoms had lessened because she was then properly taking her medication, writing, "I need to be supervised because I never take medication on my own. I forget to eat, and stay wake for two to three days at a time." Also suffering from bipolar disorder, another woman, incar-cerated for theft, commented that her mental health issues had stabilized and, "Again, I realized I had bipolar and needed meds." A combination of access to medica-tion and mental health services also contributed to improved mental health. One woman who was incarcerated for manslaughter wrote, "They've given me more accurate diagnosis now and have gotten me on better medication for me." Similarly, another participant wrote, "My mental health is better only because I see a doctor and take meds."

My Head Is Clearer, and I'm Free From Drugs. Access to drug and alcohol treatment and forced sobriety (being *clean*) also resulted in improved mental health for many women. One 39-year-old woman convicted of robbery wrote, "My mental health has definitely gotten better. I am off drugs and alcohol and working on my negative issues trying to be a better person." Another woman commented, "My mental health is better because I can't get high [take illegal drugs] to deal with life." Some women identified that their minds were "clearer" and less "cloudy" without drugs and alcohol. One 40-year-old participant explained, "The length of time I've been here has given me time to clear my head and body of heroin and, with help from the treatment program, I've actually made some changes." Another woman also commented, "My mind is much clearer off of drugs. And I am able [to] focus on myself, my rehabilitation, and the goals that I am setting for myself." A 20-year-old participant wrote, "I'm beginning to be get stronger and I'm able to think better because I'm clean from drugs and drugs ruined my life." Finally, a 22-year-old woman wrote, "I'm clean and on the right track. I'm thinking more clearly and level-headed and ready to be released into society with a better head on my shoulders."

I'm Working on My Issues. Many women who participated in mental health counseling and supportive programming described improvement in their mental health. Treatment programs available in the study institution addressed issues such as addiction, past victimization, and violence prevention, often via cognitive behavioral approaches. One participant wrote, "I've been lucky enough to finally (after 20+ years of treatment) find a good therapist. I still have tons of issues, but now I can manage them." The ability to work on issues from the past was deemed valuable to inmates. Women learned behavioral skills, such as talking about their issues and relaxation techniques, which helped them cope and adapt to the prison environment.

One 43-year-old woman, convicted of aggravated assault, described how she was able to discontinue her medication because of techniques she learned in group, writing, "I have been off all psych meds about 5 or 6 years. I still have mental issues, but I learned to stop and breathe first and journal and talk about my issues in a mental health group." Similarly, another participant wrote, "I see the psych doctor once a month. The environment is controlled and the structure here forces a person to talk about their problems. The only other option is to be self-destructive." One woman also described, "I've learned to really think things through, choose wisely and keep my circle tight, express how I feel all the time, focus on 'what is' and truly worry about making myself better."

Some women described that they were able to "work through issues" or "talk through tough issues" in groups, including issues related to past victimization and exposure to other traumatic experiences. One sexual assault victim wrote,

> Every day is a struggle, coping skills aside, to feel physically and emotionally fit. But I feel better. I have taken full advantage of the programs and groups available in order to gain a better understanding of my emotional disorders. I have used this prison time for me to learn, change, and love me. Things I didn't really make time for outside this gate. My priority was always others. I'm still learning/changing yet I'm content and have come a long way. Besides groups, I also utilize the mental health unit when I need to reach-out for it.

One 48-year-old woman, convicted of a drug-related crime, had been sexually assaulted by a family member as a child. She commented, "My mental health is better due to the programs I've been in to help with my past abuse issues. They have been great." Another woman, convicted of murder, explained:

> I'm a lifer [sentenced to serve the remainder of her life in prison]. I am so ashamed of what I did. I was so damn angry and I stayed angry for years. I finally got into counseling and they saved my life. I needed to come face to face with my issues. Issues I didn't even know that I had.

It helped me make it through the tough times. I did the abuse program and it was like I was set free. I deal with a lot of issues all the time. I see psych here. All I have to do is write him a request or call him and he is right on it. But everybody don't have that.

Another participant identified that her mental health had improved because she was in a program in which they were "able to talk about things that caused mental health problems." One such event this woman needed to talk about was witnessing the suicide of a fellow inmate, which occurred in her housing unit. Indeed, several women in this study described needing to "talk to someone" about this specific incident.

Another program viewed positively by participants was the "puppy program," which allowed incarcerated women to train service dogs. Women who trained the puppies and women who lived in the same housing unit as the puppies identified this program as having a positive impact on their mental health. One woman, convicted of murder, described that participating in the puppy program allowed her to "keep her mind off of being in prison." She commented, "My puppy helps me with everything. In some ways it helps me block everything out. I go to work. I see my friends. I sometimes forget that, oh yeah, I am in a maximum-security prison." Another woman, also convicted of murder, offered this description:

> You are so cut off with contact with people, like little stuff like hugs, and it just helps. My puppy is always happy to see me. It's nice having that affection and to cuddle with. I could be having a bad day and I have her and it's not so bad. It gives you something to look forward to every day. The dogs remind me of home. That I'm normal. Not in prison.

One woman, who was not a puppy trainer but lived in the same unit as the puppies, commented,

> At first, I didn't want to move in with the puppies. I didn't want all their hair on me and licking me. But once I was in here, I learned that

animals, especially the dogs, will make you fall in love with them. I didn't want to fall in love with these damn dogs. But I love them!

I'm Safe Now. Although we did not focus our investigation specifically on trauma, more than 90% of the women who completed our full survey identified that they had experienced a traumatic event in their lives, with almost half meeting the diagnostic criteria for PTSD at Stage One. Several women commented that being in prison got them away from the violence in their personal lives and kept them "safe from the violence on the street." One woman, incarcerated for murder, wrote, "I'm not being abused by my ex-husband anymore. Confinement in prison is so much better than the confinement he had me in." Another woman, also incarcerated for murder, wrote, "My mental health has gotten better because I am no longer in an emotionally abusive relationship. I don't have to worry about being forced to have sex or be verbally abused." Similarly, another participant, convicted of drunk driving, noted that time in prison had allowed her to file for divorce from her abusive husband and to "get help with abuse issues."

I'm Getting Closer to God. Becoming *closer to God* during incarceration resulted in improved mental health for some women. One 40-year-old woman, incarcerated for murder, wrote, "I now have a relationship with God and strive to be a better person." Another participant, who returned to prison after she was found living in a boarded up abandoned building (and thus violating her probation), stated,

> If it had not been for the chapel service here, I would not have made it. There is very little mental health services here in prison. Going to the chapel and finding Jesus saved my life. It has taken a lot of mental strength. I would have cut my throat long before I got to grounds if not for the chapel. I am not saying that for pity, because I am a lot stronger than that. The pastor over there teaches you that you matter. But it is a fight to get to the chapel. The ones who come in new need it the most and get it the least.

Distraught over the death of the nearly three dozen animals in her care (many were taken by Animal Control after she was convicted), one woman wrote,

> My animals in my care were like my children, each with its own personality and endearments. . . . In attending both Protestant and Catholic services and speaking with some of the chaplains, I have reconciled—for the most part—my anger at God for "allowing" so many trials to happen in my life and the death of the animals he placed into my care. I now have a better relationship with God.

Time Helps/Time Heals. Several women attributed their improved mental health to a function of time: time healing old wounds, time helping them to mature as individuals, and time helping them adapt to their new lives behind bars. The process of adaptation was especially evident in women sentenced to longer prison terms:

> I was in a tender mental place when I first came here. In the first evaluation I had when I got here, I had a mental break. There is an adjustment period for long-termers and lifers. Knowing you are doing ten to twenty years is overwhelming. There is a difference between doing a year to two and doing a life sentence. It may not hit you right away. It may take a year or two for you to realize what this place means. You are numb for the first year. You just exist when you first get here. You just eat and sleep. I had to work. I needed the repetition. There are little things that you struggle with, like going to the bathroom in front of a human being. It is emotionally draining. But you learn to appreciate the small things in life. There is always something beautiful every day in here. You just have to work to find it. You have to find a purpose. You let it out and let it go. As they say, "We're not going anywhere." But it's a struggle inside. I had to work myself to this point.

Several women identified that their mental health had improved over time and that they no longer needed psychotropic medication. One woman who had been incarcerated for more than 15 years for murder described this:

> I was deeply depressed when I get here, and I was put on medication for it. I've been off medication since 1995. I did take medicine in 1997 and 1999, but not long. My mind was racing those two times and my thoughts had to be slowed down. No medicine since, and I feel fine.

Another woman, incarcerated for more than 7 years, wrote, "My mental health has gotten better. I was on prescribed medications for depression, anxiety, and sleep upon entering prison. I currently take no medications and haven't for the last 5 years." A 31-year-old participant convicted of murder noted,

> My mental health is better because I don't need my meds and I'm staying alert of [or to] everything. Yeah, it's logical that we all get depressed and sad here and there. Especially a person like me with a long bid [prison sentence].

No Change in Mental Health

For some women, mental health issues remained unchanged as a result of incarceration. Many women documented that their mental health was simply "the same." Some identified that they did not suffer from any mental health issues prior to or during incarceration. For other women, their mental health was relatively the same in that they still experienced mental health issues; however, the specific nature of these issues changed as a result of incarceration. For example, one 32-year-old woman wrote, "It was a trade. I was stressed about the unknown on the outside but now I am stressed about my kids on the inside." Similarly, another woman identified, "Since I have been here I was diagnosed with situational depression and grief. On the streets I was diagnosed with depression and anxiety. Not really sure if it's gotten worse; it's about the same."

Discussion

Findings from this investigation add to our understanding of the complex ways in which women's mental health is affected by incarceration. In many instances, our results mirror those of other investigators (Douglas et al., 2009) and suggest that women's mental health can worsen, improve, or remain the same during incarceration. Although presented as isolated themes in this article, it is likely that this is a false trichotomy. Indeed, the impact of imprisonment on mental health is likely more fluid in nature, with women's own physical health, social support, access to resources, maturity level, and life experiences playing significant roles in their immediate perceptions of mental health. Similarly, adaptation to incarceration, especially among women serving long sentences, likely plays a role in women's perceptions of their mental health.

It is important to identify that imprisonment resulted in improved mental health for some women, which has also been described by other investigators (Douglas et al., 2009). For some, access to services prior to incarceration, including mental health care, medication management, and addiction treatment programs, was either limited or inadequate. For others, prison provided a safe place relative to their lives on the street, a phenomenon identified by Bradley and Davino (2002). Indeed, prison did serve as a safety net for women experiencing what one participant described as "the worst-case scenario." However, the fact that women benefited in any way from imprisonment is by itself an alarming commentary on the status of women's health and safety in the United States. These women's accounts expose the larger social issue of the link between disparities in women's health, especially among women experiencing the worst-case scenario (poverty, addiction, serious mental illness, and victimization), and imprisonment.

The women's responses also allow us to evaluate the prison system and the professionals within the system using the principles of the trauma-informed framework (Harris & Fallot, 2001). Women's accounts reflect an institutional milieu that was not fully trauma-informed and reveal the institution's limited understanding of trauma, Harris and Fallot's first principle. Although both health and correctional professionals likely knew that many of the women in their care had experienced victimization, an understanding of trauma did not appear to be fully integrated into institutional procedures. For example, women were clearly distraught by the violent event that occurred just prior to our focus groups. Many described fearing for their own safety. Women identified warning signs prior to the event but, for myriad reasons, felt too helpless and

fearful to report their suspicions to officials. Some were even too scared to report the violent event as it was taking place because they feared they could not be protected from later reprisal by the perpetrator. Without an official update from the institution after the event, women were left to reconstruct what had transpired during the chaos, often based on the inaccurate and escalating rumor mill and conversations overheard between correctional officers. These false reconstructions compounded women's sense of powerlessness, helplessness, and fear, themes that might have replicated past traumatic experiences and resulted in retraumatization.

An institution that fully understood trauma might have better anticipated the emotional disruption such a violent event might cause and restored a sense of security and safety for all women. Although women living in the unit in which the violent incident occurred were offered timely crisis mental health treatment, women housed in other units had limited access to similar services. These women, too, bore witness to the violent event, albeit in different ways: They watched the helicopter land within the institution and felt fear. They overheard officers and other staff discuss and respond to the violent event and felt powerless. This fear and powerlessness was still palpable during our focus groups. A broader institutional response during this time of crisis might have benefited the mental health of these women, as well as contributed positively to the institutional mission of safety and security.

Understanding the survivor, Harris and Fallot's (2001) second principle, necessitates that systems and professionals relate to women from a holistic perspective. Women in this study frequently described being labeled and "lumped together" as "addicts," "lifers," "drug seekers," or medical "frequent flyers" by health and correctional professionals. These labels not only described a specific negative characteristic of the woman but, at times, seemed linked to access to care [as well]. For example, women serving life sentences (lifers) reported that they were always "last on the list" to participate in mental health programs because they were "not going anywhere." These labels might have also provided a context for how a woman's health symptoms were perceived within the institution. For example, pain experienced by drug seekers and addicts was often invalidated by health professionals. These labels have the potential to additionally damage women's poor self-images. In fact, these negative labels were often transferred down to, and reinforced by, the women themselves. They were, at times, used to describe other women ("Oh, she's just a junkie") and at other times, used to describe themselves ("I'm just an inmate").

Even the label of *inmate*, although factually accurate, carried not only the negative connotation of someone who had committed a crime but also served to reinforce a gender-neutral stance that equated the circumstances and needs of incarcerated women with their male counterparts. For example, women described being subject to the same policies and procedures used in men's institutions, including routine strip searches before visitation. Women identified the irony of being required to attend a *violence prevention program* when in actuality, most had been victims of violent crimes. And finally, women were angered by policies designed for sexual offenders, most of whom were men, which barred children from sitting on their laps after a certain age.

Data from this investigation provide insight into Harris and Fallot's (2001) third principle, understanding available services. Many women described prison mental health services as primarily crisis oriented and designed for "the worst-case scenarios." Despite this orientation, some women did identify both mental health providers and specific programs that contributed to improved mental health. The most often cited beneficial programs included those that specifically addressed victimization and addiction and those that taught and reinforced positive skill-building techniques (journaling, stopping and thinking, relaxation, deep breathing, and so forth). Although not specifically a mental health program, women who participated in the puppy program, as well as women who simply lived in the same unit as the puppies, expressed that involvement in the program improved their mental health. It is important to note, however, that although these programs were viewed by some women as successful, access was often limited because of inadequate resources. Although women acknowledged that providers were overburdened by the increasing acuity and rapid growth in the inmate population, many remained steadfast in their belief that they deserved and needed care, regardless of institutional circumstances.

Finally, women characterized their relationships with service professionals, including health and correctional professionals, as largely disempowered. Only rarely were these relationships portrayed by women as mutual or collaborative. Women described having limited voice or control in their care and identified that their opinions were largely unappreciated. Their views of their symptoms and their knowledge of their own bodies was rarely considered accurate or valuable by health professionals. Despite being dissatisfied with care, some women did not voice their opinions or question health professionals because they were concerned they would be labeled a *troublemaker* and feared such a label would result in worse care. Unlike nonincarcerated women, women in prison were powerless to seek care elsewhere.

Many women believed they had been ignored and abandoned by the correctional health care system. The copayment system was particularly burdensome for most of the women in our study, and [it] might have reduced women's use of health-related services, a finding that was also identified by Fisher and Hatton (2010). Women expressed lack of confidence and trust in health professionals and were anxious over unfamiliar medical terms and diagnoses they neither understood nor fully believed were accurate. Women yearned to be able to *talk with someone* about their issues and were stymied when they were told their medical symptoms were not severe enough or their abuse not traumatic enough to merit care.

Limitations

Despite remarkably good access to most of the prison population, several key groups of incarcerated women were not allowed to participate in the study. As noted, we did not have access to women in high-security areas, such as the RHU or the MHU. It is possible that these women, by virtue of their classification in the institution, might have different (and likely more negative) responses [from] women housed in the general prison population. It is also possible that women in the general prison population who suffered significant difficulties while incarcerated might have had more incentive to share their negative experiences than women who had more positive experiences, thus, skewing the data negatively. Because the PHS was written in English and the focus groups were conducted in English, non-English speakers might also be underrepresented in our study. It is possible that non-English speakers might have different experiences in prison [from] native English speakers. As with any cross-sectional study, our data provide only snapshots of an overall picture of how women's mental health is affected by incarceration. Data collected at different points in time (Mother's Day, Christmas, a month before release) might result in different findings. Finally, these findings are specific to women incarcerated in one particular institution and might not be generalizable to other women incarcerated in other prisons and jails.

Recommendations

Research

Although our research question was focused broadly on mental health, future investigators might be interested in specific aspects of mental health, such as barriers to care, mental health and stigma, and the process of adaptation to imprisonment. It would also be valuable to better understand the key features of treatment programs and other therapeutic modalities that women in our study felt improved mental health. What are the necessary elements that make a program successful, and how do women (and DOC professionals) measure success? Do certain populations of women (such as women serving life sentences) have different needs [from] women serving shorter sentences?

In light of access to limited resources, investigators should also consider the effectiveness of innovative, alternative modes of delivering mental health treatment, such as using MP3 players (which are allowed in some correctional institutions) to teach inmates relaxation techniques or to provide skill-building exercises. In addition to improving women's mental health, the establishment of evidence-based mental health treatment programs that can be used safely and successfully in women's correctional institutions might have the potential to reduce recidivism, which would be important at individual, community, and societal levels.

Although in this investigation we focused specifically on incarcerated women's perceptions of their mental health, understanding the experiences of correctional, medical, and mental health professionals working in correctional institutions might provide important insight; in many respects, these individuals are also institutionalized.

If receptive to beginning a dialogue, these professionals are in a unique position to provide valuable insight into what "works" in prison and, equally important, what does not. It is possible that improvements in inmate well-being might result in a less stressful work environment for institutional professionals. As some women commented, a reduction in staff stress levels might result in a better institutional milieu for women in prison.

Several investigators (Fisher & Hatton, 2010; Hatton & Fisher, 2011; Martin, Murphy, Chan, et al., 2009; Martin, Murphy, Hanson, et al., 2009) have partnered with incarcerated women in the design, conduct, analysis, and dissemination of research addressing the needs of incarcerated women. Collaborating with incarcerated women as coinvestigators is one way researchers can acknowledge incarcerated women's expertise and engage them in developing research that is meaningful to them. Furthermore, this partnering has the possibility of reducing unintentional exploitation and addressing power imbalances in the research process.

Practice

Because most of the women in prison have experienced trauma, it is vital that both correctional systems and the professionals they employ approach the women they serve from a trauma-informed perspective. Harris and Fallot (2001) argued for an administrative commitment to change, including "integrating knowledge about violence and abuse into the service delivery practices of the organization" (p. 5). Knowledge can be integrated in a variety of ways, such as developing specific educational programs for staff, as well as incorporating trauma awareness into an organization's mission statement. Harris and Fallot also urged organizations to adopt a policy of universal screening for trauma among all individuals seeking services. They also argued that organizations should hire individuals who already have a basic understanding of trauma, as well as train and educate all service personnel with introductory information about trauma. Finally, Harris and Fallot identified that organizations should review existing policies and procedures with the goal of identifying anything that might potentially be harmful to or might retraumatize survivors.

The presence of a dedicated trauma treatment program, as well as institutional support of trauma-based research, signifies our study institution's positive movement toward a more trauma-informed model of care. However, women's accounts of their experiences in prison point to the continued need for trauma-based training programs targeting all professionals working in the institution. It is reasonable to believe that correctional officers and health professionals can still maintain custody and control within the institution without degrading the women they serve. Even commonplace actions, such as referring to women by their inmate identification number (often referred to as their *con number*), referring to patients as *inmates* in clinical notes, or describing women as "needy," "drug seeking," or "manipulative" are inconsistent with the trauma-informed perspective of care and should be discouraged.

Prison officials, in conjunction with experts in women's trauma, should also thoroughly examine existing policies and procedures from the perspectives of both gender and trauma. Incarcerated women are not men, and many of the policies that direct common institutional procedures might not be relevant to incarcerated women. Furthermore, these procedures might be unnecessarily traumatogenic. While examining existing policies and procedures that might be harmful to women, it is also important to identify situations that might necessitate the development of new trauma-informed policies. These procedures might be especially relevant in situations that require both security action as well as mental health intervention for victims and bystanders, such as violent events in the institution, medical emergencies, and institutional suicides.

/// DISCUSSION QUESTIONS

1. Which factors led women to believe that prison had a negative effect on their mental health status?

2. Which factors led women to believe that prison had a positive effect on their mental health status?

3. For those women that believed that prison did not impact their mental health status, what factors made this population different from the others?

References

Bradley, R. G., & Davino, K. M. (2002). Women's perceptions of the prison environment: When prison is "the safest place I've ever been." *Psychology of Women Quarterly, 26,* 351–359. doi:10.1111/1471-6402.t01-2-00074

Braithwaite, R. L., Treadwell, H. M., & Arriola, K. R. J. (2008). Health disparities and incarcerated women: A population ignored. *American Journal of Public Health, 98*(Suppl. 1), S173–S175. doi:10.2105/AJPH.2005.065375

Covington, S. S. (1998). Women in prison: Approaches in the treatment of our most invisible population. *Women & Therapy, 21,* 141–155. doi:10.1300/J015v21n01_03

Douglas, N., Plugge, E., & Fitzpatrick, R. (2009). The impact of imprisonment on health: What do women prisoners say? *Journal of Epidemiology and Community Health, 63,* 749–754. doi:10.1136/jech.2008.080713

Fisher, A. A., & Hatton, D. C. (2010). A study of women prisoners' use of co-payments for health care: Issues of access. *Women's Health Issues, 20,* 185–192. doi:10.1016/j.whi.2010.01.005

Harner, H. M., & Burgess, A. W. (2011). Using a trauma-informed framework to care for incarcerated women. *Journal of Obstetric,*

Gynecologic, and Neonatal Nursing, 40, 469–476. doi:10.1111/j.1552–6909.2011.01259.x

Harner, H. M., Hanlon, A., & Garfinkel, M. (2010). The effect of Iyengar yoga on the mental health of incarcerated women: A feasibility study. *Nursing Research, 59,* 389–399. doi:10.1097/NNR.0b013e3181f2e6ff

Harner, H. M., Hentz, P., & Evangelista, M. C. (2011). Grief interrupted: The experience of loss among incarcerated women. *Qualitative Health Research, 21,* 454–464. doi:10.1177/1049732310373257

Harris, M., & Fallot, R. D. (2001). Envisioning a trauma informed service system: A vital paradigm shift. *New Directions for Mental Health Services, 89,* 3–22. doi:10.1002/ yd.23320018903

Hatton, D. C., & Fisher, A. A. (2011). Using participatory methods to examine policy and women prisoners' health. *Policy, Politics, & Nursing Practice, 12,* 119–125. doi:10.1177/1527154411412384

James, D., & Glaze, L. (2006). Mental health problems of prisons and jail inmates, Retrieved from http://bjs.ojp.usdoj. gov/content/pub/pdf/mhppji.pdf

Kim, S. (2003). Incarcerated women in life context. *Women's Studies International Forum, 26*(1), 95–100. doi:10.1016/ S0277-5395(02)00358-8

Martin, R. E., Murphy, K., Chan, R., Ramsden, V. R., Granger-Brown, A., Macaulay, A. C., & Hislop, T. G. (2009). Primary health care: Applying the principles within a community-based participatory health research project that began in a Canadian women's prison. *Global Health Promotion, 16*(4), 43–53. doi:10.1177/1757975909348114

Martin, R. E., Murphy, K., Hanson, D., Hemingway, C., Ramsden, V., Buxton, J., & Espinoza-Magana, N. (2009). The development of participatory health research among incarcerated women in a Canadian prison. *International Journal of Prisoner Health, 5,* 95–107. doi:10.1080/174492 00902884021

Nurse, J., Woodcock, P., & Ormsby, J. (2003). Influence of environmental factors on mental health within prisons: Focus group study. *British Medical Journal, 327,* 1–5. doi:10.1136/bmj.327.7413.480

Young, D. S. (2000). Women's perceptions of health care in prison. *Health Care for Women International, 21,* 219–234. doi:10.1080/073993300245276

Women Professionals and the Criminal Justice System
Police, Corrections, and Offender Services

Section Highlights

- The gendered experience of women employed in the criminal justice system
- Challenges for women in victim services, policing, corrections, probation, and parole
- Future directions for females working in the criminal justice system

Throughout history, criminal justice occupations have been dominated by men. Whether the job was that of a police officer or working within the field of corrections, the common perception was that the duties of apprehending and managing dangerous felons was outside the perceptions of what women could—or should—do. Women first began to appear in criminal justice occupations within police organizations in the early 20th century. However, their early presence within the academy was significantly limited, because many believed that policing was a *man's job* and therefore unsuitable as an occupation for women. The duties in these occupations focused on traditional masculine traits, such as aggression, physical skill, and being tough—traits that many argued were lacking for women, making them inherently less capable of doing the job (Appier, 1998).

Society generally assumes that work in the criminal justice system is dominated by events that are dangerous, exciting, and violent. These themes are echoed and reinforced in examples of popular culture, such as television, film, and news outlets, by stories of dangerous offenders and crimes that destroy peaceful communities (Lersch & Bazley, 2012). Certainly criminal justice officials in fields such as policing, corrections, and probation and parole can and do face dangerous situations during their careers. However these extreme examples misrepresent the reality of criminal justice work, which often involves long delays, extensive paperwork, and spending time talking with residents of the community. Unlike the adrenaline rush that is depicted in the media, criminal justice personnel spend significant portions of their time dealing with situations that require empathy, compassion, and nurturing—traits that are stereotypically classified as *feminine* characteristics. For example, the typical duties of a police officer are not limited to the pursuit and capturing of the "bad guys" and more often include responding to victims of a crime and dealing with the welfare of community members. Given the various skills and traits required in criminal justice professions, has the number of women increased in these fields? How does gender contribute to these professions? Are there other differences in how women are hired, do their jobs, and establish careers in criminal justice? This section follows these issues through the fields of policing, corrections, and offender services.

Women in Policing

An examination of the history of policing indicates that the work of moral reformers was instrumental in the emergence of policewomen. During the late 19th century, women's advocacy groups were heavily involved in social issues. Examples of their efforts include the creation of a separate court for juvenile offenders as well as crime prevention outreach related to the protection of young women from immoral sexual influences. However, women were not a formal part of the justice system and served as informal advocates and, when employed, as paid social workers.

With the start of the 20th century, women entered the police force as bona fide, sworn officers. However, there is some debate as to who was the first female police officer. One report indicates that the first female police officer may have been **Marie Owens**. She was a Chicago factory inspector who transferred to the police department in 1891 and served 32 years with the city (Mastony, 2010). Other scholars point to **Lola Baldwin**, who was reportedly hired in 1908 by the Portland, Oregon, police department as a supervisor to a group of social workers (Corsianos, 2009). However, it is unclear whether Baldwin served as a sworn officer (Los Angeles Almanac, 2012). But it is **Alice Stebbins Wells**, who was hired by the Los Angeles Police Department (LAPD) in 1910, who is most often cited as the first sworn female police officer in the United States. At the time of her hiring, her job duties revolved around working with female offenders and juvenile cases. Her philosophy as a female police officer reinforced the ideal of feminine traits of policing when she stated, "I don't want to make arrests. I want to keep people from needing to be arrested, especially young people" (Appier, 1998, p. 9). As a result of the national and international attention of her hiring, she traveled the country promoting the benefits of hiring women in municipal policing agencies. As an officer with the LAPD, Wells advocated the protection of children and women, particularly when it came to sexual education. As part of her duties, she inspected dance halls, movie theaters, and locations for public recreation throughout the city. When she came into contact with girls of questionable moral status, she would lecture them on the dangers of premarital sex and advocate for the importance of purity.

Following in the footsteps of Alice Stebbins Wells, many women sought out positions as police officers. The hiring of women by police agencies throughout the early 20th century did not mean that these women were assigned the same duties as male police officers. Rather, these policewomen were essentially social workers armed with a badge. Their duties focused on preventing crime rather than responding to criminal activity. While hundreds of women joined the ranks of local law enforcement agencies between 1910 and 1920, they were a minority within most departments. Female officers were generally limited to working with juvenile and female offenders, and the male officers resented their presence in the

▲ **Photo 12.1** Captain Edyth Totten and the Women Police Reserve, New York City, 1918.

department. In an effort to distinguish the work of policewomen, many cities created separate branches within their organization. These women's bureaus were tasked with servicing the needs of women and girls in the community. Many of these bureaus were housed outside of the walls of the city police department in an attempt to create a more welcoming environment for citizens in need. Some scholars suggest that by making women's bureaus look more like a home, rather than a bureaucratic institution, women and children would be more comfortable and therefore more likely to seek out the services and advice of policewomen.

The mid-20th century saw significant growth in the numbers of women in policing. In 1922, there were approximately 500 policewomen in the United States—by 1960, more than 5,600 women were employed as officers (Schulz, 1995). Throughout this time, the majority of these policewomen remained limited in their duties, due in large part to a traditional policing (i.e., male) model. Policewomen were not permitted to engage in the same duties as policemen, out of fear that it was too dangerous and that women would not be able to adequately serve in these positions. Most important, the "all boys club" that existed in most departments simply did not want or welcome women intruding on their territory.

Despite these issues, women occasionally found themselves receiving expanded duties, particularly during times of war. With the decrease in manpower during World War I and II, many women found themselves placed in positions normally reserved for male officers, such as traffic control. In an effort to maintain adequate staffing levels during this period, the number of women hired within police agencies increased. However, the end of these wars saw the return of men to their policing posts and the displacement of women back to their gendered roles and **gendered assignments** within their respective departments (Snow, 2010).

As in many other fields during the 1960s, the civil rights and women's movements had a tremendous effect on the presence of women in policing. Legal challenges paved the way toward gendered equality in policing by opening doors to allow women to serve in more active police capacities, such as patrol. In 1964, **Liz Coffal** and **Betty Blankenship** of the Indianapolis Police Department became the first women in the United States to serve as patrol officers, an assignment that was previously restricted to male officers throughout the country. As policewomen, Coffal and Blankenship were resented by their male colleagues, who believed that the work of a police officer was too dangerous for women. Coffal and Blankenship received little training for their new positions and often had to learn things on their own. They found that dispatch often gave them the mundane and undesirable tasks, such as hospital transports. It soon became clear to Blankenship and Coffal that the likelihood of being requested for any sort of pursuit or arrest cases was slim. In an effort to gain increased experience in their position, they began to respond to calls at their own discretion. Armed with their police radio, they learned to interpret radio codes and began to respond to cases in their vicinity. They successfully navigated calls that most male officers believed they could not handle. As a result of their positive performances in often tense situations, Coffal and Blankenship began to gain some respect from their male colleagues. However, they knew that any accolades could be short lived—one mistake and they ran the risk of being removed from their patrol status, and the traditional philosophy of "police work isn't for women" would be justified. While they eventually returned to some of the "traditional feminine roles" for women in policing, their experiences in patrol set the stage for significant changes for future policewomen (Snow, 2010).

In addition to the differences in their duties, policewomen were historically subjected to different qualification standards for their positions. At the 1922 annual conference of the International Association of the Chiefs of Police, members suggested that policewomen should have completed college or nursing school (Snow, 2010). This standard is particularly ironic, given that male officers were not required to have even a high school diploma in most jurisdictions until the 1950s and 1960s. As a result, the career path of policewomen attracted women of higher educational and intellectual standing.

Not only were policewomen limited by their roles and duties within the department they faced significant barriers as well in terms of the benefits and conditions of their employment. Like in many other fields, policewomen were paid less for their work compared to policemen, even though these women often had higher levels of education than their male colleagues. In addition, the advancement and promotional opportunities for women were significantly limited, because most departments did not allow women to participate in the exam process that would grant them access to promotional opportunities. Generally speaking, the highest position that a policewoman could hold during this time was the commander of the women's bureau. Still, many agencies disagreed with that level of leadership, suggesting that women did not have the necessary skills or abilities to supervise officers or run a division. In some jurisdictions, women were forced to quit their positions when they got married, because many felt that women did not have enough time to care for a home, care for their husband, and fulfill their job duties. As one male officer explained it, "when they marry they have to resign. You see, we might want them for some job or other when they have to be home cooking their husband's dinner. That would not be much use to us, would it?" (Snow, 2010, p. 23).

In 1967, the President's Commission on Law Enforcement and the Administration of Justice advocated expanding the numbers of policewomen and diversifying their duties beyond the traditional female roles to which they were typically assigned. In 1967, the commission wrote, "The value should not be considered as limited to staff functions or police work with juveniles; women should also serve regularly in patrol, vice and investigative functions" (p. 125). Despite these assertions, few departments followed these recommendations, arguing that as members of a uniformed police patrol, officers required significant levels of upper-body strength in order to detain resistant offenders. In addition, many agency administrators argued that the job was simply too dangerous for women.

Until the 1970s, women represented only 1% of all sworn officers in the United States (Appier, 1998). However, new legislation and legal challenges in the 1960s and 1970s led to further changes involving the presence and role of policewomen. While the **Civil Rights Bill of 1964** was generally focused on eliminating racial discrimination, the word *sex* was added to the bill during the eleventh hour by House members, who hoped that this inclusion would raise objections among legislators and prohibit its passing. To the dismay of these dissenters, the bill was signed into law. In 1969, President Richard Nixon signed legislation that prohibited the use of sex as a requirement for hiring—meaning that jobs could not be restricted to men only (or women only). In addition, the Law Enforcement Assistance Administration (LEAA) mandated that agencies with federal funding (and police departments fell under this category) were prohibited from engaging in discriminatory hiring practices based on sex. While sex was now a protected category in terms of employment discrimination, the bill did little on its face to increase the presence of women in sworn policing roles. While the act prohibited discriminatory hiring practices, it had little effect on the types of assignments that were given to women once they joined the police force.

The passage of the Civil Rights Bill began a trend within departments to introduce women into ranks that were previously reserved exclusively for men. While several departments took the initiative to place women into patrol positions, many men in these departments issued strong objections against the practice. Thus, women in these positions often found themselves ostracized, with little support from their colleagues. Eight years later, in 1972, the Civil Rights Act was amended to extend employment protections to state and municipal government agencies, which opened the door to allow women to apply to all law enforcement jurisdictions as sworn officers without restrictions. While these changes increased the number of positions available to women (and to minorities), they also shifted the roles of policing away from the social service orientation that had been historically characteristic for women in policing. Their jobs now included the duties of crime fighting and the maintenance of order and public safety, just like their male counterparts (Schulz, 1995).

Over the past four decades, there have been significant increases in the number of women employed as sworn law enforcement officers. In 1922, there were approximately 500 policewomen in the United States—by 1960, more than 5,600 women were employed as officers, approximately 1.1% of all sworn officers (Rabe-Hemp, 2008; Schulz, 1995). By 1986, approximately 8.8% of municipal officers were female (Rabe-Hemp, 2008), a proportion that almost doubles by 2008 (15.2%). Women are more likely to be employed in larger jurisdictions (22%) and federal agencies (24%) compared to smaller jurisdictions (defined as departments with fewer than 500 officers) where women make up 8% of all sworn personnel (Langton, 2010). Unfortunately, these few women that serve in rural communities are relegated to lower positions within the agency and experience higher degrees of discrimination compared to women in larger metropolitan departments (Rabe-Hemp, 2008).

Why is the representation of women so low in the field of policing? While legal challenges have mandated equal access to employment and promotional opportunities for women in policing, research indicates that the overemphasis on the physical fitness skills component of the hiring process excludes a number of qualified women from employment (Lonsway, Carrington, et al., 2002). Physical fitness tests typical of law enforcement positions have been criticized as a tool to exclude women from policing, despite evidence that it is not the physical abilities of officers that are most desirable. Rather, it is their communication skills that are the best asset for the job. The number of push-ups that a woman can complete compared to a man says little about how well each will complete their duties. Yet standards such as these are used as evidence to suggest that women are inferior to their male colleagues. Women who are able to achieve the male standard of physical fitness are viewed more favorably by male colleagues, compared to women who satisfy only the basic requirements for their gender (Schulze, 2012).

While some agencies have embraced the inclusion of women on the force, women as sworn police officers still experience discrimination and isolation within some agencies. Some male officers still refuse to accept female officers, while others are indifferent to the presence of women on the force. Research indicates that younger male officers and male officers of color are more likely to accept women among the ranks compared to older and/or White officers (Renzetti, Goodstein, & Miller, 2006).

▲ **Photo 12.2** Legal changes have increased opportunities in policing for both women and people of color. Today, police officers reflect a greater diversity among the force than in the past. However, women continue to struggle in this male-dominated field.

Despite the continued increase of women in policing, the majority of these women serve within the general ranks because the upper management positions within agencies are still dominated by men. While court rulings in the 1970s opened the possibilities for promotion for policewomen, few women have successfully navigated their way to the top position of police chief. In 2009, there were 212 women serving in the top-ranking position in their departments nationwide (O'Connor, 2012). Most of these women serve in small communities or lead agencies with a specific focus, such as university police divisions or transit authorities (Schulz, 2003). Within metropolitan agencies (more than 100 sworn officers), only 7.3% of the top-level positions and 9.6% of supervisory positions are held by women. Additionally, women of color make up only 4.8% of sworn officers, and minority women are even less likely to appear in upper-level management positions, with only 1.6% of top-level positions and 3.1% of supervisory roles filled by a woman of color. The situation is even bleaker for small and rural agencies, where only 3.4% of the top-level positions are staffed by women (Lonsway, Carrington, et al., 2002). At the Federal level it wasn't until 2003 that a woman led a major Federal law enforcement agency with the appointment of Karen P. Tandy, who served as the lead administrator for the Drug Enforcement Administration (Schulz, 2004). One explanation for the limited number of women in supervisory positions is that there is low turnover generally in higher ranking positions. Limited turnover means limited opportunities for women and minorities to advance to these positions. In agencies such as the NYPD, there has been an overall reduction in the number of supervisory positions. So even when you have qualified women who score highly on promotion exams, there is a limited number of positions to place qualified candidates (Guajardo, 2016). In some cases, female candidates may be unaware of promotion opportunities (Yu, 2015). Finally, it is plausible that women are choosing not to advance, either due to limited mentoring opportunities or concerns over work-life balance (Harrington & Lonsway, 2004; Schulz, 2004). Indeed, women are more likely to choose to stay in their current positions rather than promote through the ranks due to family issues, compared to men (Rabe-Hemp, 2008). Other studies have noted a lack of mentoring for female officers (Yu, 2015). Such programs would not only assist in the recruitment and retention of female officers but would also create support for officers as they pursue opportunities for career growth and promotion.

Given the historical context of women in policing, it is not surprising that attributes such as compassion, fear, or anything else that is considered *feminine* are historically maligned, particularly by male officers. Given this masculine subculture that exists in policing, how does this affect women who are employed within the agency? What does it mean to be a woman in law enforcement?

Although women in policing have made significant advances over the past century, research is mixed on whether the contemporary situation is improving for women in law enforcement. Female officers today note that the lack of respect by their male colleagues continues to be the greatest barrier for women in law enforcement. A quarter of female officers in Federal agencies state that such negativity is pervasive and makes it difficult to manage daily life on the job (Yu, 2015). While legal challenges have required equal access to employment and promotion within law enforcement, research indicates that many women continue to be *passed over* for positions that were ultimately filled by a male officer. In many cases, women felt that they continually had to prove themselves to their male colleagues, regardless of the number of years that they spent within an organization (Rabe-Hemp, 2012).

In many jurisdictions, female officers acknowledge that sexual harassment by their male peers and superior officers is part of the landscape of policing. Studies note that 40% of Federal officers have experienced sexual discrimination or sexual harassment in the workplace (Yu, 2015). For example, one female officer was often told by a male superior, "Why don't you go home and be a normal woman barefoot and in the kitchen," and another was "slapped . . . across my ass after he told me that he likes women on their knees in front of him" (Lonsway, Paynich, & Hall, 2013, p. 191, 193). Many of these cases go unreported (Yu, 2015). Research indicates that women in higher ranking positions are less willing to tolerate sexual harassment and discrimination. While some younger officers dealt with sexual harassment by avoiding and ignoring the behaviors, others confronted their colleagues in an effort to end such behaviors early in their tenure (Haarr & Morash, 2013). Still, many others ignored the behavior because they feared retaliation or believed that nothing would be done (Lonsway et al., 2013).

Despite reports of discrimination and harassment within their agencies, they acknowledge that the culture of policing has become more accepting to women throughout their careers and that such experiences do not deter them from the field (Yu, 2015). However, these ideals of peace were not easily won and required daily support and maintenance by the women. Female officers reduce the stress of sexual harassment by developing strong social bonds with other officers within their departments (Harrison, 2012). While such an approach may not reduce or eliminate the presence of harassment, it can help mediate its effects. Research by Rabe-Hemp (2008) identifies three additional ways in which policewomen gain acceptance within the **masculine culture** of policing: (1) experiences in violent confrontations requiring the use of force, (2) achieving a high rank within the department structure, and (3) distinguishing themselves as different from their male counterparts in terms of their skills and experience. Female police officers acknowledge that acceptance in the male-dominated police culture often comes with significant costs to their personal life and ideals. In many cases, policewomen talk about putting up with disrespect and harassment in order to achieve their goals. For others, they renegotiate their original goals and settle for "second best."

While the historical acceptance of women in policing was less than enthusiastic, there have been a few trends in policing, which have emphasized characteristics that are traditionally feminine. One such example is the emergence of community policing philosophies in the 1990s, which provided a shift in police culture that increased

Spotlight on Pregnancy and Policing

To date, there is limited research on how many policewomen become pregnant or give birth. When we consider the increasing participation of women in policing, coupled with data that there are 43.5 million mothers in the United States, it is not surprising to think that these two populations would join together (U.S. Census, 2016). Historically, pregnant officers were either forced to take time off without pay or would leave the police force. In 1983, the *New York Times* published an article on the work-life challenges for women in policing. At the time, women made up only 6% of the sworn officers on the NYPD force. The article highlighted that the department had recently come out with a new maternity uniform to accommodate a growing number of women on the force who were pregnant. What was unique about this shift is that the NYPD was the first major police force in the country to create a maternity uniform for its officers (NY Times, 1983). This was significant progress compared to the challenges that pregnant officers had historically experienced. In 1978, two female officers were victorious in a wrongful termination case against the NYPD. Rather than assess whether these officers were able to return to their regular duties on the force following giving birth, the agency disqualified the women on the basis of their status as mothers. Both officers were reinstated and provided back pay (New York Times, 1978).

The Pregnancy Discrimination Act of 1978 prohibits the denial of employment because of pregnancy. Pregnancy is considered a temporary disability under the law and employers cannot discriminate against someone due to a disability. However, many companies and agencies, including police departments, have struggled with how to manage pregnancy for active duty officers. During the mid-1980s, many agencies implemented drug screening tests for both police recruits and current officers as part of their personnel processes. In 1987, police officials in Washington, DC, confirmed that women who applied for positions with the agency were tested for pregnancy without their consent. When testing candidates for drug use, the lab was also directed to test the female candidates to see if they were pregnant. One woman who applied for the position was informed by the agency that she was pregnant and was told that she "would have to reapply after her pregnancy." While the practice of testing female candidates began in 1985 out of concern that the physical training could be dangerous to the woman or her fetus, the practice was never recorded as an official policy, nor were potential candidates notified that they would be screened for pregnancy (Churchville, 1987). Despite concerns that such policies could open the agency up to legal challenges on the basis of discrimination, the practice continued within DC police until the early-2000's. Today, the Metropolitan Police Department allows for limited duty work assignments throughout the course of pregnancy.

In a study on maternity policies from the top 25 U.S. police departments of female sworn officers, Rabe-Hemp and Humiston (2015) noted that while 82% of the departments they surveyed had written maternity policies, a third of these policies were discretionary, meaning that the implementation of the policy was left up to the administration. In addition, only two-thirds of these policies had been updated in the last five years.

In acknowledging the need for policy revision, the Women in Federal Law Enforcement (2011) and the International Association of Chiefs of Police (2010) drafted model policies for agencies, which encourages departments to develop opportunities to retain female officers in meaningful assignments throughout their pregnancies. Examples such as this are evidence of progress toward family-friendly policies in policing. However, there is still work to be done. In 2016, The Justice Department proposed a resolution in a case involving the city of Florence, Kentucky, who was sued by two female officers who were denied a light duty assignment during their pregnancy. Prior to this decision, the department had limited their light duty policy to cases of on-the-job injury. The policy of distinguishing between pregnancy and on-the-job injury for cases of light duty assignments was ruled as discriminatory. Given that many officers today resign from active duty or from policing altogether because of family issues, the implementation of policies on pregnancy, light work duty, and work-life balance is important in ensuring that police agencies have opportunities for pregnant and familied women who wish to continue to serve in the same capacities as they did prior to becoming a parent (Rabe-Hemp, 2011).

the number of women working in the field. The values of **community policing** emphasize relationships, care, and communication between officers and citizens. It allows officers to develop rapport with members of their community and respond to their concerns. Effective community policing strategies have led to improved relationships and respect of officers by residents. Research indicates that policewomen have been particularly successful within models of community policing because of their enhanced problem-solving skills through communication (Lersch & Bazley, 2012). These traditionally female skills serve as an asset to departments that include community-oriented and problem-oriented policing characteristics as part of their mission as well as in dealing with certain offenders such as juveniles and women who have been victimized (Rabe-Hemp, 2009). Even though they may bring a different set of skills to the job, many female officers believe that they do the job just as well as their male counterparts, albeit in different ways. Many female officers argued that their feminine traits served them well on the job. As one officer notes:

> I think they [female officers] are very similar to male officers. They do their job. They just handle it differently. They handle calls differently. Where maybe a male might use strength, I think a female might use strength up here [pointing to her head], you know and strength here [pointing to her mouth]. (Morash & Haarr, 2012, p. 13)

Rather than feel that these female traits made them less competent, some research indicates that female officers believed that their male counterparts appreciated the value of feminine qualities in police work (Morash & Haarr, 2012). For example, women officers may have better relationships with members of their community, have fewer citizen complaints compared to their male counterparts, and are less likely to "jump" to physical interventions (Harrington & Lonsway, 2004; Lonsway, Wood, et al., 2002; Rabe-Hemp, 2009). Feminine traits, such as care and compassion, were also viewed as an asset particularly when dealing with victims, although some female officers resisted the label that they possessed these traits because of their gender (Morash & Haarr, 2012). While feminine traits are viewed as an asset in some realms of policing, some scholars have noted that being perceived as more feminine can also impact mentoring experiences and feelings of job satisfaction. Research by Barratt, Bergman, and Thompson (2014) found that women who exhibited more masculine traits received better mentoring than officers who are viewed as feminine, particularly when they are assigned a male mentor. In addition, officers who are more masculine report higher levels of job satisfaction (Swan, 2016). Such patterns highlight the need for improving both the quality of mixed gender mentoring relationships as well as increasing the number of female mentors.

Gender also impacts how officers approach their job as officers. In addition to the communication and problem solving skills that many female officers use in their daily experiences, women officers are typically not involved in cases of police brutality and corruption. Research indicates that male officers are more than 8.5 times more likely than female officers to be accused of excessive force (Lonsway, Wood, et al., 2002). Female officers are more likely to be engaged in education and service on topics where victims are disproportionately female. Female officers are more likely to pursue education on issues such as sexual assault, while only one-third of officers reported attending more than 30 hours of such specialized education, compared to two-thirds of female officers. Female officers are also more likely to collaborate with victim advocates (Rich & Seffrin, 2014).

Perhaps the most masculine of all policing environments is the SWAT (Special Weapons and Tactics) team. Few women serve in these environments, and their participation within these ranks is a fairly new phenomenon. Because SWAT is one of the most physically demanding assignments in policing, some have suggested that few women possess the abilities to work within such an intense setting (Snow, 2010). Indeed, there are significant barriers (both perceived and real) that limit the number of women who may seek out and accept these types of positions. First, many female officers view SWAT as the pinnacle of hypermasculinity in policing that would exclude women from its ranks. Second, the nature of SWAT includes physical challenges and abilities that may discourage many women from applying. Here, many of the women acknowledged that they believed they would be accepted by the *team* if they were strong enough. Finally, both male and female officers see that women would be challenged by the male SWAT officers and need to prove that they had the skills necessary to do the job, not unlike the early experiences of women in policing:

> I would see it as a constant, day-to-day battle. Any woman in that type of unit would be forced to "do more and do it better" in order to prove herself to the men in the group. This is how women were first initiated into police work, and that type of probative acceptance continues and may even be more pronounced in units such as SWAT. (Dodge, Valcore, & Klinger, 2010, p. 229)

Despite the significant increases that women have made in the realm of policing, female officers are still viewed differently from their male counterparts. For example, female officers often prefer male officers to another female as backup. This may not reflect a distrust of their fellow female officers but rather serve as a way to distance themselves from a feminine identity and reinforce their validity in a male-dominated arena (Carlan, Nored, & Downey, 2011). At the same time, many women still struggle to separate themselves from the stereotypes of days gone by in many ways, in that they are well suited to dealing with cases involving women, children, and victims in general. These perceptions influence not only beliefs about the abilities of female officers but also ultimately have an impact on the types of work assignments that they receive (Kurtz, Linnemann, & Williams, 2012).

Women in Corrections

Correctional officers are a central component of the criminal justice system. Responsible for the security of the correctional institution and the safety of the inmates housed within its walls, correctional officers are involved with every aspect of the inmate life. Indeed, correctional officers play an important part in the lives of the inmates as a result of their constant interaction. Contrary to other work assignments within the criminal justice field, the position of the correctional officer is integrated into every aspect of the daily life of prisoners. Duties of the correctional officer range from enforcing the rules and regulations of the facility to responding to inmate needs, to diffusing inmate conflicts, and to supervising the daily movement and activities of the inmate (Britton, 2003).

Historically, the workforce of corrections has been largely male and White, regardless of the race or gender of the offender. As discussed earlier, the treatment of female offenders by male guards during the early days of the prison led to significant acts of neglect and abuse of female inmates. These acts of abuse resulted in the hiring of female matrons to supervise the incarcerated female population. However, these early positions differed significantly from the duties of male officers assigned to supervise male inmates, and opportunities for female staff to work outside the population of female-only inmates were rare. For those women who were successful in gaining employment in a male institution, job duties were significantly limited. In particular, prison policies did not allow female correctional officers to work in direct supervision roles with male offenders. As in the realm of policing, the culture within correctional occupations reflected a masculine identity, and administrators believed it was too dangerous to assign a woman to supervise male inmates. In male facilities, female guards were restricted to positions that had little to no inmate contact, such as administrative positions, entry and control booths, and general surveillance (Britton, 2003).

Despite the increased access to employment opportunities for women through the 1970s, many female guards resented these gendered restrictions on their job duties and filed suit with the courts, alleging that the restriction of duties because they were women constituted sex discrimination. While many cases alleged that the restriction of female guards from male units was done to maintain issues of privacy for the offenders, the courts rejected the majority of these arguments. In *Griffin v. Michigan Department of Corrections* (654 F. Supp. 690, 1982), the court held that inmates do not possess any rights to be protected against being viewed in stages of undress or naked by a correctional officer, regardless of gender. In addition, the court held that the positive aspects of offender rehabilitation outweighed any potential risks of assault for female correctional officers; therefore, they should not be barred from working with a male incarcerated population. Other cases such as *Grummett v. Rushen* (779 F.2d 491, 1985) have concluded that the pat-down search of a male inmate (including their groin area) does not violate the Fourth Amendment protection against unreasonable search and seizure. However, the courts have held that the inverse gender relationship can be considered offensive. In *Jordan v. Gardner* (986 F.2d 1137, 1992), the court found that pat-down policies designed to control the introduction of contraband into a facility could be viewed as unconstitutional if conducted by male staff members against female inmates. Here, the court held that a cross sex search could amount to a deliberate indifference with the potential for psychological pain (under the Eighth Amendment) given the high likelihood of a female offender's history of physical and sexual abuse.

As a result of equal employment opportunity legislation, the doors of prison employment have been opened for women to serve as correctional officers. Today, women are increasingly involved in all areas of supervision of both male and female offenders, and all ranks and positions today. Many women choose corrections as a career out of interest in the rehabilitation services, as well as a perception that such a career provides job security (Hurst & Hurst, 1997). According to the 2007 Directory of Adult and Juvenile Correctional Departments, Institutions and Agencies and Probation and Parole Authorities, women made up 37% of correctional officers in state adult facilities and 51% of juvenile correctional officers (American Correctional Association, 2007). Within these facilities, both men and women are assigned to same-sex as well as cross sex supervision positions. In addition, more women are working as correctional officers in exclusively male facilities, where they constitute 24.5% of the correctional personnel in these institutions (DiMarino, 2009).

Despite significant backlash and criticism against women in corrections, research indicates that the integration of women into the correctional field has significant benefits for prison culture. First, female correctional officers are less likely than male officers to be victimized by inmates. This finding contradicts traditional concerns that women would be at risk for harm if they were responsible for the direct supervision of male offenders (Tewksbury & Collins, 2006). However, women are more likely to fear victimization by inmates (Gordon, Proulx, & Grant, 2013). Second, women officers are more likely than male officers to use communication skills, rather than physical acts of force, to obtain compliance from inmates. Finally, female officers indicate a greater level of satisfaction from their work than male officers (Tewksbury & Collins, 2006).

How does gender affect the perceptions of work in a correctional setting? As with criminal justice occupations, how do female correctional officers "do" gender in the context of their job duties? Many female correctional officers are hyperaware of their status as women and how gender affects interactions with both fellow staff and inmates. In some cases, female officers utilize skills and techniques that many scholars identify as feminine traits—communication and care for the inmates, mutual respect between inmates and staff, and so on. Female staff members often

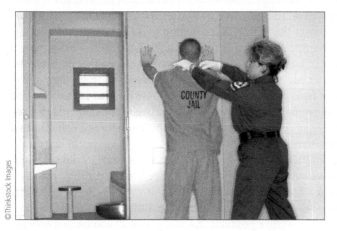

©Thinkstock Images

▲ **Photo 12.3** In the early history of prisons, women were hired to work only with female inmates. In response to equal opportunity policies and lawsuits by women in correctional fields, women today are now assigned to all types of supervision duties within the prison. Here, a female correctional officer engages in a "pat-down" search of an inmate to look for weapons or other contraband items.

become very aware of their physical status as a woman, particularly when working with male offenders, and respond by dressing down, wearing baggier clothing (in facilities where officers are not required to dress in uniform), and donning understated hairstyles and makeup to limit physical displays of gender in the workplace.

Women working in the correctional field are more likely to emphasize the "social worker" aspects of the job, compared to their male counterparts (Stohr, Mays, Lovrich, & Gallegos, 1996). Here, women use their gender to their advantage; by drawing on their communication skills, they are able to defuse potentially dangerous situations before violence ensues. However, it is important to find balance between the feminine traits and masculine traits; too much communication between staff and inmates can be viewed negatively, out of fear that staff will grow too close to an inmate and risk being taken advantage of (Britton, 2003). At the same time, some female correctional officers perceive that they are not promoted because they are viewed as less capable than their male counterparts (Matthews, Monk-Turner, & Sumter, 2010). Research indicates that gender can affect how officers approach their position, regardless of the inmate's sex. For women involved in the supervision of male inmates, their philosophies often differ significantly from that of male officers. For example, Britton (2003) found that, whereas male officers functioned within a paramilitary role and were ready to use force if necessary, women saw their role as mentors and mothers, and they focused on the rehabilitation of the inmates.

Given the increase of the prison population and the opportunities for employment, it is important for facilities to recognize the strengths and weaknesses for women who work in this field and their relationships with the incarcerated population.

However, women still struggle in this masculine, male-dominated environment. Research indicates that female correctional officers are frequent targets of sexual harassment (Chapman, 2009). The **good ol' boy network** remains quite pervasive in many facilities. Many women in leadership positions face significant challenges navigating this culture. For example, as one female officer puts it, "Men will perceive being assertive as a good quality in a guy, [but for women] they will still say, 'oh she's such a bitch.' So you need to couch what you're saying a little differently so as not to offend these poor guys over here" (Greer, 2008, p. 5). However, the perpetration of sexual harassment is not limited to other staff members. Female officers indicate that they experience persistent occurrences of sexual harassment by inmates. However, studies suggest these experiences do not affect female officers' job satisfaction—indeed many accept that incidents of sexual harassment come with the territory of being a woman working in a male-dominated arena (Chapman, 2009).

Given these challenges, are women happy working in the correctional field? Research tells us that women do tend to like their job in corrections more than their male counterparts. This is particularly interesting given that corrections is a male-dominated field, and many women have had to battle for their presence in the correctional setting (Lambert, Paoline, Hogan, & Baker, 2007). There are a number of interacting variables that determine things such as job stress and job satisfaction. For example, female correctional officers report higher levels of job stress than male officers. But what factors influence this stress? Cheeseman and Downey (2012) indicate that women who have low levels of job satisfaction will report higher levels of job-related stress. Even in cases where men and women experience on the job stress, the source of this stress varies by gender. While both men and women relate an increased stress level to lower levels of trust in their supervisor, men are more concerned with their abilities of their supervisor to effectively assess their job performance. In comparison, women are more likely to believe that their supervisors place unreasonable expectations on them and treat them poorly in the context of the work environment (Lambert, Hogan, Altheimer, & Wareham, 2010). Women are also more likely to experience increased stress when they have ambiguity within their role (clear rules and expectations, and an understanding about their authority and responsibilities) (Paoline, Lambert, & Hogan, 2015).

While much of the literature on women in corrections focuses on career trajectories and on the job challenges, some scholars also look at how the inmate population can have gendered implications on the work environment. Inmates often have conflicting perceptions about women working in the correctional field. Studies indicate that on their first interactions, male inmates draw on stereotypical assumptions regarding female officers. Yet women in these positions possess the unique opportunity to offer a positive image of women (Cheeseman & Worley, 2006). In addition, many line officers express disdain when they are assigned to work with female offenders. They suggest that girls are much more difficult to work with than the boys and state that the female inmates are more dramatic, manipulative, needy, emotional, and time consuming. Research by Pollock (1986) provides details on why male and female correctional officers believe that working with women is less desirable than supervising men. While both male and female staff members believe that women inmates are more demanding, defiant, and complaining, male officers also express concerns about being accused of inappropriate behaviors against female inmates. Female officers express that they would prefer to work with male inmates because they feel that they are more likely to be respected and appreciated by the male inmates than female inmates. Belief systems such as these have a significant impact on perceptions of working with female offenders and translate into a belief that working with women is an undesirable assignment (Rasche, 2012). Research indicates that among both male and female correctional officers (and regardless of rank), there appears to be a **male inmate preference**, despite the increased risks for violence associated with this population.

Community Corrections: Female Probation and Parole Officers

While there has been a fair amount of research on women in policing and corrections, the same cannot be said for women who work as parole and probation officers. While probation and parole agents are sworn officials like police officers, their work focuses only on convicted offender populations, whereas police officers deal with the general population as well. Given the high demand on probation services as a tool of the correctional system, it is fair to say that probation officers deal with the largest criminal justice population.

The origins of probation date back to the Middle Ages and English criminal law. In the United States, John Augustus became the first volunteer probation officer in 1841. In 1925, the federal government passed the National Probation Act and established the U.S. Federal Probation Service. By 1951, probation departments were established in every state. One of the earliest female probation officers was Catherine F. Brattan, who has been referenced as the first woman probation officer in California in 1910 (Sawyers, 1922). In contrast, parole was first implemented in the United States by Zebulon Brockway in 1876 and was implemented nationwide by 1942 (Peterselia, 2000) Indeed, like some of the early women in policing, many of these early women in probation and parole were charged with supervising juvenile offenders and, later, female offenders. In 1970, most states limited the caseloads of female parole officers to female offenders. Following the passage of the Civil Rights Act, states began to allow for cross sex supervision (Schoonmaker & Brooks, 1975). In 2012, there were 90,300 probation officers and correctional treatment specialists in the United States (Bureau of Labor Statistics [BLS], 2014). However, it is unclear how many of these positions are held by women.

As you learned earlier in this section, there has been a significant body of work investigating the cultural environment of women in policing and corrections and the challenges that they face. Could the same be said for women who work in probation and parole? Do they face these same challenges in this male-dominated environment? The answer to this question is yes. Research indicates that women in parole have similar experiences with sexual harassment and marginalization as do women in policing (Ireland & Berg, 2008). Working with highly intense populations also means extensive exposure to acts of violence. Over time, this exposure can desensitize probation officers (Petrillo, 2007).

In addition, women experience high levels of stress as part of their job duties. The presence of stress can be found in four different areas of the job: internal organizational stress, external organizational stress, job and/or task-related stress, and personal stress. Research indicates that male and female probation officers experience different categories of stress. Female probation officers register higher levels of physical stress, whereas male probation officers register high levels of internal organization, job-related, and personal stress. However, each of these types of stress was greater for officers in supervisory positions (and men were more likely to serve in these roles). At the same time, it is possible that women have lower registered levels of stress because they are more likely to be aware of the early warning signs of stress and take action (Wells, Colbert, & Slate, 2006). Despite this, many women acknowledge that these stressful on-the-job experiences often spill over into their lives. Much of the literature on criminal justice occupations (such as policing and corrections) focuses on the masculine nature of these careers and the challenges that women face within these environments. However, literature on parole officers indicates that female officers utilize gendered strategies as part of their management strategies. Like female police officers, communication skills were invaluable in the daily aspects of their job as a parole officer. As one female parole agent expressed,

> We have to have good communication skills; we have to be able to recognize volatile situations; and you have to be able to know how to handle those situations by using your communication skills. I have been involved in situations that could have easily turned volatile, but my manner, my demeanor, my communication skills, and the manner in which I dealt with these individuals has made a very big difference in the way they have responded to me. (Ireland & Berg, 2008, p. 483)

Developing rapport with their clients was also an important skill that contributed to their on-the-job safety. While male officers were more likely to use force in their cases (a reflection of their identity with policing), female agents aligned themselves with a social worker mentality, which allowed for more of a rehabilitative focus (Ireland & Berg, 2008). Particularly in cases where female officers were involved in supervising male offenders, gender became a way to challenge the offender's perceptions and stereotypes about women. However, male offenders would often challenge these female officers, using tricks from intimidation to flirting to regain some power over the situation. At the same time, their interactions with these offenders gave a unique insight as to how victims experience interactions with these offenders, particularly in cases of intimate partner violence and sexual offenses (Petrillo, 2007). In addition, female officers emphasized the role of respect between themselves and their parolees as a way to manage their caseload. "Parolees, if you treat them well and you do your job, even when you have to lock them up, they will respect you and understand that you are just doing your job. If you treat them like a piece of crap, that's what you're going to get back" (Ireland & Berg, 2008, p. 485).

While parole officers appear to engage in cross-sex supervision, probation officers are often assigned caseloads that are specialized, such as around a particular offense (drug crimes, sexual offending), need (mental health treatment), or gender of the offender. Since female probation officers are more likely to be assigned to supervise female offenders, this creates an opportunity to engage in gendered strategies. While these approaches reflect the needs of the offender, it may also be related to how officers do their job. For example, female officers are more likely to engage with their clients on an emotional level and build relationships with their clients. In this way, the probation officer serves as a positive role model for her clients (Wyse, 2013).

Conclusion

At the heart of the research for each of these fields, two major themes emerge: (1) Gender can affect the way in which women who work in these fields satisfy the demands of their positions, and (2) gender affects the experiences that they have within their jobs. These factors are multiplied for women of color, whereby race serves as yet another variable through which discrimination and other challenges can persist. For some of the most masculine positions, such as policing and corrections, women must fight against firmly held beliefs that such jobs are inappropriate for women. While equal employment opportunity legislation has opened the doors for access for women in these traditionally male-dominated fields, women still face an uphill battle because they have been denied opportunities and promotions throughout history. Despite these struggles, women remain an important presence in these fields with significant contributions that need to be encouraged and acknowledged, particularly for future generations of women in these fields.

/// SUMMARY

- Traditional male occupations, such as policing and corrections, historically excluded employment options for women on the grounds that the work was too dangerous.

- Early policewomen were involved in crime prevention efforts, primarily with juvenile and female populations.

- While equal opportunity legislation may have opened access for women in policing and corrections, institutional cultures and standards continued to create barriers for women in these occupations for entry and advancement.

- Women in police, corrections, and community supervision use different tools and techniques in their daily experiences in their positions, compared to male officers.

- Few women have successfully navigated to the top levels of their fields in law enforcement and corrections.

- As workers in these fields, women are subjected to issues with job satisfaction, stress, and burnout.

- There are more females employed in probation than any other law enforcement or correctional environment.

/// KEY TERMS

Baldwin, Lola 516

Blankenship, Betty 517

Civil Rights Bill 518

Coffal, Liz 517

Community policing 522

Gendered assignments 517

Good ol' boy network 525

Griffin v. Michigan Department of Corrections 523

Grummett v. Rushen 524

Jordan v. Gardner 524

Male inmate preference 526

Masculine culture 520

Owens, Marie 516

Wells, Alice Stebbins 516

/// DISCUSSION QUESTIONS

1. Based on the research, how do women do gender within traditional male-dominated criminal justice occupations?

2. What challenges do women who work in criminal justice occupations face that their male counterparts do not?

3. What suggestions can be made to improve the status of women within criminal justice occupations?

/// WEB RESOURCES

American Correctional Association: http://www.aca.org

Association of Women Executives in Corrections: http://www.awec.us

National Center for Women and Policing: http://www.womenandpolicing.org

 Visit **study.sagepub.com/mallicoat3e** to access additional study tools, including eFlashcards, web quizzes, web resources, video resources, and SAGE journal articles.

READING /// 23

As you learned in the section, many women in policing experience sexual harassment on the job. As a minority in this male-dominated occupation, the source of this harassment often comes from within the department. This article by Robin Haarr and Merry Morash explores how women police officers deploy coping strategies in addressing issues of workplace discrimination and harassment and how these strategies differ based on their rank within the organization.

The Effect of Rank on Police Women Coping With Discrimination and Harassment

Robin N. Haarr and Merry Morash

Numerous studies show that police women experience particularly high levels of coworker and supervisor gender-related prejudices, stereotyping, discrimination, and harassment (e.g., Brown & Grovel, 1998; Franklin, 2005; Hassell & Brandl, 2009; Morash, Haarr, & Kwak, 2006; Rabe-Hemp, 2008, 2009; Seklecki & Paynich, 2007). As a result, they receive less social support on the job (Davis, 1984; Fry & Greenfield, 1980; Greene & del Carmen, 2002; Morash & Haarr, 1995; Worden, 1993). Research on multiple occupations confirms very negative outcomes of such gender-related prejudice and discrimination on health and productivity of female employees (McDonald, 2012). For instance, women who feel they have not been promoted at work due to gender bias disproportionately suffer poor health (Nelson, Campbell Quick, Hitt, & Moesel, 1990; Nelson & Quick, 1985; Morrison & Glinow, 1990), and sexual harassment contributes to poor physical and mental health and symptoms of post-traumatic stress disorder (Willness, Steel, & Lee, 2007). Work-related stress additionally contributes to the negative organizational outcomes, including low productivity, turnover, and absenteeism (Cooper & Payne, 1988; Cooper, Kirkcaldy, & Brown, 1994; Moyle & Parkes, 1999; Parker & Sprigg, 1999; Parkes, 1990; Willness, Steel, & Lee, 2007).

Substantial scholarship carried out to test and develop a seminal psychological theory, the transactional theory of stress and coping (Lazarus & Folkman, 1984), focuses on coping with stressful interactions at work (and elsewhere). Transactional theory explains whether and how individuals perceive actions as harassment or discrimination, and how they react when they see such negativity. Even though the theory includes propositions linking status-related resources to people's vulnerability to perceived stressors (Fitzgerald, Hulin, & Drasgow, 1994), few studies have considered how status affects women's reactions to gender-related affronts at work.

When research conducted within a variety of theoretical frameworks explores women's responses to negativity at work, it usually ignores women's heterogeneity in characteristics such as status in the workplace (Gyllensten & Palmer, 2005). Thus, the present qualitative study provides detailed information on how, during their careers, policewomen differing in rank responded to negative coworker actions and attitudes toward women. Nationally, the proportion of sworn police who are women remains small, at 11.8% overall, though differently sized jurisdictions vary, and women make up 18.1% of sworn police in the 10 largest cities (Sourcebook of Criminal Justice Statistics, 2010). The most recent available

SOURCE: Haarr, R. N., & Morash, M. (2013). The effect of rank on police women coping with discrimination and harassment. *Police Quarterly, 16*(4), 395–419.

statistics show that women are further underrepresented in police promotions to high ranks (National Center for Women in Policing, 2002; Silvestri, 2006). One study (Silvestri, 2007) demonstrates that women in police leadership tend to promote transformational change more than men. Of particular interest in the present study is whether the power that comes with rank leads policewomen to take on unique approaches to addressing discrimination and harassment, thereby having unique effects on police organizations.

Such knowledge has utility. Over time, perhaps as they gain rank and experience, women officers may shift toward using previously untried or unavailable methods of confronting and changing hostile work environments. Rank brings legitimate and expert power (French & Raven, 1959) that may enable women to confront gender-related problems at work. Alternatively, particular coping strategies may enable women to move up in rank within a department, or may cause the retention of women and thus their longer tenure (Rabe-Hemp, 2009). Thus, the research can provide insight into whether or not rank frees women to confront undesirable workplace conditions in particularly effective ways, or whether certain approaches to coping with bias against women characterize those who obtain high rank. The study may illustrate the organizational benefits of having an increased number of women in leadership positions within a very male-dominated organization and occupation, and the personal advantages of some forms of coping for achieving high rank.

Relevant Literature

Research establishes two broad categories of response to stressful workplace interactions—addressing the event and disengaging from it (Compas, Connor, Saltzman, Thomsen, & Wadsworth, 2001). Addressing problematic interactions includes expressing emotions, trying to control these emotions, or trying to stop such events from occurring again to avoid being a future target of prejudice (Miller & Kaiser, 2001). Based on a review of the relatively limited prior research, Kaiser and Miller (2004) concluded that women typically do not confront perpetrators or tell people in a position of authority about even blatant discrimination or prejudice. However, these findings have

questionable generalizability to women with rank and/or tenure in police departments. Many study samples in prior research consisted of young college students. Higher status women and women working in an occupation such as policing, which requires assertiveness to, for example, make an arrest or direct people in an emergency, may behave quite differently.

In addition, interaction with and observation of other female employees in the workplace and repeated harmful events at work appear to shape responses to harassment and discrimination. Seasoned employees' model, support, or teach alternative responses. The effect is to influence less seasoned employees to shift away from avoiding or disengaging and toward more direct efforts to stop negative events (Lazarus, Dunkel-Schetter, DeLongis, & Gruen, 1986; Lazarus & Folkman, 1984; Tomaka, Blascovich, Kelsey, & Leitten, 1993). In addition, research suggests that over time, women who observe pervasive discrimination change their reactions from disengagement to active strategies (Foster, 2009).

Understanding contemporary policewomen requires data collection in contemporary agencies. In a unique recent study of the connection of tenure to police women's workplace experiences, Rabe-Hemp (2008) found that even though women with 10 to 30 years as police described negative early-career events, with time they found acceptance by coworkers and many moved up substantially in rank. She emphasized that in recent years, women with rank and tenure experience less extreme forms of antiwoman behavior than police in previous times, and that in some departments "enlightened men" grew in number and the "boys club" weakened (p. 263). Changes in workplace stressors, women's increased rank, and more women with longer tenure create a fairly complex, recent departmental context in which to examine women's experience of and coping with stressors emanating from gender harassment and prejudice.

Research on occupations other than policing suggest that occupational status and position within a place of employment affect how women respond to negative work environments. Specifically, the female–male differences in coping strategies for confronting stressors at work found in some research (Gianakos, 2000, 2002; Parasuraman & Cleek, 1984; Vitaliano, Russo, Carr, Maiuro, & Becker, 1985) are not confirmed in studies that compare

Race-ethnicity	Rank	
	Low rank $n = 13$	High rank $n = 8$
Caucasian	2 (15.4%)	6 (75.0%)
African American	3 (23.1%)	2 (25.0%)
Latina	5 (38.5%)	0 (0.0%)
Asian	3 (23.1%)	0 (0.0%)
Years on the force		
6 to 8 years	3 (23.1%)	0 (0.0%)
10 to 15 years	6 (46.2%)	3 (37.5%)
17 to 20 years	2 (15.4%)	4 (50.0%)
30+ years	2 (15.4%)	1 (12.5%)

Table 1 • Race-Ethnicity and Years on the Force by Rank for Sample of Female Police Officers

women and men with similar positions, occupations, and education (Greenglass, 1988; Korabik & Van Kampen, 1995; Long, 1990; McDonald & Korabik, 1991; Torkelson & Muhonen, 2004). Rank and type of occupation may empower women to use a greater range of strategies. For instance, in one study, compared to clerical workers, women in managerial positions had more resources for coping with stress at work, felt more control over workplace stressors, and more directly addressed problems (Long, 1998). Our emphasis on responses to negative work experiences of women currently employed as police, but varying in rank as well as tenure, contributes to prior work on both police and other occupations through its focus on rank and changes that women describe over the course of their careers.

Method

Sample

Study participants included 21 police women from two departments in a metropolitan area of a southwestern (U.S.) state. The participants ranged from 6 to 31 years tenure working as police, though some had changed departments during their career. The sample was purposively diversified to provide variation in rank and tenure. So that study participants could talk about several years of experience as police and some would have achieved relatively high rank, the purposive sample was limited to women with at least 6 years on the force. Efforts also were made to have a sample that was diverse in race and ethnicity to reflect the study setting, two departments in a metropolitan area of a southwestern state. The final sample included eight White, five Latina, five Black, and three Asian women. Despite efforts to have each racial and ethnic group represented equivalently in the subgroups differentiated by rank and tenure, primarily for Caucasian women, among the study participants, more years in policing translated into being at a higher rank. Black women were less likely to have moved up in rank despite their years on the force. Although Latinas had been employed for several years, none held higher ranking positions. They were least likely to have advanced in rank over time. Asian women were relatively new to police work, so they were concentrated in low ranks.

To recognize the unique identity and social location of each woman we quote in the section on findings, we note her description of her racial and ethnic identity in addition to rank and tenure either in the text or in parentheses after long quotes. Also, each woman is identified with a unique number so that it is possible to see whether the same or different women are quoted at various points throughout the manuscript.

Data Collection

Haarr conducted the in-depth, career-course interviews with each of the 21 women. The structured interview schedule of open-ended questions (appendix) asked for detailed information about women's experiences and the positions and ranks from their entry into the training academy to the present, the effects of gender and race and ethnicity on their work life, their experiences with discrimination and harassment, and their strategies for coping with workplace problems. In answering questions, some women disclosed their lesbian sexual orientation and explained its effect on experiences at work, so this information is noted in findings when it is relevant to women's stressors. Note that appropriate probes were added to the basic schedule during the interview process to obtain as complete a narrative of career experiences as possible. Also, study participants often provided information unprompted by particular questions, and these responses became part of the data.

The present article focuses on responses to questions in three specific information domains covered in the interview: *discrimination in police work* (e.g., coworker questions about capabilities to do the job, overprotection or failure magnification by coworkers, being made to feel inadequate by coworkers, and limited career opportunities); *harassment in the workplace* (e.g., unwanted and inappropriate comments, sexual and racial jokes, and sexual harassment); and *coping strategies* (e.g., self-identified strategies for coping with workplace discrimination and harassment). Since the study concerned women's subjective perceptions, the questions and follow-up probes allowed and encouraged participants to elaborate on their experiences.

Participants chose the interview locations, which included the police agency and the researchers' home and office. Most interviews took about 2 hours, and all were tape recorded with participants' consent and transcribed verbatim.

Analysis

Repeated review of the transcripts led to inductive identification of a wide variety of approaches that women had used to cope with instances of workplace discrimination and harassment. Women did not always associate the use of a coping approach with a point in their career or a period when they held a certain rank, but when they did, we coded the coping approach to reflect whether it was used in the academy, while assigned to a training officer, after the completion of training, while a sergeant, or after promotion to a position higher than sergeant. We also coded passages to reflect whether women associated an approach with the first years on the force or the period after they had worked as police for several years.

Several analytical approaches were used to shed light on how rank was related to the methods women used to cope with a negative work environment. First, we counted the number and the types of coping approaches for women differing in rank and the potentially confounding, associated characteristic, years in policing. Also, for each of the primary coping strategies analysis examined the career points the strategy was associated with for low- and high-ranking women, for example whether the strategy was used while in the academy, working as an officer, after promotion to sergeant, after promotion to higher ranks, after many years in policing, or more generally across the career. Finally, we examined women's statements about how their approaches to coping with workplace affronts changed over time, and how gaining power (through rank or tenure) affected their coping methods. The aim was to draw on these multiple types of information to contextualize and lend credibility to findings.

High-ranking women held positions of lieutenant, commander, and deputy chief. Low-ranking women were sergeants, held specialized positions such as Drug Abuse Resistance Education (DARE) officers, and worked on patrol. All women with 8 or fewer years on the force were at the lower rank, and five of the eight women (62.5%) with 10 to 15 years were at the lower rank. Of the nine women with 17 or more years of experience, five (55.5%) were high rank. When women explicitly tied their years on the force or their rank to a coping strategy, it was possible to present their assessments of whether rank, tenure, or both influenced the choice of strategy. In addition, we note the connection of the primary strategies to both current rank and to tenure to show whether strategies are connected to each.

The analysis focused on the most commonly used coping strategies for either or both low- and high-ranking women. Small numbers of women in both groups used other strategies, such as seeing a psychologist (one person), refusing to do certain tasks (three), and hiding their emotions (two). These less frequent approaches were not our focus. Consistent with the intersectional nature of gender, sexual orientation, race, and ethnic group identity and related discrimination (Bolton, 2003; Hassell & Brandl, 2009; He, Zhao, & Ren, 2005; Morash et al., 2006; Morash, Haarr, & Gonyea, 2006; for nonpolicing jobs, see Bowleg, 2008), women sometimes spoke of combined reasons for their negative treatment (e.g., race and gender), so findings presented below reflect this reality.

Findings

The presentation of findings first covers the number of different strategies women described using and differences by rank and tenure. Then it presents common strategies that women used regardless of rank. The section on common strategies is followed by findings associated with either low or high rank. The discussions of each coping approach include study participants' insights into how rank or tenure influenced their choice of strategy.

Number of Strategies

Especially if they had higher rank or long tenure, women reported using many different approaches to addressing perceived discrimination, prejudice, and harassment. Of the high-ranking women, 75% had used seven, eight, or nine different coping approaches, whereas over 75% of the low-ranking women had used between four and six different strategies.

Common Strategies

Straight Talk. Nearly all women (85.7% or 18) described voicing their concerns and criticisms in "straight talk" when they felt mistreated due to gender, race, or ethnicity. A slightly higher proportion of high-ranking women than those with low rank described using this approach (100.0% of the eight high-ranking, and 76.9% of the

13 low-ranking women). Consistent with findings for rank, just two of the four women with 8 or fewer years of police experience described using straight talk, and all but one (94.1%) of the women with 10 or more years of police experience gave examples of how they used "straight talk."

Women defined straight talk as being direct and standing up to their male coworkers and, when confronted with hostility, even "giving it right back to them" (#8, White, high rank, 17–20). Consistent with research in other settings (Kaiser & Miller, 2004, p. 168), they directly confronted discrimination, for instance by saying that a remark was "discriminatory" and "objectionable." A high-ranking woman (#4, White, 10–15 years) described using straight talk when male colleagues would not let her do parts of her job,

> And I would have to remind them, you know what? Let me do this. I don't need your help and if I do I'll call you, but let me do it. But I didn't take it as they were trying to keep me from doing my job. They just do it all. [Q: What effect did that have though when you would say let me do it?] [They would say] okay, okay, okay go ahead and do it. Most of them would back right off. But I would have to be really, really aggressive to get them to back off.

Most accounts of straight talk pertained to actions of coworkers and supervisors during police work on the streets. Three quarters of the eight high-ranking women and almost half of the 13 low-ranking women had used straight talk to address problems that arose when doing patrol work.

An even higher proportion (seven of eight) of high-ranking women talked about using straight talk to stop sexual and racial jokes and inappropriate comments (i.e., about personal life and physical appearance). They described telling male coworkers they did not appreciate such jokes and comments and that they should not tell such jokes or make such comments again. A high-ranking officer explained, "I'd say, I'd prefer that you not say that. It didn't make me feel demeaned or degraded. It just, to me, is inappropriate and it's not appropriate in the workplace" (#13, Black, 10–15 years). She further explained, "It made me feel like I was standing up for all the women of the world, and I know that sounds so canned, but if we don't speak up for each other, who's gonna speak up for us?" Another high-ranking officer (#21, White, 17–20 years) similarly reacted to sexual jokes or comments demeaning to women and to racial jokes. For instance, she said, "Nice joke, but would you tell this to your mother? Would you tell this to your wife? And then people are like, ugh, sorry."

Five of the eight high-ranking women spoke about using straight talk in their role as a supervisor. One explained how she addressed racially offensive comments,

> I would usually pull somebody aside and say, hey, what you said back there is blah, blah, blah. If somebody made a racial comment in a group setting and say I'm a sergeant and it's a briefing and it—all officers, you know, they criticize people in public. I would, so, criticize in public. Hey, I don't know if you think that's appropriate, but let me set the record straight for everybody. That is not appropriate, and the next time I hear you say that, you and I will be sitting in my office, and you'll be getting a notice of investigation. That will not fly here. Got it? (#21, White, 17–20 years)

In addition to rank, tenure seemed to enable women to impose their standards for behavior on other officers. An Asian woman (#1, low rank, 10–15 years) explained that if an incident similar to a superior saying early in her career that she joined the force to find a husband occurred now that she was a sergeant, which she had protested at the time by having a discussion with her superior, would lead to a simpler, more direct comment: "I would basically say, 'you're out of line.'" Early in her career, a high-ranking officer (#12, White, 30+ years) ignored coworkers' calling her "baby" and "gorgeous." She attributed her growing intolerance of this behavior to maturity, having the "guts," awareness of how inappropriate this was, becoming a supervisor, and knowledge of women's suits for harassment against departments nationwide. She took on responsibility for training on sexual harassment and EEO (Equal Employment Opportunity legislation) in the organization, leading to her handling of incidents very directly. She confronted a man who called her "baby,"

I had a peer at my rank currently who called me gorgeous every time he saw me. Finally, I stopped him one day and said, you know, that makes me very uncomfortable. Don't do that. [He said,] well, I call everybody that. And I'm like, you don't call me that. Not anymore. (#12, White, 30+ years)

With time on the job, one woman (#11, Latina, low rank, 10–15 years) became bold enough to change from having "a little discussion" after men were sent to do jobs that were her responsibility to usually talk to the supervisor hoping for the response, "Yeah, you're right, I didn't give you a chance. Next time, I'll give you the opportunity."

Besides a higher proportion of high-ranking women mentioning using straight talk when they were supervisors, a higher proportion described using straight talk early in their careers (75.0% rather than 46.2%). Also, a higher proportion provided descriptions of straight talk that they did not tie to any specific career stage (75.0% vs. 30.8%). Possibly straight talk enabled women to move up in rank, and that rank gave them the power that comes with supervisor status to use straight talk to make changes.

Alternatively, harassment and discrimination may have been so much worse in past years, when females first started performing patrol work, that women felt they had to confront issues directly. Two high-ranking women talked about the concentration of problems with "overprotection" in their earliest years of employment. Two others talked about extreme overt discrimination; in one case, a superior officer indicated that no decent women would become police officers, and in another a superior ordered an officer not to be seen with her sister, who provided transportation to work, because the sister had an "afro" hair style that the superior thought others would see as a sign of radical group membership.

Hard Work and Good Work to Prove Abilities to Do the Job. The same proportion of women that used straight talk, and the majority of women in both the high- and low-rank groups, described how at some point or at multiple points, they worked hard to prove they could do police work when others questioned their capabilities. Indeed, 17 of the 21 officers told us about using both straight talk and hard/good work. In the group with 8 or fewer years' experience, in the middle experience level group, and in the group with 17 or more years, over three quarters of women described how they confronted harassment and discrimination with hard work and efforts to prove their worth as police.

Regardless of rank, several women spoke of moments when they demonstrated their physical capabilities. A woman (#6) with low rank, who joined the department as one of the first minority women 30 years before, hid the pain caused by a recent Caesarian delivery and went on a run at the training academy. When she tripped over an obstacle, she tore out her stitches and required hospitalization. She believed her superiors would not care "whether or not I came to them with my little sympathetic stories, well, I just had a baby, I had a C-section." She thought they'd just conclude, "You can't handle this, you need to go home."

Women recruited more recently talked about less extreme conditions in which they felt they had to prove their physical similarity to men, for example by being athletic enough to excel in the academy's physical training, or jumping into fights and making arrests while on patrol. One woman recalled,

> It was very easy [to prove my physical capabilities]. I just kind of threw him on the ground and got on top of him, handcuffed him, rolled him over, stood up, and took him to the back of my car. That's what you hope for [the opportunity to prove yourself physically] because you get your chance and then they [male coworkers and supervisors] get to learn that they didn't need to think that you're gonna fail." (#21, White, high rank, 17–20 years).

One officer who held a high rank at the time of the interview (#8, White, 17–20 years) described how early in her career, she sought out opportunities to demonstrate her physical capability to make a resisted arrest, "And I know women that wanna get it over with early, so just jump in, or you know, or go to that physical-arrest mode quicker instead of finding the easy way, the other way, the better way. Because you wanna prove that you can do it." She recognized that she had better ways to handle resisted arrests than by physically overpowering the citizen, but she conformed to perceived pressures to show she could and would physically restrain someone.

Consistent with prior research on police women (Martin & Jurik, 2007), multiple women told of repeated "tests" and "retests" scattered throughout their careers in which they were called on to assuage other police officers' doubts that they had the abilities and emotional makeup needed for police work. Nine of them used the term, "test," to describe how coworkers prodded women to show whether females, in some cases specifically minority females, could be effective police. Particular tests determined whether they would make correct decisions, bear gruesome scenes, command a squad, or avoid preferential treatment of citizens of the same minority group as themselves. One officer (#19, White, low rank, 10–15 years) said that after a stint as a DARE officer, "I better be able to scale the fence. That's the bottom line. I better be able to chase those bad guys down. I better be able to perform as I did when I was on patrol six, seven, eight years ago." A high rank officer with over 30 years on the force (#12, White) said, "But every new job I ever had, it was like starting over and proving again, okay, I can be in this fight, I can run this mile, I can go over this wall, I can do whatever." Only one woman (#6), a Black, low rank officer with over 30 years on the force, felt her good reputation followed her after she protected a White coworker from a threatened attack by a group of Black men early in her career, and then worked with street gangs and the confrontation squad. More typical, a high-ranking officer (#4, White, 10–15 years) witnessed repeated testing of women. She asked the interviewer, "Do we do that to the men?" She answered the question herself, "No!"

Consistent with the prevalence of repeated testing, half of the eight high-ranking women felt they proved their capacity to make decisions and use police powers, and a quarter said they demonstrated their ability by getting a graduate university education. One (#2, Black, 17–20 years) indicated that especially women needed more than an undergraduate education to "compete" and be successful "in spite of who you are," since sometimes "people judge us by gender and by race." The time order of proving oneself and moving up in rank was not necessarily that rank came after "proof." For instance, one high-ranking Black woman (#13, 10–15 years) explained that whenever being Black and female enabled her to get a promotion, "I've always proven that I was the best fit for the job."

Putting Up With the Stressful Work Environment. Two-thirds of women told of times when they dealt with negative conditions by just putting up with them. There was no clear relationship of tenure in the department to whether women described this strategy during the interview (three or 75% of women with 8 or fewer years of experience, four or 50% of women in the middle experiential group, and six or 66.7% of those with 10 or more years). However, nearly all women talked about "putting up" as a coping strategy early in their careers, particularly during academy and field training as well as the probationary period, to cope with inappropriate and unwanted comments, sexual and racial jokes, and sexual harassment. Two examples from several high-ranking women who looked back at these periods and reflected on their reasoning and the results follow,

> I'm on probation, so I'm concerned about retaliation, and so a lot of times that is a big important factor. You don't have the department's support. I believe you can be discriminated against, but you won't seek help because of fear of retaliation. (#2, Black, 17–20 years)

> Actually, most of the time, back in the first year or two, especially when you're on probation, it was a silent anger. And other internalized anger, because I wasn't sure I belonged here, and maybe I too was looking for how I fit in. And really, I had to spend some time, even though I'd get angry, well are they right? Do I not belong here? Can I not do this? I'm much better at verbalizing now than I was back then. I mean, back then, I was just pretty grateful that they let me work here at all. (#12, White, high rank, 30+ years)

This study participant went on to say she attributed her earlier nonconfrontational stance to the period when women working on the force "was a real change and for everybody, I mean, we were all finding our place, and there were no clear lines of what was right and what was wrong." Other high-ranking officers explained that at the beginning of their careers, they wanted to fit in and be accepted by their coworkers, or they desperately needed the salary that police work provided, so they put up with affronts.

The low-ranking officers, many of whom were relatively new to the force, did not mention unclear guidelines for appropriate behavior toward women police. They instead echoed concerns about getting through the academy, being accepted, and "not causing waves." For instance, one woman reasoned,

> We were all under so much stress, and I'm thinking, is this really important? Is this something worth mentioning? I don't know where I should go with this and we didn't have a female RTO [Recruitment Training Officer]; I didn't feel comfortable talking to my RTO about it. I just didn't feel like, it really didn't bug me. At that point, I just wanted to keep my nose clean and not do anything to screw up my chances of getting through the [academy] because I had already been through hell." (#5, Asian, low rank, 6–8 years).

Another low-ranking woman said, "You just laugh it off, just do not make a big deal of it, because you don't want to cause waves, because you know if you do, the guys would find out and they would turn against you" (#20, White, low rank, 6–8 years).

Mentors. About half of the women talked about mentors' assistance in addressing negative work situations and department or academy environments. Women's comments about having or using a mentor varied little based upon rank or years on the force or on the career point they were talking about. Instead, there were similarities in women's descriptions of the important qualities that mentors possess (e.g., the ability to listen; and having a positive influence on one's career by assisting them with career planning, career advancement, and workplace problems). Mentors often served as people that a woman could "bounce ideas off of" and that could help them "to critically look at situations."

Most accounts of how mentors affected women illustrated how mentors encouraged or enabled women to challenge existing arrangements. Even in the training academy, one officer's (#21, White, high rank, 17–20 years) mentor advised her to further her career advancement by not staying too long in any assignment; later in her career, another mentor put her in situations where she could develop her teaching and training skills. One officer (#14, Latina, low rank, 6–8 years) regarded her husband as a mentor because he pushed and encouraged her to seek promotions. A woman (#18, White, 10–15 years) who now held a high rank said her female mentor helped her by demonstrating a "we're [women are] gonna make a difference attitude." Another person's mentor helped her when she complained that her coworkers were "beating the shit out of me" (#4, White, high rank, 10–15 years) by saying, "just stay the course because some day they'll all be working for you." Some mentors intervened with administrators to improve women's treatment at work. One low-ranking woman (#6, Black, 30+ years) described her mentor's intervention:

> I call him my rescuer. He used to kinda be like my savior. It was just one thing after another and I was always whining and complaining that they were doing this to me, they were doing that to me, and he was kind of a center for me. I would call him anytime I had a problem, and he helped me through the crisis or because he had some rank [Lieutenant]. He would talk to other people of rank and say, you know, they're doing this to her and I don't think this is really right. As a matter of fact, he helped me a lot, so he was kind of like my mentor.

In many ways, mentors counteracted or contradicted disempowering responses of other people to women. In addition to serving as listeners and advisors, mentors modeled what women could achieve, suggested to women that they could "make a difference," and gave advice, opportunity, and encouragement about career advancement that could place women in positions of influence.

Strategies of Low-Ranking Women

A common strategy noted by several low (61.5% or eight of 13) but few high-ranking women (25.0% or two of eight) was accepting help and protection from male coworkers. The longer women worked as police, the less likely they were to present acceptance of help and protection from men as one of their strategies for coping with harassment and discrimination. Specifically, 75%

(three) of the women with the least tenure, 50% (four) in the middle group, and 44.4% (four) with 10 or more years said that they used this approach at one or more points in their careers. Interestingly, three of the four high-ranking women who described using this strategy said they avoided using it earlier in their careers, but relied on it at some points after moving up in rank, often to deal with physical challenges that became harder with age, for example when confronted with an obstacle course at the National Law Enforcement Training Academy.

Low-ranking women discussed their willingness to accept help from their male coworkers during the training period and while working patrol. For instance, one woman (#10, Black, 17–20 years) appreciated that her training officer treated her like a daughter, "kind of gingerly and like, I'm gonna get you through everything." Another (#7, Latina, 30+ years) recounted that both at the beginning of the career and recently, she appreciated men helping her to carry things, or helping her in other ways, saying "The more help, the better."

Another officer noted that early in her career she took offense and rejected her male coworkers' attempts to help her. Later in her career, particularly when she became a patrol sergeant, she was much more willing to accept male coworkers' help. She viewed their willingness to help her as a compliment, a reflection of the fact that she was part of a patrol working group.

> Well, I used to be very offended—I can take care of myself, I can open my own door. Yeah, that guy's starting to back talk to me, but I can take care of the situation. Just leave me alone. So, I would talk to them later about it and say, quit doing that, don't do that, I can take care of myself. Now when somebody disrespects me or talks back to me or shows any kind of aggression and a guy steps in, honestly, I take that as a compliment. So, I kind of changed my way of thinking. I don't know if it's because of the supervisor thing [her status as a sergeant], because officers will come in and step in and defend their supervisor. So, I don't know if it's that or even as an officer, towards the end I'd have some officers that would say, we're your partner and we got along great, and they'll

defend you. I took it as a compliment." (#11, Latina, 10–15 years).

Another woman explained,

Depending on what's going on, I might say I'll go in first or I'll do a search, but it depends. Sometimes it feels good to have a big guy go in the door first and have me watch his back. So, it just depends. But you know, opening the car door, I don't get mad if they do that. Walking next to be on the curb so a car would hit him, not me. I think a lot of it is more how they [male coworkers] were raised or brought up, and I think a lot of it is the military. Three of the men I can think of off-hand are all military guys; that's just the way they are." (#20, White, low rank, 6–8 years)

Strategies of High-Ranking Women

Compared to low-ranking women, a higher proportion of those at high rank used three coping strategies: (a) avoid and disengage from problem people, situations, and departments (75% of high and 46% of low-ranking women), (b) rely on their own definition and assessment of themselves as police officers (87.5% of high vs. 23.1% of low-ranking woman), and (c) use unions, legal counsel, or formal grievances to address workplace problems (62.5% of high vs. 15.4% of low-ranking women). Women with 10-plus years of experience more often coped with negative work conditions through avoidance and disengagement; but there was no clear pattern of differences related to years employed in policing either for self-definition and assessment, or for reliance on formal sources of help.

Avoid and Disengage. Avoidance ranged from being person and situation specific, such as avoiding interactions with certain officers, to changing one's career, for instance by changing jobs in a department or by getting a job in another department. Starting with the more specific actions, one low-ranking officer who used this approach (#1, Asian, 10–15 years) left the room every time her colleagues began to tell offensive jokes. A woman who held a high rank had become a DARE officer earlier in her career so she could avoid spending time with the "Neanderthals" in her department (#4, White, 10–15

years). Most extreme in our sample, one officer (#11, Latina, low rank, 10–15 years) transferred to another department when she realized that as a female, she "wasn't going to go anywhere in that department."

> The mentality was you can work sex crimes, you know, deal with all the child issues, you know, the police force officers, you know, all the positions they feel a female should be able to handle. Other than that, you will never take on a supervisor role. You know, you can be in charge for a little while, but [not] to make any major decisions let alone any type of any tactical situations.

Avoiding interactions, changing jobs, and changing departments allowed women to act in their best interests and resist and escape negative treatment and biases. One high-ranking woman explained how she looked into leaving the police department to cope with a supervisor that was discriminating against her. As she told it,

> I finally put him [her supervisor] on ignore a lot. I looked into the Secret Service and my commander finally stepped up and started putting a buffer in between us and eventually when rumor got around that I had applied for the Secret Service, I got called up to the chief's office and he gave him a direct order that he was never to speak to me again. (#4, White, high rank, 17–20 years)

Another high-ranking woman (#18, White, 10–15 years) took a demotion after the chief made it clear that he would not force early retirement for a superior officer who was biased against her. Later, she was repromoted to Lieutenant. Similar to the process of self-defining that is described next, getting out of bad situations and interactions or refusing to participate in selected interactions insulated women from negative effects and placed them in a more positive work environment. Such actions did not, however, seem to alter the negative work environment by making it more positive for women in general.

Self-Define and Assess. Rank also differentiated the women who challenged notions of policing and their organizations by deciding for themselves what constituted quality police work, and therefore deciding that they were very able police officers. Several of them described their independence and strength. For example, one officer said that as one of just two girls in a family with seven siblings, she didn't like being a girl growing up, but now "I'm a strong Black woman and it's, I don't know, what can I say, it's phenomenal to be a woman now, you know." She went on to explain her relationship with coworkers:

I think it was just the living with those guys for eight years or so. And all the, I say, trauma that they put me through and you know, and then just deciding, you know, that I am here, and I'm a force to be dealt with and you're gonna deal with me whether you wanna deal with me or not. We may not come out of here friends, but you know what, I'm here and I'm not leaving just because you don't want me here. (#6, Black, low rank, 30+ years)

Another officer similarly noted her independence from her coworkers,

I got to a place a long time ago where it's my mirror that matters in the morning. How I see myself, whether I know I've done what's right, whether I know I'm doing a good job, whether I know if I can still like myself in the morning. I'm really okay with that. And I'm a real people person, and I used to really be needy, need to be loved, need to be liked, need to be about everybody, and I learned that doesn't work. (#12, White, high rank, 30+ years)

She went on to describe a period when all but two people in the department avoided her and criticized her for being single and pregnant, claiming she would never be promoted and that she was a poor role model for women. At that point, she realized "you are really on your own." As a result, she said, "I will not leave myself open to relying on other people." In her eyes, lacking a mentor was "very good for my career" because,

I have done it on my own and people, people don't accuse me anymore of getting jobs because

I'm a girl, because of who I know, because of who I've slept with, because of whatever the reasons may be. What did my boss call me? A free agent or something.

Women equated defining themselves and recognizing their worth with having confidence in their abilities and not allowing others to define or belittle them.

Women used self-definition to cope with negative comments. One said, "I know that I know how to do the job, no matter what people say about me. It's okay, because I am very confident with me. I know what I'm doing and what I'm not doing, so most of the time I'll just laugh it off" (#13, Black, high rank, 10–15 years). She added, "I've learned to really know me and to like me and my strengths and weaknesses, and my abilities and inabilities." One high-ranking woman (#2, Black, 17–20 years) explained how not allowing other people to "define" her and the roles she could have in her career gave her more control, "I know that others will define you if you allow them to define you, but others don't have control over you. I have no more control over your life than you have over mine, until I allow you to have control." Women talked about how they gained confidence in their strengths and abilities over time, often by meeting challenges, for example by resisting a supervisor's efforts to "make me quit."

More than one of the women who "self-defined" and "self-assessed" clarified that this strategy evolved over time. They rejected dependence on others for approval and acceptance. For instance, one said,

You can't worry about how and what everybody thinks. You have your group of people that matter to you and those are the people that are your friends, and those are the people that you go and move toward, try to be a good person, try to be a reputable leader. Try to do those sorts of things and maybe you wake up intermittently and go hey, I'm doing pretty good. I suppose it's in the back of your mind to get to this point and to be respected, but I think it's something that will be a by-product of all these other good behaviors. (#15, White, high rank, 17–20 years)

This officer developed self-sufficiency when she spent less time with colleagues due to the time demands of returning to school. She found,

> I was happy because I was meeting my own needs and I was recognizing the priorities that I had for myself. I think that kind of brings you into an evolution of you don't need the judgment of others to make you happy, as long as you yourself judge yourself as doing what you do well. Then you're okay.

Formal Action. One-third (seven) of the women had taken at least one formal action (e.g., filing a grievance or report of inappropriate coworker actions, seeking assistance from a union or attorney, suing the department). The proportion was much higher for the high-ranking women (five or 62.5%) than those at low rank (two or 15.4%). The specific formal actions and the number taking each one were: report the problem to a supervisor (five); threaten to file a complaint with the EEO Office (two); hire an attorney and sue the department (two); and report the problem to the union (one). During their careers, women sometimes used more than one formal action to deal with one or more workplace problems. Just one of the four women with the least years on the force had taken formal action compared with three of the eight with 10 to 15 years, and three of the nine with over 15 years.

It is possible that discrimination was so common when women with many years on the force or with rank (groups that often overlapped) began their careers, no alternatives to formal action existed for intractable problems. Two women, including one who still was at a low rank at the point of the interview, reported hiring an attorney and suing the department for discrimination, in one case allegedly due to gender and sexual orientation, and in the other because of sexual orientation. The officer who attributed discrimination to both gender and sexual orientation said,

> There was no state statute for the law or anything to protect gays and lesbians. And they [the police department] were actually quoting different individuals from throughout the state that had been fired for that reason. So, I knew my life

was over. The chief at the time said to an officer that he was going to rid the department of all the lesbians and that he could start with [officer name], meaning me. You know, I'm just this little person. What have I ever done to deserve this? And I mean it was just a terrible dark, dark time in my life. This went on for about six months and I really wanted to quit. We ended up basically suing the department for my civil rights violations, contract violations, because what happened between she [her female partner] and I had no effect on my ability to perform a job as a law enforcement officer. And that was our contention, that what happens inside the home shouldn't affect who I am inside the building. But the department didn't see it that way, and they didn't care. (#19, White, low rank, 10–15 years)

When asked what happened, she went on,

> We started all the depositions and it's interesting because when we started deposing some of the other command staff, a lot of dirt started surfacing on these other people and suddenly they wanted to settle. We met with the city attorney. They finally said king's axe [King's X] we give up. You know, we're gonna stop this, just bring [officer's name] back to work now. We're gonna sweep this all under the carpet, pretend it never happened. So, we went into this meeting and signed all these contracts that I would not reveal any of this to the media. That it's all gone away and I was gonna go back to work with no discipline on my record and all that. So, I'm literally signing these contracts and at the same time they're physically driving my file down to the state governing board. They delivered it to them requesting that they review it because they thought my certification should've been stripped. So even though I'm signing these contracts saying it's all over and it's forgiven, they're still behind the scenes sending this down to say, well, now strip her of her certification. That's evil. We found that out and my attorney turned to one of the lieutenants and

said, you know, we're done playing with you guys. I'm taking you off at the knees. And he started the whole process again of litigation. But, it was resolved. The department later came out with a policy reference: We would not discriminate against sexual orientation.

More typical, five women formally complained to supervisors about sexual harassment and discrimination by coworkers. One (#15, high rank, 17–20 years) said that after she complained, her sergeant retaliated by giving her bad reviews and practicing karate chops while they talked, and that she knew that someone was going through her desk on a regular basis. She handled this by leaving a closed folder with EEO federal guidelines for reporting sexual harassment on her desk, after which she felt there was a "buffer" for her to get through the hostility. Nonresponsive supervisors and officials often limited the change that women could effect through formal actions, but formal actions did offer protection or escape from particularly egregious harassment and bias.

Over half (58.3%, or seven) of the 12 women who avoided and disengaged from people and situations that they viewed as discriminatory also had taken some formal action during their careers. Formal action was evoked by the most negative experiences women had; avoiding and disengaging may have served as self-protection through these difficult experiences or as an earlier strategy that was not fully effective. For example, the woman (#4) who volunteered to work as a DARE officer to avoid interaction with the "Neanderthals" in her department eventually decided that she could not develop a meaningful career in the restricted roles available to her. She therefore joined another department where she could be a "street cop," which was her goal. It is important to recognize that, consistent with Foster (2009), women often use a mixture of strategies to address negative work conditions and they shift to formal actions when other approaches fail.

Discussion

The research location and the small purposively chosen sample limit generalization beyond participants. Another limitation of the research was that the sample size precluded examining sergeants as a separate, middle-ranking

group. Findings of differences in coping between women at different ranks may have been even clearer if we had been able to consider finer distinctions in rank. Finally, it may be that policies and procedures have reduced workplace problems to those that women did not bring up as forms of discrimination and harassment. Despite these shortcomings, the detailed data, which pertained to the prerecruitment period to the time of the interview for each woman, and the variation in rank and tenure allowed us to compare and examine coping approaches by point in career and by current rank. More broadly, the findings suggest that when transactional theory is used to guide research designed to increase understanding of gender and the workplace, it is essential to consider the status of workers as an element that may explain the use of certain strategies as well as the effects of using certain strategies.

High rank characterized the women who avoided and disengaged from negativity at work, who relied on their personal sense of worth and belief in their capacity to do police work to confront coworkers who treated them badly, and who resorted to official actions when bias was especially extreme. These strategies provided some individual-level protections from assaults on their identities and, in some cases, staved off some of the negative treatment they received. The findings complement research results (Morash & Haarr, 2012) showing that women police officers value their own characteristics and often do not passively accept coworkers' attacks on their positive sense of self. However, with the possible exception that some departments took steps to avoid being sued for failing to abide by EEO legislation, none of these strategies forced permanent or widespread organizational changes.

Especially as they gained rank and tenure, but for high proportions of all the groups of women we compared, speaking one's mind to coworkers seemed to stop affronts by individuals in the officers' immediate context, which sometimes was limited to an officer's interactions with just one person. Consistent with the hierarchical nature of a police department, women's span of influence increased when they used straight talk as supervisors, at which point they often used it to end sexual and racial jokes and inappropriate comments by a group of officers. However, again, even with an increased span of influence, these strategies did not ensure lasting changes throughout the organization.

Using straight talk from the start of a career in policing may enable some women to move to high rank.

Relying on help from male officers early in the career may impede moving up in rank. Further exploration of the effects of coping strategies early in career is needed to reach conclusions that have more generalizability than ours. Empirical evidence and theory to explain why women are so underrepresented at the higher ranks of police is very limited, and often focuses on individual characteristics of women officers (Archbold & Hassell, 2009; Archbold, Hassell, & Stichman, 2010; Dick & Metcalfe, 2007). However, such research has potential to show how the interaction of antiwoman contexts in police departments with women's coping approaches explain how and why only a small proportion of women move up in rank. It may, therefore, show that organizational conditions that require women to "cope" are the problem, combined with how they do cope, rather than individual propensities and characteristics of women.

Most women seemed to abandon simply putting up with harassment and bias after their earliest years in policing. In contrast, even if they gained rank and tenure, most women felt compelled to repeatedly respond to other officers' tests of their abilities by working hard and working well to prove their abilities. Smaller proportions received help from mentors, especially in steering themselves along a successful career path in police departments, but in a few cases in challenging existing organizational practices. All of the findings together lead to our conclusion that the women who took part in our research do double duty as they repeatedly demonstrate their abilities. However, straight talk and the magnification of its effects that result from moving up in rank increase the scope of the interactions and behaviors they can influence and the standards they can set for other officers. Moving up in rank also is associated with relying on one's own view of self and ability as an officer, though it is not clear whether this reliance produces promotions or results from them.

Our findings illustrate that police departments like those where the interviewed women worked remain highly gendered. Women had special problems due to bias and harassment, and except for putting up with them, usually at the beginning of their careers, they coped with these through multiple individual means. The present study did not consider collective approaches to making change, and that focus is an important area for future research. At the level of the individual, the ongoing nature of men "testing" women officers and women's responsive efforts to prove themselves, and the need to use straight talk to confront discrimination, or to withdraw from group interactions and rely on oneself for evidence of capability, indicates the persistence of the gendered nature of the organizations. Aker (1990, p. 146) described the gendered organization as marked by "advantage and disadvantage, exploitation and control, action and emotion, meaning and identity . . . patterned through and in terms of a distinction between male and female, masculine and feminine." The small proportions of women with influence that is increased by high rank most likely severely limits women's ability to address persistent gender discrimination and just how far a police department can deviate from a heavily gendered organization.

The demands on police women to individually work to change negative work conditions and constantly prove themselves, and the known negative results of such demands, show the need for more widespread organizational leadership to free women to focus their energies on doing police work rather than contending with coworkers. The unchanging small proportion of women constituting police forces and holding leadership positions most likely impede this type of organizational change. Recent national statistics on trends in the proportion of police who are women and who hold high rank, however, are generally unavailable, especially for small departments. This lack of data makes it difficult to show failures or successes in hiring, retention, and promotion of underrepresented groups, and thus impedes the development of effective policies.

/// DISCUSSION QUESTIONS

1. Discuss some of the strategies that women used to cope with instances of sexual harassment and discrimination.

2. How did the coping strategies differ for low ranking women compared to high ranking women?

What types of behaviors were most frequently experienced by female police officers?

2. Discuss the similarities and differences between gender harassment, unwanted sexual attention, and quid pro quo harassment.

3. What are the different outcomes that female officers experienced when they reported sexual harassment by a fellow officer?

References

Acker, J. (1990). Hierarchies, jobs, bodies: A theory of gendered organizations. *Gender & Society, 4*, 139–158.

Archbold, C. A., & Hassell, K. D. (2009). Paying a marriage tax: An examination of the barriers to the promotion of female police officers. *Policing, 32*, 56–74.

Archbold, C. A., Hassell, K. D., & Stichman, A. J. (2010). Comparing promotion aspirations among female and male police officers. *International Journal of Police Science & Management, 12*, 287–303.

Bolton, K. (2003). Shared perceptions: Black officers discuss continuing barriers in policing. *Policing: An International Journal of Policing Strategies & Management, 26*, 386–399.

Bowleg, L. (2008). Bringing home more than a paycheck: An exploratory analysis of Black lesbians' experience of stress and coping in the workplace. *Journal of Lesbian Studies, 12*, 69–85.

Brown, J., & Grovel, J. (1998). Stress and the woman sergeant. *Police Journal, 71*, 47–54.

Compas, B. E., Connor, J. K., Saltzman, H., Thomsen, A. H., & Wadsworth, M. E. (2001). Coping with stress during childhood and adolescence: Problems, progress and potential in theory and research. *Psychological Bulletin, 127*, 87–127.

Cooper, C. L., & Payne, R. L. (1988). *Cause, coping, and consequences of stress at work*. London, UK: Wiley.

Cooper, C. L., Kirkcaldy, B. D., & Brown, J. (1994). A model of job stress and physical health: The role of individual differences. *Personality and Individual Differences, 16*, 653–655.

Davis, J. A. (1984). Perspectives on policewomen in Texas and Oklahoma. *Journal of Police Science and Administration, 12*, 395–403.

Dick, G., & Metcalfe, B. (2007). The progress of female police officers? *International Journal of Public Sector Management, 20*, 81–100.

Fitzgerald, L. F., Hulin, C. L., & Drasgow, F. (1994). The antecedents and consequences of sexual harassment in organization: An integrated model. In L. Fitzgerald, C. L. Hulin, & F. Grasgow (Eds.), *Job Stress in a changing workforce: Investigating gender, diversity, and family issues* (pp. 55–73). Washington, DC: American Psychological Association.

Foster, M. D. (2009). Perceiving pervasive discrimination over time: Implications for coping. *Psychology of Women Quarterly, 33*, 172–182.

Franklin, C. A. (2005). Male peer support and the Police culture: Understanding the resistance and opposition to women in policing. *Women and Criminal Justice, 16*, 1–25.

French, J. R. P., & Raven, B. (1959). The bases of social power. In D. Cartwright & A. Zander (Eds.), *Group dynamics* (pp. 150–167). New York, NY: Harper & Row.

Fry, L., & Greenfield, S. (1980). An examination of attitudinal differences between police women and policemen. *Journal of Applied Psychology, 65*, 123–126.

Gianakos, I. (2000). Gender roles and coping with work stress. *Sex Roles, 42*(11/12), 1059–1079.

Gianakos, I. (2002) Predictors of coping with work stress: The influences of sex, gender role, social desirability, and locus of control. *Sex Roles, 46*(5/6), 149–158.

Greene, H. T., & del Carmen, A. (2002). Female police officers in Texas: Perceptions of colleagues and stress. *Policing: An International Journal of Police Strategies & Management, 25*, 385–398.

Greenglass, E. R. (1988). Type A behavior and coping strategies in female and male supervisors. *Applied Psychology: An International Review, 37*, 271–288.

Gyllensten, K., & Palmer, S. (2005). The role of gender in workplace stress: A critical literature review. *Health Education Journal, 64*, 271–288.

Hassell, K. D., & Brandl, S. G. (2009). An examination of the workplace experiences of police patrol officers: The role of race, sex, and sexual orientation. *Police Quarterly, 12*, 408–430.

He, N., Zhao, J., & Ren, L. (2005). Do race and gender matter in police stress? A preliminary assessment of the interactive effects. *Journal of Criminal Justice, 33*, 535–547.

Kaiser, C. R., & Miller, C. T. (2004). A stress and coping perspective on confronting sexism. *Psychology of Women Quarterly, 28*, 168–178.

Korabik, K., & Van Kampen, J. (1995). Gender, social support, and coping with work stressors among managers. *Journal of Social Behavior and Personality, 10*(6), 135–148.

Lazarus, R. S., & Folkman, S. (1984). *Stress, appraisal, and coping*. New York, NY: Springer.

Lazarus, R. S., Dunkel-Schetter, C., DeLongis, A., & Gruen, R. (1986). The dynamics of a stressful encounter: Cognitive appraisal, coping, and encounter outcomes. *Journal of Personality and Social Psychology, 50*, 992–1003.

Long, B. C. (1990). Relation between coping strategies, sex-typed traits, and environmental characteristics: A comparison of male and female managers. *Journal of Counseling Psychology, 37*, 185–194.

Long, B. C. (1998). Coping with workplace stress: A multiple-group comparison of female managers and clerical workers. *Journal of Counseling Psychology, 45*, 65–78.

Martin, S. E., & Jurik, N. C. (2007). *Doing justice, doing gender: Women in legal and criminal justice occupations.* Thousand Oaks, CA: SAGE.

McDonald, P. (2012). Workplace sexual harassment 30 years on: A review of the literature. *International Journal of Management Reviews, 14,* 1–17.

McDonald, L. M., & Korabik, K. (1991). Sources of stress and ways of coping among male and female managers. *Canadian Journal of Administrative Sciences, 8,* 231–238.

Miller, C. T., & Kaiser, C. R. (2001). A theoretical perspective on coping with stigma. *Journal of Social Issues, 57,* 73–92.

Morash, M., & Haarr, R. N. (1995). Gender, workplace problems, and stress in policing. *Justice Quarterly, 12,* 113–140.

Morash, M., & Haarr, R. N. (2012). Doing, redoing, and undoing gender: Variation in gender identities of women working as police officers. *Feminist Criminology, 7,* 3–23.

Morash, M., Haarr, R. N., & Gonyea, D. P. (2006). Workplace problems in police departments and methods of coping: Women at the intersection. In C. M. Renzetti, L. Goodstein, & S. L. Miller (Eds.), *Rethinking gender, crime & justice: Feminist readings* (pp. 213–227). Los Angeles, CA: Roxbury.

Morash, M., Haarr, R. N., & Kwak, D. H. (2006). Multilevel influences on police stress. *Journal of Contemporary Criminal Justice, 22,* 26–43.

Morrison, A. M., & Von Glinow, M. A. (1990). Women and minorities in management. *American Psychologist, 45,* 200–208.

Moyle, P., & Parkes, K. (1999). The effects of transition stress: A relocation study. *Journal of Organizational Behavior, 20,* 625–646.

National Center for Women and Policing. (2002). *Equality denied: The status of women in policing: 2001.* Los Angeles, CA: Author.

Nelson, D. L., & Quick, J. C. (1985). Professional women: Are distress and disease inevitable? *Academy of Management Review, 10,* 206–218.

Nelson, D., Campbell Quick, J., Hitt, M. A., & Moesel, D. (1990). Politics, lack of career progress, and work/home conflict: Stress and strain for working women. *Sex Roles, 23,* 169–183.

Parasuraman, S., & Cleek, M. A. (1984). Coping behaviors and managers' affective reactions to role stressors. *Journal of Vocational Behavior, 24,* 179–193.

Parker, S. K., & Sprigg, C. A. (1999). Minimizing strain and maximizing learning: The role of job demands, job control, and proactive personality. *Journal of Applied Psychology, 84,* 925–939.

Parkes, K. R. (1990). Coping, negative affectivity, and the work environment: Additive and interactive predictors of mental health. *Journal of Applied Psychology, 75,* 399–409.

Rabe-Hemp, C. E. (2008). Survival in an "all-boys club": Policewomen and their fight for acceptance. *Policing: An International Journal of Police Strategies and Management, 31,* 251–270.

Rabe-Hemp, C. E. (2009). POLICEwomen or PoliceWOMEN? Doing gender and police work. *Feminist Criminology, 4,* 114–129.

Seklecki, R., & Paynich, R. (2007). A national survey of female police officers: An overview of findings. *Police Practice and Research, 8,* 17–30.

Silvestri, M. (2006). Doing time: Becoming a police leader. *International Journal of Police Science & Management, 8,* 266–281.

Silvestri, M. (2007). "Doing" police leadership: Enter the "new smart macho." *Policing & Society, 17,* 38–58.

Sourcebook of Criminal Justice Statistics. (2010). Retrieved from http://www.albany.edu/ sourcebook/pdf/t1682010.pdf

Tomaka, J., Blascovich, J., Kelsey, R. M., & Leitten, C. L. (1993). Subjective, psychological, and behavioral effects of threat and challenge appraisal. *Journal of Personality and Social Psychology, 65,* 248–260.

Torkelson, E., & Muhonen, T. (2004). The role of gender and job level in coping with occupational stress. *Work and Stress: An International Journal of Work, Health and Organizations, 18,* 267–274.

Vitaliano, P. P., Russo, J., Carr, J. E., Maiuro, R. D., & Becker, J. (1985). The ways of coping checklist: Revisions and psychometric properties. *Multivariate Behavioral Research, 20,* 3–26.

Willness, C. R., Steel, P., & Lee, K. (2007). A meta-analysis of the antecedents and consequences of workplace sexual harassment. *Personnel Psychology, 60,* 127–162.

Worden, A. P. (1993). The attitudes of women and men in policing: Testing conventional and contemporary wisdom. *Criminology, 31,* 203–241.

READING /// 24

As in policing, women in corrections have been the minority within an occupation dominated by men. While the number of women in corrections has increased significantly in lower ranks, there continues to be few women in the upper ranks. What factors impact their success in moving up the chain of command? This article uses qualitative research methods to assess the factors that female correctional officers perceive have limited their opportunities to promote to upper level positions.

Promotional Opportunities
How Women in Corrections
Perceive Their Chances for Advancement at Work

Cassandra Matthews, Elizabeth Monk-Turner, and Melvina Sumter

Women are in a distinct minority among correctional officers, especially at more advanced ranks; however, Lambert et al. [22] projected that women would soon comprise [sic] half of the correctional workforce. In 2005, male correctional officers outnumbered women by a ratio of 2:1 [30]. The greatest gender disparity in correctional officers was at federal facilities where only 13% of correctional officers were women; however, in state facilities, women accounted for 26% of all correctional officers [30]. Much research in criminology and criminal justice has explored the representation of women in corrections; however, less work examines how women themselves perceive their opportunities for advancement in the field of corrections.[1] This work aims to add to this growing body of research.

The first female to head a correctional facility in the United States was Mary Weed [26]. Weed filled her husband's position as warden of Philadelphia's Walnut Street Jail after his death, serving as warden from 1793 to 1796 [26]. Traditionally, females served in administrative and clerical roles within the correctional field in gender segregated facilities. In 1970, California became the first state to employ female correctional officers in male institutions [29]. By 1978, Jurik [18] reported that thirty-three states

assigned females to work as correctional officers in males' prisons. By the end of the 1980s, the integration of female officers in male institutions had occurred in almost every system [5, 12, 29].

Prior research has documented that women who work in corrections face negative perceptions by coworkers, problems in being a token "woman" within the correctional hierarchy, harassment, and balancing a home life with a work life [6, 19, 24]. Griffin et al. [15] argued that female correctional workers tend to be perceived negatively by male co-workers and supervisors. Especially in institutional settings, some employees hold the perspective that females cannot perform the job as well or in the same manner as their male counterparts [3, 4]. On the other hand, there is also the perception that females who work in corrections are more of a nurturer or caregiver compared to males [3]. In fact, Crewe [8] maintained that male correctional officers "tend to perceive female officers as a calming, moderating, and a normalizing force, in effect suggesting that certain 'feminine' traits may be advantageous to prison officer work" (397). Further, Crewe [8] argued that male officers oftentimes feel protective of female officers, suggesting "that females are naturally less capable than men at doing the job" (397). In

SOURCE: Matthews, C., Monk-Turner, E., & Sumter, M. (2010). Promotional opportunities: How women in corrections perceive their chances for advancement at work. *Gender Issues, 27*, 53–66. Copyright © 2010, Springer Science+Business Media, LLC. Reprinted with permission.

the field of corrections, such perceptions could negatively impact success, suggesting that women were too soft, pushovers, or in need of protection by others [3].

In addition to negative perceptions, harassment at work is a central concern for women in corrections. Griffin et al. [15] found that male officers viewed females who enter corrections as subject to ridicule, discrimination, and harassment. In fact, Savicki et al. [28] argued that harassment from coworkers was a primary reason people left the field of corrections. Examples of harassment include but are not limited to sexual jokes, sexual innuendos, and/or unwanted physical touching. Savicki et al. [28] found that females in the correctional field were likely to experience sexual harassment in this male-dominant environment [28]. They found that "gender was at least four times as likely to be identified as the primary source of harassment over race, national origin, and religion" (611). Similarly, Kim et al. [20] maintained that female correctional officers encounter sexual harassment from both male prisoners and male co-workers. Likewise, Rader [27] argued that women experience sexual harassment, sexual innuendos, and verbal abuse from male prisoners. Such harassment may affect work performance and self-esteem which impacts promotional opportunities [24, 27, 31].

Female correctional officers face unique problems in balancing work and home life [14]. Cassirer and Reskin [6] argued that employed women continue to feel responsible for domestic work and child care [1, 16, 18]. Lambert et al. [21] concluded that work and family roles remain unbalanced, especially for women in corrections, because these roles are in conflict. Lambert et al. [21] argued that "correctional officers may treat their spouses and children like inmates, barking orders to them and questioning their activities" (148). Further, Lambert et al. [21] maintained that if women correctional officers do not successfully balance home and work roles, then their chance of obtaining a promotion are reduced. Further, given the responsibilities of "home work," some women may not wish to seek promotions since advancement at work would most likely entail less flexible work hours and additional work responsibilities [21].

Promotional Opportunities

Goodman et al. [13] argued that the higher the percentage of lower level management jobs filled by women, the more likely an organization will have women in top management positions. Goodman et al. [13] also found that high turnover in management tended to increase the likelihood that women would be in top management positions. Further, women were more likely to be in top management positions if organizational salaries were lower than average [13]. Notably, if an organization emphasized promotion and development, then the chances of having more females in management increased [13].

Maume [23] found that women managers had fewer promotional opportunities in female than male-dominated job environments. Notably, women who worked with men were more likely to be promoted than those who worked mostly with other women. Maume's [23] work is essentially at odds with Kanter's [19] reasoning that gender promotional gaps should be widest in male-dominated work environments. In sum, Maume [23] argued that promotional opportunities came easier for white men than others. Specifically, Maume [23] said one could think of "a glass escalator' for white men, a 'glass ceiling' for others . . ." when conceptualizing promotional opportunities by gender and race (483).

The glass ceiling hypothesis proposed than [sic] an invisible barrier blocks women's upward mobility into the higher reaches of occupational hierarchies [17, 25]. England and Farkas [10] explored structured mobility ladders or internal labor markets. Their work expanded the discussion of promotional gaps by recognizing that mobility opportunities in certain jobs are structurally restricted. In other words, regardless of the quality of work one does or individual motivation to advance at work, the chances for upward mobility are poor if the ladders to advance within the organization are not in place [9]. The primary focus of this study is to better understand how women who work in corrections perceive promotional opportunities in the field (both community and institutional).

Methods

This work utilizes a qualitative method in order to better understand how women perceive promotional opportunities in corrections. After gaining human subject approval, semi-structured phone interviews with women who work or have worked in community and/or institutional corrections in the state of Virginia were conducted between December 2007 and June 2008. Initially, a gatekeeper was identified which allowed us to gain access to additional women who worked in the field. Thus, from this key individual, a snowball sample ensued. Individuals in the sample represent women who work in city, federal, and state correctional facilities. Further, they include women who work at various ranks within corrections including correctional officers, managers and supervisors, and directors.

Each of the women identified agreed to be interviewed. To maintain confidentiality, names, descriptive characteristics of the participants, and the organization they previously or currently worked for were not collected during the interview process. Also, each respondent was given a pseudonym. Each participant was advised at the beginning of the conversation that the information provided would remain confidential. Participants were also advised, and all agreed, that the interview would be taped. Data were collected using a semi-structured interviewing schedule. Respondents were asked a series of questions in order to better understand how women perceived promotional opportunities in the field of corrections. Focus centered on better understanding perceptions regarding promotion in general, how gender differences in the workplace shaped perceptions of promotional opportunities, how women felt about harassment issues at work, and how they perceived problems in balancing home and work life.

Limitations of Methods and Data

Qualitative research techniques allow researchers to better understand problems from the point of view of those offering the information or data. Instead of asking many respondents a multitude of questions, usually with closed-ended response options, qualitative researchers aim to collect more detailed data from a relatively few individuals. The goal in qualitative work is to get to the heart of the matter at hand—to really understand something well as opposed to a superficial gloss of a problem. Thus, qualitative work typically relies on small samples, which poses a thorny issue for methodologists; however, as Creswell [7] writes, one really understands qualitative methods when they know that there is no answer to the question of how large the sample should be. Thus, the primary focus of this work is to better understand, from the perspective of a few female correctional officers, how they understand and feel about opportunities for advancement at work. Clearly, by opting to gather detailed information from a few respondents, this work rests on a convenience sample that was not randomly drawn. Therefore, it is important for the reader to keep in

mind that the experiences of these women cannot be generalized to the population of all female correctional officers. Nevertheless, the richness and complexities of experiences these women have related help us all better understand issues related to women's advancement in corrections.

Findings

Of the fourteen women interviewed, the median age was 46 with a range of 34–65 years old. Equal numbers (6 each) of respondents identified their racial background as white and African American/black. One respondent identified as Asian and another in the other race category. One respondent reported being single, another was single but in a monogamous relationship, seven were married, another was separated, and four were divorced. The vast majority (12) of participants had children. The age of these women's children ranged from 7 to 37, with the average age being 24. All but one participant had received their bachelor's degree; the participant who had not received her bachelor's degree will be graduating later this year.

When asked about their experience with the Department of Corrections, all fourteen work or have worked within the state department. Two women work or have worked in the federal system, and one of the fourteen works or has worked in the local government. Ten women work or have worked in the institutional section of corrections, and another five work or have worked in the community corrections field.

Promotional Experiences

Most (10) of the women in the sample had been promoted at least once while employed in the correctional field. Of the four participants that had not been promoted, each said "yes" when asked if they foresaw promotional opportunities in the future. When asked why they perceived promotions in their future, most said that they had satisfied a requirement necessary for a promotion such as additional training to gain more experience or more education. When the ten participants that had been promoted were asked if they expected additional promotions, one did not give an answer, while four said "yes," three said that they were "unsure" and two said "no" because both were retired.

When asked if there had ever been any person that they felt deserved a promotion but did not receive one while working in the correctional setting, thirteen of the participants said "yes." Most respondents felt that deserving individuals had not been promoted primarily because the process was political and that, for women, the odds of being promoted were simply against them because of their gender. For example, Jennifer said, "It does help to know the right people." Lucy and Marcia said that promotions can be "political;" specifically, Lucy said that "as I changed positions, it seemed to get more political." Likewise, Marcia stated, "It seems whenever a new opportunity comes available, you have to play the game, it's all politics." The participant, Sarah, who said "no," had the following answer, "I feel that everyone that gets a promotion deserves it for one reason or another."

Most (12) respondents felt men had greater promotional opportunities compared to women. Only two women felt promotional opportunities were equal between the genders. None of the respondents felt that women have greater opportunities for promotions in the correctional setting.

Respondents felt men were promoted more than women because they dominated supervisory and managerial positions. For example, Paige stated, "Men [receive more promotions because], they're more dominant in the field." In agreement, Marcia stated, "I would say males because they outnumber the number of women in corrections." Others responded that men knew the right people and that there is a "stigma that women cannot do the job as well as a man." For example, Sarah stated,

> If I had to choose, I would say men. First, because they do dominate the field and secondly, because they usually have that seriousness to them and can be more intimidating to others and a little more forceful in getting a job done.

Jody agreed with the idea that men might be promoted more because they were perceived as capable stating,

> From my experience I've seen more men be promoted than women but I don't think that necessarily means that men have more chances than women, I think they might fill the shoes a little better.

When asked if a promotion was important to them, all of the participants said "yes." For example, Kelly explained, "Yes [promotions are important], I want to keep climbing the ladder and try to encourage others to do so." Charlotte echoed similar sentiments when she said, "Yes, [promotions are important], I like the money and responsibility and I'd like more of both."

To better understand how the type of job held shaped a woman's feeling about promotional opportunities, responses were broken down into several broad categories. Of the fourteen respondents, ten were in a higher position of authority (positions ranged from director to assistant director to assistant superintendent to manager to supervisor). All of these women supervised others (management positions). The other four women in our sample were correctional officers (and one intake counselor) with no supervisory responsibilities (general positions).

Within the "general position" group, all saw a promotion in their future. Each said that in order to get this promotion, more training or education was needed. Four women in management positions were unsure about further promotions (three were unsure, one did not answer, and two were retired). Everyone except Natasha, who was classified as being in a general position, reported that they knew someone who desired a promotion but did not get it.

Of the fourteen respondents, the two (Kelly and Britney) who thought that men and women had equal opportunities for advancement were both in a general position. The other twelve felt that men have a greater chance of receiving a promotion. Again, the recurring theme as to why men had greater opportunities for promotion than women was that men simply outnumbered women and that there is and always would be a stigma that women cannot do the job as well as men.

Interactions With Others at Work

Respondents were asked about the amount of interaction while at work with male co-workers. All of these women worked with both men and women on a daily basis; however, the majority of interactions while at work were with men. For example, Jennifer stated that she worked

> "pretty much daily [with women], but we're always outnumbered by the men." Another participant, Lucy, said, that she worked with women "pretty frequently. But there was always more interaction with men."

Most interactions with men at work were strictly professional; however, some respondents were friendlier with male officers because a friendship was formed outside of work. For instance, Kelly (in a management position) stated,

> They're [her interactions with men are] almost always kept professional but there are a few men I work with that I became friends with outside of work and those usually are more friendly.

Another interviewee, Paige (in a general position), said,

> There are some officers that intermingle outside of work and become friends but while on duty everyone stays professional for the most part. It could be dangerous if we're not.

When interactions with men were compared to interactions with other women in the correctional setting, respondents reported being more comfortable and friendlier with other women workers. Angelina (in a management position) put it this way,

> They're [her interactions with women are] usually more friendly than with men for the most part but we're still all there for a job so we try to keep things professional.

And Paige stated,

> I tend to be friendlier or just more comfortable with women sometimes than men but it tends to stay professional also.

Women, in our sample, clearly felt in a minority, or token, position in [the] workplace, consistently reporting a sense that men were dominant in corrections.

Understandings of Sexual Harassment

Respondents were asked to define sexual harassment. While responses differed, most respondents included the terms *sexist jokes, unwanted touching, sexual comments, sexual innuendos*, and *unwanted sexual encounters* in their definitions (see Reading Table 24.1).

Respondents were asked if they had ever experienced sexual harassment. Of the fourteen women in our sample,

eight said that they had experienced sexual harassment while employed in the correctional setting. Two of these eight women reported that these encounters of sexual harassment affected their perceptions of promotional opportunities in the correctional setting. Sarah and Marcia, both in management positions, felt that if they had said something about a sexual harassment encounter that the male co-workers would have looked down on them and [that] they probably would not have been promoted. For instance, Sarah said,

> I think if I would've fought back or just did something that would look like I could outdo a male counterpart, I don't think I would've been promoted.

While Marcia agreed,

> I think maybe going back to the question you just asked me, if I would've done something like file a complaint or something, I'm not sure if I would've been promoted. In my experience, it's better to keep a tight lip about some things and just deal with it. I think if I would've done something then I don't know if I would've been trusted to have a higher rank.

Previous literature held that sexual harassment was the most common form of harassment women encounter [28]. This holds for the women in this sample as all have heard about instances of harassment and/or been a victim of sexual harassment. Britney related her concerns about harassment in this way,

> A counseling session [that] was going on; it was a juvenile offender, his family and a two officers . . . one male and a female counselor. During this meeting the male counselor said something to the effect of "you're just a woman"—" the boy isn't going to see it your way"—he said this to the other female counselor. I think they were talking to the offender and his family on what he can do to stay out of trouble and excel in school . . .

Half of the women interviewed had encountered sexist jokes and/or comments on a weekly or sometimes

Reading Table 24.1 ● Witness and Definitions of Sexual Harassment and Position

	Witnessed It?	Example/Explanation
Interviewee Managerial Position		
Lucy	No	"But I know it went on. When I was director, sexual harassment was not tolerated. I know it happened, but it never happened in front of me, and I was a bit slow at realizing it if it did."
Kelly	Yes	"Well, who hasn't in this day and age? The jokes are pretty common, you know, in the locker room or the break room. Um, I wouldn't say I hear them every day, but I would say at least once a week there's always some dirty joke buzzing around. They're not really taken too seriously; I think people know they're not there to hurt anyone's feelings."
Jennifer	No	"I've never personally witnessed anything. I've overheard jokes and heard officers and other colleagues talking amongst themselves, but that was probably me eavesdropping when I shouldn't have."
Marcia	Yes	"Well, who hasn't? Of course, in a male dominated field I have heard the raunchy jokes and sexist comments; I have seen the unnecessary flirting and such."
Sarah	Yes	"I've noticed other coworkers deal with it from other coworkers, but I've never seen an offender step out of line. Um, like the touching or I guess grabbing or like a pat on another person's rear." "I've heard the jokes and the sexist comments; I doubt those will ever go away. Well, I had this one time, a long time ago, where a male correctional officer said something like, 'oh I'll do it, since the woman doesn't want to.'"
Stella	No	"I've never witnessed anything like that; I've had my suspicions, but I don't know if it does actually happen."
Jody	No	"I've heard the stories or the rumors really, but I've never witnessed anything like that."
Nicole	No	"I've never personally witnessed it, but I don't doubt that it never happened."
Britney	No	"I have never personally witnessed it. I've heard the stories and been to the trainings at work about it. I've heard the stories that buzz around. Well, one story I've heard is when a counseling session was going on, it was a juvenile offender, his family and two officers, well, they are more like counselors then but it was one male and a female counselor.
		But during this meeting the male counselor said something to the effect of you're just a woman—the boy isn't going to see it your way—he said this to the other female counselor. I think they were talking to the offender and his family on what the juvenile can do to stay out of trouble and excel in school. I'm pretty sure he made his comment in front of the family and the offender. I know the female counselor filed a complaint, but I'm not sure if anything ever came of it. But that's what I heard happened, and I heard it down the line a bit, so I'm not exactly positive what exactly happened."
General Position		
Paige	No	*
Natasha	Yes	"I've heard some sexual jokes at work, but that's not uncommon, you know. I haven't heard anything that I have really found too offensive. And I haven't seen or heard of anything dealing with unnecessary touching or anything like that off the top of my head."
Charlotte	Yes	"I've heard jokes around the office every so often."
Candice	Yes	"Of course, I've heard the jokes and I've seen hugging and friendly touching among other workers but I'm not sure if those people were or are in a relationship or not, I think maybe they were but I don't know."

* No answer

daily basis. For example, in Marcia's interview, she almost sounds sarcastic when she's replying to the question, "Have you ever witnessed another female encountering sexual harassment in the correctional setting"; she stated, "Well, who hasn't?" Her response also suggests that sexual harassment and negative perceptions about women in the correctional field are common. Results support Rader [27] and McMahon [24] who both argued that women were teased, verbally abused, and harassed by male co-workers because of their gender and [that] this by itself can affect the promotional opportunities for women in the correctional field.

Discussion and Policy Implications

Most (12) of the women in the sample felt that men were promoted more than women in the correctional field. For instance, when asked who had greater opportunities for promotions, Lucy stated,

> I would say men because the field is male dominated and there will always be that idea; that stigma that women cannot do the job as well as a man.

None of the women felt that women were in an advantaged position with regard to being promoted at work. Cassirer and Reskin [6] found that women did not place as much importance on promotions as men did. Their research was consistent with Kanter's [19] thesis that men placed a greater emphasis on promotions than women.

Notably, all of the women said that a promotion was important to them. For example, Angelina said, "Yes, without a doubt." Sarah stated, "Yes, of course . . ." And Jennifer affirmed,

> Oh yes . . . when I supervise some officers, I push them—I try to encourage officers . . . [to] work toward being promoted.

Women perceived that men received more promotions and were more likely to be promoted than women. Notably, several women said they felt that if they complained about harassment, their male colleagues would look down on them and [that] they may not be promoted

because of that. Also of concern, women related that the belief continues to hold that men fill the shoes better when in position of higher authority. Nicole put it this way:

> Men do the job that a man can do—there are not a lot of times where a man will admit that a woman can do the same job especially in this field.

This work provides support for Griffin, Armstrong, and Hepburn's [15] argument that harassment at work was problematic for women in corrections. All of [the] women in this sample were either a victim and/or a witness of sexual harassment. Further, for some, there was a sense that if such harassment was reported, then the chance for a promotion in corrections would be diminished. It appears essential for correctional institutions to be sensitive to potential sexual harassment problems at work. Regular workshops focusing on this issue would be worthwhile. Supporting those who bring concerns forward is critical if women are to feel comfortable expressing problems at work. Clearly, women who wish to advance in correctional careers should not be penalized for ever having raised sexual harassment concerns.

Given that women represent a distinct minority among correctional officers, it seems imperative for policy makers to initiate programs to help advance women into these positions. Several initiatives like the following might make a difference. First, women who hold positions of leadership in correctional institutions might officially "mentor" other women and help them think about different promotional opportunities. They could share how they have reached the position they currently hold and what they believed helped in attaining this position. Second, women who express an interest in moving up the career ladder in correctional institutions might receive educational incentives to help attain this goal. Some institutions help those who wish to advance [by offering] the opportunity to attain more education and by providing financial support and attractive work schedules, in return for a time commitment (once the education is complete) to the supporting institution. Finally, if the lack of representation appears entrenched and no improvement in gender diversity is seen across time, it might be appropriate to set guidelines and timetables to reach the goal of gender diversity in corrections. Implementing educational and child care support, such as suggested above, might ensure that women enter these positions which would then lead to other women seeing themselves in such positions and following in their steps. Little research in the correctional field addresses how women feel about their promotional opportunities. This study helps provide some insight and adds to current literature in the field.

/// DISCUSSION QUESTIONS

1. Which three reasons do female correctional officers believe have impacted their ability to be promoted?

2. How do female correctional officers perceive their abilities on the job compared to male correctional officers?

3. How do women in corrections experience sexual harassment?

Note

1. In this work, the term *corrections* or the *correctional setting* is conceptualized as being the employment area for the participants, whether it is community, institutional, or administrational. The terms encompass various staff roles that are available, such as counselors, correctional officers, supervisors, superintendents, or directors. Promotional opportunities are defined as job advancements which may or may not include a pay increase and/or supervision of other employees. These promotions can be at a vertical level as well as at a horizontal level.

References

Armytage, P., Martyres, K., & Feiner, M. (2000). *Females in corrections: Getting the balance right.* Presented at the Women in Corrections: Staff and Clients Conference convened by the Australian Institute of Criminology in conjunction with the Department for Correctional Services SA, October/ November, Adelaide.

Camp, S. D., & Langan, N. P. (2005). Perceptions about minority and female opportunities for job advancements: Are beliefs about equal opportunities fixed? *The Prison Journal, 85,* 399–419.

Camp, S. D., Steifer, T. L., & Batchelder, J. A. (1995). *Perceptions of job advancement opportunities: A multilevel investigation of race and gender effects.* Washington, DC: Federal Bureau of Prisons & Indiana State University.

Carlson, J. R., Thomas, G., & Anson, R. H. (2004). Cross-gender perceptions of corrections officers in gender-segregated prisons. *Journal of Offender Rehabilitation, 39,* 83–103.

Cassirer, N., & Reskin, B. (2000). High hopes: Organizational position, employment experiences, and women's and men's promotion aspirations. *Work and Occupations, 27,* 438.

Creswell, J. W. (1994). *Research design: Qualitative and quantitative approaches.* Thousand Oaks, CA: Sage.

Crewe, B. (2006). Male prisoners' orientations towards women officers in an English prison. *Punishment & Society, 8,* 395–421.

Doeringer, P., & Piore, M. J. (1971). *Internal labor markets and manpower analysis.* Lexington, MA: D.C. Heath.

England, P., & Farkas, G. (1986). *Households, employment, and gender.* NY: Aldine.

Fry, L., & Glaser, D. (1987). Gender differences in work adjustment of prison employees. *Journal of Offender Counseling, Services, & Rehabilitation, 12,* 39–52.

Goodman, J. S., Fields, D. L., & Blum, T. C. (2003). Cracks in the glass ceiling: In what kind of organizations do women make it to the top? *Group and Organization Management, 28,* 475–501.

Griffin, M. (2007). Women as breadwinners. *Women and Criminal Justice, 17,* 1–25.

Griffin, M. L., Armstrong, G. S., & Hepburn, J. R. (2005). Correctional officer's perceptions of equitable treatment in the masculinized prison environment. *Criminal Justice Review, 30,* 189–206.

Grube-Farrell, B. (2002). Women, work, and occupational segregation in the uniformed services. *AFFILIA, 17,* 332–353.

Hulton, M. (2003). Some take the glass escalator, some hit the glass ceiling. *Work and Occupations, 30,* 30–61.

Jurik, N. C. (1985). An officer and a lady: Organizational barriers to women working as correctional officers in men's prisons. *Social Problems, 32,* 375–388.

Kanter, R. M. (1977). *Men and women of the corporation.* New York: Basic Books, Inc.

Kim, A.-S., Devalve, M., Elizabeth, Q. D., & Johnson, W. W. (2003). Women wardens: Results from a national survey of state correctional executives. *The Prison Journal, 83,* 406–425.

Lambert, E. G., Hogan, N. L., & Barton, S. M. (2004). The nature of work-family conflict among correctional staff: An exploratory examination. *Criminal Justice Review, 29,* 145–172.

Lambert, E. G., Paoline, E. A., III, Hogan, N. L., & Baker, D. N. (2007). Gender similarities and differences in correctional staff work attitudes and perceptions of the work environment. *Western Criminology Review, 8*, 16–31.

Maume, D. J., Jr. (1999). Glass ceilings and glass escalators: Occupational segregation and race and sex differences in managerial promotions. *Work and Occupations, 26*, 483–509.

McMahon, M. (1999). *Women on guard: Discrimination and harassment in corrections.* Toronto, Canada: University of Toronto Press Inc.

Morrison, A. (1987). *Breaking the glass ceiling.* NY: Addison-Wesley.

Morton, J. (1980). *A study of employment of women correctional officers in state level adult male correctional institutions.* Unpublished doctoral dissertation, University of Georgia, Athens.

Rader, N. (2005). Surrendering the solidarity: Considering the relationships among women correctional officers. *Women & Criminal Justice, 16*, 27–42.

Savicki, V., Colley, E., & Gjesvold, J. (2003). Harassment as a predictor of job burnout in correctional officers. *Criminal Justice and Behavior, 30*, 602–619.

Tewksbury, R., & Collins, S. C. (2006). Aggression levels among correctional officers. *The Prison Journal, 86*, 327–343.

U.S. Department of Justice. (2008). *Correctional officers, April 2007.* Washington, DC: Bureau of Statistics.

Zimmer, L. E. (1986). *Women guarding men.* Chicago: The University of Chicago Press.

Women Professionals and the Criminal Justice System

Courts and Victim Services

Section Highlights

- The gendered experience of women employed in the legal field
- Future directions for females working in courts and the law
- The role of victims' advocates in rape-crisis and domestic violence agencies

Women and the Law

Like women in many of the occupations discussed in Section XII, women in the legal field have historically been underrepresented. The 1800s saw several notable examples of women in these occupations. In 1869, Belle Mansfield became the first woman admitted to a state bar (Iowa) in the U.S (Morello, 1986; Robinson, 1890). Charlotte E. Ray became the first African American woman admitted to the bar for the District of Columbia in 1872 (Law Library of Congress, n.d.; Robinson, 1890). By 1879, antidiscrimination laws had changed, and Belva Ann Lockwood became the first woman to practice law before the U.S. Supreme Court (Cook, 1997; Law Library of Congress (n.d.); Smith, 1998). However, it was not until 1918 that the first women—Mary B. Grossman of Cleveland, OH and Mary Florence Lathrop of Denver, CO were admitted to the American Bar Association. These appearances by women into the legal profession were rare, and most of these women held positions with low prestige (Drachman, 1998). In the 21st century, the Presidency of the American Bar Association has been filled by a woman in six of the past sixteen terms. While times have improved significantly for women in this field, they still endure several challenges based on gender.

Today, women have reached near parity in terms of law school enrollment and faculty positions. Women make up almost half of all students enrolled in law school (49.3% in 2014-2015) with 13.2% of these women identifying as women of color, compared to 10.4% men of color (American Bar Association [ABA], 2017). This equality is also

▲ **Photo 13.1** The number of women in the legal field is increasing. Here, a female lawyer talks with a witness during a trial.

reflected in women's representation on law reviews, where women make up 54% of those in leadership positions and 49% of the editors-in-chief positions. Women also make up a significant presence among law school faculty. According to the American Bar Association (2010), women make up 54.6% of the tenured, tenure-track, or visiting full-time faculty at law schools across the nation. In addition, more women are finding their way into the top administrative positions within these schools. While women are less likely than men to hold the highest office (31.1% of dean positions are staffed by women), they are more likely than men to hold the office of associate or vice dean (60.6%) and assistant dean or director (69.7%).

While women have moved up the ranks within the legal academy, the number of male attorneys far exceeds the number of female attorneys in the United States. According to the American Bar Association (2017), only 36% of practicing attorneys in the United States are female. In addition, many positions are inaccessible for women. Women make up only 2% of the managing partners within the 200 largest law firms in the United States. Within Fortune 500 corporations with in-house counsel, women make up 24.8% of these positions and only a small proportion (13%) of these are staffed by women of color (National Association for Law Placement, 2010; National Association of Women Lawyers, 2009, 2010, ABA, 2017). In addition, women are less likely to make partner than men (Noonan, Corcoran, & Courant, 2008). Women make up 21% of partners at major U.S. law firms. Women of color are even more underrepresented in these roles—only 2.55% of these positions are filled by women of color (NALP, 2015). This contributes to disparities in pay between men and women. However, things are improving significantly. In 2009, female lawyers made 75% of the salaries of men. In 2015, this increased to 90%. This means that male lawyers today make approximately 10% more than their female counterparts, a significant improvement compared to just a few years ago when the disparity equaled 25% (ABA, 2017). However, not all ranks show this level of improvement because the typical female partner in a top-earning firm continues to make 20% less in compensation compared to her male colleagues.

The number of women in the legal field is increasing; over a five-year period between 2012 and 2017, the proportion of female practicing attorneys increased 5% from 31% to 36% and the number of women serving as in-house counsel with Fortune 500 companies increased 6.8%. As more women enter the profession, there will be more women seeking upper level positions. What remains to be seen is whether women within the legal field will face some of the same challenges that you learned about in sections XII with limited turnover in the upper ranks, which creates fewer opportunities for women to move into these higher ranked positions. Currently, women make up almost half of the associates positions in private practice (45%) (ABA, 2017).

Consider the organizational structure of high-profile private firms. Traditionally, the ranks of private law firms were divided into three categories. Associates, or the entry tier, is filled with new lawyers fresh out of law school who are battling for a place within the firm. Associates spend five to seven years with 80-hour work weeks in an effort to demonstrate that they should be selected as a partner. These positions are often probationary and those who are not selected for a partnership are let go. Partnership offers both financial and job security. However, this structure has shifted in recent decades. Nonequity partnerships were introduced into the mix. Lawyers at this rank have demonstrated their success as an associate but have not advanced to an equity partnership, meaning that they do not share in the firm's financial successes. Similar non-partner track positions such as staff attorneys and career associates were also created. It is not surprising that these lower paid positions were more likely to be staffed by women (Sterling, 2016).

Like many of the fields within the criminal justice system, women in the legal profession also face challenges with balancing the needs of their career with the demands of motherhood and family life. Within the corporate model of the legal system, the emphasis on billable hours requires attorneys to work long hours, both during the week and on weekends. In recent decades, the demand for billable hours by firms on their associates has increased significantly. Even with these high demands, billable hours are only part of the daily work that lawyers might engage in. The demands of this type of position often conflict with family responsibilities. For many women, the work-life conflict results in either delaying the start of a family or choosing their career over motherhood entirely. Others choose to leave their legal positions prior to making partner or leave their positions for ones that are less stressful and afford greater flexibility. In many cases, for women who exercise part-time options in an effort to create **work-family balance,** work and family life are often viewed as less ambitious compared to the male (and other female) counterparts.

While firms may offer opportunities for part-time work, research indicates that few women avail themselves of these opportunities for fear that doing so would damage their potential for career advancement. For those women who chose these career trajectories, research indicates that these positions did not necessarily involve compensatory reductions in workload, forcing many to bring their work home with them, work for which they do not receive compensation. In addition, these women often believed that a reduction in time spent in the office could ultimately affect their chances for promotion and earning potential, and it also fostered negative assumptions regarding their work ethic and level of commitment among their colleagues (Bacik & Drew, 2006). One suggestion to remedy the demands created by the billable hours model is to move toward a value billing (where the costs of the legal work are based on the nature and complexity of the case) or fixed fee (costs are quoted up front for the project) billing system. Both of these models create work efficiency and allow for a greater work-life balance (Durrani & Singh, 2011).

As women in private law practice become discouraged regarding their likelihood of achieving partner status, many make the decision to leave their positions. Indeed, men are two to three times more likely to become partners than women and also earn significantly higher salaries (ABA, 2011). While the decisions to get married, have children, and take time away from their jobs, or reduce their employment status to part-time, do not have a significant effect for men or women in their likelihood to leave private practice, these variables are associated with levels of satisfaction surrounding the balance of work and family needs. Here, satisfaction is the key, not their decisions regarding family status (Noonan & Corcoran, 2008, Kay, Alarie, & Adjei, 2013).

The majority of research on women in the legal profession lacks any discussion of how race and ethnicity interact with gender for women of color. What is available indicates that race and ethnicity have significant effects on the gendered nature of legal work. Generally speaking, men were more likely to be assigned high-profile cases, whereas women were assigned cases related to educational and other social issues. In addition, one respondent indicated that although White women and women of other minority groups were more likely to be viewed as "good attorneys," Chicanas were less likely to be viewed as valuable professionals in their field. Here, women of color are put in a position wherein they need to constantly prove themselves to their colleagues. As one female of color commented, "They just didn't appreciate me; (they) didn't think I was capable" (Garcia-Lopez, 2008, p. 598). In addition, Chicana women were more likely than White women to be overburdened with larger, lower profile caseloads. They also felt as though they were the key representatives and spokespersons for their racial-ethnic group. As another observed, "It's like they expect you to answer for the entire Latino population; like you should know everything there is to know about Latinos" (p. 601). Unlike other racial, ethnic, and gender groups, Chicana women attorneys did not define their success by financial achievements. Rather, social justice and helping people in their community play a key function in their concept of success and happiness with their lives and careers (Garcia-Lopez, 2008). In addition, many Latina law associates believe that the **glass ceiling** exists and can limit opportunities for promotion based on their gender and ethnic identity (Foley, Kidder, & Powell, 2002).

Scholars debate whether or not women can achieve equality in the legal profession. Some suggest that as older (and mostly male) partners retire, younger attorneys will be more likely to include a greater representation of women, given the increase in the number of women who attend and graduate from law school (French, 2000). Others argue that this theory neglects the fact that any change in the culture of the law firm will be slow in coming due to the small numbers of women who choose to work within these types of positions and are successful on the partnership track (Reichman & Sterling, 2001).

Spotlight on Women in Politics

In 1894, Colorado was the first state in the nation to elect a woman to a state legislative post. In fact, they elected three—Clara Cressingham, Carrie Clyde Holly, and Frances Klock. All three women were involved in political activity around improving the lives of girls and women. Both Cressingham and Klock supported bills to create homes for delinquent and destitute girls. But it was Holly who was perhaps the most active on women's rights. She was the nation's first woman to sponsor a bill and championed equal rights for men and women. She also worked to raise the age of sexual consent from 16 to 18 (NWHM, n.d.). Today, 1,830 women make up 24.8% of the elected representatives to the state legislatures. Women who are elected at the state level are more likely to be members of the Democratic Party (15%) compared to the Republican Party (9%) (NCSL, 2017).

At the federal level, Jeannette Rankin (MT) was the first woman elected to Congress in the House of Representatives in 1922. Her tenure lasted one day. It wasn't until 1931 when Hattie Caraway was first elected to succeed her husband and was subsequently reelected to a six-year term (Manning, Brudnick, & Shogan, 2015). Today, women comprise 19.6% of the elected officials (105 of the 535 members). Twenty-one women are members of the Senate (21%) and 84 (19.3%) represent their states in the House of Representatives. There are also five female delegates in the House who represent the District of Columbia and U.S. Territories. As in state legislatures, women in Congress are more likely to be Democrats. Women in Congress are also more likely to represent diverse backgrounds, because 38 of the 104 are women of color (CAWP, 2017). In comparison, only 64 of the men in Congress are members of a minority group (Marcos, 2016).

The 2016 election saw three newly elected women to the U.S. Senate. Tammy Duckworth (IL) is a retired U.S. Army Lieutenant Colonel and the first disabled woman to be elected to Congress. She lost both of her legs in combat during the Iraq War in 2004. Catherine Cortez Masto (NV) previously served as the Attorney General of Nevada and is the first Latina to serve in the Senate. Like Cortez-Masto, Kamala Harris (CA) also served as the Attorney General prior to joining the Senate. Harris is the first Indian American to serve in the U.S. Senate. All three women represent the Democratic Party and have been very active since their entry to Washington. Duckworth introduced the Friendly Airports for Mothers Act in June, which calls for medium and large sized airports to provide lactation rooms for breastfeeding mothers (S. 1110). In July 2017, Harris (joined by Senators Booker (NJ), Durbin (IL) and Warren (MA)) cosponsored the Dignity for Incarcerated Women Act, which would require federal prisons to provide free tampons and sanitary pads to women. It would ban the shackling of pregnant women or placing them in solitary confinement. The bill would assist in maintaining ties between an incarcerated woman and her family by considering the location of children when determining where she will be housed for her sentence. It would also create policies that would extend the visiting time and eliminate phone charges for women and the families (S. 1524).

There is an extensive amount of research on the legislative actions of women. Much of these findings note that women are traditionally involved in political activity (sponsor and vote) on female-centric legislation.

Examples of these activities include bills that promote women's rights, increased care and resources for families and children, and increased equality for women. Even when female legislators differ in their ideological views (Democratic vs. Republican), both sides agree that they have an obligation to represent women and will often work across party lines to accomplish these goals (Hawkesworth, Casey, Jenkins, & Kleeman, 2001). While many of these issues are often framed as "women's issues," the reality is that legislation on issues such as families, education, and social welfare are gender-neutral issues that impact both men and women. Research has noted that when there are more women serving in leadership roles in the political arena, there is an increase in the number of laws on women's issues. There is also an increase in the gendered content of these laws. However, success of these laws is dependent on their male colleagues offering their support (Wittmer & Bouche, 2013). In addition to their successes on passing laws in favor of women's rights, female participation within the legislature can help prevent antiwomen legislation (Berkman & O'Connor, 1993). Given the current makeup of legislatures both at the state and Federal level, it's clear that women are making a significant impact on the lives of men, women, and children.

Women and the Judiciary

In the judiciary, the representation of women has grown substantially over the last several decades. Although most of the conversations about women in the judiciary focus on the women that have been appointed to the U.S. Supreme Court, we have seen increases in the number of women appointed to the judiciary at all levels in recent times for both the state and federal legal systems. In light of these changes, how is this reflected in the proportion of women who serve in these positions? What is the current status of women in the judiciary?

Most female judges are assigned to courts of general jurisdiction. For example, 92% of women judges in California serve in trial courts (Williams, 2007). Similar trends are noted in the nationwide data, where 84% of women judges serve in courts at the trial level (National Association of Women Lawyers, 2010). While this might seem staggering in terms of the number of women that have been relegated to these lower level positions, we need to think about these data within the context of the number of positions at each level. For example, the majority of all justices (regardless of gender) serve in these general (and other lower level) jurisdiction courts, simply because there are so many opportunities (and high demand) for these positions. In contrast, there are few justices at the appellate and higher levels, which means fewer positions for women in general. However, the proportion of women in these positions is increasing. Nationwide, women represent 34.6% of the judges at the state supreme court level and 34.7% at the intermediate appellate jurisdiction courts. Overall, women occupy 5,596 of the 18,006 positions in state court judicial positions across the United States. Within the federal level, women occupy 60 of the 167 available positions in the Federal Circuit Court of Appeals (35.9%)

▲ **Photo 13.2** The four women of the U.S. Supreme Court. From left to right: Sandra Day O'Connor, Sandra Sotomayor, Ruth Bader Ginsburg, and Elena Kagan.

Steve Petteway, photographer for the Supreme Court of the United States.

and 33% in the District Courts (ABA, 2017). So, while the physical number of women in these positions is somewhat small, their effect is significant given the few positions that exist at this level.

What factors affect the appointment of women to the judiciary? Williams (2007) suggests that more women receive a judicial appointment as a result of a nonpartisan election, compared to partisan elections. Liberal states are more likely to have women in judicial positions, compared to conservative states. In addition, the presence of female attorneys in the state also increases the representation of women as judges in the trial courts. At the appellate level, three variables affect the representation of women in these positions: (1) As more seats are generally available on the appellate bench, the representation of women at this level increases; (2) as the number of female attorneys in a state increases, so does the number of women judges at the appellate level; (3) states that use the merit selection process to fill seats have an increased number of women on the bench, compared to those states that rely on a partisan election to fill these positions. In addition, research indicates that women in the judiciary have a greater interest in elevating their career trajectory than male judges (Jensen & Martinek, 2009).

Spotlight on Women and the Supreme Court

The U.S. Supreme Court is an institution unlike any other in the nation. The first Court was established in 1789 with six members: a chief justice and five associate justices. Today, there are a total of nine justices—eight associates plus the chief justice. Over the past 211 years, there have been 112 justices and 17 chief justices. Turnover on the Court is a slow process as members of the Supreme Court are appointed for life (and many serve until their death; Supreme Court, n.d.). The presence of women on the Supreme Court is a new practice. It wasn't until 1981 that the first female justice was appointed to the Court. To date, there have been only four women to serve on the Supreme Court: Sandra Day O'Connor, Ruth Bader Ginsburg, Sonia Sotomayor, and Elena Kagan.

In 1981, President Ronald Reagan appointed Sandra Day O'Connor as the first woman to grace the Supreme Court's bench. At the time of her appointment, there were few women in high-ranking judicial positions at the state and federal level. O'Connor began her tenure on the Court as a conservative voice, and she voted with her conservative colleagues in the overwhelming majority of her decisions ("Nine Justices," 2004). While she was initially appointed as a conservative voice on the Court, she was not always aligned with the political right and became the swing vote alongside more liberal justices in some high-profile cases before the Court. For example, in *Lawrence v. Texas* (2003), she ruled with her liberal colleagues that laws banning sodomy for homosexuals but not for heterosexuals were unconstitutional. She retired from the Court in January 2006.

O'Connor remained the lone woman on the Court until 1993, when Clinton appointed a second woman to the Court—Ruth Bader Ginsburg. During her tenure as a lawyer, she appeared before the Court on six separate occasions in cases involving women's rights. She was first appointed to the federal bench by President Carter in 1981 to serve on the U.S. Court of Appeals. During her tenure on the Court, Ginsburg has presented a balanced view in her decision making—sometimes voting with her liberal colleagues and other times serving as the swing vote for the conservative voice. One of her noted decisions on gender equality involved the case of *United States v. Virginia* (1996), which involved a challenge against the single-sex admission policy of Virginia Military Institute. In writing for the majority opinion, Ginsburg stated that "neither federal nor state government acts compatibly with equal protection when a law or official policy denies to women, simply because they are women, full citizenship stature—equal opportunity to aspire, achieve, participate in and contribute to society based on their individual talents and capacities" (518 U.S. 515, 532).

Recently, Ginsburg has been joined by two additional female justices: Sonia Sotomayor (2009) and Elena Kagan (2010). Their appointments mark a shift in the judiciary of the highest Court in the land. Sotomayor is the first woman of color, a Latina, to serve on the Supreme Court, and the inclusion of Kagan creates a historical first, because this is the first time in history that three women have served simultaneously on the Court.

Sotomayor began her career as a prosecutor and spent time in private practice before she was appointed to the judiciary (federal district court) by President George H. W. Bush in 1991. She was elevated to the Second [U.S. Circuit] Court of Appeals by President Clinton in 1997. Perhaps her most famous decision came in 1995 when she ruled against the administrators of Major League Baseball and subsequently ended the baseball strike ("Sonia Sotomayor," 2012). As the first appointment of President Obama in 2009, she has been involved in several landmark decisions, including health care reform and immigration laws. While a moderate voice early in her career, on the Court she has served as a liberal voice and is often viewed as a champion for the rights of the downtrodden (Savage, 2009).

Few presidents have the opportunity to nominate even one member to the Supreme Court. During his tenure, President Obama has made two appointments. His second appointment came in 2010 with the confirmation of Elena Kagan (Center for American Women and Politics, n.d.). Kagan's career included a variety of positions in private practice, tenure at University of Chicago Law and even a stint in the White House as a deputy domestic policy advisor under President Clinton. She became a professor at Harvard Law School and was later named its first woman dean. In 2009, President Obama appointed Kagan to serve as the solicitor general. However, this position was short lived because she was nominated and confirmed to the Supreme Court in 2010. While some viewed her lack of experience in the judiciary as a negative, she has positioned herself as one of the more influential leaders on the Court. Indeed, she has participated in two of the recent landmark decisions by the Court involving gay marriage: *Hollingsworth v. Perry* (2013; overturned California's Prop. 8) and *U.S. v. Windsor* (overturned the Defense of Marriage Act). In each of these cases, Kagan sided with the majority opinion in support of gay marriage as a component of fairness and dignity.

With three female justices on the Court, Ginsburg, Sotomayor, and Kagan make history and represent a significant increase of women in the judiciary. While the progress is certainly significant, the long tenure of justices may mean that the addition of more women to the Court will not occur in the near future. However, as new appointees, the voices of Sotomayor and Kagan will certainly shape the decisions of the Court for a significant future.

Does being female affect the way in which judges make decisions? In a study involving hypothetical vignettes, the findings indicated several areas where gender differences existed among judges who participated in the survey. In most of the scenarios, the female judges imposed longer sentences in cases of simple assault and were less likely to award civil damages for these cases. However, when damages were to be awarded, female judges awarded significantly higher monetary levels compared to male judges (Coontz, 2000). When reviewing outcomes in real-life cases, the results are mixed. Research by Steffensmeier and Hebert (1999) finds that women judges tend to be harsher in their sentencing decisions than their male counterparts. Controlling for offender characteristics, the presence of a woman on the bench increases both the likelihood of prison time for offenders (10%) and the length of their sentences (+5 months longer). In addition, property offenders and repeat offenders are the ones most likely to bear the brunt of this increased severity when facing a female judge. In contrast, research by McCall (2007) indicates that female judges are generally more liberal in their decision making. Similar research on gender differences in sentencing by Songer, Davis, and Haire (1994) indicates that male and female judges do not differ in judicial decision making in federal cases involving obscenity charges or criminal search and seizure cases, but female judges were significantly more likely to decide in favor of the victim in cases of employment discrimination. At the state supreme court level, research indicates that not only do women tend to vote more liberally in death penalty and obscenity cases but also that the presence of a woman on the court increases the likelihood that the male judges will vote in a liberal fashion (Songer & Crews-Meyer, 2000).

Women and Work in Victim Services

A violation of the criminal law is considered a crime against the state, regardless of the offense or the harm to the victim. Victims have generally played a minor role throughout the criminal justice process and have had limited rights. For example, victims were not entitled to information about the case, nor were they invited to take an active role in the process. The fight for victims' rights began to emerge during the 1970s as a grassroots effort. One of the first victim services programs was the Bay Area Women Against Rape in San Francisco, which was the first rape-crisis center. In 1975, the National Organization for Victim Assistance (NOVA) was created as a resource for victims' rights groups across the United States and provides a voice to the needs of victims of crime (Young & Stein, 2004).

With the increased attention on victims' rights at the national level, the number of agencies began to multiply. While some of these groups were nonprofit community-based organizations, there was also a push for victims' services within local and state government bureaus. The funding source varies from organization to organization. While many of these programs receive state and federal funds, these resources alone are not enough to support the needs of the organization. As a result, many programs seek out grants and private subsidies to sustain their efforts (California Emergency Management Agency [Cal EMA], 2011).

While crime and victimizations cut across race, class, and gender lines (as well as other demographic identities), women are disproportionately represented within certain categories of crime, such as rape, sexual assault, and intimate partner abuse. One of the unique factors of many victim service organizations that focus on these particular types of victims is that the workforce tends to be predominantly female. In addition, many of these workers identify as survivors of these crimes. This feminine dynamic within the workplace brings a unique perspective to these agencies, particularly compared to the majority of occupations affiliated with the criminal justice system that are male dominated. Within the victims' services field, feminine traits, such as compassion, care, and support, are a critical part of the daily work environment. This concept of survivor-as-advocate or survivor-to-survivor model began during the battered women shelter movement whereby individuals who had successfully terminated a violent relationship were available to support those who were currently going through the process (Ferraro, 1981). As the work within intimate partner violence organizations began to become more professionalized, the personal experiences of workers continued to serve as a calling to the work. For others, work within the IPV field was a reflection of their social justice philosophy (Wood, 2017). At the same time, formal education in fields such as victimology, psychology, criminology, social work, and sociology

▲ **Photo 13.3** Many women are drawn to work in the field of victims' services. Here, a counselor provides support to a young girl at a domestic violence center.

as well as specialized training on issues such as victim services, law, and the criminal justice system are invaluable for this field (Neff, Patterson, & Johnson, 2012).

However, it is important to consider that victimization is a highly sensitive experience, and the people that work within these fields are often faced with high exposure to emotion within the context of their work. Over time, this can take its toll. The following sections highlight some of the challenges that **victim advocates** face in the workplace with agencies that provide services for victims of intimate partner violence and sexual assault.

Advocates for Intimate Partner Abuse

The decision to seek out assistance in cases of intimate partner abuse can be difficult for many victims. As you learned in Section IV, victims may experience fear and shame as a part of their abuse, believe that nothing can be done to change the situation, or may fail to even identify themselves as a victim. Despite these challenges, the demand for services for victims of these crimes is in high demand. Advocates in these cases may involve a variety of duties, including providing services (or referrals for services), helping victims secure temporary and transitional housing and providing support in legal cases (Camacho & Alarid, 2008; Slattery & Goodman, 2009).

Within the context of their daily work, advocates are exposed to stories filled with episodes of physical, sexual, and psychological abuse. In addition, advocates deal with clients in emergent and pressure-filled situations. The intensity of these events can take their toll on advocates and lead to **burnout**. Not only may advocates experience emotional exhaustion because of the high levels of on-the-job stress, these experiences can lead advocates to become less connected to their work and their clients. As a result, many may question whether these costs are worth it and whether it makes a difference (Babin, Palazzolo, & Rivera, 2012). It is when an advocate feels that they are ineffective that the risk for burnout is at its highest. To a certain extent, these feelings of efficacy are perpetuated by the cycle of violence. Victims of intimate partner abuse often leave several times before they are able to completely sever their relationship. When a victim returns to her batterer, the advocate may feel that she has failed. Over time, this can have a significant impact on whether the advocate has sympathy for her client, which in turn can limit delivery of services (Kolb, 2011). In an effort to continue to support their clients, advocates will often excuse or justify their clients' actions so as to not take this decision as a personal rejection. One advocate expressed this experience in the following way:

> It takes the heat off (the client) and it makes it easier, especially with abusers, to say that we made them do it, we made them take out the charges. It's frustrating, but that's what an advocate does. (Kolb, 2011, p. 110)

For survivor-advocates, working in support for victims can represent a way of giving back to the support systems that personally helped them. Some advocates would use their individual experiences with victimization to connect with their clients. For others, working with victims provided a unique mirror of their own pathways to healing.

> I guess when you kind of get a little sidetracked and you see women and how they struggle with being independent and getting all the assistance they need, it kind of makes me realize how far I've come along and just reminds me to remember where I was at one point and it helps me to understand that I have healed and that I'm in a better place now. And it also motivates me to try to help them so they can one day feel the same way that I do now. That's my goal. (Wood, 2017 p. 321)

The emotional nature of work as a domestic violence advocate can have a significant impact on his or her mental health. Advocates may experience their own psychological strain or secondary trauma stress. **Secondary trauma stress** is similar to post-traumatic stress disorder (PTSD) and is defined as "stress resulting from helping or wanting to help a traumatized or suffering person" (Figley, 1995, p. 7). One of the greatest predictors of secondary trauma stress is whether advocates have a history of their own intimate partner abuse (Slattery & Goodman, 2009). Since many advocates in the field have a personal history of victimization by an intimate partner, this is important to consider because it can create challenges in setting boundaries and lead to emotional triggers that can be harmful for both the worker and their client (Wood, 2017). However, organizational support structures within the workplace can serve as a protective factor against developing secondary trauma stress (Slattery & Goodman, 2009). Examples of these include fostering an environment of peer-to-peer support among the workers as well as developing formal mentor programs for new employees (Babin et al., 2012).

Spotlight on Self-care for Victim Advocates

The concept of self-care involves activities and practices that help with stress management and the mainte-nance of our physical and emotional wellbeing. Self-care can involve a variety of different activities, including exercise, healthy living, mindfulness activities such as meditation, social activities with friends and family, and engagement in spiritual activity. Working with victims of crime can be an intense and emotional experience day in and day out. As a result, individuals who work within these fields often suffer from secondary trauma vic-timization, compassion fatigue, and burnout. Given these challenges, self-care becomes incredibly important in both the health and well-being of individual workers and volunteers, as well as the structure of the organization.

One area that has garnered attention on self-care for individuals who work with victims of intimate partner violence and sexual assault is art therapy. Art therapy can take a variety of different approaches such as view-ing and creating paintings, spoken word poetry, dance, and theater. Even within service oriented populations, reaching out can internalized as appearing incompetent in their position (Taylor & Furlonger, 2011). Art therapy can provide nonverbal ways to manage compassion fatigue. It can also create new mediums for expression and communication (Huet & Holttum, 2016). These shared experiences can also create peer connections between col-leagues (Ifrach & Miller, 2016). These connections and coping skills can help support each other in their daily work.

One of the greatest challenges for individuals is recognizing the early signs of STS, compassion fatigue, and burnout. Not only is self-care important in terms of employee retention, but such traumas could also impact the delivery of services to victims. It is also important for workers to be able to admit when they need help. Organizations need to create safe spaces for employees and volunteers to be able to reach out. Many organi-zations include discussions of personal well-being into their training programs or create opportunities for prac-tices such as "wellness days" with coordinated activities designed to foster support within the group (Howlett & Collins, 2014).

Rape-Crisis Workers

As one of the first examples of victims' services in the 1970s, rape-crisis organizations began as community-based grassroots agencies. Initially, these organizations were run primarily by a volunteer and female workforce. Many of these women had survived a rape or sexual assault at some point in their lifetime (Mallicoat, Marquez, & Rosenbaum, 2007). In addition to providing support for victims of sexual assault, many of these early centers worked on legisla-tive actions in pursuit of victims' rights in sexual assault cases (Maier, 2011). During the 1980s and 1990s, rape-crisis organizations began to collaborate with other service providers, such as hospitals, police departments, and other community-based services. While much of the collaboration was driven by the budget cuts and the need to develop new ways to share resources, the effect was a professionalization of these agencies and their missions (Mallicoat et al., 2007). In addition, state governments began to take an interest in making sure that crime victims had access to services (Maier, 2011). As a result, contemporary rape-crisis organizations can provide a variety of services, including crisis hotlines (many of which are staffed 24 hours a day), crisis counseling, and legal and medical advocates for victims (Ullman & Townsend, 2007) as well as services for non-English speakers and proactive education on rape and sexual assault (Maier, 2011). While work within these organizations has become a full-time professional occupation, organizations must call on volunteers to help serve the needs of the community (Mallicoat et al., 2007). In addition, today's rape-crisis centers are usually less focused on the political activism that was a core component of the early rape-crisis centers of the 1970s (Maier, 2011).

There is significant variability within the different types of rape-crisis organizations in terms of the types of populations they serve (rural vs. urban and multicultural populations), the types of services that are provided (direct services vs. community outreach), and their connection to other community agencies (Gornick, Burt, & Pitman, 1985). Despite these differences, rape-crisis organizations have a similar philosophy that places victim advocacy as a primary focus (Mallicoat et al., 2007).

Earlier in this section, you learned that the majority of the workforce within a rape-crisis center is female and that many of these women are survivors of sexual victimization. Survivors of these crimes may be drawn to work within this field for a variety of reasons. Many volunteers see working in a rape-crisis organization as a way of giving back to a community that assisted them with their own victimization experience or use it to continue to work through their own victim experience (Mallicoat et al., 2007). As well, many rape-crisis workers believe that it is their purpose to empower their clients by creating opportunities for the victims to be in control of their lives, which is something that was taken away during their assault (Ullman & Townsend, 2008).

Rape-crisis workers also help limit or prevent secondary victimization. As you learned in Section II, secondary victimization occurs when victims of sexual assault have a negative experience with the interventions, and these experiences can cause further trauma to the victim as a result. How does this revictimization occur? The process of a police investigation can further traumatize victims; they are often required to provide the details of their attack multiple times. While the intent of this process is to document the assault in detail, victims can potentially feel that they are blamed for the assault. Other stages of the investigation also carry the risk for potential revictimization, such as the rape exam, which is an extensive process. The rape exam requires specific training of professionals (such as a sexual nurse examiner) in order to ensure that evidence is collected in the correct manner. Errors in this process can not only jeopardize the case but can also cause additional emotional trauma for the victim (Maier, 2008a). As a case moves forward in the criminal justice system, victims may experience additional acts of revictimization. They may receive little information about their case as it moves through the system. They may have to "re-live" the assault when testifying as witness and, in cases where a plea bargain is offered, be denied the opportunity to confront their accuser in court (Kelleher & McGilloway, 2009). However, the presence of an advocate appears to positively impact these difficult events because victims indicate that they encounter less distress as a result of their interactions with the police and medical professionals. Victims also receive an enhanced standard of care by hospital staff when a crisis counselor is present (Campbell, 2006).

While rape-crisis counselors and advocates provide valuable services for victims and the community, these workers can face a number of barriers in their attempts to deliver services. In Section III, you learned about rape myths and how this can lead to misperceptions in society about the reality of these crimes. Research by Ullman and Townsend (2007) acknowledges that this can make it difficult to provide support for the victim. In addition, budget constrictions can limit the ability of a rape-crisis organization to provide services for the victims. Finally, many victims do not know where to turn for help. It is important that rape-crisis organizations not only conduct outreach to let victims know where they can turn for help but also engage in public education to help dismantle these misperceptions about rape and sexual assault (Kelleher & McGilloway, 2009).

Rape and sexual assault exists in every community. However, the availability of services can vary from organization to organization. Those agencies with the largest budgets (and largest staff and number of volunteers) are able to provide the most resources. Most of these agencies are located in larger urban areas. For victims in rural communities, accessible resources may be limited, and workers in these communities face their own set of unique challenges. Consider that in rural communities, anonymity about people and their lives is rare. Everyone knows everybody (and their business), which can limit privacy and jeopardize confidentiality in these cases. Victims may be less likely to report these assaults, particularly when cases involve a family member or when victims experience backlash and blame for their victimization (Annan, 2011). Victim blaming practices are heavily influenced by cultural factors, such as the acceptance of traditional gender roles or conservative religious values, in these rural communities (McGrath, Johnson, & Miller, 2012). Finally, there can be significant challenges in the delivery of services for these victims. Given that rural agencies may draw from a large geographical area, poverty and a lack of available transportation can significantly limit the delivery of support and resources to some communities (McGrath et al., 2012). Despite these challenges, rape-crisis workers in rural communities do see assets to their small stature as they can provide consistent care and attention to their clients as their cases move throughout the system. There is less of a risk that their cases will get handed off to other professionals or get lost within the system. In addition, the tight-knit community allows advocates to develop close relationships with related practitioners, which improves the continuum of care for victims (Annan, 2011).

In Section III, you learned about how women of color have different experiences of sexual assault, which demonstrated in a variety of ways, including prevalence rates, reporting behaviors, disclosure practices, help-seeking behaviors, and responses by the justice system. First, race, ethnicity, and culture have a significant impact on reporting sexual assault. For example, victims in Hindu Indian cultures believe that to be sexually assaulted means that they are no longer "pure," which is a high status symbol within the community. Rather than bring shame to their family, the women have chosen to remain silent and not report these victimizations. Second, the limited availability of resources designed for victims from different races, ethnicities, and cultures can reduce the likelihood that victims will seek out assistance. In addition, many advocates expressed that many victims seemed to accept their victimization, as if this is a normal experience within their community and that it is not necessary to make a big deal about it. Finally, racism can lead to differential treatment of victims of color by the criminal justice system, particularly for cases of interracial victimization. In the words of one advocate,

> If a woman of color is assaulted by a White man there is almost a guarantee of hopelessness—nothing is going to happen. If a White woman is assaulted by a person of color, the whole thing changes. It is going to be on the front page of the news. (Maier, 2008b, p. 311)

Like other occupations within the criminal justice field, rape-crisis workers are faced with issues such as job satisfaction and burnout. While many advocates in this field express high levels of job satisfaction in their work with victims (despite comparatively low salaries), the emotionally taxing nature of the work can lead to high levels of burnout. Earlier in this section, you learned about issues of burnout and secondary trauma for domestic violence advocates. Not surprising, rape-crisis counselors deal with many of the same issues in the context of their work environments. Indeed, the physical and emotional toll for advocates can be significantly taxing :

> Having to dedicate energies on such issues has, at times, created a critical event for me, placing me under such stress that I have suffered insomnia and sleep deprivation, urinary nocturnal frequency, migraines, lack of time to attend to exercise, etc.

> The awareness that there are perpetrators who live, work, and "play" among us who are capable of inflicting such atrocities for pleasure, for power and control, and/or for profit if they are engaged in pedophilic/adult pornographic crime scene exploitation created a deep change in men, physically, psychologically, and cognitively. (Coles, Astbury, Dartnall, & Limherwala, 2014, p. 101–102)

Research notes that age can be a significant predictor in secondary traumatic stress (STS) because younger advocates experience higher levels of STS. Organizational structure can also impact STS. Advocates who have high caseloads or who work in organizations with limited structure and supervision are at a greater risk for secondary trauma stress (Dworkin, Sorell, & Allen, 2016). As a result, it is important that workers balance the demands of work with healthy physical and emotional outlets outside of the workplace (Mallicoat et al., 2007).

Conclusion

Despite the gains of women in traditionally male-dominated criminal justice occupations, they continue to confront a glass ceiling in terms of equal representation, compensation, and opportunity within these fields. In cases such as the legal field, women in these fields become a symbol for all things gender. In other examples such as domestic violence and rape-crisis advocacy work, the organization itself becomes gendered in response to its feminist foundations, and many women are drawn to work within these environments as a result. While equal employment opportunity legislation has opened the doors for access for women in these traditionally male-dominated fields, women still face an uphill battle because they have been denied opportunity and promotion throughout history. In occupations such as attorneys and judges, the proportion of women in these fields has significantly increased in recent decades. While women are represented at both upper and lower levels of the judiciary, their presence may still be as token females. In the case of victims' services agencies, the majority of these organizations are female-centric, creating a unique environment. However, many advocates in these fields suffer from emotional burdens and challenges to gender normative values that can impact their ability to deliver services to victims. Despite these struggles, women remain an important presence in these fields with significant contributions that need to be encouraged and acknowledged, particularly for future generations of women in these fields.

/// SUMMARY

- Women in the legal field struggle with balancing work demands with family life. These struggles can affect the advancement of women in their field.

- While the number of women in the judiciary has increased, the majority of these positions are at the lower levels.

- Many rape-crisis and intimate partner violence organizations are predominantly staffed by women.

- Many women who serve as victims' advocates have their own personal experience with victimization.

- Victim advocates face issues of burnout and secondary trauma that can affect not only their levels of job satisfaction but also their abilities to offer care to victims and survivors of these crimes.

- Advocates working with victims of color need to consider the cultural issues in these communities when providing services and outreach.

- Rural communities face unique considerations in providing services and support for victims of crime.

/// KEY TERMS

Burnout 563

Glass ceiling 557

Secondary trauma stress 563

Victim advocates 563

Work-family balance 557

DISCUSSION QUESTIONS

1. Based on the research, how do women do gender within the traditional male-dominated legal occupations?

2. What challenges do women who work in law-related occupations face that their male counterparts do not?

3. What suggestions can be made to improve the status of women within law-related occupations?

4. How can organizations help support women in these occupations to improve job satisfaction and limit burnout?

5. How do the challenges for specialized populations (race/ethnicity, culture, and rural environments) impact the delivery of services for victims?

 ## WEB RESOURCES

International Association of Women Judges: http://www.iawj.org

National Association of Women Judges: http://www.nawj.org

National Association of Women Lawyers: http://www.nawl.org

> online resources Visit **study.sagepub.com/mallicoat3e** to access additional study tools, including eFlashcards, web quizzes, web resources, video resources, and SAGE journal articles.

READING /// 25

The presence of women and minorities on the bench has been steadily increasing. Given this growing diversity, how do issues of race and gender impact judicial decision making within the trial courts? This article by Christina L. Boyd highlights how diversity on the bench impacts court outcomes.

Representation on the Courts?
The Effects of Trial Judges' Sex and Race

Christina L. Boyd

Representation and its connection to diversity among political elites is as important today as ever before. Whether discussing legislators, bureaucrats, judges, or other elites, how well these actors represent the citizenry's diverse characteristics and interests—both in terms of composition and outputs—has significant implications for our political institutions' function, membership, and legitimacy. To date, the results of diversity-in-politics research indicate, for example, that black and female state legislative representatives pursue representative policies (Bratton & Haynie, 1999), female federal administrative agency bureaucrats support more female-friendly policies than their male counterparts (Dolan, 2000), and that female and black appellate court judges decide diversity-specific cases differently from their white, male colleagues and affect their colleagues' decision making (Boyd, Epstein, & Martin, 2010; Kastellec, 2013).

Although these insights are noteworthy, much remains unknown about the presence and degree of diversity representation within many of our political institutions today. To see this in one particular political institution, one need look no further than the behavior and words of the Obama Administration. Between taking office in 2009 and July 2016, President Obama successfully appointed more than ninety minority and 100 female federal trial court judges. Appointed to life tenure positions under Article III of the Constitution, these newly selected judges make up nearly 62 percent of Obama's trial court selections, by far the highest percentage of diverse judges appointed by a U.S. president.[1]

Although Obama's pride in diversifying the federal trial courts is clear, what is less clear is what impact, if any, this large number of diverse appointments is likely to have on our nation's trial courts and the decisions made therein.

The Obama Administration argues that these new judges serve as descriptive representatives of diverse communities in the United States and that their presence encourages the public to view the courts as legitimate. As Senior Counsel to the President Chris Kang (2013) notes,

> [t]hese "firsts" are important, not because these judges will consider cases differently, but because a judiciary that better resembles our nation instills even greater confidence in our justice system, and because these judges will serve as role models for generations of lawyers to come.

Descriptive representation and instilling confidence in the judiciary are undoubtedly important, but is the Obama White House correct that these diverse trial judges are not likely to decide cases distinctly from their more traditional (white and male) judicial colleagues?

SOURCE: Boyd, C. L. (2016). Representation on the courts? The effects of trial judges' sex and race. *Political Research Quarterly*, 69(4), 788-799.

Previous empirical research on the impact of diversity characteristics on trial judge behavior provides little to no help in definitively answering this important question. Although over half of the studies on the subject find no statistical support to indicate that female and racial minority trial judges decide differently from their male and white counterparts, a nontrivial number report differences. This study endeavors to bring clarity to this issue. To do so, it adopts a research design that directly addresses trial courts' unique institutional environment and the varying decision-making roles embodied by trial court judges. Namely, this project uses a newly collected and publicly available data-set of employment discrimination cases brought by the Equal Employment Opportunity Commission (EEOC) into the federal district courts. In contrast to many previous trial court-diversity studies, these data are focused on dispositive motions rather than final case outcomes or judicial opinions, they filter out those cases that are most likely to be classified as frivolous in nature, and they are narrowly focused on specific issue areas of interest to diversity theory. As the statistical results indicate after an analysis of these data, there is substantial support for diversity judging theory in federal trial court judicial behavior. Female judges are more likely than their male colleagues to decide motions in sex discrimination-related cases in favor of the discrimination-alleging plaintiff. Similarly, black judges are significantly more likely to decide in favor of the plaintiff in motions in both race-related and sex-related discrimination cases than their white counterpart district judges. These sizable results provide some of the first systematic evidence that, in cases that directly relate to their personal area of diversity, whether race or sex, diverse trial court judges make decisions on motions that are significantly more protective of plaintiffs than their colleagues.

How Diversity May Affect Trial Judging

Scholars and policy makers have long sought to discover whether diverse judges, be they females or racial minorities, behave and make decisions differently than more descriptively traditional male and white judges. And with good reason. Judges, and particularly trial judges, are well positioned to affect their assigned cases and the way that they progress. This has tremendous implications in trial courts for outcomes, settlements, costs, appeals, the distribution of resources after a case, and even the decision of litigants to file their cases and seek adjudicated remedies at all. In short, if diverse trial judges behave differently from their colleagues, we should expect substantive differences in the outputs of the judiciary.

Diversity Theories and Trial Judging

With so much interest in diverse judges, numerous prominent accounts theorizing why and when female and racial minority judges will behave differently from their traditional colleagues on the bench have emerged. These include different voice, informational, representational, balance, and organizational theories. A brief discussion of each is provided below.

Established by Gilligan (1982), the different voice theory applies primarily to males and females and rests on the idea that the two sexes think, communicate, and view the world differently from one another. Gilligan argues that the male voice is distinctly masculine and committed to concepts like logic and justice. By contrast, the female voice is much more devoted to obligations, relationships, and problem solving through personal communication. Applied to judging, the different voice theory expects to see a "feminine perspective" that extends to females' decisions as judges across "all aspects of society, whether or not they affect men and women differently" (Sherry, 1986, p. 160).

Informational theory argues that female and black judges bring a unique knowledge base and expertise to the bench in key areas such as traditional sex and race employment discrimination issues, respectively. This expertise and information is "credible and persuasive" (Boyd, Epstein, & Martin, 2010, p. 392) and yields from a combination of their professional background and their distinctive group-influenced experiences and challenges (Gryski, Main, & Dixon, 1986) that their modal male, white judge colleagues simply do not have.

Still others believe that female and minority decision makers serve as high-profile, substantive representatives of others of their class working to advance their group's interests through their decisions (e.g., Farhang & Wawro, 2004; Kastellec, 2013; Pitkin. 1967). For female judges, this means that they "will seize decision-making opportunities to liberate other women" (Cook, 1981, p. 216). For black judges, a strong race-based social identity will likely encourage strong in-group closeness and racial consciousness (McClain et al., 2009). In turn, this should affect black judge decision making on racially salient topics particularly because, as federal judge Edwards (2002, p. 328) notes, "it is safe to assume that a disproportionate number of blacks grow up with a heightened awareness of the problems that pertain to" racial discrimination "areas of the law."[2]

Importantly, while all three of these accounts—different voice, informational, and representational—sometimes vary in their empirical implications at the margins (see Boyd, Epstein, & Martin, 2010), they converge when it comes to individual judge behavior in issue areas closely connected to the judge's diversity characteristic(s). Indeed, all three anticipate that, with all other things being equal, female judges will be more likely to support sex discrimination claimants than male judges and black judges will be more likely to favor race discrimination or affirmative action plaintiffs than white judges.

Balance theory goes even further than these theories. It expects that for minority decision makers, their group's historical experience with discrimination is likely to make them more sympathetic to others facing discrimination, even if that discrimination is not based on race (Bratton & Haynie, 1999; Heider, 1958). As Kulik, Perry, and Pepper (2003, p. 71) note, since "people of color [are] at greater risk of harassment ... [t]his increased vulnerability might make members of minority groups especially sensitive to the harassment of others." Applied to diversity judging, Crowe (1999, p. 115) argues that while "female judges [may] not generalize [their identification with] sex discrimination plaintiffs to other types of discrimination plaintiffs," black judges may have a broader desire to support discrimination plaintiffs.

Of course, not all theoretical accounts expect that diverse judges should be expected to behave distinctly from white and male judges on the bench. Under organizational theory, some scholars argue that all judges—white, minority, male, and female—undergo the same professionalization and training before acquiring their judicial employment (Kritzer & Uhlman, 1977). These judges' decisions must rely on the same laws and norms, something that may be particularly constraining in trial

courts. In effect, the "powerful 'organizational' influences of selection and socialization to the judicial role" along with "adherence to prevailing norms, practices, and precedents" can offset any pre-officeholding biological, socialization, psychological, or experiential differences of the judges (Steffensmeier & Britt 2001, p. 752–753). For adherents to this organizational theory, judicial diversity characteristics like sex and race are thus expected to have no systematic effects on trial judge behavior. This is likely to sit well with those, like the Obama White House, who have argued that the addition of diverse judges to the federal judiciary has nothing to do with outcomes and everything to do with descriptive and symbolic representation—the belief that "democratic institutions in heterogeneous societies should reflect the make-up of society" (Cameron & Cummings, 2003, p. 28).

One important assumption of the above discussion of diversity judging theory is that judges hold the discretion and opportunities necessary to behave in ways to implement their preferred outcomes. In other words, female and black judges, should they be so inclined, have enough decision-making flexibility to allow them to make decisions that favor sex and race discrimination plaintiffs. For appellate court judging, there is little question that this is present (P. M. Collins & Martinek, 2011; Hettinger, Lindquist, & Martinek, 2006; Klein, 2002; Scott, 2006; Wahlbeck, 1997). However, when it comes to trial court judges, much debate and discussion exists on this subject. Many trial court scholars hold firmly to the belief that trial judges are primarily administrators, appliers of law, and organizational bureaucrats, spending their time in rote activities like holding hearings and supervising jury trials. Scholars often fail to find evidence that trial judges' identities—including things like their ideological preferences—affect outcomes (e.g., Dumas & Haynie, 2012; Keele et al., 2009). If this view of trial judging is correct and generalizable, when applied to diversity judging, it could very well mean that even if diverse trial judges wish to favor diverse plaintiffs, their hands are often tied. Empirically, it would be nearly impossible to disentangle these trial judges from those who behave according to organizational theory's expectations (i.e., who, even unconstrained, do not behave differently from their traditional colleagues).

The more likely scenario, however, is that trial judges hold numerous discretion-filled behavioral opportunities—that is, decisions rivaling those made by their appellate court brethren in most cases—but these opportunities get overshadowed or diluted by the many other rote parts of trial judging. With careful isolation of district judging roles, it should therefore be possible to focus solely on the parts of trial judging that leave room for judges' identities and preferences to matter. Which trial judging jobs provide the most discretionary behavior opportunities? The most obvious examples are decisions made during bench trials and on dispositive motions. In both instances, the judge serves as the fact finder and the law applier and also holds real potential to interpret the law. By comparison, while serving as a case manager (e.g., holding status and settlement conferences), supervising jury trials, or deciding whether to transfer a case, trial judges hold less decision-making discretion that could affect outcomes toward their preferred direction (e.g., Williams & George, 2013). This is not to say, of course, that trial judges have no discretion in these parts of their jobs, but the important point is that the discretion that is present is, at best, indirectly linked to the case's outcome and being able to drive that outcome toward favoring one party over another.

The Empirical Evidence So Far

Moving from diversity theory to empirics, which side of the theoretical divide receives the bulk of the support? When it comes to trial courts, little consensus exists.[3] For judge race, nearly half of the projects' results indicate no statistically significant impact from a trial judge's race on his or her decision-making behavior (e.g., Ashenfelter, Eisenberg, & Schwab, 1995; Kulik, Perry, & Pepper, 2003; Segal, 2000; Spohn, 1990; Walker & Barrow, 1985). Another set of these studies finds that minority trial judges are more likely to support liberal positions than their white colleagues (e.g., Chew & Kelley, 2009; Schanzenbach, 2005; Sisk, Heise, & Morriss, 1998; Weinberg & Nielsen, 2012; Welch, Combs, &d Gruhl, 1988). Only a small handful of judge-race trial judging studies find that minority judges behave contrary to all expectations by regularly supporting a conservative position more frequently than white judges, with, for example, both Steffensmeier and Britt (2001) and Uhlman (1978) finding that black judges have harsher sentencing behavior than white judges.

For judge sex, the research findings on trial judge behavior are perhaps even more convoluted. The majority of these studies find no evidence that female trial judges behave differently than male judges across a range of issue areas, from sentencing to sexual harassment claims and employment discrimination disputes (e.g., Ashenfelter, Eisenberg, & Schwab, 1995; Chew & Kelley, 2009; Gruhl, Spohn, & Welch, 1981; Kulik, Perry, & Pepper, 2003; Sisk, Heise, & Morriss, 1998; Weinberg & Nielsen, 2012). A smaller, but nontrivial, set of studies have found that female judges tend to behave more conservatively than their male counterparts in the trial courts. This includes being less likely to support women's issues like personal liberties, maternity rights, reproductive freedom, custody, and equal employment than male judges (Segal, 2000; Walker & Barrow, 1985) and being more likely to harshly sentence criminal defendants (P. M. Collins, Manning, & Carp, 2010; Spohn, 1990). Another small set of studies, however, have found that female judges behave more liberally than their male trial court colleagues (e.g., Johnson, 2014; Manning, 2004).

Research Design and Data

Looking for Diversity Effects in Trial Courts

As the above discussion indicates, when it comes to what the current literature has to say about diversity and judicial decision making in trial courts, uncertainty reigns. Before embarking on yet another study of diversity in trial judging and simply adding to the confusion, it is necessary to address the unique considerations for diversity trial court judging that present empirical challenges and may share responsibility for the state of the literature. The three key factors are as follows: the unit of analysis for judge decision making, the large number of frivolous trial court cases, and narrow diversity-centric issue area data. For a study on the subject to yield reliable results, these features must be taken into account in the research design.

First, trial courts are the courts of first instance, where litigation begins, develops a factual record, provides the initial application of law to those facts, and permits the regular and often years' long interaction between trial judges and case participants. As a product of this design, and quite distinctly from appellate courts, trial court judges have numerous opportunities to make important decisions throughout a case. Of note, most civil cases develop through motions practice, with the judge's decision to grant or deny the motion having critical implications for how the case will proceed (Hoffman, Izenman, & Lidicker, 2007; Kim et al., 2009). It is these decisions on significant motions throughout a case rather than simply a trial judge's case-terminating opinion, should one exist, that present the most fruitful opportunity to examine trial court judicial behavior. Take, for example, a sex discrimination case being litigated in the trial court where the case ultimately terminates via a pro-defendant jury verdict. An outcome-only or opinion-only focus would not study this case, because no judge decision on the verdict exists.[4] However, a motions focus may reveal that prior to the trial, the judge denied the defendant's motion to dismiss and motion for summary judgment. The judicial decisions on these motions are pro-discrimination claimant rulings in the case, albeit not ones that serve to conclude the litigation or that necessarily lead to published judicial opinions.

Second, many trial court cases, particularly in civil litigation, involve weak, potentially frivolous claims. As Epstein, Landes, and Posner (2013, p. 232) put it, "many cases are filed by pro se or emotional litigants and by litigants represented by inept or inexperienced lawyers." Most of these cases will be dismissed or abandoned no matter who the judge is. Any trial court dataset that includes a high proportion of these inherently weak cases is therefore likely biased against finding judge-specific effects due to the swamping effect of these "easy" cases and the motions practice that lies within them. Such concerns may be particularly salient in diversity-connected issue areas like employment discrimination where many worry about high numbers of frivolous lawsuits (Nielsen & Nelson, 2005).

Finally, the above-discussed theories predicting diversity effects on judging are generally issue area specific. As such, any test of them needs narrowly defined data that fit squarely within or outside of those issue areas. This means that trial court datasets focused on broad issue areas like "civil rights" or "civil liberties" may not be precise enough to detect differences in underlying judging behavior because the cases include not only those that fall within traditional women's issues and minority issues but also those extending well beyond (e.g., assault, housing discrimination, immigration).

Data

This project uses the Kim, Schlanger, and Martin (2013) newly collected dataset of EEOC-brought federal trial court employment discrimination lawsuits. The Kim, Schlanger, and Martin data sample more than 2,300 EEOC cases filed between 1997 and 2006. They permit the above concerns inherent in most trial court-diversity judging research designs to be directly addressed.

First, the EEOC dataset is motion centered rather than opinion or case outcome-centric. Coded from case docket sheets and documents, the data include every dispositive and substantive motion that takes place within a case's district court life. Each observation in the resulting data is a judge's decision on the motion.[5] This project focuses on a subset of the data which excludes motions that are not directly related to the case's potential disposition or its merits like discovery motions,[6] motions by a private complainant to intervene in the EEOC's lawsuit, and motions to relate or consolidate multiple lawsuits together. This study also excludes motions filed with the consent of both parties because these motions strip trial judges of decision-making discretion. The data also exclude observations in which no judge decision was recorded, something that occurs when the case settles prior to the motion decision, and those in which the deciding judge was a magistrate judge or Article I district judge rather than an Article III district judge.

Second, the Kim, Schlanger, and Martin (2013) dataset's inclusion of only those cases brought into the federal district courts by the EEOC has important implications for the type of cases that are in the dataset. The EEOC has statutory authority through the 1972 Equal Employment Opportunity Act to sue private employers to enforce Title VII of the Civil Rights Act of 1964 (which bans employment discrimination on the basis of sex, race, religion, and national origin), the Age Discrimination in Employment Act, and the Americans with Disabilities Act. Prior to bringing federal lawsuits to enforce these statutes, the EEOC conducts internal administrative review of discrimination complaints.[7] For many complaints, the EEOC chooses to not file a federal lawsuit. The U.S. EEOC (2014) describes its decision whether to file a federal district court lawsuit as follows:

When deciding whether to file a lawsuit, EEOC will consider several factors, including the seriousness of the violation, the type of legal issues in the case, and the wider impact the lawsuit could have on EEOC efforts to combat workplace discrimination.

In other words, the EEOC's decision to file a federal lawsuit is not random, but rather one that is based on their extensive internal investigation indicating the high quality and importance of pursuing a particular case into federal court (Hirsh, 2008). As an illustration of the EEOC's significant filtering, in fiscal year 2001, the EEOC reported that 80,840 individual charges were filed with its office. During the same year, the EEOC filed just 428 federal district courts enforcement lawsuits. For purposes of this current project, the presence of this EEOC filtering means that, unlike most civil litigation, the likelihood of weak, frivolous cases littering the data and drowning any judge identity effects is low.

Third, the EEOC dataset codes the types of alleged discrimination present in a case. This permits the examination of a subset of employment discrimination cases that is narrowly focused on the diversity characteristics of interest here (sex and race). This is a particularly important point for a study of diversity in judging for two reasons. First, many of the diversity theories described above generally only anticipate diverse judges to behave differently from their colleagues in cases directly related to their diversity characteristic, meaning that overly broad data will prove inadequate for theory testing. Second, without this data narrowness, any statistical results are likely to be deceptively deflated or nonexistent. Here, these data are parsed down into two types of categories: sex and pregnancy discrimination[8] and race and color discrimination.[9] The data exclude sex discrimination claims brought on behalf of male plaintiffs and race discrimination claims brought on behalf of white plaintiffs.

Variables

The dependent variable for the study is Pro-plaintiff Outcome. Pro-plaintiff Outcome is coded as 1 if the judge's ruling on the motion provides the EEOC and/or a private plaintiff a clear victory on the motion and 0 if the judge's ruling clearly favors the defendant. These motions are, for example, motions for summary judgment in which a party asks the judge for a pretrial victory because "no genuine dispute as to any material fact" exists and, therefore, he or she "is entitled to judgment as a matter of law" (Federal Rules of Civil Procedure Rule [FRCP] 56) or motions to dismiss in which the defendant argues that the district court lacks the necessary jurisdiction to hear the case (FRCP 12[b]). Any time the judge issues a partial ruling, such as granting a motion for summary judgment in part and denying it in part, the case is excluded from the data.[10]

The primary independent variables in the study are the race and sex of the judge deciding the motion. Drawn from the Federal Judicial Center (2011), Female Judge is coded as 1 if the judge deciding the motion is a female, 0 otherwise. Black judge is coded as 1 if the judge deciding the motion is an African American racial minority, and 0 if he is white.[11]

This study also controls for a host of judicial, case, and legal variables that may affect the outcome of substantive motions in EEOC cases. These variables and their measurement are fully detailed in the online appendix. Briefly, the control variables include judge ideology measures for the district judge deciding the motion along with the ideology and ideological variance of his supervising court of appeals (Epstein et al., 2007; Giles, Hettinger, & Peppers, 2001). It is also important to control for the type of motion. Earlier stage motions should be more nonmovant favorable than later stage motions. Similarly, as motions practice is designed to favor the nonmoving party, controlling for the identity of the movant is important. So is accounting for whether the nonmoving party opposed the motion in writing, something that, when present, may increase the odds of denial. At the case level, the study also controls for the major issue or issues alleged in the complaint and for whether the underlying case has one or more than one complainant.

Results

To statistically examine whether a federal trial judge's sex and race affect his or her decision making, we turn to a logistic regression analysis of the two sub-datasets of interest—that is, sex and pregnancy employment discrimination case motions and race and color employment discrimination case motions. To address concerns about

Table 1 • Logistic Regression Results for Whether a Motion's Outcome Is Decided in a Pro-plaintiff Direction

Variables	Model 1: Sex discrimination case motions	Model 2: Race discrimination case motions
Female judge	0.795** (0.35)	0.794 (0.73)
Black judge	1.471** (0.52)	1.655** (0.76)
Ideology controls	Included	Included
Motion controls	Included	Included
Complainant number control	Included	Included
Issue(s) alleged controls	Included	Included
Constant	−1.257 (1.67)	−1.806 (2.45)
Observations	450	186
Percent reduction in error	15.60%	23.53%

Standard errors are robust, clustered on the individual case, and presented in parentheses. The baseline motion type is Summary Judgment Motion. Full regression results including all control variables are provided in the online appendix.

**p < .05 (two-tailed).

independence of observations, the modeling includes robust standard errors clustered on the individual case. The results from the modeling for the two issue area datasets are provided in Table 1 (see Online Appendix Table A2 for the full regression results).[12] Let us begin with the results for the effect of judge sex on trial court decision making. Model 1 provides these results for sex and pregnancy discrimination case motions. Recall that many diversity theorists anticipate that female judges will be much more likely than male judges to rule in favor of the plaintiff in these sex discrimination cases. As the results indicate, this is exactly what we find. Female Judge is positive and statistically significant.

The substantive effect of this variable is further explored in Figure 1. There, the left side figure plots the predicted probability of a male (open circle) judge and female (solid circle) judge ruling in favor of the EEOC or the private plaintiff in the motion. All other variables in the model are held at their median (for continuous variables) and modal (for dichotomous variables) values. For female trial judges, the average predicted probability of

ruling for the sex discrimination plaintiff is.35. For the male, this number is only.20. As the accompanying right side figure indicates, this difference in the average predicted probability is.15 and is statistically different from 0. This result thus provides substantial evidence that female trial judges do indeed behave distinctly from their male colleagues when faced with decision-making opportunities firmly triggering "women's issues."

When it comes to race discrimination case motions, however, there is no statistical evidence that male and female judges systematically behave distinctly from one another. The Female Judge variable is positive in the second regression model, but it does not reach statistically significant levels. This point is driven home by the large confidence interval (CI) on the plotted difference in Figure 1's right side panel that clearly overlaps 0 (CI = [−0.16, 0.53]). This lack of result for Female Judge in the race discrimination dataset is not surprising. Diversity theory expects that female judges will generally only behave differently from their male colleagues when acting as substantive representatives of their class or when using their unique professional experience and knowledge related to being a woman—that is, things that are certainly put into play in sex discrimination cases but likely not in most race discrimination cases.

Turning now to an examination of the effect of judge race on trial court decision making, it makes sense to first focus on Model 2 (race discrimination case motions). Just as with judge sex and sex discrimination cases, there is much theory in support of the expectation that black trial judges will be much more likely to support race discrimination claimants than white trial judges. The positive and statistically significant coefficient for black judge in Model 2 empirically supports this. Figure 2 once again plots the substantive effect. As the bottom portion of the left-hand plot indicates, the average predicted probability of a black judge ruling in favor of the race discrimination plaintiff is .70. This number is only .31 for similarly situated white trial judges. The average difference in this predicted probability is .39 and is statistically different from 0 (see right side of Figure 2), meaning that there is a 126 percent increase in the likelihood of a black trial judge ruling in favor of the EEOC's race discrimination claim in a dispositive motion over a white trial judge.

Interestingly, there is also a positive and statistically significant effect from a judge's race on voting behavior in sex discrimination case motions. This is apparent by examining black judge in Model 1 and the top section of Figure 2. As the figure shows, black trial judges have an average predicted probability of ruling in a pro-plaintiff manner on sex discrimination case motions of .514; for white judges, this number is .195. This difference, nearly .32, is again impressively large and both substantively and statistically significant. This large effect for black trial judges deciding sex discrimination case motions may be explained by the above-discussed balance theory—that is, the idea that black judges are sensitive to others facing discrimination.

Finally, for the control variables (see the online appendix), in both the sex and race discrimination data, the variable capturing the fact that the defendant is the movant is positive and significant. This result reflects that the nonmoving party holds an advantage in district court motions practice. In the sex discrimination data, the results also indicate that multiple types of motions are significantly more likely to lead to pro-plaintiff outcomes than the baseline type of motions, Summary Judgment

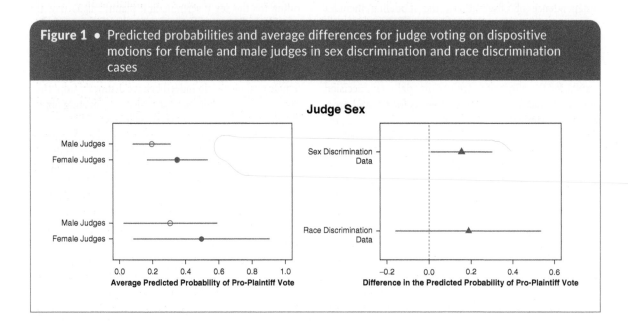

Figure 1 • Predicted probabilities and average differences for judge voting on dispositive motions for female and male judges in sex discrimination and race discrimination cases

Figure 2 • Predicted probabilities and average differences for judge voting on dispositive motions for black and white judges in sex discrimination and race discrimination cases

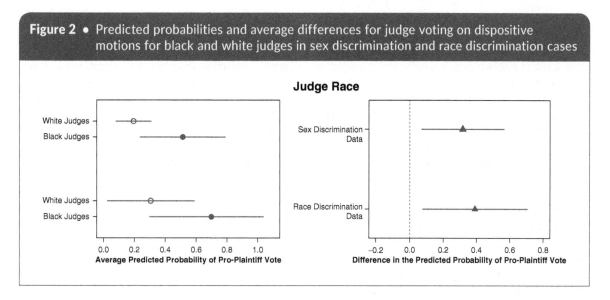

Motions. In neither dataset is district judge ideology statistically significant. This nonresult is robust to the measurement of district judges' preferences, with Party of the Appointing President substituted for District Judge Ideology yielding no difference in effect. Although this may come as a surprise to some political scientists used to seeing attitudinal results in judicial behavior, a lack of effect is not uncommon in many district court studies (e.g., Howard, 2002; Keele et al., 2009; Walker, 1972; Zorn & Bowie, 2010).

Discussion

As noted in the outset of this project, previous attempts to find diversity effects in judging in the trial courts have been largely unsuccessful. By reexamining the research design used for analyzing diversity in judging in trial courts and focusing on data generated from judicial decisions on motions rather than simply case outcomes or published opinions, data that filter out frivolous cases, and data that are narrowly focused on individual issue areas of theoretical interest to diversity theory, this project has been able to bring new clarity to this important issue. Indeed, the results here provide some of the first

consistent, systematic evidence that female and racial minority trial judges do indeed behave differently, and rather substantially, from their traditional colleagues. Female trial court judges, when deciding dispositive motions in sex discrimination cases, are about 15 percent more likely to rule in favor of the discrimination claimant than male judges. Similarly, in race discrimination cases, black trial court judges are about 39 percent more likely to decide in favor of the race discrimination plaintiff than white judges. These results thus join other recent work finding strong diversity judging effects in certain settings, whether that be outcomes in federal appellate courts (Boyd, Epstein, & Martin, 2010; Kastellec, 2013), opinion crafting, oral argument questions, conference behavior, and the hiring of clerks and office staff in appellate courts (e.g., Haire, Moyer, &d Treier, 2013; Kaheny et al., 2015), or nonmerits trial judging activities like whether to actively encourage settlement (Boyd 2013) or what decisions to make during in-court administrative proceedings such as arraignment and bail requests (Fox & Sickel, 2000).

Although the findings here provide important insight into trial court judging, particularly in the diversity context, there are inherent limitations in the project's generalizability that merit note. One of these stems from the focus of the underlying database only on those cases brought by the EEOC into the federal district courts. As discussed in detail above, the EEOC focus serves many empirical and research design benefits and is similar in scope to other recent studies examining one type of case—whether that be, for example, cases only brought by the Solicitor General (Black & Owens, 2012, 2013; Zorn, 2002) or amicus curiae (P. M. Collins, 2004, 2007; Collins & Martinek, 2010) or only those that eventually lead to an appeal (Randazzo, 2008). Here, just like many of these other litigants and cases, the EEOC is not an average, typical plaintiff in trial courts but rather is a strong repeat player that makes smart decisions regarding which cases to file and which cases not to file. Would we observe the same results by examining employment discrimination lawsuits filed by all types of plaintiffs? Although only future research can answer this question with certainty, the EEOC focus in this project means that the results here are most likely to be generalizable to other plaintiff-brought lawsuits that are filtered and well-crafted, meaning that, for example, an average individual employment discrimination plaintiff bringing a lawsuit declined by the EEOC will probably be less likely to hold the same advantage before diverse judges.

A second data-linked limitation of this project rests with its inability to speak directly to the important issue of intersectionality—that is, the idea that, as once stated by Crenshaw (1992, p. 1467–1468), black women face the "dual vulnerability" of racism and sexism that intersect "to create experiences that are sometimes unique." Applied to judges, T. Collins and Moyer (2008, p. 225) argue that "minority women have a distinctive identity" that affects their behavior. For trial court judges, this could, in theory, lead to black female judges being more likely to support female sex discrimination plaintiffs, black race discrimination plaintiffs, or black female plaintiffs raising sex and race discrimination claims simultaneously. Indeed, a disproportionate number of the early sex harassment lawsuits were filed by black women (MacKinnon, 1979, p. 53), and some discrimination lawsuits even today include both race and sex discrimination claims (see Note 9). Unfortunately, the current study's number of black female judge observations is too small to provide an empirical test of intersectionality. There are just three total black female judges in the data and not a single black female judge observation in which the judge presides over

a motion with both a race and sex discrimination claim in the underlying lawsuit.[13] Only future research, aided by a larger sample of data and the ever-growing number of female, racial minority judges on the bench, will be able to fully tackle this issue at the district court level.

In addition, the data used here focus on two types of cases—race employment discrimination and sex employment discrimination. As such, this project cannot be confidently applied to other issue areas like criminal sentencing, abortion, family law matters, or beyond. The theory of difference in diversity judging is much less uniform in these areas, largely because it is not as easy to connect a judge's race or sex with expected preferences over issues not directly linked to sex or race. Although female and black trial judges may behave differently from their colleagues in other issue areas, only future empirical tests can provide confirmation. Similarly, this project's data, by design, do not represent all parts of a district judge's job. As discussed above, many of a district judge's duties are not discretionary and likely do not leave room for her preferred outcomes to be implemented into behavior.

Even after acknowledging these limitations, the implications of the diversity effect found here are vast. Federal trial courts are now responsible for hearing more than 300,000 cases per year—a number that far exceeds those heard by U.S. Courts of Appeals and the U.S. Supreme Court—and composed of nearly 32 percent female judges and more than 13 percent black judges. The fact that some trial court cases are affected so drastically by the identity of the judge has repercussions not just for the outcome of the immediate case and the likelihood of the plaintiff being successful. Rather, such an influence reverberates through the judicial hierarchy and beyond (Baum, 1997, 2006). Although the federal district court loser retains the right to appeal, fewer than 20 percent do so (Eisenberg, 2004). And, when they do appeal, the appellate courts are generally required to be quite deferential to the lower court decision. In other words, what happens in trial court judging matters.

Finally, in returning to this paper's introduction, this project is particularly timely given President Obama's judicial appointment priorities. Recall that the Obama Administration has argued that while diversifying the federal trial courts is important for creating a judiciary that "resembles our nation" (Kang, 2013), it does not mean that these judges will consider cases differently from traditional judges. The evidence provided here strongly disputes this point, meaning that President Obama has not only been altering the descriptive identity of the nation's federal trial courts through his diverse appointments but also affecting the resulting substantive policy and law—now and well into the future given the lifetime tenure held by these appointees.

/// DISCUSSION QUESTIONS

1. How does the racial/ethnic identity of judges influence decision making in cases of sexual and racial discrimination?

2. How does sex influence decision making in cases of sexual and racial discrimination?

3. What are the implications of the findings of this study given the increasing diversity in judicial appointments across the United States?

Notes

1. By comparison, previous presidents had the following diversity appointment percentages to the federal district courts: 33 percent (Carter), 16 percent (Reagan), 36 percent (G. H. Bush), 52 percent (Clinton), and 34 percent (G. W. Bush). These calculated percentages include all judges who were female, minority, or both and do not double count female and racial minorities.

2. Recent scholarship calls for the testing of the intersection of race and sex in diversity judging (intersectionality). This topic is tackled in further detail below in Note 9 and in the "Discussion" section.

3. By contrast, for appellate courts, research paints an increasingly consistent picture: judge diversity matters, but generally only in issue areas directly connected to the diversity characteristic. For female judges, that means a higher likelihood to favor claimants in women's issue-type cases like sexual discrimination and sexual harassment (e.g., Boyd, Epstein, & Martin, 2010; Crowe, 1999; Farhang & Wawro, 2004; Haire & Moyer, 2014; Peresie, 2005; Songer, Davis, & Haire, 1994). For nonwhite judges, areas like voting rights, race discrimination, affirmative action, and some criminal matters tend to produce differential judicial behavior (e.g., Cox & Miles, 2008; Crowe, 1999; Kastellec, 2013; Scherer, 2004).

4. As Siegelman and Donohue (1990) find, less than one out of four employment discrimination cases yield publicly available opinions. Those opinions that are available are not representative of broader discrimination litigation.

5. More than 29 percent of the cases in the Kim, Schlanger, and Martin (2013) data have no recorded motions.

6. Including discovery motions in the statistical analysis below does not alter the results reported.

7. Statutory and administrative procedure requires nearly all employment discrimination complaints that may eventually be brought into federal court to first be filed with the Equal Employment Opportunity Commission (EEOC).

8. The Pregnancy Discrimination Act of 1978 prohibits "sex discrimination on the basis of pregnancy." This project includes workplace pregnancy discrimination allegations with sex discrimination. The results do not change if pregnancy discrimination cases are excluded.

9. Plaintiffs can plead multiple types of discrimination in their district court complaints. Within the Kim, Schlanger, and Martin (2013) data, multiple claim pleading is relatively rare. For example, in the sex discrimination data, less than 10 percent of the case motion observations include another form of discrimination. Although all major discrimination claim types within the Kim, Schlanger, and Martin (2013) data (race, national origin, age, disability, and religion) are paired with sex discrimination claims at least once, race is the most common (about 8.5% of all sex discrimination observations).

10. An alternative coding scheme for these partial decisions is to include them in the data and code them as a loss for the movant. Although the moving party received some relief, the judge's decision denying the motion in part results in the case continuing despite the movant's efforts to the contrary. The inclusion of these additional observations does not change the statistical results for the key judge sex and race variables.

11. This variable's coding excludes from the data those district judges that are neither black nor white. Previous work suggests that black judges are distinct from other minority judges in these cases. Here, these nonblack minority judges amount to a handful of observations, and alternative coding schemes, including grouping these judges with white judges

(Kastellec, 2013) or with black judges (T. Collins & Moyer, 2008), have no effect on the results reported below.

12. Additional modeling confirms the robustness of the results. Following propensity score nearest-neighbor matching (Ho et al., 2006), the estimated differences were statistically significant and in the expected direction for judge race and sex. Only descriptive (noncausal) inference is possible in this study of individual judge behavior (Rubin, 2006). Multilevel modeling with motions nested within cases, while not ideal here due to a relatively small number of observations and an average of only two motions per case, also confirms the results reported in the main text.

13. As initial evidence on the effect of black female judges in the data, the statistical results reported below remain unchanged after excluding the small number of these judges from the data.

References

Ashenfelter, O., Eisenberg, T., & Schwab, S. J. (1995). Politics and the judiciary: The influence of judicial background on case outcomes. *Journal of Legal Studies, 24* (2): 257–281.

Baum, L. (1997). *The puzzle of judicial behavior.* Ann Arbor: University of Michigan Press.

Baum, L. (2006). *Judges and their audiences: A perspective on judicial behavior.* Princeton: Princeton University Press.

Black, R, C., & Owens, R. J. (2012). *The Solicitor General and the United States Supreme Court: Executive branch influence and judicial decisions.* Cambridge: Cambridge University Press.

Black, R. C., & Owens, R. J. (2013). A built-in advantage: The office of the Solicitor General and the U.S. Supreme Court. *Political Research Quarterly, 66*:454–466.

Boyd, C. L. (2013). She'll settle it?" *Journal of Law and Courts, 1*:193–219.

Boyd, C. L., Epstein, L., & Martin, A. D. (2010). Untangling the causal effects of sex on judging. *American Journal of Political Science, 54* (2): 389–411.

Bratton, K. A., Haynie, K. L. (1999). Agenda setting and legislative success in state legislatures: The effects of gender and race. *Journal of Politics, 61*:658–679.

Cameron, C., & Cummings, C. (2003). Diversity and judicial decision making: Evidence from affirmative action cases in the Federal Courts of Appeals, 1971–1999. Paper presented at the Crafting and Operating Institutions Conference, Yale University, April 11–13.

Chew, P. K., & Kelley, R. E. (2009). Myth of the color-blind judge: An empirical analysis of racial harassment cases. *Washington University Law Review, 86*:1117–1166.

Collins, P. M., Jr. (2004). Friends of the Court: Examining the influence of amicus curiae participation in U.S. Supreme Court litigation. *Law & Society Review, 38* (4): 807–832.

Collins, P. M., Jr. (2007). Lobbyists before the U.S. Supreme Court: Investigating the influence of amicus curiae briefs. *Political Research Quarterly, 60* (1): 55–70.

Collins, P. M., Jr., Manning, K. L., & Carp, R. A. (2010). Gender, critical mass, and judicial decision making. *Law & Policy, 32*:260–281.

Collins, P. M., Jr., & Martinek, W. L. (2010). Friends of the circuits: Interest group influence on decision making in the U.S. Courts of Appeals. *Social Science Quarterly, 91*:397–414.

Collins, P. M., Jr., & Martinek, W. L. (2011). The small group context: Designated district court judges in the U.S. Courts of Appeals. *Journal of Empirical Legal Studies, 8*:177–205.

Collins, T., & Moyer, L. (2008). Gender, race, and intersectionality on the federal appellate bench. *Political Research Quarterly, 61*:219–227.

Cook, B. B. (1981). Will women judges make a difference in women's legal rights? In M. Rendel (Ed.), *Women, power, and political systems* (pp. 216–239). London: Croom Helm.

Cox, A. B., & Miles, T. J. (2008). Judging the Voting Rights Act. *Columbia Law Review, 108* (1): 1–54.

Crenshaw, K. (1992). Race, gender, and sexual harassment. *Southern California Law Review, 65*:1467–1476.

Crowe, N. (1999). The effects of judges' sex and race on judicial decision making on the U.S. Courts of Appeals, 1981–1996. PhD diss., University of Chicago.

Dolan, J. (2000). The senior executive service: Gender, attitudes, and representative bureaucracy. *Journal of Public Administration Research and Theory, 3*:513–529.

Dumas, T, L., & Haynie, S. L. (2012). Building an integrated model of trial court decision making: Predicting plaintiff success and awards across circuits. *State Politics & Policy Quarterly, 12*: 103–126.

Edwards, H, T. (2002). Race and the judiciary. *Yale Law & Policy Review, 20*:325–330.

Eisenberg, T. (2004). Appeal rates and outcomes in tried and non-tried cases: Further exploration of anti-plaintiff appellate outcomes. *Journal of Empirical Legal Studies, 1*:659–688.

Epstein, L., Landes, W. M., & Posner, R. M. (2013). *The behavior of federal judges: A theoretical and empirical study of rational choice.* Cambridge: Harvard University Press.

Epstein, L., Martin, A. D., Segal, J. A., & Westerland, C. (2007). The judicial common space. *Journal of Law, Economics, & Organization, 23* (2): 303–325.

Farhang, S., & Wawro, G. (2004). Institutional dynamics on the U.S. Court of Appeals: Minority representation under panel decision making. *Journal of Law, Economics, & Organization, 20*: 299–330.

Federal Judicial Center. (2011). History of the federal judiciary: Federal judges biographical database." Retrieved from http:// www.fjc. gov/public/home.nsf/hisj

Fox, R., & Van Sickel, R. (2000). Gender dynamics and judicial behavior in criminal trial courts: An exploratory study. *Justice System Journal, 21* (3): 261–280.

Giles, M. W., Hettinger, V. A., & Peppers, T. (2001). Picking federal judges: A note on policy and partisan selection agendas. *Political Research Quarterly, 54* (3): 623–641.

Gilligan, C. (1982). *In a different voice: Psychological theory and women's development.* Cambridge: Harvard University Press.

Gruhl, J., Spohn, C., & Welch, S. (1981). Women as policymakers: The case of trial judges. *American Journal of Political Science, 25* (2): 308–322.

Gryski, G., Main, E. C., & Dixon, W. J. (1986). Models of state high court decision making in sex discrimination cases. *Journal of Politics, 48:*143–155.

Haire, S. B., & Moyer, L. P. (2014). *Does diversity matter? Judicial policy making in the U.S. Courts of Appeals.* Charlottesville: University of Virginia Press.

Haire, S. B., Moyer, L. P., & Treier, S. (2013). Diversity, deliberation, and judicial opinion writing. *Journal of Law and Courts, 1:* 303–330.

Heider, F. (1958). *The psychology of interpersonal relations.* New York: Wiley.

Hettinger, V. A., Lindquist, S. A., & Martinek, W. L. (2006). *Judging on a collegial court.* Charlottesville: University of Virginia Press.

Hirsh, C. E. (2008). Settling for less? Organizational determinants of discrimination-charge outcomes. *Law & Society Review, 42:*239–274.

Ho, D., Imai, K., King, G., & Stuart, E. (2006). MatchIt: Nonparametric preprocessing for parametric casual inference. R package version 2.2–11. Retrieved from http://gking .harvard.edu/matchit

Hoffman, D. A., Izenman, A. J., & Lidicker, J. R. (2007). Docketology, district courts, and doctrine. *Washington University Law Review, 85:*681–751.

Howard, R. M. (2002). Litigation, courts, and bureaucratic policy: Equity, efficiency, and the Internal Revenue Service. *American Politics Research, 30:*583–607.

Johnson, B. D. (2014). Judges on trial: A reexamination of judicial race and gender effects across modes of conviction. *Criminal Justice Policy Review, 25:* 159–184.

Kaheny, E. B., Szmer, J., Hansen, M., & Scheurer, K. (2015). High court recruitment of female clerks: A comparative analysis of the U.S. Supreme Court and the Supreme Court of Canada. *Judicature, 36:*355–377.

Kang, C. (2013). President Obama nominates four distinguished women to serve as federal judges. The White House. Retrieved from http://www.whitehouse.gov/blog/2013/05/17/president-obama-nominates-four-distinguished-women serve-federal-judges.

Kastellec, J. P. (2013). Racial diversity and judicial influence on appellate courts. *American Journal of Political Science, 57* (1): 167–183.

Keele, D. M., Malmsheimer, R. W., Floyd, D. W., & Zhang, L. (2009). An analysis of ideological effects in published versus unpublished judicial opinions. *Journal of Empirical Legal Studies, 6* (1): 213–239.

Kim, P. T., Schlanger, M., Boyd, C. L., & Martin, A. D. (2009). How should we study district judge decision-making? *Washington University Journal of Law & Policy, 29:*83–112.

Kim, P. T., Schlanger, M., & Martin, A. D. (2013). EEOC Litigation Project. Washington University in St. Louis, MO. Retrieved from http://eeoclitigation.wustl.edu/

Klein, D. E. (2002). *Making law in the United States Courts of Appeals.* New York: Cambridge University Press.

Kritzer, H. M., & Uhlman, T. M. (1977). Sisterhood in the courtroom: Sex of judge and defendant in criminal case disposition. *Social Sciences Journal, 14:*77–88.

Kulik, C. T., Perry, E. L., & Pepper, M. (2003). Here comes the judge: The influence of judge personal characteristics on federal sexual harassment case outcomes. *Law and Human Behavior, 27:* 69–86.

MacKinnon, C. A. (1979). *Sexual harassment of working women: A case of sex discrimination.* New Haven: Yale University Press.

Manning, K. L. (2004). Como decide? Decision-making by Latino judges in the federal courts. Paper presented at 2004 Midwest Political Science Association Annual Meeting, Chicago, IL, March 16-21.

McClain, P. D., Johnson Carew, J. D., Walton, E., Jr., & Watts, C. S. (2009). Group membership, group identity, and group consciousness: Measures of racial identity in American politics? *Annual Review of Political Science, 12:*471–485.

Nielsen, L. B., & Nelson, R. L. (2005). Rights realized? An empirical analysis of employment discrimination litigation as a claiming system. *Wisconsin Law Review, 2005:*663–711.

Peresie, J. L. (2005). Female judges matter: Gender and collegial decision making in the federal appellate courts. *Yale Law Journal, 114* (7): 1759–1790.

Pitkin, H. (1967). *The concept of representation.* Berkeley: University of California Press.

Randazzo, K. A. (2008). Strategic anticipation and the hierarchy of justice in U.S. district courts. *American Politics Research, 36:*669–693.

Rubin, D. B. (2006). *Matched sampling for causal effects.* New York: Cambridge University Press.

Schanzenbach, M. M. (2005). Racial and sex disparities in prison sentences: The effect of district-level judicial demographics. *Journal of Legal Studies, 34:*57–92.

Scherer, N. (2004). Blacks on the bench. *Political Science Quarterly, 119:*655–672.

Scott, K M. (2006). Understanding judicial hierarchy: Reversals and the behavior of intermediate appellate judges. *Law & Society Review, 40:*163–192.

Segal, J. A. (2000). Representative decision making on the federal bench: Clinton's district court appointees. *Political Research Quarterly, 53* (1): 137–150.

Sherry, S. (1986). "Civic virtue and the feminine voice in constitutional adjudication. *Virginia Law Review, 72:*543–616.

Siegelman, P. R., & Donohue, J., III. (1990). Studying the iceberg from its tip: A comparison of published and unpublished employment discrimination cases. *Law & Society Review*, 24:1133–1170.

Sisk, G. C., Heise, M., & Morriss, A. P. (1998). Charting the influences on the judicial mind: An empirical study of judicial reasoning. *New York Law Review*, 73:1377–1500.

Songer, D. R., Davis, S., & Haire, S. (1994). A reappraisal of diversification in the federal courts: Gender effects in the Courts of Appeals. *Journal of Politics*, 56 (2): 425–439.

Spohn, C. (1990). Decision making in sexual assault cases: Do Black and female judges make a difference? *Women & Criminal Justice*. 2:83–105.

Steffensmeier, D., & Britt, C. L. (2001). Judges' race and judicial decision making: Do Black judges sentence differently? *Social Science Quarterly*, 82:749–764.

Uhlman, T. M. (1978). Black elite decision making: The case of trial judges. *American Journal of Political Science*, 22:884–895.

U.S. Equal Employment Opportunity Commission. (2014). Litigation procedures. Retrieved from http://www.eeoc.gov/eeoc/litigation/procedures.cfm

Wahlbeck, P. J. (1997). The life of the law: Judicial politics and legal change. *Journal of Politics*, 59:778–802.

Walker, T. G. (1972). Note concerning partisan influences on trial-judge decision making. *Law & Society Review*, 6:645–650.

Walker, T. G., & Barrow, D. J. (1985). The diversification of the federal bench: Policy and process ramifications. *Journal of Politics*, 47 (2): 596–617.

Weinberg, J. D., & Nielsen, L. B. (2012). Examining empathy: Discrimination, experience, and judicial decision making. *Southern California Law Review*, 85: 313–352.

Welch, S., Combs, M., & Gruhl, J. (1988). Do Black judges make a difference? *American Journal of Political Science*, 32 (1): 126–136.

Williams, M. S., & George, T. E. (2013). Who will manage complex civil litigation? The decision to transfer and consolidate multidistrict litigation. *Journal of Empirical Legal Studies*, 10: 424–461.

Zorn, C. J. W. (2002). U.S. government litigation strategies in the federal appellate courts. *Political Research Quarterly*, 55: 145–166.

Zorn, C. J. W., & Barnes Bowie, J. (2010). Ideological influences on decision making in the federal judicial hierarchy: An empirical assessment. *Journal of Politics*, 72 (4): 1212–1221.

READING /// 26

In an effort to meet the needs of crime victims, many agencies began as community-based movements to serve the needs of particular crime victims, such as intimate partner violence or rape and sexual assault. This article by Sarah Ullman and Stephanie Townsend looks at the challenges that rape crisis workers face in the delivery of services to victims.

Barriers to Working With Sexual Assault Survivors
A Qualitative Study of Rape Crisis Center Workers

Sarah E. Ullman and Stephanie M. Townsend

Rape crisis centers are uniquely situated to respond to the physical, emotional, and social needs of survivors. Their services focus on three critical areas: 24-hour crisis hotlines, individual and group counseling (often on a short-term basis only), and legal and medical advocacy (Campbell & Martin, 2001). Although there have been few explicit studies on the benefits of receiving rape crisis services, there is evidence that rape crisis

SOURCE: Ullman, S. E., & Townsend, S. M. (2007). Barriers to working with sexual assault survivors: A qualitative study of rape crisis center workers. *Violence Against Women*, 14(4), 412–443.

NOTE: This article was partially written while the first author was a faculty scholar at the University of Illinois at Chicago, Great Cities Institute. Earlier portions of this article were presented at the 2003 and 2004 American Society of Criminology meetings. We thank anonymous reviewers of this article for helpful comments.

center advocates do help victims obtain services from the legal, medical, and mental health systems. In a study of survivors' postassault experie Campbell et al. (1999) found that survivors who worked with a rape crisis center advocate experienced significantly less distress than those who did not. In community studies, rape crisis centers are rated as most helpful of a range of support sources by victims seeking help after assault (Filipas & Ullman, 2001; Golding, Siegel, Sorenson, Burnam, & Stein, 1989). A recent study of more than 1,000 sexual assault survivors recruited from the community in a large metropolitan area showed that 16% sought rape crisis services and 79.3% rated them as helpful—a higher percentage than any of 10 informal and formal support sources assessed (Ullman, Filipas, Townsend, & Starzynski, in press). Despite the potential benefit of crisis services, only 1 in 5 survivors in their sample received these services. Similarly, the numbers of survivors accessing the legal, mental health, and criminal justice systems are also low. Representative community data show that only 11.0% have contact with the legal system, 9.3% seek medical care, and 16.1% obtain mental health services (Golding et al., 1989). Recent convenience samples show higher rates of contact, with 20% to 39% contacting the legal system, 20% to 43% seeking medical care, and 39% to 60% obtaining mental health care (Campbell et al., 1999; Ullman, 1996; Ullman et al., in press). Even the highest of these estimates reflects a relatively low proportion of survivors accessing services that can potentially benefit from them in coping with the physical and psychological effects of sexual violence. This raises questions about whether there are barriers to services that could be mitigated. Specific services for rape victims can be obtained from mental health, medical, and police or legal sources following the crime. Martin (2005) has provided a detailed description of all formal service providers and their roles in relation to serving rape victims. Martin argues that some service providers pose barriers for victims and their advocates because of unique organizational goals that conflict with the goal of enhancing victim recovery. For example, Martin has shown how organizational goals such as police' and prosecutors' need for victims to serve as credible witnesses and hospital personnel's treatment of victims as patients with physical injuries lead them to treat victims in an unresponsive manner. Other work with rape survivors shows that they experience harmful

treatment from medical and legal institutions that often revictimize them with negative social reactions (Campbell, 1998; Campbell, Wasco, Ahrens, Sefl, & Barnes, 2001). This evidence suggests that organizational or system barriers lead to harmful responses to victims and likely a lack of therapeutic services. The existence of barriers is further supported by Logan, Evans, Stevenson, and Jordan's (2005) recent focus groups with 30 female clients from rural and urban rape crisis centers that showed barriers of lack of access, availability, and knowledge of services, and unacceptable and/or revictimizing experiences with service providers (e.g., lack of sensitivity by mental health, medical, and criminal justice personnel). These findings regarding secondary victimization are consistent with many other studies of sexual assault victims, showing that survivors report a variety of negative social reactions both from informal and especially from formal support providers. Furthermore, studies show these reactions have harmful effects on psychological symptoms of survivors, including posttraumatic stress disorder (PTSD; Campbell et al., 1999; Davis, Brickman, & Baker, 1991; Ullman, 1996; Ullman et al., in press; Ullman & Filipas, 2001).

Reports from victims are an important source of information regarding barriers to accessing support. An alternative approach is to seek the perspectives of advocates whose role is both to provide direct support and to help victims access resources from other systems. Advocates may be a useful source of information in at least three ways. First, they can help to identify barriers victims face. This approach was used by Campbell (1998), who interviewed rape crisis advocates about their most recent case. Advocates were asked about victims' experiences with the legal, medical, and mental health systems, including what actions were taken by each system, whether those actions fit what the victim wanted, and how readily available the services were. Analyses indicated that there were three patterns in victims' experiences. One group had positive experiences with all three systems, a second group had positive experiences only with the medical system, and a third group had difficult experiences with all three systems. This study revealed differential patterns of responses based on community-level, assault-related, and individual-level variables. It also demonstrated that advocates could be an important source of information about the experiences victims have when seeking support services.

Second, advocates may also be important sources of information about the challenges service providers face when assisting survivors. Burnout and vicarious trauma have been documented as problems in past studies of rape crisis workers (Baird & Jenkins, 2003; Ghahramanlou & Brodbeck, 2000; Schauben & Frazier, 1996) and crime victim support workers generally (see Salston & Figley, 2003, for a review). Yet most research has only studied these psychological symptoms in relation to worker characteristics and client caseloads. It is also important to understand organizational and system-related barriers from the vantage point of those who interface with many survivors during long periods. Social service providers' perspectives in their own words can provide additional insights into the institutional barriers that limit the availability and efficacy of services. Such information may help in understanding the larger context of rape crisis work that contributes to vicarious trauma and burnout in workers.

Third, understanding the perspectives of service providers on service-related barriers can help researchers who are attempting to do collaborative research on sexual violence. Collaborative methods for research and evaluation are especially appropriate when working with violence against women organizations because of the fact that workers in such organizations possess critical knowledge about issues such as client safety and confidentiality (Wasco et al., 2004). It is also beneficial for practitioners who cite benefits of collaboration that include identification of promising practices, validation of local program experiences, obtaining data to support funding requests, and evaluation of client services and programs, whereas researchers cite benefits of gaining new perspectives, generating research ideas, improving project design, and interpreting research findings (National Violence Against Women Prevention Research Center, 2001). However, there are numerous challenges to collaboration between researchers and service providers, including differing priorities, different organizational cultures, and a diversity of professional backgrounds, that give rise to different terminologies (Riger, 1999). Overcoming these challenges and negotiating tensions first requires that researchers understand the context in which service providers work. To foster effective collaborations, it is particularly important that researchers understand the barriers that service providers may face in their work. This can

sensitize researchers to the complexities of service provision, thereby allowing for better communication and collaboration.

In summary, although some research has documented barriers faced by survivors to getting help (Campbell, 1998; Campbell et al., 2001; Martin, 2005), further work is needed from service provider perspectives on the barriers they face in advocating for survivors. Therefore, a qualitative interview study was conducted of victim advocates from various rape crisis centers in a large urban area. This was a grounded theory, exploratory study to identify barriers advocates face in their work and how those barriers affect survivors' ability to receive support. Implications for future research and practice with sexual assault survivors are discussed.

Method

Sample

The sample was composed of 25 women who were current or former rape victim advocates working at rape crisis centers in a large Midwestern metropolitan area. This sample is part of a larger study of both clinicians and advocates working at a variety of social service agencies, including rape crisis centers (see Ullman, 2005, for a description of the first author's experience doing these interviews). Participants were recruited using multiple methods. Letters were sent to 60 people working in agencies in the metropolitan area who were listed as participants at the most recent national conference on sexual violence prevention. All persons who called the researcher or responded to the researcher's phone calls did participate in the study. In response to these letters, 14 interviews were conducted (a 23% response rate). Although the sexual violence conference is a selective source to sample, many eligible participants could be easily identified from that list with contact information for many metropolitan area rape crisis workers who attended the conference. In addition, 10 interviewees were identified by participants referring the interviewer to other people who had worked in the rape crisis field in the area, and one person was located by a chance meeting at a professional function. This resulted in a total sample of 25 advocates, representing 10 distinct agency locations, with an average of 2.80 persons interviewed per location. Nineteen participants were currently working as advocates doing advocacy, referral, and/or crisis counseling at rape crisis centers. Six were former advocates who had worked at rape crisis centers, generally within the past year. Most advocates had done medical advocacy and/or crisis counseling. Two had done primarily legal advocacy, one had done health education, and six had also done administrative work (e.g., volunteer coordinator, director, supervisor) in addition to advocacy. Eight rape crisis centers were free-standing organizations, two programs were contained within a larger social service agency or community mental health center, and one participant worked both on a rape crisis hotline and in a university counseling and advocacy setting. All women had experience working with sexual assault survivors, ranging from 1.5 to 16 years of experience, with an average of 5.14 years of experience (s = 3.83). Eleven workers also had mental health experience doing crisis counseling or other types of therapy with sexual assault survivors, with an average of 3.64 years of experience (s = 6.00). Participants were asked to indicate if they had any or all of four types of training (sexual assault, domestic violence, child abuse, violence against women). Thirteen had all 4 types of training, and 12 had from 1 to 3 types of training. All had training on sexual assault. No further detail was specifically asked about the nature and extent of participants' training. In terms of practice location, 4 worked in suburban locations, 19 worked in the city, and 2 worked in both city and suburban settings. Women were asked to check off all applicable items in a checklist that characterized their treatment orientation. Seventeen endorsed a feminist orientation in their approach to working with survivors, whereas 12 endorsed various other treatment orientations such as client-centered and cognitive-behavioral. All participants were women. In terms of education, 1 had a PhD, 7 had master's degrees, 14 had bachelor's degrees, and 3 had some college or an associate's degree. Most women were White (n = 12), followed by Hispanic (n = 6), Black (n = 5), Asian (n = 1), and multiracial (n = 1). Women's average age was 33.04 years (s = 9.20 years). Most women (n = 12) were in their 20s, with a range of 25 to 58 years. Two had incomes of $10,000 to $20,000, 11 had incomes from $20,000 to $30,000 per year, 8 earned $30,000 to $40,000 per year, 3 had incomes of $60,000 or more, and 1 refused to provide her income.

Agencies

Services for rape victims in the area from which participants were sampled include a 24-hour hotline for the entire metropolitan area that is run out of the largest rape crisis center in the city. The hotline is coordinated by full-time employees and staffed by trained volunteers 24 hours a day. Other services provided by the area's rape crisis centers include medical and legal advocacy, crisis counseling and referral to other social and mental health services, prevention education, and training to other agencies including police and state's attorneys. Agencies where workers were employed included two large rape crisis centers, one of which had satellite offices in both city and suburban locations. Both of these rape crisis centers had administrative and supervisory staff, advocates, and counselors, with a smaller core of paid, full-time staff and a larger core of volunteer victim advocates who typically went on emergency room calls when rape victims were taken there by police following an assault.

Some workers mainly did crisis counseling and gave referrals to survivors of sexual assault, whereas others did longer-term therapy with survivors or administrative work and supervision of other employees in their agencies. Most advocates did crisis counseling and medical advocacy, with two advocates primarily doing legal advocacy and prevention education to area schools and colleges. Typically, those doing mostly counseling also worked on advocacy needs with clients, some of whom were also receiving therapy from mental health professionals outside of the rape crisis center. Smaller agencies were typically more mental health focused and were often part of community mental health centers, although they still identified as rape crisis centers. They provided the same advocacy and counseling services, but the larger organizations where they were housed also served other populations, such as child victims or clients with general mental health needs. Agencies varied in geographic location and both provider and client demographic characteristics, partially reflecting the agency, its philosophy, and the client population of the specific agency location. For example, agencies in predominantly Black or Hispanic neighborhoods had more staff with similar ethnic backgrounds, whereas agencies located in the downtown central city had a greater proportion of White staff.

Obviously, our study is limited by a small sample from a subset of centers in one metropolitan area, some of whom were former advocates with negative experiences that may have motivated them to participate. No rural advocates were included in this study, which is a limitation because rape crisis center services are much more limited in rural areas (Martin, 2005) and barriers that advocates and victims face may differ in rural areas (Logan et al., 2005). In addition, only a couple of open-ended questions were asked about barriers advocates faced in working with survivors and in their organizations specifically, which were followed up with probes. Detailed questions were not asked about a predetermined list of specific barriers, which may have led to underreporting of certain barriers or more discussion by advocates of the most salient barriers they face. Because only the first author conducted these interviews, age and race matching with advocates was not possible. The first author is a White, middle-aged female, which may have led to fewer or poorer quality data from advocates with different age and ethnic characteristics (see Ullman, 2005, for a discussion of her perceptions of how this may have affected interviews with older, ethnic minority women, in particular).

Procedure

Participants completed in-person interviews at a time and location convenient for them. Most interviews were conducted at their work offices (20) at a convenient time for the women, but 5 preferred to be interviewed at other locations. Interviews were conducted from November 2002 through May 2003 by the first author. Interviews ranged from 45 minutes to 1 hour and 20 minutes in length, with the average interview length of 65.36 minutes (s = 13.36 minutes), and a modal interview length of 1 hour.

Semistructured interviews asked about women's training and work experience with survivors of sexual assault and other relevant work experience, how disclosures of sexual assault tended to occur, how interviewees typically respond to disclosures, difficult and rewarding aspects of working with survivors, barriers to working with survivors and to survivors' obtaining services, and solutions that might improve services to this population. Participants were also asked about their views about the role of mental health professionals in working with sexual assault survivors. Only the data on barriers were analyzed in the current study.

Analysis Strategy

A grounded theory approach was used for data analysis. Four stages of analysis were used. The first stage consisted of open and axial coding (Strauss & Corbin, 1998). Open codes emerged from the text to break the data into discrete parts. Axial coding extended the analysis from the textual level to the conceptual level. The second stage of analysis involved construction of a meta-matrix, which is a master chart that compiles descriptive data from each case into a standard format (Miles & Huberman, 1994). Column headings identified key variables and each row represented a program. This process allowed for the identification of themes that were common to many programs and those that were unique to a small number of programs. The third stage of analysis was the manipulation of the meta-matrix to create submatrices that were conceptually ordered according to key variables (Miles & Huberman, 1994). This process allowed for identification of patterns between variables. The final stage was the creation of analysis forms that summarized the submatrices. In completing these forms, both within-case and cross-case analyses were done, in which the content of codes within and then across cases were compared. The goal was to identify and interpret any themes or patterns that could answer the research question of what barriers interfere with survivors receiving help following a sexual assault. The results as described in the following section were based on the final stage of analysis.

Results and Discussion

Advocates identified multiple barriers to their work with survivors at their organizations and in the social systems (e.g., medical, criminal justice) from which survivors seek help. In the sections that follow, each barrier is described by advocates reporting them and how the barrier affected advocates' ability to work with survivors and help them access needed services. To frame the organization of these barriers, Reading Figure 26.1 shows how these themes may be organized hierarchically to show their interrelationships.

Broader societal attitudes discussed first can be viewed as influencing several subgroups of barriers occurring at levels of the (a) organization, (b) staff, and (c) direct services.

Societal Attitudes

Barriers to service provision exist within a larger societal context. At the macro level, it is important to consider how societal attitudes may be reflected in the responses that societal institutions make to rape survivors. Some advocates (36%) spoke about attitudes toward rape manifested in system responses that interfered with advocacy. For example, one advocate discussed the larger barrier of societal denial of the problem of rape:

We still haven't reached a point in our society where you can even acknowledge this problem for what it is and that's why people can't get over it. I don't care if they're sitting in an office an hour a week and somebody says, yes you have a right to all these feelings, everything else in the world, tells them that they don't. Until we acknowledge that, that's never gonna happen! (Advocate 36)

Race and class biases are also societal barriers reflected in organizations, including rape crisis centers and in institutions that respond to survivors' needs. These types of biases were noted by 56% of participants.

So, it's all based on the story that night what's the story? How credible is the witness? the victim? How credible is the perp? Well, you know racism plays into account, classism plays into account, I mean you name it, it's there. Sexism plays a role, too. (Advocate 3)

There's always this doubt. I've never heard a person who wasn't of color told: "Well, you can take it back if you want, you know if you tell me that you made it up, then we'll let you go if you try to press charges." They bully young people and particularly young people of color by saying, "I'm giving you a chance to take this back." Police say I'm giving you a chance to tell me the

truth, if you're not telling me the truth then you know, you can take it back now, but if we go through with this and we try and prosecute and we find out that you're lying, then you're gonna go to jail, you know? It's like a script. I haven't heard like an older person told that, I've never heard a person who wasn't of color asked those things so, and when I say older, I mean like people in their 40's or 50's unless there was a situation where maybe they were mentally ill or they were a substance abuser. It's always people who are disenfranchised in some form or fashion who are completely silenced and not believed. (Advocate 25)

One participant continued to explain further the ways survivors are treated differently based on gender and sexual orientation:

It's even sexist because male survivors are treated horribly. They don't even take it seriously and act like they deserve it. The impression I've gotten is not as if they're saying that it didn't happen, it was just they deserved it or they must have been doing something to condone it or they must be homosexual so it's because of their lifestyle. I've seen survivors who were not homosexual openly say, well you know, I'm not gay, but all the questioning was geared around that. Did you know the guy, were you in a relationship with him? Why does that matter so? People still have in their minds what the ideal rape victim looks like, behaves like, what type of lifestyle they have. It's amazing to me that we haven't gotten past that. I think it's partly the media and it's partly about just wanting to remain in your comfort zone. (Advocate 25)

Another advocate spoke of problems that survivors with disabilities and immigrants have in getting appropriate responses from service systems:

I think the hardest work that I've done is with people with any type of disability and with elder people and not because they put up a barrier. It's

Reading Figure 26.1 ● Organization of Barrier Themes Identified by Rape Victim Advocates

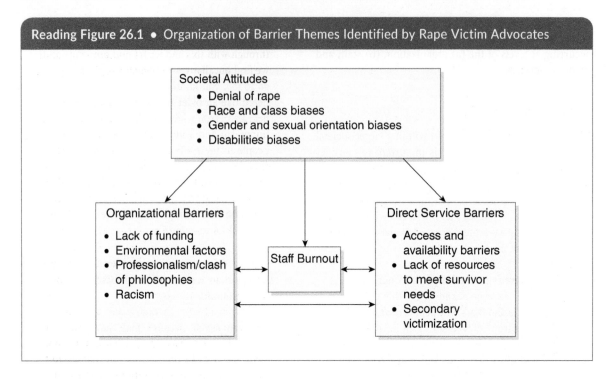

hard also to work with people with mental illness because it's hard to work with them, and it's hard to make the system to understand them and respect them and their rights. It's also hard with immigrants for the same reason and because law enforcement doesn't cooperate with them and thinks what they're saying or what they think is because of their ethnicity. (Advocate 32)

Clearly, these attitudes make it even more difficult for advocates to help survivors from marginalized groups who suffer from multiple sources of stigmatization and devaluation in the eyes of social institutions that deal with rape victims. It is much more difficult for advocates to combat not only rape stereotypes affecting all rape survivors but also additional stereotypes about "less deserving" rape victims who because of age, race, sexual orientation, occupation, mental illness, or immigration status are viewed as unworthy of the system's attention or response. These attitudes about specific groups of people are ingrained in all members of society to varying degrees

and may be more unconscious and well accepted. This may make them even harder for advocates to challenge than rape stereotypes, which probably are less socially acceptable to admit adhering to. These broad societal attitudes undergird specific barriers that are seen at the levels of the organization and staff, and they contribute to barriers that victims face when seeking direct services.

Organizational Barriers

The high prevalence of rape in combination with widespread denial of this problem contributes to the underresourcing of agencies that serve victims. As a result, rape crisis centers face organizational-level barriers to providing an adequate response to victims' needs. Barriers at this level include a lack of funding and environmental stressors. In the effort to obtain more funding and resources, agencies have come under pressure to adopt organizational practices that are seen as more professional but that in some cases redefine the agencies' focus on advocacy. In addition, organizations are not immune from societal attitudes such as racism that may be manifest in their own practices. Each of these barriers was articulated by participants in this study.

Lack of Funding

The lack of funding was an issue mentioned by 64% of participants. Some described funding as precluding advocates from making a long-term commitment to rape crisis work. This may directly contribute to staff turnover and, therefore, to lower quality services for survivors.

> It's hard to think about making a RCC [rape crisis center] a career for a long time, cause it's impossible, it's very hard to imagine spending the rest of your life working for no more than $35,000 a year and that's after being at an agency for a long time. Especially, I mean I remember that they just made a decision that nobody was going to advance, they were only going to have supervisors that had master's degrees, so everybody that had a BA or BS, that was sort of then the ground level. Some were sort of faced with this dilemma, because there's obviously nowhere else to advance in the agency without having a master's degree but the money and time it would take to get a master's degree and then come back, even the supervisory level is really only going to make $4,000 more. But I went for my master's last year, it would be financially prohibitive even in a supervisory position. So, I think that they can also value sort of experience in the field. (Advocate 35)

> I know I'm glad we're getting money, I'm glad to have this done but it's just I think there were some of the people at [Agency X] who left because they had children and the agency doesn't provide child care, you know you can't bring your child, too. I understand that, and so it's cheaper to stay at home with your children than to have day care and work at [Agency X]. The pay is that low for some of the positions, and I don't understand how in a feminist organization why people have to leave a job. (Advocate 35)

In addition to low salaries, which may contribute to staff turnover, the lack of funding raises the possibility of competition between agencies for available funds. This was a concern of 16% of participants. One advocate spoke of this in relation to the competition between domestic violence and sexual assault providers for the same dollars:

> I think sometimes you run into that sort of change in focus [from rape to domestic violence], I think other times it's really just vying for the same funding. I think the whole DV/sexual assault thing is that domestic violence has always just been sort of ahead of the ball in terms of getting the funding, the awareness, and getting more people to recognize it as an issue. Plus, I think just in general it's [domestic violence] easier for people to talk about than anything that has to do with sex. That kind of puts you down a couple of notches in terms of who's gonna want to talk to you about it, fund you, and let you into their schools to talk about it. So, I think that there has always sort of been that challenge distinguishing sexual assault from domestic violence and getting sexual assault recognized, also a very serious concern that needs attention. (Advocate 10)

The scarcity and competitiveness of funds were also discussed in terms of how it shapes the approaches agencies take to doing their work. One such effect is that agencies may take on new projects because they fear losing the support of grantors, even though the new projects are beyond the scope of what the agency can handle. For example, an advocate complained of a situation when her agency director agreed to provide advocacy to more area hospitals, when advocate resources were already stretched to the limit in covering their existing contracts:

> I'm sure it has to do with funding, but I think that there's also a way in which we, as in "we" as a part of this agency get so scared that we're gonna lose funding or not be able to expand services that we start agreeing to things that are not helpful to the agency. (Advocate 35)

Part of the problem may be that grantors do not recognize the larger context of providing services or the preliminary steps needed to launch an initiative. This can create a mismatch between grantors' expectations and what is actually necessary to carry out community initiatives. One advocate explained this in the context of outreach she did to the [ethnic group name] community:

> The [ethnic group name] services program was funded when I started working at the agency and they had staff that was funded by [the state coalition], but the funding was strictly for counseling, and the entire time that I was there, they had a total of 3 or 4 clients, because the outreach had not been done. You can't just open your doors and expect that people are gonna come. What ended up happening with that program was that everyone was aware that we were in danger of losing that funding, and so the manager asked me to come in and make a last-minute push to try and drum up some clients. But it was a little late, and actually that was a time when I felt like I was ready to transition into something else anyway, so I said okay, fine, but the more I started working on that, the more I felt like this is just not something that I care to save, because this program was of course conceived in a way that had no consideration or respect for the communities that it was presuming to serve. If the funding was really what it should be, it should be funded to be purely outreach and that's it. We shouldn't even have been funded for counseling at that point in time, which they would have known if they had talked to anybody within those communities. (Advocate 37)

A former advocate with many years in the field explained her broader view of funding in relation to other government priorities. She spoke of federal changes in terms of a shift from funding victim services to funding criminal justice and prosecution-based strategies and a wholesale shift of funds away from violence against women toward issues of gangs and drugs:

> There's so many different levels to that because nationally there's nothing available because the funding has been diverted over the last 5 years from victim services into prosecution. And so there's less and less money available to victim services, so a lot of the money comes from things like the Violence Against Women Act and some other kinds of victims' services. But in order to deal with the crime, the current administration strategy is to shift away [from] putting victim services money into prosecution. But the problem is that prosecution money has been transferred into prosecution of gangs and drugs, so the prosecution level of sexual assault, domestic violence, or child sexual abuse has not necessarily increased in correlation with extra money they put into prosecution. (Advocate 38)

She also spoke of the problematic structure of services where duplicate services have been developed in parallel, instead of having centralized services, where common resources can be shared by many different constituencies. Her comments on this matter are especially notable because they contrast with other participants who expressed more concern with maintaining their own agencies' programs and services. This former advocate, however, proposed a centralization of services as a way to make better use of limited funds:

> Right now is there are a lot of dollars spent on duplication of services, but what I would like to see is an actual kind of centralization of services that a lot of these violence against women agencies need, so you have a centralization of services that offer legal advocates so that not everybody has these positions. You could have a centralized database where you allow common resources to be funded commonly and collectively and then people can utilize the resources. So if you've got a curriculum development person who's actually being funded from eight different agencies, each of those agencies has to spend less money, but they can all utilize the curricula developed by that kind of a practice system. I think it's what's necessary and I think it's the next part of the maturation process of these agencies. (Advocate 38)

Environmental Factors

Limited funding may also lead to less than ideal settings in which to provide services. Environmental factors within rape crisis centers were cited as barriers to providing services by 8% of advocates. This problem may be greater, however, at smaller agencies and satellite offices. Those mentioning positive environmental characteristics of their work settings (e.g., spacious, peaceful, welcoming) all worked in larger agencies, whereas most of the small number of participants mentioning problems with the work environment (3 out of 4) worked in these smaller settings. Specifically, they talked about problems with lack of privacy and limited space for doing advocacy in their workplace. For example,

> In terms of counseling, I've only had about 3 clients coming into the office for legal advocacy where there's no real privacy. I have the cubicle where I sit, but there's no real privacy for a client to come in and talk to me. (Advocate 22)

A related issue regarding the physical work environment was safety concerns, mentioned by one advocate working at a larger agency in the city:

> For the first month I was working there, there was no lock on the office door, so I couldn't even lock myself in, and I just remember being terrified at night and being told by the agency that we don't have enough money and there's too many people coming in and out to deal with this problem. (Advocate 35)

Although few advocates in this study mentioned environmental factors, likely because they were not specifically asked about these factors, they seemed important to mention because they may affect advocates in their work with victims. Martin (2005) notes that smaller agencies, particularly rape crisis centers, may be less able to be responsive to victims' needs generally because of their limited resources.

Professionalization of Rape Crisis Centers

Another important organizational characteristic that may affect the ability of advocates to help survivors is the professionalization of rape crisis centers, which was mentioned by 16% of advocates. Research has documented that as many rape crisis centers have become more

institutionalized, they have focused more on counseling and advocacy for individual survivors and less on political action and institutional advocacy, as in the past (Campbell, Baker, & Mazurek, 1998). In this study, a major barrier raised by some advocates was professionalization of rape crisis centers. Professionalization and standardization of services has its benefits, such as ensuring that survivors receive quality treatment (e.g., counseling) by well-trained professionals who have specific educational credentials. However, it may also have disadvantages, such as minimizing the traditional feminist or social change perspective, that may be important for challenging systems that fail to meet victims' needs.

Advocates presented two conflicting views on the impact of professionalization of rape crisis centers on survivors receiving their services. Three advocates argued that professionalization (e.g., requiring specific educational credentials) was harmful because it (a) excluded many women who had a vital contribution to make helping rape survivors and (b) led rape crisis centers to hire professionals who were nonfeminist or even antifeminist in their orientation). Another perspective voiced by one advocate in particular was that professionalization (defined as appropriate professional training and demeanor) is important to encourage in rape crisis centers, so that survivors are appropriately treated and the field is taken seriously and supported by external funders. However, this approach may also narrow the range of people whose skills are employed in the field. In this sample, concerns about professionalization were noted more by those workers endorsing a feminist orientation. The advocates quoted below described the manifestation of professionalization of rape crisis work occurring at the organizational level:

> There's a lot of issues like professionalization of the movement that I think is a big problem. Everything is so focused on services. You have people at [Agency X], they had this awesome very powerful woman working there, she'd been doing the work for several years and she was let go, they got rid of her position. We had heard it was because she doesn't have a college degree and that's [Agency X's] formal policy is you have to have a college degree to do the work. I think that just excludes a lot of very amazing people. (Advocate 29)

There are ways that agencies could think more about how they are marketing their services, who their staff are, what their priorities are in terms of staffing and where centers and satellites are going to be located, but I think that's not the kind of thing that happens. This is where I start to get really angry because I feel as though I've seen the agencies get more and more professionalized and become more of a system. They all work together more, so they become more and more alike, and it's frustrating because there's this move to say we want all of our counselors to have master's degrees. On the one hand, yeah you would like your sexual assault survivors to get sort of the best kind of counseling that they can, but the master's is not always the best measure of who's best able to provide 10 weeks of crisis counseling. (Advocate 35)

This latter point is likely valid given research showing no correlation of professional training with psychotherapeutic effectiveness (Luborsky et al., 1986; Stein & Lambert, 1984). Professional technical expertise and knowledge do not necessarily predict success. Instead, effective therapists and other support sources have qualities of warmth, empathy, and genuineness (Frank & Frank, 1991), which may not come from professional training or certification.

Limiting staff to those with graduate degrees can also narrow the focus of rape crisis centers. Specifically, the need for activism and social advocacy, not simply counseling, was identified as important for empowering survivors:

We have to move toward thinking about social advocacy and making change. I see a lot more counselors who are just trained as counselors and don't think about activism. If you're in there empowering your clients, think about how much they can advocate for themselves. Not just with family members or partners, but society. . . . Writing a letter to the editor can be a part of the counseling or therapy, but that gets lost when they're more traditional, and that's not being stressed in the training. (Advocate 35)

Unfortunately, as agencies professionalize and require more educational credentials, they lose a broader activist focus, which is critical for fighting rape and for empowering survivors, and end up with a narrower, apolitical, individual counseling approach.

Another advocate described the problem of supervisors with clinical credentials who are nonfeminist and yet are hired at rape crisis centers that traditionally espoused and often still espouse a feminist commitment to addressing violence against women:

They hired a clinical supervisor who was not a feminist, who said that she doesn't understand what feminism's about. But how can you work in a RCC and not be a feminist? I remember one time she came to talk to me about a client she had. She said the woman had gone to make a phone call at like three in the morning, and this woman said, "Well don't you just think that was stupid, I mean that was just asking to get raped." And I said, "I cannot believe you are the clinical supervisor at this agency!" (Advocate 35)

Clearly, such statements are problematic coming from a leader in an organization devoted to eradicating violence against women and sensitive treatment of rape survivors. This may not only affect survivors who have contact with the staff person but also communicate a negative and demoralizing message to advocates about how their organization's leaders view sexual assault survivors.

Although these concerns about professionalization and especially about the hiring of staff based on narrow criteria were shared by many of the advocates, an alternative view was also expressed. An advocate who had left rape crisis work to work on behalf of rape victims in another arena presented a very different view of professionalization. She argued for a "professionalism" that referred to the need for professional behavior in rape crisis centers. This was distinct from the issue of professionalization of rape crisis centers by requiring workers to have advanced degrees:

A controversial thing that I've said before, and people get mad at me all the time, is I think a lot of victim service agencies adopt a victim mentality of "woe is us, there's nothing we can do, there's too much to be done, we can't do it all, we're stressed out." There is a lack of professionalism in these agencies. . . . I think part of it is, you've gotta professionalize the profession in a way that it hasn't been. I mean we just have not done it and I don't think it has to be that damn stressful as people make it out to be. I think there is a way to do this and I think it has to do with leadership. One of the things I have fought very hard for at [Agency X] is to say, look, if it stresses you out that much, don't do it! (Advocate 38)

I asked how this kind of professionalism differed from the negative side of professionalization of agencies that other advocates expressed to me. She elaborated on the problem:

Sometimes you hear these young, passionate people are very feminist or who have very strong politics who feel like the model is very apolitical or very service oriented and doesn't have that kind of analysis. But the thing about it is, and maybe this is just me getting older too, is that passion that you find in the college age population. . . . You can't build a workforce on that, cause guess what, those kids grow up and when they hit 25, they quit cause they wanna make more money. I think the problem is people want to build a lot on trying to harness that energy, but that is a fleeting kind of energy, it is not a permanent energy, and so what you have to do is you have to create a channel in which you capture that energy but that can't be the permanent fuel that you run on. The permanent fuel that you run on has to be based on professionals who are in it for the long haul. (Advocate 38)

This quote suggests that both conditions of the work (e.g., low pay) and who it attracts (e.g., young feminists) may lead to staff turnover because of lack of career advancement opportunities in rape crisis centers. She spoke of how she envisioned developing services to address specific functions that agencies sought to fulfill and that such a model would lead to long-term growth instead of functioning in survival mode in the context of limited government resources directed at the problem.

We need staff people to fulfill these functions. What are the functions that should be fulfilled from a staff perspective, what are the functions from a volunteer perspective and how can we professionalize the whole process so that we're putting appropriate responsibilities on staff, appropriate responsibilities on volunteers, appropriate responsibilities on the boards of directors, appropriate responsibilities on leadership, and we've created some really strong selection tools, retention tools, leadership development tools, so that people in these positions are people who wanna be in these positions for the long haul, and we're actually developing the skills necessary for them to become better as they go along. . . . It's a difference between surviving and thinking about long-term growth. I think the way that these organizations are constructed right now is all based on a survival model. I absolutely think this issue [rape] is one of the most underfunded issues in our country, and it's one of the most prevalent issues in our country, and we don't deal with it. But until the rest of the world comes around, we have to do better with what we have. (Advocate 38)

Racism in Rape Crisis Centers

Racism is an issue that has been critically important in the contemporary women's movement generally and in relation to the issue of rape and rape crisis centers specifically (Campbell et al., 2001; Matthews, 1994; Scott, 1998). Racism is not only an issue that must be confronted in the broader society. It must also be confronted within rape crisis centers themselves. If left unaddressed, it undermines an agency's ability to provide quality services to victims of color and replicates within the agency dynamics of oppression that are related to the cultural causes of violence against women. Racism was spontaneously noted to be a problem in rape crisis organizations by 24% of advocates in this study:

I think the whole rape crisis center thing is still a "White feminist" women's movement thing, and I think it's still painfully obvious. Especially at a center like X which for the most part is White women. (Advocate 30)

Another advocate voiced her perception that her organization tried to be nonracist by sponsoring events related to women of color, but that action was not tantamount to a thorough organizational critical self-examination and attempt to be truly nonracist in everyday practices:

> We just had this event focused on women of color, which I think is good, but I think in some way it's almost like, well you know, we did that event kind of a thing like, we're not racist, we did that event! (Advocate 29)

Another advocate discussed a systemic issue that she perceived affected workers in her satellite office. The workers all happened to be women of color and were treated with distrust by the manager at the main office of the organization, who was White:

> There was, in my mind, a ridiculous conflict with our manager who had a basic lack of trust in people in our office, many of whom had conflicts with her in the past. A lot of us perceived that this was related to the fact that everyone who worked in our office were people of color. (Advocate 37)

Another more structural manifestation of racism was the geographic distribution of services, which resulted in disproportionately poorer access to rape crisis services for women living in predominantly ethnic minority neighborhoods.

> Downtown and the north side is where most services are! There are less on south side, yet huge populations reside there. There are not enough funds to publicize resources or to understand what people want or need. Many White feminists in the field who are college educated need to not "poo-poo" religion. We don't understand different cultural responses. (Advocate 33)

Another former advocate who was an administrator and worked for many years in the [city]

rape crisis movement explained the larger context of racism in rape crisis centers. The civil rights movement and the feminist movement really were on parallel but unconnected charts, whether it's the NAACP or the Urban League and the victims' organizations. Different institutions came out of the civil rights movement and civil rights history and then there's sexual assault and domestic violence that really came out of the feminist movement. So now you've got these organizations that are trying to go back and deal with some of these issues. Because they were segregationist in their thinking, which translated into a lot of segregation in their practices. They're trying to heal some of that, but a lot of Black women in their communities don't want to have anything to do with you, because they say: you have not been here for us when we needed you. (Advocate 38)

Although the issue of racism was not mentioned by the majority of advocates in terms of how they were treated by rape crisis centers or as a barrier to their work with survivors, it was mentioned by a few White and ethnic minority women despite the fact that no questions in the interview focused on this topic specifically. This suggests that issues of racism are likely of concern for many advocates working in rape crisis centers. Some women perceive that their organizations have not dealt with this issue fully, which is likely a reflection of the larger context in which racism continues to afflict society and the feminist movement more generally. Insofar as racism alienates ethnic minority women advocates and causes them job stress in working at their organizations, this is a problem that may lead to burnout for these workers and may also indirectly negatively affect their ability to help survivors.

Staff Burnout

Both organizational barriers and the nature of rape crisis centers' work may affect advocates' ability to help survivors by causing stress and burnout. Research has shown vicarious traumatization and burnout are problems for many counselors and advocates working with sexual assault survivors (Baird & Jenkins, 2003; Ghahramanlou & Brodbeck, 2000; Schauben & Frazier, 1995; Wasco &

Campbell, 2002), although existing studies have not examined how organizations may specifically contribute to these problems. Not surprisingly, 44% of advocates, particularly ex-advocates (4 out of 6), mentioned factors associated with stress and burnout among workers that were caused by their agency's working conditions.

> There's burnout and that can be difficult. But I think that's in any social service setting required to witness everybody else's pain and the impact of that. (Advocate 25)

> I think it starts at the top. Funders want you to do as much as you can with as little. And they certainly don't want you to have downtime. They don't see that downtime is actually recovery time so that you can sustain it long term. I think that the way that the jobs are set up is to do this 100% of the time and not to take part time stuff. And I think that's why people get into private practice, because they're so sick of this nonprofit stuff where you just burn your workers out. You exploit either their sense of giving, their naivete or their age. I think young idealistic workers get easily crapped on because they are so passionate. I was so passionate and now I'm like totally cynical and rekindling my passion, but only because I've had a year off already to sort of recover and think about this. (Advocate 31)

Multiple causes of burnout were identified by the advocates. First, a number of them, especially those who had left their agencies because of burnout, cited inadequate supervision as a factor contributing to burnout.

> I think it's because there's a lot of supervision problems in rape crisis work and we have supervisors who don't know what our jobs are. Maybe they've done medical [advocacy]. A lot of the executive directors in [city] haven't done any direct service work. My supervisor has done medical, but she has not done legal [advocacy]. There's low accountability in the centers, you have people who are super burnt out and not fired. There are legal advocates who don't do anything, there's a lot of people who don't do

anything. Counselors who don't do anything, don't see anyone, you know. (Advocate 29)

> I just feel how much can they care about survivors when the frontline people working directly with survivors are treated with blatant disregard for their well-being. I mean that's sort of my cynical perspective at this point. . . . They would say, "Yeah we hear what you're saying and we're working on it," which was the response for 2 years during which they were not working on it. I never felt like I was blamed necessarily, but it certainly was not like, "Oh you're right, we're gonna fix this tomorrow, because this is a problem and you know we see that." It was never like that. Everything was this huge long process, and most things that were addressed were never taken care of or fixed. (Advocate 30)

Other organizational problems that may be related to staff burnout raised mostly by former advocates included lack of adequate pay, lack of support, lack of accountability for work, and even outright abuse of workers that may actually characterize inadequately funded human service agencies in general (Glisson, 2000; Webster & Hackett, 1999).

> I don't have to have somebody who's exploiting me, disempowering, abusing me basically, not paying me anything, I mean the money is a part of that too because nobody wants to work for crap. We tell clients we're trained to empower people, but who do we as social workers empower, everybody but ourselves. We're just these little doormats for everybody, and we're encouraged to be that way, because when we speak out, our agencies don't want to hear it. I think there's a problem with social work as a whole that the people who are in the nonprofit and advocacy/victim services are sort of qualitatively poorer than they could be. (Advocate 31)

> I mean I don't really know how to frame it, but there are problems of not like getting support, and when people aren't supported, you have a lot of people who don't like their jobs. For instance, someone called and she said, "I tried

to work with the legal advocate at this other center on the north side, she had no idea what I was talking about, so can you help me?" I gave her a bunch of information and she asked: "What are you talking about?" Who is talking to this legal advocate and finding out why she doesn't know what her job is? I mean it's because she's not getting training or support. Why isn't someone addressing it? I think training and support would create better advocacy skills and reduce burnout. (Advocate 29)

When the executive director first came to the agency, she said, I'm gonna do this, this, and this. And we were like, great! And then nothing changed. She didn't do any of what she said she was gonna do. I've said the relationship with the agency, it's like an abusive relationship. The agency's the abuser and the worker is the victim. I felt like there was so many times where I thought, am I crazy? Is it me? It takes a long time to leave and realize that you deserve better! It was so similar, it's really scary looking back at it, it was like a cycle of violence. (Advocate 30)

Organizational factors such as time constraints imposed by rigid work demands and inflexibility in rape crisis centers were also cited as a barrier to advocates' own professional development and their ability to sustain themselves in doing such stressful work. One advocate who had burnt out and left her agency noted,

There's this national women of color against violence conference, and we were told that time volunteering there couldn't be work time which was frustrating because we were networking. It's sort of an inflexibility that became more institutionalized on the grant-making level. You have to count how everyone's time is being spent, but that fails to count how workers sitting around chatting for 2 hours is an important part of self-care and sustaining morale. . . . I just think that there are ways in which the agency doesn't always want to be flexible in terms of hours, yet they expect you to be flexible. They need someone that's gonna stay until 8:00, but they're the same people saying that you can't come in when it's convenient for you. (Advocate 35)

Although past research has suggested that supportive organizations may directly and indirectly promote workers' self-care (Wasco, Campbell, & Clark, 2002), which may reduce stress and burnout, researchers have not directly studied workers' perceptions of how organizations may be unsupportive. This may be partially because of past studies recruiting workers through their organizations (e.g., via executive directors), whereas in this study, workers were recruited directly, not through their organizations, as were former advocates who, not surprisingly, were more negative about their former employers.

It is very important to note that despite these negative aspects of agencies raised by workers, rape crisis centers do extremely positive work with few resources. Comments such as those noted here would likely be reflective of workers' perceptions in any human services organization. These issues may in fact be common yet unlikely to be voiced by workers who are still in the field, as evidenced by the fact that only one current advocate in this study (who was working off site at a hospital doing advocacy) clearly raised these negative criticisms about her organization. This led to interviews with former advocates, all of whom more fully elaborated on this theme. It is not surprising that current workers, most of whom were interviewed at their agencies, would be hesitant to raise these controversial issues.

Barriers to Direct Services

Although societal attitudes, organizational-level variables, and staff burnout affect the availability and quality of services, their effects may not always directly affect individual victims. However, there are barriers to service provision that directly affect individual victims who may be in need of or who may seek services from rape crisis centers and from the legal, medical, and mental health systems. Barriers that occur in the course of providing direct services to victims include limited access to services, the unavailability of specific services, a lack of resources to meet victims' needs, and secondary victimization when services are sought.

Access and Availability of Services to Meet Survivor Needs

The ability to access support services is the starting point for victims to get formal help in coping with sexual assault. However, barriers to survivors' connecting with existing services were noted by many (44%) of the advocates interviewed. These barriers included stigma of receiving services, geographic location, cost of services, and inadequate availability of services. Some of these barriers appeared to be related to race and geographic location, suggesting that they may differentially affect subgroups of survivors. For example, the stigma of seeking mental health services and geographic location of services were noted as barriers for ethnic minority women. In discussing how ethnic minority women might perceive her agency, one advocate explained,

> Why do I want to come downtown to some ritzy, all White counseling center where they're gonna tell me I'm crazy? You know the stereotype. Well, counseling doesn't mean you're the crazy one. Just because we're downtown doesn't mean we're ritzy or we're all Caucasian or all straight or whatever it may be. Many people of communities that are oppressed do not want to come to the services, they want the services to come to them. So, we must go out to their communities and meet them on their turf, go into their schools and show that I'm not afraid to come meet you where you're at. I'm not afraid as a White woman to come into your neighborhood. (Advocate 3)

Clearly, if ethnic minority women perceive that going to services means they could be labeled mentally ill or that the service providers will be White, middle-class women who will not identify with them or understand their concerns, this may be enough of a barrier to prevent them from accessing available services. In addition, there may be practical difficulties associated with traveling to organizations that provide services outside survivors' neighborhoods, especially for women who rely on public transportation.

Another frequently cited barrier was the availability of affordable or free services:

> One of the most obvious barriers for many survivors is needing resources that are affordable or free. We're really fortunate that all of our services are free because it makes sense that somebody who's the victim of a crime shouldn't have to pay. That's a big worry to survivors that I've worked with—how am I gonna pay for this? Fortunately, in the emergency rooms we can tell them that the law [Sexual Assault Survivors Emergency Treatment Act] pays for your care through the [state] Department of Public Aid. We tell them, if you get a bill, call me, we'll fix it. (Advocate 8)

Unfortunately, advocates also noted that many victims do not realize that rape crisis services are available free of charge, so they may not seek help believing they would have to pay for services they cannot afford. Inadequate availability of services was cited with regard to basic rape crisis services for specific subpopulations and for related needs extending beyond rape crisis including bilingual services and services for disabled women. For example, the lack of bilingual services prevents some women from being able to access formal support, as one advocate described:

> The other [barrier] that comes up immediately is living in a city as diverse as [city] is the limited language capabilities that we have and so we serve clients obviously in English. We do have sort of a backup system. And there are several other agencies that do bilingual ... we have crisis intervention services. So, we feel pretty well equipped to handle calls that are monolingual Spanish speakers. But [city] has a large population of Latino people and Polish people and we just can't serve them. (Advocate 6)

The pressing need for bilingual services to serve survivors and their family and friends is clear from the area's demographics. According to the 2000 census, 26% of this urban area's population was Hispanic. In addition, the area has a very large Polish-speaking population.

However, rape crisis services in languages other than English are not widely available.

Several advocates also noted the limited services for disabled survivors:

> There are limited resources available for people with disabilities. There is the deaf and hard of hearing community that some people describe as disabled. Some people don't see that as a disability, but certainly the resources available for that community are very limited. (Advocate 6)

> I am surprised for such a big city there are not rape crisis centers with a focus on disabilities. I just surely thought that there would be all these great programs. I think there was a grant out there a couple of years ago, but the program failed and I don't know why. I think that's sad. (Advocate 1)

The limited availability of services for disabled survivors is particularly notable in light of data showing that disabled persons are at equal or greater risk of sexual victimization than others (Young, Nosek, Howland, Chanpong, & Rintala, 1997).

Resource Barriers That Reduce Direct Services

Resource issues mentioned by 28% of advocates that affect rape crisis centers' capacity to provide direct services included funding constraints, agency inefficiency in using funds, and paperwork required by funders. In addition, the scarcity of resources appears to have resulted in problems with the way organizations are structured and how they treat employees, both of which affect their ability to serve survivors. These organizational issues included poor supervision, unresponsiveness to employees' needs, and inflexibility of organizations.

The most commonly mentioned resource barrier, noted by all of those interviewed, was the sheer lack of funding for rape crisis centers. As one advocate put it,

> It really comes down to funding. I mean we can't expand our programs any further. We have

waiting lists of hospitals that want us in. We have waiting lists of high schools and colleges that want us doing our prevention programs. We don't have enough people to go out to police stations and be a face that the police officers recognize. We don't have enough people in courthouses that are court watchers to know how judges are ruling, so that we could know who to vote in or vote out. If we had more funding to expand some of our programs, we could make a bigger impact for all victims as a whole. (Advocate 3)

Another frequently cited (52%) problem was that the funding restricts the range of activities in which rape crisis centers can engage. This may mean that survivors in certain areas are unserved or that necessary work is not funded:

> One of the biggest barriers is definitely how funding is set up. For your funding to have a boundary is very frustrating. Even for just basic mental health counseling, you can't see anybody past [a certain street]. But if there's really nothing there for those people, where do they go? There have been times when I've wanted to do a little more community outreach, but my funding only lets me do 1% so it gets a little frustrating, so I think more flexibility would be good. (Advocate 16)

> I think the expectation is higher than what can be provided in the amount of time that the funds allot for it. They don't provide enough up-front time for advertising, getting the word out, going into the community before you're supposed to be showing results. Then you're not successful and they take the money away, give it to someone else, and then they run into the same problem. So, I think it's sort of a two-fold problem. One coming from the funder's restrictions and then the other just trying to be creative, thinking outside the box of different ways of providing the service. (Advocate 10)

> External funding also requires accountability and reporting to the funder. Although only a couple of advocates mentioned burdensome

paperwork, they aptly described how it could conflict with efforts to provide crisis advocacy to survivors:

There was an argument always between the street staff and management (who had to actually answer to funders), and they want to know exactly what this victim's age was, and what that relationship is—if that information is not available. There's a four-page form that you have called an intake form and on there you put the exact time you spent with them, all the medication that they were given—you know just things that you have to know. I understood the need for it but, my other need was greater [i.e., to be there for her client]. (Advocate 36)

I know one of their biggest frustrations is time and the sheer amount of paperwork you have to do for a client. I've had a couple of them tell me, if I didn't have to go and do all that paperwork, I could probably see an extra client a day. . . . I think funders are too concerned about numbers. They always want to know how many people? How much money? How many hours? And it doesn't always boil down to that and I think they just don't seem to get that. (Advocate 16)

Secondary Victimization

The final direct services barrier affecting victims noted by advocates was secondary victimization. Because sexual violence has emotional, medical, and legal ramifications, survivors often come into contact with multiple community systems. Navigating these systems can be challenging and, at times, retraumatizing. Often, a main function of advocates is to work on behalf of survivors to ensure that their rights are respected and that they receive all of the assistance to which they are entitled. Consequently, advocates face barriers to working with survivors not only in the context of their own agencies and funders but also in their interactions with other systems. A major barrier mentioned by most (72%) of those interviewed was that survivors experience negative or revictimizing reactions, such as being blamed or disbelieved when telling other people about the assault or seeking formal services. Hospitals were frequently cited as a common first contact for

survivors and as a place where they may face unpredictable responses:

There are certain hospitals in this city that are wonderful. I mean I haven't dealt with very many yet, but I've heard the stories. I mean there are certain ERs that if I had a friend that was raped, I would probably send them to that ER first, even if it was 5 miles out of the way because their staff is compassionate, they're prepared to deal with this issue, they just take a good approach to it. And then you have other hospitals—it just depends on the luck of the draw. I mean if you've got a physician that's tired or cranky or doesn't want to deal with this or feels like this person has lied or the victim happens to be a prostitute. (Advocate 7)

Certainly, one of the barriers is how people treat people who've been sexually assaulted and all the myths that they come to the table with. If the victim's first interaction with whomever they're disclosing to is negative, then that could sort of stop them from seeking other help. If their first contact is the hospital ER and a nurse or a doctor is rude or inappropriate or doesn't believe them, that could just end it right there. They're not gonna want to get help in any other way, they'll forget it, not want to tell anybody else feeling that no one will believe me. If it's the police who respond negatively initially, maybe they won't go on to get medical help. That's a huge barrier. (Advocate 10)

When you do encourage survivors to get help, you're sort of sending them into the lion's den almost. I mean this is a scary thing to go to the hospital and it's kind of a gamble, whether or not the experience is going to go well. It's even worse to have your case taken into the legal system and frankly, I don't know. If I were raped right now, I don't know if I would go to the hospital. I certainly would not prosecute and there's no way I would go to court. So, I was beginning to feel while I was there even [at the agency]—how can I be doing this work, telling people what they should do with their case when I wouldn't do it myself? (Advocate 30)

A lot of times they [formal support sources] don't say things in front of the [victims]. But out of the room, nurses and law enforcement would make comments to me that always are out of line, they say too much to me and that's when I get really frustrated. It happens a lot of times where nurses are revictimizing my clients, saying, "Girl, what are you thinking? What were you doing like at 9:00 at night up there?" (Advocate 32)

These reactions to victims by the medical system make it difficult for advocates because they often are unable to protect survivors from further trauma following the rape caused by these negative social reactions from service providers, which research shows are associated with greater PTSD symptoms in survivors (Campbell et al., 1999; Ullman & Filipas, 2001). Because victims need these systems' services and advocates have less power than medical personnel, advocates are put in a bind if they try to confront personnel making negative reactions to victims. Advocates have to work with service providers on an ongoing basis, and although they may try to educate them as best they can, they must walk a fine line in doing so, as they can receive defensive reactions and hostility from these personnel. Even worse, providers' hostility may be taken out on survivors who may subsequently be treated even more poorly. Clearly, this problem adds to advocates' burden because they have to try to support survivors regarding not only the rape and its effects but also the revictimization they are experiencing from system personnel.

Because of problems of secondary victimization within the medical system, advocates also suggested that training of medical personnel was needed. However, pointing this out to those providers often led to anger or denial by personnel who did not appreciate advocates' viewpoints about system responses to survivors.

I mean the hospital situation could also be equally frustrating with people not really knowing how to do exams very well and doctors and nurses that just weren't really trained in how to

do these things and didn't really have the bedside manner that we would have liked. We have contracts with various hospitals and we would try to go into hospitals and do trainings with folks in ERs and not only is it hard to do trainings, but when you get there, they're like, "We know how to do our job, we don't need you people having to tell us how to do our jobs." And we would say well actually, we have all these cases where evidence was tampered with or a client is saying that this happened. That shouldn't have happened. So, we knew that stuff was happening. And that was often frustrating too. (Advocate 30)

As a consequence of these attitudes, advocates are often unable to effectively ensure that victims' rights are fulfilled and that they get appropriate medical care and proper collection of forensic evidence in the rape kit.

The legal and criminal justice systems were also identified as sources of secondary victimization for survivors.

I think another huge barrier is just the mythology that's out there and is so pervasive. Victim blame is, in my perception, the number one barrier to prosecution that victims face. If they're willing and want to prosecute, what law enforcement looks at primarily is how credible is this person and how credible is their story? Because if they're not credible, this isn't going to stand up in court and we don't want to take it. And there are 101 billion ways to discredit somebody, and I've seen and heard them all. What we know is that people are targeted [for rape] because of their vulnerability and their inability to be credible or tell the story in the way that law enforcement needs it to be told. (Advocate 8)

I get very frustrated with felony review in the state's attorney's office in the sense that unless there is a statement from the offender, we can't charge this individual. The system doesn't like to give options. I've been in with state's attorneys who want the case to go a certain way and they don't give victims all their options and that is one of my jobs—to make sure they're aware of all their options. But sometimes that doesn't sit well with the state's attorney's office. (Advocate 20)

I promised her that she doesn't have to see him [the offender]. She didn't want to press charges, she didn't want him in her life. They had already put him out of the house. He had snuck in. We go to the police station, there's a woman detective who I already knew, I had a history with her, she was awful, awful. She questioned the woman [survivor] in the same room with the suspect handcuffed to a piece of wood on the wall. So, we're at the other end of this conference table and he's right there the whole time. It was so unnecessarily abusive. (Advocate 36)

The court system is really awful. If you get a good state's attorney, and there are some out there, that's fine. But most of the time and especially with sexual assault, they don't want to deal with it. We've been training people in the state's attorney's office, but they didn't even want to sit through the training. (Advocate 16)

A former advocate summarized the problems with entering the legal system for rape survivors most clearly:

We still have a system where it's extremely tough for women to come out and allege a rape, let alone go through the process of a trial.... I understand the profound expectations people have when they press charges and I know 9 times out of 10 it'll be plea bargained out and you don't get your moment in court. If it does go to trial, you don't ever get to tell your story the way you want to, so I think expectations women have of what it means to go to court are derived from our popular cultural ideal of standing up in court, pointing at somebody and saying he raped me and that of course does not happen. I've said, you know your job as a survivor now is to get stronger and here are all the different options you can use to get stronger. Don't let

anybody tell you that the only way to get stronger is through the legal system, 'cause it will probably not be the result. So, I'm much more brutally honest with them and I think there's a lot of advocates who kind of feed into the mythology of what it means to press charges and that you have to press charges to get rapists off the streets. We're not gettin' 'em off the street! If we do get 'em off the street, it will be for 5 to 6 months and, from what I've seen, chances are if a man rapes women, he is either going to participate as a rapist or be victimized by sexual assault in jail. When he gets back on the street, he's a much more dangerous rapist than he was before. I have no faith in the legal system to solve this issue. (Advocate 38).

In summary, secondary victimization from police and legal personnel makes it difficult for advocates to help survivors get any kind of real justice or accountability from the criminal justice system. Advocates can try to support survivors who choose to pursue a criminal case by helping keep them informed about their case and going to court with them, but they have little control over whether a case will be deemed credible and worthy of the prosecutor's time and effort in the first place. Police may also poorly treat survivors, violate their rights, and retraumatize them when they perceive that certain survivors have less value, such as young, ethnic minority women. This makes it extremely difficult for advocates whose goal is to try to empower survivors within an inherently antivictim criminal justice system.

Conclusions and Study Implications

This study identified a number of barriers that workers in rape crisis centers perceive that survivors face getting services. Consistent with past research on survivors, advocates noted numerous problems with access, availability, affordability, and acceptability of services (Campbell, 1998; Campbell et al., 2001; Logan et al., 2005; Martin, 2005). Our sample of rape crisis center workers mentioned barriers of access and availability to services, funding, and resource problems at both organization and system levels, and secondary victimization or insensitivity of service providers, notably medical and criminal justice system personnel. Many interviewees mentioned problems of underfunding of rape crisis centers and difficulty securing help among women in disadvantaged groups such as the homeless, prostitutes, the disabled, and mentally ill. Some barriers also varied by workers' demographic or treatment orientation. Those with higher degrees reported fewer problems with services being insensitive or structural barriers generally. Workers with less formal education cited more structural barriers and services insensitivity and fewer survivor-related barriers. It is unclear if these perceptions were because of the jobs of workers in the organization or differences in individuals with these different degrees. Views about the causes of social problems may also differ for those who elect to gain higher degrees, who may have a greater investment and belief in the system than those who do not.

Most advocates mentioned the problems of secondary victimization by the systems that are supposed to help women obtain medical treatment and justice. However, workers doing primarily advocacy were more likely than those doing counseling to mention racism and sexism as barriers and service providers' insensitivity toward minorities specifically. Not surprisingly, those endorsing a feminist orientation were more likely to mention barriers related to race, class, and gender bias; professionalization of rape crisis centers; rape myths or societal denial of rape; language barriers; and lack of culturally competent services than were those endorsing nonfeminist treatment orientations. Although both Whites and minorities mentioned issues of racism generally as barriers, ethnic minorities were more likely to mention racist biases of the system specifically, particularly if they were young, compared to Whites. In addition, Latinas mentioned language barriers and familial, cultural, or immigration issues more than others. This finding is consistent with past studies of sexual assault victims who frequently note problems of receiving negative social reactions when seeking help from formal systems (Campbell et al., 1999, 2001; Ullman, 1996; Ullman & Filipas, 2001). In our study, workers also identified barriers associated with language, ethnic minority race, family or culture, immigration, disability, mental illness, prostitution, and young age to be associated with poorer access to services and more secondary victimization by formal service providers, especially

medical and criminal justice personnel. Racism was noted in our study as a barrier particularly for younger women in how they were treated as rape victims. Young, ethnic minority women were viewed as being subject to greater police harassment and secondary victimization by medical and criminal justice system personnel.

Although Logan et al.'s (2005) sample mentioned bureaucratic problems and staff incompetence as barriers for women seeking services, these were discussed in relationship to medical and criminal justice systems, not rape crisis centers themselves. Other research by Campbell and Martin (Campbell et al., 2001; Martin, 2005) has also documented problems, particularly with the medical and criminal justice or legal systems' responses to rape victims. Survivors in Logan et al.'s study did not mention any of the numerous problems found in our study, [those] noted by advocates we interviewed in these organizations. This may be because of a number of factors. They may not have had awareness of these problems, given that their contact is more limited than employees of centers studied here. The women were recruited by rape crisis centers, and the focus groups were conducted at the centers, which may have made any problems that arose with those agencies less likely to be mentioned. Women with negative experiences may also have been less likely to have been referred to the study by rape crisis center staff. Finally, their study did not ask women about problems with getting help from rape crisis centers specifically.

However, our study found that various organizational barriers to doing advocacy were professionalization, racism, inflexibility of rape crisis centers, physical space limitations, structure of programs, burnout, and vicarious trauma related to poor supervision; and lack of accountability and caretaking of staff by agencies, corruption, lack of respect for clients in one agency, and paperwork demands. Past research has clearly documented the serious problem of vicarious trauma and burnout in those who work with traumatized populations, including sexual assault survivors (Salston & Figley, 2003; Schauben & Frazier, 1995; Wasco & Campbell, 2002). Racism has also been documented by others studying rape crisis centers (Campbell et al., 2001; Matthews, 1994; Scott, 1998). Professionalization has been noted by other researchers who study rape crisis centers as leading to changes in these organizations (Campbell et al., 1998) such as being less political, which were noted as negative by a number of younger advocates in this study. Clearly, some of the organizational problems noted are related to funding limitations, but others, such as racism, may be associated with professionalization.

These problems did not characterize all agencies, and the worst problems were mentioned by former advocates who likely felt freer to talk about problems in their past work settings but also may have had worse experiences than other employees. Clearly, the small convenience sample of metropolitan area advocates studied presents biases that may not reflect what a random sampling of rape crisis center employees and former employees might report. Further research is needed to determine how widespread these perceptions are and how these issues may be better addressed in rape crisis centers in the future. We caution that these findings should not be taken to mean that rape crisis centers are not doing extremely positive work on behalf of survivors of sexual assault in the community. These problems more likely reflect widely shared, yet often unspoken, experiences of workers in low-paid human service organizations, all of whom provide critically needed services without adequate funding and societal support (Glisson, 2000; Webster & Hackett, 1999).

Community studies suggest that rape crisis centers are typically rated as one of the most helpful support sources by sexual assault survivors (Filipas & Ullman, 2001; Golding et al., 1989), compared with other formal sources such as mental health, medical, and criminal justice, which are typically rated less favorably. In addition, a recent preliminary descriptive evaluation of rape crisis services in Illinois found that they were an effective use of taxpayer money (Wasco et al., 2004). Despite the findings here of problems in these organizations, some of which were noted to a greater extent by former advocates in the sample, it does not necessarily imply that many survivors are not receiving excellent help from these agencies. Human service agencies, including rape crisis centers, typically receive less funding than needed to serve their client populations and often cannot afford to pay or support workers as much as they ideally would like to. Although efficient use of limited resources is one way to overcome such limitations, clearly sheer amounts of funding and support for providing such services to a population in crisis is a major task that cannot simply be managed by better fiscal management.

More attention is needed for addressing problems related to less-than-optimal resources and support for advocates in particular working in rape crisis centers, and these problems are unlikely to be limited to centers in the metropolitan area studied here. However, it is known that this line of work is related to high burnout, and many current employees mentioned the problems of high turnover in these agencies that offer little chance for promotion or pay increases. Future research on secondary trauma and burnout in rape crisis workers should go beyond studying worker characteristics, training, and work roles and also study organizational characteristics that may also contribute to these negative outcomes.

Martin (2005) has persuasively argued that organizational constraints and goals often result in secondary victimization of rape victims because workers in medical and criminal justice systems follow rules required to do their jobs, which entails practices that often conflict with the needs of rape victims. This implies that organizational change, not only training or education of service system personnel, will be needed to improve rape victims' treatment. Clearly, this exploratory study suggests that more research is needed to understand how rape crisis workers may be better supported in their organizations and in their advocacy efforts generally for survivors in the systems with which they interface. Researchers need to be aware of the stresses faced by rape crisis centers and their workers if they wish to collaborate with them in work that may help to respond to rape in the community. This study's results may also help researchers to better understand the larger context in which survivors attempt to get help from rape crisis centers, the medical system, and the criminal justice system. Without an understanding of the larger context of survivors' help-seeking experiences from both survivors' and service providers' perspectives, researchers may be less able to fully understand how survivors navigate their recovery and their support-seeking experiences following sexual assault. The findings suggest many barriers that rape crisis centers need to address to enhance their advocates' ability to help rape survivors. However, increased resources to these organizations are urgently needed to enable them to make these changes. This is vital given that rape crisis centers are the only support system whose goal is to help victims navigate their recovery and to obtain help from other service systems. Beyond this, the larger societal context of rape and other organizations that deal with rape victims (e.g., hospitals, criminal justice) also need to be adapted or transformed in some way to improve responses to victims following sexual assault.

/// DISCUSSION QUESTIONS

1. Discuss how each of the organizational barriers can limit how rape crisis advocates engage in victim assistance.

2. How has the professionalization of rape crisis centers affected their ability to engage in advocacy work?

3. What barriers exist in providing direct services to victims? How do rape-crisis advocates respond to these challenges?

Note

1. The rape kit involves collecting data from a variety of different places in search of DNA that may have been left from the offender and includes a pelvic exam, scraping under the fingernails, combing for hairs in the pubic region, and oral swabbing.

References

Baird, S., & Jenkins, S. R. (2003). Vicarious traumatization, secondary traumatic stress, and burnout in sexual assault and domestic violence agency staff. *Violence and Victims, 18,* 71–86.

Campbell, R. (1998). The community response to rape: Victims' experiences with the legal, medical, and mental health systems. *American Journal of Community Psychology, 26,* 355–379.

Campbell, R., Baker, C. K., & Mazurek, T. L. (1998). Remaining radical? Organizational predictors of rape crisis centers' social change initiatives. *American Journal of Community Psychology, 26,* 457–483.

Campbell, R., & Martin, P. Y. (2001). Services for sexual assault survivors: The role of rape crisis centers. In C. M. Renzetti, J. L. Edelson, & R. K. Bergen (Eds.), *Sourcebook on violence against women* (pp. 227–241). Thousand Oaks, CA: Sage.

Campbell, R., Sefl, T., Barnes, H. E., Ahrens, C. E., Wasco, S. M., & Zaragoza-Diesfeld, Y. (1999). Community services for rape survivors: Enhancing psychological well-being or increasing trauma? *Journal of Consulting and Clinical Psychology, 67,* 847–858.

Campbell, R., Wasco, S. M., Ahrens, C. E., Sefl, T., & Barnes, H. E. (2001). Preventing the "second rape": Rape survivors' experiences with community service providers. *Journal of Interpersonal Violence, 16,* 1239–1259.

Davis, R. C., Brickman, E. R., & Baker, T. (1991). Effects of supportive and unsupportive responses of others to rape victims: Effects on concurrent victim adjustment. *American Journal of Community Psychology, 19,* 443–451.

Filipas, H. H., & Ullman, S. E. (2001). Social reactions to sexual assault victims from various support sources. *Violence & Victims, 16,* 673–692.

Frank, J. D., & Frank, J. B. (1991). *Persuasion and healing: A comparative study of psychotherapy* (3rd ed.). Baltimore: Johns Hopkins University Press.

Ghahramanlou, M., & Brodbeck, C. (2000). Predictors of secondary trauma in sexual assault trauma counselors. *International Journal of Emergency Medicine, 2,* 229–240.

Glisson, C. (2000). Organizational climate and culture. In R. Patti (Ed.), *Handbook of social welfare administration* (pp. 195–218). Thousand Oaks, CA: Sage.

Golding, J. M., Siegel, J. M., Sorenson, S. B., Burnam, M. A., & Stein, J. A. (1989). Social support sources following sexual assault. *Journal of Community Psychology, 17,* 92–107.

Logan, T. K., Evans, L., Stevenson, E., & Jordan, C. (2005). Barriers to services for rural and urban rape survivors. *Journal of Interpersonal Violence, 20,* 591–616.

Luborsky, L., Crit, S., Christoph, P., McLellan, A. T., Woody, G., Piper, W., et al. (1986). Do therapists vary much in their success? Findings from four outcome studies. *American Journal of Orthopsychiatry, 56,* 501–512.

Martin, P. Y. (2005). *Rape work: Victims, gender, and emotions in organization and community context.* New York: Routledge.

Matthews, N. (1994). *Confronting rape: The feminist anti-rape movement and the state.* London: Routledge.

Miles, M. B., & Huberman, A. M. (1994). *Qualitative data analysis* (2nd ed.). Thousand Oaks, CA: Sage.

National Violence Against Women Prevention Research Center. (2001, May). *Fostering collaborations to prevent violence against women: Integrating findings from practitioner and researcher focus groups.* Charleston, SC: Author.

Riger, S. (1999). Working together: Challenges in collaborative research on violence against women. *Violence Against Women, 5,* 1099–1117.

Salston, M., & Figley, C. R. (2003). Secondary traumatic stress effects of working with survivors of criminal victimization. *Journal of Traumatic Stress, 16,* 167–174.

Schauben, L. J., & Frazier, P. A. (1995). Vicarious trauma: The effects on female counselors of working with sexual violence survivors. *Psychology of Women Quarterly, 19,* 49–64.

Scott, E. K. (1998). Creating partnerships for change: Alliances and betrayals in the racial politics of two feminist organizations. *Gender & Society, 12,* 400–423.

Stein, D. M., & Lambert, M. J. (1984). On the relationship between therapist experience and psychotherapy outcome. *Clinical Psychology Review, 4,* 127–142.

Strauss, A. L., & Corbin, J. M. (1998). *Basics of qualitative research: Techniques and procedures for developing grounded theory.* Newbury Park, CA: Sage.

Ullman, S. E. (1996). Do social reactions to sexual assault victims vary by support provider? *Violence and Victims, 11,* 143–156.

Ullman, S. E. (2005). Interviewing clinicians and advocates who work with sexual assault survivors: A personal perspective on moving from quantitative to qualitative methods. *Violence Against Women, 11,* 1–27.

Ullman, S. E., & Filipas, H. H. (2001). Predictors of PTSD symptom severity and social reactions in sexual assault victims. *Journal of Traumatic Stress, 14,* 369–389.

Ullman, S. E., Filipas, H. H., Townsend, S. M., & Starzynski, L. L. (in press). Psychosocial correlates of PTSD symptom severity in sexual assault survivors. *Journal of Traumatic Stress.*

Wasco, S. M., & Campbell, R. (2002). Emotional reactions of rape victim advocates: A multiple case study of anger and fear. *Psychology of Women Quarterly, 26,* 120–130.

Wasco, S. M., Campbell, R., & Clark, M. (2002). A multiple case study of rape victim advocates' self-care routines: The influence of organizational context. *American Journal of Community Psychology, 30,* 731–760.

Wasco, S. M., Campbell, R., Howard, A., Mason, G., Staggs, S., Schewe, P., & Riger, S. (2004). A statewide evaluation of services provided to rape survivors. *Journal of Interpersonal Violence, 19,* 252–263.

Webster, L., & Hackett, R. K. (1999). Burnout and leadership in community mental health systems. *Administration and Policy in Mental Health, 26,* 387–399.

Young, M. E., Nosek, M. A., Howland, C. A., Chanpong, G., & Rintala, D. H. (1997). Prevalence of abuse of women with disabilities. *Archives of Physical Medicine and Rehabilitation, 78*(Suppl.), S34–S38.

Glossary

Acquaintance rape: the victim knows the perpetrator; it usually accounts for the majority of rape and sexual assault cases.

Adler, Freda: her works were inspired by the emancipation of women that resulted from the effects of the second wave of feminism. Adler suggested that women's rates of violent crime would increase.

Age-of-consent campaign: designed to protect young women from men who preyed on the innocence of girls by raising the age of sexual consent to 16 or 18 in all states by 1920.

Altruistic: one explanation for infanticide where the mother believes that it is in the best interest of her child to be dead and that the mother is doing a good thing by killing her child.

Attachment: the bond that people have with the values of society as a result of their relationships with family, friends, and social institutions.

Baldwin, Lola: hired in 1908 by the Portland, Oregon, police department to provide supervisory assistance to a group of social workers. Her employment sparked debates as to whether she was a sworn officer or a social worker.

Barefield v. Leach (1974): held that states could not justify disparities in the programs for female inmates based on a smaller female incarcerated population and the costs of program delivery.

Battered women's movement: shelters and counseling programs established throughout the United States to help women in need as a result of the feminist movements in the 1960s and 1970s. It led to systemic changes in how the police and courts handled cases of domestic violence.

Belief: a general acceptance of society's rules.

Blankenship, Betty: one of the first women in the United States to serve as a patrol officer; she worked for the Indianapolis Police Department in 1964, and she helped set the stage for significant changes for the future of policewomen.

Bootstrapping: modern-day practice of institutionalizing girls for status offenses.

Burnout: the feeling of being under high levels of emotional and physical duress. This feeling is often categorized into three stages: (1) emotional exhaustion due to stress, (2) depersonalization, and (3) reduced personal accomplishment.

Campus sexual assault: refers to acts of rape and sexual assault that occur during the collegiate experience. Can involve, but is not limited to, crimes that occur on a college campus

Canterino v. Wilson (1982): males and females must be treated equally unless there is a substantial reason that requires a distinction be made.

Chivalry: instances in which women receive preferential treatment by the justice system.

Civil Rights Bill of 1964: focused on eliminating racial discrimination; however, the word *sex* was added to the bill, prohibiting the use of sex as a requirement for hiring.

Coffal, Liz: one of the first women in the United States to serve as a patrol officer for the Indianapolis Police Department in 1964; she helped set the stage for significant changes for the future of policewomen.

Commitment: the investment that an individual has to the normative values of society.

Community policing: a policing strategy that is based on the idea that the community is extremely important in achieving shared goals; it emphasizes community support from its members, which can help reduce crime and fear.

Cooper v. Morin (1980): held that the equal protection clause prevents prison administrators from justifying the disparate treatment of women on the grounds that providing such services for women is inconvenient.

Core rights of victims: vary by jurisdiction; however, the following core rights have been found in many state constitutions: right to attend, right to compensation, right to be heard, right to be informed, right to protection, right to restitution, right to return of property, right to a speedy trial, and right to enforcement.

Custodial institutions: similar to male institutions, women are warehoused and little programming or treatment is offered to the inmates.

Cyberstalking: incidents of stalking that use electronic forms of technology such as e-mail, text, GPS, and the Internet.

Cycle of victimization and offending: explains how young girls often run away from home in an attempt to escape from an abusive situation, usually ending up as offenders themselves.

Cycle of violence: conceptualized by Lenore Walker in 1979 to help explain how perpetrators of intimate partner abuse maintain control over their victims over time. The cycle is made up of three distinct time frames: tension building, the abusive incident, and the honeymoon period.

Dark figure of crime: crimes that are not reported to the police and therefore not represented in official crime statistics, such as the Uniform Crime Reports and the National Incident-Based Reporting System.

Dating violence: intimate partner abuse in relationships where people are unmarried and may or may not be living together; violence that occurs between two people who are unmarried; teenagers are seen as the most at-risk population.

Debt bondage: a form of forced labor trafficking that requires victims to pay off debt through labor.

Differential association theory: focuses on the influence that one's social relationships may have in encouraging delinquent behavior. This theory also incorporated various characteristics of the social learning theory, suggesting that criminality is a learned behavior.

Discretionary arrest: police officers have the option to arrest or not arrest the offender based on their free choice within the context of their professional judgment.

Drug-facilitated rape: an unwanted sexual act that occurs after a victim voluntarily or involuntarily consumes drugs or alcohol.

Economic abuse: refers to acts of intimate partner abuse that involve control over personal finances (such as denial of money, prohibitions on work).

Emotional abuse: refers to acts of intimate partner abuse that involve tools of emotional or psychological control rather than physical.

Evil woman hypothesis: women are punished not only for violating the law but also for breaking the socialized norms of gender-role expectations.

Extralegal factors: can include the type of attorney (private or public defender), which can significantly affect the likelihood of pretrial release for women.

Fear of victimization: a gendered experience where women experience higher rates of fear of crime compared to males. This idea is based on the distorted portrayal of the criminal justice system by the media.

Femicide: the killing of women based on gender discrimination. The murders often involve sexual torture and body mutilation.

Feminism: a series of social and political movements (also referred to as the *three waves of feminism*) that advocated for women's rights and gender equality.

Feminist criminology: developed as a reaction against traditional criminology, which failed to address women and girls in research. It reflects several of the themes of gender roles and socialization that resulted from the second wave of feminism.

Feminist pathways perspective: provides some of the best understanding of how women find themselves stuck in a cycle that begins with victimization and leads to offending.

Feminist research methods: process of gathering research that involves placing gender at the center of the conversation, giving women a voice, and changing the relationship between the researcher and the subject to one of care and concern versus objectivity.

Filicide: the homicide of children older than one year of age by their parent.

Formal processing: a petition is filed requesting a court hearing, which can initiate the designation of being labeled as a delinquent.

Fry, Elizabeth: a key figure in the crusade to improve the conditions of incarcerated women in the United Kingdom and an inspiration for the American women's prison reform movement.

Gender gap: refers to the differences in male and female offending for different types of offenses.

Gender-responsive programming: creates parity in offender programming and is designed to meet the unique needs of women. Generally involves consideration of six key principles: gender, environment, relationships, services and supervision, socioeconomic status, and community.

Gender-specific programming: must be able to address the wide variety of needs of the delinquent girl. Efforts by Congress have been made to allocate the resources necessary for analyzing, planning, and implementing these services.

Gendered assignments: job duties that were usually assigned to officers based on their gender; female officers were more inclined to receive social service positions rather than patrol and crime-fighting positions.

Gendered justice: also referred to as *injustice*; it is the discrimination of individuals based on their gender. This idea is often seen in the criminal justice system where females' needs and unique experiences go unmet because of the fact that the theories of offending have come from the male perspective.

Genital mutilation: also known as female circumcision and involves the vandalism or removal of female genitalia for the purposes of protecting girls' virginity and eliminating the potential for sexual pleasure.

Glass ceiling: a term used to describe the invisible barriers that limit the ability of women and minorities from achieving high rank opportunities in the workplace.

Glover v. Johnson (1979): held that the state must provide the same opportunities for education, rehabilitation, and vocational training for female offenders as provided for male offenders.

Good ol' boy network: a social network of people who provide access and grant favors to each other. It is usually made up of elite White males, and they tend to exclude other members of their community.

Griffin v. Michigan Department of Corrections (1982): held that inmates do not possess any rights to be protected against being viewed in stages of undress or naked by a correctional officer, regardless of gender.

Grummett v. Rushen (1985): the pat-down search of a male inmate (including the groin area) does not violate one's Fourth Amendment protection against unreasonable search and seizure.

Hagan, John: developed the power control theory; his research focused on the roles within the family unit, especially that of patriarchy.

Harassment: acts that are indicative of stalking behaviors but do not ignite feelings of fear in the victim.

Hirschi, Travis: proposed the social bonds theory; his research focused primarily on delinquency and the reasons why people may not become involved in criminal activity.

Honor-based violence: murders that are executed by a male family member and are a response to a belief that the woman has offended a family's honor and has brought shame to the family.

Human trafficking: the exploitation and forced labor of individuals for the purposes of prostitution, domestic servitude, and other forms of involuntary servitude in agricultural and factory industries.

Incapacitated rape: an unwanted sexual act that occurs after a victim voluntarily consumes drugs or alcohol.

Incarcerated mothers: have a significant effect on children. The geographical location of the prison and length of sentencing determine whether mothers can have ties with their children; in many cases, the children are either cared for by family members or are placed in foster care.

Infanticide: an act in which a parent kills his or her child within the first year.

Intimate partner abuse: abuse that occurs between individuals who currently have, or have previously had, an intimate relationship.

Involvement: one's level of participation in conventional activities (studying, playing sports, or participating in extracurricular activities).

Jail the offender and protect the victim models: prioritization is given to the prosecution of offenders over the needs of the victims; however, these models are widely criticized due to their limitations and inability to deter individuals from participating in the offenses.

Jordan v. Gardner (1992): the pat-down policy designed to control the introduction of contraband into the facility could be viewed as unconstitutional if conducted by male staff members against female inmates.

Just world hypothesis: society has a need to believe that people deserve whatever comes to them; this paradigm is linked to patterns of victim blaming.

Juvenile delinquency: the repeated committing of crimes by young children and adolescents.

Juvenile Justice and Delinquency Prevention (JJDP) Act of 1974: provides funding for state and local governments to help decrease the number of juvenile delinquents and to help provide community and rehabilitative programs to offenders.

Labor trafficking: the recruitment, harboring, transportation, provision, or obtaining of a person for labor or services, through the use of force, fraud, or coercion for the purpose of subjection to involuntary servitude, peonage, debt bondage, or slavery.

Laub, John: codeveloped the life course theory; his research has primarily focused on the following criminological and sociological topics: deviance, the life course, and juvenile delinquency and justice.

Legal factors: have an impact on the decision-making process for both males and females in different ways. They vary from jurisdiction to jurisdiction and they can range from criminal history to offense severity.

Level of Service Inventory-Revised (LSI-R): a risk assessment tool used for correctional populations.

Life course theory: examines how adverse life events impact criminality over time and can provide insight on both female and male offending patterns.

Lifestyle theory: developed to explore the risks of victimization from personal crimes and seeks to relate the patterns of one's everyday activities to the potential for victimization.

Lombroso, Cesare, and William Ferrero: the first criminologists to investigate the nature of the female offender; they worked together to publish *The Female Offender* in 1985.

Male inmate preference: women inmates are perceived as more demanding, defiant, and harder to work with, so male and female officers would much rather work with male inmates.

Mandatory arrest: surfaced during the 1980s and 1990s with the intention to stop domestic violence by deterring offenders. It clarified the roles of police officers when dealing with domestic violence calls and removed the responsibility of arrest from the victim.

Masculine culture: also known as the *male-dominated police culture*; while attempting to gain acceptance into this culture, females are often disrespected and harassed by their male counterparts.

Masked criminality of women: Otto Pollak's theory that suggested that women gain power by deceiving men through sexual playacting, faked sexual responses, and menstruation.

Mendelsohn, Benjamin: distinguished categories of victims based on the responsibility of the victim and the degree to which the victim had the power to make decisions that could alter his or her likelihood of victimization.

Minneapolis Domestic Violence Experiment: helped show the decrease in recidivism rates when an actual arrest was made in misdemeanor domestic violence incidents, in comparison to when a police officer just counseled the aggressor.

National Crime Victimization Survey (NCVS): gathers additional data about crimes to help fill in the gap between reported and unreported crime (also known as the dark figure of crime).

National Incident-Based Reporting System (NIBRS): An incident-based system of crimes reported to the police. The system is administered by the Federal Bureau of Investigation as part of the annual Uniform Crime Reports.

National Intimate Partner and Sexual Violence Survey (NISVS): An annual survey by the Centers for Disease Control and Prevention designed to measure the prevalence of intimate partner violence, sexual violence, and stalking.

National Violence Against Women Survey (NVAWS): A telephone survey of 8,000 men and 8,000 women in the United States (English and Spanish speaking) that was conducted by the Centers for Policy Research to measure the prevalence of violence against women.

Neonaticide: an act of homicide of an infant during the first 24 hours after the birth of the child.

Net widening: refers to the practice whereby programs such as diversion were developed to inhibit the introduction of youth into the juvenile justice system. However, these programs expanded the reach of the juvenile court and increased the number of youth under the general reach of the system, both informally and formally.

No-drop policies: developed in response to a victim's lack of participation in the prosecution of her batterer; these policies have led to the disempowering of victims.

Owens, Marie: a contender for the title of first female police officer; she worked as a Chicago factory inspector, transferred to the police department in 1891, and allegedly served on the force for 32 years.

Parens patriae: originated in the English Chancery Courts; this practice gives the state custody of children in cases where the child has no parents or the parents are deemed unfit care providers.

Parole: (1) a form of post-incarceration supervision of offenders in the community; (2) a method of releasing offenders from prison prior to the conclusion of their sentence.

Pollak, Otto: wrote *The Criminality of Women* in 1961 to further explain his belief that crime data sources failed to reflect the true extent of female crime.

Post-traumatic stress disorder (PTSD): may develop after a person experiences a traumatic life event. PTSD can include flashbacks, avoidance of emotional contexts, and recurrent nightmares and may inhibit normal daily functioning abilities.

Power control theory: looks at the effects of patriarchy within the family unit as a tool of socialization for gender roles.

Probation: a form of community-based supervision that imposes restrictions and regulations on offenders but allows for them to serve their sentence in the community compared to jail or prison.

Pseudo-families: the relationship among individuals who are not related; these relationships are common in the prison system and are often created as a means to provide emotional support to one another during their imprisonment.

Pulling a train: also known as *sexed in*; example of the gang initiation process that requires sexual assault by multiple male members.

Rape: sexual intercourse under force, threat of force, or without the legal consent of the individual. In many jurisdictions, the term *rape* specifically applies in cases of penile-vaginal forced intercourse.

Rape myth acceptance: false beliefs that are seen as justifiable causes for sexual aggression against women.

Reauthorization of the Juvenile Justice and Delinquency Prevention (JJDP) Act (1992): acknowledged the need to provide gender-specific services to address the unique needs of female offenders.

Reentry: the transition from an incarcerated setting to the community; it usually involves meetings with parole officers who provide referrals to receive treatment; unsuccessful reentry often leads to recidivism.

Reformatory: a new concept that saw incarceration as an institution designed with the intent to rehabilitate women from their immoral ways.

Resiliency: also known as *protective factors*; these can enable female victims and female offenders to succeed.

Restraining order: available in every jurisdiction; it is designed to provide the victim with the opportunity to separate from the batterer and prohibit the batterer from contacting the victim.

Risk factors for female delinquency: include a poor family relationship, a history of abuse, poor school performance, negative peer relationships, and issues with substance abuse.

Routine activities theory: created to discuss the risk of victimization in property crimes. It suggests that the likelihood of a criminal act or the likelihood of victimization occurs when an offender, a potential victim, and the absence of a guardian that would deter said offender from making contact with the victim are combined.

Same-sex intimate partner abuse: intimate partner abuse that occurs in a same-sex relationship. Research is significantly limited on this issue, and many victims fear reporting these acts or seeking help because of concerns of being "outed" or concerns about homophobia.

Same-sex sexual assault: often refers to male-on-male assault, because of the limited research on woman-on-woman sexual violence.

Sampson, Robert: codeveloped the *life course theory*; his research has focused on a variety of topics within the fields of criminology and sociology.

Secondary trauma stress (STS): high levels of stress that results from the need and/or desire to help a victim; victim advocates are often affected by this type of stress.

Secondary victimization: the idea that victims become more traumatized after the primary victimization. It can stem from victim blaming or from the process of collecting evidence (physical or testimonial).

Sentencing guidelines: created in conjunction with the Sentencing Reform Act of 1984; the only factors to be considered in imposing a sentence were offense committed, the presence of aggravating or mitigating circumstances, and the criminal history of the offender.

Sexual assault: often used as an umbrella term for all forms of unwanted sexual activity other than rape, sexual assault includes acts, such as penetration other than vaginal-penile penetration, penetration by objects, sodomy, forced oral copulation, sexual touching, and other lewd acts.

Simon, Rita: hypothesized that women would make up a greater proportion of property crimes as a result of their "liberation" from traditional gender roles and restrictions.

Social bond theory: focused on four criteria, or bonds, which prevent people from acting on potential criminological impulses or desires. Travis Hirschi identified these bonds as attachment, commitment, involvement, and belief.

Spousal rape: involves emotional coercion or physical force against a spouse to achieve nonconsensual sexual intercourse; it can often lead to domestic violence.

Stalking: a course of conduct directed at a reasonable person that could cause them to feel fearful. It includes acts such as unwanted phone calls or messages, being followed or spied on, and making unannounced visits.

Status offenses: noncriminal behaviors such as running away, immorality, truancy, and indecent conduct that allowed youth to come under the jurisdiction of the juvenile court.

Statutory rape: sexual activity that is unlawful because it is prohibited by stature or code; it generally involves someone who is not of legal age to give consent.

Stranger rape: the perpetrator is unknown to the victim and is usually associated with a lack of safety, such as walking home at night or not locking the doors.

Street prostitution: an illegal form of prostitution that takes place in public places.

Sutherland, Edwin: proposed the differential association theory; his research focused on one's social relationships and their influence on delinquent behavior.

Symbolic assailant: a perpetrator, often of minority ethnicity, who hides in dark shadows awaiting the abduction, rape, or murder of unknown innocents. He or she attacks at random, is unprovoked, and is difficult to apprehend.

Trafficking Victims Protection Act of 2000: designed to punish traffickers, protect victims, and facilitate prevention efforts in the community to fight against human trafficking.

T-visa: visas issued by the United States for victims; the T-visa is issued for human trafficking victims.

Uniform Crime Reports (UCR): An annual collection of reported crime data from police departments. It is compiled by the Federal Bureau of Investigation.

Victim advocates: trained professionals who support victims of a crime. Victim advocates can provide emotional support, knowledge about the legal process and the rights of crime victims, and provide information and resources for services and assistance.

Victim blaming: shifting the blame of rape from the offender to the victim; by doing so, the confrontation of the realities of victimization is avoided.

Violence Against Women Act (VAWA): passed in 1994; this federal law provides funding for training and research on intimate partner abuse as well as sets forth policies for restitution and civil redress. VAWA established the Office on Violence Against Women within the Department of Justice; it provided funding for battered women's shelters and outreach education, funding for domestic violence training for police and court personnel, and the opportunity for victims to sue for civil damages as a result of violent acts perpetuated against them.

von Hentig, Hans: his theory of victimization highlights 13 categories of victims and focuses on how personal factors such as biological, social, and psychological characteristics influence risk factors for victimization.

Walking the line: gang initiation process for girls in which they are subjected to assault by their fellow gang members.

Welfare Reform Act of 1996: Section 115 of this act bans women with a felony drug conviction from collecting welfare benefits and food stamps.

Wells, Alice Stebbins: the first female police officer hired in the United States by the Los Angeles Police Department in 1920; she advocated for the protection of children and women, especially when it came to sexual education.

Work-family balance: a term used to describe the prioritization of family life (marriage, children, and lifestyle) within the demands of the workplace.

Wraparound services: holistic and culturally sensitive plans for each woman that draw on a coordinated range of services within her community, such as public and mental health systems, addiction recovery, welfare, emergency shelter organizations, and educational and vocational services.

References

Abad-Santos, A. (2013, January 3). Everything you need to know about Steubenville High School football "rape crew." *The Wire*. Retrieved from http://www.thewire.com/national/2013/01/steubenville-high-football-rape-crew/60554/

Abe-Kim, J., Takeuchi, D. T., Hong, S., Zane, N., Sue, S., Spencer, M. S., . . . & Alegría, M. (2007). Use of mental health-related services among immigrant and U.S.-born Asian Americans: Results from the National Latino and Asian American Study. *American Journal of Public Health, 97*(1), 91.

Abdul, M., Joarder, M., & Miller, P. W. (2014). The experiences of migrants trafficked from Bangladesh. *The ANNALS of the American Academy of Political and Social Science, 653*(1): 141–161.

Acoca, L., & Dedel, K. (1997). *Identifying the needs of young women in the juvenile justice system.* San Francisco, CA: National Council on Crime and Delinquency.

Acoca, L., & Dedel, K. (1998a). *Identifying the needs of young women in the juvenile justice system.* San Francisco, CA: National Council on Crime and Delinquency.

Acoca, L., & Dedel, K. (1998b). *No place to hide: Understanding and meeting the needs of girls in the California juvenile justice system.* San Francisco, CA: National Council on Crime and Delinquency.

Adler, F. (1975). *Sisters in crime: The rise of the new female criminal.* New York: McGraw-Hill.

After court order, Madonna faces accused in stalker case. (1996, January 4.). *New York Times*. Retrieved from http://www.nytimes.com/1996/01/04/us/after-court-order-madonna-faces-accused-in-stalker-case.html

Agnew, R. (1992). Foundation for a general strain theory of crime and delinquency. *Criminology, 30,* 47–88.

Agosin, M. (2006). *Secrets in the sand: The young women of Juarez.* New York: White Pine Press.

Air Force Times. (2012, December 2). Sex assault victims seeking help sooner. Retrieved from http://www.airforcetimes.com/article/20121202/NEWS/212020308/

Akintunde, D. O. (2010). Female genital mutilation: A socio-cultural gang up against womanhood. *Feminist Theology, 18*(2), 192–205.

Alabama Coalition Against Domestic Violence (ACADV). (n.d.). *Dating violence.* Retrieved from http://www.acadv.org/dating.html

Albonetti, C. A. (1986). Criminality, prosecutorial screening, and uncertainty: Toward a theory of discretionary decision making in felony case processing. *Criminology, 24*(4), 623–645.

Alderden, M., & Long, L. (2016). Sexual assault victim participation in police investigations and prosecution. *Violence and Victims, 31*(5): 819–836.

Alexy, E. M., Burgess, A. W., Baker, T., & Smoyak, S. A. (2005). Perceptions of cyberstalking among college students. *Brief Treatment and Crisis Intervention, 5*(3), 279–289.

Alpert, E. (2013, February 18). Murder charges filed after woman burned alive in Papua New Guinea. *Los Angeles Times*. Retrieved from http://articles.latimes.com/2013/feb/18/world/la-fg-wn-woman-burned-alive-papua-new-guinea-20130218

Althaus, D. (2010). Ciudad Juarez women still being tortured by killers. *Houston Chronicle.* Retrieved from http://www.chron.com/news/nation-world/article/Ciudad-Juarez-women-still-being-tortured-by-1703010.php

Alvarez, L. (2011, July 5). Casey Anthony not guilty in slaying of daughter. *New York Times.* Retrieved from http://www.nytimes.com/2011/07/06/us/06casey.html?pagewanted=all&_r=0

American Bar Association (ABA). (2010). *Law school staff by gender and ethnicity.* Retrieved from http://www.americanbar.org/content/dam/aba/migrated/legaled/statistics/charts/facultyinformationbygender.authcheckdam.pdf

American Bar Association (ABA). (2011). *A current glance at women in the law, 2011.* Retrieved from http://www.americanbar.org/content/dam/aba/marketing/women/current_glance_statistics_2011.authcheckdam.pdf

American Bar Association (ABA). (2017). *A current glance at women in the law, 2011.* Retrieved from http://www.americanbar.org/content/dam/aba/marketing/women/current_glance_statistics_january2017.authcheckdam.pdf

American Bar Association (ABA). (2012). *Goal III Report: An annual report on women's advancement into leadership positions in the American Bar Association.* Retrieved from http://www.americanbar.org/content/dam/aba/administrative/women/2012_goa13_women.authcheckdam.pdf

American Bar Association Commission on Domestic Violence. (2008). *Domestic violence Civil Protection Orders (CPOs) by state*. Retrieved from http://www.americanbar.org/content/dam/aba/migrated/domviol/pdfs/CPO_Protections_for_LGBT_Victims_7_08.authcheckdam.pdf

American Correctional Association. (2007). *Directory of adult and juvenile correctional departments, institutions and agencies and probation and parole authorities*. Alexandria, VA: Author.

American Society of Criminology (ASC). (n.d.). *History of the American Society of Criminology*. Retrieved from http://www.asc41.com

Americans for the Arts. (2000). Arts facts: Arts programs for at-risk youth. Retrieved from http://www.americansforthearts.org/sites/default/files/pdf/get_involved/advocacy/research/2008/youth_at_risk08.pdf

Amnesty International. (1999). *Document—Pakistan: Violence against women in the name of honour*. Retrieved from http://amnesty.org/en/library/asset/ASA33/017/1999/en/53f9cc64-e0f2-11dd-be39-2d4003be4450/asa330171999en.html

Amy Elizabeth Fisher. (2014). The Biography.com website. Retrieved from http://www.biography.com/people/amy-fisher-235415.

Anderson, T. L. (2006). Issues facing women prisoners in the early twenty-first century. In C. Renzetti, L. Goodstein, & S. L. Miller (Eds.), *Rethinking gender, crime and justice* (pp. 200–212). Los Angeles: Roxbury.

Annan, S. L. (2011). "It's not just a job. This is where we live. This is our backyard": The experiences of expert legal and advocate providers with sexually assaulted women in rural areas. *Journal of the American Psychiatric Nurses Association, 17*(2), 139–147.

Anuforo, P. O., Oyedele, L., & Pacquiao, D. F. (2004). Comparative study of meanings, beliefs, and practices of female circumcision among three Nigerian tribes in the United States and Nigeria. *Journal of Transcultural Nursing, 15*(2), 103–113.

Appier, J. (1998). *Policing women: The sexual politics of law enforcement and the LAPD*. Philadelphia: Temple University Press.

Arin, C. (2001). Femicide in the Name of Honor in Turkey. *Violence against women, 7*(7), 821–825.

Associated Press. (2012, July 21). Air Force instructor sentenced to 20 years in prison after raping female recruit and sexually assaulting several other women. Retrieved from http://www.dailymail.co.uk/news/article-2177097/Lackland-Air-Force-instructor-Luis-Walker-sentenced-20-years-prison-guilty-rape-sexual-assault.html

Atchison, A. J., & Heide, K. M. (2011). Charles Manson and the family: The application of sociological theories to multiple murder. *International Journal of Offender Therapy and Comparative Criminology* 55(5): 771–798.

Australian Bureau of Statistics (ABS). (2016). Recorded crime—Offenders. Retrieved from http://www.abs.gov.au/ausstats/abs@.nsf/Lookup/by%20Subject/4519.0~2012-13~Main%20Features~Offenders,%20Australia~4

Babin, E. A., Palazzolo, K. E., & Rivera, K. D. (2012). Communication skills, social support, and burnout among advocates in a domestic violence agency. *Journal of Applied Communication Research, 40*(2), 147–166.

Bachman, R., Zaykowski, H., Lanier, C., Poteyeva, M., & Kallmyer, R. (2010). Estimating the magnitude of rape and sexual assault against American Indian and Alaska Native (AIAN) women. *Australian & New Zealand Journal of Criminology, 43*(2), 199–222.

Bacik, I., & Drew, E. (2006). Struggling with juggling: Gender and work/life balance in the legal professions. *Women's Studies International Forum, 29,* 136–146.

Baillargeon, J., Binswanger, I. A., Penn, J. V., Williams, B. A., & Murray, O. J. (2009). Psychiatric disorders and repeat incarcerations: The revolving prison door. *American Journal of Psychiatry, 166,* 103–109.

Baker, C. K., Holditch Niolon, P., & Oliphant, H. (2009). A descriptive analysis of transitional housing programs for survivors of intimate partner violence in the United States. *Violence Against Women, 15*(4), 460–481.

Ball, J. D., & Bostaph, L. G. (2009). He versus she: A gender-specific analysis of legal and extralegal effects on pretrial release for felony defendants. *Women and Criminal Justice, 19*(2), 95–119.

Balsam, K. F., Molina, Y., Blayney, J. A., Dillworth, T., Zimmerman, L., & Kaysen, D. (2015). Racial/ethnic differences in identity and mental health outcomes among young sexual minority women. *Cultural Diversity and Ethnicy Minority Psychology, 21*(3): 380–390.

Banyard, V. L., Moynihan M. M., & Plante, E. G. (2007). Sexual violence prevention through bystander education: An experimental evaluation. *Journal of Community Psychology, 35*(4): 463–481.

Barata, P. C., & Schneider, F. (2004). Battered women add their voices to the debate about the merits of mandatory arrest. *Women's Studies Quarterly, 32*(3/4), 148–163.

Barefield v. Leach, Civ. Act. No. 10282 (D.N.M. 1974).

Barratt, C. L., Bergman, M. E., & Thompson, R. J. (2014). Women in federal enforcement: The role of gender role orientations and sexual orientation in mentoring. *Sex Roles, 71*(1–2): 21–32.

Barrick, K., Lattimore, P. K., Pitts, W. J., & Zhang, S. X. (2014). When farmworkers and advocates see trafficking but law enforcement does not: Challenges in identifying labor trafficking in North Carolina. *Crime, Law, and Social Change, 61*: 205–214.

Bates, K. A., Bader, C. D., & Mencken, F. C. (2003). Family structure, power-control theory, and deviance: Extending power-control theory to include alternate family forms. *Western Criminological Review, 4*(3), 170–190.

Baum, K., Catalano, S., Rand, M., & Rose, K. (2009). *Stalking victimization in the United States*. U.S. Department of Justice, Bureau of Justice Statistics. Retrieved from http://ojp.usdoj.gov/content/pub/pdf/svus.pdf

BBC. (2013, May 7). Profile: Amanda Berry, Georgina De Jesus and Michelle Knight. Retrieved from http://www.bbc.co.uk/news/world-us-canada-22433057

Beck, A. J., Harrison, P. M., & Guerino, P. (2010). Sexual victimization in juvenile facilities reported by youth, 2008–2009. U.S. Department of Justice, Bureau of Justice Statistics. Retrieved from http://bjs.ojp.usdoj.gov/content/pub/pdf/svjfry09.pdfNALS of

Belanger, D. (2014). Labor migration and trafficking among Vietnamese migrants in Asia. *The ANNALS of the American Academy of Political and Social Science* 653(1): 87–106.

Belenko, S., & Houser, K. A. (2012). Gender differences in prison-based drug treatment participation. *International Journal of Offender Therapy and Comparative Criminology, 56*(5), 790–810.

Belknap, J. (2007). *The invisible woman: Gender, crime and justice.* Belmont, CA: Thomson-Wadsworth.

Belknap, J., Dunn, M., & Holsinger, K. (1997). *Moving toward juvenile justice and youth serving systems that address the distinct experience of the adolescent female* (Report to the Governor). Columbus, OH: Office of Criminal Justice Services.

Belknap, J., & Holsinger, K. (1998). An overview of delinquent girls: How theory and practice failed and the need for innovative change. In R. Zaplin (Ed.), *Female crime and delinquency: Critical perspectives and effective interventions* (pp. 31–64). Gaithersburg, MD: Aspen.

Belknap, J., & Holsinger, K. (2006). The gendered nature of risk factors for delinquency, *Feminist Criminology, 1*(1), 48–71.

Bennett, L., Riger, S., Schewe, P., Howard, A., & Wasco, S. (2004). Effectiveness of hotline, advocacy, counseling, and shelter services for victims of domestic violence: A statewide evaluation. *Journal of Interpersonal Violence, 19*(7), 815–829.

Bennett-Smith, M. (2013, February 7). Accused "witch" Kepari Leniata burned alive by mob in Papua New Guinea. *Huffington Post.* Retrieved from http://www.huffingtonpost.com/2013/02/07/kepari-leniata-young-mother-burned-alive-mob-sorcery-papua-new-guinea_n2638431.html

Bennice, J. A., & Resick, P. A. (2003). Marital rape history, research, and practice. *Trauma, Violence, & Abuse, 4*(3), 228–246.

Bent-Goodley, T. B. (2004). Perceptions of domestic violence: A dialogue with African American women. *Health and Social Work, 29*(4), 307–316.

Berg, A. (2011, September 4). Stop shackling pregnant prisoners. *The Daily Beast.* Retrieved from http://www.thedailybeast.com/articles/2011/09/04/stop-shackling-pregnant-prisoners-new-push-to-ban-controversial-practice.html

Berkman, M. B., & O'Connor, R. E. (1993). Do women legislators matter? Female legislators and state abortion policy. *American Politics Quarterly, 21*(1): 102–124.

Bernard, T. J. (1992). *The cycle of juvenile justice.* New York: Oxford University Press.

Bernhard, L. A. (2000). Physical and sexual violence experienced by lesbian and heterosexual women. *Violence Against Women, 6*(1), 68–79.

Beynon, C. M., McVeigh, C., McVeigh, J., Leavey, C., & Bellis, M. A. (2008). The involvement of drugs and alcohol in drug-facilitated sexual assault: A systematic review of the evidence. *Trauma, Violence, & Abuse, 9*(3), 178–188.

Black, M. C., Basile, K. C., Breiding, M. J., Smith, S. G., Walters, M. L., Merrick, M. T., . . . Stevens, M. R. (2011). *The National Intimate Partner and Sexual Violence Survey (NISVS): 2010 summary report.* Atlanta, GA: National Center for Injury Prevention and Control, Centers for Disease Control and Prevention. Retrieved from http://www.cdc.gov/ViolencePrevention/pdf/NISVS_Report2010-a.pdf

Blackburn, A. G., Pfeffer, R. D., & Harris, J. A. (2016). Serious about change: A gendered examination of the impact of offense type on parole success. *Women & Criminal Justice, 26*(5): 340–353.

Blackwell, B. S., Holleran, D., & Finn, M. A. (2008). The impact of the Pennsylvania sentencing guidelines on sex differences in sentencing. *Journal of Contemporary Criminal Justice, 24*(4), 399–418.

Blackwell, D. B. (2012, June 15). Through my eyes: Surviving sexual assault. Retrieved from http://www.usafa.af.mil/shared/media/document/AFD-120619-023.pdf

Block, C. R. (2003). How can practitioners help an abused woman lower her risk of death? *National Institute of Justice (NIJ) Journal, 250*, 4–7. Retrieved from http://www.ncjrs.gov/pdffiles1/jr000250c.pdf

Block, K. J. (1999). Bringing scouting to prison: Programs and challenges. *The Prison Journal, 79*(2), 269–283.

Block, K. J., & Potthast, M. J. (1998). Girl Scouts Beyond Bars: Facilitating parent-child contact in correctional settings. *Child Welfare, 77*(5), 561–579.

Bloom, B., Owen, B., & Covington, S. (2003). *Gender-responsive strategies: Research, practice, and guiding principles for women offenders.* Washington, DC: National Institute of Corrections. U.S. Department of Justice. Retrieved from http://nicic.gov/pubs/2003/018017.pdf

Bloom, B., Owen, B., & Covington, S. (2004). Women offenders and the gendered effects of public policy. *Review of Policy Research, 21*(1), 31–48.

Bloom, B., Owen, B., Deschenes, E. P., & Rosenbaum, J. (2002a). Improving juvenile justice for females: A statewide assessment in California. *Crime and Delinquency, 48*(4), 526–552.

Bloom, B., Owen, B., Deschenes, E. P., & Rosenbaum, J. (2002b). Moving toward justice for female offenders in the new millennium: Modeling gender-specific policies and programs. *Journal of Contemporary Criminal Justice, 18*(1), 37–56.

Blumberg, J. (2007, October 24). A brief history of the Salem witch trials. *The Smithsonian.* Retrieved from http://www.smithsonianmag.com/history/a-brief-history-of-the-salem-witch-trials-175162489/

Boivin, R., & Leclerc, C. (2016). Domestic violence reported to the police: Correlates of victims' reporting behavior and support to legal proceedings. *Violence and Victims, 31*(3): 402–415.

Bond, C., & Jeffries, S. (2009). Does indigeneity matter? Sentencing indigenous offenders in South Australia's higher courts. *Australian & New Zealand journal of Criminology, 42, 47–71.*

Bond, C. E. W., & Jeffries, S. (2012). Harsher sentences?: Indigeneity and prison sentence length in Western Australia's higher courts. *Journal of Sociology, 48*(3), 266–286.

Boone, R. (March 2, 2017). School collected evidence before alerting authorities in locker-room sex assault of disabled black teen. *Chicago Tribune.* Retrieved from http://www.chicagotribune.com/news/nationworld/ct-coat-hanger-assault-disabled-black-teen-20170302-story.html

Bornstein, D. R., Fawcett, J., Sullivan, M., Senturia, K. D., & Shiu-Thornton, S. (2006). Understanding the experiences of lesbian, bisexual and trans survivors of domestic violence. *Journal of Homosexuality, 51*(1), 159–181.

Bourduin, C. M., & Ronis, S. T. (2012). Research note: Individual, family, peer, and academic characteristics of female serious juvenile offenders. *Youth Violence and Juvenile Justice, 10*(4), 386–400.

Bowles, M. A., DeHart, D., & Webb, J. R. (2012). Family influences on female offenders' substance use: The role of adverse childhood events among incarcerated women. *Journal of Family Violence, 27,* 681–686.

Boyd, C. (2001). The implications and effects of theories of intergenerational transmission of violence for boys who live with domestic violence. *Australian Domestic & Family Violence Clearinghouse Newsletter, 6,* 6–8.

Boykins, A. D., Alvanzo, A. A., Carson, S., Forte, J., Leisey, M., & Plichta, S. B. (2010). Minority women victims of recent sexual violence: Disparities in incident history. *Journal of Women's Health, 19*(3), 453–461.

Boyle, E. H., McMorris, B. J., & Gomez, M. (2002). Local conformity to international norms: The case of female genital cutting. *International Sociology, 17*(1), 5–33.

Bozelko, C. (January 11, 2017). Give working prisoners dignity—and decent wages. *National Review.* Retrieved from www.nationalreview.com/article/443747/prison-labor-laws-wages-make-it-close-slavery

Branum, D. (2013, January 8). USAFA reports show increased trust in system, better reporting. *Air Force Print News Today.* Retrieved from http://www.usafa.af.mil/news/story_print.asp?id=123331120

Brennan, P. K. (2006). Sentencing female misdemeanants: An examination of the direct and indirect effects of race/ethnicity. *Justice Quarterly, 23*(1), 60–95.

Brennan, T., Breitenbach, M., Dieterich, W., Salisbury, E. J., & van Voorhis, P. (2012). Women's pathways to serious and habitual crime: A person-centered analysis incorporating gender responsive factors. *Criminal Justice and Behavior, 39*(11), 1481–1508.

Brents, B. G., & Hausbeck, K. (2005). Violence and legalized brothel prostitution in Nevada: Examining safety, risk, and prostitution policy. *Journal of Interpersonal Violence, 20*(3), 270–295.

Bright, C. L., Ward, S. K., & Negi, N. J. (2011). "The chain has to be broken": A qualitative investigation of the experiences of young women following juvenile court involvement. *Feminist Criminology, 6*(1), 32–53.

Britton, D. M. (2003). *At work in the iron cage: The prison as a gendered organization.* New York: New York University Press.

Broidy, L., & Agnew, R. (1997). Gender and crime: A general strain theory perspective. *Journal of Research in Crime and Delinquency, 34,* 275–306.

Brown v. Plata, 563 U.S. 493 (2011).

Brown, L. M., Chesney-Lind, M., & Stein, N. (2007). Patriarchy matters: Toward a gendered theory of teen violence and victimization. *Violence Against Women, 13*(12), 1249–1273.

Brown, M., & Bloom, B. (2009). Reentry and renegotiating motherhood: Maternal identity and success on parole. *Crime & Delinquency, 55*(2), 313–336.

Brown, M. J., & Groscup, J. (2009). Perceptions of same-sex domestic violence among crisis center staff. *Journal of Family Violence, 24,* 87–93.

Brumfield, B., & Simpson, D. (2013, October 9). Malala Yousafzai: Accolades, applause and a grim milestone. CNN. Retrieved from http://www.cnn.com/2013/10/09/world/asia/malal-shooting-anniversary/

Brunovskis, A., & Surtees, R. (2012). Coming home: Challenges in family reintegration for trafficked women. *Qualitative Social Work, 12*(4), 454–472.

Brunson, R., & Miller, J. (2006). Gender, race, and urban policing: The experience of African American youths. *Gender & Society, 20,* 531–552.

Bryant-Davis, T., Chung, H., & Tillman, S. (2009). From the margins to the center ethnic minority women and the mental health effects of sexual assault. *Trauma, Violence, & Abuse, 10*(4), 330–357.

Bui, H. (2007). The limitations of current approaches to domestic violence. In R. Muraskin (Ed.), *It's a crime* (4th ed., pp. 261–276). Upper Saddle River, NJ: Pearson Prentice Hall.

Bui, H., & Morash, M. (2008). Immigration, masculinity, and intimate partner violence from the standpoint of domestic violence service providers and Vietnamese-origin women. *Feminist Criminology, 3*(3), 191–215.

Bunch, J., Clay-Warner, J., & Lei, M. (2012, December 6). Demographic characteristics and victimization risk: Testing the mediating effects of routine activities. *Crime & Delinquency.* Advance online publication. Retrieved from http://cad.sagepub.com/content/early/2012/12/05/0011128712466932.full.pdf+html

Bundeskriminalamt (BKA). (2015). *Police crime statistics 2015.* Retrieved from https://www.bka.de/EN/CurrentInformation/PoliceCrimeStatistics/2015/pcs2015.html?nn=39580

Bureau of Justice Statistics (BLS). (2006). *Intimate partner violence.* Office of Justice Programs. Retrieved from http://bjs.ojp.usdoj.gov/content/pub/press/ipvpr.cfm

Bureau of Labor Statistics (BLS). (2009). Median weekly earnings of full-time wage and salary workers by detailed occupation and sex. Retrieved from www.bls.gov/cps/cpsaat39.pdf

Bureau of Labor Statistics (BLS). (2014). *Occupational outlook handbook, 2014–15 Edition*. Probation Officers and Correctional Treatment Specialists. Retrieved from http://www.bls.gov/ooh/community-and-social-service/probation-officers-and-correctional-treatment-specialists.htm

Burgess-Jackson, K. (Ed.). (1999). *A most detestable crime: New philosophical essays on rape*. New York: Oxford University Press.

Burgess-Proctor, A. (2006). Intersections of race, class, gender and crime: Future directions for feminist criminology. *Feminist Criminology, 1*(1), 27–47.

Burgess-Proctor, A., Pickett, S. M., Parkhill, M. R., Hamill, T. S., Kirwan, M., & Kozak, A. T. (2016). College women's perception of and inclination to use campus sexual assault resources: Comparing the views of students with and without sexual victimization histories. *Criminal Justice Review, 41*(2): 204–218.

Burgess-Proctor, A. (2012). Backfire: Lessons learned when the criminal justice system fails help-seeking battered women. *Journal of Crime and Justice, 35*(1), 68–92.

Burke, J. (2012, November 2). Kashmir parents accused of killing daughter in acid attack. *The Guardian*. Retrieved from http://www.theguardian.com/world/2012/nov/02/paresnts-accused-kashmir-acid-attack

Burks, A. C., Cramer, R. J., Henderson, C. E., Stroud, C. H., Crosby, J. W., & Graham, J. (2015). Frequency, nature, and correlates of hate crime victimization experiences in an urban sample of lesbian, gay, and bisexual community members. *Journal of Interpersonal Violence*. DOI: 10.1177/0886260515605298.

Burton, V. S., Cullen, F. T., Evans, D., Alarid, L. F., & Dunaway, G. (1998). Gender, self-control, and crime. *Journal of Research in Crime and Delinquency, 35*(2), 123–147.

Bush, G. W. (2004). State of the Union Address. Prisoner Reentry Initiative. Available at https://georgewbush-whitehouse.archives.gov/government/fbci/pri.html

Bush-Baskette, S. (1998). The war on drugs as a war on Black women. In S. L. Miller (Ed.), *Crime control and women* (pp. 113–129). Thousand Oaks, CA: Sage.

Bush-Baskette, S. (1999). The war on drugs: A war against women? In S. Cook & S. Davies (Eds.), *Harsh punishment: International experiences of women's imprisonment* (pp. 211–229). Boston, MA: Northeastern University Press.

Bush-Baskette, S. R. (2000, December). The war on drugs and the incarceration of mothers. *Journal of Drug Issues, 30*, 919–928.

Bush-Baskette, S. R. (2010). *Misguided justice: The war on drugs and the incarceration of Black women*. New York: iUniverse.

Bush-Baskette, S. R., & Smith, V. C. (2012). Is meth the new crack for women in the war on drugs? Factors affecting sentencing outcomes for women and parallels between meth and crack. *Feminist Criminology, 7*(1), 48–69.

Cable News Network (CNN). (2001). Patty Hearst profile. Retrieved from http://www.cnn.com/CNN/Programs/people/shows/hearst/profile.html

Calderon Gamboa, J. (2007, Winter). Seeking integral reparations for the murders and disappearances of women in Ciudad Juárez: A gender and cultural perspective. *Human Rights Brief, 14*(2), 31–35. Retrieved from http://www.wcl.american.edu/hrbrief/14/2calderon.pdf

California Department of Corrections and Rehabilitation (CDCR) (2013). Prison Census Data as of June 30, 2013. Table 10 Prison Census Data, Total Institution Population. Offenders by Sentence Status and Gender. Retrieved from www.cdcr.ca.gov/Reports_Research/Offender_Information_Services_Branch/Annual/Census/CENSUSd1306.pdf

California Department of Corrections and Rehabilitation (CDCR) (n.d.). How to send money to an inmate. Retrieved from www.cdcr.ca.gov/visitors/sending-money-to-inmates.html.

California Emergency Management Agency (Cal EMA). (2011). Victim services programs. Retrieved from http://www.calema.ca.gov/PublicSafetyandVictimServices/Pages/Victim-Services-Programs.aspx

Camacho, C. M., & Alarid, L. F. (2008). The significance of the victim advocate for domestic violence victims in Municipal Court. *Violence and Victims, 23*(3), 288–300.

Campbell, A. (1984). *The girls in the gang*. New Brunswick, NJ: Rutgers University Press.

Campbell, A. (1995). Female participation in gangs. In M.W. Klein, C. L. Maxson, & J. Miller (Eds.), *The modern gang reader* (pp. 70–77). Los Angeles, CA: Roxbury.

Campbell, J., & Carlson. J. R. (2012). Correctional administrators' perceptions of prison nurseries. *Criminal Justice and Behavior, 39*(8), 1063–1074.

Campbell, J. C., Webster, D., Koziol-McLain, J., Block, C. R., Campbell, D., Curry, M. A., . . . & Wilt, S. (2003). Assessing risk factors for intimate partner homicide. *National Institute of Justice (NIJ) Journal, 250*, 14–19. Retrieved from http://www.ncjrs.gov/pdffiles1/jr000250e.pdf

Campbell, N. D. (2000). *Using women: Gender, drug policy and social justice*. New York: Routledge.

Campbell, R. (2006). Rape survivors' experiences with the legal and medical systems: Do rape victim advocates make a difference? *Violence Against Women, 12*(1), 30–45.

Campbell, R., Ahrens, C. E., Sefl, T., Wasco, S. M., & Barnes, H. E. (2001). Social reactions to rape victims: Healing and hurtful effects on psychological and physical health outcomes. *Violence and Victims, 16*, 287–302

Canada honor killing trial verdict: Shafia family found guilty. (2012, January 29). *Huffington Post*. Retrieved from http://www.huffingtonpost.com/2012/01/29/canada-honor-killing-shafia-family-guilty_n_1240268.html

Canterino v. Wilson, 546 F. Supp. 174 (W.D. Ky. 1982).

Caputo, G. A., & King, A. (2011). Shoplifting: Work, agency, and gender. *Feminist Criminology, 6*(3), 159–177.

Carbone-Lopez, K., Gatewood Owens, J., & Miller, J. (2012). Women's "storylines" of methamphetamine initiation in the Midwest. *Journal of Drug Issues, 42*(3), 226–246.

Carey, K. B., Durney, S. E., Shepardson, R. L, & Carey, M. P. (2015). Incapacitated and forcible rape of college women: Prevalence across the first year. *Journal of Adolescent Health, 56*: 678–680.

Carlan, P. E., Nored, L. S., & Downey, R. A. (2011). Officer preferences for male backup: The influence of gender and police partnering. *Journal of Police and Criminal Psychology, 26*(1), 4–10.

Carr, N. T., Hudson, K., Hanks, R. S., & Hunt, A. N. (2008). Gender effects along the juvenile justice system: Evidence of a gendered organization. *Feminist Criminology, 3*(1), 25–43.

Carson, E. A., & Anderson, E. (2016). Prisoners in 2015. U.S. Department of Justice, Office of Justice Programs, Bureau of Justice Statistics. Retrieved from https://www.bjs.gov.content/pub/pdf/p15.pdf

Carson, E. A., & Golinelli, D. (2013). Prisoners in 2012—Advance counts. U.S. Department of Justice, Bureau of Justice Statistics. Retrieved from http://www.bjs.gov/content/pub/pdf/p12ac.pdf

Casey Anthony. (2014). The Biography.com website. Retrieved from http://www.biography.com/people/casey-anthony-20660183.

Cass, A., & Mallicoat, S. L. (2014). College student perceptions of victim action: Will targets of stalking report to police? *American Journal of Criminal Justice*. doi: 10.1007/s12103-014-9252-8

Catalano, S. (2007). *Intimate partner violence in the United States.* Bureau of Justice Statistics. Washington, DC: U.S. Department of Justice. Retrieved from http://bjs.ojp.usdoj.gov/content/pub/pdf/IPAus.pdf

Catalano, S. (2012). *Intimate partner violence in the United States.* Bureau of Justice Statistics, Office of Justice Programs. Retrieved from http://bjs.ojp.usdoj.gov/content/intimate/ipv.cfm

Catterall, J. S., Dumais, S. A., & Hampden-Thompson, G. (2012). The Arts and achievement in at-risk youth: Findings from four longitudinal studies. National Endowment for the Arts. Retrieved from http://arts.gov/sites/default/files/Arts-At-Risk-Youth.pdf

CBSLA.com. July 3, 2013). Woman recently released from prison for killing abusive boyfriend speaks out. Retrieved from http://losangeles.cbslocal.com/2013/07/03/women-recently-released-from-prison-for-killing-abusive-boyfriend-speaks-out/

CBS News. (2009, February 11). Air Force rape scandal grows. Retrieved from http://www.cbsnews.com/2100-201_162-543490.html

Center for American Women and politics. (n.d.). Women on the U.S. Supreme Court. Retrieved from http://www.cawp.rutgers.edu/fast_facts/levels_of_office/USSupremeCourt.php

Center for American Women and Politics. (2017). Women in the U.S. Congress 2017. Retrieved from www.cawp.rutgers.edu/women-us-congress-2017.

Centers for Disease Control and Prevention (CDC). (1992–2004). Youth risk behavior surveillance—United States 1991–2004. CDC surveillance summaries. Department of Health and Human Services. Retrieved from http://www.cdc.gov/

Centers for Disease Control and Prevention (CDC). (2003). *Costs of intimate partner violence against women in the United States: 2003.* Atlanta, GA: National Centers for Injury Prevention and Control.

Centers for Disease Control and Prevention (CDC). (n.d.). *Intimate partner violence.* Retrieved from http://www.cdc.gov/Violence Prevention/intimatepartnerviolence/definitions.html

Centers for Disease Control and Prevention (CDC). 1991-2015 High School Youth Risk Behavior Survey Data. Retrieved from http://nccd.cdc.gov/youthonline/

Cerulli, C., Kothari, C., Dichter, M., Marcus, S., Kim, T. K. Wiley, J., & Rhodes, K. V. (2015). Help-seeking patterns among women experiencing intimate partner violence: Do they forgo the criminal justice system if their adjudication wishers are not met? *Violence nd Victims, 30*(1): 16–31.

Chamberlain, L. (2007, March 28). 2 cities and 4 bridges where commerce flows. *New York Times, 28.*

Chancer, L. (2016). Introduction to special 10th anniversary issue of feminist criminology: Is criminology still male dominated? *Feminist Criminology, 11*(4): 307–310.

Chapman, S. B. (2009). *Inmate-perpetrated harassment: Exploring the gender-specific experience of female correctional officers.* (Doctoral dissertation). City University of New York, New York. Retrieved from ProQuest Dissertations and Theses database, http://media.proquest.com/media/pq/classic/doc/1679173831/fmt/ai/rep/NPDF?_s=uODFIQqrVIzWJxoNj7uj9lddn8I%3D

Chasmar, J. (2013, June 10). Teacher publically tortured, beheaded for witchcraft in Papua New Guinea. *Washington Times.* Retrieved from http://www.washingtontimes.com/news/2013/jun/10/teacher-publicly-tortured-beheaded-witchcraft-papu/

Cheeseman, K. A., & Downey, R. A. (2012). Talking 'bout my generation: The effect on "generation" on correctional employee perceptions of work stress ad job satisfaction. *The Prison Journal, 92*(1), 24–44.

Cheeseman, K. A., & Worley, R. M. (2006). A "captive" audience: Legal responses and remedies to the sexual abuse of female inmates. *Criminal Law Bulletin–Boston, 42*(4), 439.

Chesler, P. (2010). Worldwide trends in honor killings. *Middle East Quarterly, 17*(2), 3–11.

Chesney-Lind, M. (1973). Judicial enforcement of the female sex role. *Issues in Criminology, 8*, 51–70.

Chesney-Lind, M. (1997). *The female offender: Girls, women and crime.* Thousand Oaks, CA: Sage.

Chesney-Lind, M. (2006). Patriarchy, crime and justice: Feminist criminology in an era of backlash. *Feminist Criminology, 1*(1), 6–26.

Chesney-Lind, M., & Chagnon, N. (2016). Criminology, gender, and race: A case study of privilege in the academy. *Feminist Criminology, 11*(4): 311–333.

Chesney-Lind, M., & Shelden, R. G. (2004). *Girls, delinquency and juvenile justice.* Belmont, CA: West/Wadsworth.

Chika, I. S. (2011). Legalization of marital rape in Neigeria: a gross violation of women's health and reproductive rights. *Journal of Social Welfare & Family Law, 33*(1): 39–46.

Chiricos, T., Padgett, K., & Gertz, M. (2000). Fear, TV news and the reality of crime. *Criminology, 38*(3), 755–786.

Cho, H. (2012a). Intimate partner violence among Asian Americans: Risk factor differences across ethnic subgroups. *Journal of Family Violence, 27*(3): 215–224.

Cho, H. (2012b). Use of mental health services among Asian and latino victims of intimate partner violence. *Violence Against Women, 18*(4): 404–419.

Cho, S-Y, Dreher, A., & Neumayer, E. (2011). *The spread of anti-trafficking policies—Evidence from a new index.* Cege Discussion Paper Series No. 119, Georg-August-University of Goettingen, Germany.

Churchville, V. (November 5, 1987). Applicants for D.C. Police secretly tested for pregnancy: Officials reassess policy after complaint D.C. Police reassess pregnancy test policy. *The Washington Post,* p. A1.

Ciong, Z. B., & Huang, J. (2011). Predicting Hmong male and female youth's delinquent behavior: An exploratory study. *Hmong Studies Journal, 12,* 1–34. Retrieved from http://www.hmong studies.org/XiongandHuangHSJ12.pdf

CISION. (2012, October 5). Assaulted, betrayed and jailed but ultimately triumphant, Brenda Clubine fights for abused women. Retrieved from http://www.prnewswire.com/news-releases/assaulted-betrayed-and-jailed-but-ultimately-triumphant-brenda-clubine-fights-for-abused-women-172869521.html

Clear, T., & Frost, N. (2007). Informing public policy. *Criminology & Public Policy, 6*(4), 633–640.

Clements-Nolle, K., Wolden, M., & Bargmann-Losche, J. (2009). Childhood trauma and risk for past and future suicide attempts among women in prison. *Women's Health Issues, 19,* 185–192.

Cloud, J. (2011, June 16). How the Casey Anthony murder case became the social media trial of the century. *Time Magazine.* Retrieved from http://content.time.com/time/nation/article/0,8599,2077969,00.html

Cobbina, J. E., Huebner, B. M., & Berg, M. T. (2012). Men, women and postrelease offending: An examination of the nature of the link between relational ties and recidivism. *Crime & Delinquency, 58*(3), 331–361.

Cobbina, J. E., & Oselin, S. S. (2011). It's not only for the money: An analysis of adolescent versus adult entry into street prostitution. *Sociological Inquiry, 81*(3): 310–332.

Coles, J., Astbury, J., Dartnall, E., & Limjerwala, S. (2014). A qualitative exploration of research trauma and researchers' reporpnses to investigating sexual violence. *Violence Against Women, 20*(1): 95–117.

Coffman, K. (2012, April 30). Dougherty gang sentenced in Colorado for police shootout. *Reuters.* Retrieved from http://news.yahoo .com/dougherty-gang-sentenced-colorado-police-shootout-230049502.html

Cohen, A. K. (1955). *Delinquent boys.* Glencoe, IL: Free Press.

Cohen, L. E., & Felson, M. (1979). Social change and crime rate trends: A routine activity approach. *American Sociological Review,* 588–608.

Connor, T. (2013, October 16). Ariel Castro victim reparations bill gets initial approval. *NBC News.* Retrieved from http://usnews .nbcnews.com/_news/2013/10/16/20988996-ariel-castro-victim-reparations-bill-gets-initial-approval?lite

Contreras, R. (2009). "Damn, yo—Who's that girl?" An ethnographic analysis of masculinity in drug robberies. *Journal of Contemporary Ethnography, 38*(4), 465–492.

Cook, C. L., & Fox, K. A. (2012). Testing the relative importance of contemporaneous offenses: The impacts of fear of sexual assault versus fear of physical harm among men and women. *Journal of Criminal Justice 40*(2), 142–151.

Cook, F. A. (1997). Belva Ann Lockwood: For peace, justice, and president. Stanford, CA: Women's Legal History Biography Project, Robert Crown Law Library, Stanford Law School. Retrieved from http://wlh-static.law.stanford.edu/papers/LockwoodB-Cook97.pdf

Cook, J. A., & Fonow, M. M. (1986). Knowledge and women's interests: Issues of epistemology and methodology in feminist sociological research. *Sociological Inquiry, 56,* 2–29.

Coontz, P. (2000). Gender and judicial decisions: Do female judges decide cases differently than male judges? *Gender Issues, 18*(4), 59–73.

Cooper, A., & Smith, E. L. (2011). Homicide trends in the United States. Annual rates for 2009 and 2010. U.S. Department of Justice. Retrieved from http://bjs.ojp.usdoj.gov/content/pub/pdf/htus8008.pdf

Cooper, H. (2017, March 15). Reports of sexual assault increase at two military academies. *The New York Times.* Retrieved from https://www.nytimes.com/2017/03/15/us/politics/sexual-assault-military-west-point-annapolis.html?_r=0

Cooper v. Morin, 49 N.Y.2d 69 (1979).

Copp, J. E., Giordano, P. C., Longmore, M. A., & Manning, W. D. (2015). Stay or leave decision making in nonviolent and violent dating relationships. *Violence and Victims, 30*(4): 581–599.

Cops, D., & Pleysier, S. (2011). "Doing Gender" in fear of crime: The impact of gender identity on reported levels of fear of crime in adolescents and young adults. *British Journal of Criminology, 51*(1), 58–74.

Corman, H., Dave, D. M., & Reichman, N. E. (2014). Effects of welfare reform on women's crime. *International Review of Law and Economics, 40:* 1–14.

Corsianos, M. (2009). *Policing and gendered justice: Examining the possibilities.* Toronto, Canada: UTP Higher Education.

Covington, S. (1999). *Helping women recover: A program for treating substance abuse.* San Francisco, CA: Jossey-Bass.

Cox, L., & Speziale, B. (2009). Survivors of stalking: Their voices and lived experiences. *Affilia: Journal of Women and Social Work, 24*(1), 5–18.

Crandall, M., Senturia, K., Sullivan, M., & Shiu-Thornton, S. (2005). No way out: Russian-speaking women's experiences with domestic violence. *Journal of Interpersonal Violence, 20*(8), 941–958.

Crime in the United States 2010 (CIUS). (2010). Forcible rape. Uniform Crime Reports. U.S. Department of Justice, Federal Bureau of Investigation. Retrieved from http://www.fbi.gov/about-us/cjis/ucr/crime-in-the-u.s/2010/crime-in-the-u.s.-2010/violent-crime/rapemain

Crime in the United States 2012 (CIUS). (2012). About crime in the U.S. Uniform Crime Reports. U.S. Department of Justice, Federal Bureau of Investigation. Retrieved from http://www.fbi.gov/about-us/cjis/ucr/crime-in-the-u.s/2012/crime-in-the-u.s.-2012

Crime in the United States (CIUS). (2015). 10-year UCR arrest trends. Retrieved from: https://ucr.fbi.gov/crime-in-the-u.s/2015/crime-in-the-u.s.-2015

Crosnoe, R., Erickson, K. G., & Dornbusch, S. M. (2002). Protective functions of family relationships and school factors on the deviant behavior of adolescent boys and girls. *Youth and Society, 33*(4), 515–544.

Curry, G. D., Ball, R. A., & Fox, R. J. (1994). *Gang crime and law enforcement recordkeeping. Research in brief.* Washington, DC: U.S. Department of Justice, Office of Justice Programs, National Institute of Justice. Retrieved from http://www.ncjrs.gov/txtfiles/gcrime.txt

Dahl, J. (2012, May 16). Fla. woman Marissa Alexander gets 20 years for "warning shot": Did she stand her ground? CBS News. Retrieved from http://www.cbsnews.com/news/fla-woman-marissa-alexander-gets-20-years-for-warning-shot-did-she-stand-her-ground/

Daigle, L. E., Cullen, F. T., & Wright, J. P. (2007). Gender differences in the predictors of juvenile delinquency: Assessing the generality-specificity debate. *Youth Violence and Juvenile Justice, 5*(3), 254–286.

Dalla, R. L. (2000). Exposing the "pretty woman" myth: A qualitative examination of the lives of female streetwalking prostitutes. *Journal of Sex Research, 37*(4), 344–353.

Dalla, R. L., Xia, Y., & Kennedy, H. (2003). "You just give them what they want and pray they don't kill you": Street-level workers' reports of victimization, personal resources and coping strategies. *Violence Against Women, 9*(11), 1367–1394.

Daly, K. (1994). *Gender, crime, and punishment.* New Haven, CT: Yale University Press.

Daly, K., & Chesney-Lind, M. (1988). Feminism and criminology. *Justice Quarterly, 5*(4), 497–538.

Danner, M. J. E. (2003). Three strikes and it's women who are out: The hidden consequences for women of criminal justice policy reforms. In R. Muraskin (Ed.), *It's a crime: Women and justice* (2nd ed., Chapter 44). Upper Saddle River, NJ: Prentice-Hall.

Davidson, J. T. (2011). Managing risk in the community: How gender matters. In R. Sheehan, G. McIvor, & C. Trotter (Eds.), *Working with women offenders in the community.* New York: Willan.

Davies, K., Block, C. R., & Campbell, J. (2007). Seeking help from the police: Battered women's decisions and experiences. *Criminal Justice Studies, 20*(1), 15–41.

Davis, C. P. (2007). At risk girls and delinquency: Career pathways. *Crime and Delinquency, 53*(3), 408–435.

Davis, K. E., Coker, A. L., & Sanderson, M. (2002). Physical and mental health effects of being stalked for men and women. *Violence and Victims, 17*(4), 429–443.

Day, J. C., Zahn, M. A., & Tichavsky, L. R. (2015). What works for whom? The effects of gender responsive programming on girls and boys in secure detention. *Journal of Research in Crime and Delinquency, 52*(1): 93–129.

De Atley, R. (2013, October 28). Sara Kruzan: If sentenced today, hers would be a different story. *The Press-Enterprise.* Retrieved from http://www.pe.com/local-news/local-news-headlines/20131028-kruzan-if-sentenced-today-hers-would-be-a-different-story.ece

De Groof, S. (2008). And my mama said. . . . The (relative) parental influence on fear of crime among adolescent boys and girls. *Youth & Society, 39*(3), 267–293.

DeHart, D., Lynch, S., Belknap, J., Dass-Brailsford, P., & Green, B. (2014). Life history models of female offending: The roles of serious mental illness and trauma in women's pathways to jail. *Psychology of Women Quarterly, 38*(1): 138–151.

De Vaus, D., & Wise, S. (1996, Autumn). Parent's concern for the safety of their children. *Family Matters, 43,* 34–38.

DeHart, D., & Moran, M. (2015). Poly-victimization among girls in the justice system: Trajectories of risk and association to juvenile offending. *Violence Against Women, 21*(3): 291–312.

DeJong, C., Burgess-Proctor, A., & Elis, L. (2008). Police officer perceptions of intimate partner violence: An analysis of observational data. *Violence and Victims, 23,* 683–696.

DeLisi, M., Beaver, K. M., Vaughn, M. G., Trulson, C. R., Kisloski, A. E., Drury, A. J., & Wright, J. P. (2010). Personality, gender, and self-control theory revisited: Results from a sample of institutionalized juvenile delinquents. *Applied Psychology in Criminal Justice, 6*(1), 31–46.

Deluca, M. (2013, August 1). Ariel Castro victim Michelle Knight: "Your hell is just beginning." Retrieved from http://usnews.nbcnews.com/_news/2013/08/01/19813977-ariel-castro-victim-michelle-knight-your-hell-is-just-beginning?lite

Demuth, S., & Steffensmeier, D. (2004). The impact of gender and race-ethnicity in the pretrial release process. *Social Problems, 51*(2), 222–242.

Dennis, M. L., Scott, C. K., Funk, R., & Foss, M. A. (2005). The duration and correlates of addiction and treatment careers. *Journal of Substance Abuse Treatment, 28*(2), S51–S62.

Department of Defense (2017). DOD annual report on sexual harassment and violence at the military service academies, academic program year 2015–2016. Retrieved from http://www.sapr.mil/public/docs/reports/MSA/APY_15-16/APY_15-16_MSA_InfoPaper.pdf

Dershowitz, A. (2011, July 7). Casey Anthony: The system worked. *Wall Street Journal*. Retrieved from http://online.wsj.com/news/articles/SB10001424052702303544604576429783247016492

Diep, F. (2013, June 10). Mississippi will test teen mom babies for statutory rape evidence. *Popular Science*. Retrieved from http://www.popsci.com/science/article/2013–06/new-mississippi-teen-moms-babies-statutory-rape

Dietz, N. A., & Martin, P. Y. (2007). Women who are stalked: Questioning the fear standard. *Violence Against Women, 13*(7), 750–776.

DiMarino, F. (2009). Women as corrections professionals. *Corrections.com*. Retrieved from http://www.corrections.com/articles/21703-women-as-corrections-professionals

Dimond, J. P., Fiesler, C., & Bruckman, A. S. (2011). Domestic violence and information communication technologies. *Interacting With Computers, 23*, 413–421.

Dinan, E. (2005, February 27). Where the Smart boys are 14 years later. *Portsmouth Herald*. Retrieved from http://www.hampton.lib.nh.us/hampton/biog/pamsmart/20050227PH.htm

Dissell, R. (2012, September 2). Rape charges against high school players divide football town of Steubenville, Ohio. Cleveland.com. Retrieved from http://www.cleveland.com/metro/index.ssf/2012/09/rape_charges_divide_football_t.html

Dobash, R., & Dobash, R. E. (1992). *Women, violence and social change*. New York: Routledge.

Dodderidge, J. (1632). *The lawes resolutions of women's rights: Or, the law's provision for women*. London, UK: John More, Rare Book and Special Collections Division, Library of Congress.

Dodge, M. Valcore, L., & Klinger, D. A. (2010). Maintaining separate spheres in policing: Women on SWAT teams. *Women & Criminal Justice, 20*(3), 218–238.

Donovan, P. (1996). Can statutory rape laws be effective in preventing adolescent pregnancy? *Family Planning Perspectives, 29*(1). Retrieved from http://www.guttmacher.org/pubs/journals/2903097.html

Dooley, S., Scott, T., Ng, C., & Effron, L. (July 8, 2016). Jaycee Dugard on reclaiming her life after being held captive for 18 years: "I have lived a lot of lifetimes." ABC News. Retrieved from http://abcnews.go.com/US/jaycee-dugard-reclaiming-life-held-captive-18-years/story?id=40280031

Dowler, K. (2003). Media consumption and public attitudes toward crime and justice: The relationship between fear of crime, punitive attitudes, and perceived police effectiveness. *Journal of Criminal Justice and Popular Culture, 10*(2), 109–126.

Downey, M. (2007, October 28). Genarlow Wilson is free . . . But other victims of Georgia's sweeping sex offender laws are not. *Atlanta Journal-Constitution*, B1.

Drabble, L., Trocki, K. F., Hughes, T. L., Korcha, R. A., & Lown, A. E. (2013). Sexual orientation differences in the relationship between victimization and hazardous drinking among women in the National Alcohol Survey. *Psychology of Addictive Behaviors, 27*(3), 639–648.

Drachman, V. G. (1998). *Sisters in law: Women lawyers in modern American history*. Cambridge, MA: Harvard University Press.

Dugan, L, Nagin, D., & Rosenfeld, R. (2003). Exposure reduction or retaliation: Domestic violence resources on intimate-partner homicide. *Law & Society Review, 37*(1), 169–198.

Durrani, S., & Singh, P. (2011). Women, private practice and billable hours: Time for a total rewards strategy? *Compensation & Benefits Review, 43*(5), 300–305.

Dworkin, E. R., Sorell, N. R., & Allen, N. E. (2016). Individual-and-setting-level correlates of secondary traumatic stress in rape crisis center staff. *Journal of Internpersonal Violence*

Dye, M. H., & Aday, R. H. (2013). "I just wanted to die": Preprison and current suicide ideation among women serving life sentences. *Criminal justice and Behavior, 40*(8), 832–849.

Egelko, B. (March 16, 2016). Court rejects suit by kidnap survivor Jaycee Duggard. SF Gate. Retrieved from http://www.sfgate.com/crime/article/Court-rejects-suit-by-kidnap-survivor-Jaycee-6892232.php

Eghigian, M., & Kirby, K. (2006). Girls in gangs: On the rise in America. *Corrections Today, 68*(2), 48–50.

Eigenberg, H., & Garland, R. (2008). Victim blaming. In L. J. Moriarty (Ed.), *Controversies in victimology* (pp. 21–36). Newark, NJ: Elsevier Press.

Einat, T., & Chen. G. (2012). What's love got to do with it? Sex in a female maximum security prison. *The Prison Journal, 92*(4), 484–505.

England, L. (2008, March 17). Rumsfeld knew. *Stern Magazine*. Retrieved from http://www.stern.de/politik/ausland/lynndie-england-rumsfeld-knew-614356.html?nv=ct_cb

Esbensen, F. A., & Carson, D. C. (2012). Who are the gangsters? An examination of the age, race/ethnicity, sex and immigration status of self-reported gang members in a seven-city study of American youth. *Journal of Contemporary Criminal Justice, 28*(4), 465–481.

Esbensen, F. A., Deschenes, E. P., & Winfree, L. T., Jr. (1999). Differences between gang girls and gang boys: Results from a multisite survey. *Youth and Society, 31*(1), 27–53.

Esfandiari, G. (2006). Afghanistan: Rights watchdog alarmed at continuing "honor killings." Women's United Nations Report Network. Retrieved from http://www.wunrn.com/news/2006/09_25_06/100106_afghanistan_violence.htm

Estrada, F., & Nilsson A. (2012). Does it cost more to be a female offender? A life-course study of childhood circumstances, crime, drug abuse, and living conditions. *Feminist Criminology, 7*(3), 196–219.

Ewoldt, C. A., Monson, C. M., & Langhinrichsen-Rohling, J. (2000). Attributions about rape in a continuum of dissolving marital relationships. *Journal of Interpersonal Violence, 15*(11), 1175–1183.

Ezell, M., & Levy, M. (2003). An evaluation of an arts program for incarcerated juvenile offenders. *Journal of Correctional Education, 54*(3), 108–114.

Fagel, M. (2013, March 8). Jury questions to Jodi Arias illustrate their frustration with her story. *Huffington Post.* Retrieved from http://www.huffingtonpost.com/mari-fagel/jodi-arias-jury-questions_b_2825167.html

Farid, M. (2014, January 13). On the shelves: "I am Malala": Her first-hand story. *The Jakarta Post.* Retrieved from http://www.thejakartapost.com/news/2014/01/13/on-shelves-i-am-malala-her-first-hand-story.html-0

Farley, M. (2004). "Bad for the body, bad for the heart": Prostitution harms women even if legalized or decriminalized. *Violence Against Women, 10*(10), 1087–1125.

Farley, M., & Barkin, H. (1998). Prostitution, violence, and post-traumatic stress disorder. *Women and Health, 27*(3), 37–49.

Farley, M., & Kelly, V. (2000). Prostitution: A critical review of the medical and social sciences literature. *Women and Criminal Justice, 11*(4), 29–64.

Farrell, A., McDevitt, J., & Fahy, S. (2010). Where are all the victims? Understanding the determinants of official identification of human trafficking incidents. *Criminology & Public Policy, 9*, 201–233.

Farrell, A., Owens, C., McDevitt, J. (2014). New laws but few cases: Understanding the challenges to the investigation and prosecution of human trafficking cases. *Crime, Law and Social Change, 61*: 139–168.

Fattah, E. A., & Sacco, V. F. (1989). *Crime and victimization of the elderly.* New York: Springer-Verlag.

Federal Bureau of Investigation (FBI). (2003). Bank crime statistics 2003. Retrieved from http://www.fbi.gov/stats-services/publications/bank-crime-statistics-2003/bank-crime-statistics-bcs-2003

Federal Bureau of Investigation (FBI). (2011). *Crime in the U.S. 2010: Uniform Crime Reports.* Retrieved from http://www.fbi.gov/about-us/cjis/ucr/crime-in-the-u.s/2010/crime-in-the-u.s.-2010

Federal Bureau of Investigation (FBI). (2012a, January 6). Attorney General Eric Holder announces revisions to the Uniform Crime Report's definition of rape: Data reported on rape will better reflect state criminal codes, victim experiences [Press release]. U.S. Department of Justice, Uniform Crime Reports. Retrieved from http://www.fbi.gov/news/pressrel/press-releases/attorney-general-eric-holder-announces-revisions-to-the-uniform-crime-reports-definition-of-rape

Federal Bureau of Investigation (FBI). (2012b). Crime in the United States, 2012. Retrieved from http://www.fbi.gov/about-us/cjis/ucr/crime-in-the-u.s/2012/crime-in-the-u.s.-2012/cius_home

Federal Bureau of Investigation (FBI). (2012c). UCR program changes definition of rape: Includes all victims and omits requirement of physical force. Criminal Justice Information Service, U. S. Department of Justice. Retrieved from http://www.fbi.gov/about-us/cjis/cjis-link/march-2012/ucr-program-changes-definition-of-rape

Feld, B. C. (2009). Violent girls or relabeled status offenders? An alternative interpretation of the data. *Crime and Delinquency, 55*(2), 241–265.

Felix, Q. (2005). Human rights in Pakistan: Violence and misery for children and women. *Asia News.* Retrieved from http://www.asianews.it/news-en/Human-rights-in-Pakistan:-violence-and-misery-for-children-and-women-2554.html

Fellner, J. (2010). Sexually abused: The nightmare of juveniles in confinement. *Huffington Post.* Retrieved from http://www.huffingtonpost.com/jamie-fellner/sexually-abused-the-night_b_444240.html

Ferraro, K. J. (1981). *Battered women and the shelter movement* (Doctoral dissertation). Arizona State University, Tempe.

Ferro, C., Cermele, J., & Saltzman, A. (2008). Current perceptions of marital rape: Some good and not-so-good news. *Journal of Interpersonal Violence, 23*(6): 764–779

Ferszt, G. G. (2011). Who will speak for me? Advocating for pregnant women in prison. *Policy, Politics & Nursing Practice, 12*(4), 254–256.

Figley, C. R. (1995). Compassion fatigue: Toward a new understanding of the costs of caring. In B. H. Stamm (Ed.), *Secondary traumatic stress: Self-care issues for clinicians, researchers, and educators* (2nd ed., pp. 3–28). Lutherville, MD: Sidran.

Fisher, B. S., Cullen, F. T., & Turner, M. G. (2000). The sexual victimization of college women. Series: Research report. *NCJ.* Retrieved from https://www.ncjrs.gov/txtfiles1/nij/182369.txt

Fisher, B. S., Daigle, L. E., & Cullen, F. T. (2010). What distinguishes single from recurrent sexual victims? The role of lifestyle-routine activities and first-incident characteristics. *Justice Quarterly, 27*(1), 102–129.

Fisher, B. S., Daigle, L. E., Cullen, F. T., & Turner, M. G. (2003). Reporting sexual victimization to the police and others: Results from a national-level study of college women. *Criminal Justice and Behavior, 30*(1), 6–38.

Fisher, B. S., & May, D. (2009). College students' crime-related fears on campus: Are fear-provoking cues gendered? *Journal of Contemporary Criminal Justice, 25*(3), 300–321.

Fisher, B. S., & Sloan, J. J. (2003). Unraveling the fear of sexual victimization among college women: Is the "shadow of sexual assault" hypothesis supported? *Justice Quarterly, 20*, 633–659.

Fleisher, M. S., & Krienert, J. L. (2004). Life-course events, social networks, and the emergence of violence among female gang members. *Journal of Community Psychology, 32*(5), 607–622.

Fleury-Steiner, R., Bybee, D., Sullivan, C. M., Belknap, J., & Melton, H. C. (2006). Contextual factors impacting battered women's intentions to reuse the criminal legal system. *Journal of Community Psychology, 34*(3), 327–342.

Foley, S., Kidder, D. L., & Powell, G. N. (2002). The perceived glass ceiling and justice perceptions: An investigation of Hispanic law associates. *Journal of Management, 28*(4), 471–496.

Ford, M. (2017, May 12). Jeff Sessions reinvigorates the drug war. *The Atlantic*. Retrieved from https://www.theatlantic.com/politics/archive/2017/05/sessions-sentencing-memo/526029/

Foundation for Women's Health, Research and Development (FORWARD). (2012). *Female genital mutilation*. Retrieved from http://www.forwarduk.org.uk/key-issues/fgm

Fox News. (2014, January 7). One of two teens convicted in Steubenville rape case released. Retrieved from http://www.foxnews.com/us/2014/01/07/one-two-teens-convicted-in-steubenville-rape-case-released/

Franiuk, R., Seefelt, J. L., Cepress, S. L., & Vandello, J. A. (2008). Prevalence and effects of rape myths in the media: The Kobe Bryant case. *Violence Against Women, 14*, 287–309.

Freedman, E. B. (1981). *Their sisters' keepers: Women's prison reform in America, 1830–1930*. Ann Arbor: University of Michigan Press.

Freeman, H. (2013, June 18). Nigella Lawson: From domestic goddess to the face of domestic violence. *The Guardian*. Retrieved from http://www.theguardian.com/commentisfree/2013/jun/18/nigella-lawson-domestic-goddess-violence

Freiburger, T. L., & Burke, A. S. (2011). Status offenders in the juvenile court: The effects of gender, race and ethnicity on the adjudication decision. *Youth Violence and Juvenile Justice, 9*(4), 352–365.

Freiburger, T. L., & Hilinski, C. M. (2010). The impact of race, gender, and age on the pretrial decision. *Criminal Justice Review, 35*(3), 318–334.

French, S. (2000). Of problems, pitfalls and possibilities: A comprehensive look at female attorneys and law firm partnership. *Women's Rights Law Reporter, 21*(3), 189–216.

Frost, N. A., & Clear, T. R. (2007). Doctoral education in criminology and criminal justice. *Journal of Criminal Justice Education, 18*, 35–52.

Frost, N. A., & Phillips, N. D. (2011): Talking heads: Crime reporting on cable news. *Justice Quarterly, 28*(1), 87–112.

Fus, T. (2006, March). Criminalizing marital rape: A comparison of judicial and legislative approaches. *Vanderbilt Journal of Transnational Law, 39*(2), 481–517.

Gaarder, E., & Belknap, J. (2002). Tenuous borders: Girls transferred to adult court. *Criminology, 40*(3), 481–518.

Garcia, C. A., & Lane, J. (2010). Looking in the rearview mirror: What incarcerated women think girls need from the system. *Feminist Criminology, 5*(3), 227–243.

Garcia, C. A., & Lane, J. (2012). Dealing with the fall-out: Identifying and addressing the role that relationship strain plays in the lives of girls in the juvenile justice system. *Journal of Criminal Justice, 40*, 259–267.

Garcia-Lopez, G. (2008). Nunca te toman en cuenta [They never take you into account]: The challenges of inclusion and strategies for success of Chicana attorneys. *Gender and Society, 22*(5), 590–612.

Gartner, R., & Kruttschnitt, C. (2004). A brief history of doing time: The California Institution for Women in the 1960's and the 1990's. *Law and Society Review, 38*(2), 267–304.

Gast, P. (2011, August 10). Siblings wanted in bank robbery, shootout arrested after chase. CNN. Retrieved from http://www.cnn.com/2011/CRIME/08/11/georgia.three.siblings.manhunt.archives/index.html?iref=allsearch

Gavazzi, S. M., Yarcheck, C. M., & Lim, J.-Y. (2005). Ethnicity, gender, and global risk indicators in the lives of status offenders coming to the attention of the juvenile court. *International Journal of Offender Therapy and Comparative Criminology, 49*(6), 696–710.

Gehring, K., & Van Voorhis, P. (2014). Needs and pretrial failure: Additional risk factors for female and male pretrial defendants. *Criminal Justice and Behavior, 41*(8): 943–970.

Gehring, K., Van Voorhis, P., & Bell, V. (2010). "What Works" for female probationers? An evaluation of the *Moving On* program. *Women, Girls and Criminal Justice, 11*(1), 6–10.

General Accounting Office (GAO). (1999). *Women in prison: Issues and challenges confronting U.S. correctional systems*. Washington, DC: U.S. Department of Justice.

Gerbner, G., & Gross, L. (1980, Summer). The "Mainstreaming" of America: Violence profile no. 11. *Journal of Communication, 30*, 10–29.

Giaris, H. (September 8, 2014). Don't watch the Ray Rice video. Don't ask why Janay Palmer married him. Ask why anyone would blame a victim. *The Guardian*. Retrieved from https://www.theguardian.com/commentisfree/2014/sep/08/ray-rice-domestic-violence-video-janay-palmer-victim-blaming

Gidycz, C. A., Orchowski, L. M., King, C. R., & Rich, C. L. (2008). Sexual victimization and health-risk behaviors: A prospective analysis of college women. *Journal of Interpersonal Violence, 23*(6), 744–763.

Gilbert, E. (2001). Women, race and criminal justice processing. In C. Renzetti & L. Goodstein (Eds.), *Women, crime, and criminal justice: Original feminist readings*. Los Angeles, CA: Roxbury.

Gilfus, M. E. (1992). From victims to survivors to offenders: Women's routes of entry and immersion into street crime. *Women and Criminal Justice, 4*(1), 63–89.

Gillum, T. L. (2008). Community response and needs of African American female survivors of domestic violence. *Journal of Interpersonal Violence, 23*(1), 39–57.

Gillum, T. L. (2009). Improving services to African American survivors of IPV: From the voices of recipients of culturally specific services. *Violence Against Women, 15*(1), 57–80.

Girard, A. L., & Senn, C. Y. (2008). The role of the new "date rape drugs" in attributions about date rape. *Journal of Interpersonal Violence, 23*(1), 3–20.

Girl Scouts of America (GSA). (2008). *Third-year evaluation of Girl Scouts Beyond Bars final report*. Retrieved from http://www.girlscouts.org/research.pdf/gsbb_report.pdf

Girls Incorporated. (1996). *Prevention and parity: Girls in juvenile justice.* Indianapolis, IN: Girls Incorporated National Resource Center & Office of Juvenile Justice and Delinquency Prevention.

Girshick, L. B. (2002). No sugar, no spice: Reflections on research on woman-to-woman sexual violence. *Violence Against Women, 8*(12), 1500–1520.

Glaze, L., & Maruschak, L. (2008). *Parents in prison and their minor children.* Washington, DC: U.S. Department of Justice.

Glover v. Johnson, 478 F. Supp. 1075 (1979).

Goddard, C., & Bedi, G. (2010). Intimate partner violence and child abuse: A child-centered perspective. *Child Abuse Review, 19,* 5–20.

Goulette, N., Wooldredge, J., Frank, J., & Travis III, L. (2015). From initial appearance to sentencing: Do female defendants experience disparate treatment? *Journal of Criminal Justice, 43*: 406–417.

Glueck, S., & Glueck, E. (1934). *Five hundred delinquent women.* New York: Alfred A. Knopf.

Gordon, J. A., Proulx, B., & Grant, P. H. (2013). Trepidation among the "keepers": Gendered perceptions of fear and risk of victimization among corrections officers. *American Journal of Criminal Justice, 38,* 245–265.

Gormley, P. (2007). The historical role and views toward victims and the evolution of prosecution policies in domestic violence. In R. Muraskin (Ed.), *It's a crime: Women and Justice* (4th ed., Ch. 13). Upper Saddle River, NJ: Pearson Prentice Hall.

Gornick, J., Burt, M. J., & Pitman, P. J. (1985). Structures and activities of rape crisis centers in the early 1980s. *Crime and Delinquency, 31,* 247–268.

Gottfredson, M., & Hirschi, T. (1990). *A general theory of crime.* Palo Alto, CA: Stanford University Press.

Gover, A. R., Brank, E. M., & MacDonald, J. M. (2007). A specialized domestic violence court in South Carolina: An example of procedural justice for victims and defendants. *Violence Against Women, 13*(6), 603–626.

Gover, A. R., Welton-Mitchell, C., Belknap, J., & Deprince, A. P. (2013). When abuse happens again: Women's reasons for not reporting new incidents of intimate partner abuse to law enforcement. *Women & Criminal Justice, 23,* 99–120.

Gracia, E., & Tomas, JM. (2014). Correlates of victim-blaming attitudes regarding partner violence against women among the Spanish general population. *Violence Against Women, 20*(1): 26–41.

Greenfeld, L. A. (1997). *Sex offenses and offenders: An analysis of data on rape and sexual assault.* Washington, DC: U.S. Department of Justice, Office of Justice Programs.

Greenfeld, L. A., & Snell, T. L. (2000). *Women offenders.* Washington, DC: Bureau of Justice Statistics. Retrieved from http://bjs.ojp.usdoj.gov/content/pub/pdf/wo.pdf

Greer, K. (2008). When women hold the keys: Gender, leadership and correctional policy. Management and Training Institute. Retrieved from http://nicic.gov/Library/023347

Grella, C. E., & Rodriguez, L. (2011). Motivation for treatment among women offenders in prison-based treatment and longitudinal outcomes among those who participate in community aftercare. *Journal of Psychoactive Drugs, 43*(1), 58–67.

Grella, C. E., Lovinger, K., & Warda, U. S. (2013). Relationships among trauma exposure, familiar characteristics, and PTSD: A case-control study of women in prison and in the general population. *Women & Criminal Justice, 23*(1): 63–79.

Griffin v. Michigan Department of Corrections, 654 F. Supp. 690 (1982).

Griffin, T., & Wooldredge, J. (2006). Sex-based disparities in felony dispositions before versus after sentencing reform in Ohio. *Criminology, 44*(4), 893–923.

Grossman, S. F., & Lundy, M. (2011). Characteristics of women who do and do not receive onsite shelter services from domestic violence programs. *Violence Against Women, 17*(8), 1024–1045.

Grossman, S. F., Lundy, M., George, C. C., & Crabtree-Nelson, S. (2010). Shelter and service receipt for victims of domestic violence in Illinois. *Journal of Interpersonal Violence, 25*(11), 2077–2093.

Grothoff, G. E., Kempf-Leonard, K., & Mullins, C. (2014). Gender and juvenile drug abuse: A general strain theory perspective. *Women & Criminal Justice, 24*: 22–43.

Grubb, A., & Turner, E. (2012). Attribution of blame in rape cases: A review of the impact of rape myth acceptance, gender role conformity and substance use on victim blaming. *Aggression and Violent Behvior, 17*(5), 443–452.

Grummett v. Rushen, 779 F.2d 491 (1985).

Guajardo, S. A. (2016). Women in policing: A longitudinal assessment of female officers in supervisory positions in the New York City Police Deparment. *Women & Criminal Justice, 26*(1): 20–36.

Guerino, P., Harrison, P. M., & Sabol, W. J. (2011). Prisoners in 2010. U.S. Department of Justice, Bureau of Justice Statistics. Retrieved from http://www.bjs.gov/content/pub/pdf/p10.pdf

Guevara, L., Herz, D., & Spohn, C. (2008). Race, gender, and legal counsel: Differential outcomes in two juvenile courts. *Youth Violence and Juvenile Justice, 6*(1), 83–104.

Gyimah-Brempong, K., & Price, G. N. (2006). Crime and punishment: And skin hue too? *American Economic Association, 96*(2), 246–250.

Haarr, R. N., & Morash, M. (2013). The effect of rank on police women coping with discrimination and harassment. *Police Quarterly, 16*(4), 395–419.

Hagan, J. (1989). *Structural criminology.* New Brunswick, NJ: Rutgers University Press.

Hall, M., Golder, S., Conley, C. L., & Sawning, S. (2013). Designing programming and interventions for women in the criminal justice system. *American Journal of Criminal Justice, 38,* 27–50.

Hannan, L. (2014, January 10). Marissa Alexander can remain free on bond, but judge clearly upset with home-detention supervisor. *The Florida Times Union.* Retrieved from http://jacksonville.com/breaking-news/2014-01-10/story/marissa-alexander-can-remain-free-bond-judge-clearly-upset-home

Hardesty, J. L., Oswald, R. F., Khaw, L., & Fonseca, C. (2011). Lesbian/bisexual mothers and intimate partner violence: Help seeking in the context of social and legal vulnerability. *Violence Against Women, 17*(1), 28–46.

Harlow, P. (2013, March 17). Guilty verdict in Steubenville rape trial. CNN Transcripts. Retrieved from http://transcripts.cnn.com/TRANSCRIPTS/1303/17/rs.01.html

Harner, H. M., & Riley, S. (2013). The impact of incarceration on women's mental health: Responses from women in a maximum-security prison. *Qualitative Health Research, 23*(1), 26–42.

Harner, H. M., Wyant, B. R., & DaSilva, D. (2017). "Prison ain't free like everyone thinks": Financial stressors faced by incarcerated women. *Qualitative Health Research, 27*(5): 688–699.

Harrington, P., & Lonsway, K. A. (2004). Current barriers and future promise for women in policing. In B. R. Price & N. J. Sokoloff (Eds.), *The criminal justice system and women: Offenders, prisoners, victims, & workers* (3rd ed., pp. 495–510). Boston, MA: McGraw Hill.

Harris, K. M., & Edlund, M. J. (2005). Self-medication of mental health problems: New evidence from a national survey. *Health Services Research, 40*(1), 117–134.

Harrison, J. (2012). Women in law enforcement: Subverting sexual harassment with social bonds. *Women & Criminal Justice, 22*(3), 226–238. doi: 10.1080/08974454.2012.687964

Harrison, P. M., & Beck, A. J. (2006). Prison and Jail inmates at midyear 2005 [*BJS Bulletin*]. http://bjs.ojp.usdoj.gov/content/pub/pdf/pjim05.pdf

Hart, T. C., & Rennison, C. M. (2003). *Special report: National Crime Victimization Survey: Reporting crime to the police.* Bureau of Justice Statistics. Retrieved from http://bjs.ojp.usdoj.gov/index.cfm?ty=pbdetail&iid=1142

Hassouneh, D., & Glass, N. (2008). The influence of gender-role stereotyping on female same-sex intimate partner violence. *Violence Against Women, 14*(3), 310–325.

Hastings, D. (October 10, 1993). National Spokeswoman for battered women: Is she telling the truth? California: Brenda Clubine's description of the events that precipitated killing of her husband doesn't match her murder trial testimony. Gov. Pete Wilson denied her bid for clemency, saying she has "repeatedly lied." *Los Angeles Times.* Retrieved from http://articles.latimes.com/1993-10-10/local/me-44254_1_brenda-clubine-sue-osthoff-murder-trial-testimony

Hauser, C. (February 7, 2017). Florida woman whose "Stand Your Ground" defense was rejected is released. *New York Times.* Retrieved from https://www.nytimes.com/2017/02/07/us/marissa-alexander-released-stand-your-ground.html

Hawkesworth, M., Casey, K. J., Jenkins, K., & Kleeman, K. E. (2001). Legislating by and for women: A comparison of the 103rd and 104th Congresses. Center for American Women and Politics. Retrieved from www.capwip.org/readingroom/women_103_104.pdf

Haynes, D. F. (2004). Used abused, arrested and deported: Extending immigration benefits to protect the victims of trafficking and to secure the prosecution of traffickers. *Human Rights Quarterly, 26*(2), 221–272.

Heidensohn, F. M. (1985). *Women and crime: The life of the female offender.* New York: New York University Press.

Heimer, K. (1996). Gender, interaction and delinquency: Testing a theory of differential social control. *Social Psychology Quarterly, 59*, 339–361.

Hennessey, M., Ford, J. D., Mahoney, K., Ko, S. J., & Siegfried, C. B. (2004). Trauma among girls in the juvenile justice system. National Child Traumatic Stress Network Juvenile Justice Working Group. Retrieved from http://www.nctsn.org/nctsn_assets/pdfs/edu_materials/trauma_among_girls_in_jjsys.pdf

Hensley, J (March 3, 2017). Does Brandon Marshall become an exception to Ravens' domestic violence stance? *ESPN.* Retrieved from http://www.espn.com/blog/nflnation/post/_/id/232290/does-brandon-marshall-become-an-exception-to-ravens-domestic-violence-stance

Henry, L. (2013, September 17). A death needlessly sad, exorbitantly expensive. Retrieved from http://www.bakersfield.com/columnists/lois-henry-a-death-needlessly-sad-exorbitantly-expensive/article_2614a651-2f64-5c3d-b264-8f5238b4ca35.html

Hersh, S. M. (2004, May 10). Torture at Abu Ghraib. *The New Yorker.* Retrieved from http://www.newyorker.com/archive/2004/05/10/040510fa_fact?currentPage=all

Hessy-Biber, S. N. (2004). *Feminist perspectives on social research.* New York: Oxford University Press.

Higdon, M. (2008). Queer teens and legislative bullies: The cruel and invidious discrimination behind heterosexist statutory rape laws. *UC Davis Law Review, 42*, 195.

Hillard, G. (2012, October 5). Domestic abuse victims get chance at freedom. *NPR.* Retrieved from http://www.prnewswire.com/news-releases/assaulted-betrayed-and-jailed-but-ultimately-triumphant-brenda-clubine-fights-for-abused-women-172869521.html

Hindelang, M. J., Gottfredson, M. R., & Garofalo, J. (1978). *Victims of personal crime: An empirical foundation for a theory of personal victimization.* Cambridge, MA: Ballinger.

Hines, D. A., Armstrong, J. L., Reed, K. P., & Cameron, A. Y. (2012). Gender differences in sexual assault victimization among college students. *Violence & Victims, 27*(6), 922–940.

Hirsch, A. E. (2001). Bringing back shame: Women, welfare reform and criminal justice. In P. J. Schram & B. Koons-Witt (Eds.), *Gendered (in)justice: Theory and practice in feminist criminology* (pp. 270–286). Long Grove, IL: Waveland Press.

Hirschel, D. (2008). *Domestic violence cases: What research shows about arrest and dual arrest rates.* National Institute of Justice. Retrieved from http://www.nij.gov/nij/publications/dv-dual-arrest-222679/dv-dual-arrest.pdf

Hirschel, D., Buzawa, E., Pattavina, A., Faggiani, D., & Reuland, M. (2007). *Explaining the prevalence, context and consequences of dual arrest in intimate partner cases.* U.S. Department of Justice. Retrieved from https://www.ncjrs.gov/pdffiles1/nij/grants/218355.pdf

Hirschi, T. (1969). *Causes of delinquency*. Berkeley: University of California Press.

Hockenberry, S., & Puzzanchera, C. (2017). *Juvenile Court Statistics 2014*. Pittsburgh: National Center for Juvenile Justice. Retrieved from http://www.ncjj.org/pdf/jcsreports/jcs2014.pdf.

Hollingsworth v. Perry, 133 S.Ct. 2652 (2013).

Holsinger, K., & Holsinger, A. M. (2005). Differential pathways to violence and self-injurious behavior: African American and White girls in the juvenile justice system. *Journal of Research in Crime & Delinquency, 42*(2), 211–242.

Howlett, S. L., & Collins, A. (2014). Vicarious traumatization: Risk and resilience among crisis support volunteers in a community organization. *South African Journal of Psychology, 44*(2): 180–190.

Hsu, H., & Wu, B. (2011). Female defendants and criminal courts in Taiwan: An observation study. *Asian Criminology, 6*, 1–14.

Huebner, A. J., & Betts, S. C. (2002). Exploring the utility of social control theory for youth development: Issues of attachment, involvement, and gender. *Youth & Society, 34*(2), 123–145.

Huebner, B. M., DeJong, C., & Cobbina, J. (2010). Women coming home: Long-term patterns of recidivism. *Justice Quarterly, 27*(2), 225–254.

Huebner, B. M., & Pleggenkuhle, B. (2015). Residential location, household composition, and recidivism: An analysis by gender. *Justice Quarterly, 32*(5): 818–844.

Huet, V., & Holttum, S. (2016). Art therapists with experience of mental distress: Implications for art therapy training and practice. *International Journal of Art Therapy, 21*(3): 95–103.

Huffington Post. (2013, November 25). Steubenville grand jury investigation: Four more school employees indicted. Retrieved from http://www.huffingtonpost.com/2013/11/25/steubenville-grand-jury-investigation_n_4337646.html?utm_hp_ref=steubenville-rape

Human Rights Campaign. (2014). A guide to state-level advocacy following enactment of the Matthew Shepard and James Byrd, Jr. Hate Crimes Prevention Act. Retrieved from http://hrc-assets.s3-website-us-east-1.amazonaws.com/files/assets/resources/HRC-Hate-Crimes-Guide-2014.pdf

Human Rights Watch. (2006). Custody and control: Conditions of confinement in New York's juvenile prisons for girls. Retrieved from http://www.hrw.org/sites/default/files/reports/us0906webwcover.pdf

Human Rights Watch (2017a). Demogratic Republic of Congo. Retrieved from https://www.hrw.org/africa/democratic-republic-congo

Human Rights Watch (2017b). DR Congo: Ensure justice for killings in the Kasais. Retrieved from https://www.hrw.org/news/2017/02/24/dr-congo-ensure-justice-killings-kasais

Hunt, G., & Joe-Laidler, K. (2001). Situations of violence in the lives of girl gang members. *Health Care for Women International, 22*, 363–384.

Hurst, T. E., & Hurst, M. M. (1997). Gender differences in mediation of severe occupational stress among correctional officers. *American Journal of Criminal Justice, 22*(1), 121–137.

Ifrach, E, R., & Miller, A. (2016). Social action art therapy as an intervention for compassion fatigue. *The Arts in Psychotherapy, 50*: 34–39.

Inciardi, J. A., Lockwood, D., & Pottiger, A. E. (1993). *Women and crack-cocaine*. Toronto, Canada: Maxwell Macmillian.

Ingram, E. M. (2007). A comparison of help seeking between Latino and non-Latino victims of intimate partner violence. *Violence Against Women, 13*(2), 159–171.

Inter-American Commission on Human Rights. (2003). The situation of the rights of women in Ciudad Juárez, Mexico: The right to be free from violence and discrimination. Retrieved from http://www.cidh.org/annualrep/2002eng/chap.vi.juarez.htm

International Association of Chiefs of Police. (2010). Pregnancy & policing: A new policy makes them more compatible. Retrieved from www.aele.org/los2010kruger-pregnancy.pdf

International Labour Organization. (2005). *A global alliance against forced labour*. Geneva, Switzerland: United Nations.

Ireland, C., & Berg, B. (2008). Women in parole: Respect and rapport. *International Journal of Offender Therapy and Comparative Criminology, 52*(4), 474–491.

Irwin, J. (2008). (Dis)counted stories: Domestic violence and lesbians. *Qualitative Social Work, 7*(2), 199–215.

Jablonski, R. (January 8, 2015). Steubenville rape convict Trent Mays released from juvenile detention. Retrieved from http://www.cleveland.com/metro/index.ssf/2015/01/steubenville_rape_convict_tren.html

Jacobs, A. (2000). *Give 'em a fighting chance: The challenges for women offenders trying to succeed in the community*. Retrieved from http://www.wpaonline.org/pdf/WPA_FightingChance.pdf

James, D. J., & Glaze, L. E. (2006). *Bureau of Justice Statistics Special Report: Mental Health Problems of Prison and Jail Inmates* (NCJ No. 213600). Washington, DC: U.S. Department of Justice, Office of Justice Programs.

James, S. E., Herman, J. L., Rankin, S., Keisling, M., Mottet, L., & Anafi, M. (2016). *The Report of the 2015 U.S. Transgender Survey*. Washington, DC: National Center for Transgender Equality. Retrieved from http://www.transequality.org/sites/default/files/docs/usts/USTS%20Full%20Report%20-%20FINAL%201.6.17.pdf

Javdani, S., & Allen, N.E. (2016). An ecological model for intervention for juvenile justice-involved girls: Development and preliminary prospective evaluation. *Feminist Criminology, 11*(2): 135–162.

Jefferies, M. (2013, June 19). Nigella Lawson photos: Charles Saatchi reveals why he accepted police caution but makes no public apology. *The Mirror*. Retrieved from http://www.mirror.co.uk/news/uk-news/nigella-lawson-photos-charles-saatchi-1960358

Jensen, J. M., & Martinek, W. L. (2009). The effects of race and gender on the judicial ambitions of state trial court judges. *Political Research Quarterly, 62*(2), 379–392.

Jo, Y., & Bouffard, L. (2014). Stability of self-control and gender. *Journal of Criminal Justice, 42*(4): 356–365.

Joe, K., & Chesney-Lind, M. (1995). Just every mother's angel: An analysis of gender and ethnic variation in youth gang membership. *Gender and Society, 9*(4), 408–430.

Johnson, H. (2004). Drugs and crime: A study of incarcerated female offenders. *Australian Institute of Criminology, 63*. Retrieved from http://www.aic.gov.au/documents/E/B/8/%7BEB8A400C-E611-42BF-9B9F-B58E7C5A0694%7DRPP63.pdf

Johnson, I. M. (2007). Victims' perceptions of police response to domestic violence incidents. *Journal of Criminal Justice, 35,* 498–510.

Johnson, J. E., Esposito-Smythers, C., Miranda, R., Rizzo, C. J., Justus, A. N., & Clum, G. (2011). Gender, social support, and depression in criminal justice-involved adolescents. *International Journal of Offender Therapy and Comparative Criminology, 55*(7), 1096–1109.

Johnson, K., Scott, J., Rughita, B., Kisielewski, M., Asher, J., Ong, R., & Lawry, L. (2010). Association of sexual violence and human rights violations with physical and mental health in territories of the Eastern Democratic Republic of the Congo. *Journal of the American Medical Aossociation. 304*(5): 553–562.

Jones-Brown, D. (2007). Forever the symbolic assailant: The more things change, the more they stay the same. *Criminology & Public Policy, 6*(1), 103–121.

Jordan v. Gardner, 986 F.2d 1137 (1992).

Just Detention International (JDI). (2009). Incarcerated youth at extreme risk of sexual abuse. Retrieved from http://www.just detention.org/en/factsheets/jdifactsheetyouth.pdf

Justice Research and Statistics Association (JRSA). (n.d.). Background and status of incident-based reporting and NIBRS. Retrieved from http://www.jrsa.org/ibrrc/background-status/nibrs_states.shtml

Karakurt, G., & Silver, K. E. (2013). Emotional abuse in intimate relationships: The role of gender and age. *Violence and Victims, 28*(5), 804–821.

Karandikar, S., Gezinski, L. B., & Meshelemiah, J. C. A. (2013). A qualitative examination of women involved in prostitution in Mumbai, India: The role of family and acquaintances. *International Social Work, 56*(4), 496–515.

Kardam, N. (2005). The dynamics of honor killings in Turkey: Prospects for action. United Nations Development Programme. Retrieved from http://www.unfpa.org/public/publications/pid/383

Kaeble, D., & Bonczar, T. P. (2016). Probation and Parole in the United States. U.S. Department of Justice, Office of Justice Programs, Bureau of Justice Statistics. Retrieved from https://www.bjs.gov/content/pub/pdf/ppus15.pdf

Katz, J., & Moore, J. (2013). Bystander education training for capus sexual assault prevention: An initial meta-analysis. *Violence and Victims, 28*(6): 1054–1067.

Katz, C. M., & Spohn, C. (1995). The effect of race and gender and bail outcomes: A test of an interactive model. *American Journal of Criminal Justice, 19,* 161–184.

Kaukinen, C. (2004). Status compatibility, physical violence, and emotional abuse in intimate relationships. *Journal of Marriage and Family, 66*(2), 452–471.

Kaukinen, C., & DeMaris, A. (2009). Sexual assault and current mental health: The role of help-seeking and police response. *Violence Against Women, 15*(11), 1331–1357.

Kay, F. M., Alarie, S., & Adjei, J. (2013). Leaving private practice: How organizational context, time, pressures, and structural inflexibilities share departures from private law practice. *Indiana J. Glob. Leg. Stud.,* 20: 1223–1260.

KBOI News Staff (2016, September 1). Charges dropped against one teen in alleged Dietrich sexual assault case. Retrieved from http://kboi2.com/news/local/charges-dropped-against-teen-in-alleged-dietrich-sexual-assault-case

Kelleher, C., & McGilloway, S. (2009). "Nobody ever chooses this . . .": A qualitative study of service providers working in the sexual violence sector—Key issues and challenges. *Health and Social Care in the Community, 17*(3), 295–303.

Kellermann, A. L., & Mercy, J. A. (1992). Men, women, and murder: Gender-specific differences in rates of fatal violence and victimization. *The Journal of Trauma, 33*(1), 1–5.

Kernsmith, P. (2005). Exerting power or striking back: A gendered comparison of motivations for domestic violence perpetration. *Violence and Victims, 20,* 173–185.

Kiefer, M. (2015, April 13). Jodi Arias sentence: Natural life, no chance of release. Retrieved from www.azcentral.com/story/news/local/mesa/2015/04/13/jodi-arias-faces0life-sentence-to-day-murder-travis-alexander/25608085/

Kilpatrick, D. G., Resnick, H. S., Ruggiero, K. J., Conoscenti, L. M., & McCauley, J. (2007). *Drug-facilitated, incapacitated, and forcible rape: A national study.* Charleston, SC: Medical University of South Carolina, National Crime Victims Research & Treatment Center.

Kim, B., Gerber, J., Henderson, C., & Kim, Y. (2012). Applicability of general power-control theory to prosocial and antisocial risk taking behaviors among women in South Korea. *The Prison Journal, 92*(1), 125–150.

Kim B., Hawkins P. M. (2013). Who's getting cited: Representation of women and non-white scholars in major American criminology and criminal justice journals between 1986–2005. *International Journal of Criminology and Sociology, 2,* 306–321.

Kim, B., & Merlo, A. (2012). In her own voice: Presentations on women, crime, and criminal justice at American Society of Criminology meetings from 1999–2008. *Women and Criminal Justice, 22*(1), 66–88.

Kirkwood, M. K., & Cecil, D. K. (2001). Marital rape: A student assessment of rape laws and the marital exemption. *Violence Against Women, 7*(11): 1234–1253.

Kitty, J. M. (2012). "It's like they don't want you to get better": Psy control of women in the carceral context. *Feminism & Psychology, 22*(2), 162–182.

Klein, A. R. (2004). *The criminal justice response to domestic violence.* Belmont, CA: Wadsworth Thomson Learning.

Knoll, C., & Sickmund, M. (2010). *Delinquency cases in juvenile court, 2007*. Office of Justice Programs. Office of Juvenile Justice and Delinquency Prevention. Retrieved from http://www.ncjrs.gov/pdffiles1/ojjdp/230168.pdf

Knoll, C., & Sickmund, M. (2012). *Delinquency cases in juvenile court, 2009*. Office of Juvenile Justice and Delinquency Prevention. Retrieved from http://www.ojjdp.gov/pubs/239081.pdf

Koeppel, M. D. H. (2012, November 28). Gender sentencing of rural property offenders in Iowa. *Criminal Justice Policy Review.* Advance online publication. doi:10.1177/0887403412465308

Kohsin Wang, S., & Rowley, E. (2007). *Rape: How women, the community and the health sector respond*. Geneva, Switzerland: World Health Organization/Sexual Violence Research Initiative

Kolb, K. H. (2011). Sympathy work: Identity and emotion management among victim-advocates and counselors. *Qualitative Sociology, 34*, 101–119.

Konradi, A. (2016). Can justice be served on campus? An examination of due process and victim protection policies in the campus adjudication of sexual assault in Maryland. *Humanity & Society,* 1-32. DOI: 10.1177/0160597616651657.

Koons-Witt, B. (2006). Decision to incarcerate before and after the introduction of sentencing guidelines. *Criminology, 40*(2), 297–328.

Koons-Witt, B. A., Sevigny, E. L., Burrow, J. D., & Hester, R. (2012). Gender and sentencing outcomes in South Carolina: Examining the interactions with race, age, and offense type. *Criminal Justice Police Review, 10*, 1–26.

Koren, M. (2016, June 17). Why the Stanford judge gave Brock Turner six months. *The Atlantic.* Retrieved from https://www.theatlantic.com/news/archive/2016/06/stanford-rape-case-judge/487415/

Kraaij, V., Arensman, E., Garnefski, N., & Kremers, I. (2007). The role of cognitive coping in female victims of stalking. *Journal of Interpersonal Violence, 22*(12), 1603–1612.

Krouse, P. (2013, July 26). Ariel Castro agrees to plea deal: Life in prison, no parole, plus 1,000 years. Retrieved from http://www.cleveland.com/metro/index.ssf/2013/07/ariel_castro_agrees_to_plea_de.html

Kruttschnitt, C., & Savolianen, J. (2009). Ages of chivalry, places of paternalism: Gender and criminal sentencing in Finland. *European Journal of Criminology, 6*(3), 225–247.

Kuriakose, D. (2013, October 9). Malala Yousafzai: From blogger to Nobel Peace Prize nominee—Timeline. *The Guardian.* Retrieved from http://www.theguardian.com/world/interactive/2013/oct/09/malala-yousafzai-timeline

Kurshan, N. (2000). *Women and imprisonment in the United States: History and current reality*. Retrieved from http://www.prison-activist.org/archive/women/women-and-imprisonment.html

Kurtz, D. L., Linnemann, T., & Williams, L. S. (2012). Reinventing the matron: The continued importance of gendered images and division of labor in modern policing. *Women & Criminal Justice, 22*(3), 239–263.

Kyckelhahn, T., Beck, A. J., & Cohen, T. H. (2009). Characteristics of suspected human trafficking incidents. Retrieved from http://www.ojp.usdoj.gov/bjs/abstract/cshti08.htm

La Ganga, M. L. (2017, February 24). Idaho judge rules attack on high scholl football player was "not a rape" or racist. *The Guardian* Retrieved from https://www.theguardian.com/us-news/2017/feb/24/idaho-football-player-rape-case-coat-hanger-light-sentence

LaGrange, T. C., & Silverman, R. A. (1999). Low self-control and opportunity: Testing the general theory of crime as an explanation of gender differences in delinquency. *Criminology, 37*(1), 41–72.

Lambert, E. G., Hogan, N. L., Altheimer, I., & Wareham, J. (2010). The effects of different aspects of supervision among female and male correctional staff: A preliminary study. *Criminal Justice Review, 35*, 492–513. doi: 10.1177/0734016810372068

Lambert, E. G., Paoline, E. A. Hogan, N. L., & Baker, D. N. (2007). Gender similarities and differences in correctional staff work attitudes and perceptions of the work environment. *Western Criminology Review, 8*(1), 16–31.

Lambert, E. G., Smith, B., & Geistman, J. (2013). Do men and women differ in the perceptions of stalking: An exploratory study among college students. *Violence and Victims, 28*(2), 195–209.

Lane, J., Gover, A. R., & Dahod, S. (2009). Fear of violent crime among men and women on campus: The impact of perceived risk and fear of sexual assault. *Violence and Victims, 24*(2), 172–192.

Langenderfer-Magruder, L., Walls, N. E., Kattari, S. K., Whitfield, D. L., & Ramos, D. (2016). Sexual victimization and subsequent police reporting by gender identity among lesbian, gay, bisexual, transgendered, and queer adults. *Violence and Victims, 31*(2): 320–331.

Langhinrichsen-Rohling, J., & Monson, C. M. (1998). Marital rape: Is the crime taken seriously without co-occurring physical abuse? *Journal of Family Violence, 13*(4): 433–443.

Langton, L. (2010). Crime data brief: Women in law enforcement. Bureau of Justice Statistics. Retrieved from http://bjs.ojp.usdoj.gov/content/pub/pdf/wle8708.pdf

LaVigne, N. G., Brooks, L. E., & Shollenberger, T. L. (2009). Women on the outside: Understanding the experiences of female prisoners returning to Houston, Texas. Urban Institute Justice Policy Center. Retrieved from http://www.urban.org/sites/default/files/publication/30401/411902-Women-on-the-Outside-Understanding-the-Experiences-of-Female-Prisoners-Returning-to-Houston-Texas.PDF

Law Library of Congress (n.d.). Women lawyers and state bar admission. The Library of Congress. Retrieved from http://memory.loc.gov/ammem/awhhtml/awlaw3/women_lawyers.html

Lawrence v. Texas, 539 U.S. 558 (2003).

Learner, S. (2012). Scarred for life. *Nursing Standard, 26*(18), 20–21.

LeBlanc, P. (2017, June 16). The text messages that led up to teen's suicide. CNN. Retrieved from www.cnn.com/2017/06/08/us/text-message-suicide-michelle-carter-conrad-roy/index.html

Lee, J., Pomeroy, E. C., Yoo, S. K., & Rheinboldt, K. T. (2005). Attitudes toward rape: A comparison between Asian and Caucasian college students. *Violence Against Women, 11*(2): 177–196.

Lee, M. Y., & Law, P. F. M. (2001). Perception of sexual violence against women in Asian American communities. *Journal of Ethnic and Cultural Diversity in Social Work, 10*(2): 3–25.

Lee, R. K. (1998). Romantic and electronic stalking in a college context. *William and Mary Journal of Women and the Law, 4,* 373–466.

Legal Action Center. (2011). State TANF options drug felon ban. Retrieved from http://www.lac.org/doc_library/lac/publications/HIRE_Network_State_TANF_Options_Drug_Felony_Ban.pdf

Leiber, M., Brubaker, S., & Fox, K. (2009). A closer look at the individual and joint effects of gender and race in juvenile justice decision making. *Feminist Criminology, 4,* 333–358.

Leonard, E. B. (1982). *Women, crime, and society.* New York: Longman.

Lerner, M. J. (1980). *The belief in a just world: A fundamental delusion.* New York: Plenum Press.

Lersch, K. M., & Bazley, T. (2012). A paler shade of blue? Women and the police subculture. In R. Muraskin (Ed.), *Women and justice: It's a crime* (5th ed., pp. 514–526). Upper Saddle River, NJ: Prentice-Hall.

Leung, R. (2009, February 11). Abuse of Iraqi POWs by GIs probed. *60 Minutes.* CBS News. Retrieved from http://www.cbsnews.com/stories/2004/04/27/60ii/main614063.shtml

Liang, B., Lu, H., & Taylor, M. (2009). Female drug abusers, narcotic offenders, and legal punishment in China. *Journal of Criminal Justice, 37,* 133–141.

Like-Haislip, T. Z., & Miofsky, K. (2011). Race, ethnicity, gender, and violent victimization. *Race and Justice, 1*(3), 254–276.

Lindgren, J., Stanglin, D., & Alcindor, Y. (2013, August 7). Ariel Castro's house of horror demolished in Cleveland. *USA Today.* Retrieved from http://www.usatoday.com/story/news/nation/2013/08/07/ariel-castro-cleveland-house-abduction/2626855/

Lipari, R. N., Cook, P. J., Rock, L., & Matos, K. (2008). 2006 gender relations survey of active duty members (DMDC Report No. 2007–022). Arlington, VA: Defense Manpower Data Center.

Lipsky, S., Caetano, R., Field, C. A., & Larkin, G. L. (2006). The role of intimate partner violence, race, and ethnicity in help-seeking behaviors. *Ethnicity and Health, 11*(1), 81–100.

Littleton, H., Breitkopf, C. R., & Berenson, A. (2008). Beyond the campus: Unacknowledged rape among low-income women. *Violence Against Women, 14*(3), 269–286.

Logan, T. K., Evans, L., Stevenson, E., & Jordan, C. E. (2005). Barriers to services for rural and urban survivors of rape. *Journal of Interpersonal Violence, 20*(5), 591–616.

Lombroso, C. (2006). *Criminal man* (M. Gibson & N. Hahn Rafter, Trans.). Durham, NC: Duke University Press.

Lombroso, C., & Ferrero, W. (1895). *The female offender.* New York: Barnes.

Long, L., & Ullman, S. E. (2013). The impact of multiple traumatic victimization on disclosure and coping mechanisms for Black women. *Feminist Criminology, 8*(4), 295–319.

Lonsway, K. A., & Fitzgerald, L. F. (1994). Rape myths in review. *Psychology of women quarterly, 18*(2), 133–164.

Lonsway, K. A., Paynich, R., & Hall, J. N. (2013). Sexual harassment in law enforcement: Incidence, impact, and perception. *Police Quarterly, 16*(2), 177–210.

Lonsway, K., Carrington, S., Aguirre, P., Wood, M., Moore, M., Harrington, P., . . . Spillar, K. (2002). *Equality denied: The status of women in policing: 2001.* The National Center for Women and Policing. Retrieved from http://www.womenandpolicing.org/PDF/2002_Status_Report.pdf

Lonsway, K., Wood, M., Fickling, M., De Leon, A., Moore, M., Harrington, P., . . . Spillar, K. (2002). *Men, women and police excessive force: A tale of two genders: A content analysis of civil liability cases, sustained allegations and citizen complaints.* The National Center for Women and Policing. Retrieved from http://www.womenandpolicing.org/PDF/2002_Excessive_Force.pdf

Lopez, A. (2012). Scott signs "historic" anti-shackling bill for incarcerated pregnant women. *Florida Independent.* Retrieved from http://floridaindependent.com/74661/rick-scott-anti-shackling-bill

Lopez, A. J. (2007). Expert: Victims' path rockier than celebrities'. *Rocky Mountain News.* Retrieved from http://therocky.com/news/2007/mar/15/expert-victims-path-rockier-than-celebrities/

Los Angeles Almanac. (2012). LAPD had the nation's first police woman. Retrieved from http://www.laalmanac.com/crime/cr73b.htm

Lowe, N. C., May, D. C., & Elrod, P. (2008). Theoretical predictors of delinquency among public school students in a mid-southern state: The roles of context and gender. *Youth Violence and Juvenile Justice, 6*(4), 343–362.

Lyons, C. (2006, April 20). "Media circus" atmosphere aggravated case. Retrieved from http://www.hampton.lib.nh.us/hampton/biog/pamsmart/equinox2006_4.htm

Ma, F. (June 24, 2013). Domestic abse victim Glenda Virgil is freed. *SFGate.* Retrieved from http://www.sfgate.com/opinion/openforum/article/Domestic-abuse-victim-Glenda-Virgil-is-freed-4619772.php

MacIntosh, J. (2011, August 9). "Rack" and ruin: Stripper goes on "crime spree" with brothers. *New York Post.* Retrieved from http://www.nypost.com/p/news/national/vixen_faces_rack_ruin_q5hnBQ1AlZJrIImUY4CHCP

Maggard. S. R., Higgins, J. L., & Chappell, A. T. (2013). Predispositional juvenile detention: An analysis of race, gender and intersectionality. *Journal of Crime and Justice, 36*(1), 67–86.

Maguire, B. (1988). Image vs. reality: An analysis of prime-time television crime and police programs. *Journal of Crime and Justice, 11*(1), 165–188.

Maher, L. (1996). Hidden in the light: Occupational norms among crack-using street level sex workers. *Journal of Drug Issues, 26,* 143–173.

Maher, L. (2004a). A reserve army: Women and the drug market. In B. Price & N. Sokoloff (Eds.), *The criminal justice system and women: Offenders, prisoners, victims and workers* (3rd ed., pp. 127–146). New York, NY: McGraw-Hill.

Maher L. (2004b). "Hooked on heroin: Drugs and drifters in a globalized world." *Addiction, 99*, 929–930.

Mahoney, J. (2013, May 9). Death penalty possible for alleged Cleveland kidnapper, prosecutor says. *The Globe and Mail*. Retrieved from http://web.archive.org/web/20130509221120/ http://www.theglobeandmail.com/news/world/kidnap-suspect-ariel-castro-due-in-cleveland-court/article11810618/?cmpid=rss1

Mahoney, J. L., Cairns, B. D., & Farmer, T. W. (2003). Promoting interpersonal competence and educational success through extracurricular activity participation. *Journal of Educational Psychology, 95*(2), 409–418.

Maier, S. L. (2008a). "I have heard terrible stories . . ": Rape victim advocates' perceptions of the revictimization of rape victims by the police and medical system. *Violence Against Women, 14*(7), 786–808.

Maier, S. L. (2008b). Rape victim advocates' perception of the influence of race and ethnicity on victims' responses to rape. *Journal of Ethnicity and Criminal Justice, 6*(4), 295–326.

Maier, S. L. (2011). "We belong to them": The costs of funding for rape crisis centers. *Violence Against Women, 17*(11), 1383–1408.

Mallicoat, S. L. (2006, August). *Mary Magdalene project: Kester program evaluation*. Paper presented at the Program Committee of the Mary Magdalene Project, Van Nuys, CA.

Mallicoat, S. L. (2007). Gendered justice: Attributional differences between males and females in the juvenile courts. *Feminist Criminology, 2*(1), 4–30.

Mallicoat, S. L. (2011). Lives in transition: A needs assessment of women exiting from prostitution. In R. Muraskin (Ed.), *It's a crime: Women and justice* (4th ed., pp. 241–255). Upper Saddle River, NJ: Prentice-Hall.

Mallicoat, S. L., Marquez, S. A., & Rosenbaum, J. L. (2007). Guiding philosophies for rape crisis centers. In R. Muraskin (Ed.), *It's a crime: Women and criminal justice* (4th ed., pp. 217–225). Upper Saddle River, NJ: Prentice-Hall.

Mandal, S. (2014) The impossibility of marital rape: Contestations around marriage, sex, violence and the law in contemporary India. *Australia Feminist Studies, 29*(81): 255–272.

Mann, M., Menih, H., & Smith, C. (2014). There is 'hope for you yet': The female drug offender in sentencing discourse. *Australian & New Zealand Journal of Criminology, 47*(3): 355–373.

Manning, J. E., Brudnick, I. A., & Shogan, C. J. (2015). Women in Congress: Historical overview, tables, and discussion. Congressional Research Service. Retrieved from https://fas.org/sgp/crs/misc/R43244.pdf

Marcos, C. (2016, November 17). 115th Congress will be the most racially diverse in history. *The Hill*. Retrieved from www.thehill.com/homenews/house/306480-115th-congress-will-be-the-most-racially-diverse-in-history

Marcotte, A. (2014, September 11). Ray Rice defenders have found their argument: He's a victim too. *Slate*.. Retrieved from http://www.slate.com/blogs/xx_factor/2014/09/11/ray_rice_and_janay_rice_do_not_share_the_blame_at_al.html

Marks, P. (1993, November 16). Buttafuoco is sentenced to 6 months for rape. *The New York Times*. http://www.nytimes.com/1993/11/16/nyregion/buttafuoco-is-sentenced-to-6-months-for-rape.html

Marshall, T., Simpson S., & Stevens, A. (2001). Use of health services by prison inmates: Comparisons with the community. *Journal of Epidemiology and Community Health, 55*(5): 364–365.

Martin, E. K., Taft, C. T., & Resick, P. A. (2007). A review of marital rape. *Aggression and Violent Behavior, 12*(3), 329–347.

Martin, L. (1991). *A report on the glass ceiling commission*. Washington, DC: U.S. Department of Labor.

Maruschak, L., & Parks, E. R. (2012). Probation and parole in the United States, 2011. U.S. Department of Justice, Bureau of Justice Statistics. Retrieved from http://www.bjs.gov/content/pub/pdf/ppus11.pdf

Mary Katherine Schmitz. (2014). The Biography.com website. Retrieved from http://www.biography.com/people/mary-kay-letourneau-9542379.

Maslin, J. (1987, September 17). Fatal attraction [Review]. Retrieved from http://www.nytimes.com/movie/review?res=9B0DE-3DE163CF93BA2575AC0A961948260

Mastony, C. (2010). Was Chicago home to the country's 1st female cop? Researcher uncovers the story of Sgt. Marie Owens. *Chicago Tribune*. Retrieved from http://articles.chicagotribune.com/2010-09-01/news/ct-met-first-police-woman-20100901_1_female-officer-police-officer-female-cop

Mastony, C. (2012, May 23). $4.1 million settlement set for pregnant inmates who said they were shackled before giving birth. *Chicago Tribune*. Retrieved from http://articles.chica gotribune.com/2012-05-23/news/ct-met-shackled-pregnant-women-20120523_1_pregnant-women-pregnant-inmates-shackles-and-belly-chains

Matsueda, R. (1992). Reflected appraisals, parental labeling, and delinquency: Specifying a symbolic interactionist theory. *American Journal of Sociology, 97*(6), 1577.

Matthews, C., Monk-Turner, E., & Sumter, M. (2010). Promotional opportunities: How women in corrections perceive their chances for advancement at work. *Gender Issues, 27*, 53–66.

Mauer, M. (2013). The changing racial dynamics of women's incarceration. The Sentencing Project. Retrieved from http://www.sentencingproject.org/doc/advocacy/Changing%20Racial%20Dynamics%20Webinar%20Slides.pdf

Mayell, H. (2002, February 12). Thousands of women killed for family honor. *National Geographic News, 12*.

McAtee, J (2017, March 15). Charges against LA Rams DE Ethan Westbrooks dropped in domestic violence case. SBNation. Retrievedathttp://www.turfshowtimes.com/2017/3/15/14937898/la-rams-de-ethan-westbrooks-charges-dropped-domestic-violence-case

McCall, M. (2007). Structuring gender's impact: Judicial voting across criminal justice cases. *American Politics Research, 36*(2), 264–296.

McCann, A. (2014, August 28). The NFL's uneven history of punishing domestic violence. FiveThirtyEight. Retrieved from https://fivethirtyeight.com/features/nfl-domestic-violence-policy-suspensions/

McCartan, L. M., & Gunnison, E. (2010). Individual and relationship factors that differentiate female offenders with and without a sexual abuse history. *Journal of Interpersonal Violence, 25*(8), 1449–1469.

McCoy, L. A., & Miller, H. A. (2013). Comparing gender across risk and recidivism in nonviolent offenders. *Women & Criminal Justice, 23*(2), 143–162.

McGrath, S. A., Johnson, M., & Miller, M. H. (2012). The social ecological challenges of rural victim advocacy: An exploratory study. *Journal of Community Psychology, 40*(5), 588–606.

McKnight, L. R., & Loper, A. B. (2002). The effect of risk and resilience factors on the prediction of delinquency in adolescent girls. *School Psychology International, 23*(2), 186–198.

Mears, D. P., Cochran, J. C., & Bales, W. D. (2012). Gender differences in the effects of prison on recidivism. *Journal of Criminal Justice, 40*, 370–378.

Melton, H. C. (2007). Predicting the occurrence of stalking in relationships characterized by domestic violence. *Journal of Interpersonal Violence, 22*(1), 3–25.

Mendelsohn, B. (1956). A new branch of bio-psychological science: La Victimology. *Revue Internationale de Criminologie et de Police Technique 10*, 782–789.

Merolla, D. (2008). The war on drugs and the gender gap in arrests: A critical perspective. *Critical Sociology, 34*(2), 355–270.

Merton, R. K. (1938). Social structure and anomie. *American Sociological Review, 3*(5), 672–682.

Messina, N., Grella, C. E., Cartier, J., & Torres, S. (2010). A randomized experimental study of gender-responsive substance abuse treatment for women in prison. *Journal of Substance Abuse Treatment, 39*, 97–107.

Meyer, C. L., & Oberman, M. (2001). *Mothers who kill their children: Understanding the acts of moms from Susan Smith to the "Prom mom."* New York: University Press.

Millar, G., Stermac, L., & Addison, M. (2002). Immediate and delayed treatment seeking among adult sexual assault victims. *Women & Health, 35*(1), 53–64.

Miller, J. (1994). An examination of disposition decision-making for delinquent girls. In M. Schwartz & D. Milovanivoc (Eds.), *Race, gender, and class in criminology: The intersections* (pp. 219–246). New York: Garland.

Miller, J. (1998a). Gender and victimization risk among young women in gangs. *Journal of Research in Crime and Delinquency, 35*, 429–453.

Miller, J. (1998b). Up it up: Gender and the accomplishment of street robbery. *Criminology, 36*(1), 37–66.

Miller, J. (2000). *One of the guys: Girls, gangs and gender.* Oxford, UK: Oxford University Press.

Miller, L. J. (2003). Denial of pregnancy. In M. G. Spinelli (Ed.), *Infanticide: Psychosocial and legal perspectives on mothers who kill* (pp. 81–104). Washington, DC: American Psychiatric Publishing, Inc..

Miller, M. E. (2016, June 6). "A steep price to pay for 20 minutes of action": Dad defends Stanford sex offender. *Washington Post.* Retrieved from https://www.washingtonpost.com/news/morning-mix/wp/2016/06/06/a-steep-price-to-pay-for-20-minutes-of-action-dad-defends-stanford-sex-offender/?utm_term=.448ccd755a77

Miller, S. (2005). Victims as offenders: The paradox of women's violence in relationships. New Brunswick, NJ: Rutgers University Press.

Miller, S., Loeber, R., & Hipwell, A. (2009). Peer deviance, parenting and disruptive behavior among young girls. *Journal of Abnormal Child Psychology, 37*(2), 139–152.

Miller, S. L., & Meloy, M. L. (2006). Women's use of force: Voices of women arrested for domestic violence. *Violence Against Women, 12*(1), 89–115.

Miller, S. L., & Peterson, E. S. L. (2007). The impact of law enforcement policies on victims of intimate partner violence. In R. Muraskin (Ed.), *It's a crime: Women and criminal justice* (4th ed., Chapt. 14). Upper Saddle River, NJ: Pearson Prentice Hall.

Ministry of Labour in cooperation with the Ministry of Justice and the Ministry of Health and Social Affairs, Government of Sweden. (1998). *Fact sheet.* Stockholm, Sweden: Secretariat for Information and Communication, Ministry of Labour.

Mintz, Z. (2013, June 10). Witch hunts in Papua New Guinea on the rise, killings connected to economic growth and jealousy. *International Business Times.* Retrieved from http://www.ibtimes.com/witch-hunts-papua-new-guinea-rise-killings-connected-economic-growth-jealousy-1298363

Moe, A. M. (2007). Silenced voices and structured survival: Battered women's help seeking. *Violence Against Women, 13*(7), 676–699.

Moe, A. M. (2009). Battered women, children, and the end of abusive relationships. *Afilia: Journal of Women and Social Work, 24*(3), 244–256.

Moffitt, T. E., Caspi, A., Rutter, M., & Silva, P. A. (2001). Sex differences in antisocial behavior: Conduct disorder, delinquency and violence in the Dunedin Longitudinal Study. New York: Cambridge University Press.

Molidor, C. E. (1996). Female gang members: A profile of aggression and victimization. *Social Work, 41*(3), 251–257.

Moon, B., & Morash, M. (2017). Gender and general strain theory: A comparison of strains, mediating, and moderating effects explaining three types of delinquency. *Youth & Society, 49*(4): 484–504.

Moore, J. W. (1991). *Going down to the barrio: Homeboys and homegirls in change.* Philadelphia: Temple University Press.

Moore, J., & Terrett, C. P. (1998). *Highlights of the 1996 National Youth Gang Survey. Fact sheet.* Washington, DC: U.S. Department of Justice, Office of Justice Programs, Office of Juvenile Justice and Delinquency Prevention.

Morash, M., & Haarr, R. N. (2012). Doing, redoing, and undoing gender: Variation in gender identities of women working as police officers. *Feminist Criminology, 7*(1), 3–23.

Morash, M., Stevens, T., & Yingling, J. (2014). Focus on the family: Juvenile court responses to girls and their caretakers. *Feminist Criminology, 9*(4): 298–322.

Morello, K. (1986). *The invisible bar: The woman lawyer in America 1638 to the present.* New York: Random House.

Morgan, K. D. (2013). Issues in female inmate health: Results from a southeastern state. *Women & Criminal Justice, 23,* 121–142.

Moses, M. (1995). "Girl Scouts Beyond Bars"—A synergistic solution for children of incarcerated parents. *Corrections Today, 57*(7), 124–127.

Munge, B. A., Pomerantz, A. M., Pettibone, J. C., & Falconer, J. W. (2007). The influence of length of marriage and fidelity status on perception of marital rape. *Journal of Interpersonal Violence, 22*(10): 1332–1339.

Mungin, L., & Alsup, D. (2013, September 4). Cleveland kidnapper Ariel Castro dead: Commits suicide in prison. CNN Justice. Retrieved from http://www.cnn.com/2013/09/04/justice/ariel-castro-cleveland-kidnapper-death/

Murtha, T. (2013, March 19). From Big Dan's to Steubenville: A generation later, media coverage of rape still awful. RH Reality Check. Retrieved from http://rhrealitycheck.org/article/2013/03/19/from-big-dans-to-steubenville-a-generation-later-media-coverage-of-rape-still-awful/

Mustaine, E. E., & Tewksbury, R. (2002). Sexual assault of college women: A feminist interpretation of a routine activities analysis. *Criminal Justice Review, 27*(1), 89–123.

Myers, R. K., Nelson, D. B., & Forke, C. M. (2016). Occurrence of stalking behaviors among female and male undergraduate students. *Journal of College Student Development, 57*(2): 213–218.

Nagel, I., & Hagan, J. (1983). Gender and crime: Offense patterns and criminal court sanctions. In N. Morris and M. Tonry (Eds.), *Crime and justice* (Vol. 4, pp. 91–144). Chicago, IL: University of Chicago Press.

Nagel, I. H., & Johnson, B. L. (2004). The role of gender in a structured sentencing system: Equal treatment, policy choices and the sentencing of female offenders. In P. Schram & B. Koons-Witt (Eds.), *Gendered (in)justice: Theory and practice in feminist criminology.* Long Grove, IL: Waveland Press.

Nanivazo, M. (2012, May 24). Sexual violence in the Democratic Republic of the Congo. United Nations University. Retrieved from https://unu.edu/publications/articles/sexual-violence-in-the-democratic-republic-of-the-congo.html

Nash, S. T. (2006). Through Black eyes: African American women's constructions of their experiences with intimate male partner violence. *Violence Against Women, 11*(11), 1420–1440.

National Asian Women's Health Organization. (2002). *Silent epidemic: A survey of violence among young Asian American women.* Retrieved from http://www.nawho.org/pubs/NAWHOSilentEpidemic.pdf

National Association for Law Placement. (2010). *Law firm diversity among associates erodes in 2010.* National Association for Law Placement. Retrieved from www.nalp.org/uploads/PressReleases/10NALPWomenMinoritiesPressRel.pdf

National Association for Law Placement (NALP). (2015).*Women black/African-American associates lose ground at manor U.S. law firms.* Retrieved from www.nalp.org/lawfirmdiversity_nov2015

National Association of Women Lawyers and The NAWL Foundation. (2009). *Report of the Fourth Annual National Survey on Retention and Promotion of Women in Law Firms.* Retrieved from http://nawl.timberlakepublishing.com/files/2009%20Survey%20Report%20FINAL.pdf

National Association of Women Lawyers and The NAWL Foundation. (2010). *Report of the Fifth Annual National Survey on Retention and Promotion of Women in Law Firms.* Retrieved from http://nawl.timberlakepublishing.com/files/NAWL%202010%20Final(1).pdf

National Coalition Against Domestic Violence. (n.d.). Mission statement and purpose. Retrieved from www.ncadv.org

National Coalition Against Domestic Violence. (2006). Comparison of VAWA 1994, VAWA 2000 and VAWA 2005 Reauthorization Bill. Retrieved from http://www.ncadv.org/files/VAWA_94_00_05.pdf

National Conference of State Legislatures. (2017). Women in State Legislatures for 2017. Retrieved from www.ncsl.org/legislators-staff/legislators/womens-legislative-network/women-ion-state-legislatures-for-2017.aspx

National Drug Intelligence Center. (n.d.). Drug-facilitated sexual assault fast facts. Retrieved from http://www.justice.gov/archive/ndic/pubs8/8872/index.htm#Top

National Incident Based Reporting System. (2016a). Summary of NIBRS, 2015. Retrieved from https://ucr.fbi.gov/nibrs/2015/resource-pages/nibrs-2015_summary_final-1.pdf

National Incident Based Reporting System. (2016b). Arrestees, Sex by Arrest Offense Category, 2015. Retrieved from https://ucr.fbi.gov/nibrs/2015/tables/data-tables

National Incident Based Reporting System (NIBRS). (2015). Summary of NIBRS 2015. Retrieved from https://ucr.fbi.gov/nibrs/2015/resource-pages/nibrs-2015_summary_final-1.pdf

National Public Radio. (n.d.). Timeline: America's war on drugs. Retrieved from http://www.npr.org/templates/story/story.php?storyId=9252490

National Women's History Museum (NWHM). (n.d). Women wielding power: Pioneer female state legislators. Retrieved from https://www.nwhm.org/org/online-exhibits/legislators/Colorado.hmtl

National Youth Gang Center. (2009). *National Youth Gang Survey analysis.* Retrieved from http://www.nationalgangcenter.gov/Survey-Analysis

Navarro, J. N., & Jasinski, J. L. (2013). Why girls? Using routine activities theory to predict cyberbullying experiences between girls and boys. *Women & Criminal Justice, 23,* 286–303.

Neff, J. L., Patterson, M. M., & Johnson, S. (2012). Meeting the training needs of those who meet the needs of victims: Assessing service providers. *Violence and Victims, 27*(4), 609–632.

New York Times. (1978, February 22). 2 officers win case on issue of pregnancy. Pg. B3.

New York Times. (1983, February 21). Women balance police work at home. Pg. C18.

Newton, M. (2003). Ciudad Juarez: The serial killer's playground. Retrieved from http://www.trutv.com/library/crime/serial_killers/predators/ciudad_juarez/11.html

Ng, C. (2013, March 17). Steubenville, Ohio, football players convicted in rape trial. ABC News. Retrieved from http://abcnews.go.com/US/steubenville-football-players-guilty-ohio-rape-trial/story?id=18748493

Nguyen, H. V., Kaysen, D., Dillworth, T. M., Brajcich, M., & Larimer, M. E. (2010). Incapacitated rape and alcohol use in White and Asian American college women. *Violence Against Women, 16*(8): 919–933.

Nine justices, ten years: A statistical retrospective. (2004). *Harvard Law Review, 118*(1), 521. Retrieved from http://web.archive.org/web/20060327053526/http://www.harvardlawreview.org/issues/118/Nov04/Nine_Justices_Ten_YearsFTX.pdf

Nixon, K., Tutty, L., Downe, P., Gorkoff, K., & Ursel, J. (2002).The everyday occurrence: Violence in the lives of girls exploited through prostitution. *Violence Against Women, 8*(9), 1016–1043.

Nokomis Foundation. (2002). We can do better: Helping prostituted women and girls in Grand Rapids make healthy choices: A prostitution round table report to the community. Retrieved from http://www.nokomisfoundation.org/documents/WeCanDoBetter.pdf

Noonan, M. C., & Corcoran, M. E. (2008). The mommy track and partnership: Temporary delay or dead end? *Annals of the American Academy of Political and Social Science, 596,* 130–150.

Noonan, M. C., Corcoran, M. E., & Courant, P. N. (2008). Is the partnership gap closing for women? Cohort differences in the sex gap in partnership chances. *Social Science Research, 37,* 156–179.

Norton-Hawk, M. (2004). A comparison of pimp-and non-pimp-controlled women. *Violence Against Women, 10*(2), 189–194.

NY Daily News. (2013, December 20). Congress passed defense bill with provision to crack down on sexual assault in the military. Retrieved from http://www.nydailynews.com/news/politics/sen-gillibrand-military-sexual-assault-bill-passes-article-1.1553722

O'Connor, M. L. (2012). Early policing in the United States: "Help wanted—Women need not apply!" In R. Muraskin (Ed.), *Women and justice: It's a crime* (5th ed., pp. 487–499). Upper Saddle River, NJ: Prentice-Hall.

Odem, M. E. (1995). *Delinquent daughters: Protecting and policing adolescent female sexuality in the United States, 1885–1920.* Chapel Hill: University of North Carolina Press.

O'Donnell, P., Richards, M., Pearce, S., & Romero, E. (2012). Gender differences in monitoring and deviant peers as predictors of delinquent behavior among low-income urban African American youth. *Journal of Early Adolescence, 32*(3), 431–459.

Office for National Statistics. (2014). *Crime in England and Wales, year ending December 2013.* Retrieved from http://www.ons.gov.uk/ons/dcp171778_360216.pdf

Office of Civil Rights, Department of Education. (2011, April 4). Dear Colleague letter. Retrieved from https://www2.ed.gov/about/offices/list/ocr/letters/colleague-201104.pdf

Office on Violence Against Women (OVW). (n.d.). Home. U.S. Department of Justice. Retrieved from http://www.ovw.usdoj.gov

Office on Violence Against Women. (n.d.). VAWA 2013 summary: Changes to OVW-administered grant programs. Retrieved from http://www.ncdsv.org/images/OVW_VAWA+2013+summary+changes+to+OVW-administered+Grant+Programs.pdf

O'Keefe, E. (2013, December 19). Congress approves reforms to address sexual assault, rape in military. *Washington Post.* Retrieved from http://www.washingtonpost.com/politics/congress-poised-to-approve-reforms-to-address-sexual-assault-rape-in-military/2013/12/19/bbd34afa-68c9-11e3-a0b9-249bbb34602c_story.html

Oppel, R. A. (2013, March 17). Ohio teenagers guilty in rape that social media brought to light. *The New York Times.* Retrieved from http://www.nytimes.com/2013/03/18/us/teenagers-found-guilty-in-rape-in-steubenville-ohio.html?pagewanted=all&_r=0

Ortiz, N. R., & Spohn, C. (2014). Mitigating the effect of a criminal record at sentencing: Local life circumstances and substantial assistance departures among recidivists in federal court. *Criminal Justice Policy Review, 25*(1), 3–28.

Otis, M. D. (2007). Perceptions of victimization risk and fear of crime among lesbians and gay men. *Journal of Interpersonal Violence, 22*(2): 198–217.

Owen, B., & Bloom B. (1998). *Modeling gender-specific services in juvenile justice: Final report to the office of criminal justice planning.* Sacramento, CA: OCJP.

OXFAM. (n.d.). Protecting the accused: Sorcery in PNG. Retrieved from http://www.oxfam.org.nz/what-we-do/where-we-work/papua-new-guinea/gender-justice/confronting-sorcery

OXFAM. (2010, October 15). Sorcery beliefs and practices in Gumine: A source of conflict and insecurity. Retrieved from http://www.oxfam.org.nz/sites/default/files/reports/Sorcery_report_FINAL.pdf

Oxman-Martinez, J., & Hanley, J. (2003, February 20). Human smuggling and trafficking: Achieving the goals of the UN protocols? *Cross Border Perspectives: Human Trafficking, 20.*

Ozbay, O., & Ozcan Y. Z. (2008). A test of Hirschi's social bonding theory: A comparison of male and female delinquency. *Internal Journal of Offender Therapy and Comparative Criminology, 52*(2), 134–157.

Pakes, F. (2005). Penalization and retreat: The changing face of Dutch criminal justice. *Criminal Justice, 5*(2), 145–161.

Palmer, B. (2001). Women in the American judiciary: Their influence and impact. *Women and Politics, 23*(3), 91–101.

Panchanadeswaran, S., & Koverola, C. (2005). Voices of battered women in India. *Violence Against Women, 11*(6), 736–758.

Paoline, E. A., Lambert, E. G., & Hogan, N. L. (2015). Job stress and job satisfaction among jail staff: Exploring gendered effects. *Women & Criminal Justice, 25*(5): 339–359.

Parsons, J., & Bergin, T. (2010). The impact of criminal justice involvement on victims' mental health. *Journal of Traumatic Stress, 23*(2), 182–188. doi:10.1002/jts.20505

Patel, S., & Gadit, A. M. (2008). Karo-kari: A form of honour killing in Pakistan. *Transcultural Psychiatry, 45*(4), 683–694.

Pathe, M., & Mullen, P. E. (1997). The impact of stalkers on their victims. *British Journal of Psychiatry, 170,* 12–17.

Patterson, D., & Campbell, R. (2010). Why rape survivors participate in the criminal justice system. *Journal of Community Psychology, 38*(2), 191–205.

Pelissero, T. (2014, August 28). NFL toughens its stance on domestic violence. *USA Today.* Retrieved from https://www.usatoday .com/story/sports/nfl/2014/08/28/nfl-toughens-its-stance-on-domestic-violence/14746187/

Perona, A. R., Bottoms, B. L., & Sorenson, E. (2006). Research-based guidelines for child forensic interviews. *Journal of Aggression, Maltreatment & Trauma, 12*(3/4), 81–130.

Perry, D. (2010). *The girls of Murder City: Fame, lust, and the beautiful killers who inspired* Chicago. New York: Penguin Group/ Viking Press.

Peterman, A., Palermo, T., & Bredenkamp, C. (2011). Estimates and determinants of sexual violence in the democratic Republic of the Congo. *American Journal of Public Health*

Peterselia, J. (2000). Parole and prisoner reentry in the United States. Perspectives. American Probation and Parole Association. Retrieved from http://www.appa-net.org/eweb/resources/ pppsw_ 2013/history.htm

Peterson, F. (2012, July 21). Luis Walker, Lackland boot camp instructor, convicted of rape and sexual assault. *Global Post.* Retrieved from http://www.globalpost.com/dispatch/news/ regions/americas/united-states/120721/luis-walker-rape-sex-assault-lackland-texas-sexual-air-force-military-boot

Petrillo, M. (2007). Power struggle: Gender issues for female probation officers in the supervision of high risk offenders. *Probation Journal: The Journal of Community and Criminal Justice, 54*(4), 394–406.

The Pew Charitable Trusts and the John D. and Catherine T. MacArthur Foundation. (2014). State prison health care spending: An examination. Retreved from http://www.pewtrusts. org/~/media/assets/2014/07/stateprisonhealthcarespendingreport.pdf

Phillips, D. (2017, March 6). Marines shared illicit images of female peers. *The New York Times.* Retrieved from https://www .nytimes.com/2017/03/06/us/inquiry-opens-into-how-30000-marines-shared-illicit-images-of-female-peers.html

Pilon, M. (2017, January 31). Inside the NFL's domestic violence punishment problem. B/R Mag. Retrieved from http://mag .bleacherreport.com/nfl-domestic-violence-policy-suspensions/

Pinchevsky, G. M., & Steiner, B. (2016). Sex-Based disparities in pretrial release decisions and outcomes. *Crime and Delinquency, 62*(3), 308–340.

Piquero, N. L., Gover, A. R., MacDonald, J. M., & Piquero, A. R. (2005). The influence of delinquent peers on delinquency: Does gender matter? *Youth & Society, 36*(3), 251–275.

Planty, M., Langton, L., Krebs, C., Berzofsky, M., & Smiley-McDonald, H. (2013). Female victims of sexual violence, 1994–2010. U.S. Department of Justice, Bureau of Justice Statistics. Retrieved from http://www.bjs.gov/content/pub/pdf/ fvsv9410.pdf

Platt, A. M. (1969). *The child savers.* IL: University of Chicago Press.

Pollak, O. (1950). *Criminality of women.* Baltimore, MD: University of Pennsylvania Press.

Pollak, O. (1961). *The criminality of women.* New York: A. S. Barnes.

Pollak, S. (2013, February 7). Woman burned alive for witchcraft in Papua New Guinea. *Time.* Retrieved from http://newsfeed.time .com/2013/02/07/Woman-burned-alive-for-witchcraft-in-Papua-New-Guinea

Pollock, J. M. (1986). *Sex and supervision: Guarding male and female inmates.* New York: Greenwood Press.

Postmus, J. L., Plummer, S., & Stylianou, A. M. (2016). Measuring economic abuse in the lives of survivors: Revising the scale of economic abuse. *Violence Against Women, 22*(6): 692–703.

Potter, G., & Kappeler, V. (2006). *Constructing crime: Perspectives on making news and social problems* (2nd ed.). Long Grove, IL: Waveland Press.

Potter, H. (2015). *Intersectionality and criminality: Disrupting and revolutionizing studies of crime.* New York: Routledge.

Potter, H. (2006). An argument for Black feminist criminology. *Feminist Criminology, 1*(2), 106–124.

Potter, H. (2007a). Battered Black women's use of religious services and spirituality for assistance in leaving abusive relationships. *Violence Against Women, 13*(3), 262–284.

Potter, H. (2007b). *Battle cries: Understanding and confronting intimate partner abuse against African-American women.* New York: New York University Press.

President's Commission on Law Enforcement and the Administration of Justice. (1967). *The challenge of crime in a free society.* Washington, DC: U.S. Government Printing Office.

Proano-Raps, T. C., & Meyer, C. L. (2003). Postpartum syndrome and the legal system. In R. Muraskin (Ed.), *It's a crime: Women and justice* (3rd ed., pp. 53–76). Upper Saddle River, NJ: Prentice-Hall.

Pryor, D. W., & Hughes, M. R. (2013). Fear of rape among college women: A social psychological analysis. *Violence and Victims, 28*(3), 443–465.

Quinn, B. (2013, March 19). Taliban victim Malala Yousafzai starts school in UK. *The Guardian.* Retrieved from http://www .theguardian.com/world/2013/mar/20/taliban-victim-malala-yousafzai-school

Rabe-Hemp, C. (2012). The career trajectories of female police executives. In R. Muraskin (Ed.), *Women and justice: It's a crime* (5th ed., pp. 527–543). Upper Saddle River, NJ: Prentice-Hall.

Rabe-Hemp, C. (2011). Exploring administrators' perceptions of light-duty assignment. *Police Quarterly, 14*(2): 124–141.

Rabe-Hemp. C., & Humiston, G. S. (2015). A survey of maternity policies and pregnancy accommodations in American police deparments. *Police Practice and Research, 16*(3): 239–253.

Rabe-Hemp, C. E. (2008). Survival in an "all boys club": Policewomen and their fight for acceptance. *Policing: An International Journal of Police Strategies and Management, 31*(2), 251–270.

Rabe-Hemp, C. E. (2009). POLICEwomen or PoliceWOMEN? Doing gender and police work. *Feminist Criminology, 4*(2), 114–129.

Raeder, M. S. (1995). The forgotten offender: The effect of the sentencing guidelines and mandatory minimums on women and their children. *Federal Sentencing Reporter, 8*, 157.

Rafferty, Y. (2007). Children for sale: Child trafficking in Southeast Asia. *Child Abuse Review, 16*(6), 401–422.

Rafter, N. H. (1985). *Partial justice: Women in state prisons 1800–1935.* Boston: New England University Press.

Raphael, J. (2000). *Saving Bernice: Battered women, welfare, and poverty.* Boston: Northeastern University Press.

Raphael, J. (2004). *Listening to Olivia: Violence, poverty, and prostitution.* Boston: Northeastern University Press.

Raphael, J., & Shapiro, D. L. (2004). Violence in indoor and outdoor venues. *Violence Against Women, 10*(2), 126–139.

Raphael, K. G. (2005). Childhood abuse and pain in adulthood: More than a modest relationship? *The Clinical Journal of Pain, 21*(5), 371–373.

Rasche, C. E. (2012). The dislike of female offenders among correctional officers: A need for specialized training. In R. Muraskin (Ed.), *Women and justice: It's a crime* (5th ed., pp. 544–562). Upper Saddle River, NJ: Prentice-Hall.

Rathbone, C. (2005). *A world apart: Women, prison, and life behind bars.* New York: Random House.

Raymond, J. G. (2004). Prostitution on demand: Legalizing the buyers as sexual consumers. *Violence Against Women, 10*(10), 1156–1186.

Reichman, N. J., & Sterling, J. S. (2001). Recasting the brass ring: Deconstructing and reconstructing workplace opportunities for women lawyers. *Capital University Law Review, 29*, 923–977.

Reinharz, S. (1992). *Feminist methods in social research.* New York: Oxford University Press.

Rennison, C. M. (2009). A new look at the gender gap in offending. *Women and Criminal Justice, 19*, 171–190.

Renzetti, C. M., Goodstein, L., & Miller, S. E. (2006). *Rethinking gender, crime, and justice: Feminist readings.* New York: Oxford University Press.

Resnick, H., Acierno, R., Holmes, M., Dammeyer, M., & Kilpatrick, D. (2000). Emergency evaluation and intervention with female victims of rape and other violence. *Journal of Clinical Psychology, 56*(10), 1317–1333.

Resnick, P. J. (1970). Murder of the newborn: A psychiatric review of neonaticide. *American Journal of Psychiatry, 126*, 1414–1420.

Revolutionary Worker. (2002). The disappearing women of Juarez. Retrieved from http://revcom.us/a/v24/1161-1170/1166/juarez.htm

Reyns, B. W., & Englebrecht, C. M. (2012). The fear factor: Exploring predictors of fear among stalking victims throughout the stalking encounter. *Crime & Delinquency, 59*(5), 788–808.

Reyns, B. W., Burek, M. W., Henson, B., & Fisher, B. S. (2013). The unintended consequences of digital technology: Exploring the relationship between sexting and cybervictimization. *Journal of Crime and Justice, 36*(1), 1–17.

Rice, S. K., Terry, K. J., Miller, H. V., & Ackerman, A. R. (2007). Research trajectories of female scholars in criminology and criminal justice. *Journal of Criminal Justice Education, 18*(3), 360–384.

Rich, K., & Seffrin, P. (2014). Birds of a feather or fish out of water? Policewomen taking rape reports. *Feminist Criminology, 9*(2): 137–159.

Rickert, V. I., Wiemann, C. M., & Vaughan, R. D. (2005). Disclosure of date/acquaintance rape: Who reports and when. *Journal of Pediatric and Adolescent Gynecology, 18*(1), 17–24.

Rideout, M. (2007). May 1, 1990: The shocking death that started a sensation in N.H. Keene Equinox. Retrieved from http://www.hampton.lib.nh.us/hampton/biog/pamsmart/equinox2006_1.htm

Ritchie, B. E. (2001). Challenges incarcerated women face as they return to their communities: Findings from life history interviews. *Crime and Delinquency, 47*(3), 368–389.

Robinson, L. (1890). Woman lawyers in the United States. *The Green Bag, 2*, 10.

Robison, S. M. (1966). A critical review of the Uniform Crime Reports. *Michigan Law Review, 64*(6), 1031–1054.

Rodriguez, S. F., Curry, T. R., & Lee, G. (2006). Gender differences in criminal sentencing: Do effects vary across violent, property, and drug offenses? *Social Science Quarterly, 87*(2), 318–339.

Roe-Sepowitz, D. E. (2012). Juvenile entry into prostitution: The role of emotional abuse. *Violence Against Women, 18*(5), 562–579.

Romero-Daza, N., Weeks, M., & Singer, M. (2003). "Nobody gives a damn if I live or die": Violence, drugs, and street-level prostitution in inner city Hartford, Connecticut. *Medical Anthropology, 22*, 233–259.

Rosenbaum, A. (2009). Batterer intervention programs: A report from the field. *Violence and Victims, 24*(6), 757–770.

Rosenbaum, J. L. (1989). Family dysfunction and female delinquency. *Crime and Delinquency, 35*, 31–44.

Rosenbaum, J. L., & Spivack, S. (2013). *Implementing a gender-based arts program for juvenile offenders.* Waltham, MA: Elsevier.

Ross, E. (2013, May 10). Air Force sex scandal heats up. Retrieved from http://www.koaa.com/news/air-force-sex-scandal-heats-up/

Rumney, P. N. S. 1999. When rape isn't rape: Court of appeal sentencing practice in cases of marital and relationship rape. *Oxford Journal of Legal Studies, 19* (2): 243–270.

Ryder, J. A., & Brisgone, R. E. (2013). Cracked perspectives: Reflections of women and girls in the aftermath of the crack cocaine era. *Feminist Criminology, 8*(1), 40–62.

Ryon, S. B. (2013). Gender as social threat: A study of offender sex, situational factors, gender dynamics and social control. *Journal of Criminal Justice, 41*, 426–437.

S. v. Modise (2007). South Africa: North West High Court, Mafikeng. ZANWHC 73. As cited in Mandal, S. (2014). The impossibility of marital rape: Contestations around marriage, sex, violence and the law in contemporary India. *Australia Feminist Studies, 29*(81): 255–272.

Sabina, C., Cuevas, C. A., & Schally, J. L. (2012). Help-seeking in a national sample of victimized Latino women: The influence of victimization types. *Journal of Interpersonal Violence, 27*(1), 40–61.

Sacks, M., & Ackerman, A. (2014). Bail and sentencing: Does pretrial detention lead to harsher punishment? *Criminal Justice Policy Review, 25*(1): 59–77.

Salisbury, E. J., Van Voorhis, P., Wright, E., M., & Bauman, A. (2009). Changing probation experiences for female offenders based on women's needs and risk assessment project findings. *Women, Girls and Criminal Justice, 10*(6), 83–84, 92–95.

Salonga, R. (2016, August 11). Jaycee Dugard TV interview: On her daughters, "Room" and the $20 million settlement. *The Mercury News.* Retrieved from http://www.mercurynews.com/2016/07/08/jaycee-dugard-tv-interview-on-her-daughters-room-and-the-20-million-settlement/

SAMHSA. (2009). Substance abuse treatment: Addressing the specific needs of women. A treatment improvement protocol TIP 51. Center for Substance Abuse Treatment. Retrieved from http://mentalhealth.samhsa.gov/cmhs/CommunitySupport/women_violence/default.asphttp://bjs.ojp.usdoj.gov/index.cfm?ty=tp&tid=35

Sampson, R. (2003). Acquaintance rape of college students. *Public Health Resources, 92.*

Sampson, R., & Laub, J. (1993). *Crime in the making: Pathways and turning points through life.* Cambridge, MA: Harvard University Press.

Sanchez, R., & Lance, N. (2017, June 17). Judge finds Michelle Carter guilty of manslaughter in texting suicide case. CNN. Retrieved from www.cnn.com/2017/06/16/michelle-carter-texting-case/index.html

Sandifer, J. L. (2008). Evaluating the efficacy of a parenting program for incarcerated mothers. *The Prison Journal, 88*(3), 423–445.

Saulters-Tubbs, C. (1993). Prosecutorial and judicial treatment of female offenders. *Federal Probation, 37–42.*

Savage, D. G. (2009). Sotomayor takes her seat. *American Bar Association Journals, 95*(10), 24–25.

Sawyers, E. T. (1922). History of Santa Clara County, California. Retrieved from http://www.mariposaresearch.net/santaclararesearch/SCBIOS/cfbrattan.html

Schadee, J. (2003). Passport to healthy families. *Corrections Today, 65*(3), 64.

Schalet, A., Hunt, G., & Joe-Laidler, K. (2003). Respectability and autonomy: The articulation and meaning of sexuality among girls in the gang. *Journal of Contemporary Ethnography, 32*(1), 108–143.

Schemo, D. J. (2003, August 29). Rate of rape at academy is put at 12% in survey. Retrieved from http://www.nytimes.com/2003/08/29/national/29ACAD.html?th

Schoonmaker, M. H., & Brooks, J.S. (1975). Women in probation and parole, 1974. *Crime & Delinquency, 21*(2), 109–115.

Schoot, E., & Goswami, S. (2001). *Prostitution: A violent reality of homelessness.* IL: Chicago Coalition for the Homeless.

Schulz, D. M. (1995). *From social worker to crime fighter: Women in United States municipal policing.* Westport, CT: Praeger.

Schulz, D. M. (2003). Women police chiefs: A statistical profile. *Police Quarterly, 6*(3), 330–345.

Schulz, D. M. (2004). Invisible no more: A social history of women in U.S. policing. In B. R. Price & N. J. Sokologg (Eds.), *The criminal justice system and women* (pp. 483-494). New York: McGraw-Hill.

Schulze, C. (2012). The policies of United States police departments: Equal access, equal treatment. In R. Muraskin (Ed.), *Women and justice: It's a crime* (5th ed., pp. 500–513). Upper Saddle River, NJ: Prentice-Hall.

Schwartz, M. D., & DeKeseredy, W. S. (2008). Interpersonal violence against women: The role of men. *Journal of Contemporary Criminal Justice, 24*(2), 178–185.

Schwartz, M. D., DeKeseredy, W. S., Tait, D., & Alvi, S. (2001). Male peer support and a feminist routing activities theory: Understanding sexual assault on the college campus. *Justice Quarterly, 18*(3), 623–649.

Scott-Ham, M., & Burton, F. C. (2005). Toxicological findings in cases of alleged drug-facilitated sexual assault in the United Kingdom over a 3-year period. *Journal of Clinical Forensic Medicine, 12*(4), 175.

The Second Chance Act (H.R. 1593). Available at https://www.congress.gov/bill/110th-congress/house-bill/1593/text

Sedlak, A. J., McPherson, K. S., & Basena, M. (2013). Nature and risk of victimization: Findings from the survey of youth in residential placement [Bulletin]. Office of Juvenile Justice and Delinquency Prevention. Retrieved from http://www.ojjdp.gov/pubs/240703.pdf

Seelye, K. Q., & Bidgood, J. (2017). Guilty verdict for young woman who urged friend to kill himself. *New York Times.* Retrieved from https://www.nytimes/2017/06/16/us/suicide-texting-trial-michelle -carter-conrad-roy.html

Seghetti, L. M., & Bjelopera, J. P. (2012). The Violence Against Women Act: Overview, legislation and federal funding. Congressional Research Service. Retrieved from http://www.fas.org/sgp/crs/misc/R42499.pdf

Sellers, C., & Bromley, M. (1996). Violent behavior in college student dating relationships. *Journal of Contemporary Criminal Justice, 12*(1), 1–27.

Sengstock, M. C. (1976). *Culpable victims in Mendelsohn's typology.* Retrieved from https://www.ncjrs.gov/App/publications/Abstract.aspx?id=48998

Sentencing Project. (2006). *Life sentences: Denying welfare benefits to women convicted of drug offenses.* Retrieved from http://www.sentencingproject.org/doc/publications/women_smy_lifesentences.pdf

Severance, T. A. (2005). "You know who you can go to": Cooperation and exchange between incarcerated women. *The Prison Journal, 85*(3), 343–367.

Shackling pregnant inmates banned under California law, but many states allow the practice. (2012, October 11). *Huffington Post.* Retrieved from http://www.huffingtonpost.com/2012/10/11/pregnant-women-shackles-giving-birth-two-thirds-33-states_n_1958319.html

Shannon-Lewy, C., & Dull, V. T. (2005). The response of Christian clergy to domestic violence: Help or hindrance? *Aggression and Violent Behavior, 10*(6), 647–659.

Sharma, A. (2013, October 31). Sara Kruzan released from prison 18 years after killing pimp as teen. Retrieved from http://www.kpbs.org/news/2013/oct/31/sara-kruzan-killed-pimp-teen-goes-free/

Sharp, S. F., Peck, B. M., & Hartsfield, J. (2012). Childhood adversity and substance use of women prisoners: A general strain theory approach. *Journal of Criminal Justice, 40*, 202–211.

Sharpe, G. (2009). The trouble with girls today: Professional perspectives on young women's offending. *Youth Justice, 9*(3), 254–269.

Sheeran, T. J. (2013, July 17). Ariel Castro pleads not guilty to 977 counts in Ohio kidnapping indictment. *Huffington Post.* Retrieved from http://www.huffingtonpost.com/2013/07/17/ariel-castro-arraignment-charges_n_3609793.html

Shekarkhar, Z., & Gibson, C. L. (2011). Gender, self-control, and offending behaviors among Latino youth. *Journal of Contemporary Criminal Justice, 27*(1), 63–80.

Shelden, R. G. (1981). Sex discrimination in the juvenile justice system: Memphis, Tennessee, 1900–1917. In M. Q. Warren (Ed.), *Comparing male and female offenders* (pp. 52–72). Beverly Hills, CA: Sage.

Shenoy, D. P., Neranartkomol, R., Ashok, M., Chiang, A., Lam, A. G., & Trieu, S. L. (2010). Breaking down the silence: A study examining patterns of sexual assault and subsequent disclosure among ethnic groups of Asian American college women. *Californian Journal of Health Promotion, 7*(2): 78–91.

Shepherd, S. M., Luebbers, S., & Dolan, M. (2013, April–June). Identifying gender differences in an Australian youth offender population. *Sage Open, 3*, 1–12.

Sherman, L. W., & Berk, R. A. (1984). The Minneapolis Domestic Violence Experiment. *Police Foundation Reports.* Retrieved from http://www.policefoundation.org/pdf/minneapolisdve.pdf

Sholchet, C. (2013, May). Jodi Arias guilty of first degree murder: Death penalty possible. CNN. Retrieved from http://www.cnn.com/2013/05/08/justice/arizona-jodi-arias-verdict/

Shorey, R. C., Cornelius, T. L., & Strauss, C. (2015). Stalking in college student dating relationships: A descriptive investigation. *Journal of Family Violence, 30*: 935–942.

Shufelt, J. L., & Cocozza, J. J. (2006). Youth with mental health disorders in the juvenile justice system: Results from a multi-state prevalence study. National Center for Mental Health and Juvenile Justice. Retrieved from http://www.ncmhjj.com/pdfs/publications/PrevalenceRPB.pdf

Sigurvinsdottir, R., & Ullman S. E. (2015). The role of sexual orientation in the victimization and recovery of sexual assault survivors. *Violence and Victims, 3* (4): 636–648.

Silva, S. A., Pires, A. P., Guerreiro, C., & Cardoso, A. (2012). Balancing motherhood and drug addiction: The transition to parenthood of addicted mothers. *Journal of Health Psychology, 18*(3), 359–367.

Silverman, J. G., Raj, A., Mucci, L. A., & Hathaway, J. E. (2001). Dating violence against adolescent girls and associated substance use, unhealthy weight control, sexual risk behavior, pregnancy, and suicidality. *Journal of American Medical Association, 285*(5), 572–579.

Silverman, J. R., & Caldwell, R. M. (2008). Peer relationships and violence among female juvenile offenders: An exploration of differences among four racial/ethnic populations. *Criminal Justice and Behavior, 35*(3), 333–343.

Simkhada, P. (2008). Life histories and survival strategies amongst sexually trafficked girls in Nepal. *Children and Society, 22*, 235–248.

Simmons, W. P. (2006, Spring). Remedies for the women of Ciudad Juárez through the Inter-American Court of Human Rights. *Northwestern Journal of International Human Rights, 4*(3). Retrieved from http://www.law.northwestern.edu/journals/jihr/v4/n3/2/Simmons. pdf

Simon, R. (1975). *Women and crime.* Lexington, MA: D. C. Heath.

Skolnick, J. (1966). *Justice without trial.* New York: Wiley.

Slattery, S. M., & Goodman, L. A. (2009). Secondary traumatic stress among domestic violence advocates: Workplace risk and protective factors. *Violence Against Women, 15*(11), 1358–1379.

Smith, E. L., & Farole, D. J., Jr. (2009). *Profile of intimate partner violence cases in large urban counties.* Bureau of Justice Statistics, U.S. Department of Justice. Retrieved from http://bjs.ojp.usdoj.gov/content/pub/pdf/pipvcluc.pdf

Smith, J. C. (1998). *Rebels in law: Voices in history of Black women lawyers* (KF299.A35 R43 1998). Ann Arbor: University of Michigan.

Smith-Spark, L., & Nyberg, P. (2013, July 31). Nigella Lawson and Charles Saatchi take step toward divorce. CNN. Retrieved at http://www.cnn.com/2013/07/31/world/europe/nigella-lawson-saatchi-divorce/

Smoyer, A. B. (2015). Feedling relationships: Foodways and social networks in a women's prison. *Affilia: Journal of Women and Social Work, 30*(1): 26–39.

Smude, L. (2012). Realignment: A new frontier for California criminal justice. In C. Gardiner & S. Mallicoat (Eds.), *California's criminal justice system* (pp. 153–168). Durham, NC: Carolina Academic Press.

Snedker, K. A. (2012). Explaining the gender gap in fear of crime: Assessments of risk and vulnerability among New York City residents. *Feminist Criminology, 7*(2), 75–111.

Snell, C., Sorenson, J., Rodriguez, J. J., & Kuanliang, A. (2009). Gender differences in research productivity among criminal justice and criminology scholars. *Journal of Criminal Justice, 37*(3), 288–295.

Snow, R. L. (2010). *Policewomen who made history: Breaking through the ranks.* Lanham, MD: Rowman and Littlefield.

Snyder, H. N., & Sickmund, M. (2006). *Juvenile offenders and victims: 2006 national report.* National Center for Juvenile Justice. Office of Juvenile Justice and Delinquency Prevention. Retrieved from http://www.ojjdp.gov/ojstatbb/nr2006/

Snyder, J. A., Fisher, B. S., Scherer, H. L, & Daigle, L. E. (2012). Unsafe in the camouflage tower: Sexual victimization and perceptions of military academy leadership. *Journal of Interpersonal Violence, 27*(16), 3171–3194.

Snyder, Z. K. (2009). Keeping families together: The importance of maintaining mother-child contact for incarcerated women. *Women & Criminal Justice, 19*, 37–59.

Sokoloff, N. J. (2004). Domestic violence at the crossroads: Violence against poor women and women of color. *Women Studies Quarterly, 32*(3/4), 139–147.

Songer, D. R., & Crews-Meyer, K. A. (2000). Does judge gender matter? Decision making in state supreme courts. *Social Science Quarterly, 8*(3), 750–762.

Songer, D. R., Davis, S., & Haire, S. (1994). A reappraisal of diversification in the federal courts: Gender effects in the court of appeals. *Journal of Politics, 56*(2), 425–439.

Sonia Sotomayor. (2012). *The New York Times.* Retrieved from http://topics.nytimes.com/top/reference/timestopics/people/s/sonia_sotomayor/index.html?8qa

Spears, J. W., & Spohn, C. C. (1996). The genuine victim and prosecutors' charging decisions in sexual assault cases. *American Journal of Criminal Justice, 20*, 183–205.

Spencer, G. C. (2004/2005). Her body is a battlefield: The applicability of the Alien Tort Statute to corporate human rights abuses in Juarez, Mexico. *Gonzaga Law Review, 40*, 503.

Spinelli, M. G. (2004). Maternal infanticide associated with mental illness: Prevention and the promise of saved lives. *American Journal of Psychiatry, 161*, 1548–1557.

Spitzberg, B. H. (2016). Acknowledgment of unwanted pursuit, threats, assault, and stalking in a college population. *Psychology of Violence* Advance online publication. http://dx.doi.org/10.1037/a0040205

Spitzberg, B. H., & Cupach, W. R. (2003). What mad pursuit? Obsessive relational intrusion and stalking related phenomena. *Aggression and Violent Behavior, 8*, 345–375.

Spohn, C., & Beichner, D. (2000). Is preferential treatment of female offenders a thing of the past? A multisite study of gender, race, and imprisonment. *Criminal Justice Policy Review, 11*(2), 149–184.

Spohn, C., & Belenko, S. (2013). Do the drugs do the time? The effect of drug abuse on sentences imposed on drug offenders in three U.S. District Courts. *Criminal Justice and Behavior, 40*(6), 646–670.

Spohn, C., & Brennan, P. K. (2011). The joint effects of offender race/ethnicity and gender on substantial assistance departures in federal courts. *Race and Justice 1*(1), 49–78.

Spohn, C., Gruhl, J., & Welch, S. (1987). The impact of the ethnicity and gender of defendants on the decision to reject or dismiss felony charges. *Criminology, 25*(1), 175–192

Sports Illustrated (2017, February 17). Former NFL RB Trent Richardson arrested on domestic violence charge. Retrieved from https://www.si.com/nfl/2017/02/17/trent-richardson-arrested-domestic-violence-charge-alabama

Srinivas, T., & DePrince, A. P. (2015). Links between the police response and women's psychological outcomes following intimate partner violence. *Violence and Victims, 30*(1): 32–48.

St. John, P. (2013, October 26). Jerry Brown freedom for woman imprisoned at 16 for killing pimp. *Los Angeles Times.* Retrieved from http://articles.latimes.com/2013/oct/26/local/la-me-ff-kruzan-20131027

Stacy, M. (2012, May 19). Marissa Alexander gets 20 years for firing warning shot. *Huffington Post.* Retrieved from http://www.huffingtonpost.com/2012/05/19/marissa-alexander-gets-20_n_1530035.html

Stalens, L. J., & Finn, M. A. (2000). Gender differences in officers' perceptions and decisions about domestic violence cases. *Women and Criminal Justice, 11*(3), 1–24.

Stangle, H. L. (2008). Murderous Madonna: Femininity, violence, and the myth of postpartum mental disorder in cases of maternal infanticide and filicide. *William and Mary Law Review, 50*, 699–734.

Starzynski, L. L., Ullman, S. E., Townsend, S. M., Long, L. M., & Long, S. M. (2007). What factors predict women's disclosure of sexual assault to mental health professionals? *Journal of Community Psychology, 35*(5), 619–638.

Stattin, H., & Magnusson, D. (1990). *Pubertal maturation in female development* (Vol. 2). Hillsdale, NJ: Erlbaum.

Steer, J. (2013, May 6). Cleveland police: Missing teens Amanda Berry and Gina DeJesus found alive, appear to be OK. Retrieved from http://www.newsnet5.com/news/local-news/cleveland-metro/cleveland-police-dispatch-missing-teens-amanda-berry-and-gina-dejesus-found-alive

Steffensmeier, D., & Allan, E. (1996). Gender and crime: Toward a gendered theory of female offending. *American Review of Sociology, 22*, 459–487.

Steffensmeier, D., & Hebert, C. (1999). Women and men policymakers: Does the judge's gender affect the sentencing of criminal defendants? *Social Forces, 77*(3), 1163–1196.

Steffensmeier, D., Kramer, J., & Streifel, C. (1993). Gender and imprisonment decisions. *Criminology, 31*, 411–446.

Steffensmeier, D., Schwartz, J., Zhong, H., & Ackerman, J. (2005). An assessment of recent trends in girls' violence using diverse longitudinal sources: Is the gender gap closing? *Criminology, 43,* 355–405.

Steffensmeier, D., Zhong, H., Ackerman, J., Schwartz, J., & Agha, S. (2006). Gender gap trends for violent crimes, 1980 to 2003: A UCR-NCVS comparison. *Feminist Criminology, 1*(1), 72–98.

Stephens, E., & Melton, H. (2016). The impact of children on intimate partner abuse victims' service-seeking. *Women & Criminal Justice.* DOI: 10.1080/08974454.2016.1247773

Sterling, J. S., & Reich,an, N. (2016). Overlooked and undervalued: Women in private law practice. *Annual Review of Law and Social Science, 12*: 373–393.

Stevenson, T., & Love, C. (1999). *Her story of domestic violence: A timeline of the battered women's movement.* Safework: California's Domestic Violence Resource. Retrieved from http://www.mincava.umn.edu/documents/herstory/herstory .html

Stewart, C. C., Langan, D., & Hannem, S. (2013). Victim experiences and perspectives on police responses to verbal violence in domestic settings. *Feminist Criminology, 8*(4), 269–294.

Stohr, M. K., Mays, G. L., Lovrich, N. P., & Gallegos, A. M. (1996). *Parallel perceptions: Gender, job enrichment and job satisfaction among correctional officers in women's jails.* Paper presented at the Annual Meeting of the Academy of Criminal Justice Sciences, Las Vegas, Nevada.

Stotzer, R. L. (2014). Law enforcement and criminal justice personnel interactions with transgender people in the United States: A literature review. *Aggression and Violent Behavior, 19*(3), 263–277.

Strachan, M. (2013, October 29). Target to drop criminal background questions in job applications. *Huffington Post.* Retrieved from http://www.huffingtonpost.com/2013/10/29/target-criminal-history-questions_n_4175407.html

Stringer, E. C., & Barnes, S. L. (2012). Mothering while imprisoned: The effects of family and child dynamics on mothering attitudes. *Family Relations, 61*, 313–326.

Strom, K. J., Warner, T. D., Tichavsky, L., & Zahn, M. A. (2010, September 8). Policing juveniles: Domestic violence arrest policies, gender, and police response to child-parent violence. *Crime & Delinquency.* Advance online publication. Retrieved from http://www.sagepub.com/journals/Journal200959

Suerth, J. (2017, June 16). After guilty verdit in texting suicide case, what's next for Michelle Carter? CNN. Retrieved from www.cnn .com/2017/06/16/us/michelle-carter-whats-next/index.html.

Sullivan, M., Senturia, K., Negash, T., Shiu-Thornton, S., & Giday, B. (2005). For us it's like living in the dark: Ethiopian women's experiences with domestic violence. *Journal of Interpersonal Violence, 20*(8), 922–940.

Supreme Court. (n.d.). The Supreme Court of the United States—History. Retrieved from http://www.judiciary.senate.gov/ nominations/SupremeCourt/SupremeCourtHistory.cfm

Surette, R. (2003). The media, the public, and criminal justice policy. *Journal of the Institute of Justice & International Studies, 2,* 39–52.

Sutherland, E., & Cressey, D. (1974). *Criminology* (9th ed.). Philadelphia: H. B. Lippincott.

Sutton, J. R. (1988). Stubborn children: Controlling delinquency in the United States, 1640–1981. Berkeley: University of California Press.

Svensson, R. (2003). Gender differences in adolescent drug use. *Youth and Society, 34,* 300–329.

Svensson, R. (2004). Shame as a consequence of the parent-child relationship: A study of gender differences in juvenile delinquency. *European Journal of Criminology, 1*(4), 477–504.

Swan, A. A. (2016). Masculine, feminine, or androgynous: The influence of gender identity on job satisfaction among female police officers. *Women & Criminal Justice, 26*(1): 1-19.

Tamborra, T. L. (2012). Poor, urban, battered women who are stalked: How can we include their experiences. *Feminist Criminology, 7*(2), 112–129.

Tasca, M., Zatz, M., & Rodriguez, N. (2012). Girls' experiences with violence: An analysis of violence against and by at-risk girls. *Violence Against Women, 18*(6), 672–680.

Taylor, S. C., & Norma, C. (2012). The "symbolic protest" behind women's reporting of sexual assault crime to the police. *Feminist Criminology, 7*(1), 24–47.

Taylor, W., & Furlonger, B. (2011). A review of vicarious traumatization and supervision among Australian telephone and online counsellors. *Austrailian Journal of Guidance and Counselling, 21*: 225–235.

Testa, R. J., Sciacca, L. M., Wang, F., Hendricks, M. L., Goldblum, P., Bradford, J., & Bongar, B. (2012). Effect of violence on transgender people. *Professional Psychology: Research and Practice, 43*(5): 452–459.

Tewksbury, R., & Collins, S. C. (2006). Aggression levels among correctional officers. *The Prison Journal, 86*(3), 327–343.

Tewksbury, R., Connor, D. P., Chesseman, K., & Rivera, B. L. (2012). Female sex offenders' anticipations for reentry: Do they really know what they're in for? *Journal of Crime and Justice, 35*(3), 451–463.

The Florida Senate. (2011). Examine Florida's "Romeo and Juliet" law (Issue brief 2012–2014). Retrieved from http://www .flsenate.gov/PublishedContent/Session/2012/InterimReports/ 2012–214cj.pdf

Thompson, D. (2017, June 22). Parole deined for Manson follower Krenwinkle in California. ABC News. Retrieved from http:// abcnews.go.com/US/wireStory/manson-follower-longest-serving-female-inmate-seeks-parole-48211374

Thompson, M., & Petrovic, M. (2009). Gendered transitions: Within-person changes in employment, family, and illicit drug use. *Journal of Research in Crime and Delinquency, 46*(3), 377–408.

Tiby, E. (2001). Victimization and fear among lesbians and gay men in Stockholm. *International Review of Victimiology, 8*: 217–243

Tille, J. E., & Rose, J. C. (2007). Emotional and behavioral problems of 13-to-18 year-old incarcerated female first-time offenders and recidivists. *Youth Violence and Juvenile Justice, 5*(4), 426–435.

Tillman, S., Bryant-Davis, T., Smith, K., & Marks, A. (2010). Shattering silence: Exploring barriers to disclosure for African American sexual assault survivors. *Trauma, Violence, & Abuse, 11*(2), 59–70.

Tillyer, R., Hartley, R. D., & Ward, J. T. (2015). Differential treatment of female defendants sentence length: Does criminal history moderate the effects of gender on in Federal narcotics cases? *Criminal Justice and Behavior, 42*(7): 703–721.

Tjaden, P. G., & Thoennes, N. (2006). *Extent, nature, and consequences of rape victimization: Findings from the National Violence Against Women Survey*. Washington, DC: U.S. Department of Justice, Office of Justice Programs, National Institute of Justice.

Tonsing, J., & Barn, R. (2016). Intimate partner violence in South Asian communities: Exploring the notion of "shame" to promote understandings of migrant women's experiences. *International Social Work*. DOI: 10.1177/0020872816655868

Topping, A., & Quinn, B. (2013, June 18). Nigella Lawson assault: Charles Saatchi accepts police caution. *The Guardian*. Retrieved from http://www.theguardian.com/uk/2013/jun/18/saatchi-lawson-police-caution-assault?guni=Article:in%20body%20 1ink

Torre, I. (2013, October 9). Oakistan's educational challenges. CNN. Retrieved from http://www.cnn.com/2013/10/09/world/asia/infographic-pakistan-education/index.html?iid=article_sidebar

Truman, J. L. (2011). *Criminal victimization, 2010*. Washington, DC: Bureau of Justice Statistics.

Truman, J. L., & Morgan, R. E. (2016). Criminal Victimization, 2015. U.S. Department of Justice, Bureau of Justice Statistics. Retrieved from https://www.bjs.gov/content/pub/pdf/cv15.pdf

Turrell, S. C., & Cornell-Swanson, L. (2005). Not all alike: Within-group differences in seeking help for same-sex relationship abuses. *Journal of Gay & Lesbian Social Services, 18*(1), 77–88.

Turvill, W. (2013, November 1). Saatchi decides not to sue Nigella and reveal the "truth" over their break-up as he "wants to get on with his life." *Daily Mail*. Retrieved from http://www.dailymail.co.uk/news/article-2483393/Charles-Saatchi-wont-sue-Nigella-Lawson-divorce-truth.html

Ullman, S. E., & Townsend, S. M. (2007). Barriers to working with sexual assault providers. *Violence Against Women, 13*(4), 412–443.

Ullman, S. E., & Townsend, S. M. (2008). What is an empowerment approach to working with sexual assault survivors? *Journal of Community Psychology, 36*(3), 299–312.

United Nations. (2000). *Protocol to prevent, suppress and punish trafficking in persons, especially women and children*. Geneva, Switzerland: Author.

United Nations. (2008). UN-backed container exhibit spotlights plight of sex trafficking victims. UN News Centre. Retrieved from http://www.un.org/apps/news/story.asp?NewsID=25524&Cr=trafficking&Cr1

United Nations. (2010). Impunity for domestic violence, "honor killings" cannot continue. UN News Centre. Retrieved from http://www.un.org/apps/news/story.asp?NewsID=33971&Cr=violence+against+women&Cr1

United Nations Office on Drugs and Crime (UNODC) (2017). United Nations Survey of Crime Trends and Operations of Criminal Justice Systems (2016 UN-CTS). Retrieved from https://www.unodc.org/unodc/en/data-and-analysis/statistics/crime/cts-data-collection.html

United Nations Office on Drugs and Crime (UNODC). (2016). Global Report on Trafficking in Persons 2016 Retrieved from http://www.unodc.org/documents/data-and-analysis/glotip/2016_Global_Report_on_Trafficking_in_Persons.pdf

United Nations Office of the Special Representative of the Secretary General for Sexual Violence in Conflict. (2015). Democratic Republic of the Congo. Retrieved from http://www.un.org/sexualviolenceinconflict/countries/democratic-republic-of-the-congo/

UN News Centre. (2013, May 31). UN human rights office regrets Papua New Guinea's decision to resume death penalty. Retrieved from http://www.un.org/apps/news/story.asp?NewsID=45049&Cr=death+penalty&Cr1=&Kw1=sorcery&Kw2=&Kw3=#.UtR6byjiOI4

UN: "Sorcery" murders must end. (2013, April 13). *New Zealand Herald*. Retrieved from http://www.nzherald.co.nz/world/news/article.cfm?c_id=2&objectid=10877300

U.S. Bureau of the Census. (2000). Profiles of general demographic characteristics. Retrieved from http://www2.census.gov/census_2000/datasets/demographic_profile/0_United_States/2kh00.pdf

U.S. Census. (2013). Quick facts, Stubenville, OH. Retrieved from http://quickfacts.census.gov/qfd/states/39/3974608.html

U.S. Census (2016). Facts for Features, Mother's Day. Retrieved from https://www.census.gov/newsroom/facts-for-features/2016/cb-16-ff09.html

U.S. Department of Defense. (2010). *DoD fiscal year (FY) 2009 annual report on sexual assaults in the military services*. Washington, DC: Office of the Secretary of Defense, Sexual Assault Prevention and Response Office. Retrieved from http://www.sapr.mil/media/pdf/reports/fy09_annual_report.pdf

U.S. Department of Health and Human Services. (2011). *National human trafficking resource center fact sheet*. U.S. Department of Health and Human Services. Retrieved from http://www.hhs.gov/

U.S. Department of Justice, Office of Justice Programs. (1998). *New directions from the field: Victims' rights and services for the 21st century*. Washington, DC: U.S. Government Printing Office.

U.S. Department of Justice. (2003). *Criminal victimization, 2003*. Washington, DC: Author.

U.S. Department of Labor (2008). Ready4Work: Final Research Project. Retrieved from https://wdr.doleta.gov/research/FullText_Documents/Ready4Work%20Final%20Research%20Report.pdf

U.S. Department of State. (2008). *Trafficking in Persons Report*. U.S. Department of State. Retrieved from http://www.state.gov

U.S. Department of State. (2009). *Trafficking in Persons Report 2009.* U.S. Department of State. Retrieved from http://www.state.gov

U.S. Department of State. (2011). *Trafficking in Persons Report 2011.* U.S. Department of State. Retrieved from http://www.state.gov/j/tip/rls/tiprpt/2010/index.htm

U.S. Department of State. (2012). *Trafficking in Persons Report 2012.* U.S. Department of State. Retrieved from http://www.state.gov

U.S. Department of State. (2013). *Trafficking in Persons Report 2013.* U.S. Department of State. Retrieved from http://www.state.gov/documents/organization/210737.pdf

U.S. v. Cabell, 890 F. Supp. 13, 19 [D.D.C. 1995].

U.S. v. Johnson, 964 F.2d 124 (2d Cir. 1992).

United States v. Virginia, 518 U.S. 515, 532 (1996).

U.S. v. Windsor, 133 S.Ct. 2675 (2013).

Valera, R. J., Sawyer, R. G., & Schiraldi, G. R. (2000). Violence and post traumatic stress disorder in a sample of inner city street prostitutes. *American Journal of Health Studies, 16*(3), 149–155.

van der Put, C. E., Dekovic, M., Hoeve, M., Stams, G., van der Laan, P. H., & Langewouters, F. (2014). Risk assessment of girls: Are there any sex differences in risk factors for re-offending and in risk profiles? *Crime and Delinquency, 60*(7): 1033–1056.

Van Outtsel, J., Ponnet, K., & Walrave, M. (2016). Cyber dating abuse victimization among secondary school students from a life-style-routine activities theory perspective. *Journal of Interpersonal Violence.* DOI: 10.1177/08862605166293990

Vanassche, S., Sodermans, A. K., Matthijs, K., & Swicegood, G. (2014). The effects of family type, family relationships and parental role models on delinquency and alcohol use among Flemish adolescents. *Journal of Child and Family Studies, 23*(1): 128–143.

Van Voorhis, P., Salisbury, E., Wright, E., & Bauman, A. (2008). *Achieving accurate pictures of risk and identifying gender responsive needs: Two new assessments for women offenders.* Washington, DC: United States Department of Justice, National Institute of Corrections.

Van Wormer, K. S., & Bartollas, C. (2010). *Women and the criminal justice system.* Boston: Allyn and Bacon.

Ventura Miller, H., Miller, J. M., & Barnes, J. C. (2016). Reentry programming for opioid and opiate involved female offenders: Findings from a mixed methods evaluation. *Journal of Criminal Justice,* 129–136.

VictimLaw (n.d.). About victims' rights. Retrieved from https://www.victimlaw.org/victimlaw/pages/victimsRight.jsp

Viglione, J., Hannon, L., & DeFina, R. (2011). The impact of light skin on prison time for Black female offenders. *The Social Science Journal, 48,* 250–258.

Villagran, L. (n.d.). The victims' movement in Mexico. Retrieved from https://www.wilsoncenter.org/sites/default/files/05_victims_movement_villagran.pdf

Visher, C. A. (1983). Gender, police arrest decisions, and notions of chivalry. *Criminology, 21,* 5–28.

von Hentig, H. (1948). *The criminal and his victim: Studies in the sociobiology of crime.* Cambridge, MA: Yale University Press.

Wagenaar, H. (2006). Democracy and prostitution: Deliberating the legalization of brothels in the Netherlands. *Administration and Society, 38*(2), 198–235.

Walker, L. E. (1979). *The battered woman.* New York: Harper and Row.

Walsh, D. (2012, October 9). Taliban gun down girl who spoke up for rights. *New York Times.* Retrieved from http://www.nytimes.com/2012/10/10/world/asia/teen-school-activist-malala-yousafzai-survives-hit-by-pakistani-taliban.html?pagewant-ed+all&_r=0

Walters, M. L., Chen, J., & Breiding, M. J. (2013). The National Intimate Partner and Sexual *Violence Survey (NISVS): 2010 Findings on victimization by sexual orientation.* Atlanta, GA: National Center for Injury Prevention and Control, Centers for Disease Control and Prevention.

Wang, M. C., Horne, S. G., Levitt, H. M., & Klesges, L. M. (2009). Christian women in IPV relationships: An exploratory study of religious factors. *Journal of Psychology and Christianity, 28*(3), 224–235.

Wang, Y. (2011). Voices from the margin: A case study of a rural lesbian's experience with woman-to-woman sexual violence. *Journal of Lesbian Studies, 15*(2), 166–175.

Ward, J. T., Hartley, R. D., & Tillyer, R. (2016). Unpacking gender and racial/ethnic biases in the federal sentencing of drug offenders: A causal mediation approach. *Journal of Criminal Justice, 46*: 196–206.

Warr, M. (1984). Fear of victimization: Why are women and the elderly more afraid. *Social Science Quarterly, 65*(3), 681–702.

Warr, M. (1985). Fear of rape among urban women. *Social Problems, 32*(3), 238–250.

Warshaw, R. (1994). *I never called it rape.* New York: Harper Perennial.

Washington, P. A. (2001). Disclosure patterns of Black female sexual assault survivors. *Violence Against Women, 7*(11), 1254–1283.

Watterson, K. (1996). *Women in prison: Inside the concrete womb.* Boston: Northeastern University Press.

Webster v. Reproductive Health Services, 492 U.S. 490 (1989).

Weerman, F. M., & Hoeve, M. (2012). Peers and delinquency: Are sex differences in delinquency explained by peer factors? *European Journal of Criminology, 9*(3), 228–244.

Wells, T., Colbert, S., & Slate, R. N. (2006). Gender matters: Differences in state probation officer stress. *Journal of Contemporary Criminal Justice, 22*(1), 63–79.

Welsh-Huggins, A. (2013a, March 17). Teen in Steubenville rape case: "I could not remember anything." *Huffington Post.* Retrieved from http://www.huffingtonpost.com/2013/03/16/steubenville-rape-case-teen-cant-recall-assault_n_2893398.html?utm_hp_ref=steubenville-rape

Welsh-Huggins, A. (2013b, May 2). Steubenville Rape: Teen girls guilty of threatening rape victim on Twitter. *Huffington Post.* Retrieved from http://www.huffingtonpost.com/2013/05/02/steubenville-rape-teen-girls-guilty-threats-twitter_n_3204301.html

Wesely, J. K. (2006). Considering the context of women's violence: Gender, lived experiences, and cumulative victimization. *Feminist Criminology, 1*(4), 303–328.

West, C. M. (2004). Black women and intimate partner violence: New directions for research. *Journal of Interpersonal Violence, 19*(12), 1487–1493.

West, D. A., & Lichtenstein, B. (2006). Andrea Yates and the criminalization of the filicidal maternal body. *Feminist Criminology, 1*(3), 173–187.

Westervelt, S. D., & Cook, K. J. (2007). Feminist research methods in theory and action: Learning from death row exonerees. In S. Miller (Ed.), *Criminal justice research and practice: Diverse voices from the field* (pp. 21–37). Boston: University Press of New England.

Westmarland, N. (2001). The quantitative/qualitative debate and feminist research: A subjective view of objectivity. *Forum: Qualitative Social Research, 2*(1). Retrieved from http://www.qualitative-research.net/index.php/fqs/article/view/974/2125

Weymouth, M. (2014, September 9). Wait, people are still victim blaming Janay Rice? *Philadelphia Magazine.* Retrieved from http://www.phillymag.com/news/2014/09/09/people-still-victim-blaming-janay-rice/

Whaley, R. B., Hayes-Smith, J., & Hayes-Smith, R. (2010). Gendered pathways? Gender, mediating factors, and the gap in boys' and girls' substance use. *Crime and Delinquency, 59*(5), 651–669.

Whaley, R. B., Hayes, R., & Smith, J. M. (2014). Differential reactions to schools bonds, peers, and victimization in the case of adolescent substance use: The moderating effect of sex. *Crime & Delinquency, 62*(10): 1263–1285.

Whitaker, M. (2014, April 2). Marissa Alexander in court, seeking "stand your ground" immunity. MSNBC. Retrieved from http://www.msnbc.com/politicsnation/florida-mom-seeks-stand-your-ground

Widom, C. S. (1989). The cycle of violence. *Science, 244,* 160–166.

Wies, J. R. (2008). Professionalizing human services: A case of domestic violence shelter advocates. *Human Communication, 67*(2), 221–233.

Williams, M. (2007). Women's representation on state trial and appellate courts. *Social Science Quarterly, 88*(5), 1192–1204.

Wiltz, T. (2016, August 9). More states lift welfare restrictions for drug felons. Stateline. The PEW Charitable Trusts. Retrieved from www.pewtrusts.org/en/research-and-analysis/blogs/stateline/2016/08/09/more-states-life-welfare-restrictions-for-drug-felons

Wismont, J. M. (2000). The lived pregnancy experience of women in prison. *Journal of Midwifery and Women's Health, 45*(4), 292–300.

Wittmer, D. E., & Bouche, V. (2013). The limits of gendered leadership: Policy implications of female leadership on "women's issues." *Politics & Gender, 9:* 245–275.

Women in Federal Law Enforcement. (2011). Pregnancy guidelines for federal law enforcement. Retrieved from www.wifle.org/pregnancyguidelines.pdf

Women's Health. (2004). *UMHS Women's Health Program.* Retrieved from http://www.med.umich.edu/whp/newsletters/summer04/p03-dating.html

Women's Prison Association (WPA). (2003). *WPA focus on women and justice: A portrait of women in prison.* Retrieved from http://www.wpaonline.org/pdf/Focus_December 2003.pdf

Women's Prison Association (WPA). (2008). *Mentoring women in reentry.* Retrieved from http://www.wpaon line.org

Women's Prison Association (WPA). (2009a). *Quick facts: Women and criminal justice 2009.* Retrieved from http://www.wpaon line.org

Women's Prison Association (WPA). (2009b). Mothers, infants and imprisonment: A national look at prison nurseries and community-based alternatives. Retrieved from http://www.wpaoline.com

Women's Prison Association. (n.d.) History & Mission. Retrieved from http://www.wpaonline.org/about/history

Women's Prison Association. (WPA). (n.d.). Laws banning shackling during childbirth gaining momentum nationwide. Retrieved from http://66.29.139.159/pdf/Shackling%20Brief_final.pdf

Wood, L. (2017). "I look across from me and I see me": Survivors as advocates in intimate partner violence agencies. *Violence Against Women, 23*(3): 309–329.

Wooditch, A. (2011). The efficacy of the *Trafficking in Persons Report*: A review of the evidence. *Criminal Justice Policy Review, 22*(4), 471–493.

Woodlock, D. (2017). The abuse of technology in domestic violence and stalking. *Violence Against Women, 23*(5): 584–602.

Wooldredge, J., & Griffin, T. (2005). Displaced discretion under Ohio sentencing guidelines. *Journal of Criminal Justice, 33,* 301–316.

World Health Organization. (2012). *Sexual and reproductive health.* Retrieved from http://www.who.int/reproductivehealth/about_us/en/index.html.

World Law Direct (2011). Shackling laws. Retrieved from http://www.worldlawdirect.com/forum/law-wiki/43470-shackling-laws.html

Wright, E. M., DeHart, D. D., Koons-Witt, B. A., & Crittenden, C. A. (2013). "Buffers" against crime? Exploring the roles and limitations of positive relationships among women in prison. *Punishment & Society, 15*(1), 71–95.

Wyse, J. J. B. (2013). Rehabilitating criminal selves: Gendered strategies in community corrections. *Gender & Society, 27*(2), 231–255.

Yacoubian, G. S., Urbach, B. J., Larsen, K. L., Johnson, R. J., & Peters, R. J. (2000). A comparison of drug use between prostitutes and other female arrestees. *Journal of Alcohol and Drug Education, 46*(2), 12–26.

Yahne, C. E., Miller, W. R., Irvin-Vitela, L., & Tonigan, J. S. (2002). Magdalena Pilot Project: Motivational outreach to substance abusing women street sex workers. *Journal of Substance Abuse Treatment, 23*(1), 49–53.

Yavuz, N., & Welch, E. W. (2010). Addressing fear of crime in public space: Gender differences in reaction to safety measures in train transit. *Urban Studies, 47*(12), 2491–2515.

Yesberg, J. A., Scanlan, J. M., Hanby, L, J., Serin, R. C., & Polaschek, D. L. L. (2015). Predicting women's recidivism: Validating a dynamic community-based "gender-neutral" tool. *Probation Journal, 62*(1): 33–48.

Yeum, E. B. B. (2010). Eleventh annual review of gender and sexuality law: Criminal law chapter: Rape, sexual assault and evidentiary matters. *Georgetown Journal of Gender & the Law, 11*, 191–869.

Yirga, W. S., Kassa, N. A., Gebremichael, M. W., & Aro, A. R. (2012). Female genital mutilation: Prevalence, perceptions, and effect on women's health in Kersa district of Ethiopia. *International Journal of Women's Health, 4*(1), 45–54.

Yoshihama, M., Ramakrishnon, A., Hammock, A. C., & Khaliq, M. (2012). Intimate partner violence prevention program in an Asian immigrant community: Integrating theories, data, and community. *Violence Against Women, 18*(7): 763–783.

Young, M., & Stein, J. (2004). *The history of the crime victims' movement in the United States: A component of the Office for Victims of Crime Oral History Project.* Washington DC: U.S. Department of Justice. Retrieved from https://www.ncjrs.gov/ovc_archives/ncvrw/2005/pdf/historyofcrime.pdf

Yu, H. (2015). An examiniation of women in federal law enforcement: An exploratory analysis of the challenges they face in the work environment. *Feminist Criminology, 10*(3): 259–278.

Zaitzow, B. H., & Thomas, J. (2003). *Women in prison: Gender and social control.* Boulder, CO: Lynne Rienner.

Zaykowski, H., & Gunter, W. D. (2013). Gender differences in victimization risk: Exploring the role of deviant lifestyles. *Violence and Victims, 28*(2), 341–356.

Zettler, H. R., & Morris, R. G. (2015). An exploratory assessment of race and gender-specific predictors of failure to appear in court among defendants released via a pretrial services agency. *Criminal Justice Review, 40*(4): 417–430.

Index

About the Author

Stacy L. Mallicoat is a Professor of Criminal Justice and Chair of the Division of Politics, Administration and Justice at California State University, Fullerton. She earned her BA in Legal Studies and Sociology from Pacific Lutheran University and her PhD from the University of Colorado Boulder in Sociology. She is the author of several books, including *Crime and Criminal Justice: Concepts and Controversies, Women, Gender and Crime: Core Concepts,* and *Criminal Justice Policy.* Her work also appears in a number of peer-reviewed journals and edited volumes. She is an active member of the American Society of Criminology, the ASC's Division on Women and Crime, and the Academy of Criminal Justice Sciences.